SPORTS LAW: Cases and Materials

SIXTH EDITION

RAY YASSER
Professor of Law
University of Tulsa College of Law

JAMES R. MCCURDY
Professor of Law
Gonzaga University School of Law

C. PETER GOPLERUD
Dean & Professor of Law
Florida Coastal School of Law

MAUREEN A. WESTON
Professor of Law
Pepperdine University School of Law

Library of Congress Cataloging-in-Publication Data

Sports law : cases and materials / Ray Yasser . . . [et a.l.]. — 6th ed.
p. cm.
Rev. ed. of: Constitutional law / Donald E. Lively . . . [et al.]. c1996.
Includes index.
ISBN 0-8205-7037-0 (hard cover)
1. Sports — Law and legislation — United States — Cases. I. Yasser, Ray.
KF3989.A7Y37 2006
344.73'099 — dc22 2006035130

Editorial Offices
744 Broad Street, Newark, NJ 07102 (973) 820-2000
201 Mission St., San Francisco, CA 94105-1831 (415) 908-3200
701 East Water Street, Charlottesville, VA 22902-7587 (804) 972-7600
www.lexis.com

(Pub.3568)

PREFACE

While recognizing that Sports Law issues are burgeoning, we made the unconventional and at-first-glance counterintuitive decision to downsize the book, resting on the theory that the right kind of "less" can be "more." With this Sixth Edition, we commit more than ever to the major cases and the established legal doctrine. We trust that the trimmed down materials presented will provide sufficient grist for anything that might come up. Recent events (like those involving Ron Artest, Barry Bonds, Duke Lacrosse and Floyd Landis, to name just a few) are more often than not best understood in the context of established law. So we concede this is not a current events book, and at the same time contend it is a very current book.

We have tried to cull extraneous or repetitive materials in the interest of efficiency. For example, the privacy tort of appropriation receives coverage in the torts materials, but extended treatment in the chapter on intellectual property. As another illustration, the trial court's opinion in Hackbart is deleted while the appellate opinion is retained because it best reflects the prevailing view about tort liability of one participant to another.

One new feature of the Sixth Edition is an annotated Web Directory which will facilitate information gathering and ease any inconvenience related to the decision to downsize. For example, the NBA Standard Player Contract is readily available from the NBA Player's Association website. Collective bargaining agreements and NCAA regulations are also generally accessible off internet sites. We will also update and expand the teacher's manual, which contains a variety of skills exercises.

Our hope is that those of you who have used our book before will agree that the new edition delivers more with fewer words. Once again, we welcome any comments from our colleagues.

January 2007
Ray Yasser
James R. McCurdy
C. Peter Goplerud
Maureen A. Weston

ACKNOWLEDGMENTS

I want to thank my long-time (but still very youthful) Faculty Assistant Cyndee Jones for her cheerful all-purpose enabling. I don't know what I will do without her, and I'm hoping that I will retire before she leaves.

I would also like to thank my Student Research Assistant Chris Wilson for his stalwart assistance in preparing the Sixth Edition revisions. Chris' future is indeed bright.

Professor McCurdy wishes to acknowledge the excellent and enthusiastic assistance of Robbie McMillian, a Phi Beta Kappa in residence at Gonzaga University Law School.

Dean Goplerud would like to express his thanks and appreciation to Kate Ellis, a 2006 graduate of Florida Coastal School of Law, for her research work on the Sixth Edition.

Professor Weston would like to thank Maidie E. Oliveau, Los Angeles sports lawyer and arbitrator for the Court of Arbitration for Sport, for her helpful contributions to CAS materials.

We would like to acknowledge, too, the extraordinarily able assistance of Jennifer Beszley, our managing editor at Lexis Nexis.

TABLE OF CONTENTS

PART I

AMATEUR SPORTS AND THE LAW

> Student-athletes shall be amateurs in an intercollegiate sport, and their participation should be motivated primarily by education and by the physical, mental and social benefits to be derived. Student participation in intercollegiate athletics is an avocation, and student-athletes should be protected from exploitation by professional and commercial enterprises.

National Collegiate Athletic Association, Division I Manual, 2.9 (2006-07) [Hereinafter Division I Manual].

A. INTRODUCTION TO AMATEURISM

The crucial factor distinguishing the amateur athlete from the professional athlete is that the former actually pays to play while the latter plays for pay. The distinction is, however, often ambiguous, if not illusory. As a practical matter, "amateur" sports really exist on two not so distinct planes — the pure and spurious. Examples of various forms of pure amateurs abound, ranging from the Little Leaguer to the individual and team players in organized tennis tournaments, to the "weekend warrior" running in the occasional ten-kilometer road race. On the other hand, spurious amateur athletes, such as big time college athletes in the major sports of football and basketball, are arguably compensated through benefits and exposure they receive because of their participation in athletics. For college athletes, the over-the-table pay is the scholarship. Off the books, compensation may include jobs and pay without work, athletic wear, special academic support, food and travel, cash for tickets, unsecured loans, cut-rate deals, and other assorted freebies. (Such examples now extend beyond the so-called major sports. Several schools have been sanctioned by the National Collegiate Athletic Association in recent years for so-called "extra benefits" violations in tennis, track and field, and golf.) Unlike most pure amateurs, athletes in major collegiate programs also generate substantial revenues and are subject to an elaborate regime of participation rules and eligibility requirements in order to play.

B. ADMINISTRATION OF AMATEUR ATHLETICS AND THE ROLE OF ATHLETIC ASSOCIATIONS

Various organizations administer amateur athletic competitions for both pure recreational and major amateur athletic competitions. A number of institutions administer amateur sports by the specific sport, such as Little League

Baseball, Inc., which establishes policies, rules of play, and eligibility for youth baseball at the local and international levels. Other major organizations govern amateur athletic competition, such as a state inter-scholastic athletic association or the National Collegiate Athletic Association, which governs major intercollegiate athletic competitions but whose members are public and private collegiate institutions. Each of these organizations have promulgated various regulations defining "amateurism," setting forth rules for eligibility, and outside activity and denying eligibility to those who fail to qualify as "amateurs." The rules vary from one amateur sports organization to another and there are certain difficulties in applying the rules.

Disputes between the athletes and the actions of the governing amateur athletic associations and its members occur at all levels. The materials that follow explore the rights, obligations, and legal relationships between these athletes and governing athletic institutions, which control access and eligibility to participate. A primary consideration in this study is determining the legal status of the particular athletic association for purposes of determining application of Constitutional requirements of due process and equal protection, of statutory mandates, and other common law relationships.

There is, however, a theoretical bottom line. An amateur is one who engages in athletic competition as an "avocation" as distinguished from a "vocation." It is interesting to note that until recently these rules, and their application, have not been extensively tested in the courts. In recent years the line between professionalism and amateurism has blurred, and legal issues have surfaced more frequently. This portion of the book will explore the various issues that may arise in the context of amateurism. It will also look at a variety of legal relationships, in amateur and international sports, including contractual, constitutional, and statutorily created relationships.

C. THE NATIONAL COLLEGIATE ATHLETIC ASSOCIATION: AN OVERVIEW

1. The NCAA

The National Collegiate Athletic Association (NCAA) is a voluntary association of about 1,200 colleges and universities, athletic conferences and sports organizations devoted to the sound administration of intercollegiate athletics.[1] It is headquartered in Indianapolis, Indiana and is operated on a daily basis by a large professional staff. The NCAA regulates athletic competition among its members, sets rules for eligibility to participate, establishes restrictions and guidelines for recruitment of prospective student-athletes, conducts several dozen championship events in the sports sanctioned by the association, enters

---

[1] NCAA Home, *Governance Organization*, <ncaa.org/membership/governance/ org_chart.html>.

into television and promotional contracts relating to these championship events, and enters into agreements to license the NCAA name and logos.

2. NCAA Structure

Within the NCAA, there are separate divisions for members. The association is divided essentially into three divisions: Division I, Division II and Division III. Division I is composed of the major athletic powers in the country, as well as many other institutions that choose to compete at the major college level. Division I is divided into Division I-A and Division I-AA for purposes of regulating football.

The members govern the organization through the establishment of rules designed to further its purposes and goals. The operating structure is that of three federations, with legislation developed in different ways, depending upon the division. Day to day operation of the organization is overseen by a governance hierarchy led by the 20 member Executive Committee. The Executive Committee is composed of institutional chief executive officers charged with ensuring that each division operates with the purposes, policies and principles of the association. In addition to its governing members, the NCAA also has a permanent professional staff, with individual departments for administration, business, championships, communications, compliance services enforcement, legislative services and publishing.

The legislative process within the NCAA has been evolving. Formerly the association enacted all legislation in the context of the Annual Convention. Since the creation of the current structure, Division I has developed legislation through a separate process.

3. Jurisdiction and Responsibilities of the NCAA

The NCAA's duties and responsibilities cover a wide range of activities, including athlete eligibility, recruiting, championships, rules of competition, and enforcement. The professional staff administers the rules and regulations of the association. Membership Services oversees the bulk of the administration, while the enforcement department handles investigation and prosecution of violations of the rules.

It is important to remember that the two concepts at the core of the NCAA are those relating to amateurism and the importance of education. All NCAA student-athletes are to be amateurs and the association's regulations set out explicit definitions of amateurism and specific prohibitions on the acceptance of extra benefits by student-athletes. They further define "pay" to include many items beyond the obvious salary or stipend. It is thus a violation of the rules on amateurism for benefits to be provided to the parents or close relatives of student-athletes. Amateur status is forfeited in most situations where an athlete retains an agent or declares himself eligible for a professional sports draft.

(Eligibility may be restored for a basketball or football player not taken in the NBA or NFL draft.) The association has established an Amateurism Clearinghouse to analyze questions raised regarding participation in junior sports, particularly outside the United States, by prospective student-athletes. There are also restrictions on athletes involved in promotional activities that benefit them solely because of their athletic abilities. Finally, there are restrictions on employment for athletes on full scholarship. The NCAA has set up opportunities for athletes to access funds for personal or family emergencies, as well as to respond to particular hardship situations. This funding is supplemental to the scholarship.

The NCAA's focus on education is best exemplified by the following:

> Intercollegiate athletics shall be maintained as a vital component of the educational program, and student-athletes shall be an integral part of the student body. The admission, academic standing and academic progress of student-athletes shall be consistent with the policies and standards adopted by the institution for the student body in general.

Division I Manual § 2.5. The association establishes standards for initial eligibility of athletes entering member institutions. The bylaws set specific thresholds for scores on standardized tests and the satisfactory completion of a minimum number of core courses in high school. These rules have been the subject of controversy and litigation documented elsewhere in this book. The NCAA also sets forth specific requirements for "satisfactory progress towards a degree" that the athletes must maintain. Student-athletes have typically four years of eligibility and must complete those four years within a five-year period. (There are limited exceptions to both requirements.) There are, of course, procedures in place for athletes ruled ineligible under any of these provisions to appeal those determinations.

In most sports at the Division I level there is intense recruitment of the student-athletes prior to their enrollment in a member institution. The NCAA bylaws set out a very explicit framework for the recruitment process. The regulations limit, among other things, the number of visits made by coaches to athletes, the number of visits to campuses made by the athletes, the number and types of contacts made by coaches, and the times of year that contacts may be made. The rules also severely restrict the participation of alumni and boosters in the recruitment process.

Once the athlete has enrolled at a member institution and is part of one of the athletic teams, there are restrictions on the number of hours set for practice, the times of year for competition, and the number of contests. In addition, the NCAA conducts and regulates post-season competition in more than twenty sports for men and women.

A final point that should be noted is the concept of "institutional control." The NCAA bylaws require that each institution control its program in a manner consistent with the rules and regulations of the association. The CEO of the institution is ultimately responsible for maintaining this control. This includes the responsibility for watching over the conduct of athletic administrators, coaches, faculty, and supporters of the program. The most serious violation that the university can commit is "failure to maintain institutional control."

Notes and Comments

Numerous other organizations are involved in the regulation and governance of athletics at the amateur or international level. Each state has an organization that governs high school athletic competition and there is a national organization, the National Federation of State High School Associations. *See* www.nfhs.org. The United States Olympic Committee was created and granted a charter by Congress to be the organization charged with the exclusive jurisdiction and authority over participation and representation of the United States in the Olympic Games. 36 U.S.C. Section 371, et seq. The USOC also has the responsibility for the oversight of U.S. participation in such competitions as the Pan American Games and the ParaOlympics. The USOC oversees the activities of the various national governing bodies (NGBs) of each of the individual sports sanctioned by the International Olympic Committee. (*See* www.USOC.org. and **Chapter 16**, *infra.*)

Chapter 1

LEGAL RELATIONSHIPS IN AMATEUR SPORTS

A. ATHLETES' RIGHTS

1. Rights Arising From the Athletic Scholarship

Athletic scholarships are awarded to both men and women at the collegiate level in a wide variety of sports. All of the major collegiate regulatory bodies, the NCAA, National Association of Intercollegiate Athletics (NAIA), and the National Junior College Athletic Association (NJCAA) regulate the details of the scholarship process, including the number of scholarships available and the terms of the scholarships. For example, the NCAA Division I full scholarship includes a maximum of tuition, fees, room and board, and books. There are also academic requirements that must be met before the student-athlete qualifies for a scholarship. The materials below explore the legal relationships arising from the athletic scholarship.

PROBLEM

Barney Moore is a student-athlete at Southern State University. He plays basketball for the school and is just finishing his freshman year at the school. When he was in high school he was highly recruited, with most of the prominent basketball schools offering him a full scholarship. The schools were all impressed with his abilities as a point guard and his general leadership qualities. All made extensive promises to him concerning his role at their school. Southern State was no different. The assistant coaches who visited with Barney and his parents all stated that if he came to Southern State he not only would play for four years, but he would start for four years at point guard. The coaches actually went further with assurances that he would be groomed for stardom in the National Basketball Association. They noted several other Southern State players, point guards to be exact, who had gone on to fame and fortune in the NBA. In addition, they promised extensive tutoring and other assistance with his educational experience.

Barney Moore was convinced by the sales talk of the Southern State coaches and was truly excited about going to school there. It was therefore quite shocking to him when the head coach abruptly resigned one week after Barney signed his letter of intent to go to SSU. Under the NCAA system he was bound to SSU by the letter of intent and could not go to another school without sitting out a season. The new coaching staff came on board near the end of the spring and all during the summer prior to the beginning of Moore's freshman year were on the telephone and in his home assuring him that everything the prior coaching staff had promised would happen. Barney, however, asked for release from the letter of intent so he could go to another school. The coaches refused to release him and his only options were to stay or transfer and lose a year of eligibility. Reluctantly he decided to honor his end of the scholarship agreement and arrived on time for the beginning of classes.

Once informal workouts and then regular practice began, it became clear to Moore that there was another point guard, a junior college transfer brought in late in the summer, that was catching the eyes of the coaching staff. Once the season began, the other player was the starter, and during the season Moore averaged 8 minutes of playing time per game and only scored 2 points per game. He was extremely disappointed and depressed about the situation. He decided to transfer.

Upon discussing this with the coaches he was told that they really wanted to "red shirt" him the following year and groom him for the starting role the year after, when the current starter would be gone. He did not want to sit out and lose more ground. Even though transferring would require him to sit out also, it would at least be in a better environment. In the end he did transfer to Northern State University.

He has now come to see you about the possibility of legal action against SSU for damages suffered as a result of the whole experience. What do you advise and why? The cases and materials below should be helpful in resolving the matter.

Case File

TAYLOR v. WAKE FOREST UNIVERSITY
191 S.E.2d 379 (N.C. Ct. App. 1972)

This action was instituted for the recovery of educational expenses incurred by George J. Taylor, father, and Gregg F. Taylor, son, after alleged wrongful termination of an athletic scholarship issued to Gregg F. Taylor by Wake Forest University.

As early as December 1965, football coaches at Wake Forest were in communication with Gregg Taylor soliciting his enrollment at Wake Forest. This interest was engendered by the football playing ability of Gregg Taylor. Not only was Wake Forest interested in him, but other colleges and universities were likewise showing an interest. As a result of this interest and negotiations, Gregg Taylor and his father, George Taylor, on 27 February 1967, submitted an application entitled, "Atlantic Coast Conference Application For A Football Grant-In-Aid Or A Scholarship."

This application was accepted by Wake Forest on 24 May 1967. It provided in part:

> "This Grant, if awarded, will be for 4 years provided I conduct myself in accordance with the rules of the Conference, the NCAA, and the Institution. I agree to maintain eligibility for intercollegiate athletics under both Conference and Institutional rules. Training rules for intercollegiate athletics are considered rules of the Institution, and I agree to abide by them.
>
> If injured while participating in athletics supervised by a member of the coaching staff, the Grant or Scholarship will be honored; and the medical expenses will be paid by the Athletic Department.
>
> * * *
>
> This grant, when approved, is awarded for academic and athletic achievement and is not to be interpreted as employment in any manner whatsoever."

At the time of the execution of the agreement between the Taylors and Wake Forest, some of the rules of the NCAA prohibited:

> "(a) Gradation or cancellation of institutional aid during the period of its award on the basis of a student-athlete's prowess or his contribution to a team's success.
>
> (b) Gradation or cancellation of institutional aid during the period of its award because of an injury which prevents the recipient from participating in athletics.
>
> (c) Gradation or cancellation of institutional aid during the period of its award for any other athletic reason, except that such aid may be gradated or canceled if the recipient (1) voluntarily renders himself ineligible for intercollegiate competition, or (2) fraudulently misrepresents any information on his application, letter of intent or tender, or (3) engages in serious misconduct warranting substantial disciplinary penalty.
>
> Any such gradation or cancellation of aid is permissible only if (1) such action is taken by the regular disciplinary and/or scholarship awards authorities of the institution, (2) the student has had an opportunity for a hearing, and (3) the action is based on institutional policy applicable to the general student body."

At the time the contract was entered into Wake Forest did not have a written Grant-ln Aid policy. This policy was not put in writing until January 1969. One of the written policy provisions was to the effect that financial aid could be terminated for "[r]efusal to attend practice sessions or scheduled work-outs that are a part of the athletic program or to act in such a manner as to disrupt these sessions." The Wake Forest Athletic Director set out in an affidavit:

> "[T]he policy of requiring student athletes to regularly attend practice sessions was in effect at the defendant university when the first scholarship was granted more than 30 years ago."

In compliance with the contract entered into, Gregg Taylor enrolled and became a student at Wake Forest at the beginning of the Fall Session 1967. He participated in the football program during the Fall of 1967.

At the end of that semester, his grade average was 1.0 out of a possible 4.0. Wake Forest required a 1.35 grade average after freshman year, a 1.65 grade average after sophomore year, and a 1.85 grade average after junior year. The 1.0 grade average received by Gregg Taylor for the first semester of his freshman year in the Fall of 1967 was thus below the grade average required by Wake Forest. Gregg Taylor notified the football coach on 6 February 1968 that he would not participate in regular practice sessions of the football team during the Spring of 1968 until his grades had improved. For the second semester of his freshman year, which was the Spring of 1968, Gregg Taylor obtained a 1.9 grade average. This brought his grade average above what Wake Forest required even after junior year. Despite this improvement in his grade average, Gregg Taylor decided that he would not further participate in the football program, and in the fall of his sophomore year, which was the Fall of 1968, Gregg Taylor attained a 2.4 grade average. Gregg Taylor continued in his refusal to participate in the football program.

Wake Forest notified Gregg Taylor on or about 1 May 1969 that a hearing would be held on 14 May 1969 before the Faculty Athletic Committee as to whether his scholarship should be terminated. At this hearing Gregg Taylor was notified that the Faculty Athletic Committee would recommend to the Scholarship Committee that his scholarship be terminated because of his failure to participate in the football program at Wake Forest. Thereafter, the Scholarship Committee of Wake Forest accepted the recommendation of the Faculty Athletic Committee, and on 10 July 1969, the Scholarship Committee notified Gregg Taylor that his scholarship had been terminated as of the end of the 1968-1969 academic year, which was the end of Gregg Taylor's sophomore year.

Gregg Taylor continued to attend Wake Forest during the 1969-1970 academic year, which was his junior year, and likewise, the academic year of 1970-1971, which was his senior year; and he received an undergraduate degree from Wake Forest in June 1971.

As a result of the termination of the scholarship, expenses in the amount of $5500 were incurred during those two academic years. It is for this sum of $5500 that his action was instituted.

The defendant Wake Forest moved for summary judgment pursuant to Rule 56 of the Rules of Civil Procedure on the ground that there was no genuine issue as to any material fact and that the defendant was entitled to judgment as a matter of law. This motion was allowed, and the plaintiffs appealed.

CAMPBELL, Judge.

* * *

Plaintiffs contend that there was a genuine issue as to a material fact and that a jury should determine whether Gregg Taylor acted reasonably and in good faith in refusing to participate in the football program at Wake Forest when such participation interfered with reasonable academic progress.

The plaintiff's position depends upon a construction of the contractual agreement between plaintiffs and Wake Forest. As stated in the affidavit of George J. Taylor, the position of the plaintiffs is that it was orally agreed between plaintiffs and the representative of Wake Forest that:

> "[I]n the event of any conflict between educational achievement and athletic involvement, participation in athletic activities could be limited or eliminated to the extent necessary to assure reasonable academic progress."

And plaintiffs were to be the judge as to what "reasonable academic progress" constituted.

We do not agree with the position taken by plaintiffs. The scholarship application filed by Gregg Taylor provided:

> ". . .I agree to maintain eligibility for intercollegiate athletics under both Conference and Institutional rules. Training rules for intercollegiate athletics are considered rules of the Institution, and I agree to abide by them."

Both Gregg Taylor and his father knew that the application was for "Football Grant-In-Aid Or A Scholarship," and that the scholarship was "awarded for academic and athletic achievement." It would be a strained construction of the contract that would enable the plaintiffs to determine the "reasonable academic progress" of Gregg Taylor. Gregg Taylor, in consideration of the scholarship award, agreed to maintain his athletic eligibility and this meant both physically and scholastically. As long as his grade average equaled or exceeded the requirements of Wake Forest, he was maintaining his scholastic eligibility for athletics. Participation in and attendance at practice were required to maintain his physical eligibility. When he refused to do so in the absence of any injury or excuse other than to devote more time to studies, he was not complying with his contractual obligations.

The record disclosed that Wake Forest fully complied with its agreement and that Gregg Taylor failed to do so. There was no "genuine issue as to any material fact" and summary judgment was proper.

ROSS v. CREIGHTON UNIVERSITY

957 F.2d 410 (7th Cir. 1992)

Before RIPPLE and KANNE, Circuit Judges, and ESCHBACH, Senior Circuit Judge.

RIPPLE, Circuit Judge.

Kevin Ross filed suit against Creighton University (Creighton or the University) for negligence and breach of contract arising from Creighton's alleged failure to educate him. The district court dismissed Mr. Ross' complaint for failure to state a claim. For the following reasons we affirm in part and reverse in part the judgment of the district court.

I

BACKGROUND

A. Facts

* * *

In the spring of 1978, Mr. Ross was a promising senior basketball player at Wyandotte High School in Kansas City, Kansas. Sometime during his senior year in high school, he accepted an athletic scholarship to attend Creighton and to play on its varsity basketball team.

Creighton is an academically superior university. Mr. Ross comes from an academically disadvantaged background. At the time of his enrollment at Creighton, Mr. Ross was at an academic level far below that of the average Creighton student. For example, he scored in the bottom fifth percentile of college-bound seniors taking the American College Test, while the average freshman admitted to Creighton with him scored in the upper twenty-seven percent. According to the complaint, Creighton realized Mr. Ross' academic limitations when it admitted him, and, to induce him to attend and play basketball, Creighton assured Mr. Ross that he would receive sufficient tutoring so that he "would receive a meaningful education while at Creighton." . . .

Mr. Ross attended Creighton from 1978 until 1982. During that time he maintained a D average and acquired 96 of the 128 credits needed to graduate. However, many of these credits were in courses such as Marksmanship and Theory of Basketball, and did not count towards a university degree. Mr. Ross alleges that he took these courses on the advice of Creighton's Athletic Department, and that the department also employed a secretary to read his assignments and prepare and type his papers. Mr. Ross also asserts that Creighton failed to provide him with sufficient and competent tutoring that it had promised.

When he left Creighton, Mr. Ross had the overall language skills of a fourth grader and the reading skills of a seventh grader. Consequently, Mr. Ross enrolled, at Creighton's expense, for a year of remedial education at the Westside Preparatory School in Chicago. At Westside, Mr. Ross attended classes with grade school children. He later entered Roosevelt University in Chicago, but was forced to withdraw because of a lack of funds. In July 1987, Mr. Ross suffered what he terms a "major depressive episode," during which he barricaded himself in a Chicago motel room and threw furniture out the window. . . . To Mr. Ross, this furniture "symbolized" Creighton employees who had wronged him. . . .

B. District Court Proceedings

Mr. Ross filed suit against Creighton in Cook County (Illinois) Circuit Court for negligence and breach of contract. Creighton, which is located in Omaha, Nebraska, removed the case to federal court on diversity grounds, pursuant to 28 U.S.C. §§ 1332 and 1441.

Mr. Ross' complaint advances three separate theories of how Creighton was negligent towards him. First, he contends that Creighton committed "educational malpractice" by not providing him with a meaningful education and preparing him for employment after college. Second, Mr. Ross claims that Creighton negligently inflicted emotional distress upon him by enrolling him in a stressful university environment for which he was not prepared, and then by failing to provide remedial programs that would have helped him survive there. Third, Mr. Ross urges the court to adopt a new cause of action for the tort of "negligent admission," which would allow recovery when an institution admits, and then does not adequately assist, a woefully unprepared student. The complaint also sets forth a contract claim, alleging that Creighton contracted to provide Mr. Ross "an opportunity . . . to obtain a meaningful college education and degree, and to do what was reasonably necessary . . . to enable [Mr. Ross] to obtain a meaningful college education and degree." . . . It goes on to assert that Creighton breached this contract by failing to provide Mr. Ross adequate tutoring; by not requiring Mr. Ross to attend tutoring sessions; by not allowing him to "red-shirt," that is, to forego a year of basketball, in order to work on academics; and by failing to afford Mr. Ross a reasonable opportunity to take advantage of tutoring services. Mr. Ross also alleges that Creighton breached a promise it had made to him to pay for a college education.

Creighton moved to dismiss the complaint under Federal Rule of Civil Procedure 12(b)(6), and the district court granted this motion. *Ross v. Creighton Univ.*, 740 F. Supp. 1319 (N.D. Ill. 1990). . . . With regard to the negligence claims, the court held that the first of Mr. Ross' negligence theories — educational malpractice — would not be allowed by the Illinois Supreme Court if it faced such a claim as a matter of first impression. *Id.* at 1329. Characterizing this theory as one "beloved of commentators, but not of courts," the court reasoned that the difficulties in determining causation and the duty owed, the intensely collaborative nature of education, and the possibility of a deluge of educational malpractice claims would compel Illinois to reject this cause of action. *Id.* at 1327-29. The court also held that a claim for negligent infliction of emotional distress exists in Illinois only if the plaintiff was physically harmed by the negligent act, within the "zone of danger" of physical harm, or the victim of a traditional tort such as medical malpractice. Since Mr. Ross' claim did not fit any of these categories, the court denied his claim on that theory. *Id.* at 1329-30. Finally, the court held that Illinois would refuse on policy grounds to permit Mr. Ross' newly fashioned claim for negligent admission to Creighton. The court reasoned that allowing this cause of action would unduly burden universities and also endanger the college prospects of many marginal students by requiring schools to factor into their admissions decisions the costs of tort damages resulting from a negligent admission. *Id.* at 1330.

With regard to the contract claims, the court recognized that the relationship between a student and a university is at least partly contractual. . . . However, the court concluded that a breach of contract action could be maintained only for the breach of a specific contractual promise that did not require the court to assess the general quality of the education. In the district court's view, none of Mr. Ross' allegations met these criteria. Consequently, the contractual counts were dismissed.

II

ANALYSIS

* * *

B. The Negligence Claims

[The court rejected the negligence claims of the plaintiff, based essentially on the principle that there are no adequate standards against which to measure such a claim.]

* * *

C. The Contract Claims

In counts two and three of his complaint, Mr. Ross alleges that Creighton breached an oral or a written contract that it had with him. When read as a totality, these allegations fairly allege that Creighton agreed, in exchange for Mr. Ross' promise to play on its basketball team, to allow him an opportunity to participate, in a meaningful way, in the academic program of the University despite his deficient academic background. The complaint further alleges, when read as a totality, that Creighton breached this contract and denied Mr. Ross any real opportunity to participate in and benefit from the University's academic program when it failed to perform five commitments made to Ross: (1) "to provide adequate and competent tutoring services," (2) "to require [Mr. Ross] to attend tutoring sessions," (3) to afford Mr. Ross "a reasonable opportunity to take full advantage of tutoring services," (4) to allow Mr. Ross to red-shirt, and (5) to provide funds to allow Mr. Ross to complete his college education.

It is held generally in the United States that the "basic legal relation between a student and a private university or college is contractual in nature. The catalogues, bulletins, circulars, and regulations of the institution made available to the matriculant become a part of the contract." *Zumbrun v. University of*

Southern California, 25 Cal. App. 3d 1, 101 Cal. Rptr. 499, 504 (1972) (collecting cases from numerous states). Indeed, there seems to be "no dissent" from this proposition. *Wickstrom v. North Idaho College*, 111 Idaho 450, 452, 725 P.2d 155, 157 (1986). . . . As the district court correctly noted, Illinois recognizes that the relationship between a student and an educational institution is, in some of its aspects, contractual. *See Steinberg v. Chicago Medical School*, 69 Ill. 2d 320, 13 Ill. Dec. 699, 371 N.E.2d 634 (1977) (agreement that medical school application would be evaluated according to the criteria described by the medical school in its literature); *DeMarco v. University of Health Sciences,* 40 Ill. App. 3d 474, 352 N.E.2d 356 (1976) (refusal to award M.D. degree for reasons unrelated to academic qualifications constitutes breach of contract). It is quite clear, however, that Illinois would not recognize all aspects of a university-student relationship as subject to remedy through a contract action. *DeMarco* makes the point quite clearly. "A contract between a private institution and a student confers duties upon both parties which cannot be arbitrarily disregarded and may be judicially enforced." *DeMarco*, 352 N.E.2d at 361–62. However, "a decision of the school authorities relating to the academic qualification of the students will not be reviewed. . . . [C]ourts are not qualified to pass an opinion as to the attainments of a student . . . and . . . courts will not review a decision of the school authorities relating to academic qualifications of the students." *Id.*

There is no question, we believe, that Illinois would adhere to the great weight of authority and bar any attempt to repackage an educational malpractice claim as a contract claim. As several courts have noted, the policy concerns that preclude a cause of action for educational malpractice apply with equal force to bar a breach of contract claim attacking the general quality of an education. . . . "Where the essence of the complaint is that the school breached its agreement by failing to provide an effective education, the court is again asked to evaluate the course of instruction . . . [and] is similarly called upon to review the soundness of the method of teaching that has been adopted by an educational institution." *Paladino v. Adelphi Univ.*, 89 A.D.2d 85, 454 N.Y.S.2d 868, 872 (1982).

To state a claim for breach of contract, the plaintiff must do more than simply allege that the education was not good enough. Instead, he must point to an identifiable contractual promise that the defendant failed to honor. Thus, as was suggested in *Paladino*, if the defendant took tuition money and then provided no education, or alternately, promised a set number of hours of instruction and then failed to deliver, a breach of contract action may be available. *Paladino*, 454 N.Y.S.2d at 873. . . . Similarly, a breach of contract action might exist if a student enrolled in a course explicitly promising instruction that would qualify him as a journeyman, but in which the fundamentals necessary to attain that skill were not even presented. *See Wickstrom*, 725 P.2d at 156-58. In these cases, the essence of the plaintiff's complaint would not be that the institution failed to perform adequately a promised educational service, but rather that it failed to perform that service at all. Ruling on this issue would not require an inquiry into the nuances of educational processes and theories, but rather an objective assessment of whether the institution made a good faith effort to perform on its promise.

We read Mr. Ross' complaint to allege more than a failure of the University to provide him with an education of a certain quality. Rather, he alleges that the University knew that he was not qualified academically to participate in its curriculum. Nevertheless, it made a specific promise that he would be able to participate in a meaningful way in that program because it would provide certain specific services to him. Finally, he alleges that the University breached its promise by reneging on its commitment to provide those services and, consequently, effectively cutting him off from any participation in and benefit from the University's academic program. To adjudicate such a claim, the court would not be required to determine whether Creighton had breached its contract with Mr. Ross by providing deficient academic services. Rather, its inquiry would be limited to whether the University had provided any real access to its academic curriculum at all.

Accordingly, we must disagree respectfully with our colleague in the district court as to whether the contract counts of the complaint can be dismissed at the pleadings stage. In our view, the allegations of the complaint are sufficient to warrant further proceedings. We emphasize, however, the narrow ground of our disagreement. We agree — indeed we emphasize — that courts should not "take on the job of supervising the relationship between colleges and student athletes or creating in effect a new relationship between them." *Ross,* 740 F. Supp. at 1332. We also recognize a formal university student contract is rarely employed and, consequently, "the general nature and terms of the agreement are usually implied, with specific terms to be found in the university bulletin and other publications; custom and usages can also become specific terms by implication." *Wickstrom*, 725 P.2d at 157 (quoting *Peretti*, 464 F. Supp. at 786).

Nevertheless, we believe that the district court can adjudicate Mr. Ross' specific and narrow claim that he was barred from any participation in and benefit from the University's academic program without second-guessing the professional judgment of the University faculty on academic matters.

Conclusion

Accordingly, the judgment of the district court is affirmed in part and reversed and remanded in part for proceedings consistent with this opinion

AFFIRMED in part, REVERSED in part and REMANDED.

NOTES AND COMMENTS

1. The NCAA defines an amateur student athlete as one who engages in a particular sport for the educational, physical, mental and social benefits derived therefrom and to whom participation in that sport is an avocation. The International Olympic Committee has in the past defined an amateur as one who participated in sports as an avocation and who did not receive remuneration for her efforts. In particular sports it was left to the international governing bodies to specifically define amateur. The need for such definitions appears to be dwindling, as most sports have opened their Olympic competitions to professionals.

The NCAA continues to tinker with issues relating to amateurism. The association still allows a student-athlete to make inquiry as to his value to a professional sports organization. If he has been drafted in baseball, he may even conduct negotiations, so long as an agent is not involved. But, if the professional sport requires the athlete to make an affirmative indication of his interest in being drafted, the student-athlete would lose his amateur status by so indicating. However, if the sport is basketball, it is acceptable to place one's name on the draft list without jeopardizing eligibility so long as the individual is not selected by a team in the draft and declares his or her intent to resume intercollegiate competition within 30 days of the draft. This declaration of intent must be submitted in writing to the athlete's director of athletics. Division I Manual, 12.2.4.2.1 (2005-06). A football player may also enter the NFL draft and retain his eligibility if he is not drafted and does not sign an agreement with an agent.

There are countless bizarre anecdotes concerning athletes and the rules on amateurism. Players have been suspended for receiving benefits from agents, as well as for appearing in promotional materials for charitable organizations. There have been issues with athletes who, prior to entering college, have had experience as professional models. In the spring of 2002, world-class free style skier Jeremy Bloom announced that he would accept an offer to attend the University of Colorado and play football for the school. Following an inquiry by Bloom and the university, the NCAA indicated that he would be eligible to play football only if he would agree to cancel his endorsement contracts with several equipment and apparel manufacturers. Freestyle skiing is not an NCAA sport. Bloom went to court seeking an injunction against the NCAA. The trial court denied the request for injunctive relief and Bloom elected to play football and at least temporarily forfeit several hundred thousand dollars in endorsements. In February 2003 Bloom filed an appeal with the Colorado Court of Appeals, which was not successful. [**For further discussion of the Bloom case, *see* Chapter 4, *infra*.**]

2. Problem. Billy Smith is a freshman in college at a midwest university which is a major sports power. He is a football player who was highly recruited by several schools during his senior year in high school. You are approached by Smith for legal advice concerning some activity which occurred during the recruitment process. During a recruiting visit in the fall he was at a local restaurant with a booster of the school. At some point in the meeting he was nudged under the table by the booster and given something which Smith stuck in his sock. He later discovered that it was $400 in cash. He knew immediately that this was the school he wanted to attend. Later he was given a sheet of paper detailing other things boosters intended to give him for playing for the school. The various payments, jobs, clothing and other gifts totaled nearly

$40,000 over the four years of his college career. At no time were any members of the athletic department staff involved in these transactions. Smith believes that nothing is wrong with these transactions since most involved a member of the school's board of trustees. Is he still an amateur? What steps will you take to deal with the matter?

3. *See Fortay v. University of Miami*, 1994 U.S. Dist. LEXIS 1865 (D.N.J. 1994), in which a football player brought an action claiming breach of contract due to promises allegedly made during the recruitment process which apparently never bore fruit. What advice should an athletic director give to her coaches regarding promises made during the recruitment process? What process should be utilized to train and educate coaches about such promises or commitments?

4. *See Jackson v. Drake University,* 778 F. Supp. 1490 (S.D. Iowa 1991). *Jackson* raises claims similar to those raised in *Ross.* The plaintiff was a recruited basketball player for Drake University and contended the university breached its contract with him and committed educational malpractice. Specifically, he asserted the school failed to provide the education and educational assistance promised during his recruitment, and instead of encouraging progress toward a degree, the coaching staff urged him to register for easy irrelevant classes that would allow him to remain eligible to play. As was the case in *Ross,* the court declined to recognize educational malpractice as a valid cause of action. Unlike *Ross,* there was no finding by the court of misrepresentation or breach of contract.

2. Workers' Compensation

This section explores the general issue of whether athletes are workers for workers' compensation purposes. In order to understand how injured athletes fit into various workers' compensation schemes, it is first necessary to understand how such schemes typically operate.

Every state has its own workers' compensation statute. These statutes all reflect a type of bargain struck between employers and employees. The gist of the bargain is that injured employees give up their rights to pursue common law tort claims (with the promise of full recovery but with the concomitant danger of no recovery) in exchange for a more certain, albeit limited, recovery under the workers' compensation act. The employer, in turn, relinquishes common law defenses to tort actions (like contributory negligence and assumption of risk) but enjoys the assurance that damage awards will be limited. Typically, the scheme is funded by insurance paid by the employer into a fund administered by a specialized agency empowered to process claims. In deference to this common sense political bargain, most courts tend to liberally construe workers' compensation schemes to bring as many workers as reasonably possible under the law's umbrella, and to defer to the judgment of the specialized agency.

Generally, a workers' compensation law makes the employer strictly liable for an injury to an employee that occurs in the course of employment. Eligibility for benefits is based upon the employer-employee relationship. An employee is defined as a person in the service of another under a contract of hire, written or implied. The threshold inquiry is whether the injured worker fits the state's definition of an employee. A recurring question that arises is whether a particular worker is an employee (and thus covered) or an independent contractor (who would fall outside the coverage of the act).

Each state has developed its own tests for making this determination in cases where the worker-employer relationship is not entirely clear. The tests adopted appear to fall into two basic categories — the "nature of the work" test and the "right to control" test.

Under the "nature of the work" test, the court focuses upon whether the worker's efforts are inextricably linked to a significant aspect of the employer's business.

Under the "right of control" test, the focus is upon the employer's ability to manipulate the efforts of the worker. A greater understanding of the tests used can be better achieved in the context of a particular case arising in a specific jurisdiction. Obviously, it is important to be familiar with the law of the applicable jurisdiction.

Assuming that the injured worker is regarded as an employee, the next question is whether the personal injury "arose out of" or was "in the course of" the employment. These phrases have been the focus of more than a considerable amount of litigation. As a general rule, the courts tend to look for a causal connection between the injury and the employment. The test of causation is met if it is the employment which brings the worker into the orbit of the risk that in fact resulted in the injury.

The basic elements of recovery under most acts include medical expenses and lost earnings. Medical expenses are compensable if reasonably incurred. In regard to lost earnings (and impaired earning capacity), the basis for the amount of available benefits turns on the employee's average weekly wage just prior to the injury. Incapacity to work is classified as temporarily total, temporarily partial, permanently partial, or permanently total. Benefits are paid as a percentage of the average weekly wage. The percentage varies from state to state, and is often accompanied by a statewide cap on both periodic payments and the overall amount payable. The acts also provide for additional benefits for injuries which result in specific consequences, like the loss of the use of a limb, or the loss of sight. Benefits are payable to dependents in cases of worker death. While workers' compensation laws are generally premised on some common grounds, it must be kept in mind that each state's scheme has its own nuances. Workers' compensation law is very much a matter of well developed, particularized and vibrant state law.

The athletic scholarship is fundamental to the modern American amateur sports milieu. The athlete's acceptance of the athletic scholarship creates a legal relationship between the athlete and the educational institution that grants the award. In a series of cases, scholarship athletes have sought to recover for their injuries under workers' compensation laws. The important issue in such litigation is whether scholarship athletes are employees of the educational institution which provides them with the scholarship. The problem that follows explores this and related issues.

PROBLEM

The senior partner in your law firm has asked for your assistance in evaluating a case. The preliminary investigation has been completed and the partner has asked you to help her decide whether the firm should pursue the claim. In preparing for your meeting with the partner, you can assume that the Oklanois Workers' Compensation Statute is identical in every respect to the Michigan Statute referred to in *Coleman*, reproduced below, but that the Oklanois Courts have not yet ruled on the athlete as worker issue. Feel free to engage in a free-wheeling, open discussion with the partner at the meeting. As of this time, no action has been taken on the case.

The case involves the workers' compensation claim of Tommy Monday. The facts are not in dispute. Mr. Monday is a 22-year-old senior at Oklanois State University who suffered a catastrophic injury last month while competing in a wrestling match for the university. At the time of the injury, Monday was on full scholarship, which included full tuition, room and board, and books. As part of his scholarship, he also received $100 per month expense money, consistent with NCAA rules in regard to permissible scholarship assistance. The injury occurred during a home match with wrestling rival Iowa State University. Mr. Monday suffered a broken neck, which crushed his spinal cord, while attempting a difficult and dangerous "bridging" maneuver. Monday is now paralyzed from the neck down, and doctors give him no objective hope for recovery.

Wrestling is a revenue-producing sport at Oklanois State University. In fact, over 6,000 fans paid to attend the so-called "Bedlam" match against Iowa State University. The match was televised regionally and Oklanois State University receives $10,000 for the television rights to the annual "Bedlam" competition. Many wrestling fans believed the number 1 national rating hinged on the outcome of this match.

WALDREP v. TEXAS EMPLOYERS INSURANCE ASSOCIATION

21 S.W.3d 692 (Tex. App. 2000)

LEE YEAKEL.

Appellant Alvis Kent Waldrep, Jr. was awarded workers' compensation benefits by the Texas Workers' Compensation Commission (the "Commission") for an injury he sustained while playing football for Texas Christian University ("TCU"). Appellee Texas Employers Insurance Association, in receivership, Texas Property and Casualty Insurance Guaranty Association appealed the award to the district court. Following a trial *de novo*, a jury found that Waldrep had failed to prove that he was an employee of TCU at the time of his injury. The district court rendered judgment that Waldrep take nothing against TEIA. Waldrep appeals the judgment, claiming that (1) he was an employee as a matter of law and (2) the district court erred in admitting and excluding certain evidence at trial. We will affirm the district court's judgment.

BACKGROUND

Waldrep graduated from high school in Alvin, Texas in 1972. During his junior and senior years, TCU was among many schools interested in recruiting Waldrep, a young man known for his athletic ability as well as his good academic record. Tommy Runnels, a TCU assistant football coach, visited Waldrep frequently at his home and school, attempting to interest Waldrep in TCU's football and academic programs. During one home visit, Waldrep's mother asked Runnels what would happen if Waldrep were injured during his football career at TCU. Runnels assured Waldrep and his family that TCU would "take care of them" and emphasized that Waldrep would keep his scholarship even if he were injured and could not play football.

Waldrep was very impressed with the facilities at TCU and believed that his abilities would fit in well with TCU's football program. He was also aware that recruitment and his future involvement in athletics at TCU were governed by the rules of the Southwest Athletic Conference ("Southwest Conference") and the National Collegiate Athletic Association ("NCAA"). To affirm his intent to attend school at TCU and participate in TCU's football program, Waldrep signed two documents. First, Waldrep signed a pre-enrollment form ("Letter of Intent"),[4] which demonstrated his formal desire to play football for TCU

---

[4] The Letter of Intent provided in pertinent part:

> This is to express my desire to participate in the athletic program at Texas Christian University and to certify my intention to enroll at that institution on August, 1972. My decision is subject to acceptance by this institution, the fulfillment of its admission requirements and scholastic requirement for athletic awards.
>
> . . .Regulations and Procedures for Pre-Enrollment Applications.
>
> Financial aid is awarded by Southwest Conference members on the basis of a student-athlete's desire to participate in the athletic program of the institution making the award.

and penalized him if he decided to enter a different school within the Southwest Conference. Waldrep later signed a financial aid agreement ("Financial Aid Agreement"), ensuring that Waldrep's room, board, and tuition would be paid while attending TCU and that Waldrep would receive ten dollars per month for incidentals. This cash payment was generally referred to as "laundry money." Both documents were contingent on Waldrep's meeting TCU's admission and scholastic requirements for athletic awards.

In August 1972, Waldrep enrolled at TCU. In October 1974, while playing football for TCU against the University of Alabama, Waldrep was critically injured. He sustained a severe injury to his spinal cord and was paralyzed below the neck. Today, Waldrep has no sensation below his upper chest. In 1991, Waldrep filed a workers' compensation claim for his injury. The Commission entered an award in his favor. TEIA appealed this decision to the district court. In a trial *de novo*, a jury found that Waldrep was not an employee of TCU at the time of his injury. The district court rendered judgment in favor of TEIA. On appeal, Waldrep presents five issues. The first addresses whether, as a matter of law, Waldrep was an employee of TCU The final four challenge various evidentiary rulings made by the district court.

DISCUSSION

Status as an Employee for Workers' Compensation Purposes

By his first issue, Waldrep asserts that at the time of his injury he was an employee of TCU *as a matter of law*. We begin by noting that Waldrep is attacking the legal sufficiency of an adverse answer to a jury question on which he had the burden of proof. After hearing all of the evidence, the jury declined to find that Waldrep was an employee of TCU at the time of his injury. . . .

We are confronted with a situation novel to Texas jurisprudence: whether, for workers' compensation law purposes, a recipient of a scholarship or financial aid from a university becomes that university's employee by agreeing in return to participate in a university-sponsored program. Cases decided under the various workers' compensation statutes in effect from time to time have almost uniformly determined the existence of an employer-employee relationship by an analysis of whether the claimant of workers' compensation benefits was an *employee* as distinguished from an *independent contractor*. . . . These authorities do not conveniently overlay the facts presented here, as there is no allegation that Waldrep was an independent contractor. Yet they are instructive in one significant aspect: one may receive a benefit from another in return for services and not become an employee.

The jury charge defined "employee" as "a person in the service of another under a contract of hire, express or implied, oral or written, whereby the employer

---

> By the signing of the Letter of Intent, the student-athlete pledges that he will participate to the best of his ability in the athletic program of the signing institution.

Southwest Athletic Conference, *Pre-Enrollment Application* (1972).

has the right to direct the means or details of the work and not merely the result to be accomplished." Thus, in failing to find that Waldrep was TCU's employee, the jury may have believed that there was no contract of hire between Waldrep and TCU or, if there was, it did not give TCU the right to direct the means or details of Waldrep's "work." We will examine both possibilities.

Existence of Contract of Hire

For the purpose of workers' compensation law, the employer-employee relationship may be created *only* by a contract. Waldrep strongly urges that the Letter of Intent and Financial Aid Agreement are express contracts of hire that set forth the terms of Waldrep's "employment." However, we do not find these documents to be so clear. At best, they only partially set forth the relationship between Waldrep and TCU. By their terms, they generally bound Waldrep to TCU to the exclusion of other Southwest Conference schools, if he intended to participate in athletics, and extended him financial aid so long as he complied with the admission and scholastic requirements of TCU and the rules and regulations of both TCU and the Southwest Conference. These requirements, rules, and regulations are not specifically described in either of the agreements. Nor does the record in this case set them forth in any detail. The Letter of Intent and Financial Aid Agreement are also silent with regard to whether any rules or regulations of the NCAA would apply to Waldrep or affect his relationship with TCU. Yet it is undisputed that before Waldrep signed the Letter of Intent and Financial Aid Agreement, both he and TCU understood that his recruitment and future football career at TCU would be governed by and subject to the rules of the NCAA.

TEIA, on the other hand, posits that Waldrep clearly and simply did not have a contract of hire. TEIA directs us to *Travelers Insurance Co. v. Brown*, 395 S.W.2d 701 (Tex. Civ. App. — Texarkana 1965, writ ref'd n.r.e.), and *Carnes v. Transport Insurance Co.*, 615 S.W.2d 909 (Tex. Civ. App. — El Paso 1981, writ ref'd n.r.e.), to support its proposition. However, both involve the intervention of a third party and are therefore distinguishable from the case before us. In *Brown*, Louis contracted with Smith to clean the interior walls of a building. Louis then hired Brown to actually do the work. The court of civil appeals held that Brown was not Smith's employee because there was no evidence "of an intention on Smith's part to empower Louis to employ workmen for Smith." *Brown*, 395 S.W.2d at 702. In *Carnes*, Carnes was held not to be an employee of Thrasher while driving a truck leased by Courtney to Thrasher when there was no evidence that Thrasher would pay Carnes, either directly or through Courtney, for Carnes's operation of the vehicle. *See Carnes*, 615 S.W.2d at 912. Neither case, when applied to the facts of Waldrep's relationship with TCU, leads inexorably to the conclusion that there was no contract of hire.

Mindful of the district court's definition of employee, the jury was left to determine if there was a "contract of hire" between Waldrep and TCU. We observe that "the most basic policy of contract law . . . is the protection of the justified expectations of the parties." . . . Was it the expectation of Waldrep and

TCU that Waldrep would become TCU's employee? To form a contract, the parties must mutually assent to its terms. Whether there is such assent is determined "based on objective standards of what the parties said and did and not on their alleged subjective states of mind." . . . Because the Letter of Intent and Financial Aid Agreement do not evidence the entire agreement between Waldrep and TCU, we consider them against "the background of circumstances surrounding [their] execution." . . . We may also look to the parties' conduct after execution of the documents, and such conduct "may be a strong factor in determining just what the real agreement contemplated." [Citation omitted.]

On the facts of this record, any contract of hire must have been a contract whereby TCU hired Waldrep to attend the university, remain in good standing academically, and play football. However, if Waldrep played football for pay, he would have been a professional, not an amateur.

The evidence reflects that the actions of both Waldrep and TCU were consistent with a joint intention that Waldrep be considered an amateur and not a professional. It is undisputed that before Waldrep signed the Letter of Intent and Financial Aid Agreement, both he and TCU understood that his recruitment and future football career at TCU would be governed by and subject to the rules of the NCAA. The record indicates that the NCAA's policies and rules in effect at that time exhibited a concerted effort to ensure that each school governed by these rules made certain that student-athletes were not employees. Indeed, the rules declared that the fundamental policy of the NCAA was "to maintain intercollegiate athletics as an integral part of the educational program and the athlete as an integral part of the student body, and, by so doing, retain a clear line of demarcation between college athletics and professional sports." *NCAA Manual* at 5. Following its policy, the evidence reflects that the NCAA rules made the principle of amateurism foremost and established several requirements to ensure that the student-athlete would not be considered a professional. *See NCAA Manual* at 6. For example, the NCAA had strict rules against student-athletes taking pay for participation in sports, and student-athletes were ineligible to participate if they were receiving or had received a salary from a professional sports organization. *See NCAA Manual* at 5-6.

Additionally, the record reflects that Waldrep and TCU did not treat the financial aid Waldrep received as "pay" or "income." First, as previously noted, the NCAA rules provided that student-athletes would be ineligible if they used their skill for pay in any form; however, that same rule goes on to state that "a student-athlete may accept scholarships or educational grants-in-aid from his institution" as these benefits do not conflict with the NCAA rules. *Id.* As the NCAA rules were based upon a principle of amateurism and strictly prohibited payment for play, these two provisions together indicate that the NCAA and its participating institutions did not consider the acceptance of financial aid from the institution to be "taking pay." Moreover, the rules provided that any financial aid that exceeded tuition and fees, room and board, required course-related supplies and books, and incidental expenses of fifteen dollars per month would be considered "pay" for participation in intercollegiate athletics. *See NCAA Manual* at 8. TCU gave Waldrep financial aid for these items but nothing more, indicating that TCU did not intend to pay Waldrep for his participation. Of equal significance, TCU never placed Waldrep on its payroll, never paid him a salary, and never told him that he would be paid a salary. There is no evidence that Waldrep expected a salary. No social security or income tax was withheld from Waldrep's grant-in-aid. *See Continental Ins. Co. v. Wolford*, 526 S.W.2d 539, 540 (Tex. 1975) (withholding taxes is *indicia* of employee status). Waldrep never filed a tax return reporting his financial aid. *See Anchor Cas. Co. v. Hartsfield*, 390 S.W.2d 469, 470 (Tex. 1965); *Mayo v. Southern Farm Bureau Cas. Ins. Co.*, 688 S.W.2d 241, 243 (Tex. App. — Amarillo 1985, writ ref'd n.r.e.).[12, 13]

The evidence further reflects that Waldrep and TCU intended that Waldrep participate at TCU as a *student*, not as an *employee*. During the recruitment process, TCU never told Waldrep that he would be an employee, and Waldrep never told TCU that he considered himself to be employed. Moreover, a basic purpose of the NCAA, which governed Waldrep's intercollegiate football career, was to make the student-athlete an integral part of the student body. *See NCAA Manual* at 5. According to the NCAA rules, "an amateur student-athlete is one who engages in athletics for the education, physical, mental and social benefits he derives therefrom, and to whom athletics is an avocation." *NCAA Manual* at 6. Of importance is the evidence that Waldrep was aware when he signed the Letter of Intent and Financial Aid Agreement that he would still receive financial aid even if hurt or unable to play football, as long as he complied with the

12 Waldrep requested the district court to take judicial notice "that at all times relevant to this case . . . athletics scholarships were excluded from taxable income and were not required to be reported to the Internal Revenue Service" and directed the court to section 117 of the Internal Revenue Code. The court responded, "I will take notice of it. I think it's something that at least I ought to consider. And if you all want to have some kind of stipulation read or instruction to the jury, that's fine with me." The record discloses no stipulation or instruction. The Internal Revenue Code provision in effect at the time Waldrep attended TCU provided, *inter alia*: "In the case of an individual, gross income does not include . . . any amount received . . . as a scholarship at an educational institution . . . or . . . as a fellowship grant, including the value of contributed services and accommodations. . . ." Internal Revenue Code of 1954, ch. 736, 68A Stat. 38 (codified as amended at I.R.C. § 117(a) (West Supp. 1999)). This provision does not eliminate how Waldrep and TCU treated Waldrep's grant-in-aid for tax purposes as an *indicia* of employment.

Whether a scholarship or fellowship is includable in the recipient's taxable income is based on the particular circumstances of the grant. *See, e.g., Hembree v. U.S.*, 464 F.2d 1262, 1264 (4th Cir. 1972) ("primary purpose of the payment made to the taxpayer" is controlling); *Burstein v. U.S.*, 224 Ct. Cl. 1, 622 F.2d 529, 537 (Ct. Cl. 1980) ("A purpose of section 117 is to avoid the exclusion of money received as compensation for services but labeled as a 'scholarship' or 'fellowship.'"); *Quast v. U.S.*, 293 F. Supp. 56, 59 (D. Minn. 1968) ("The character of the payments . . . is determined fundamentally by the usual test of the parties' intent. The question is did the parties intend a scholarship or a fellowship, or in the alternative a salary.").

13 *Mayo* sets forth several factors relevant in establishing employment: (1) the right to hire and discharge the worker, (2) the carrying of the worker on social security and income tax withholding records, (3) the providing of equipment, (4) the responsibility to pay wages, and (5) the right to control the specifics of a worker's performance. *See Mayo v. Southern Farm Bureau Cas. Ins. Co.*, 688 S.W.2d 241, 243 (Tex. App. — Amarillo 1985, writ ref'd n.r.e.).

rules of the Southwest Conference. Thus, TCU could not "fire" Waldrep as it could an employee. *See Mayo*, 688 S.W.2d at 243. In addition, when Waldrep signed the agreements, he still had to meet the scholastic requirements for athletic awards and qualify for admission to TCU in order to enroll and participate in the football program. Waldrep testified that he knew when he signed the agreements that in order to play football at TCU he would have to maintain certain academic requirements as a student. Thus, his academic responsibilities dictated whether he could continue to play football.

Financial-aid awards are given to many college and university students based on their abilities in various areas, including music, academics, art, and athletics. Sometimes these students are required to participate in certain programs or activities in return for this aid. But, as the Supreme Court of Indiana observed, "scholarship recipients are considered to be students seeking advanced educational opportunities and are not considered to be professional athletes, musicians or artists employed by the university for their skill in their respective areas." *Rensing v. Indiana State Univ. Bd. of Trustees*, 444 N.E.2d 1170, 1174 (Ind. 1983).

Although the record in this case contains facts from which the jury could have found that Waldrep and TCU were parties to a contract of hire, there is also probative evidence to the contrary. Viewing the evidence in the light most favorable to the jury's verdict, we hold that the record before us reflects more than a mere scintilla of evidence that Waldrep was not in the service of TCU under a contract of hire.

Right to Direct the Means or Details of Waldrep's Work

If, however, we assume the jury found that a contract existed between Waldrep and TCU, we must determine whether there is some evidence concerning TCU's right to direct the means or details of Waldrep's "work." The definition of "employee" submitted to the jury correctly states the recognized test to determine whether an employer-employee relationship exists: the *right* of the employer to direct or control the means or details of the employee's work. *See Mayo*, 688 S.W.2d at 243 (ultimate test in deciding employment question is right of alleged employer to control specifics of worker's performance) (citing *Hartsfield*, 390 S.W.2d at 471). To determine whether there is a right of control, "we first must look to the terms of the employment contract." *Allstate Ins. Co. v. Scott*, 511 S.W.2d 412, 414 (Tex. Civ. App. — El Paso 1974, writ ref'd n.r.e.). Where there is no express contract or where the terms of the contract are indefinite, the *exercise* of control "may be the best evidence available to show the actual terms of the contract." *Newspapers, Inc. v. Love*, 380 S.W.2d 582, 590 (Tex. 1964); *see Scott*, 511 S.W.2d at 414. However, "'the *right* to control' remains the supreme test and the 'exercise of control' necessarily presupposes a right to control which must be related to some agreement expressed or implied." *Love*, 380 S.W.2d at 590 (emphasis added); *see Scott*, 511 S.W.2d at 414 ("the exercise of control, while evidentiary only and not the true test, is the best evidence available in determining the right of control").

The record reflects that TCU *exercised* direction and control over all of the athletes in its football program, including non-scholarship players, while they were participating in the *football program*. Waldrep admitted that his high school coaches exercised the same type of control over his participation in sports as the coaches at TCU. Waldrep further testified that he did everything that the coaches told him to do because he wanted to, because he loved the game, and because he wanted to be the best, not because he had to. The evidence is clear that TCU did not have the right to direct or control all of Waldrep's activities during his tenure at the school. The NCAA rules protected Waldrep's financial-aid award even if his physical condition prevented him from playing football for any reason. *See NCAA Manual* at 8. Moreover, TCU could not simply cancel Waldrep's grant-in-aid based on his "athletic ability or his contribution to [the] team's success," or even, in certain circumstances, if he quit. *Id.*

The fact that the athletic department at TCU established practice and meeting times to be observed by those playing football does not establish that TCU had the *right* to direct and control all aspects of the players' activities while enrolled in the university. *See Hartford Accident & Indem. Co. v. Hooten*, 531 S.W.2d 365, 368 (Tex. Civ. App. — San Antonio 1975, writ ref'd n.r.e.) (fact that hospital established regulations and rules to be observed by private-duty nurses is no evidence of existence of employer-employee relationship). Waldrep's acceptance of financial aid from TCU did not subject him to any extraordinary degree of control over his academic activities.

Waldrep clearly presented evidence that TCU *exercised* direction or control over some of his activities while a student at the university. Perhaps the jury might have found this sufficient to prove that TCU had the *right* to direct the means or details of Waldrep's activities, but the jury declined to do so. Viewing the evidence in the light most favorable to the jury's verdict, we hold that the record before us reflects more than a mere scintilla of evidence disputing TCU's right of control.

On appeal, Waldrep bears a heavy burden in seeking reversal and rendition based on an adverse finding to a jury issue on which he had the burden of proof. The record before us reflects evidence both for and against the jury's finding. The district court properly left the jury to determine the issue of employment. The circumstances presented in the record before us do not establish an employer-employee relationship as a matter of law. We hold that there is some evidence to support the jury's verdict declining to find that Waldrep was an employee of TCU at the time of his injury. Waldrep has failed to satisfy *Sterner's* first prong. *See Sterner, 767 S.W.2d at 690.* Therefore, we overrule Waldrep's first issue.

[The court then ruled adverse to Waldrep on several evidentiary issues.]

CONCLUSION

In conclusion, we note that we are aware college athletics has changed dramatically over the years since Waldrep's injury. Our decision today is based on facts and circumstances as they existed almost twenty-six years ago. We express no opinion as to whether our decision would be the same in an analogous situation arising today; therefore, our opinion should not be read too broadly. Having disposed of all of the issues before us, we affirm the district court's judgment.

NOTES AND COMMENTS

1. Have we allowed for a catastrophically injured student-athlete to "fall through the cracks" by not providing some type of assured compensation for the injury? Should universities be required to carry long-term medical and disability insurance for injured athletes? This is a solution suggested by *Workers' Compensation and College Athletics: Should Universities Be Responsible for Athletes Who Incur Serious Injuries?,* 10 J.C. & U.L. 197 (1983-1984).

2. Scholarship athletes as university employees? The litmus test of whether a college athlete should be considered an employee for workers' compensation purposes is the existence of a quid pro quo arrangement. When competent evidence shows that the student's performance of athletic services is given as consideration for financial aid, the courts should recognize the student's status as a student-employee.

An objective appraisal of the relevant cases reveals the better reasoned approach: the ordinary athletic scholarship does indeed create an employer-employee relationship.

For a variety of unarticulated reasons — foremost among them the fear of uncharted waters — it is not surprising that the courts have tended to refuse to hold that the amateur athletes are really employees. It is an uncomfortable and unsettling realization that our scholarship athletes are really employees, but it is a conclusion that an honest appraisal compels. And it is a conclusion from which a number of beneficial consequences will undoubtedly flow, contributing to the reform of a system much in need of constructive change.

a. One immediate consequence of course is that athletes in Monday's position will be compensated for athletic injuries. As things stand now, athletes such as Monday on our college campuses can only recover for injuries suffered by either pursuing tort remedies or counting on the largesse of the university community. The tort remedy will often be unavailable because of the absence of negligence. The availability of voluntary assistance is haphazard. The workers' compensation model is the obvious mechanism for granting relief. Some kind of insurance fund for injured athletes must be provided.

b. If scholarship athletes really are university employees, they are not "amateurs" as that term is commonly defined. To a certain extent this means that big-time college sports will be openly professionalized. In the eyes of many who have studied the current system, this would be a healthy development. The American Council on Education, for example, issued an internal report following a study of the American amateur sports system. The Council is a research group representing some 1,400 colleges and universities. The Council, after noting the "corruption" that is rampant in major college football and basketball programs, suggested that a solution is for the major college football and basketball powers to shed the facade of amateurism, pay athletes over the table, and not even require them to be students. The report stated that the situation was beyond the control of the National Collegiate Athletic Association. College presidents, according to the report, faced three options: (1) a return to amateurism (this option, however, was regarded as "not really viable" because of economic pressures and demands from alumni and other supporters for winning teams); (2) continuing the present situation (the council noted that continuing the status quo meant drifting toward professionalism and an increased credibility gap between the pretenses of the student-athlete model and the realities of money, corruption, and professionalism); or (3) an open move to professionalism (this entails a situation in which blue-chip athletes would be paid a market wage rather than an artificially constrained amount with all the attendant pressures for under-the-table payments).

The Council favored the third option, which in turn would create an environment in which true amateurism could be reborn. Schools that do not desire professional teams could opt for a genuine amateur model and build organizations capable of being administered in a principled manner.

Which option do you regard as most desirable? Why? What are the likely consequences of openly professionalizing big time college football and basketball? How would professional intercollegiate sports differ from the existing "amateur" model? Is this a desirable change?

3. Can athletic scholarships be distinguished from other kinds of scholarships based upon special skills? Richard (Digger) Phelps, former basketball coach at the University of Notre Dame, asked: "Does that mean if a chemistry student is on scholarship and the lab blows up, he or she is eligible for workman's compensation?" NAT'L L.J., Monday, July 5, 1982, page 6. How do you respond to Digger?

4. Problem. You have been asked to testify before an Oklanois State legislative committee which is considering legislation to amend the state's workers' compensation law to include scholarship athletes within the definition of employee. Be prepared to deliver your remarks and to participate in the discussion at the legislative hearing. Feel free to assume the role of a state legislator (either in favor of or against the legislation), a faculty representative to the NCAA from Oklanois State University (who has been instructed by the President of O.S.U. to oppose the legislation), a trial lawyer, a coach, an administrator, or an injured athlete.

5. Disability or Sports Accident Insurance. Educational institutions typically are insured for claims against the university. The NCAA Catastrophic Injury Insurance Program also covers student-athletes who are catastrophically injured while participating in a covered intercollegiate athletic activity. The NCAA pays the entire premium for the policy, which has a $10,000 death benefit and a maximum benefit of $20 million with a $50,000 deductible. This program, however, typically covers players with very serious injuries and not the many other types of injuries that occur as a result of competitive play. Should student-athletes be required to carry insurance? Some states, such as California, require that students have insurance if they want to play interscholastic athletics.

6. For more detailed discussion of the treatment of student-athletes within the university, *see* Christopher W. Haden, *Chalk Talk: Foul! The Exploitation of the Student-Athletes: Student-Athletes Deserve Compensation for Their Play in the College Athletic Arena*, 30 J.L & EDUC. 673 (2001); Jason Gurdus, Note, *Protection Off of thePlaying Field: Student Athletes Should Be Considered University Employees for Purposes of Workers' Compensation,* 29 HOFSTRA L. REV. 907 (2001); Michelle D. McGirt, Comment, *Do Universities Have a Special Duty of Care to Protect Student-Athletes From Injury?*, 6 VILL. SPORTS & ENT. L.J. 219 (1999).

B. COACHING AND INSTITUTIONAL CONTRACTS

1. Coaching Contracts

PROBLEM

You represent Harry Jones, a basketball coach. Harry is 42 years old and has been a head coach at both the collegiate and professional levels for 12 years. Included in this experience are two collegiate positions which he held for three years each, and two professional positions. Most recently, he has been the coach of an NBA team. He has held this position for two years. Harry has been offered the head coaching job for the University of Oklanois, a Division I school which formerly was a basketball power. The president of the university would like for the school to be a force in basketball once again and sees Jones as the key to this. Jones has produced winners in each job he has held. You are to draft a proposal for a contract to be presented to the president.

Obviously the contract must be constructed so as to maximize the benefits and protections most important to Jones. You should also anticipate the university's concerns.

Case File

RODGERS v. GEORGIA TECH ATHLETIC ASSOCIATION

303 S.E.2d 467 (Ga. Ct. App. 1983)

Pope, Judge.

Franklin C. "Pepper" Rodgers brought this breach of contract action against the Georgia Tech Athletic Association to recover the value of certain perquisites which had been made available to him as the head coach of football at the Georgia Institute of Technology. . . . The issue presented for resolution by this appeal is whether Rodgers is entitled to recover the value of certain perquisites or "fringe benefits" of his position as head coach of football under the terms of his contract of employment with the Association.

Rodgers was removed from his coaching position by vote of the Association's Board of Trustees on December 18, 1979, notwithstanding a written contract of employment through December 31, 1981. In addition to an annual salary, the contract provided that Rodgers, as an employee of the Association, would be entitled "to various insurance and pension benefits and perquisites" as he became eligible therefor. Rodgers makes no claim for base salary, health insurance and pension plan benefits, all of which were provided voluntarily by the Association through December 31, 1981, the expiration date of the contract. Rather, his claim is solely for the value of the aforesaid "perquisites," to which he claims entitlement under this employment contract.

Rodgers lists some 29 separate items as such perquisites. In support of his motion for summary judgment, Rodgers categorized these items into two groups: A. Items provided directly to him by the Association but discontinued when Rodgers was relieved of his duties, and B. Items provided by sources other than the Association by virtue of his position as head coach of football. These items are listed in the Appendix to this opinion.

The subject contract was in the form of a letter from the Association dated April 20, 1977 offering Rodgers the position of head coach of football for three years at an annual salary plus certain benefits and perquisites. This contract provided that Rodgers could be terminated for illness or other incapacity continuing for three months, death, or "any conduct or activity involving moral turpitude or which in the opinion of [the Board of Trustees] would constitute an embarrassment to the school." Rodgers accepted this contract on April 25, 1977. This contract was extended until January 1, 1982 by a subsequent letter agreement between the parties. At its December 18, 1979 meeting, the Association's Board of Trustees determined that a change should be made in the position of head coach of football. The following statement was approved and released to the press: "The Board of Trustees of the Georgia Tech Athletic Association met at its regular December meeting this morning. After full discussion, the Board determined that in the best interest of Georgia Tech, with full respect for Coach

Pepper Rodgers, a change should be made in the position of Head Coach of Football. The Board stated that it would, of course, honor the financial contractual obligation to Coach Rodgers and that Doug Weaver, the Athletic Director, had been directed to immediately pursue the obtaining of a new head coach."

1. Rodgers asserts essentially two theories of recovery: (a) breach of contract, and (b) appropriation of a "property right."

[The court summarily disposed of the second theory and proceeded to resolve the breach of contract issue.] . . .

2. Rodgers contends that he was terminated or fired from his employment by the Association.

However, the evidence of record supports the Association's view that Rodgers was merely relieved of his duties as the head coach of football yet remained an employee of the Association, albeit without any function or duties, for the duration of his contract. In either event, this disassociation of Rodgers from his position and duties was not "for cause" pursuant to the terms of the contract. Therefore, the Association was obligated to pay Rodgers that part of the amount set forth in the contract "which he himself was entitled to receive as compensation for his services." *Southern Cotton Oil Co. v. Yarborough,* 26 Ga. App. 766, 770, 107 S.E. 366 (1921); *see also Dinnan v. Totis,* 159 Ga. App. 352(1), 283 S.E.2d 321 (1981).

In addition to a salary, health insurance and pension benefits, the contract provided that Rodgers, as an employee of the Association, was entitled to "perquisites" as he became eligible therefor. The term "perquisites" is defined as "[e]moluments or incidental profits attaching to an office or official position, beyond the salary or regular fees." BLACK'S LAW DICTIONARY 1299 (4th ed. 1968). The term is also defined as "a privilege, gain, or profit incidental to an employment in addition to regular salary or wages; esp. one expected or promised [e.g.,] the [perquisites] of the college president include a home and car. . . ." WEBSTER'S THIRD NEW INTERNATIONAL DICTIONARY 1685 (1981). Thus, Rodgers was entitled to the perquisites (or their value) for which he was eligible during the duration of his contract. The problem presented here for resolution is to determine whether any of the items listed in the Appendix were indeed perquisites to which Rodgers was entitled pursuant to his contract.

First, we must determine the intention of the parties as to the scope of the perquisites to which Rodgers was entitled under the contract. . . . The pertinent language of the contract provides: "You, as Head Coach of Football, will devote your time, attention, skill, and efforts to the performance of your duties as Head Coach under the policies established by the Athletic Board and the Athletic Director, and you will receive compensation at [an] annual rate of $35,175.00 payable in equal monthly installments. In addition, as an employee of the Association, you will be entitled to various . . . perquisites as you become eligible therefor." The Association contends that the language "as an employee of the Association" limited Rodgers' eligibility for perquisites to those items common to all Association employees. Rodgers argues that he was not only entitled to those perquisites common to all Association employees, but that he was also entitled to additional perquisites for which he became eligible as the head coach of football. Since the contract is susceptible to either construction, it is ambiguous. This ambiguity may be resolved by applying the appropriate rules of construction.

"If a contract is so framed as to be susceptible of two constructions, that interpretation which is least favorable to the author . . . should generally be accepted. . . . 'When it is possible to do so without contravening any rule of law, the courts will construe a contract as binding on both the parties, where, from the language of the contract, the conduct of the parties, and all the attendant circumstances, it appears that the intention of the parties was that both should be bound [thereby], and substantial justice requires that the contract be given effect.'" [Citations ommitted.] *Bridges v. Home Guano Co.*, 33 Ga. App. 305, 309, 125 S.E. 872 (1924). . . . The subject contract was drafted by the Association. Moreover, the record discloses that Rodgers, during his tenure as head coach of football, did receive perquisites in addition to those received by other Association employees. Accordingly, we conclude that the parties intended that Rodgers would receive perquisites, as he became eligible therefor, based upon his position as head coach of football and not merely as an employee of the Association.

We must next determine the nature of the items for which Rodgers seeks damages, *i.e.*, whether the items listed in the Appendix are perquisites vel non. We will first address ourselves to those items listed in Section A of the Appendix and address separately those items listed in Section B.

(a) The Association asserts that Rodgers was not entitled to any of the items listed in Section A because they were expense account items — "tools" to enable him to more effectively execute his duties as head coach of football. Rodgers counters that those items were an integral part of the total compensation package that he received as head coach of football and constituted consideration for his contract of employment. We certainly agree with the Association that Rodgers would be entitled to recover only "compensatory damages that he suffered by reason of the breach of his contract; in other words, that the proper measure of damages arising from the breach of the contract of employment was actual loss sustained by the breach, and not the gross amount of [his] wages and expenses [under the contract]." [Citations omitted.] However, the evidence offered as to the nature of the items in Section A was in considerable dispute. The fact that these items were not reported as taxable income by Rodgers is not conclusive as to their nature . . . nor is the fact that Rodgers reimbursed the Association for occasional "personal" expenses which it had paid. Thus, with three exceptions, we cannot say as a matter of law either that Rodgers was entitled to the items listed in Section A as perquisites of his employment, or that he was not.

The three exceptions to this finding are the services of a secretary, the services of an administrative assistant, and the cost of trips to football conventions, clinics, etc. The undisputed purpose of the services of the secretary and administrative assistant was to assist Rodgers in fulfilling his duties under the contract. Since Rodgers had been relieved of his duties as head coach of football, and, thus, had no responsibilities under the contract, he had no need for these support services. This is true even though the secretary and administrative assistant may have occasionally provided personal services to Rodgers beyond their duties to him as head coach of football since, as Rodgers admits, their primary functions were to provide services to the head coach of football. Also, since Rodgers had been relieved of his coaching duties, the Association was not obligated to pay his expenses for trips to various football related activities, these costs clearly being business-related and not in the nature of compensation.

(b) We turn our attention finally to those items in Section B of the Appendix — items which Rodgers asserts were perquisites he received from sources other than the Association by virtue of his position as head coach of football at Georgia Tech. The Association argues that Rodgers' claim for recovery of these items was in the nature of a tort claim for humiliation and injury to feelings. Rodgers counters that these items were perquisites within the contemplation of the parties which constituted part of the consideration for the contract even though they were provided by sources other than the Association.

. . . [W]e must now determine whether Rodgers may recover the items in Section B under his breach of contract theory.

"[T]he consideration of a contract need not flow directly from the promis[or] [here, the Association], but may be the promise or undertaking of one or more third persons." . . . "Damages growing out of a breach of contract, in order to form the basis of a recovery, must be such as can be traced solely to the breach, must be capable of exact computation, must have arisen naturally and according to the usual course of things from such breach, and must be such as the parties contemplated as a probable result of the breach." *Sanford-Brown Co. v. Patent Scaffolding Co.*, 199 Ga. 41, 33 S.E.2d 422 (1945). "As a general rule, a party is entitled to recover profits that would have resulted from a breach of a contract into which he has entered, where the breach is the result of the other party's fault. And while a breach of the original contract will not ordinarily entitle a plaintiff to recover as damages the profits of collateral enterprises or subcontracts, yet where the knowledge of the subcontract [or collateral enterprise] is within the contemplation of the parties when the original contract is made, and is known to have been made with reference thereto, anticipated profits shown to be certain, fixed in amount, and the direct fruit of the contract, are recoverable. Profits are excluded only when there are no criteria, definite and certain, upon which an adjudication can be based. They then become speculative and imaginary." *Carolina Portland Cement Co. v. Columbia Improvement Co.*, 3 Ga. App. 483(2), 60 S.E. 279 (1908).

We will apply the foregoing legal principles to the facts of record. Can Rodgers' loss of the items in Section B be traced solely to the Association's breach of the contract? Rodgers testified that he received these perquisites as a result of his being head coach of football at Georgia Tech. The record discloses, however, that the items relating to housing and the cost of premiums on a life insurance policy were discontinued several years prior to the Association's breach of contract and were, in fact, not related to the breach. Thus, these items were properly excluded by the trial court. The remaining items were discontinued as the direct result of Rodgers being relieved of his duties as head coach of football.

Are the remaining items in Section B capable of exact computation? A "gift" is defined as "[a] voluntary transfer of personal property without consideration." BLACK'S LAW DICTIONARY 817 (4th ed. 1968). A gift, then, being a voluntary transaction and without consideration, can not form an enforceable part of the consideration of a contract. Although Rodgers may have received gifts of money and personalty during his tenure as head coach of football, such voluntary contributions to his financial well-being are totally incapable of exact computation, for a gift made in one year is no assurance of a similar gift in the next. In fact, Rodgers concedes that he did not receive these gifts each year. Thus, the item which listed various financial gifts was properly excluded from recovery. The items now remaining are sufficiently capable of computation. *See generally Hoffman v. Louis L. Battey Post etc. Am. Legion*, 74 Ga. App. 403, 410-11, 39 S.E.2d 889 (1946).

Did these remaining items arise naturally and according to the usual course of things, and were they such as the parties contemplated as a probable result of a breach? There is no evidence of record showing that the Association had any knowledge of Rodgers' free lodging at certain Holiday Inns or of his membership in Terminus International Tennis Club. Thus, the loss of these items could not be such as was contemplated as a probable result of a breach of the contract. The evidence was in dispute as to the remaining items — profits from his television and radio shows and from his summer football camp plus the loss of use of a new automobile and tickets to professional sporting events — *i.e.,* whether such items were contemplated by the parties at the time the contract was executed as perquisites or fringe benefits to which Rodgers would be entitled as the result of his position as head coach of football at Georgia Tech. These items are of the type commonly provided to head coaches at major colleges and universities. There was some evidence that the Association knew that Rodgers would receive (and, in fact, did receive) these benefits as the result of his head coaching position and that his removal from that position would result in the loss of these benefits. In fact, some members of the Association assisted Rodgers in obtaining many of these items. Also, there was at least some evidence by which the amount of these items could be fixed. Therefore, summary judgment in favor of the Association as to these items was inappropriate. . . . For these same reasons, summary judgment in favor of Rodgers was properly denied.

In summary, a question of fact remains as to whether Rodgers is entitled to recover those items listed in Section A of the Appendix not excluded in this opinion and also those items in Section B not heretofore excluded, any recovery being subject to proof of the amount of his damages as set forth in this opinion. All items which have been excluded are denoted by asterisks in the Appendix.

Judgment affirmed in part; reversed in part.

DEEN, P.J., and SOGNIER, J., concur.

APPENDIX

A. Benefits and Perquisites Received by Rodgers Directly from the Georgia Tech Athletic Association.

(1) gas, oil, maintenance, repairs, other auto mobile expenses;

(2) automobile liability and collision insurance;

(3) general expense money;

(4) meals available at the Georgia Tech training table;

(5) eight season tickets to Georgia Tech home football games during all of 1980 and 1981;

(6) two reserved booths, consisting of approximately 40 seats at Georgia Tech home football games during fall of 1980 and 1981;

(7) six season tickets to Georgia Tech home basketball games for 1980 and 1981;

(8) four season tickets to Atlanta Falcon home football games for 1980 and 1981;

(9) four game tickets to each out-of-town Georgia Tech football game during fall of 1980 and 1981;

(10) pocket money at each home football game during fall of 1980 and 1981;

(11) pocket money at each out-of-town Georgia Tech football game during fall of 1980 and 1981;

(12) parking privileges at all Georgia Tech home sporting events;

*(13) the services of a secretary;

*(14) the services of an administrative assistant;

(15) the cost of admission to Georgia Tech home baseball games during spring of 1980 and 1981;

*(16) the cost of trips to football coaches' conventions, clinics, and meetings and to observe football practice sessions of professional and college football teams;

(17) initiation fee, dues, monthly bills, and cost of membership at the Capital City Club;

(18) initiation fee, dues, monthly bills, and cost of membership at the Cherokee Country Club;

(19) initiation fee and dues at the East Lake Country Club.

B. Benefits and Perquisites Received by Rodgers from Sources Other Than the Georgia Tech Athletic Association by Virtue of Being Head Coach of Football.

(1) profits from Rodgers' television football show, "The Pepper Rodgers Show," on Station WSB-TV in Atlanta for the fall of 1980 and 1981;

(2) profits from Rodgers' radio football show on Station WGST in Atlanta for the fall of 1980 and 1981;

(3) use of a new Cadillac automobile during 1980 and 1981;

(4) profits from Rodgers' summer football camp, known as the "Pepper Rodgers Football School," for June, 1980 and June, 1981;

*(5) financial gifts from alumni and supporters of Georgia Tech for 1980 and 1981;

*(6) lodging at any of the Holiday Inns owned by Topeka Inn Management, Inc. of Topeka, Kansas, for the time period from December 18, 1979 through December 31, 1981;

*(7) the cost of membership in Terminus International Tennis Club in Atlanta for 1980 and 1981;

(8) individual game tickets to Hawk basketball and Braves baseball games during 1980 and 1981 seasons;

*(9) housing for Rodgers and his family in Atlanta for the period from December 18, 1979 through December 31, 1981;

(10) the cost of premiums of a $400,000.00 policy on the life of Rodgers for the time period from December 18, 1979 through December 31, 1981.

O'BRIEN v. THE OHIO STATE UNIVERSITY

2006 Ohio Misc. LEXIS 52 (Ct. of Claims 2006)

Opinion By: Joseph T. Clark

FACTS

On April 12, 1997, plaintiff was hired by defendant as the head coach of the men's basketball team. Plaintiff had worked as a basketball coach for more than 20 years prior to his taking the position. Defendant is a member of the National Collegiate Athletic Association (NCAA), a voluntary association governing the conduct of intercollegiate athletic programs of member institutions.

* * *

On May 14, 1998, Alex Radojevic, a 21-year-old basketball player from Yugoslavia, arrived on the campus of The Ohio State University for an unofficial visit. . . . By all accounts, Radojevic was a prized recruit, a "difference maker."

In early September . . . Radojevic received word that his father had passed away. According to plaintiff, Radojevic was distraught by the news of his father's death and he had expressed concern for his mother who was living in a war-torn region of Yugoslavia. Radojevic was unable to offer her any financial assistance and he could not return home for fear of being forced into military service.

In late September or early October plaintiff learned that in 1996 Radojevic had signed a contract to play professional basketball for a Yugoslavian team and had received some of the compensation due him under the contract. Although Radojevic played only sparingly with the team, plaintiff learned that the team had tendered additional payments which Radojevic reportedly refused to accept. Plaintiff testified that based upon this information he concluded that Radojevic was a professional basketball player and that he was not eligible to play college basketball.

Although plaintiff and his staff were aware of the professional contract, they continued to recruit Radojevic. On November 11, 1998, Radojevic signed a document known as a National Letter of Intent (NLI) which is utilized by NCAA member institutions to establish the commitment of a prospect to attend a particular institution.

On December 13, 1998, Radojevic arrived in Columbus for his "official visit." Radojevic's student-sponsor for the visit was Slobodan Savovic, a player on the men's basketball team who also hailed from Yugoslavia. The visit lasted two days during which time Radojevic attended a basketball game and some other events. The activities and the expenses associated with the visit were documented by defendant in accordance with NCAA rules.

At some time in mid-to-late December 1998, plaintiff was asked to provide financial assistance to the Radojevic family. While the details surrounding the request are sketchy, it appears that the request originated from a man by the name of Spomenko Patrovic, a Yugoslavian national who worked as a waiter in New York City and who claimed to be either Radojevic's relative or his legal guardian. Plaintiff testified that in late December 1998 or early January 1999 he removed $6,000 in cash from a drawer in his office desk and placed it in an unmarked envelope. He gave the envelope to then assistant coach, Paul Biancardi, with instructions to deliver the envelope to Patrovic in New York City. Patrovic was to have the money delivered to the Radojevic family in Yugoslavia.

Plaintiff has characterized the transaction as a loan. He has acknowledged, however, that there was no written loan agreement and that the terms for repayment were not discussed. Plaintiff maintains that it was Radojevic's dire family circumstances and not his interest in Radojevic as a potential college player that prompted him to provide the loan. He testified that he was certain that the loan did not violate NCAA rules because Radojevic had surrendered his amateur status in 1996. Plaintiff was also certain that there was no NCAA prohibition against lending money to the family of a professional basketball player.

In February 1999, an NCAA student-athlete reinstatement representative notified defendant that Radojevic had signed a professional basketball contract in 1996. When Ferdinand "Andy" Geiger, defendant's athletic director, approached plaintiff and the coaching staff with this information he was assured that the circumstances surrounding the 1996 contract were such that Radojevic could regain his amateur status by applying to the NCAA for reinstatement. Defendant immediately declared Radojevic ineligible for competition in accordance with an NCAA directive and on March 24, 1999, defendant filed an application for his reinstatement. The application was denied and on May 24, 1999, the NCAA subcommittee denied the appeal from that decision.

Radojevic never enrolled as a student-athlete at defendant's institution and he never played basketball for defendant's team. He entered the 1999 NBA draft and was selected by the Toronto Raptors as the 12th pick in the first round.

Approximately three months later, on September 15, 1999, plaintiff signed an NCAA Certificate of Compliance certifying that during the 1998-1999 academic year he had "reported through the appropriate individuals * * * any knowledge of violations of NCAA legislation involving [the] institution."

In March 1999, defendant's men's basketball team completed one of its most successful seasons in recent memory. The team had won 27 games, a Big Ten conference title, and had advanced to the Final Four in the NCAA tournament. Plaintiff won several post-season awards for his coaching, including national coach-of-the-year honors.

On the heels of this great success, Andy Geiger felt so enthusiastic about the basketball program and its head coach that he initiated discussions with plaintiff regarding a new contract. . . . The new agreement took effect September 12, 1999. Everyone involved in the negotiation process agreed that the terms of plaintiff's new contract were much more favorable to plaintiff than those contained in his prior agreement. For example, under the new agreement plaintiff received an eight-year extension through the 2007 season and a substantial increase in compensation. The contract also contained financial incentives based upon team performance, coaching honors, and graduation rates. The new agreement also placed significant limitations upon defendant's right to terminate plaintiff's employment.

On April 24, 2004, defendant held its annual spring football game at Ohio Stadium. Geiger had asked plaintiff to attend the game so that he could address a gathering of alumni. Just prior to the time that Geiger was to make his remarks, plaintiff pulled him aside and informed him about the financial assistance he had provided to the Radojevic family in 1998. He told Geiger that he had provided the assistance because of the serious financial hardships facing Radojevic's family and that his motives were purely humanitarian. Plaintiff explained that the transaction would likely be revealed to the public in a lawsuit that had been filed by a woman named Kathy Salyers. Plaintiff wanted Geiger to hear about the loan from him personally rather than from the press.

On cross-examination at trial, Geiger acknowledged that during this conversation he told plaintiff "we will try to work through this together." Geiger also testified that he believed that plaintiff's motivation for making the loan was purely humanitarian and that he had referred to the loan as a "noble act." Geiger claimed that plaintiff admitted that the loan was made in violation of NCAA rules. Both plaintiff and Geiger have testified that the conversation was brief, lasting no more than five minutes. However, plaintiff strongly disagreed with Geiger's assertion that he had admitted violating NCAA rules.

Some time in May 2004, Vanatta obtained transcripts of deposition testimony filed in the Saylers' lawsuit and reviewed the testimony with Geiger. It was at that time that Geiger learned of Saylers' allegation that she had provided improper benefits to Slobodan Savovic throughout his playing career. After returning to Columbus, Ohio, Geiger summoned plaintiff to meet with him and Vanatta on May 26, 2004. During a five or ten minute meeting, Geiger told plaintiff that the loan had been reported to the NCAA and that there was going to be an investigation. Geiger also suggested that plaintiff hire an attorney. Plaintiff contacted Geiger on the following day and asked him if he was going to be fired. According to plaintiff, Geiger told him he was not going to be fired. Plaintiff testified that he apologized to Geiger for putting him in an "awkward position" and offered to talk about resigning his coaching position if the university felt that public knowledge of the loan would harm the basketball program. Plaintiff, however, refused to discuss the allegations regarding Slobodan Savovic.

At approximately 7:30 a.m. on June 8, 2004, plaintiff was summoned to Geiger's office for a meeting. At 8:30 a.m., Geiger handed plaintiff a letter notifying him of defendant's intention to terminate his employment as head coach of the men's basketball team and informing him that his dismissal would be announced at a news conference that afternoon. Plaintiff was given an option to resign his employment in lieu of termination.

Later that morning, plaintiff's counsel contacted Geiger's office seeking more time for plaintiff to consider his options and for an opportunity to discuss the issue. Geiger declined to speak with plaintiff's counsel and plaintiff refused to resign. At an afternoon press conference Geiger announced plaintiff's dismissal, effective immediately.

On May 13, 2005, more than 11 months after plaintiff's dismissal, defendant received a "Notice of Allegations" from the NCAA. The notice contained enumerated allegations against the men's basketball program, the women's basketball program, and the men's football program. Six of the violations involved Slobodan Savovic and three concerned the loan to the Radojevic family.

ANALYSIS

Plaintiff brought this action against defendant alleging a single claim for breach of contract. In order to recover for breach of contract, plaintiff must prove the following elements: existence of a contract, performance by the plaintiff, breach by the defendant, and damages or loss as the result of the breach.

Existence and Performance of Contract

There is no dispute in this case that the relationship between the parties is governed by plaintiff's 1999 employment contract. * * * [The court found that there was substantial performance by the plaintiff.]

Breach of Contract

Defendant notified plaintiff of its intention to terminate his employment and cited the contractual provisions upon which defendant relied in Geiger's letter of June 8, 2004. That letter reads in pertinent part as follows:

> "Dear Jim:
>
> "As you know, you informed me on April 24, 2004, that you had paid approximately six thousand dollars ($6,000) to Radojevic, a men's basketball prospective student-athlete. You admitted that you gave him this money sometime after Mr. Radojevic signed his National Letter of Intent to attend The Ohio State University (November 11, 1998), but before May 24, 1999, the date that Mr. Radojevic's request for reinstatement to the NCAA was denied by the NCAA's Subcommittee on Student-Athlete Reinstatement. Although you explained that you gave him the money to assist him with his family's dire financial situation in light of the Serbian war, that reason, however noble, does not excuse your action.
>
> "In our discussion on April 24, 2004, you admitted that you knew your action was a violation of NCAA rules, and you are correct. In particular, it is a recruiting inducement in violation of NCAA Bylaw 13.2.1. Despite the fact that the University was no longer actively recruiting Mr. Radojevic after he signed his National Letter of Intent, he is considered a 'prospect' according to NCAA rules until he officially registers and enrolls in a minimum full-time program of studies and attends classes for autumn quarter. Furthermore, for each of the past five years, you violated NCAA Bylaw 30.3.5 which, by your signature on the annual NCAA Certification of Compliance form, requires you to confirm that you have self-reported your knowledge of any NCAA violations. We

have self-reported this matter and other allegations related to the program to the NCAA.

"Section 4.1(d) of your employment agreement requires you to 'know, recognize and comply' with all applicable rules and regulations of the NCAA and to 'immediately report to the Director [of Athletics] and to the Department of Athletics Compliance Office' if you have 'reasonable cause to believe that any person * * * has violated * * * such laws, policies, rules or regulations.' You have materially breached this important term of your contract.

"Unfortunately, your admitted wrongdoings leave the University no choice. Pursuant to Section 5.1(a) of your employment agreement, we intend to terminate such agreement *for cause,* effective at 5:00 p.m. today, June 8, 2004. Rather than being terminated *for cause,* you may choose to terminate your employment agreement (including your Letter of Agreement regarding supplemental compensation for appearing on radio and television programs, and for summer basketball camps and miscellaneous bonuses and benefits) and resign from your position as head men's basketball coach provided that you agree to continue to cooperate fully with the University and the NCAA in our investigation of issues related to the men's basketball program. Under either scenario, the University has no obligation to provide compensation or benefits (other than the availability of continued health benefits) to you past the effective date of such termination or resignation.

"I deeply regret that we have come to this circumstance. After we have celebrated so much success together, this is very hard."

* * *

The letter clearly identifies the contractual provisions upon which defendant relies in exercising its right of termination. Specifically, defendant claims that plaintiff breached Section 4.1 which provides in relevant part:

"4.1 In consideration of the compensation specified in this agreement, Coach shall:

* * *

"(d) Know, recognize and comply with all applicable laws, policies, rules and regulations of Ohio State, the Big 10 Conference and the NCAA; supervise and take appropriate steps to ensure that Coach's assistant coaches, any other employees for whom Coach is administratively responsible and the members of the Team know, recognize and comply with all such laws, policies, rules and regulations; and *immediately report to the Director and to the Department of Athletics Compliance Office if Coach has reasonable cause to believe that any person or entity, including without limitation, representatives of Ohio State's athletic interests, has violated or is likely to violate any such laws, policies, rules or regulations.* Coach shall cooperate fully with the Department's Compliance Office at all times." (Emphasis added.)

Upon review of the language used by the parties in Section 4.1(d), the court finds that plaintiff could breach his duties thereunder if either he fails to comply with NCAA rules *or* he has reasonable cause to believe that an NCAA violation has occurred and that he fails to immediately report it to the director. As written, Section 4.1(d) could be breached by plaintiff without the actual commission of an infraction so long as plaintiff had reasonable grounds to believe that an infraction had or was likely to occur.

NCAA Rules

There is no question in this case that plaintiff failed to immediately report the loan to either defendant's director or its Department of Athletics Compliance. In fact, plaintiff told no one about the loan for almost five years. Thus, at the outset the court must determine whether plaintiff had reasonable cause to believe that he had violated an NCAA rule when he loaned money to the Radojevic family.

* * *

In the June 8, 2004, letter, defendant identified NCAA Bylaw 13.2.1 as the primary violation. That Bylaw provides in pertinent part:

> "13.2.1 General Regulation. An institution's staff member or any representative of its athletics interests shall not be involved, directly or indirectly, in making arrangements for or giving, or offering to give any financial aid or other benefits to the prospect or the prospect's relatives or friends, other than expressly permitted by NCAA regulations."

* * *

Plaintiff's position is that the loan to the Radojevic family did not violate Bylaw 13.2.1 because Alex Radojevic was a professional athlete at the time the loan was made. Plaintiff testified:

* * *

> [Both parties presented expert testimony concerning the interpretation of the applicable NCAA Rules and whether the actions of the plaintiff would constitute a violation of the rules.]

* * *

Ultimately, the determination whether plaintiff committed a major infraction of NCAA rules and what sanctions, if any, may be imposed upon defendant will be made by the NCAA Committee on Infractions and not this court. As of the date of publication of this decision, the NCAA has yet to decide the issue. In this case, in order to determine that plaintiff breached Section 4.1(d) of the employment agreement, the court need only find that plaintiff had reasonable cause to believe that he committed an infraction when he made the loan to the Radojevic family. The circumstances surrounding plaintiff's decision to make the loan combined with plaintiff's subsequent words and conduct convince the court that plaintiff had reasonable cause to believe that he had committed an infraction.

Plaintiff testified that he found out about the professional contract in September 1998 and that he was certain at that time that Radojevic was not eligible to play college basketball. Yet Radojevic signed an NLI and he was brought in for an official visit. Professor Swank [the plaintiff's expert] was unable to think of any reason why Radojevic would be offered an NLI and invited to make an official visit to the school if plaintiff were convinced that Radojevic was ineligible to play.

Plaintiff also chose not to seek the guidance of his own compliance office prior to making the loan even though he was aware that the compliance office was available to answer his inquiries with reasoned responses. Similar services were available to plaintiff at the Big Ten conference level and from the NCAA itself. The court finds that plaintiff ignored these resources not because he was certain that the loan complied with NCAA rules but because the Radojevic family desperately needed his help and because he believed that giving help was the right thing to do.

After making the loan to the Radojevic family in December, plaintiff and his coaching staff assured Geiger that reinstatement was possible and actively participated in the reinstatement process. The testimony of Geiger and Heather Lyke Catalano, defendant's chief compliance officer, was that plaintiff was genuinely upset and frustrated with the NCAA when he learned that the appeal had been denied.

Plaintiff's words and conduct are not those of a person who was sure that Radojevic would never play college basketball. Indeed, plaintiff acknowledged on cross-examination that if Radojevic had been reinstated, he would not have been eligible to play because of the loan plaintiff made to his family. Plaintiff testified that he would have had to reveal the loan if reinstatement had been granted.

In consideration of all of the evidence presented, the court finds that in December 1998 plaintiff had reasonable grounds to believe that he had violated NCAA Recruiting Bylaw 13.02.1 by making a loan to the family of Alex Radojevic. Plaintiff's conduct in making the loan and then failing to report it to the director was a breach of Section 4.1(d) of the contract.

Materiality and Termination for Cause

As stated above, plaintiff's 1999 employment contract placed significant limitations upon defendant's right to terminate plaintiff's employment. For example, defendant was obligated to pay plaintiff a substantial portion of his remaining salary if plaintiff were terminated other than for cause. Conversely, if plaintiff were terminated for cause, defendant would be under no obligation to pay plaintiff any further compensation. Furthermore, it is clear from the plain language of the agreement that not every failure of performance by plaintiff provides cause for termination. The specific language of the contract at issue is Section 5.1 which states:

> "5.1 Terminations for Cause — Ohio State may terminate this agreement at any time for *cause,* which, for the purpose of this agreement, shall be limited to the occurrence of one or more of the following:
>
> > "(a) a material breach of this agreement by Coach, which Coach fails to remedy to OSU's reasonable satisfaction, within a reasonable time period, not to exceed thirty (30) days, after receipt of a written notice from Ohio State specifying the act(s), conduct or omission(s) constituting such breach;
> >
> > "(b) a violation by Coach (or a violation by a men's basketball program staff member about which Coach knew or should have known and did not report to appropriate Ohio State personnel) of applicable law, policy, rule or regulation of the NCAA or the Big Ten Conference which leads to a 'major' infraction investigation by the NCAA or the Big Ten Conference and which results in a finding by the NCAA or the Big Ten Conference of lack of institutional control over the men's basketball program or which results in Ohio State being sanctioned by the NCAA or the Big Ten Conference. . . .
> >
> > * * *
> >
> > "(c) any criminal conduct by Coach that constitutes moral turpitude or other improper conduct that, in Ohio State's reasonable judgment, reflects adversely on Ohio State or its athletic programs."

Defendant does not contend that plaintiff's termination for cause can be justified either by Section 5.1(b) or 5.1(c). The notice of termination references only Section 5.1(a). Thus, in deciding whether plaintiff's employment was terminated for cause, the court need only consider whether plaintiff's breach was "material".

Under common law, "a 'material breach' is a failure to do something that is so fundamental to a contract that the failure to perform that obligation defeats the essential purpose of the contract or makes it impossible for the other party to perform under the contract." . . . Defendant contends that plaintiff's conduct in violating NCAA rules and thereafter failing to immediately report the violation constitutes a "material breach" of the employment agreement and provides defendant with sufficient cause to terminate plaintiff's employment pursuant to paragraph 5.1(a).

* * *

Section 4.1(d)

. . . [I]n view of the language used in Section 4.1(d) of the contract it is clear that defendant reasonably expected plaintiff to refrain from violating NCAA rules, to monitor assistant coaches and players to assure their compliance with those rules, to exercise a reasonable degree of vigilance to uncover any violations, and to immediately report any suspected violations.

The specific conduct allegedly constituting plaintiff's breach of contract was described by Julie Vanatta as follows:

> "A. And it's the University's belief that everything in conjunction with the payment to Alex Radojevic and the reinstatement appeal of Alex Radojevic is a violation of 4.1(d)."

Defendant argues that plaintiff's breach of Section 4.1(d) deprived it of the benefit it reasonably expected from the employment agreement in three ways: subjecting defendant to NCAA sanctions; adversely affecting defendant's reputation in the community; and breaching the trust between plaintiff and defendant's athletic director.

Sanctions

In assessing the potential harm to defendant in the form of NCAA sanctions, the court is mindful that the NCAA notice of allegations lists a total of seven violations in the men's basketball program; six of those allegations involve a player other than Alex Radojevic. Thus, the extent of the harm to defendant in the form of NCAA sanctions that can be fairly attributed to the Radojevic matter is difficult to predict.

Moreover, a defense based upon the four-year limitation period is clearly available to defendant with respect to the Radojevic matter. The court finds that even though defendant has elected not to avail itself of this defense in proceedings before the NCAA, the availability of this defense is a mitigating factor in determining the extent that defendant is or will be deprived of the expected benefit of Section 4.1(d).

Finally, the NCAA has not sought any sanctions arising from plaintiff's execution of allegedly false NCAA compliance certificates and the evidence shows that the NCAA rarely penalizes member institutions for such violations.

With respect to self-imposed sanctions, Heather Lyke Catalano testified that member institutions, such as defendant, frequently self-impose penalties in advance of the NCAA findings in an effort to demonstrate good faith. The hope is that the NCAA will ultimately conclude that the self-imposed sanctions are sufficient and that no further penalty will be imposed.

In September 2004, defendant self-imposed sanctions in response to the NCAA allegations. Those sanctions included the forfeiture of two scholarships in the 2005 recruiting class and a post-season ban for the 2004-2005 season. There was no testimony in this case whether those sanctions were imposed solely as a result of the Radojevic matter. However, even if the court were to assume that all of the sanctions relate to the alleged recruiting violation involving Radojevic, the evidence shows that these sanctions are not as debilitating to defendant's basketball program as defendant suggests. Michelle Willis testified that at the time the post-season ban was imposed, she did not believe that the team was good enough to merit a post-season tournament invitation. With regard to the two scholarships forfeited by defendant for the 2005 recruiting class, the evidence demonstrates that the loss may not result in significant harm to the basketball program given defendant's expectation that the recruiting class for the 2005-2006 year will be one of the best in its history.

* * *

Trust

* * *

The court is convinced that plaintiff's failure to disclose the loan until he was forced by circumstances to do so, damaged the relationship between himself and Geiger. The trial testimony of these two individuals established that prior to the night of April 24, 2004, they had forged a strong working relationship built upon a foundation of mutual respect, admiration, and trust. The court finds that both men cared deeply about the university, the basketball program, and the student-athletes involved in the program. The evidence shows that for seven years plaintiff and Geiger had worked effectively toward a shared goal of improving the quality of the men's basketball program. In the course of their labor, the two became friends.

The court notes, however, that the issue of trust about which Geiger testified so emphatically during his direct examination was not referenced in the parties' written agreement. It was also absent from the June 8, 2004, letter notifying plaintiff of defendant's intention to terminate plaintiff's employment.

Given the detail with which other important aspects of the parties' relationship were set out in the language of the agreement, it is certainly reasonable to assume that if defendant believed that the trust of the athletic director were of critical importance to the transaction, there would have been some provision in the agreement concerning that issue. After all, it was defendant who initiated the process of reshaping plaintiff's contractual provisions, and there has been no suggestion in this case that defendant lacked sophistication in either the negotiation or the drafting of coaching contracts. Thus, the only reasonable conclusion to draw from the omission of such a provision is that defendant bargained away its right to terminate plaintiff's employment on the basis of some subjective evaluation made by defendant's athletic director.

At best, the issue of trust is an implied term of the parties' agreement. The question in this case is whether this implied term is so fundamental to the contract that a single isolated breach by plaintiff can defeat the essential purpose of the contract or make it impossible for defendant to perform. While the court agrees that a good working relationship between the athletic director and the coach is an important aspect of this agreement, the court finds that the loss of trust caused by plaintiff's failure of performance was not as profound and debilitating as defendant contends.

* * *

Good Faith

The extent to which plaintiff's failure to perform comports with good faith and fair dealing is the final circumstance the court must consider in determining materiality. Defendant argues that plaintiff acted in bad faith by paying a recruit and then engaging in a "cover-up" designed to prevent defendant from discovering his misconduct. The evidence does not support such a sinister view of plaintiff's conduct.

The court has found that plaintiff had reasonable cause to believe that he had committed an NCAA infraction when he made the loan and that he breached Section 4.1(d) of the agreement by doing so. Thus, it follows that plaintiff's failure to disclose the loan was not completely consistent with good faith and fair dealing.

The court is mindful, however, that the loan was made for humanitarian purposes and not for the purpose of gaining an improper recruiting advantage. Moreover, as the court has already observed, Professor Swank testified that it was reasonable for plaintiff to believe that he could make a loan without committing an infraction of NCAA Bylaws. Thus, plaintiff's conduct does not demonstrate the degree of willfulness normally associated with bad faith.

Additionally, the drafters of the Restatement of Contracts have stated that "the obligation of good faith and fair dealing extends to the assertion, settlement and litigation of contract claims and defenses." *See* Restatement of Contracts 2d, Section 205, Comment e. As stated above, after plaintiff disclosed the loan to Geiger he expressed regret for putting his Athletic Director and the University in an "awkward position." And, prior to the point in time when he was told by Geiger that the process had become adversarial, plaintiff offered to discuss his resignation. Plaintiff also gave assurances to defendant, both personally and through counsel, that he would cooperate in any subsequent NCAA proceedings.

On the other hand, the evidence reveals conduct on the part of defendant that was not consistent with good faith and fair dealing. For example, after plaintiff's revelation of April 24, 2004, Geiger either failed or refused to work with plaintiff toward a resolution even though he had stated that he would do so. Furthermore, after Geiger informed plaintiff that the process was going to become adversarial and encouraged plaintiff to retain legal counsel, Geiger did not permit counsel the opportunity to discuss the issue with him. Finally, Geiger allowed plaintiff only four hours to consider his fate after delivering the June 8, 2004, letter.

Upon consideration of the relevant circumstances for determining materiality, the court finds that plaintiff's failure of performance was not material. Although plaintiff breached Section 4.1(d) by making and then failing to timely disclose a loan, the extent to which defendant was deprived of the benefit it reasonably expected from the employment agreement was not as significant as defendant contends. For example, the evidence shows that the NCAA sanctions and the injury to defendant's reputation that can be fairly attributed to the loan are relatively minor. Additionally, while plaintiff may not be able to cure either the reputational injury or the NCAA sanctions, the evidence shows that the breach of trust could have been repaired. In comparison, plaintiff's forfeiture of salary and benefits is substantial. Furthermore, while plaintiff's conduct prior to disclosing the loan was not completely consistent with good faith and fair dealing, plaintiff did make a good faith effort to resolve the dispute. Defendant chose a course that was adversarial.

Because plaintiff's failure of performance was not material, defendant did not have cause for termination. Because defendant did not have cause for termination, defendant was contractually obligated to pay plaintiff in accordance with the provisions relating to termination other than for cause. Defendant breached the contract by refusing to pay plaintiff.

* * *

Compliance

With respect to Section 4.1(d) of the instant agreement, it is clear to the court that NCAA compliance is important to defendant; it is one of the specified duties of the coach. However, Section 5.1(b) of the contract contemplates a chain of events whereby plaintiff could retain his employment in the face of an ongoing major infractions investigation by the NCAA and that he could remain so employed absent the imposition of certain serious sanctions. From this language the court concludes that the parties did not consider plaintiff's performance under Section 4.1(d) of the contract to be so critical that a failure of any kind would justify immediate termination for cause. If defendant reasonably expected perfect compliance, Section 5.1(b) would not have been made part of the agreement.

Similarly, Section 5.5 of the agreement provides the court with insight into the relative importance of absolute NCAA compliance. Section 5.5 provides:

> "5.5 Suspension of Other Disciplinary Action. If Coach is found to have violated any law, policy, rule or regulation of the NCAA, the Big Ten Conference or Ohio State, Coach may be subject to suspension or other disciplinary or corrective action as set forth in the applicable enforcement procedures (subject to the provisions of Section 5.6 hereof)."

Reading such provision in conjunction with Section 5.1(b) it is clear that a violation of NCAA rules, even a major infraction, will not justify termination for cause under Section 5.1(a) unless that violation has some independent significance which prevents future performance.

Geiger testified that, in his opinion, defendant had no choice but to immediately terminate plaintiff's employment. Suspension, Geiger explained, was not a viable option. "A. We're now in the 19th month of the NCAA process. Having a coach in limbo or having a coach suspended would be grossly unfair to the young people that play basketball at Ohio State, would have arrested any development of our program, and that is — that was an untenable solution." (Trial Transcript, Page 783, Line 21 through Page 784, Line 1.)

It is difficult to square Geiger's testimony with the language of the parties' agreement. Although Geiger testified that suspending plaintiff for the pendency of the NCAA investigation was an "untenable solution," the agreement entered into by the parties clearly contemplates such action. Moreover, at the time the parties entered into the 1999 employment agreement Geiger was aware that NCAA investigations proceed very slowly. When asked if he had told plaintiff that the NCAA investigation would move at a snail's pace he answered: "I probably did because they always do." Based upon the language of the agreement, and the evidence admitted in this case, the court finds that defendant bargained away its right to immediately dismiss plaintiff simply because of the inconvenience occasioned by a protracted NCAA investigation.

CONCLUSION

In summary, Geiger's June 8, 2004, letter speaks to a single, isolated recruiting infraction by plaintiff and plaintiff's failure to timely disclose that violation. The evidence shows that the violation consists of a loan made to the family of a prospect for humanitarian reasons. The evidence also demonstrates that such prospect was ineligible to participate in intercollegiate athletics at the time that the loan was made. Although plaintiff breached his contract by making the loan under these circumstances, the court is persuaded, given the contract language, that this single, isolated failure of performance was not so egregious as to frustrate the essential purpose of that contract and thus render future performance by defendant impossible. Because the breach by plaintiff was not a material breach, defendant did not have cause to terminate plaintiff's employment. Defendant's decision to do so without any compensation to plaintiff was a breach of the parties' agreement.

For the foregoing reasons, the court finds that plaintiff has proven his claim of breach of contract by a preponderance of the evidence and accordingly, judgment shall be rendered in favor of plaintiff. [The court subsequently ruled that O'Brien was entitled to $2.4 million in damages. The university has appealed the case.]

NOTES AND COMMENTS

1. Coaching contracts are far different today than in previous times. There was a time when coaches were hired with a handshake agreement or, in the more complicated situations, a brief letter agreement. The university administrator and the coach today, particularly in the revenue producing sports, frequently engage in complex negotiations resulting in multi-page contracts. Concern over early termination and details of outside income agreements has caused both coaches and university officials to desire intricate written contracts. In drafting such contracts there should be a number of key considerations, important to both sides of the agreement. These include such items as:

a. the term of the agreement;

b. the compensation and the source of compensation;

c. the duties and responsibilities of the coach (specific details are desirable);

d. an indication that the coach may be reassigned to other duties if his or her coaching duties are terminated;

e. a liquidated damages clause covering early termination by the coach;

f. description of the reasons for termination by the university, including intentional or major violations of NCAA rules (some schools include in this clause an option to terminate if the coach is found to have violated rules while at a previous school);

g. provisions relating to outside income, including limitations and reporting requirements (outside income generally would be from summer camps, endorsements, radio and television shows, and shoe contracts);

h. clauses relating to the hiring of assistant coaches and scheduling (the head coach's role in both tasks should be spelled out in the contract); and

i. fringe benefits, including expense accounts, retirement, insurance, season tickets, and any other standard university benefits.

For a detailed description of collegiate coaching contracts *see* GREENBERG & GRAY, SPORTS LAW PRACTICE Ch. 6 (2d ed. 1998). *See also* Robert W. Ferguson, *Slam Dunk: Negotiating Coaching Contracts for Women's College Basketball Programs*, 19 SPG ENT. & SPORTS LAW 8 (2001); Edward N. Stoner II & Arlie R. Nogay, *The Model University Coaching Contract ("MCC"): A Better Starting Point for Your Next Negotiation*, 16 J.C. & U.L. 43 (1989).

2. For cases and discussion of gender based issues arising from coaching contracts or raised in connection with dismissal of coaches, *see* **Chapter 3**, *infra*.

3. Despite improved clarity and detail in coaching contracts there continue to be disputes when a contract is terminated — by either side. Gerry DiNardo, the head football coach at Louisiana State University was sued by his former employer, Vanderbilt University as a result of his decision to take the LSU job when he still had several years remaining on his contract at Vanderbilt. The Sixth Circuit ruled that a liquidated damages clause in the contract was enforceable and that damages should be awarded to Vanderbilt. *Vanderbilt University* *v. DiNardo*, 174 F.3d 751 (6th Cir. 1999). The case was settled prior to trial for an undisclosed amount in May, 2000. DiNardo moved on to become the head coach at the University of Indiana. He is currently a broadcaster.

4. Coaches, as with any employees, enjoy the various protections provided by federal and state law against discrimination, slander, and other injurious actions taken by an employer. For example, universities must be cautious when terminating the contract of an older coach. A jury found against the University of Notre Dame in an action filed by Joseph Moore, a former football coach who was fired from his job as an assistant at the age of 64. The official reason given was that he "did not measure up to the standards of Notre Dame." There was evidence introduced at trial, including comments made by the head coach who fired Moore that age was a strong factor in the termination. *Moore v. The University of Notre Dame*, 22 F. Supp. 2d 896 (N.D. Ind. 1998); *Moore v. The University of Notre Dame*, 968 F. Supp. 1330 (N.D. Ind. 1997).

5. University administrators have a variety of avenues open to them in dealing with coaches and their employment relationships in times of difficulty. For example, the University of Alabama fined its head football coach $360,000 and reduced the length of his contract from five years to three years following his admission of certain actions amounting to an improper relationship with a university employee. The university took this action simultaneous with the settlement of a sexual harassment action filed by the employee. *Alabama Upholds DuBose Penalties*, ATLANTA CONSTITUTION, August 13, 1999, p.5D.

Termination of contracts will often be preceded by varying degrees of due process, depending upon whether the school involved is a public institution and depending upon institutional or state governmental requirements. *See e.g.*, *Weaver v. Nebo School Dist.*, 29 F. Supp. 2d 1279 (D. Utah 1998) (decision not to assign a teacher as volleyball coach because of her candor concerning her sexual orientation constituted retaliation for exercise of First Amendment rights); *Lancaster v. Independent School Dist. No. 5*, 149 F.3d 1228 (10th Cir. 1998) (teacher's coaching responsibilities not part of his teaching duties and therefore not protected by due process).

2. Institutional and Conference Contracts and Licensing Agreements

Another area where university administrators and legal counsel must be concerned with contractual matters is in connection with radio and television broadcast of athletic events involving the school's teams. The school's rights and obligations, as well as those of the broadcaster, must be clearly spelled out in the contract. Such items as the description and location of the production facilities, promotional responsibilities, distribution rights, advertising rights, and compensation must be articulated.

Schools must also be careful in drafting agreements simply to engage in an athletic contest with another school. Items such as provision of officials, the site of the game, share of gate receipts, fixed guarantees for playing the game, broadcast rights, and ticket allocation must be clearly spelled out in any agreement. See generally the course materials from Legal Issues in Intercollegiate Athletics (Second Annual National Conference on Current Issues in Sports Law, DePaul University College of Law, 1990).

The specific provisions of a contract for a game have recently come into conflict in a matter involving two television networks, two colleges, and two Major League Baseball teams. On Saturday, September 21, 1996, San Diego State University and the University of Oklahoma were scheduled to play a football game in Jack Murphy Stadium in San Diego at 1:00 p.m., with the game carried as a regional telecast by ABC Sports. Later that day the San Diego Padres were to play the Los Angeles Dodgers at 8:00 p.m. In late August, the Fox Broadcasting Network announced that it would show the Padres-Dodgers game as its Saturday Game of the Week in a national broadcast pursuant to its contract with Major League Baseball. Game time was set to be 12:30 p.m. setting up a serious conflict with the football game. Major League Baseball and the Padres claimed to have priority at Jack Murphy Stadium, but the City of San Diego, owner of the stadium, initially sided with the university. Ultimately ABC decided, in the course of discussions with all of the parties, to drop the game from its scheduled telecasts. The football game was then re-scheduled for 8:05 p.m. and the baseball game was carried as per FOX's plans as the Game of the Week.

In this era of "Superconferences," and teams jumping from long established relationships with other schools, even conference agreements must be carefully drafted. Typically, leagues will have a constitution and by-laws that govern the operation and administration of the conference.

At the end of the 90s and the beginning of the new century there was considerable instability among the major collegiate athletic conferences. Institutions changed conference affiliation in large numbers, some amicably and some in a climate of hostility. The most prevalent reason for this shift was economics, largely driven by the opportunity for lucrative television contracts for football and men's basketball. There was sporadic litigation, but ultimately economic settlements were reached and the institutions moved on, literally and figuratively. *See Trustees of Boston College v. Big East Conference*, 2004 Mass. Super LEXIS 298 (Sup. Ct. Mass. 2004); Jim Terhune, *Settlement Keeps U of L in Conference USA*, LOUISVILLE COURIER JOURNAL, p.1A, (June 26, 1996). The settlement produced several changes in the conference's bylaws, among which was a provision setting up binding arbitration as a step in settling future disputes among the league's member schools.

A final area where contractual language is critical for collegiate athletic programs is licensing. It has become critical because, like so many other aspects of intercollegiate athletics it has become big business. In 1995, revenues from officially licensed collegiate products exceeded $2.5 billion. Robert Lattinville, *Logo Cops: the Law and Business of Collegiate Licensing*, 5 KAN. J.L. & PUB. POL'Y 81 (1996). In order to enter into the necessary contracts for exploitation and protection purposes, a thorough understanding of the Lanham Act is necessary. (15 U.S.C. § 1051, et seq.) An understanding of trademarks, the function of trademarks, and the registration of trademarks is necessary. Then it will be important to have a thorough comprehension of the law and business of licensing trademarks and logos. *See* **Chapter 13**, *infra*. *See also* GREENBERG & GRAY, SPORTS LAW PRACTICE, Ch. 8 (2d ed. 1998).

NOTES AND COMMENTS

1. The alliance of conferences creating the Bowl Championship Series (BCS) has raised some questions relating to television contracts, selection process and antitrust law. No legal challenges have been presented but the conferences and schools outside the six conferences in the BCS alliance carefully watch the selection process at the end of every football season for potential causes of action. Do you see any?

2. For an additional case involving a school that attempted to leave a collegiate conference, *see Mid-Atlantic Conference v. NEIU*, 721 N.E.2d 805 (Ill. App. 1999).

Chapter 2

AMATEUR SPORTS ASSOCIATIONS: RULES, PROCEDURES, ELIGIBILITY, AND OTHER ISSUES

A wide range of regulations affects the lives of amateur athletes. In a very real sense, athletes, particularly those involved in team sports, are treated like soldiers. Generally, those who administer amateur athletics value regimentation and discipline highly. The result is a regulatory scheme touching upon aspects of the athlete's life which perhaps would be viewed as inappropriate if applied to a "civilian." Regulations dealing with hair length, for example, still can be found in the sports setting. At some high schools, athletes who marry lose their amateur status and can no longer participate. The regulators are the individuals, organizations, and institutions responsible for the conduct of the athletic competition.

How courts review the rules that are adopted by those responsible for the conduct of athletic competition depends largely upon whether the regulatory entity is categorized as governmental or private. The government is, of course, constrained by the Constitution. The private actor is not. When government's rules are challenged, the basic principles that will be applicable usually involve equal protection and due process. When the actions of a private entity are challenged, the basic principles that apply emanate not from the Constitution but from the rather amorphous body of private association law. Traditionally, the courts have only intervened in the affairs of private associations where the organization's actions violate its own rules or where its acts constitute fraud or illegality or are arbitrary and unreasonable. In situations other than these, the courts historically have been hesitant to interfere.

A. THRESHOLD CONSTITUTIONAL ISSUES

In American constitutional theory the distinction between governmental action and non-governmental action is crucial. Nearly all of the Constitution's guarantees of individual freedom protect individuals from governmental action. Generally, individuals are simply unable to deprive other individuals of their constitutional rights. With few exceptions, it is only the action of the government which is constrained by those portions of the Constitution which define individual freedom. The language and structure of the Constitution make this point virtually unassailable. Thus, a person who alleges a denial of constitutionally protected rights must at the outset demonstrate that it is indeed the action of the government that is being challenged. In fact, the merits of the claim will not be reached unless it can be shown that, somehow, the government has acted. This is the so-called "state action" requirement.

In some cases it is very easy to see the governmental action. For example, a person challenging the constitutionality of a state statute under the equal protection clause will have little difficulty meeting the state action requirement. Clearly, the state acts when it passes a statute. Similarly, in some cases it will be very easy to conclude that the state is really not involved in the controversy. Purely private disputes ordinarily do not raise constitutional issues no matter how egregious the private act. The difficulty arises in cases where state action is not apparent but where the state is nonetheless somehow involved. The boundaries separating the acts of the government from the acts of the individual are not always so clear in a society where government plays a pervasive role.

The context of amateur athletics provides a good setting for the more difficult state action cases. Although many amateur athletic organizations (*e.g.,* the National Collegiate Athletic Association and the United States Olympic Committee) are "private" in the sense that they are not formal creatures of the state, they arguably perform state-like functions and the state itself is inevitably somehow involved with their operations — directly or indirectly — by providing money, services, facilities, permission or encouragement. If the putatively private actor is really performing a public function, then perhaps it ought to be treated as though it were the state. Or, if the level of state involvement is significant, then perhaps the action of the private organization ought to be treated as state action. The following cases are illustrative of the problems associated with the state action threshold in the area of constitutional challenges to various sports association regulations. As you work through the problem and materials, remember that the constitutional issues will not even be considered in the absence of state action.

Assuming that the state action requirement is met, the court will assess the merits of the plaintiff's claim. Although the approaches vary widely, common threads run through the process of constitutional decision-making. It is, after all, a process that requires the accommodation of competing interests. On the one hand, the court will evaluate the nature of the constitutionally protected interest that has been arguably invaded or infringed upon by the state actor. How serious is the invasion? How significant is the plaintiff's loss? Was the harm intended or incidental? On the other hand, the court will look at what the state actor was trying to achieve. What was the purpose of the action? Was it designed to achieve some important goal? Was it successful in achieving that goal? It is this process of accommodating important competing interests that is at the heart of constitutional decision-making. The ultimate decision that is reached inevitably reflects the cultural values that loom over the process.

Problem

The Green County Soccer Association (GCSA) is part of a long chain of amateur soccer organizations in Oklanois. At the bottom level are the area clubs — Shadow Mountain Soccer Club, Shawnee Soccer Club, etc. — of which there are approximately ten. Each child who belongs to one of these clubs pays a membership fee. Each club pays a certain amount per child to the GCSA. The GCSA then pays a fee per child to the Oklanois Soccer Association (OSA) an organization headquartered in the state capital and chartered under state law. The OSA pays a certain fee per child to the United States Youth Soccer Association (USYSA), which in turn is a division of the United States Soccer Federation (USSF), an organization chartered by Congress. The USSF is in turn a member of the Federation Internationale Football Association (FIFA).

In case of injury to an athlete, a series of administrative remedies must be exhausted at each level before the higher authority can be petitioned to hear a grievance. With an elaborate chain of remedies such as this, an athlete's grievance rarely makes it to court.

If such a grievance were to make it to court, a determination of whether state action existed would be necessary, if constitutional questions were involved. Would the action of the GCSA be state action? The USYSA? The USSF? The FIFA? What additional facts are necessary to resolve the question?

Case File

DEFRANTZ v. UNITED STATES OLYMPIC COMMITTEE

492 F. Supp. 118 (D.D.C. 1980)

John H. Pratt, District Judge.

MEMORANDUM OPINION

Plaintiffs, 25 athletes and one member of the Executive Board of defendant United States Olympic Committee (USOC), have moved for an injunction barring defendant USOC from carrying out a resolution, adopted by the USOC House of Delegates on April 12, 1980, not to send an American team to participate in the Games of the XXIInd Olympiad to be held in Moscow in the summer of 1980. Plaintiffs allege that in preventing American athletes from competing in the Summer Olympics, defendant has exceeded its statutory powers and has abridged plaintiffs' constitutional rights.

For the reasons discussed below, we find that plaintiffs have failed to state a claim upon which relief can be granted. Accordingly, we deny plaintiffs' claim for injunctive and declaratory relief and dismiss the action.

THE FACTS

In essence, the action before us involves a dispute between athletes who wish to compete in the Olympic Games to be held in Moscow this summer, and the United States Olympic Committee, which has denied them that opportunity in the wake of the invasion and continued occupation of Afghanistan by Soviet military forces Because this dispute confronts us with questions concerning the statutory authority of the USOC, its place and appropriate role in the international Olympic movement, and its relationship to the United States Government and with certain United States officials, we begin with a brief discussion of the organizational structure of the Olympic Games and the facts which have brought this action before us. These facts are not in dispute.

According to its Rules and By-laws, the International Olympic Committee (IOC) governs the Olympic movement and owns the rights of the Olympic games. IOC Rules provide that National Olympic Committees (NOC) may be established "as the sole authorities responsible for the representation of the respective countries at the Olympic Games," so long as the NOC's rules and regulations are approved by the IOC. The USOC is one such National Olympic Committee.

The USOC is a corporation created and granted a federal charter by Congress in 1950. . . . This charter was revised by the Amateur Sports Act of 1978. . . . Under this statute, defendant USOC has "exclusive jurisdiction" and authority over participation and representation of the United States in the Olympic Games.

The routine procedure initiating the participation of a national team in Olympic competition is the acceptance by the NOC of an invitation from the Olympic Organizing Committee for the particular games. In accordance with this routine procedure under IOC Rules, the Moscow Olympic Organizing Committee extended an invitation to the USOC to participate in the summer games. Recent international and domestic events, however, have made acceptance of this invitation, which must come on or before May 24, 1980, anything but routine.

On December 27, 1979, the Soviet Union launched an invasion of its neighbor, Afghanistan. That country's ruler was deposed and killed and a new government was installed. Fighting has been at times intense, casualties have been high, and hundreds of thousands of Afghan citizens have fled their homeland. At present, an estimated 100,000 Soviet troops remain in Afghanistan, and fighting continues.

President Carter termed the invasion a threat to the security of the Persian Gulf area as well as a threat to world peace and stability and he moved to take direct sanctions against the Soviet Union. These sanctions included a curtailment of agricultural and high technology exports to the Soviet Union, and restrictions on commerce with the Soviets. The Administration also turned its attention to a boycott of the summer Olympic Games as a further sanction against the Soviet Union.

As the affidavit of then Acting Secretary of State Warren Christopher makes clear, the Administration was concerned that "[t]he presence of American competitors would be taken by the Soviets as evidence that their invasion had faded from memory or was not a matter of great consequence or concern to this nation." . . . The Administration's concern was sharpened because "[t]he Soviet Union has made clear that it intends the Games to serve important national political ends. For the U.S.S.R., international sports competition is an instrument of government policy and a means to advance foreign policy goals."

With the concerns in mind, the Administration strenuously urged a boycott of the Moscow games. On January 20, 1980, President Carter wrote the President of the United States Olympic Committee to urge that the USOC propose to the IOC that the 1980 summer games be transferred from Moscow, postponed, or cancelled if the Soviet forces were not withdrawn within a month. On January 23, 1980, the President delivered his State of the Union Message, in which he said that he would not support sending American athletes to Moscow while Soviet military forces remained in Afghanistan.

Following these statements, the United States House of Representatives passed, by a vote of 386 to 12, a Concurrent Resolution opposing participation by United States athletes in the Moscow Games unless Soviet troops were withdrawn from Afghanistan by February 20th. The Senate passed a similar resolution by a vote of 88 to 4.

As this was unfolding, the USOC's 86 member Executive Board held a meeting in Colorado Springs on January 26, 1980, inviting White House counsel Lloyd Cutler to address them "because no officer or any member of the Board was knowledgeable about the far-reaching implications of the Soviet invasion." . . . According to USOC President Kane, in early January some USOC officers became concerned that sending American athletes to Moscow could expose them to danger if hostility erupted at the games, and that acceptance of the invitation could be seen as tacit approval of or at least acceptance of the Soviet invasion. Mr. Cutler also met with USOC officers at least twice in February to discuss the matter further. On each occasion, according to the Kane affidavit, Mr. Cutler urged Mr. Kane to convene an emergency meeting of the USOC Executive Board to act on the Moscow problem. However, legal counsel for the USOC advised Mr. Kane that only the House of Delegates and not the USOC Executive Board could decide whether or not to send a team to Moscow.

On March 21, 1980, President Carter told members of the Athletes Advisory Council, an official body of the USOC, that American athletes will not participate in the Moscow summer games. On April 8, 1980, the President sent a telegram to the president and officers of the USOC and to its House of Delegates, urging the USOC to vote against sending an American team to Moscow.

In an April 10th speech, the President said that "if legal actions are necessary to enforce [my] decision not to send a team to Moscow, then I will take those legal actions." . . .On April 10 and 11, 1980, the 13 member Administrative Committee of the USOC met in Colorado Springs and voted to support a resolution against sending a team to Moscow. Only Anita DeFrantz, a plaintiff in this action, dissented.

At the President's request and over initial objections by the USOC, Vice President Mondale addressed the assembled House of Delegates prior to their vote on April 12, 1980. The Vice President strongly and vigorously urged the House of Delegates to support a resolution rejecting American participation in the summer games in Moscow.

After what USOC President Kane describes in his affidavit as "full, open, complete and orderly debate by advocates of each motion," the House of Delegates, on a secret ballot, passed by a vote of 1,604 to 798, a resolution which provided in pertinent part:

> RESOLVED that since the President of the United States has advised the United States Olympic Committee that in light of international events the national security of the country is threatened, the USOC has decided not to send a team to the 1980 Summer Games in Moscow. . . .
>
> FURTHER RESOLVED, that if the President of the United States advises the United States Olympic Committee, on or before May 20, 1980, that international events have become compatible with the national interest and the national security is no longer threatened, the USOC will enter its athletes in the 1980 Summer Games.

Plaintiffs describe these attempts by the Administration to persuade the USOC to vote not to send an American team to Moscow as "a campaign to coerce defendant USOC into compliance with the President's demand for a boycott of the Olympic Games." . . . In addition, plaintiffs' complaint alleges that the President and other Executive Branch officials threatened to terminate federal funding of the USOC and that they raised the possibility of revoking the federal income tax exemption of the USOC if the USOC did not support the President's decision to boycott the 1980 Games. The complaint also alleges that these officials stated that the Federal government would provide increased funding to the USOC if the USOC supported a boycott.

Plaintiffs state three causes of action in their complaint. The first, a statutory claim, is that defendant violated the Amateur Sports Act of 1978, *supra,* in the following respects:

a. Defendant exercised a power it does not have — to decide that no United States amateur athletes shall participate in the 1980 Games.

b. Defendant breached a duty to organize, finance and control participation in the events and competitions of the Olympic Games by United States athletes.

c. Defendant denied to United States amateur athletes the opportunity to compete in these Games on a basis other than their want of athletic merit, or for a sports related reason.

d. Defendant yielded its exclusive jurisdiction over Olympic matters to the political leaders of the nation.

e. Defendant acted in a political manner.

f. Defendant yielded its autonomy and has succumbed to political and economic pressure.

Plaintiffs' second cause of action, a constitutional claim, alleges that defendant's action constituted "governmental action" which abridged plaintiffs' rights of liberty, self-expression, personal autonomy and privacy guaranteed by the First, Fifth and Ninth Amendments to the United States Constitution.

Plaintiffs' third cause of action is that the USOC has violated its Constitution, By-laws and governing statute, injuring the USOC and violating the rights of plaintiff Shaw, a member of the USOC's Executive Board, and that defendant is subject to an action to compel compliance with its Constitution, By-laws and governing statute.

Plaintiffs allege that unredressed, these violations will result in great and irreparable injury to the athletes. "Many would lose a once-in-a-lifetime opportunity to participate in the Olympic Games, and the honor and prestige that such participation affords. Most of the class members are at or near their physical peaks at the present time and will not physically be capable of reaching the same or higher levels at a later period of their lives." . . .

In summary, plaintiffs ask this court to declare the April 12, 1980 resolution of the USOC House of Delegates null and void because it violated statutory authority and constitutional provisions and to permanently enjoin the USOC from carrying out that resolution.

Defendant and the Government have moved to dismiss . . . on several grounds. . . . As for the constitutional claims, they argue that the decision of the USOC was not "state action" and therefore, that plaintiffs have no cognizable constitutional claims. They further argue that even if the action of the USOC could be considered "state action," no rights guaranteed to plaintiffs under the Constitution were abridged.

* * *

ANALYSIS

This action presents us with several issues for decisions, falling into two distinct categories; one is statutory and the other is constitutional. [The Court denied relief under the Amateur Sport Act of 1978.]

* * *

2. Constitutional Claims

Plaintiffs have alleged that the decision of the USOC not to enter an American team in the summer Olympics has violated certain rights guaranteed to plaintiffs under the First, Fifth and Ninth Amendments to the United States Constitution. This presents us with two questions: (1) whether the USOC's decision was "governmental action" (state action), and, assuming state action is found, (2) whether the USOC's decision abridged any constitutionally protected rights.

(a) State Action

Although federally chartered, defendant is a private organization. Because the Due Process Clause of the Fifth Amendment, on which plaintiffs place great reliance, applies only to actions by the federal government, plaintiffs must show that the USOC vote is a "governmental act," *i.e.,* state action. In defining state action, the courts have fashioned two guidelines. The first involves an inquiry into whether the state:

> . . . has so far insinuated itself into a position of interdependence with [the private entity] that it must be recognized as a joint participant in the challenged activity.

Burton v. Wilmington Parking Authority, 365 U.S. 715, 725 (1961).

In *Burton,* the Supreme Court found state action, but it did so on wholly different facts than those existing here. The private entity charged with racially discriminating against plaintiff was a restaurant which was physically and financially an integral part of a public building, built and maintained with public funds, devoted to a public parking service, and owned and operated by an agency of the State of Delaware for public purposes. Noting the obvious and deep enmeshment of defendant and the state, the court found that the state was a joint participant in the operation of the restaurant, and accordingly found state action. Here, there is no such intermingling, and there is no factual justification for finding that the federal government and the USOC enjoyed the "symbiotic relationship" which courts have required to find state action. The USOC has received no federal funding and it exists and operates independently of the federal government. Its chartering statute gives it "exclusive jurisdiction" over "all matters pertaining to the participation of the United States in the Olympic Games. . . ." . . . To be sure, the Act does link the USOC and the federal government to the extent it requires the USOC to submit an annual report to the President and the Congress. But this hardly converts such an independent relationship to a "joint participation."

The second guideline fashioned by the courts involves an inquiry of whether:

> . . .there is a sufficiently close nexus between the state and the challenged action of the regulated entity so that the action of the latter may be fairly treated as that of the state itself.

Jackson v. Metropolitan Edison Co., 419 U.S. 345, 351 (1974).

Jackson provides an indication of how close this nexus must be in order to find state action. In that case, the Supreme Court found there was no state action even though the defendant was a utility closely regulated by the state, and even though the action complained of (the procedure for termination of electrical services) had been approved by the state utility commission. In the instant case, there was no requirement that any federal government body approve actions by the USOC before they become effective.

Plaintiffs clearly recognize this, but they argue that by the actions of certain federal officials, the federal government initiated, encouraged, and approved of the result reached (*i.e.,* the vote of the USOC not to send an American team to the summer Olympics). Plaintiffs advance a novel theory. Essentially, their argument is that the campaign of governmental persuasion, personally led by President Carter, crossed the line from "governmental recommendation," which plaintiffs find acceptable and presumably necessary to the operation of our form of government, into the area of "affirmative pressure that effectively places the government's prestige behind the challenged action," and thus, results in state action. We cannot agree.

Plaintiff can point to no case outside the area of discrimination law which in any way supports their theory, and we can find none. Furthermore, this Circuit's Court of Appeals has addressed what level of governmental involvement is necessary to find state action in cases not involving discrimination.

> Each party cites numerous cases dealing with the amount of governmental involvement which is necessary before a private entity becomes sufficiently entangled with governmental functions that federal jurisdiction attaches. If any principle emerges from these cases, it would appear to be that, at least where race is not involved, *it is necessary to show that the Government exercises some form of control over the actions of the private party*. (Emphasis supplied.)

* * *

Here there is no such control. The USOC is an independent body, and nothing in its chartering statute gives the federal government the right to control that body or its officers. Furthermore, the facts here do not indicate that the federal government was able to exercise any type of "de facto" control over the USOC. The USOC decided by a secret ballot of its House of Delegates. The federal government may have had the power to prevent the athletes from participating in the Olympics even if the USOC had voted to allow them to participate, but it did not have the power to make them vote in a certain way. All it had was the power of persuasion. We cannot equate this with control. To do so in cases of this type would be to open the door and usher the courts into what we believe is a largely nonjusticiable realm, where they would find themselves in the untenable position of determining whether a certain level, intensity, or type of "Presidential" or "Administration" or "political" pressure amounts to sufficient control over a private entity so as to invoke federal jurisdiction.

We accordingly find that the decision of the USOC not to send an American team to the summer Olympics was not state action, and therefore, does not give rise to an actionable claim for the infringements of the constitutional rights alleged.

* * *

At this point, we find it appropriate to note that we have respect and admiration for the discipline, sacrifice, and perseverance which earns young men and women the opportunity to compete in the Olympic Games. Ordinarily, talent alone has determined whether an American would have the privilege of participating in the Olympics. This year, unexpectedly, things are different. We express no view on the merits of the decision made. We do express our understanding of the deep disappointment and frustrations felt by thousands of American athletes.

In doing so, we also recognize that the responsibilities of citizenship often fall more heavily on some than on others. Some are called to military duty. Others never serve. Some return from military service unscathed. Others never return. These are the simple, although harsh, facts of life, and they are immutable.

NATIONAL COLLEGIATE ATHLETIC ASSOCIATION v. TARKANIAN

488 U.S. 179 (1988)

* * *

JUSTICE STEVENS delivered the opinion of the Court.

When he became head basketball coach at University of Nevada, Las Vegas (UNLV) in 1973, Jerry Tarkanian inherited a team with a mediocre 14-14 record. . . . Four years later the team won 29 out of 32 games and placed third in the championship tournament sponsored by the National Collegiate Athletic Association (NCAA), to which UNLV belongs.

Yet in September 1977 UNLV informed Tarkanian that it was going to suspend him. No dissatisfaction with Tarkanian, once described as "the 'winningest' active basketball coach," motivated his suspension. Rather, the impetus was a report by the NCAA detailing 38 violations of NCAA rules by UNLV personnel, including 10 involving Tarkanian. The NCAA had placed the University's basketball team on probation for two years and ordered UNLV to show cause why the NCAA should not impose further penalties unless UNLV severed all ties during the probation between its intercollegiate athletic program and Tarkanian.

Facing demotion and a drastic cut in pay, Tarkanian brought suit in Nevada state court, alleging that he had been deprived of his Fourteenth Amendment due process rights in violation of 42 U.S.C. § 1983. Ultimately Tarkanian obtained injunctive relief and an award of attorney's fees against both UNLV and the NCAA. . . . NCAA's liability may be upheld only if its participation in the events that led to Tarkanian's suspension constituted "state action" prohibited by the Fourteenth Amendment and were performed "under color of" state law within the meaning of § 1983. We granted certiorari to review the Nevada Supreme Court's holding that the NCAA engaged in state action when it conducted its investigation and recommended that Tarkanian be disciplined. . . . We now reverse.

I

In order to understand the four separate proceedings that gave rise to the question we must decide, it is useful to begin with a description of the relationship among the three parties — Tarkanian, UNLV, and the NCAA.

Tarkanian initially was employed on a year-to-year basis but became a tenured professor in 1977. He receives an annual salary with valuable fringe benefits, and his status as a highly successful coach enables him to earn substantial additional income from sports-related activities such as broadcasting and the sponsorship of products.

UNLV is a branch of the University of Nevada, a state-funded institution. . . . In performing their official functions, the executives of UNLV unquestionably act under color of state law.

The NCAA is an unincorporated association of approximately 960 members, including virtually all public and private universities and four-year colleges conducting major athletic programs in the United States. Basic policies of the NCAA are determined by the members at annual conventions. Between conventions, the Association is governed by its Council, which appoints various committees to implement specific programs.

One of the NCAA's fundamental policies "is to maintain intercollegiate athletics as an integral part of the educational program and the athlete as an integral part of the student body, and by so doing, retain a clear line of demarcation between college athletics and professional sports." . . . It has therefore adopted rules, which it calls "legislation," governing the conduct of the intercollegiate athletic programs of its members. This NCAA legislation applies to a variety of issues, such as academic standards for eligibility, admissions, financial aid, and the recruiting of student athletes. By joining the NCAA, each agrees to abide by and to enforce such rules.

The NCAA's bylaws provide that its enforcement program shall be administered by a Committee on Infractions. The Committee supervises an investigative staff, makes factual determinations concerning alleged rule violations, and is expressly authorized to "impose appropriate penalties on a member found to be in violation, or recommend to the Council suspension or termination of membership." In particular, the Committee may order a member institution to show cause why that member should not suffer further penalties unless it imposes a prescribed discipline on an employee; it is not authorized, however, to sanction a member institution's employees directly. The bylaws also provide that representatives of member institutions "are expected to cooperate fully" with the administration of the enforcement program. . . . The bylaws do not purport to confer any subpoena power on the Committee or its investigators. They state:

> "The enforcement procedures are an essential part of the intercollegiate athletic program of each member institution and require full and complete disclosure by all institutional representatives of any relevant information requested by the NCAA investigative staff, Committee on Infractions or Council during the course of an inquiry."

During its investigation of UNLV, the Committee on Infractions included three law professors, a mathematics professor, and the dean of a graduate school. Four of them were on the faculties of state institutions; one represented a private university.

The NCAA Investigation of UNLV

On November 28, 1972, the Committee on Infractions notified UNLV's president that it was initiating a preliminary inquiry into alleged violations of NCAA requirements by UNLV. As a result of that preliminary inquiry, some three years later the Committee decided that an "Official Inquiry" was warranted and so advised the UNLV president on February 25, 1976. That advice included a series of detailed allegations concerning the recruitment of student athletes during the period between 1971 and 1975. Many of the allegations implicated Tarkanian. It requested UNLV to investigate and provide detailed information concerning each alleged incident.

With the assistance of the Attorney General of Nevada and private counsel, UNLV conducted a thorough investigation of the charges. On October 27, 1976, it filed a comprehensive response containing voluminous exhibits and sworn affidavits. The response denied all of the allegations and specifically concluded that Tarkanian was completely innocent of wrongdoing. Thereafter, the Committee conducted four days of hearings at which counsel for UNLV and Tarkanian presented their views of the facts and challenged the credibility of the NCAA investigators and their informants. Ultimately the Committee decided that many of the charges could not be supported, but it did find 38 violations of NCAA rules, including 10 committed by Tarkanian. Most serious was the finding that Tarkanian had violated the University's obligation to provide full cooperation with the NCAA investigation. . . .

The Committee proposed a series of sanctions against UNLV, including a two-year period of probation during which its basketball team could not participate in post-season games or appear on television. The Committee also requested UNLV to show cause why additional penalties should not be imposed against UNLV if it failed to discipline Tarkanian by removing him completely from the University's intercollegiate athletic program during the probation period. UNLV appealed most of the Committee's findings and proposed sanctions to the NCAA Council. After hearing arguments from attorneys representing UNLV and Tarkanian, the Council on August 25, 1977 unanimously approved the Committee's investigation and hearing process and adopted all its recommendations.

UNLV's Discipline of Tarkanian

Promptly after receiving the NCAA report, the president of UNLV directed the University's vice president to schedule a hearing to determine whether the Committee's recommended sanctions should be applied. Tarkanian and UNLV were represented at that hearing, the NCAA was not. Although the vice president expressed doubt concerning the sufficiency of the evidence supporting the Committee's findings, he concluded that "given the terms of our adherence to the NCAA we cannot substitute — biased as we must be — our own judgment on the credibility of witnesses for that of the infractions committee and the Council." . . . With respect to the proposed sanctions, he advised the president that he had three options.

> "1. Reject the sanction requiring us to disassociate Coach Tarkanian from the athletic program and take the risk of still heavier sanctions, *e.g.*, possible extra years of probation.
>
> "2. Recognize the University's delegation to the NCAA of the power to act as ultimate arbiter of these matters, thus reassigning Mr. Tarkanian from his present position — though tenured and without adequate notice — even while believing that the NCAA was wrong.
>
> "3. Pull out of the NCAA completely on the grounds that you will not execute what you hold to be their unjust judgments." . . .

Pursuant to the vice president's recommendation, the president accepted the second option and notified Tarkanian that he was to be completely severed of any and all relations, formal or informal, with the University's Intercollegiate athletic program during the period of the University's NCAA probation.

Tarkanian's Lawsuit Against UNLV

The day before his suspension was to become effective, Tarkanian filed an action in Nevada state court for declaratory and injunctive relief against UNLV and a number of its officers.

He alleged that these defendants had, in violation of 42 U.S.C. § 1983, deprived him of property and liberty without the due process of law guaranteed by the Fourteenth Amendment to the United States Constitution. Based on a stipulation of facts and the testimony offered by Tarkanian, the trial court enjoined UNLV from suspending Tarkanian on the ground that he had been denied procedural and substantive due process of law. UNLV appealed.

The NCAA, which had not been joined as a party, filed an amicus curiae brief arguing that there was no actual controversy between Tarkanian and UNLV; thus, the suit should be dismissed. Alternatively, the NCAA contended that the trial court had exceeded its jurisdiction by effectively invalidating the enforcement proceedings of the NCAA, even though the Association was not a party to the suit. Should a controversy exist, the NCAA argued, it was a necessary party to litigate the scope of any relief. Finally, it contested the trial court's conclusion that Tarkanian had been denied due process. The Nevada Supreme Court concluded that there was an actual controversy but agreed that the NCAA was a necessary party and therefore reversed and remanded to permit joinder of the NCAA. *University of Nevada v. Tarkanian*, 95 Nev. 389, 594 P.2d 1159 (1979).

The Lawsuit Against NCAA

Tarkanian consequently filed a second amended complaint adding the NCAA. . . . After a four-year delay, the trial judge conducted a two-week bench trial and resolved the issues in Tarkanian's favor. The court concluded that NCAA's conduct constituted state action for jurisdictional and constitutional purposes, and that its decision was arbitrary and capricious. It reaffirmed its earlier injunction barring UNLV from disciplining Tarkanian or otherwise enforcing the Confidential Report. Additionally, it enjoined the NCAA from conducting "any further proceedings against the University," from enforcing its show-cause order, and from taking any other action against the University that had been recommended in the Confidential Report. . . .

* * *

The Nevada Supreme Court agreed that Tarkanian had been deprived of both property and liberty protected by the Constitution and that he was not afforded due process before suspension. It thus affirmed the trial court's injunction insofar as it pertained to Tarkanian, but narrowed its scope "only to prohibit enforcement of the penalties imposed upon Tarkanian in Confidential Report No. 123(47) and UNLV's adoption of those penalties." . . . The court also reduced the award of attorney's fees.

As a predicate for its disposition, the State Supreme Court held that the NCAA had engaged in state action. Several strands of arguments supported this holding. First, the court assumed that it was reviewing "UNLV's and the NCAA's imposition of penalties against Tarkanian,". . . rather than the NCAA's proposed sanctions against UNLV if it failed to discipline Tarkanian appropriately. Second, it regarded the NCAA's regulatory activities as state action because "many NCAA member institutions were either public or government supported.". . . Third, it stated that the right to discipline a public employee "is traditionally the exclusive prerogative of the state" and that UNLV could not escape its responsibility for such disciplinary action by delegating that duty to a private entity. . . . The court next pointed to our opinion in *Lugar v. Edmondson Oil Co.*, 457 U.S. 922, 937 (1982), in which we held that the deprivation of a federal right may be attributed to the state if it resulted from a state-created rule and the party charged with the deprivation can fairly be said to [be] a state actor. Summing up its holding that the NCAA's activities constituted state action, the Nevada Supreme Court stated:

"The first prong [of *Lugar*] is met because no third party could impose disciplinary sanctions upon a state university employee unless the third party received the right or privilege from the university. Thus, the deprivation which Tarkanian alleges is caused by the exercise of a right or privilege created by the state. Also, in the instant case, both UNLV and the NCAA must be considered state actors. By delegating authority to the NCAA over athletic personnel decisions and by imposing the NCAA sanctions against Tarkanian, UNLV acted jointly with the NCAA."

II

Embedded in our Fourteenth Amendment jurisprudence is a dichotomy between state action, which is subject to scrutiny under the Amendment's Due Process Clause, and private conduct, against which the Amendment affords no shield, no matter how unfair that conduct may be. . . . As a general matter the protections of the Fourteenth Amendment do not extend to "private conduct abridging individual rights." . . .

* * *

In this case Tarkanian argues that the NCAA was a state actor because it misused power that it possessed by virtue of state law. He claims specifically that UNLV delegated its own functions to the NCAA, clothing the Association with authority both to adopt rules governing UNLV's athletic programs and to enforce those rules on behalf of UNLV. Similarly, the Nevada Supreme Court held that UNLV had delegated its authority over personnel decisions to the NCAA. Therefore, the court reasoned, the two entities acted jointly to deprive Tarkanian of liberty and property interests, making the NCAA as well as UNLV a state actor.

These contentions fundamentally misconstrue the facts of this case. In the typical case raising a state action issue, a private party has taken the decisive conduct as state action. This may occur if the State creates the legal framework governing the conduct . . . if it delegates its authority to the private actor . . . or sometimes if it knowingly accepts the benefits derived from unconstitutional behavior. . . . Thus, in the usual case we ask whether the State provided a mantle of authority that enhanced the power of the harm-causing individual actor.

This case uniquely mirrors the traditional state action case. Here the final act challenged by Tarkanian — his suspension — was committed by UNLV. When it decides to impose a serious disciplinary sanction upon one of its tenured employees, it must comply with the terms of the Due Process Clause of the Fourteenth Amendment to the Federal Constitution. . . . Thus when UNLV notified Tarkanian that he was being separated from all relations with the University's basketball program, it acted under color of state law. . . .

The mirror image presented in this case requires us to step through an analytical looking glass to resolve it. Clearly UNLV's conduct was influenced by the rules and recommendations of the NCAA, the private party. But it was UNLV, the state entity, that actually suspended Tarkanian. Thus the question is not whether UNLV participated to a critical extent in the NCAA's activities, but whether UNLV's actions in compliance with the NCAA rules and recommendations turned the NCAA's conduct into state action.

We examine first the relationship between UNLV and the NCAA regarding the NCAA's rule-making. UNLV is among the NCAA's members and participated in promulgating the Association's rules; it must be assumed, therefore, that Nevada had some impact on the NCAA's policy determinations. Yet the NCAA's several hundred other public and private member institutions each similarly affected those policies. Those institutions, the vast majority of which were located in States other than Nevada, did not act under color of Nevada law. It necessarily follows that the source of the legislation adopted by the NCAA is not Nevada but the collective membership, speaking through an organization that is independent of any particular State[13] . . .

State action nonetheless might lie if UNLV, by embracing the NCAA's rules, transformed them into state rules and the NCAA into a state actor. . . . UNLV engaged in state action when it adopted the NCAA's rules to govern its own behavior, but that would be true even if UNLV had taken no part in the promulgation of those rules. In *Bates v. State Bar of Arizona*, 433 U.S. 350 (1977), we established that the State Supreme Court's enforcement of disciplinary rules transgressed by members of its own bar was state action. Those rules had been adopted in toto from the American Bar Association Code of Professional Responsibility. It does not follow, however, that the ABA's formulation of those disciplinary rules was state action. The State Supreme Court retained plenary power to reexamine those standards and, if necessary, to reject them and promulgate its own. . . . So here, UNLV retained the authority to withdraw from the NCAA and establish its own standards. The University alternatively could have stayed in the Association and worked through the Association's legislative process to amend rules or standards it deemed harsh, unfair, or unwieldy. Neither UNLV's decision to adopt the NCAA's standards nor its minor role in their formulation is a sufficient reason for concluding that the NCAA was acting under color of Nevada law when it promulgated standards governing athlete recruitment, eligibility, and academic performance.

Tarkanian further asserts that the NCAA's investigation, enforcement proceedings, and consequent recommendations constituted state action because they resulted from a delegation of power by UNLV. UNLV, as an NCAA member, subscribed to the statement in the Association's bylaws that NCAA "enforcement procedures are an essential part of the intercollegiate athletic program of

---

13 The situation would, of course, be different if the membership consisted entirely of institutions located within the same State, many of them public institutions created by the same sovereign. *See Clark v. Arizona Interscholastic Association,* 695 F.2d 1126 (9th Cir. 1982), *cert. denied,* 464 U.S. 818 (1983); *Louisiana High School Athletic Association v. St. Augustine High School,* 396 F.2d 224 (5th Cir. 1968). The dissent apparently agrees that the NCAA was not acting under color of state law in its relationships with private universities, which constitute the bulk of its membership.

each member institution." . . . It is, of course, true that a state may delegate authority to a private party and thereby make that party a state actor. . . . But UNLV delegated no power to the NCAA to take specific action against any University employee. The commitment by UNLV to adhere to NCAA enforcement procedures was enforceable only by sanctions that the NCAA might impose on UNLV itself.

Indeed, the notion that UNLV's promise to cooperate in the NCAA enforcement proceedings was tantamount to a partnership agreement or the transfer of certain University powers to the NCAA is belied by the history of this case. It is quite obvious that UNLV used its best efforts to retain its winning coach — a goal diametrically opposed to the NCAA's interest in ascertaining the truth of its investigators' reports. During the several years that the NCAA investigated the alleged violations, the NCAA and UNLV acted much more like adversaries than like partners engaged in a dispassionate search for the truth. The NCAA cannot be regarded as an agent of UNLV for purposes of that proceeding. It is more correctly characterized as an agent of its remaining members which, as competitors of UNLV, had an interest in the effective and evenhanded enforcement of NCAA's recruitment standards. Just as a state-compensated public defender acts in a private capacity when she represents a private client in a conflict against the State, . . . the NCAA is properly viewed as a private actor at odds with the State when it represents the interests of its entire membership in an investigation of one public university.

The NCAA enjoyed no governmental powers to facilitate its investigation.[17] It had no power to subpoena witnesses, to impose contempt sanctions, or to assert sovereign authority over any individual. Its greatest authority was to threaten sanctions against UNLV, with the ultimate sanction being expulsion of

---

[17] In *Dennis v. Sparks,* 449 U.S. 24 (1980), on which the dissent relies, the parties had entered into a corrupt agreement to perform a judicial act. As we explained:

> "[H]ere the allegations were that an official act of the defendant judge was the product of a corrupt conspiracy involving bribery of the judge. Under these allegations, the private parties conspiring with the judge were acting under color of state law; and it is of no consequence in this respect that the judge himself is immune from damages liability. Immunity does not change the character of the judge's action or that of his co-conspirators. Indeed, his immunity is dependent on the challenged conduct being an official judicial act within his statutory jurisdiction, broadly construed. Private parties who corruptly conspire with a judge in connection with such conduct are thus acting under color of law. . . ."

Id. at 28-29 (footnote and citations omitted).

In this case there is no suggestion of any impropriety respecting the agreement between the NCAA and UNLV. Indeed the dissent seems to assume that NCAA's liability as a state actor depended not on its initial agreement with UNLV, but on whether UNLV ultimately accepted the NCAA's recommended discipline of Tarkanian. See *post*, at 203. In contrast, the conspirators in *Dennis* became state actors when they formed the corrupt bargain with the judge, and remained so through completion of the conspiracy's objectives. Cf. *Adickes v. Kress & Co.,* 398 U.S. 144, 149-150 & n.5 (1970) (private restaurant that denied plaintiff service in violation of federal law would be liable as state actor upon proof that it conspired with police officer to deprive plaintiff of her constitutional rights).

the University from membership. Contrary to the premise of the Nevada Supreme Court's opinion, the NCAA did not — indeed, could not — directly discipline Tarkanian or any other state university employee.[18] The express terms of the Confidential Report did not demand the suspension unconditionally; rather, it requested "the University . . . to show cause" why the NCAA should not impose additional penalties if UNLV declines to suspend Tarkanian. . . . Even the University's vice president acknowledged that the Report gave the University options other than suspension: UNLV could have retained Tarkanian and risked additional sanctions, perhaps even expulsion from the NCAA, or it could have withdrawn voluntarily from the Association.

Finally, Tarkanian argues that the power of the NCAA is so great that the UNLV had no practical alternative to compliance with its demands We are not at all sure this is true,[19] but even if we assume that a private monopolist can impose its will on a state agency by a threatened refusal to deal with it, it does not follow that such a private party is therefore acting under color of state law. . . .

In final analysis the question is whether "the conduct allegedly causing the deprivation of a federal right [can] be fairly attributable to the State." . . . It would be ironic indeed to conclude that the NCAA's imposition of sanctions against UNLV — sanctions that UNLV and its counsel, including the Attorney General of Nevada, steadfastly opposed during protracted adversary proceedings — is fairly attributable to the State of Nevada. It would be more appropriate to conclude that UNLV has conducted its athletic program under color of the policies adopted by the NCAA, rather than that those policies were developed and enforced under color of Nevada law.

---

[18] Tarkanian urges us to hold, as did the Nevada Supreme Court, that the NCAA by its rules and enforcement procedures has usurped a traditional, essential state function. Quite properly, he does not point to the NCAA's overriding function of fostering amateur athletics at the college level. For while we have described that function as "critical," *NCAA v. Board of Regents of the University of Oklahoma,* 468 U.S. 85, 120 (1984), by no means is it a traditional, let alone an exclusive, state function. Tarkanian argues instead that the NCAA has assumed the state's traditional and exclusive power to discipline its employees.

"[A]s to state employees connected with intercollegiate athletics, the NCAA requires that its standards, procedures and determinations *become* the State's standards, procedures and determinations for disciplining state employees," he contends. "The State is *obligated* to impose NCAA standards, procedures and determinations making the NCAA a joint participant in the State's suspension of Tarkanian." Brief for Respondent 34-35 (emphases in original).

This argument overlooks the fact that the NCAA's own legislation prohibits it from taking any direct action against Tarkanian. Moreover, suspension of Tarkanian is one of many recommendations in the Confidential Report. Those recommendations as a whole were intended to bring UNLV's basketball program into compliance with NCAA rules. Suspension of Tarkanian was but one means toward achieving that goal.

[19] The University's desire to remain a powerhouse among the nation's college basketball teams is understandable, and nonmembership in the NCAA obviously would thwart that goal. But that UNLV's options were unpalatable does not mean that they were nonexistent.

The judgment of the Nevada Supreme Court is reversed and the case is remanded to that court for further proceedings not inconsistent with this opinion.

It is so ordered.

JUSTICE WHITE, with whom JUSTICE BRENNAN, JUSTICE MARSHALL, and JUSTICE O'CONNOR join, dissenting. [Dissent omitted]

* * *

BRENTWOOD ACADEMY v. TENNESSEE SECONDARY SCHOOL ATHLETIC ASSOCIATION

531 U.S. 288 (2001)

JUSTICE SOUTER delivered the opinion of the Court.

The issue is whether a statewide association incorporated to regulate interscholastic athletic competition among public and private secondary schools may be regarded as engaging in state action when it enforces a rule against a member school. The association in question here includes most public schools located within the State, acts through their representatives, draws its officers from them, is largely funded by their dues and income received in their stead, and has historically been seen to regulate in lieu of the State Board of Education's exercise of its own authority. We hold that the association's regulatory activity may and should be treated as state action owing to the pervasive entwinement of state school officials in the structure of the association, there being no offsetting reason to see the association's acts in any other way.

I

Respondent Tennessee Secondary School Athletic Association (Association) is a not-for-profit membership corporation organized to regulate interscholastic sport among the public and private high schools in Tennessee that belong to it. No school is forced to join, but without any other authority actually regulating interscholastic athletics, it enjoys the memberships of almost all the State's public high schools (some 290 of them or 84% of the Association's voting membership), far outnumbering the 55 private schools that belong. A member school's team may play or scrimmage only against the team of another member, absent a dispensation.

The Association's rulemaking arm is its legislative council, while its board of control tends to administration. The voting membership of each of these nine-person committees is limited under the Association's bylaws to high school principals, assistant principals, and superintendents elected by the member schools, and the public school administrators who so serve typically attend meetings during regular school hours. Although the Association's staff members are not paid by the State, they are eligible to join the State's public retirement system for its employees. Member schools pay dues to the Association, though the bulk of its revenue is gate receipts at member teams' football and basketball tournaments, many of them held in public arenas rented by the Association.

The constitution, bylaws, and rules of the Association set standards of school membership and the eligibility of students to play in interscholastic games. Each school, for example, is regulated in awarding financial aid, most coaches must have a Tennessee state teaching license, and players must meet minimum academic standards and hew to limits on student employment. Under the bylaws, "in all matters pertaining to the athletic relations of his school," the principal is responsible to the Association, which has the power "to suspend, to fine, or otherwise penalize any member school for the violation of any of the rules of the Association or for other just cause."

Ever since the Association was incorporated in 1925, Tennessee's State Board of Education (State Board) has (to use its own words) acknowledged the corporation's functions "in providing standards, rules and regulations for interscholastic competition in the public schools of Tennessee." More recently, the State Board cited its statutory authority, when it adopted language expressing the relationship between the Association and the Board. Specifically, in 1972, it went so far as to adopt a rule expressly "designating" the Association as "the organization to supervise and regulate the athletic activities in which the public junior and senior high schools in Tennessee participate on an interscholastic basis." . . . The Rule provided that "the authority granted herein shall remain in effect until revoked" and instructed the State Board's chairman to "designate a person or persons to serve in an ex-officio capacity on the [Association's governing bodies]." That same year, the State Board specifically approved the Association's rules and regulations, while reserving the right to review future changes. Thus, on several occasions over the next 20 years, the State Board reviewed, approved, or reaffirmed its approval of the recruiting Rule at issue in this case. In 1996, however, the State Board dropped the original Rule . . . expressly designating the Association as regulator; it substituted a statement "recognizing the value of participation in interscholastic athletics and the role of [the Association] in coordinating interscholastic athletic competition," while "authorizing the public schools of the state to voluntarily maintain membership in [the Association]."

The action before us responds to a 1997 regulatory enforcement proceeding brought against petitioner, Brentwood Academy, a private parochial high school member of the Association. The Association's board of control found that Brentwood violated a rule prohibiting "undue influence" in recruiting athletes, when it wrote to incoming students and their parents about spring football practice. The Association accordingly placed Brentwood's athletic program on probation for four years, declared its football and boys' basketball teams ineligible to compete in playoffs for two years, and imposed a $ 3,000 fine. When these penalties were imposed, all the voting members of the board of control and legislative council were public school administrators.

Brentwood sued the Association and its executive director in federal court under Rev. Stat. § 1979, 42 U.S.C. § 1983, claiming that enforcement of the Rule was state action and a violation of the First and Fourteenth Amendments. The District Court entered summary judgment for Brentwood and enjoined the Association from enforcing the Rule. . . . In holding the Association to be a state actor under § 1983 and the Fourteenth Amendment, the District Court found that the State had delegated authority over high school athletics to the Association, characterized the relationship between the Association and its public school members as symbiotic, and emphasized the predominantly public character of the Association's membership and leadership. . . .

The United States Court of Appeals for the Sixth Circuit reversed. It recognized that there is no single test to identify state actions and state actors but applied three criteria derived from *Blum* v. *Yaretsky*, 457 U.S. 991(1982), *Lugar* v. *Edmondson Oil Co.*, 457 U.S. 922 (1982), and *Rendell-Baker* v. *Kohn*, 457 U.S. 830 (1982), and found no state action under any of them. It said the District Court was mistaken in seeing a symbiotic relationship between the State and the Association, it emphasized that the Association was neither engaging in a traditional and exclusive public function nor responding to state compulsion. . . . We granted certiorari to resolve the conflict and now reverse.

II

A

Our cases try to plot a line between state action subject to Fourteenth Amendment scrutiny and private conduct (however exceptionable) that is not. . . . The judicial obligation is not only to " 'preserve an area of individual freedom by limiting the reach of federal law' and avoi[d] the imposition of responsibility on a State for conduct it could not control," . . . but also to assure that constitutional standards are invoked "when it can be said that the State is *responsible* for the specific conduct of which the plaintiff complains." If the Fourteenth Amendment is not to be displaced, therefore, its ambit cannot be a simple line between States and people operating outside formally governmental organizations, and the deed of an ostensibly private organization or individual is to be treated sometimes as if a State had caused it to be performed. Thus, we say that state action may be found if, though only if, there is such a "close nexus between the State and the challenged action" that seemingly private behavior "may be fairly treated as that of the State itself."

* * *

Our cases have identified a host of facts that can bear on the fairness of such an attribution. We have, for example, held that a challenged activity may be state action when it results from the State's exercise of "coercive power," when the State provides "significant encouragement, either overt or covert," or when a private actor operates as a "willful participant in joint activity with the State or its agents[.]" . . . We have treated a nominally private entity as a state actor when it is controlled by an "agency of the State," . . . when it has been delegated a public function by the State, when it is "entwined with governmental policies" or when government is "entwined in [its] management or control[.]" . . .

Amidst such variety, examples may be the best teachers, and examples from our cases are unequivocal in showing that the character of a legal entity is determined neither by its expressly private characterization in statutory law, nor by the failure of the law to acknowledge the entity's inseparability from recognized government officials or agencies. *Lebron* v. *National Railroad Passenger Corporation*, 513 U.S. 374 (1995), held that Amtrak was the Government for constitutional purposes, regardless of its congressional designation as private; it was organized under federal law to attain governmental objectives and was directed and controlled by federal appointees. *Pennsylvania* v. *Board of Directors of City Trusts of Philadelphia* held the privately endowed Gerard College to be a state actor and enforcement of its private founder's limitation of admission to whites attributable to the State, because, consistent with the terms of the settlor's gift, the college's board of directors was a state agency established by state law. Ostensibly the converse situation occurred in *Evans* v. *Newton*, which held that private trustees to whom a city had transferred a park were nonetheless state actors barred from enforcing racial segregation, since the park served the public purpose of providing community recreation, and "the municipality remained entwined in [its] management [and] control[.]"

These examples of public entwinement in the management and control of ostensibly separate trusts or corporations foreshadow this case, as this Court itself anticipated in [*National Collegiate Athletic Association v.*] *Tarkanian*, *supra*. *Tarkanian* arose when an undoubtedly state actor, the University of Nevada, suspended its basketball coach, Tarkanian, in order to comply with rules and recommendations of the National Collegiate Athletic Association (NCAA). The coach charged the NCAA with state action, arguing that the state university had delegated its own functions to the NCAA, clothing the latter with authority to make and apply the university's rules, the result being joint action making the NCAA a state actor.

To be sure, it is not the strict holding in *Tarkanian* that points to our view of this case, for we found no state action on the part of the NCAA. We could see, on the one hand, that the university had some part in setting the NCAA's rules, and the Supreme Court of Nevada had gone so far as to hold that the NCAA had been delegated the university's traditionally exclusive public authority over personnel. But on the other side, the NCAA's policies were shaped not by the University of Nevada alone, but by several hundred member institutions, most of them having no connection with Nevada, and exhibiting no color of Nevada law. Since it was difficult to see the NCAA, not as a collective membership, but as surrogate for the one State, we held the organization's connection with Nevada too insubstantial to ground a state action claim.

But dictum in *Tarkanian* pointed to a contrary result on facts like ours, with an organization whose member public schools are all within a single State.

"The situation would, of course, be different if the [Association's] membership consisted entirely of institutions located within the same State, many of them public institutions created by the same sovereign." To support our surmise, we approvingly cited two cases: *Clark v. Arizona Interscholastic Assn.*, 695 F.2d 1126 (9th Cir. 1982), a challenge to a state high school athletic association that kept boys from playing on girls' interscholastic volleyball teams in Arizona; and *Louisiana High School Athletic Assn. v. St. Augustine High School*, 396 F.2d 224 (5th Cir. 1968), a parochial school's attack on the racially segregated system of interscholastic high school athletics maintained by the athletic association. In each instance, the Court of Appeals treated the athletic association as a state actor.

B

Just as we foresaw in *Tarkanian*, the "necessarily fact-bound inquiry," leads to the conclusion of state action here. The nominally private character of the Association is overborne by the pervasive entwinement of public institutions and public officials in its composition and workings, and there is no substantial reason to claim unfairness in applying constitutional standards to it.

The Association is not an organization of natural persons acting on their own, but of schools, and of public schools to the extent of 84% of the total. Under the Association's bylaws, each member school is represented by its principal or a faculty member, who has a vote in selecting members of the governing legislative council and board of control from eligible principals, assistant principals and superintendents.

Although the findings and prior opinions in this case include no express conclusion of law that public school officials act within the scope of their duties when they represent their institutions, no other view would be rational, the official nature of their involvement being shown in any number of ways. Interscholastic athletics obviously play an integral part in the public education of Tennessee, where nearly every public high school spends money on competitions among schools. Since a pickup system of interscholastic games would not do, these public teams need some mechanism to produce rules and regulate competition. The mechanism is an organization overwhelmingly composed of public school officials who select representatives (all of them public officials at the time in question here), who in turn adopt and enforce the rules that make the system work. Thus, by giving these jobs to the Association, the 290 public schools of Tennessee belonging to it can sensibly be seen as exercising their own authority to meet their own responsibilities. Unsurprisingly, then, the record indicates that half the council or board meetings documented here were held during official school hours, and that public schools have largely provided for the Association's financial support. A small portion of the Association's revenue comes from membership dues paid by the schools, and the principal part from gate receipts at tournaments among the member schools. Unlike mere public buyers of contract services, whose payments for services rendered do not convert the service providers into public actors, the schools here obtain membership in the service organization and give up sources of their own income to their collective association. The Association thus exercises the authority of the predominantly public schools to charge for admission to their games; the Association does not receive this money from the schools, but enjoys the schools' moneymaking capacity as its own.

In sum, to the extent of 84% of its membership, the Association is an organization of public schools represented by their officials acting in their official capacity to provide an integral element of secondary public schooling. There would be no recognizable Association, legal or tangible, without the public school officials, who do not merely control but overwhelmingly perform all but the purely ministerial acts by which the Association exists and functions in practical terms. Only the 16% minority of private school memberships prevents this entwinement of the Association and the public school system from being total and their identities totally indistinguishable.

To complement the entwinement of public school officials with the Association from the bottom up, the State of Tennessee has provided for entwinement from top down. State Board members are assigned ex officio to serve as members of the board of control and legislative council, and the Association's ministerial employees are treated as state employees to the extent of being eligible for membership in the state retirement system.

It is, of course, true that the time is long past when the close relationship between the surrogate association and its public members and public officials acting as such was attested frankly. As mentioned, the terms of the State Board's Rule expressly designating the Association as regulator of interscholastic athletics in public schools was deleted in 1996, the year after a Federal District Court held that the Association was a state actor because its rules were "caused, directed and controlled by the Tennessee Board of Education," *Graham* v. *TSSAA*, 1995 WL 115890 (E.D. Tenn., Feb. 20, 1995).

But the removal of the designation language from Rule 0520-1-2-.08 affected nothing but words. Today the State Board's member-designees continue to sit on the Association's committees as nonvoting members, and the State continues to welcome Association employees in its retirement scheme. The close relationship is confirmed by the Association's enforcement of the same preamendment rules and regulations reviewed and approved by the State Board (including the recruiting Rule challenged by Brentwood), and by the State Board's continued willingness to allow students to satisfy its physical education requirement by taking part in interscholastic athletics sponsored by the Association. The most one can say on the evidence is that the State Board once freely acknowledged the Association's official character but now does it by winks and nods. The amendment to the Rule in 1996 affected candor but not the "momentum" of the Association's prior involvement with the State Board. *Evans v. Newton*, 382 U.S. at 301. The District Court spoke to this point in finding that because of "custom and practice," "the conduct of the parties has not materially changed" since

1996, "the connections between TSSAA and the State [being] still pervasive and entwined."

The entwinement down from the State Board is therefore unmistakable, just as the entwinement up from the member public schools is overwhelming. Entwinement will support a conclusion that an ostensibly private organization ought to be charged with a public character and judged by constitutional standards; entwinement to the degree shown here requires it.

C

Entwinement is also the answer to the Association's several arguments offered to persuade us that the facts would not support a finding of state action under various criteria applied in other cases. These arguments are beside the point, simply because the facts justify a conclusion of state action under the criterion of entwinement, a conclusion in no sense unsettled merely because other criteria of state action may not be satisfied by the same facts.

The Association places great stress, for example, on the application of a public function test, as exemplified in *Rendell-Baker* v. *Kohn*, 457 U.S. 830 (1982). There, an apparently private school provided education for students whose special needs made it difficult for them to finish high school. The record, however, failed to show any tradition of providing public special education to students unable to cope with a regular school, who had historically been cared for (or ignored) according to private choice. It was true that various public school districts had adopted the practice of referring students to the school and paying their tuition, and no one disputed that providing the instruction aimed at a proper public objective and conferred a public benefit. But we held that the performance of such a public function did not permit a finding of state action on the part of the school unless the function performed was exclusively and traditionally public, as it was not in that case. The Association argues that application of the public function criterion would produce the same result here, and we will assume, *arguendo,* that it would. But this case does not turn on a public function test, any more than *Rendell-Baker* had anything to do with entwinement of public officials in the special school.

For the same reason, it avails the Association nothing to stress that the State neither coerced nor encouraged the actions complained of. "Coercion" and "encouragement" are like "entwinement" in referring to kinds of facts that can justify characterizing an ostensibly private action as public instead. Facts that address any of these criteria are significant, but no one criterion must necessarily be applied. When, therefore, the relevant facts show pervasive entwinement to the point of largely overlapping identity, the implication of state action is not affected by pointing out that the facts might not loom large under a different test.

D

This is not to say that all of the Association's arguments are rendered beside the point by the public officials' involvement in the Association, for after application of the entwinement criterion, or any other, there is a further potential issue, and the Association raises it. Even facts that suffice to show public action (or, standing alone, would require such a finding) may be outweighed in the name of some value at odds with finding public accountability in the circumstances. In *Polk County*, 454 U.S. at 322, a defense lawyer's actions were deemed private even though she was employed by the county and was acting within the scope of her duty as a public defender. Full-time public employment would be conclusive of state action for some purposes, but not when the employee is doing a defense lawyer's primary job; then, the public defender does "not act on behalf of the State; he is the State's adversary." The state-action doctrine does not convert opponents into virtual agents.

The assertion of such a countervailing value is the nub of each of the Association's two remaining arguments, neither of which, however, persuades us. The Association suggests, first, that reversing the judgment here will somehow trigger an epidemic of unprecedented federal litigation. Even if that might be counted as a good reason for a *Polk County* decision to call the Association's action private, the record raises no reason for alarm here. Save for the Sixth Circuit, every Court of Appeals to consider a statewide athletic association like the one here has found it a state actor. This majority view began taking shape even before *Tarkanian*, which cited two such decisions approvingly . . . (and this was six years after *Blum*, *Rendell-Baker*, and *Lugar*, on which the Sixth Circuit relied here). No one, however, has pointed to any explosion of § 1983 cases against interscholastic athletic associations in the affected jurisdictions. Not to put too fine a point on it, two District Courts in Tennessee have previously held the Association itself to be a state actor, see *Graham*, 1995 WL 115890, but there is no evident wave of litigation working its way across the State. A reversal of the judgment here portends nothing more than the harmony of an outlying Circuit with precedent otherwise uniform.

Nor do we think there is anything to be said for the Association's contention that there is no need to treat it as a state actor since any public school applying the Association's rules is itself subject to suit under § 1983 or Title IX of the Education Amendments of 1972. If Brentwood's claim were pushing at the edge of the class of possible defendant state actors, an argument about the social utility of expanding that class would at least be on point, but because we are nowhere near the margin in this case, the Association is really asking for nothing less than a dispensation for itself. Its position boils down to saying that the Association should not be dressed in state clothes because other, concededly public actors are; that Brentwood should be kept out of court because a different plaintiff raising a different claim in a different case may find the courthouse open. Pleas for special treatment are hard to sell, although saying that does not, of course, imply anything about the merits of Brentwood's complaint; the issue here is merely whether Brentwood properly names the Association as a § 1983 defendant, not whether it should win on its claim.

The judgment of the Court of Appeals for the Sixth Circuit is reversed, and the case is remanded for further proceedings consistent with this opinion. It is so ordered.

JUSTICE THOMAS, with whom THE CHIEF JUSTICE, JUSTICE SCALIA, and JUSTICE KENNEDY join, dissenting. [Opinion omitted.]

NOTES AND COMMENTS

1. Prior to the Supreme Court's decision in *Tarkanian*, the lower courts had viewed the NCAA as a "state" actor for a number of years, almost without exception. *See, e.g., Howard University v. National Collegiate Athletic Association*, 510 F.2d 213 (D.C. Cir 1975); *Parish v. National Collegiate Athletic Association*, 506 F.2d 1028 (5th Cir. 1975). This trend ended with the decision in *Arlosoroff v. National Collegiate Athletic Association*, 746 F.2d 1019 (4th Cir. 1984), which followed the Supreme Court's reasoning in non-sports association cases, holding that the actions of the NCAA were not equivalent state action. (*Blum v. Yaretsky*, 457 U.S. 991 (1982) and *Rendell-Baker v. Kohn,* 457 U.S. 830 (1982)).

Does *Tarkanian* spell the end for constitutional challenges to action taken by the NCAA? Would a case brought by an athlete who had been harmed by NCAA action be distinguishable?

It may well be that the best approach for an athlete challenging the NCAA will be to utilize the law of private associations or contractual theories such as presented in the materials in **Chapter 1**, *supra*. The law of private associations essentially prevents courts from interfering in the internal workings of a voluntary private association, such as the NCAA. However, courts will intervene if a decision of an organization is contrary to its own laws or rules, or not authorized by its constitution or bylaws. *Mozingo v. Oklahoma Secondary School Activities Association,* 575 P.2d 1379 (Okla. Ct. App. 1978); *California State U., Hayward v. NCAA*, 121 Cal. Rptr. 85 (Cal. Ct. App. 1975).

In the aftermath of *Tarkanian*, Illinois, Florida, Nevada, and Nebraska enacted legislation purporting to require the NCAA to provide very specific due process in the context of its enforcement actions. The Nevada statute was challenged by the NCAA and ultimately declared unconstitutional as a violation of the Commerce Clause. *National Collegiate Athletic Association v. Miller,* 10 F.3d 633 (9th Cir. 1993). At about this same time the NCAA promulgated significant changes for its enforcement procedures that provided greater due process than prior to the amendments. *See* Division I Manual, Article 32 (2003). *Query*: What other theories are available to athletes to challenge actions of the NCAA related to eligibility, enforcement, or other issues?

2. In *Lafler v. Athletic Board of Control*, 536 F. Supp. 104 (W.D. Mich. 1982), the court relied upon *DeFrantz* to find that no state action was involved in denying the plaintiff, a woman, the opportunity to compete in the Golden Gloves boxing competition. Judge Miles showed dazzling footwork as he shadowboxed the state action issue:

> The plaintiff admits that her application to compete was submitted to the Golden Gloves competition, which is a private, not a state, organization. All parties appear to agree that the rule which prohibits the plaintiff from participating in the competition was promulgated by the United States of America Amateur Boxing Federation (USA/ABF) and adopted by the Michigan Amateur Boxing Federation. It appears unlikely, based upon the decision and reasoning of the court in *DeFrantz* v. *United States Olympic Committee* . . . that either of these entities could be considered agencies or arms of the state or federal government. The most that the plaintiff can show that . . . the Athletic Board of Control . . . ha[s] done, is to acquiesce in some way in the Boxing Federation's enforcement of its own rules. This acquiescence, or even approval, without more, does not constitute state action. *Jackson v. Metropolitan Edison Co.*, 419 U.S. 345 (1974). Therefore, the plaintiff has not shown a likelihood of success under the Equal Protection Clause because of the probable absence of any state action.

Id. at 105-06.

Is this conclusion justified? Wouldn't you like to know more about what the Athletic Board of Control does and how it is constituted?

3. The 10th Circuit has ruled that the governing organization of amateur basketball in the United States, ABA/USA, is not a governmental actor for constitutional purposes, following *Tarkanian* and *DeFrantz*. *Behagen v. Amateur Basketball Association of the United States of America,* 884 F.2d 524 (10th Cir. 1989).

4. In its 5-4 decision, the U.S. Supreme Court in *Brentwood Academy* held that the TSSA was a state actor. Why? What distinguishes a state high school athletic association from the NCAA or USOC? Does such a distinction warrant varied application of Constitutional principles? What is the status of *Tarkanian* and *DeFrantz* following *Brentwood*?

B. NATIONAL COLLEGIATE ATHLETIC ASSOCIATION ENFORCEMENT AND ELIGIBILITY ISSUES

1. Enforcement Process and the Role of the Attorney

PROBLEM 1

You are an attorney in Norsa, Oklanois, which is the location of Oklanois State University, a public university which is a Division I member of the NCAA.

You have represented the university in the past in matters involving its athletic program.

The school was on NCAA probation three years ago for recruiting violations in basketball. The program has a new head coach, who brought in three new assistant coaches. The reputation of the program is that it is "clean," operating within the NCAA rules. Of course, if any sport at the school is determined to have committed a "major" violation within five years of the previous violation, the school will be deemed a repeat violator and the "death penalty" could be imposed on the offending sport. This would mean at least a one year suspension of that sport.

You have been approached by the Athletic Director at OSU concerning a preliminary inquiry letter received by the university from the NCAA indicating the Association has conducted an investigation into allegation of irregularities surrounding the school's athletic program. He assumes that it is nothing serious and must be about some program other than basketball. He simply wants to let you know of the NCAA's actions in case it becomes more serious.

A few days later the president of OSU receives an Official Inquiry Letter from the assistant executive director of the NCAA informing the university of the matter under investigation and requesting cooperation. The letter sets out ten allegations against the basketball program, some serious and some not so serious. The president, the athletic director, and the basketball coach are extremely upset and inform you that they do not want to cooperate.

The specifics of the allegations are as follows:

1. Improper contact of a basketball recruit after the player had signed a letter of intent.
2. Improper contact of parents and prospective athlete by an institutional staff member not allowed to scout off-campus.
3. Contact of a recruit by phone during the 48 hour "dead period" prior to and after National Letter of Intent signing day.
4. Improper contact with a prospective student athlete prior to a basketball game during a day in which he was to be a participant in the competition.
5. A former assistant coach demonstrated a knowing and willful effort to violate NCAA rules and regulations.
6. An assistant coach sent a prospective student athlete a package containing $500 in cash.
7. A "booster" of the school's program arranged for travel expenses for a basketball player's parents to all of the school's games during the previous season.

8. Several prospective and enrolled players' lodging and credit arrangements were contrary to normal university housing policies and of a type not available to all students.

9. An athletic department representative provided round trip car transportation for a prospective student athlete and a friend to a basketball game. They both received a free hat, t-shirt and tickets to the game.

10. A former assistant coach arranged for or provided a student athlete with a monthly allowance that ranged from $50 to $200.

11. A student athlete competed in regular and post season competition on behalf of the institution while failing to make satisfactory progress towards a degree.

You are to advise the university of the appropriate course to take with regard to the investigation. Describe the methods which you would employ to thoroughly represent the university. Bear in mind that the death penalty lurks in the background of this case and the fact that this is a big money program.

PROBLEM 2

You represent Midwestern State University and have been contacted by the President and the Athletic Director regarding a problem which has just come to their attention. Two of the school's former football players may have been ineligible during their just completed senior seasons as a result of signing contracts with an agent. The President is reasonably convinced that the two players both signed with the agent just prior to the start of their senior year and may have received money from the agent as well. The two players were high draft choices and are just now beginning their rookie years in the NFL.

The agent involved has been surrounded by controversy for the last several years, but has never actually encountered legal difficulties. The President is concerned about the ramifications for the school's sports programs and would also like to take some action against the agent. Discuss the problems which may face the school and the possible courses of action regarding both the school and the agent.

PROBLEM 3

You are a legislative aide in a southwestern state. All of the four major state universities in your state currently have athletic programs which are under various NCAA sanctions. Your boss, the chair of the state senate's education committee, has asked you to draft a bill which would deal with sleazy recruiting practices by college coaches and supporters of athletic programs, as well as activities of sports agents. What approach would you take and what language would have to be used? Do you see any problems that might arise from this type of legislation?

Case File

The NCAA, as noted in the **Introduction** to **Part I**, is the most significant governing body for collegiate athletics. Its membership includes, particularly at the Division I level, all of the major collegiate athletic programs in the country. It regulates recruitment and eligibility and operates championships, among other things. Its elaborate and quite complex rules relating to eligibility, amateurism, recruitment, financial aid and championships are frequently subject to interpretation and occasionally violated.

The NCAA Infractions Process. When a member institution is alleged to have violated a provision of the NCAA's rules, the association's enforcement staff will commence an investigation. There are a number of ways in which alleged violations come to the attention of the NCAA. Frequently they are a result of self-reporting by the institutions. There are also instances of investigations being initiated as a result of information provided by opposing schools, recruits, and reporters. All investigations are treated as confidential until announcements are made according to the prescribed procedures. If the enforcement staff has reasonably reliable information indicating an institution has acted in violation of the association's governing legislation it will serve a Notice of Inquiry on the CEO of the institution. This notice will detail the potential violations, the sport and the individuals involved. Following the preliminary investigation, the process can go one of three directions: the case may be closed for lack of evidence; a major violation may be found and summary disposal discussions begin with the school; and a less or secondary violation may be found and appropriate penalties are then discussed and imposed.

If the enforcement staff has "sufficient information to warrant" a Notice of Allegations will be issued to the CEO of the institution. This notice will detail the allegations with perhaps even more specificity than the Notice of Inquiry. The institution will then conduct its own investigation, often utilizing outside counsel and investigators. Outside counsel will advise the institution that it must cooperate with the NCAA in the process and must not expect that the adversarial climate and tactics normally found in civil litigation will be tolerated in the NCAA process. Failure to cooperate is itself a violation of the rules. (Another significant violation, frequently found in these matters, is lack of institutional control of the athletic program.) Individual coaches and athletes may also have their own legal representation.

Following the investigation the Committee on Infractions will conduct a hearing to determine findings and any penalties deemed appropriate. This hearing will involve the institution's representatives, involved parties, the enforcement staff, and, where appropriate, the report of an independent hearing officer. Following the hearing, the Committee on Infractions will issue its report, which will include penalties. Potential penalties range from public censure and reprimand to the "death penalty," the total shut-down of a program or particular sport for a set time. In between are such sanctions as reduction in scholarships allowed, forfeiture of tournament money, and ineligibility for television appearances. The school has the opportunity to appeal the ruling to the Infractions Appeals Committee. This appellate body will receive written "briefs" from the institution and from the Committee on Infractions. It will also hold a hearing involving all interested parties. This process has on occasion produced modified findings and penalties.

Further details concerning the process and reports of decisions by the Committee on Infractions may be found at www.ncaa.org. *See also* Division I Manual, Article 32 (2006).

2. National Collegiate Athletic Association Eligibility Issues

NCAA v. YEO

171 S.W.3d 863 (Tex. 2005)

OPINION BY: NATHAN L. HECHT

Construing the Texas Constitution's guarantee of due course of law, we held twenty years ago . . . that "students do not possess a constitutionally protected interest in their participation in extracurricular activities." . . . Respondent nevertheless contends that because of her unique situation as "the most decorated athlete in the history of the Republic of Singapore", to disqualify her from participating in an intercollegiate swimming competition would deprive her of protected property and liberty interests in her reputation and existing and future financial opportunities in violation of the Texas Constitution. The lower courts agreed, distinguishing this case from *Stamos*. We conclude that the rule in *Stamos* applies and therefore reverse the judgment of the court of appeals and render judgment that respondent take nothing.

When Coach Michael Walker recruited Joscelin Yeo, a high school student in the Republic of Singapore, to enroll at the University of California at Berkeley, she had already achieved fame in her country as a swimmer. At Berkeley, she won numerous All-American awards and was a member of a world-record-setting relay team in 1999. Before the 2000-2001 school year, Walker left Berkeley for the University of Texas at Austin ("UT-Austin"). He was helping coach the Singapore Olympic team, of which Yeo was a member, and she went with him to UT-Austin. Berkeley and UT-Austin are both members of the National Collegiate Athletic Association ("NCAA"), which prescribes rules for determining the eligibility of student athletes to engage in competition. A member that violates these rules is subject to sanctions. NCAA rules generally prohibit a student who transfers from one four-year member institution to another from participating in intercollegiate athletic competitions for one full academic year, but this restriction may be waived under certain circumstances if the former institution does not object. Berkeley refused to waive the restriction, and thus Yeo was ineligible to compete at UT-Austin for an academic year.

As permitted by NCAA rules, Yeo did not enroll in classes for the fall semester of 2000 in order to compete in the Olympics. In compliance with the one-year restriction, she did not participate in intercollegiate events during that semester or the spring semester, when she was enrolled in classes. UT-Austin mistakenly believed that Yeo's first semester had counted toward satisfying the restriction and that she was free to engage in competition beginning the fall semester of 2001. After Yeo competed in four events, Berkeley complained to the NCAA. UT-Austin confessed its error and agreed that Yeo would sit out the remainder of the semester, but the NCAA required that she not participate in the first four events the following spring, to match the four events in which she had been disqualified. Yeo did not know of UT-Austin's discussions with the NCAA and simply did as UT-Austin told her.

UT-Austin then added three swimming events at the beginning of its spring semester schedule. After Yeo had sat out those events and a fourth one, UT-Austin allowed her to rejoin the swim team, but Berkeley again complained, arguing that the added events could not be used to satisfy the one-year restriction. NCAA staff agreed and on March 6 issued a decision that Yeo not participate in the next three regularly scheduled events, including the 2002 NCAA women's swimming and diving championship on March 22. UT-Austin immediately appealed the staff decision to the NCAA Student-Athlete Reinstatement Committee ("the SARC"), and a telephonic hearing was scheduled for the next day. For the first time, UT-Austin told Yeo of the problem and advised her simply to plea for sympathy. She did, but at the conclusion of the hearing, the SARC upheld the staff decision. At UT-Austin's suggestion, Yeo then obtained legal counsel, who persuaded Berkeley on March 15 to waive Yeo's one-year restriction, something it had refused to do before. Counsel moved the SARC to reconsider, especially in light of this development, but it refused.

On March 20, Yeo sued UT-Austin and its vice president for institutional relations and legal affairs, Patricia Ohlendorf, to enjoin them from disqualifying her from competing in the championship meet two days later and for a declaration that UT-Austin had denied her procedural due process as guaranteed by the Texas Constitution. That same day, the trial court issued a temporary restraining order granting Yeo the injunctive relief requested. On March 21, the NCAA intervened in the action, but Yeo moved to strike the intervention, and after a hearing later that day, the trial court granted Yeo's motion. The next morning, the NCAA sought mandamus relief from the court of appeals, and UT-Austin appealed from the temporary restraining order. That afternoon, the court of appeals denied the petition for mandamus and dismissed the interlocutory appeal for want of jurisdiction. Yeo competed in the championship meet.

In November 2002, after a trial to the bench, the trial court rendered judgment for Yeo, declaring that UT-Austin had denied Yeo procedural due process guaranteed by the Texas Constitution, thereby depriving her of protected liberty and property interests. The court permanently enjoined UT-Austin from declaring Yeo ineligible in the future without affording her due process and from punishing her for participating in past competitions, including the 2002 women's championship. The trial court also awarded Yeo $ 164,755.50 in attorney fees through an appeal to this Court. The NCAA appealed from the order striking its intervention, and UT-Austin appealed from the judgment. The court of appeals affirmed. We granted the NCAA's and UT-Austin's petitions for review.

Since the championship meet in March 2002, Yeo has, of course, moved on. When briefs were filed in this case, we were told that Yeo had graduated from UT-Austin, received a Rhodes Scholarship, and ended her college swimming career. But none of the parties argues that the case has become moot, because the injunction prevents the NCAA from imposing retroactive sanctions under its "Restitution Rule". We agree that the case is not moot. We first consider whether Yeo has an interest protected by due course of law under article I, section 19 of the Texas Constitution. In so doing, we look as usual to cases construing the federal constitutional guarantee of due process as persuasive authority. The parties have not identified any difference between the state and federal guarantees material to the issues in this case.

Yeo does not challenge our holding in *Stamos* that a student has no interest in participating in extracurricular activities that is protected by the Texas Constitution's guarantee of due course of law. Nor does she dispute that under NCAA rules, she was ineligible to participate in the 2002 NCAA women's swimming and diving championship. Yeo argues that she was entitled to notice and a meaningful hearing before NCAA rules were applied to her because of her unique reputation and earning potential. Had she been disqualified from competing in the championship meet, she contends, people would have suspected that it was for her own misconduct and not for UT-Austin's mistakes in attempting to comply with NCAA rules. Yeo acknowledges that the United States Supreme Court has held that reputation alone is not a protected liberty or property interest. But it is the degree of her interests, Yeo contends, and not merely their character, that bring them within constitutional protection. A student-athlete with a lesser reputation or less certain of her earning potential, she concedes, would not have the same rights. The court of appeals agreed:

> In connection with the permanent injunction, the trial court made several material findings of fact that are essentially unchallenged: (1) Yeo had already established a world-class reputation and her "good name, outstanding reputation, high standing in her community, her unblemished integrity and honor are particularly important in the Republic of Singapore and in light of her cultural background"; (2) if NCAA rules did not prohibit athletes from accepting professional compensation while competing in NCAA sanctioned events, Yeo "would be immediately

eligible to capitalize on her public persona by entering into lucrative endorsement and marketing opportunities as well as being eligible for prize winnings due to her performance as a member of Singapore's national team"; and (3) "UT-Austin represented to [Yeo] at the time she transferred from [Cal-Berkeley] to become a student-athlete at UT-Austin that UT-Austin would not jeopardize or compromise [Yeo's] eligibility to compete on behalf of UT-Austin in NCAA athletic competition."

These findings of fact support Yeo's theory that her athletic reputation, which was established *even before* she began attending Cal-Berkeley and competing under NCAA regulations, constitutes a protected interest for purposes of due course of law. Yeo had competed in two Olympic games before attending college and had been named sportswoman of the year and Olympic flag-bearer for her native country, Singapore. At both the temporary restraining order and permanent injunction hearings, Yeo represented that it was this continuing interest in her athletic and professional reputation that UT-Austin had damaged by its actions.

* * *

Here, Yeo presented testimony from multiple witnesses indicating that she had established a reputation as a world-class athlete in her home country of Singapore *separate and apart from her intercollegiate swimming career*. As a result, much of her reputation had been built outside of the United States and the structure of NCAA intercollegiate athletics. We cannot say that the trial court erred in holding that Yeo had a protected interest under these facts.

UT-Austin, joined by various *amici curiae*, contends that an affirmance in this case will create a protected interest in every intercollegiate student-athlete to participate in athletic events. We reject this argument and note that we reach this decision because of the unique fact pattern with which we are presented. Based upon the largely undisputed findings of fact, Yeo had already established a protected interest in her reputation as an athlete long before she came to this country to swim competitively as a student-athlete under NCAA rules. Our holding that Yeo, under these facts, has a protected interest should not be read as extending that same protection to every other intercollegiate athlete. The determination of whether a student-athlete has a protected interest is necessarily fact-specific, depending on that athlete's specific situation and reputation. Each such case must be decided on its own merits, in light of the financial realities of contemporary athletic competition. We hold that Yeo's established liberty interest in her reputation as an athlete is entitled to due course of law protection and we affirm the trial court's decision in that regard. [114 S.W. 3d at 596-598]

We reject Yeo's argument and the court of appeals' holding. The United States Supreme Court has stated, and we agree, that whether an interest is protected by due process depends not on its *weight* but on its *nature*.[1]

Yeo does not take issue with this principle but argues in effect that the weight of an interest can determine its nature. A stellar reputation like hers, Yeo contends and the court of appeals concluded, is categorically different from a more modest reputation. We disagree. The loss of either may be, to its owner, substantial. The court of appeals held that whether a reputation is constitutionally protected must be decided case by case, but it did not suggest a measure for distinguishing one case from another, and neither does Yeo. We see none, which convinces us that the *nature* of one's interest in a good reputation is the same no matter how good the reputation is.

Yeo's claimed interest in future financial opportunities is too speculative for due process protection. There must be an actual legal entitlement. While student-athletes remain amateurs, their future financial opportunities remain expectations.

Yeo argues that her reputation and future financial interests are entitled to constitutional protection under our decision in *University of Texas Medical School v. Than*.[2] There we held that a medical student charged with academic dishonesty had a protected liberty interest in a graduate education. But since *Than* we have refused to accord a student's interest in athletics the same protection. We decline to equate an interest in intercollegiate athletics with an interest in graduate education.

Accordingly, we hold that Yeo has asserted no interests protected by article I, section 19 of the Texas Constitution. The case must therefore be dismissed. While we need not reach the NCAA's arguments that it should have been permitted to intervene, we expressly disapprove the court of appeals' conclusions that the NCAA's interests were not sufficiently implicated to warrant intervention, and that intervention would have unduly complicated the case.

We have twice reminded the lower courts that "judicial intervention in [student athletic disputes] often does more harm than good." As the Fifth Circuit has said, judges are not "super referees". Along the same vein, the United States

---

1 *Board of Regents of State Colleges v. Roth*, 408 U.S. 564, 570-571, 33 L. Ed. 2d 548, 92 S. Ct. 2701 (1972) ("But, to determine whether due process requirements apply in the first place, we must look not to the 'weight' but to the nature of the interest at stake. We must look to see if the interest is within the Fourteenth Amendment's protection of liberty and property.") (citation omitted); *Goss v. Lopez*, 419 U.S. 565, 575-576, 42 L. Ed. 2d 725, 95 S. Ct. 729 (1975) ("In determining 'whether due process requirements apply in the first place, we must look not to the "weight" but to the *nature* of the interest at stake.' [Id. at 570-571.] . . . The Court's view has been that as long as a property deprivation is not *de minimis*, its gravity is irrelevant to the question whether account must be taken of the Due Process Clause. *Sniadach v. Family Finance Corp.*, 395 U.S. 337, 342, 23 L. Ed. 2d 349, 89 S. Ct. 1820 (1969) (Harlan, J., concurring); *Boddie v. Connecticut*, 401 U.S. 371, 378-379, 28 L. Ed. 2d 113, 91 S. Ct. 780 (1971); [Roth, 408 U.S. at 570 n.8].").

2 901 S.W.2d 926, 38 Tex. Sup. Ct. J. 910 (Tex. 1995).

Supreme Court has observed: "Courts do not and cannot intervene in the resolution of conflicts which arise in the daily operation of school systems and which do not directly and sharply implicate basic constitutional values." We reiterate this counsel to the trial courts and courts of appeals.

The judgment of the court of appeals is reversed, and judgment is rendered that Yeo take nothing.

BLOOM v. NATIONAL COLLEGIATE ATHLETIC ASSOCIATION

93 P.3d 621 (Colo. App. 2004)

OPINION BY: DAILEY

In this dispute concerning eligibility to play college football, plaintiff, Jeremy Bloom, appeals the trial court's order denying his request for a preliminary injunction against defendants, the National Collegiate Athletic Association (NCAA) and the University of Colorado (CU). We affirm.

I. Background

* * *

Bloom, a high school football and track star, was recruited to play football at CU. Before enrolling there, however, he competed in Olympic and professional World Cup skiing events, becoming the World Cup champion in freestyle moguls. During the Olympics, Bloom appeared on MTV, and thereafter was offered various paid entertainment opportunities, including a chance to host a show on Nickelodeon. Bloom also agreed to endorse commercially certain ski equipment, and he contracted to model clothing for Tommy Hilfiger.

Bloom became concerned that his endorsements and entertainment activities might interfere with his eligibility to compete in intercollegiate football. On Bloom's behalf, CU first requested waivers of NCAA rules restricting student-athlete endorsement and media activities and, then, a favorable interpretation of the NCAA rule restricting media activities.

The NCAA denied CU's requests, and Bloom discontinued his endorsement, modeling, and media activities to play football for CU during the 2002 fall season. However, Bloom instituted this action against the NCAA for declaratory and injunctive relief, asserting that his endorsement, modeling, and media activities were necessary to support his professional skiing career, something which the NCAA rules permitted.

In his complaint, Bloom alleged: (1) as a third-party beneficiary of the contract between the NCAA and its members, he was entitled to enforce NCAA bylaws permitting him to engage in and receive remuneration from a professional sport different from his amateur sport; (2) as applied to the facts of this case, the NCAA's restrictions on endorsements and media appearances were arbitrary and capricious; and (3) those restrictions constituted improper and unconscionable restraints of trade.

For these reasons, Bloom requested that the NCAA restrictions be declared inapplicable, and that the NCAA and CU be enjoined from applying them, to activities originating prior to his enrollment at CU or wholly unrelated to his prowess as a football player.

The trial court ordered CU joined as an indispensable party in the case, and CU aligned with the NCAA as an involuntary defendant. After an evidentiary hearing, the trial court determined that, although Bloom was a third-party beneficiary of NCAA bylaws, he was not entitled to preliminary injunctive relief under the six-part test of *Rathke v. MacFarlane*, 648 P.2d 648, 653-54 (Colo. 1982). The trial court found that Bloom had satisfied three parts of the test: (1) there is a danger of real, immediate, and irreparable injury which may be prevented by injunctive relief; (2) no plain, speedy, and adequate remedy is available at law; and (3) the injunction would preserve the status quo pending trial on the merits. However, the trial court found that Bloom had not satisfied the other parts of the test: (4) there is a reasonable probability of success on the merits; (5) granting a preliminary injunction would not disserve the public interest; and (6) the balance of equities favors the injunction.

Bloom appeals the trial court's ruling under C.A.R. 1(a)(3).

II. Standard of Review

[The court discussed the standard of review for injunctive relief.]

III. Claims on Appeal

Initially, we limit our consideration on appeal to Bloom's claims of breach of contract and arbitrary and capricious action by the NCAA.

* * *

IV. Standing

We reject the NCAA's assertion that Bloom lacked standing to pursue claims for breach of contract or arbitrary and capricious action on the part of the NCAA.

A party has standing to seek relief when he or she has suffered actual injury to a legally protected interest. *Turkey Creek, LLC v. Rosania*, 953 P.2d 1306, 1314 (Colo. App. 1998).

A person not a party to an express contract may bring an action on the contract if the parties to the agreement intended to benefit the nonparty, provided that the benefit claimed is a direct and not merely incidental benefit of the contract. While the intent to benefit the nonparty need not be expressly recited in the contract, the intent must be apparent from the terms of the agreement, the surrounding circumstances, or both. *Parrish Chiropractic Ctrs., P.C. v. Progressive Cas. Ins. Co.*, 874 P.2d 1049, 1056 (Colo. 1994). Here, the trial court found, and we agree, that the NCAA's constitution, bylaws, and regulations evidence a clear intent to benefit student-athletes. And because each student-athlete's eligibility to compete is determined by the NCAA, we conclude that Bloom had standing in a preliminary injunction hearing to contest the meaning or applicability of NCAA eligibility restrictions. . . .

With respect to a claim of arbitrary and capricious action, the Kentucky Supreme Court observed that "relief from our judicial system should be available if voluntary athletic associations act arbitrarily and capriciously toward student-athletes." *NCAA v. Lasege*, 53 S.W.3d 77, 83 (Ky. 2001). The basis upon which the court made that observation, however, is not altogether clear. There is some suggestion in Lasege that judicial review was justified because the NCAA occupied the role of a quasi-state actor with respect to individual student-athletes. . . . However, in an analogous circumstance, the United States Supreme Court concluded that the NCAA is not a state actor and that a state university's adherence to NCAA rules does not implicate the "state action" necessary to trigger a civil rights claim. See *NCAA v. Tarkanian*, 488 U.S. 179 (1988). . .

Courts are reluctant to intervene, except on the most limited grounds, in the internal affairs of voluntary associations. . . . Even then, it would appear that a plaintiff must ordinarily allege an invasion of some type of civil or property right to have standing. . .

Here, Bloom is not a member of the NCAA, and he does not have a constitutional right to engage in amateur intercollegiate athletics at CU. . . . Nor does he assert any property interest in playing football for CU.

However, to the extent Bloom's claim of arbitrary and capricious action asserts a violation of the duty of good faith and fair dealing that is implied in the contractual relationship between the NCAA and its members, his position as a third-party beneficiary of that contractual relationship affords him standing to pursue this claim. . . .

In sum, we conclude that Bloom has third-party beneficiary standing to pursue what in essence are two claims for violation of his contractual rights.

V. Probability of Success

Bloom contends that the trial court erred in assessing the probability of success on his contract claims. We disagree.

Initially, we note that, as a third-party beneficiary, Bloom has rights no greater than those of the parties to the contract itself, here, the NCAA and its member institutions.

A. Interpretation of NCAA Bylaws

In interpreting a contract, we seek to give effect to the intent and the reasonable expectations of the parties. . . . To determine the intent and expectations of the parties, we view the contract in its entirety, not in isolated portions . . .

and we give words and phrases their plain meaning according to common usage. If its meaning is clear and unambiguous, the contract is enforced as written. If, however, the contract is susceptible of more than one reasonable interpretation, it is ambiguous, and its meaning must be determined as an issue of fact. In resolving an ambiguity, a court will follow the construction placed upon it by the parties themselves before the controversy arose.

Bloom relies on NCAA Bylaw 12.1.2, which states that "[a] professional athlete in one sport may represent a member institution in a different sport." He asserts that, because a professional is one who "gets paid" for a sport, a student-athlete is entitled to earn whatever income is customary for his or her professional sport, which, in the case of professional skiers, primarily comes from endorsements and paid media opportunities.

We recognize that, like many others involved in individual professional sports such as golf, tennis, and boxing, professional skiers obtain much of their income from sponsors. We note, however, that none of the NCAA's bylaws mentions, much less explicitly establishes, a right to receive "customary income" for a sport.

To the contrary, the NCAA bylaws prohibit every student-athlete from receiving money for advertisements and endorsements. In this regard, NCAA Bylaw 12.5.2.1 states:

> Subsequent to becoming a student-athlete, an individual shall not be eligible for participation in intercollegiate athletics if the individual: (a) Accepts any remuneration for or permits the use of his or her name or picture to advertise, recommend or promote directly the sale or use of a commercial product or service of any kind, or (b) Receives remuneration for endorsing a commercial product or service through the individual's use of such product or service.

Additionally, while NCAA Bylaw 12.5.1.3 permits a student-athlete to continue to receive remuneration for activity initiated prior to enrollment in which his or her name or picture is used, this remuneration is only allowed, if, as pertinent here, "the individual became involved in such activities for reasons independent of athletics ability; . . . no reference is made in these activities to the individual's name or involvement in intercollegiate athletics; [and] . . . the individual does not endorse the commercial product."

Further, NCAA Bylaw 12.4.1.1 prohibits a student-athlete from receiving "any remuneration for value or utility that the student-athlete may have for the employer because of the publicity, reputation, fame or personal following that he or she has obtained because of athletics ability." Unlike other NCAA bylaws, the endorsements and media appearance bylaws do not contain any sport-specific qualifiers. See, e.g., NCAA Bylaw 12.3.1 (ineligibility of student-athlete to compete in intercollegiate sport based on agreement with agent to market athlete's athletic ability or reputation "in that sport").

In our view, when read together, the NCAA bylaws express a clear and unambiguous intent to prohibit student-athletes from engaging in endorsements and paid media appearances, without regard to: (1) when the opportunity for such activities originated; (2) whether the opportunity arose or exists for reasons unrelated to participation in an amateur sport; and (3) whether income derived from the opportunity is customary for any particular professional sport.

The clear import of the bylaws is that, although student-athletes have the right to be professional athletes, they do not have the right to simultaneously engage in endorsement or paid media activity and maintain their eligibility to participate in amateur competition. And we may not disregard the clear meaning of the bylaws simply because they may disproportionately affect those who participate in individual professional sports.

Further, the record contains ample evidence supporting the trial court's conclusion that this interpretation is consistent with both the NCAA's and its member institutions' construction of the bylaws. An NCAA official testified that both the endorsement and media appearance provisions have been consistently applied and interpreted in a nonsport-specific manner. Indeed, another NCAA official related that association members had resisted efforts to change the endorsement rule to be sport-specific. Although the evidence is conflicting, the record supports the trial court's conclusion that, from the beginning, CU understood that the endorsement and media activity rules were nonsport-specific in scope.

Thus, even if the bylaws were viewed as ambiguous, the record supports the trial court's conclusion that the bylaws would ultimately be interpreted in accordance with the NCAA's and its member institutions' construction of those bylaws.

B. Application of Bylaws to Bloom

The United States Supreme Court has recognized the NCAA as "the guardian of an important American tradition," namely, amateurism in intercollegiate athletics. See *NCAA v. Bd. of Regents*, 468 U.S. 85, 101 (1984).

Under that tradition, "college sports provided an important opportunity for teaching people about character, motivation, endurance, loyalty, and the attainment of one's personal best — all qualities of great value in citizens. In this sense, competitive athletics were viewed as an extracurricular activity, justified by the university as part of its ideal objective of educating the whole person." James J. Duderstadt, Intercollegiate Athletics and the American University 70 (Univ. Mich. Press 2003).

The NCAA's "Principle of Amateurism" states:

> Student-athletes shall be amateurs in an intercollegiate sport, and their participation should be motivated primarily by education and by the physical, mental and social benefits to be derived. Student participation in intercollegiate athletics is an avocation, and student-athletes should be protected from exploitation by professional and commercial enterprises.

NCAA Const. art. 2.9.

The NCAA's purpose, in this regard, is not only "to maintain intercollegiate athletics as an integral part of the educational program," but also to "retain a clear line of demarcation between intercollegiate athletics and professional sports." NCAA Const. art. 1, § 1.3.1.

Here, the trial court found that application of the endorsement and media appearance rules in Bloom's case was rationally related to the legitimate purpose of retaining the "clear line of demarcation between intercollegiate athletics and professional sports."

The trial court noted that salaries and bonuses are an acceptable means for attaining income from professional sports, but endorsement income is not acceptable if a student-athlete wishes to preserve amateur eligibility. According to NCAA officials: (1) endorsements invoke concerns about "the commercial exploitation of student-athletes and the promotion of commercial products"; and (2) it is not possible to distinguish the precise capacity in which endorsements are made. A CU official related that generally, the endorsement rule prevents students from becoming billboards for commercialism, and in Bloom's case, there would "be no way to tell whether he is receiving pay commensurate with his . . . football ability or skiing ability."

In this respect, the trial court observed:

> In an honest world where there is no attempt to avoid an ideal, there wouldn't be an impact on amateurism if Mr. Bloom was allowed to be compensated as is customary for professional skiers; however, it's naive to think that we live in such a world. There are those who would be less than honest and seek profit for profit's sake. . . .

If Mr. Bloom was allowed to receive the [endorsement] income that is customary for professional skiers, it is not difficult for me to imagine that some in other professional sports would decide that in addition to direct monetary compensation . . . endorsements or promotion of goods would become customary.

Similar concerns underlie the NCAA's prohibition on paid entertainment activity. Paid entertainment activity may impinge upon the amateur ideal if the opportunity were obtained or advanced because of the student's athletic ability or prestige, even though that activity may further the education of student-athletes such as Bloom, a communications major. As the trial court noted, there are "various shades of gray within which such events could fall." And, as should be evident, the NCAA does not prohibit unpaid internships, externships, or other educational opportunities in the entertainment field.

In this case, Bloom presented evidence that some of his acting opportunities arose not as a result of his athletic ability but because of his good looks and on-camera presence. However, the record contains evidence that Bloom's agent and the Tommy Hilfiger company marketed Bloom as a talented multi-sport athlete, and a representative from a talent agency intimated that Bloom's reputation as an athlete would be advantageous in obtaining auditions for various entertainment opportunities. Further, the NCAA indicated, when asked to interpret its rules, that it was unable, due to insufficient information, to determine which of Bloom's requested media activities were, in fact, unrelated to his athletic ability or prestige.

Under these circumstances, we perceive no abuse of the trial court's discretion in failing to fault the NCAA for refusing to waive its rules, as requested by CU, to permit Bloom "to pursue any television and film opportunities while he is a student-athlete at CU." See *Cole v. NCAA*, 120 F. Supp. 2d 1060, 1071-72 (N.D. Ga. 2000) (NCAA decisions regarding "challenges of student-athletes are entitled to considerable deference," and courts are reluctant to replace the NCAA as the "decision-maker on private waiver applications"); see also NCAA v. Lasege, *supra*, 53 S.W.3d at 83 (voluntary athletic associations "should be allowed to 'paddle their own canoe' without unwarranted interference from the courts").

Bloom also asserts that the NCAA is arbitrary in its application of the endorsement and media bylaws. He notes that, while the NCAA would bar him from accepting commercial endorsements, it will allow colleges to commercially endorse athletic equipment by having students wear the equipment, with identifying logos and insignias, while engaged in intercollegiate competition. But the trial court determined, and we agree, that this application of the bylaws has a rational basis in economic necessity: financial benefits inure not to any single student-athlete but to member schools and thus to all student-athletes, including those who participate in programs that generate no revenue.

Bloom further argues that the NCAA is arbitrary in the way it applies its bylaws among individual students. Bloom presented evidence that, in one instance, a student-athlete was permitted to make an unpaid, minor appearance in a single film. But the NCAA could rationally conclude that this situation was different: Bloom did not seek permission to make an unpaid appearance in one specific instance; he wanted to take advantage of any number of television and film opportunities, and he wanted to be paid. Bloom also presented evidence that a second student-athlete was permitted to appear on television while he participated in his professional sport. But Bloom did not show that the NCAA would prohibit him from appearing on television while participating in his professional sport.

* * *

Bloom has thus failed to demonstrate any inconsistency in application which would lead us to conclude that the NCAA was arbitrarily applying its rules.

Finally, we are not convinced that the NCAA treated Bloom unfairly in the manner in which it denied the requests to waive or interpret its rules.

Although Bloom is correct that he was not permitted to personally petition the NCAA, he effectively submitted three petitions to the NCAA with the full assistance and support of CU. The trial court's finding that Bloom had "an ability to fully present his . . . position through the membership institution" is amply supported by the record.

Further, the court found, with record support, that the NCAA requested additional information on CU's petition (evidencing that the NCAA was not acting arbitrarily or capriciously), and that there was no evidence that the NCAA gave CU's petition any less consideration than its other "hundreds of administrative and waiver requests."

The record thus supports the trial court's findings that the NCAA's administrative review process is reasonable in general and that it was reasonably applied in this case. As such, these findings, as well as those with respect to the NCAA's application of its bylaws, are not manifestly arbitrary, unreasonable, or unfair. See *Bd. of County Comm'rs v. Fixed Base Operators, Inc., supra*, 939 P.2d at 467.

For these reasons, we agree with the trial court that Bloom failed to demonstrate a reasonable probability of success on the merits.

VI. Other Issues

As noted earlier, to obtain a preliminary injunction, Bloom had to satisfy every part of the *Rathke v. McFarlane* test. Because he failed to satisfy the part requiring a reasonable probability of success on the merits, Bloom was not entitled to a preliminary injunction. . . .

Accordingly, the trial court's order is affirmed.

NOTES AND COMMENTS

1. Following *Tarkanian,* the NCAA task force on due process and enforcement procedures recommended a series of changes in the NCAA's enforcement procedures. The committee determined that the basic structure was fundamentally sound and fair, but outlined eleven recommendations for change. At the 1993 NCAA Convention these and several other changes were approved by the delegates.

The following changes were adopted by the delegates of the 1993 Convention:

> The Committee on Infractions was expanded to include two members from the general public. Division I Manual, 19.1. A new Infractions

> Appeals Committee was created to hear and act upon appeals of the findings of major violations by the Committee on Infractions. The five member Infractions Appeals Committee is to have at least one member from the general public, not connected with a collegiate institution, conference or professional or similar sports organization, or representative of coaches or players in any capacity. Division I Manual, 19.3.

Changes were made regarding proper notice to an institution which has been charged with a violation. The new language provides in pertinent part:

> Whenever possible, the notice shall contain the following information regarding potential violations:
>
> a) The involved sport;
>
> b) The approximate time period during which the alleged violations occurred;
>
> c) The identity of the involved individuals;
>
> d) An approximate time frame for the investigation;
>
> e) A statement indicating that the institution and involved individuals may be represented by legal counsel at all stages of the proceeding;
>
> f) A statement requesting that the individuals associated with the institution not discuss the case prior to interviews by the enforcement staff and institution except for reasonable campus communications not intended to impede the investigation of the allegations and except for consultation with legal counsel;
>
> g) A statement indicating that other facts may be developed during the course of the investigation that may relate to additional violations; and
>
> h) A statement regarding the obligation of the institution to cooperate in the case.

Division I Manual, 32.2.2.4.

The delegates adopted a provision which provides that any enforcement staff member with a conflict of interest should refrain from participating in an investigation. Division I Manual, 32.2.2.5. The convention also approved the use of tape recorders by investigators. The delegates also adopted a provision which affords more liberal discovery options than previously available:

> Subsequent to the filing of an official inquiry in an infractions case, the enforcement staff shall provide to the member institution and the involved individuals reasonable access to pertinent information, including tape recordings of interviews and documentary evidence, that will be used by the enforcement staff in the infractions hearing.

Division I Manual, 32.5.3, 32.5.4.

Finally, as noted, the appeals process has been modified to some extent. The changes represent a positive response to concerns of critics, but do not go as far as some have suggested. *See* C. Peter Goplerud III, *NCAA Enforcement Process: A Call for Procedural Fairness*, 20 CAP. U. L. REV. 543 (1991).

2. An institution under investigation by the Association is advised to cooperate every step of the way with the enforcement staff. One attorney with extensive experience representing schools before the NCAA, Michael Glazier of Kansas City, actually tells clients before taking a case that he will "out-NCAA the NCAA." The end results of a number of specific cases indicates that the penalties for schools will be less severe in cases where there is early and extensive cooperation.

3. The most severe penalty available to the Association is the so-called death penalty. This may be imposed where an institution is a "repeat violator," that is there is a major violation within five years of a previous major violation. The death penalty results in the suspension, for at least one year, of the sport involved in the latest violation. To date, this has been imposed once, against Southern Methodist University in 1987.

4. The *Tarkanian* decision makes judicial review of the NCAA enforcement process problematic. It would appear that only a challenge to the procedures utilized in a particular investigation under the laws of private associations would have a chance for success.

5. The confidential nature of the NCAA's investigative process was also challenged in *Combined Communications Corp. of Oklahoma v. Boger*, 689 F. Supp. 1065 (W.D. Okla. 1988). The case arose out of separate, but contemporaneous, investigations into the football programs at the University of Oklahoma and Oklahoma State University. Corporations operating a newspaper and a television station filed the action in an attempt to gain access to the Official Letter of Inquiry sent by the Association to the two schools. The University of Oklahoma settled their portion of the matter, but Oklahoma State succeeded on a motion to dismiss. The media plaintiffs sought the letter under the First and Fourteenth Amendments and the Oklahoma Open Records Act. The court found no constitutional right of access to this type of information.

Under similar circumstances, but with a state law which might have required disclosure at an early stage, the University of Florida waived its right to receive an Official Letter of Inquiry at the early portion of the 1989 investigation into both its football and basketball programs. The school did this apparently in order to be able to "quietly" conduct its own investigation with some hope of confidentiality. *See also Kneeland v. National Collegiate Athletic Association*, 850 F.2d 224 (5th Cir. 1988); *University of Kentucky v. Courier-Journal & Louisville Times Co.*, 830 S.W.2d 373 (Ky. 1992); *Berst v. Chipman*, 653 P.2d 107 (Kan. 1982).

What impact would it have on the NCAA's ability to investigate alleged infractions if the process was a matter of public record? *See* Note, *Statutory*

Law: The Oklahoma Open Records Act: Are NCAA Investigation Records Accessible?, 42 OKLA. L. REV. 145 (1989). *See also Greene v. Athletic Council of Iowa State University*, 251 N.W.2d 559 (Iowa 1977).

For two cases involving the media's right to acquire information relating to coaches' salaries and contracts, see *Cremins v. The Atlanta Journal and The Atlanta Constitution*, 405 S.E.2d 675 (Ga. 1991) and *Dooley v. Davidson*, 397 S.E.2d 922 (Ga. 1990).

6. Occasionally the NCAA also faces challenges to its role as an operator of championship events. A school dissatisfied with the selection process used to determine the field for the Division I-AA football playoffs attempted to utilize the judicial system to rectify the situation. *See Howard University v. NCAA*, 675 F. Supp. 652 (D.D.C. 1987).

A state district court judge ruled against the UNLV basketball team in its quest to have its NCAA sanctions lifted in order to allow them to play in the 1992 NCAA basketball tournament. The players had claimed that agreements reached between UNLV and the NCAA, and Jerry Tarkanian and the NCAA postponed penalties against the school until 1992. The players claimed that the agreements were based on an unfair process and were designed to unjustly enrich the defendants UNLV, Tarkanian, and the NCAA. The court ruled that the players had no legally protected right to participate in post-season competition. In its most basic sense, the decision indicates that the players simply had no cause of action. *L.A. Times*, March 12, 1992, p.2C.

C. GENERAL ELIGIBILITY ISSUES

Although the *Tarkanian* case seemingly marks the end of constitutional challenges to actions of the NCAA due to lack of state action, athletes may be successful in raising constitutional issues where the defendant is a true state actor. The following cases and materials involve claims against state supported universities and public high schools. All clearly involve state action. Resolution of the state action question in favor of the athlete is only the starting point. In order to be successful the athlete must then proceed with a claim that a constitutional right has been infringed. Usually, the claim involves procedural due process or equal protection, but other constitutionally protected rights (like speech or privacy, for example) are occasionally raised. The cases and materials that follow explore these constitutional rights issues.

PROBLEM 1

Billy Rogers is a basketball player at Oklanois State University. He is the type athlete who can get a basketball to do almost anything for him except his school work. He has recently run into some academic problems which are threatening to derail a promising professional career. Rogers is a senior and has been evaluated by professional scouts as a potential first round pick in the draft, if he has a good senior season. If the draft were now, or for some reason Rogers did not play his final season, he would not be drafted in either of the two rounds of the NBA draft.

You are in private practice and Rogers has come to you seeking advice with regard to his latest academic mishap. His troubles began last spring. To remain eligible for the team, he had to meet three requirements: maintain passing grades, accumulate credits and enroll in a degree program. He met the first two, earning a C average in rudimentary courses in Oklanois's open admissions program. He ran afoul of the third requirement when he applied for acceptance to the University's New School, a special degree program for students who propose independent-study projects, and was rejected. Last summer he went to summer school in an attempt to gain admission to a degree program. He tried to obtain entrance into the general college, which allows students to design their own majors. Again he was rejected.

At the beginning of the fall semester, desperate for a major, Rogers renewed his application for independent study. After he was rebuffed, he learned that his case had been handled in an irregular fashion. The admissions committee had twice voted to accept him. But each time school officials vetoed the decision after hearing charges from the dean that Rogers had handed in work prepared by other students and had withdrawn from several courses that he was failing. As a result of the denial, Rogers was declared ineligible for athletic competition for his final season.

What advice do you give him? What legal approaches are available to him? If asserting a constitutional claim, does Rogers have a legally protected interest? What strategy do you suggest?

PROBLEM 2

Will and Phil Vanderbilt, seven foot tall twins, are high school seniors who are standout basketball players. They have not played on the same team since grade school due to various family problems.

Will has recently moved from the high school district where his parents live to a neighboring district to live with a family friend. The old district has a poor basketball program and the new one has a strong program. The state high school athletic association, as a part of its transfer rules, has a provision which causes a student to lose one year of eligibility if he or she transfers from one school district to another and is not living with a parent or guardian. Will has thus jeopardized his last year of high school eligibility and could lose opportunities for college coaches to watch him play and be evaluated for scholarships.

Phil currently attends school in a district in which an aunt lives. He has recently become extremely religious and wants to attend a Catholic high school outside his district. The transfer rule would make him ineligible for basketball.

It should be noted that the transfer rule has an exception allowing citywide attendance at parochial schools in the state's largest city. Phil lives in another city. There is a Catholic school in his district but its basketball program is only average.

Will and Phil have approached you about their eligibility questions. What advice do you have for them?

CASE FILE

INDIANA HIGH SCHOOL ATHLETIC ASSOCIATION, INC. v. AVANT

650 N.E.2d 1164 (Ind. Ct. App. 1995)

GARRARD, Judge; HOFFMAN, J. and DARDEN, J. Concur.

GARRARD, Judge

The Indiana High School Athletic Association, Inc. (IHSAA) ruled that Bilal Avant (Avant) was ineligible to participate in varsity athletics at Roosevelt High School his senior year under the IHSAA's Transfer Rule. The trial court disagreed with the IHSAA's determination and issued a preliminary injunction enjoining the IHSAA from rendering Avant ineligible for any varsity team during the 1993/1994 basketball season. IHSAA appeals.

FACTS

During the summer following his junior year in high school, Avant transferred from Andrean High School (Andrean), a private high school located in Merrillville, to Roosevelt High School (Roosevelt), a public high school in Gary. Avant's parents did not change their residence; rather, Avant moved from a private school to a public school located in the same school district. Avant played basketball and baseball at Andrean during 9th grade, 10th grade and 11th grade. In fact, he played on the varsity teams in these sports his junior year, and he was characterized as an "outstanding" athlete and player. After transferring to Roosevelt, Avant hoped to continue participating in sports.

Both Andrean and Roosevelt are members of the IHSAA and are subject to the association's athletic eligibility rules. The primary purpose of the IHSAA Transfer Rule is to eliminate school jumping and recruitment. This rule provides, in substance, that a student who transfers to a member school with a change of residence by the student's parents will have immediate full (varsity) eligibility at the new school. However, a transfer without an accompanied move by parents will result in ineligibility during the first 365 days following transfer, unless the student qualifies under a listed exception. The rules also provide for limited (junior-varsity) eligibility when a student transfers without a corresponding change of residence by the parents. On the contrary, a student who transfers for "primarily athletic reasons" will be ineligible for all athletics for the first 365 days after enrollment at the new school. The IHSAA Hardship Rule mediates the harsh effects of the eligibility rules in limited situations.

Avant completed a Transfer Report as required by the IHSAA Rules. The IHSAA Executive Committee then held a hearing on November 12, 1993 to determine Avant's eligibility for interscholastic sports. The committee's written decision found that Avant was ineligible for varsity athletics during the 1993/1994 school year. Not only did he fail to qualify for full eligibility under the IHSAA rules, Avant also failed to establish that application of the Transfer Rule to him constituted an undue hardship. The committee granted Avant limited eligibility to participate in junior-varsity athletics at Roosevelt.

On December 3, 1993, Avant filed a complaint for injunctive relief and jury demand against the IHSAA and Roosevelt. The trial court immediately issued a temporary restraining order against the IHSAA and Roosevelt. After a hearing, the trial court enjoined the IHSAA from preventing Avant from participation on any varsity athletic team at Roosevelt. The court further ordered that the IHSAA could impose no penalty on Roosevelt for allowing Avant to participate on its varsity teams, nor could the IHSAA take action against any school against which Avant played. The trial court found that it could review the IHSAA decision to determine if it was "arbitrary or capricious," and for violations of Article I § 23 of the Indiana Constitution. In granting the injunction, the court stated that Avant had shown a likelihood of success on the merits; however, it failed to identify the claim upon which Avant was likely to succeed. This interlocutory appeal followed.

ISSUES

I. Whether the trial court properly reviewed the decisions of the IHSAA regarding Avant's eligibility.

   A. Whether judicial review of the actions of a private voluntary association is proper without first establishing a civil or property right.

   B. Whether the IHSAA acted arbitrarily or capriciously in granting Avant only limited eligibility.

II. Whether the trial court properly reviewed the actions of the IHSAA for violations of Article I § 23 of the Indiana Constitution.

   A. Whether Article I § 23 applies only to actions of the general assembly.

   B. Whether the IHSAA is involved in state action.

   C. Whether the IHSAA violated Article I § 23 by rendering Avant ineligible to participate in varsity athletics at Roosevelt.

III. Whether the trial court erred by enjoining the IHSAA from applying its Restitution Rule should the court's injunction be reversed.

DISCUSSION AND DECISION

I.

A. Whether Judicial Review is Available.

The IHSAA's first argument is that the trial court erred by concluding that the IHSAA's decisions were judicially reviewable. The IHSAA relies upon *State ex rel. Givens v. Superior Court of Marion County* (1954), 233 Ind. 235, 117 N.E.2d 553, for the position that courts may review actions of a voluntary association like the IHSAA only if a civil or property right has been invaded. The IHSAA contends that it affected no civil or property right of Avant's, and thus its decision was not reviewable by the trial court.

The general rule in Indiana as to voluntary associations is that courts will not ordinarily interfere to control the administration of their constitutions or by-laws, or to enforce rights springing therefrom. Our supreme court described this rule in *State ex rel. Givens* as follows:

> A voluntary association may, without direction or interference by the courts, for its government, adopt a constitution, by-laws, rules and regulations which will control as to all questions of discipline, or internal policy and management, and its right to interpret and administer the same is as sacred as the right to make them. *Id.* at 555.

In *Givens,* certain members of a voluntary trade union sought by injunctive relief to force the holding of an election of officers of an association and the submission of their names as candidates at such election. The supreme court found that any attempt by the judiciary to compel the officers of the union to perform their duties as to the election of officers would be an unlawful interference with the association's internal affairs. *Id.* The court stated that "unless plaintiffs' complaint is based upon, and seeks the protection of, some civil or property right," the trial court here was without jurisdiction to grant relief. *Id.* Finding no civil or property right present, the court held that the trial court was without subject-matter jurisdiction. *Id.* at 556.

We find disposition of this issue, however, to be governed by *Haas v. South Bend Community School Corporation* (1972), 259 Ind. 515, 289 N.E.2d 495. In *Haas*, our supreme court held that the IHSAA's rule prohibiting male and female students from competing on the same team or against each other denied equal protection as guaranteed by the Fourteenth Amendment to the Federal Constitution and Article 1 § 23 of the Indiana Constitution. *Id.* at 501. Before addressing the constitutional issue, however, the Court deemed it necessary to "dispose of the apparent obstacle presented by [*State ex rel. IHSAA v. Lawrence Circuit Court* (1959), 240 Ind. 114, 162 N.E.2d 250]." *Id.* at 497. The *Lawrence* case held that students have no constitutional right to participate in interscholastic athletics, and thus found the trial court to be without jurisdiction over the matter. *State ex rel. IHSAA v. Lawrence*, 240 Ind. at 124, 162 N.E.2d at 255. In 1972, *Haas* overruled the portion of *Lawrence* holding that the actions of the IHSAA were not judicially reviewable.[2] The Court indicated that a student cannot be arbitrarily denied the opportunity to qualify to participate in interscholastic athletic competition. *Haas*, 289 N.E.2d at 497. Thus, the IHSAA's decisions are reviewable under the arbitrary and capricious standard.

B. Whether the IHSAA Acted Arbitrarily and Capriciously.

The IHSAA next contends that it did not act arbitrarily and capriciously when it denied Avant full eligibility for interscholastic athletics after he transferred from Andrean to Roosevelt. Avant does not contest the finding that his actions violated the Transfer Rule, thus rendering him ineligible for varsity athletics. Instead, he argues that using his technical violation of the rule to disqualify him is arbitrary and capricious since he was not recruited by Roosevelt and the basis for his decision to transfer was financial and personal hardship rather than athletics.

The motivation behind Avant's transfer to Roosevelt was a factual issue before the IHSAA. The Court of Appeals will not judge the credibility of witnesses or weigh evidence that was before the IHSAA on factual issues. Therefore, we will affirm the IHSAA's factual determinations if supported by substantial evidence of probative value.

The IHSAA determined that while the evidence was inconclusive to prove Avant's transfer was primarily for athletic purposes, the evidence sufficiently established athletics as a factor.

The IHSAA noted that Avant did not mention financial hardship when leaving Andrean or on his Transfer Report. Moreover, Avant did not follow up on the Andrean athletic director's offer to help Avant secure employment or available financial aid. Evidence indicated that Avant had disagreements with the Andrean basketball coach, as he did with all his coaches, and that he "had to put up with" the coaches' philosophy for three years. Before learning he could not play on the junior-varsity team, Avant's decision to transfer was attributed to his being unhappy at Andrean.

The IHSAA concluded that Avant did not qualify for relief under the IHSAA Hardship Rule. This rule gives the IHSAA authority to set aside the effect of any rule when:

a. Strict enforcement of the Rule in the particular case will not serve to accomplish the purpose of the Rule;

b. The spirit of the Rule has not been violated; and

---

2 *Haas* reaffirmed the Court's prior ruling that a student has no constitutional right to participate in interscholastic athletics. *Haas*, 289 N.E.2d at 498.

c. There exists in the particular case circumstances showing an undue hardship which would result from enforcement of the Rule.

The general consideration section of the hardship rule contains the following language:

> Likewise, a change in financial condition of the student or a student's family may be considered a hardship, however, such conditions or changes in conditions must be permanent, substantial and significantly beyond the control of the student or the student's family.

While the IHSAA noted that attending Andrean did create a hardship on Avant's family, this financial hardship had existed since Avant's freshman year. Furthermore, the IHSAA found no change in the family's circumstances which would cause an undue hardship. Substantial evidence of probative value supported the IHSAA's factual determination that Avant was ineligible for varsity athletics due to his transfer. The IHSAA's decision was not arbitrary or capricious.

II.

A. Whether Art. I § 23 Applies Only to the General Assembly.

The IHSAA contends that the language of Art. I § 23 of Indiana's Constitution is limited to acts of the general assembly. Art. I § 23 states:

> The General Assembly shall not grant to any citizen, or class of citizens, privileges or immunities which, upon the same terms, shall not equally belong to all citizens.

The IHSAA admits that our supreme court in *Haas* applied Art. I § 23 to the IHSAA, a private entity. However, it argues that the court did not explain its extension of this provision to nonpublic entities.

As the state intermediate appellate court, we are of course obliged to follow the holdings of our supreme court, whether or not the rationale or the constitutional implications of a decision are explained to the satisfaction of litigants. Since the *Haas* decision, the supreme court has not limited application of Art. I § 23 to actions of the general assembly. Therefore, when the state is sufficiently involved to treat decisive conduct as state action, Art. I § 23 applies.

B. State Action.

The IHSAA next argues that we should reevaluate whether it engages in state action under the *Blum / Rendell-Baker* analysis.[7] Although Indiana courts

---

[7] The U.S. Supreme Court moved away from the entanglement theory of state action and set out a three-step analysis in *Rendell-Baker v. Kohn* (1982), 457 U.S. 830, and *Blum v. Yaretsky* (1982), 457 U.S. 991, as follows:

(a) To what extent is the business subject to state regulations?

(b) Is there a sufficiently close nexus between the state and the challenged action of the

have found previously that the IHSAA engages in state action, appellant asks us to reconsider this issue in light of the *Blum / Rendell-Baker* test and a line of cases holding that the NCAA does not engage in state action. Appellant reasons that "the composition, function and rules of the NCAA are substantially similar, and the reasoning of the NCAA cases are equally applicable to the IHSAA."

This court has already rejected the IHSAA's analogy between the NCAA and state high school associations. *IHSAA v. Schafer*, 598 N.E.2d at 550. In *Schafer*, the court noted that the U.S. Supreme Court placed an important footnote after holding that the NCAA does not engage in state action. That footnote stated:

> The situation would, of course, be different if the membership consisted entirely of institutions located within the same State, many of them public institutions created by the same sovereign. (citations omitted) *Id.* at 549.

Thus, an important distinction between the NCAA and the IHSAA is that the NCAA represents schools at a national level while the members of the IHSAA are all secondary schools in Indiana.

Based upon this footnote and our existing case law, we previously concluded that the IHSAA engages in state action subject to judicial review in making and enforcing its rules. *Id.* at 550. The IHSAA has failed to persuade us differently.

C. Application of Article I § 23.

Because we have affirmed that Art. I § 23 applies to the IHSAA, we must determine whether application of the Transfer Rule to Avant violated this provision. Our analytical methodology is governed by a recent decision of the Indiana Supreme Court.

On November 28, 1994, the Indiana Supreme Court affirmed the decision of the full Workers' Compensation Board of Indiana that the statutory agricultural exemption to the Indiana Workers' Compensation Act did not violate Art. I § 23. *Collins v. Day,* 644 N.E.2d 72, 82 (Ind. 1994). In doing so, the court held that claims under Art. I § 23 should be interpreted and applied independently from federal equal protection analysis. *Id.* at 75. The court articulated two requirements which must be met by legislation granting unequal privileges or immunities in order to withstand constitutional scrutiny: (1) the classification must be based upon distinctive, inherent characteristics which rationally distinguish the unequally treated class, and the disparate treatment accorded by the legislation must be reasonably related to such distinguishing characteristics; and (2) the classification must be open to any and all persons who share the inher-

---

private entity so that the action of the entity may be fairly treated as that of the state itself?

(c) Does the private decision involve such coercive power or significant encouragement, either overt or covert, by the state that the choice must in law be deemed to be that of the state?

ent characteristics which distinguish and justify the classification, with the special treatment accorded to any particular classification extended equally to all such persons. *Id.* at 79. In applying this two-part standard, courts must accord considerable deference to the manner in which the legislature has balanced the competing interests involved. *Id.* at 79-80.

We first address whether the treatment of transfer students without a corresponding change of residence by their parents separately from students transferring with a change of residence by their parents is a classification based upon distinctive, inherent characteristics and, if so, whether the unequal treatment is reasonably related to such distinguishing characteristics. The Transfer Rule is designed to eliminate school jumping and recruitment of student athletes. Transfers not accompanied by a change in residence (or falling outside the thirteen exceptions) are suspect in that they are subject to substantial manipulation. The Transfer Rule deters unscrupulous students and parents from manufacturing all sorts of reasons for a transfer, thereby thinly disguising athletically motivated transfers. The distinctions between these classifications are reasonably related to achieving the IHSAA's purpose in deterring school jumping and recruitment.

Furthermore, we find that the Transfer Rule applies equally to all persons similarly situated.

If a student transferring without a change in residence by his/her parents does not fit one of the thirteen listed exceptions or qualify as an "undue hardship," then the student is ineligible for varsity athletics.

We conclude that application of the two-part standard reveals no violation of Art. I § 23 in the present case.

* * *

CONCLUSION

We conclude that the trial court erred by enjoining the IHSAA from rendering Avant ineligible to participate in varsity athletics at Roosevelt. Although the court had jurisdiction to review the IHSAA's decision concerning Avant's eligibility, the IHSAA did not act arbitrarily or capriciously in granting Avant only limited eligibility. Moreover, the IHSAA's actions did not constitute a violation of privileges or immunities under the Indiana Constitution.

HOFFMAN, J. and DARDEN, J. concur.

TIFFANY v. ARIZONA INTERSCHOLASTIC ASSOCIATION, INC.

726 P.2d 231 (Ariz. Ct. App. 1986)

OPINION

MEYERSON, Judge.

Does a high school student have a constitutional right to participate in interscholastic athletic competition during his senior year in high school? This is the primary question raised in this appeal. As explained more fully herein, we hold that defendant-appellant Arizona Interscholastic Association, Inc. (AIA) did not violate the due process clause of the fourteenth amendment when it refused to grant plaintiff-appellee John Tiffany a hardship waiver from its nineteen-year-old eligibility rule. We concur with the trial court, however, that AIA acted unlawfully by failing to follow its own bylaws in considering the request for the waiver.

I. FACTS

Tiffany began his senior year at St. Mary's High School in Phoenix during the 1983-84 school term. He had been held back in kindergarten and first grade because of a learning disability.

Thus, he turned nineteen years of age on August 5, 1983, the month before his senior year would begin. Tiffany had participated in athletics throughout grade school and during high school. He wanted to participate in athletic competition during his senior year.

AIA is a voluntary association composed of all public and most private high schools in Arizona. AIA formulates and promulgates rules and regulations pertaining to, among other things, interscholastic athletic competition among its members. Under AIA's bylaws, if a student turns nineteen before September 1 of the school year, he is not eligible to participate in interscholastic athletics. AIA bylaws provide, however, that:

> The Executive Board in individual cases may, at its discretion and upon such terms and conditions as it may impose, waive or modify any eligibility rule when in its opinion there are circumstances beyond the control of the student or parent whereby enforcement of the rule would work an undue hardship on the student. . . .

The parties have stipulated that the decision to hold Tiffany back in the early grades was made by his teachers and school administrators with his parents' approval. AIA does not contest that these circumstances were beyond the control of Tiffany and his parents.

At a hearing before the Executive Board of AIA, Tiffany presented evidence that he very much enjoyed his participation in interscholastic athletics, the friendship of those with whom he would compete, and the benefits from the discipline and regulation involved in playing varsity athletics. Tiffany indicated to the Executive Board that his motivation in studying came from the fact that in order to be eligible for interscholastic athletics a certain grade point average must be maintained. The Executive Board denied the request for the waiver. It is agreed by the parties that AIA has a policy of not making any exceptions to the nineteen-year-old eligibility rule.

Tiffany subsequently filed a complaint requesting that AIA be enjoined from disqualifying him from interscholastic athletic competition. He requested that AIA's actions be declared unconstitutional as a denial of due process. The trial court granted a preliminary injunction allowing Tiffany to play during the 1983-84 school year. Final judgment was entered in 1985. Because Tiffany requested attorney's fees, the trial court determined that the controversy was not moot.

The trial court held that AIA's Executive Board acted "unreasonably, capriciously and arbitrarily" when it failed to exercise its discretion in considering Tiffany's request for a waiver. The trial court also ruled that Tiffany possessed a "sufficient liberty or property interest or personal stake in participating in high school athletics" such that AIA's actions violated his constitutional rights. . . .

II. CONSTITUTIONAL CLAIMS

To succeed in an action under 42 U.S.C. § 1983, a plaintiff must establish that the defendant acted under color of law to deprive the plaintiff of a right, privilege or immunity secured by the constitution or laws of the United States. It is uncontested that AIA's actions are under color of law within the meaning of 42 U.S.C. § 1983. . . . AIA disputes, however, that its conduct in this case deprived Tiffany of any interest cognizable under this statute.

In order to decide whether Tiffany's exclusion from interscholastic athletics during his senior year in high school violated due process (and therefore 42 U.S.C. § 1983), it first must be determined whether Tiffany had any property or liberty interest in participating in high school sports during the 1983-84 school year. The beginning point in analyzing this constitutional issue is the decision of the United States Supreme Court in *Goss v. Lopez*, 419 U.S. 565 (1975). In *Goss*, the Supreme Court held that a school could not suspend a student for ten days without insuring due process safeguards. The Court reasoned that a "State is constrained to recognize a student's legitimate entitlement to a public education as a property interest which is protected by the Due Process Clause and which may not be taken away for misconduct without adherence to the minimum procedures required by that Clause."

"[E]ducation is perhaps the most important function of state and local governments," and the total exclusion from the educational process for more than a trivial period, and certainly if the suspension is for ten days, is a serious event in the life of the suspended child. Neither the property interest in educational benefits temporarily denied nor the liberty interest in reputation, which is also implicated, is so insubstantial that suspensions may constitutionally be imposed by any procedure the school chooses, no matter how arbitrary. . . . We now proceed to apply the ruling of *Goss* to the case before us.

Most courts which have considered this issue have declined to hold that participation in a single year of high school athletic competition rises to the level of a constitutionally protectable property interest. For example, in *Albach v. Odle*, 531 F.2d 983 (10th Cir. 1976), the plaintiff challenged a rule automatically barring from interscholastic high school athletic competition for one year any student who transferred from his home district to a boarding school or from a boarding school to his home district. The court found that the ruling in *Goss v. Lopez* was limited to the "educational process." In language which has been cited repeatedly by other courts, the court declared:

> The educational process is a broad and comprehensive concept with a variable and indefinite meaning. It is not limited to classroom attendance but includes innumerable separate components, such as participation in athletic activity and participation in school clubs and social groups, which combine to provide an atmosphere of intellectual and moral advancement We do not read *Goss* to establish a property interest subject to constitutional protection in each of these separate components.

* * *

Under certain limited circumstances, however, courts have found that participation in interscholastic sports rises to the level of a constitutionally protected property interest. For example, in *Boyd v. Board of Directors*, 612 F. Supp. 86 (E.D. Ark. 1985), the court held that a student could not be suspended from the high school football team without procedural due process of law protections. The court found that the plaintiff-student was an outstanding athlete and that the 1983 season was his last opportunity to participate in football at the high school level. The testimony indicated that participation in high school sports was "vital and indispensable to a college scholarship and, in essence, a college education." The court found that his participation in interscholastic athletics must be deemed a property interest protected by the due process clause of the fourteenth amendment. . . .

In *Florida High School Activities Ass'n, Inc. v. Bryant*, 313 So. 2d 57 (Fla. Dist. Ct. App. 1975), the court affirmed the trial court which ordered the defendant to allow the plaintiff to participate in athletics during the 1974-75 school year. Although the court did not express its ruling in due process terms, it accepted the trial court's finding that basketball was an important and vital part of the plaintiff's life " 'providing an impetus to his general scholastic and social development and rehabilitation from his prior problems as a juvenile delinquent.' "

As the above cases demonstrate, in the realm of constitutional law, there are very few absolutes. We are persuaded that under certain circumstances a high school student can properly establish an entitlement to due process protection in connection with a suspension or exclusion from high school athletics.

We believe that an appropriate extension of the holding in *Goss v. Lopez* was expressed by the court in *Pegram v. Nelson*, 469 F. Supp. 1134 (M.D.N.C. 1979). In that case, a high school student was suspended from school for ten days and was also excluded from after-school activities for a period of four months. The court acknowledged that the "opportunity to participate in extracurricular activities is not, by and in itself, a property interest." The court recognized, however, that:

> Total exclusion from participation in that part of the educational process designated as extracurricular activities for a lengthy period of time could, depending upon the particular circumstances, be a sufficient deprivation to implicate due process.

It is not necessary in this case to define the precise parameters of the circumstances under which due process must be afforded to a student excluded from high school athletics. This is so because Tiffany has not asserted any cognizable interest beyond his claim to mere participation in one year of interscholastic sports. Tiffany argues that he very much enjoys his participation in athletics, the friendship of those that he competes with and the benefit he derives from the discipline and regulation involved in playing varsity sports. Such interests, albeit important to him, simply do not rise to the level of constitutional magnitude necessary to invoke the protection of the due process clause. We likewise conclude that the scholastic benefit derived from the incentive to maintain a certain grade point average to remain eligible for athletic competition is also an interest which is outside the scope of constitutional protection. Unlike the "deprivation of a previously granted scholarship [which] would invoke the protections of procedural due process," . . . the educational stimulus Tiffany claims to derive from athletic participation is, in constitutional terms, a "mere subjective 'expectation,'" . . .and not protected by procedural due process. In short, Tiffany has failed to demonstrate the type of serious damage to his "later opportunities for high education and employment,". . . which would raise his interest in interscholastic athletics to a level warranting the safeguards of the due process clause.

III. FAILURE TO EXERCISE DISCRETION

Although we reject Tiffany's constitutional claim, we sustain the trial court's ruling that the Executive Board of AIA acted unlawfully when it failed to exercise its discretion at the eligibility hearing. As noted above, despite the fact that AIA's bylaws specifically provide that its Executive Board will exercise discretion in considering hardship waivers to its eligibility rules, it is undisputed that the Executive Board has adopted a policy of not making any exceptions to the nineteen-year-old eligibility requirement.

It is hornbook law that an administrative board must follow its own rules and regulations. . . . An administrative agency's failure to follow its own rules and regulations does not create a constitutional due process right on behalf of a party who suffers some wrong at the hands of the administrative body. . . .

Rather, the obligation of such a body to follow its own rules and regulations is founded in principles of administrative law. . . .

In Arizona, the procedure by which one can compel an administrative board to exercise its discretion is through the filing of a mandamus. . . . Although Tiffany's complaint was not denominated a special action, the record of the trial court proceedings reflects that the mandamus issue was implicitly tried by the parties. We hold that the trial court was correct in concluding that the Executive Board of AIA acted "unreasonably, capriciously and arbitrarily" when it failed to exercise its discretion in considering Tiffany's request for a waiver.

* * *

Affirmed in part, reversed in part.

GREER, P.J. and KLEINSCHMIDT, J. concur.

NOTES AND COMMENTS

1. Eligibility questions arise in a variety of settings. Such things as restrictions on transfer students, marriage, hair length, and alcohol and drug usage have been the subject of litigation by athletes. *See, e.g., Robbins v. Indiana High School Athletic Ass'n,* 941 F. Supp. 786 (S.D. Ind. 1996) (transfer rule does not violate constitution even where transfer motivated by religious conversion); *Jordan v. O'Fallon Township High School Dist.*, 706 N.E.2d 137 (Ill. Ct. App. 1999); *Fusato v. Washington Interscholastic Activities Ass'n*, 970 P.2d 774 (Wash. Ct. App. 1999) (narrow construction against foreign exchange student of hardship exception on transfer eligibility violates equal protection); and *Indiana High School Athletic Ass'n v. Carlberg*, 694 N.E.2d 222 (Ind. 1998) (transfer rule advances legitimate association interest); *Moran v. School District #7, Yellowstone County*, 350 F. Supp. 1180 (D. Mont. 1972) (prohibition on married students participating in interscholastic athletics held invalid); *Long v. Zopp*, 476 F.2d 180 (4th Cir. 1973) (limitation on hair length reasonable, but only during the playing season and only for health and safety reasons); and *Bunger v. Iowa High School Athletic Ass'n*, 197 N.W.2d 555 (Iowa 1972) (rule prohibiting use of alcohol outside the school year for athletes beyond the scope of authority of high school athletic association); *Conard v. The University of Washington,* 834 P.2d 17 (Wash. 1992) (football players dismissed from team do not have protected interest in their athletic scholarships).

2. Freedom of expression may also become an issue in athletics. In *Williams v. Eaton*, 468 F.2d 1079 (10th Cir. 1972), several black athletes were dismissed from the University of Wyoming football team following a dispute over their plan to wear black armbands during a game with Brigham Young University. The armbands were intended to express opposition to religious beliefs of the Church of Jesus Christ of Latter-Day Saints on racial matters. The court ruled in favor of the university stating that had the university permitted the armbands it would have been "violative of the First Amendment establishment clause and its requirement of neutrality on expressions relating to religion." The court thus found that the athletes' First Amendment free speech rights were not violated by the actions of the university.

See also Menora v. Illinois High School Ass'n, 683 F.2d 1030 (7th Cir. 1982) (ban on basketball players wearing hats as applied to Jewish athletes wearing yarmulkes during games upheld against First Amendment challenge); *Marcum v. Dahl*, 658 F.2d 731 (10th Cir. 1981) (permissible to dismiss two members of the women's basketball team at the University of Oklahoma for making disparaging remarks about the coach); *Hysaw v. Washburn University,* 690 F. Supp. 940 (D. Kan. 1987) (football players who boycotted team claiming racial discrimination and were removed from team raise free speech and other issues under Section 1983).

3. In raising constitutional issues, athletes must establish basic constitutional thresholds. Initially, they must prove the action taken against them is "state action." *Compare Tarkanian* and *Brentwood Academy*. Second, the athletes must demonstrate a constitutionally protected liberty or property interest in athletic participation. Upon what grounds is a property right in athletic participation established? *Compare Goss v. Lopez*, 419 U.S. 565 (1975) (holding that a student's legitimate entitlement to a public education is a protected property interest) and *Haas*, *supra* (recognizing an interest in the opportunity to participate) with *Board of Regents v. Roth*, 408 U.S. 564 (1972) (stating that property rights" are created and their dimensions are defined by existing rules or understandings that stem from an independent source such as state law) and *Lawrence* (no constitutional property interest in participation). *See also Indiana High School Athletic Ass'n v. Carlberg*, 694 N.E.2d 222 (Ind. 1998) (no protected interest in athletic participation at the high school level under either federal or state constitution); *Jordan v. O'Fallon Township High School District*, 706 N.E.2d 137 (Ill. App. Ct. 1999) (no protected interest in athletic participation, despite an interest in obtaining a college scholarship); and *Fusato v. Washington Interscholastic Activities Ass'n*, 970 P.2d 774 (Wash. Ct. App. 1999) (no fundamental right to participate in athletics for equal protection purposes). Should recognition of a property interest depend on the skill level of a particular plaintiff?

Chapter 3
GENDER EQUITY IN AMATEUR ATHLETICS

A. INTRODUCTION

This chapter examines the important and often controversial question of what is the meaning of "gender equity" in amateur athletics, and how such equity is to be measured and attained. Does gender equity consist of treating both sexes in exactly the same manner when it comes to participation in athletes? There are, after all, relevant differences between the sexes in both ability, and perhaps, interest. Arguably, a profound inequality would result from rigid adherence to the notion that sexual distinctions should be obliterated. Do you agree?

In the sports context, difficult questions arise as one endeavors to create a sports structure that does not unfairly discriminate on the basis of sex. Must a female be afforded an opportunity to try out for the "men's team"? Does it matter that a "women's team" already exists in that sport? Does it matter that although no "women's team" exists, the sport is a violent, contact sport? Must a male be afforded an opportunity to try out for the "women's team" in a sport for which there is no "men's team"?

Prior to 1970, few law suits challenged sexual discrimination in athletics. Social consciousness and the women's movement changed matters dramatically. Beginning in the early 1970s, suits by women alleging sexual discrimination violative of the Fourteenth Amendment began to emerge. The passage of Title IX of the Educational Amendments Act of 1972 provided women with a statutory remedy to complement the constitutional theories. In relevant part, Title IX provides:

> No person in the United States shall, on the basis of sex, be excluded from participation in, be denied the benefits of, or be subjected to discrimination under any education program or activity receiving federal financial assistance. . . .

20 U.S.C. § 1681(a). Title IX has resulted in substantial increases in programs for women, but also the elimination of certain men's programs. Has the tide of Title IX shifted too far?

The following cases and materials examine gender equity issues in sports both from a constitutional perspective, as well as within the meaning and application of Title IX. The materials also consider other remedies that might be available in the gender equity context.

B. CONSTITUTIONAL ISSUES

PROBLEM 1

Shirley Wynn is a 16-year-old high school junior. She is an extremely talented tennis player, enjoying a very high national junior ranking. Her high school has a girls' tennis team on which she played last year, but she wants to play on the boys' team this year. Her argument is that she will have better competition if she plays against boys and thus will better prepare herself for collegiate and professional competition which appears likely to be in her future. The state high school athletic association prohibits girls from competing on boys' teams and vice versa. Shirley wants to take whatever action may be necessary to be allowed to play against the male competition. What advice would you give her and what action would you take?

PROBLEM 2

Liz Zimmer, an athletically talented 16-year-old high school sophomore, wants to try out for her high school football team. The Washahoma State High School Athletic Association regulations prohibit female participation on boys' teams in all contact sports. The regulations specify that football, basketball, ice hockey, and wrestling are contact sports. By all accounts, Liz is physically capable of playing high school football. She is bigger and stronger, and a better all around athlete, than many of the boys who are on the team. The coach, citing the regulation, has refused to allow her to try out.

Liz has appealed to the school's principal to be allowed to play on the team. You are the school board attorney and have been contacted by the principal for advice.

CASE FILE

HOOVER v. MEIKLEJOHN

430 F. Supp. 164 (D. Colo. 1977)

MEMORANDUM OPINION AND ORDER

MATSCH, Judge.

In this class action under Rule 23(b)(2), Donna Hoover through her mother and next friend, representing all female persons of high school age or younger in the State of Colorado who are or may be affected by Rule XXI of the Colorado High School Activities Association, has invoked the jurisdiction granted by 28 U.S.C. § 1343(3) to seek a judgment declaring that rule to be unconstitutional, an order enjoining its enforcement, and mandatory affirmative relief under 28 U.S.C. § 2201 and 42 U.S.C. § 1983. The defendants concede jurisdiction and admit that their actions are under color of state law. They also agree that the prerequisites of Rule 23(a) have been met.

The plaintiff is 16 years old and a student in the eleventh grade at Golden High School, one of twelve senior high schools operated by Jefferson County School District R-1. The named defendants include all members of the board of education who govern that district.

The plaintiff is 5'4" tall, weighs 120 pounds, and is in excellent physical condition. In the fall of 1976, Golden High School had a varsity soccer team which engaged in interscholastic competition with other public high schools in Colorado. The teacher-coach, Tracy Fifer, permitted participation by Donna Hoover as the only female on the team. She engaged in the conditioning and skills drills at the team's practice sessions and she played in junior varsity games, which were unofficial contests played between the same schools whose varsity teams met in sanctioned competition. These junior varsity matches were to assist the skills development of those who had not yet shown sufficient proficiency to play on the varsity team. Donna Hoover was the only female playing in those junior varsity games. Although she was stunned on one occasion as a result of a collision with a much larger player, she did not suffer any disabling injury in the games or in any practice sessions.

On or about September 28, 1976, the principal of Golden High School directed that the plaintiff be removed from the soccer team because her participation was in violation of Rule XXI, § 3 of the Colorado High School Activities Association. That is a voluntary, non-profit, unincorporated association of public high schools (together with some private schools as associate members) which is governed by a board of control composed of professional educators elected from eight districts. The purpose of the organization is stated in Article II of its constitution:

> The purpose of the Association is to approve, promote, develop and direct all activities among its member schools, that will contribute to, or be a part of a well rounded and meaningful educational experience at the secondary school level. The Association shall strive to develop a unified and coordinated activities plan, without destroying the identity of any specific activity.
>
> The Association shall be an instrumentality of the member schools for the accomplishment of the foregoing objectives.

The Association sanctions interscholastic competition in many sports, including soccer. While schools may participate in programs which are not sanctioned by the Association, its official sanction is required for state tournaments and the Association promulgates rules governing eligibility, qualification of coaches and officials, and the official rules of play for each sanctioned sport. Additionally, a low cost insurance program is made available through the Association.

While the Association has no sex classification for cross country and baseball, the sport of soccer is limited by Rule XXI, § 3, as follows:

> Participation in this activity shall be limited to members of the male sex.
>
> NOTE: Because inordinate injury risk jeopardizes the health and safety of the female athlete, participation in this activity is limited to members of the male sex.

Soccer is a relatively new sport in Colorado high schools. It was first sanctioned five years ago and the state championship program was developed only two years ago. The decision to limit soccer to males resulted from consultation with a committee of the Colorado Medical Society designated as "Medical Aspects of Sports Committee." That group consists of seven physicians, from different geographical areas, whose practice involves pediatrics and orthopedics. Members of that committee testified at the trial of this case that the recommendation to classify soccer as a contact sport and to prohibit mixed sex play was the result of a perception of physiological differences which would subject the female players to an inordinate risk of injury.

Primarily, the committee was concerned with risks attendant upon collisions in the course of play. While the rules of soccer prohibit body contact (except for a brush-type shoulder block when moving toward the ball), there are frequent instances when players collide in their endeavors to "head" the ball. In those instances, contact is generally in the upper body area.

There is agreement that after puberty the female body has a higher ratio of adipose tissue to lean body weight as compared with the male, and females have less bone density than males. It is also true that, when matured, the male skeletal construct provides a natural advantage over females in the mechanics of running. Accordingly, applying the formula of force equals mass times acceleration, a collision between a male and a female of equal weights, running at full speed, would tend to be to the disadvantage of the female. It is also true that while males as a class tend to have an advantage in strength and speed over females as a class, the range of differences among individuals in both sexes is greater than the average differences between the sexes. The association has not established any eligibility criteria for participation in interscholastic soccer, excepting for sex. Accordingly, any male of any size and weight has the opportunity to be on an interscholastic team and no female is allowed to play, regardless of her size, weight, condition or skill.

Interscholastic athletic competition is an integral part of the educational program of public high schools in Colorado. The prevalent view is set forth in Section 1 of the association's by-laws:

> The program of the interscholastic athletics in high schools shall be so organized and administered as to contribute to the health, worthy use of leisure time, citizenship and character objectives of secondary education.

The defendants on the board of education and the professional educators in control of the activities association have concluded that the game of soccer is among those which serve an educational purpose and governmental funds have been provided for it. It is a matter of common knowledge that athletics are a recognized aspect of the educational program offered at American colleges and universities and that many of them offer scholarships to males and females for their agreement to participate in intercollegiate sports competition. Such offers result from organized recruiting programs directed toward those who have demonstrated their abilities on high school teams. Accordingly, the chance to play in athletic games may have an importance to the individual far greater than the obvious momentary pleasure of the game.

Accordingly, the claim of the plaintiff class in this case is properly characterized as a denial of an equal educational opportunity. . . .

* * *

This case has been presented and argued by both counsel within the framework of the two-tiered analysis familiar to equal protection decisions. If a "fundamental" right or interest is denied or impaired or if a classification is made on a "suspect" basis, the court must look with "strict scrutiny" to determine whether there is justification by a "compelling" state interest. Where there is neither a "fundamental" interest nor a "suspect" classification, a difference in the effects of state action is constitutionally permitted if it is "rationally related" to a "legitimate" state objective.

The defendants have argued and the plaintiff concedes that the Supreme Court has excluded education from "fundamental" rights by reserving that category to those which are explicitly or implicitly recognized in the language of the Constitution. . . .

The Supreme Court has exhibited an obvious reluctance to label sex as a "suspect" classification because the consequences of the application of the many "invidious" discrimination precedents to all separations by sex could lead to some absurd results. For example, would the Constitution preclude separate public toilets?

* * *

In a very recent Supreme Court opinion, *Craig v. Boren*, 429 U.S. 190 (1976), Mr. Justice Brennan, writing for the Court, attempted to define a new standard of review, saying:

> To withstand constitutional challenge, previous cases establish that classifications by gender must serve important governmental objectives and must be substantially related to achievement of those objectives. . . .

That language may be considered a "middle-tier approach" requiring something between "legitimate" and "compelling," viz, "important," and something more than a "rational" relationship but less perhaps than "strict scrutiny," viz, "substantially" related.

The artificiality of screening issues of constitutional moment through such a latticework of labels is becoming increasingly apparent. . . .

[I]n his concurring opinion in *Craig, supra,* Mr. Justice Stevens frankly expressed his own dissatisfaction with the majority analysis in these words:

> There is only one Equal Protection Clause. It requires every State to govern impartially. It does not direct the courts to apply one standard of review in some cases and a different standard in other cases. Whatever criticism may be leveled at a judicial opinion implying that there are at least three such standards applies with the same force to a double standard.
>
> I am inclined to believe that what has become known as the two tiered analysis of equal protection claims does not describe a completely logical method of deciding cases, but rather is a method the Court has employed to explain decisions that actually apply a single standard in a reasonably consistent fashion. I also suspect that a careful explanation of the reasons motivating particular decisions may contribute more to an identification of that standard than an attempt to articulate it in all-encompassing terms. . . .

Mr. Justice Powell also wrote a concurring opinion in *Craig*, in which he shared his fellow Justices' uneasiness with the familiar analysis. Although recognizing that the two-tiered approach now has substantial precedential support, he acknowledged that there are valid reasons for dissatisfaction with an approach which is "viewed by many as a result-oriented substitute for more critical analysis." . . . For a thoughtful discussion of equal protection analysis, he referred to an article by J. Harvie Wilkinson III, *The Supreme Court, the Equal Protection Clause, and the Three Faces of Constitutional Equality,* 61 VA. L. REV. 945 (1975).

In that writing, Professor Wilkinson has made this constructive suggestion:

> The constitutional inquiry to test governmental denials of equal opportunity ought to weigh and to balance carefully the following elements: (1) the importance of the opportunity being unequally burdened or denied; (2) the strength of the state interest served in denying it; and (3) the character of the groups whose opportunities are denied. [footnote omitted] The test is very different from the present suspect classification inquiry which focuses almost exclusively on the third element, purportedly ignores the first altogether if no suspect class is involved, and scrutinizes state interests only in two widely variant categories of rational and compelling.

61 VA. L. REV. at 991.

* * *

1. The importance of the opportunity being unequally burdened or denied.

The opportunity not merely burdened but completely denied to the plaintiff and the class she represents is the chance to compete in soccer as a part of a high school educational experience. Whether such games should be made available at public expense is not an issue. The content of an educational program is completely within the majoritarian control through the representatives on the school board. But, whether it is algebra or athletics, that which is provided must be open to all. The Court in *Brown* expressed a constitutional concern for equality in educational opportunity and this controversy is squarely within that area of concern. Accordingly, without reference to any label that would place this opportunity on one of two or more "tiers," it must be given a great importance to Donna Hoover and every other individual within her class. Surely it is of greater significance than the buying of beer, considered in *Craig*, supra.

2. The strength of the state interest served in denying it.

The defendants in this case have sought to support the exclusionary rule by asserting the state interest in the protection of females from injury in this sport. While the evidence in this case has shown that males as a class tend to have an advantage in strength and speed over females as a class and that a collision between a male and a female would tend to be to the disadvantage of the female, the evidence also shows that the range of differences among individuals in both sexes is greater than the average differences between the sexes. The failure to establish any physical criteria to protect small or weak males from the injurious effects of competition with larger or stronger males destroys the credibility of the reasoning urged in support of the sex classification. Accordingly, to the extent that governmental concern for the health and safety of anyone who knowingly and voluntarily exposes himself or herself to possible injury can ever be an acceptable area of intrusion on individual liberty, there is no rationality in limiting this patronizing protection to females who want to play soccer.

3. The character of the group whose opportunities are denied.

Women and girls constitute a majority of the people in this country. To be effective citizens, they must be permitted full participation in the educational programs designed for that purpose. To deny females equal access to athletics supported by public funds is to permit manipulation of governmental power for a masculine advantage.

Egalitarianism is the philosophical foundation of our political process and the principle which energizes the equal protection clause of the Fourteenth Amendment. The emergence of female interest in an active involvement in all aspects of our society requires abandonment of many historical stereotypes. Any notion that young women are so inherently weak, delicate or physically inadequate that the state must protect them from the folly of participation in vigorous athletics is a cultural anachronism unrelated to reality. The Constitution does not permit the use of governmental power to control or limit cultural changes or to prescribe masculine and feminine roles.

It is an inescapable conclusion that the complete denial of any opportunity to play interscholastic soccer is a violation of the plaintiffs right to equal protection of the law under the Fourteenth Amendment. This same conclusion would be required under even the minimal "rational relationship" standard of review applied to classifications which are not suspect and do not involve fundamental rights. The governmental purpose in fielding a soccer team is to enhance the secondary school educational experience. The exclusion of girls to protect them from injury cannot be considered to be in furtherance of that education objective. If the purpose of the exclusionary rule is the protection of health, safety and welfare of the students, it is arbitrary to consider only the general physiological differences between males and females as classes without any regard for the wide range of individual variants within each class. . . .

While Rule XXI is invalid under either method of analysis, there is a difference between them which is revealed in considering both the remedy required here and the possible ramifications of this case for future controversies.

There is no contention in this case that the Constitution compels soccer competition with teams composed of the best players, regardless of sex. Donna Hoover sought a chance to play on the boys' team only because there is no girls' team. The parties here agree that the effective equalization of athletic opportunities for members of both sexes would be better served by comparable teams for members of each sex and that under current circumstances mixed-sex teams would probably be dominated by males. Accordingly, it is conceded that "separate but equal" teams would satisfy the equality of opportunity required by the Constitution. The "separate but equal" doctrine was articulated in *Plessy v. Ferguson*, 163 U.S. 537 (1896), approving racial separation in transportation facilities. The doctrine was rejected for education in *Brown*, supra, upon the conclusion that racial separation was inherently unequal because it involved a stigmatizing inferiority for the minority race. No such effect is conceivable for a separation of athletic teams by sex.

The Colorado High School Activities Association has sanctioned separate sex teams for basketball, gymnastics, swimming, tennis and track on a separate but equal basis pursuant to the following stated philosophy in the by-laws:

> Section 2
>
> The Colorado High School Activities Association, in order to effectively equalize athletic opportunities for members of both sexes, promotes and encourages the use of comparable athletic teams for members of each sex where selection for such teams is based upon competitive skills. This effort is to promote and encourage the growth of female involvement in athletic programs sponsored by this organization.

> The term "competitive skills" as used in this context refers to those skill [sic] presently possessed by athletes as a class composed of male athletes, as compared to the class of female athletes.

Given the lack of athletic opportunity for females in past years, the encouragement of female involvement in sports is a legitimate objective and separation of teams may promote that purpose. . . . It may also justify the sanction of some sports only for females, of which volleyball may be an example.

Separate soccer teams for males and females would meet the constitutional requirement of equal opportunity if the teams were given substantially equal support and if they had substantially comparable programs. There may be differences depending upon the effects of such neutral factors as the level of student interest and geographic locations. Accordingly, the standard should be one of comparability, not absolute equality.

In arriving at the conclusion that the defendants are in violation of the Fourteenth Amendment by providing interscholastic soccer only for male high school students, I am aware that there will be many concerned about the ramifications of this ruling. Football, ice hockey and wrestling are also made available only for males in Colorado, and volleyball is provided only for females. While there is now no reason to rule beyond the specific controversy presented by the evidence, it would seem appropriate to make some general observations about constitutional concerns in athletic programs supported by public funds.

The applicability of so fundamental a constitutional principle as equal educational opportunity should not depend upon anything so mutable as customs, usages, protective equipment and rules of play. The courts do not have competence to determine what games are appropriate for the schools or which, if any, teams should be separated by sex. What the courts can and must do is to insure that those who do make those decisions act with an awareness of what the Constitution does and does not require of them. Accordingly, it must be made clear that there is no constitutional requirement for the schools to provide any athletic program, as it is clear that there is no constitutional requirement to provide any public education. What is required is that whatever opportunity is made available be open to all on equal terms.

It must also be made clear that the mandate of equality of opportunity does not dictate a disregard of differences in talents and abilities among individuals. There is no right to a position on an athletic team. There is a right to compete for it on equal terms.

Adherence to the traditional equal protection analysis in these school sports cases can cause an unwelcome intrusion into issues which should be beyond the court's concern. It may here be observed that the flexibility which is suggested by common sense would be precluded by strict adherence to the two-tiered analysis if sex classifications are considered "suspect" or if some level of justification higher than "rational relationship" is required. In *Cape v. Tennessee Secondary School Athletic Association*, 424 F. Supp. 792 (E.D. Tenn. 1976), the holding was that the United States Constitution was violated because Tennessee high school girls could not play the same game of full court basketball permitted by the rules governing boys' teams. Is the full court dribble a matter of constitutional importance? In *Brendan v. Independent School District*, 477 F.2d 1292 (8th Cir. 1973), the court emphasized that "non-contact" sports were involved. Should equality of opportunity be measured according to style of play? Must there be "measure for measure" in each sport? Will girls be hurt by playing soccer with boys? The courtroom is not the place and the adversary process is not the method by which these questions should be answered. Fundamental principles of participatory democracy must not be trivialized by elevating every public controversy to a constitutional level.

This case has been kept within the confines of a particular sport because that is the way the parties chose to present it. If future controversies arise in other areas of athletic competition, it may be well to consider a broader perspective and to address the constitutional issue of equality of opportunity in the manner suggested by Professor Wilkinson. The importance of an opportunity for both sexes to participate in a total athletic program presenting a variety of choices for those with differing interests and abilities is far different from the importance of an opportunity for a boy to play volleyball or a girl to play football. The strength of the state interest and the character of the groups affected will also differ according to the scope of the total program.

Accordingly, whatever may be the validity of the two-tiered analysis to other questions of equal protection, it should be avoided in athletics as education to keep the courts out of the thicket of an acute analysis of rules and games. The question should not be whether there is a basis for each classification; but what is the relative importance of the individual interest affected compared with the governmental objective.

The plaintiff has asked for an order requiring the school board to permit her to play on the Golden High School soccer team and to enjoin the other defendants from imposing any penalty or other sanction upon that high school or any competing team because of that permission. Because there is no obligation to provide any soccer program and because equal opportunity can be given to the plaintiff class either by mixed-sex or comparable separate-sex teams, the defendants have a choice of actions to be taken. They may decide to discontinue soccer as an interscholastic athletic activity; they may decide to field separate teams for males and females, with substantial equality in funding, coaching, officiating and opportunity to play; or they may decide to permit both sexes to compete on the same team. Any of these actions would satisfy the equal protection requirements of the Constitution. What the defendants may not do is to continue to make interscholastic soccer available only to male students.

Upon the foregoing, it is

ORDERED and ADJUDGED that Rule XXI, Section 3 of the Colorado High School Activities Association is facially unconstitutional and that the defendants' exclusion of Donna Hoover and the class she represents from participation in any form of interscholastic soccer competition while male students are permitted to participate in such competition is a denial of equal educational opportunity, and, it is

ORDERED, that the defendants are permanently enjoined from the enforcement of or adherence to Rule XXI, Section 3 of the Colorado High School Activities Association and from providing interscholastic soccer only for male high school students.

WILLIAMS v. SCHOOL DISTRICT OF BETHLEHEM

998 F.2d 168 (3d Cir. 1993)

Before: SLOVITER, Chief Judge, MANSMANN and SCIRICA, Circuit Judges

SLOVITER, Chief Judge.

Can high school field hockey be considered a contact sport? The district court held that it could not as a matter of law. On this ground and others, we disagree with the trial court's entry of summary judgment against the School District, and remand because there are material fact issues to be resolved.

I. Facts and Procedural History

When John Williams was fourteen years old and in ninth grade, he presented himself for the girls' field hockey team tryouts at Liberty High School, a public school in the School District of Bethlehem, Pennsylvania. He had played intramural coed field hockey when he was in eighth grade at a middle school in the School District, but the high school has only a girls' field hockey team. After the tryouts, the coach made tentative position and team assignments based on each player's abilities. John, whose skills were average, would probably have played goalie on the junior varsity team. However, after school officials learned that John and another boy had been issued uniforms, the boys were instructed that they could not play on the girls' field hockey team.

John's parents, plaintiffs Sarah and Wayne Williams, filed this action in October 1990 against the School District of Bethlehem, challenging John's exclusion from the girls' field hockey team. They made claims alleging violations of title IX of the Education Amendments of 1972, 20 U.S.C. § 1681 (1988), and its implementing regulation, 34 C.F.R. § 106.41 (1990); the Equal Protection and Due Process clauses of the federal Constitution, under 42 U.S.C. § 1983 (1988); and the Equal Rights Amendment to the Pennsylvania Constitution (E.R.A.), Pa. Const. art. I, § 28.

Plaintiffs sought a permanent injunction, attorneys' fees, and costs. While the litigation was pending, they reached an agreement with the School District that for the fall 1991 sports season, John, then a sophomore, would be permitted to practice with the girls' field hockey team but not to play in interscholastic games.

Based on the undisputed facts that the School District limits player participation on the field hockey team to females and that John was not permitted to be a part of the Liberty High School team only because of that policy, the district court granted summary judgment on July 14, 1992 in favor of the plaintiffs, permanently enjoining the School District from excluding John from the Liberty High School girls' field hockey team. In holding that the School District violated title IX, the court held as a matter of law that field hockey is not a "contact sport" and that males "have previously been denied athletic opportunities," App. at 66, thereby holding inapplicable the exception in the implementing regulation for those situations. *See* 34 C.F.R. § 106.41(b) (1990). In sustaining the plaintiffs' federal Equal Protection claim, the district court held, inter alia, that the School District's exclusionary policy was not necessary to preserve girls' athletic opportunities and that it was not justified by the goal of rectifying past discrimination against girls in athletics.

In addition, without resolving what standard of scrutiny applied, the district court held that the Pennsylvania E.R.A. was violated because its coverage is "at least as stringent" as the federal Equal Protection clause, which it had already found was violated. After the grant of the permanent injunction, John, by then a junior, rejoined the field hockey team as a full participant for the fall 1992 season. The School District appeals.

II. Discussion

A. Title IX

[The court reversed the trial court's grant of summary judgment for the plaintiff on the Title IX issue.]

B. Federal Constitutional Claims

In an extended discussion, the district court upheld the plaintiffs' claim that the School District's policy precluding boys from playing field hockey violated the federal Constitution's Equal Protection clause. The School District argues that the plaintiffs' constitutional claims under 42 U.S.C. § 1983 are precluded because they are based on a matter fully addressed by the comprehensive scheme in title IX.

The Supreme Court has made clear that where a federal statute provides its own comprehensive enforcement scheme, Congress intended to foreclose a right of action under section 1983. *Middlesex County Sewerage Auth. v. National Sea Clammers Ass'n*, 453 U.S. 1, 20-21 (1981). This court recently addressed the applicability of the *Sea Clammers* doctrine to cases in which plaintiff asserts a claim under title IX and the federal Constitution. In *Pfeiffer v. Marion Center Area School District*, 917 F.2d 779, 789 (3d Cir. 1990), we held that the constitutional claims are "subsumed" in title IX, and that the district court, having addressed the title IX claim, properly refused to hear plaintiff's section 1983 claim. Plaintiffs argue that the *Sea Clammers* doctrine is inapplicable where an injunction is sought, but in *Pfeiffer* plaintiff also sought an injunction, and we are bound by that holding.

The district court in the instant case acknowledged that *Sea Clammers* rendered its discussion of the constitutional claims unnecessary, but chose to proceed, *inter alia,* "for the sake of completeness." . . . The court should have been guided instead by the Supreme Court's admonition that courts should exercise restraint before reaching federal constitutional claims. We will therefore not reach the constitutional issues, and will vacate the district court's judgment on the section 1983 claim.

C. Pennsylvania Equal Rights Amendment

In granting the plaintiffs' motion for summary judgment, the district court did not separately discuss the Pennsylvania E.R.A. claim because it concluded that once it found that the School District violated the federal Equal Protection clause, the School District necessarily violated the Pennsylvania E.R.A. We will therefore review the court's federal Equal Protection analysis as if it were made in the Pennsylvania E.R.A. context, and apply the same plenary review as we have done on the other claims.

The Pennsylvania E.R.A. provides that "[e]quality of rights under the law shall not be denied or abridged in the Commonwealth of Pennsylvania because of the sex of the individual. Pa. Const. art. I, § 28. The provision applies equally to men and to women, *see Swidzinski v.Schultz*, 493 A.2d 93, 95-96 (Pa. Super. 1985), and, according to the Supreme Court of Pennsylvania, its purpose is to insure equality of rights under the law and to eliminate sex as a basis for distinction. The sex of citizens of this Commonwealth is no longer a permissible factor in the determination of their legal rights and legal responsibilities. The law will not impose different benefits or different burdens upon the members of a society based on the fact that they may be man or woman. *Henderson v. Henderson*, 327 A.2d 60, 62 (Pa. 1974) (invalidating statute permitting only women to receive alimony after divorce).

The Court has stated, "In this Commonwealth, sex may no longer be accepted as an exclusive classifying tool."

Although the Supreme Court of Pennsylvania has not addressed the E.R.A. in the context of interscholastic athletics, in a thoughtful opinion the Commonwealth Court made clear that if the classification between boys and girls in connection with team sports is based on impermissible assumptions and stereotypes about the comparative characteristics or abilities of boys and girls, the E.R.A. will be violated. However, after the Commonwealth Court's decision in *Packel,* the Pennsylvania Supreme Court decided *Fischer v. Department of Public Welfare*, 502 A.2d 114 (Pa. 1985), where it accepted the view prevailing among jurisdictions with a state E.R.A. that

> the E.R.A. does not prohibit differential treatment among the sexes when, as here[,] that treatment is reasonably and genuinely based on physical characteristics unique to one sex.

Id. 502 A.2d at 125 (quotation omitted).

In defending the E.R.A. claim, the School District argued that because of the undeniable physical differences between girls and boys of high school age, sex was the only classification feasible for accomplishing, inter alia, the legitimate and substantial interest of promoting athletic opportunities for girls. As we noted in our discussion of title IX, the parties introduced conflicting evidence on the extent of physical differences between boys and girls at the high school level. Some of the evidence supports the School District's argument that the differences between the sexes increase dramatically through high school, and that by age sixteen, these differences are substantial.

The validity of the School District's policy excluding boys from the field hockey team depends on whether there are "physical characteristics unique to [boys]" which warrant differential treatment. If there are real physical differences between high school boys and high school girls, then the sexes are "not similarly situated as they enter into most athletic endeavors," *Petrie v. Illinois High School Ass'n*, 394 N.E.2d 855, 863 (Ill. App. Ct. 1979), and exclusion based on sex may be justified, *see Bartholomew ex rel. Bartholomew v. Foster*, 541 A.2d 393, 397 (Pa. Commw. 1988) ("The only types of sexual discrimination . . . permitted in this Commonwealth are those which are reasonably and genuinely based on physical characteristics unique to one sex.") (quotation omitted), aff'd without opinion, 563 A.2d 1390 (Pa. 1989).

The district court found resolution of the dispute on physical differences "completely unnecessary" because there was no evidence to suggest that more than a handful of boys would ever express interest in playing field hockey. Only four girls have ever tried out for boys' teams in the School District (two for football and two for soccer), and only two boys, including John Williams, have tried out for girls' teams (field hockey).

We believe that resolution of this factual dispute cannot be avoided. Whether boys will be interested in trying out for the field hockey team is irrelevant to the issue whether real physical differences between boys and girls justify differential treatment, in this case, the exclusion of boys from the girls' teams but not girls from the boys' teams. Under Pennsylvania law, as expressed most recently by the state's Supreme Court in *Fischer,* the legality of the School District's policy can only be resolved by deciding whether there are genuine physical differences between boys and girls or whether, instead, the policy is based on unwarranted and stereotyped assumptions about the sexes. That issue raises a fact question which precludes summary judgment.

A related dispute between the parties concerns whether permitting boys to play on the girls' teams will result in boys' eclipsing girls' athletic opportunities in the School District. Plaintiffs pointed out, as noted above, that few students have tried out for or joined teams designated for the other sex. They also contended that, far from negatively affecting girls' athletic opportunities, allowing boys on the team will increase those opportunities because, during at least one sports season, Liberty High School had "barely" the minimum number of female players to field a team. Finally, plaintiffs asserted that because field hockey at Liberty High School is a "no cut" team, boys can never displace girls from the team.

The School District countered with the argument that if more boys are allowed on the team and permitted to play, more girls will warm the bench during the field hockey matches. It also presented the testimony of Villani that if positions on the field hockey team were open to girls and boys, "eventually boys would dominate, eliminating the opportunities of females." . . . Gros agreed that male players' physical characteristics give them a significant competitive advantage over female players.

Nonetheless, the district court, again relying on the facts that few boys have expressed an interest in the sport and that no cuts are made from the Liberty High School field hockey team, found that admitting boys would not displace girls from play. In our view, the district court must resolve the factual issue as to physical differences before it can determine whether boys are likely to displace girls from the team. *Compare Cape v. Tennessee Secondary Sch. Athletic Ass'n,* 563 F.2d 793, 795 (6th Cir. 1977) ("[i]t takes little imagination to realize that were play and competition not separated by sex, the great bulk of the females would quickly be eliminated from participation and denied any meaningful opportunity for athletic involvement") and *Gil,* No. 85-E-646, slip op. at 26 ("Boys, as a class, are undoubtedly better physiologically equipped to play field hockey than are girls.") with *Attorney Gen. v. Massachusetts Interscholastic Athletic Ass'n*, 393 N.E.2d 284, 293 (Mass. 1979) ("No doubt biological circumstance does contribute to some overall male advantages. But we think the differences are not so clear or uniform as to justify a rule in which sex is sought to be used as a kind of 'proxy' for a functional classification."). For reasons we have already explained, this issue must be resolved at trial.

Ultimately, the validity of the classification will depend on the relationship between the classification and the government interest. . . .

* * *

We will therefore remand the E.R.A. claim to the district court for fact-finding as to whether there are any real physical differences between boys and girls that warrant different treatment, and whether boys are likely to dominate the school's athletic program if admitted to the girls' teams. Only then will it be possible to determine whether the School District's policy of excluding boys from girls' teams is necessary to the School District's recognized interest in preserving meaningful athletic opportunities for girls, *see Petrie*, 75 Ill. App. 3d 980, 31 Ill. Dec. 653, 394 N.E.2d at 862-64, and/or whether there is a current need to rectify the admittedly pervasive past discrimination against female high school students with respect to athletic opportunities, *see Clark*, 695 F.2d at 1131.

III. Conclusion

In summary, the district court's order granting summary judgment for the plaintiffs will be reversed. We do not foreclose the School District from moving for summary judgment on the title IX claim based on its affidavits, thereby shifting the burden to the plaintiffs to produce evidence demonstrating a genuine issue of material fact precluding summary judgment. If the district court determines that the School District is entitled to summary judgment on the title IX claim, then our precedent would counsel dismissal of the pendent E.R.A. claim which could then be maintained in state court.

* * *

NOTES AND COMMENTS

1. The United States Supreme Court has analyzed the standards for determining an equal protection violation where the questioned classification was gender based. In *United States v. Virginia*, 518 U.S. 515 (1996), the Court found that the establishment of a single sex public military school in Virginia denied equal protection of the laws to women. The Court reiterated that gender classifications are subject to heightened scrutiny and that parties seeking to defend gender based governmental action must demonstrate an "exceedingly persuasive justification." Any challenged classification must serve an important governmental objective and the means developed must be substantially related to achieving that objective. Under this intermediate scrutiny standard, justifications must be real, not concocted for purposes of responding to litigation.

2. The sex discrimination issue has arisen in a wide variety of contexts. The cases have involved situations where there was a men's team and no women's team, a women's team and no men's team, separate but allegedly unequal teams for men and women, teams in the same sport but playing under different rules, and teams in the same sport but playing in different seasons. *See Libby v. Illinois High School Association,* 921 F.2d 96 (7th Cir. 1990); *Habetz by Habetz v. Louisiana High School Athletic Association,* 915 F.2d 164 (5th Cir. 1990).

3. Is there a valid claim of sex discrimination when a state high school athletic association authorizes separate seasons of play for high school athletic teams separated or substantially separated according to gender? For example, what is the result if boys play tennis in the spring and girls play tennis in the fall? *See Streibel v. Minnesota State High School League*, 321 N.W.2d 400 (Minn. 1982) (holding that league's policy of separate seasons for boys' and girls' athletic teams was constitutional).

4. What is the appropriate approach for a court to take when a boy wants to play on a girls' team in a noncontact sport in which there is no boys' team? *See*

Clark v. Arizona Interscholastic Association, 695 F.2d 1126 (9th Cir. 1982) (a girls-only volleyball team promotes a strong government interest in supporting equal opportunities for females in athletics and redressing past inequities); and *Gomes v. Rhode Island Interscholastic League,* 469 F. Supp. 659 (D.R.I. 1979), *vacated as moot,* 604 F.2d 733 (1st Cir. 1979) (boy allowed to play on girls' volleyball team where previously no opportunity for boys to play the sport). *See also, Kleczek v. Rhode Island Interscholastic League, Inc.*, 768 F. Supp. 951 (D.R.I. 1991).

5. To what extent do you think that the decisions of the courts are motivated by the type of relief sought? Female athletes as plaintiffs could request 1) the opportunity to participate on an exclusively male team; 2) the creation of an exclusively female team; or 3) the opportunity to participate on an exclusively male team despite the existence of a female team.

Would Donna Hoover have been afforded an opportunity to play on the boys' soccer team if the school had fielded a girls' team? Male plaintiffs could request similar relief. Would a male plaintiff be successful if he sought the creation of, for example, a boys' volleyball team where there was only a girls' team?

It is also important to remember that the defendant, a school district or university, can shape the ultimate relief given to the plaintiff. In *Hoover,* the court points out that the school district has the option to either allow the female plaintiff to participate on the boys' team, create an exclusively girls' team, or not offer the particular sport at all. However, as we will see in the second part of this chapter, the school may not have all of these options if Title IX issues are raised by a plaintiff.

6. The opportunity to participate on a particular athletic team has not been the only relief sought by female athletes. Consider the claim that rule variations in the same sport violate the Equal Protection Clause.

In *Cape v. Tennessee Secondary Sch. Athletic Association,* 563 F.2d 792 (6th Cir. 1977) (per curiam), *reversing,* 424 F. Supp. 732 (E.D. Tenn. 1976), the court reversed the trial court's finding that the difference between rules for high school girls' and boys' basketball did violate equal protection. The rules for the girls' teams mandated six players per team, and three of the six players (forwards) were required to stay on the offensive end of the court and the other three players (guards) stayed on the defensive end. Only forwards were allowed to shoot. Since her coach made her play guard, the plaintiff claimed that she was at a disadvantage in obtaining a college scholarship in basketball because she could not develop her skills (e.g., shooting) to play the full court game. The court reasoned that since no challenge was made to the separation of boys and girls in basketball teams, there must be, for purposes of this case, some difference in physical abilities between boys and girls. Therefore, according to the court, there was no reason why the rules could not "be tailored to accommodate [the physical differences]." *Id.* at 795. A similar result was reached in *Jones v. Oklahoma Secondary Sch. Activities Association,* 453 F. Supp. 150 (W.D. Okla. 1977).

Compare Cape and *Jones* with *Dodson v. Arkansas Activities Association,* 468 F. Supp. 395 (E.D. Ark. 1979). In *Dodson*, the court noted the decisions in *Cape* and *Jones*, but declined to follow them. In doing so, the court said: "To the extent that the reasoning of those cases is contrary to this opinion, the Court respectfully disagrees. They are not binding authority here, and their reasoning seems, with deference, unpersuasive." *Dodson*, 468 F. Supp. at 398-99.

C. TITLE IX

Title IX is a statutory remedy for gender based classifications in education. It applies to athletics in educational settings, notably intercollegiate and interscholastic athletics. It provides a cause of action separate and apart from constitutional challenges.

As noted above, Title IX of the Education Amendments of 1972 to the Civil Rights Act of 1964 provides that:

> No person in the United States shall, on the basis of sex, be excluded from participation in, be denied the benefits of, or be subjected to discrimination under any education program or activity receiving federal financial assistance. . . .

20 U.S.C. § 1681(a). The Department of Health, Education, and Welfare (HEW) was charged with implementing the act. Regulations were finally issued and became effective in 1975, nearly three years following passage of the law. (45 C.F.R. Part 86.) Schools were to be in compliance with the act and regulations by July of 1978. Confusion abounded as to coverage of the act and the appropriate interpretation of the regulations. As a result, HEW issued a policy interpretation in December of 1979. 44 Fed. Reg. 71,413 (1979).

HEW's Office of Civil Rights (OCR) was charged with enforcing the act and participated in drafting the policy interpretation. According to OCR, the test for compliance would be a comparison of:

> Availability, quality and kinds of benefits, opportunities and treatment of the members of both sexes. Institutions will be in compliance if the compared program components are equivalent, that is, equal or equal in effect. Under this standard, identical benefits, opportunities or treatment are not required, provided the overall effect of any differences is negligible.

44 Fed. Reg. 71,413-15 (1979).

In order to understand the factors and policies of gender equity, it is necessary to understand the history of this relatively young statute. In *Cannon v. University of Chicago*, 441 U.S. 677 (1979), the Supreme Court held that even though there is no express provision in the act authorizing private individuals to bring actions, there is an implied right of action. Five years later in *Grove City College v. Bell*, 465 U.S. 444 (1984), the Court held that Title IX was "program specific." In other words, the act applied only to particular programs of a university or public school. Under this interpretation athletic programs were subject to Title IX scrutiny only if they received federal funding. Since most athletic programs do not receive federal funding directly, the net result of *Grove City* was that Title IX became neglected and ineffective. Several years later Congress put teeth back into the act when it passed the Civil Rights Restoration Act of 1987. (20 U.S.C. §§ 1687-88). In this legislation Congress extended the full reach of Title IX to any program of any institution or public school that accepts federal funding. Thus, there was a legislative overruling of *Grove City*.

The next significant development in Title IX history came in the decision in *Franklin v. Gwinnett County Public Schools*, 503 U.S. 60 (1992). In this case the Supreme Court ruled that monetary damages are available in actions pursuant to Title IX, at least for those involving intentional violations of the act.

As a result of the above judicial decisions and the 1987 legislation, nearly all colleges, universities, community colleges, and elementary and secondary school districts are covered by the Act. Federal funding of any sort received by the institution or school district, even if unrelated to athletics, will cause the athletic program to come under the coverage of the act.

Today the Department of Education is responsible for enforcement of Title IX.

Specific enforcement activities are carried out by its Office of Civil Rights. The original regulations and the 1979 policy interpretation are still the law of the land. 34 C.F.R. Part 106. The 1979 policy interpretation and 1996 and 1998 clarifications of the policy interpretation have been critical to the enforcement of the act. The policy interpretation called for the investigators to evaluate the following areas: 1) athletic financial assistance (34 C.F.R. § 106.37(c)); 2) equivalency in other athletic benefits and opportunities (34 C.F.R. § 106.41(c)(2)-(10)); and 3) effective accommodation of student interests and abilities (34 C.F.R. § 106.41(c)(1)). The interpretation also directs investigators to evaluate the following factors within athletic programs when attempting to determine compliance:

1. Whether the selection of sports and levels of competition effectively accommodate the interests and abilities of members of both sexes;
2. The provision of equipment and supplies;
3. Scheduling of games and practice time;
4. Travel and per diem allowance;
5. Opportunity to receive coaching and academic tutoring;
6. Assignment and compensation of coaches and tutors;
7. Provision of locker rooms, practice and competitive facilities;
8. Provision of medical and training facilities and services;

9. Provision of housing and dining facilities and services;

10. Publicity.

34 C.F.R. § 106.41(c) (1998).

As noted in the cases included in the case file, several courts have focused their analyses on the so-called three part test set out in the policy interpretation to determine, at least threshold, compliance. This test provides, in essence, three ways in which a school may be found to be in compliance. The court will look to one of these benchmarks: (1) whether intercollegiate level participation opportunities for male and female students are provided in numbers substantially proportionate to their respective enrollments; (2) where the members of one sex have been and are underrepresented among intercollegiate athletes, whether the institution can show a history and continuing practice of program expansion which is demonstrably responsive to the developing interest and abilities of the members of that sex; or (3) where the members of one sex are underrepresented among intercollegiate athletes, and the institution cannot show a continuing practice of program expansion such as cited above, whether it can be demonstrated that the interests and abilities of the members of that sex have been fully and effectively accommodated by the present program. 44 Fed. Reg. 71,413-18 (1979).

PROBLEM

You are counsel for a small, private university with a total enrollment of approximately 4,500 students. More than 2,000 of the students receive federal educational loans or loan guarantees. Several of the university's buildings, including the administration building (in which the office of the athletic director is located), were built with the help of federal funds. The school has a work-study program which is funded in part with federal monies. The school is a Division I member of the NCAA and participates in a number of varsity sports.

It is summertime, and in the brief lull between the end of the basketball season and the start of the football season, you receive a series of memorandums from the athletic director, Joe Daniels, to wit:

June 15

The Athletic Department has recently become concerned about Title IX and its possible impact on our programs, particularly the threat to our football and basketball teams. We would like to know if you think there are any legitimate issues to cause us concern.

June 18

Per our telephone conversation on June 16, in which you requested more information, the following is pertinent data for your consideration:

Men's Sports*	Scholarships	Participants	Funding**
baseball	11	35	$ 675,000
golf	4	8	205,000
tennis	4	8	205,000
track/cross country	12	35	481,000
hockey	18	35	816,000
swimming	9	25	340,000
TOTAL	58	146	$2,722,000

Women's Sports	Scholarships	Participants	Funding
golf	4	8	$ 205,000
tennis	4	8	205,000
basketball	13	15	911,000
swimming	12	20	357,000
volleyball	12	15	360,000
track	10	28	420,000
soccer	10	20	430,000
crew	10	18	350,000
TOTAL	75	132	$3,2385,000

* I have not included the men's football and basketball teams in these figures because they are revenue-producing sports. Women's basketball also produces a minimal amount of revenue.

** The funding figures represent the total operating budget for each sport, including, but not limited to, expenditures for scholarships, coaches' salaries, equipment, travel, recruitment, and overhead.

June 25

Per our telephone conversation on June 22, it is our view and the view of many other schools, that revenue-producing sports shouldn't be included in Title IX figures because they generate money, while the other sports do not. However, if you insist on having them, here they are: In football we have 85 scholarships, 115 participants, and $5,825,000 in expenditures. The football program brings in $17,500,000 per year in revenues. In basketball, we have 13 scholarships, 15 participants, $2,235,000 in expenditures and $7,500,000 in revenues. Stadium and operational costs are not included.

Also, per your request, some additional information: The football team practices and plays home games at the University Stadium, where its training facilities and locker rooms are also located. The men's basketball and women's basketball, swimming and volleyball teams all practice and play in the new sports center, which has one basketball court. The only conflict over practice times has been in scheduling basketball team practices. The men have the court from 2 p.m. to 5 p.m weekdays, the women from 7 a.m. to 10 a.m. We have received some complaints about this, because a few of the women basketball players had class conflicts.

All of the men's and women's teams (except football and men's basketball) travel to and from games in university vans, and usually do not spend the night at away game locations. When they're at tournaments or have to spend the night, they stay at a Motel Six or other comparable facilities.

The football and basketball teams travel by air and generally stay overnight in the away-game locations for at least one night.

The football team keeps a local orthopedist on retainer to treat injuries incurred in practice and games. Athletes on the other teams rely on the services of the student health clinic.

We have a tutoring program available to all athletes. Our experience has shown that members of the football and basketball teams usually need tutorial help far more often than members of the other teams.

Our coaches for football and men's basketball are full-time and each makes $125,000 per year. The baseball coach is also full-time, and makes a salary of $95,000 per year. The women's basketball coach makes $125,000 per year. The total compensation packages for each of the above coaches is greater than listed due to additional radio and television, shoe, automobile, and miscellaneous outside perks associated with the position.

We conducted a survey of students last fall and received approximately 900 responses: 700 from men (who account for 2,000 of the total student body) and 200 from women (who account for 2,500 of the total number of students). Generally, the students appeared to be satisfied with the school's athletic program, but expressed an interest in women's soccer and gymnastics. We have recently added soccer to our program for women.

Two female athletes recently complained to me about the athletic program and threatened to file a Title IX complaint with the Department of Education. I explained to them that such an action would virtually destroy our school's football and (men's) basketball teams, and they backed down.

Last fall a female student from Argentina who had extensive soccer experience wanted to try out as a place kicker for our football team. The coach told her no women were allowed on the team.

Prepare a memorandum to the Athletic Director answering these questions:

1. Is the athletic department bound by Title IX? Why or why not?

2. If Title IX pertains to the athletic department, is the school in compliance with Title IX? What, if any, violations do you see?

3. If the school is not in compliance, what actions must be taken to eliminate the violations?

4. As a practical matter, what advice do you give Mr. Daniels concerning Title IX?

CASE FILE

COHEN v. BROWN UNIVERSITY

101 F.3d 155 (1st Cir. 1996)

BOWNES, Senior Circuit Judge.

This is a class action lawsuit charging Brown University, its president, and its athletics director (collectively "Brown") with discrimination against women in the operation of its intercollegiate athletics program, in violation of Title IX of the Education Amendments of 1972, 20 U.S.C. §§ 1681-1688 ("Title IX"), and its implementing regulations, 34 C.F.R. §§ 106.1-106.71. The plaintiff class comprises all present, future, and potential Brown University women students who participate, seek to participate, and/or are deterred from participating in intercollegiate athletics funded by Brown.

This suit was initiated in response to the demotion in May 1991 of Brown's women's gymnastics and volleyball teams from university-funded varsity status to donor-funded varsity status. Contemporaneously, Brown demoted two men's teams, water polo and golf, from university-funded to donor-funded varsity status. As a consequence of these demotions, all four teams lost, not only their university funding, but most of the support and privileges that accompany university-funded varsity status at Brown.

. . . [T]he district court granted plaintiffs' motion for a preliminary injunction, ordering, inter alia, that the women's gymnastics and volleyball teams be reinstated to university-funded varsity status, and prohibiting Brown from eliminating or reducing the status or funding of any existing women's intercollegiate varsity team until the case was resolved on the merits. *Cohen v. Brown Univ.*, 809 F. Supp. 978, 1001 (D.R.I. 1992) ("*Cohen I*"). A panel of this court affirmed the district court's decision granting a preliminary injunction to the plaintiffs. *Cohen v. Brown Univ.*, 991 F.2d 888, 907 (1st Cir. 1993) ("*Cohen II*"). In so doing, we upheld the district court's analysis and ruled that an institution violates Title IX if it ineffectively accommodates its students' interests and abilities in athletics under 34 C.F.R. § 106.41(c)(1) (1995), regardless of its performance with respect to other Title IX areas. *Id.* at 897.

On remand, the district court determined after a lengthy bench trial that Brown's intercollegiate athletics program violates Title IX and its supporting regulations. *Cohen v. Brown Univ.*, 879 F. Supp. 185, 214 (D.R.I. 1995) ("*Cohen III*"). [Hereinafter citations to the previous *Cohen* opinions have been omitted except where relevant to lengthy quotations.] The district court ordered Brown to submit within 120 days a comprehensive plan for complying with Title IX, but stayed that portion of the order pending appeal. *Id.* The district court subsequently issued a modified order, requiring Brown to submit a compliance plan within 60 days. Modified Order of May 4, 1995. This action was taken to ensure that the Order was "final" for purposes of this court's jurisdiction, and to expedite the appeal process. *Id.* Finding that Brown's proposed compliance plan was not comprehensive and that it failed to comply with the opinion and order of *Cohen III*, the district court rejected the plan and ordered in its place specific relief consistent with Brown's stated objectives in formulating the plan. . . . The court's remedial order required Brown to elevate and maintain at university-funded varsity status the women's gymnastics, fencing, skiing, and water polo teams. The district court's decision to fashion specific relief was made, in part, to avoid protracted litigation over the compliance plan and to expedite the appeal on the issue of liability. The district court entered final judgment on September 1, 1995, and on September 27, 1995, denied Brown's motion for additional findings of fact and to amend the judgment. This appeal followed.

* * *

Brown contends that we are free to disregard the prior panel's explication of the law in *Cohen II*. Brown's efforts to circumvent the controlling effect of *Cohen II* are unavailing, however, because, under the law of the case doctrine, we are bound in this appeal, as was the district court on remand, by the prior panel's rulings of law. . . .

I.

* * *

Brown operates a two-tiered intercollegiate athletics program with respect to funding: although Brown provides the financial resources required to maintain its university-funded varsity teams, donor-funded varsity athletes must themselves raise the funds necessary to support their teams through private donations. The district court noted that the four demoted teams were eligible for NCAA competition, provided that they were able to raise the funds necessary to maintain a sufficient level of competitiveness, and provided that they continued to comply with NCAA requirements. The court found, however, that it is difficult for donor-funded varsity athletes to maintain a level of competitiveness commensurate with their abilities and that these athletes operate at a competitive disadvantage in comparison to university-funded varsity athletes. *Id.* at 189. For example, the district court found that some schools are reluctant to include donor-funded teams in their varsity schedules and that donor-funded teams are unable to obtain varsity-level coaching, recruits, and funds for travel, equipment, and post-season competition.

Brown's decision to demote the women's volleyball and gymnastics teams and the men's water polo and golf teams from university-funded varsity status was apparently made in response to a university-wide cost-cutting directive. The district court found that Brown saved $62,028 by demoting the women's teams and $15,795 by demoting the men's teams, but that the demotions "did not appreciably affect the athletic participation gender ratio."

Plaintiffs alleged that, at the time of the demotions, the men students at Brown already enjoyed the benefits of a disproportionately large share of both the university resources allocated to athletics and the intercollegiate participation opportunities afforded to student athletes. Thus, plaintiffs contended, what appeared to be the even-handed demotions of two men's and two women's teams, in fact, perpetuated Brown's discriminatory treatment of women in the administration of its intercollegiate athletics program. In the course of the preliminary injunction hearing, the district court found that, in the academic year 1990-91, Brown funded 31 intercollegiate varsity teams, 16 men's teams and 15 women's teams, and that, of the 894 undergraduate students competing on these teams, 63.3% (566) were men and 36.7% (328) were women. During the same academic year, Brown's undergraduate enrollment comprised 52.4% (2,951) men and 47.6% (2,683) women. The district court also summarized the history of athletics at Brown, finding, inter alia, that, while nearly all of the men's varsity teams were established before 1927, virtually all of the women's varsity teams were created between 1971 and 1977, after Brown's merger with Pembroke College. The only women's varsity team created after this period was winter track, in 1982.

In the course of the trial on the merits, the district court found that, in 1993-94, there were 897 students participating in intercollegiate varsity athletics, of which 61.87% (555) were men and 38.13% (342) were women. During the same period, Brown's undergraduate enrollment comprised 5,722 students, of which 48.86% (2,796) were men and 51.14% (2,926) were women. The district court found that, in 1993-94, Brown's intercollegiate athletics program consisted of 32 teams, 16 men's teams and 16 women's teams. Of the university-funded teams, 12 were men's teams and 13 were women's teams; of the donor-funded teams, three were women's teams and four were men's teams. At the time of trial, Brown offered 479 university-funded varsity positions for men, as compared to 312 for women; and 76 donor-funded varsity positions for men, as compared to 30 for women. In 1993-94, then, Brown's varsity program — including both university — and donor-funded sports — afforded over 200 more positions for men than for women. Accordingly, the district court found that Brown maintained a 13.01% disparity between female participation in intercollegiate athletics and female student enrollment, and that "although the number of varsity sports offered to men and women are equal, the selection of sports offered to each gender generates far more individual positions for male athletes than for female athletes."

In computing these figures, the district court counted as participants in intercollegiate athletics for purposes of Title IX analysis those athletes who were members of varsity teams for the majority of the last complete season. Brown argued at trial that "there is no consistent measure of actual participation rates because team size varies throughout the athletic season," and that "there is no consistent measure of actual participation rates because there are alternative definitions of 'participant' that yield very different participation totals." Reasoning that "where both the athlete and coach determine that there is a place on the team for a student, it is not for this Court to second-guess their judgment and impose its own, or anyone else's, definition of a valuable or genuine varsity experience," the district court concluded that "every varsity team member is therefore a varsity 'participant.'" Thus, the district court held that

> the "participation opportunities" offered by an institution are measured by counting the actual participants on intercollegiate teams. The number of participants in Brown's varsity athletic program accurately reflects the number of participation opportunities Brown offers because the University, through its practices "predetermines" the number of athletic positions available to each gender. *Id.* at 202-03.

The district court found from extensive testimony that the donor-funded women's gymnastics, women's fencing and women's ski teams, as well as at least one women's club team, the water polo team, had demonstrated the interest and ability to compete at the top varsity level and would benefit from university funding.

The district court did not find that full and effective accommodation of the athletics interests and abilities of Brown's female students would disadvantage Brown's male students.

II.

Title IX provides that "no person in the United States shall, on the basis of sex, be excluded from participation in, be denied the benefits of, or be subjected to discrimination under any education program or activity receiving Federal financial assistance." 20 U.S.C.A. § 1681(a) (West 1990). As a private institution that receives federal financial assistance, Brown is required to comply with Title IX.

Title IX also specifies that its prohibition against gender discrimination shall not "be interpreted to require any educational institution to grant preferential or disparate treatment to the members of one sex on account of an imbalance which may exist" between the total number or percentage of persons of that sex participating in any federally supported program or activity, and "the total number or percentage of persons of that sex in any community, State, section, or other area." 20 U.S.C.A. § 1681(b) (West 1990). Subsection (b) also provides, however, that it "shall not be construed to prevent the consideration in any . . . proceeding under this chapter of statistical evidence tending to show that such an imbalance exists with respect to the participation in, or receipt of the benefits of, any such program or activity by the members of one sex." *Id.*

Applying § 1681(b), the prior panel held that Title IX "does not mandate strict numerical equality between the gender balance of a college's athletic program and the gender balance of its student body." The panel explained that, while evidence of a gender-based disparity in an institution's athletics program is relevant to a determination of noncompliance, "a court assessing Title IX compliance may not find a violation solely because there is a disparity between the gender composition of an educational institution's student constituency, on the one hand, and its athletic programs, on the other hand."

* * *

Title IX was passed with two objectives in mind: "to avoid the use of federal resources to support discriminatory practices," and "to provide individual citizens effective protection against those practices." *Cannon v. University of Chicago*, 441 U.S. 677, 704 (1979). . . .

In 1978, several years after the promulgation of the regulations, OCR [Office of Civil Rights of the Department of Education] published a proposed "Policy Interpretation," the purpose of which was to clarify the obligations of federal aid recipients under Title IX to provide equal opportunities in athletics programs. "In particular, this Policy Interpretation provides a means to assess an institution's compliance with the equal opportunity requirements of the regulation which are set forth at [34 C.F.R. §§ 106.37(c) and 106.41(c)]." 44 Fed. Reg. at 71,415. After considering a large number of public comments, OCR published the final Policy Interpretation. 44 Fed. Reg. 71,413–71,423 (1979). While the Policy Interpretation covers other areas, this litigation focuses on the "Effective Accommodation" section, which interprets 34 C.F.R. § 106.41(c)(1), the first of the non-exhaustive list of ten factors to be considered in determining whether equal athletics opportunities are available to both genders. The Policy Interpretation establishes a three-part test, a two-part test, and factors to be considered in determining compliance under 34 C.F.R. § 106.41(c)(1). At issue in this appeal is the proper interpretation of the first of these, the so-called three-part test, which inquires as follows:

(1) Whether intercollegiate level participation opportunities for male and female students are provided in numbers substantially proportionate to their respective enrollments; or

(2) Where the members of one sex have been and are underrepresented among intercollegiate athletes, whether the institution can show a history and continuing practice of program expansion which is demonstrably responsive to the developing interest and abilities of the members of that sex; or

(3) Where the members of one sex are underrepresented among intercollegiate athletes, and the institution cannot show a continuing practice of program expansion such as that cited above, whether it can be demonstrated that the interests and abilities of the members of that sex have been fully and effectively accommodated by the present program.

44 Fed. Reg. at 71,418.

The district court held that, "because Brown maintains a 13.01% disparity between female participation in intercollegiate athletics and female student enrollment, it cannot gain the protection of prong one." Nor did Brown satisfy prong two. While acknowledging that Brown "has an impressive history of program expansion," the district court found that Brown failed to demonstrate that it has "maintained a continuing practice of intercollegiate program expansion for women, the underrepresented sex." The court noted further that, because merely reducing program offerings to the overrepresented gender does not constitute program expansion for the underrepresented gender, the fact that Brown has eliminated or demoted several men's teams does not amount to a continuing practice of program expansion for women. As to prong three, the district court found that Brown had not "fully and effectively accommodated the interest and ability of the underrepresented sex 'to the extent necessary to provide equal opportunity in the selection of sports and levels of competition available to members of both sexes.'"

On January 16, 1996, DED released a "Clarification Memorandum," which does not change the existing standards for compliance, but which does provide further information and guidelines for assessing compliance under the three-part test. The Clarification Memorandum contains many examples illustrating how institutions may meet each prong of the three-part test and explains how participation opportunities are to be counted under Title IX.

* * *

III.

[The court rejected Brown's assertion that it should review issues decided in *Cohen II*. It held that the law of the case doctrine precludes relitigation of these issues.]

IV.

Brown contends that the district court misconstrued and misapplied the three-part test. Specifically, Brown argues that the district court's interpretation and application of the test is irreconcilable with the statute, the regulation, and the agency's interpretation of the law, and effectively renders Title IX an "affirmative action statute" that mandates preferential treatment for women by imposing quotas in excess of women's relative interests and abilities in athletics. Brown asserts, in the alternative, that if the district court properly construed the test, then the test itself violates Title IX and the United States Constitution.

We emphasize two points at the outset. First, notwithstanding Brown's persistent invocation of the inflammatory terms "affirmative action," "preference," and "quota," this is not an affirmative action case. Second, Brown's efforts to evade the controlling authority of *Cohen II* by recasting its core legal arguments as challenges to the "district court's interpretation" of the law are unavailing; the primary arguments raised here have already been litigated and decided adversely to Brown in the prior appeal.

A.

[The court discussed Brown's contention that the district court was requiring affirmative action in violation of the constitution. The court dismissed this argument.]

B.

Cohen II squarely rejected Brown's interpretation of the three-part test and carefully delineated its own, which is now the law of this circuit as well as the law of this case. . . . Brown's rehashed statutory challenge is foreclosed by the law of the case doctrine and we are therefore bound by the prior panel's interpretation of the statute, the regulation, and the relevant agency pronouncements.

* * *

Cohen II held that the Policy Interpretation is entitled to substantial deference because it is the enforcing agency's "considered interpretation of the regulation." . . .

* * *

C.

As previously noted, the district court held that, for purposes of the three-part test, the intercollegiate athletics participation opportunities offered by an institution are properly measured by counting the number of actual participants on intercollegiate teams. The Policy Interpretation was designed specifically for intercollegiate athletics. Because the athletics regulation distinguishes between club sports and intercollegiate sports, under the Policy Interpretation, "club teams will not be considered to be intercollegiate teams except in those instances where they regularly participate at the varsity level." Accordingly, the district court excluded club varsity teams from the definition of "intercollegiate teams" and, therefore, from the calculation of participation opportunities, because the evidence was inadequate to show that the club teams regularly participated in varsity competition.

The district court's definition of athletics participation opportunities comports with the agency's own definition. *See* Clarification Memorandum at 2 ("In determining participation opportunities, OCR counts the number of actual athletes participating in the athletic program."). We find no error in the district court's definition and calculation of the intercollegiate athletics participation opportunities afforded to Brown students, and no error in the court's finding of a 13.01% disparity between the percentage of women participating in intercollegiate varsity athletics at Brown and the percentage of women in Brown's undergraduate student body.

D.

Brown contends that an athletics program equally accommodates both genders and complies with Title IX if it accommodates the relative interests and abilities of its male and female students. This "relative interests" approach posits that an institution satisfies prong three of the three-part test by meeting the interests and abilities of the underrepresented gender only to the extent that it meets the interests and abilities of the overrepresented gender.

Brown maintains that the district court's decision imposes upon universities the obligation to engage in preferential treatment by requiring quotas in excess of women's relative interests and abilities. With respect to prong three, Brown asserts that the district court's interpretation of the word "fully" "requires universities to favor women's teams and treat them better than men's [teams]. . . . forces them to eliminate or cap men's teams. . . . [and] forces universities to impose athletic quotas in excess of relative interests and abilities." Appellant's Br. at 55.

The prior panel considered and rejected Brown's approach, observing that "Brown reads the 'full' out of the duty to accommodate 'fully and effectively.'" *Cohen II*, 991 F.2d at 899. Under *Cohen II*'s controlling interpretation, prong three "demands not merely some accommodation, but full and effective accommodation. If there is sufficient interest and ability among members of the statistically underrepresented gender, not slaked by existing programs, an institution necessarily fails this prong of the test." *Id.* at 898.

Brown's interpretation of full and effective accommodation is "simply not the law." We agree with the prior panel and the district court that Brown's relative interests approach "cannot withstand scrutiny on either legal or policy grounds," because it "disadvantages women and undermines the remedial purposes of Title IX by limiting required program expansion for the underrepresented sex to the status quo level of relative interests". After *Cohen II*, it cannot be maintained that the relative interests approach is compatible with Title IX's equal accommodation principle as it has been interpreted by this circuit.

Brown argues that the district court's interpretation of the three-part test requires numerical proportionality, thus imposing a gender-based quota scheme in contravention of the statute. This argument rests, in part, upon Brown's reading of 20 U.S.C. § 1681(b) as a categorical proscription against consideration of gender parity. Section 1681(b) provides:

> Nothing contained in subsection (a) of this section shall be interpreted to require any educational institution to grant preferential or disparate treatment to the members of one sex on account of an imbalance which may exist with respect to the total number or percentage of persons of that sex participating in or receiving the benefits of any federally supported program or activity, in comparison with the total number or percentage of persons of that sex in any community, State, section or other area. . . .

20 U.S.C.A. § 1681(b) (West 1990).

The prior panel, like Brown, assumed without analysis that § 1681(b) applies unequivocally to intercollegiate athletics programs. We do not question *Cohen II*'s application of §1681(b). We think it important to bear in mind, however, the congressional concerns that inform the proper interpretation of this provision. Section 1681(b) was patterned after § 703(j) of Title VII, 42 U.S.C. § 2000e-2(j), and was specifically designed to prohibit quotas in university admissions and hiring, based upon the percentage of individuals of one gender in a geographical community. See H.R. Rep. No. 554, 92d Cong., 1st Sess. (1971), reprinted in 1972 U.S.C.C.A.N. 2462, 2590-92 (Additional Views); 117 Cong. Rec. 39,261-62 (1971) (remarks of Rep. Quie); 117 Cong. Rec. 30,406, 30,409 (remarks of Sen. Bayh); 117 Cong. Rec. 39,251-52 (remarks of Rep. Mink and Rep. Green). Thus, the legislative history strongly suggests that the underscored language defines what is proscribed (in the contexts of admissions and hiring) in terms of a geographical area, beyond the institution, and does not refer to an imbalance within the university, with respect to the representation of each gender in intercollegiate athletics, as compared to the gender makeup of the student body.

In any event, the three-part test is, on its face, entirely consistent with § 1681(b) because the test does not require preferential or disparate treatment for either gender. Neither the Policy Interpretation's three-part test, nor the district court's interpretation of it, mandates statistical balancing; "rather, the policy interpretation merely creates a presumption that a school is in compliance with Title IX and the applicable regulation when it achieves such a statistical balance."

The test is also entirely consistent with § 1681(b) as applied by the prior panel and by the district court. As previously noted, *Cohen II* expressly held that "a court assessing Title IX compliance may not find a violation solely because there is a disparity between the gender composition of an educational institution's student constituency, on the one hand, and its athletic programs, on the other hand." The panel then carefully delineated the burden of proof, which requires a Title IX plaintiff to show, not only "disparity between the gender composition of the institution's student body and its athletic program, thereby proving that there is an underrepresented gender," but also "that a second element — unmet interest — is present," meaning that the underrepresented gender has not been fully and effectively accommodated by the institution's present athletic program. Only where the plaintiff meets the burden of proof on these elements and the institution fails to show as an affirmative defense a history and continuing practice of program expansion responsive to the interests and abilities of the underrepresented gender will liability be established. Surely this is a far cry from a one-step imposition of a gender-based quota.

Brown simply ignores the fact that it is required to accommodate fully the interests and abilities of the underrepresented gender, not because the three-part test mandates preferential treatment for women ab initio, but because Brown has been found (under prong one) to have allocated its athletics participation opportunities so as to create a significant gender-based disparity with respect to these opportunities, and has failed (under prong two) to show a history and continuing practice of expansion of opportunities for the underrepresented gender. Brown's interpretation conflates prongs one and three and distorts the three-part test by reducing it to an abstract, mechanical determination of strict numerical proportionality. In short, Brown treats the three-part test for compliance as a one-part test for strict liability.

Brown also fails to recognize that Title IX's remedial focus is, quite properly, not on the overrepresented gender, but on the underrepresented gender; in this case, women. Title IX and its implementing regulations protect the class for whose special benefit the statute was enacted. It is women and not men who have historically and who continue to be underrepresented in sports, not only at Brown, but at universities nationwide. *See Williams v. School Dist. of Bethlehem, Pa.*, 998 F.2d 168, 175 (1993) (observing that, although Title IX and its regulations apply equally to boys and girls, "it would require blinders to ignore that the motivation for promulgation of the regulation on athletics was the historic emphasis on boys' athletic programs to the exclusion of girls' athletic programs in high schools as well as colleges").

The prior panel held that "the fact that the overrepresented gender is less than fully accommodated will not, in and of itself, excuse a shortfall in the provision of opportunities for the underrepresented gender." Instead, the law requires that, absent a demonstration of continuing program expansion for the underrepresented gender under prong two of the three-part test, an institution must either provide opportunities in proportion to the gender composition of the student body so as to satisfy prong one, or fully accommodate the interests and abilities of athletes of the underrepresented gender under prong three. In other words,

> If a school, like Brown, eschews the first two benchmarks of the accommodation test, electing to stray from substantial proportionality and failing to march uninterruptedly in the direction of equal athletic opportunity, it must comply with the third benchmark. To do so, the school must fully and effectively accommodate the underrepresented gender's interests and abilities, even if that requires it to give the underrepresented gender (in this case, women) what amounts to a larger slice of a shrinking athletic-opportunity pie.

Id. at 906.

We think it clear that neither the Title IX framework nor the district court's interpretation of it mandates a gender-based quota scheme. In our view, it is Brown's relative interests approach to the three-part test, rather than the district court's interpretation, that contravenes the language and purpose of the test and of the statute itself. To adopt the relative interests approach would be, not only to overrule *Cohen II*, but to rewrite the enforcing agency's interpretation of its own regulation so as to incorporate an entirely different standard for Title IX compliance. This relative interests standard would entrench and fix by law the significant gender-based disparity in athletics opportunities found by the district court to exist at Brown, a finding we have held to be not clearly erroneous. According to Brown's relative interests interpretation of the equal accommodation principle, the gender-based disparity in athletics participation opportunities at Brown is due to a lack of interest on the part of its female students, rather than to discrimination, and any attempt to remedy the disparity is, by definition, an unlawful quota. This approach is entirely contrary to "Congress's unmistakably clear mandate that educational institutions not use federal monies to perpetuate gender-based discrimination," and makes it virtually impossible to effectuate Congress's intent to eliminate sex discrimination in intercollegiate athletics.

E.

Brown also claims error in the district court's failure to apply Title VII standards to its analysis of whether Brown's intercollegiate athletics program complies with Title IX. The district court rejected the analogy to Title VII, noting that, while Title VII "seeks to determine whether gender-neutral job openings have been filled without regard to gender[,] Title IX . . . was designed to address the reality that sports teams, unlike the vast majority of jobs, do have official gender requirements, and this statute accordingly approaches the concept of discrimination differently from Title VII."

* * *

We find no error in the district court's refusal to apply Title VII standards in its inquiry into whether Brown's intercollegiate athletics program complies with Title IX. *See Cohen II*, 991 F.2d at 901 ("There is no need to search for analogies where, as in the Title IX milieu, the controlling statutes and regulations are clear."). We conclude that the district court's application of the three-part test does not create a gender-based quota and is consistent with Title IX, 34 C.F.R. § 106.41(b) (1995), the Policy Interpretation, and the mandate of *Cohen II*.

F.

Brown has contended throughout this litigation that the significant disparity in athletics opportunities for men and women at Brown is the result of a gender-based differential in the level of interest in sports and that the district court's application of the three-part test requires universities to provide athletics opportunities for women to an extent that exceeds their relative interests and abilities in sports. Thus, at the heart of this litigation is the question whether Title IX permits Brown to deny its female students equal opportunity to participate in sports, based upon its unproven assertion that the district court's finding of a significant disparity in athletics opportunities for male and female students reflects, not discrimination in Brown's intercollegiate athletics program, but a lack of interest on the part of its female students that is unrelated to a lack of opportunities.

We view Brown's argument that women are less interested than men in participating in intercollegiate athletics, as well as its conclusion that institutions should be required to accommodate the interests and abilities of its female students only to the extent that it accommodates the interests and abilities of its male students, with great suspicion. To assert that Title IX permits institutions to provide fewer athletics participation opportunities for women than for men, based upon the premise that women are less interested in sports than are men, is (among other things) to ignore the fact that Title IX was enacted in order to remedy discrimination that results from stereotyped notions of women's interests and abilities.

Interest and ability rarely develop in a vacuum; they evolve as a function of opportunity and experience. The Policy Interpretation recognizes that women's lower rate of participation in athletics reflects women's historical lack of opportunities to participate in sports. *See* 44 Fed. Reg. at 71,419 ("Participation in intercollegiate sports has historically been emphasized for men but not women. Partially as a consequence of this, participation rates of women are far below those of men.").

Moreover, the Supreme Court has repeatedly condemned gender-based discrimination based upon "archaic and overbroad generalizations" about women. . . . The Court has been especially critical of the use of statistical evidence offered to prove generalized, stereotypical notions about men and women. For example, in holding that Oklahoma's 3.2% beer statute invidiously discriminated against males 18-20 years of age, the Court in *Craig v. Boren*, 429 U.S. 190, 208-09 (1976), stressed that "the principles embodied in the Equal Protection Clause are not to be rendered inapplicable by statistically measured but loose-fitting generalities." . . .

Thus, there exists the danger that, rather than providing a true measure of women's interest in sports, statistical evidence purporting to reflect women's interest instead provides only a measure of the very discrimination that is and has been the basis for women's lack of opportunity to participate in sports. Prong three requires some kind of evidence of interest in athletics, and the Title IX framework permits the use of statistical evidence in assessing the level of interest in sports.[15] Nevertheless, to allow a numbers-based lack-of-interest

---

[15] Under the Policy Interpretation,

> Institutions may determine the athletic interests and abilities of students by nondiscriminatory methods of their choosing provided:

defense to become the instrument of further discrimination against the underrepresented gender would pervert the remedial purpose of Title IX. We conclude that, even if it can be empirically demonstrated that, at a particular time, women have less interest in sports than do men, such evidence, standing alone, cannot justify providing fewer athletics opportunities for women than for men. Furthermore, such evidence is completely irrelevant where, as here, viable and successful women's varsity teams have been demoted or eliminated. We emphasize that, on the facts of this case, Brown's lack-of-interest arguments are of no consequence. As the prior panel recognized, while the question of full and effective accommodation of athletics interests and abilities is potentially a complicated issue where plaintiffs seek to create a new team or to elevate to varsity status a team that has never competed in varsity competition, no such difficulty is presented here, where plaintiffs seek to reinstate what were successful university-funded teams right up until the moment the teams were demoted.

On these facts, Brown's failure to accommodate fully and effectively the interests and abilities of the underrepresented gender is clearly established. See Clarification Memorandum at 8 ("If an institution has recently eliminated a viable team from the intercollegiate program, OCR will find that there is sufficient interest, ability, and available competition to sustain an intercollegiate team in that sport unless an institution can provide strong evidence that interest, ability or available competition no longer exists."); *id.* at 8-9 n.2 ("While [other] indications of interest may be helpful to OCR in ascertaining likely

---

a. The processes take into account the nationally increasing levels of women's interests and abilities;

b. The methods of determining interest and ability do not disadvantage the members of an underrepresented sex;

c. The methods of determining ability take into account team performance records; and

d. The methods are responsive to the expressed interests of students capable of intercollegiate competition who are members of an underrepresented sex.

44 Fed. Reg. at 71,417.

The 1990 version of the Title IX Athletics Investigator's Manual, an internal agency document, instructs investigating officials to consider, inter alia, the following: (i) any institutional surveys or assessments of students' athletics interests and abilities, *see* Valerie M. Bonnette & Lamar Daniel, Department of Education, Title IX Athletics Investigator's Manual at 22 (1990); (ii) the "expressed interests" of the underrepresented gender, *id.* at 25; (iii) other programs indicative of interests and abilities, such as club and intramural sports, sports programs at "feeder" schools, community and regional sports programs, and physical education classes, *id.*

As the district court noted, however, the agency characterizes surveys as a "simple way to identify which additional sports might appropriately be created to achieve compliance. . . . Thus, a survey of interests would follow a determination that an institution does not satisfy prong three; it would not be utilized to make that determination in the first instance." *Cohen III*, 897 F. Supp. at 210 n.51; *see* 1990 Investigator's Manual at 27 (explaining that a survey or assessment of interests and abilities is not required by the Title IX regulation or the Policy Interpretation but may be required as part of a remedy when OCR has concluded that an institution's current program does not equally effectively accommodate the interests and abilities of students). (We note that the text of the 1990 Investigator's Manual cited herein at page 25 was apparently at page 27 of the copy of the Manual before the district court.)

interest on campus, particularly in the absence of more direct indicia[,] an institution is expected to meet the actual interests and abilities of its students and admitted students."). Under these circumstances, the district court's finding that there are interested women able to compete at the university-funded varsity level, is clearly correct. Finally, the tremendous growth in women's participation in sports since Title IX was enacted disproves Brown's argument that women are less interested in sports for reasons unrelated to lack of opportunity.

Brown's relative interests approach is not a reasonable interpretation of the three-part test. This approach contravenes the purpose of the statute and the regulation because it does not permit an institution or a district court to remedy a gender-based disparity in athletics participation opportunities. Instead, this approach freezes that disparity by law, thereby disadvantaging further the underrepresented gender. Had Congress intended to entrench, rather than change, the status quo — with its historical emphasis on men's participation opportunities to the detriment of women's opportunities — it need not have gone to all the trouble of enacting Title IX.

V.

In the first appeal, this court rejected Brown's Fifth Amendment equal protection challenge to the statutory scheme. *Cohen II*, 991 F.2d at 900-01. Here, Brown argues that its challenge is to the decision of the district court. As Brown puts it, "the [equal protection] violation arises from the court's holding that Title IX requires the imposition of quotas, preferential treatment, and disparate treatment in the absence of a compelling state interest and a determination that the remedial measure is 'narrowly tailored' to serve that interest."

[The court again rejected Brown's Equal Protection challenge, stating that the prior panel's reliance on *Metro Broadcasting* has not been undermined by the Supreme Court's subsequent ruling in *Adarand*.]

* * *

VI.

[Brown raised two issues regarding excluded testimony which the court found to be harmless error.]

VII.

It does not follow from our statutory and constitutional analyses that we endorse the district court's remedial order. Although we decline Brown's invitation to find that the district court's remedy was an abuse of discretion, we do find that the district court erred in substituting its own specific relief in place of Brown's statutorily permissible proposal to comply with Title IX by cutting men's teams until substantial proportionality was achieved.

* * *

The district court itself pointed out that Brown may achieve compliance with Title IX in a number of ways:

> It may eliminate its athletic program altogether, it may elevate or create the requisite number of women's positions, it may demote or eliminate the requisite number of men's positions, or it may implement a combination of these remedies. I leave it entirely to Brown's discretion to decide how it will balance its program to provide equal opportunities for its men and women athletes. I recognize the financial constraints Brown faces; however, its own priorities will necessarily determine the path to compliance it elects to take.

Cohen III, 879 F. Supp. at 214; *see also Cohen II*, 991 F.2d at 898 n.15 (noting that a school may achieve compliance with Title IX by "reducing opportunities for the overrepresented gender").

[The court analyzed Brown's submitted plan and generally agreed with the district court that it did not represent a good faith effort to comply with the dictates of Title IX. However the court held that the district court erroneously substituted its own plan rather than accepting Brown's alternative plan of reducing men's sports until proportionality was achieved.]

VIII.

* * *

Affirmed in part, reversed in part, and remanded for further proceedings. No costs on appeal to either party.

TORRUELLA, Chief Judge (Dissenting). Because I am not persuaded that the majority's view represents the state of the law today, I respectfully dissent. [Chief Judge Torruella's dissent argued the majority and District Court's interpretation of the law was inconsistent with recent rulings in *Adarand* and *United States v. Virginia*, 135 L. Ed. 2d 735, 116 S. Ct. 2264 (1996).]

PEDERSON v. LOUISIANA STATE UNIVERSITY

213 F.3d 858 (5th Cir. 2000)

CARL E. STEWART, Circuit Judge:

We must today determine whether the largest public university in Louisiana has discriminated against women under Title IX in the provision of facilities and teams for intercollegiate athletic competition. . . . [W]e conclude that LSU violated Title IX by failing to accommodate effectively the interests and abilities of certain female students and that its discrimination against these students was intentional.

I. Procedural & Factual History

On March 23, 1994, three female undergraduate students attending LSU — Beth Pederson, Lisa Ollar, and Samantha Clark ("Pederson Plaintiffs") — filed suit in the United States District Court for the Middle District of Louisiana, alleging that LSU had violated and continued to violate Title IX of the Education Amendments Act of 1972, 20 U.S.C. §§ 1681-1688 (1994) ("Title IX"), and the Equal Protection Clause of the United States Constitution by denying them equal opportunity to participate in intercollegiate athletics, equal opportunity to compete for and to receive athletic scholarships, and equal access to the benefits and services that LSU provides to its varsity intercollegiate athletes, and by discriminating against women in the provision of athletic scholarships and in the compensation paid coaches.[1] The Pederson Plaintiffs sought declaratory, injunctive, and monetary relief on behalf of themselves and all those similarly situated. . . .

Subsequently, plaintiffs Cindy and Karla Pineda ("Pineda Plaintiffs" and, together with Pederson Plaintiffs, "Appellants") sought to intervene in the original action. The motion to intervene was denied, and the Pineda Plaintiffs filed suit on behalf of themselves and a class of those similarly situated in the Eastern District of Louisiana on January 3, 1995. Appellees transferred the Pineda action to the Middle District of Louisiana and moved to consolidate the Pineda action with the Pederson action. The district court granted the motion, and Appellants filed an amended complaint merging the actions.

In the course of the litigation, the district court denied Appellants' motions for preliminary injunctions. On September 14, 1995, it granted Appellees' motion for partial summary judgment, dismissing for lack of standing Appellants' claims for equal treatment in the areas of coaches' salaries, budgets, facilities, training, and travel, on the ground that Appellants could not demonstrate injury-in-fact related to existing varsity athletic programs in which they had never sought to participate. On the same date, the district court dismissed Appellants' 42 U.S.C. § 1983 claims against defendants Davis and Dean in their individual capacities on the basis of qualified immunity, and also dismissed the remaining § 1983 and Fourteenth Amendment claims. The district court also entered an order provisionally certifying the following class:

> Those female students enrolled at LSU since 1993 and any time thereafter who have sought or seek to participate in varsity intercollegiate athletics at LSU but who are or were not allowed such participation due to LSU's failure to field teams in said female varsity athletics.

. . . On January 12, 1996, the district court entered its opinion on the merits finding that Appellees were in violation of Title IX. The district court ruled, however, that Appellees did not intentionally violate Title IX and therefore would not

---

[1] Pederson, Ollar, and Clark all play soccer. Pederson enrolled at LSU beginning in the autumn term of 1992. Ollar enrolled at LSU beginning with the autumn term of 1990. Clark enrolled at LSU beginning in the autumn term of 1990 through December 1994. The district court found that, when LSU implemented a soccer team in the autumn term of 1995, Pederson tried out for and made the team but ultimately did not participate because of financial difficulties and lack of necessary skill, and Ollar and Clark did not participate because they had no remaining college eligibility.

be liable for monetary damages. The district court also dismissed the claims of the Pederson Plaintiffs for lack of standing. As a result of its finding that Appellees were in violation of Title IX, the district court ordered Appellees to submit a plan for compliance with the statute (the "Compliance Plan").

. . . On July 24, 1997, Appellants collectively filed a notice of appeal from the final judgment entered on July 1, 1997. In this consolidated appeal, Appellants challenge the district court's decision to decertify the class, the district court's conclusion that Appellees did not intentionally violate Title IX, the district court's decision to dismiss the Pederson Plaintiffs' claims for lack of standing, and the district court's conclusion that Appellants lacked standing to pursue their claims alleging a lack of equal treatment in existing LSU varsity sports.

Prior to the entry of final judgment against Appellees, the Supreme Court decided *Seminole Tribe v. Florida*, 517 U.S. 44 (1996). In their answer to both complaints, Appellees had pled the affirmative defense of Eleventh Amendment immunity. In light of Seminole Tribe, Appellees filed a Rule 12(b)(1) motion to dismiss on May 14, 1996, contending that Eleventh Amendment sovereign immunity deprived the court of subject matter jurisdiction. On March 4, 1997, the district court denied Appellees' motion. On March 19, 1997, Appellees filed a notice of appeal of the district court's denial of their 12(b)(1) motion. On June 9, 1997, Appellees appealed from the district court's May 9, 1997 order approving the Compliance Plan. The notice of appeal encompassed all of the district court's earlier rulings, including the district court's finding that LSU is or was in violation of Title IX. On July 7, 1997, Appellees filed another notice of appeal from the final judgment entered on July 1, 1997. On appeal, Appellees challenge the district court's denial of their 12(b)(1) motion to dismiss, the district court's conclusion that Appellees were in violation of Title IX, and the district court's ordered injunctive relief on the ground that it is overbroad.

II. Jurisdiction

[The court discussed and ruled on a series of jurisdictional issues raised and remanded several for further action by the district court.]

III. Title IX

We now turn to the merits of this dispute, and we will address the underlying issues in Parts III and IV of this opinion. In this Part, we affirm the district court's judgment that LSU violated Title IX and reverse the district court's judgment that LSU did not intentionally discriminate against women in the provision of athletics.

A. Background

Title IX proscribes gender discrimination in education programs or other activities receiving federal financial assistance. Patterned after Title VI of the Civil Rights Act of 1964, 42 U.S.C. § 2000d (1994), Title IX, as amended,

> No person in the United States shall, on the basis of sex, be excluded from participation in, be denied the benefits of, or be subjected to discrimination under any education program or activity receiving Federal financial assistance. . . .

§ 901(a), 20 U.S.C. § 1681(a). The second core provision relates to enforcement. Section 902 of Title IX authorizes each agency awarding federal financial assistance to any education program to promulgate regulations "ensuring that aid recipients adhere to § 901(a)'s mandate." The "ultimate sanction" for noncompliance is termination of federal funding or the denial of future federal grants to the offending institution. *Id.* Like § 901, § 902 is program-specific:

> Such termination or refusal shall be limited to the particular political entity, or part thereof, or other recipient as to whom such a finding [of noncompliance] has been made, and shall be limited in its effect to the particular program, or part thereof, in which such noncompliance has been so found. . . . § 902, 20 U.S.C. § 1682.

Beginning in the mid-1970's, the Department of Health, Education and Welfare, and its successor, the Department of Education, have relied on their § 902 power to promulgate regulations governing the operation of federally-funded education programs. These regulations encompass not only athletics policies, but also actions by funding recipients in the areas of, inter alia, admissions, textbooks, and employment. *See, e.g.,* 34 C.F.R. §§ 106.21 (admissions), 106.42 (textbooks), 106.51 (employment) (1999). The regulation most pertinent to the instant controversy requires that

> No person shall, on the basis of sex, be excluded from participation in, be denied the benefits of, be treated differently from another person or otherwise be discriminated against in any interscholastic, intercollegiate, club or intramural athletics offered by a recipient, and no recipient shall provide any such athletics separately on such basis.

34 C.F.R. § 106.41(a) (1999). The regulations further provide that

> A recipient which operates or sponsors interscholastic, intercollegiate, club or intramural athletics shall provide equal athletic opportunity for members of both sexes. In determining whether equal opportunities are available the Director will consider, among other factors:
>
> (1) Whether the selection of sports and levels of competition effectively accommodate the interests and abilities of members of both sexes;
>
> (2) The provision of equipment and supplies;
>
> (3) Scheduling of games and practice time;
>
> (4) Travel and per diem allowance;
>
> (5) Opportunity to receive coaching and academic tutoring;
>
> (6) Assignment and compensation of coaches and tutors;

> (7) Provision of locker rooms, practice and competitive facilities;
>
> (8) Provision of medical and training facilities and services;
>
> (9) Provision of housing and dining facilities and services;
>
> (10) Publicity.
>
> Unequal aggregate expenditures for members of each sex or unequal expenditures for male and female teams if a recipient operates or sponsors separate teams will not constitute noncompliance with this section, but the Assistant Secretary may consider the failure to provide necessary funds for teams for one sex in assessing equality of opportunity for members of each sex.

34 C.F.R. § 106.41(c).

B. Title IX Violation

Appellees argue brazenly that the evidence did not demonstrate sufficient interest and ability in fast-pitch softball at LSU and that, therefore, they cannot be liable under Title IX. The heart of this contention is that an institution with no coach, no facilities, no varsity team, no scholarships, and no recruiting in a given sport must have on campus enough national-caliber athletes to field a competitive varsity team in that sport before a court can find sufficient interest and abilities to exist. It should go without saying that adopting this criteria would eliminate an effective accommodation claim by any plaintiff, at any time. In any event, the district court's finding that the requisite level of interest existed is a finding of fact subject to review for clear error. Having reviewed the record, we determine that the district court did not clearly err because there was ample indication of an interest by women in fast-pitch softball.

Appellees argue that the district court applied the wrong legal framework to assess Appellees' liability by placing the evidentiary burden upon them to explain the reason for their 1983 decision to disband the women's fast-pitch softball team. They argue for de novo review of that decision, but we agree with Appellants and the record supports that the district court considered all the evidence of interest and ability at LSU before concluding that Appellees were in violation of Title IX, not merely the fact that LSU disbanded its team in 1983.

Appellees would have us hold that, although the student population of LSU is 51% male and 49% female, the population participating in athletics is 71% male and 29% female. Given this breakdown, they argue that it is improper to consider proportionality, because to do so would be to impose quotas, and that the evidence shows that female students are less interested in participating in sports than male students. The law suggests otherwise. Title IX provides that the district court may consider disproportionality when finding a Title IX violation:

> This subsection shall not be construed to prevent the consideration in any hearing or proceeding under this chapter of statistical evidence

tending to show that such an imbalance exists with respect to the participation in or receipt of the benefits of, any such program or activity by the members of one sex.

20 U.S.C. § 1681(b). LSU's hubris in advancing this argument is remarkable, since of course fewer women participate in sports, given the voluminous evidence that LSU has discriminated against women in refusing to offer them comparable athletic opportunities to those it offers its male students.

Nevertheless, Appellees persist in their argument by suggesting that the district court's reliance on the fact that LSU fields a men's baseball team as evidence of discrimination was improper because there is no requirement that the same sports be offered for both men and women and because LSU offers nine sports for women and only seven for men. We find that it was indeed proper for the district court to consider the fact that LSU fields a men's baseball team while declining to field a comparable team for women despite evidence of interest and ability in fast-pitch softball at LSU.

Appellees finally contest the district court's determination that LSU's decision to add fastpitch softball and soccer was not for the purpose of encouraging women's athletics. They challenge the district court's finding that LSU did not attempt to determine the interest and ability level of its female student population, contending that there is evidence in the record that shows that LSU does analyze the interest level of its female student athletes. Our review of the record demonstrates no such analysis on the part of LSU. The proper analytical framework for assessing a Title IX claim can be found in the Policy Interpretations to Title IX, which require an analysis of the disproportionality between the university's male and female participation, the university's history of expanding opportunities for women, and whether the university effectively accommodates the interests of its female students. *See* Title IX of the Education Amendments of 1972, Policy Interpretation, 44 Fed. Reg. 71,413, 71,414 (1979). Specifically, the Policy Interpretation explains that Title IX's application to athletic programs covers three general subject areas: scholarships, equivalent treatment, and equal accommodation. As a matter of law, a Title IX violation "may be shown by proof of a substantial violation in any one of the three major areas of investigation set out in the Policy Interpretation." *Roberts v. Colorado St. Univ.*, 814 F. Supp. 1507, 1511 (D. Colo.). Credible evidence supports the conclusion that LSU failed all three prongs. Nevertheless, addressing merely the accommodation prong, regulations adopted by the Department of Education in 1997 also support the district court's conclusions. *See* 34 C.F.R. § 106.37(c)(1) (providing that recipients that award athletic scholarships must do so with a view toward reasonable opportunities for such awards to members of both sexes); *id.* § 106.41(c)(1) (declaring that "[a] recipient which operates or sponsors interscholastic, intercollegiate, club or intramural athletics shall provide equal athletic opportunity for members of both sexes"); 45 C.F.R. § 86.41(c)(1) (requiring the consideration of "whether the selection of sports and levels of competition effectively accommodate the interests and abilities of members of both sexes"). Applying this framework, as the Supreme Court has indicated that we should, the district court correctly found that LSU did not have a history of expanding women's athletic programs and had not presented credible evidence regarding the interests and abilities of its student body. These findings were not clearly erroneous. Regardless, our independent review of the record supports the district court's conclusion that Appellees failed to accommodate effectively its female students. Proper evaluation of the district court's conclusion that Appellees violated Title IX required a careful consideration of the evidence presented at trial. Based on that review, we believe that the district court did not commit clear error in its factual conclusions or legal error in the standards that it applied.

C. Intentional Discrimination

The district court found that LSU had violated and continued to violate the prescriptions of Title IX. The trial judge further concluded that, notwithstanding this threshold finding, a Title IX claimant must additionally prove intentional discrimination on the part of a recipient before she may recover monetary damages. With respect to the claims at issue in this case, the district court considered the question to be a "very close one" but eventually held that LSU did not intentionally violate Title IX. 912 F. Supp. at 918. Having carefully reviewed the trial record we hold that the district court erred in its legal conclusion. We find that LSU did intentionally violate Title IX, thus we reverse that ruling.

The district court stated that Appellees' actions were not a result of intentional discrimination but rather of "arrogant ignorance, confusion regarding the practical requirements of the law, and a remarkably outdated view of women and athletics which created the by-product of resistance to change." Id. The district court reasoned, inter alia, that, because Athletic Director Dean testified that he believes that his "women's athletics" program is "wonderful" and because he was ignorant of the program's state of compliance with Title IX, Appellees did not intentionally discriminate against women. *See id.* at 919.

The district court's decision finding LSU to have unintentionally violated Title IX by not effectively accommodating their female student-athletes simply does not withstand scrutiny.

The district court stated that

> Rather than taking notice of the enormous social change which has taken place in the past 25 years, LSU has continued to assume athletics is as it once was, a traditionally male domain, and its women students did not want to participate in athletics in the same manner and to the same extent as its mean, and acted accordingly.

912 F. Supp. at 920. If an institution makes a decision not to provide equal athletic opportunities for its female students because of paternalism and stereotypical assumptions about their interests and abilities, that institution intended to treat women differently because of their sex. Moreover, Appellees' ignorance

about whether they are violating Title IX does not excuse their intentional decision not to accommodate effectively the interests of their female students by not providing sufficient athletic opportunities.

Apparently, Dean "believed his program to be so wonderful that he invited an investigator from the Department of Education's Office of Civil Rights to visit LSU to evaluate the athletics program's compliance with Title IX." *Id.* That representative's findings confirmed Dean's ignorance of the actual state of compliance with Title IX by his athletic program, *see id.*, but the district court nonetheless reasoned that Dean's testimony was "credible" because "otherwise he would not have invited OCR to LSU to assess the program." *Id.* This conclusion ignores the fact that, already on notice of potential violations, Dean and others continued to adhere to deprecatory nomenclature when referring to female athletes, refused to authorize additional sports for women, and instead seemed content that the "women's teams fielded [by LSU] during the relevant time frame performed well in competition." *Id.* This assessment of the athletics program is not merely "arrogance," as the district court concluded, *see id.*; it belies an intent to treat women differently in violation of the law.

It bears noting that the provisions of Title IX and its attendant regulations are not merely hortatory; they exist, as does any law, to sculpt the relevant playing field. Consequently, Appellees' alleged ignorance of the law does not preclude our finding that LSU acted intentionally. Appellees need not have intended to violate Title IX, but need only have intended to treat women differently. Appellees' outdated attitudes about women amply demonstrate this intention to discriminate, and the district court squarely found that LSU's treatment of women athletes was "remarkably outdated," "archaic," and "outmoded." Well-established Supreme Court precedent demonstrates that archaic assumptions such as those firmly held by LSU constitute intentional gender discrimination. *See, e.g., United States v. Virginia*, 518 U.S. 515 (1996) (holding that an institution's refusal to admit women is intentional gender discrimination in violation of the Equal Protection Clause because, inter alia, of "overbroad generalizations about the different talents, capacities, or preferences of males and females"); *Roberts v. United States Jaycees*, 468 U.S. 609 (1984) (warning of the dangers posed by gender discrimination based on "archaic and overbroad assumptions"). We conclude that, because classifications based on "archaic" assumptions are facially discriminatory, actions resulting from an application of these attitudes constitutes intentional discrimination.

In addition to the district court's evaluation of LSU's attitudes as "archaic," our independent evaluation of the record and the evidence adduced at trial supports the conclusion that Appellees persisted in a systematic, intentional, differential treatment of women. For instance, in meetings to discuss the possibility of a varsity women's soccer team, Dean referred to Lisa Ollar repeatedly as "honey," "sweetie," and "cutie" and negotiated with her by stating that "I'd love to help a cute little girl like you." Dean also opined that soccer, a "more feminine sport," deserved consideration for varsity status because female soccer players "would look cute running around in their soccer shorts." Dean, charismatically defending LSU's chivalry, later told the coach of the women's club soccer team that he would not voluntarily add more women's sports at LSU but would "if forced to." Among many other examples, Karla Pineda testified that, when she met with representatives of the Sports and Leisure Department to request the implementation of an intramural fast-pitch softball team, she was told that LSU would not sponsor fast-pitch softball because "the women might get hurt."

LSU perpetuated antiquated stereotypes and fashioned a grossly discriminatory athletics system in many other ways. For example, LSU appointed a low-level male athletics department staff member to the position of "Senior Women's Athletic Administrator," which the NCAA defines as the most senior women in an athletic department. LSU consistently approved larger budgets for travel, personnel, and training facilities for men's teams versus women's teams. The university consistently compensated coaches of women's team's at a rate far below that of its male team coaches.

Appellees have not even attempted to offer a legitimate, nondiscriminatory explanation for this blatantly differential treatment of male and female athletes, and men's and women's athletics in general; they merely urge that "archaic" values do not equate to intentional discrimination. Instead, LSU makes its mantra the contention that it was either ignorant of or confused by Title IX and thus cannot be held intentionally to have discriminated. To support this dubious argument, LSU turns for support to cases that deal with the standard for school liability for sexual harassment under Title IX. A series of cases, crowned by Supreme Court pronouncements in the last two terms, hold that schools sued for harassment under Title IX must have actual knowledge of the harassment and cannot be liable on a theory of strict liability. Where the school has control over the harasser but acts with deliberate indifference to the harassment or otherwise fails to remedy it, liability will lie under Title IX. LSU seeks to apply these holdings to the case at bar, arguing that, before a finding of intentional discrimination is warranted, Appellees must have been aware that they were discriminating on the basis of sex by not effectively accommodating the interests and abilities of its female student-athletes.

We conclude that the Title IX sexual harassment cases discussed above have little relevance in determining whether LSU intentionally discriminated here. Indeed, the most significant of the sexual harassment holdings actually supports Appellants' argument: LSU arguably acted with deliberate indifference to the condition of its female athletics program. In any event, the requirement in the sexual harassment cases — that the academic institution have actual knowledge of the sexual harassment — is not applicable for purposes of determining whether an academic institution intentionally discriminated on the basis of sex by denying females equal athletic opportunity. In the sexual harassment cases, the issue was whether the school district should be liable for the discriminatory acts of harassment committed by its employees. These cases hold that school districts must themselves have actual discriminatory intent before they will be liable for the discriminatory acts of their employees. In the instant case, it is the institution itself that is discriminating. The proper test is not whether it knew of or is responsible for the actions of others, but is whether Appellees intended to treat women differently on the basis of their sex by providing them unequal athletic opportunity, and, as we noted above, we are convinced that they did. Our review of the record convinces us that an intent to discriminate, albeit one motivated by chauvinist notions as opposed to one fueled by enmity, drove LSU's decisions regarding athletic opportunities for its female students.

The judgment of the district court is REVERSED and the case REMANDED with instruction to proceed to Stage II.

* * *

1) We HOLD that this suit is not barred by the Eleventh Amendment.

2) We HOLD that to establish standing under a Title IX effective accommodation claim of the sort presented here, a party need only demonstrate that she is able and ready to compete for a position on the unfielded team.

3) With regard to Appellants, we REVERSE the district court's ruling that the Pederson Plaintiffs lacked standing to challenge LSU's failure to field a varsity soccer team and REVERSE its subsequent judgment dismissing their claims with prejudice. We AFFIRM the district court's ruling that Appellants lacked standing to challenge the entire LSU varsity program.

We HOLD that Appellants' damages claims, and the questions of Title IX violation and intentional discrimination underlying them, are not moot as to the named Appellants. We further HOLD that the issue of injunctive relief is moot as to the named Appellants. We REMAND to the district court to determine the merits of the Pederson Plaintiffs' claims before proceeding to Stage II of trial, the damages phase.

4) With regard to the putative class, we HOLD that the numerosity prong of Rule 23(a) was satisfied and a class was necessary, if any such requirement exists. Accordingly, we VACATE the district court's decertification order, REVERSE the district court's judgment dismissing the claims for class relief, and REMAND with instructions to consider further the certification of the putative class in light of this opinion. We HOLD that the issue of injunctive relief is not moot as to the putative class.

5) With regard to the merit issues, we AFFIRM the district court's judgment that Appellees violated Title IX. We REVERSE the district court's finding that Appellees did not intentionally discriminate, VACATE its subsequent judgment denying the Pineda Plaintiffs' damages claims, and REMAND to the district court with instructions to proceed to Stage II of trial. We HOLD that we lack jurisdiction to address the district court's injunctive relief order and VACATE

that order, leaving the district court free to reinstate so much of the order and subsequent rulings as it deems necessary, if and when a class is finally certified.

KELLEY v. BOARD OF TRUSTEES OF THE UNIVERSITY OF ILLINOIS

35 F.3d 265 (7th Cir. 1994)

CUMMINGS, Circuit Judge.

On May 7, 1993, the University of Illinois announced that it intended to terminate four varsity athletic programs, including the men's swimming program, effective July 1, 1993. On May 25, 1993, the plaintiffs, all members of the University of Illinois' men's swimming team prior to its termination, brought suit against the Board of Trustees of the University, its chancellor, athletic director and associate athletic director ("defendants"), alleging that defendants violated Title IX of the Education Amendments of 1972 (20 U.S.C. § 1681) and the Equal Protection Clause of the Fourteenth Amendment. Plaintiffs' complaint sought damages, as well as an injunction prohibiting the defendants from terminating the men's swimming program, under 42 U.S.C. § 1983 and 42 U.S.C. § 1985(3). In response, defendants filed a motion to dismiss, which the parties agreed to convert to a motion for summary judgment. Plaintiffs moved for a preliminary injunction. After hearing testimony in support of plaintiffs' request for a preliminary injunction and receiving affidavits in support of defendants' motion for summary judgment, the district court granted summary judgment in favor of the defendants and found that the request for a preliminary injunction was therefore moot. Plaintiffs now appeal.

I.

[The court begins the opinion with a thorough discussion of the history of Title IX, the regulations implementing the statute, the 1979 Interpretation, and the "three part test."]

II.

In 1982, the Office of Civil Rights of the United States Department of Education determined that the University of Illinois had denied its female students equal athletic opportunities. Relying on the University's representations that it would remedy the disparity within a reasonable period of time, the Office of Civil Rights concluded that the school was not in violation of Title IX. A decade later, however, female participation in intercollegiate athletics at the University of Illinois continued to be disproportionate to female undergraduate enrollment. Thus in 1993, for example, while women comprised 44 percent of the student body of the University, they accounted for only 23.4 percent of the school's intercollegiate athletes.

It was against this backdrop that the decision to cut the men's swimming program was made. Faced with a significant deficit in its athletic budget —

$600,000 before the receipt of substantial, unanticipated income from a college football bowl game — the University determined that it would need to reduce athletic costs significantly. Determined to field only teams "capable of competing for championships in the Big Ten Conference and the National Collegiate Athletic Association" the University concluded that it would have to discontinue certain intercollegiate teams in order to eliminate its deficit.

While the University's decision to reduce its athletic offerings was motivated by budget considerations, other considerations — including the need to comply with Title IX — influenced the selection of particular programs to be terminated. The final selection of the teams to be eliminated was made by defendant Morton Weir, then chancellor of the University's Urbana-Champaign Campus. In reaching his decision, Chancellor Weir relied on the recommendation of the Athletic Board of Control, a body that advises the chancellor on athletic issues. The Athletic Board of Control, in turn, relied on advice from the University's Athletic Director, defendant Ronald Guenther. In making his recommendation, Guenther evaluated all 19 sports offered by the University against seven criteria: (1) whether or not the Big Ten Conference and the National Collegiate Athletic Association sponsored a championship in the sport; (2) the tradition of success of the sport at the University; (3) the level of interest and participation in the sport at the high school level; (4) the adequacy of the University's facilities for the sport; (5) the level of spectator interest in the sport; (6) gender and ethnic issues; and (7) the cost of the sport. Guenther recommended that four teams — men's swimming, men's fencing, and men's and women's diving — be cut, a recommendation adopted by Chancellor Weir.

Men's swimming was selected for termination because, among other things, the program was historically weak, swimming is not a widely offered athletic activity in high schools, and it does not have a large spectator following. The University did not eliminate the women's swimming program because the school's legal counsel advised that such action would put the University at risk of violating Title IX.

III.

The University's decision not to terminate woman's swimming program was — given the requirements of Title IX and the applicable regulation and policy interpretation — extremely prudent.

The percentage of women involved in intercollegiate athletics at the University of Illinois is substantially lower than the percentage of women enrolled at the school. If the University had terminated the women's swimming program, it would have been vulnerable to a finding that it was in violation of Title IX. Female participation would have continued to be substantially disproportionate to female enrollment, and women with a demonstrated interest in an intercollegiate athletic activity and demonstrated ability to compete at the intercollegiate level would be left without an opportunity to participate in their sport. The University could, however, eliminate the men's swimming program without violating Title IX since even after eliminating the program, men's participation in athletics would continue to be more than substantially proportionate to their presence in the University's student body. And as the caselaw makes clear, if the percentage of student-athletes of a particular sex is substantially proportionate to the percentage of students of that sex in the general student population, the athletic interests of that sex are presumed to have been accommodated. The University's decision to retain the women's swimming program — even though budget constraints required that the men's program be terminated — was a reasonable response to the requirements of the applicable regulation and policy interpretation.

Plaintiffs contend, however, that the applicable regulation, 34 C.F.R. § 106.41, and policy interpretation, 44 Fed. Reg. 71,418 (1979), pervert Title IX.[4] Title IX, plaintiffs contend, "has through some alchemy of bureaucratic regulation been transformed from a statute which prohibits discrimination on the basis of sex into a statute that mandates discrimination against males. . . ." Or, as plaintiffs put it later: "If a university is required by Title IX to eliminate men from varsity athletic competition. . . , then the same Title IX should require the university to eliminate women from the academic departments where they are over[-]represented and men from departments where they have been over[-]represented. Such a result would be ridiculous."

We agree that such a result would be ridiculous. But Congress itself recognized that addressing discrimination in athletics presented a unique set of problems not raised in areas such as employment and academics. Congress therefore specifically directed the agency in charge of administering Title IX to issue, with respect to "intercollegiate athletic activities," regulations containing "reasonable provisions considering the nature of particular sports." And where Congress has specifically delegated to an agency the responsibility to articulate standards governing a particular area, we must accord the ensuing regulation considerable deference.

The regulation at issue here is neither "arbitrary . . . nor manifestly contrary to the statute." *Cf. id.* The regulation provides that notwithstanding Title IX's requirement that "no person . . . shall, on the basis of sex, be excluded from participation in . . . any . . . activity," a school may "sponsor separate teams for members of each sex where selection for such teams is based upon competitive skill or the activity involved is a contact sport." 34 C.F.R. § 106.41(a), (b). Such a provision is not at odds with the purpose of Title IX and we do not understand plaintiffs to argue that it is. And since 34 C.F.R. § 106.41 is not manifestly contrary to the objectives of Title IX, this Court must accord it deference.

---

[4] Plaintiffs also contend that Title IX prohibited the University, when deciding which athletic programs to terminate, from taking gender into account. Plaintiffs, however, do not contend that the University considered gender any more than it was required to by the applicable regulation and policy interpretation — nor would the record support such a contention if made. Thus the plaintiffs' claim is, in essence, a claim that the relevant regulation and policy interpretation violate Title IX.

Plaintiffs, while they concede the validity of 34 C.F.R. § 106.41, argue that the substantial proportionality test contained in the agency's policy interpretation of that regulation establishes a gender-based quota system, a scheme they allege is contrary to the mandates of Title IX. But the policy interpretation does not, as plaintiffs suggest, mandate statistical balancing.

Rather the policy interpretation merely creates a presumption that a school is in compliance with Title IX and the applicable regulation when it achieves such a statistical balance. Even if substantial proportionality has not been achieved, a school may establish that it is in compliance by demonstrating either that it has a continuing practice of increasing the athletic opportunities of the underrepresented sex or that its existing programs effectively accommodate the interests of that sex.

Moreover, once it is agreed Title IX does not require that all teams be co-ed — a point the plaintiffs concede — and that 34 C.F.R. § 106.41 is therefore a valid regulation, schools must be provided some means of establishing that despite offering single-sex teams, they have provided "equal athletic opportunities . . . for both sexes." Undoubtedly the agency responsible for enforcement of the statute could have required schools to sponsor a women's program for every men's program offered and vice versa. Requiring parallel teams would certainly have been the simplest method of ensuring equality of opportunity — and plaintiffs would doubtless have preferred this approach since, had it been adopted, the men's swimming program would likely have been saved. It was not unreasonable, however, for the agency to reject this course of action. Requiring parallel teams is a rigid approach that denies schools the flexibility to respond to the differing athletic interests of men and women. It was perfectly acceptable, therefore, for the agency to chart a different course and adopt an enforcement scheme that measures compliance by analyzing how a school has allocated its various athletic resources.

This Court must defer to an agency's interpretation of its regulations if the interpretation is reasonable, a standard the policy interpretation at issue here meets. Measuring compliance through an evaluation of a school's allocation of its athletic resources allows schools flexibility in meeting the athletic interests of their students and increases the chance that the actual interests of those students will be met. And if compliance with Title IX is to be measured through this sort of analysis, it is only practical that schools be given some clear way to establish that they have satisfied the requirements of the statute. The substantial proportionality contained in Benchmark 1 merely establishes such a safe harbor.

Since the policy interpretation maps out a reasonable approach to measuring compliance with Title IX, this Court does not have the authority to condemn it. Plaintiffs' claim that the University of Illinois violated Title IX when it terminated the men's swimming program is, therefore, rejected. The University's actions were consistent with the statute and the applicable regulation and policy interpretation. And despite plaintiffs' assertions to the contrary, neither the regulation nor the policy interpretation run afoul of the dictates of Title IX.

IV.

Plaintiffs' final argument is that the defendants' decision to eliminate the men's swimming program while retaining the women's program denied them equal protection of law as guaranteed by the Fourteenth Amendment. We do not agree. First, the record makes clear that the University considered gender solely to ensure that its actions did not violate federal law. And insofar as the University actions were taken in an attempt to comply with the requirements of Title IX, plaintiffs' attack on those actions is merely a collateral attack on the statute and regulations and is therefore impermissible.

To the extent that plaintiffs' argument is that Title IX and the applicable regulation — rather than the actions of the defendants — are unconstitutional, it is without merit. While the effect of Title IX and the relevant regulation and policy interpretation is that institutions will sometimes consider gender when decreasing their athletic offerings, this limited consideration of sex does not violate the Constitution. Congress has broad powers under the Due Process Clause of the Fifth Amendment to remedy past discrimination. Even absent a specific finding that discrimination has occurred, remedial measures mandated by Congress are "constitutionally permissible to the extent that they serve important governmental objectives . . . and are substantially related to achievement of those ends." There is no doubt but that removing the legacy of sexual discrimination — including discrimination in the provision of extra-curricular offerings such as athletics — from our nation's educational institutions is an important governmental objective. We do not understand plaintiffs to argue otherwise.

Plaintiffs' complaint appears, instead, to be that the remedial measures required by Title IX and the applicable regulation and policy interpretation are not substantially related to their purported goal. Plaintiffs contend that the applicable rules allow "the University to . . . improve[ ] its statistics without adding any opportunities for women . . .", an outcome they suggest is unconstitutional. But to survive constitutional scrutiny, Title IX need not require — as plaintiffs would have us believe — that the opportunities for the underrepresented group be continually expanded. Title IX's stated objective is not to ensure that the athletic opportunities available to women increase. Rather its avowed purpose is to prohibit educational institutions from discriminating on the basis of sex. And the remedial scheme established by Title IX and the applicable regulation and policy interpretation are clearly substantially related to this end. Allowing a school to consider gender when determining which athletic programs to terminate ensures that in instances where overall athletic opportunities decrease, the actual opportunities available to the underrepresented gender do not. And since the remedial scheme here at issue directly protects the interests of the disproportionately burdened gender, it passes constitutional muster.

V.

Since the district court correctly determined that the University of Illinois decision to terminate the men's swimming program did not violate Title IX or the Equal Protection Clause, its decision is affirmed.

NOTES AND COMMENTS

1. *See generally,* K.L. Tokarz, *Sex Discrimination in Amateur and Professional Sports, in* 2 LAW OF PROFESSIONAL AND AMATEUR SPORTS ch. 13 (G.A. Uberstine, ed., Clark Boardman Ltd. 1988). *See also,* Rodney K. Smith, *When Ignorance is Not Bliss: In Search of Racial and Gender Equity in Intercollegiate Athletics,* 61 MO. L. REV. 329 (1996); Diane Heckman, *Women & Athletics: A Twenty Year Retrospective on Title IX,* 9 U. MIAMI ENT. & SPORTS L. REV. 1 (1992); Walter B. Connolly, Jr. & Jeffrey D. Adelman, *A University's Defense to a Title IX Gender Equity in Athletics Lawsuit: Congress Never Intended Gender Based Equity on Student Body Ratios*, 71 U. DET. MERCY L. REV. 845 (1994).

2. *Cohen* went through several stages in both the district court and the circuit court prior to the opinion above. *See Cohen v. Brown University*, 991 F.2d 888 (1st Cir. 1993). Following the opinion in the principal case, the Supreme Court denied certiorari, *Brown Univ. v. Cohen,* 520 U.S. 1186 (1997). The case was remanded to the district court, and ultimately the university and the plaintiffs settled the matter, with the university agreeing to specific improvements and additions to its women's athletic program.

The Supreme Court has also had the opportunity to evaluate the impact of the act on the NCAA. In *NCAA v. Smith*, 525 U.S. 459 (1999), the Court held that the receipt of dues by the association from its members who receive federal funds does not make the NCAA subject to Title IX. The Court, however, left open two questions regarding the impact of the act on the NCAA. First, it refused to rule on whether the NCAA directly or indirectly receives federal funding through the National Youth Sports Program (NYSP) the association administers. Second, the Court declined an opportunity to rule on the effect of a federal funds recipient ceding controlling authority over a federally funded program. Specifically, the athlete had argued that the action of member institutions, virtually all of which are recipients of federal funds, in turning over governing authority to the NCAA makes the association subject to the act. On remand, the district court ruled against the plaintiff on both issues. The Third Circuit, however, found that the allegations regarding the relationship between the NYSP and the NCAA, coupled with the receipt of federal funds by the NYSP, if proven would subject the NCAA to the act. *Smith v. NCAA*, 266 F.3d 152 (3d Cir. 2001). The matter is now back in the district court.

The Fourth Circuit, in *Mercer v. Duke University*, 19 F.3d 643 (4th Cir. 1999), has held in a case interpreting the regulations implementing Title IX, that where a university permits members of the opposite sex to try out for a single sex contact sports team, Title IX will protect the athlete against discriminatory treatment. *See* 34 C.F.R. § 106.41. This interpretation would, however, allow a school to deny participation opportunities in the contact sport without subjecting itself to liability. In this case Duke University had allowed a female athlete to try out for the football team as a walk-on kicker. Following one academic year of practicing and working with the team, she was told by the kicking coach that she had made the team. During the subsequent season she claims that she was the subject of discriminatory treatment and ultimately she was told that she was dropped from the team. Her claim is that she was dropped because of her sex. The matter was remanded to the district court. The trial produced a verdict in favor of *Mercer* for one dollar in compensatory damages and two million dollars in punitive damages. The Fourth Circuit vacated the award of punitive damages finding them not available in actions brought to enforce Title IX. *Mercer v. Duke University*, 190 F.3d 643 (4th Cir. 2002).

See also, Barnett v. Texas Wrestling Ass'n, 16 F. Supp. 2d 690 (N.D. Tex. 1998) (state association not in violation of Title IX for its exclusion of females from wrestling matches against males).

It has also been held that when a high school athletic association holds championships for boys and girls in the same sport, but in different seasons, a violation of Title IX will be found if the girls are found to be at a significant disadvantage with regard to college recruitment. *McCormick v. School Dist. of Mamaroneck,* 370 F.3d 275 (2d Cir. 2004).

3. In addition to the *Kelley* case, there have been other instances of men raising Title IX issues, particularly where sports programs are cut in an effort to accommodate women's sports teams. *See also, Neal v. Board of Trustees of the California State University*, 2002 U.S. App. LEXIS 24451 (9th Cir. 2002); *Miami Univ. Wrestling Club v. Miami Univ.*, 302 F.3d 608 (6th Cir. 2002); *Chalenor v. Univ. of N.D.*, 291 F.3d 1042 (8th Cir. 2002); and *Gonyo v. Drake University*, 879 F. Supp. (S.D. Iowa 1995).

The National Wrestling Coaches Association filed suit in early 2002 against the United States Department of Education contending it is enforcing Title IX in a manner that unlawfully discriminates against men. Specifically, the association contended that the Department's Three Part Test for determining compliance with the participation opportunities portion of Title IX exceeded the authority granted by the statute. The D.C. Circuit dismissed the case, finding the association lacked standing to bring the action. *National Wrestling Coaches Ass'n v. Dept. of Education,* 366 F.3d 930 (D. C. Cir. 2004); *cert. den.* 2005 U.S. LEXIS 4519 (2005).

4. In 2002, the Secretary of Education appointed a Commission to study Title IX and recommend any needed changes in the manner in which the act is administered and enforced. In February 2003, the Commission on Opportunity in Athletics presented its report to the Secretary. The report set forth 23 recommendations, including proposals to clarify or change the way in which the

Three Part Test is administered. The full report may be viewed at http://www.ed.gov/pubs/titleixat30/index.html. In July of 2003, a clarification letter was issued by Assistant Secretary of Education Gerald Reynolds indicating, among other points, that the 3 Part Test would continue to be applied. The Department of Education also pledged aggressive enforcement of Title IX and announced very clearly that there is not a requirement that schools eliminate or reduce teams in order to comply. www.ed.gov/about/offices/list/ocr/title9guidanceFinal.pdf.

Then in March of 2005, with no advance notice, a further clarification was issued by the Department. This letter allows schools to use email surveys to determine whether they are fully and effectively accommodating interests of students, thus complying with Part 3 of the 3 Part Test. Apparently these surveys, with no further investigation, will be sufficient to satisfy the test. www.ed.gov/about/offices/list/ocr/docs/title9guidanceadditional.html This action has been heavily criticized and produced a Senate hearing that elicited opposition from advocates for women's sports. http://commerce.senate.gov/hearings/witnesslist.cfm?id=1732.

5. Much of the national publicity concerning Title IX cases has focused on collegiate programs. However, during the latter part of the 1990s there has been a significant increase in the volume of litigation involving high school and middle school programs. Indeed, in one state, Oklahoma, there have been ten separate cases filed in a three-year time period. Most of these cases have focused on equal treatment and benefits, particularly facilities and quality of coaching. *See* Ray Yasser & Samuel J. Schiller, *Gender Equity In Interscholastic Sports: The Final Saga: The Fight for Attorneys' Fees*, 34 TULSA L.J. 85 (1998); Ray Yasser & Samuel J. Schiller, *Gender Equity In Interscholastic Sports: A Case Study*, 33 TULSA L.J. 273 (1997); Ray Yasser & Samuel J. Schiller, *Gender Equity in Athletics: The New Battleground of Interscholastic Sports,* 15 CARDOZO ARTS & ENT. L.J. 371 (1997).

6. In 1994 Congress enacted the Equity in Athletics Disclosure Act, Pub. L. No. 103-382, 108 Stat. 3969, codified at 20 U.S.C. § 1092(g). The act requires schools with intercollegiate athletic programs to prepare and disseminate a report annually containing the following information:

a. the number of male and female undergraduate students attending the institution;

b. a listing of the varsity sports teams, including the number of participants per team, total operating expenses, whether the head coach is male or female, the number of assistant coaches and how many are male and female;

c. the total amount of money spent on athletically related student aid;

d. the ratio of athletically related student aid awarded male athletes to that awarded to female athletes;

e. the total amount of expenditures spent on recruiting, broken down for men's and women's teams;

f. the total annual revenues generated for all men's teams and for all women's teams;

g. the average salary of head coaches for men's teams and the average salary of head coaches for women's teams;

h. the average salary for assistant coaches of men's teams and the average salary for assistant coaches of women's teams.

The first such reports were published October 1, 1996, with the information pertaining to the 1995-96 academic year. Similar reports have been published each year. *See* 34 C.F.R. Part 668.

D. EMPLOYMENT DISCRIMINATION

The materials in the prior sections have focused on the claims of participants under the federal Constitution, state constitutions, and Title IX. In this section the focus shifts to coaches and claims they may have under appropriate circumstances under Title IX, the Equal Pay Act of 1963 (29 U.S.C. § 206(d)), and Title VII of the Civil Rights Act of 1964 (42 U.S.C. § 2000e et seq.).

PROBLEM

Bernie Johnson was hired as women's basketball coach at Eastern Oklanois University, a public institution that is a Division I member of the NCAA. After about 18 months on the job he began to have discussions with the Athletic Director about the manner in which his program, and women's athletics in general, was being treated. He believed the university was in violation of Title IX and said so. The Athletic Director told him to concentrate on his job as coach, citing a 4-21 record the previous season and the fact that the team was about to begin a new season that did not look promising.

During the second season Johnson continued to complain about unequal treatment for his team, even at times making such comments to the press. Following that season, in which the team struggled to a 9-16 record, the school informed him that his contract would not be renewed. Johnson has come to you seeking advice as to whether he has any legal recourse.

Case File

STANLEY v. UNIVERSITY OF SOUTHERN CALIFORNIA

178 F.3d 1069 (9th Cir. 1999), *cert. denied*, 528 U.S. 1022 (1999)

Hug, Chief Judge:

Appellant Marianne Stanley appeals from the district court's order granting summary judgment in favor of defendants University of Southern California and Michael Garrett on Stanley's claims of discrimination and breach of employment contract. Stanley also appeals the denial of her motion to recuse Judge Davies, and her motion to re-tax costs. Appellants move for an award of sanctions against Stanley for filing the latter two appeals.

FACTUAL AND PROCEDURAL BACKGROUND

Marianne Stanley was hired as head coach of the women's basketball team for the University of Southern California ("USC") in 1989. Her initial contract, signed in July of that year, was for a four-year term, expiring June 30, 1993. The contract provided that she would make a base salary of $60,000 per year. This base salary was increased to $62,000 per year in 1992. The women's basketball program at USC enjoyed much success during Stanley's tenure.

Defendant Michael Garrett is the Athletic Director at USC. On April 20, 1993, two months prior to the expiration of Stanley's contract, Stanley and Garrett had an initial meeting to negotiate a new contract. The parties disagree over what took place at this meeting. Stanley contends that on that date she entered into a contract for a salary equivalent to that of George Raveling, the USC men's basketball coach. It is undisputed that Garrett expressly stated that USC could not pay her that salary, but that he would make her a formal offer in writing shortly after that meeting.

On April 27, 1993, Garrett offered Stanley, in writing, a three-year contract providing $80,000 in year one, $90,000 in year two, and $100,000 in year three, with a $6,000 per year housing allowance for each of the three years. The parties met again on May 27, 1993, at which point Garrett claims that Stanley rejected the April 27 offer because she insisted that her compensation should be equivalent to Raveling's. Stanley argues that she never rejected this offer, but simply disagreed as to the amount of compensation, because the April 27 offer was inconsistent with the April 20 offer — for Raveling's salary level — that she already had accepted.

On June 7, 1993, Stanley proposed a three-year contract providing $96,000 per year for the first eighteen months, and a salary equivalent to that of Raveling for the remainder of the term. Garrett rejected this offer. Stanley then retained an attorney who, on June 18, 1993, proposed to Garrett a three-year contract with an automatic two-year renewal provision, and total compensation of $88,000 for year one, $97,000 for year two, and $112,000 for year three, plus additional incentives. Garrett rejected this offer and withdrew the April 27 offer.

On June 21, 1993, Garrett sent to Stanley's attorney a written offer for a one-year contract for $96,000. Stanley's existing contract expired on June 30, 1993, but Stanley continued to perform her duties. On July 13, while on a recruiting trip, Stanley asked Garrett if he would still offer her a multi-year contract. He indicated that his June 21 one-year contract offer was USC's final offer, and that Stanley would have to accept or reject it by the end of the day. Stanley did not respond, but sent a memo to Garrett on July 14 requesting additional time to consider the offer. On July 15 Garrett revoked the offer, informed Stanley that he was seeking a new coach for the team, and requested that Stanley perform no further services for USC.

On August 5, 1993, Stanley initiated this action in Los Angeles County Superior Court, making claims of sex discrimination and retaliatory discharge. On August 6, 1993, the Superior Court granted Stanley's request for a temporary restraining order reinstating Stanley as head coach of the women's team at $96,000 per year pending the hearing on Stanley's motion for preliminary injunction. On that same day, defendants removed the action to federal court on the ground that the complaint stated claims arising under federal law.

On August 30, 1993, the district court denied the motion for preliminary injunction, and Stanley appealed. This court affirmed the denial of the preliminary injunction in an opinion filed January 6, 1994. *Stanley v. University of Southern California*, 13 F.3d 1313 (9th Cir. 1994) ("*Stanley I*"). Between September 1993 and February 1994, Stanley amended her complaint several times, and defendants' motions to dismiss were granted as to several claims. Stanley's Third Amended Complaint alleges the following causes of action: (1) violation of the Equal Pay Act, 29 U.S.C. § 206(d)(1) and California Fair Employment and Housing Act ("FEHA"); (2) violation of Article I, § 8 of the California Constitution; (3) violation of Title IX of the Civil Rights Act of 1972, 20 U.S.C. § 1681; (4) retaliation; (5) wrongful discharge in violation of public policy; (6) breach of express contract; (7) breach of implied-in-fact contract; and (8) breach of implied covenant of good faith and fair dealing. Stanley sought reinstatement, declaratory relief, injunctive relief preventing USC from further discriminating against her, back pay, three million dollars in compensatory damages, and five million dollars in punitive damages.

On October 17, 1994, defendants filed a motion for summary judgment. After Stanley was allowed additional time to conduct discovery, on March 10, 1995, the district court granted summary judgment for USC and Garrett. This appeal followed.

DISCUSSION

I. Discrimination Claims

* * *

A. Equal Pay Act Claim

The Equal Pay Act provides in relevant part:

> No employer having employees subject to any provisions of this section shall discriminate, within any establishment in which such employees are employed, between employees on the basis of sex by paying wages to employees . . . at a rate less than the rate at which he pays wages to employees of the opposite sex in such establishment for equal work on jobs the performance of which requires equal skill, effort, and responsibility, and which are performed under similar working conditions. . . .

29 U.S.C. § 206(d)(1).

In an Equal Pay Act case, the plaintiff has the burden of establishing a prima facie case of discrimination by showing that employees of the opposite sex were paid different wages for equal work. The prima facie case is limited to a comparison of the jobs in question, and does not involve a comparison of the individuals who hold the jobs. . . . To make out a prima facie case, the plaintiff bears the burden of showing that the jobs being compared are "substantially equal." . . . Significantly, under the Act, the plaintiff need not demonstrate that the jobs in question are identical; she must show only that the jobs are substantially equal.

Because we are reviewing an appeal from the grant of summary judgment, the question is whether, viewing the evidence in the light most favorable to Stanley, and resolving all inferences in her favor, a genuine issue of material fact exists regarding the substantial equality of the jobs. . . .

Circuit courts employ a two-step "substantially equal" analysis in Equal Pay Act cases. In *Brobst v. Columbus Srvs. Int'l*, 761 F.2d 148, 156 (3d Cir. 1985), the Third Circuit described this approach, writing that "the crucial finding on the equal work issue is whether the jobs to be compared have a 'common core' of tasks, i.e., whether a significant portion of the two jobs is identical." When a plaintiff establishes such a "common core of tasks," the court must then determine whether any additional tasks, incumbent on one job but not the other, make the two jobs "substantially different." *Id.* Both the Seventh and Fourth Circuits have also adopted this approach to Equal Pay Act cases. *See Fallon v. State of Illinois*, 882 F.2d 1206, 1209 (7th Cir. 1989); *Brewster v. Barnes*, 788 F.2d 985, 991 (4th Cir. 1986).

Here, we may assume that the men's and women's coaching jobs share a common core of tasks. Garrett — U.S.C.'s athletic director and a defendant in this case — has acknowledged that the women's and men's coaches "have the same basic responsibilities" with regard to recruiting athletes and administering the basketball programs. In his declaration, Garrett also stated:

> Both the women's and men's head basketball coaches have the following general duties and responsibilities: basketball program; coaching and discipline of team members; general supervision over the personal and academic lives of the student athletes; and supervision over assistant coaches, part-time coaches and other athletic department personnel involved in the women's and men's basketball programs.

The parties are in serious dispute, however, as to whether the additional responsibilities borne by the men's coach, but not by the women's coach, suffice to make the two jobs "substantially different." The defendants point out that the men's coach bears greater revenue generating responsibilities, that he is under greater media and spectator pressure to produce a winning program, and that he actually generates more revenue for the University.

Stanley claims that the differences between the two jobs are attributable to previous gender-based decisions on the part of the University. Essentially, Stanley claims that the differences between the two jobs result from the University's historically disparate treatment of male and female teams; namely, its decisions to invest in and promote the men's program more than the women's program. She then claims that because the differences between the jobs derive from previous gender-based decisions on the part of the University, the differences cannot be relied on to determine that the jobs are "substantially different."

The University, on the other hand, argues that the differences between the two jobs are not attributable to anything it has done or failed to do in the past. According to USC, the reason that women's basketball does not generate the same amount of revenue as men's basketball, and that the women's coach is not under the same pressure as the men's coach, is that there simply is not a sufficient spectator or media market for women's basketball games. Accordingly, it contends that the differences in responsibilities in the two jobs legitimately suffice to make them "substantially different."

We need not decide which party is correct regarding the reason for the differences that exist. Even assuming that Stanley has succeeded in raising a genuine issue of fact as to this question, the University is entitled to summary judgment on other grounds. A defendant may rebut a prima facie case by showing that the disparity in pay is a "differential based on any . . . factor other than sex." 29 U.S.C. § 206(d)(1). Defendants here assert an affirmative defense (that is, a nondiscriminatory reason for the pay differential) based on Stanley and Raveling's markedly disparate levels of experience and qualifications. The record convincingly supports their claim. When Raveling began coaching at U.S.C., he had thirty-one years of coaching experience. He had been the coach of the men's Olympic basketball team. He had been *twice* named national coach of the year, and *twice* named PAC-10 coach of the year. On top of his coaching experience, Raveling also had nine years of marketing and promotional experience, and was the author of several books on basketball. When Stanley started coaching at U.S.C., three years after Raveling became head coach of the men's team, she had seventeen years of experience coaching basketball, or *fourteen years less experience* than Raveling. She never coached an Olympic team. She had no marketing or promotional experience other than that she gained as a coach. She had never published a book about basketball.

The EEOC Notice cited above, on which *the plaintiff* relies extensively, recognizes this type of affirmative defense, stating that "superior experience, education, and ability may justify pay disparities if distinctions based on these criteria are not gender based." EEOC Notice at 23. In *Stanley I*, moreover, we wrote that "employers may reward professional experience and education without violating the EPA." *Stanley I*, 13 F.3d at 1322. Coaches with substantially more experience and significantly superior qualifications may, of course, be paid more than their less experienced and qualified counterparts, even when it is the male coach who has the greater level of experience and qualifications. By alleging that the pay differential at issue here was due to Stanley and Raveling's markedly different levels of experience and qualifications, the defendants have proffered a factor "other than sex," 29 U.S.C. § 206(d)(1), to explain the difference in pay. *See also*, *Harker v. Utica College of Syracuse Univ.*, 885 F. Supp. 378 (N.D.N.Y. 1995) (nine year experience differential between women's and men's basketball coaches justifies pay differential).

Garrett's testimony, moreover, supports the University's explanation. In explaining the disparity between Raveling and Stanley's salaries, Garrett referred extensively to the coaches' divergent levels of experience and differences in qualifications. He stressed Raveling's thirty-one years of experience, his experience as an Olympic coach, his nine years in marketing and promotion positions, and his authorship of several books on basketball. Garrett highlighted the fact that Raveling had been twice honored as national coach of the year, twice voted PAC-10 coach of the year, and was "widely recognized as one of the top basketball recruiters in the nation." Garrett then contrasted Stanley's lesser experience and qualifications. While he mentioned some of Stanley's accomplishments, he pointed out that she had only seventeen years coaching experience, had never coached an Olympic team, and had never authored any books on basketball.

Where the defendant demonstrates that a pay differential was based on a factor other than sex, the employee may prevail by showing that the employer's proffered nondiscriminatory reason is a "pretext for discrimination." On this appeal, Stanley bears the burden of demonstrating a material fact regarding pretext in order to survive summary judgment.

Stanley's pretext argument, however, fails to meet even this minimal burden. In her briefs, Stanley disputes that Raveling had greater qualifications and experience than she. For example, Stanley states that "Mr. Raveling does not have substantially different qualifications and experience than Ms. Stanley." Unsupported allegations made in briefs are not sufficient, however, to defeat a motion for summary judgment. Stanley has conspicuously failed, moreover, to present any meaningful evidence in support of her claim that she and Raveling had comparable levels of experience. Stanley points first to her deposition testimony that she was responsible for securing donors for the women's team. Such evidence, while important in assessing Stanley's revenue raising responsibilities, says nothing of her relative level of experience. She next points to her testimony that she worked briefly as a color analyst on a Philadelphia cable station. Again, this evidence does not undermine the University's claim that Raveling possessed far greater experience as a coach and marketer than Stanley. Stanley also argues that Raveling's marketing abilities are in dispute because "Raveling was not able to successfully promote nor market a summer basketball [camp] during his entire employment at USC." However, Raveling's ability to market this camp sheds no light on his previous *experience* in marketing. Stanley, moreover, does not dispute the fact that Raveling has nine years of experience in marketing, while she had no work experience outside coaching.

In the end, therefore, we are left with these *undisputed* facts: Stanley had far less relevant experience and qualifications than Raveling. She had fourteen years less experience as a basketball coach. She, unlike Raveling, never coached the Olympic team. She had no marketing experience outside coaching. She had never written any books on basketball. Accordingly, Stanley has failed to raise a genuine issue of fact as to Raveling's markedly "superior experience," and qualifications. *EEOC Notice* at 23. In short, she has failed to raise a genuine issue of fact as to the University's non-discriminatory reason for paying Raveling a higher salary.

Accordingly, we affirm the district court's decision to grant the defendants' motion for summary judgment on the Equal Pay Act claim.

[The court then rejected Stanley's arguments based on California statutes, Title IX and retaliation. It also upheld the district court's granting of summary judgment on several contractual claims. The court further affirmed the lower court's ruling on recusal of the trial judge. The court did find the district court had abused its discretion in awarding excessive costs to the defendants and remanded the case for re-taxing of costs.]

PREGERSON, dissenting:

By focusing on the differences between Stanley's and Raveling's qualifications, the majority skips over the many ways in which gender discrimination insidiously affected the University's treatment of the women's basketball program and Stanley as its Head Coach. The University's half-hearted promotion of the women's basketball program, its intensive marketing of the men's basketball program, and the formidable obstacles Stanley faced as a woman athlete in a male-dominated profession contributed to this disparate treatment.

It is hard for me to square these realities with the majority's ruling denying Stanley relief without a trial.

Therefore, I dissent.

BOWERS v. BAYLOR UNIVERSITY

862 F. Supp. 142 (W.D. Tex. 1994)

WALTER S. SMITH, JR.

I. Background

Plaintiff, Pam Bowers ("Bowers"), was hired by Baylor University ("Baylor") to coach its women's basketball team in 1979. In 1989, Bowers began to complain about the disparate allocation of resources in the men's and women's basketball programs, including but not limited to the disparate terms and conditions of her employment versus the terms and conditions of employment by and between Baylor and the men's basketball coach. Her first contact with the Office of Civil Rights of the Department of Education was in March of 1989, and Baylor was aware of plaintiff's complaints at or about the same time.

Bowers' employment was initially terminated by Baylor in 1993. Bowers alleges that the termination was premised on alleged violations of NCAA and Southwest Conference rules, and that her win-loss record was not even mentioned. After her termination, Bowers filed a complaint with the Office of Civil Rights and the Equal Employment Opportunity Commission. Immediately after filing the complaint, Bowers was notified that she would be reinstated (1) on the same terms under which she had been employed the previous 14 years, or (2) on a two year written contract. Bowers alleges that she was forced to accept the first offer because the terms of the written contract were vague and ambiguous and Baylor refused to discuss them.

Despite her reinstatement, Bowers continued to pursue her employment complaints with the federal agencies. In an employment evaluation of August 30, 1993, Bowers' win-loss record was mentioned, and she was informed that she needed to achieve a winning season. On or about March 28, 1994, Bowers was notified in writing that her employment would be terminated as of May 31, 1994 because of her unsuccessful win-loss record throughout her employment at Baylor.

Bowers' claims are asserted exclusively under Title IX of the Education Amendments of 1972. 20 U.S.C. §§ 1681-88. She raises no claim under Title VII of the Civil Rights Act of 1964, as amended, 42 U.S.C. § 2000e to 2000e-17, under the Equal Pay Act, 29 U.S.C. § 206(d), or under state law. She contends that Baylor and various members of its administration violated Title IX by discriminating against her on the basis of sex and by retaliating against her for challenging Baylor's allegedly discriminatory conduct.

Bowers seeks a declaratory judgment that Baylor's practices were unlawful, a permanent injunction to restrain further discrimination, a mandatory injunction to reinstate her as Baylor's head women's basketball coach, back pay and benefits, compensatory damages of $1 million, and punitive damages in excess of $3 million. Bowers' claims are not based upon an express remedy found in

Title IX, but rather on a theory that she has an implied cause of action under Title IX.

* * *

III. Discussion

A. Baylor's Motion

Baylor believes that Bowers'Title IX claims should be dismissed for lack of subject matter jurisdiction and for failure to state a claim for which relief can be granted. Specifically, Baylor argues that Title IX does not provide employees such as Bowers with a private cause of action for damages. Bowers disagrees, and believes that Supreme Court precedent, although not directly on point, dictates that this motion be denied.

* * *

Title IX does not expressly authorize an employee to file a private suit for damages. In fact, Title IX contains no mention of employees or employment discrimination at all. Likewise, Title IX contains no mention of damages and no mention of lawsuits to be brought by private citizens.

The Supreme Court was first confronted with the issue of whether a private cause of action was implicit in Title IX in *Cannon v. University of Chicago*, 441 U.S. 677 (1979). In that case, a university student brought suit alleging that she had been excluded from the medical education program on the basis of her gender. The district court dismissed her case, holding that the proper remedy was loss of federal funds by the institution. The Supreme Court disagreed, and after analyzing the four factors of *Cort v. Ash*, 422 U.S. 66 (1975), held that the female student could maintain her lawsuit despite the absence of any express authorization for it in Title IX.[2]

Over the dissenting voices of three justices, the Supreme Court went one step further in *Franklin v. Gwinnett County Public Schools*, 112 S. Ct. 1028, 117 L. Ed. 2d 208 (1992). In *Franklin*, a female high school student brought suit against her school district under Title IX because she had been subjected to sexual harassment by a male coach at the school. The district court dismissed the case on the ground that Title IX does not authorize an award of monetary dam-

---

[2] The four factors that a court must analyze to determine whether Congress intended a statute to create a remedy for a specific class of persons was set forth in *Cort*. These factors are:

(a) whether the statute was enacted for the benefit of a special class of which the plaintiff is a member;

(b) whether there is any indication of legislative intent to create a private remedy;

(c) whether implication of such a remedy is consistent with the underlying purposes of the legislative scheme; and

(d) whether implying a federal remedy is inappropriate because the subject matter involves an area basically of concern to the States.

Cort at 78.

ages. The Supreme Court reversed, and held that not only did Title IX create an implied cause of action for the plaintiff, as the Court had recognized in *Cannon*, but it also authorized monetary damages as a remedy. The Court focused upon the long standing rule that "where legal rights have been invaded, and a federal statute provides for a general right to sue for such invasion, federal courts may use any available remedy to make good the wrong done." *Franklin* at 1033 (citing *Bell v. Hood*, 327 U.S. 678 (1946), and *J.I. Case Co. v. Borak*, 377 U.S. 426 (1964)).

Neither the Fifth Circuit Court of Appeals nor the Supreme Court has directly addressed the issue of whether an employee of a school receiving federal funds has a private cause of action for damages under Title IX. The Supreme Court tangentially addressed the issue in *North Haven Board of Education v. Bell*, 456 U.S. 512 (1982). At issue in that case was the validity of regulations promulgated by the Department of Education pursuant to Title IX prohibiting federally funded education programs from discriminating on the basis of gender with respect to employment *See* 34 C.F.R. §§106.51-106.61 (1980).

The Supreme Court first analyzed the broad directive in Title IX that "no person" may be discriminated against on the basis of gender, and held that employees who directly participate in federal programs or who directly benefit from federal grants, loans, or contracts clearly fall within Title IX. *North Haven Board of Education* at 520. The Court stated:

> Because [Title IX] neither expressly nor impliedly excludes employees from its reach, we should interpret the provision as covering and protecting these 'persons' unless other considerations counsel to the contrary. After all, Congress easily could have substituted 'student' or 'beneficiary' for the word 'person' if it had wished to restrict the scope of [Title IX].

Id. at 521. Based upon these three Supreme Court decisions, this Court is of the opinion that a private cause of action for damages under Title IX does exist in this case, and Baylor's Motion to Dismiss should be denied. Baylor's brief is quite thorough in its discussion to the contrary, and is similar to Supreme Court dissents in the above cases. While this Court and a minority of Supreme Court justices might agree with Baylor's reasoning, current precedent dictates a ruling in favor of the plaintiff. The Supreme Court's approval of the regulations in *North Haven Board of Education*, and the Supreme Court's decisions in *Cannon* and *Franklin*, lead this Court to the conclusion that the Supreme Court would take the next logical step of recognizing Bowers' cause of action under Title IX.

B. Individual Defendant's Motion

The individual defendants ask that the claims against them be dismissed in their entireties because Title IX does not permit claims against individuals who are administrators or employees of separately incorporated educational institutions. The individual defendants cite three district court cases that have so held. *See Doe v. Petaluma City School District*, 830 F. Supp. 1560 (N.D. Cal. 1993); *Bougher v. University of Pittsburgh*, 713 F. Supp. 139 (W.D. Pa. 1989), *aff'd,* 882 F.2d 74 (3d. Cir. 1989); *Bagley v. Hooper*, Civ. A. No. 81-1126-Z, 1985 WL 17643 (D. Mass. 1985).

The plaintiff argues that her retaliation cause of action should withstand dismissal because under the regulations promulgated pursuant to Title VI, "no recipient or other person shall intimidate, threaten, coerce, or discriminate against any individual for the purpose of interfering with any right or privilege secured [by this Act]." 34 C.F.R. § 100.7(e). The plaintiff notes that this provision, along with the other Title VI procedural guarantees, are incorporated by reference into Title IX by 34 C.F.R. § 106.71.

Even assuming that 34 C.F.R. § 106.71 mandates the incorporation of the procedural safeguards of Title VI, the Court is of the opinion that extending its reach to cover individual defendants would amount to a substantive change, not a procedural change. Even the plaintiff fails to set forth any authority for the proposition that Title IX can be applied to individuals, or that 34 C.F.R. § 100.7(e) creates a private Title IX cause of action for retaliation against individual defendants. The one case cited by the plaintiff, *Tyler v. Howard University*, does not even address the issue.

This Court agrees with the individual defendants' position, and is particularly persuaded by the reasoning of *Doe v. Petaluma City School District*. The individual defendants are administrators and employees of Baylor, and do not constitute educational institutions in and of themselves. The Court does not accept the plaintiff's reasoning, and is of the opinion that § 100.7(e) is not a procedural provision. Therefore, they should be dismissed with prejudice, leaving only Baylor as a defendant in this case.

IV. Conclusion

Based upon the foregoing, the Court is of the opinion that the plaintiff has alleged a cause of action under Title IX against Baylor University, but has failed to state a cause of action against the individual defendants. Accordingly, it is

ORDERED that the Motion of Defendant Baylor University to Dismiss Plaintiff's Claims is DENIED.

NOTES AND COMMENTS

1. The position taken by the court in Bowers was affirmed by the Supreme Court in *Jackson v. Birmingham Bd. of Education*, 544 U.S. 167 (2005) (Coach fired because of complaints he lodged against a school regarding gender equity violations has a cause of action for retaliation pursuant to Title IX).

2. *See Bartges v. University of North Carolina, Charlotte*, 908 F. Supp. 1312 (D.N.C. 1995), in which the court focuses on both Title VII and Title IX claims surrounding the dismissal of a coach who had raised concerns about gender discrimination in the athletic program. *See also*, *Clay v. Board of Trustees of Neosho Cty. Community College*, 905 F. Supp. 1488 (D. Kan. 1995).

3. *Deli v. University of Minnesota*, 863 F. Supp. 958 (D. Minn. 1994), raises equal pay issues under both Title VII and Title IX. The court determined that the plaintiff female coach of the women's gymnastics team had failed to demonstrate that her position was substantially equal to the positions of coaches of men's teams. It also held that Title VII and the Equal Pay Act do not prohibit salary discrimination based on the gender of athletes being coached. *See also*, *Bedard v. Roger Williams University*, 989 F. Supp. 94 (D.R.I. 1997) (associate athletic director had no cause of action for discrimination pursuant to Title IX when she was terminated).

4. *See also* Terry W. Dodds, *Equal Pay in College Coaching: A Summary of Recent Decisions*, 24 S. ILL. U. L.J. 319 (2000); Comment, *Pay Equity for Intercollegiate Coaches: Exploring the EEOC Enforcement Guidelines*, 13 MARQ. SPORTS L. REV. 149 (2002).

5. Additional cases include: *Perdue v. City of New York*, 13 F. Supp. 2d 326 (E.D.N.Y. 1998) (ruling that former women's basketball coach provided substantial evidence to support jury determination of equal pay violation and Title VII intentional discrimination claim, awarded $85,000 in compensatory damages, $135,829 in back pay, and $134, 829 in liquidated damages — based on the willfulness finding — pursuant to the EPA, plus attorney's fees and costs provided for by both the EPA and Title VII); *Lowrey v. Texas A&M University System*, 11 F. Supp. 2d 895 (S.D. Tex. 1998) (denying defendant's motion for summary judgment on female athletic coordinator's retaliation claims under Title VII and Title IX).

Chapter 4

AMATEUR SPORTS AND ANTITRUST LAW

A. INTRODUCTION

The antitrust laws have played a very significant role in shaping sports in this country. Another section of the book explores the relationship between professional sports and antitrust laws. This chapter focuses upon the antitrust status of the organizations, particularly the NCAA, which regulate amateur sports activities.

Beginning with the passage of the Sherman Act in 1890, Congress has enacted legislation designed to protect and foster the competitive process in the American marketplace. The body of antitrust law consists of this legislation, along with cases interpreting the legislation. The law applies to activity which involves or affects interstate commerce. According to the 1955 Report of the Attorney General's National Committee to Study the Antitrust Laws:

> The general objective of the antitrust laws is promotion of competition in open markets. This policy is a primary feature of private enterprise. Most Americans have long recognized that opportunity for market access and fostering of market rivalry are basic tenets of our faith in competition as a form of economic organization.

At the risk of gross oversimplification, the general objective of the antitrust law — the promotion of competition in open markets — can be thwarted in two fundamental ways. First, economic rivals can act collusively to reduce competition. Second, the market structure itself can be such that competition is restricted. Thus, antitrust law aims at: (a) eliminating anti-competitive collusion and (b) preventing monopolistic and oligopolistic market structures.

The language of the Sherman Act reflects these twin aims. Under Section 1 of the Act, "every contract, combination . . . or conspiracy" which restrains trade is prohibited. 15 U.S.C. § 1 (1989). A violation of this section requires action by more than one person. In theory, a firm acting on its own will not violate Section 1. The gist of a Section 1 offense is an agreement among business entities or persons which seeks to limit or destroy competition. This would be labeled an unreasonable restraint of trade. Section 2 declares that "every person who shall monopolize, or attempt to monopolize, or combine or conspire . . . to monopolize" is guilty of an offense. 15 U.S.C. § 2 (1989). In theory, a Section 2 violation may result from either an agreement among firms to control the market or from the actions of a single firm. Thus, duality is not a requirement of a Section 2 violation.

A number of extremely complex questions arise as one attempts to apply antitrust principles to the activities of amateur sports organizations. The threshold requirement for the application of the Sherman Act is that the activity must involve or affect interstate commerce. Can one argue that the Sherman Act ought to apply only to purely commercial enterprises and not to nonprofit amateur sports organizations? Or, is there reason to distinguish one nonprofit amateur sports organization from another for purposes of deciding whether the antitrust laws apply? Does the nature of the activity determine whether the antitrust laws apply? If the Sherman Act does apply, what is the nature of the court's analysis? For purposes of meeting the Section 1 duality requirement, is an amateur sports organization one firm or an amalgam of separate entities? How do you determine if a restraint is "unreasonable"? What is a monopoly? To what extent must one control a market in order to permit the conclusion that a monopoly exists? How do you define the relevant market? As you read the following cases and materials, consider these questions.

B. COLLEGIATE SPORTS ANTITRUST ISSUES

PROBLEM 1

Jimmy Spencer is the head basketball coach at Southwest State University. He is very successful. He is 40 years old and is in his fourteenth year as a head basketball coach, the last ten at SSU. He has taken SSU to the NCAA tournament six times in ten years and to the Final Four twice.

Spencer is in the second year of a four year contract. The school pays him $175,000 per year. He has a television show which pays $200,000 annually, a radio talk show which pays $50,000, and a contract with All-Pro shoes which pays $200,000. Additional income from camps, clinics, speaking engagements and endorsements totals $300,000. He also is provided with two cars by local dealers, has a $900,000 home which was purchased with no money down and with a 6 percent 30 year mortgage. If he stays at SSU for 15 years the house becomes his with no further obligation under the mortgage agreement. He also has a complimentary country club membership.

The NCAA has just passed a new regulation limiting outside income for coaches. The association is evidently concerned with over-commercialization of college sports. Coaches must report all athletically related income to the chief executive officer of the school and must turn over to the university any amount in excess of $15,000 received from equipment manufacturers. There is a total limitation on outside income of 50 percent of the base salary from the school.

The All-Pro contract requires SSU players to wear All-Pro shoes during all regular season and tournament games. Spencer must also appear at clinics sponsored by All-Pro five times per year. Spencer's personal camp is also sponsored by All-Pro. Spalding provides compensation and basketballs and Gatorade provides liquids and compensation.

Spencer seeks your advice. He wants to know how the rule will affect him and whether there is any way, either through litigation or other avenues, that he can challenge or circumvent the rule.

PROBLEM 2

Bobby Spikes is a world-class short track speed skater. He is 18 years old and is an early favorite for a gold medal in the next Winter Olympics. Speed skating at this level is a professional sport. The prize money on the World Cup circuit is not significant, by comparison to other sports. Bobby has signed several endorsement deals with skate manufacturers, a sunglass company, and a resort in Idaho. He is also a very talented football player and has been offered a scholarship to play at Western State University, a Division I member of the NCAA. He is very interested in playing for WSU, but has just learned that the NCAA will not certify him as eligible because of his endorsement contracts and the other prize money he has won on the World Cup tour. He has contacted you for advice. He is willing to give up the endorsements but is concerned about the limits placed on NCAA scholarships. He is not sure he can afford to take the scholarship. Does he have any recourse against the NCAA? The pertinent NCAA rules concerning this issue may be found at www.NCAA.org.

CASE FILE

NATIONAL COLLEGIATE ATHLETIC ASSOCIATION v. BOARD OF REGENTS OF THE UNIVERSITY OF OKLAHOMA

468 U.S. 85 (1983)

JUSTICE STEVENS delivered the opinion of the Court.

The University of Oklahoma and the University of Georgia contend that the National Collegiate Athletic Association has unreasonably restrained trade in the televising of college football games. After an extended trial, the District Court found that the NCAA had violated § 1 of the Sherman Act and granted injunctive relief. 546 F. Supp. 1276 (W.D. Okla. 1982). The Court of Appeals agreed that the statute had been violated but modified the remedy in some respects. 707 F.2d 1147 (10th Cir. 1983). We granted certiorari, 464 U.S. 913 (1983), and now affirm.

I. The NCAA

Since its inception in 1905, the NCAA has played an important role in the regulation of amateur collegiate sports. It has adopted and promulgated playing rules, standards of amateurism, standards for academic eligibility, regulations concerning recruitment of athletes, and rules governing the size of athletic squads and coaching staffs. In some sports, such as baseball, swimming, basketball, wrestling, and track, it has sponsored and conducted national tournaments. It has not done so in the sport of football, however. With the exception of football, the NCAA has not undertaken any regulation of the televising of athletic events.

The NCAA has approximately 850 voting members. The regular members are classified into separate divisions to reflect differences in size and scope of their athletic programs. Division I includes 276 colleges with major athletic programs; in this group only 187 play intercollegiate football. Divisions II and III include approximately 500 colleges with major athletic programs. Division I has been subdivided into Divisions I-A and I-AA for football.

Some years ago, five major conferences together with major football-playing independent institutions organized the College Football Association (CFA). The original purpose of the CFA was to promote the interests of major football-playing schools within the NCAA structure. The Universities of Oklahoma and Georgia, respondents in this Court, are members of the CFA.

History of the NCAA Television Plan

In 1938, the University of Pennsylvania televised one of its home games. From 1940 through the 1950 season all of Pennsylvania's home games were televised. That was the beginning of the relationship between television and college football.

On January 11, 1951, a three-person "Television Committee," appointed during the preceding year, delivered a report to the NCAA's annual convention in Dallas. Based on preliminary surveys, the committee had concluded that "television does have an adverse effect on college football attendance and unless brought under some control threatens to seriously harm the nation's overall athletic and physical system." The report emphasized that "the television problem is truly a national one and requires collective action by the colleges." As a result, the NCAA decided to retain the National Opinion Research Center (NORC) to study the impact of television on live attendance, and to declare a moratorium on the televising of football games. A television committee was appointed to implement the decision and to develop an NCAA television plan for 1951.

The committee's 1951 plan provided that only one game a week could be telecast in each area, with a total blackout on 3 of the 10 Saturdays during the season. A team could appear on television only twice during a season. The plan also provided that the NORC would conduct a systematic study of the effects of the program on attendance. The plan received the virtually unanimous support of the NCAA membership; only the University of Pennsylvania challenged it. Pennsylvania announced that it would televise all its home games. The council of the NCAA thereafter declared Pennsylvania a member in bad standing and the four institutions scheduled to play at Pennsylvania in 1951 refused to do so. Pennsylvania then reconsidered its decision and abided by the NCAA plan.

During each of the succeeding five seasons, studies were made which tended to indicate that television had an adverse effect on attendance at college football games. During those years the NCAA continued to exercise complete control over the number of games that could be televised.

From 1952 through 1977 the NCAA television committee followed essentially the same procedure for developing its television plans. It would first circulate a questionnaire to the membership and then use the responses as a basis for formulating a plan for the ensuing season. The plan was then submitted to a vote by means of a mail referendum. Once approved, the plan formed the basis for NCAA's negotiations with the networks. Throughout this period the plans retained the essential purposes of the original plan. Until 1977 the contracts were all for either 1- or 2-year terms. In 1977 the NCAA adopted "principles of negotiation" for the future and discontinued the practice of submitting each plan for membership approval. Then the NCAA also entered into its first 4-year contract granting exclusive rights to the American Broadcasting Co. (ABC) for the 1978-1981 seasons. ABC had held the exclusive rights to network telecasts of NCAA football games since 1965.

The Current Plan

The plan adopted in 1981 for the 1982-1985 seasons is at issue in this case. This plan, like each of its predecessors, recites that it is intended to reduce, insofar as possible, the adverse effects of live television upon football game attendance.[6] It provides that "all forms of television of the football games of NCAA member institutions during the Plan control periods shall be in accordance with this Plan." The plan recites that the television committee has awarded rights to negotiate and contract for the telecasting of college football games of members of the NCAA to two "carrying networks." In addition to the principal award of rights to the carrying networks, the plan also describes rights for a "supplementary series" that had been awarded for the 1982 and 1983 seasons,[7] as well as a procedure for permitting specific "exception telecasts."[8]

6 "The purposes of this Plan shall be to reduce, insofar as possible, the adverse effects of live television upon football game attendance and, in turn, upon the athletic and related educational programs dependent upon the proceeds therefrom to spread football television participation among as many colleges as practicable; to reflect properly the image of universities as educational institutions; to promote college football through the use of television, to advance the overall interests of intercollegiate athletics, and to provide college football television to the public to the extent compatible with these other objectives." *Id.* at 35 (parenthetical omitted).

7 The supplementary series is described in a separate article of the plan. It is to consist of no more than 36 exposures in each of the first two years and no more than 40 exposures in the third and fourth years of the plan. Those exposures are to be scheduled on Saturday evenings or at other times that do not conflict with the principal football series that is scheduled for Saturday afternoons. *Id.* at 86-92.

8 An "exception" telecast is permitted in the home team's market of games that are sold out, and in the visiting team's market of games played more than 400 miles from the visiting team's campus, but in both cases only if the broadcast would not be shown in an area where another college football game is to be played. *Id.* at 62-72. Also, Division II and Division III institutions are allowed complete freedom to televise their games, except that the games may not appear on a network of more than five stations without the permission of the NCAA. *Id.* at 73-74.

In separate agreements with each of the carrying networks, ABC and the Columbia Broadcasting System (CBS), the NCAA granted each the right to telecast the 14 live "exposures" described in the plan, in accordance with the "ground rules" set forth therein.[9] Each of the networks agreed to pay a specified "minimum aggregate compensation to the participating NCAA member institutions" during the 4-year period in an amount that totaled $131,750,000. In essence the agreement authorized each network to negotiate directly with member schools for the right to televise their games. The agreement itself does not describe the method of computing the compensation for each game, but the practice that has developed over the years and that the District Court found would be followed under the current agreement involved the setting of a recommended fee by a representative of the NCAA for different types of telecasts, with national telecasts being the most valuable, regional telecasts being less valuable, and Division II or Division III games commanding a still lower price.[10] The aggregate of all these payments presumably equals the total minimum aggregate compensation set forth in the basic agreement.

Except for differences in payment between national and regional telecasts, and with respect to Division II and Division III games, the amount that any team receives does not change with the size of the viewing audience, the number of markets in which the game is telecast, or the particular characteristic of the game or the participating teams. Instead, the "ground rules" provide that the carrying networks make alternate selections of those games they wish to televise, and thereby obtain the exclusive right to submit a bid at an essentially fixed price to the institutions involved.

The plan also contains "appearance requirements" and "appearance limitations" which pertain to each of the 2-year periods that the plan is in effect. The basic requirement imposed on each of the two networks is that it must schedule appearances for at least 82 different member institutions during each 2-year period. Under the appearance limitations no member institution is eligible to appear on television more than a total of six times and more than four times nationally, with the appearances to be divided equally between the two carrying networks. The number of exposures specified in the contracts also sets an absolute maximum on the number of games that can be broadcast.

---

[9] In addition to its contracts with the carrying networks, the NCAA has contracted with Turner Broadcasting System, Inc. (TBS), for the exclusive right to cablecast NCAA football games. The minimum aggregate fee for the initial 2-year period of the TBS contract is $17,696,000. 546 F. Supp. at 1291-1292.

[10] The football television committee's briefing book for 1981 recites that a fee of $600,000 was paid for each of the 12 national games telecast by ABC during the regular fall season and $426,779 was paid for each of the 46 regional telecasts in 1980. App. 250. The report further recites: "Division I members received $27,842,185 from 1980 football television revenue, 89.8 percent of the total. Division II's share was $625,195 (2.0 percent), while Division III received $385,195 (1.3 percent) and the NCAA $2,147,425 (6.9 percent)." *Id.* at 251.

Thus, although the current plan is more elaborate than any of its predecessors, it retains the essential features of each of them. It limits the total amount of televised intercollegiate football and the number of games that any one team may televise. No member is permitted to make any sale of television rights except in accordance with the basic plan.

Background of this Controversy

Beginning in 1979 CFA members began to advocate that colleges with major football programs should have a greater voice in the formulation of football television policy than they had in the NCAA. CFA therefore investigated the possibility of negotiating a television agreement of its own, developed an independent plan, and obtained a contract offer from the National Broadcasting Co. (NBC). This contract, which it signed in August 1981, would have allowed a more liberal number of appearances for each institution, and would have increased the overall revenues realized by CFA members.

In response the NCAA publicly announced that it would take disciplinary action against any CFA member that complied with the CFA-NBC contract The NCAA made it clear that sanctions would not be limited to the football programs of CFA members, but would apply to other sports as well. On September 8, 1981, respondents commenced this action in the United States District Court for the Western District of Oklahoma and obtained a preliminary injunction preventing the NCAA from initiating disciplinary proceedings or otherwise interfering with CFA's efforts to perform its agreement with NBC. Notwithstanding the entry of the injunction, most CFA members were unwilling to commit themselves to the new contractual arrangement with NBC in the face of the threatened sanctions and therefore the agreement was never consummated.

Decision of the District Court

After a full trial, the District Court held that the controls exercised by the NCAA over the televising of college football games violated the Sherman Act. The District Court defined the relevant market as "live college football television" because it found that alternative programming has a significantly different and lesser audience appeal. The District Court then concluded that the NCAA controls over college football are those of a "classic cartel" with an

> "almost absolute control over the supply of college football which is made available to the networks, to television advertisers, and ultimately to the viewing public. Like all other cartels, NCAA members have sought and achieved a price for their product which is, in most instances, artificially high. The NCAA cartel imposes production limits on its members, and maintains mechanisms for punishing cartel members who seek to stray from these production quotas. The cartel has established a uniform price for the products of each of the member producers, with no regard for the differing quality of these products or the consumer demand for these various products." The District Court found that competition in the relevant market had been restrained in three

> ways: (1) NCAA fixed the price for particular telecasts; (2) its exclusive network contracts were tantamount to a group boycott of all other potential broadcasters and its threat of sanctions against its own members constituted a threatened boycott of potential competitors; and (3) its plan placed an artificial limit on the production of televised college football.

In the District Court the NCAA offered two principal justifications for its television policies; that they protected the gate attendance of its members and that they tended to preserve a competitive balance among the football programs of the various schools. The District Court rejected the first justification because the evidence did not support the claim that college football television adversely affected gate attendance. With respect to the "competitive balance" argument, the District Court found that the evidence failed to show that the NCAA regulations on matters such as recruitment and the standards for preserving amateurism were not sufficient to maintain an appropriate balance.

Decision of the Court of Appeals

The Court of Appeals held that the NCAA television plan constituted illegal per se price fixing. It rejected each of the three arguments advanced by NCAA to establish the procompetitive character of its plan. First, the court rejected the argument that the television plan promoted live attendance, noting that since the plan involved a concomitant reduction in viewership the plan did not result in a net increase in output and hence was not procompetitive. Second, the Court of Appeals rejected as illegitimate the NCAA's purpose of promoting athletically balanced competition. It held that such a consideration amounted to an argument that "competition will destroy the market" — a position inconsistent with the policy of the Sherman Act. Moreover, assuming arguendo that the justification was legitimate, the court agreed with the District Court's finding "that any contribution the plan made to athletic balance could be achieved by less restrictive means." Third, the Court of Appeals refused to view the NCAA plan as competitively justified by the need to compete effectively with other types of television programming, since it entirely eliminated competition between producers of football and hence was illegal *per se.*

Finally, the Court of Appeals concluded that even if the television plan were not per se illegal, its anticompetitive limitation on price and output was not offset by any procompetitive justification sufficient to save the plan even when the totality of the circumstances was examined. The case was remanded to the District Court for an appropriate modification in its injunctive decree.

II

There can be no doubt that the challenged practices of the NCAA constitute a "restraint of trade" in the sense that they limit members' freedom to negotiate and enter into their own television contracts. In that sense, however, every contract is a restraint of trade, and as we have repeatedly recognized, the Sherman Act was intended to prohibit only unreasonable restraints of trade.

It is also undeniable that these practices share characteristics of restraints we have previously held unreasonable. The NCAA is an association of schools which compete against each other to attract television revenues, not to mention fans and athletes. As the District Court found, the policies of the NCAA with respect to television rights are ultimately controlled by the vote of member institutions. By participating in an association which prevents member institutions from competing against each other on the basis of price or kind of television rights that can be offered to broadcasters, the NCAA member institutions have created a horizontal restraint — an agreement among competitors on the way in which they will compete with one another. A restraint of this type has often been held to be unreasonable as a matter of law. Because it places a ceiling on the number of games member institutions may televise, the horizontal agreement places an artificial limit on the quantity of televised football that is available to broadcasters and consumers. By restraining the quantity of television rights available for sale, the challenged practices create a limitation output; our cases have held that such limitations are unreasonable restraints of trade. Moreover, the District Court found that the minimum aggregate price in fact operates to preclude any price negotiation between broadcasters and institutions, thereby constituting horizontal price fixing, perhaps the paradigm of an unreasonable restraint of trade.

Horizontal price fixing and output limitation are ordinarily condemned as a matter of law under an "illegal *per se*" approach because the probability that these practices are anticompetitive is so high; a *per se* rule is applied when "the practice facially appears to be one that would always or almost always tend to restrict competition and decrease output." In such circumstances a restraint is presumed unreasonable without inquiry into the particular market context in which it is found. Nevertheless, we have decided that it would be inappropriate to apply a *per se* rule to this case. This decision is not based on a lack of judicial experience with this type of arrangement, on the fact that the NCAA is organized as a nonprofit entity, or on our respect for the NCAA's historic role in the preservation and encouragement of intercollegiate amateur athletics. Rather, what is critical is that this case involves an industry in which horizontal restraints on competition are essential if the product is to be available at all.

As Judge Bork has noted: "[S]ome activities can only be carried out jointly. Perhaps the leading example is league sports. When a league of professional lacrosse teams is formed, it would be pointless to declare their cooperation illegal on the ground that there are no other professional lacrosse teams." R. BORK, THE ANTITRUST PARADOX 278 (1978). What the NCAA and its member institutions market in this case is competition itself — contests between competing institutions. Of course, this would be completely ineffective if there were no rules on which the competitors agreed to create and define the competition to be marketed. A myriad of rules affecting such matters as the size of the field, the number of players on a team, and the extent to which physical violence is to be encouraged or proscribed, all must be agreed upon, and all restrain the manner in which institutions compete. Moreover, the NCAA seeks to market a particular brand of football — college football. The identification of this "product" with an academic tradition differentiates college football from and makes it more popular than professional sports to which it might otherwise be comparable, such as, for example, minor league baseball. In order to preserve the character and quality of the "product," athletes must not be paid, must be required to attend class, and the like. And the integrity of the "product" cannot be preserved except by mutual agreement; if an institution adopted such restrictions unilaterally, its effectiveness as a competitor on the playing field might soon be destroyed. Thus, the NCAA plays a vital role in enabling college football to preserve its character, and as a result enables a product to be marketed which might otherwise be unavailable. In performing this role, its actions widen consumer choice — not only the choices available to sports fans but also those available to athletes — and hence can be viewed as procompetitive.

Broadcast Music squarely holds that a joint selling arrangement may be so efficient that it will increase sellers' aggregate output and thus be procompetitive. *See* 441 U.S. at 18-23. Similarly, as we indicated in *Continental T.V., Inc v. GTE Sylvania Inc.*, 433 U.S. 36, 51-57 (1977), a restraint in a limited aspect of a market may actually enhance marketwide competition. Respondents concede that the great majority of the NCAA's regulations enhance competition among member institutions. Thus, despite the fact that this case involves restraints on the ability of member institutions to compete in terms of price and output, a fair evaluation of their competitive character requires consideration of the NCAA's justifications for the restraints.

Our analysis of the case under the Rule of Reason, of course, does not change the ultimate focus of our inquiry. Both *per se* rules and the Rule of Reason are employed "to form a judgment about the competitive significance of the restraint." *National Society of Professional Engineers v. United States*, 435 U.S. 679, 692 (1978). A conclusion that a restraint of trade is unreasonable may be "based either (1) on the nature or character of the contracts, or (2) on surrounding circumstances giving rise to the inference or presumption that they were intended to restrain trade and enhance prices. Under either branch of the test, the inquiry is confined to a consideration of impact on competitive conditions." *Id.* at 690 (footnotes omitted).

Per se rules are invoked when surrounding circumstances make the likelihood of anticompetitive conduct so great as to render unjustified further examination of the challenged conduct. But whether the ultimate finding is the product of a presumption or actual market analysis, the essential inquiry remains the same whether or not the challenged restraint enhances competition. Under the Sherman Act the criterion to be used in judging the validity of a restraint on trade is its impact on competition.

III

Because it restrains price and output, the NCAA's television plan has a significant potential for anticompetitive effects. The findings of the District Court indicate that this potential has been realized. The District Court found that if member institutions were free to sell television rights, many more games would be shown on television, and that the NCAA's output restriction has the effect of raising the price the networks pay for television rights. Moreover, the court found that by fixing a price for television rights to all games, the NCAA creates a price structure that is unresponsive to viewer demand and unrelated to the prices that would prevail in a competitive market. And, of course, since as a practical matter all member institutions need NCAA approval, members have no real choice but to adhere to the NCAA's television controls.

The anticompetitive consequences of this arrangement are apparent. Individual competitors lose their freedom to compete. Price is higher and output lower than they would otherwise be, and both are unresponsive to consumer preference. This latter point is perhaps the most significant, since "Congress designed the Sherman Act as a 'consumer welfare prescription.'" . . . A restraint that has the effect of reducing the importance of consumer preference in setting price and output is not consistent with this fundamental goal of antitrust law. Restrictions on price and output are the paradigmatic examples of restraints of trade that the Sherman Act was intended to prohibit. . . . At the same time, the television plan eliminates competitors from the market, since only those broadcasters able to bid on television rights covering the entire NCAA can compete. Thus, as the District Court found, many telecasts that would occur in a competitive market are foreclosed by the NCAA's plan.

Petitioner argues, however, that its television plan can have no significant anticompetitive effect since the record indicates that it has no market power — no ability to alter the interaction of supply and demand in the market. We must reject this argument for two reasons, one legal, one factual.

As a matter of law, the absence of proof of market power does not justify a naked restriction on price or output. To the contrary, when there is an agreement not to compete in terms of price or output, "no elaborate industry analysis is required to demonstrate the anticompetitive character of such an agreement." . . . Petitioner does not quarrel with the District Court's finding that price and output are not responsive to demand. Thus the plan is inconsistent with the Sherman Act's command that price and supply be responsive to consumer preference. We have never required proof of market power in such a case. This naked restraint on price and output requires some competitive justification even in the absence of a detailed market analysis.

As a factual matter, it is evident that petitioner does possess market power. The District Court employed the correct test for determining whether college football broadcasts constitute a separate market — whether there are other products that are reasonably substitutable for televised NCAA football games. Petitioner's argument that it cannot obtain supra-competitive prices from broadcasters since advertisers, and hence broadcasters, can switch from college football to other types of programming simply ignores the findings of the District Court. It found that intercollegiate football telecasts generate an audience uniquely attractive to advertisers and that competitors are unable to offer programming that can attract a similar audience. These findings amply support its conclusion that the NCAA possesses market power. Indeed, the District Court's subsidiary finding that advertisers will pay a premium price per viewer to reach audiences watching college football because of their demographic characteristics is vivid evidence of the uniqueness of this product. . . . It inexorably follows that if college football broadcasts be defined as a separate market — and we are convinced they are — then the NCAA's complete control over those broadcasts provides a solid basis for the District Court's conclusion that the NCAA possesses market power with respect to those broadcasts. . . .

Thus, the NCAA television plan on its face constitutes a restraint upon the operation of a free market, and the findings of the District Court establish that it has operated to raise prices and reduce output. Under the Rule of Reason, these hallmarks of anticompetitive behavior place upon petitioner a heavy burden of establishing an affirmative defense which competitively justifies this apparent deviation from the operations of a free market. . . . We turn now to the NCAA's proffered justifications.

IV

Relying on *Broadcast Music*, petitioner argues that its television plan constitutes a cooperative "joint venture" which assists in the marketing of broadcast rights and hence is procompetitive. While joint ventures have no immunity from the antitrust laws, as *Broadcast Music* indicates, a joint selling arrangement may "mak[e] possible a new product by reaping otherwise unattainable efficiencies." . . . The essential contribution made by the NCAA's arrangement is to define the number of games that may be televised, to establish the price for each exposure, and to define the basic terms of each contract between the network and a home team. The NCAA does not, however, act as a selling agent for any school or for any conference of schools. The selection of individual games, and the negotiation of particular agreements, are matters left to the networks and the individual schools. Thus, the effect of the network plan is not to eliminate individual sales of broadcasts, since these still occur, albeit subject to fixed prices and output limitations. Unlike *Broadcast Music*'s blanket license covering broadcast rights to a large number of individual compositions, here the same rights are still sold on an individual basis, only in a noncompetitive market.

The District Court did not find that the NCAA's television plan produced any procompetitive efficiencies which enhanced the competitiveness of college football television rights; to the contrary it concluded that NCAA football could be marketed just as effectively without the television plan. There is therefore no predicate in the findings for petitioner's efficiency justification. Indeed, petitioner's argument is refuted by the District Court's finding concerning price and output. If the NCAA's television plan produced procompetitive efficiencies, the plan would increase output and reduce the price of televised games. The District Court's contrary findings accordingly undermine petitioner's position. In light of these findings, it cannot be said that "the agreement on price is necessary to market the product at all." In *Broadcast Music*, the availability of a package product that no individual could offer enhanced the total volume of music that was sold. Unlike this case, there was no limit of any kind placed on the volume that might be sold in the entire market and each individual remained free to sell his own music without restraint. Here production has been limited, not enhanced. No individual school is free to televise its own games without restraint. The NCAA's efficiency justification is not supported by the record.

Neither is the NCAA's television plan necessary to enable the NCAA to penetrate the market through an attractive package sale. Since broadcasting rights to college football constitute a unique product for which there is no ready substitute, there is no need for collective action in order to enable the product to compete against its nonexistent competitors. This is borne out by the District Court's finding that the NCAA's television plan reduces the volume of television rights sold.

V

Throughout the history of its regulation of intercollegiate football telecasts, the NCAA has indicated its concern with protecting live attendance. This concern, it should be noted, is not with protecting live attendance at games which are shown on television; that type of interest is not at issue in this case. Rather, the concern is that fan interest in a televised game may adversely affect ticket sales for games that will not appear on television.

Although the NORC studies in the 1950's provided some support for the thesis that live attendance would suffer if unlimited television were permitted, the District Court found that there was no evidence to support that theory in today's market. Moreover, as the District Court found, the television plan has evolved in a manner inconsistent with its original design to protect gate attendance. Under the current plan, games are shown on television during all hours that college football games are played. The plan simply does not protect live attendance by ensuring that games will not be shown on television at the same time as live events.

There is, however, a more fundamental reason for rejecting this defense. The NCAA's argument that its television plan is necessary to protect live attendance is not based on a desire to maintain the integrity of college football as a distinct and attractive product, but rather on a fear that the product will not prove sufficiently attractive to draw live attendance when faced with competition from televised games. At bottom the NCAA's position is that ticket sales for most college games are unable to compete in a free market. The television plan protects ticket sales by limiting output — just as any monopolist increases revenues by reducing output. By seeking to insulate live ticket sales from the full spectrum of competition because of its assumption that the product itself is insufficiently attractive to consumers, petitioner forwards a justification that is inconsistent with the basic policy of the Sherman Act. . . .

VI

Petitioner argues that the interest in maintaining a competitive balance among amateur athletic teams is legitimate and important and that it justifies the regulations challenged in this case. We agree with the first part of the argument but not the second.

Our decision not to apply a per se rule to this case rests in large part on our recognition that a certain degree of cooperation is necessary if the type of competition that petitioner and its member institutions seek to market is to be preserved. It is reasonable to assume that most of the regulatory controls of the NCAA are justifiable means of fostering competition among amateur athletic teams and therefore procompetitive because they enhance public interest in intercollegiate athletics. The specific restraints on football telecasts that are challenged in this case do not, however, fit into the same mold as do rules defining the conditions of the contest, the eligibility of participants, or the manner in which members of a joint enterprise shall share the responsibilities and the benefits of the total venture.

The NCAA does not claim that its television plan has equalized or is intended to equalize competition within any one league. The plan is nationwide in scope and there is no single league or tournament in which all college football teams compete. There is no evidence of any intent to equalize the strength of teams in Division I-A with those in Division II or Division III, and not even a colorable basis for giving colleges that have no football program at all a voice in the management of the revenues generated by the football programs at other schools. The interest in maintaining a competitive balance that is asserted by the NCAA as a justification for regulating all television of intercollegiate football is not related to any neutral standard or to any readily identifiable group of competitors.

The television plan is not even arguably tailored to serve such an interest. It does not regulate the amount of money that any college may spend on its football program, nor the way in which the colleges may use the revenues that are generated by their football programs, whether derived from the sale of television rights, the sale of tickets, or the sale of concessions or program advertising. The plan simply imposes a restriction on one source of revenue that is more important to some colleges than to others. There is no evidence that this restriction produces any greater measure of equality throughout the NCAA than would a restriction on alumni donations, tuition rates, or any other revenue-producing activity. At the same time, as the District Court found, the NCAA imposes a variety of other restrictions designed to preserve amateurism which are much better tailored to the goal of competitive balance than is the television plan, and which are "clearly sufficient" to preserve competitive balance to the extent it is within the NCAA's power to do so. And much more than speculation supported the District Court's findings on this score. No other NCAA sport employs a similar plan, and in particular the court found that in the most closely analogous sport, college basketball, competitive balance has been maintained without resort to a restrictive television plan.

Perhaps the most important reason for rejecting the argument that the interest in competitive balance is served by the television plan is the District Court's unambiguous and well supported finding that many more games would be televised in a free market than under the NCAA plan. The hypothesis that legitimates the maintenance of competitive balance as a procompetitive justification under the Rule of Reason is that equal competition will maximize consumer demand for the product. The finding that consumption will materially increase if the controls are removed is a compelling demonstration that they do not in fact serve any such legitimate purpose.

VII

The NCAA plays a critical role in the maintenance of a revered tradition of amateurism in college sports. There can be no question but that it needs ample latitude to play that role, or that the preservation of the student-athlete in higher education adds richness and diversity to intercollegiate athletics and is entirely consistent with the goals of the Sherman Act. But consistent with the Sherman Act, the role of the NCAA must be to preserve a tradition that might otherwise die; rules that restrict output are hardly consistent with this role. Today we hold only that the record supports the District Court's conclusion that by curtailing output and blunting the ability of member institutions to respond to consumer preference, the NCAA has restricted rather than enhanced the place of intercollegiate athletics in the Nation's life. Accordingly, the judgment of the Court of Appeals is Affirmed.

JUSTICE WHITE, with whom JUSTICE REHNQUIST joins, dissenting.

[Although] some of the NCAA's activities, viewed in isolation, bear a resemblance to those undertaken by professional sports leagues and associations, the Court errs in treating intercollegiate athletics under the NCAA's control as a purely commercial venture in which colleges and universities participate solely, or even primarily, in the pursuit of profits. Accordingly, I dissent.

I

"While it would be fanciful to suggest that colleges are not concerned about the profitability of their ventures, it is clear that other, noncommercial goals play a central role in their sports programs." . . . The NCAA's member institutions have designed their competitive athletic programs "to be a vital part of the educational system." . . . Deviations from this goal, produced by a persistent and perhaps inevitable desire to "win at all costs," have in the past led, and continue to lead, to a wide range of competitive excesses that prove harmful to students and institutions alike. . . . The fundamental policy underlying the NCAA's regulatory program, therefore, is to minimize such deviations and "to maintain intercollegiate athletics as an integral part of the student body and, by so doing, retain a clear line of demarcation between college athletics and professional Sports." . . .

The NCAA, in short, "exist[s] primarily to enhance the contribution made by amateur athletic competition to the process of higher education as distinguished from realizing maximum return on it as an entertainment commodity." . . . In pursuing this goal, the organization and its members seek to provide a public good — a viable system of amateur athletics — that most likely could not be provided in a perfectly competitive market. . . . "Without regulation, the desire of member institutions to remain athletically competitive would lead them to engage in activities that deny amateurism to the public. No single institution could confidently enforce its own standards since it could not trust its competitors to do the same." . . . The history of intercollegiate athletics prior to the advent of the NCAA provides ample support for this conclusion. By mitigating what appears to be a clear failure of the free market to serve the ends and goals of high education, the NCAA ensures the continued availability of a unique and valuable product, the very existence of which might well be threatened by unbridled competition in the economic sphere.

In pursuit of its fundamental goal and others related to it, the NCAA imposes numerous controls on intercollegiate athletic competition among its members, many of which "are similar to those which are summarily condemned when undertaken in a more traditional business setting."

[Thus], the NCAA has promulgated and enforced rules limiting both the compensation of student athletes, . . . and the number of coaches a school may hire for its football and basketball programs, . . . restricted the number of athletic scholarships its members may award, and established minimum academic standards for recipients of those scholarships; and it has pervasively regulated the recruitment process, student eligibility, practice schedules, squad size, the number of games played, and many other aspects of inter-collegiate athletics. . . . One clear effect of most, if not all, of these regulations is to prevent institutions with competitively and economically successful programs from taking advantage of their success by expanding their programs, improving the quality of the product they offer, and increasing their sports revenues. Yet each of these regulations represents a desirable and legitimate attempt "to keep university athletics from becoming professionalized to the extent that profit making objectives would overshadow educational objectives." . . . Significantly, neither the Court of Appeals nor this Court questions the validity of these regulations under the Rule of Reason. . . .

Notwithstanding the contrary conclusion of the District Court, and the majority, I do not believe that the restraint under consideration in this case — the NCAA's television plan — differs fundamentally for antitrust purposes from the other seemingly anticompetitive aspects of the organization's broader program of self-regulation.

* * *

In affirming the Court of Appeals, the Court first holds that the television plan has sufficient redeeming virtues to escape condemnation as a *per se* violation of the Sherman Act, this because of the inherent characteristics of competitive athletics and the justifiable role of the NCAA in regulation college athletics. It nevertheless affirms the Court of Appeals' judgment that the NCAA plan is an unreasonable restraint of trade because of what it deems to be the plan's price-fixing and output-limiting aspects. As I shall explain, in reaching this result, the Court traps itself in commercial antitrust rhetoric and ideology and ignores the context in which the restraints have been imposed. But it is essential at this point to emphasize that neither the Court of Appeals nor this Court purports to hold that the NCAA may not (1) require its members who televise their games to pool and share the compensation received among themselves with other schools and with the NCAA; (2) limit the number of times any member may arrange to have its games shown on television; or (3) enforce reasonable blackout rules to avoid head-to-head competition for television audiences. As I shall demonstrate, the Court wisely and correctly does not condemn such regulations. What the Court does affirm is the Court of Appeals' judgment that the NCAA may not limit the number of games that are broadcast on television and that it may not contract for an overall price that has the effect of setting the price for individual game broadcast rights. I disagree with the Court in these respects.

II

"In a competitive market," the District Court observed, "each football-playing institution would be an independent seller of the right to telecast its football games. Each seller would be free to sell that right to any entity it chose," and "for whatever price it could get." . . . Under the NCAA's television plan, member institutions' competitive freedom is restrained because, for the most part, television rights are bought and sold, not on a per-game basis, but as a package deal. With limited exceptions not particularly relevant to antitrust scrutiny of the plan, broadcasters wishing to televise college football must be willing and able to purchase a package of television rights without knowing in advance the particular games to which those rights apply. The real negotiations over price and terms take place between the broadcasters and the NCAA rather than between the broadcasters and individual schools. Knowing that some games will be worth more to them than others, the networks undoubtedly exercise whatever bargaining power they possess to ensure that the minimum aggregate compensation they agree to provide for the package bears some relation to the average value to them of the games they anticipate televising. Because some schools' games contribute disproportionately to the total value of the package, the manner in which the minimum aggregate compensation is distributed among schools whose games are televised has given rise to a situation under which less prominent schools receive more in rights fees than they would receive in a competitive market and football powers like respondents receive less.

As I have said, the Court does not hold, nor did the Court of Appeals hold, that this redistributive effect alone would be sufficient to subject the television plan to condemnation under § 1 of the Sherman Act. Nor should it, for an agreement to share football revenues to a certain extent is an essential aspect of maintaining some balance of strength among competing colleges and of minimizing the tendency to professionalism in the dominant schools. Sharing with the NCAA itself is also a price legitimately exacted in exchange for the numerous benefits of membership in the NCAA, including its many-faceted efforts to maintain a system of competitive, amateur athletics. For the same reasons, limiting the number of television appearances by any college is an essential attribute of a balanced amateur athletic system. Even with shared television revenues, unlimited appearances by a few schools would inevitably give them an insuperable advantage over all others and in the end defeat any efforts to maintain a system of athletic competition among amateurs who measure up to college scholastic requirements.

The Court relies instead primarily on the District Court's findings that (1) the television plan restricts output; and (2) the plan creates a noncompetitive price structure that is unresponsive to viewer demand. . . . These findings notwithstanding, I am unconvinced that the television plan has a substantial anticompetitive effect.

First, it is not clear to me that the District Court employed the proper measure of output. I am not prepared to say that the District Court's finding that "many more college football games would be televised" in the absence of the NCAA controls, . . . is clearly erroneous. To the extent that output is measured solely in terms of the number of televised games, I need not deny that it is reduced by the NCAA's television plan. But this measure of output is not the proper one. The District Court found that eliminating the plan would reduce the number of games on network television and increase the number of games shown locally and regionally. . . . It made no finding concerning the effect of the plan on total viewership, which is the more appropriate measure of output or, at least, of the claimed anticompetitive effects of the NCAA plan. This is the NCAA's position, and it seems likely to me that the television plan, by increasing network coverage at the expense of local broadcasts, actually expands the total television audience for NCAA football. The NCAA would surely be an irrational "profit maximizer" if this were not the case. In the absence of a contrary finding by the District Court, I cannot conclude that respondents carried their burden of showing that the television plan has an adverse effect on output and is therefore anticompetitive.

Second, and even more important, I am unconvinced that respondents have proved that any reduction in the number of televised college football games brought about by the NCAA's television plan has resulted in an anticompetitive increase in the price of television rights. The District Court found, of course, that "the networks are actually paying the large fees because the NCAA agrees to limit production. If the NCAA would not agree to limit production, the networks would not pay so large a fee." . . . Undoubtedly, this is true. But the market for television rights to college football competitions should not be equated to the markets for wheat or widgets. Reductions in output by monopolists in most product markets enable producers to exact a higher price for the same product. By restricting the number of games that can be televised, however, the NCAA creates a new product — exclusive television rights — that are more valuable to networks than the products that its individual members could market independently.

The television plan makes a certain number of games available for purchase by television networks and limits the incidence of head-to-head competition between football telecasts for the available viewers. Because competition is limited, the purchasing network can count on a larger share of the audience, which translates into greater advertising revenues and, accordingly, into larger payments per game to the televised teams. There is thus a relationship between the size of the rights payments and the value of the product being purchased by the networks; a network purchasing a series of games under the plan is willing to pay more than would one purchasing the same games in the absence of the plan since the plan enables the network to deliver a larger share of the available audience to advertisers and thus to increase its own revenues. In short, by focusing only on the price paid by the networks for television rights rather than on the nature and quality of the product delivered by the NCAA and its member institutions, the District Court, and this Court as well, may well have deemed anticompetitive a rise in price that more properly should be attributed to an increase in output, measured in terms of viewership.

Third, the District Court's emphasis on the prices paid for particular games seems misdirected and erroneous as a matter of law. The distribution of the minimum aggregate fees among participants in the television plan is, of course, not wholly based on a competitive price structure that is responsive to viewer demand and is only partially related to the value those schools contribute to the total package the networks agree to buy. But as I have already indicated, . . . this "redistribution" of total television revenues is a wholly justifiable, even necessary, aspect of maintaining a system of truly competitive college teams. As long as the NCAA cannot artificially fix the price of the entire package and demand supercompetitive prices, this aspect of the plan should be of little concern. And I find little, if anything, in the record to support the notion that the NCAA has power to extract from the television networks more than the Broadcasting rights are worth in the marketplace.

III

Even if I were convinced that the District Court did not err in failing to look to total viewership, as opposed to the number of televised games, when measuring output and anticompetitive effect and in failing fully to consider whether the NCAA possesses power to fix the package price, as opposed to the distribution of that package price among participating teams, I would nevertheless hold that the television plan passes muster under the Rule of Reason. The

NCAA argues strenuously that the plan and the network contracts "are part of a joint venture among many of the nation's universities to create a product — high-quality college football — and offer that product in a way attractive to both fans in the stadiums and viewers on [television]. The cooperation in producing the product makes it more competitive against other [television] (and live) attractions." . . . The Court recognizes that, "[i]f the NCAA faced 'interbrand' competition from available substitutes, then certain forms of collective action might be appropriate in order to enhance its ability to compete." . . . It rejects the NCAA's proffered pro-competitive justification, however, on the ground that college football is a unique product for which there are no available substitutes and "there is no need for collective action in order to enable the product to compete against its nonexistent competitors." . . . This proposition is singularly unpersuasive.

It is one thing to say that "NCAA football is a unique product," . . . that "intercollegiate football telecasts generate an audience uniquely attractive to advertisers and that competitors are unable to offer programming that can attract a similar audience." . . . It is quite another, in my view, to say that maintenance or enhancement of the quality of NCAA football telecasts is unnecessary to enable those telecasts to compete effectively against other forms of entertainment. The NCAA has no monopoly power when competing against other types of entertainment. Should the quality of the NCAA's product "deteriorate to any perceptible degree or should the cost of 'using' its product rise, some fans undoubtedly would turn to another form of entertainment. . . . Because of the broad possibilities for alternative forms of entertainment," the NCAA "properly belongs in the broader 'entertainment' market rather than in . . . [a] narrower marke[t]" like sports or football. . . .

The NCAA has suggested a number of plausible ways in which its television plan might enhance the ability of college football telecasts to compete against other forms of entertainment. . . . Although the District Court did conclude that the plan is "not necessary for effective marketing of the product," . . . its finding was directed only at the question whether college football telecast would continue in the absence of the plan. It made no explicit findings concerning the effect of the plan on viewership and thus did not reject the factual premise of the NCAA's argument that the plan might enhance competition by increasing the market penetration of NCAA football. . . . The District Court's finding that network coverage of NCAA football would likely decrease if the plan were struck down, . . . in fact, strongly suggests the validity of the NCAA's position. On the record now before the Court, therefore, I am not prepared to conclude that the restraints imposed by the NCAA's television plan are "such as may suppress or even destroy competition" rather than "such as merely regulat[e] and perhaps thereby promot[e] competition." . . .

IV

Finally, I return to the point with which I began — the essentially noneconomic nature of the NCAA's program of self regulation. Like Judge Barrett, who dissented in the Court of Appeals, I believe that the lower courts "erred by subjugating the NCAA's educational goals (and, incidentally, those which Oklahoma and Georgia insist must be maintained in any event) to the purely competitive commercialism of [an] 'every school for itself' approach to television contract bargaining." . . . Although the NCAA does not enjoy blanket immunity from the antitrust laws, . . . it is important to remember that the Sherman Act "is aimed primarily at combinations having commercial objectives and is applied only to a very limited extent to organizations . . . which normally have other objectives." . . .

The fact that a restraint operates on nonprofit educational institutions as distinguished from business entities is as "relevant in determining whether that particular restraint violates the Sherman Act" as is the fact that a restraint affects a profession rather than a business. . . . The legitimate noneconomic goals of colleges and universities should not be ignored in analyzing restraints imposed by associations of such institutions on their members, and these noneconomic goals "may require that a particular practice, which could properly be viewed as a violation of the Sherman Act in another context, be treated differently." . . . The Court of Appeals, like the District Court, flatly refused to consider what it termed "noneconomic" justifications advanced by the NCAA in support of the television plan. It was of the view that our decision in *National Society of Professional Engineers v. United States*, 435 U.S. 679 (1978), precludes reliance on noneconomic factors in assessing the reasonableness of the television plan. . . . This view was mistaken, and I note that the Court does not in so many words repeat this error.

Professional Engineers did make clear that antitrust analysis usually turns on "competitive conditions" and "economic conceptions." . . . Ordinarily, "the inquiry mandated by the Rule of Reason is whether the challenged agreement is one that promotes competition or one that suppresses competition." The purpose of antitrust analysis, the Court emphasized, "is to form a judgment about the competitive significance of the restraint; it is not to decide whether a policy favoring competition is in the public interest, or in the interest of the members of an industry." Broadly read, these statements suggest that noneconomic values like the promotion of amateurism and fundamental educational objectives could not save the television plan from condemnation under the Sherman Act. But these statements were made in response to "public interest" justifications proffered in defense of a ban on competitive bidding imposed by practitioners engaged in standard, profit-motivated commercial activities. The primarily noneconomic values pursued by educational institutions differ fundamentally from the "overriding commercial purpose of [the] day-to-day activities" of engineers, lawyers, doctors, and businessmen, . . . And neither *professional engineers* nor any other decision of this court suggests that associations of nonprofit educational institutions must defend their self-regulatory restraints solely in terms of their competitive impact, without regard for the legitimate noneconomic values they promote.

When these values are factored into the balance, the NCAA's television plan seems eminently reasonable. Most fundamentally, the plan fosters the goal of amateurism by spreading revenues among various schools and reducing the financial incentives toward professionalism. As the Court observes, the NCAA imposes a variety of restrictions perhaps better suited than the television plan for the preservation of amateurism. Although the NCAA does attempt vigorously to enforce these restrictions, the vast potential for abuse suggests that measures, like the television plan, designed to limit the rewards of professionalism are fully consistent with, and essential to the attainment of, the NCAA's objectives. In short, "[t]he restraints upon Oklahoma and Georgia and other colleges and universities with excellent football programs insure that they confine those programs within the principles of amateurism so that intercollegiate athletics supplement, rather than inhibit, educational achievement." . . . The collateral consequences of the spreading of regional and national appearances among a number of schools are many: the television plan, like the ban on compensating student-athletes, may well encourage students to choose their schools, at least in part, on the basis of educational quality by reducing the perceived economic element of the choice, . . . it helps ensure the economic viability of athletic programs at a wide variety of schools with weaker football teams; and it "promot[es] competitive football among many and varied amateur teams nationwide." . . . These important contributions, I believe, are sufficient to offset any minimal anticompetitive effects of the television plan.

For all of these reasons, I would reverse the judgment of the Court of Appeals. At the very least, the Court of Appeals should be directed to vacate the injunction of the District Court pending the further proceedings that will be necessary to amend the outstanding injunction to accommodate the substantial remaining authority of the NCAA to regulate the telecasting of its members' football games.

LAW v. NATIONAL COLLEGIATE ATHLETIC ASSOCIATION

134 F.3d 1010 (10th Cir. 1998)

EBEL, Circuit Judge.

Defendant-Appellant the National Collegiate Athletic Association ("NCAA") promulgated a rule limiting annual compensation of certain Division I entry-level coaches to $16,000. Basketball coaches affected by the rule filed a class action challenging the restriction under Section 1 of the Sherman Antitrust Act. The district court granted summary judgment on the issue of liability to the coaches and issued a permanent injunction restraining the NCAA from promulgating this or any other rules embodying similar compensation restrictions. The NCAA now appeals, and we affirm.

I. Background

The NCAA is a voluntary unincorporated association of approximately 1,100 educational institutions. The association coordinates the intercollegiate athletic programs of its members by adopting and promulgating playing rules, standards of amateurism, standards for academic eligibility, regulations concerning recruitment of student athletes, rules governing the size of athletic squads and coaching staffs, and the like. The NCAA aims to "promote opportunity for equity in competition to assure that individual student-athletes and institutions will not be prevented unfairly from achieving the benefits inherent in participation in intercollegiate athletics."

The NCAA classifies sports programs into separate divisions to reflect differences in program size and scope. NCAA Division I basketball programs are generally of a higher stature and have more visibility than Division II and III basketball programs. Over 300 schools play in Division I, and each Division I member hires and employs its own basketball coaches.

During the 1980s, the NCAA became concerned over the steadily rising costs of maintaining competitive athletic programs, especially in light of the requirements imposed by Title IX of the 1972 Education Amendments Act to increase support for women's athletic programs. The NCAA observed that some college presidents had to close academic departments, fire tenured faculty, and reduce the number of sports offered to students due to economic constraints. At the same time, many institutions felt pressure to "keep up with the Joneses" by increasing spending on recruiting talented players and coaches and on other aspects of their sports programs in order to remain competitive with rival schools. In addition, a report commissioned by the NCAA known as the "Raiborn Report" found that in 1985 42% of NCAA Division I schools reported deficits in their overall athletic program budgets, with the deficit averaging $824,000 per school. The Raiborn Report noted that athletic expenses at all Division I institutions rose more than 100% over the eight-year period from 1978 to 1985. Finally, the Report stated that 51% of Division I schools responding to NCAA inquiries on the subject suffered a net loss in their basketball programs alone that averaged $145,000 per school.

Part of the problem identified by the NCAA involved the costs associated with part-time assistant coaches. The NCAA allowed Division I basketball teams to employ three full-time coaches, including one head coach and two assistant coaches, and two part-time coaches. The part-time positions could be filled by part-time assistants, graduate assistants, or volunteer coaches. The NCAA imposed salary restrictions on all of the part-time positions. A volunteer coach could not receive any compensation from a member institution's athletic department. A graduate assistant coach was required to be enrolled in a graduate studies program of a member institution and could only receive compensation equal to the value of the cost of the educational experience (grant-in-aid) depending on the coach's residential status (*i.e.*, a non-resident graduate assistant coach could receive greater compensation to reflect the higher cost of out-of-state tuition than could an in-state student). The NCAA limited compensation to part-time assistants to the value of full grant-in-aid compensation based on the value of out-of-state graduate studies.

Despite the salary caps, many of these part-time coaches earned $60,000 or $70,000 per year. Athletic departments circumvented the compensation limits by employing these part-time coaches in lucrative summer jobs at profitable sports camps run by the school or by hiring them for part-time jobs in the physical education department in addition to the coaching position. Further, many of these positions were filled with seasoned and experienced coaches, not the type of student assistant envisioned by the rule.

In January of 1989, the NCAA established a Cost Reduction Committee (the "Committee") to consider means and strategies for reducing the costs of intercollegiate athletics "without disturbing the competitive balance" among NCAA member institutions. The Committee included financial aid personnel, inter-collegiate athletic administrators, college presidents, university faculty members, and a university chancellor. In his initial letter to Committee members, the Chairman of the Committee thanked participants for joining "this gigantic attempt to save intercollegiate athletics from itself." It was felt that only a collaborative effort could reduce costs effectively while maintaining a level playing field because individual schools could not afford to make unilateral spending cuts in sports programs for fear that doing so would unduly hamstring that school's ability to compete against other institutions that spent more money on athletics. In January of 1990, the Chairman told NCAA members that the goal of the Committee was to "cut costs and save money." It became the consensus of the Committee that reducing the total number of coaching positions would reduce the cost of intercollegiate athletic programs.

The Committee proposed an array of recommendations to amend the NCAA's bylaws, including proposed Bylaw 11.6.4 that would limit Division I basketball coaching staffs to four members — one head coach, two assistant coaches, and one entry-level coach called a "restricted-earnings coach." The restricted-earnings coach category was created to replace the positions of part-time assistant, graduate assistant, and volunteer coach. The Committee believed that doing so would resolve the inequity that existed between those schools with graduate programs that could hire graduate assistant coaches and those who could not while reducing the overall amount spent on coaching salaries.

A second proposed rule, Bylaw 11.02.3, restricted compensation of restricted-earnings coaches in all Division I sports other than football to a total of $12,000 for the academic year and $4,000 for the summer months (the "REC Rule" for restricted-earnings coaches).[4] The Committee determined that the $16,000 per

---

[4] Bylaw 11.02.3 provided:

> Restricted-Earnings Coach. A restricted-earnings coach is any coach who is designated by the institution's athletics department to perform coaching duties and who serves in that capacity on a volunteer or paid basis with the following limitations on earnings derived from the member institution:

year total figure approximated the cost of out-of-state tuition for graduate schools at public institutions and the average graduate school tuition at private institutions, and was thus roughly equivalent to the salaries previously paid to part-time graduate assistant coaches. The REC Rule did allow restricted-earnings coaches to receive additional compensation for performing duties for another department of the institution provided that (1) such compensation is commensurate with that received by others performing the same or similar assignments, (2) the ratio of compensation received for coaching duties and any other duties is directly proportional to the amount of time devoted to the two areas of assignment, and (3) the individual is qualified for and actually performs the duties outside the athletic department for which the individual is compensated. The REC Rule did not prevent member institutions from using savings gained by reducing the number and salary of basketball coaches to increase expenditures on other aspects of their athletic programs.

Supporting adoption of the REC Rule, the Committee stated:

> The largest expense item in the athletics budget is personnel. Currently, only football and basketball have limits on the number of coaches who may be employed, and the existing categorical designations of part-time graduate student and volunteer coach have not been effective in

---

(a) During the academic year, a restricted-earnings coach may receive compensation or remuneration from the institution's athletics department that is not in excess of either $12,000 or the actual cost of educational expenses incurred as a graduate student.

(b) During the summer, a restricted-earnings coach may receive compensation or remuneration (total remuneration shall not exceed $4,000) from:

(1) The institution's athletics department or any organization funded in whole or in part by the athletics department or that is involved primarily in the promotion of the institution's athletics program (*e.g.*, booster club, athletics foundation association);

(2) The institution's camp or clinic;

(3) Camps or clinics owned or operated by institutional employees; or

(4) Another member institution's summer camp.

(c) During the summer or the academic year, the restricted-earnings coach may receive compensation for performing duties for another department or office of the institution, provided:

(1) The compensation received for those duties outside the athletic department is commensurate with that received by others performing those same or similar assignments;

(2) The ratio of compensation received for coaching duties and any other duties is directly proportionate to the amount of time devoted to the two areas of assignment; and

(3) The individual is qualified for and is performing the duties outside the athletic department for which the individual is compensated.

(d) Compensation for employment from a source outside the institution during the academic year or from sources other than those specified under 11.02.3-(b) and 11.02.3-(c) above during the summer shall be excluded from the individual's limit on remuneration.

> reducing the number of full-time paid employees associated with the sport. In addition, the committee recognizes the recent proliferation of part-time personnel associated with many Division I sports.
>
> Proposed limitations reflect an effort to (1) reduce the number of coaches associated with each sport by at least one full-time-equivalent position; (2) establish an "unrestricted" head or assistant coach category that will accommodate any type of volunteer, paid, full-time or part-time coach; and (3) establish a "restricted earnings" category that will encourage the development of new coaches while more effectively limiting compensation to such coaches.

"Report of the NCAA Special Committee on Cost Reduction," Part Two, ¶ 1.

The NCAA adopted the proposed rules, including the REC Rule, by majority vote in January of 1991, and the rules became effective on August 1, 1992. The rules bind all Division I members of the NCAA that employ basketball coaches. The schools normally compete with each other in the labor market for coaching services.

In this case, plaintiffs-appellees were restricted-earnings men's basketball coaches at NCAA Division I institutions in the academic year 1992-93. They challenged the REC Rule's limitation on compensation under section 1 of the Sherman Antitrust Act, 15 U.S.C. § 1 (1990), as an unlawful "contract, combination . . . or conspiracy, in restraint of trade." They did not challenge other rules promulgated by the NCAA, including the restriction on the number of coaches. The district court exercised jurisdiction pursuant to 28 U.S.C. § 1337 (1993) and 15 U.S.C. §§ 15 and 26 (1982).

The district court addressed the issue of liability before addressing issues of class certification and damages. Ruling on cross-motions for summary judgment, the court found the NCAA liable for violating section 1. Following the ruling, an administrative committee of the NCAA rescinded the compensation limits. However, the rescission was subject to ratification by NCAA members at their January 1996 meeting, and the appellate record does not reflect that such ratification ever occurred. Prior to the meeting, a new rule was proposed that would have eliminated the restricted-earnings coach position and replaced it with a position having similar compensation restrictions. On January 5, 1996, the district court, pursuant to 15 U.S.C. § 26, permanently enjoined the NCAA from enforcing or attempting to enforce any restricted earnings coach salary limitations against the named plaintiffs, and it further enjoined the NCAA from "reenacting the compensation limitations embodied in [the REC Rule]." The NCAA appeals the permanent injunction.

Rule of Reason Analysis

Section 1 of the Sherman Act provides, "Every contract, combination in the form of trust or otherwise, or conspiracy, in restraint of trade or commerce among the several States, or with foreign nations, is hereby declared to be illegal." 15 U.S.C. § 1. Because nearly every contract that binds the parties to an agreed course of conduct "is a restraint of trade" of some sort, the Supreme Court has limited the restrictions contained in section 1 to bar only "unreasonable restraints of trade." *NCAA v. Board of Regents*, 468 U.S. 85, 98 (1984); *see also Standard Oil Co. v. United States*, 221 U.S. 1, 52-60 (1911). To prevail on a section 1 claim under the Sherman Act, the coaches needed to prove that the NCAA (1) participated in an agreement that (2) unreasonably restrained trade in the relevant market. The NCAA does not dispute that the REC Rule resulted from an agreement among its members. However, the NCAA does contest the district court's finding that on the record before it, there was no genuine dispute of fact that the REC Rule is an unreasonable restraint of trade.

Two analytical approaches are used to determine whether a defendant's conduct unreasonably restrains trade: the *per se* rule and the rule of reason. The per se rule condemns practices that "are entirely void of redeeming competitive rationales." Once a practice is identified as illegal *per se*, a court need not examine the practice's impact on the market or the procompetitive justifications for the practice advanced by a defendant before finding a violation of antitrust law. Rule of reason analysis, on the other hand, requires an analysis of the restraint's effect on competition. *See National Soc'y of Prof'l Engineers v. United States*, 435 U.S. 679, 695 (1978). A rule of reason analysis first requires a determination of whether the challenged restraint has a substantially adverse effect on competition. The inquiry then shifts to an evaluation of whether the procompetitive virtues of the alleged wrongful conduct justifies the otherwise anticompetitive impacts. The district court applied the rule of reason standard to its analysis of the REC Rule.

Horizontal price-fixing is normally a practice condemned as illegal *per se*. By agreeing to limit the price which NCAA members may pay for the services of restricted-earnings coaches, the REC Rule fixes the cost of one of the component items used by NCAA members to produce the product of Division I basketball. As a result, the REC Rule constitutes the type of naked horizontal agreement among competitive purchasers to fix prices usually found to be illegal *per se*. *See, e.g., Mandeville Island Farms, Inc. v. American Crystal Sugar Co.*, 334 U.S. 219, 235 (1948) (complaint alleging conspiracy among sugar refiners to purchase sugar-beets at agreed-upon prices sufficient to survive a motion for dismissal because the challenged conduct is precisely the type of activity condemned by section 1 of the Sherman Act); *National Macaroni Mfrs. Ass'n v. FTC*, 345 F.2d 421, 426-27 (7th Cir. 1965) (agreement among macaroni producers to limit amount of premium priced durum wheat purchased and to substitute specified percentage of inferior wheat in finished macaroni *per se* illegal because effect of restriction was effectively to reduce price of durum wheat that had risen as a result of a recent shortage).

However, the Supreme Court recognized in *Broadcast Music, Inc. v. Columbia Broadcasting Sys., Inc.*, 441 U.S. 1, 23 (1979), that certain products require horizontal restraints, including horizontal price-fixing, in order to exist at all.

Faced with such a product — the ASCAP blanket music license which could not exist absent an agreement among artists to sell their rights at uniform prices — the Court held that a rule of reason analysis should be applied to the restraint. *Id.* at 24.

Subsequently, the Supreme Court in *NCAA v. Board of Regents* departed from the general treatment given to horizontal price-fixing agreements by refusing to apply a per se rule and instead adopting a rule of reason approach in reviewing an NCAA plan for televising college football that involved both limits on output and price-fixing. *See* 468 U.S. at 99-103. The Court explained:

> Horizontal price fixing and output limitation are ordinarily condemned as a matter of law under an "illegal *per se*" approach because the probability that these practices are anticompetitive is so high; a *per se* rule is applied "when the practice facially appears to be one that would always or almost always tend to restrict competition and decrease output." In such circumstances a restraint is presumed unreasonable without inquiry into the particular market context in which it is found.
>
> Nevertheless, we have decided that it would be inappropriate to apply a *per se* rule to this case. This decision is not based on a lack of judicial experience with this type of arrangement, on the fact that the NCAA is organized as a nonprofit entity, or on our respect for the NCAA's historic role in the preservation and encouragement of intercollegiate amateur athletics. *Rather, what is critical is that this case involves an industry in which horizontal restraints on competition are essential if the product is to be available at all.*

468 U.S. at 100-01 (quoting *Broadcast Music*, 441 U.S. at 19-20) (footnotes omitted and emphasis added).

The "product" made available by the NCAA in this case is college basketball; the horizontal restraints necessary for the product to exist include rules such as those forbidding payments to athletes and those requiring that athletes attend class, etc. *See* 468 U.S. at 101-02 (what a sports league and its members "market . . . is competition itself. . . . Of course, this would be completely ineffective if there were no rules . . . to create and define the competition to be marketed."). Because some horizontal restraints serve the procompetitive purpose of making college sports available, the Supreme Court subjected even the price and output restrictions at issue in *Board of Regents* to a rule of reason analysis. *See id.* at 103; *see also Hairston v. Pacific 10 Conference*, 101 F.3d 1315, 1318-19 (9th Cir. 1996) (employing rule of reason analysis and finding that imposing sanctions for violations of NCAA rules did not violate section 1 of the Sherman Act); *Banks v. NCAA*, 977 F.2d 1081, 1088-94 (7th Cir. 1992) (upholding nodraft and no-agent eligibility rules for student athletes under rule of reason analysis); *Justice v. NCAA*, 577 F. Supp. 356, 379-82 (D. Ariz. 1983) (NCAA sanctions against member institution imposed for violations of NCAA rule barring compensation of student athletes did not violate antitrust laws under rule of reason analysis).

Plaintiff coaches cite the Supreme Court's refusal to create exceptions to the per se treatment of price-fixing schemes in cases such as *Superior Court Trial Lawyers and Arizona v. Maricopa County Medical Soc'y*, 457 U.S. 332, 342 (1982), and urge us to apply a *per se* analysis to the NCAA rule at issue in this case. Since neither case dealt with a "product" such as college sports that requires horizontal restraints to exist, the cases are not persuasive here in light of the Supreme Court's analysis of NCAA price-fixing under a rule of reason in *Board of Regents*.

The coaches also argue that *Board of Regents* is distinguishable because the agreement in that case went to marketing the product itself — college sports — and because that agreement was closer to a joint venture because it involved a "joint selling arrangement." By contrast, they contend (1) that the hiring of coaches involves the market for coaching services, an input, rather than college sports, the output, and (2) that the price-fixing at issue in this case does not involve "joint buying" because each school independently hires its own coaches. The second point does not distinguish this case from *Board of Regents*. In *Board of Regents*, like the present case, each school negotiated individually with television networks within the constraints of price agreements. *See* 468 U.S. at 93. The first point is similarly unpersuasive. *Board of Regents* does not turn on whether the agreement in question is based on input components or output products. Rather, *Board of Regents* more generally concluded that because horizontal agreements are necessary for sports competition, all horizontal agreements among NCAA members, even those as egregious as price-fixing, should be subject to a rule of reason analysis. *See* 468 U.S. at 101-03.

Finally, the Supreme Court has made it clear that the per se rule is a "demanding" standard that should be applied only in clear cut cases. As a result, courts consistently have analyzed challenged conduct under the rule of reason when dealing with an industry in which some horizontal restraints are necessary for the availability of a product, even if such restraints involve horizontal price-fixing agreements. Thus, we apply the rule of reason approach in this case.

Courts have imposed a consistent structure on rule of reason analysis by casting it in terms of shifting burdens of proof. Under this approach, the plaintiff bears the initial burden of showing that an agreement had a substantially adverse effect on competition. If the plaintiff meets this burden, the burden shifts to the defendant to come forward with evidence of the procompetitive virtues of the alleged wrongful conduct. If the defendant is able to demonstrate procompetitive effects, the plaintiff then must prove that the challenged conduct is not reasonably necessary to achieve the legitimate objectives or that those objectives can be achieved in a substantially less restrictive manner. Ultimately, if these steps are met, the harms and benefits must be weighed against each other in order to judge whether the challenged behavior is, on balance, reasonable.

A. Anticompetitive Effect

We first review whether the coaches in this case demonstrated anticompetitive effect so conclusively that summary judgment on the issue was appropriate.

A plaintiff may establish anticompetitive effect indirectly by proving that the defendant possessed the requisite market power within a defined market or directly by showing actual anticompetitive effects, such as control over output or price. A naked, effective restraint on market price or volume can establish anticompetitive effect under a truncated rule of reason analysis.

The NCAA argues that the district court erred by failing to define the relevant market and by failing to find that the NCAA possesses power in that market. The NCAA urges that the relevant market in this case is the entire market for men's basketball coaching services, and it presented evidence demonstrating that positions as restricted-earnings basketball coaches make up, at most, 8% of that market. Thus, the NCAA argues it has at least created a genuine issue of material fact about whether it possesses market power and that summary judgment was therefore inappropriate.

The NCAA misapprehends the purpose in antitrust law of market definition, which is not an end unto itself but rather exists to illuminate a practice's effect on competition. In *Board of Regents*, the Court rejected a nearly identical argument from the NCAA that a plan to sell television rights could not be condemned under the antitrust laws absent proof that the NCAA had power in the market for television programming. *See* 468 U.S. at 109. "As a matter of law, the absence of proof of market power does not justify a naked restriction on price or output. To the contrary, when there is an agreement not to compete in terms of price or output, 'no elaborate industry analysis is required to demonstrate the anticompetitive character of such an agreement.'" *Id.* (quoting *National Soc'y of Prof'l Engineers,* 435 U.S. at 692). No "proof of market power" is required where the very purpose and effect of a horizontal agreement is to fix prices so as to make them unresponsive to a competitive marketplace. *See* 468 U.S. at 110. Thus, where a practice has obvious anticompetitive effects — as does price-fixing — there is no need to prove that the defendant possesses market power. Rather, the court is justified in proceeding directly to the question of whether the procompetitive justifications advanced for the restraint outweigh the anticompetitive effects under a "quick look" rule of reason.

We find it appropriate to adopt such a quick look rule of reason in this case. Under a quick look rule of reason analysis, anticompetitive effect is established, even without a determination of the relevant market, where the plaintiff shows that a horizontal agreement to fix prices exists, that the agreement is effective, and that the price set by such an agreement is more favorable to the defendant than otherwise would have resulted from the operation of market forces. Under this standard, the undisputed evidence supports a finding of anticompetitive effect. The NCAA adopted the REC Rule to reduce the high cost of part-time coaches' salaries, over $60,000 annually in some cases, by limiting compensation to entry-level coaches to $16,000 per year. The NCAA does not dispute that the cost-reduction has effectively reduced restricted-earnings coaches' salaries. Because the REC Rule was successful in artificially lowering the price of coaching services, no further evidence or analysis is required to find market power to set prices. Thus, in the case at bar, the district court did not need to resolve issues of fact pertaining to the definition of the relevant market in order to support its decision on summary judgment that the REC Rule is a naked price restraint.

The NCAA contends that the district court misapplied *Board of Regents*, a case in which the Court had before it detailed factual findings that resulted from a trial. The NCAA is right about the procedural posture of *Board of Regents*, but wrong about its significance. In *Board of Regents* the Supreme Court relied on the district court's findings that the television plan in fact resulted in horizontal price restraints. Because the REC Rule is a horizontal price restraint on its face, similar factual findings are not required in this case. Further, although in *Board of Regents* the Court found that the parties had proven factually that the NCAA had market power in the defined market of college football, the Court said that as a matter of law it did not need to analyze market power because horizontal price restraints are so obviously anticompetitive.

Finally, the NCAA cites *Hennessey v. NCAA*, 564 F.2d 1136 (5th Cir. 1977) (per curiam). In *Hennessey*, assistant football and basketball coaches challenged a NCAA bylaw limiting the number of assistant coaches member institutions could employ at any one time. *See id.* at 1141-42. The Fifth Circuit upheld the rule, concluding that the plaintiff failed to show that the rule was an unreasonable restraint of trade after weighing the anticompetitive effects with the procompetitive benefits of the restriction. *See id.* at 1153-54.

Hennessey is not controlling for a variety of reasons. First, the REC Rule is distinguishable from the agreement at issue in *Hennessey*. *Hennessey* addresses a restriction on the number of assistant coaches that a Division I school could employ whereas the REC Rule limits salary of a certain category of coaches. Therefore, the analysis of the reasonableness of the restraint in *Hennessey*, which did not involve a naked restriction on price, will not control the analysis of the reasonableness of the REC Rule.

Second, the *Hennessey* court placed the burden of showing the unreasonableness of the coaching restriction in that case on the plaintiff and then found that the plaintiff could not make such a showing because the rule had only recently been implemented. In our analysis, the plaintiff only has the burden of establishing the anticompetitive effect of the restraint at issue. Once the plaintiff meets that burden, which the coaches have done in this case by showing the naked and effective price-fixing character of the agreement, the burden shifts to the defendant to justify the restraint as a "reasonable" one. *See* I ABA Section of Antitrust Law, *supra*, at 66 (citing cases). It is on this step that the defendant NCAA stumbles. Thus, we disagree with the Fifth Circuit's allocation of the burden of proof in *Hennessey*, and we note that this shift in the burden of proof could explain the difference in outcome between our case and *Hennessey*.

Third, *Hennessey* predates the Supreme Court's opinion in *Board of Regents*. The Fifth Circuit very well may have reached a different result in *Hennessey* if it had the benefit of that precedent, because *Board of Regents* suggests a less deferential approach to the NCAA than the approach taken in *Hennessey*. Finally, of course, *Hennessey* is not Tenth Circuit precedent, and accordingly is not binding authority on us.

B. Procompetitive Rationales

Under a rule of reason analysis, an agreement to restrain trade may still survive scrutiny under section 1 if the procompetitive benefits of the restraint justify the anticompetitive effects. Justifications offered under the rule of reason may be considered only to the extent that they tend to show that, on balance, "the challenged restraint enhances competition."

In *Board of Regents* the Supreme Court recognized that certain horizontal restraints, such as the conditions of the contest and the eligibility of participants, are justifiable under the antitrust laws because they are necessary to create the product of competitive college sports. Thus, the only legitimate rationales that we will recognize in support of the REC Rule are those necessary to produce competitive intercollegiate sports. The NCAA advanced three justifications for the salary limits: retaining entry-level coaching positions; reducing costs; and maintaining competitive equity. We address each of them in turn.

1. Retention of Entry-Level Positions

The NCAA argues that the plan serves the procompetitive goal of retaining an entry-level coaching position. The NCAA asserts that the plan will allow younger, less experienced coaches entry into Division I coaching positions. While opening up coaching positions for younger people may have social value apart from its affect on competition, we may not consider such values unless they impact upon competition. *See Superior Court Trial Lawyers*, 493 U.S. at 423-24 (rejecting argument by trial lawyers that boycott of court-appointed work was justified to promote the social value of increasing the quality of representation); *FTC v. Indiana Fed'n of Dentists*, 476 U.S. 447 (1986) (refusing to consider ethical policy of insuring proper dental care as a valid procompetitive end); *Board of Regents*, 468 U.S. at 117 (rejecting justifications offered to support a challenged restraint that do not promote competition as "inconsistent with the basic policy of the Sherman Act"); *National Soc'y of Prof'l Engineers*, 435 U.S. at 695-96 (holding that policy goals such as protecting public safety and promoting ethical behavior do not qualify as legitimate procompetitive objectives unless they serve to "regulate and promote" competition); *see also* Areeda, *supra*, P 1504, at 381 (courts should "not inquire whether the restraint promotes the 'public interest' but only whether it increases competition.").[14]

---

14 Similarly, the NCAA cannot be heard to argue that the REC Rule fosters the amateurism that serves as the hallmark of NCAA competition. While courts should afford the NCAA plenty of room under the antitrust laws to preserve the amateur character of intercollegiate athletics, *see Banks*, 977 F.2d at 1089-93, courts have only legitimized rules designed to ensure the amateur status of student athletes, not coaches.

The NCAA also contends that limiting one of the four available coaching positions on a Division I basketball team to an entry level position will create more balanced competition by barring some teams from hiring four experienced coaches instead of three. However, the REC Rule contained no restrictions other than salary designed to insure that the position would be filled by entry-level applicants; it could be filled with experienced applicants. In addition, under the REC Rule, schools can still pay restricted-earnings coaches more than $16,000 per year by hiring them for physical education or other teaching positions. In fact, the evidence in the record tends to demonstrate that at least some schools designated persons with many years of experience as the restricted-earnings coach. The NCAA did not present any evidence showing that restricted-earnings positions have been filled by entry-level applicants or that the rules will be effective over time in accomplishing this goal. Nothing in the record suggests that the salary limits for restricted-earnings coaches will be effective at creating entry-level positions. Thus, the NCAA failed to present a triable issue of fact as to whether preserving entry-level positions served a legitimate procompetitive end of balancing competition.

2. Cost Reduction

The NCAA next advances the justification that the plan will cut costs. However, cost-cutting by itself is not a valid procompetitive justification. If it were, any group of competing buyers could agree on maximum prices. Lower prices cannot justify a cartel's control of prices charged by suppliers, because the cartel ultimately robs the suppliers of the normal fruits of their enterprises. Further, setting maximum prices reduces the incentive among suppliers to improve their products. Likewise, in our case, coaches have less incentive to improve their performance if their salaries are capped. As the Supreme Court reiterated in *Superior Court Trial Lawyers*, 493 U.S. at 423, "the Sherman Act reflects a legislative judgment that ultimately competition will produce not only lower prices, but also better goods and services. . . . This judgment recognizes that all elements of a bargain — quality, service, safety, and durability — and not just the immediate cost, are favorably affected by the free opportunity to select among alternative offers." (Internal quotations omitted.)

The NCAA adopted the REC Rule because without it competition would lead to higher prices. The REC Rule was proposed as a way to prevent Division I schools from engaging in behavior the association termed "keeping up with the Joneses," *i.e.*, competing. However, the NCAA cannot argue that competition for coaches is an evil because the Sherman Act "precludes inquiry into the question whether competition is good or bad." *National Soc'y of Prof'l Engineers*, 435 U.S. at 695.

While increasing output, creating operating efficiencies, making a new product available, enhancing product or service quality, and widening consumer choice have been accepted by courts as justifications for otherwise anticompetitive agreements, mere profitability or cost savings have not qualified as a defense under the antitrust laws. *See* I ABA Section of Antitrust Law, *supra*, at

66-67 (citing cases). The NCAA's cost containment justification is illegitimate because the NCAA:

> Improperly assumes that antitrust law should not apply to condemn the creation of market power in an input market. The exercise of market power by a group of buyers virtually always results in lower costs to the buyers — a consequence which arguably is beneficial to the members of the industry and ultimately their consumers. If holding down costs by the exercise of market power over suppliers, rather than just by increased efficiency, is a procompetitive effect justifying joint conduct, then section 1 can never apply to input markets or buyer cartels. That is not and cannot be the law. Reducing costs for member institutions, without more, does not justify the anticompetitive effects of the REC Rule.

The NCAA argues that reducing costs can be considered a procompetitive justification because doing so is necessary to maintain the existence of competitive intercollegiate sports. Emphasizing the deficits many college sports programs faced prior to the adoption of the REC Rule, the NCAA quotes with approval language from the opinion in *Hennessey* to support its claim that reducing costs serves as a procompetitive benefit:

> Colleges with more successful programs, both competitively and economically, were seen as taking advantage of their success by expanding their programs, to the ultimate detriment of the whole system of intercollegiate athletics. Financial pressures upon many members, not merely to "catch up," but to "keep up," were beginning to threaten both the competitive, and the amateur, nature of the programs, leading quite possibly to abandonment by many. "Minor" and "minority" sports were viewed as imperiled by concentration upon the "money makers," such as varsity football and basketball.
>
> Bylaw 12-1 [the rule at issue in *Hennessey*] was, with other rules adopted at the same time, intended to be an "economy measure." In this sense it was both in design and effect one having commercial impact. But the fundamental objective in mind was to preserve and foster competition in intercollegiate athletics — by curtailing, as it were, potentially monopolistic practices by the more powerful — and to reorient the programs into their traditional role as amateur sports operating as part of the educational process.

564 F.2d at 1153.

We are dubious that the goal of cost reductions can serve as a legally sufficient justification for a buyers' agreement to fix prices even if such cost reductions are necessary to save inefficient or unsuccessful competitors from failure. Nevertheless, we need not consider whether cost reductions may have been required to "save" intercollegiate athletics and whether such an objective served as a legitimate procompetitive end because the NCAA presents no evidence that limits on restricted-earning coaches' salaries would be successful in reducing deficits, let alone that such reductions were necessary to save college basketball. Moreover, the REC Rule does not equalize the overall amount of money Division I schools are permitted to spend on their basketball programs. There is no reason to think that the money saved by a school on the salary of a restricted-earnings coach will not be put into another aspect of the school's basketball program, such as equipment or even another coach's salary, thereby increasing inequity in that area. *Accord Board of Regents*, 468 U.S. at 118-19 (rejecting NCAA's argument that television rights plan would increase competitive equity among NCAA teams where the plan did not "regulate the amount of money that any college may spend on its football program").

3. Maintaining Competitiveness

We note that the NCAA must be able to ensure some competitive equity between member institutions in order to produce a marketable product: a "team must try to establish itself as a winner, but it must not win so often and so convincingly that the outcome will never be in doubt, or else there will be no marketable 'competition.'" Michael Jay Kaplan, Annotation, *Application of Federal Antitrust Laws to Professional Sports*, 18 A.L.R. FED. 489 § 2(a) (1974). The NCAA asserts that the REC Rule will help to maintain competitive equity by preventing wealthier schools from placing a more experienced, higher-priced coach in the position of restricted-earnings coach. The NCAA again cites Hennessey to support its position, and again we find *Hennessey* to be unpersuasive for the reasons previously articulated.

While the REC Rule will equalize the salaries paid to entry-level coaches in Division I schools, it is not clear that the REC Rule will equalize the experience level of such coaches.[15] Nowhere does the NCAA prove that the salary restrictions enhance competition, level an uneven playing field, or reduce coaching inequities. Rather, the NCAA only presented evidence that the cost reductions would be achieved in such a way so as to maintain without "significantly altering," "adversely affecting," or "disturbing" the existing competitive balance. The undisputed record reveals that the REC Rule is nothing more than a cost-cutting measure and shows that the only consideration the NCAA gave to competitive balance was simply to structure the rule so as not to exacerbate competitive imbalance. Thus, on its face, the REC Rule is not directed towards competitive balance nor is the nexus between the rule and a compelling need to maintain competitive balance sufficiently clear on this record to withstand a motion for summary judgment.

---

[15] For example, some more experienced coaches may take restricted-earnings coach positions with programs such as those at Duke or North Carolina, despite the lower salary, because of the national prominence of those programs. In fact, absent the REC Rule, the market might produce greater equity in coaching talent, because a school with a less-prominent basketball program might be able to entice a more-experienced coach away from a prominent program by offering a higher salary.

4. Wait and See

In the alternative, the NCAA argues that even if evidence of the procompetitive benefits of the REC Rule are not forthcoming at the moment, we should follow the advice of the court in *Hennessey* and adopt a "wait and see" approach to give the rule time to succeed. *See* 564 F.2d at 1153-54 (refusing to place the burden on the NCAA to prove that the procompetitive benefits of the challenged restraint in that case outweighed its negative effects because doing so would "foreclose . . . any opportunity to build up experience on which the issue ultimately could be judged"). However, we believe that the court in Hennessey erred as a matter of law to the extent that the court tried to free the NCAA as the defendant from its burden of showing that the procompetitive justifications for a restraint on trade outweigh its anticompetitive effects. The Supreme Court in *Board of Regents* made it clear that the NCAA still shoulders that burden, and we hold that the NCAA failed to provide sufficient evidence to carry its burden in this case.

IV. Conclusion

For the reasons discussed above, we AFFIRM the district court's order granting a permanent injunction barring the NCAA from reenacting compensation limits such as those contained in the REC Rule based on its order granting summary judgment to the plaintiffs on the issue of antitrust liability.

WORLDWIDE BASKETBALL AND SPORT TOURS, INC. v. NATIONAL COLLEGIATE ATHLETIC ASSOCIATION

388 F.3d 955 (6th Cir. 2004), *cert. denied*, 126 S. Ct. 334 (2005)

ALICE M. BATCHELDER, Circuit Judge.

The National Collegiate Athletic Association, (the "NCAA"), appeals the district court's order declaring that the NCAA's "Two in Four Rule" violates Section I of the Sherman Antitrust Act, 15 U.S.C. § 1, and permanently enjoining the enforcement of that rule. Because we conclude that the district court erred in applying an abbreviated or "quick-look" analysis and in its definition of the market for purposes of antitrust analysis, and because the record does not contain evidence to support a proper market definition, we REVERSE the judgment of the district court.

I.

. . . Of concern in this case is a portion of the NCAA Division I men's basketball regulations, specifically because of a restriction on the type and number of games individual schools are permitted to play.

Men's Division I basketball is divided into conferences; within each conference the member schools individually play each other. Each school, however, makes its own schedule and may seek several non-conference games. The NCAA sets the maximum number of games that each team may play per year. Throughout the year, there are various tournaments in which a school's team may participate, some of which are "certified" and some of which are not. Certified tournament events are multiple-game early season tournaments. These events were originally introduced as a means of encouraging scheduled games with schools in Alaska and Hawaii that traditionally had difficulty scheduling games because of their inconvenient locations. In recent years, the NCAA has become concerned that the more "powerful" basketball schools (i.e., members of the "Big Six" conferences) were disproportionately taking advantage of the certified events. To address this concern, the NCAA adopted Proposal 98- 92 ("98-92"), which increases to 28 the number of allowed games per season for each team, provides that a team's participation in a certified event, regardless of how many games the team actually plays as part of that event, counts as one game toward the NCAA regular season maximum, and permits each team to participate in "not more than one certified basketball event in one academic year, and not more than two certified basketball events every four years." As stated in the text of 98-92, the rationale of the rule is to:

> address competitive equity concerns by giving many Division I institutions an opportunity to compete in certified events, particularly those outside the continental United States, so that the inherent recruiting and competitive advantages are distributed equally among Division I institutions. This proposal will provide Division I men's and women's basketball programs greater flexibility in the scheduling of basketball contests. It will permit institutions the opportunity to participate in certified contests in accordance with the legislation or to add additional contests to the institution's regular-season schedules during those years in which the institution either is not permitted to engage in a certified contest or chooses not to participate in such an event.

The plaintiffs in this case are promoters of outside certified tournament events (the "Promoters"). They allege that the NCAA is less concerned with the disproportionate advantage to the Big Six Conferences than it is with the monies that the outside promoters of certified events are able to make in connection with these events. The Promoters contend that the Two in Four Rule, the prong of 98-92 that limits teams to two certified events every four years, was adopted purely to deny outside promoters the opportunity to make money from the certified events.

Complaining that the application of this rule limited their ability to schedule events with schools having the most powerful and famous basketball programs, which in turn hampered their ability to sell tickets and make broadcast contracts, the Promoters initiated this suit on December 21, 2000, alleging that the Two in Four rule is a violation of the Sherman Antitrust Act. On August 6, 2001, they filed a motion for preliminary injunction under § 16 of the Clayton Act; that motion was then consolidated with a motion for permanent injunction.

The district court issued an Opinion and Order on July 19, 2002, holding that because the rule had not been in effect long enough to permit its effect to be accurately evaluated, the motion for preliminary injunction was denied and the motion for permanent injunction would be held in abeyance. The plaintiffs renewed their request for a permanent injunction on February 29, 2003, asserting that there was by then enough evidence to justify the injunction. The district court granted the permanent injunction on July 28, 2003. *Worldwide Basketball and Sports Tours, Inc. v. NCAA*, 273 F. Supp. 2d 933, 954-55 (S.D. Ohio 2003). The NCAA timely appealed, and because of the nature of the injunction, the NCAA sought and obtained from this court a stay and order for expedited appeal.

II.

* * *

Section One of the Sherman Act provides that:

> Every contract, combination in the form of trust or otherwise, or conspiracy, in restraint of trade or commerce among the several States, or with foreign nations, is declared to be illegal. Every person who shall make any contract or engage in any combination or conspiracy hereby declared to be illegal shall be deemed guilty of a felony, and, on conviction thereof, shall be punished by fine not exceeding $ 10,000,000 if a corporation, or, if any other person, $ 350,000, or by imprisonment not exceeding three years, or by both said punishments, in the discretion of the court.

15 U.S.C. § 1. By its plain language, this section applies to the Two in Four rule only if the rule is commercial in nature. The NCAA maintains that the rule is academically directed and motivated and its commercial impact is negligible. The Promoters and the district court, on the other hand, assume that the Two in Four rule involves a "restraint of trade or commerce." *Id.*

The dispositive inquiry in this regard is whether the rule itself is commercial, not whether the entity promulgating the rule is commercial. . . . At least some NCAA rules have been held to be commercial and hence subject to antitrust scrutiny. *See National Collegiate Athletic Ass'n v. Board of Regents*, 468 U.S. 85, 98, 82 L. Ed. 2d 70, 104 S. Ct. 2948 (1984) ("*Bd. of Regents*") (finding NCAA rules limiting live broadcasting of college football games subject to scrutiny under Sherman Act). One of our sister circuits has held that NCAA rules governing eligibility for participating in collegiate sports are not commercial, *see Smith v. NCAA*, 139 F.3d 180, 184-85 (3rd Cir. 1998), *vacated on other grounds by NCAA v. Smith*, 525 U.S. 459, 142 L. Ed. 2d 929, 119 S. Ct. 924 (1999), but this circuit has not yet addressed the commercial or non-commercial nature of particular NCAA rules.

We think it apparent that the Two in Four rule has some commercial impact insofar as it regulates games that constitute sources of revenue for both the member schools and the Promoters. We therefore assume that the district court's implicit finding that the Two in Four rule is commercial is supported by the evidence and we proceed on that basis.

In order to establish their claim under Section 1 of the Sherman Act, the Promoters must prove that the NCAA "(1) participated in an agreement that (2) unreasonably restrained trade in the relevant market." *Nat'l Hockey League Players' Assoc. v. Plymouth Whalers Hockey Club*, 325 F.3d 712, 718 (6th Cir. 2003). The NCAA does not dispute the Promoters' claim that the Two in Four Rule represents an agreement in which the NCAA participated. The NCAA vigorously contests the district court's conclusion that the Two in Four agreement unreasonably restrains trade in the relevant market.

A.

. . . It is well-established that cases involving industries "in which horizontal restraints on competition are essential if the product is to be available at all" should be analyzed using the rule of reason. . . .

Under the rule of reason analysis, the plaintiff bears the burden of establishing that the conduct complained of "produces significant anticompetitive effects within the relevant product and geographic markets." *Nat'l Hockey League*, 325 F.3d at 718. If the plaintiff is able to meet that burden, the defendant must provide evidence to establish that the restraint complained of has procompetitive effects sufficient to justify the injury resulting from the anticompetitive effects of the restraint. *Id.* The plaintiff is then left to prove that the legitimate procompetitive objectives can be achieved in a substantially less restrictive manner. *Id.* . . .

When applying the rule of reason, the courts have occasionally applied what has come to be called an abbreviated or "quick-look" analysis. Accordingly, in analyzing a restriction on the number of NCAA football games which could be televised in *Bd. of Regents*, the Supreme Court held that a "naked restraint on price and output requires some competitive justification even in the absence of a detailed market analysis." *Bd. of Regents*, 468 U.S. at 110. Similarly, in *FTC v. Indiana Fed'n of Dentists*, 476 U.S. 447, 90 L. Ed. 2d 445, 106 S. Ct. 2009 (1986), the Court found that "no elaborate industry analysis is required to demonstrate the anticompetitive character" of a horizontal agreement among dentists to withhold X-Rays from insurers for use in benefit determinations. *Id.* at 459 (quoting *National Soc. of Professional Engineers v. United States*, 435 U.S. 679, 692, 55 L. Ed. 2d 637, 98 S. Ct. 1355 (1978)). Recently, in *California Dental Assoc. v. FTC*, 526 U.S. 756, 143 L. Ed. 2d 935, 119 S. Ct. 1604 (1999), the Supreme Court granted certiorari to address when abbreviated or quick-look rule of reason is appropriate. *Id.* at 764-65. The Court reasoned that:

> there is generally no categorical line to be drawn between restraints that give rise to an intuitively obvious inference of anticompetitive effect and those that call for more detailed treatment. What is required, rather, is an enquiry meet for the case, looking to the circumstances, details, and

> logic of a restraint. The object is to see whether the experience of the market has been so clear, or necessarily will be, that a confident conclusion about the principal tendency of a restriction will follow from a quick (or at least quicker) look, in place of a more sedulous one.

Id. at 780-81. In analyzing cases such as *Bd of Regents, Indiana Fed'n of Dentists, and Nat'l Soc. of Prof'l Eng'rs* in which an abbreviated or quick-look analysis was applied, the Court found that "in each of these cases . . . an observer with even a rudimentary understanding of economics could conclude that the arrangements in question would have an anticompetitive effect on customers and markets." *Id.* at 770. In its 2002 decision denying a preliminary injunction, the district court found application of the quick-look rule of reason inappropriate, stating that "the two in four rule simply does not have the 'obvious anticompetitive effects' as the rule at issue in *Board of Regents* [did,] so as to dispense with the full rule of reason analysis." In its 2003 decision granting a preliminary injunction, the court again suggested that it was applying the full rule of reason analysis. *See Worldwide Basketball & Sports Tours*, 273 F. Supp. 2d at 948. After accurately announcing the requirements of the full rule of reason, however, the district court stated that "if a Plaintiff can show that the restraint has actually produced significant anti-competitive effects, such as a reduction in output, a formal market analysis is unnecessary." *Id.* at 949-50. . . . This is, in fact, an able exposition of the quick-look standard. . . .

We believe that the district court was correct the first time: this is not a case which is suitable for quick-look analysis. Far from being a case in which "an observer with even a rudimentary understanding of economics could conclude that the arrangements in question would have an anticompetitive effect on *customers* and *markets*," *id.* (emphasis added), here the relevant market is not readily apparent and the Plaintiffs have failed to adequately define a relevant market, thereby making it impossible to assess the effect of 98-92 on customers rather than merely on competitors. While it is true that "the rule of reason can sometimes be applied in the twinkling of an eye," *Bd. of Regents*, 468 U.S. at 109 n.39 . . . this abbreviated or "quick-look" analysis may only be done where the contours of the market and, where relevant, submarket, are sufficiently well-known or defined to permit the court to ascertain without the aid of extensive market analysis whether the challenged practice impairs competition. Under the "quick-look" approach, extensive market and cross-elasticity analysis is not necessarily required, but where, as here, the precise product market is neither obvious nor undisputed, the failure to account for market alternatives and to analyze the dynamics of consumer choice simply will not suffice. The district court therefore erred in applying a quick-look analysis.

B.

"In considering what is the relevant market for determining the control of price and competition, no more definite rule can be declared than that commodities reasonably interchangeable by consumers for the same purposes make up that 'part of the trade or commerce', monopolization of which may be illegal."

United States v. E.I. du Pont De Nemours & Co., 351 U.S. 377, 395, 100 L. Ed. 1264, 76 S. Ct. 994 (1954). The "relevant market encompasses notions of geography as well as product use, quality, and description". . . Relying on du Pont, this court has found the "reasonable interchangeability" standard to be the essential test for ascertaining the relevant product market test. . . . Reasonable interchangeability "may be gauged by (1) the product uses, i.e., whether the substitute products or services can perform the same function, and/or (2) consumer response (cross-elasticity); that is, consumer sensitivity to price levels at which they elect substitutes for the defendant's product or service." *Id.* . . .

The Supreme Court has long recognized that within a product market, "well-defined submarkets may exist which, in themselves, constitute product markets for antitrust purposes.". . . . "The boundaries of such a submarket may be determined by examining such practical indicia as industry or public recognition of the submarket as a separate economic entity, the product's peculiar characteristics and uses, unique production facilities, distinct customers, distinct prices, sensitivity to price changes, and specialized vendors."

A submarket "merely provides several new factors, in addition to [the existing ones of selling price, uses, and physical characteristics, which the court may use in determining interchangeability between different products." . . . However, "a submarket analysis incorporates, but does not replace, the standard market test. It merely adds new factors to that test so as to more precisely define the market affected by the defendant's actions." The burden is on the antitrust plaintiff to define the relevant market within which the alleged anti-competitive effects of the defendant's actions occur. "Failure to identify a relevant market is a proper ground for dismissing a Sherman Act claim." . . .

The district court found the relevant market in this case to be Division I mens' college basketball, and noted that both the Promoters and the NCAA agreed with this definition of the relevant market. Although the NCAA does not appear to have disputed the Promoters' view that the relevant market is Division I Men's Basketball as a whole, the basis for that view is not developed in the record. Indeed, the district court had no factual circumstances to which it could apply the legal test, since the Promoters presented no evidence of "products or services that are either (1) identical to or (2) available substitutes for the defendant's product or service." Dr. Tollison, the Promoters' expert witness, admitted that he did not look at those in competition with the Promoters (their "competitors"), the competitors' output, or their output relative to the Promoters. And he did no test to determine which events are in competition with others. Finally, Dr. Tollison, when pressed, admitted that his testimony regarding the Big Six market was instead derived from "common sense."

Furthermore, the district court concedes that Dr. Tollison "did not perform a study on the effect of the Two in Four Rule on consumers of Division I mens' games. According to Tollison, the loss of games necessarily constitutes a loss to consumers in the relevant market because college basketball events are not fungible." However products need not be fungible to be market competitors for the purposes of antitrust analysis. The Supreme Court has repeatedly held that "it is improper 'to require that products be fungible to be considered in the relevant market.'" *United States v. Continental Can Co.*, 378 U.S. 441, 449, 12 L. Ed. 2d 953, 84 S. Ct. 1738 (1964) (quoting *E. I. du Pont De Nemours & Co.*, 351 U.S. at 394). Rather than fungibility, the proper analysis "is an appraisal of the 'cross-elasticity' of demand in the trade." *E. I. du Pont De Nemours & Co.*, 351 U.S. at 394. Indeed, Dr. Tollison admitted that a cross-elasticity study is necessary to determine the relevant market, yet he concedes that he failed to perform such an analysis. The district court, however, did not base its decision that the Two in Four Rule is anticompetitive simply on the Division I Mens' College Basketball market taken as a whole. Instead, the court held that "it is undisputed that the relevant market in this case is Division I mens' college basketball together with the appropriate submarket consisting of school-scheduled games," where school-scheduled games are defined as games that a team is not required to play but rather are selected by a school's scheduling coach.

Contrary to the district court's findings, however, the record suggests that the submarket is not undisputed.

Dr. Tollison did not testify that school-scheduled games are the relevant submarket, nor did he provide any basis for arriving at that conclusion. Rather, he opined that the relevant submarket is pre- and post-season tournaments, but because Tollison failed to provide any basis for that opinion, the district court correctly found it unreliable. Because the Promoters' failed to define the relevant market, and with it the submarket, the district court had ample basis to dismiss their claim. Instead, however, the district court relied on what it found to be the opinion of the defendant's expert, Mr. Guth — that the relevant submarket is school-scheduled games — an opinion with which the court said Dr. Tollison had agreed. However, it is less than clear that Mr. Guth defines school-scheduled games as the relevant submarket. Admittedly, there is some evidence in the record which would support this proposition. For example, Mr. Guth stated that "in my view, the relevant market appears to be overall men's Division I basketball, and in particular, where the close substitution takes place in school-scheduled games and not solely in terms of the impact on the plaintiff promoter group." He also produced a report in which he stated that "the most important product, for purposes of this litigation, should be defined as school-scheduled games." At trial, however, when he was pointedly asked by counsel whether by this he was saying that the relevant market is school-scheduled games, Guth responded: "Neither in words nor in intent." Mr. Guth then clarified that while he believed that "the most important product, that is the close substitutes, in this litigation should be defined as school-scheduled games[,]" he nonetheless was "not saying that there is a school-scheduled game relevant market as that term is used by economists with antitrust matters." Given this record, it would be difficult to conclude that Mr. Guth named school-scheduled games as the relevant submarket. Accordingly, we decline to relieve the Promoters of their burden based on such a dubious stipulation by the defendant's expert. Because the Promoters failed to define the relevant market within which the significance of the allegedly anti-competitive effects can be gauged, and the record is not sufficient to support the district court's holding with respect to the relevant market, the Promoters cannot prevail on their claim that the Two in Four Rule violates Section 1 of the Sherman Act. Accordingly, we need not reach the question of whether the NCAA's Two in Four rule is anticompetitive or satisfies the rule of reason test. . . .

For the foregoing reasons, we REVERSE the judgment of the district court.

JULIA SMITH GIBBONS, Circuit Judge, concurring. [omitted]

NOTES AND COMMENTS

1. On May 29, 1996, Judge Vratil issued a lengthy order imposing sanctions against the NCAA in connection with the discovery process. She also ordered the member institutions to respond to plaintiffs' interrogatories, inasmuch as the institutions were "real parties in interest." *Law v. NCAA*, 167 F.R.D. 464 (D. Kan. 1996). State college and university Division I members of the NCAA appealed the order, contending they are not parties to the action who can be ordered to respond to interrogatories and that they are entitled to Eleventh Amendment immunity from being treated as parties for discovery purposes. The Tenth Circuit agreed with the schools on both counts and vacated the district court's reference to them as real parties in interest and vacated the order requiring them to respond to the interrogatories. The order did not provide any relief for the NCAA itself and also did not apply to private universities. *University of Texas at Austin v. Vratil,* 1996 U.S. App. LEXIS 24451 (10th Cir. 1996).

In 1999, the NCAA entered into a $54.5 million settlement with approximately 2,000 Division I assistant coaches who filed suit against the NCAA alleging the restricted earnings rule violated federal antitrust laws.

2. Could a pair of athletic conferences enter into a contract with one of the post season bowl games which would prohibit schools in the conferences from appearing in contests which were played on the same day and at the same time? What about the validity of an agreement with six of the post season bowl games and several conferences to provide teams exclusively to those bowls? How would such an arrangement have to be structured to avoid antitrust problems?

3. Shortly after the NCAA television case was decided the College Football Association, a group of the major football powers, and ABC entered into a lucrative television contract. A smaller group of schools, the members of the Pacific-10 and Big Ten Conferences, signed a contract with CBS. Shortly thereafter the smaller group filed suit against ABC, the CFA, and two members of the CFA. The suit sought an injunction prohibiting Nebraska and Notre Dame from refusing to allow television coverage of one of each of their games solely on the basis of the exclusivity of their contract with ABC and the CFA. The key restriction in the CFA-ABC contract barred the broadcast of CFA member games on other networks even when the opposing team was not a member of the CFA. The court found the agreement to be an unreasonable horizontal restraint. The court found the arrangement intentionally reduced output along with the imposition of sharp restraints on individual school competition. *Regents of University of California v. ABC, Inc.*, 747 F.2d 511 (9th Cir. 1984).

4. A group of Southern Methodist University alumni, football players, and cheerleaders brought an antitrust action following the imposition of the death penalty by the NCAA in 1987. The gist of the claim was that the action of the NCAA violated the antitrust and civil rights laws by restricting the benefits that may be awarded athletes. The action was dismissed because several of the plaintiffs lacked standing and the others had failed to state a claim upon which relief could be granted. *McCormack v. NCAA*, 845 F.2d 1338 (5th Cir. 1988). *See* Comment, McCormack v. National Collegiate Athletic Association: *College Athletics Sanctions from an Antitrust and Civil Rights Perspective,* 15 J.C. & U.L. 459 (1989).

5. For further comments on the NCAA television case, *see* Sims, NCAA v. Board of Regents *and a Truncated Rule of Reason: Retaining Flexibility Without Sacrificing Efficiency,* 27 ARIZ. L. REV. 193 (1985); Note, *Antitrust Law — NCAA Thrown for a Loss by Court's Traditional Antitrust Blitz* — NCAA v. Board of Regents of the University of Oklahoma, 104 S. Ct. 2948 (1984), 18 CREIGHTON L. REV. 917 (1985); and Note, Board of Regents of the University of Oklahoma v. National Collegiate Athletic Association: *Antitrust Violations in College Football*, 29 ST. LOUIS U. L.J. 207 (1984).

6. In *Kupec v. Atlantic Coast Conference*, 399 F. Supp. 1377 (M.D.N.C. 1975), the plaintiff, a college quarterback, made the following allegation in his complaint:

> The actions of the member institutions of the Atlantic Coast Conference in combining to set maximum compensation to be received by student athletes . . . have unreasonably restrained . . . commerce . . . in violation of the Sherman Act. . . .

Kupec's antitrust claim was never addressed on the merits. How would you decide it? Would it be impacted by the decision in *Law v. NCAA*? In light of *Law*, consider the entire NCAA Manual and discuss possible antitrust claims.

Two cases pending at press time of this edition raise antitrust claims over limitations placed on the number of scholarships a school may award in football and the total value of the scholarship. The case involving the limit on the number of scholarships was filed by a group of walk-on players. The plaintiffs survived an initial motion to dismiss, but the court denied their motion to certify a class for the case. *In re NCAA 1-A Walk-On Football Player Litigation,* 2006 U.S. LEXIS 28824 (W.D. Wash. 2006). The other case, brought by former Division I football and basketball players, focuses on the limitations of the scholarship itself. *White v. NCAA*, Case No. CV-0999 RGK (C.D. Cal. 2006)

7. Antitrust claims were also raised in *Behagen v. Amateur Basketball Association of the United States of America*, 884 F.2d 542 (10th Cir. 1989). The plaintiff charged that the actions of ABA/USA in refusing to reinstate his amateur status so that he could play basketball in Europe were an unreasonable restraint of trade in violation of the Sherman Act. The court held that the association was exempt from the Sherman Act as a direct result of the intent of Congress expressed in the Amateur Sports Act. *See also*, Nafziger, *The Amateur Sports Act of 1978*, B.Y.U. L. REV. 47 (1983).

8. Standards for non-wood baseball bats have spawned antitrust litigation in recent years. One bat manufacturer brought an action against the NCAA and several other manufacturers, alleging manipulation of the market by changing standards. The federal district court dismissed the matter, finding no antitrust injury had been proved. *Baum Research & Development Co. v. Hillerich & Bradsby*, 31 F. Supp. 2d 1016 (E.D. Mich. 1998). One of the defendants in that case, Easton Sports, itself filed suit against the NCAA alleging unlawful restraint of trade in its amendment of design and performance standards for baseball bats. *Easton Sports, Inc. v. NCAA*, Case No. 98-2351-KHV (D. Kan. 1998). The matter was settled in October of 1999, following the NCAA's establishment of standards and criteria for approval of bats.

9. Unlike every other NCAA sport, college football does not conduct an end of season playoff championship series. Instead, there are more than two dozen bowl games pairing schools from various conferences against one another. Most of these arrangements are the result of contractual agreements between conferences. Television contracts support the bowl games and provide substantial financial payouts for the schools involved. The Bowl Championship Series (BCS) consists of four games at the end of the postseason. This is the culmination of the college season and is an attempt to match the top eight teams in the country. The last of the four games is an attempt to create a national championship game. There are automatic entries in the BCS for the conference champions from six conferences plus the University of Notre Dame if it wins 9 games or finishes in the top 10 of the final BCS ratings. The ratings are based on a complicated formula that is revised annually. It is possible for a team outside of the six conferences to qualify, but it must finish in the top four in the final ratings. Would a school outside the BCS super-conferences that finished ranked sixth in the country have a cause of action for exclusion from the BCS?

PART II
PROFESSIONAL SPORTS ISSUES

Professional sports comprise a major portion of the multi-billion dollar sports industry in the United States. The industry includes the ever popular professional team operations, individual sports contests, such as golf and tennis, and other often overlooked endeavors from wrestling to sled dog racing. The industry encompasses not only the sports events *qua* events, but the support services that enable and also market the events. Thus, the sports lawyer may focus on corporate or tax law issues, media and advertising contracts, or concessions arrangements as often as player contracts or collective bargaining issues. Issues confronting the attorney working within the professional sports environment require full knowledge of most fields of law.

This section focuses on legal issues that are peculiar to professional sports. Notes and questions suggest the broader perspective. It will help to apply individual life experiences and knowledge of general legal principles to the problems and materials that follow. As you work through the problems, attempt to gain insights into the workings of the professional sports industry as well as the legal principles governing the industry.

Chapter 5

LEAGUE DECISION MAKING AND COMMISSIONER POWER

A. INTRODUCTORY COMMENTS

This chapter considers issues arising from the working relations of members of the various professional sports leagues. Operational concerns of leagues and member clubs comprise a significant portion of the sports law practice for the attorney. Matters essential to the individual club include all business and tax considerations, stadium arrangements, concession contracts, various broadcasting and website issues, contracts of players and coaches, merchandising of consumer goods, and marketing of the "team" through season and group ticket sales and public relations.

The working relationships between teams in a league are conducted according to provisions of league constitutions and bylaws. Recurring issues are analyzed from the internal perspective of member teams in a league. Disputes often arise between rival leagues, thus necessitating analysis of league governance from an external perspective. The common ground for attack is found in application of the antitrust laws; joined with contract and other theories. The antitrust laws as they apply to employment matters are presented at **Chapter 6**, *infra*, but the application to league decisionmaking is considered in this chapter, including the historic baseball antitrust exemption. The materials of **Section E,** *infra*, develop the plaintiff's case under Section 1 of the Sherman Antitrust Act and other theories; **Section F** requires the formulation of antitrust defenses; and **Section G** focuses on the question of "antitrust injury." The chapter also addresses issues concerning the exercise of authority by league commissioners.

B. SPORTS LEAGUE OPERATIONS — FUNDAMENTAL CHARACTERISTICS

As indicated by the problems and cases below, sports leagues are unique entities in the world of business. The teams appear to the average fan as individual firms competing both on and off the field. Many aspects of club operations, however, are conducted jointly with other teams in the league. More importantly, it is the league, not the teams, that generates the fundamental market opportunity to produce professional sports games within the league territories. The league transfers derivative rights in the naked market opportunity, a property interest, to enable the member clubs to gain economic rewards by enhancing the inherent value of the business opportunity through team marketing and other operations.

It is noteworthy that no matter how many professional sports teams were organized independently historically, the clubs gained market opportunities by obtaining them from various leagues. A club could purchase an inaugural or expansion franchise in a league, or an existing franchise from a team owner with league approval. Sometimes teams would merge with a different league to gain the market opportunities. Even if teams form independently to join in creating a league, the market opportunity arises and exists as a league asset, just as does cash from operations and other property. A team cannot play a game without other teams.

The clubs of a league are joined together, and with the league, pursuant to the terms of a Constitution & By-laws. Thus, the clubs and leagues enjoy contractual relationships, and, of course, are governed by the law of torts in their interactions, including decisions made by league directors. As you will observe from reading the cases below, the traditional approach of litigants and the resulting judicial scrutiny focuses on contract and tort claims, including fiduciary duties. Plaintiffs regularly utilize statutory schemes, including the antitrust laws, for the basis of their arguments. Parties rarely discern and debate rights and duties that emanate from the property interests at stake. But the fixed treatment of professional sports entities as business organizations tied only by contract to league operations diverts focus from the basic characteristics of the market opportunity, the core property interest, shared by the league and member teams. Weistart and Lowell, in THE LAW OF SPORTS 307-08 (1979) [*citing, Metropolitan Base Ball Association v. Simmons,* 1 Pa. County Ct. 134, 17 Phila. 419 (1885)], anticipate the conflict:

> [F]or the purpose of analyzing most private law issues, it can be said that the basic relationship between the clubs within a league is one of contract. . . . While this sort of contract analysis represents the approach most typically taken to intraleague controversies, the courts have indicated that other principles may be applied in appropriate circumstances. For example, it is often held that membership in an association such as a league gives rise to property interests which are entitled to protection. . . . This characterization may be particularly apt in the sports context since the league serves a basic business function, and actions of the league may have impact upon a member's access to certain "property" in the form of economic rewards.

Viewing the league-club relationships from the property law perspective generates a distinct approach to recurring legal issues. For example, a question arises whether a team owner has purchased the sticks in the bundle of property rights that enables sale or relocation of the team operations. In the area of antitrust, the argument may be made that the league exists as a "single entity," incapable of conspiracy in restraint of trade.

Within the jural relationship between leagues and clubs, league constituent members possess distinct duties to protect market opportunities of the league as a whole, as well as protect individual club operations. The inherent opportunity for clubs to place team interests above league interests reveals a "tragedy of the commons" phenomenon whereby the pursuit of maximum benefits by individual entities results in a ruination of the whole. The phenomenon is described in the classic writing of Hardin, "Tragedy of the Commons," 162 Science 1243 (1968). Hardin envisioned a common grazing area utilized by individual animal owners. It is to the benefit of each individual animal owner to introduce an additional animal unit to the commons. But, the increased use of the common property resource leads to overgrazing and detriment to all. The tragic result occurs because the individual animal owners did not take into account the costs or benefits to others, including the community, in deciding to increase the grazing burden. The ignored costs or benefits, existing outside the decision-making formula, are referred to as "externalities."

The conflict arises in at least three contexts: the individual team pursuit of players and/or geographic locations or ownership groups that benefit the individual club, but not the long-term interests of the league as a whole. Neglect of the costs and benefits to the league generates an externality problem that leads to market failure. Costs threatening the public good, "fan interest," for example, may arise by loss of competitive balance in the player market. It may also occur by saturation of market support infrastructure, including fan interest, advertising, sponsorship capital, media contracts, and merchandising. League constraints on club relocation, transfer of ownership, and player movement are designed to internalize the external costs in order to prevent the tragedy of partial or total league failure. The tragedy can also arise as a result of interleague warfare, as is explored at **Section H**, *infra*.

As you work through the problems below, attempt to identify the "common property resources" that are vulnerable to the tragedy in the particular circumstance, and the manner in which the league constraints address the potential peril. Consider whether actions in contract, tort, or antitrust serve to provide suitable remedies to the alleged grievances.

C. BASEBALL ANTITRUST EXEMPTION — PROLOGUE

1. The Curt Flood Act of 1998

In late 1998, both houses of Congress unanimously passed the Curt Flood Act of 1998, and forwarded the bill for Presidential signature. The Act is the only Congressional legislation relating to the historical baseball antitrust exemption recognized by the United States Supreme Court in 1922. Both the Major League Baseball Players Association and Major League Baseball encouraged Congress to seek removal of the exemption as it relates to major league labor matters. (Basic Agreement, Article XXVIII.) Removal of the exemption in this context enables major league baseball players to enjoy the same rights under antitrust laws as do other professional athletes. The rights of non-baseball professional athletes were established by the United States Supreme Court in *Brown v. Pro Football, Inc.*, 518 U.S. 231 (1996) (*see* **Case File** at **Chapter 6**). The case holds that the "non-statutory labor exemption" compels organized labor to rely on the labor laws, not the antitrust laws, in bargaining after expiration of a collective bargaining agreement and past *impasse*. Apparently, only by an act of "decertification" of the union are workers able to utilize the antitrust laws as weapons in disputes with management.

The original bill, S.53, was introduced by Senator Hatch to amend the Clayton Act (15 U.S.C. §§ 12 et seq.) to extend application of the antitrust laws to major league baseball. It specifically provided that the amendment shall not be construed to affect the applicability or nonapplicability to the amateur draft, the minor league reserve clause, the Professional Baseball Agreement between the major and minor leagues, other minor league matters, any restraint by professional baseball on franchise relocation, and the application of the Sports Broadcasting Act of 1961. The National Association of Professional Baseball Leagues, the minor league umbrella organization, quickly became involved in the debate. The NAPBL desired to protect its 17 leagues and 175 clubs located in the United States from ancillary impact resulting from the loosely worded bill. After considerable deliberations and what Professor Roberts calls a "long, rancorous, and difficult process," the Curt Flood Act of 1998 provides for extension of the antitrust laws to the narrow area of activity "directly relating to or affecting employment of major league baseball players to play baseball at the major league level. . . ." 15 U.S.C. § 27(a). *See generally*, Roberts, *A Brief Appraisal of the Curt Flood Act of 1998 from the Minor League Perspective*, 9 MARQ. SPORTS L.J. 413, 416-19 (1999). The Act further provides that it does not extend the reach of the antitrust laws to baseball matters not relating to major league employment. The activities include minor league employment, and both major and minor league non-labor activities. For a comprehensive analysis of Congressional treatment of the historical baseball antitrust exemption, including the legislative dynamics behind the passage of the Curt Flood Act of 1998, *see* DUQUETTE, REGULATING THE NATIONAL PASTIME (1999). Questions concerning the scope of the Curt Flood Act of 1998, and the nature of the judicially derived baseball antitrust exemption surviving the Act are explored in the **Problem** below. *See also* EDMONDS & MANZ, BASEBALL AND ANTITRUST: THE LEGISLATIVE HISTORY OF THE CURT FLOOD ACT OF 1998 (2001).

2. The Historical Baseball Antitrust Exemption

The historical baseball antitrust exemption emanates from Justice Holmes' opinion in *Federal Baseball Club v. National League*, 259 U.S. 200 (1922). The National League, formed in 1876, successfully countered economic opposition by competing leagues during the 1800s, including the American Association (1881), Union Association (1884), and the Players' League (1889). *See generally* RADER, BASEBALL: A HISTORY OF AMERICA'S GAME (2D ED. 2002); ROSS, THE NATIONAL GAME (2000). In 1901, the Western League, a minor league, moved into Cleveland, a city recently abandoned by the National League, and several east coast cities. The Western League proclaimed itself the American League and began to raid National League rosters. After fierce litigation and economic battle, the National and American Leagues joined in the National Agreement in 1903, to protect the respective rosters and other common interests. *See* Sowell, JULY 2, 1903 (1992), for a description of the events surrounding the competition between the two leagues.

In 1913, the Federal League formed and attempted to sign professional players in both the American and National Leagues. After the 1915 season, the American and National Leagues agreed to pay a sizable sum of money to the Federal League owners for a dissolution of the League, and enabled some Federal League members to purchase American or National League franchises. The Baltimore club of the Federal League filed suit alleging the parties to the agreement conspired to monopolize the baseball business in violation of the Sherman Act. "[Plaintiff] alleges that the defendants destroyed the Federal League by buying up some of the constituent clubs and in one way or another inducing all of those clubs except the plaintiff to leave their League, and that the three persons connected with the Federal League and named as defendants, one of them being the President of the League, took part in the conspiracy." *Id.* In *Federal Baseball*, the United States Supreme Court ruled that baseball was not subject to the reach of the antitrust laws, but was merely the business of "giving exhibitions of baseball, which are purely state affairs . . . ," and was "not a subject of commerce." *Id.* at 201.

As indicated in the 1972 *Flood* opinion in the Case File below, baseball maintained its judicially recognized exemption from the antitrust laws despite judicial challenges and intense Congressional scrutiny during the 1950s, 60s and 70s. During the same period, the U.S. Supreme Court declined to extend the exemption to other sports, such as football, boxing, and basketball. In *Flood*, the Court reaffirmed the exemption, although noting that baseball is a business and is engaged in interstate commerce. The Court emphasized that baseball since 1922 has been allowed to develop and expand unhindered by federal legislative action. It further stated that the established and recognized aberration is entitled to the benefit of *stare decisis*.

3. Modern Scrutiny of the Exemption

Events of the past years generated a renewed focus upon the traditionally recognized baseball antitrust exemption. The Major League Baseball strike of 1994 compelled Congress to reexamine the validity and scope of the exemption. The recurring relocation of NFL clubs from existing cities and publicly owned facilities to competing locations further motivated Congress to consider the exemption during the 1995 and 1996 sessions. Interestingly, in the latter instance, Congressional committees contemplated the creation of an express exemption similar to that of baseball enabling the NFL, NBA and other professional sports leagues to prevent the movement of a club from one city to another. Congress returned to focus on the exemption as a result of Major League Baseball's contemplated "contraction" of the Minnesota Twins and Montreal Expos in 2001, and the concurrent labor negotiations that resulted in a collective bargaining agreement. In the judicial arena, a federal district court in Pennsylvania and the state courts of Florida restricted the scope of the *Flood / Federal Baseball* precedent to player reserve clause matters. The *Piazza* case is found in the **Case File** below. The Minnesota Supreme Court and the Eleventh Circuit Court of Appeals both rejected the *Piazza* analysis. (*See* **Note 2**, *infra.*) Thus, the nature, scope, and appropriateness of the baseball antitrust exemption continues as a significant sports law debate, after the passage of the Curt Flood Act of 1998.

PROBLEM

The United States Senate Judiciary Committee plans to schedule hearings for review of the baseball antitrust exemption during the next session of Congress. The Committee desires to consider extending the exemption to other professional sports. The Committee Chair requests that the Chief Counsel and legal staff prepare a memorandum outlining and discussing the baseball antitrust exemption. The Chief Counsel for the Committee assigned the task to you, and specifically instructs as follows:

1. Prepare a preliminary draft report analyzing the nature and scope of the historical baseball antitrust exemption.
2. Should the exemption be limited to the "reserve clause," or should it extend to the "business of baseball?"
3. What are the limits of a "business of baseball" definition?
4. Outline the elements of the Curt Flood Act of 1998.
5. What is the impact of the Curt Flood Act on the baseball antitrust exemption?
6. Are the minor leagues and current major league cities protected under the resulting law?

Case File

FLOOD v. KUHN
407 U.S. 258 (1972)

Mr. Justice Blackmun delivered the opinion of the Court.

For the third time in 50 years the Court is asked specifically to rule that professional baseball's reserve system is within the reach of the federal antitrust laws. Collateral issues of state law and of federal labor policy are also advanced.

I. The Game

It is a century and a quarter since the New York Nine defeated the Knickerbockers 23 to 1 on Hoboken's Elysian Fields June 19, 1846, with Alexander Jay Cartwright as the instigator and the umpire. The teams were amateur, but the contest marked a significant date in baseball's beginnings. That early game led ultimately to the development of professional baseball and its tightly organized structure.

The Cincinnati Red Stockings came into existence in 1869 upon an outpouring of local pride. With only one Cincinnatian on the payroll, this professional team traveled over 11,000 miles that summer, winning 56 games and tying one. Shortly thereafter, on St. Patrick's Day in 1871, The National Association of Professional Baseball Players was founded and the professional league was born.

The ensuing colorful days are well known. The ardent follower and the student of baseball know of General Abner Doubleday; the formation of the National League in 1876; Chicago's supremacy in the first year's competition under the leadership of Al Spalding and with Cap Anson at third base; the formation of the American Association and then of the Union Association in the 1880's; the introduction of Sunday baseball; interleague warfare with cutrate admission prices and player raiding; the development of the reserve "clause"; the emergence in 1885 of the Brotherhood of Professional Ball Players, and in 1890 of the Players League; the appearance of the American League, or "junior circuit" in 1901, rising from the minor Western Association; the first World Series in 1903, disruption in 1904, and the Series' resumption in 1905; the short-lived Federal League on the majors' scene during World War I years; the troublesome and discouraging episode of the 1919 Series; the home run ball; the shifting of franchises; the expansion of the leagues; the installation in 1965 of the major league draft of potential new players; and the formation of the Major League Baseball Players Association in 1966.

Then there are the many names, celebrated for one reason or another, that have sparked the diamond . . . and that have provided tinder for recaptured thrills, for reminiscence and comparisons, and for conversation and anticipation in season and off season. . . . The list seems endless.

And one recalls the appropriate reference to the "World Series," attributed to Ring Lardner, Sr.; Ernest L. Thayer's "Casey at the Bat"; the ring of "Tinker to Evers to Chance"; and all the other happenings, habits, and superstitions about and around baseball that made it the "national pastime" or, depending upon the point of view, "the great American tragedy."

II. The Petitioner

The petitioner, Curtis Charles Flood, born in 1938, began his major league career in 1956 when he signed a contract with the Cincinnati Reds for a salary of $4,000 for the season. He had no attorney or agent to advise him on that occasion. He was traded to the St. Louis Cardinals before the 1958 season. Flood rose to fame as a center fielder with the Cardinals during the years 1958-1969. In those 12 seasons he compiled a batting average of .293. His best offensive season was 1967 when he achieved .335. He was .301 or better in six of the 12 St. Louis years. He participated in the 1964, 1967, and 1968 World Series. He played errorless ball in the field in 1966, and once enjoyed 223 consecutive errorless games. Flood has received seven Golden Glove Awards. He was co-captain of his team from 1965-1969. He ranks among the 10 major league outfielders possessing the highest lifetime fielding averages.

* * *

But at the age of 31, in October 1969, Flood was traded to the Philadelphia Phillies of the National League in a multi-player transaction. He was not consulted about the trade. He was informed by telephone and received formal notice only after the deal had been consummated. In December he complained to the Commissioner of Baseball and asked that he be made a free agent and be placed at liberty to strike his own bargain with any other major league team. His request was denied.

Flood then instituted this antitrust suit in January 1970 in federal court for the Southern District of New York. The defendants (although not all were named in each cause of action) were the Commissioner of Baseball, the presidents of two major leagues, and the 24 major league clubs. In general, the complaint charged violations of the federal antitrust laws and civil rights statutes, violation of state statutes and the common law, and the imposition of a form of peonage and involuntary servitude contrary to the Thirteenth Amendment and 42 U.S.C. § 1994, 18 U.S.C. § 1581, and 29 U.S.C. §§ 102 and 103. Petitioner sought declaratory and injunctive relief and treble damages.

Flood declined to play for Philadelphia in 1970, despite a $100,000 salary offer, and he sat out the year. After the season was concluded, Philadelphia sold its rights to Flood to the Washington Senators. Washington and the petitioner were able to come to terms for 1971 at a salary of $110,000. Flood started the season but, apparently because he was dissatisfied with his performance, he left the Washington club on April 27, early in the campaign. He has not played baseball since then.

III. The Present Litigation

Judge Cooper, in a detailed opinion, first denied a preliminary injunction, 309 F. Supp. 793 (S.D. N.Y. 1970), observing on the way:

> "Baseball has been the national pastime for over one hundred years and enjoys a unique place in our American heritage. Major league professional baseball is avidly followed by millions of fans, looked upon with fervor and pride and provides a special source of inspiration and competitive team spirit especially for the young.
>
> "Baseball's status in the life of the nation is so pervasive that it would not strain credulity to say the Court can take judicial notice that baseball is everybody's business. To put it mildly and with restraint, it would be unfortunate indeed if a fine sport and profession, which brings surcease from daily travail and an escape from the ordinary to most inhabitants of this land, were to suffer in the least because of undue concentration by any one or any group on commercial and profit considerations. The game is on higher ground; it behooves every one to keep it there."

309 F. Supp. at 797. Flood's application for an early trial was granted. The court next deferred until trial its decision on the defendants' motions to dismiss the primary causes of action, but granted a defense motion for summary judgment on an additional cause of action. 312 F. Supp. 404 (S.D.N.Y. 1970).

Trial to the court took place in May and June 1970. An extensive record was developed. In an ensuing opinion, 316 F. Supp. 271 (S.D.N.Y. 1970), Judge Cooper first noted that:

> "Plaintiff's witnesses in the main concede that some form of reserve on players is a necessary element of the organization of baseball as a league sport, but contend that the present all-embracing system is needlessly restrictive and offer various alternatives which in their view might loosen the bonds without sacrifice to the game. . . .
>
> "Clearly the preponderance of credible proof does not favor elimination of the reserve clause. With the sole exception of plaintiff himself, it shows that even plaintiff's witnesses do not contend that it is wholly undesirable; in fact they regard substantial portions meritorious. . . ."

316 F. Supp. at 275-76. He then held that *Federal Baseball Club v. National League,* 259 U.S. 200 (1922), and *Toolson v. New York Yankees, Inc.*, 346 U.S. 356 (1953), were controlling; that it was not necessary to reach the issue whether exemption from the antitrust laws would result because aspects of baseball now are a subject of collective bargaining; that the plaintiffs state-law claims, those based on common law as well as on statute, were to be denied because baseball was not "a matter which admits of diversity of treatment," 316 F. Supp. at 280; that the involuntary servitude claim failed because of the absence of "the essential element of this cause of action, a showing of the compulsory

service;" 316 F. Supp. at 281-82; and that judgment was to be entered for the defendants. Judge Cooper included a statement of personal conviction to the effect that "negotiations could produce an accommodation on the reserve system which would be eminently fair and equitable to all concerned" and that "the reserve clause can be fashioned so as to find acceptance by player and club." 316 F. Supp. at 282 and 284.

On appeal, the Second Circuit felt "compelled to affirm." 443 F.2d 264, 265 (1971). It regarded the issue of state law as one of first impression, but concluded that the Commerce Clause precluded its application. Judge Moore added a concurring opinion in which he predicted, with respect to the suggested overruling of *Federal Baseball* and *Toolson*, that "there is no likelihood that such an event will occur." 443 F.2d. at 268, 272.

We granted certiorari in order to look once again at this troublesome and unusual situation. 404 U.S. 880 (1971).

IV. The Legal Background

A. *Federal Baseball Club v. National League,* 259 U.S. 200 (1922), was a suit for treble damages instituted by a member of the Federal League (Baltimore) against the National and American Leagues and others. The plaintiff obtained a verdict in the trial court, but the Court of Appeals reversed. The main brief filed by the plaintiff with this Court discloses that it was strenuously argued, among other things, that the business in which the defendants were engaged was interstate commerce; that the interstate relationship among the several clubs, located as they were in different States, was predominant; that organized baseball represented an investment of colossal wealth; that it was an engagement in moneymaking; that the gate receipts were divided by agreement between the home club and the visiting club; and that the business of baseball was to be distinguished from the mere playing of the game as a sport for physical exercise and diversion. *See also* 259 U.S. at 201-06.

Mr. Justice Holmes, in speaking succinctly for a unanimous Court, said:

> "The business is giving exhibitions of baseball, which are purely state affairs. . . . But the fact that in order to give the exhibitions the Leagues must induce free persons to cross state lines and must arrange and pay for their doing so is not enough to change the character of the business. . . . [T]he transport is a mere incident, not the essential thing. That to which it is incident, the exhibition, although made for money would not be called trade or commerce in the commonly accepted use of those words. As it is put by the defendants, personal effort, not related to production, is not a subject of commerce. That which in its consummation is not commerce does not become commerce among the States because the transportation that we have mentioned takes place. To repeat the illustrations given by the Court below, a firm of lawyers sending out a member to argue a case, or the Chautauqua lecture

bureau sending out lecturers, does not engage in such commerce because the lawyer or lecturer goes to another State.

"If we are right the plaintiff's business is to be described in the same way and the restrictions by contract that prevented the plaintiff from getting players to break their bargains and the other conduct charged against the defendants were not an interference with commerce among the States."

259 U.S. at 208-09.

* * *

B. In the years that followed, baseball continued to be subject to intermittent antitrust attack. The courts, however, rejected these challenges on the authority of *Federal Baseball.* In some cases stress was laid, although unsuccessfully, on new factors such as the development of radio and television with their substantial additional revenues to baseball. For the most part, however, the Holmes opinion was generally and necessarily accepted as controlling authority. And in the 1952 Report of the Subcommittee on Study of Monopoly Power of the House Committee on the Judiciary, H.R. Rep. No. 2002, 82d Cong., 2d Sess., 229, it was said, in conclusion:

> "On the other hand the overwhelming preponderance of the evidence established baseball's need for some sort of reserve clause. Baseball's history shows that chaotic conditions prevailed when there was no reserve clause. Experience points to no feasible substitute to protect the integrity of the game or to guarantee a comparatively even competitive struggle. The evidence adduced at the hearings would clearly not justify the enactment of legislation flatly condemning the reserve clause."

C. The Court granted certiorari, 345 U.S. 963 (1953), in the *Toolson, Kowalski,* and *Corbett* cases, cited in nn.12 and 13, *supra*, and, by a short *per curiam* (Warren, C.J., and Black, Frankfurter, Douglas, Jackson, Clark, and Minton, JJ.), affirmed the judgments of the respective courts of appeals in those three cases. *Toolson v. New York Yankees, Inc.,* 346 U.S. 356 (1953). *Federal Baseball* was cited as holding "that the business of providing public baseball games for profit between clubs of professional baseball players was not within the scope of the federal antitrust laws," 346 U.S. at 357, and:

> "Congress has had the ruling under consideration but has not seen fit to bring such business under these laws by legislation having prospective effect. The business has thus been left for thirty years to develop, on the understanding that it was not subject to existing antitrust legislation. The present cases ask us to overrule the prior decision and, with retrospective effect, hold the legislation applicable. We think that if there are evils in this field which now warrant application to it of the antitrust laws it should be by legislation. Without re-examination of the underlying issues, the judgments below are affirmed on the authority of

Federal Baseball Club of Baltimore v. National League of Professional Baseball Clubs, supra, so far as that decision determines that Congress had no intention of including the business of baseball within the scope of the federal antitrust laws."

Id. This quotation reveals four reasons for the Court's affirmance of *Toolson* and its companion cases: (a) Congressional awareness for three decades of the Court's ruling in *Federal Baseball*, coupled with congressional inaction. (b) The fact that baseball was left alone to develop for that period upon the understanding that the reserve system was not subject to the existing federal antitrust laws. (c) A reluctance to overrule *Federal Baseball* with consequent retroactive effect. (d) A professed desire that any needed remedy be provided by legislation rather than by court decree. The emphasis in *Toolson* was on the determination, attributed even to *Federal Baseball*, that Congress had no intention to include baseball within the reach of the federal antitrust laws. Two Justices (Burton and Reed, JJ.) dissented, stressing the factual aspects, revenue sources, and the absence of an express exemption of organized baseball from the Sherman Act. 346 U.S. at 357. The 1952 congressional study was mentioned. *Id.* at 358, 359, 361.

It is of interest to note that in *Toolson* the petitioner had argued flatly that *Federal Baseball* "is wrong and must be overruled," Brief for Petitioner, No. 18, O.T. 1953, p. 19, and that Thomas Reed Powell, a constitutional scholar of no small stature, urged, as counsel for an *amicus*, that "baseball is a unique enterprise," Brief for Boston American League Base Ball Club Co. as Amicus Curiae 2, and that "unbridled competition as applied to baseball would not be in the public interest." *Id.* at 14.

D. *United States v. Shubert*, 348 U.S. 222 (1955), was a civil antitrust action against defendants engaged in the production of legitimate theatrical attractions throughout the United States and in operating theaters for the presentation of such attractions. The District Court had dismissed the complaint on the authority of *Federal Baseball* and *Toolson*. 120 F. Supp. 15 (S.D.N.Y. 1953). This Court reversed. Mr. Chief Justice Warren noted the Court's broad conception of "trade or commerce" in the antitrust statutes and the types of enterprises already held to be within the reach of that phrase. He stated that *Federal Baseball* and *Toolson* afforded no basis for a conclusion that businesses built around the performance of local exhibitions are exempt from the antitrust laws. 348 U.S. at 227. He then went on to elucidate the holding in *Toolson* by meticulously spelling out the factors mentioned above:

"In *Federal Baseball*, the Court, speaking through Mr. Justice Holmes, was dealing with the business of baseball and nothing else. . . . The travel, the Court concluded, was a 'mere incident, not the essential thing.' . . .

"In *Toolson*, where the issue was the same as in *Federal Baseball*, the Court was confronted with a unique combination of circumstances. For over 30 years there had stood a decision of this Court specifically fixing the status of the baseball business under the antitrust laws and more particularly the validity of the so called

'reserve clause.' During this period, in reliance on the *Federal Baseball* precedent, the baseball business had grown and developed. . . . And Congress, although it had actively considered the ruling, had not seen fit to reject it by amendatory legislation. Against this background, the Court in *Toolson* was asked to overrule *Federal Baseball* on the ground that it was out of step with subsequent decisions reflecting present-day concepts of interstate commerce. The Court, in view of the circumstances of the case, declined to do so. But neither did the Court necessarily reaffirm all that was said in *Federal Baseball*. Instead, '[w]ithout reexamination of the underlying issues; the Court adhered to *Federal Baseball* so far as that decision determines that Congress had no intention of including the business of baseball within the scope of the federal antitrust laws.' 346 U.S. at 357. In short, *Toolson* was a narrow application of the rule of *stare decisis*.

". . . If the *Toolson* holding is to be expanded — or contracted — the appropriate remedy lies with Congress."

348 U.S. at 228-30.

E. *United States v. International Boxing Club,* 348 U.S. 236 (1955), was a companion to *Shubert* and was decided the same day. This was a civil anti-trust action against defendants engaged in the business of promoting professional championship boxing contests. Here again the District Court had dismissed the complaint in reliance upon *Federal Baseball* and *Toolson*. The Chief Justice observed that "if it were not for *Federal Baseball* and *Toolson*, we think that it would be too clear for dispute that the Government's allegations bring the defendants within the scope of the Act." 348 U.S. at 240-41. He pointed out that the defendants relied on the two baseball cases but also would have been content with a more restrictive interpretation of them than the *Shubert* defendants, for the boxing defendants argued that the cases immunized only businesses that involve exhibitions of an athletic nature. The Court accepted neither argument. It again noted, 348 U.S. at 242, that "*Toolson* neither overruled *Federal Baseball* nor necessarily reaffirmed all that was said in Federal Baseball." It stated:

"The controlling consideration in *Federal Baseball* and *Hart* was, instead, a very practical one — the degree of interstate activity involved in the particular business under review. It follows that *stare decisis* cannot help the defendants here; for, contrary to their argument, *Federal Baseball* did not hold that all businesses based on professional sports were outside the scope of the antitrust laws. The issue confronting us is, therefore, not whether a previously granted exemption should continue, but whether an exemption should be granted in the first instance. And that issue is for Congress to resolve, not this Court."

348 U.S. at 243. The Court noted the presence then in Congress of various bills forbidding the application of the antitrust laws to "organized professional sports enterprises"; the holding of extensive hearings on some of these; subcommittee opposition; a postponement recommendation as to baseball; and the fact that "Congress thus left intact the then-existing coverage of the antitrust laws." 348 U.S. at 243-44.

Mr. Justice Frankfurter, joined by Mr. Justice Minton, dissented. "It would baffle the subtlest ingenuity," he said, "to find a single differentiating factor between other sporting exhibitions . . . and baseball insofar as the conduct of the sport is relevant to the criteria or considerations by which the Sherman Law becomes applicable to a 'trade or commerce.'" 348 U.S. at 248. He went on:

> "The Court decided as it did in the *Toolson* case as an application of the doctrine of *stare decisis*. That doctrine is not, to be sure, an imprisonment of reason. But neither is it a whimsy. It can hardly be that this Court gave a preferred position to baseball because it is the great American sport. . . . If *stare decisis* be one aspect of law, as it is, to disregard it in identical situations is mere caprice.
>
> "Congress, on the other hand, may yield to sentiment and be capricious, subject only to due process. . . .
>
> "Between them, this case and *Shubert* illustrate that nice but rational distinctions are inevitable in adjudication. I agree with the Court's opinion in *Shubert* for precisely the reason that constrains me to dissent in this case."

348 U.S. at 249-50. Mr. Justice Minton also separately dissented on the ground that boxing is not trade or commerce. He added the comment that "Congress has not attempted" to control baseball and boxing. 348 U.S. at 251, 253. The two dissenting Justices, thus, did not call for the overruling of *Federal Baseball* and *Toolson*; they merely felt that boxing should be under the same umbrella of freedom as was baseball and, as Mr. Justice Frankfurter said, 348 U.S. at 250, they could not exempt baseball "to the exclusion of every other sport different not one legal jot or tittle from it."

F. The parade marched on. *Radovich v. National Football League*, 352 U.S. 445 (1957), was a civil Clayton Act case testing the application of the antitrust laws to professional football. The District Court dismissed. The Ninth Circuit affirmed in part on the basis of *Federal Baseball* and *Toolson*. The court did not hesitate to "confess that the strength of the pull" of the baseball cases and of *International Boxing* "is about equal," but then observed that "[f]ootball is a team sport" and boxing an individual one. 231 F.2d 620, 622.

This Court reversed with an opinion by Mr. Justice Clark. He said that the Court made its ruling in *Toolson* "because it was concluded that more harm would be done in overruling *Federal Baseball* than in upholding a ruling which at best was of dubious validity." 352 U.S. at 450. He noted that Congress had not acted. He then said:

> "All this, combined with the flood of litigation that would follow its repudiation, the harassment that would ensue, and the retroactive effect of such a decision, led the Court to the practical result that it should sustain the unequivocal line of authority reaching over many years.
>
> "[S]ince *Toolson* and *Federal Baseball* are still cited as controlling authority in antitrust actions involving other fields of business, we now specifically limit the rule there established to the facts there involved, *i.e.,* the business of organized professional baseball. As long as the Congress continues to acquiesce we should adhere to — but not extend — the interpretation of the Act made in those cases. . . .
>
> "If this ruling is unrealistic, inconsistent, or illogical, it is sufficient to answer, aside from the distinctions between the businesses, that were we considering the question of baseball for the first time upon a clean slate we would have no doubts. But *Federal Baseball* held the business of baseball outside the scope of the Act. No other business claiming the coverage of those cases has such an adjudication. We, therefore, conclude that the orderly way to eliminate error or discrimination, if any there be, is by legislation and not by court decision. Congressional processes are more accommodative, affording the whole industry hearings and an opportunity to assist in the formulation of new legislation. The resulting product is therefore more likely to protect the industry and the public alike. The whole scope of congressional action would be known long in advance and effective dates for the legislation could be set in the future without the injustices of retroactivity and surprise which might follow court action."

352 U.S. at 450-52. Mr. Justice Frankfurter dissented essentially for the reasons stated in his dissent in *International Boxing,* 352 U.S. at 455. Mr. Justice Harlan, joined by Mr. Justice Brennan, also dissented because he, too, was "unable to distinguish football from baseball." 352 U.S. at 456. Here again the dissenting Justices did not call for the overruling of the baseball decisions. They merely could not distinguish the two sports and, out of respect for *stare decisis*, voted to affirm.

G. Finally, in *Haywood v. National Basketball Ass'n.*, 401 U.S. 1204 (1971), Mr. Justice Douglas, in his capacity as Circuit Justice, reinstated a District Court's injunction *pendente lite* in favor of a professional basketball player and said, "Basketball . . . does not enjoy exemption from the antitrust law." 401 U.S. at 1205.

H. This series of decisions understandably spawned extensive commentary, some of it mildly critical and much of it not; nearly all of it looked to Congress for any remedy that might be deemed essential.

I. Legislative proposals have been numerous and persistent. Since *Toolson* more than 50 bills have been introduced in Congress relative to the applicability or nonapplicability of the antitrust laws to baseball. A few of these passed one house or the other. Those that did would have expanded, not restricted, the reserve system's exemption to other professional league sports. And the Act of Sept 30, 1961, Pub. L. 87-331, 75 Stat. 732, and the merger addition thereto effected by the Act of Nov. 8, 1966, Pub. L. 89-800, § 6(b), 80 Stat. 1515, 15 U.S.C. §§ 1291-1295, were also expansive.

V

In view of all this, it seems appropriate now to say that:

1. Professional baseball is a business and it is engaged in interstate commerce.

2. With its reserve system enjoying exemption from the federal antitrust laws, baseball is, in a very distinct sense, an exception and an anomaly. *Federal Baseball* and *Toolson* have become an aberration confined to baseball.

3. Even though others might regard this as "unrealistic, inconsistent, or illogical," *see Radovich*, 352 U.S. at 452, the aberration is an established one, and one that has been recognized not only in *Federal Baseball* and *Toolson*, but in *Shubert, International Boxing*, and *Radovich*, as well, a total of five consecutive cases in this Court. It is an aberration that has been with us now for half a century, one heretofore deemed fully entitled to the benefit of *stare decisis*, and one that has survived the Court's expanding concept of interstate commerce. It rests on a recognition and an acceptance of baseball's unique characteristics and needs.

4. Other professional sports operating interstate — football, boxing, basketball, and, presumably, hockey and golf — are not so exempt.

5. The advent of radio and television, with their consequent increased coverage and additional revenues, has not occasioned an overruling of *Federal Baseball* and *Toolson*.

6. The Court has emphasized that since 1922 baseball, with full and continuing congressional awareness, has been allowed to develop and to expand unhindered by federal legislative action. Remedial legislation has been introduced repeatedly in Congress but none has ever been enacted. The Court, accordingly, has concluded that Congress as yet has had no intention to subject baseball's reserve system to the reach of the antitrust statutes. This, obviously, has been deemed to be something other than mere congressional silence and passivity.

7. The Court has expressed concern about the confusion and the retroactivity problems that inevitably would result with a judicial overturning of *Federal Baseball*. It has voiced a preference that if any change is to be made, it come by legislative action that, by its nature, is only prospective in operation.

8. The Court noted in *Radovich*, 352 U.S. at 452, that the slate with respect to baseball is not clean. Indeed, it has not been clean for half a century.

This emphasis and this concern are still with us. We continue to be loath, 50 years after *Federal Baseball* and almost two decades after *Toolson*, to overturn those cases judicially when Congress, by its positive inaction, has allowed those decisions to stand for so long and, far beyond mere inference and implication, has clearly evinced a desire not to disapprove them legislatively.

Accordingly, we adhere once again to *Federal Baseball* and *Toolson* and to their application to professional baseball. We adhere also to *International Boxing* and *Radovich* and to their respective applications to professional boxing and professional football. If there is any inconsistency or illogic in all this, it is an inconsistency and illogic of long standing that is to be remedied by the Congress and not by this Court. If we were to act otherwise, we would be withdrawing from the conclusion as to congressional intent made in *Toolson* and from the concerns as to retrospectivity therein expressed. Under these circumstances, there is merit in consistency even though some might claim that beneath that consistency is a layer of inconsistency.

* * *

The conclusion we have reached makes it unnecessary for us to consider the respondents' additional argument that the reserve system is a mandatory subject of collective bargaining and that federal labor policy therefore exempts the reserve system from the operation of federal antitrust laws.

We repeat for this case what was said in *Toolson*:

> "Without re-examination of the underlying issues, the [judgment] below [is] affirmed on the authority of *Federal Baseball Club of Baltimore v. National League of Professional Baseball Clubs, supra*, so far as that decision determines that Congress had no intention of including the business of baseball within the scope of the federal antitrust laws."

346 U.S. at 357. And what the Court said in *Federal Baseball* in 1922 and what it said in *Toolson* in 1953, we say again here in 1972: the remedy, if any is indicated, is for congressional, and not judicial, action.

The judgment of the Court of Appeals is

Affirmed.

THE CHIEF JUSTICE and MR. JUSTICE WHITE join in the judgment of the Court, and in all but Part I of the Court's opinion.

MR. JUSTICE POWELL took no part in the consideration or decision of this case.

MR. CHIEF JUSTICE BURGER, concurring.

I concur in all but Part I of the Court's opinion but, like MR. JUSTICE DOUGLAS, I have grave reservations as to the correctness of *Toolson v. New York Yankees, Inc.*, 346 U.S. 356 (1953); as he notes in his dissent, he joined that holding but has "lived to regret it." The error, if such it be, is one on which the affairs of a great many people have rested for a long time.

Courts are not the forum in which this tangled web ought to be unsnarled. I agree with Mr. Justice Douglas that congressional inaction is not a solid base, but the least undesirable course now is to let the matter rest with Congress; it is time the Congress acted to solve this problem.

MR. JUSTICE DOUGLAS, with whom MR. JUSTICE BRENNAN concurs, dissenting.

This Court's decision in *Federal Baseball Club v. National League*, 259 U.S. 200, made in 1922, is a derelict in the stream of the law that we, its creator, should remove. Only a romantic view of a rather dismal business . . . over the last 50 years would keep that derelict in midstream.

In 1922 the Court had a narrow, parochial view of commerce. With the demise of the old landmarks of that era, particularly *United States v. Knight Co.,* 156 U.S. 1, *Hammer v. Dagenhart,* 247 U.S. 251, and *Paul v. Virginia,* 8 Wall. 168, the whole concept of commerce has changed.

Under the modern decisions such as *Mandeville Island Farms v. American Crystal Sugar Co.,* 334 U.S. 219, *United States v. Darby,* 312 U.S. 100, *Wickard v. Filburn,* 317 U.S. 111, *United States v. South-Eastern Underwriters Assn.,* 322 U.S. 533, the power of Congress was recognized as broad enough to reach all phases of the vast operations of our national industrial system. An industry so dependent on radio and television as is baseball and gleaning vast interstate revenues (see H.R. Rep. No. 2002, 82d Cong., 2d Sess., 4, 5 (1952)) would be hard put today to say with the Court in the *Federal Baseball Club* case that baseball was only a local exhibition, not trade or commerce.

Baseball is today big business that is packaged with beer, with broadcasting, and with other industries. The beneficiaries of the *Federal Baseball Club* decision are not the Babe Ruths, Ty Cobbs, and Lou Gehrigs.

The owners, whose records many say reveal a proclivity for predatory practices, do not come to us with equities. The equities are with the victims of the reserve clause. I use the word "victims" in the Sherman Act sense, since a contract which forbids anyone to practice his calling is commonly called an unreasonable restraint of trade. *Gardella v. Chandler,* 172 F.2d 402 (2d Cir.). And *see Haywood v. National Baseball Assn.,* 401 U.S. 1204 (Douglas, J., in chambers).

If congressional inaction is our guide, we should rely upon the fact that Congress has refused to enact bills broadly exempting professional sports from antitrust regulation. H.R. Rep. No. 2002, 82d Cong., 2d Sess. (1952). The only statutory exemption granted by Congress to professional sports concerns broadcasting rights. 15 U.S.C. §§ 1291-1295. I would not ascribe a broader exemption through inaction than Congress has seen fit to grant explicitly.

There can be no doubt "that were we considering the question of baseball for the first time upon a clean slate" we would hold it to be subject to federal antitrust regulation. *Radovich v. National Football League,* 353 U.S. 445, 452. The unbroken silence of Congress should not prevent us from correcting our own mistakes.

MR. JUSTICE MARSHALL, with whom MR. JUSTICE BRENNAN joins, dissenting.

* * *

This is a difficult case because we are torn between the principle of *stare decisis* and the knowledge that the decisions in *Federal Baseball Club v. National League,* 259 U.S. 200 (1922), and *Toolson v. New York Yankees, Inc.,* 346 U.S. 356 (1953), are totally at odds with more recent and better reasoned cases. In *Federal Baseball Club,* a team in the Federal League brought an antitrust action against the National and American Leagues and others. In his opinion for a unanimous Court, Mr. Justice Holmes wrote that the business being considered was "giving exhibitions of baseball, which are purely state affairs." 259 U.S. at 208. Hence, the Court held that baseball was not within the purview of the antitrust laws. Thirty-one years later, the Court reaffirmed this decision, without re-examining it, in *Toolson,* a one-paragraph *per curiam* opinion. Like this case, *Toolson* involved an attack on the reserve system. The Court said:

> "The business has . . . been left for thirty years to develop, on the understanding that it was not subject to existing antitrust legislation. The present cases ask us to overrule the prior decision and, with retrospective effect, hold the legislation applicable. We think that if there are evils in this field which now warrant application to it of the antitrust laws it should be by legislation."

Id. at 357. Much more time has passed since *Toolson* and Congress has not acted. We must now decide whether to adhere to the reasoning of *Toolson — i.e.,* to refuse to re-examine the underlying basis of *Federal Baseball Club* — or to proceed with a reexamination and let the chips fall where they may.

In his answer to petitioner's complaint, the Commissioner of Baseball "admits that under present concepts of interstate commerce defendants are engaged therein." App. 40. There can be no doubt that the admission is warranted by today's reality. Since baseball is interstate commerce, if we re-examine baseball's antitrust exemption, the Court's decisions in *United States v. Shubert,* 348 U.S. 222 (1955), *United States v. International Boxing Club,* 348 U.S. 236 (1955), and *Radovich v. National Football League,* 352 U.S. 445 (1957), require that we bring baseball within the coverage of the antitrust laws. *See also, Haywood v. National Basketball Assn.,* 401 U.S. 1204 (Douglas, J., in chambers).

We have only recently had occasion to comment that:

> "Antitrust laws in general, and the Sherman Act in particular, are the Magna Carta of free enterprise. They are as important to the preservation of economic freedom and our free-enterprise system as the Bill of Rights is to the protection of our fundamental personal freedoms. . . . Implicit in such freedom is the notion that it cannot be foreclosed with

respect to one sector of the economy because certain private citizens or groups believe that such foreclosure might promote greater competition in a more important sector of the economy."

United States v. Topco Associates Inc., 405 U.S. 596, 610 (1972). The importance of the antitrust laws to every citizen must not be minimized. They are as important to baseball players as they are to football players, lawyers, doctors, or members of any other class of workers. Baseball players cannot be denied the benefits of competition merely because club owners view other economic interests as being more important, unless Congress says so.

Has Congress acquiesced in our decisions in *Federal Baseball Club* and *Toolson*? I think not. Had the Court been consistent and treated all sports in the same way baseball was treated, Congress might have become concerned enough to take action. But, the Court was inconsistent, and baseball was isolated and distinguished from all other sports. In *Toolson* the Court refused to act because Congress had been silent. But the Court may have read too much into this legislative inaction.

* * *

We do not lightly overrule our prior constructions of federal statutes, but when our errors deny substantial federal rights, like the right to compete freely and effectively to the best of one's ability as guaranteed by the antitrust laws, we must admit our error and correct it. We have done so before and we should do so again here.

To the extent that there is concern over any reliance interests that club owners may assert, they can be satisfied by making our decision prospective only. Baseball should be covered by the antitrust laws beginning with this case and henceforth, unless Congress decides otherwise.

Accordingly, I would overrule *Federal Baseball Club* and *Toolson* and reverse the decision of the Court of Appeals. This does not mean that petitioner would necessarily prevail, however. Lurking in the background is a hurdle of recent vintage that petitioner still must overcome. In 1966, the Major League Players Association was formed. It is the collective-bargaining representative for all major league baseball players. Respondents argue that the reserve system is now part and parcel of the collective bargaining agreement and that because it is a mandatory subject of bargaining, the federal labor statutes are applicable, not the federal antitrust laws. The lower courts did not rule on this argument, having decided the case solely on the basis of the antitrust exemption.

* * *

PIAZZA v. MAJOR LEAGUE BASEBALL

831 F. Supp. 420 (E.D. Pa. 1993)

PADOVA, J.

Plaintiffs allege that the organizations of professional major league baseball and an affiliated individual frustrated their efforts to purchase the San Francisco Giants baseball club (the "Giants") and relocate it to Tampa Bay, Florida. Plaintiffs charge these defendants with infringing upon their rights under the United States Constitution and violating federal antitrust laws and several state laws in the process.

Asserting that this Court lacks subject matter jurisdiction over plaintiffs' federal and state claims and that plaintiffs' federal claims fail to state a cause of action, defendants move to dismiss this suit. With regard to plaintiffs' federal antitrust claims, defendants also claim exemption from antitrust liability under *Federal Baseball Club of Baltimore, Inc. v. National League of Professional Baseball Clubs,* 259 U.S. 200 (1922), and its progeny. For the following reasons, I will grant defendants' motion as to plaintiffs' direct claims under the Constitution: but I will deny defendants' motion in all other repsects. As to defendants' assertion of exemption from antitrust liability, I hold that the exemption created by *Federal Baseball* is inapplicable here because it is limited to baseball's "reserve system."

I. BACKGROUND

A. The Allegations

Plaintiffs are Vincent M. Piazza and Vincent N. Tirendi, both Pennsylvania residents, and PT Baseball, Inc. ("PTB"), a Pennsylvania corporation wholly owned by Piazza and Tirendi. Pursuant to a written Memorandum of Understanding ("Memorandum") dated August 18, 1992, Piazza and Tirendi agreed with four other individuals, all Florida residents, to organize a limited partnership for the purpose of acquiring the Giants. (The parties to the Memorandum will be referred to collectively as the "Investors.")

* * *

Earlier, on August 6, 1992, the Investors had executed a Letter of Intent with Robert Lurie, the owner of the Giants, to purchase the Giants for $115 million. Pursuant to this Letter of Intent, Lurie agreed not to negotiate with other potential buyers of the Giants and to use his best efforts to secure from defendant Major League Baseball approval of the sale of the Giants to the Partnership and transfer of the team to the Suncoast Dome, located in St. Petersburg, Florida.

As required by the rules of Major League Baseball, the Partnership submitted an application to that organization on September 4, 1992 to purchase the Giants and move the team to St. Petersburg. In connection with this application, Major League Baseball and its "Ownership Committee" undertook or purported to undertake a personal background check on the Investors. On September 10, 1992, defendant Ed [*sic*] Kuhlmann, Chairman of the Ownership Committee, stated at a press conference that, among other things, the personal background check on the Investors had raised a "serious question in terms of some of the people who were part of that group" and that "a couple of investors will not be in the group." Kuhlmann elaborated that there was a "background" question about two of the investors rather than a question of financial capability and that something had shown up on a "security check." Kuhlmann also stated that the "money" of the two investors "would not have been accepted." Immediately following Kuhlmann at the news conference, Jerry Reinsdorf, a member of the Ownership Committee, added that the Ownership Committee's concern related to the "out-of-state" money and that the "Pennsylvania People" had "dropped out."

As the only principals of the Partnership who reside in Pennsylvania, Piazza and Tirendi aver that the clear implication of Kuhlmann's and Reinsdorf's comments, combined with the fact that Piazza and Tirendi are of Italian descent, was that the personal background check had associated them with the Mafia and/or other criminal or organized criminal activity. Piazza and Tirendi further allege that they have never been involved in such activity; nor had they "dropped out" of the Partnership. They also allege that they were never apprised by Baseball or anyone else of the charges against them nor given an opportunity to be heard.

On September 11, 1992, plaintiffs' counsel sent letters to Major League Baseball, Kuhlmann, and Reinsdorf requesting immediate correction of these statements and their implications. Plaintiffs' counsel never received a response to these letters, but on September 12, 1992, defendant Kuhlmann admitted to some members of the media that "there was no problem with the security check."

On the same day that the Partnership submitted its application to purchase and relocate the franchise, Kuhlmann directed Lurie to consider other offers to purchase the Giants, in knowing violation of Lurie's exclusive agreement with the Partnership. On September 9, 1992, Bill White, President of the National League, invited George Shinn, a North Carolina resident, to make an alternative bid to purchase the Giants in order to keep the team in San Francisco. An alternative offer was ultimately made by other investors to keep the Giants in San Francisco. Even though this offer was $15 million less than the $115 million offer made by the Partnership, Major League Baseball formally rejected the proposal to relocate the Giants to the Tampa Bay area on November 10, 1992.

Plaintiffs allege that Baseball never intended to permit the Giants to relocate to Florida and failed to evaluate fairly and in good faith their application to do so. They claim that to avoid relocation of the Giants, Baseball set out to "destroy the financial capability of the Partnership by vilifying plaintiffs." And in addition to preventing plaintiffs' purchase and relocation of the Giants, plaintiffs allege that Baseball's allegedly defamatory statements cost them the loss of a significant contract in connection with one of their other businesses, which depends upon impeccable personal reputations."

B. The Claims

1. Federal claims

* * *

Plaintiffs' final federal claim asserts violations of sections 1 and 2 of the Sherman Antitrust Act, 15 U.S.C.A. §§ 1 and 2 (West 1973 & Supp. 1993). Plaintiffs claim that Baseball has monopolized the market for Major League Baseball teams and that Baseball has placed direct and indirect restraints on the purchase, sale, transfer, relocation of, and competition for such teams. Plaintiffs allege that these actions have unlawfully restrained and impeded plaintiffs' opportunities to engage in the business of Major League Baseball.

II. DISCUSSION

* * *

D. Antitrust

* * *

3. Exemption from Antitrust Liability

I now turn to the heart of Baseball's motion to dismiss plaintiffs' Sherman Act claim — that in *Federal Baseball Club of Baltimore, Inc. v. National League of Professional Baseball Clubs, Inc.,* 259 U.S. 200 (1922); *Toolson v. New York Yankees,* 346 U.S. 356 (1953); and *Flood v. Kuhn,* 407 U.S. 258 (1972), the United States Supreme Court exempted Baseball from liability under the federal antitrust laws. Plaintiffs do not deny that these cases recognize some form of exemption from antitrust liability related to the game of baseball, but argue alternatively that the exemption either does not apply in this case, cannot be applied as a matter of law to the facts of this case, or should no longer be recognized at all.

* * *

b. Discussion

(i) Scope of the exemption

In each of the three cases in which the Supreme Court directly addressed the exemption, the factual context involved the reserve clause. Plaintiffs argue that the exemption is confined to that circumstance, which is not presented here. Baseball, on the other hand, argues that the exemption applies to the "business of baseball" generally, not to one particular facet of the game.

Between 1922 and 1972, Baseball's expansive view may have been correct. Although *Federal Baseball* involved the reserve clause, that decision was based upon the proposition that the business of exhibiting baseball games, as opposed to the business of moving players and their equipment, was not interstate commerce and thus not subject to the Sherman Act. *Toolson* ,also a reserve clause case, spoke in terms of the "business of baseball" enjoying the exemption. *Toolson,* 346 U.S. at 357. Likewise, *Radovich,* a 1957 decision concerning football, recognized the exemption as extending to the "business of organized professional baseball." *Radovich,* 352 U.S. 450-53.

In 1972, however, the Court in *Flood v. Kuhn* stripped from *Federal Baseball* and *Toolson* any precedential value those cases may have had beyond the particular facts there involved, *i.e.,* the reserve clause. The *Flood* Court employed a two-prong approach in doing so. First, the Court examined the analytical underpinnings of *Federal Baseball* — that the business of exhibiting baseball games is not interstate commerce. In the clearest possible terms, the Court rejected this reasoning, removing any doubt that "[p]rofessional baseball is a business . . . engaged in interstate commerce." *Flood,* 407 U.S. at 282.

Having entirely undercut the precedential value of the reasoning of *Federal Baseball,* the Court next set out to justify the continued precedential value of the result of that decision. To do this, the Court first looked back to *Toolson* and uncovered the following four reasons why the Court there had followed *Federal Baseball*:

> (a) Congressional awareness for three decades of the Court's ruling in *Federal Baseball*, coupled with congressional inaction. (b) *The fact that baseball was left alone to develop for that period upon the understanding that the reserve system was not subject to existing antitrust laws.* (c) A reluctance to overrule *Federal Baseball* with consequent retroactive effect. (d) A professed desire that any needed remedy be provided by legislation rather than court decree.

Id. at 273-74 (emphasis added). The emphasized text indicates that the *Flood* Court viewed the disposition in *Federal Baseball* and *Toolson* as being limited to the reserve system, for baseball developed between 1922 and 1953 with the understanding that its reserve system, not the game generally, was exempt from the antitrust laws. This reading of *Flood* is buttressed by (1) the reaffirmation in *Flood* of a prior statement of the Court that "'*Toolson* was a narrow application of the doctrine of *stare decisis*,'" *id.* at 276 (quoting *Shubert,* 348 U.S. at 228-30); and (2) the *Flood* Court's own characterization, in the first sentence of its opinion, of the *Federal Baseball, Toolson,* and *Flood* decisions: "For the third time in 50 years the Court is asked *specifically* to rule that professional baseball's *reserve system* is within the reach of the antitrust laws." *Id.* at 259 (emphasis added) (footnote omitted).

Viewing the dispositions in *Federal Baseball* and *Toolson* as limited to the reserve clause, the *Flood* Court then turned to the reasons why, even though analytically vitiated, the precise results in *Federal Baseball* and *Toolson* were to be accorded the continuing benefit of stare decisis. Like *Toolson,* the *Flood* Court laid its emphasis on continued positive congressional inaction and concerns over retroactivity. *Id.* at 283-84. In particular, the *Flood* Court "concluded that Congress as yet has had no intention to subject baseball's *reserve system* to the reach of the antitrust statutes." *Id.* at 983 (emphasis added). Finally, the Court acknowledged that "[w]ith its *reserve system* enjoying exemption from the federal antitrust laws, baseball is, in a very distinct sense, an exception and an anomaly. *Federal Baseball* and *Toolson* have become an aberration confined to baseball." *Id.* at 282 (emphasis added). Thus in 1972, the Supreme Court made clear that the *Federal Baseball* exemption is limited to the reserve clause.

Relying primarily upon *Charles O. Finley & Co. v. Kuhn,* 569 F.2d 527 (7th Cir. 1978), *cert. denied,* 439 U.S. 876 (1978), defendant Baseball offers a different reading of *Flood.* The plaintiff in that case, Charles O. Finley & Co. ("Finley"), owned the Oakland Athletics ("Oakland") baseball club. *Finley*, 569 F.2d at 530. In June of 1976, Oakland negotiated tentative agreements to sell Oakland's contract rights in three players to other teams. *Id.* at 531. Defendant Commissioner of Baseball Bowie Kuhn disapproved of the sale, and Finley subsequently brought suit, claiming, among other things, that the Commissioner conspired with others in violation of the antitrust laws. *Id.* Finding the Commissioner exempt from the antitrust laws under *Federal Baseball,* the district court granted summary judgment in favor of the Commissioner, and Finley appealed.

Like plaintiffs here, Finley argued on appeal that the exemption applies only to the reserve system. The Seventh Circuit disagreed, finding that "[d]espite the *two* references in the *Flood* case to the reserve system, it appears clear from the entire opinions in the three baseball cases, as well as from *Radovich,* that the Supreme Court intended to exempt the business of baseball, not any particular facet of that business, from the federal antitrust laws." *Id.* at 541 (emphasis added) (footnotes omitted).

In reaching this conclusion, the Seventh Circuit looked back to *Federal Baseball, Toolson,* and *Radovich,* as I have done here, and concluded that the Court had focused in those cases upon the business of baseball, not just the reserve clause. Then the court discussed *Flood*:

> In *Flood v. Kuhn,* the Court said that "Professional baseball is engaged in interstate commerce" and "we adhere once again to *Federal Baseball* and *Toolson* and to their application to professional baseball."

Id. (citation omitted). This single paragraph represents the Seventh Circuit's entire substantive discussion of *Flood* — the Supreme Court's most recent and most thorough explanation of the *Federal Baseball* exemption. The court discounted two references in *Flood* to the reserve clause and made no mention of the fact that *Flood* refers to the reserve clause at least *four* times, the two not discussed by the court indicating that (1) the Supreme Court reads *Federal Baseball* and *Toolson* as reserve clause cases, *Flood,* 407 U.S. at 273-74; and (2) the Court continues to follow the precise disposition of those decisions because

Congress continues to express no intention of subjecting the reserve clause to the antitrust laws, *id.* at 283.

But there is an even more significant flaw in the Seventh Circuit's analysis of *Flood* than in failing to note the extent to which that decision turned upon the reserve clause: Application of the doctrine of *stare decisis* simply permits no other way to read *Flood* than as confining the precedential value of *Federal Baseball* and *Toolson* to the precise facts there involved. To understand why this is so, one must fully understand the doctrine of *stare decisis* and its application by lower courts to Supreme Court decisions. The Third Circuit recently offered the following explanation:

> [Supreme Court] . . . opinions usually include two major aspects. First, the Court provides the legal standard or test that is applicable to laws implicating a particular . . . provision. This is part of the reasoning of the decision, the *ratio decidendi*. Second, the Court applies that standard or test to the particular facts of the case that the Court is confronting — in other words, it reaches a specific result using the standard or test.
>
> As a lower court, we are bound by both the Supreme Court's choice of legal standard or test and by the result it reaches under the standard or test. As Justice Kennedy has stated, courts are bound to adhere not only to results of cases, but also "to their explications of the governing rules of law." Our system of precedent or *stare decisis* is thus based on adherence to both the reasoning and result of a case, and not simply to the result alone. This distinguishes the American system of precedent, sometimes called "rule *stare decisis*," from the English system, which historically has been limited to following the results or disposition based on the facts of a case and thus referred to as "result *stare decisis*."
>
> Like lower courts, the Supreme Court applies principles of *stare decisis* and recognizes an obligation to respect both the standard announced and the result reached in its prior cases. Unlike lower courts, the Supreme Court is free to change the standard or result from one of its earlier cases when it finds it to be "unsound in principle [or] unworkable in practice."

Planned Parenthood of Southeastern Pa. v. Casey, 947 F.2d 682, 691-92 (3d Cir. 1991) (citations omitted), *aff'd in part and rev'd in part on other grounds,* 112 S.Ct. 2791 (1992).

Applying these principles of stare decisis here, it becomes clear that, before *Flood*, lower courts were bound by both the rule of *Federal Baseball* and *Toolson* (that the business of baseball is not interstate commerce and thus not within the Sherman Act) and the result of those decisions (that baseball's reserve system is exempt from the antitrust laws). The Court's decision in *Flood*, however, effectively created the circumstance referred to by the Third Circuit as "result *stare decisis*," from the English system. In *Flood*, the Supreme

Court exercised its discretion to invalidate the rule of *Federal Baseball* and *Toolson*. Thus no rule from those cases binds the lower courts as a matter of *stare decisis*. The only aspect of *Federal Baseball* and *Toolson* that remains to be followed is the result or disposition based upon the facts there involved, which the Court in *Flood* determined to be the exemption of the reserve system from the antitrust laws.

Neither *Finley* nor any other case cited by Baseball in support of its view of the exemption has undertaken such an analysis of the Supreme Court's baseball trilogy. And as none of these decisions is binding upon this Court, I will not follow them. It is well settled that exemptions from the antitrust laws are to be narrowly construed. *See Group Life & Health Ins. Co. v. Royal Drug Co.,* 440 U.S. 205, 231 (1979). Application of this principle is particularly appropriate, if not absolutely critical, in this case because the exemption at issue has been characterized by its own creator as an "anomaly" and an "aberration." *Flood*, 407 U.S. at 282; *see also id.* at 286 (*Federal Baseball* is a "derelict in the stream of the law." (DOUGLAS, J. dissenting)). For these reasons, I conclude that the antitrust exemption created by *Federal Baseball* is limited to baseball's reserve system, and because the parties agree that the reserve system is not at issue in this case, I reject Baseball's argument that it is exempt from antitrust liability in this case.

(ii) Nature of the exemption

Although it would be appropriate to end here my discussion of the *Federal Baseball* exemption, for the purpose of providing a complete record of decision in the event of certification for immediate appeal under 28 U.S.C.A. § 1292(b) (West Supp.1993), I will press on to consider the implications of applying "rule *stare decisis*" to *Federal Baseball* and plaintiffs' complaint.

Assuming, as Baseball would have it, that *Finley* is correct and the exemption extends beyond the reserve system, I must determine exactly how far the exemption reaches. I find that stating, as did the *Finley* court, that the exemption covers the "business of baseball" does little to delineate the contours of the exemption.

As mentioned above, to state a claim under the Sherman Act, plaintiffs must allege injury to competition in a relevant product market. *See Mid-South Grizzlies*, 720 F.2d at 785. Although the Supreme Court has not couched its explanation of the exemption in these terms, I believe that the only arguably surviving rule to be gleaned from the Court's baseball trilogy is that if the relevant product market involved is the market defined as the "business of baseball," injury to competition in that market may not be redressed under the Sherman Act. Cf *Henderson Broadcasting Corp. v. Houston Sports Ass'n.,* 541 F. Supp. 263 (S.D. Tex. 1982) (exemption does not apply to market for broadcast of baseball games). *Federal Baseball* itself made this clear. The focus in that case was upon competition in two different businesses or markets. The first was defined as the business of "giving exhibitions of base ball [*sic*]." *Federal Base-*

ball, 259 U.S. at 208. The second was defined as the business of "moving players and their paraphernalia from place to place." D.C. Opinion, 269 F. at 686. The Sherman Act was held not to apply to restraints in the first market because that market did not implicate interstate commerce. *Federal Baseball,* 259 U.S. at 208-09. Restraints in the second market, however, were redressable under the Sherman Act because that market did implicate interstate commerce. D.C. Opinion, 269 F. at 687-88. Thus, assuming the validity of *Finley,* the *Federal Baseball* exemption is one related to a particular market — the market comprised of the exhibition of baseball games — not a particular type of restraint (such as the reserve clause) or a particular entity (such as Major League Baseball).

It follows from having expressed the exemption as relating to a particular market that the next question is whether the plaintiffs in this case seek relief for restraints in that market or some other market. If Baseball's allegedly unlawful conduct merely restrained competition in the market comprised of baseball exhibitions, Baseball is immune from liability under the Act. If some other market was involved, however, even the expansive version of the *Federal Baseball* exemption would not apply.

A "market" may be defined as "any grouping of sales whose sellers, if unified by a hypothetical cartel or merger, could raise prices significantly above the competitive level." PHILIP E. AREEDA & HERBERT HOVENKAMP, ANTITRUST LAW ¶ 518.1b (Supp. 1991) (footnote omitted). As stated above, plaintiffs allege that the relevant product market in this case is the market for ownership of existing major league professional baseball teams. Reduced to its essentials, one can infer at this stage of the proceedings that this market has the following components: (1) the product being sold is an ownership interest in professional baseball teams; (2) the sellers are team owners; and (3) the buyers are those who would like to become team owners. Viewing the complaint in the light most favorable to plaintiffs, it would not be unreasonable also to infer that if the team owners combined, they could increase the price of teams considerably and control the conditions of sale.

The market to which the expansive version of the *Federal Baseball* exemption applies, on the other hand, has the following components: (1) the product is the exhibition of baseball games; (2) the sellers, as with the market defined by plaintiffs, are team owners; and (3) the buyers are fans and, perhaps, the broadcast industry. Thus the two markets have different products — baseball teams versus baseball games — and different consumers.

Although not expressed in market terms, the Court of Appeals in *Federal Baseball* attributed great weight to such differences. The court distinguished for Sherman Act purposes between the business that encompassed the exhibition of baseball games (the "game exhibition market") and the business that involved the movement of players and their paraphernalia (the "player transportation market"). D.C. Opinion, 269 F. at 686. The focus of the exemption was on the exhibition of games only, which Justice Holmes characterized in affirming the

Court of Appeals as "purely state affairs." *Federal Baseball,* 259 U.S. at 208. Other aspects of a baseball team's business — interstate aspects distinguishable from but nonetheless related to the games such as the movement of players and equipment — were not part of the exemption. Thus the anticompetitive nature of the reserve clause in the game exhibition market was found not to violate the Sherman Act, but could have given rise to a claim under the Act had it directly affected other markets. A similar distinction may be made here. The plaintiffs in this case target not anticompetitive activity in the market for the exhibition of baseball games; but anticompetitive activity in market for the sale of ownership interests in baseball teams — a market seemingly as distinguishable from the game exhibition market as the player transportation market.

Recent courts construing the expansive version of the exemption, although not focusing upon the distinction made by the Court of Appeals in *Federal Baseball,* have defined the exempted market (characterized as the "business of baseball") as that which is central to the "'unique characteristics and needs'" of baseball. *Postema v. National League of Professional Baseball Clubs,* 799 F. Supp. 1475, 1488 (S.D.N.Y. 1992) (quoting *Flood,* 407 U.S. at 282), *rev'd on other grounds,* 1993 WL 240824 (2d Cir. July 6, 1993); *Henderson,* 541 F. Supp. at 268-69, 271 (*Federal Baseball* exemption not applicable to market for broadcast of baseball games). There seems to be agreement among these courts and others that, defined in this way, the exempted market includes (1) the reserve system and (2) matters of league structure. *See, e.g., Professional Baseball Schools and Clubs, Inc. v. Kuhn,* 693 F.2d 1085 (11th Cir. 1982); *Postema,* 799 F. Supp. at 1489; *Henderson,* 541 F. Supp. at 269; *State v. Milwaukee Braves, Inc.,* 31 Wis. 2d 699, 144 N.W.2d 1, 15 (1966), *cert. denied,* 385 U.S. 990 (1966).

I do not view these decisions as conflicting with the analysis of the Court of Appeals in *Federal Baseball.* Applying their logic, the Court of Appeals can be understood as essentially viewing the movement of players and their equipment from game to game as a market activity not central to the unique characteristics and needs of exhibiting baseball games. Thus, when these decisions are considered together, the following list of activities or markets that are not within the exempted market can be generated: (1) the movement of players and their equipment from game to game; (2) the broadcast of baseball games; and, perhaps, (3) employment relations between organized professional baseball and nonplayers.

No court, however, has analyzed or applied the expansive view of the *Federal Baseball* exemption to the market for ownership interests in existing baseball teams. Thus I must determine whether this market is central to the unique characteristics and needs of baseball exhibitions. I conclude that such a determination is not possible without a factual record, and that, viewing plaintiffs' complaint in their favor, plaintiffs may be able to demonstrate that team ownership is not central to baseball's unique characteristics.

Plaintiffs plead that they were attempting to acquire an interest in a business owned by Robert Lurie engaged in the exhibition of baseball games — the San

Francisco Giants. As stated above, the products being sold in this market (teams) are different from those being sold in the exempted market (games).

And acquiring an ownership interest in team may very well be no more unique to the exhibition of baseball games than is moving players and their equipment from game to game. Although players and their equipment are, beyond doubt, uniquely necessary to a baseball game, the Court of Appeals in *Federal Baseball* found, on a trial record, that their movement — which essentially involves the transportation of men and equipment — was not. Likewise, although teams, as business entities engaged in exhibiting baseball games, are undoubtedly a unique necessity to the game, the transfer of ownership interests in such entities may not be so unique. Moreover, anticompetitive conduct toward those who seek to purchase existing teams has never been considered by any court to be an essential part of the exhibition of baseball games.

On the other hand, it is conceivable that, although the precise products in plaintiffs' market and the exempted market are different, these markets nonetheless overlap to such an extent that they should be treated identically for purposes of the expansive view of *Federal Baseball*. In other words, the acquisition of a business that is engaged in baseball exhibitions may be central in some way not apparent on the face of the complaint to the unique characteristics of baseball exhibitions. Without a factual record, I would be engaged in mere speculation in deciding now whether it is or is not.

Accordingly, I conclude that if "rule *stare decisis*" and the *Finley* expansive view were applied, this case would not be ripe for determination of whether the *Federal Baseball* exemption applies. Thus, even under this analysis, Baseball's motion would be denied. One additional observation bears mentioning. I have considered plaintiffs' complaint in the light most favorable to plaintiffs and have accepted their definition of the relevant market as the market for team ownership. But the gravamen of plaintiffs' case may be Baseball's interference with plaintiffs' efforts to acquire and relocate the Giants to Florida. As stated earlier, matters of league structure have been viewed by other courts as being unique to baseball. The physical relocation of a team and Baseball's decisions regarding such a relocation could implicate matters of league structure, and thus be covered by the exemption. If, therefore, the expansive view of *Federal Baseball* were applied and a factual record were developed showing that this case concerns only restraints on the market for ownership and relocation of the Giants as inseparable activities, "rule *stare decisis*" could require application of the exemption.

III. CONCLUSION

Baseball's motion to dismiss is granted in part and denied in part. Plaintiffs' direct claims under the U.S. Constitution are dismissed. In all other respects the motion is denied. Because I have not dismissed all of plaintiffs' claims over which this Court has original jurisdiction, I will continue to exercise supplemental jurisdiction over plaintiffs' state law claims. . . .

CURT FLOOD ACT OF 1998

Pub. L. No. 105-297, 112 Stat. 2824

January 27, 1998

An Act

To require the general application of the antitrust laws to major league baseball, and for other purposes.

Be it enacted by the Senate and House of Representatives of the United States of America in Congress assembled,

SECTION 1. SHORT TITLE.

This Act may be cited as the "Curt Flood Act of 1998".

SECTION 2. PURPOSE.

It is the purpose of this legislation to state that major league baseball players are covered under the antitrust laws (*i.e.*, that major league baseball players will have the same rights under the antitrust laws as do other professional athletes, *e.g.*, football and basketball players), along with a provision that makes it clear that the passage of this Act does not change the application of the antitrust laws in any other context or with respect to any other person or entity.

SECTION 3. APPLICATION OF THE ANTITRUST LAWS TO PROFESSIONAL MAJOR LEAGUE BASEBALL.

The Clayton Act (15 U.S.C. § 12 et seq.) is amended by adding at the end the following new section:

"SEC. 27. (a) Subject to subsections (b) through (d), the conduct, acts, practices, or agreements of persons in the business of organized professional major league baseball directly relating to or affecting employment of major league baseball players to play baseball at the major league level are subject to the antitrust laws to the same extent such conduct, acts, practices, or agreements would be subject to the antitrust laws if engaged in by persons in any other professional sports business affecting interstate commerce.

"(b) No court shall rely on the enactment of this section as a basis for changing the application of the antitrust laws to any conduct, acts, practices, or agreements other than those set forth in subsection (a). This section does not create, permit or imply a cause of action by which to challenge under the antitrust laws, or otherwise apply the antitrust laws to, any conduct, acts, practices, or agreements that do not directly relate to or affect employment of major league baseball players to play baseball at the major league level, including but not limited to —

"(1) any conduct, acts, practices, or agreements of persons engaging in, conducting or participating in the business of organized professional baseball relating to or affecting employment to play baseball at the minor league level, any organized professional baseball amateur or first-year player draft, or any reserve clause as applied to minor league players;

"(2) the agreement between organized professional major league baseball teams and the teams of the National Association of Professional Baseball Leagues, commonly known as the `Professional Baseball Agreement', the relationship between organized professional major league baseball and organized professional minor league baseball, or any other matter relating to organized professional baseball's minor leagues;

"(3) any conduct, acts, practices, or agreements of persons engaging in, conducting or participating in the business of organized professional baseball relating to or affecting franchise expansion, location or relocation, franchise ownership issues, including ownership transfers, the relationship between the Office of the Commissioner and franchise owners, the marketing or sales of the entertainment product of organized professional baseball and the licensing of intellectual property rights owned or held by organized professional baseball teams individually or collectively;

"(4) any conduct, acts, practices, or agreements protected by Public Law 87-331 (15 U.S.C. § 1291 et seq.) (commonly known as the 'Sports Broadcasting Act of 1961');

"(5) the relationship between persons in the business of organized professional baseball and umpires or other individuals who are employed in the business of organized professional baseball by such persons; or

"(6) any conduct, acts, practices, or agreements of persons not in the business of organized professional major league baseball.

"(c) Only a major league baseball player has standing to sue under this section. For the purposes of this section, a major league baseball player is —

"(1) a person who is a party to a major league player's contract, or is playing baseball at the major league level; or

"(2) a person who was a party to a major league player's contract or playing baseball at the major league level at the time of the injury that is the subject of the complaint; or

"(3) a person who has been a party to a major league player's contract or who has played baseball at the major league level, and who claims he has been injured in his efforts to secure a subsequent major league player's contract by an alleged violation of the antitrust laws: Provided however, That for the purposes of this paragraph, the alleged antitrust violation shall not include any conduct, acts, practices, or agreements of persons in the business of organized professional baseball relating to or affecting employment to play baseball at the minor league level, including any organized professional baseball amateur or first-year player draft, or any reserve clause as applied to minor league players; or

"(4) a person who was a party to a major league player's contract or who was playing baseball at the major league level at the conclusion of the last full championship season immediately preceding the expiration of the last collective bargaining agreement between persons in the business of organized professional major league baseball and the exclusive collective bargaining representative of major league baseball players.

"(d)(1) As used in this section, 'person' means any entity, including an individual, partnership, corporation, trust or unincorporated association or any combination or association thereof. As used in this section, the National Association of Professional Baseball Leagues, its member leagues and the clubs of those leagues, are not 'in the business of organized professional major league baseball'.

"(2) In cases involving conduct, acts, practices, or agreements that directly relate to or affect both employment of major league baseball players to play baseball at the major league level and also relate to or affect any other aspect of organized professional baseball, including but not limited to employment to play baseball at the minor league level and the other areas set forth in subsection (b), only those components, portions or aspects of such conduct, acts, practices, or agreements that directly relate to or affect employment of major league players to play baseball at the major league level may be challenged under subsection (a) and then only to the extent that they directly relate to or affect employment of major league baseball players to play baseball at the major league level.

"(3) As used in subsection (a), interpretation of the term 'directly' shall not be governed by any interpretation of section 151 et seq. of title 29, United States Code (as amended).

"(4) Nothing in this section shall be construed to affect the application to organized professional baseball of the nonstatutory labor exemption from the antitrust laws.

"(5) The scope of the conduct, acts, practices, or agreements covered by subsection (b) shall not be strictly or narrowly construed".

NOTES AND COMMENTS

1. The baseball exemption to the application of antitrust laws is also discussed further in this chapter, and at **Chapter 6**, *infra,* as it relates to employment/labor issues. The question of whether professional sports activities other than baseball should be regarded as exempt from the antitrust statutes recurs in various contexts, as discussed in **Note 4**, *infra.* Interestingly, economists have long recognized the peculiar workings of markets in the professional sports area that result in monopoly leagues. *See, e.g.,* Neale, *The Peculiar Economics of Professional* Sports, 78 QUARTERLY J. OF ECON. 1-14 (1964). A traditional professional sports league model, developed by El-Hodiri and Quirk, relies on Rottenberg's pioneering work which concludes that the player contract reserve clause and amateur draft do not inhibit the feared movement of players to the highest bidders. Rottenberg, *The Baseball Player's Labor Market,* 64 J. POL. ECON. 242, 255 (1956). The Coase Theorem assures that the ownership of property rights should not alter the allocation of resources. Coase, *The Problem of Social* Cost, 3 J. LAW & ECO. 1 (1960). Thus, where players can be bought and sold, league constraints will not deter movement of players from weak to strong markets. El-Hodiri and Quirk recommended that league rules prohibiting the sale of players should be exempt from the antitrust laws, due to the externalities peculiar to professional sports. El-Hodiri and Quirk, *An Economic Model of a Professional Sports League,* 79 J. POL. ECON. 1302 (1971).

2. The *Piazza* case was followed in two Florida court decisions, *Butterworth v. National League of Professional Baseball Clubs,* 644 So. 2d 1021 (Fla. 1994), *affirmed,* 2003 WL 21212629 (11th Cir. 2003), and *Morsani v. Major League Baseball,* 663 Fla. App. 553 (1995), but rejected in *Major League Baseball v. Butterworth,* 181 F. Supp. 2d 1316 (N.D. Fla. 2001), ("The Court determined that the decision whether to terminate baseball's antitrust exemption should be made by Congress, not by the Court. . . . The Court's rationale remains every bit as valid today as it was when *Flood* was decided.") and *Minnesota Twins Partnership v. State ex. rel. Hatch,* 592 N.W.2d 847 (Minn. 1999) ("*Piazza* ignores what is clear about *Flood* — that the Supreme Court had no intention of overruling *Federal Baseball* or *Toolson. . . .*"). *See also, Major League Baseball v. Crist,* 331 F.3d 1177 (11th Cir. 2003) ("Lest there be any doubt about the matter, the district court forcefully destroyed the notion that the antitrust exemption should be narrowly cabined to the reserve system."). For a commentary describing the "flawed analysis" of *Piazza, see* Scibilia, *Baseball Franchise Stability and Consumer Welfare: An Argument for Reaffirming Baseball's Antitrust Exemption with Regard to its Franchise Relocation Rules,* 6 SETON HALL J. SPORT L. 409 (1996).

3. Review *Flood v. Kuhn.* Can you identify precedent for the *stare decisis* principle enunciated in *Flood*? Did the United States Supreme Court abdicate its responsibility in *Flood v. Kuhn*? Can the result be justified in light of the application of antitrust statutes to other professional sports? The Holmes opinion in *Federal Baseball Club v. National League,* 259 U.S. 200 (1922), although criticized, is probably not so erroneous for its day. The early twentieth century marked the last days of a perceived *laissez-faire* period in the nation's history. Remember, *Plessy v. Ferguson* was the law of the land.

The *Flood* Court, conversely, had fifty years of antitrust and commercial law development to aid its analysis. The national perspective changed drastically during the fifty year period between *Federal Baseball Club* and *Flood.* Can the *Flood* opinion be explained as a "romanticism" of professional baseball? One aspect of the inquiry that had not changed was "baseball's unique characteristics and needs." The uniqueness of organized baseball is further explored at **Note 9**, below. *See generally*, Abrams, *Before the Flood: The History of Baseball's Antitrust Exemption*, 9 MARQ. SPORTS L.J. 307 (1999).

4. The fact that Congress had refused to legislatively repeal the baseball antitrust exemption, although given the opportunity, had significant bearing on the *Flood* decision.

The *Flood* opinion recognizes that baseball, "with full and continuing Congressional awareness," has developed and expanded unhindered by federal legislative regulation. Does the Supreme Court limit the parameters of development and expansion to "reserve clause" matters, as suggested by the *Piazza* court?

Congress' passage of the Curt Flood Act of 1998, expressly removing the exemption in the limited area of major league labor relations, is an opportunity in which Congress chose not to legislatively repeal the exemption in other areas. Congress considers granting the antitrust exemption to non-baseball professional sports leagues to generate further protection of cities from the losses stemming from franchise relocations. *See, e.g.* S. 952 (introduced May 4, 1999). For an analysis of other bills providing antitrust exemption to non-baseball sports conditioned upon league-based franchise relocation constraints, *see* Cotrupe, *Curbing Franchise Free Agency: The Professional Sports Franchise Relocation Act of 1998*, 9 DEPAUL-LCA J. ART & ENT. L. 165 (1998).

Both the House and Senate regularly revisited the baseball antitrust exemption in past years. For a comprehensive treatment of Congressional activity, *see* DUQUETTE, REGULATING THE NATIONAL PASTIME (1999).

5. Is the *Piazza* court accurate in its statement that *Federal Baseball* involved the reserve clause? What was the basis for the plaintiff's cause of action in *Federal Baseball*? What are the underlying elements of plaintiffs' causes of action in *Piazza*? *See National League v. Federal Baseball Club*, 269 Fed. 681 (D.C. Cir. 1920) (Plaintiff claims National Agreement between major leagues and minor league association, including reserve clause, produced monopolization of professional baseball). *See also American Baseball Club of Chicago v. Chase*, 149 N.Y. Supp. 6 (1914).

6. Is the *Piazza* court correct in concluding that the U.S. Supreme Court in *Flood* limited the precedential scope of *Federal Baseball* and *Toolson* to the reserve clause? What is the rationale of the *Flood* Court's adherence to *Toolson*? What is the basis of Justice Burger's concurrence? Did the U.S. Supreme Court, in *Flood*, recognize the doctrine of "reliance" as an alternative rationale for the 1953 *Toolson* case? *Compare* the Court's statement in *Radovich*:

> Vast efforts had gone into the development and organization of baseball since that [Federal Baseball] decision and enormous capital had been invested in reliance on its permanence. Congress had chosen to make no change. All this, combined with the flood of litigation that would follow its repudiation, the harassment that would ensue, and the retroactive effect of such a decision, led the Court to the practical result that it should sustain the unequivocal line of authority reaching over many years.

Radovich v. National Football League, 352 U.S. 445, 450-51 (1957).

7. Does the *Piazza* court accurately state and apply the principle of *stare decisis*?

Is it clear that the Supreme Court invalidated the "governing rules" underlying *Federal Baseball* and *Toolson*, thus enabling the lower court to utilize the English rule of "result *stare decisis*," rather than the American system of "rule *stare decisis*?" *See Planned Parenthood of Southeastern Pennsylvania v. Casey*, 505 U.S. 833 (1992) (where original rationale for a rule has ceased to exist, continuation of the rule may be justified due to reliance); *Rappa v. New Castle County*, 18 F.3d 1043, 1061 (3d Cir. 1994) (where lower courts are unable to derive governing standards from plurality opinions, result *stare decisis* may be utilized); *Salerno v. American League of Professional Baseball Clubs*, 429 F.2d 1003 (2d Cir. 1970) (possible overruling of Supreme Court holdings is the exclusive privilege of the Supreme Court). Does the Judge Padova adopt the "result" envisioned by the Supreme Court in *Flood*?

8. Does the analysis of the *Piazza* opinion survive the passage of the Curt Flood Act of 1998? For an article suggesting the presence of a "slight crack" for the application of *Piazza* and its offspring, *see* Edmonds, *The Curt Flood Act of 1998: A Hollow Gesture After All These Years?*, 9 MARQ. SPORTS L.J. 315 (1999). *See generally*, *Symposium: The Curt Flood Act*, 9 MARQ. SPORTS L.J. (1999). *See also*, *Major League Baseball v. Butterworth*, 181 F. Supp. 2d 1316, 1331 n.16 (N.D. Fla. 2001), *affirmed,* 2003 WL 21212629 (11th Cir. 2003) (Congress explicitly indicated its intention not to affect issues other than direct employment matters). *But see*, Myers, *Shaking Up the Line-Up: Generating Principles for an Electrifying Economic Structure for Major League Baseball*, 12 MARQ. SPORTS L. REV. 631, 639 (2002) (Congress enumerates a nonexclusive list of issues that do not "directly relate to or affect" major leaguers as defined in the Act, and further limits standing to major league players). For an article suggesting that the player-management bargaining relationship was not effectively changed by the language of the Curt Flood Act, *see* Kaiser, *Revisiting the Impact of the Curt Flood Act of 1998 on the Bargaining Relationship between Players & Management in Major League Baseball,"* 1 DEPAUL J. SPORTS L. & CONTEMP. PROBS 230 (2004).

9. The existence of the minor leagues distinguishes organized baseball from other professional sports. Is minor league baseball included in the various courts' analyses of the baseball antitrust exemption? Do the "business of baseball" or "reserve clause" definitions of the exemption encompass the minor leagues, or the hierarchy of agreements forming the structure of the minor leagues?

The longstanding contractual relationship between the minor leagues and Major League Baseball is unique to professional baseball, although professional hockey has developed a similar structure. Contemporaneously with and subsequent to the *Federal Baseball* decision in 1922, the major and minor leagues constructed a more than 75-year contractual relationship to develop players of major league quality and provide baseball entertainment for fans in North America. Branch Rickey, in 1921, began to successively develop the farm system approach to player development (others, including the Cleveland Indians had tried it before). Commissioner Landis initially opposed the farm system. Necessities over time moved the minor leagues from a position of relative independence in 1921 to a state of dependence on major league sharing of expenses in modern times. Without the antitrust exemption, the farm system of "organized baseball" is subject to attack under the Sherman and Clayton Acts. The baseball antitrust exemption enabled investment in the minor league system by major league clubs, minor leagues and clubs, and minor league communities to develop unhindered by challenges under the antitrust laws and costs of litigation. For historical descriptions of the minor leagues and development of the farm system, *see* LEIFER, MAKING THE MAJORS 80, 91, 195-96 (1995); SULLIVAN, MINORS (1990).

The contractual arrangements of "organized baseball" are structured as follows:

a. National Association Agreement — 20 minor leagues (orig. 1901)

b. Major League Agreement — National & American Leagues (1921)

c. Professional Baseball Agreement — Major League Baseball and National Association of Professional Baseball Leagues

d. Uniform Player Development Contract between Major and Minor League Clubs

e. Uniform Minor League Contract between Major League Club and Minor League Player

Both the National Association Agreement and Professional Baseball Agreement establish protected territorial rights and other joint arrangements. Under the Professional Baseball Agreement, the Major League club pays a specified number of player salaries (based on league classification: AAA, AA, A, Short-A, Rookie); salary packages for manager, coaches, and trainer; share in costs of bats and balls; and other expenses. The Minor League club/league assumes the cost of umpires, umpire development program, transportation costs, specified hotel costs, and all game and facility costs. A minor league player, who is drafted or signed as a free agent, may be obligated to the signing club for a period of six years. However, if the player is not on the 40-player roster at the end of three years, the player may be drafted by another Major League club.

10. Courts have consistently held that the baseball antitrust exemption is applicable to cases involving minor league baseball. *See, e.g., Triple-A Baseball Club Assoc. v. Northeastern Baseball, Inc.,* 832 F.2d 214 (1st Cir. 1987); *Professional Baseball Schools & Clubs, Inc. v. Kuhn,* 693 F.2d 1085 (11th Cir. 1982); *Portland Baseball Club v. Kuhn,* 491 F.2d 1101 (9th Cir. 1974); *New Orleans Pelicans Baseball, Inc. v. National Association of Professional Baseball Leagues, Inc.*, 1994 WL 631144 (E.D. La. 1994). The Congressional testimony of "Bud" Selig and Stan Brand, as well as others throughout the years, affirms that some minor league business operations will fail in the event the antitrust exemption is removed. *Testimony of Allan H. "Bud" Selig, President of the Milwaukee Brewers Baseball Club and Chair of the Major League Executive Council*, before the Economic and Commercial Law Subcommittee of the Committee on the Judiciary, U. S. House of Representatives, Sept. 22, 1994; *Testimony of Stanley M. Brand, Vice-President, National Association of Professional Baseball Leagues, Inc.,* before the Subcommittee on Labor-Management Relations of the Committee on Education and Labor, U. S. House of Representatives, Sept. 29, 1994. Do aggrieved parties possess standing to prosecute a Fifth Amendment "regulatory takings" claim? *See Lucas v. South Carolina Coastal Council*, 505 U.S. 1003 (1992) (where regulations diminish value of property, a court considers "[t]he economic impact of the regulation on the claimant . . . the extent to which the regulation has interfered with distinct investment-backed expectations").

11. Several courts have previously enunciated limits to the reach of the baseball antitrust exemption. A radio broadcaster brought suit against the owner of the Houston Astros and another broadcaster alleging that cancellation of a broadcast contract was a violation of the antitrust laws. The court held that suit was not barred by the baseball exemption. *Henderson Broadcasting Corp. v. Houston Sports Ass'n, Inc.,* 541 F. Supp. 263, 271 (S.D. Tex. 1982). *See also Postema v. National League of Professional Baseball Clubs*, 799 F. Supp. 1475 (S.D.N.Y. 1992) (umpires); *Twin City Sportservice, Inc. v. Charles O. Finley*, 365 F. Supp. 235 (N.D. Cal. 1972), *rev'd on other grounds*, 512 F.2d 1264 (9th Cir. 1975) (concessions); *Fleer v. Topps Chewing Gum & Major League Baseball Players Ass'n*, 658 F.2d 139 (3d Cir. 1981) (baseball cards).

12. The baseball antitrust exemption, existing as a matter of federal law, preempts state antitrust law to the contrary. *See Major League Baseball v. Butterworth,* 181 F. Supp. 2d 1316 (N.D. Fla. 2001), *affirmed,* 2003 U.S. App. LEXIS 10487 (11th Cir. 2003); *State v. Milwaukee Braves, Inc.,* 144 N.W.2d 1 (Wis. 1966).

13. For arguments that the baseball antitrust exemption results in adverse effects on consumers, *see* Ross, *The Effect of Baseball's Status as a Legal "Anomaly and Aberration,* in LEGAL ISSUES IN PROFESSIONAL BASEBALL 215 (Kurlantizick ed. 2005). *Compare*, Nathanson, *The Irrelevance of Baseball's Antitrust Exemption,* 58 Rutgers L. Rev. 1 (2005) (baseball antitrust exemption is largely irrelevant to the actual workings of the business of baseball); Ostertag, *Baseball's Antitrust Exemption: Its History & Continuing Importance*, 4 VA. SPORTS & ENT. L.J. 54 (2004)(exemption plays its most important role ever in contributing to the preservation of the overall health of the sport).

D. LEAGUE DECISION MAKING — GENERALLY

Each professional sports league possesses a distinct organizational form established by the league's governing documents. Some leagues operate within the typical business corporation structure, and others utilize the non-profit status for the conduct of league affairs. Other leagues exist as unincorporated associations. Regardless of form, league operations require centralized decision making. A typical league decision making structure includes a "board of directors" type committee of owners, joined by a league president or commissioner with varying powers. The NFL, for example, is an unincorporated association, not operated for profit. The NFL Properties, Inc. is the profit making arm of the League. The NFL Executive Committee includes one representative from each member club and possesses general decision making powers as provided by the NFL Constitution. *See* NFL Const. and ByLaws, Art. VI. The NFL Commissioner is present at meetings of the Executive Committee, and likely wields considerable influence. *See generally* Harris, THE LEAGUE: THE RISE AND DECLINE OF THE NFL (1986).

Both the NBA and NHL are also unincorporated associations, with respective Commissioners, "Boards of Governors," and separate "Properties" entities. *See* NBA Const. and Bylaws, Section 2; NHL Const. and ByLaws, Section 2. The National League and American League, as noted above, are independent leagues with distinct Constitutions. *See* Constitution & Rules of The National League of Professional Baseball Clubs, Section 2; Constitution of The American League of Professional Baseball Clubs, Section 2. The two major leagues are joined by the Major League Agreement. *See* MLA, Art. I. The Major League Agreement establishes the Office of the Commissioner (MLA, Art. I, Sec. 1). League-wide merchandising efforts are performed by Major League Baseball Properties, Inc.

Each of the minor baseball leagues possesses a Constitution and Bylaws that delegates decision making powers to a Board of Directors and League President. As revealed in the *New Orleans Pelicans* case below, some decisions of minor baseball leagues require interim ratification by the President of the National Association of Professional Baseball Leagues and oversight of the Office of the Commissioner. *See generally* Professional Baseball Agreement; National Association Agreement.

Professional sports leagues function as private associations. Courts are reluctant to scrutinize actions of private associations, except where the league activities are deemed to lack fundamental fairness, or are considered arbitrary and capricious.

Leagues, of course, must conduct the decision process according to the terms of the leagues' governing documents. The law of private associations as applied in amateur sports is discussed at **Chapter 2**, **Section B**, *supra*. Courts regularly review league decision making for compliance with the antitrust laws. The application of the antitrust statutes to amateur sports, including an introduction of the Sherman Act, is addressed at **Chapter 4**, **Section A**, *supra*. Most league governing documents, including collective bargaining agreements, provide for arbitration of intra-league disputes.

League directors, sitting as governing board members of the league entity, possess fiduciary duties of care and loyalty. *See e.g.,* RUPA § 404; Gervitz, CORPORATION LAW, § 4.1-.2 (2000). As one court recognizes at **Note 5**, *infra*, league directors must make decisions for the league as a whole and may not act in their own self-interest to the detriment of the league. League decisions, in order to protect the market opportunity, must make efforts to include all costs, including externalities, in the decision formula to avoid the tragedy of the commons phenomenon. Given that the league has delegated certain autonomous property rights in the league's market opportunity, clubs possesses potential conflicts of interest in given situations. As you will observe from the cases and materials below, although the fiduciary relationship is generally recognized, the fiduciary principles are yet to play a significant role in legal challenges to league decision making.

E. LEAGUE DECISION MAKING — MEMBERSHIP

Professional sports leagues traditionally restrict membership by and through formal and informal rules requiring approval of franchise sales and further prohibiting certain classes of ownership. The National Football League, for example, requires approval by 3/4 of club owners of all transfers of ownership interests in an NFL club, other than transfers within a family. NFL Const. and ByLaws, art. 3.5. Although the organizational structure of an NFL member may exist as a sole proprietorship, association, partnership, or corporation, the entity must be organized for purposes of operating a professional football club. NFL Const. and ByLaws, art. 3.1-3.9. The provisions were interpreted by former NFL Commissioner, Pete Rozelle, as requiring organization solely for the purpose of operating a football team. *See generally* GREENBERG & GRAY, 1 SPORTS LAW PRACTICE § 11.06(4)(a) (2d ed. 2005). The NFL has traditionally respected an uncodified policy barring the sale of ownership interests in an NFL club to the public through offerings of publicly traded stock. *See Sullivan v. National Football League*, 34 F.3d 1091 (1st Cir. 1994).

League approval processes are designed to assure that (1) member club operations are adequately capitalized; 2) *pro forma* budgets are reasonably projected; 3) the new ownership and club are otherwise economically secure; and 4) owners are of sound moral character and otherwise compatible with league members. Approval is required for the sale of clubs by members of the league, and for sale of expansion franchises by the league. League Directors must act in the best interests of the league as a whole, thereby assuring that all costs are internalized within the decision making. As the *Levin* case, *infra*, indicates, leagues owners sometimes utilize "subjective" criteria in scrutinizing prospective members.

As you work on the Problem below, attempt to identify the impact that a league membership decision may have on the integrity and stability of the league-generated market opportunity. Roger Noll emphasizes that a poorly managed team affects other clubs in the league, and the league as a whole. If a club is not operated efficiently, its games with other teams may be unpopular, affecting the financial status of all clubs. Because revenues are shared, the return is less than optimal. The league also has an interest in the integrity of operations. Noll, *The Economics of Sports Leagues*, 1 LAW OF AMATEUR & PROFESSIONAL SPORTS, ch. 19 (Uberstine ed. 2005).

PROBLEM

A large media-based corporation desires to purchase an NFL club and an NBA team. The corporation contemplates securing ownership interests in either existing franchises or expansion clubs. The corporation hired your law firm to assist in the needed transactions.

The senior partner assigned the matter to you. She instructed you to review the cases in the **Case File,** *infra*, and write a memorandum outlining the law as it applies to sports league decision making. She further directed you to assume that each of the relevant leagues requires approval of the sale of a franchise by a 3/4 vote of league members. Also assume that each league has a rule prohibiting ownership of more than one professional sports franchise. The senior partner anticipates difficulties in gaining approval of the sales transactions. She specifically asks for the following information:

1. What general legal constraints, incuding contract, tort, and fiduciary principles, apply to league owners in their league decision making roles?
2. Identify the essential elements of an antitrust claim for use in the event of league rejection of a sale of a franchise.

3. What additional elements, if any, are required to maintain an antitrust action challenging the cross-ownership rule?

4. What evidentiary matters are significant in the contemplated antitrust actions? Develop a checklist of needed data for your trial notebook.

CASE FILE

MORSANI v. MAJOR LEAGUE BASEBALL

663 So. 2d 653 (Fla. Dist. Ct. App. 1995)

RYDER, Acting Chief Judge.

Frank Morsani and the Tampa Bay Baseball Group (TBBG) seek review of the trial court's dismissal of their complaint alleging tortious interference with advantageous contractual and business relationships . . . in connection with their attempt to acquire a major league baseball team. We hold that the trial court erred in its dismissal for failure to state a cause of action for tortious interference because the complaint sufficiently alleged that the appellees exceeded the scope of their approval rights. . . . Accordingly, we reverse the dismissal and remand for further proceedings consistent with this opinion.

Appellants were plaintiffs in a multi-count suit against sixty defendants, nearly all of whom were associated with major league baseball in one capacity or another at the relevant times. The complaint alleged that the defendants had tortiously interfered with various contractual rights and advantageous business relationships which the plaintiffs had developed over the years in their efforts to acquire ownership of a major league baseball team in Tampa, Florida. . . .

The trial court dismissed the complaint as to fifty-eight of the sixty defendants pursuant to a motion for failure to state a cause of action pursuant to Florida Rule of Civil Procedure 1.140(b)(6). The plaintiffs and the remaining two defendants stipulated without prejudice to the plaintiffs' rights to challenge the propriety of the final judgment itself, that the two defendants would be deemed included in the order of dismissal.

Counts I through III of the complaint alleging tortious interference correspond to the plaintiffs' attempts to purchase a team through negotiations with owners of Minnesota Twins, Inc. and Texas Rangers, Ltd. and to acquire an expansion team, respectively. . . . Our function when reviewing an order of dismissal entered pursuant to Rule 1.140(b), Florida Rules of Civil Procedure, is confined to whether the trial court properly concluded that the complaint did not state a cause of action. In reaching that determination, we must take the pleaded facts as true and we are not concerned with the quality of the allegations or how they will ultimately be proved. . . .

The complaint alleges that in 1982, Morsani attended the major league baseball winter meetings, expressed his desire to purchase a major league baseball team and sought advice from various defendants concerning the team's purchase and relocation to the Tampa Bay area. Upon the defendants' advice, TBBG was formed. Various defendants told the plaintiffs that they would support and approve the sale of the Minnesota Twins, Inc. to them if they would secure a site to build a major league baseball stadium in the Tampa Bay area. At an expense in excess of $2 million, the plaintiffs secured a long-term lease with the Tampa Sports Authority for the construction of a baseball stadium and entered into negotiations with the shareholders of Minnesota Twins, Inc. for the purchase of their stock.

In 1984, the owners of 51% of the stock of Minnesota Twins, Inc., Calvin Griffith and Thelma Griffith-Haynes, agreed to sell their controlling interest to the plaintiffs for approximately $24 million on condition that they first buy H. Gabriel Murphy's 42.14% minority interest in the corporation. The plaintiffs then negotiated and entered into a fully-executed written contract with Murphy for the purchase of his interest, at a purchase price of $11.5 million. The contract provided that its closing was conditioned upon prior approval by the owners of other American League teams, as the Constitution of the American League required, and any other approvals which might validly be required. Thereafter, with full knowledge of these agreements, various of the defendants conspired together and used improper means to prevent the plaintiffs from consummating their purchase. They caused Griffith and Griffith-Haynes to sell their 51% interest to Carl Pohlad. They also demanded that the plaintiffs assign their contract with Murphy to Pohlad, and that Murphy consent to the assignment. At the time this assignment was demanded, the value of the minority interest purchased by the plaintiffs had increased from $11.5 million to $25 million.

The plaintiffs balked at the demand and sought payment for the $13.5 million increase in value of the contract, as well as reimbursement of the $2 million previously expended, as a condition to assigning the contract to Pohlad. The relevant defendants then threatened the plaintiffs. These threats were that plaintiffs would never own an interest in a major league baseball team, and that there would never be a major league baseball team in the Tampa Bay area, unless the plaintiffs assigned the contract as demanded and accepted only $250,000.00 for the assignment, and, further, that they agree to forbear pursuing any legal remedies for the additional $15 million plus in damages in exchange for obtaining an ownership interest in another major league baseball team in time to begin the 1993 season. In exchange for the promise of another team, the plaintiffs assigned their contract to Pohlad.

The complaint also alleged that in 1988, several defendants informed the plaintiffs that they would support and approve the sale of Texas Rangers, Ltd. to the plaintiffs. The plaintiffs then reached an agreement with Eddie Gaylord for the purchase of his 33% interest in the partnership, and entered into a written contract with Eddie Chiles for the purchase of his 58% controlling interest in the partnership. Thereafter, with full knowledge of these agreements, various defendants conspired together and used improper means to prevent the plaintiffs from consummating their purchase. They caused both Gaylord and Chiles to breach their agreements with the plaintiffs in favor of a Texas investor. They then, again, threatened the plaintiffs that they would never own an interest in a major league baseball team, and that there would never be a major league baseball team in the Tampa Bay area, unless the plaintiffs agreed to forbear pursuing any legal remedies in exchange for obtaining an ownership interest in another major league baseball team in time to begin the 1993 season. In exchange for the renewed and continuing promise of another team, the plaintiffs once again withheld their claims.

Some of the defendants informed the plaintiffs in 1988 that, consistent with the prior promises made to obtain their forbearance, the plaintiffs would be awarded an expansion team in time to begin the 1993 season. Thereafter, various defendants conspired together and used improper means to prevent the plaintiffs from obtaining the promised team. In 1989, they interfered with the plaintiffs' advantageous business relationships by demanding that one of the investors in TBBG relinquish his interest as a condition of obtaining the team, and thereby reduced the corporation's financial viability. The defendants then prohibited the plaintiffs from obtaining any additional financial backing from persons or entities not located in the Tampa Bay area, including Sam Walton. These interferences reduced the financial viability of the plaintiffs well below that of a competitor group led by H. Wayne Huizenga, and effectively eliminated the plaintiffs from contention for the promised expansion team which began the 1993 season as The Florida Marlins in Miami.

To establish the tort of interference with a contractual or business relationship, the plaintiff must allege and prove (1) the existence of a business relationship under which the plaintiff has legal rights, (2) an intentional and unjustified interference with that relationship by the defendant and (3) damage to the plaintiff as a result of the breach of the business relationship. . . .

The appellants acknowledge that a cause of action for tortious interference does not exist against one who is himself a party to the contract allegedly interfered with. . . . They urge, however, that none of the defendants except Calvin Griffith and Thelma Griffith-Haynes owned stock in Minnesota Twins, Inc., and only they and Gabriel Murphy could contract to sell their stock in the Twins to the plaintiffs. They further contend that the various defendants' approval rights do not make them parties to the contract.

The trial court concluded that the existence of the defendants' approval rights made them, as the leagues and teams, the source of the business opportunity allegedly interfered with, and, therefore, were incapable of interference. See *Genet Co. v. Annheuser-Busch, Inc.*, 498 So. 2d 683 (Fla. App. 1986). *Genet*, however, is distinguishable because the brewer's decision to disapprove the proposed transfer was based entirely on business considerations. No malice was shown. Here, the appellants have alleged the use of threats, intimidation and conspiratorial conduct.

[I]t is clear that the privilege to interfere in a contract because of a financial interest is not unlimited. *Frank Coulson, Inc.-Buick v. General Motors Corp.*, 488 F.2d 202 (5th Cir. 1974). The better view is that it is necessary for the interfering party to have a financial interest in the business of the third party which is in the nature of an investment in order to justify the interference. . . . Furthermore, a privilege to interfere with a third party's conduct does not include the purposeful causing of a breach of contract. *Yoder v. Shell Oil Co.,* 405 So. 2d 743, 744 (Fla. App. 1981), *review denied,* 412 So. 2d 470 (Fla. 1982).

Where there is a qualified privilege to interfere with a business relationship, the privilege carries with it the obligation to employ means that are not improper. *McCurdy v. Collins*, 508 So. 2d 380, 384 (Fla. App. 1987). As the appellants have pleaded their cause of action, the defendants' approval rights were exercised outside the context of the proper exercise of their rights. *See Peacock v. General Motors Acceptance Corp.*, 432 So. 2d 142 (Fla. App. 1983).

We conclude, therefore, that Counts I, II and III state a cause of action for tortious interference with advantageous contractual and business relationships and reverse their dismissal.

* * *

DANAHY and LAZZARA, JJ., concur.

NEW ORLEANS PELICANS BASEBALL CLUB, INC. v. NATIONAL ASSOCIATION OF PROFESSIONAL BASEBALL LEAGUES, INC.

1994 U.S. Dist. LEXIS 21468 (E.D. La. 1994)

FELDMAN, District Judge.

Defendants move the Court to grant summary judgment in their favor on all counts of the complaint and to dismiss the complaint with prejudice. For the reasons that follow, the Court DENIES defendants' motion except as to plaintiff's state and federal antitrust claims, which the Court GRANTS.

Background

This case involves the unsuccessful attempt of plaintiff to purchase and relocate a AA Southern League baseball club to New Orleans. The National League added two expansion teams for 1993, the Colorado Rockies, and the Florida Marlins. Likewise, the AAA International League added two clubs, in Ottawa, Canada and Charlotte, North Carolina. These changes displaced minor league clubs previously operating in those cities. Consequently, the AAA Denver Zephyrs and the AAA Charlotte Knights needed to find new homes. In search of a new home, the Zephyrs explored the possibility of relocating to New

Orleans. The plaintiff claims, however, that the Zephyrs abandoned this idea due to lack of financing.

This litigation arises from the attempts by the New Orleans Pelicans, Inc. to purchase the Charlotte Knights from Charlotte Baseball Inc. and relocate the team to the New Orleans area. The plaintiff and Charlotte Baseball Inc were brought together by the President of the Southern League, Jimmy Bragan. . . . In August 1992, the plaintiff signed a letter of intent to purchase the Charlotte Knights of the Southern League, and conditioned the purchase on the ability of the Pelicans to move the club to the New Orleans territory. . . .

On November 2, 1992, President Moore gave written approval of the Control Interest Transfer. Three days later, on November 5, he issued a conditional written approval of the relocation of the Charlotte club to New Orleans "subject to the possibility of (1) a protest by another League, or [and here is the spark that fueled the dispute] (2) the submissions of notice by a club of a League of higher classification of its protection of, or request to relocate to, territory that would include any portion of your proposed relocation territory." This letter required that such a notice be in writing and received by the close of business on November 20, 1992. . . .

On November 18, 1992, the Zephyrs, who play in the American Association, submitted a written request for the New Orleans territory; President Moore notified plaintiff of this change of events the following day.

On November 20, 1992, the American Association are said to have voted, in a conference call, 7 to 1 in favor of the Zephyr's relocation to New Orleans. The result of this vote was, defendants claim, communicated orally to Mr. Moore by a representative of the American Association, Branch Rickey, that same day. Plaintiff disputes whether this vote was taken in accordance with the American Association's by-laws, and whether the result of the vote was communicated orally to Mr. Moore before the November 20, 1992 deadline.

On November 23, 1992, Mr. Moore announced three requirements that the Zephyrs had to meet by December 1, 1992 in order to receive consideration of their desire to try to relocate to the New Orleans territory. Specifically, he required permission of the American Association for relocation and approval of the proposed playing facility; a copy of a lease on a facility in which the franchise would play; and approval of the major league team affiliate of the relocation and proposed playing facility.

On December 6, despite the Zephyr's failure to comply with the December 1, 1992 deadline, Moore granted Denver's request to relocate, and thus, thwarted the application of the plaintiff. Then Moore denied an appeal by the Southern League and the PBEC refused to review the Moore decision or the entire history of the transaction.

The Pelicans never purchased the Charlotte club. The plaintiff, of course, blames this on the defendants. The Charlotte club has since been sold to another and is playing temporarily in Nashville, Tennessee. The Zephyrs did relocate to New Orleans and played their 1993 home games at UNO.

II. Arbitrary and Capricious Conduct

This Court stated the following in its Order and Reasons, dated April 30, 1992, denying defendants' motion to dismiss:

> To be entitled to relief, the plaintiff must prove: (1) that the New Orleans territory was open at the time the Pelicans claimed it, but was thereafter protected and the Pelicans were entitled to protection by the defendants after it was granted to them; (2) that the defendants violated their own rules and expanded their rules to benefit the Zephyrs; (3) that the defendants' actions were intentional, arbitrary and capricious; (4) that the New Orleans territory was never properly claimed by the Zephyrs and was properly awarded to the Pelicans; (5) that the New Orleans territory was never properly claimed by the League to which the Zephyrs belong; and (6) that after the Zephyrs claimed the territory, the defendants acted improperly because they did not enforce their own rules, requirements and deadlines.

Defendants claim that the plaintiff's suit must fail because the Pelicans never had territorial rights protected by the PBA or the NAA and the defendants properly awarded those rights to the Zephyrs. In support of this argument, the defendants maintain that the November 2, 1992 letter merely approved the Pelicans' Application for Control Interest Transfer, the ownership rights, but did not approve the team's relocation to New Orleans. They further argue that the November 5, 1992 letter properly set forth the requirements of Rule 34(E) and that those requirements were satisfied when the Zephyrs submitted, on November 18, 1992, a written application for the New Orleans territory, which the League approved on November 20, 1992. . . .

Plaintiff asserts that material facts are in dispute as to whether defendants acted arbitrarily and capriciously by allowing the Zephyrs to relocate to the New Orleans area. Specifically, plaintiff claims first, that there are material questions of fact regarding the effect of the November 2, 1992 letter. . . . Second, plaintiff asserts that material questions of fact abound regarding whether Moore exceeded the scope of his authority under the rules of baseball in his November 5th letter and whether the conditions of that letter were properly satisfied. . . .

A. Analysis

Under Louisiana law, courts will generally not interfere with the internal judgments of a private association, except in cases in which the action complained of is arbitrary, capricious or unjustly discriminatory. . . . That test drives this analysis, and it will be a central feature of pre-jury submission motion practice at the close of some or all of the evidence.

The question before the Court, therefore, is whether there is a genuine issue of a material fact that the defendants acted arbitrarily and capriciously in this case. A genuine issue of material facts exists where the evidence is such that a reasonable jury could find that the defendants acted arbitrarily and capriciously. Reviewing the evidence in a light most favorable to the plaintiff, the Court finds that the defendants are not entitled to summary relief.

Two fact issues trump summary judgment. First, the meaning of the letter of November 2, 1992. That letter explicitly approved the Application for Control Interest Transfer; however, the letter may also have awarded the plaintiff territorial rights in the New Orleans territory. The text itself is inconclusive. . . .

Next, the Court finds that the controversial letter of November 5, 1992 and the circumstances that followed present the strongest reasons for denying summary judgment. In fact, the success or failure of plaintiff's case will ride on the letter of November 5, 1992. It provides in part:

> . . . I hereby approve the proposed relocation subject to the possibility of (1) a protest by another League, or (2) the submission of notice by a club of a league of higher classification of its protection of, or request to relocate to, territory that would include any portion of your proposed relocation territory. To be effective, any such protest or notice must be in writing and received by the National Association office before 5:00 p.m. on November 20, 1992.

At first blush, it seems that President Moore's second condition departs from the textual grant of Rule 34, which controls the relocation of teams. Rule 34 says:

> . . . The Commissioner and the President of the Minor League Association shall have fifteen (15) days from the date of approval of the proposed expansion or relocation to grant permission for the occupation of the territory, and during that fifteen (15) day period a *League of higher classification* that applies for the rights to the same territory shall be given preference. (emphasis added)

President Moore's letter states, however, that a club of a higher classification may also express an interest in an area; in contrast, Rule 34 states only that a league of a higher classification may express such an interest. This distinction takes on significant meaning given what ensued after the fifteen day deadline was triggered. It is this tension that animates the fight.

It is undisputed that the Zephyrs expressed interest in the New Orleans area in writing on November 18, 1992. It is further undisputed that the American Association, in a 7 to 1 vote, approved the Zephyrs' request on November 20, 1992.

The defendants' first and basic problem with these events is that the Zephyrs are most assuredly a club, not a league. Moore has admitted that his authority comes from the rules of baseball and that he cannot legislate. Thus, a material question of fact remains regarding whether the conditions set forth in the letter of November 5, 1992 were within Moore's authority as President of the National Association.

Defendants argue that all this is irrelevant because the American Association approved the Zephyrs' move on November 20, 1992, and orally notified President Moore of their vote later that day. Plaintiff correctly points out that the record is far from clear as to whether President Moore received notice of the vote on November 20. Moreover, President Moore's letter expressly required that any notice had to be in writing. Instead, it was given orally. Accordingly, even if the notice was given on November 20, 1992, it was arguably not given in accordance with the guidelines set forth by President Moore himself. These unresolved fact issues could give content to the arbitrary and capricious characterization of unwelcomed conduct and must be resolved at trial.

Consequently, the Court DENIES defendants' motion for summary judgment on plaintiff's claims relating to the arbitrary and capricious conduct of defendants.

III. Remedies

1. Specific Performance

Defendants maintain that, even if arbitrary and capricious conduct is proved, plaintiff has no right to specific performance. The defendants claim that no territorial rights can accrue until and unless the relocation has the approval of the League, the President of the NAPBL, and consideration by the Commissioner. Defendants claim that the only specific performance that could be awarded would be to order the Commissioner's Office to consider whether to disapprove the Pelicans' relocation request.

Plaintiff maintains that it is entitled to specific performance of its rights to the New Orleans territory. The right to the New Orleans territory, plaintiff claims, would return plaintiff to the status quo as it was prior to the arbitrary and capricious acts complained of, thereby enabling it to attempt to bring a professional baseball team to New Orleans. Moreover, if the Pelicans were entitled to the territory, plaintiff says, the team is entitled to be compensated for the value of the territory as a result of the actions of the National Association that awarded the territory to the Zephyrs.

A. Analysis

If plaintiff proves that the arbitrary and capricious decisions of defendants caused it to lose its rights to the New Orleans territory, plaintiff will be entitled to specific performance, in the form of being granted rights to the New Orleans territory. That is the only way to return plaintiff to the status quo prior to the arbitrary and capricious acts complained of, unless compensation is a provable alternative.

Ultimately, the Court agrees with plaintiff that it would be inappropriate for the Court to attempt to speculate on what might happen if plaintiff wins.

Accordingly, the Court rejects defendants' argument that plaintiff is not entitled to specific performance.

2. Baseball Rules Benefit Only Leagues and Clubs

Defendants argue that the rules of baseball exist for the benefit of the Leagues and the Clubs that are subject to the NAA and PBA. Defendants argument focuses on the fact that, because the Pelicans do not own a club within a NAPBL member league, they are not capable of relocating to New Orleans.

Plaintiff asserts that this argument incorrectly assumes that the Pelicans never had rights to the New Orleans territory. They claim that defendants' argument puts the cart before the horse. These arguments echo those to which the Court has already spoken.

A. Analysis

The Court still agrees with plaintiff. Defendants' argument overlooks plaintiff's theory in this case. Plaintiff's case turns on whether the Pelicans were awarded rights to the New Orleans territory; if a jury finds that they were awarded those rights, then plaintiff is entitled to relief in some form, regardless of the present ownership status of the AA team. Whether the Pelicans own a team today is irrelevant to whether defendants deprived that team of their rights to the New Orleans territory.

PIAZZA v. MAJOR LEAGUE BASEBALL

831 F. Supp. 420 (E.D. Pa. 1993)

[The facts of this case are found *supra* at **Section C**, with the materials relating to the baseball antitrust exemption.]

PADOVA, J.

D. Antitrust

Baseball next moves to dismiss plaintiffs' claims under sections 1 and 2 of the Sherman Anti-Trust Act ("Sherman Act"), 15 U.S.C.A. §§ 1 and 2 (West 1973 & Supp.1993), and offers the following . . . reasons why these claims should be dismissed: (1) plaintiffs have failed to allege that Baseball's actions restrained competition in a relevant market; (2) plaintiffs have no standing to assert a Sherman Act claim; . . . .

1. Relevant Market

Absent a per se violation, which neither party argues has been alleged here, a cause of action under the Sherman Act requires, inter alia, an allegation of injury to competition in relevant product and geographic markets. *See Mid-South Grizzlies v. National Football League*, 720 F.2d 772, 785-88 (3d Cir.1983), *cert. denied*, 467 U.S. 1215 (1984); *Fleer Corp. v. Topps Chewing Gum, Inc.*, 658 F.2d 139, 147 (3d Cir. 1981). Baseball argues that plaintiffs have not alleged an injury to competition in a relevant product market because plaintiffs were seeking to join Baseball, rather than compete with it.

In support of this proposition, Baseball relies heavily upon the Third Circuit's holding in *Mid-South Grizzlies*. Plaintiffs in that case, the Mid-South Grizzlies (the "Grizzlies"), were a joint venture located in Memphis, Tennessee that owned a team in the World Football League ("WFL"). *Mid-South Grizzlies*, 720 F.2d at 775-76. After the WFL's demise, the Grizzlies applied for admission to the National Football League ("NFL"). *Id.* The NFL rejected the Grizzlies' application, and the Grizzlies subsequently brought suit against the NFL under sections 1 and 2 of the Sherman Act. *Id.* The Third Circuit affirmed the district court's entry of summary judgment in favor of the NFL because, inter alia, "the Grizzlies [had] shown no actual or potential injury to competition resulting from the rejection of their application for an NFL franchise." *Id.* at 787.

The Grizzlies had identified the relevant product market for Sherman Act purposes as "major-league professional football." *Id.* at 783. The NFL argued that denial of the Grizzlies' franchise application could not have injured competition in this product market because there was no economic competition among league members capable of injury. *Id.* at 786. The Third Circuit agreed in part, finding on the record before it no evidence of economic competition between a potential NFL franchise located in Memphis, Tennessee and the nearest team geographically (280 miles away in St. Louis, Missouri). The court expressly declined, however, to hold that there could never be intra-league competition, noting that it was conceivable that "within certain geographic submarkets two league members [could] compete with one another for ticket buyers, for local broadcast revenue, and for sale of the concession items like food and beverages and team paraphernalia." *Id.* at 787 (footnote omitted). Baseball argues on the basis of this decision that it could not have injured competition in a relevant product market. I disagree.

There are two important distinctions between *Mid-South Grizzlies* and the instant case. First, unlike the Grizzlies, plaintiffs here were not seeking to join Major League Baseball through creation of a franchise but were attempting to purchase an existing team. The import of this distinction turns upon the second distinction, which is that also unlike the Grizzlies, who identified the relevant product market as major-league professional football generally, plaintiffs here have identified the relevant product market as the market for existing American League and National League baseball teams. In other words, plaintiffs allege injury to competition in the team franchise market (the market for ownership of professional baseball teams, and the market for ownership of the Giants in particular). They do not seek to redress injury to an intra-league market comprised of Major League Baseball generally, which plaintiffs sought to join through the purchase of a franchise, and which may or may not include competition among present franchise owners. Plaintiffs aver that they were competing in the team franchise market with other potential investors located primarily outside of Major League Baseball for ownership of the Giants, and that Baseball interfered directly and substantially with competition in that market. I therefore reject Baseball's contention that plaintiffs have failed to allege a restraint on competition in a relevant product market. *See Fishman v. Estate of Wirtz*, 807 F.2d 520, 532 n.9 (7th Cir. 1986) (stating in antitrust action brought by jilted suitors of the Chicago Bulls basketball team that the "national sports franchise market could be a relevant market" for Sherman Act purposes) (dictum)). *Mid-South Grizzlies* is therefore entirely distinguishable from the instant case.

* * *

2. Standing

The principles of standing applicable to alleged violations of sections 1 and 2 of the Sherman Act are the same as those applicable to questions of standing under section 4 of the Clayton Act, 15 U.S.C.A. § 15 (West Supp. 1993). *See Bogus v. American Speech & Hearing Ass'n,* 582 F.2d 277, 288 n.13 (3d Cir. 1978). "In addressing the 'standing' of parties to bring a claim under § 4 of the Clayton Act, the Supreme Court has focused on the nexus between the antitrust violation and the plaintiff's harm and on whether the harm alleged is of the type for which Congress provides a remedy." *In re: Lower Lake Erie Iron Ore Antitrust Litig.,* 998 F.2d 1144, 1163 (3d Cir. 1993, as corrected June 15, 1993). In *Associated Gen. Contractors, Inc. v. California State Council of Carpenters*, 459 U.S. 519, 545 (1983) ("*AGC*"), the Supreme Court outlined a multi-factor inquiry to analyze nexus questions for purposes of standing under § 4 of the Clayton Act. As characterized recently by the Third Circuit, the *AGC* standing factors are as follows: (1) the causal connection between the antitrust violation and the harm to the plaintiff and the intent by the defendant to cause that harm, with neither factor alone conferring standing; (2) whether the plaintiff's alleged injury is of the type for which the antitrust laws were intended to provide redress; (3) the directness of the injury, which addresses the concerns that liberal application of standing principles might produce speculative claims; (4) the existence of more direct victims of the alleged antitrust violations; and (5) the potential for duplicative recovery or complex apportionment of damages. *Lower Lake Erie* at 1165-66. These factors must be considered and balanced in light of the unique circumstances of each case. *See Merican, Inc. v. Caterpillar Tractor Co.,* 713 F.2d 958, 965 (3d Cir. 1983), *cert. denied,* 465 U.S. 1024 (1984).

Without directly addressing the *AGC* factors, Baseball posits two reasons why plaintiffs lack Sherman Act standing. First, Baseball contends that plaintiffs' antitrust claim can be boiled down to Baseball's rejection of the Partnership's application to acquire and transfer the Giants. Thus, Baseball argues, any claim arising out of an alleged restraint on competition belongs only to the Partnership entity, not plaintiffs individually. Second, Baseball asserts that the only direct harm allegedly suffered by plaintiffs independent of their interest in the Partnership was the alleged injury to their reputation, a harm not actionable under the Sherman Act. I view the first of Baseball's arguments as focusing upon the first, third and fourth *AGC* factors, and the second of Baseball's arguments as focusing upon the second *AGC* factor.

a. Directness of injury, causation and other victims

The directness of injury and causation for antitrust standing purposes depends upon whether the plaintiff has alleged a direct causal connection between the defendant's purported antitrust activity and the plaintiff's alleged harm. *See AGC*, 459 U.S. at 540-42; *Lower Lake Erie* at 1166-67. Plaintiffs identify the antitrust activity here as Baseball's alleged conspiracy to intentionally monopolize and restrain competition in the market for ownership of Major League Baseball teams, the Giants in particular. Plaintiffs allege that these unlawful activities have resulted in (1) the elimination of plaintiffs and organizations in which plaintiffs owned majority interests from competition in this market; (2) the exclusion of plaintiffs and their organizations from engaging in the business of Major League Baseball; and (3) loss of plaintiffs' contractual and property rights.

Baseball argues that plaintiffs' alleged injury is, at best, indirect because only the Partnership, not plaintiffs, could have been affected. Although this contention may prove factually correct after the case has developed, I cannot find sufficient support in plaintiffs' complaint to agree. Plaintiffs plead that they were individually excluded by Baseball from the relevant product market and suffered damages as a result. For example, plaintiffs Piazza and Tirendi allege that Baseball schemed to prevent the transfer of the Giants to Florida by unlawfully excluding them first individually, as the financial backbone of the Partnership, from the market for the Giants (and other Major League Baseball teams), only later to target the financially weakened Partnership and the remaining Investors. Thus the plaintiffs, not just the Partnership, sustained the injuries for which they seek redress.

In support of its position that the Partnership is a more direct victim, Baseball relies upon several decisions that stand for the familiar proposition that [a] stockholder of a corporation does not acquire standing to maintain an [antitrust] action in his own right, as a shareholder, when the alleged injury is inflicted upon the corporation and the only injury to the shareholder is the indirect harm which consists in the diminution in value of his corporate shares resulting from the impairment of corporate assets. *Kauffman v. Dreyfus Fund, Inc.*, 434 F.2d 727, 732 (3d Cir. 1970), *cert. denied,* 401 U.S. 974 (1971). *See also, e.g., Rand v. Anaconda-Ericsson, Inc.*, 794 F.2d 843, 849 (2d Cir.), *cert. denied,* 479 U.S. 987 (1986). But such decisions, even if they apply with equal force to partners and partnership entities, are inapposite. It is true that plaintiffs cite injury to the Partnership as a consequence of Baseball's antitrust behavior; but they also identify unique, particularized injury to themselves. As I read their complaint, plaintiffs do not seek to redress a diminution in the value of their interest in the Partnership or any other wrong that befell the Partnership per se. They seek to redress Baseball's allegedly unlawful exclusion of Vincent Piazza, Vincent Tirendi, and PTB from competing in a relevant market. I therefore find that the first, third, and fourth *AGC* factors weigh strongly in plaintiffs' favor.

b. Goal of antitrust laws

Baseball next contends that the only harm plaintiffs allege independent of the Partnership is harm to their reputations. Again, I must disagree. As discussed above, plaintiffs seek to redress damages sustained as a result of Baseball's alleged exclusion of them from a relevant market. Such injuries are clearly of the type that Congress sought to redress through the antitrust laws. The Supreme Court has repeatedly stated that a central purpose of the Sherman Act is to protect "the economic freedom of participants in the relevant market." *AGC*, 459 U.S. at 538. Thus, the second *AGC* factor favors plaintiffs.

c. Duplicative recovery and complex apportionment

Although the parties do not address the fifth *AGC* factor — the potential for duplicative recovery or complex apportionment of damages — I conclude that this factor, too, weighs in favor of plaintiffs. Were plaintiffs suing on behalf of the Partnership, I can conceive of a situation where multiple recoveries would be possible to the extent that the other Investors are not parties to this litigation. As noted above, however, that is not the case. Plaintiffs seek to redress their own particular injuries; thus there appears no risk of duplicative recoveries or complex apportionment of damages. Finding that each of the *AGC* factors weighs in favor of plaintiffs, I therefore reject Baseball's contention that plaintiffs lack standing to press a Sherman Act claim.

LEVIN v. NATIONAL BASKETBALL ASSOCIATION

385 F. Supp. 149 (S.D.N.Y. 1974)

OWEN, District Judge.

* * *

The plaintiffs, two businessmen, in 1972 had an agreement to buy the Boston Celtics basketball team, one of the 17-member National Basketball Association.

N.B.A., as its constitution recites, is a joint venture "organized to operate a league consisting of professional basketball teams each of which shall be operated by a member of the Association." It has been in existence since 1946. Each of its joint ventures holds a franchise to operate a team. While the teams compete vigorously on the basketball court, the joint venturers are dependent upon one another as partners in the league format to make it possible. N.B.A. operates through its Board of Governors which consists of one governor designated by each member. Action by the Board on a transfer of membership requires the affirmative vote of three quarters of the members of the Board.

When plaintiffs applied to the N.B.A. . . . that motion failed to carry at the meeting of the Board of Governors on June 15, 1972, there being two votes in favor, thirteen votes opposed and one not present.

Plaintiffs immediately demanded and were granted a personal hearing before the Board. Following the presentation of their case a second vote was taken. It was, however, to identical effect.

There is a sharp dispute on the reason for the rejection. Plaintiffs contend that they were rejected because of their friendship and business associations with one Sam Schulman, owner of the Seattle SuperSonics, who was an anathema to the other members of the league. Plaintiff Levin testified in a deposition that he was told the "real" reason by Basketball Commissioner Kennedy and Richard Bloch, President of the Phoenix Suns and Chairman of the N.B.A. Finance Committee. According to Levin, Kennedy said:

> "I don't have to draw you a picture. . . . They are obviously worried that if you fellows are also owners, that you will side with Sam Schulman in all matters in the future and cause the league more troubles than they now have with Sam as it is."

* * *

[A]ccording to Levin, Bloch said:

> "You are with Sam Schulman. . . . They are obviously worried that you fellows, being close to Sam, are going to be siding with him on any matters that come up before the NBA."

On the other hand, the reason given by the N.B.A. for the rejection was that the business association between the plaintiffs and Schulman violated the "conflict of interest" provision of the N.B.A. constitution. That provision reads: A member shall not exercise control directly or indirectly, over any other member of the Association. This provision is necessary, N.B.A. claims, in order that the league may enjoy public support because there is in fact, and the public believes there is, intense competition in the league framework between the *teams* operated by the N.B.A. members.

In any event plaintiffs, rejected, sold their rights in the Celtics elsewhere and commenced this action.

In order to survive defendants' motion for summary judgment, plaintiffs must demonstrate that the conduct complained of is a violation of the antitrust laws. While it is true that the antitrust laws apply to a professional athletic league, and that joint action by members of a league can have antitrust implications this is not such a case. Here the plaintiffs wanted to *join* with those unwilling to accept them, *not to compete with them,* but to be partners in the operation of a sports league for plaintiffs' profit. Further, no matter which reason one credits for the rejection, it was not an anti-competitive reason. Finally, regardless of the financial impact of this rejection upon the plaintiffs, if any, the exclusion of the plaintiffs from membership in the league did not have an anti-competitive effect nor an effect upon the public interest. The Celtics continue as an operating club, and indeed are this year's champion.

The law is well established that it is competition, and not individual competitors, that is protected by the antitrust laws.

It is also clear that where the action the plaintiffs attack, the rejection from copartnership, has neither anti-competitive intent nor effect, that conduct is not violative of the antitrust laws.

* * *

Since there was no exclusion of plaintiffs from competition with the alleged excluders, nor anti-competitive acts by them and no public injury occasioned thereby, the defendants' acts did not constitute a violation of the antitrust laws and defendants' motion for summary judgment is granted. . . .

NOTES AND COMMENTS

1. For discussion of the application of antitrust and other legal principles to the various leagues' decision making processes, *see* GREENBERG & GRAY, 1 SPORTS LAW PRACTICE §§ 11.04, 11.06 (2d ed. 2005); Roberts, *Antitrust Issues in Professional Sports, in* 3 LAW OF PROFESSIONAL AND AMATEUR SPORTS Ch. 21 (Uberstine ed., 2005). *See* **Chapter 6**, *infra,* for treatment of antitrust law as applied to professional sports league player restraints.

2. The "tragedy of the commons" concept is regularly applied in many contexts. *See generally*, Revesz, FOUNDATIONS OF ENVIRONMENTAL LAW & POLICY (1997) (environment); Lipton, *Information Property: Rights & Responsibilities*, 56 FLA. L. REV. 135 (2004) (public information); Holman & McGregor, *The Internet as Commons: The Issue of Access*, 10 COMM. L. & POL'Y 267 (2005) (cyberspace); Bessendorf, *Game in the Hothouse: Theoretical Dimensions in Climate Change*, 28 SUFFOLK TRANSNAT'L L. REV. 325 (2005) (climate change); Symposium Issue, 22 YALE J. ON REG. (2005) (regulation of radio waves); and Vinciguerra, *The Dialectic Relationship Between Different Concepts of Property Rights & Its Significance on Intellectual Property Rights*, 10 TECH. L. L& POL'Y 155 (2005) (health care).

Society utilizes various mechanisms that serve to internalize costs or benefits to avoid the tragedy. Hardin advocated "mutual coercion agreed upon," which suggests regulation and/or consensual arrangements. Hardin, *Tragedy of the Commons*, 162 *Science* 1243 (1968). Demsetz urges the use of property rights to deal with externalities. Demsetz, *Toward a Theory of Property Rights*, 57 J. AMER. ECON. REV. 347, 348 (1967). Calabresi & Malamed encourage the use of property rights, rules of liability, and the power of eminent domain. Calabresi & Malamed, *Property Rules, Liability Rules & Inalienability: One View of the Cathedral*, 85 HARV. L. REV. 1089, 1094-95 (1972). Pigou strongly favors the use of taxation as a means of internalizing externalities. Pigou, THE ECONOMICS OF WELFARE (1920).

3. Is the *Morsani* court's recognition of the tortious interference with a contractual relationship claim persuasive? Is the defendant accurate in arguing that Major League Baseball is a party to the contract and thus cannot interfere with the contract? Does MLB exist as a party due to its approval power status? Which party may be said to "own" the Minnesota Twins franchise? In *Hollywood Baseball Association v. Commissioner*, 42 T.C. 234 (1964), the U.S. Tax Court described the relationship of the Pacific Coast League and its members, as follows:

> The P.C.L. had the exclusive right to play monopoly baseball in certain areas of the west coast of the United States, including Los Angeles and San Francisco. This exclusive right to play establishment baseball in the relevant areas was inherent in the P.C.L.'s membership in the general system of organized professional baseball.
>
> The member teams of the P.C.L. had *derivative rights* from the league under the general entity scheme of organized baseball. A franchise membership in the P.C.L. entitled the holder to operate a P.C.L. team within the territory controlled by the league and granted the right to play P.C.L. baseball as a member of the league. . . . It bestowed on the member an equal share of the P.C.L. exclusive territorial rights within the baseball monopoly, including allocable rights to televise and radiocast games played against home teams in the P.C.L. area. It entitled the franchise holder to the privilege of being an equal partner in the league, including all league assets and property rights.
>
> Separate, distinct, and divisible from rights derived from the P.C.L. franchise ownership were so-called territorial rights. The league territorial right was the right to play exclusive entity baseball in several areas. A team territorial right was the right to play home games within a certain area. . . . (Emphasis added)

Must an applicant for league membership secure a transfer of "derivative rights" (market opportunity) from the league? Does the *Morsani* court indicate that a party to a contract may nevertheless tortiously interfere where the party employs "improper means," including malice, in its process for approval? Can similar arguments be made on the basis of the implied covenant to fairly deal with applicants for league membership?

A question that has remained dormant in judicial scrutiny of professional sports league decisions focuses upon the exact nature of the "derivative rights" that the league assigns to the club operators. As explained above, the naked market opportunity is a property interest generated by the league. The league could choose to conduct games as a syndicate or private concern, as did the National League at the turn of the twentieth century. The league could relocate the team, expand or contract, or sell the opportunity outright. But, the syndicated approach proved unpopular with the fans. *See*, Scully, THE BUSINESS OF MAJOR LEAGUE BASEBALL 4 (1989). Instead, the leagues assign the "derivative rights" to team operators. Definition of the nature of the assigned interests may be aided by Hohfeldian analysis. *See*, Hohfeld, *Some Fundamental Legal Conceptions as Applied in Judicial Reasoning*, 23 YALE L.J. 16 (1913); *Fundamental Legal Conceptions as Applied in Judicial Reasoning*, 26 YALE L.J. 710 (1917). The club owner purchases some sticks in the market opportunity "bundle of sticks," but not the stick enabling the operator to sell the franchise. The league retains the stick that provides the right to alienate the opportunity. The operator possesses, in Hohfeldian terminology, only a "privilege" to suggest sale to a new operator. The team owners have "privileges," thinking they are "rights," and the courts generally do not see the difference. The typical approach of litigants and the resulting judicial examination treats the issues as if the team operator obtains all of the sticks in the bundle, and then contracts or regrants away some rights. Viewing the league-team relationship from a property perspective generates interesting questions regarding the respective rights and duties of the parties, standing, and whether the league is a "single entity" for antitrust purposes.

For an example of a seemingly confused judicial analysis of the rights and duties of the league and teams with respect to sale of a franchise, *see Triple-A Baseball Club Associates v. Northeastern Baseball, Inc.*, 655 F. Supp. 513, *aff'd in part, rev'd in part,* 832 F.2d 214 (1st Cir. 1987). The International League Constitution required that membership in the League could only be assigned upon the approval of five League Directors. The International League argued at trial that the league transfers membership and the attendant rights at the time the League Directors approve of the suggested assignment. The trial court construed the language of the Constitution to empower the club owner with the "exclusive power to do the actual assigning." "[T]he league's only role in the process is to grant its approval and thereby confer upon the member the power to effectively assign." *Id.* at 544. Thus, the court ruled that the club owner has the "exclusive" right to alienate the market opportunity, but cannot exercise the right until the league has conferred the power to do so. Arguably, an exclusive right without the power to exercise it does not fit well within Hohfeldian property law concepts. A better approach may be found through isolation of the sticks in the bundle. For a detailed analysis utilizing the Hohfeldian construct, *see* McCurdy, *The Fundamental Nature of Professional Sports Leagues, Constituent Clubs, and Mutual Duties to Protect Market Opportunities: Organized Baseball Case Study*, in LEGAL ISSUES IN PROFESSIONAL BASEBALL (Kurlantzick ed. 2005) 129-142.

4. In *Fishman v. Estate of Wirtz,* 594 F. Supp. 853 (N.D. Ill. 1984), the plaintiff succeeded in proving that the defendant violated the antitrust laws by preventing the closing of a contract to purchase the Chicago Bulls of the NBA. Defendant actions also violated state law as a tortious interference with a contract. It is noteworthy that the alleged NBA coconspirators reached settlement with the plaintiff prior to trial. The *Fishman* case provides exhaustive treatment of damage issues in antitrust actions as applied to professional sports.

5. Do fiduciary duties limit the discretion of league owners to approve or reject the sale of member clubs? *See Professional Hockey Corporation v. World Hockey Association,* 191 Cal. Rptr. 773 (Cal. Ct. App. 1973). League directors possess fiduciary duties to make decisions for the league as a whole, including the duty of loyalty. Thus, league owners may not act in their own self-interest to the detriment of the league. *See also Triple-A Baseball Club Association v. Northeastern Baseball, Inc.*, 655 F. Supp. 513 (D. Maine 1987), *rev'd on other grounds*, 832 F.2d 214 (1st Cir. 1987) (directors and officers of a corporation owe a fiduciary duty to the corporation, including a duty to deal in good faith with the interests of those in a minority position with regard to any particular issue); The *Raiders II* court, **Section F, Note 13**, *infra*, determined that NFL directors owed members of the league an implied contractual duty of "good faith and fair dealing" when acting on behalf of the league. Watson, *What's "Love" got to do with It?: Potential Fiduciary Duties Among Professional Sports Team Owners,* 9 SPORTS LAW. J. 152 (2002).

6. Historically, owners of franchises in a specific professional sports league have also possessed ownership interests in franchises in other leagues. An NFL rule banning "cross-ownership" was successfully challenged as a violation of Section 1 of the Sherman Antitrust Act. *North American Soccer League v. National Football League*, 670 F.2d 1249 (2d Cir. 1982). The Second Restatement of Trusts states that a fiduciary has a duty not to profit at the expense of the beneficiary and not to enter into competition with the beneficiary. Restatement (Second) of Trusts § 170 cmt. A (1959). The question of whether ownership of a franchise in another league constitutes competition likely depends on evidence of cross-elasticity of demand and other factors. The opportunity to operate competing sports operations within the league territory may lead to ruinous competition, depleting the common pool of resources, such as fan interest and loyalty. In the event the market possesses the ability to support an additional sports operation, the opportunity may exist for league expansion. The "cross-owner" may be seen as seizing the league's expansion opportunity for the director's own benefit, arguably a violation of the duty of loyalty. *See generally*, Laby, *Resolving Conflicts of Duty in Fiduciary Relationships*, 54 Amer. U. L. Rev. 75 (2004).

7. Do league owners possess duties benefiting parties who are not contractually related with them as league members, but desire to join the league? Do the league owner's duties to league members, including the prospective seller of a franchise, extend to prospective buyers through a third party beneficiary theory? Does the filing of a non-refundable application fee create an express contract between the league and applicant for membership? In any event, does a prospective buyer of a league franchise enjoy an implied contract with league owners? Does there exist an implied trust relationship between the league and applicant? Which party has better standing to bring suit against the league, prospective buyer or seller?

8. Can you identify legal principles serving to constrain a rejected applicant's claim that the league decision was arbitrary and capricious? Is the use of informal or non-codified rules by league owners always subject to the arbitrary and capricious argument? What should be the standard of review? In the *Pelicans* case, Mike Moore interpreted Rule 34 of the National Association Agreement. Does the court's holding indicate that construction of a formal rule made by league owners is subject to question according to principles of "contract law"? "Statutory construction"?

9. Most leagues utilize various exculpatory clauses in the applications for prospective league members. Typical clauses include:

A. Waiver of recourse statements;

B. Indemnity clauses; and

C. Liquidated damages provisions.

Applications generally recite that the decision by the league is made in the league's "sole and absolute discretion, and may be based on subjective and objective criteria." Waiver of recourse paragraphs provide that "the league and its officers and directors shall not be liable to the applicant for any claim arising out of or in any way related to the proposed transfer of the club to the applicant. Applicant further covenants to indemnify the league, its directors and officers, employees, and agents for payment of any attorney's fees, court costs, and expenses incurred in defense of any claim brought against them relating to the application, process, and approval or disapproval of the application or any individual applicants." Finally, a liquidated damages provision stipulates that "the sole and exclusive remedy against the league, its directors and officers, employees or agents shall be for the return of any application fee paid to the league."

League applications require submission of biographical and financial information regarding all individuals and entities included in the prospective ownership group. Applications regularly require applicants to agree to "indemnify and hold harmless the league, its directors and officers, employees, agents, clubs, and designees" from any and all claims, obligations, liabilities, proceedings, judgments, damages, costs, and expenses, including attorney's fees, incurred by any of the indemnified parties and arising out of or related in any way to the release of any information or credit reports."

Are the typical exculpatory clauses adequate to shield the league and its owners from litigation by rejected applicants? What arguments can be used to circumvent the insulation sought by the provisions? Should a league require indemnification by the club owner seeking to transfer membership? For a case in which plaintiff challenged the adequacy of a "release" provision, claimed the release was secured as a result of economic duress, and argued the release was a "part and parcel" of the alleged conspiracy and therefore unenforceable, *see V.K.K. Corporation v. National Football League*, discussed and cited at **Note 21**, *infra*.

10. Is the *Pelicans* court accurate in suggesting that specific performance is available as a remedy for the plaintiff? If so, to what *status quo* shall the plaintiff be returned?

11. The National Association Agreement, Sec. 10.06, governing minor league baseball clubs and leagues, provides for territorial protection for each franchise, as follows:

> **(A) League Control of Territories.** Each League shall have control of its clubs' territories until its membership is terminated.
>
> **(B) Territorial Protection.** Each club shall be granted protected territorial rights covering a specific geographical area ('territory') within which only that club may operate and play its home games. . . . [Protected area is defined as the county in which the club operates; another National Association club may not operate within a fifteen mile 'buffer' located in counties surrounding the protected county, unless written permission is granted by the protected club, or an exception is granted pursuant to Sec. 10.06(E).]

The Durham Bulls, now of the International League (Class AAA), has been one of minor league baseball's most successful franchises. Raleigh, North Carolina lies only 3.7 miles from the Durham city boundary. The two cities share a single market. Raleigh is precluded by the territorial protection provision from attracting a minor league baseball club. Application of the baseball antitrust exemption to minor league baseball eliminates the possibility of suit by Raleigh. What nonjudicial alternatives are available for use by the City of Raleigh in gaining a minor league franchise?

12. The National Association Agreement, Sec. 10.08, authorizes a league of a higher classification to acquire the territory of a league and club of a lower classification. The league of higher classification that "drafts" the territory, however, must pay to the league of lower classification compensation as agreed by the parties. § 10.08(c). In the event the parties fail to agree, a board of arbitration determines the just and reasonable compensation. *Id.* What valuation methods are available for utilization in determining just and reasonable compensation?

In the arbitration of the compensation owed the Denver Zephyrs by the Colorado Rockies, the National League and Rockies advocated use of the "make whole" model. The model is designed to place the minor league owner in "as good a position as if the property had not been taken." Assuming there are only a limited number of cities that are viable major league markets, does the minor league territorial rights package include "special site value"? During the arbitration between the Pioneer Baseball League and the Salt Lake Trappers vs. the Pacific Coast League and the Portland Beavers, the Pioneer League introduced evidence addressing the impact on the league resulting from the drafting of an "anchor franchise." The evidence supported an argument that the league should be compensated for the "risk" of total or partial failure in the future. What factors are relevant to show compensation due the club and league?

13. What is the distinction between *per se* violations of the antitrust laws and violations of the "rule of reason"? For discussion of the competing rules in player restraint cases, *see* **Chapter 6**, *infra*.

14. The *Piazza* court, in recognizing plaintiffs' standing to maintain a claim under Section 4 of the Clayton Act, recited four factors for consideration. Is the alleged injury to plaintiffs the type for which the antitrust laws were intended to redress? Can the *Piazza* court's answer be reconciled with that of the *Levin* court? How does a plaintiff construct the argument that a formal rule requiring owner approval of a prospective member restrains the economic freedom of or excludes the plaintiff in a relevant market? Review the questions of standing presented in **Chapter 4**, *supra*, concerning amateur sports and the antitrust laws; **Note 21** below; **Section F, Note 4** (relocation cases); and **Section G, Note 2** (broadcasting constraint issues). *See also*, Roberts, *Antitrust Issues in Professional Sports*, *in* 3 THE LAW OF PROFESSIONAL AND AMATEUR SPORTS ch. 21 (Uberstine ed. 2005).

In *Baseball at Trotwood, LLC v. Dayton Professional Baseball Club, LLC*, 113 F. Supp. 1 (S.D. Ohio 1999), plaintiffs alleged that their lack of success in gaining approval to purchase the Michigan Battle Cats and relocate to the Dayton, Ohio area was a result of concerted activities of numerous defendants, including the competing buyers, the Midwest League, NAPBL, Cincinnati Reds, and owner Marge Schott. In granting defendants' Motion to Dismiss the antitrust claims, Chief Judge Rice held: "Although the actions of the Defendants may have harmed one of the competitors in that endeavor, those actions, while they may constitute business torts, did not harm economic competition, insofar as the consumer is concerned, since they did not prevent the Plaintiffs from being one of two or more groups presenting minor league baseball in the Dayton market." *Id.* at page 8.

The court further explained by footnote:

> However, assuming that the Plaintiffs have alleged that the Defendants harmed competition in that market, the Court nevertheless cannot conclude that they have alleged that they have suffered an antitrust injury, since they have not alleged facts that would support a finding that consumers were harmed as a result. . . . [T]he Court . . . declines to follow *Piazza*. . . . It bears emphasis that antitrust laws were designed "to protect consumers from producers, not to protect producers from each other or to ensure that one firm gets more of the business," *citing*, *Ehredt Underground*, 90 F.3d at 240.

Id. at 11, n.24.

15. Note the importance of evidence establishing the relevant market in each case. Do you perceive any limitations on the development of market analysis in antitrust cases, outside the attorney's aptitude for creativity and the evidence rule of relevance?

16. In *Piazza*, the court distinguishes the Third Circuit's holding in *Mid-South Grizzlies*. Is the attempt to purchase an existing and operating club different from the attempt to buy an existing expansion franchise that has not yet operated? Is the relevant product market identified in *Mid-South Grizzlies*, "major-league professional football," meaningfully distinct from the *Piazza* market described as "a market for existing American and National League baseball teams"? Are either of the two formulations distinguishable from the market specified in *North American Soccer*, "the market for sports capital"? *See also Seattle Totems Hockey Club, Inc. v. National Hockey League*, 783 F.2d 1347 (9th Cir.), *cert. denied*, 479 U.S. 932 (1986) (NHL rejected plaintiff's application for expansion franchise); *Baseball at Trotwood, LLC v. Dayton Professional Baseball Club, LLC,* 113 F. Supp. 1, 8 (S.D. Ohio 1999) (court deemed factual differences to be without legal significance).

17. What is the court's basis for applying Section 1 of the Sherman Antitrust Act in *North American Soccer*?

18. Can *Levin* be explained as a result of plaintiff's failure to prove injury? Does the development of arguments in cases involving league reliance on informal rules or subjective standards differ from the effort in cases concerning formal league rules? Does the likelihood that a prospective owner may utilize the antitrust laws to force itself into a relationship with league members who have heretofore rejected it have any public policy implications for the law of private associations?

19. The "single entity" defense, discussed in *North American Soccer League*, is further addressed at **Sections F and G**, *infra*.

20. Does a defendant bear the burden of showing the absence of "less restrictive alternatives" to accomplish the objective of the league policy under review? The burden of rebutting plaintiff's evidence indicating the existence of less restrictive alternatives?

21. Does a league member who wishes to sell a club, but is not allowed to do so, possess standing to bring an antitrust claim? Is the identity of the relevant market a question of law or one of fact? In *Sullivan v. National Football League*, 34 F.3d 1091 (1st Cir. 1994), a league member successfully prosecuted an antitrust action challenging an unofficial NFL rule that restricted owners from selling shares in their teams to the public. The jury rendered a verdict in plaintiff's favor for $38 million, reduced through remittitur to $17 million, but trebled pursuant to the Sherman Act for a final judgment of $51 million.

On appeal, the NFL argued that 1) NFL clubs do not compete with each other for the sale of ownership interests, thus there can be no injury to competition, and 2) plaintiff did not present sufficient evidence to create a *prima facie* case for jury consideration. The Court of Appeals for the First Circuit ruled that the NFL's policy against public ownership restricts competition between clubs for the sale of their ownership interests, distinguishing the *Mid-South Grizzlies* restraint as merely preventing particular outsiders from joining the league. The court affirmed the jury findings of a "nationwide market for the sale and purchase of ownership interests" in NFL clubs generally, and the Patriots in particular, and that the NFL policy had an "actual harmful affect" on competition within the market. The court, determining various errors at trial, reversed and remanded for a new trial. *Id.* at 22. The second trial resulted in a hung jury. After court supervised mediation, the case was settled for a reported $11.5 million.

In a related case, Chuck Sullivan filed an antitrust action, alleging that the NFL rule against public sales of shares prevented plaintiff from securing stadium financing. The First Circuit affirmed the district court holding that plaintiff lacked standing individually and as assignee of assets of corporation, considering that the alleged injury was not an antitrust injury, injury was indirect, and any damages were highly speculative. *Sullivan v. Tagliabue*, 25 F.3d 43 (1st Cir. 1994), *affirming*, 828 F. Supp. 114 (D. Mass. 1994).

In yet another case arising from the saga of the New England Patriots, Francis Murray sued the NFL, constituent clubs, and officials, alleging the NFL violated the antitrust laws by preventing him from gaining control of the New England Patriots and moving the club to Hartford, Connecticut or St. Louis. The Murray-Kiam partnership did not fare well subsequent to the purchase of the Patriots from William Sullivan. Eventually, James Orthwein, a Murray creditor, suceeded to Murray's interest in the Patriots by consensual agreement.

Murray later filed suit alleging that the NFL's policies regarding team financing and dispute resolution violated both Sections one (conspiracy to restrain trade) and two (monopoly) of the Sherman Act. The United States District Court granted Defendants' Motion for Summary Judgment on all issues, holding that Plaintiff failed to provide evidence supporting the contention that the NFL policies caused injury to competition. *Murray v. National Football League*, 1998 WL 205596 (E.D. Pa. 1998).

Finally, Victor Kiam sued the NFL, alleging that the NFL members, including the Jacksonville Defendants, conspired to block his intended relocation of the Patriots from Boston to an area outside of New England. In 1992, the NFL membership approved Kiam's sale of the club to Orthwein, but required a "release" from Kiam and other plaintiffs that insulated the NFL from any known and unknown claims for known and unknown damages, except suit in the event the NFL allowed Orthwein to relocate the Patriots prior to 1995. Orthwein sold the club to Robert Kraft in 1994. The Patriots have operated in New England since that date. More than thirty months after signing the "release," Kiam filed the lawsuit against the NFL members, claiming that the "release" was obtained while Kiam was under economic duress caused by the NFL. After a full trial, a jury rejected Kiam's economic duress claim. After entry of judgment on the duress claim, Kiam argued that the "release" was "part and parcel" of a conspiracy and was invalid for that reason. The United States District Court granted Defendants' Motion for Summary Judgment on the issue. The case opinion contains eighty-nine evidentiary points as to which there existed no genuine issue of fact. The points provide a detailed description of the workings of the NFL. *VKK Corporation v. National Football League*, 1999 WL 432558 (S.D.N.Y. 1999). *See also*, *VKK Corporation v. National Football League*, 1999 WL 4432557 (S.D.N.Y. 1999) (Amended Complaint against Defendant, Touchdown Jacksonville, Inc., barred by statute of limitations); *VKK Corporation v. National Football League*, 1999 WL 454499 (S.D.N.Y. 1999) (Defendants' Motion for Imposition of Sanctions Against Plaintiffs' Attorneys denied).

The Court of Appeals for the Second Circuit ruled that the release was adequate to shield the NFL and member clubs; plaintiff forfeited any right to assert economic duress in execution of the release, by delay in challenging the release; "part and parcel doctrine" did not apply to the release, as release was not an integral part of the alleged conspiracy; and release was supported by consideration. The court, however, held that the release did not cover the Touchdown Jacksonville Defendants, and a question of fact existed to prohibit summary judgment on the antitrust allegations against them. *See*, Note, *Contracts and Antitrust — Economic Duress and Anti-Competitive Practices — Coercive Tactics Utilized by the National Football League to Prevent Franchise Relocation* — V.K.K. Corporation v. National Football League, *244 F.3d 114 (2d Cir. 2001)*, 12 SETON HALL J. SPORT L. 1149 (2002).

22. Clubs, including the New York Yankees, continue to consider the sale of shares to the public as a revenue generating device. The shares of stock in the Cleveland Indians, Boston Celtics, and Vancouver Canucks are publicly traded. Owners of teams in different sports suggest the packaging of the teams and regional sports networks within a public company format. *See generally*, Cheffins, *Playing the Stock Market: "Going Public" and Professional Team Sports*, 24 J. CORP. L. 641 (1999).

23. Problem: In the fall of 2001, the Commissioner of Baseball announced that MLB contemplated the contraction of the number of clubs for play in the following year, focusing primarily on the Minnesota Twins and Montreal Expos. Although the contraction did not occur and was barred by the subsequent collective bargaining agreement between MLB and the MLBPA, what arguments could be made that contraction constitutes an illegal restraint of trade under Section 1 of the Sherman Antitrust Act? What is the likely response of MLB? For a brief description of the competing antitrust arguments, *see* Alloy, *Addition by Subtraction*, in LEGAL ISSUES IN PROFESSIONAL BASEBALL (Kurlantzick ed. 2005) 64, 78-83; Day, *Labor Pains: Why Contraction is not the solution to Major League Baseball's Competitive Balance Problems*, 12 FORDHAM INTELL.PROP. MEDIA & ENT. L.J. 521 (2002). *See also* Brand & Giorgione, *The Effect of Baseball's Antitrust Exemption and Contraction on Its Minor League Baseball System: A Case Study of the Harrisburg Senators,* 10 VILL. SPORTS & ENT. L.J. 49 (2003). Assuming the ownership of the two teams targeted for contraction sell willingly, who has standing to challenge the transaction? *See* **Section F, Note 4**, *infra*.

24. For comments of Bill Veeck, the legendary owner and baseball promoter, regarding league decision making, *see* VEECK AS IN WRECK (1962); THE HUSTLER'S HANDBOOK (1966).

For further insights into the business of sports leagues, *see generally* Schuerholz, BUILT TO WIN (2006); Noll, *The Economics of Sports Leagues, in* 3 LAW OF AMATEUR AND PROFESSIONAL SPORTS, ch. 19 (Uberstine ed. 2005); VINCENT, THE LAST COMMISSIONER (2002) (memoir of past Commissioner of Baseball); WEILER, LEVELING THE PLAYING FIELD (2002) (analysis of law to make sports better for the fan); ABRAMS, LEGAL BASES: BASEBALL AND THE LAW (1998) (examination of baseball in the legal context); SHERMAN, BIG LEAGUE, BIG TIME (1998) (birth of Arizona Diamondbacks); HELYAR, LORDS OF THE REALM (1994) (History of baseball as a business); WHITFORD, PLAYING HARDBALL (1993) (Colorado Rockies and Florida Marlins expansion process); QUIRK & FORT, PAY DIRT: THE BUSINESS OF PROFESSIONAL TEAM SPORTS (1992) (Economic analysis of sports leagues, including market for sports franchises); ZIMBALIST, BASEBALL & BILLIONS (1992) (Examination of the economics of professional baseball, including the Office of the Commisioner); CRUISE & GRIFFITHS, NET WORTH: EXPLODING THE MYTHS OF PRO HOCKEY (1991) (Critical review of historical NHL decision making); SCULLY, THE BUSINESS OF MAJOR LEAGUE BASEBALL (1989) (Analysis of the structure of baseball markets and expansion); DRAPE, IN THE HORNETS' NEST: CHARLOTTE AND ITS FIRST YEAR IN THE NBA (1989) (Reflections on the NBA expansion process).

F. LEAGUE DECISION MAKING — RELOCATION

Professional sports leagues traditionally restrict the movement of a club from one location to another by and through formal and informal rules requiring approval of franchise relocation. The transfer of a league member's operations to a new locale also serves to relocate the club's "territory," within which the club is assured exclusive operations. *See Hollywood Baseball Association v. Commissioner*, *supra*, **Section E Notes and Comments, Note 3.**

League approval processes are designed to assure that (1) potential relocation sites possess adequate demographic and other characteristics needed to maintain league stability; (2) relocation does not exacerbate travel and scheduling demands; (3) the newly created "territory" does not encroach upon existing "territorial rights"; (4) approval does not undermine geographic diversity required for league-wide marketing; and (5) contractual and moral duties to cities, including notions of loyalty, are satisfied.

The league approval process serves as a mechanism to assure that all costs are internalized within the decision making by league directors. Inefficiencies resulting from the existence of "externalities" leads to the tragedy of the commons phenomenon. Various costs in utilizing the commons are likely to escape detection in relocation decisions made by individual clubs. The costs include fan loyalty to the existing team, stable relationships with communities, league-wide interest in protection of rivalries and the existence of geographic diversity, and the availability of media, advertising, and sponsorship money. As the cases below indicate, a league often permits club relocation conditioned on the payment of a "relocation fee." The "fee" includes the value of the league-generated naked market opportunity. It also covers the costs to the league as a whole and to other league members. Questions concerning the proper amount of the fee generate considerable conflict.

PROBLEM

The United States Senate Judiciary Committee plans to schedule hearings to review the application of the antitrust laws to professional sports league decision making. The Committee Chair requests that the Chief Counsel and legal staff prepare a memorandum outlining and discussing the application of the antitrust statutes to professional sports league decisions relating to franchise relocation. The Chief Counsel for the Committee assigned the task to you, and specifically instructs as follows:

1. Describe the elements of an antitrust action challenging formal and informal league rules requiring league approval of franchise movement.
2. What factors are relevant according to the *Raiders, Clippers,* and *St. Louis* cases?
3. Identify available defenses for use by professional sports leagues in antitrust cases.
4. Is Congressional action needed for protection of cities and taxpayers from harm resulting from franchise relocation? If so, what is the nature of the legislative solution?

CASE FILE

LOS ANGELES MEMORIAL COLISEUM COMMISSION v. NATIONAL FOOTBALL LEAGUE
726 F.2d 1381 (9th Cir. 1984)

J. BLAINE ANDERSON, Circuit Judge:

I. FACTS

In 1978, the owner of the Los Angeles Rams, the late Carroll Rosenbloom, decided to locate his team in a new stadium, the "Big A," in Anaheim, California. That left the Los Angeles Coliseum without a major tenant. Officials of the Coliseum then began the search for a new National Football League occupant. They inquired of the League Commissioner, Pete Rozelle, whether an expansion franchise might be located there but were told that at the time it was not possible. They also negotiated with existing teams in the hope that one might leave its home and move to Los Angeles.

The L.A. Coliseum ran into a major obstacle in its attempts to convince a team to move. That obstacle was Rule 4.3 of Article IV of the NFL Constitution. In 1978, Rule 4.3 required unanimous approval of all the 28 teams of the League whenever a team . . . seeks to relocate in the home territory of another team. Home territory is defined in Rule 4.1 as

> the city in which [a] club is located and for which it holds a franchise and plays its home games, and includes the surrounding territory to the extent of 75 miles in every direction from the exterior corporate limits of such city. . . .

In this case, the L.A. Coliseum was still in the home territory of the Rams.

The Coliseum viewed Rule 4.3 as an unlawful restraint of trade in violation of § 1 of the Sherman Act, 15 U.S.C. § 1, and brought this action in September of 1978. The district court concluded, however, that no present justiciable controversy existed because no NFL team had committed to moving to Los Angeles. 468 F.Supp. 154 (C.D.Cal. 1979).

The NFL nevertheless saw the Coliseum's suit as a sufficient threat to warrant amending Rule 4.3. In late 1978, the Executive Committee of the NFL, . . . changed the rule to require only three-quarters approval by the members of the League for a move into another team's home territory.

Soon thereafter, Al Davis, managing general partner of the Oakland Raiders franchise, stepped into view. His lease with the Oakland Coliseum had expired in 1978. He believed the facility needed substantial improvement and he was unable to persuade the Oakland officials to agree to his terms. He instead turned to the Los Angeles Coliseum.

In January, 1980, the L.A. Coliseum believed an agreement with Davis was imminent and reactivated its lawsuit against the NFL, seeking a preliminary injunction to enjoin the League from preventing the Raiders' move. The district court granted the injunction, 484 F.Supp. 1274 (1980), but this court reversed, finding that an adequate probability of irreparable injury had not been shown. 634 F.2d 1197 (1980).

On March 1, 1980, Al Davis and the Coliseum signed a "memorandum of agreement" outlining the terms of the Raiders' relocation in Los Angeles. . . . In response, the League brought a contract action in state court, obtaining an injunction preventing the move. In the meantime, the City of Oakland brought its much-publicized eminent domain action against the Raiders in its effort to keep the team in its original home. . . .

Over Davis' objection that Rule 4.3 is illegal under the antitrust laws, the NFL teams voted on March 10, 1980, 22-0 against the move, with five teams abstaining. . . .

The Los Angeles Memorial Coliseum Commission then renewed its action against the NFL and each member club. The Oakland Alameda County Coliseum, Inc. was permitted to intervene. The Oakland Raiders cross-claimed against the NFL and is currently aligned as a party plaintiff.

The action was first tried in 1981, but resulted in a hung jury and mistrial. A second trial was conducted, with strict constraints on trial time. The court was asked to determine if the NFL was a "single business entity" and as such incapable of combining or conspiring in restraint of trade. . . . The court concluded the League was not a "single entity."

The jury returned a verdict in favor of the Los Angeles Memorial Coliseum Commission and the Oakland Raiders on the antitrust claim and for the Raiders on their claim of breach of the implied promise of good faith and fair dealing. . . .

On June 14, 1982, the court issued its judgment on the liability issues, permanently enjoining the NFL and its member clubs from interfering with the transfer of the Oakland Raiders' NFL franchise from the Oakland Coliseum to the Los Angeles Memorial Coliseum. . . .

The damages trial was completed in May 1983 with the jury returning a verdict awarding the Raiders $11.55 million and the Los Angeles Coliseum $4.86 million. These awards were trebled by the district court pursuant to 15 U.S.C. § 15. . . .

II. SHERMAN ACT § 1

* * *

The rule of reason requires the fact-finder to decide whether under all the circumstances of the case the agreement imposes an unreasonable restraint on competition.

When judicial experience with a particular kind of restraint enables a court to predict with certainty that the rule of reason will condemn that restraint, the court will hold that the restraint is per se unlawful. . . .

In the present case, the district judge found that the unique nature of the business of professional football made application of a per se rule inappropriate. The court therefore instructed the jury that it was to decide whether Rule 4.3 was an unreasonable restraint of trade. The parties do not contest the appropriateness of this basic reasonableness inquiry. The NFL, however, raises two arguments against the lower court's judgment finding section 1 liability. First, the NFL contends that it is a single entity incapable of conspiring to restrain trade under section 1. Second, it insists that Rule 4.3 is not an unreasonable restraint of trade under section 1.

A. *Single Entity*

The NFL contends the league structure is in essence a single entity, akin to a partnership or joint venture, precluding application of Sherman Act section 1 which prevents only contracts, combinations or conspiracies in restraint of trade. . . .

The district court directed a verdict for plaintiffs on this issue and as a preliminary matter the NFL states the jury should have been allowed to decide the question. . . . When there is no substantial evidence to support a claim, i.e., only one conclusion can be drawn, the court must direct a verdict, even in an antitrust case.

* * *

The district court cited three reasons for rejecting the NFL's theory. Initially, the court recognized the logical extension of this argument was to make the League incapable of violating Sherman Act § 1 in every other subject restriction — yet courts have held the League violated § 1 in other areas. Secondly, other organizations have been found to violate § 1 though their product was "just as unitary . . . and requires the same kind of cooperation from the organization's members." Finally, the district court considered the argument to be based upon the false premise that the individual NFL "clubs are not separate business entities whose products have an independent value." We agree with this reasoning.

* * *

While the NFL clubs have certain common purposes, they do not operate as a single entity. NFL policies are not set by one individual or parent corporation, but by the separate teams acting jointly. . . .

Although the business interests of League members will often coincide with those of the NFL as an entity in itself, that commonality of interest exists in every cartel. . . .

Our inquiry discloses an association of teams sufficiently independent and competitive with one another to warrant rule of reason scrutiny under § 1 of the Sherman Act. The NFL clubs are, in the words of the district court, "separate business entities whose products have an independent value." The member clubs are all independently owned. Most are corporations, some are partnerships, and apparently a few are sole proprietorships. Although a large portion of League revenue, approximately 90%, is divided equally among the teams, profits and losses are not shared, a feature common to partnerships or other "single entities." In fact, profits vary widely despite the sharing of revenue. The disparity in profits can be attributed to independent management policies regarding coaches, players, management personnel, ticket prices, concessions, luxury box seats, as well as franchise location, all of which contribute to fan support and other income sources.

In addition to being independent business entities, the NFL clubs do compete with one another off the field as well as on to acquire players, coaches, and management personnel. In certain areas of the country where two teams operate in close proximity, there is also competition for fan support, local television and local radio revenues, and media space.

These attributes operate to make each team an entity in large part distinct from the NFL. . . .

Of course, the singular nature of the NFL will need to be accounted for in discussing the reasonableness of the restriction on team movement, but it is not enough to preclude § 1 scrutiny. . . .

B. *Rule of Reason*

As elaborated upon by this circuit: "Rule of reason analysis calls for a 'thorough investigation of the industry at issue and a balancing of the arrangement's positive and negative effects on competition.'" This balancing process is not applied, however, until after the plaintiff has shown the challenged conduct restrains competition. To establish a cause of action, plaintiff must prove these elements: "(1) An agreement among two or more persons or distinct business entities; (2) Which is intended to harm or unreasonably restrain competition; (3) And which actually causes injury to competition."

Our rejection of the NFL's single entity defense implicitly recognized the existence of the first element . . . we have no doubt the plaintiffs also met their burden of proving the existence of the second element. Rule 4.3 is on its face an agreement to control, if not prevent, competition among the NFL teams through territorial divisions. The third element is more troublesome.

It is in this context that we discuss the NFL's ancillary restraint argument. Also, a showing of injury to competition requires "[p]roof that the defendant's activities had an impact upon competition in a relevant market.". . .

In a quite general sense, the case presents the competing considerations of whether a group of businessmen can enforce an agreement with one of their co-contractors to the detriment of that co-contractor's right to do business where he pleases. More specifically, this lawsuit requires us to engage in the difficult task of analyzing the negative and positive effects of a business practice in an industry which does not readily fit into the antitrust context. Section 1 of the Sherman Act was designed to prevent agreements among competitors which eliminate or reduce competition and thereby harm consumers. Yet, as we discussed in the context of the single entity issue, the NFL teams are not true competitors, nor can they be.

The NFL's structure has both horizontal and vertical attributes. On the one hand, it can be viewed simply as an organization of 28 competitors, an example of a simple horizontal arrangement. On the other, and to the extent the NFL can be considered an entity separate from the team owners, a vertical relationship is disclosed. In this sense the owners are distributors of the NFL product, each with its own territorial division. In this context it is clear that the owners have a legitimate interest in protecting the integrity of the League itself. Collective action in areas such as League divisions, scheduling and rules must be allowed, as should other activity that aids in producing the most marketable product attainable. Nevertheless, legitimate collective action should not be construed to allow the owners to extract excess profits. In such a situation the owners would be acting as a classic cartel. Agreements among competitors, i.e., cartels, to fix prices or divide market territories are presumed illegal under § 1 because they give competitors the ability to charge unreasonable and arbitrary prices instead of setting prices by virtue of free market forces.

On its face, Rule 4.3 divides markets among the 28 teams, a practice presumed illegal, but, as we have noted, the unique structure of the NFL precludes application of the per se rule. Instead, we must examine Rule 4.3 to determine whether it reasonably serves the legitimate collective concerns of the owners or instead permits them to reap excess profits at the expense of the consuming public.

1. Relevant Market

The NFL contends it is entitled to judgment because plaintiffs failed to prove an adverse impact on competition in a relevant market. . . .

In the present case, the parties entered a stipulation regarding relevant market evidence because the time allowed for witnesses in the second trial was restricted by the trial court. The stipulation provided that no experts would be called to testify on the subject. Instead, the transcripts and exhibits used by the economic experts were deemed incorporated in the record and admitted in evidence at the retrial, allowing counsel to argue market issues as if the experts had testified before the jury. Our review shows, however, that neither the transcripts nor the exhibits were placed before the jury. We are surprised that in a trial of this magnitude these able attorneys would neglect such important evidence. Upon a careful review of the record, however, we find that testimony of others was sufficient to cover the subject where necessary, and to guide the jury's finding that Rule 4.3 is an unreasonable restraint of trade.

In the antitrust context, the relevant market has two components: the product market and the geographic market. . . . Two related tests are used in arriving at the product market: first, reasonable interchangeability for the same or similar uses; and second, cross-elasticity of demand, an economic term describing the responsiveness of sales of one product to price changes in another. Similar considerations determine the relevant geographic market, which describes the "economically significant" area of effective competition in which the relevant products are traded.

The Raiders attempted to prove the relevant market consists of NFL football (the product market) in the Southern California area (the geographic market). The NFL argues it competes with all forms of entertainment within the United States, not just Southern California. The L.A. Coliseum claims the relevant market is stadia offering their facilities to NFL teams (the product market) in the United States (the geographic market). The NFL agrees with this geographic market, but argues the product market involves cities competing for all forms of stadium entertainment, including NFL football teams.

That NFL football has limited substitutes from a consumer standpoint is seen from evidence that the Oakland Coliseum sold out for 10 consecutive years despite having some of the highest ticket prices in the League. A similar conclusion can be drawn from the extraordinary number of television viewers — over 100 million people — that watched the 1982 Super Bowl, the ultimate NFL product. NFL football's importance to the television networks is evidenced by the approximately $2 billion they agreed to pay the League for the right to televise the games from 1982–1986. . . .

The evidence from which the jury could have found a narrow pro football product market was balanced, however, with other evidence which tended to show the NFL competes in the first instance with other professional sports, especially those with seasons that overlap with the NFL's. On a broader level, witnesses . . . testified that NFL football competes with other television offerings for network business, as well as other local entertainment for attendance at the games.

In terms of the relevant geographic market, witnesses, testified, . . . that NFL teams compete with one another off the field for fan support in those areas where teams operate in close proximity such as New York City-New Jersey, Washington, D.C.-Baltimore, and formerly San Francisco-Oakland. . . . Also, the San Francisco Forty Niners and the New York Giants were paid $18 million because of the potential for harm from competing with the Oakland Raiders and the New York Jets, respectively, once those teams joined the NFL as a result of the merger with the American Football League. . . .

Testimony also adequately described the parameters of the stadia market. On one level, stadia do compete with one another for the tenancy of NFL teams. Such competition is shown by the Rams' move to Anaheim. . . .

It is true, as the NFL argues, that competition among stadia for the tenancy of professional football teams is presently limited. It is limited, however, because of the operation of Rule 4.3. Prior to this lawsuit, most teams were allowed to relocate only within their home territory. . . . There was evidence to the effect that the NFL in the past remained expressly noncommitted on the question of team movement. This was done to give owners a bargaining edge when they were renegotiating leases with their respective stadia. The owner could threaten a move if the lease terms were not made more favorable.

The NFL claims that it is places, not particular stadia, that compete for NFL teams. This is true to a point because the NFL grants franchises to locales (generally a city and a 75 mile radius extending from its boundary). It is the individual stadia, however, which are most directly impacted by the restrictions on team movement. A stadium is a distinct economic entity and a territory is not.

We find that this evidence taken as a whole provided the jury with an adequate basis on which to judge the reasonableness of Rule 4.3 both as it affected competition among NFL teams and among stadia.

We conclude with one additional observation. In the context of this case in particular, we believe that market evidence, while important, should not become an end in itself. Here the exceptional nature of the industry makes precise market definition especially difficult. . . . The critical question is whether the jury could have determined that Rule 4.3 reasonably served the NFL's interest in producing and promoting its product, *i.e.,* competing in the entertainment market, or whether Rule 4.3 harmed competition among the 28 teams to such an extent that any benefits to the League as a whole were outweighed. . . .

2. The History and Purpose of Rule 4.3

The NFL has awarded franchises exclusive territories since the 1930's. . . . League members saw exclusive territories as a means to aid stability, ensuring the owner who was attempting to establish an NFL team in a particular city that another would not move into the same area, potentially ruining them both.

Rule 4.3 is the result of that concern. Prior to its amendment in 1978, it required unanimous League approval for a move into another team's home territory. That, of course, gave each owner an exclusive territory and he could vote against a move into his territory solely because he was afraid the competition might reduce his revenue. . . . Currently three-quarters approval is required for all moves.

That the purpose of Rule 4.3 was to restrain competition among the 28 teams may seem obvious and it is not surprising the NFL admitted as much at trial. It instead argues that Rule 4.3 serves a variety of legitimate League needs, including ensuring franchise stability. We must keep in mind, however, that the Supreme Court has long rejected the notion that "ruinous competition" can be a defense to a restraint of trade. Conversely, anticompetitive purpose alone is not enough to condemn Rule 4.3. The rule must actually harm competition, and that harm must be evaluated in light of the procompetitive benefits the rule might foster.

3. Ancillary Restraints and the Reasonableness of Rule 4.3

The NFL's primary argument is that . . . Rule 4.3 is reasonable under the doctrine of ancillary restraints. The NFL's argument is inventive and perhaps it will breathe new life into this little used area of antitrust law, but we reject it for the following reasons.

The common-law ancillary restraint doctrine was, in effect, incorporated into Sherman Act section 1 analysis by Justice Taft in *United States v. Addyston Pipe & Steel Co.,* 85 F. 271 (6th Cir.1898), *aff'd as modified,* 175 U.S. 21 (1899). Most often discussed in the area of covenants not to compete, the doctrine teaches that some agreements which restrain competition may be valid if they are "subordinate and collateral to another legitimate transaction and necessary to make that transaction effective."

Generally, the effect of a finding of ancillarity is to "remove the *per se* label from restraints otherwise falling within that category." We assume, with no reason to doubt, that the agreement creating the NFL is valid and the territorial divisions therein are ancillary to its main purpose of producing NFL football. The ancillary restraint must then be tested under the rule of reason, *id.*, the relevance of ancillarity being it "increases the probability that the restraint will be found reasonable.". . .

The competitive harms of Rule 4.3 are plain. Exclusive territories insulate each team from competition within the NFL market, in essence allowing them to set monopoly prices to the detriment of the consuming public. The rule also effectively foreclosed free competition among stadia such as the Los Angeles Coliseum that wish to secure NFL tenants. . . . If the transfer is upheld, direct competition between the Rams and Raiders would presumably ensue to the benefit of all who consume the NFL product in the Los Angeles area.

The NFL argues, however, that territorial allocations are *inherent* in an agreement among joint venturers to produce a product. . . . We agree that the nature of NFL football requires some territorial restrictions in order both to encourage participation in the venture and to secure each venturer the legitimate fruits of that participation.

Rule 4.3 aids the League, the NFL claims, in determining its overall geographical scope, regional balance and coverage of major and minor markets. Exclusive territories aid new franchises in achieving financial stability, which protects the large initial investment an owner must make to start up a football team. Stability arguably helps ensure no one team has an undue advantage on the field. Territories foster fan loyalty which in turn promotes traditional rivalries between teams, each contributing to attendance at games and television viewing.

Joint marketing decisions are surely legitimate because of the importance of television. . . . The League must be allowed to have some control over the placement of teams to ensure NFL football is popular in a diverse group of markets.

Last, there is some legitimacy to the NFL's argument that it has an interest in preventing transfers from areas before local governments, which have made a substantial investment in stadia and other facilities, can recover their expenditures. . . .

As noted by Justice Rehnquist, a factor in determining the reasonableness of an ancillary restraint is the "possibility of less restrictive alternatives" which could serve the same purpose. See Justice Rehnquist's dissent from the denial of certiorari in *North American Soccer League,* 459 U.S. 1074, ____, 103 S.Ct. 499, 502, 74 L.Ed.2d 639, 641 (1982). Here, the district court correctly instructed the jury to take into account the existence of less restrictive alternatives when determining the reasonableness of Rule 4.3's territorial restraint. Because there was substantial evidence going to the existence of such alternatives, we find that the jury could have reasonably concluded that the NFL should have designed its "ancillary restraint" in a manner that served its needs but did not so foreclose competition.

The NFL argues that the requirement of Rule 4.3 that three-quarters of the owners approve a franchise move is reasonable because it deters unwise team transfers. While the rule does indeed protect an owner's investment in a football franchise, no standards or durational limits are incorporated into the voting requirement to make sure that concern is satisfied. Nor are factors such as fan loyalty and team rivalries necessarily considered.

The NFL claims that . . . [s]ince the owners are guided by the desire to increase profits, they will necessarily make reasonable decisions, the NFL asserts, on such issues of whether the new location can support two teams, whether marketing needs will be adversely affected, etc. Under the present Rule 4.3, however, an owner need muster only seven friendly votes to prevent three-quarters approval for the sole reason of preventing another team from entering its market, regardless of whether the market could sustain two franchises. A basic premise of the Sherman Act is that regulation of private profit is best left to the marketplace rather than private agreement. The present case is in fact a good example of how the market itself will deter unwise moves, since a team will not lightly give up an established base of support to confront another team in its home market.

The NFL's professed interest in ensuring that cities and other local governments secure a return on their investment in stadia is undercut in two ways. First, the local governments ought to be able to protect their investment through the leases they negotiate with the teams for the use of their stadia. Second, the NFL's interest on this point may not be as important as it would have us believe because the League has in the past allowed teams to threaten a transfer to another location in order to give the team leverage in lease negotiations.

Finally, the NFL made no showing that the transfer of the Raiders to Los Angeles would have any harmful effect on the League. Los Angeles is a market large enough for the successful operation of two teams, there would be no scheduling difficulties, facilities at the L.A. Coliseum are more than adequate, and no loss of future television revenue was foreseen. Also, the NFL offered no evidence that its interest in maintaining regional balance would be adversely affected by a move of a northern California team to southern California.

It is true, as the NFL claims, that the antitrust laws are primarily concerned with the promotion of *interbrand* competition. To the extent the NFL is a product which competes with other forms of entertainment, including other sports, its rules governing territorial division can be said to promote interbrand competition. Under this analysis, the territorial allocations most directly suppress intrabrand, that is, NFL team versus NFL team, competition. A more direct impact on intrabrand competition does not mean, however, the restraint is reasonable. . . .

To withstand antitrust scrutiny, restrictions on team movement should be more closely tailored to serve the needs inherent in producing the NFL "product" and competing with other forms of entertainment. An express recognition and consideration of those objective factors espoused by the NFL as important, such as population, economic projections, facilities, regional balance, etc., would be well advised. Fan loyalty and location continuity could also be considered. . . .

Some sort of procedural mechanism to ensure consideration of all the above factors may also be necessary, including an opportunity for the team proposing the move to present its case. In the present case, for example, testimony indicated that some owners, as well as Commissioner Rozelle, dislike Al Davis and consider him a maverick. Their vote against the Raiders' move could have been motivated by animosity rather than business judgment.

* * *

V. CONCLUSION

The NFL is a unique business organization to which it is difficult to apply antitrust rules which were developed in the context of arrangements between actual competitors. This does not mean that the trial court and jury were incapable of meeting the task, however. The lower court correctly applied and described the law. The reasonableness of a restraint is a "paradigm fact question," and our review of the record convinces us the jury had adequate evidence to answer that question.

We believe antitrust principles are sufficiently flexible to account for the NFL's structure. To the extent the NFL finds the law inadequate, it must look to Congress for relief.

* * *

AFFIRMED.

NATIONAL BASKETBALL ASSOCIATION v. SDC BASKETBALL CLUB, INC.

815 F.2d 562 (9th Cir.), *cert. dismissed*, 484 U.S. 960 (1987)

FERGUSON, Circuit Judge:

Once again this court must consider the application of federal antitrust law to a sports league's effort to restrain the movement of a member franchise. In this case, the league, the National Basketball Association (NBA), seeks declaratory judgment that it may restrain the movement of its franchise, the Los Angeles Clippers (nee San Diego Clippers), and that it may impose a charge upon them for the Clippers' unilateral usurpation of the "franchise opportunity" available in the Los Angeles market. . . .

I.

The Clippers currently operate a professional basketball franchise in the Los Angeles Sports Arena. The franchise is a member of the NBA. . . . In the early 1980s, the then San Diego Clippers desired to move their franchise to Los Angeles. The Clippers abandoned their effort after the NBA filed suit in the Southern District of California. . . .

In 1984, this court rendered the decision in *Raiders I*. The *Raiders I* panel found that the National Football League (NFL) was not immune from the antitrust laws as a single business entity. 726 F.2d at 1387-90. Possible antitrust violations within the league thus properly are tested by "rule of reason" antitrust analysis. . . .

The then extant clause directly governing the movement of franchises within the NBA, Article 9 of the NBA constitution, was similar to a clause abandoned by the NFL prior to the Raiders' litigation as potentially violative of federal antitrust laws. Seeing the *Raiders I* decision as a window of opportunity, the Clippers, through their president Alan Rothenberg, on May 14, 1984, announced to the NBA their move to Los Angeles. . . .

The NBA asserts that Article 9 was not the only limitation upon franchise movement. Article 9 provided that no team could move into a territory operated by another franchise without that franchise's approval. The Clippers complied with this requirement, as the Los Angeles Lakers agreed in writing to waive their rights under Article 9. The NBA argues, however, that the league as a body must be permitted to consider moves in order to give effect to a number of constitutional provisions for the exclusiveness of franchise territories. Article 9, it contends, limits the actions of the NBA as a league and does not prescribe the only strictures on franchise movement.

The NBA also began proceedings to adopt a new rule governing the consideration of franchise moves, later adopted as Article 9A. . . .

While the proper case may warrant summary judgment, in this case there remain genuine issues of fact and summary judgment should not have been granted.

The antitrust issues are directly controlled by the two *Raiders* opinions, although the district judge had the benefit only of *Raiders I* when he rendered judgment. Collectively, the *Raiders* opinions held that rule of reason analysis governed a professional sports league's efforts to restrict franchise movement. More narrowly, however, *Raiders I* merely held that a reasonable jury could have found that the NFL's application of its franchise movement rule was an unreasonable restraint of trade. *See Raiders I*, 726 F.2d at 1398. *Raiders II* confirmed that the jury's liability verdict affirmed in *Raiders I* "held Rule 4.3 [the franchise movement rule] invalid only as it was applied to the Raiders' proposed move to Los Angeles." The Clippers' and the Coliseum's efforts to characterize *Raiders I* as presenting guidelines for franchise movement rules are thus unavailing.

Neither the jury's verdict in *Raiders*, nor the court's affirmance of that verdict, held that a franchise movement rule, in and of itself, was invalid under the antitrust laws.

Raiders I did establish the law of this circuit in applying the rule of reason to a sports league's franchise relocation rule, "a business practice in an industry which does not readily fit into the antitrust context." Any antitrust plaintiff "must prove these elements: '(1) An agreement among two or more persons or distinct business entities; (2) Which is intended to harm or unreasonably restrain competition; (3) And which actually causes injury to competition.'" *Id.* (quoting *Kaplan v. Burroughs Corp.*). The *Raiders I* panel carefully examined the structure of professional football in applying the *Kaplan* standard, a structure in which the "teams are not true competitors, nor can they be." The *Raiders I* panel concluded that the relevant market for professional football, the history and purpose of the franchise movement rule, and the lack of justification of the rule under ancillary-restraint doctrine all supported the jury's verdict. In so doing, of course, the panel set down no absolute rule for sports leagues. . . .

Yet the Clippers argue, as they must to support summary judgment, that the "NBA three-quarters rule . . . is illegal under *Raiders I*" — *i.e.,* either that the NBA rule is void as a matter of law under *Raiders I,* or that the NBA has not adduced genuine issues of fact to allow the rule to stand. The Clippers assert that the rule "is illegal as applied . . . [but that under *Raiders I*], a professional sports league's club relocation rule must at least be 'closely tailored' and incorporate objective standards and criteria such as population, economic projections, playing facilities, regional balance, and television revenues." Putting to the side, for the moment, NBA's adamant and repeated assertions that such standards have been incorporated in the evaluation of franchise movements, the Clippers misperceive the effect of the *Raiders* cases. The Clippers' confusion, and that of a number of commentators, may derive from the *Raiders I* panel's painstaking efforts to guide sports leagues toward procedures that might, in all cases, withstand antitrust analysis. The objective factors and procedures recounted by the Clippers are "well advised," *id.,* and might be sufficient to demonstrate procompetitive purposes that would save the restriction from the rule of reason. They are not, however, necessary conditions to the legality of franchise relocation rules.

* * *

The NBA asserts a number of genuine issues of fact: (1) the purpose of the restraint as demonstrated by the NBA's use of a variety of criteria in evaluating franchise movement, (2) the market created by professional basketball, which the NBA alleges is substantially different from that of professional football, and (3) the actual effect the NBA's limitations on movements might have on trade. The NBA's assertions, if further documented at trial, create an entirely different factual setting than that of the Raiders and the NFL. Further, as the NBA correctly notes, the antitrust issue here is vastly different than that in the *Raiders* cases: the issue here is "whether the mere requirement that a team seek

[NBA] Board of Governor approval before it seizes a new franchise location violates the Sherman Act." The NBA here did not attempt to forbid the move. It scheduled the Clippers in the Sports Arena, and when faced with continued assertions of potential antitrust liability, brought this suit for declaratory relief. Given the *Raiders I* rejection of per se analysis for franchise movement rules of sports leagues, and the existence of genuine issues of fact regarding the reasonableness of the restraint, the judgment against the NBA must be reversed.

ST. LOUIS CONVENTION & VISITORS COMMISSION v. NATIONAL FOOTBALL LEAGUE

154 F.3d 851 (8th Cir. 1998)

MURPHY, Circuit Judge.

After St. Louis lost its professional football team to Phoenix in 1988, extensive efforts began to obtain another team and resulted in the successful relocation of the Los Angeles Rams in 1995. Many millions of dollars were spent in order to accomplish the relocation, and the St. Louis Convention and Visitors Center (CVC) sued the National Football League and twenty four of its member teams . . . alleging that these expenditures were made necessary by actions of the NFL in violation of antitrust and tort law. The cae was tried before a jury for over four weeks before it ended in a judgment in favor of the NFL. CVC appeals the dismissal of its claim for Sherman Act conspiracy and tortious interference with contract. The NFL cross appeals the refusal of the district court to rule that the league and the member teams do not amount to a single entity for antitrust purposes. We affirm the judgment.

I.

A.

The move of the St. Louis Cardinals football team to Phoenix in 1988 caused the Missouri state legislature, the city of St. Louis and the surrounding county to undertake to find a replacement by the beginning of the 1995 season. . . . The initial goal was to obtain one of the two NFL expansion franchises to be established in 1993. In order to attract a team the city resolved to build a convention center in downtown St. Louis called America's Center which would include a new football stadium. The football stadium was called the Trans World Dome, and its $258 million cost was paid from state and local government funds. The stadium lease was assigned to CVC which became its manager and initially subleased the right to present football in the dome to private parties.

Problems associated with control over the lease and the potential ownership group caused St. Louis to be passed over in the NFL's expansion voting. The new franchises were awarded to Jacksonville, Florida and Charlotte, North Carolina. This forced the St. Louis football enthusiasts to adopt another strategy, and they turned their attention toward attracting an existing team. . . . As a result a written agreement was eventually signed by CVC and the Rams.

The NFL Constitution and Bylaws require a favorable vote by three fourths of the team owners to permit relocation, and the proposal for the Rams to move was initially voted down by the owners. It was late approved after the Rams agreed to pay the NFL a $29 million relocation fee. CVC eventually agreed with the Rams to pay $20 million of this fee, despite a clause in their contract allowing CVC to cancel if the fee were to exceed $7.5 million.

The Rams began playing in St. Louis in 1995, and in that year CVC was unable to make some of the payments owed to the team. CVC then brought this suit. . . . It also made an agreement with the Rams that they would receive half of any recovery obtained in the case in return for forgiveness of the money CVC owed them. The theory CVC presented at trial was that the league's relocation rules and the way they had been applied had created an atmosphere in which teams were unwilling to relocate. It contended that this anti-relocation atmosphere had discouraged interested teams from bidding on the St. Louis lease. The result was a one buyer market which forced the CVC to give more favorable lease terms than it would have in a competitive market.

B.

* * *

When NFL members decided to create two new team franchises for 1993, representatives from various cities made presentations to team owners in order to win a franchise.

St. Louis political leaders and business people were among those who made presentations to the league. . . . But there were problems with the St. Louis application for a team. . . .

CVC's next option was to arrange for an existing team to leave its home city and relocate to St. Louis. Community members formed the civic organization FANS, Inc. in January of 1994, headed by former Senator Thomas Eagleton, to accomplish the task which they were increasingly anxious to complete. Around this time, Congressman Richard Gephardt alerted FANS that the Los Angeles Rams were considering relocating from their stadium in Anaheim, California. . . . FANS then contacted John Shaw, the Rams president, and began negotiations on a relocation agreement and stadium lease. During this period, St. Louis was competing with Hartford and Anaheim in addition to Baltimore.

FANS made an initial presentation to the Rams, but talks ended because of problems . . . over the lease. . . . Discussions resumed only after CVC gained control over the lease, and the Rams told CVC that they would discontinue any business dealings if the CVC approached any other team about moving to St. Louis. CVC never contacted any other team to solicit a bid on the lease. . . .

C.

Relocation decisions by the NFL come under Article 4.3 of the league constitution. . . . While not expressed in the governing documents, the league claims the right to assess a relocation fee on any team seeking to move. At the time CVC was dealing with the Rams, the NFL had levied one previous relocation fee; the Cardinals had been assessed $7.5 million for their move to Phoenix.

After a successful antitrust challenge to an application of Rule 4.3 to the relocation of the Oakland Raiders to Los Angeles [citation omitted], the NFL commissioner had issued procedures for obtaining league approval of any proposed relocation and nine non-exclusive factors (the guidelines) that team owners should consider in deciding how to vote on a move. No guidelines have been promulgated on the imposition or computation of a relocation fee. . . .

Owner voted down the initial application by the Rams because of disagreements between the league and the team on several of the relocation terms, including payment of a relocation fee, sharing of revenues form the sale of "personal seat licenses" (options to purchase tickets), and possible indemnification of the league for television payments it might owe as a consequence of the move. After the initial league vote, and in anticipation of the assessment of a relocation fee, CVC agreed with the Rams it would pay up to $7.5 million of any fee. . . .

The Rams and the NFL reentered negotiations, and the NFL commissioner said that the relocation could be approved if the Rams would pay a higher fee. . . . The Rams then agreed to pay a $29 million relocation fee, to forgo any share in the next two relocation fees levied by the league, to share $17 million in personal seat license revenue with the NFL, and to indemnify the league for up to $12.5 million of any extra expenses arising from the league's television contract. The Rams relocation was approved on April 12, 1995.

The agreement between CVC and the Rams about CVC's obligating itself on any relocation fee was not revealed to the NFL owners during these negotiations, and it does not appear that the owners were informed about it until after the April 12 vote. . . . The parties agreed in June of 1995 that CVC would pay $20 million of the relocation fee and that CVC would be directly liable to the NFL for its payment. CVC did not exercise the agreement's escape clause, and the Rams began playing in St. Louis in 1995. During that year CVC experienced difficulties meeting its financial obligations to the Rams and did not pay approximately $24 million of the amount due. CVC and Rams president Shaw then agreed that CVC would sue the NFL and that the Rams would receive a right to half of any recovery in place of the payments due.

II.

* * *

B.

A number of motions were brought during the pretrial period, including one by the NFL for summary judgment on the Section 1 claim. The NFL argued that the league and teams form a single economic enterprise incapable of conspiring among themselves. The court denied the motion on the basis of collateral estoppel. The Ninth Circuit had previously ruled against the NFL on the same issue in Raiders I. [Citation omitted.] The district court was not persuaded that two subsequent cases dealing with the concept of single economic enterprise required a different result. *Copperweld Corp. v. Independence Tube Corp.*, 467 U.S. 752 (1984) (parent and wholly owned subsidiary cannot conspire with each other under Section 1) and *City of Mt. Pleasant v. Associated Elec. Coop., Inc.*, 838 F.2d 268, 274-76 (8th Cir. 1988) (test is whether entities have "pursued interests diverse from those of the cooperative itself"). . . .

The court's discussion of the Section 1 claim gave direction on several legal points. It indicated that CVC could not succeed on this antitrust claim with a theory that Article 4.3 was per se anticompetitive, but instead would have to show that the alleged anticompetitive effect of the rule outweighed its procompetitive features. [Citations omitted.] . . . [C]ertain rules of sports leagues governing matters such as the number of games to be televised and the division of home territories among professional teams, while perhaps ordinarily per se anticompetitive, were necessary for the existence of the league and should therefore be judged under a rule of reason analysis. CVC would also have to offer proof that the alleged conspiracey to suppress movement of teams in fact caused the absence of competing bids on the Trans World Dome lease before a jury could be permitted to decide whether harm to competition form Article 4.3 and its enforcement outweighed the positive effects on competition. [Citation omitted.] This was because CVC's claim was unlike cases alleging damage from a direct application of a regulation. . . . There was nothing in the NFL Constitution and Bylaws or in the deposition evidence to suggest that there was an explicit ban or limit on competitive bidding for leases.

The court also denied summary judgment on CVC's Section 2 and tortious interference claims. It held that CVC could make out a Section 2 monopoly leveraging claim if it could show that the NFL used a monopoly position in the professional football market to gain an advantage in the market for stadia. More evidence was necessary in order to evaluate the NFL's claim that the stadium market was not distinct from the market for professional football. . . .

C.

CVC's case consisted largely of the testimony of various owners, league commissioner Paul Tagliabue, Rams president John Shaw, and several experts. It also presented testimony of individuals involved in the Rams relocation to St. Louis. . . . CVC focuses in this appeal on three bodies of evidence.

CVC attempted to show that past applications of Article 4.3 and the related guidelines and the NFL approach to team relocations had created an atmosphere in which teams were afraid to move and that they did not bid on CVC's lease as a result. Several team owners stated in deposition testimony that the purpose of the rules was to ensure stability, and they also testified to differing interpretations of the guidelines and of their relative importance in deciding how to vote. CVC argued that this evidence showed teams could anticipate league disapproval of any moves or use of the rules to extract concessions upon relocating and that teams would therefore not seek out and bid on opportunities to move. . . .

CVC claims that the uncertainty about imposition of a relocation fee and its amount was one reason why teams did not seek out relocation opportunities. . . . CVC offered evidence on the benefits a predictable formula for calculating the fee would have and pointed out that the NFL has not adopted one.

CVC called Rams president John Shaw in its case in chief. He explained during his testimony that the Rams would obtain a portion of any recovery in the case. . . . Shaw testified that based on his experience representing the Rams at league meetings Article 4.3 prevented team movement, that the NFL took an antagonistic approach toward relocations, and that there were high risks of alienating the league or possible penalties in any attempt to move a NFL team. . . .

Among the experts called by CVC was Professor John Siegfried, an economics professor at Vanderbilt University. . . . Siegfired said that in his opinion the relocation policies had a direct effect on the lease price. He testified that any team which challenged the regulations would be the only bidder on an available lease (in antitrust terms, a "monopsony") and could therefore extract favorable terms from a captive buyer. In a "freely competitive marketplace with full dissemination of information" he would expect teams to seek out the best lease opportunities and to bid against each other on them. He based his conclusions on "observed market behavior" and the "prospect of earning higher returns at the Trans World Dome.

CVC also used circumstantial evidence to support its argument that the NFL culture caused the lack of bidding on its lease. CVC argued that the purpose of the NFL rules was to deter relocation and that accomplished that purpose and prevented other teams from bidding on the lease. It claimed that the market would normally produce competition for a lucrative lease, and offered the testimony of Stanley "Bud" Adams, Jr., owner of the Houston Oilers football team, who stated he would have expected high competition for the lease. CVC contends in its brief that from this evidence, "a reasonable jury could infer that some external factor was disrupting free competition — and that a set of relocation policies designed and intended to frustrate team movement were the most likely candidate."

D.

The NFL moved for judgment as a matter of law at the close of CVC's case, after four weeks of evidence, and the district court granted the motion as to two of CVC's three remaining claims. The court found that CVC had failed to present evidence that the relocation fee caused a breach in its lease agreement . . . a necessary element of tortious interference. . . . CVC instead modified its agreement with the Rams to accommodate the size of the fee. . . . Judgment was granted in the NFL's favor on the Section 2 claim as well, since CVC had not shown that the NFL had a monopoly in the professional football market or that there was a secondary market in NFL stadia. CVC has not appealed the ruling on the Section 2 claim. The court permitted the Section 1 claim to proceed, despite expressing misgivings about CVC's case.

After the NFL had presented two days of evidence and was close to finishing its case, the court convened the charge conference to prepare for submission of the Section 1 claim to the jury. . . . At this point the NFL moved again for judgment as a matter of law, *see* FED. R. CIV. P. 50(a). It argued that without a showing that the NFL's rules and acions had in fact deterred bidding on the St. Louis lease, CVC's claim was in essence a per se attack on Article 4.3 and the guidelines, and the court had already indicated that the rule of reason was the proper method of analysis.

After further briefing and oral argument, the court described the critical question as whether there was evidence tending to show that "the alleged restraint arises our of 'the agreement of the teams to adopt Article 4.3 to empower the commissioner to adopt and promulgate rules in enforcing 4.3 which has resulted in conduct which has precluded teams from coming to bid competitively in St. Louis.'" In other words, in order to go to the jury CVC had to show more than a theoretical connection between the allegedly anticompetitive actions and the events surrounding the Rams move to St. Louis.

Since the court concluded that CVC had presented no evidence to show that the NFL's rule and the guidelines actually caused league teams other than the Rams to refrain from competitive bidding on the Trans World Dome lease, it granted the Rule 50 motion. CVC had not shown that it had either tried to learn if other teams might be interested in relocating, that there were teams actually interested in moving to St. Louis, or that the failure of the others to bid on the lease was due to the NFL's policies and acts. There was no showing that there had been interested teams who had failed to contact CVC or that at the time CVC was seeking a team there were team owners who had not bid because of past application of league rules or acts of the commissioner to stop relocations. Finally, the court held that CVC had failed to present evidence of antitrust injury. . . .

III.

CVC's appeal from the judgment focuses on the dismissal of its claim under Section 1 of the Sherman Act. . . . It seeks a new trial. CVC argues that its evidence was sufficient to establish a Section 1 violation, contending that it had shown a connection in fact between the NFL rules and actions and the lack of competitive bidding on the lease. . . . The NFL responds the CVC did not produce sufficient evidence and no evidence that it sought bids from other teams or that other teams were even in a position to move. The league and teams also suggest that Article 4.3 and the related guidelines could not have affected the number of bidders on the lease because the rules did not become relevant until after the agreement between the Rams and CVC was completed. . . . Finally, the

NFL artues that CVC was unable to show there were not independent reasons for the absence of other bids, especially since other owners did not know that the St. Louis lease problems which surfaced during the expansion period had been corrected or that certain acts alleged to have been take by the commissioner to prevent team relocation had occurred.

The league and teams also cross appeal. They challenge the district court ruling that they were collaterally estopped from arguing that they are a single economic enterprise incapable of conspiracy under Section 1 of the Sherman Act. They contend that the Supreme Court decision in *Copperweld* . . . , and this court's decision in *City of Mt. Pleasant* . . . have changed the law on single economic enterprise since the Ninth Circuit decision in Raiders I. . . .

A.

CVC claims that the district court failed to use the correct legal standard for Rule 50. . . . Since it presented enough evidence to survive the earlier motion for summary judgment and introduced more evidence at trial, the Rule 50 motion should have been denied and the case submitted to the jury.

The district court stated the correct legal standard at the time it granted the Rule 50 motion, and our review of the record does not lead to the conclusion that it failed to apply it. . . . Although CVC claims that the court explicitly declined to consider evidence of causation, the passages it cites in the district court opinion do not contain any such statement. Rather, the court explained in its opinion that even after weeks of trial it was not clear what legal theory CVC was proceeding with on its Section 1 claim. The court restated its consistent ruling the CVC would not be able to rely solely on the existence of the NFL rules to prove its case. That principle of law was not incorrect, and CVC does not point to any other example to support its argument that the court did not follow the standard.

The court's prior decision on summary judgment did not control the outcome of the Rule 50 motion. . . . By the time the district court ruled on the Rule 50 motion, it was able to review all the evidence in light of the legal discussions at the charge conference. It concluded that CVC had not met its burden. . . .

B.

CVC contends that its evidence was sufficient to withstand a Rule 50 motion. CVC says that the testimony of John Shaw and Professor Siegfried, together with circumstantial evidence, tended to show that the actions by the NFL caused the lack of bidding and the damages it seeks. The NFL replies that none of the evidence shows that the NFL policies, or their implementation, had the actual effect of deterring any team from making a bid on the stadium lease.

* * *

I.

In order to prevail under Section 1, CVC must prove that: (1) there was an agreement among the league and member teams in restraint of trade; (2) it was injured as a direct and proximate result; and (3) its damages are capable of ascertainment and not speculative. [Citation omitted.] The first element is established by proof that there was an agreement in restraint of trade and that the challenged action was "part of or pursuant to that agreement." [Citation omitted.] Other Section 1 challenges to rules of sports leagues have involved situations where the defendants had taken action pursuant to an allegedly anticompetitive rule and the plaintiff attacked the rule itself or the application of the rule. [Citation omitted.] [T]here was not question that the defendants were acting pursuant to an agreement in restraint of trade, and the issue was whether the agreement was unreasonable. . . . This case is different because CVC has not challenged a vote by team owners or a particular application of the rules, . . . nor was St. Louis unable to obtain a NFL team. CVC complains instead about market conditions and attributes the conditions existing at the time it was seeking a tenant to an atmosphere created by the rules and the handling of prior relocations.

CVC did not present evidence tending to show that there was even one other team besides the Rams that failed to bid on its lease because of the NFL rules and past applications of them. [Citation omitted.] In order to prove that Section 1 defendants were acting pursuant to a conspiracy, a plaintiff must present evidence that tends "to exclude the possibility that the alleged coconspirators acted independently," [citation omitted] because "conduct as consistent with permissible competition as with illegal conspiracy does not, standing alone, support an inference of antitrust conspiracy." [Citation omitted.]

CVC presented no evidence to exclude the possibility that the owners who did not bid on the St. Louis lease were acting for independent business reasons rather than pursuant to the alleged agreement in restraint of trade. Indeed, the evidence at trial was to the contrary. The deposition testimony of the owners reflected their awareness of problems with the St. Louis lease, concern for their existing leases, and loyalty to their communities. . . . Moreover, CVC did not present evidence tending to show that all NFL teams would use the same criteria to evaluate a relocation opportunity or automatically attempt to move to the city offering the most lucrative lease. CVC argues that the parties' pretrial stipulation that the league Constitution and Bylaws amounted to an agreement among the NFL and its members was all that was necessary to show the existence of a conspiracy. That evidence did not tend to prove that any team acted pursuant to a conspiracy to prevent bidding on the stadium lease, however. "[A]ntitrust law limits the range of permissible inferences from ambiguous evidence in a Section 1 case," and the trial evidence did not support an inference that NFL teams were acting pursuant to the alleged conspiracy when they declined to bid. . . .

2.

The district court rested its summary judgment on the issue of causation. In order to satisfy the causation element of a Section 1 case, CVC had to show that the NFL's anticompetitive acts were an actual, material cause of the alleged harm to competition. [Citation omitted.] Since nothing in the NFL rules expressly prevented competition among teams for leases or stated that only one team could negotiate with a leaseholder at a time, CVC had to show that past suppression of movement and the alleged antirelocation atmosphere created by previous rule applications effectively prevented all other teams from dealing with the CVC about the St. Louis lease and entering bids.

CVC argues that Shaw's testimony was sufficient to prove causation, but his testimony did not tend to prove that the rules deterred any interested owner from bidding in St. Louis or that other owners considered the rules a factor in their lack of interest in the lease. . . . Shaw was not a disinterested witness, and in the absence of other evidence his testimony was not enough to establish that the rules and its past application had created an anti-relocation atmosphere in the NFL which caused a lack of bidders, especially in light of the fact that Shaw's own team succeeded in moving after negotiatin with several cities. [Citation omitted.] Shaw was not a participant in what is alleged to have been a refusal to approach CVC. . . .

CVC contends that the testimony of its expert . . . establishes a causal link between the NFL's actions and the lack of competitive bidding on the lease. A jury may not rest its verdict on an expert's conclusion "without some underlying facts and reasons, or a logical inferential process to support the expert's opinion." [Citation omitted.] Here, there was no evidence on which the jury could have drawn a logical inference from Siegfried's opinion. Siegfried testified that he would have expected to see bidding on the lease, but there was no evidence to support a finding that there were teams that were actually able and desiring to bid, but were prevented from doing it. Moreover, Siegfried rested his conclusions on economic theory that states that in a freely competitive market NFL teams would want to move to the most advantageous lease opportunity, but there was no evidence which tended to show that this was actually the case, especially in light of admissions by CVC witnesses that several team owners would not move because of loyalty to their communities or ownership of stadia. Siegfried also testified that he had not seen any of the lease agreements involved in the case, any relocation agreement, or any documentation on the lease negotiations. Without evidence tending to show that Siegfried's economic model actually applied to the NFL and the CVC efforts to obtain a team, his testimony is insufficient to create a jury question on the issue of causation. . . .

CVC relies also on circumstantial evidence to prove causation. It claims that since the purpose of the rules was to deter team movement and there was a lack of competitive bidding . . . , it can be inferred that the rules were the cause of the harm allegedly suffered. . . . The fact that the rules were allegedly intended to discourage relocation does not support the inference that they prevented all other teams besides the Rams from pursuing a possible move to St. Louis. There were many legitimate reasons why owners may not have bid, and without evidence from those who did not bid about why they had not, the circumstantial evidence was insufficient to allow the case to be presented to the jury on causation.

* * *

Where a plaintiff has otherwise failed to present evidence of causation, he must show that he made "a demand on the defendant to allow the plaintiff to take some action or obtain some benefit, which the defendant's challenged practice is allegedly preventing the plaintiff from taking or obtaining, in order to prove that the practice caused the injury in fact." [Citation omitted.] The record shows no effort by CVC to solicit bids from other NFL teams and CVC did not contact any other NFL team to encourage it to consider the St. Louis opportunity. The negotiations between CVC and the Rams were carried out in secret, and there was undisputed evidence that CVC had made a conscious decision to negotiate with only one team. . . .

* * *

3.

The district court also ruled that CVC failed to present evidence to make out a submissible case of antitrust injury. CVC says that its evidence tended to prove that the NFL's policies caused a reduction in competitive bidding which is an antitrust injury. The NFL replies that the theory of CVC's case was that the very existence of Article 4.3 and the guidelines limited team bidding. It did not show that they operated to make CVC's financial obligations greater than they should have been, there was no antitrust injury. The league and team also argue that the rules did not result in a reduction in output of the number of NFL games, teams, or stadia which would be necessary to show antitrust injury. . . .

Antitrust injury is "injury of the type the antitrust laws were intended to prevent and flows from that which makes defendant's acts unlawful." [Citation omitted.] CVC failed to offer proof of antitrust injury because it did not present evidence to show that there was a suppression of bidding on the St. Louis lease.

* * *

V.

CVC had ample opportunity to prove the causes of action that are the subject of its appeal, and it took form four weeks to put in its evidence at trial. . . . Since CVC failed to produce sufficient evidence to make out essential elements required under Section 1 of the Sherman Act . . . , the league and the member teams were entitled to judgment as a matter of law. . . .

NOTES AND COMMENTS

1. The cases above illustrate the "fact sensitivity" of the balancing test used in antitrust analysis. Should a party ever prevail on a motion for summary judgment in a case governed by the rule of reason? Does the answer to the balancing test depend on whether the league constraints address identifiable "externalities?" For analysis of externalities and league decision making, *See* Fisher, Maxwell & Schouten, *The Economics of Sports Leagues and the Relocation of Teams: The Case of the St. Louis Rams*, 10 MARQ. SPORTS L.J. 193 (2000).

2. Does The Development Of Market Analysis Differ In The "Relocation" Cases From The Development In The "Ownership" Cases? *See Generally* Seal, *Market Definition In Antitrust Litigation In The Sports And Entertainment Industries*, 61 ANTITRUST L.J. 737 (1993); Comment, *Leveling The Playing Field: Relevant Product Market Definition In Sports Franchise Relocation Cases,* 2000 U. Chi. Legal F. 245 (2000).

3. *Compare* The Result In The *Raiders* Case With The Court's Holding In *San Francisco Seals, Ltd. v. National Hockey League*, 379 F. Supp. 966 (C.D. Cal. 1974) (NHL Member Desiring to relocate was not a competitor with defendants in an economic sense).

4. The "players" in the typical relocation case include the franchise owner desiring to relocate operations, the existing member city and facility, the relocation city and facility, and the defendants, voting league members and league entity. Which of the potential plaintiffs possess standing to maintain an antitrust claim? Are the losses suffered by the existing host city a result of league violations of the antitrust laws? For a discussion of antitrust claims by cities, including issues of standing, *see* Mitten & Burton, *Professional Sports Franchise Relocations From Private Law and Public Law Perspectives: Balancing Marketplace Competition, League Autonomy, and the Need for a Level Playing Field*, 56 MD. L. REV. 57 (1997).

In the fall of 2001, the Commissioner of Baseball announced that MLB contemplated the contraction of the Minnesota Twins and Montreal Expos. Do the two cities possess standing to challenge contraction as a violation of the antitrust laws? For a proposal of an interesting alternative to contraction, *see* Ross & Szymanski, *Open Competition in League Sports*, 2002 WIS. L. REV. 625 (2002) (suggests use of the practice of "promotion and relegation," whereby unsuccessful teams are relegated to a lower division of play).

5. The *St. Louis Convention & Visitors Commission* case focuses upon the causation requirement of a Section 1 claim. How would you reconstruct the plaintiff's case, including the offering of evidence, to establish issues proper for jury consideration? Was the *St. Louis* court correct in ruling that the testimony of Ram's president John Shaw was insufficient to establish evidence of causation? Is the admissibility of Shaw's testimony subject to objections under the Federal Rules of Evidence?

6. The NFL, in arguing for dismissal of the case pursuant to its renewed Rule 50 motion in *St. Louis*, contended that plaintiff's case was inadequate to establish evidence of conspiracy for jury consideration. The NFL relied upon the U.S. Supreme Court's holding in *Matsushita Electric Industrial Co., Ltd. v. Zenith Radio Corp.*, 475 U.S. 574 (1986). The Court explained, "[C]onduct as consistent with permissible competition as with illegal conspiracy does not standing alone, support an inference of antitrust conspiracy. . . . [A] plaintiff seeking damages for violation of Section 1 must present evidence 'that tends to exclude the possibility' that the alleged conspirators acted independently." *Id.* at 588. The NFL further quoted from the Note accompanying the ABA Sample Jury Instruction, "Thus the issue of conspiracy or mutual agreement or understanding will not go to the jury unless the court has found that plaintiff has presented evidence which tends to exclude the possibility of independent action." *St. Louis Convention & Visitors Commission*, United States District Court for the Eastern District of Missouri, Eastern Division, No. 4:95CV2443JCM, Transcript, Nov. 10, 1997, page 3441.

7. For examination of the "single entity" nature of sports leagues, *see* Roberts, *Antitrust Issues in Professional Sports, in* LAW OF PROFESSIONAL AND AMATEUR SPORTS, ch. 19 (Uberstine ed. 2005); *The Antitrust Status of Sports Leagues Revisited*, 64 TUL. L. REV. 117 (1989); *The Single Entity Status of Leagues Under Section 1 of the Sherman Act: An Alternative View*, 60 TUL. L. REV. 562 (1986); *Sports Leagues and the Sherman Act: The Use and Abuse of Section 1 to Regulate Restraints on Intraleague Rivalry*, 32 UCLA L. REV. 219 (1984) (author emphasizes that the league is the lowest indivisible economic unit capable of producing an entertainment product, but proposes that Section 1 analysis is proper in situations where a minority of clubs control league actions to the benefit of the clubs, not the league interests as a whole).

8. For the views of other commentators regarding the "single entity" defense, *see* McChesney, *Professional Sports Leagues and the Single Entity Defense,* 6 SPORTS LAW. 125 (1999); Jacobs, *Professional Sports Leagues, Antitrust, and the Single Entity Theory*, 67 IND. L.J. 25 (1991); Goldman, *Sports, Antitrust, and the Single Entity Theory*, 63 TUL. L. REV. 751 (1989); Grauer, *Recognizing the National Football League as a Single Entity under Section 1 of the Sherman Act: Implications of the Consumer Welfare Model*, 82 MICH. L. REV. 1, 7-14 (1983).

9. The argument that professional sports leagues are "single entities" whose internal decisions are not subject to antitrust scrutiny is often based on the U.S. Supreme Court's holding in *Copperweld Corp. v. Independence Tube Corp.*, 467 U.S. 752 (1984), that a parent corporation and its wholly owned subsidiary constituted a single firm for Section 1 purposes. For the opinion of one court recognizing a possibility that the NBA could be understood as "one firm," *see Chicago Professional Sports Limited Partnership v. National Basketball Association*, 1996 WL 66111 (N.D. Ill. 1996) ("Single entity" issue remanded to U.S.

District Court). *See also Seabury Management, Inc. v. Professional Golfers' Association of American, Inc.*, 52 F.3d 322, 1995 U.S. App. LEXIS 17577 (4th Cir. 1995) (unpublished disposition), *aff'g in part and rev'g in part, Seabury Management, Inc. v. PGA*, 878 F. Supp. 771 (D. Md. 1994) (PGA and member sections are "single entities").

In the *St. Louis* case, the NFL argued that its thirty member clubs operate as an integrated business producing a joint product. Any single member of the NFL cannot produce a single game. Thus, the clubs do not compete to produce games, but produce them together. In *City of Mt. Pleasant v. Associated Elec. Coop., Inc.*, 838 F.2d 268 (8th Cir. 1988), the court affirmed a grant of summary judgment, concluding that a collective of separately owned and operated electric power utilities constituted a single economic enterprise for Section 1 purposes. The members of the Mt. Pleasant cooperative, like the NFL teams, were separately owned. The NFL clubs, however, are more closely integrated in some respects than the coop members. Although the NFL clubs set individual ticket prices, as the coop members set individual power rates, the members of the league share at least 80-90 percent of their revenues and equalize many of their expenses. The NFL clubs have also jointly entered into a collective bargaining agreement with the players' union that establishes minimum salaries and salary cap. The members of the coop are linked together by supply contracts, while the NFL clubs are contractually linked pursuant to the NFL Constitution and Bylaws. Whereas the coop members generally compete among themselves for customers, only the NFL teams located in the same community compete for live fans. *See* NFL Brief at 549 PLI/Pat 665, 668 (Feb.-Mar. 1999).

10. In *Fraser v. Major League Soccer, L.L.C.*, 284 F.3d 47 (1st Cir. 2002), the court rejected the *Copperweld* rationale utilized by the U.S. District Court, and instead suggested use of a reshaped rule of reason analysis to determine the antitrust implications of the MLS structure, a hybrid arrangement somewhere between a single entity and cooperative format among existing competitors. See the discussion of *Fraser* and the "single entity" defense at **Notes 4-7, Section G**, *infra*.

11. You are appearing in a United States District Court on behalf of a client member of a professional sports league. The league was sued for violation of the antitrust laws in the league's rejection of plaintiff's application to relocate a league franchise to another city. The U.S. District Judge asks you for an off-the-cuff explanation of the "ancillary restraint doctrine." What is your response? *See* Roberts, *The Evolving Confusion of Professional Sports Antitrust, the Rule of Reason, and the Doctrine of Ancillary Restraints*, 61 S. CAL. L. REV. 943 (1988).

12. In *Sullivan v. National Football League*, 34 F.3d 1091, 1106-08 (1st Cir. 1994), the court recognized that the NFL had submitted evidence of record at trial to support the "equal involvement defense" doctrine. The defense is an absolute bar to an antitrust suit where the plaintiff bears "substantially equal responsibility for an anticompetitive restriction by creating, approving, maintaining, continually and actively supporting, relying upon, or otherwise utilizing" the restriction to the plaintiff's benefit. *Id.* at 1106-07. What evidence is available for the defendant's use in attempting to prove the defense by a preponderance in "relocation" cases? Interestingly, the owner of the Seattle Seahawks, Ken Behring, voiced, in February of 1996, his intention to relocate the Seahawks to the Los Angeles area. Mr. Behring and other NFL owners, reportedly, had previously agreed to "save" the Los Angeles territory for league expansion to benefit all NFL owners.

13. The damages portion of *Los Angeles Memorial Coliseum Comm'n v. NFL* (*Raiders II*) appears at 791 F.2d 1356 (9th Cir. 1986). The court upheld the jury's treble damage award to the Coliseum Commission in the amount of $14,580,243. The Raider's award of $34,633,146 was remanded for a determination of the amount of set-off due the NFL for the lost value of the Los Angeles area league-generated opportunity. The Court stated:

> The value of the Los Angeles opportunity arose not only from the economic potential of one of the nation's largest media markets, but also from the NFL's well-established and widely followed nationwide entertainment product. . . . If and when the NFL placed an expansion team in the Los Angeles area, the accumulated value of the Los Angeles opportunity would have been realized by the NFL through charging the new expansion team owner for the expansion opportunity.
>
> As indicated above, the value of the league's expansion opportunities belonged to the league as a whole, or in other words, was owned in part by each franchise owner. Unquestionably, when the Raiders moved to Los Angeles, they appropriated for themselves the expansion value. . . . Although by moving out of Oakland the Raiders "gave back" an expansion opportunity to the NFL, the uncontradicted testimony at trial showed the Los Angeles market to be a significantly more lucrative franchise opportunity. . . . Al Davis testified that the Raiders increased their value by some $25 million by moving to Los Angeles. . . .
>
> As a result, the injunction permitting the Raiders to play NFL football in Los Angeles . . . provided them with a windfall benefit beyond the scope of the antitrust verdict. *Id.*

The offset ruling remedied a potential defect in *Raiders* I identified by Weistart that the opinion requires the league to give to an insider what could be sold for a considerable amount to an outsider. *See* Weistart, *League Control of Market Opportunities: A Perspective on Competition and Cooperation in the Sports Industry*, 1984 DUKE L.J. 1013 (1984). The underlying premise of Professor Weistart's analysis and that of Professor Roberts' concern, *supra*, **Note 7**, is that league members have the opportunity to place team interests above league interests — a forecasting of the "tragedy of the commons." Significantly, the offset is to be applied prior to the trebling of the damages. Professor Shropshire points out that an offset of $25 million to the Raiders' actual damages of approximately $11.5 million results in Al Davis owing the NFL an amount of about

$13.5 million. Shropshire, THE SPORTS FRANCHISE GAME 40 (1995). It is little surprise that the matter was resolved by out-of-court settlement.

14. The accepted notion that the value of a relocation or an expansion site is generated by the league is fundamental to the concept of a league and its operations. In the St. Louis scenario, a part of the indemnification payment is equal to the portion of the value of the relocation site generated by the NFL. As the *St. Louis* court notes, another element of the indemnification package includes the amount of rebate owed pursuant to television and broadcast contracts resulting from the substitution of a lesser market for the existing one. What other cost elements can you identify? Draft guidelines that would serve to direct the NFL owners in constructing an indemnification payment package. *See generally* GREENBERG & GRAY, 1 SPORTS LAW PRACTICE, § 11.04(1)(b) (2005). Professor Fort constructs an expansion fee formula that combines the discounted net present values of expected team profits, expected local revenue impacts, and expected media package impacts. Fort, SPORTS ECONOMICS 135-39 (2003). The formula serves to include in the calculation external costs and benefits that would otherwise be overlooked in the decision making process, and therefore would result in an inefficient allocation of resources.

15. Do league members possess fiduciary duties which prevent the relocation of existing clubs to potential expansion cities to the detriment of the league as a whole? *See* cases cited at **Notes and Comments, Note 5, Section E,** *supra*.

16. The City of Oakland attempted to retain the Raiders through a condemnation action. *See City of Oakland v. Oakland Raiders,* 646 P.2d 835 (Cal. 1982). The California Court of Appeals upheld a lower court judgment on remand that eminent domain acquisition was invalid under the commerce clause. *City of Oakland v. Oakland Raiders,* 174 Cal. App. 3d 414, 421, 220 Cal. Rptr. 153, 157 (1985). For discussion of other cities' use of eminent domain power, *see* Greenberg, *Professional Sports Franchises: Retention Methods, Escape Clauses, and Franchise Relocation, in* 3 LAW OF AMATEUR AND PROFESSIONAL SPORTS, ch. 23 (Uberstine ed. 2005).

17. For discussion of the "relocation" issue, *see* Gordon, *Baseball's Antitrust Exemption and Franchise Relocation: Can a Team Move?,* 26 FORDHAM URB. L.J. 1201 (1999); Mitten & Burton, *Professional Sports Franchise Relocations From Private Law and Public Law Perspectives: Balancing Marketplace Competition, League Autonomy, and the Need for a Level Playing Field,* **Notes and Comments, Note 4,** *supra;* Scibilia, *Baseball Franchise Stability and Consumer Welfare: An Argument for Reaffirming Baseball's Antitrust Exemption with Regard to its Franchise Relocation Rules,* 6 SETON HALL J. SPORT L. 409 (1996).

18. Professor Zimbalist views the root of the "relocation" problem as lying in the leagues' monopoly status. He proposes a solution that creates competition between separate leagues, whereby each league attempts to occupy all viable cities before the other, expand into any markets that could support a team, and place more teams in markets that are capable of supporting multiple teams. In this manner, the "supply and demand situation would balance out." Commissoner Tagliabue, conversely, argues that cities would be protected by Congressional recognition of league exemption from antitrust scrutiny. Which of the arguments is more persuasive? Given present day economic realities, can the supply-demand equation balance as proposed? Professor Zimbalist also recognizes that demographically lesser cities, as a result of new stadium economics, can now compete with larger cities. Does the continual increase in the number of viable facilities and cities assure an imbalance with a static supply of major league quality players? In this sense, is the economic demand for professional sports teams different from consumer demand for scarce resources? Is the monopoly a "natural monopoly"? Does the answer vary according to time period and factual circumstances? *See* Noll & Zimbalist, *Economic Impact of Sports Teams & Facilities in Sports*, in JOBS & TAXES: THE ECONOMIC IMPACT OF SPORTS TEAMS & STADIUMS 65 (Noll & Zimbalist, eds. 1997); Testimony of Andrew Zimbalist before the Committee on the Judiciary, U. S. House of Representatives, Feb. 6, 1996; Piraino, Jr., *The Antitrust Rationale for the Expansion of Professional Sports Leagues*, 57 Ohio St. L.J. 1677 (1996); Ross, *Antitrust Options to Redress Anticompetitive Restraints and Monopolistic Practices by Professional Sports Leagues,* 52 CASE W. RES. L. REV. 133 (2001); QUIRK & FORT, HARD BALL Ch. 6 (1999).

19. The antitrust laws as they relate to monopoly power are further examined at **Section H**, *infra*.

20. For a case in which the league files an action to enjoin an owner from relocating a club without league approval, *see National Basketball Association v. Minnesota Professional Basketball, Limited Partnership*, 56 F.3d 866 (8th Cir. 1994).

21. Can public entities protect community interests, including taxpayers, by constructing favorable lease terms? *See* Shropshire, *Opportunistic Sports Franchise Relocations: Can Punitive Damages Based on Contract Strike a Balance?,* 22 LOY. L.A. L. REV. 569 (1989). Discussion of legal and equitable remedies available for use by public entities in stadium lease disputes appears at **Chapter 10**, *infra*.

G. LEAGUE DECISION MAKING — MERCHANDISING/BROADCASTING

Professional sports leagues commonly restrict the broadcast of league games to protect "live" game production within the home market, and otherwise assure benefits for the league as a whole. The NBA policy limiting the manner and number of games broadcast by individual team members, including a cap on "superstation" telecasts, is challenged in the *Chicago Professional Sports* (*Bulls II*) case, *infra*, as a violation of the Sherman Act.

The choice made by an individual club to broadcast its game on a national scale may not take into account the effects on other franchises and the league as a whole. The externalities are generally recognized as the impact on home games and telecasts of other teams, including the possibility of strong teams drawing fan support, television audience, and sponsorship money from weaker clubs. The customary league sharing of national broadcast revenues is designed to enable weaker clubs to compete in the market for players and assure competitive balance among teams. National broadcasting and marketing also emphasizes and promotes the "league product" and season, thus justifying league control over the area. The necessity of some league control over the delivery of games to the national audience is commonly accepted, although a questions of the proper mix of nationally delivered games generate considerable controversy. *See*, Fisher, Maxwell, & Schouten, *The Economics of Sports Leagues — The Chicago Bulls Case*, 10 Marq. Sports L.J. 1 (1999).

League members also enter into contractual arrangements enabling the joint marketing of "logo bearing" merchandise. Typically, individual club rights are assigned to a "league entity" that is empowered to license the use of the league and club marks or other identifying insignia on merchandise sales, advertising, and other promotional ventures. The league entity is usually authorized to actively promote the marketing of licensed goods, thereby gaining economies of scale in the merchandising efforts. The entity frequently sells "exclusive sponsorship rights" at a premium price. Revenues generated through the program are shared by league members on a prearranged basis.

National Football League Properties, Inc., the NFL entity administering the contractual arrangement between NFL members ("NFL Trust"), filed an action against the Dallas Cowboys, Texas Stadium Corporation, and Cowboys owner, Jerry Jones, alleging that individual sponsorship contracts made through the stadium corporation violated the joint contract, the Lanham Act, and other common law principles. *See National Football League Properties, Inc. v. Dallas Cowboys Football Club, Ltd.*, in **Case File**, *infra*. The Cowboys responded by filing a suit against the NFL Trust, challenging the arrangement as a violation of the Sherman Act. Plaintiff seeks $200 million in actual damages, trebled under the federal antitrust laws; an unspecified additional amount for alleged breach of common law duties; and $150 million in punitive damages. *Dallas Cowboys Football Club, Ltd. v. National Football League Trust*, United States District Court for the Southern District of New York, 95 Civ. 9426 (1995).

PROBLEM

The members of the Professional Rugby League established a joint marketing program, the "Rugby Trust," by entering into a contractual arrangement identical with that of the NFL (*see* **Case File** below). The generated revenue is divided evenly among the clubs after deducting expenses of the "Trust."

The program has worked well for a number of years to result in an increase in total league sales. The "Trust" further generates revenue by licensing exclusive sponsorships, such as the "official soft drink of the Rugby League," "the official ale of the Rugby League," and so forth. Expenses are projected at a lesser amount than would be expended if each club were to individually market club products. Recently, the owner of the El Paso club, Razorback James, contracted to establish exclusive sponsors of the rugby stadium, the location of the club's Professional Rugby League games. Significantly, James also owns the stadium. James regularly receives stadium sponsors as guests in his "owners suite" for games, and generates much publicity tying the sponsors to his stadium operations. The stadium revenues are not shared with other League members as revenue generated pursuant to the contractual arrangement. The revenue is available, however, for club use in hiring players and otherwise meeting club expenses.

The League hired your law firm to assist in challenging the El Paso owner's actions. The League desires to file suit to enjoin the performance of the stadium sponsorships and collect damages as allowed by law. Owner James reports that he will challenge the "Trust" arrangement as a violation of the antitrust laws. The senior partner of your firm instructed you as follows:

1. Outline and describe the causes of action available for use in the case;
2. Describe the elements of an antitrust action challenging the joint marketing arrangement;
3. Identify defenses available for use by the Professional Rugby League.

Case File

NATIONAL FOOTBALL LEAGUE PROPERTIES, INC. v. DALLAS COWBOYS FOOTBALL CLUB, LTD.

922 F. Supp. 849 (S.D.N.Y. 1996)

OPINION AND ORDER

Scheindlin, District Judge:

Defendants Dallas Cowboys Football Club, Ltd., Texas Stadium Corporation, and Jerral W. Jones (together, "Defendants") move, pursuant to Fed.R.Civ.P. 12(b)(6), to dismiss this lawsuit for failure to state a claim upon which relief can be granted. For the reasons set forth below, this motion is granted in part and denied in part.

I. Factual Background

The National Football League ("NFL") is an unincorporated association comprised of 30 Member Clubs, including the Defendant Dallas Cowboys Football

Club, Ltd. ("Cowboys Partnership"), which owns and operates the football team known as the Dallas Cowboys. Effective October 1, 1982, entities owning 26 of the then 28 Member Clubs entered into a trust agreement (the "Trust Agreement") which created the NFL Trust. The Trust Agreement provided that each Member Club would transfer to the NFL Trust the exclusive right to use its "Club Marks" for commercial purposes (with certain limited exceptions). These "Club Marks" include a team's name, helmet design, uniform design, and identifying slogans. . . . The Member Clubs also granted to the NFL Trust the exclusive right to use NFL Marks, such as the NFL Shield Design, and the names "NFL," "American Football Conference," "National Football Conference," and "Super Bowl." . . .

As soon as the NFL Trust was created, it entered into a "License Agreement" with Plaintiff NFL Properties, Inc. that provides Plaintiff with "the exclusive right to license the use of the Trust Property on all types of articles of merchandise and in connection with all types of advertising and promotional programs.". . . The Club Marks of the Cowboys Partnership, like the marks of other Member Clubs, are included in the Trust Property exclusively licensed to Plaintiff.

Plaintiff has been active in promoting the NFL and its Member Clubs, and has issued hundreds of licenses for the use of Club Marks. . . . Plaintiff has also entered into agreements with companies involved in specific product categories — such as soft drinks or charge cards — to be exclusive sponsors of the NFL and its Member Clubs. Sponsors are given the right to use the Club Marks and NFL Marks in advertising, promotion and packaging, to promote themselves as an "Official Sponsor" of the NFL and, in some cases, as an "Official Sponsor" of the Member Clubs. . . . The revenue generated from Plaintiff's sale of licensing and sponsorship rights is shared equally by the Member Clubs, which are the sole shareholders of Plaintiff. . . .

Plaintiff contends that Defendants have embarked upon a wrongful plan and scheme which violates the Trust and License Agreements and infringes upon Plaintiff's rights. Specifically, the Complaint alleges that Defendants have entered into a number of highly-publicized contractual arrangements — with Dr. Pepper, Pepsi, and NIKE — that "impermissibly exploit the Club Marks and the NFL Marks, and thus wrongfully misappropriate revenue that belongs to plaintiff and should be shared among all the Member Clubs.". . . The Complaint also alleges that Defendants are negotiating a similar contract with American Express. . . . Although all of the contractual arrangements Plaintiff mentions are nominally between the "sponsors" and Defendant Texas Stadium Corporation, Plaintiff claims that Defendants are using Texas Stadium as a "stand in" to help the Cowboys Partnership circumvent its obligations under the Trust and License Agreements. . . .

The Complaint further alleges that Defendants misappropriated Club Marks and NFL Marks in solicitation materials they submitted to potential sponsors. In particular, Plaintiff asserts that Defendants used Club Marks — including the Cowboys "Star" logo — and NFL Marks — including the NFL's "Shield" logo — in the solicitation booklet they sent to Dr. Pepper. . . . Plaintiff contends that Defendants had no right to use such marks for any purpose. . . .

The Complaint contains nine counts. Count I alleges that Defendants' actions violate § 43(a) of the Lanham Act. Counts II and III assert, respectively, that Defendants have acted in concert to cause the Cowboys Partnership to breach express provisions of the Trust and License Agreements and the implied covenant of good faith. Count IV maintains that the Cowboys Partnership has breached its obligations as a settlor of the NFL Trust and as an owner of marks licensed to Plaintiff. Count V alleges that, by engaging in the scheme set forth in the Complaint, the Cowboys Partnership and Defendant Jones have violated fiduciary duties owed to Plaintiff and the other Member Clubs. Count VI asserts that Defendants have been unjustly enriched by their scheme, Count VII that they have misappropriated revenue belonging to Plaintiff, and Count VIII that they have tortiously interfered with contractual rights granted by Plaintiff to its licensees. Finally, Count IX seeks a declaratory judgment establishing that Defendants' actions violate the law, as set forth in Counts I through VIII.

Defendants deny that their actions in any way violate either the Trust Agreement or the License Agreement. In support of their argument, Defendants have submitted copies of the contracts Texas Stadium entered into with Nike, Pepsi, and Dr. Pepper, as well as the contract it eventually entered into with American Express. Defendants maintain that none of these contracts grant sponsors the right to use any Trust Property — namely, either Club Marks or NFL Marks; indeed, they note that the contracts with Pepsi, Nike and American Express explicitly state that the sponsor is not entitled to use any Club Marks. . . . Defendants argue that all of Plaintiff's claims are based on false assertions that are refuted by the underlying contracts, and that Plaintiff's action should therefore be dismissed.

II. Legal Standard

In evaluating a motion to dismiss, courts must accept as true the factual allegations contained in the complaint. . . . All reasonable inferences must be drawn in favor of the non-moving party on such a motion. . . .

III. Analysis

Plaintiff repeatedly alleges in its Complaint that Defendants, through Texas Stadium, have granted sponsors the right to use the mark "Texas Stadium, home of the Dallas Cowboys." . . . Plaintiff also alleges that Defendants have "authoriz[ed] NIKE branded apparel to be worn on the field and on the sidelines during televised NFL games." . . . An examination of the contracts at issue reveals that they neither grant the use of the phrase "home of the Dallas Cowboys" nor authorize NIKE apparel to be worn on the Dallas Cowboys' sidelines. Defendants contend that because the contracts do not authorize the alleged misconduct, Plaintiff's entire case must be dismissed.

A. Breach of Contract

Plaintiff's claim for breach of contract withstands Defendants' motion to dismiss for a number of reasons. First, although the contracts do not contain the language discussed above, they do grant other rights which may violate the Trust and License Agreements. The Pepsi contract grants Pepsi the right to use a logo which says "Texas Stadium/Home of America's Favorite Team," which Plaintiff claims is a Club Mark. The logo licensed for use by American Express contains a star which Plaintiff claims is similar to the star that appears on the Dallas Cowboys' helmets. Accepting Plaintiff's allegation that Texas Stadium entered into these contracts as a "stand in" for the Cowboys Partnership, and drawing all inferences in favor of Plaintiff, the use of either of these logos would violate the Trust and License Agreements.

Second, the Complaint alleges that Defendants engaged in conduct which might violate the Trust and License Agreements — namely, a concerted campaign to create the impression that companies such as NIKE and Pepsi were sponsors of the Dallas Cowboys organization. During a nationally televised game, Defendant Jones, who controls both the Cowboys Partnership and Texas Stadium Corporation, allegedly escorted the CEO of NIKE to the Dallas Cowboys' sideline while both men prominently wore NIKE branded attire. . . . The Complaint further alleges that Jones ordered team personnel not to dress in apparel licensed by Plaintiff during this game, so that "[m]illions of television viewers observed no apparel brand other than NIKE" on the Cowboys' sideline. . . . Hence, despite contractual provisions to the contrary, in practice Defendants may have authorized NIKE apparel to be worn on the Dallas Cowboys' sideline, adjacent to players wearing the Club Marks.

Plaintiff also alleges that, in furtherance of their scheme to mislead the public, the Dallas Cowboys and NIKE jointly issued a press release in which the CEO of NIKE referred to the agreement as one with the "Dallas Cowboys"; and that Defendant Jones announced that the entire Cowboys organization drinks Pepsi, and posed for pictures at a press conference dressed in a "shirt emblazoned with a Cowboys Club Mark and boots emblazoned with a Pepsi logo. . . ." . . . All of the above conduct may constitute an impermissible use of Club Marks (*e.g.*, the name "Dallas Cowboys" and the team's uniforms), since under the Trust and License Agreements the Cowboys Partnership gave Plaintiff the exclusive right to use these marks for commercial purposes. At a minimum, alleging such conduct is sufficient to state a claim for breach of the implied duty of good faith, which constitutes a breach of contract under New York law. . . .

Finally, the Complaint alleges that Defendants misappropriated Club Marks and NFL Marks in solicitation materials they sent to potential sponsors. Specifically, the Complaint states that Defendants used the Club's "Star" logo and the NFL's "Shield" logo in a solicitation booklet they sent to Dr. Pepper. . . . Because the Trust and License Agreements give Plaintiff the exclusive right to use these Marks for commercial purposes, Defendants may have breached these agreements by using these Marks in a solicitation booklet. Defendants' counsel conceded that his clients' use of the Marks in solicitation materials was "[a]bsolutely inappropriate" and "probably violated their obligations. . . ." . . .

B. The Lanham Act

Plaintiff also alleges that Defendants violated § 43(a) of the Lanham Act, 15 U.S.C. § 1125(a), which provides in relevant part:

> (a)(1) Any person who, on or in connection with any goods or services, or any container for goods, uses in commerce any word, term, name, symbol, or device, or any combination thereof, or any false designation of origin, false or misleading description of fact, or false or misleading representation of fact, which —
>
> (A) is likely to cause confusion, or to cause mistake, or to deceive as to the affiliation, connection, or association of such person with another person, or as to the origin, *sponsorship, or approval* of his or her goods, services, or commercial activities of another person, . . . shall be liable in a civil action by any person who believes that he or she is or is likely to be damaged by such act (emphasis added).

Such a claim requires only a valid trademark and a likelihood of confusion on the part of the public. *See Nike, Inc. v. Just Did It Enters.,* 6 F.3d 1225, 1227 (7th Cir. 1993).

Plaintiff has the exclusive right to use NFL Marks and Club Marks for commercial purposes. Plaintiff clearly alleges that Defendants have commercially exploited Club Marks and NFL Marks by using them to solicit a sponsorship agreement and by authorizing their use in agreements with Dr. Pepper, Pepsi, NIKE. . . . As described above, Plaintiff also alleges that Defendants, through various press conferences and public appearances, have sought to create the impression that a relationship exists between the Cowboys and various sponsor companies. . . . Of course, whether the marks used by Defendants were NFL Marks or Club Marks is a question of fact.

There are decisions of this Court which suggest that an exclusive licensee of the right to distribute goods bearing a certain trademark cannot bring an action under s 43(a) of the Lanham Act against the trademark owner for permitting the use of the trademark in violation of the licensing agreement. *See L.G.B. Inc. v. Gitano Group, Inc.*, 769 F. Supp. 1243, 1249 (S.D.N.Y. 1991); *Ballet Makers, Inc. v. United States Shoe Corp.*, 633 F. Supp. 1328, 1335 (S.D.N.Y. 1986); *Silverstar Enters., Inc. v. Aday*, 537 F. Supp. 236, 241 (S.D.N.Y. 1982). The reasoning of these cases is that where the trademark owner, who is the source of the goods, authorizes the use of the mark for "genuine" goods, there can be no likelihood of confusion as to the source of the goods and, consequently, the quality of the goods.

Plaintiff's interest in the marks, however, is in authorizing the international corporate sponsorship of goods, not in selling goods. In this context the concepts of genuine goods, quality of goods, and source of goods have little significance. The quality, source, or genuineness of Pepsi or NIKE shoes, for example, are primarily reflected by their respective marks regardless of whether they are sponsored by the Cowboys or the NFL. As neither Plaintiff nor Defendants sell or manufacture goods, it makes little sense to focus on the source of the goods as the courts did in *Ballet Makers* and the other cited cases. . . . Rather, in the sponsorship context, the focus should be on the nature of Defendants' activities regarding marks which Plaintiff has the exclusive right to commercially exploit. Plaintiff has pleaded that Defendants have used NFL Marks and Club Marks in a manner which is likely to confuse the public as to Plaintiff's "sponsorship or approval" of Dr. Pepper, Pepsi, and NIKE. . . . These allegations are sufficient to state a cause of action under the broad language of § 43(a) of the Lanham Act.

C. Other Claims

Plaintiff's other claims arise out of the same set of operative facts as the breach of contract and Lanham Act claims, and are likewise not defeated by the contracts Defendants have submitted. However, Defendants have raised independent objections to several of Plaintiff's common law claims, two of which are convincing.

i. Breach of Implied Covenant of Good Faith

Defendants seek to dismiss Plaintiff's claim for breach of the implied duty of good faith because it is duplicative of Plaintiff's breach of contract claim. "Under New York law, parties to an express contract are bound by an implied duty of good faith, but breach of that duty is merely a breach of the underlying contract." *Fasolino Foods*, 961 F.2d at 1056. Plaintiff's separate claim for breach of the implied duty of good faith is therefore dismissed as redundant. . . .

ii. Breach of Obligations as Settlor of the NFL Trust Agreement and as Licensor of the Cowboys Club Marks

Defendants contend that Count IV of the Complaint should be dismissed because neither a settlor of a trust nor a licensor is under any duty — beyond that set forth in the underlying trust or licensing agreement — to refrain from taking steps that will reduce the value of the trust property or license. In support of its claim, Plaintiff cites a single case involving a settlor's deliberate interference with a trustee's efforts to fulfill his duties under the trust agreement. *See Vandyke v. Webb*, 167 A.D. 445, 152 N.Y.S. 508 (1st Dep't 1915). The cause of action recognized in *Vandyke* is nothing more than a simple breach of the implied duty of good faith. The case does not support Plaintiff's view that a settlor has any duty independent of its obligations under a trust agreement, which include the implied duty of good faith. Count IV is therefore dismissed.

iii. Misappropriation of Property

Defendants assert that the Complaint fails to state a claim for misappropriation of property because it does not adequately identify the property rights allegedly misappropriated. Further, they argue that this claim fails because

New York does not recognize a cause of action for the misappropriation of intangible assets. Neither of these arguments has merit. The first fails because the Complaint clearly alleges that Defendants have misappropriated revenue belonging to Plaintiff. . . . The second is irrelevant because revenue is not an "intangible asset."

Even if the Complaint only alleged that Defendants have misappropriated Club Marks, which are intangible, dismissal would not be warranted. Misappropriation claims that concern intangible rights are generally not recognized. . . . However, in the context of unfair competition, a plaintiff may state a cause of action for the misappropriation of an intangible asset, at least where it is ultimately embodied in a tangible product. . . .

iv. Tortious Interference

Defendants contend that the Complaint fails to allege the elements of tortious interference with contract. A plaintiff in such an action must allege that: i) a valid contract existed between plaintiff and a third party; ii) defendant knew of this contract; iii) defendant intentionally induced the third party to breach the contract or otherwise render performance impossible; and iv) plaintiff suffered damages. *See Kronis, Inc. v. AVX Corp.,* 81. N.Y.2d 90, 94, 595 N.Y.S.2d 931, 612 N.E.2d 289 (1993). . . .

Kronis suggests that a plaintiff can state a claim for tortious interference with contract without actually alleging that the third party breached its contract. However, a plaintiff must at least allege that the defendant's interference made the contract impossible to perform, or that the defendant induced the third party to render performance impossible. *See Museum Boutique Intercontinental, Ltd. v. Picasso*, 886 F. Supp. 1155, 1163 & n.19 (S.D.N.Y. 1995).

The Complaint meets this requirement. Plaintiff alleges that Defendants' intentional conduct has "interfered with and caused the violation and derogation of contractual rights granted by plaintiff to its licensees and sponsors."... Plaintiff has entered into contracts that make companies exclusive sponsors of the NFL and its Member Clubs for specific product categories. Plaintiff alleges that Defendants, by making unilateral arrangements with the direct competitors of these exclusive sponsors, have made it impossible for Plaintiff to honor its contractual obligations. Accordingly, Plaintiff's claim for tortious interference withstands Defendants' motion.

IV. Conclusion

For the reasons set forth above, Defendants' motion is granted in part and denied in part.

So Ordered.

CHICAGO PROFESSIONAL SPORTS LIMITED PARTNERSHIP v. NATIONAL BASKETBALL ASSOCIATION

95 F.3d 593 (7th Cir. 1996)

EASTERBROOK, Circuit Judge.

In the six years since they filed this antitrust suit, the Chicago Bulls have won four National Basketball Association titles and an equal number of legal victories. Suit and titles are connected. The Bulls want to broadcast more of their games over WGN television, a "superstation" carried on cable systems nationwide. The Bulls' popularity makes WGN attractive to these cable systems; the large audience makes WGN attractive to the Bulls. Since 1991 the Bulls and WGN have been authorized by injunction to broadcast 25 or 30 games per year. 754 F. Supp. 1336 (1991). We affirmed that injunction in 1992, *see* 961 F.2d 667, and the district court proceeded to determine whether WGN could carry even more games — and whether the NBA could impose a "tax" on the games broadcast to a national audience, for which other superstations have paid a pretty penny to the league. After holding a nine-week trial and receiving 512 stipulations of fact, the district court made a 30-game allowance permanent, 874 F. Supp. 844 (1995), and held the NBA's fee excessive, 1995-2 Trade Cas. para. 71,253. Both sides appeal. The Bulls want to broadcast 41 games per year over WGN; the NBA contends that the antitrust laws allow it to fix a lower number (15 or 20) and to collect the tax it proposed. With apologies to both sides, we conclude that they must suffer through still more litigation.

Our 1992 opinion rejected the league's defense based on the Sports Broadcasting Act, . . . but our rationale implied that the NBA could restructure its contracts to take advantage of that statute. 961 F.2d at 670-72. In 1993 the league tried to do so, signing a contract that transfers all broadcast rights to the National Broadcasting Company. NBC shows only 26 games during the regular season, however, and the network contract allows the league and its teams to permit telecasts at other times. Every team received the right to broadcast all 82 of its regular season games (41 over the air, 41 on cable), unless NBC telecasts a given contest. The NBANBC contract permits the league to exhibit 85 games per year on superstations. Seventy were licensed to the Turner stations (TBS and TNT), leaving 15 potentially available for WGN to license from the league. It disdained the opportunity. The Bulls sold 30 games directly to WGN, treating these as over-the-air broadcasts authorized by the NBC contract — not to mention the district court's injunction. The Bulls' only concession (perhaps more to the market than to the league) is that WGN does not broadcast a Bulls game at the same time as a basketball telecast on a Turner superstation.

Back in 1991 and 1992, the parties were debating whether the NBA's television arrangements satisfied § 1 of the Sports Broadcasting Act . . . . We held not, because the Act addresses the effects of "transfers" by a "league of clubs," and the NBA had prescribed rather than "transferred" broadcast rights. The 1993 contract was written with that distinction in mind. The league asserted title to the copyright interests arising from the games and transferred all broadcast rights to NBC; it received some back, subject to contractual restrictions. Section 1 has been satisfied. But the league did not pay enough attention to § 2, 15 U.S.C. § 1292, which reads: Section 1291 of this title shall not apply to any joint agreement described in the first sentence in such section which prohibits any person to whom such rights are sold or transferred from televising any games within any area, except within the home territory of a member club of the league on a day when such club is playing at home. The NBA-NBC contract permits each club to license the broadcast of its games, and then, through the restriction on superstation broadcasts, attempts to limit telecasts to the teams' home markets. Section 2 provides that this makes § 1 inapplicable, so the Sports Broadcasting Act leaves the antitrust laws in force. . . .

The NBA could have availed itself of the Sports Broadcasting Act by taking over licensing and by selling broadcast rights in the Bulls' games to one of the many local stations in Chicago, rather than to WGN. The statute offered other options as well. . . . By signing a contract with NBC that left the Bulls, rather than the league, with the authority to select the TV station that would broadcast the games, the NBA made its position under the Sports Broadcasting Act untenable. For as soon as the Bulls picked WGN, any effort to control cable system retransmission of the WGN signal tripped over § 2. The antitrust laws therefore apply, and we must decide what they have to say about the league's effort to curtail superstation transmissions.

Three issues were left unresolved in 1992. One was whether the Bulls and WGN, as producers, suffer antitrust injury. 961 F.2d at 669-70. The NBA has not pursued this possibility, and as it is not jurisdictional (plaintiffs suffer injury in fact), we let the question pass. The other two issues are related. We concluded in 1992 that the district court properly condemned the NBA's superstation rule under the quick-look version of the Rule of Reason, . . . because (a) the league did not argue that it should be treated as a single entity, and (b) the anti-free-riding justification for the superstation rule failed because a fee collected on nationally telecast games would compensate other teams (and the league as a whole) for the value of their contributions to the athletic contests being broadcast. 961 F.2d at 762-76. Back in the district court, the NBA argued that it is entitled to be treated as a single firm and therefore should possess the same options as other licensors of entertainment products; outside of court, the league's Board of Governors adopted a rule requiring any club that licenses broadcast rights to superstations to pay a fee based on the amount the two Turner stations pay for games they license directly from the league.

Plaintiffs say that the single-entity argument was forfeited by its omission from the first appeal, but we think not. . . .

The district court was unimpressed by the NBA's latest arguments. It held that a sports league should not be treated as a single firm unless the teams have a "complete unity of interest" — which they don't. The court also held the fee to be invalid. Our opinion compelled the judge to concede that a fee is proper in principle. 961 F.2d at 675-76. But the judge thought the NBA's fee excessive. Instead of starting with the price per game it had negotiated with Turner (some $450,000), and reducing to account for WGN's smaller number of cable outlets, as it did, the judge concluded that the league should have started with the advertising revenues WGN generated from retransmission on cable (the "outer market revenues"). Then it should have cut this figure in half, the judge held, so that the Bulls could retain "their share" of these revenues. The upshot: the judge cut the per game fee from roughly $138,000 to $39,400. . . .

The core question in antitrust is output. Unless a contract reduces output in some market, to the detriment of consumers, there is no antitrust problem. A high price is not itself a violation of the Sherman Act. . . . WGN and the Bulls argue that the league's fee is excessive, unfair, and the like. But they do not say that it will reduce output. They plan to go on broadcasting 30 games, more if the court will let them, even if they must pay $138,000 per telecast. Although the fee exceeds WGN's outer-market revenues, the station evidently obtains other benefits — for example, (i) the presence of Bulls games may increase the number of cable systems that carry the station, augmenting its revenues 'round the clock; (ii) WGN slots into Bulls games ads for its other programming; and (iii) many viewers will keep WGN on after the game and watch whatever comes next. Lack of an effect on output means that the fee does not have antitrust significance. Once antitrust issues are put aside, how much the NBA charges for national telecasts is for the league to resolve under its internal governance procedures. It is no different in principle from the question how much (if any) of the live gate goes to the visiting team, who profits from the sale of cotton candy at the stadium, and how the clubs divide revenues from merchandise bearing their logos and trademarks. Courts must respect a league's disposition of these issues, just as they respect contracts and decisions by a corporation's board of directors. . . .

According to the league, the analogy to a corporate board is apt in more ways than this. The NBA concedes that it comprises 30 juridical entities — 29 teams plus the national organization, each a separate corporation or partnership. The teams are not the league's subsidiaries; they have separate ownership. Nonetheless, the NBA submits, it functions as a single entity, creating a single product ("NBA Basketball") that competes with other basketball leagues (both college and professional), other sports ("Major League Baseball", "college football"), and other entertainments such as plays, movies, opera, TV shows, Disneyland, and Las Vegas. Separate ownership of the clubs promotes local boosterism, which increases interest; each ownership group also has a powerful incentive to field a better team, which makes the contests more exciting and thus more attractive. These functions of independent team ownership do not imply that the league is a cartel, however, any more than separate ownership of hamburger joints . . . implies that McDonald's is a cartel. Whether the best analogy is to a system of franchises (no one expects a McDonald's outlet to compete with other members of the system by offering pizza) or to a corporate holding company structure (on which *see Copperweld Corp. v. Independence Tube Corp.*, 467 U.S. 752 (1984)) does not matter from this perspective. The point is that antitrust law permits, indeed encourages, cooperation inside a business organization the better to facilitate competition between that organization and other producers. To say that participants in an organization may cooperate is to say that they may control what they make and how they sell it: the producers of Star Trek may decide to release two episodes a week and grant exclusive licenses to show them, even though this reduces the number of times episodes appear on TV in a given market, just as the NBA's superstation rule does.

The district court conceded this possibility but concluded that all cooperation among separately incorporated firms is forbidden by § 1 of the Sherman Act, except to the extent *Copperweld* permits. *Copperweld*, according to the district court, "is quite narrow, and rests solely upon the fact that a parent corporation and its wholly-owned subsidiary have a 'complete unity of interest.'" . . . Although that phrase appears in *Copperweld*, the Court offered it as a statement of fact about the parent-subsidiary relation, not as a proposition of law about the limits of permissible cooperation. As a proposition of law, it would be silly. Even a single firm contains many competing interests. One division may make inputs for another's finished goods. The first division might want to sell its products directly to the market, to maximize income (and thus the salary and bonus of the division's managers); the second division might want to get its inputs from the first at a low transfer price, which would maximize the second division's paper profits. Conflicts are endemic in any multi-stage firm, such as General Motors or IBM, . . . but they do not imply that these large firms must justify all of their acts under the Rule of Reason. Or consider a partnership for the practice of law (or accounting): some lawyers would be better off with a lock-step compensation agreement under which all partners with the same seniority have the same income, but others would prosper under an "eat what you kill" system that rewards bringing new business to the firm. Partnerships have dissolved as a result of these conflicts. Yet these wrangles — every bit as violent as the dispute among the NBA's teams about how to generate and divide broadcast revenues — do not demonstrate that law firms are cartels, or subject to scrutiny under the Rule of Reason their decisions about where to open offices or which clients to serve.

Copperweld does not hold that only conflict-free enterprises may be treated as single entities. Instead it asks why the antitrust laws distinguish between unilateral and concerted action, and then assigns a parent-subsidiary group to the "unilateral" side in light of those functions. Like a single firm, the parent-subsidiary combination cooperates internally to increase efficiency. Conduct that "deprives the marketplace of the independent centers of decisionmaking that competition assumes", . . . without the efficiencies that come with integration inside a firm, go on the "concerted" side of the line. And there are entities in the middle: "mergers, joint ventures, and various vertical agreements". . . that reduce the number of independent decisionmakers yet may improve efficiency. These are assessed under the Rule of Reason. We see no reason why a sports league cannot be treated as a single firm in this typology. It produces a single product; cooperation is essential (a league with one team would be like one hand clapping); and a league need not deprive the market of independent centers of decisionmaking. The district court's legal standard was therefore incorrect, and a judgment resting on the application of that standard is flawed.

Whether the NBA itself is more like a single firm, which would be analyzed only under § 2 of the Sherman Act, or like a joint venture, which would be subject to the Rule of Reason under § 1, is a tough question under *Copperweld*. It has characteristics of both. Unlike the colleges and universities that belong to the National Collegiate Athletic Association, which the Supreme Court treated as a joint venture in NCAA, the NBA has no existence independent of sports. It makes professional basketball; only it can make "NBA Basketball" games; and unlike the NCAA the NBA also "makes" teams. . . . All of this makes the league look like a single firm. Yet the 29 clubs, unlike GM's plants, have the right to secede . . . , and rearrange into two or three leagues. Professional sports leagues have been assembled from clubs that formerly belonged to other leagues; the National Football League and the NBA fit that description, and the teams have not surrendered their power to rearrange things yet again. Moreover, the league looks more or less like a firm depending on which facet of the business one examines. . . . From the perspective of fans and advertisers (who use sports telecasts to reach fans), "NBA Basketball" is one product from a single source even though the Chicago Bulls and Seattle Supersonics are highly distinguishable, just as General Motors is a single firm even though a Corvette differs from a Chevrolet. But from the perspective of college basketball players who seek to sell their skills, the teams are distinct, and because the human capital of players is not readily transferable to other sports (as even Michael Jordan learned) the league looks more like a group of firms acting as a monopsony. That is why the Supreme Court found it hard to characterize the National Football League in *Brown v. Pro Football, Inc.*, 116 S.Ct. 2116, 2126, 135 L.Ed.2d 521 (1996): "the clubs that make up a professional sports league are not completely independent economic competitors, as they depend upon a degree of cooperation for economic survival. . . . In the present context, however, that circumstance makes the league more like a single bargaining employer, which analogy seems irrelevant to the legal issue before us." To say that the league is "more like a single bargaining employer" than a multiemployer unit is not to say that it necessarily is one, for every purpose.

The league wants us to come to a conclusion on this subject . . . and award it the victory. Yet as we remarked in 1992, "[c]haracterization is a creative rather than exact endeavor." 961 F.2d at 672. The district court plays the leading role, followed by deferential appellate review. We are not authorized to announce and apply our own favored characterization unless the law admits of only one choice. The Supreme Court's ambivalence in *Brown*, like the disagreement among judges on similar issues, implies that more than one characterization is possible, and therefore that the district court must revisit the subject using the correct legal approach.

Most courts that have asked whether professional sports leagues should be treated like single firms or like joint ventures have preferred the joint venture characterization. . . . But Justice Rehnquist filed a strong dissent from the denial of certiorari in the soccer case, arguing that "the league competes as a unit against other forms of entertainment", *NFL v. North American Soccer League*, 459 U.S. 1074, 1077 (1982), and the fourth circuit concluded that the Professional Golf Association should be treated as one firm for antitrust purposes, even though that sport is less economically integrated than the NBA. *Seabury Management, Inc. v. PGA of America, Inc.*, 878 F. Supp. 771 (D. Md. 1994), *affirmed in relevant part,* 52 F.3d 322 (4th Cir. 1995). . . . These cases do not yield a clear principle about the proper characterization of sports leagues — and we do not think that *Copperweld* imposes one "right" characterization. Sports are sufficiently diverse that it is essential to investigate their organization and ask *Copperweld's* functional question one league at a time — and perhaps one facet of a league at a time, for we do not rule out the possibility that an organization such as the NBA is best understood as one firm when selling broadcast rights to a network in competition with a thousand other producers of entertainment, but is best understood as a joint venture when curtailing competition for players who have few other market opportunities. . . .

However this inquiry may come out on remand, we are satisfied that the NBA is sufficiently integrated that its superstation rules may not be condemned without analysis under the full Rule of Reason. We affirmed the district court's original injunction after applying the "quick look" version because the district court had characterized the NBA as something close to a cartel, and the league had not then made a *Copperweld* argument. After considering this argument, we conclude that when acting in the broadcast market the NBA is closer to a single firm than to a group of independent firms. This means that plaintiffs cannot prevail without establishing that the NBA possesses power in a relevant market, and that its exercise of this power has injured consumers. . . .

Substantial market power is an indispensable ingredient of every claim under the full Rule of Reason. . . . During the lengthy trial of this case, the NBA argued that it lacks market power, whether the buyers are understood as the viewers of games (the way the district court characterized things in *NCAA*) or as advertisers, who use games to attract viewers (the way the Supreme Court characterized a related market in *Times-Picayune Publishing Co. v. United States,* 345 U.S. 594 (1953)). College football may predominate on Saturday afternoons in the fall, but there is no time slot when NBA basketball predominates. The NBA's season lasts from November through June; games are played seven days a week. This season overlaps all of the other professional and college sports, so even sports fanatics have many other options. From advertisers' perspective — likely the right one, because advertisers are the ones who actually pay for telecasts — the market is even more competitive. Advertisers seek viewers of certain demographic characteristics, and homogeneity is highly valued. A homogeneous audience facilitates targeted ads: breakfast cereals and toys for cartoon shows, household appliances and detergents for daytime soap operas, automobiles and beer for sports. If the NBA assembled for advertisers an audience that was uniquely homogeneous, or had especially high willingness-to-buy, then it might have market power even if it represented a small portion of air-time. The parties directed considerable attention to this question at trial, but the district judge declined to make any findings of fact on the subject, deeming market power irrelevant. As we see things, market power is irrelevant only if the NBA is treated as a single firm under *Copperweld*; and given the difficulty of that issue, it may be superior to approach this as a straight Rule of Reason case, which means starting with an inquiry into market power and, if there is power, proceeding to an evaluation of competitive effects.

* * *

At all events, the judgment of the district court is vacated, and the case is remanded for proceedings consistent with this opinion. Pending further proceedings in the district court or agreement among the parties, the Bulls and WGN must respect the league's (and the NBC contract's) limitations on the maximum number of superstation telecasts.

CUDAHY, Circuit Judge, concurring:

Although I agree with the majority's firm conclusion that the "quick look" doctrine does not apply to these complex facts, I must indicate some differences in significant matters that are reached in the course of the majority opinion. Thus, in arriving at its conclusion that a full Rule of Reason analysis is required, the majority seems to be extrapolating from its discussion of whether the NBA may be a "single entity." Classification as a "single entity" means immunity from Sherman Act, § 1, considerations, a distinction much more drastic than the conclusion that the conduct in question here deserves a "quizzical look" rather than a mere "quick look." So, although it is not entirely clear, the majority seems to be saying that, since the NBA may be a single entity, its conduct certainly merits more than a quick look. Perhaps so, but, since the single entity question is unresolved, I would prefer to address the problem from a slightly different direction.

For the "quick look" approach should have a narrow application, reflecting its recent and sharply delimited origin in the *NCAA* case. *Nat'l Collegiate Athletic Ass'n v. Bd. of Regents of the Univ. of Oklahoma*. . . . That case, involving a loose alliance of colleges which had agreed on price and output restrictions on broadcast of their football games, held that under some circumstances a full analysis of market power is not required to determine that an agreement is anticompetitive. This framework should not be extended to the more highly integrated and economically unitary NBA.

The colleges which made up the NCAA were entirely separate economic entities, competing with each other in many areas unrelated to their athletic encounters. There is, of course, a sort of continuum of economic integration, with entities at different points along the continuum warranting differing levels of antitrust concern. At one end are loose alliances of economic actors having independent concerns (like the NCAA), the anticompetitive nature of whose agreements is obvious from a "quick look." At the other end are fully–integrated entities in which the economic interests of the participants are so completely aligned that antitrust scrutiny of their policies is unnecessary except where § 2 of the Sherman Act is violated. In the center is the broad range of organizations (generally like the NBA) whose separate constituents are individually owned but are closely but not completely tied economically to their organizations. These entities are capable of anticompetitive agreements, but a full Rule of Reason analysis is necessary to ensure that productive cooperation is not mistaken for anticompetitive conduct. Single entity aside, there is certainly enough concern here for the efficiency of the league as a competitor in the entertainment market to require full Rule of Reason analysis.

On a more clear-cut point, I think it was appropriate for Judge Will to examine the size of the NBA's fee for the WGN broadcasts of Bulls games. In this connection, the majority rejects considerations of fairness "and the like" and asserts that, "The core question in antitrust is output." . . . For better or for worse, under the highly reductive view that currently prevails in antitrust matters, this somewhat grating aphorism appears to be correct. The Holy Grail of consumer welfare means that more is better no matter how the more is distributed. Taking these principles as a given, it is still difficult for me to understand how output can be disjoined from cost under the circumstances of this case. In fact, Judge Will found as a fact that, "[the NBA's proposed fee] may well at some future date decrease output and distribution of Bulls games on WGN. . . ." But, particularly since output is currently constrained to 30 games, rather than whatever the market would produce, it is difficult to ascertain whether the fee is high enough to reduce output below the competitive level. Since it is not clear to me that the magnitude of Judge Will's adjustment was justified by antitrust considerations alone, I would include this issue with other matters to be considered on remand.

* * *

However, on the assumption that the "single entity" question may be reached (and presumably will be reached on remand) a number of considerations will be relevant. Assuming as I must that the sole goal of antitrust is efficiency or, put another way, the maximization of total societal wealth, the question whether a sports league is a "single entity" turns on whether the actions of the league have any potential to lessen economic competition among the separately owned teams. . . . The fact that teams compete on the floor is more or less irrelevant to whether they compete economically — it is only their economic competition which is germane to antitrust analysis. In principle, of course, a sports league could actually be a single firm and the individual teams could be under unified ownership and management. Such a firm would, of course, be subject to scrutiny only under § 2 of the Sherman Act and not under § 1. From the point of view of wealth maximization, a league of independently-owned teams, if it is no more likely than a single firm to make inefficient management decisions, should be treated as a single entity. The single entity question thus would boil down to "whether member clubs of a sports league have legitimate economic interests of their own, independent of the league and each other.". . . It follows that a sports league, no matter what its ownership structure, can make inefficient decisions only if the individual teams have some chance of economic gain at the expense of the league.

Another form of the same question is whether a sports league is more like a single firm or like a joint venture. With efficiency the sole criterion, a joint venture warrants scrutiny for at least two reasons — (1) the venture could possess market power with respect to the jointly produced product (essentially act like a single firm with monopoly power) or (2) the fact that the venturers remain competitors in other arenas might either distort the way the joint product is managed or allow the venturers to use the joint product as a smoke-screen behind which to cut deals to reduce competition in the other arenas. The most convincing "single entity" argument involving the NBA is that the teams produce only the joint product of "league basketball" and that there is thus no significant economic competition between them. . . . If this is the case, the argument goes, type (2) concerns drop out and only type (1) concerns remain. Type (1) concerns, of course, are exactly those appropriate for § 2 analysis of a single firm.

There are, however, flaws in this single entity argument. The assumption underlying it is that league sports are a different and more desirable product than a disorganized collection of independently arranged games between teams. For this reason, it is contended that joining sports teams into a league is efficiency-enhancing and desirable. I will accept this premise. . . . It is perhaps true, as argued by the NBA and many commentators, that sports are different from many joint ventures because the individual teams cannot, even in principle, produce the product — league sports. However, the fact that cooperation is necessary to produce league basketball does not imply that the league will necessarily produce its product in the most efficient fashion. There is potential for inefficient decisionmaking regarding the joint product of "league basketball" even when the individual teams engage in no economic activity outside of the league. This potential arises because the structure of the league is such that all "owners" of the league must be "owners" of individual teams and decisions are made by a vote of the teams. This means that the league will not necessarily make efficient decisions about the number of teams fielded or, more generally, the competitive balance among teams. Thus, the fact that several teams are required to make a league does not necessarily imply that the current makeup of the league is the most desirable or "efficient" one.

The NBA's justification for its restriction of Bulls broadcasts centers on the need to maintain a competitive balance among teams. Such a balance is needed to ensure that the league provides high quality entertainment throughout the season so as to optimize competition with other forms of entertainment. Competitive balance is not the only contributor to the entertainment value of NBA basketball, however. Fan enjoyment of league sports depends on both the opportunity to identify with a local or favorite team and the thrill of watching the best quality of play. A single firm owning all of the teams would presumably arrange for the number of teams and their locations efficiently to maximize fan enjoyment of the league season. There is, however, no reason to expect that the current team owners will necessarily make such decisions efficiently, given their individual economic interests in the financial health of their own teams.

It's not surprising that far-flung fans want to watch the Bulls' superstars on a superstation. The NBA argues that the broadcasting of more Bulls games to these fans will disturb the competitive balance among teams. However, one can also speculate that, since sports viewing has become more of a television activity than an "in the flesh" activity, these fans might prefer to have a league composed of fewer, better teams (like the Bulls). If this were the case, league policies designed to shore up all of the current teams would be inefficient. The point, of course, is not that this speculation is necessarily correct, but that the efficient number of teams (or, more generally, the efficient competitive balance) may not be obtained as a matter of course given the current league ownership framework.

The team owners thus retain independent economic interests. This would be the case even if they did not compete for the revenues of the league. Teams do compete for broadcast revenues, however. "A conflicting economic interest between the league and an individual club can exist only when league revenues are distributed unequally among the member clubs based on club participation in the games generating the revenue." . . . When teams receive a disproportionate share of the broadcast revenues generated by their own games, such a situation exists.

The analysis of this issue is tricky, however, since decisions about how to allocate broadcasting revenues are made by the league. It may be that "member clubs of a league do not have any legitimate independent economic interests in the league product" and "each team has an ownership interest in every game" (including an equal a priori ownership interest in the broadcast rights to every game). . . . If this assumption is correct, then whatever arrangements for revenue distribution the league decides to make will be, like bonuses to successful salespeople in an ordinary firm, presumptively efficient. If, however, broadcast rights inure initially to the two teams participating in a particular game and if, as is certainly the case, some games are more attractive to fans than others, the league cannot be presumed to have made decisions allocating those broadcast revenues efficiently.

The analogy, within the context of an ordinary firm, is to allow the salespeople to vote on the bonuses each is to get. Each salesperson has some incentive, of course, to promote the overall efficiency of the firm on which his or her salary, or perhaps the value of his or her firm stock, depends and therefore to award the larger bonuses to the most productive salespersons. However, in this scenario each salesperson has two ways of maximizing personal wealth — increasing the overall efficiency of the firm and redistributing income within the firm. The result of the vote might not be to distribute bonuses in the most efficient fashion. The potential for this type of inefficiency is particularly great when, as with the NBA, the league is "the only game in town" so that a team does not have the option of going elsewhere if it is not receiving revenues commensurate with its contribution to the overall league product. In any event, a group of team owners who do not share all revenues from all games might well make decisions that do not maximize the profit of the league as a whole.

As this discussion demonstrates, determining whether the potential for inefficient decisionmaking survives within a joint venture because of the independent economic interests of the partners is extraordinarily complex and confusing. For this reason, a simple, if not courageous, way out of the problem might be to establish a legal presumption that a single entity cannot exist without single ownership. To avoid the complexities and confusions of attempted analysis, one might simply ordain that combinations that lack diverse economic interests should opt for joint ownership of a single enterprise to avoid antitrust problems. On the other hand, judges may want to play economist to the extent of resisting simplifying assumptions.

In any event, sports leagues argue that they must maintain independent ownership of the teams because separate ownership enhances the appearance of competitiveness demanded by fans. But the leagues cannot really expect the courts to aid them in convincing consumers that competition exists if it really does not. If consumers want economic competition between sports teams, then independent ownership and preservation of independent economic interests is likely an efficient choice for a sports league. But that choice, as with other joint ventures, brings with it the attendant antitrust risks. The NBA cannot have it both ways.

Relating all of this to the majority's treatment of the single entity issue, I see two problems with the majority analysis. First, as already noted, divorcing the question of single entity from the question of ownership is likely to lead to messy and inconsistent application of antitrust law. The bottom line may be that the inquiry into whether separate economic interests are maintained by the participants in a joint enterprise is likely to be no easier than a full Rule of Reason analysis.

Second, some of the majority's discussion of independent interests is puzzling. The majority contends that the district court "concluded that all cooperation among separately incorporated firms is forbidden by § 1 of the Sherman Act, except to the extent *Copperweld* permits.". . . *Copperweld* concluded that a parent corporation and its wholly-owned subsidiary have a "complete unity of interest" and hence should be treated as a single entity. Here the district court simply concluded that the NBA, because it involved cooperation between separately owned teams, was subject to antitrust analysis. . . . This conclusion is a far cry from deciding that all cooperation among separately incorporated firms is forbidden.

I also cannot agree with the majority's analysis of the type of "unity of interest" required for single entity status. The majority states, . . . that "[e]ven a single firm contains many competing interests." The opinion goes on to cite the competition for salary and bonuses between division managers as an example. However, when *Copperweld* talks about unity of interests in the single entity context, I think it must be taken to mean unity of economic interests of the decisionmakers. . . . A single firm does not evidence diverse economic interests to the outside world because final decisions are made by the owners or stockholders, who care only about the overall performance of the firm. Only because this is the case can single firms be assumed to behave in the canonical profit-maximizing fashion. The diverse interests mentioned in the majority opinion seem as irrelevant to the antitrust analysis as is the on-court rivalry between teams in the NBA.

Thus, when *Copperweld* refers to conduct that "deprives the marketplace of the independent centers of decisionmaking that competition assumes," it does not refer to "decisionmakers" whose economic independence is only potential. The antitrust issue is really whether, as a result of some cooperative venture, economic interests which remain independent coordinate their decisions. As *Copperweld* notes, "[t]he officers of a single firm are not separate economic actors pursuing separate economic interests. . . ." . . . Therefore, their joint decisionmaking is of no antitrust concern. Employees or divisions within a firm, on the other hand, may remain separate economic actors pursuing separate economic interests but they do not make the final decisions governing the firm's operations. They may compete for shares of the firm's revenues, but they do not decree how that revenue will be shared. Thus their conflict or cooperation does not pose antitrust issues either. Joint ventures, on the other hand, are subject to antitrust scrutiny precisely because separate economic interests are joined in decisionmaking, with the potential for distorted results.

As long as teams are individually owned and revenue is not shared in fixed proportion, the teams both retain independent economic interests and make decisions in concert. Where this is the case, there is a strong argument that sports leagues should be treated as joint ventures rather than single entities because there remains a potential that league policy will be made to satisfy the independent economic interests of some group of teams, rather than to maximize the overall performance of the league. Thus, it is possible, if more Bulls games were broadcast, league profits might increase. But, if the revenue from the broadcast of Bulls games goes disproportionately to the Bulls, the other league members may not vote for this more efficient result.

There may, of course, be cases in which independent ownership of the partners in a joint venture does not pose any real possibility of inefficient decisionmaking. This would be the case if the parties did not compete in any other arena and if all revenues were shared in fixed proportions among the partners. In general, however, a plausible case can be made for the proposition that independent ownership should presumptively preclude treatment as a single entity. This certainly does not mean, of course, that "all cooperation among separately incorporated firms is forbidden by § 1 of the Sherman Act". . . . It would mean only that such cooperation must ordinarily be justified under the Rule of Reason. Justification might not be more difficult than the elusive search for treatment as a single entity.

* * *

NOTES AND COMMENTS

1. Can you discern a unified theory of antitrust law as applied to professional sports league decision making? Do the cases reveal several theories depending on the peculiar facts of each case?

2. Judge Easterbrook, in *Bulls I*, commented that the concept of "antitrust injury" is distinct from notions of "injury in fact" under Article III analysis. He further remarked:

> The antitrust laws throttle some cooperative behavior of producers to preserve the benefits of competition for consumers. Producers often complain about the efforts of business rivals, which reduce their profits. . . . Judicial relief from the real injuries caused by rivalry would harm the consumers the antitrust laws are supposed to protect. . . . The antitrust injury doctrine . . . requires every plaintiff to show that its loss comes from the acts that reduce output or raise prices to consumers.

Chicago Professional Sports Limited Partnership v. National Basketball Association, 961 F.2d 667, 669-70 (7th Cir. 1992).

The court in *Bulls II* notes that the NBA did not pursue the "antitrust injury" issue on remand and thus the court lets the "question pass." Is the court's statement accurate? What is the basis of the majority's overruling of the lower court's treatment of the NBA fee? Do both the majority and concurring opinions agree on the definition of "antitrust injury"? Does the majority's definition raise implications for ownership or relocation cases? For discussion of the historical development of the concept of "antitrust injury," *see* AREEDA & HOVENKAMP, 1 ANTITRUST LAW Ch. 1 (2d ed. 2000).

3. How does the court characterize the doctrine emanating from *Copperweld?* What is the basis of the Judge Cudahy's disagreement with the majority regarding the "single entity" issue? Review the discussion of the "single entity" defense at **Section F**, *supra*.

4. The United States Court of Appeals for the 4th Circuit relied on *Copperweld* analysis to affirm a trial court determination that the PGA and member sections were "single entities," and legally incapable of conspiracy. *Seabury Management, Inc. v. Professional Golfers' Associaton of America, Inc.*, 52 F.3d 322, 1995 WL 241379 (4th Cir. 1995) (unpublished disposition), *aff'g in part and rev'g in part, Seabury Management, Inc. v. PGA*, 878 F. Supp. 771 (D. Md. 1994). The U.S. District Court stated:

> While the MAPGA is not a wholly-owned subsidiary of the PGA and these entities are separately incorporated, the evidence at trial established that as pertinent to this case the PGA and its member sections function as a single economic unit with the PGA possessing ultimate control over the actions of individual sections.
>
> The Court finds it significant that the sections are governed by the PGA Constitution, by policies adopted either at PGA annual meetings or by the PGA Board of Directors, and by other pertinent policy documents, such as trademark licensing agreements.

Id. at 777. *See also* discussion of the "single entity" under the *Copperweld* test as applied in *City of Mt. Pleasant v. Associated Elec. Coop., Inc.*, 838 F.2d 268 (8th Cir. 1988), at **Section F, Note 9**, *supra*.

5. Major League Soccer established a limited liability company that owns all of the teams in the league, intellectual property rights, tickets, equipment, and broadcast rights. MLS establishes league schedules, enters into stadium leases, pays the salaries of referees and league personnel, and has sole responsibility for contracting with and compensating players and assigning the players to designated teams. MLS, however, relinquishes some control over team operations to certain investors (nine of twelve teams), who provide management services and operate with some degree of autonomy. In return for the services, MLS pays each operator a "management fee," equaling the sum of one-half of local ticket receipts and concessions; the first $1,125,000 of local broadcast revenues (increasing annually by a percentage rate); a 30% share (declining to 10% by 2006) of any amount above the base amount; all revenues from overseas tours; one-half share of MLS Championship Game revenues; and a share of revenues from exhibition games. Remaining revenues are distributed equally to all investors.

In 1997, eight named players sued MLS, the United States Soccer Federation, and the operator/investors, alleging violations of Sections 1 and 2 of the Sherman Antitrust Act (as well as claims under the Clayton Act) resulting from the agreement not to compete for player services. The United States District Court granted the MLS motion for summary judgment, holding that MLS and its investors comprised a single entity and, therefore, could not conspire in violation of Section 1. *Fraser v. Major League Soccer, L.L.C.*, 97 F. Supp. 2d 130 (D. Mass. 2000).

The Court of Appeals for the First Circuit, however, rejected the "single entity" rationale, viewing the MLS structure as a "hybrid arrangement, somewhere between a single company . . . and a cooperative arrangement between existing competitors." It suggested an appropriate "rule of reason" analysis, reshaped toward a body of more flexible rules for interdependent multi-party enterprises. The Court affirmed, finding the District Court's error "harmless," as the jury found that the market alleged in plaintiffs' Complaint was not proved. *Fraser v. Major League Soccer, L.L.C.*, 284 F.3d 47 (1st Cir. 2002). *See*, discussion at **Section F, Note 10**, *supra*; Waxman, Fraser v. MLS, L.L.C.*: Is There a Sham Exception to the* Copperweld *Single Entity Immunity?*, 12 MARQ. SPORTS L. REV. 487 (2001) (supports the utilization of a "sham" exception to single entity immunity).

6. Is the *Bulls* court accurate in its distinction between the nature of NCAA and the NBA operations? *See* **Chapter 4** for discussion of the antitrust laws as applied to amateur athletics. How does a "monopsony" differ from a "cartel"? What arguments concerning the "single entity" issue do you expect the parties to make on remand?

7. Problem. Draft a league constitution that structures league operations as a "single entity." Several professional leagues, including Major League Soccer (MLS), the Women's National Basketball Association (WNBA), the American Basketball League (ABL) (defunct), and the Central Baseball League (independent minor baseball league), have attempted to use the structure. For a detailed enumeration of the elements of the MLS structure, *see Fraser v. Major League Soccer, L.L.C.*, 284 F.3d 47 (1st Cir. 2002), and the lower court opinion at 97 F. Supp. 2d 130 (D. Mass. 2000). *See also*, Atherton, Fraser v. Major League Soccer (MLS)*: the Future of the Single-Entity League and the International Transfer System*, 66 UMKC L. REV. 887 (1998).

8. Both majority and concurring opinions reject use of the "quick look" doctrine in the *Bulls* case. Do the opinions recognize the doctrine as a viable mechanism for use in antitrust cases, or as one limited to the facts of *Board of Regents*? How would you explain the "quick look" doctrine in arguing for its use at trial?

9. The concurring opinion in *Bulls II* accuses the majority of extrapolating from its "single entity" analysis to construct its conclusion that "full rule of reason" inquiry is required. Does the majority infer that evidence, indicating defendants' organization is "close to a single entity," is also persuasive that the actions of the defendants are reasonable under "rule of reason" scrutiny? Should there exist a separate test for the appropriateness of actions by partners in a "joint venture" that is closer to a "single entity" than a "cartel"? *See* Deckert, *Multiple Characterizations for the Single Entity Argument? The 7th Circuit Throws an Airball in* Chicago Sports Limited Partnership v. NBA, 5 VILL. SPORTS & ENT. L.J. 73 (1998); Piraino, Jr., *Beyond Per Se, Rule of Reason or Merger Analysis: A New Antitrust Standard for Joint Ventures*, 76 MINN. L. REV. 1 (1991).

10. In the Dallas Cowboys' suit against the NFL Trust, the plaintiffs alleged that the "Trust is a classic price-fixing cartel that has eliminated competition among NFL clubs." *Dallas Cowboys Football Club, Ltd. v. National Football League Trust*, U.S. District Court, S.D.N.Y., 95-9426 (1995), at Complaint, Paragraph 1. Plaintiff identified relevant markets as follows:

> (a) the market for the rights to use the marks of major league professional football clubs and otherwise to affiliate with major league professional football for purposes of advertising and promoting goods and services ("professional football sponsorship market") and (b) the market for the rights to use the marks of major league professional football clubs on apparel and other goods ("professional football merchandise market"). [*Id.* at Complaint, Paragraph 25.]
>
> The relevant geographic market for assessing competition in the professional football sponsorship market and the professional football merchandise market is the United States. Defendants have market power and monopoly power in the professional football merchandise market. On information and belief, there are also local and regional submarkets of both the professional football sponsorship market and the professional football merchandise market. [*Id.* at Complaint, Paragraph 28.]

11. Is the antitrust claim of the Dallas Cowboys and owner, Jerry Jones, vulnerable to application of the "equal involvement defense," recognized in *Sullivan v. National Football League*, 34 F.3d 1091, 1106-08 (1st Cir. 1994)? See discussion of the "equal involvement defense" at **Note 12, Section F**, *supra*. What evidence is available for defendant's use in attempting to prove the defense in the *Cowboys* case?

The NFL (NFL Properties) and Jerry Jones settled the matter on terms acceptable to the Cowboys. For commentaries analyzing the dispute, *see* Hoffman, *Dallas' Head Cowboy Emerges Victorious in a Licensing Showdown with the NFL:* National Football League Properties v. Dallas Cowboys Football Club, et. al., 7 Seton Hall J. Sport L. 255 (1997); Hale, *Jerry Jones Versus the NFL: An Opportunity to Apply Logically the Single Entity Defense to the NFL*, 4 Sports Law. J. 1 (1997).

The Yankee Stadium-Adidas sponsorship deal (10-years; $95 million) provides a scenario similar to the Rugby League Problem and the Dallas Cowboys litigation. In that case, George Steinbrenner wore an Adidas pin on his lapel; members of the front office, groundskeepers, and stadium personnel wore Adidas gear; and Adidas signage appeared prominently at Yankee Stadium. MLB Properties objected to the sponsorship as a violation of MLB's policy (established by the 1995 Agency Agreement) of having merchandising arrangements exclusively authorized by Properties. The Yankees responded by filing suit challenging the joint marketing policy as a violation of the antitrust laws. (Interestingly, an attorney conflict of interest question arose as the New York law firm also represented Time Warner, owner of the Atlanta Braves, a defendant in the action.) Like the *Cowboys* case, the matter was settled on terms favorable to the Yankees. For analysis of the legal issues and ultimate settlement, *see*Weinberger, *Baseball Trademark Licensing and the Antitrust Exemption: An Analysis of* New York Yankees Partnership v. Major League Baseball Enterprises, Inc., 23 COLUM.-VLA J.L. & ARTS 75 (1999).

12. Are all joint commercial efforts by league members subject to attack under §1 of the Sherman Antitrust Act? Season ticket arrangements of professional ballclubs have been challenged as illegal under the antitrust laws. *See, e.g., Driskill v. Dallas Cowboys Football Club,* 498 F.2d 321 (5th Cir. 1974); *Coniglio v. Highwood Services, Inc.,* 495 F.2d 1286 (2d Cir. 1974). For an action filed for a refund of ticket prices on the basis that the club was moving, *see Stern v. Cleveland Browns Football Club, Inc.,* 1996 WL 761163 (Ohio Ct. App. 1996). For a challenge of the NFL's "blackout rule," which prohibits live local telecasts of home games that are not sold out 72 hours before game-time, but not radio broadcasts, as a violation of the Americans with Disabilities Act of 1990, 42 U.S.C. § 12182, *see Stoutenborough v. National Football League, Inc.*, 59 F.3d 580 (6th Cir. 1995) ("Blackout rule" does not violate ADA). For a discussion of league "black out" rules, *see* Fecteau, *NFL Network Blackouts: Old Law Meets New Technology with the Advent of the Satellite Dish*, 5 MARQ. SPORTS L.J. 221 (1995). *See also* Roberts, *The Legality of the Exclusive Collective Sale of Intellectual Property Rights by Sports Leagues,* 3 VA. J. SPORTS & L. 52 (2001). For a case challenging the price for satellite broadcasts under the antitrust laws, *see Shaw v. Dallas Cowboys Football Club, Ltd.*, 172 F.3d 299 (3d Cir. 1999) (Sports Broadcasting Act does not exempt from antitrust scrutiny the NFL's agreement to sell its teams' pooled television broadcast rights to a direct broadcast satellite distributor). *See generally*, Crandall, Note, *The DIRECTV NFL Sunday Ticket: An Economic Plea for Antitrust Law Immunity* 79 WASH. U. L.Q. 287 (2001).

13. For an overview of applicable trademark law to the various licensing programs, *see* Baharlias, . . . *Yes, I Think the Yankees Might Sue if We Named Our Popcorn 'Yankees Toffee Crunch': A Comprehensive Look at Trademark Infringement Defenses in the Context of the Professional and Collegiate Sports Industry*, 8 SETON HALL J. SPORT L. 99 (1998). Who owns the "real time" information generated by league games? *See National Basketball Ass'n v. Motorola, Inc.*, 105 F.3d 841 (2d Cir. 1997); Kaplan, NBA v. Motorola*: A Legislative Proposal Favoring the Nature of Property, the Survival of Sports Leagues, and the Public Interest*, 23 HASTINGS COMM. & ENT. L.J. 29 (2000). Trademark and intellectual property issues are explored at **Chapter 13**, *infra*.

H. LEAGUE VS. LEAGUE — MONOPOLY

League decision making sometimes is challenged by parties who are not members of or otherwise associated with the league. Typical suits are filed by a newly organized league against an established league. There is little question that the underlying purpose of a firm's efforts in head to head (league to league) competition in any business venture is to dominate the market. The relevant query is whether the dominant league has unfairly prevented competition to gain the market position. The attack from parties external to league operations usually focuses on Section 2 of the Sherman Act. The Act prohibits the misuse of monopoly power. Thus, a plaintiff must show that the defendant 1) possesses monopoly power, and 2) has misused the power. The plaintiff must establish the relevant "product market" and "geographic market" to prove existence of monopoly power. Defendant actions are considered to qualify as "misuse" of monopoly power where the actions illegally exclude or prevent competition.

The elements of plaintiff's antitrust action are explained in *American Football League v. National Football League,* 205 F. Supp. 60, 63 (D. Md. 1962), as follows:

> The several charges of (a) monopolization, (b) attempt to monopolize and (c) combination or conspiracy to monopolize require proof of different elements.
>
> (a) *Monopolization.* To prove monopolization . . . plaintiffs must show (1) that defendants possessed monopoly power and (2) that they undertook some course of action the consequence of which was to exclude competition or prevent competition or which was undertaken with the purpose or intent to accomplish that end. . . .
>
> (1) 'Monopoly power is the power to control prices or exclude competition.' The test of monopoly power in this case . . . is whether the NFL had sufficient power to prevent the formation or successful operation of a new league. . . .
>
> (2) A business organization which has acquired monopoly power is guilty of monopolization if it undertakes a course of action the consequences of which would be to exclude competitors or prevent competition. Proof of specific intent is not necessary. . . .
>
> (b-c). *Attempt and Conspiracy.* There may be an attempt . . . or conspiracy to monopolize without . . . monopoly power. . . . The requisite intent to monopolize must be present and predominate.

PROBLEM

The professional Rugby League is a fledgling association of member clubs located throughout the United States. The league is comprised of six geographically defined divisions. The league's regular championship season schedule consists of a fall schedule and a spring schedule. The six division champions and two "wildcard" clubs meet in a single elimination playoff series in the late spring.

The Rugby League developed as a result of marketing studies indicating that the American sports entertainment audience desires a spectator sport combining the characteristics of American football and European soccer. The marketing consultants concluded that the market is greatly enhanced by potential TV broadcasts in Canada, Mexico, Japan, and Europe. Network television contracts, suitable stadium access, and "big name" American athletes are essential to the future success of the Rugby League.

The Rugby League is in its inaugural season. Several problems confront the League. First, the league franchises are unable to secure leases of adequate stadium playing field facilities in major cities. The NFL, seemingly, has "tied-up" the stadium facilities through long-term lease arrangements. The Rugby League clubs play games in high school stadiums. Second, the league is unable to secure network or cable TV contracts. Network officials stated, "Your marketing analysis appears accurate, but we do not feel that we should risk our relationship with the NFL by contracting with the Rugby League. The spring schedule also competes with the NBA and Major League Baseball." The League has not discovered any evidence that NFL or other professional sports league officers have directly influenced the decisions of network officials. Third, NFL clubs voted to expand the active club rosters by ten additional players. The League is of the opinion that big-name college football players, who are marginal NFL players, are now sitting on the bench for NFL teams rather than playing for Rugby League teams. Evidence indicates that the NFL decided to expand club rosters in response to the Rugby League's efforts to sign college football players.

The NFL instituted what is considered by officials of the Rugby League as a "negative ad campaign," designed to denigrate the Rugby League in the eyes of the consumer. TV and radio ads promote the NFL games as follows: "Watch the actionpacked NFL matchup between ____ and the ____, unless you prefer Rugby (Voice over with English accent: 'Say old boy, can we catch the first train to London?' Background laughter)"; Coach telling player cut from the roster in training camp: "Son, I'm sorry. You're just not NFL material." Veteran player says, "Look kid, don't take it so hard. You can always play rugby." Released player looks to floor and remarks, "Yeah, where? Butte, Montana?" The veteran raises an eyebrow. (Voice over: "If you are not watching Rugby in Butte, catch the NFL Sunday action on ____").

Your firm is retained as general counsel to the Rugby League. The senior partner assigned the Rugby League file to you. Your client desires to bring an antitrust action against the NFL. A meeting is scheduled for next week to discuss the facts surrounding the Rugby League matter within the context of antitrust law. The senior partner directs you to complete the following tasks:

1. Outline the elements of an antitrust action filed by one league against another (RL v. NFL);

2. Develop arguments based on your reading of the cases below using the facts of the problem;

3. Make independent observations or analysis that you perceive as helpful in discussing the matter with your client; and

4. Be prepared to defend your analysis at the meeting.

CASE FILE

AMERICAN FOOTBALL LEAGUE v. NATIONAL FOOTBALL LEAGUE

205 F. Supp. 60 (D. Md. 1962)

THOMSEN, Chief Judge.

In this action for treble damages and injunctive relief under the antitrust laws, plaintiffs, the American Football League (AFL) and its members, charge defendants, the National Football League (NFL) and most of its members, with monopolization, attempted monopolization and conspiracy to monopolize major league professional football.

It is not disputed that all of the parties to the case are engaged in interstate commerce and subject to the provisions of the antitrust laws. At a pretrial conference the parties agreed that the trial should be conducted in two stages: that the court first hear evidence on and determine the issue of liability (including the requirement that plaintiffs prove some injury from each of the alleged violations); and, if liability is found, that the court thereafter hear evidence on and consider the issue of relief (the amount of damages or the equitable relief to which the several plaintiffs may be entitled).

The Parties

The AFL was organized in the latter half of 1959, and began play in 1960. Joe Foss has been its only Commissioner. At the time this suit was filed, October 14, 1960, its member teams or franchisees and the principal owners thereof were [8 clubs].

* * *

The NFL was organized in 1920 and since 1933 has had from 10 to 14 teams. Bert Bell served as Commissioner until his death on October 11, 1959; thereafter Austin Gunsel was Acting Commissioner until January 1960, when Pete Rozelle was elected Commissioner. As of the date of suit, its teams, their principal owners, and others who figured prominently in the evidence were [14 clubs].

* * *

Each of the leagues is an unincorporated association, with permanent franchises which remain the property of the members to whom issued unless forfeited or transferred with the approval of the league.

The Issues

The successful operation of a major league professional football team requires (1) membership in a league in which the several clubs are reasonably well matched in playing strength and are located in areas which can and will support the teams by attendance throughout the season sufficient to provide adequate revenues for both the home and visiting clubs, (2) the acquisition of a group of capable players, and (3) the sale of television rights. Plaintiffs allege that defendants monopolized, attempted to monopolize and conspired to monopolize each of these three areas of competition.

With respect to (1), plaintiffs contend that they have shown that all defendants *monopolized* and that all defendants, except the Washington Redskins, *attempted* to monopolize and *conspired* to monopolize the metropolitan areas in which franchises can successfully be located. Plaintiffs argue that the granting of NFL franchises to Dallas and to Minneapolis-St. Paul, at the times and under the circumstances shown by the evidence, and statements made with respect to a proposed franchise for Houston, constituted an exercise of monopoly power, and that those acts were done as part of an attempt or a conspiracy to monopolize. On the other hand, defendants deny that they had monopoly power, and contend that those franchises were granted and those statements were made pursuant to a policy of expansion adopted by the NFL before the AFL was organized, and that the timing was at most an effort by the NFL and its members to compete more effectively with proposed AFL teams in particular cities.

With respect to (2) above — acquisition of players — plaintiffs conceded at the close of their case that they had not proved *any* violation of the antitrust laws entitling them to recover herein.

With respect to (3), they conceded that they had not shown the requisite intent to support their charge that defendants had *attempted* to monopolize or *conspired* to monopolize with respect to the sale of TV or radio rights; but they contend that they have shown that defendants possessed monopoly power, and that the approval by the NFL Commissioner of the TV contract made by the Baltimore Colts and Pittsburgh Steelers with the National Broadcasting Company was an exercise of that power which renders defendants liable on the charge of monopolization. Defendants contend that the Commissioner was obliged to approve the contract under the principles laid down by Judge Grim in the *United States v. National Football League,* 116 F. Supp. 319 (E.D. Pa. 1953), and it was agreed that further evidence and argument on this point should await the decision of the court on the question whether the NFL had monopoly power.

Elements of Offenses Charged

The several charges of (a) monopolization, (b) attempt to monopolize and (c) combination or conspiracy to monopolize require proof of different elements.

(a) *Monopolization.* To prove monopolization in this private antitrust suit plaintiffs must show (1) that defendants possessed monopoly power and (2) that they undertook some course of action the consequence of which was to exclude competition or prevent competition in the business of major league professional football or which was undertaken with the purpose or intent to accomplish that end.

(1) "Monopoly power is the power to control prices or exclude competition." . . . [A] party has monopoly power if it has "over 'any part of the trade or commerce among the several States,' a power of controlling prices or unreasonably restricting competition."

"Monopoly is a relative word." Whether the sole business in a particular field has monopoly power depends upon the nature of the business. Those wishing to operate professional football teams must belong to a league. The test of monopoly power in this case, therefore, is whether the NFL had sufficient power to prevent the formation or successful operation of a new league. It is not sufficient that they might have had the power to exclude a new league from a particular city or group of cities, unless the power to exclude from that city or group of cities would have effectively prevented the formation or operation of a new league.

(2) A business organization which has acquired monopoly power is guilty of monopolization if it undertakes a course of action the consequence of which would be to exclude competitors or prevent competition. Proof of a specific intent is not necessary.

However, it cannot be required to forego normal competitive business methods to further legitimate business ends, as distinguished from acts which are done with the intent to create or preserve a monopoly, or which would have the consequence of excluding competitors from a relevant market.

(b)-(c). *Attempt and Conspiracy.* There may be an attempt to monopolize, or a combination or conspiracy to monopolize, without the offender or offenders actually having monopoly power. But an essential element of an attempt to monopolize, or of a combination or conspiracy to monopolize, is a specific intent to destroy competition or build monopoly. Neither rough competition nor unethical business conduct is sufficient. The requisite intent to monopolize must be present and predominant.

The intent must be to gain control over some relevant market sufficient to set prices in that market or to exclude competitors therefrom. An intent to exclude competitors from only part of the relevant market would not be sufficient to create liability for an attempt or a conspiracy, unless as plaintiffs contend in this case, defendants believed that by excluding the AFL from certain cities, *e.g.,* Dallas and Minneapolis-St. Paul, they could effectively exclude it from the entire market, and acted with that specific intent as their preponderant motive.

Relevant Market

The market which must be studied to determine whether a business organization has monopoly power will vary with the part of commerce under consideration. The "part of the trade or commerce among the several States" involved in the present action is major league professional football. Essentially, the relevant market is nationwide; but because of the nature of major league professional football, there are several areas of effective competition between plaintiffs and defendants.

The competition for players and coaches is nationwide. The competition for the sale of TV and radio rights to networks or sponsors is essentially nationwide. The competition for attendance at games, and the competition between the telecast of a game from one city and the actual playing of a game in another city, is generally confined to the area in which the game is being played. The competition between the leagues for metropolitan areas in which franchises can profitably be located is the most important aspect of the competition in this case. This area of competition is essentially nationwide, embracing all cities and metropolitan areas which may reasonably be expected to support a major league professional football team. Consideration must also be given to the fact that at least six and probably eight teams are necessary for the successful operation of a league, and that only a few cities, at most, under present conditions, can successfully support two teams.

FINDINGS OF FACT

[The facts as presented here are gleaned from the decision on appeal of this case, 323 F.2d 124 (4th Cir. 1963)].

[T]he two football leagues, American and National, are unincorporated associations. Each has a commissioner who exercises some executive and administrative authority, but, in each, ultimate control is vested in the owners of the football teams for whose benefit the league exists. In each instance, the teams are corporations, each of which was the holder of a franchise to operate a professional football team in a designated city. Most of the corporate team owners are controlled and dominated by a single individual, though in a minority of instances the role of the dominant individual is played by a small group of two or three, and in one instance of five. It is these individuals who exercise ultimate control of the leagues with which they are associated.

The National Football League was organized in 1920. For a number of years its existence was precarious. Until the last ten years, its membership was far from static, and until 1946 every major league professional football team operating in the United States was associated with it. In 1945, the All American Football Conference was organized, and it operated through the four seasons of 1946-1949 with eight teams, except that two of the teams were merged in 1949, and in the last season, there were but seven teams. Thereafter the All American Football Conference disbanded, but three of its teams were received into the National Football League, and teams franchised in those three cities, Baltimore, Cleveland and San Francisco, were operated under National League franchises when this action was commenced.

In 1959, the National Football League operated with twelve teams located in eleven cities. There were two teams in Chicago and one each in Cleveland, New York, Philadelphia, Pittsburgh, Washington, Baltimore, Detroit, Los Angeles,

San Francisco, and Green Bay, Wisconsin. In 1960 two additional franchises were placed, one in Dallas and one in Minneapolis-St. Paul, the Dallas team beginning play in 1960 and the Minneapolis-St. Paul team in 1961. In 1961, one of the Chicago teams, the Cardinals, was transferred to St. Louis.

The American Football League was organized in 1959, and began with a full schedule of games in 1960. Affiliated with it were eight teams located in eight cities, Boston, Buffalo, Houston, New York, Dallas, Denver, Los Angeles and Oakland. After the 1960 season, the Los Angeles team was moved to San Diego.

In the first half of the 1952 season, a team operated under a National League franchise in Dallas. It failed and was replaced by a team located in another city, but a few years later there was substantial interest in Texas as a fruitful area for professional football.

Many of the National league owners were interested in expanding the league. Halas, owner of the Chicago Bears, was the earliest and most ardent advocate of expansion. Early in 1956, he predicted that National would expand from twelve to sixteen teams during the period of 1960-1965. In July 1957, Bert Bell, National's Commissioner, predicted some expansion by 1960, and at National's annual meeting in January 1958, an expansion committee was appointed composed of Halas and Rooney, owner of the Pittsburgh Steelers. Marshall, of the Washington Redskins, was an implacable foe of expansion, but the District Court found, with reason, that by 1959 a majority of the owners were in favor of expansion to sixteen teams and the granting of four additional franchises, two at a time.

As the National League contemplated expansion, the interest of the owners centered on Houston, Dallas, and two or three other cities. The weather in the Southwest was particularly favorable, and, with the improvement of the financial condition of the National League teams and the increasing revenues they received from television, it was thought that Houston and Dallas, with their natural rivalry, could each support a team. Those two cities were considered by National's owners as the most likely prospects for expansion, with Minneapolis-St. Paul, Buffalo and Miami close behind.

Meanwhile, there were people actively interested in acquiring franchises to operate National League teams in Houston and Dallas. Clint Murchison, Jr. and his father, of Dallas, had sought to purchase the San Francisco 49'ers, the Washington Redskins and the Chicago Cardinals, intending, if successful in acquiring one of those teams, to move it to Dallas. In 1957 and 1958, Lamar Hunt, of Dallas, and the Houston Sports Association applied to National for franchises to operate teams in those two cities. Hunt also sought to acquire the Chicago Cardinals and move that team to Dallas. Early in 1959, Murchison and Hunt (Dallas) and Cullinan, Kirksey and Adams (Houston Sports Association) were all actively seeking National League franchises. They were given encouragement by Bell, Halas and Rooney, all of whom were talking in terms of expansion into Houston and Dallas about 1961.

In February and April 1959, Halas held press conferences to stimulate sales of tickets to a preseason game between the Chicago Bears and the Pittsburgh Steelers, scheduled to be played in Houston in August. In those press conferences, he discussed expansion plans, predicting that expansion would begin about 1960, and that the most likely cities were Houston, Dallas, Miami and Buffalo. Upon inquiry by Murchison, Halas suggested that he plan to make a formal application for a Dallas franchise to be considered at National's annual meeting in January 1960.

Meanwhile, in the spring of 1959, Hunt, of Dallas, decided that a new league was feasible and could be successfully organized. He had been told by Bell that he might submit a formal application for the Dallas franchise at the January 1960 annual meeting. However, he was either unsure of National's expansion into Dallas, of when it would occur, or of his chances of obtaining the franchise in competition with Murchison.

The remainder of 1959 was very eventful. Hunt proceeded actively with his plan to organize a new league. In July, he disclosed his intention to Commissioner Bell. On July 28, Bell with Hunt's permission, told a congressional committee of Hunt's plans, and stated that the National League owners favored organization of the new league. Early in August, Hunt and Adams publicly announced the formation of the new league, with teams owned by them to be located, respectively, in Dallas and Houston. Hunt and his associates were actively in touch with interested persons in a number of other cities. On August 22, representatives from Los Angeles, Dallas, Houston, New York, Minneapolis and Denver signed articles of association. Representatives from many other cities had been in touch with Hunt. Wilson, of Detroit, sought an American franchise for Miami, and later for Buffalo, and the Buffalo franchise was formally granted in October. In November, an application for a franchise to be placed in Boston was approved. Thus, in late November, American had tentative arrangements for teams in Houston, Dallas, Minneapolis, New York, Boston, Denver, Buffalo and Los Angeles.

In the meanwhile, Murchison, of Dallas, and Cullinan and Kirksey, who had been associated with Adams in efforts to obtain a National franchise for Houston, continued their efforts to obtain National franchises for those two cities. In late August, at their insistence, Halas, with the approval of a number of National owners, publicly announced that National's expansion committee would recommend to the 1960 meeting franchises for Dallas and Houston to begin play in 1961, the Houston franchise to be conditioned upon the availability of an adequate stadium. Construction of a new stadium in Houston was in contemplation, and there was hope that a National League team might obtain use of the Rice University Stadium until a new municipal stadium was constructed and available. Just after the death of Commissioner Bell on October 11, 1959, the National League owners met informally and agreed to adopt the announced recommendation of the expansion committee. This was followed by a widely publicized press release announcing that the National League would grant two new franchises in 1960, one of them to go to Dallas and the other to Houston if an adequate stadium was made available in Houston.

In October, however, it became known that the Rice University Stadium would not be made available for use by a National League team, and all further consideration of a National League franchise in Houston was then abandoned.

A number of people in Minnesota had been seeking a National League football team, but after Hunt's plans for a new league had been disclosed to them, Winter, Boyer and Skoglund, of Minneapolis, entered into American's Articles of Association, which were executed in August 1959. Winter, however, remained in touch with representatives of the National League, as did Johnson, an influential Minneapolis newspaperman. Johnson and Winter preferred a National League team to an American League team, but, on August 22, 1959, they had no assurance that the National League would place a franchise in Minnesota at any reasonably foreseeable date. They must have retained some hope their preference for the National League might be realized, however, when National's announcement of its intention to place a team in Houston was conditioned upon the availability of an appropriate stadium, coupled with prominent mention of Minneapolis in connection with National's later expansion to sixteen teams. When it became known that an appropriate stadium in Houston was not available, Johnson and Winter sought definite commitments from the National League. They obtained telegraphic commitments in November. Winter, Skoglund and Boyer failed to deposit the performance bond of $100,000, which was required of American League members in November, but, thereafter, Skoglund and Boyer sought to obtain leases from the Minneapolis Stadium Commission for an American league team. The Commission refused to enter into such lease arrangement until the placement of a National League team in Minneapolis-St. Paul was settled.

In January 1960, Winter, of Minneapolis, and Haugsrud, of Duluth, formally applied to the National League for a franchise. Boyer joined in its presentation a complete release and a return of the $25,000 deposit, which he, Winter and Skoglund had made. At National's annual meeting on January 28, 1960, franchises were granted to Dallas and Minneapolis-St. Paul, the grant to Minneapolis-St. Paul being conditioned upon the enlargement of the Minneapolis stadium and the sale of 25,000 season tickets for the 1961 season when play was to commence. The Dallas franchise, however, permitted it to operate in 1960, for Murchison was very anxious that his National League team commence play in Dallas in the same year Hunt's American League team commenced play there.

On the next day, the American League had its annual meeting, during which it granted a franchise to Oakland, which took the place of Minneapolis-St. Paul. The American League owners preferred Oakland to other applicants, because they wanted a second team on the West Coast and because they regarded the Oakland area as promising.

It thus came to pass that in the 1960 season, teams of the two leagues were in direct competition in New York, Dallas, Los Angeles, and in the San Francisco-Oakland area. Each league had teams in other cities in which there was no direct competition between the leagues. The two leagues were competing on a national basis for television coverage, outstanding players and coaches, and the games of each league competed for spectators with the televised broadcast of a game of the other.

Players and TV

The NFL has avoided competition among its teams for outstanding college players by its player selection system, sometimes called a draft. Such a system is probably necessary for the successful operation of a league. The AFL adopted a similar system.

The NFL has minimized competition between attendance at its games and telecasts of other NFL games by prohibiting the telecasting of NFL games into a city where an NFL game is being played. . . . The AFL adopted a similar policy.

On several occasions during the late Summer and Fall of 1959, Hunt, on behalf of the AFL, sought an agreement with the NFL which (1) provided for a common player draft and (2) would have prohibited the telecasting of any game of either league into city whether either an NFL or an AFL game was being played. This would have seriously restricted if not entirely eliminated the telecasting of "away" games of the New York, Los Angeles, and Dallas teams back to those cities and would have otherwise seriously diluted the value of the TV rights. Moreover, both proposals were of doubtful validity, at best, although plaintiffs contend that a common player draft would be a reasonable restriction on commerce, for reasons which need not be elaborated here. Both proposals were promptly and repeatedly rejected by the NFL owners.

For many years most of the NFL games have been telecast over the CBS network through arrangements made by the teams or their sponsors. On or about March 30, 1960, Pittsburgh and Baltimore reached an agreement with NBC for nationwide telecasts of their regular season games. This arrangement was opposed by the other NFL teams and by Commissioner Rozelle, and was detrimental to other NFL clubs as well as to the AFL clubs. Plaintiffs concede that this action was not taken with the specific intent to injure the AFL and it members.

The TV arrangements of the AFL were handled by an organization inexperienced in dealing with sports promotion. After presenting unsatisfactory plans to ABC and NBC, the AFL made a very profitable deal with ABC, which had been negotiating with Hunt since the middle of 1959.

Monopoly Power

Plaintiffs contend that defendants had the power to prevent or exclude competition by plaintiffs in the business of major league professional football. As we have seen, the principal areas of competition are for (1) a sufficient number of cities capable of supporting teams to form a practicable league, (2) players, and (3) the sale of TV rights.

(1) *Cities.* There are many cities in the United States capable of supporting competently managed major league professional football teams. Hunt testified that in his opinion a metropolitan area of 500,000 or more with proper management and under the right circumstances will support such a team. On all the evidence a figure of 700,000 appears more reasonable. There are 52 metropolitan areas in the United States with a population over 500,000 of which 31 have more than 700,000 and 24 more than 1,000,000.

Aside from population, the material factors in determining whether a city is a suitable location for a professional football franchise include an adequate stadium, available financial backing, weather, fan enthusiasm, and proximity to another professional football team or other competing sports.

Some problems, such as stadium inadequacies, can often be resolved once the probability of obtaining a professional football franchise has been sufficiently established. For example, Oakland and Houston are in the process of constructing new stadiums; Minneapolis and San Diego expanded the seating capacity of their existing stadiums.

It is doubtful whether under present conditions any cities except possibly New York and one or two other large metropolitan areas can support two teams. The AFL, however, had no difficulty in finding owners for the franchises Hunt wished to place in New York and Los Angeles, and had applications from several other NFL cities. There is no reason to believe that the Oakland club will not be successful, once its stadium is completed, although it is located in the San Francisco Bay area, where it must compete with the NFL 49'ers.

The owners of a franchise must be prepared to absorb a large initial loss; profit projection is speculative and eventual profits are usually small. Naturally most investors would prefer to have a franchise in an established, financially successful league rather than in a newly organized unproved league. However, the lure of owning a successful team is very attractive to many rich men, as well as to sports promoters; witness the applications received by the AFL from Vancouver, Seattle, Portland, San Francisco, San Diego, Newark, Buffalo, Kansas City, St. Louis, Louisville, New Orleans, Miami and Atlanta, as well as from the eight cities originally selected, plus Oakland.

Fan enthusiasm may be built up over the years; poor college football towns may be developed into loyal supporters of a professional team, e.g., Baltimore, where it has also been shown that established competing attractions, such as horse racing, are not fatal. Plaintiffs have failed to show any lack of sufficient qualified applicants for franchises to support a second league.

No doubt the NFL could have forced the AFL out of any particular city except New York and possibly one or two other very large cities, plus Dallas and Houston, where rich owners are determined to fight it out. But it was not financially practicable for the NFL to expand into all the cities in which the AFL might place teams. There is no evidence that the NFL has ever contemplated more than 16 teams, and it is probably not feasible to operate a larger league. Even during 1959, after the AFL was organized, the NFL owners were unwilling to weaken their own league by expanding into any area which they did not believe would prove a suitable addition to the NFL.

Plaintiffs suggest that defendants had the power to add enough new cities to the NFL to destroy the AFL, and after having destroyed it, to drop the cities the NFL did not want. But the NFL did not have the resources to add more than two new teams at once nor more than four new teams within the next five years without so weakening the existing clubs as to make such action undesirable and not practically possible.

(2) *Players*. In 1959 the NFL had most of the ablest players under contract. However, colleges graduate annually large numbers of talented players, and, because after the season starts professional football rosters are usually limited to around 35 players, many good players are released each year after the training season and are available to be signed by clubs in any league. Moreover, NFL players become free agents after a period of years.

By March 1960, the AFL clubs had submitted 365 player contracts to the AFL commissioner for approval, and an estimated 668 players had signed contracts with one of the AFL teams. Plaintiffs were able to compete successfully with the NFL and with the Canadian League for the services of many highly qualified players. AFL clubs signed six of the 12 first choices of the NFL teams in the 1959 draft, and competition from the AFL and the Canadian League deprived two NFL clubs of the services of more than half of their first 10 draft choices.

The NFL has no power to prevent the AFL from signing an adequate number of qualified players.

(3) *TV.* The evidence shows that defendants did not have the power to exclude plaintiffs from adequate television outlets.

The AFL admits that it has been notably successful in its operations, and gives promise of increasing success. Like the NFL, it has an expansion committee.

Defendants did not have the power to prevent or unreasonably to restrict competition. Therefore, they are not liable on the claim of monopolization.

Intent

Since defendants did not have monopoly power, plaintiffs must rely on their claims that defendants attempted or conspired to monopolize. To recover on either of those claims plaintiffs must show that some acts were done or some course of action undertaken with the specific intent to destroy the AFL as a competitor.

The acts relied on by plaintiffs are the offering and granting of franchises to Dallas and Minneapolis and the conditional offer of a franchise to Houston, at the times and under the circumstances those acts were done. To prove the requisite intent, plaintiffs rely particularly on (a) the August 29, 1959, announcement with respect to Dallas and Houston, (b) various proposals and suggestions made by NFL owners to AFL owners between September and November 1959, and (c) the statements and telegrams in November 1959 with respect to the Minnesota franchise.

(a) The announcement on August 29 that the committee would recommend the grant of franchises to Dallas and Houston to begin play in 1961 was in line with the general plan for the expansion of the NFL during the years 1961-1965, which had been agreed upon by most of the owners before the AFL was contemplated. As we have seen, various motives induced the several owners to go along with these plans. Some were attracted by the great enthusiasm for football in Texas, the size of the Cotton Bowl in Dallas, and the Rice Stadium and plans for a municipal stadium in Houston. The Philadelphia Eagles wanted a 16-team league with two eight-team divisions. Some felt that the good of the league, as well as the good of the sport in competition with other sports, called for expansion into areas that were clearly ready, as soon as the financial and playing strength of the NFL clubs made it feasible to stock new clubs with players, and they were being urged to do so by Hester, the attorney who was lobbying for the Sports Bill. Weather, local rivalry and scheduling convenience also made the two cities in Texas an attractive pair.

At the request of Murchison, in October 1959, the effective date of the Dallas franchise was advanced one year, from 1961 to 1960, in order to permit the NFL team to start at the same time as the AFL team. This was done for business reasons, *i.e.,* to enable the NFL team to compete more effectively with the AFL team in Dallas for season ticket sales, choice of dates in the Cotton Bowl, newspaper support and the like.

Plaintiffs note that several of the NFL owners told Hunt's attorney that they did not believe Dallas could support two teams. That does not prove that their predominant intent in granting a franchise to Dallas, or advancing the playing date to 1960, was to destroy the AFL. Their views were at least equally consistent with their claimed desire to strengthen Murchison's competitive position as against Hunt's Dallas AFL team, so that the NFL team would have a better chance to survive. Although some of the NFL owners may have felt that this competition might discourage the AFL from continuing its team in Dallas or even from continuing operations as a league, this was not a predominant or principal motive in granting the franchise or advancing the date.

(b) Pauley and Murchison were particularly anxious to avoid competing teams in their respective cities (Los Angeles and Dallas), and many of the meetings and proposals during the Fall of 1959 arose out of the desire of those NFL owners to find a solution for their special problems. Their efforts were encouraged by some of the other NFL owners and were welcomed by many of the

AFL owners, who really wanted franchises in the NFL, and in most instances would have been satisfied with a share in such a franchise. All of the owners, AFL as well as NFL, were anxious to avoid costly competition in signing players. The offers and suggestions of the NFL owners were not made with any predominant intent to destroy the AFL, but as part of the effort being made by both sides to find solutions to their mutual problems.

(c) After it was clear that the Rice Stadium in Houston would not be made available to the NFL, most of the owners agreed that Minneapolis-St. Paul should replace Houston as one of the first two franchises to be granted in accordance with the expansion policy to which all but Marshall had agreed. Undoubtedly, the November telegrams were sent at the request of Johnson and Winter to persuade Winter's associates, Boyer and Skoglund, to give up the AFL franchise, so that the NFL could come into the Twin Cities without competition there. It was obvious that Minneapolis-St. Paul could not support two teams, and the NFL wanted to have a successful team there. As in the case of Dallas, that was a business reason, different from an intent to destroy the new league. The evidence does not support plaintiffs' contention that an intent to destroy the AFL was a predominant motive of defendants.

If the NFL had had monopoly power, the course of action followed by the NFL owners might have been sufficient to create liability for monopolization, which does not require proof of specific intent; but the actual motives and intent were not such as would support liability on the claim of attempt to monopolize or the claim of conspiring to monopolize.

Injury

Houston. As a result of the expansion statement made by Halas on August 29, 1959, Adams changed his arrangement with the Houston Public School system for the lease of Jeppersen Stadium from a one-year lease at $3,000 per game, the lessee to have the parking concession, to a three-year lease at $4,000 per game, the lessor to have the parking concession.

Dallas. The granting of an NFL franchise to Dallas, which began play at the same time as Hunt's AFL team, undoubtedly has been costly to the AFL team, and may have prevented that attendance at some of the games there from passing the guarantee point, although that is doubtful because interest in and attendance at both NFL and AFL games in Dallas has been disappointing, and may indicate that the city is not as good a location for a professional football team as was generally believed.

Minneapolis. Plaintiffs' claim of injury with respect to Minneapolis is based primarily on the theory that the acts of the NFL owners required the AFL to substitute an inferior Oakland franchise for a more desirable franchise in Minneapolis. It is claimed that this substitution resulted in reduced income to the AFL and its members from both home and road games, and that other AFL clubs suffered a loss of valuable property rights from having to stock the Oakland franchise with players.

The first of these propositions is doubtful. . . . Whatever injury there may have been was contributed to by unskillful handling of the Oakland arrangements. The transfer of four or five players from each of the other clubs to Oakland probably caused some injury to the other teams, offset in a few instances by acquiring and retaining well-publicized or favorite players from the Minneapolis draft list.

Unclean Hands

Defendants contend that plaintiffs are barred from equitable relief by the doctrine of unclean hands. It is true that Hunt was not entirely candid with Bell and was devious in his dealings with some of the NFL owners, but that is a far cry from such conduct as would amount to unclean hands. Hunt and many of the other AFL owners were eager to become a part of the alleged monopoly, and also proposed to the NFL that they join in agreements of doubtful validity to keep down the amounts they would have to pay the players and to place restrictions on telecasting. Those acts of Hunt and other AFL owners would not prevent recovery, although they might properly be considered in determining the equitable relief which might be granted if defendants were guilty of any violation of the laws which would render them liable to plaintiffs.

Conclusions

1. This court has jurisdiction over the defendants and the subject matter of this action.

2. Neither individually nor in concert have the defendants monopolized any part of the trade or commerce among the several states; particularly they have not monopolized major league professional football.

3. None of the defendants has attempted to monopolize or combined or conspired with any other person or persons to monopolize major league professional football.

4. None of the defendants has engaged in a combination or conspiracy in unreasonable restraint of trade or commerce among the several states in the presentation of major league professional football games.

5. None of the plaintiffs is entitled to relief in this case against any of the defendants.

Judgment will be entered in favor of the defendants, with costs.

UNITED STATES FOOTBALL LEAGUE v. NATIONAL FOOTBALL LEAGUE

634 F. Supp. 1155 (S.D.N.Y. 1986)

LEISURE, District Judge:

The United States Football League and certain of its member clubs (collectively referred to as the "USFL") have sued the National Football League, its commissioner and certain of its member clubs (hereinafter collectively referred to as the "NFL") to obtain declaratory and injunctive relief and to recover damages resulting from alleged violations of Section 1 and 2 of the Sherman Anti Trust Act, 15 U.S.C. §§ 1 & 2, and the common law.

* * *

Contentions of the Parties

"Television is at the heart of this case.". . . The USFL alleges that its inability to obtain a network television contract for the Fall of 1986 was a result of "coercive" pressure applied by the NFL to the three networks not to agree to a Fall 1986 contract with the USFL. In addition, the USFL alleges that the existence of the NFL's three network television contracts has the effect of precluding a new major professional football league from ever having its games televised, thereby depriving it of the television revenues and nationwide exposure a new league requires to be able to compete successfully against the NFL.

The NFL contends that none of the "factual" allegations about the other professional football leagues, the prior antitrust suits against the NFL, or the events surrounding the 1961 and 1966 legislation are probative of any factual issue relating to the USFL's alleged antitrust injury and damages. . . .

Applicable Law

The USFL argues that all three violations of Section 2 — monopolization, attempted monopolization, and conspiracy to monopolize — require proof of both anticompetitive intent and analysis of the defendants' market power, including the sources of that power. . . .

The USFL contends that in appropriate cases, prior antitrust violations and the history of the relevant market are admissible to establish market power and intent. . . .

The USFL also argues that evidence of conspiratorial conduct occurring before plaintiffs' damage period is admissible to establish the intent, motive and method of the defendants' conspiracies against the USFL. . . .

AAFC and WFL Allegations

The NFL argues that there are no allegations in the complaint, nor have any facts been presented by the USFL, showing that the NFL caused the AAFC's dissolution in 1947 or the WFL's dissolution in 1975. . . .

At oral argument, the USFL conceded that the allegations concerning the AAFC appear in the pleadings for background purposes only. Accordingly, with respect to the AAFC, the motion is granted. The USFL shall make no reference, and shall offer no evidence at trial, that implies that the NFL caused the demise of the AAFC. . . . This ruling does not, however, preclude the USFL from referring to the AAFC in the context of a presentation for background purposes of the history of professional football in the United States.

Two incidents have come to the Court's attention that provide a basis for allegations that the NFL harmed or attempted to harm the WFL. The first arose out of the 1973 attendance by Robert Wussler, then President of CBS Sports, at a WFL owners meeting. The USFL claims that NFL Commissioner Rozelle let it be known to the networks that he considered Wussler's attendance to be an unfriendly act. The USFL relies upon this incident both to prove that the NFL entertained anticompetitive intent toward the WFL and to prove that in 1981-82 the NFL pressured the networks not to give the fledgling USFL a television contract. In December 1981, the USFL's publicity agent invited the President of CBS Sports to attend a January 1982 Florida meeting of prospective USFL owners. One CBS executive advised the other not to attend since Wussler's attendance at the 1973 WFL meeting "was enormously embarrassing to CBS and considered an unfriendly act by Pete [Rozelle]."

When questioned about the Wussler incident during his deposition in this case, Commissioner Rozelle recalled that he told Robert Wood, President of CBS in 1973, that Rozelle had heard that Wussler, the head of CBS Sports, had attended a WFL meeting. "I was somewhat surprised because CBS had just entered into a four year contract with us for playing Sunday." . . .

Rozelle's testimony concerning this incident raises a material question of fact as to whether there was an attempt to pressure CBS, if not the other networks, to avoid any involvement with the WFL. This is consistent with the USFL's theory that the same tactics have been used to discourage the networks from giving the USFL a contract to televise USFL games. . . .

The second instance of alleged NFL misconduct directed against the WFL is set forth in § 61(a) of the amended complaint, which alleges that in 1985 the NFL "reinstituted a policy, first developed by the defendant NFL Member Clubs when the WFL came into being and abandoned by the defendant NFL Member Clubs after the WFL's demise" to permit the signing of free agent players to NFL contracts for future seasons after the completion of the sixth weekend of play in the current season. Previously, such signings were not allowed until the end of the then current season.

While there is little or no evidence that the change in the free agent signing rule harmed the WFL, the NFL's alleged parallel response to the two leagues raises a triable issue of fact as to the NFL's monopolistic intent with respect to the WFL and later the USFL.

The decisions in *United States v. Grinnell Corp.* . . . and *Lorain Journal Co. v. United States,* support the proposition that the history of how a monopolist achieved its position is relevant. The USFL has presented specific facts demonstrating that the allegations that the NFL unlawfully caused or attempted to cause the demise of the WFL are not "fanciful." Accordingly, with respect to the WFL, the motion is denied.

AFL Allegations

The USFL's allegations concerning the AFL are also defective. . . . Paragraph 22 of the amended complaint quotes a statement by the owner of the Washington Redskins in 1960, Mr. Marshall, that the only reason for the expansion was to destroy the new AFL. In *American Football League v. National Football League* it was held that these allegations were false. The AFL's claims of monopolization, attempted monopolization and conspiracy to monopolize against the NFL were dismissed. . . .

The NFL urges that in the interests of stability in the law and judicial economy that these findings should be given collateral estoppel effect and that the USFL not be permitted to resurrect stale claims that were rejected when they were fresh . . . unless the USFL presents new, credible, persuasive evidence which could not have been presented at the original trial, the allegations concerning the AFL should not be presented to the jury. . . . Accordingly the motion is granted. Plaintiffs shall make no reference nor offer any evidence at trial concerning supposed conduct by the NFL directed at the AFL. . . .

Prior NFL Antitrust Judgments

The NFL had been named a defendant in at least eighteen antitrust lawsuits.

The NFL has moved to strike from the amended complaint any reference and to exclude from trial any evidence which pertains to previous antitrust legislation against the defendants. The USFL argues that it is appropriate in this case to consider these past Section 1 violations as relevant to proving a Section 2 violation. . . .

The NFL argues that in order for its prior antitrust lawsuits to be relevant to the instant matter, there must be a direct logical connection to the allegations in this case. . . .

The . . . authorities indicate that plaintiffs bear the burden of showing that the conduct underlying earlier Section 1 judgments against the NFL is related to the conduct at issue in this case. This can be done either by demonstrating that there is a similarity of conduct or presenting some evidence that the prior conduct has injured plaintiff. Instead, the USFL argues, in conclusory fashion, that the prior antitrust judgments supply crucial evidence of a longstanding antitrust conspiracy dating back to the 1940's, which casts light on the current antitrust conspiracy. It contends that such evidence helps to establish the intent, motive and method of defendants' conspiratorial conduct directed against the plaintiffs. The USFL, however, has not presented specific facts that connect the alleged anticompetitive activity in the instant case to the past instances of the NFL's antitrust conduct.

* * *

Even if it is assumed, *arguendo*, that any or all of these prior NFL adverse antitrust judgments are relevant to any of the issues in the instant case, they should be excluded under Fed. R. Evid. 403. Rule 403 permits the exclusion of evidence on the grounds of prejudice, confusion or waste of time. . . .

Litigation Arising from the Raiders Move

The NFL has moved to strike allegations from the amended complaint and to exclude from trial any evidence which pertains to litigation between the Los Angeles Raiders football franchise and the NFL, and between the City of Oakland, California and the Los Angeles Raiders football franchise. . . .

Even assuming that the USFL is correct that the result in the *L.A. Coliseum* case is a final judgment for purposes of issue preclusion, the Court adopts its holding with respect to the other earlier NFL antitrust litigation and holds that the result in the *L.A. Coliseum* case is irrelevant to the issues presented in the instant case. . . .

The eminent domain litigation between the City of Oakland and the Raiders is irrelevant since neither of the parties in that action are parties in the instant case. . . .

ON MOTION FOR PARTIAL SUMMARY JUDGMENT

The NFL has moved, pursuant to Fed. R. Civ. P. 56, for partial summary judgment as to:

> 1) plaintiffs' "stadium-related" claims; 2) plaintiffs' "disparagement" claims; and 3) plaintiffs' "game officials" claims. . . .

A threshold issue as to all of these motions is whether the USFL has actually stated separate and distinct claims as to stadium-related conduct, disparagement, and game officials. The USFL argues that the NFL has deliberately misconstrued the nature of the First Amended Complaint. . . . Plaintiffs maintain that the complaint pleads defendants' acts and practices not as separate causes of action, but as part of an integrated plan by defendants to "conquer the USFL." Thus, it is argued, the USFL has done nothing more than exercise the prerogative of a private antitrust plaintiff to sue on the basis of aggregate anticompetitive conduct. . . .

A review of plaintiffs' amended complaint supports the USFL's position that its antitrust claims are consciously omnibus in nature. Accordingly, the Court will not, on the present motions for summary judgment, treat individual allegations of anticompetitive conduct as separate "claims" but will endeavor only to "ascertain what material facts exist without substantial controversy.". . .

I. Stadium-Related Conduct

In essence, the USFL alleges that the NFL and its member clubs, acting separately as well as in various alliances, engaged in numerous acts directed at preventing existing and potential USFL clubs from gaining adequate access to suitable stadium facilities. . . . The USFL has also asserted a separate common law claim, for intentional interference with contractual relations, based on defendants' stadium–related conduct.

The NFL has suggested, and the USFL does not seriously contest, that the allegations may be divided into four separate groups: 1) alleged denials of access to stadia during the spring; 2) alleged denials of access to stadia during the fall (following the USFL's decision to abandon its spring schedule); 3) alleged delays in obtaining stadium leases; 4) alleged harm to USFL franchises through the granting of stadium leases with disadvantageous terms.

The NFL contends that the USFL has offered no admissible evidence that establishes either: 1) direct involvement by the NFL in the stadium lease and use arrangements negotiated by individual NFL clubs; or 2) any concerted action by NFL clubs or uniformity of position by such clubs with regard to the terms of stadium leases. To the contrary, the NFL insists, the deposition testimony of key NFL figures establishes the absence of such league involvement or concerted action. Having reviewed the record with considerable care, this Court agrees that a large portion of the evidence proffered by the USFL is either inadmissible hearsay that may not be relied upon in opposing a motion for summary judgment, or is simply immaterial to the allegations plaintiffs are seeking to prove.

Nonetheless, it may be assumed, for purposes of the ensuing discussion of *Noerr-Pennington* immunity, that the USFLs stadium-related allegations are supported by admissible evidence. . . .

A. Noerr-Pennington

It is undisputed that, in all but one instance, the USFL's allegations of denial of stadium access are directed at the failure of a state or local governmental authority to grant a lease to a potential USFL team, to grant a lease as quickly as plaintiffs would have liked, or to grant a lease on terms sufficiently favorable to the USFL lessee. Plaintiffs reject any suggestion, however, that these local governmental authorities exercised "free discretion" in considering applications by USFL clubs for stadium leases. Rather, the USFL alleges that, in numerous instances, the governmental authorities that own and operate local stadia have dealt harshly with USFL applicants as a direct result of pressure by the NFL and/or its member clubs. Such pressure, the USFL maintains, includes threats by NFL clubs to abandon certain cities and stadia; or (in cities that do not currently have NFL franchises) engaging in the practice of "franchise dangling." Not surprisingly, the USFL argues that such behavior is overtly anticompetitive.

In each of the instances in which the decision whether or not to lease to a USFL club rested with a local governmental authority, plaintiffs' allegations of misconduct invariably turn on the involvement of one or more of the NFL defendants in the lease-approval process. Usually, such involvement was manifested by the local NFL club's presentation of its viewpoint to the appropriate city body on public issues.

Such petitioning conduct, the NFL asserts, amounts to an exercise of free speech that cannot possibly give rise to liability under the federal antitrust laws. Under the *Noerr-Pennington* doctrine, "mere solicitation of governmental action through legislative processes, even though the sole purpose of the defendants is to restrain competition, is an activity which is fully protected by the First Amendment and is immune from Sherman Act liability." *Miracle Mile Associates v. City of Rochester*. . . .

The USFL contends that the *Noerr-Pennington* doctrine cannot be invoked to immunize anticompetitive activity directed at government agencies acting in a purely commercial or proprietary capacity. . . . Recent decisions by federal courts of appeal, however, suggest that the *Noerr-Pennington* doctrine should not be given such a limited construction.

The Ninth Circuit, for example, has squarely held that there is no "commercial exception" to the *Noerr-Pennington* doctrine. . . .

The Ninth Circuit's approach has been expressly adopted by the Fifth Circuit. . . .

Having reviewed the relevant authority, this Court concludes that *Noerr-Pennington* may indeed be applied to immunize petitioning conduct directed at government agencies acting in a proprietary capacity, even if such conduct may be characterized as anticompetitive.

* * *

C. Plaintiffs' Common Law Claim

In light of this Court's finding that the NFL's stadium-related conduct does not violate the federal antitrust laws, and given the likelihood that the USFL will, for the most part, be unable to introduce such conduct as "purpose or character" evidence at trial, defendants' alternative motion to sever plaintiffs' stadium-related "claims" has perhaps lost some of its urgency.

The problem is that if plaintiffs are allowed to pursue this state law claim in the present action, the door would be opened to the admission of evidence that (for reasons explained earlier) may greatly prejudice defendants with respect to plaintiffs' federal antitrust claims.

* * *

The imbalance in proof that would be caused by the retention of jurisdiction over plaintiffs' pendent claim for stadia interference, along with the concomitant jury confusion, present adequate justification for the claim's dismissal.

II. Disparagement

The USFL alleges that part of the NFL's Section 2 violation was "a deliberate and widespread campaign launched by the defendants . . . to disparage the USFL and its business prospects." Specifically, plaintiffs allege that the NFL's "defamatory campaign has involved, among other things, the dissemination of press reports reflecting negatively on the USFL to the press and the media; and the making of disparaging and threatening remarks in an attempt to . . . drive the USFL out of major league professional football in the United States."

As noted earlier, plaintiffs have not asserted a separate claim under the antitrust laws based on the NFL's "disparagement" of the USFL. Plaintiffs do maintain, however, that the jury is entitled to consider the NFL's campaign of negative publicity as an integral part of defendants' aggregate anticompetitive conduct which, taken as a whole, violates the Sherman Act. . . .

Although disparagement by itself will not give rise to a cause of action under the federal antitrust laws, . . . product disparagement coupled with the power to exclude competition may be illegal under the Sherman Act. Nonetheless, the mere dissemination of unflattering opinion or information about a competitor, unaccompanied by misstatements of fact, simply does not amount to a violation of the antitrust laws. . . .

In this case, no triable issue of fact exists concerning the truth or falsity of the opinion or information disseminated by the NFL about the USFL, since plaintiffs have identified no specific misrepresentation of fact made by any defendant. Thus, even though the NFL may have consciously denigrated the USFL in the public forum, such a pattern of behavior, unaccompanied by false statement, does not constitute predatory or anticompetitive conduct as a matter of law.

Evidence of defendants' "anti-USFL" campaign may be admissible at trial as probative of defendants' intent, or of the "purpose or character" of the NFL's anticompetitive conduct. In addition, evidence regarding the anti-USFL campaign may be relevant to plaintiffs' common law claims for intentional interference with contractual relations, a species of tort that does not require proof of false statement.

Defendants' motion for partial summary judgment as to plaintiffs' disparagement "claims" is granted to the following extent: First, plaintiffs are barred at trial from arguing that defendants have made any false statements or misrepresentations of fact about the USFL, since this Court finds that no substantial controversy exists regarding that issue. Second, whereas plaintiffs have failed to support their allegations of disparagement with any specific allegation of false statement or misrepresentation, this Court now holds that the NFL's dissemination of unflattering opinion or information about the USFL does not constitute predatory or anticompetitive conduct within the meaning of the Sherman Act.

III. Game Officials

In its amended complaint, the USFL alleges that the nationwide market for "qualified . . . game officials" is one of "several . . . distinct submarkets relevant to the plaintiffs' allegations." Plaintiffs allege that the NFL violated Section 2 by attempting to monopolize, conspiring to monopolize and actually monopolizing the market for "qualified professional football officials,". . . by refusing to permit officials employed by the NFL to officiate USFL games and by "requiring" that NFL officials observe the terms of their "full-year contracts." Plaintiffs elsewhere allege that the NFL intentionally interfered with the USFL's prospective business and contractual relations by "foreclosing the USFL from the available pool of professional football officials by requiring NFL officials to observe full-year service contracts."

B. The NFL's "Control" of the Market for Game Officials

The NFL, however, contends that this allegation does not rise to the level of a triable issue of fact, since "the NFL did not in 1983, nor does it today, control any market for qualified game officials.". . .

Plaintiffs' response to the NFL's assertion is a disturbing exercise in *ipse dixit*. "[A]t a minimum, the USFL insists, triable issues exist as to whether there is a 'market' of major league professional football game officials for the purpose of antitrust analysis, and what control the NFL exercised in that market in 1983 and today." Having made such a conclusory denial, plaintiffs simply fail to satisfy a basic obligation of a party opposing summary judgment, *i.e.*, to "bring to the district court's attention some affirmative indication that his version of relevant events is not fanciful."

The NFL's position is that a market for qualified game officials does exist, that it is nationwide, and that it may be defined as including only those individuals with ten years of experience, at least five of which have been at the college level. Quite significantly, the USFL's own complaint is consistent with the NFL's position as to the existence of a market for qualified game officials, and as to that market's geographic definition. Nonetheless, by referring to a product market of "major league professional football officials,". . . plaintiffs apparently seek to argue that the market in issue consists only of game officials with pro football experience.

For purposes of the present motion, this argument is untenable for at least two reasons. First, plaintiffs' proposed market definition is unsupported by any "specific facts or evidentiary data," or by any of "the sort of concrete particulars which [Rule 56] require[s]." Second, the NFL's definition of the qualified game officials market is demonstrably consistent with the manner in which both the NFL and the USFL have, in practice, defined this particular market. It is uncontested that the NFL regards an official with five years of college experience and ten years of overall experience to be qualified. . . .

Once the market of qualified game officials has been defined as including those officials who satisfy the five-and-ten criteria used by both the NFL and the USFL, it becomes clear that the NFL is entitled to summary judgment on the issue of market power. . . .

Perhaps more significant than the NFL's lack of monopoly power as to qualified game officials is the dearth of evidence in the record to support plaintiffs' argument that "defendants'" refusal to lend NFL officials to the USFL constitutes anticompetitive or predatory conduct in violation of the federal antitrust laws.

Analytically, the contractual restriction at issue could be treated either as a covenant not to compete or as a refusal to deal. Covenants not to compete, in the antitrust context, are generally subject to a rule of reason analysis. . . .

Applying the relevant case law to the NFL's prohibition of off-season officiating, it is not readily apparent how such a restriction, though obviously a restraint of trade in the literal sense, could possibly violate the antitrust laws. The restriction at issue is only one year in duration, and does not even extend to non-football officiating. Furthermore, although the USFL challenges the scope of the business interests served by the NFL's off-season prohibition, plaintiffs do not seriously challenge the existence of such interests. Finally, the covenant not to compete at issue in the present case relates to the ability of the NFL's game officials to seek football-related employment *during the term of their employment*. It strains credulity to suggest that the antitrust laws should be construed so as to punish a business for requiring its employees to remain loyal to their employer while they remain employed.

Although a monopolist's refusal to deal with others in the chain of distribution can give rise to liability under Section 2, . . . such cases commonly involve a plaintiff's inability to acquire the monopolist's product or resources absent cooperation by the monopolist. . . . In the instant case, the USFL's access to other available sources of supply in the qualified game officials market has been established beyond genuine dispute by the NFL. . . .

Moreover, the USFL's access to alternative sources of supply appears to preclude the possibility that plaintiffs could have successfully asserted a Section 1 claim against the NFL based on defendants' refusal to lend their officials to the USFL.

IV. CONCLUSION

First, defendants' efforts to secure advantageous stadium leases from local governmental authorities, as well as any efforts to convince such authorities not to grant stadium leases to USFL clubs, are found, as a matter of law, to constitute privileged conduct incapable of violating the Sherman Act. Second, the Court finds that plaintiffs' myriad allegations of "disparagement" of the USFL by the NFL do not include specific allegations of falsity or misstatement of fact. Therefore, no triable issue of fact exists with regard to that issue. Third, the Court finds, as a matter of law, that the NFL did not in 1983, and does not today, possess monopoly power in the market for qualified game officials. . . .

NOTES AND COMMENTS

1. In the *USFL* case, plaintiff prayed for an award of actual damages in the amount of $440,000,000 ($1,320,000,000 trebled). The USFL also sought injunctions prohibiting the NFL from impeding USFL attempts to gain TV network contracts, increasing NFL player rosters, negotiating with USFL players, entering into exclusive service contracts with game officials, making disparaging statements about the USFL, and forming exclusive stadium contracts.

The trial of the *USFL* case resulted in a jury verdict in favor of the plaintiff, finding that the NFL possessed monopoly power and was liable for damages to the USFL for willfully maintaining the power. The jury, however, awarded only $1.00 in damages (trebled to $3.00 under the Clayton Act). The Second Circuit upheld the jury award as adequate compensation. *United States Football League v. National Football League,* 842 F.2d 1335 (2d Cir. 1988), *aff 'g,* 644 F. Supp. 1040 (S.D.N.Y. 1986). The USFL recovered attorneys' fees in the amount of $5,515,290.81, and costs of $62,220.92, although the USFL was successful on only one of its antitrust claims. *United States Football League v. National Football League*, 704 F. Supp. 474 (S.D.N.Y. 1989), *aff'd*, 887 F.2d 408 (2d Cir. 1989).

2. The USFL challenged the NFL's pooled rights TV contracts with ABC, CBS, and NBC as a violation of Section One of the Sherman Act, despite the fact that none of the contracts were exclusive, and none of the networks were precluded from telecasting USFL games. The district court ruled that the existence of the three contracts did not constitute a *per se* violation of the Act, but should be examined under the rule of reason test. *United States Football League v. National Football League*, 634 F. Supp. 1155, 1165 (S.D.N.Y. 1986). In the subsequent trial of the case, the jury found that the three TV contracts did not constitute an unreasonable restraint of trade under Section 1 of the Sherman Act. *United States Football League v. National Football League*, 644 F. Supp. 1040, 1042 (S.D.N.Y. 1986), *aff 'd,* 1842 F.2d 1335 (2d Cir. 1988).

3. The National Football League argued that Congress exempted NFL television contracts from the reach of the antitrust laws. *See* 15 U.S.C. § 1291. The district court in the *USFL* case examined the face of the Act and the legislative history to conclude, "[n]othing in this opinion should be considered as indicating that an absolute antitrust exemption extends to circumstances surrounding the three NFL-network contracts." 634 F. Supp. 1155, 1165 (S.D.N.Y. 1986). *See Chicago Professional Sports Limited Partnership v. National Basketball Association*, 95 F.3d 593 (7th Cir. 1996), and discussion of television broadcasting limitations at **Section G**, *supra*.

See also United States v. National Football League, 116 F. Supp. 319 (E.D. Pa. 1953), *construed*, 196 F. Supp. 445 (E.D. Pa. 1961). The USFL argued that enactment of 15 U.S.C. § 1291 was a direct Congressional response to the 1953 and 1961 cases, and applied only to a single network contract. *United States Football League v. National Football League*, 634 F. Supp. 1155, 1157-65.

Television contracts in professional and amateur sports, including the "blackout" of games, are the subject of recurring suits under the antitrust statutes. *See*, Garrett & Hochberg, *Sports Broadcasting, in* 3 THE LAW OF AMATEUR AND PROFESSIONAL SPORTS Ch. 20 (Uberstine ed. 2002).

4. Can you make a valid argument that professional sports leagues operate in a market that is "naturally" monopolistic? What role, if any, does the "natural monopoly" doctrine play in the *AFL* and *USFL* cases? *See United States v. Aluminum Co. of America (Alcoa)*, 148 F.2d 416 (2d Cir. 1945). *See also Aspen Skiing Co. v. Aspen Highlands Skiing Corp.*, 472 U.S. 585 (1985) (monopolist's unwillingness to participate in a joint marketing scheme with its only competitor could amount to a "deliberate effort" to maintain the monopoly); *Independent Entertainment Group, Inc. v. National Basketball Association*, 853 F. Supp. 333 (C.D. Cal. 1994) (monopolist is not required to share employees with a competitor). *Compare*, *Verizon Communications, Inc. v. Law Offices of Curtis V. Trinko, LLP (Trinko)*, 540 U.S. 398 (2004)(opinion suggests monopolist's sacrifice of short-term profits is a necessary element of exclusionary conduct). *See*, Lao, *Aspen Skiing and Trinko: Antitrust Intent and "Sacrafice,"* 73 Antitrust L.J. 171 (2005).

5. Economists have long recognized that markets do not work to support two or more independent and competing major sports leagues, but result in monopoly leagues. *See* Neale, *The Peculiar Economics of Professional Sports*, 78 Quarterly J. of Econ. 1-14 (1964); Quirk & Fort, PAY DIRT: THE BUSINESS OF PROFESSIONAL TEAM SPORTS 298 (1992). One writer explains:

> "[T]he free market has historically failed to sustain multiple premier leagues competing against one another in the same sport. Multiple-league competition has consistently failed absent a partial merger or acquisition because in a multi-league model, one league eventually gains a comparative advantage and drives the others out of business. This is true even when all the leagues begin operating at the same time and with similar resources.

Edelman, *How to Curb Professional Sports' Bargaining Power Vis-à-Vis the American City*, 2 VA. SPORTS & ENT. L.J. 280 (2003), at 301.

The failure of free markets to work efficiently in the professional sports league context is attributed to the existence of "externalities" that are not included in the profit-loss calculus of competing agents. Without agreement, the leagues do not possess mutual mechanisms to assure the internalization of the costs and benefits not taken into account. The resulting failure is a "tragedy of the commons" phenomenon discussed earlier. The phenomenon occurs in a market-based economy where parties utilize common resources. In attempting to maximize their individual best interests, the efforts produce outcomes that are to the long-term detriment of all. The actions of competing interests in inter-league warfare impact at least two commons: market support and the player talent pool. The recognized commons are comprised of several sub-commons, and may be interrelated. Fan interest, for example, is the core element of the market support infrastructure, which includes advertising and sponsorship capital, media contracts, and merchandising. Unrestricted competition in the market for players may lead to dilution of the player talent pool, also leading to loss of fan support. *See* Whitney, *Bidding Till Bankrupt: Destructive Competition in Professional Team* Sports, 31 ECONOMIC INQUIRY 100, 113 (1993). The existence of and competition between rival leagues has historically saturated the market to result in the tragedy. After some time, the leagues fail or come together to make the necessary agreements, allocate the property rights, and establish rules necessary for successful league operations.

6. The tragedy of the commons is a collective action problem that in game theory analysis fits within the traditional "prisoners' dilemma" game. The social dilemma or trap results where individual rationality can lead to group irrationality or poor outcomes, leaving parties worse off than if they had cooperated. *See generally*, Baird, Gertner & Picker, GAME THEORY & THE LAW 34, 49, 316-17 (2004). *See also*, Raiffa, Richardson & Metcalfe, NEGOTIATION ANALYSIS: THE SCIENCE & ART OF COLLABERATIVE DECISION MAKING 67 (2002); Ostrom, GOVERNING THE COMMONS: THE EVOLUTION OF INSTITUTIONS FOR COLLECTIVE ACTION (1990). Much of the game theory analysis that is useful for collective action scenarios was developed by Nobel Laureate John Nash. The concept of the "Nash equilibrium" is based on the principle that the combination of strategies that players are likely to choose is the combination in which no player could do better by selecting a different strategy given the strategy choices of other players. In a large class of games, there exist multiple equilibrium points, depending on the choices made by the parties. For application of the concept of "Nash equilibrium" in the professional sports context, *see* Szymanski, *Professional Team Sports Are Only a Game: The Walrasian Fixed-Supply Conjecture Model, Contest-Nash Equilibrium, and the Invariance Principle*, 5 J. Sports Econ. 111 (2004). For a description of the Nash perspective and its development, *see* Nasar, A BEAUTIFUL MIND 88-91 (1998).

7. How did the plaintiff's case in *AFL* differ from plaintiffs case in *USFL*. How do you explain that the NFL was held to possess monopoly power in *USFL*, but was held not to possess monopoly power in *AFL*?

8. The NFL and AFL merged in 1966. Does the fact of the merger aid in the action brought by the USFL? The merger of professional sports leagues is exempted from the reach of the antitrust laws by operation of 15 U.S.C. § 1291.

9. In many geographic areas, only one (if any) facility exists which can adequately accommodate the needs of competing professional sports franchises. An existing professional sports franchise in the area likely either owns the facility or possesses an exclusive lease to utilize the facility. A club's exclusive control of the only available playing site, of course, is relevant to the question of the relative market position of the established league under § 2 monopoly analysis. Exclusive control also generates restraint of trade questions under §§ 1 and 3 of the Sherman Act. The seemingly endless litigation concerning the Washington Redskins' control of RFK Stadium in Washington, D.C., is instructive. *Hecht v. Pro-Football, Inc. (I)*, 444 F.2d 931 (D.C. Cir. 1971), *cert. denied*, 404 U.S. 1047 (1972); *Hecht v. Pro-Football, Inc. (II)*, 570 F.2d 982 (D.C. Cir. 1977). Plaintiffs in *Hecht I* and *II* contend that a restrictive covenant in the RFK lease enjoyed by the Washington Redskins violates the antitrust laws. Plaintiffs claim that inability to gain access to the stadium prevented the plaintiffs from gaining an AFL franchise for the D.C. area.

In *Hecht I*, the district court granted summary judgment for the defendant, on the basis that the District of Columbia Armory Board's leasing of RFK Stadium was governmental action immune from the antitrust laws. The D.C. Circuit Court reversed and remanded for trial on the merits, concluding that Congress had evinced no intention to confer the immunity. 570 F.2d 982.

In *Hecht II*, the case was tried to a jury, which rendered a verdict for defendants. Plaintiff appealed, challenging numerous instructions and evidentiary rulings. The D.C. Circuit Court reversed and remanded for a new trial.

In addition to discussing the usual antitrust issues, the court recognized the "essential facilities" doctrine:

> [W]here facilities cannot practicably be duplicated by would-be competitors, those in possession of them must allow them to be shared on fair terms. It is illegal restraint of trade to foreclose the scarce facility.

Id. at 992. A facility is "essential" where duplication is economically infeasible and denial of facility use inflicts a severe handicap on potential market entrants. The doctrine does not operate where sharing of the facility would be impractical or would inhibit defendant's ability to serve its customers adequately. *Id. Compare,* Hawker, *Open Windows: The Essential Facilities Doctrine and Microsoft,* 25 OHIO N.U. L. REV. 115 (1999).

10. The D.C. Circuit Court in *Hecht II* suggested that the trial court utilize special jury interrogatories in antitrust cases, rather than the usual general verdict, lest the case appear before the court a third time. What jury instructions are needed? What expert testimony is required to prove a *prima facie* case?

11. For a case in which the plaintiff failed in challenging the Minnesota Vikings' exclusive lease of the Metrodome, *see Scallen v. Minnesota Vikings Football Club, Inc.*, 574 F. Supp. 278 (D. Minn. 1983). For a case in which plaintiff alleged that defendants exclusively controlled the Rosemont Horizon, an "essential facility" for the booking and promotion of pop, rock, and rhythm and blues concerts in the Chicago area, see *Flip Side Productions, Inc. v. Jam Productions, Ltd.*, 843 F.2d 1024 (7th Cir. 1988) (Indoor arena not an "essential facility" and plaintiff lacked standing to bring claim under RICO).

12. In *Fraser v. Major League Soccer, L.L.C.*, 284 F.3d 47 (1st Cir. 2002), the Circuit Court of Appeals affirmed the lower court rulings in the trial including plaintiff's Section 2 monopoly claims. Plaintiff alleged that MLS monopolized the market for Division I professional soccer in the United States; attempted to monopolize the market; and conspired with the United States Soccer Foundation to monopolize the market. The jury returned a verdict that plaintiff failed to prove the alleged relevant market as limited to the United States (compared with a worldwide market definition). Thus, the court entered judgment for the defendant.

13. In late December of 1998, the American Basketball League, a women's professional league, announced it was bankrupt and had suspended operations. The collapse of the ABL left the Women's National Basketball Association (WNBA) as the only women's professional basketball league in the United States. From the start, the ABL reportedly lacked the financial and marketing support that the WNBA enjoyed from its parent league, the NBA. The ABL attempted to market its product as having the best players, but could not compete with the WNBA's advertising campaigns and television exposure on NBC, ESPN, and Lifetime. The ABL season ran from November through March, whereas the WNBAschedule operated in the summer months. The ABL failed to secure a TV deal. ABL co-founder and CEO, Gary Cavalli, remarked, "At this point, the league is out of money. While this is an extremely painful decision, we had no choice but to shut down. . . . It became clear that, although we had the best product, we could not find enough people willing to confront the NBA and give us the major sponsorships and TV contracts we needed." Shipley, *ABL Says It is Bankrupt, Shuts Down*, www.washingtonpost.com/wpsrv/sports/abl/daily/dec98/23/ablfolds23.htm. Can you identify arguments that the ABL possesses a cause of action against the WNBA pursuant to Section 2? Does the WNBA bear the responsibility of taking active steps to assure continued operations of its sole competitor?

I. AUTHORITY OF LEAGUE COMMISSIONERS

The commissioners and/or presidents of the various professional sports leagues notoriously possess dominant powers in governing league matters. As the *Finley v. Kuhn* case below reveals, the perceived value of unfettered "commissioner power" arose amidst the chaos generated by the "Black Sox" scandal. The vesting of broad governing authority in a commissioner, however, is not limited to professional baseball. The commissioner of the National Football League possesses similar powers, as do the commissioners of the NBA and other leagues. Legendary NFL Commissioner, Pete Rozelle, for example, imposed the "Rozelle Rule," discussed at **Chapter 6**, *infra. See also Dryer v. Los Angeles Rams,* **Chapter 7,** *infra,* for a challenge of the commissioner's authority in grievance arbitration proceedings.

The source of the commissioner's powers is the league constitution and by-laws. Thus, a dispute concerning the scope of a commissioner's authority requires construction of the intent of league members in drafting and adopting the league constitution.

The collective bargaining agreement between management and labor may modify, limit, or otherwise affect the power of the commissioner as established by the league constitution. For example, Commissioner decisions in player disciplinary matters are usually subject to review through arbitration. *See* **Note 4**, *infra*. The attorney must gain a working knowledge of the scope of authority vested in the commissioner of the league in which the attorney operates. The constitutions and by-laws of most professional sports leagues broadly authorize the commissioners to take discretionary action in the following areas:

1. Approval of player contracts;

2. Resolution of disputes between player and club;

3. Resolution of disputes between clubs;

4. Resolution of disputes between player or club and the league;

5. Disciplinary matters, involving players, clubs, front office personnel, owners, and others; and

6. Rulemaking authority.

The following problem and case file are designed to acquaint you with trouble cases involving the awesome power of the commissioner. As you work through the problem, attempt to identify non-legal alternatives for resolution of the matter. Remember the admonition of Fisher & Ury, **Chapter 9**, *infra*: "Effective negotiators convert competitive positional bargaining to mutual joint problem solving."

PROBLEM

Andrew Cverko is Commissioner of the professional Rugby League. The Constitution and By-Laws of the Rugby League enable the Commissioner to exercise authority, as follows:

> Art. 8 — The Commissioner shall have full, complete, and final jurisdiction and authority to arbitrate:
>
> a. Any dispute involving two or more members of the League;
>
> b. Any dispute involving players, coaches and/or other employees and members of the League;
>
> c. Any dispute between a player and any official of the League;
>
> d. Any dispute involving a member of the League or any employees of the members of the League, or any combination

> thereof, that in the opinion of the Commissioner constitutes conduct detrimental to the best interests of the League and professional rugby.

Art. 9 — The Commissioner shall interpret and from time to time establish policy and procedure in respect to the provisions of the Constitution and Bylaws and any enforcement thereof.

Art. 10 — The Commissioner is authorized to hire legal counsel and take or adopt appropriate legal action or such other steps as he deems necessary and proper in the best interests of the League and professional rugby, whenever any party not a member of the League, or a member thereof, is guilty of any conduct detrimental either to the League, its member clubs or employees, or to professional rugby.

Art. 11 — Whenever the Commissioner, after notice and hearing, decides that an owner, shareholder, player, coach, officer, or other person has either violated the Constitution and By-Laws of the League, or has been or is guilty of conduct detrimental to the welfare of the League or professional rugby, the Commissioner shall have complete authority to:

1. Suspend for a prescribed period of time and/or fine a person in amount not in excess of $5,000.00;
2. Cancel any contract or agreement;
3. Cancel or require forfeiture of any interest in a franchise;
4. Impose other such additional punishment as the Commissioner shall deem appropriate.

Cverko is concerned that the traditional lifestyles employed by rugby players is not consonant with the values of American families. He feels that it is essential that the professional rugby players limit their aggressiveness and passion to the playing field in order to capture the hearts of the American viewing public. Cverko unilaterally promulgated rules of conduct applicable to players, owners, and front office officials. The rules prohibit 1) excess drinking of alcohol; 2) drug use; 3) bawdy songs; 4) immoral activities; and 5) conduct not in the best interests of the League and professional rugby.

Cverko completed his first investigation and issued a notice of disciplinary proceeding to Thomas "The Big Hit" O'Leary. The investigation revealed that O'Leary is the official beer drinking and bawdy song leader of the Spokane River, a member club. He openly dates the estranged wife of a state attorney general. Recently, an after game party created a disturbance in Spokane. O'Leary was arrested along with fifteen other persons for disturbing the peace, malicious mischief, contributing to the delinquency of minors, and assault on a police officer. Cverko also has received several complaints from member clubs alleging that O'Leary has on numerous occasions utilized dangerous tackling methods in violation of the league rules. Cverko desires to use the O'Leary disciplinary proceeding to establish his power base as commissioner. Your law firm is general counsel to the Rugby League. You anticipate that O'Leary will seek to enjoin the disciplinary proceeding. Advise Cverko and the League concerning the Commissioner's authority under the provisions of the League Constitution above. Map out a strategy for use by Cverko in the O'Leary matter. Specifically describe all limitations on the exercise of the commissioner's authority.

CASE FILE

CHARLES O. FINLEY & CO., INC. v. KUHN

569 F.2d 527 (7th Cir. 1978)

SPRECHER, Circuit Judge.

* * *

The two important questions raised by this appeal are whether the Commissioner of baseball is contractually authorized to disapprove player assignments which he finds to be "not in the best interests of baseball" where neither moral turpitude nor violation of a Major League Rule is involved, and whether the provision in the Major League Agreement whereby the parties agree to waive recourse to the courts is valid and enforceable.

I

Joe Rudi, Rollie Fingers and Vida Blue were members of the active playing roster of the Oakland A's baseball club and were contractually bound to play for Oakland through the end of the 1976 baseball season. On or about June 15, 1976, Oakland and Blue entered a contract whereby Blue would play for Oakland through the 1979 season, but Rudi and Fingers had not at that time signed contracts for the period beyond the 1976 season.

If Rudi and Fingers had not signed contracts to play with Oakland by the conclusion of the 1976 season, they would at that time have become free agents eligible thereafter to negotiate with any major league club, subject to certain limitations on their right to do so that were then being negotiated by the major league clubs with the Players Association.

On June 14 and 15, 1976, Oakland negotiated tentative agreements to sell the club's contract rights for the services of Rudi and Fingers to the Boston Red Sox for $2 million and for the services of Blue to the New York Yankees for $1.5 million. . . .

The defendant Bowie K. Kuhn is the Commissioner of baseball (Commissioner), having held that position since 1969. On June 18, 1976, the Commissioner disapproved the assignments of the contracts of Rudi, Fingers and Blue to the Red Sox and Yankees "as inconsistent with the best interests of baseball, the integrity of the game and the maintenance of public confidence in it." The Commissioner expressed his concern for (1) the debilitation of the Oakland club, (2) the lessening of the competitive balance of professional baseball through the buying of success by the more affluent clubs, and (3) "the present unsettled circumstances of baseball's reserve system."

Thereafter on June 25, 1976, Oakland instituted this suit principally challenging, as beyond the scope of the Commissioner's authority and, in any event, as arbitrary and capricious, the Commissioner's disapproval of the Rudi, Fingers and Blue assignments. The complaint set forth seven causes of action: (I) that the Commissioner breached his employment contract with Oakland by acting arbitrarily, discriminatorily and unreasonably; (II) that the Commissioner, acting in concert with others, conspired to eliminate Oakland from baseball in violation of federal antitrust laws; (III) that Oakland's constitutional rights of due process and equal protection were violated; (IV) that Oakland's constitutional rights were violated by the first disapproval of a player assignment where no major league rule was violated; (V) that the defendants (the Commissioner, the National and American Leagues and the Major League Executive Council) induced the breach of Oakland's contracts with Boston and New York; (VI) that the Commissioner did not have the authority to disapprove Oakland's assignments "in the best interests of baseball"; and (VII) that Oakland have specific performance of its contracts of assignment with Boston and New York.

On September 7, 1976, the district court granted the Commissioner's motion for summary judgment as to Counts II, III and IV. Count II was dismissed on the ground that the business of baseball is not subject to the federal antitrust laws. Counts III and IV were dismissed on the ground that Oakland did not allege sufficient nexus between the state and the complained of activity to constitute state action.

A bench trial took place as a result of which judgment on the remaining four counts of the complaint was entered in favor of the Commissioner on March 17, 1977.

* * *

II

Basic to the underlying suit brought by Oakland and to this appeal is whether the Commissioner of baseball is vested by contract with the authority to disapprove player assignments which he finds to be "not in the best interests of baseball." In assessing the measure and extent of the Commissioner's power and authority, consideration must be given to the circumstances attending the creation of the office of Commissioner, the language employed by the parties in drafting their contractual understanding, changes and amendments adopted from time to time, and the interpretation given by the parties to their contractual language throughout the period of its existence.

Prior to 1921, professional baseball was governed by a three-man National Commission formed in 1903. . . . Between 1915 and 1921, a series of events and controversies contributed to a growing dissatisfaction with the National Commission. . . .

On September 28, 1920, an indictment issued charging that an effort had been made to "fix" the 1919 World Series by several Chicago White Sox players. Popularly known as the "Black Sox Scandal," this event rocked the game of professional baseball and proved the catalyst that brought about the establishment of a single, neutral Commissioner of baseball.

In November, 1920, the major league club owners unanimously elected federal Judge Kenesaw Mountain Landis as the sole Commissioner of baseball and appointed a committee of owners to draft a charter setting forth the Commissioner's authority. In one of the drafting sessions an attempt was made to place limitations on the Commissioner's authority. Judge Landis responded by refusing to accept the office of Commissioner.

On January 19, 1921, Landis told a meeting of club owners that he had agreed to accept the position upon the clear understanding that the owners had sought "an authority . . . outside of your own business, and that a part of that authority would be a control over whatever and whomever had to do with baseball." Thereupon, the owners voted unanimously to reject the proposed limitation upon the Commissioner's authority, they all signed what they called the Major League Agreement. . . . The agreement, a contract between the constituent clubs of the National and American Leagues, is the basic charter under which major league baseball operates.

The Major League Agreement provides that "[t]he functions of the Commissioner shall be . . . to investigate . . . any act, transaction or practice . . . not in the best interests of the national game of Baseball" and "to determine what preventative, remedial or punitive action is appropriate in the premises, and to take such action. . . ." Art. 1, Sec. 2(a) and (b).

The Major League Rules, which govern many aspects of the game of baseball, are promulgated by vote of major league club owners. Major League Rule 12(a) provides that "no . . . [assignment of players] shall be recognized as valid unless . . . approved by the Commissioner."

The Major Leagues and their constituent clubs severally agreed to be bound by the decisions of the Commissioner and by the discipline imposed by him. They further agreed to "waive such right of recourse to the courts as would otherwise have existed in their favor." Major League Agreement, Art. VII, Sec. 2.

Upon Judge Landis' death in 1944, the Major League Agreement was amended in two respects to limit the Commissioner's authority. First, the parties deleted the provision by which they had agreed to waive their right of recourse to the courts to challenge actions of the Commissioner. Second, the parties added the following language to Article 1, Section 3:

> No Major League Rule or other joint action of the two Major Leagues, and no action or procedure taken in compliance with any such Major League Rule or joint action of the two Major Leagues shall be considered or construed to be detrimental to Baseball.

The district court found that this addition had the effect of precluding the Commissioner from finding an act that complied with the Major League Rules to be detrimental to the best interests of baseball.

[I]n 1964, . . . the parties adopted three amendments to the Major League Agreement: (1) the language added in 1944 preventing the Commissioner from finding any act or practice "taken in compliance" with a Major League Rule to be "detrimental to baseball" was removed; (2) the provision deleted in 1944 waiving any right of recourse to the courts . . . was restored; and (3) in places where the language "detrimental to the best interests of the national game of baseball" or "detrimental to baseball" appeared those words were changed to "not in the best interests of the national game of Baseball" or "not in the best interests of Baseball."

* * *

The Commissioner has been given broad power in unambiguous language to investigate any act, transaction or practice not in the best interests of baseball, to determine what preventative, remedial or punitive action is appropriate in the premises, and to take that action. He has also been given the express power to approve or disapprove the assignments of players. . . . [I]ndicative of the nature of the Commissioner's authority is the provision whereby the parties agree to be bound by his decisions and discipline imposed and to waive recourse to the courts.

The Major League Agreement also provides that "[i]n the case of conduct by Major Leagues, Major League Clubs, officers, employees or players . . . action by the Commissioner for each offense *may include*" a reprimand, deprivation of a club of representation at joint meetings, suspension or removal of non-players, temporary or permanent ineligibility of players, and a fine not to exceed $5,000 in the case of a league or club and not to exceed $500 in the case of an individual. Art. 1. Sec. 3.

* * *

The court concluded that the enumeration does not purport to be exclusive and provides that the Commissioner may act in one of the listed ways without limiting him to those ways.

The court further concluded that the principles of construction that the specific controls the general, or that the expression of some kinds of authority operates to exclude unexpressed kinds, do not apply since the Commissioner is empowered to determine what preventative, remedial or punitive action is appropriate in a particular case and the listed sanctions are punitive only. . . .

[W]e agree with the district court that Section 3 does not purport to limit that authority.

III

Despite the Commissioner's broad authority . . . Oakland has attacked the Commissioner's disapproval of the Rudi-Fingers-Blue transactions on a variety of theories which seem to express a similar thrust in differing language.

The complaint alleged that the "action of Kuhn was arbitrary, capricious, unreasonable, discriminatory, directly contrary to historical precedent, baseball tradition, and prior rulings and actions of the Commissioner.". . .

The plaintiff has argued that it is a fundamental rule of law that the decisions of the head of a private association must be procedurally fair. Plaintiff then argued that it was "procedurally unfair" for the Commissioner to fail to warn the plaintiff that he would "disapprove large cash assignments of star players even if they complied with the Major League Rules."

In the first place it must be recalled that prior to the assignments involved here drastic changes had commenced to occur in the reserve system and in the creation of free agents. In his opinion disapproving the Rudi, Fingers and Blue assignments, the Commissioner said that "while I am of course aware that there have been cash sales of player contracts in the past, there has been no instance in my judgment which had the potential for harm to our game as do these assignments, particularly in the present unsettled circumstances of baseball's reserve system and in the highly competitive circumstances we find in today's sports and entertainment world."

* * *

In the second place, baseball cannot be analogized to any other business or even to any other sport or entertainment. Baseball's relation to the federal antitrust laws has been characterized by the Supreme Court as an "exception," an "anomaly" and an "aberration." Baseball's management through a commissioner is equally an exception, anomaly and aberration. . . . Standards such as the best interests of baseball, the interests of the morale of the players and the honor of the game, or "sportsmanship which accepts the umpire's decision without complaint," are not necessarily familiar to courts and obviously require some expertise in their application. While it is true that professional baseball selected as its first Commissioner a federal judge, it intended only him and not the judiciary as a whole to be its umpire and governor.

As we have seen . . . the Commissioner was vested with broad authority and that authority was not to be limited in its exercise to situations where Major League Rules or moral turpitude was involved. . . .

During his almost 25 years as Commissioner, Judge Landis found many acts, transactions and practices to be detrimental to the best interests of baseball in situations where neither moral turpitude nor a Major League Rule violation was involved, and he disapproved several player assignments.

On numerous occasions since he became Commissioner of Baseball in February 1969, Kuhn has exercised broad authority under the best interests clause of the Major League Agreement. . . .

On several occasions Charles O. Finley, the principal owner of the plaintiff corporation and the general manager of the Oakland baseball club, has himself espoused that the Commissioner has the authority to exercise broad powers pursuant to the best interests clause, even where there is no violation of the Major League Rules and no moral turpitude is involved.

* * *

Oakland relied upon Major League Rule 21, which deals, in Oakland's characterization of it, with "(a) throwing or soliciting the throwing of ball games, (b) bribery by or of players or persons connected with clubs or (c) umpires, (d) betting on ball games, and (e) physical violence and other unsportsmanlike conduct" as indicating the limits of what is "not in the best interests of baseball." However, Rule 21(f) expressly states:

> Nothing herein contained shall be construed as exclusively defining or otherwise limiting acts, transactions, practices or conduct not to be in the best interests of Baseball; and any and all other acts, transactions, practices or conduct not to be in the best interests of Baseball are prohibited, and shall be subject to such penalties including permanent ineligibility, as the facts in the particular case may warrant.

[W]e agree with the district court's finding that "[t]he history of the adoption of the Major League Agreement in 1921 and the operation of baseball for more than 50 years under it, including: the circumstances preceding and precipitating the adoption of the Agreement; the numerous exercises of broad authority under the best interests clause by Judge Landis and . . . Commissioner Kuhn; the amendments to the Agreement in 1964 restoring and broadening the authority of the Commissioner; . . . and most important the express language of the Agreement itself — are all to the effect that the Commissioner has the authority to determine whether any act, transaction or practice is not in the best interests of baseball.". . . .

[W]e agree with the district court's finding and conclusion that the Commissioner "acted in good faith, after investigation, consultation and deliberation, in a manner which he determined to be in the best interests of baseball" and that "[w]hether he was right or wrong is beyond the competence and the jurisdiction of this court to decide."

* * *

Oakland has argued that the district court erred in not finding on the issue of procedural fairness. To the extent that Oakland made this an issue during the course of the trial, the court responded with adequate findings . . . .

Finally, Oakland has also argued that the court excluded evidence which tended to show the Commissioner's malice toward Mr. Finley. Finley's own testimony on this subject, as well as the Commissioner's deposition covering the subject, were admitted as part of the record. When counsel for the Commissioner attempted to cross-examine Finley in regard to the same subject, Oakland's counsel objected on the ground of relevancy and the court sustained the objection on the ground that the Commissioner's motivation was not a serious issue in the case. When the Commissioner was being cross-examined the same objection was sustained. . . . The court made an express finding that the Commissioner had not been motivated by malice.

IV

The district court granted the defendant's motion for summary judgment as to Count II of the complaint, which sought to establish a violation of the Sherman Antitrust Act. The court said that "Baseball, anomaly of the antitrust law, is not subject to the provisions of that Act." The plaintiff on appeal has argued that any exemption which professional baseball might enjoy from federal antitrust laws applies only to the reserve system.

* * *

The Supreme Court has held three times that "the business of baseball" is exempt from the federal antitrust laws.

[I]t appears clear from the entire opinions in the three baseball cases, . . . that the Supreme Court intended to exempt the business of baseball, not any particular facet of that business, from the federal antitrust laws.

V

In this part we consider the district court's judgment of August 29, 1977, granting the Commissioner's counterclaim for a declaratory judgment that the waiver of recourse clause is valid and enforceable.

* * *

Even in the absence of a waiver of recourse provision in an association charter, "[i]t is generally held that courts . . . will not intervene in questions involving the enforcement of bylaws and matters of discipline in voluntary associations."

. . . [T]he waiver of recourse clause contested here seems to add little if anything to the common law nonreviewability of private association actions. This clause can be upheld as coinciding with the common law standard disallowing court interference. We view its inclusion in the Major League Agreement merely as a manifestation of the intent of the contracting parties to insulate from review decisions made by the Commissioner concerning the subject matter of actions taken in accordance with his grant of powers.

A second situation in which the waiver of recourse clause must be tested is in conjunction with the provision immediately preceding it which provides that "[a]ll disputes and controversies related in any way to professional baseball between clubs . . . shall be submitted to the Commissioner, as Arbitrator who, after hearing, shall have the sole and exclusive right to decide such disputes and controversies." Art. VII, Sec. 1. These clauses combine to place the Commissioner in the role of binding arbitrator between disputing parties as compared to his power to act upon his own initiative in the best interests of baseball as in the present case.

Considering the waiver of recourse clause in its function of requiring arbitration by the Commissioner, its validity cannot be seriously questioned. Illinois has adopted the Uniform Arbitration Act allowing contracting parties to require that all existing and future disputes be determined by arbitration. . . . Moreover, it has been made clear that the United States Arbitration Act, 9 U.S.C. §§ 1-14, provides for arbitration of future disputes concerning contracts evidencing transactions in interstate commerce and that this federal law controls state law to the contrary. . . . We conclude that the waiver of recourse clause is valid when viewed as requiring binding arbitration by the Commissioner for disputes between clubs.

Even if the waiver of recourse clause is divorced from its setting in the charter of a private, voluntary association and even if its relationship with the arbitration clause in the agreement is ignored, we think that it is valid under the circumstances here involved. Oakland claims that such clauses are invalid as against public policy. This is true, however, only under circumstances where the waiver of rights is not voluntary, knowing or intelligent, or was not freely negotiated by parties occupying equal bargaining positions. . . .

Although the waiver of recourse clause is generally valid for the reasons discussed above, we do not believe that it forecloses access to the courts under all circumstances. Thus, the general rule of nonreviewability which governs the actions of private associations is subject to exceptions 1) where the rules, regulations or judgments of the association are in contravention to the laws of the land or in disregard of the charter or bylaws of the association and 2) where the association has failed to follow the basic rudiments of due process of law. Similar exceptions exist for avoiding the requirements of arbitration under the United States Arbitration Act. . . .

Notes and Comments

1. The scope of the Commissioner's authority is defined by the league constitution and by-laws read *in pari materia* with the collective bargaining agreement. Thus, a common question is whether commissioner actions are *ultra* *vires*. The commissioner must also follow procedures set forth in the enabling documents. *See National Hockey League Players' Association v. Bettman,* 1994 WL 738835 (S.D.N.Y. 1994); *Professional Sports, Ltd. v. Virginia Squires Basketball Club*, 373 F. Supp. 946 (W.D. Tex. 1974). *See also Riko Enterprises, Inc. v. Seattle SuperSonics Corp.*, 357 F. Supp. 521 (S.D.N.Y. 1973); *American League Baseball Club of New York v. Johnson*, 179 N.Y.S. 498 (Sup. Ct. 1919), *aff'd*, 179 N.Y.S. 898 (1920).

2. A Commissioner usually possesses broad authority to take unilateral action in governing league matters, including the power to promulgate rules. For a case in which imposition of a fine system by the Commissioner constituted an unfair labor practice, *see National Football League Players Association v. NLRB*, 503 F.2d 12 (8th Cir. 1974).

3. League constitutions and by-laws generally vest the Commissioner with adjudicatory authority to arbitrate disputes between clubs. Most league documents provide a procedure for the "protest" of games. Thus, a club may "protest" a game, alleging a violation of league rules. A threshold question concerns the standing of the club to protest. The party protesting the game must follow the procedures set forth in the league constitution. The Salt Lake City Trappers, for example, attempted to protest a game played between the Butte Copper Kings and Great Falls Dodgers. The question of standing was not reached by the Pioneer League president as the Trappers failed to follow "protest" procedures set forth by the constitution. Issues concerning the role of the Commissioner as arbitrator are discussed at **Chapter 7**, *infra*.

4. Commissioner authority in disciplinary matters traditionally has been "plenary" in nature. The commissioner's power, however, may be limited by provisions of the league constitution. *See, e.g.*, *In the Matter Between the Major League Baseball Players Association and the Commissioner of Major League Baseball (John Rocker), Decision of Arbitration Panel*, 638 PLI/Pat 765 (2001) (Commissioner fine of John Rocker in the amount of $20,000, reduced to $500.00, the maximum fine allowed for conduct deemed not in the best interests of baseball pursuant to Article 1, Section 3(a) of the Major League Agreement); *Atlanta National League Baseball Club, Inc. v. Kuhn*, 432 F. Supp. 1213 (N.D. Ga. 1977) (suspension of owner Ted Turner upheld, but Commissioner's decision to deprive club of first round draft choice held to be *ultra vires*). *See generally*, Arkell, *National Hockey League Jurisprudence: Past, Present and Future*, 8 SETON HALL J. SPORT L. 135, 138-57 (1998) (NHL Commissioner's authority limited by NHL Constitution and By Laws, collective bargaining agreement, and applicable case law).

5. The collective bargaining agreement often makes Commissioner decisions in disciplinary matters subject to review through an arbitration mechanism. Most collective bargaining agreements, including those in the non-sports industry context, contain a requirement of "just cause" for worker discipline. *See, e.g.*, *In the Matter Between the Major League Players Association and the Commissioner of Major League Baseball (John Rocker), Decision of Arbitration Panel*

(Das, Chair), 638 PLI/Pat 765 (2001) (arbitrator reduces suspension applying "just cause" standard); *In the Matter of Arbitration Between National Basketball Players Association on Behalf of Player Latrell Sprewell and Warriors Basketball Club and National Basketball Association* (Feerick, Arb., March 4, 1998) (arbitrator reduces punishment for workplace violence, reading together the "just cause" and "arbitrary and capricious" provisions of the collective bargaining agreement). For an examination of the power of a commissioner in disciplinary matters and the impact of review through arbitration, *see* Pollack, *Take My Arbitrator, Please: Commissioner "Best Interests" Disciplinary Authority in Professional Sports*, 67 FORDHAM L. REV. 1645 (1999) (argues that to properly maintain the integrity of professional baseball and basketball, the MLBPA and NBPA should recognize that commissioners need non-reviewable authority to make disciplinary decisions). See discussion of grievance arbitration at **Chapter 7, Section G**, *infra*.

6. Commissioner of Baseball Peter V. Ueberroth and then Commissioner-elect A. Bartlett Giamatti initiated an investigation regarding allegations that Cincinnati Reds Manager Pete Rose wagered on major league baseball games in violation of league rules. Giamatti retained John M. Dowd as Special Counsel for the purpose of conducting an investigation of the matter. On May 9, 1989, Dowd submitted a report to Giamatti summarizing the evidence obtained during the investigation. Commissioner Giamatti scheduled a hearing on the matter for June 26, 1989. Rose responded by filing suit in state court seeking a temporary restraining order and injunction prohibiting Giamatti from conducting the disciplinary proceedings. Rose alleged seven causes of action under state common law, as follows:

1. breach of contract;
2. breach of an implied covenant of good faith and fair dealing;
3. breach of fiduciary duty;
4. promissory estoppel;
5. tortious interference with contract;
6. negligence; and
7. common law of "due process and natural justice."

The crux of the complaint contended that Rose was denied the right to a fair hearing by an unbiased decisionmaker. Subsequent to issuance of the temporary restraining order, defendants removed the case to the United States District Court, alleging diversity jurisdiction. Rose filed a motion to remand to state court. The district court denied Rose's motion. *Rose v. Giamatti*, 721 F. Supp. 906 (S.D. Ohio 1989). The case opinion contains an excellent review of the history of the Commissioner's Office, and the current procedures utilized by the Commissioner. The injunction was continued pending appeal. *Rose v. Giamatti*, 721 F. Supp. 924 (S.D. Ohio 1989). The parties settled the matter without further court action. *See generally* RESTON, COLLISION AT HOMEPLATE (1991).

The *Rose* case presents the question of whether principles, external to league governing documents, constrain the exercise of power by the Commissioner. Can you identify common law or other principles that are appropriately applied to Commissioner actions? Does the *Finley v. Kuhn* case establish limitations applicable to the *Rose* case? Is the league process mandating that the Commissioner serve as investigator, prosecutor, and judge subject to attack as "fundamentally unfair"? What is the likely impact of the "waiver of recourse" clause on Rose's arguments? Compare the disciplinary process utilized by professional sports leagues with the process of administrative agencies.

The Dowd Report (Investigation of Pete Rose), which was filed with the Office of the Commissioner, is provided at 68 MISS. L.J. 915 (1999).

7. George Steinbrenner, owner of the New York Yankees, agreed to a lifetime ban from major league baseball as part of a settlement in a case initiated by Commissioner Vincent under Art. I, Sec. 2(a) and (b), Major League Agreement. Steinbrenner allegedly paid gambler Howard Spira $40,000 for information on then Yankee outfielder Dave Winfield. After investigation of the matter, Vincent and Steinbrenner agreed as follows:

1. Steinbrenner must resign as general partner of the New York Yankees and appoint a new one, subject to approval by the Commissioner;
2. Steinbrenner must reduce his ownership in the Yankees to less than 50% (transfer to member of his family subject to approval of the Commissioner);
3. Steinbrenner may remain as a limited partner;
4. Steinbrenner may participate in certain business affairs of the Yankees, subject to approval of the Commissioner (TV or radio contracts, concession leases & agreements);
5. Steinbrenner cannot visit the clubhouse, offices, owners' box or pressbox at Yankee Stadium, or the Spring Training facility without the approval of the Commissioner;
6. Steinbrenner cannot be involved in day-to-day baseball operations or personnel matters;
7. Steinbrenner cannot sue Major League Baseball or otherwise challenge the sanctions in court;
8. The Yankees must certify every six months that there has been no unauthorized contact;
9. The Yankees must gain league approval for hiring, firing, promotion, demotion or reassignment of any officer of the club for five years.

A suit to enjoin enforcement of the agreement between Vincent and Steinbrenner was filed by two Yankee limited partners, despite the "waiver of recourse" provision. The suspension of George Steinbrenner concerning the Spira matter ended on July 24, 1992 (suspension lifted effective March 1993). For a case describing the investigation and process utilized by the Office of the Commissioner, *see Steinbrenner v. Esquire Reporting Co.*, 1991 WL 102540 (S.D.N.Y. 1991). George Steinbrenner was again suspended in May of 1997, by the executive council, ruling in lieu of a Commissioner, as a result of the Yankee's deal with Adidas and the Yankee's suit filed against MLB. The council prohibited Steinbrenner and the Yankees from participation on all of baseball's governing committees. The suspension did not bar Steinbrenner from running the Yankees. For discussion of the Adidas matter and ultimate settlement, *see* **Note 11, Section G,** *supra*.

8. On July 7, 1992, the Chicago Cubs sued Commissioner Vincent, contending the Commissioner exceeded his authority under the Major League Agreement by ordering geographic realignment of the National League divisions. The National League Constitution provides that no club may be realigned without the club's consent.

On March 4, 1992, ten National League clubs voted to approve realignment of the Chicago Cubs, St. Louis Cardinals, Cincinnati Reds, and Atlanta Braves. The New York Mets and Chicago Cubs voted in the negative, with the Cubs vetoing the change under the National League Constitution. Commissioner Vincent ordered the realignment "in the best interests of baseball," claiming authority under Art. I, Sec. 2, Major League Agreement. Are general Commissioner powers vested under the Major League Agreement paramount to express provisions of the National and American League Constitutions?

The United States District Court granted a temporary injunction prohibiting Commissioner-ordered realignment. The court ruled that Art. VIII of the Major League Agreement limits Commissioner exercise of Art. I power to disputes "other than those whose resolution is expressly provided for by another means in this Agreement, the Major League Rules, the Constitution of either Major League or the Basic Agreement. . . ." Art. VIII, Sec. 1. The Commissioner resigned office shortly thereafter, and Major League Baseball did not further challenge the ruling. *Chicago National League Baseball Club, Inc. v. Vincent*, No. 92 C 4398 (N.D. III. 1992) (Findings of Fact, Conclusions of Law, and Order withdrawn and vacated; Preliminary Injunction dissolved, Action dismissed, Sept. 24, 1992).

9. In August of 1992, Major League Baseball owners directed a vote of "no confidence" to Commissioner Vincent, and asked for his resignation. The Commissioner responded that Art. IX of the Major League Agreement prevented his termination:

> "Each of the parties hereto subscribes to this Agreement in consideration of the promises of all the others that no diminution of the com-

pensation or powers of the present or any succeeding Commissioner shall be made during his term of office."

Subsequently, Commissioner Vincent resigned the office to preserve the "best interests of baseball." Does Art IX prohibit the firing of the Commissioner? The altering of Commissioner duties? Do fans or other parties possess standing to challenge owner action pursuant to a "private commissioner" theory? Given the political and perhaps economic power of club owners, do commissioners possess the awesome authority traditionally associated with the office?

10. In 1994, Major League Baseball club owners restructured the powers of the Commissioner. Article I of the Major League Agreement was modified by the addition of a new Section 5, which made clear that the Commissioner possessed no authority under the best interests of baseball power to intervene in any matter relating to a subject of collective bargaining between the clubs and the Major League Baseball Players Association. The section overturns precedent established by former Commissioners Bowie Kuhn and Peter Ueberroth. The owners, however, amended Article I, Section 2(a) to make the Commissioner the Chair of the Player Relations Committee, the negotiating arm of MLB in labor matters. Thus, the Commissioner is no longer authorized to act unilaterally and independently in labor negotiations, but retains an integral position as Chair of the negotiation committee. A new Section 4 was also added to Article I to prohibit the Commissioner from utilizing the best interests of baseball power to resolve issues that are properly resolved by the member clubs pursuant to the Major League Agreement and League Constitutions. An express exception enables the Commissioner to act in cases involving the integrity of, or public confidence in, the national game of baseball. Article V, Section 2(e) was amended to state, "All League specific matters shall be decided by a vote of the Member Clubs of such League pursuant to the League Constitution." Interestingly, no mention is made of the authority of owners to remove the Commissioner from office, although the dismissal of League Presidents is provided for in a new Article I, Section 10. For the conflicting views of commentators as to the effect of the amendments on the role of the Commissioner, *see* Arcella, *Major League Baseball's Disempowered Commissioner: Judicial Ramifications of the 1994 Restructuring*, 97 COLUM. L. REV. 2420, 2421 (1997) (Commissioner power curtailed); Reinsdorf, *The Powers of the Commissioner in Baseball*, 7 MARQ. SPORTS L.J. 211, 231-35 (1996) (Commissioner power enhanced).

11. Marge Schott, former owner of the Cincinnati Reds, was suspended on two occasions for making comments considered inappropriate under the "best interests" standard. She joined Rose and Steinbrenner in receiving sanctions formulated through negotiation. Can you identify limitations on the power of the Commissioner's Office under the "best interests" standard? Does the authority extend to internal club operations? Should speech, even if "politically incorrect" speech, be protected from sanction? Does the "best interests" power of the commissioner extend to private matters? *See* Jefferson, *The NFL and Domestic Violence: The Commissioner's Power to Punish Domestic Abusers*, 7 SETON HALL J. SPORT L. 353 (1997).

Commissioner discipline of players for speech-related conduct is generally subject to the "just cause" standard expressed in the collective bargaining agreement, discussed in **Note 5**, *supra*. The standard is applied according to the "common law of the workplace," regarding employee discipline for speech, both within and outside the workplace. *See generally*, Gershenfeld, *Discipline & Discharge*, in COMMON LAW OF THE WORKPLACE: THE VIEWS OF ARBITRATORS, ch. 6 (Antoine ed. 2005); Abrams, *Off His Rocker: Sports Discipline and Labor Arbitration*, 11 MARQ. SPORTS L. REV. 167 (2001).

12. The Cincinnati Bengals of the National Football League included a "loyalty clause" in players' contracts that requires the forfeiture of part or all of signing bonuses if "in the Club's sole judgement [sic] Player at any time makes any public comment to the media, . . . that is derogatory of or criticizing teammates, Club coaches, Club management or the Club's operation or policies. . . ." The National Football League Players Association filed a grievance, contending the clause violates terms of the collective bargaining agreement establishing a maximum discipline schedule. The arbitrator found that the separately negotiated bonus provision requiring forfeiture of monies does not conflict with the collective bargaining act provisions because it seeks to regulate conduct that is also subject to fines under the CBA. *In the Matter of Arbitration Between National Football League Players Association on Behalf of the Cincinnati Bengals Players and National Football League Management Council on Behalf of the Cincinnati Bengals (Bloch, Arb.)*, Jan. 17, 2001.

Can you identify other legal arguments to check the power of the clubs to limit the free speech of players as a condition of contract? *See* Fielder, *Keep Your Mouth Shut and Listen: The NFL Player's Right of Free Expression*, 10 U. MIAMI BUS. L. REV. 547 (2002); Fuhrman, Comment, *Can Discrimination Law Affect the Imposition of a Minimum Age Requirement for Employment in the National Basketball Association?*, 3 U. PA. J. LAB. & EMP. L. 585 (2001); Dean, *Can the NBA Punish Dennis Rodman? An Analysis of First Amendment Rights in Professional Basketball*, 23 VT. L. REV. 157 (1998). The National Basketball Association announced a dress code for the leagues players. The dress code prohibits "sneakers, sandals, flip-flops, or work boots . . . sleeveless shirts, shorts, T-shirts, jerseys . . . headgear of any kind . . . chains, pendants, or medallions worn over the players' clothes . . . sunglasses worn indoors, headphones (other than on team bus, plane, or in locker room)." The dress code applies only to team and league activities. Can you identify legal arguments that limit the power of employers to control the dress of employees while on the job?

Chapter 6

LABOR RELATIONS IN PROFESSIONAL SPORTS

A. INTRODUCTORY COMMENTS

This chapter examines the collective bargaining process utilized by professional sports leagues and player unions to structure the relationships between players and ballclubs. Player associations first formed in the 1800s, but evolved into player labor unions later. Labor relationships in professional sports provide a colorful chapter in the history of the industry, including work stoppages, intense negotiations, and public debate regarding the affect the drama has on the nature and integrity of the games. Not only did Major League Baseball cancel a World Series during a strike period, but the National Hockey League lost an entire season due to a 302-day lockout.

A working knowledge of the collective bargaining agreements of each professional league, including an understanding of the processes by which the agreements were formed, is essential for attorneys representing players and team management. The collective bargaining system established pursuant to the National Labor Relations Act is explored at **Section B**, *infra*. The importance of the interrelationship of labor law and antitrust statutes becomes evident as you read the materials. Although early negotiations centered on traditional wage and conditions of employment issues, such as pensions and insurance, the modern paradigm pits millionaire players and millionaire owners in battles over the division and distribution of the economic rewards derived from the leagues' market opportunities. Thus, the dynamics of the collective bargaining process may be quite different than experienced in the typical non-sports employer-employee negotiations.

Collective bargaining in professional sports focuses upon two primary areas. The first is distributive in nature, as it relates to the division of the revenue pie between owners and players. The second respects the desire of the parties to assure competitive balance, and therefore the general health of the league and its market opportunity.

In recent collective bargaining efforts, parties agreed to guarantee a fixed percentage of gross league revenues for salary distribution to the players. The 1983 NBA-NBPA agreement assured players of receiving 53% of gross revenues, but increased to 55% in the 1999 CBA. The 1993 NFL-NFLPA agreement promised players 58% of revenues. In 2005, the NHL and NHLPA joined to initially allocate 54% of gross league revenues to player salaries, with step ladder increases in future years. The agreements often include "salary caps" which join with the fixed salary percentage obligations to work within sometimes widely varying complex mathematical models. The "cap" also has the effect of limiting player movement among teams. It can be a "soft cap" where the clubs can readily circumvent the restrictions. The 1983 and 1988 NBA caps proved to be quite soft, but the salary limitation was hardened in the 1999 CBA, although some exceptions remained. The NFL CBA, in 1993, produced a "hard cap." The 2005 NHL-NHLPA CBA includes a hard cap. The amount an individual player may earn is capped at 20% of the maximum team payroll. The Basic Agreement negotiated by the MLBPA and Major League Baseball eschewed the "salary cap" for the "payroll or luxury tax." The 2003 Basic Agreement implements a "competitive balance tax" that imposes a burden on clubs whose salary obligations exceed a fixed "tax threshold" in a given season. Most, if not all, leagues include "revenue sharing" as an element in the agreed upon mix of mechanisms designed to protect the economic welfare of league operations.

Professional sports leagues, from the beginning, have utilized various devices to restrict player movement from club to club. Leagues contend that unrestricted competition in the market for player talent may lead to a dilution of the talent pool and result in the reduction of competitive balance among league teams, and the attendant loss of fan support. The ruinous competition for players is a "tragedy of the commons" phenomenon, whereby the interrelated commons, *player talent pool* and *fan interest*, are overgrazed to the detriment of the league as a whole. The economic principles underlying the use of player movement restrictions are presented at **Section D**, *infra*.

The most popular schemes include the "reserve clause," "option clause," draft system, no tampering rules, and free agent compensation arrangements. The reserve clause provides the club an exclusive right to a player's services for succeeding seasons. The option clause allows a club to renew player contracts at the option of the club, usually enabling for exercise of the option at salary reduction. Draft systems divide the amateur or professional supply of players among the clubs of a league, awarding each club the exclusive right to contract with the player drafted. Free agent compensation schemes often require compensation in the form of players or draft choices to a team losing a player to another club.

Players, in the 1970s, successfully challenged the league constraints on player movement as violations of the Sherman Act. *See, e.g., Mackey v. National Football League*, **Case File**, *infra*; *Kapp v. National Football League*, 586 F.2d 644 (9th Cir. 1978); *Smith v. Pro-Football, Inc.*, 593 F.2d 1173 (D.C. Cir. 1978); *Robertson v. National Basketball Ass'n*, **Case File**, *infra*; *Philadelphia World Hockey Club, Inc. v. Philadelphia Hockey Club, Inc.*, 451 F. Supp. 462 (E.D. Pa. 1972); *Boston Professional Hockey Association, Inc. v. Cheevers*, 348 F. Supp. 261, *rem. on other grounds*, 472 F.2d 127 (1st Cir. 1972). Since that time, most of the customary constraints on player movement have been preserved as part of the collective bargaining agreements made pursuant to the National Labor Relations Act. The terms of collective bargaining agreements are insulated from antitrust attack by the non-statutory labor exemption, addressed at **Section C**, *infra*, and the **Case File** below. A recurring question considers whether the restrictions are adequately addressed in the CBA. Another queries whether a unilateral imposition of constraints is appropriate within the context of collective bargaining pursuant to the National Labor Relations Act.

B. COLLECTIVE BARGAINING — GENERALLY

Collective bargaining is a process by which a group of workers of an industry bargain or negotiate as a collective whole (unit) with the management to determine the working conditions, benefits, and salaries of the industry. The process is governed by the National Labor Relations Act. Interestingly, in professional sports, parties to the collective bargaining agreements retain the power to individually negotiate significant elements of the employment contract.

Paul D. Staudohar
PLAYING FOR DOLLARS: LABOR RELATIONS AND THE SPORTS BUSINESS 7-13 (1996)*

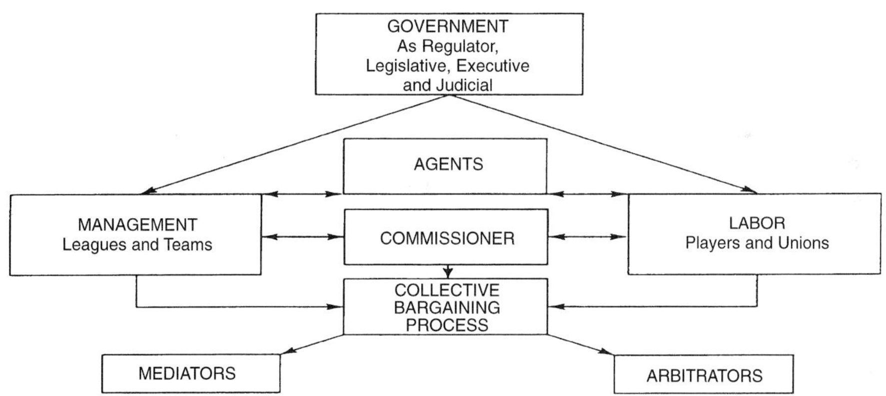

Figure 1.1 Model of Labor Relations in the Sports Industry

Sports Industry Model

A simple model illustrating the key elements of labor relations in the sports industry is shown in Figure 1.1. Underlying this model is the proposition that industrial relations includes the institutions, theories, and processes for resolving contending money and power claims in the employment relationship. The

* Reprinted from Paul D. Staudohar: PLAYING FOR DOLLARS: LABOR RELATIONS AND THE SPORTS BUSINESS. Copyright © 1996 Cornell University. Used by permission of the publisher, Cornell University Press.

three principal participants in the industrial relations function are government, management, and labor, and government's role is primarily that of regulator of the other two institutions.

The federal government performs the regulatory function under its legislative, executive, and judicial branches. Labor relations in sports are formalized under a system of union representation and collective bargaining, and therefore the National Labor Relations Act of 1935 provides a basic legal framework that carries with it a half-century of experience in other areas of American commerce. Hundreds of decisions by the National Labor Relations Board and federal courts, which interpret and apply the law to collective bargaining, right to strike, and antitrust policy, have substantial effects on the sports industry.

Management, operating through league structures and team ownership, provides for the planning, supervision, and control of corporate enterprise decisions. The leagues have the responsibility for such functions as negotiating collective bargaining agreements, setting rules for drafting of players, determining policies for the enforcement of management rights, and negotiating national television agreements. Owners of clubs give up much of their authority to the league offices but retain decision-making authority in areas such as negotiating individual player contracts, movement of players to other teams (subject to negotiated agreement with the union), hiring coaches and front office personnel, and entering into local television contracts.

Labor refers to the players and their unions. The principal objective of the sports union is to promote its effectiveness in collective bargaining. In achieving its objectives, the union (1) engages in organizing its membership for solidarity, (2) negotiates contracts applicable to all players, (3) uses pressure tactics such as strikes and picketing, if necessary, (4) enforces the terms of the negotiated agreement through the grievance procedure, and (5) serves an internal governmental function in conducting meetings, voting on contracts negotiated, and providing other means of communication to members. Since nearly all players at the major league level pay substantial dues to their unions, these organizations constitute a formidable presence in collective bargaining.

As shown in Figure 1.1, two other participants interact with management and labor in sports: the commissioner and agents. The role of the commissioner varies among sports. Theoretically, the commissioner is supposed to serve both management and labor and be a public spokesperson. As a practical matter, in that they are selected, paid, and retained at the discretion of management, commissioners tend to line up more on the side of management on contentious issues. Nonetheless, commissioners serve as a kind of buffer between the two sides in areas of dispute and seek to represent the interests of both in areas of mutual benefit.

In contract, agents are clearly a thorn in the side of management. As the representatives of players in individual salary contract negotiations, agents have added a powerful impetus to raising average salaries to dizzying heights. Some agents also represent players in managing their assets and in outside commercial ventures such as television commercials. Management resents the intrusion of agents in matters of their control over players, and some impartial observers view agents as a destructive force in sports. But their success in enhancing the economic welfare of their clients is undeniable, and agents will retain their influential role unless the players' unions take over the individual contract negotiating function. A possible compromise, which is currently being done in football and basketball, is the screening of agents to help avoid players being taken advantage of by unscrupulous agents.

The figure does not depict a role for agents in the collective bargaining process. They are involved only in the limited sense of handling individual salary negotiations, which may include incentives and bonuses but not for all players as a group. In contrast, minimum player salaries, meal money, playoff play, pensions, and other compensation issues are negotiated by the unions for all players.

There are two additional participants shown in Figure 1.1 who may become involved in the collective bargaining process: mediators and arbitrators. These are neutrals who assist in the resolution of disputes, either negotiation impasses or grievances. Until recently, many of the battles between management and labor in sports have been fought in the courts. As labor relations in sports evolves and becomes more mature, third-party neutrals are taking on a more varied and important role than in the past.

Collective Bargaining

National Labor Relations Act

Workers involved in interstate commerce, which includes professional team sports, are covered by the National Labor Relations Act (NLRA), as amended. Section 7 of this law provides three basic rights that form the heart of labor relations policy in the United States: (1) the right to self-organization, to form, join, or assist labor organizations; (2) the right to bargain collectively through representatives of their own choosing; and (3) the right to engage in "concerted activities" for employees' mutual aid or protection. In short, workers are permitted to unionize, bargain collectively, and use pressure tactics (e.g., strike and picket) to achieve their legitimate objectives. Administration is carried out by the National Labor Relations Board (NLRB) and the federal courts.

The NLRB enforces the law by policing unfair labor practices committed by either labor or management. For example, the employer and union are forbidden from interfering with employees' rights under section 7, and allegations of such violations are handled by the NLRB. Also administered by the NLRB is a machinery for determining appropriate units or groups of employees qualified to vote in a union representation election and for conducting such elections by secret ballot vote. Finally, the NLRB reviews questions concerning what issues are subject to negotiation under the law. The NLRB is not currently active in the administration of unit determination and elections in the major sports, although it may become so if a new league is formed. Units include active players, and elections involving players have resulted in the choice of an exclusive bargaining agency. Most of the NLRB's current work in sports involves unfair labor practices and scope of bargaining.

On unfair labor practices, two common allegations in sports are that the employer has disciplined or discharged players for engaging in union activities and that the employer has refused to bargain in "good faith." Good faith bargaining requires that the parties communicate through proposals and counterproposals and that they make every reasonable effort to reach agreement. In certain cases, employers must furnish basic information about finances and budgets in order to comply with good faith dictates. There has been recurring conflict over this issue in sports, since owners are reluctant to disclose financial data to unions.

The scope of bargaining is defined in the NLRA as including wages, hours, and working conditions. Wages include pay, fringe benefits, and bonus payments; hours refer to time spent on the job; and working conditions are factors influencing the work environment, such as work rules, safety, and seniority. These topics are considered by the NLRB to be mandatory subjects for bargaining that must be negotiated in good faith. So-called permissive subjects for bargaining are those on which management is not obligated to negotiate but may do so if it wishes. This includes management rights or prerogatives that the employer has an exclusive right to determine. Illegal subjects are those the law prohibits from being negotiated. From time to time, the NLRB has been asked to rule in a sports industry case on whether a subject, such as wage scales or use of artificial turf, is negotiable.

The Structure of Bargaining

The characteristics of bargaining units are generally the same throughout the team sports. All active league players are in the unit, and nearly all players are members of their respective unions. Clubs join together in bargaining with unions so that the negotiated contract in each sport applies to all teams uniformly. The formal bargaining structure influences the diversity of individual and organizational interests that must be accommodated during the negotiation of an agreement. Conflict is inherent in nearly all negotiating situations, both between the parties and within the union or team management.

For most private industry and public employment, bargaining is limited to a single union dealing with a single firm or government employer. In several industries, however, contracts are negotiated on a national basis, applying to employees throughout the country. Because of the weakening of some firms in major American industries, the traditional style of pattern bargaining — in which agreements reached with a target firm have a substantial influence on agreements reached by the same union with other firms in the industry — is becoming less important. In the United States about one-sixth of all collective bargaining agreements are negotiated by associations of private employers. Mutliemployer bargaining is found in the lumber, coal, construction, longshoring, railroad, trucking, hotel, and retail grocery industries. It is also found in professional sports, in which individual teams band together through the league format to negotiate a contract with the players' union that applies equally to all teams. The agreements reached in professional sports are not industry-wide, however, because each of the sports has a separate contract with union. Another feature that makes sports unique is the multilateral nature of bargaining. The clubs bargain as a group with unions over certain aspects of wages, hours, and working conditions, but the most important issue — individual salary — is negotiated between the club and player. The significance of this distinctive element of the structure of sports bargaining will be evident in several examples offered in later chapters to illustrate the dynamics of the process. Unions have been actively involved in clearing the way for greater labor market freedom for players to negotiate individual contracts, but their role is indirect in that they are not responsible for reaching agreement on individual salaries.

Jack Barbash calls bargaining a "love-hate," "cooperation-conflict" relationship. The parties realize their common interest in maximizing the income that finances their respective shares. But conflict arises over division of the economic pie. Most American managers and union leaders, and particularly in professional sports, view negotiations as a contest in which the "smart player" wins. Negotiation *strategy* is the overall plan of how to proceed at the bargaining table — at one pole is taking the "hard line," while at the other end is cooperating. *Tactics* are the specific methods that a party uses to implement its strategy, for example, adopting unrealistic positions, trading off issues, or such pressure tactics as strikes and lockouts. The adversarial strategy thus sets the tone for the labor-management relationship and the kinds of tactics that are employed.

Tactically, both sides usually adopt extreme positions. The union has its "shopping list," in which it asks for gains on many issues far beyond what it thinks realistically possible. Management typically offers very little at the outset. Both parties recognize the need to bluff and make dire threats with no real intention of carrying them out. Although the union is ordinarily the moving party in making demands at the outset of negotiations, an effective position for management is making high, hard demands of its own at the outset. Underlying this tactic is the adage that the best defense is a good offense. In recent years, throughout American industry and increasingly in professional sports, management has been trying to get unions to accept give-backs that reduce benefits gained under the previous contract. This tactic has been generally successful in much of U.S. industry, but did not produce significant retrenchment in sports until 1995, when concessions occurred in hockey as a result of a lengthy lockout. Negotiators are keenly aware that they must ultimately secure the approval of their principals for whatever they tentatively agree on. Rejections create serious problems for both parties, who must then return to the bargaining table for further efforts at shaping acceptable compromise.

Contents of Agreements

Typical collective bargaining agreements contain many pages of legalistic language spelling out the formal relationship between the parties. Key areas of these agreements include:

1. Specification of contract length. The duration is usually from one to five years, with three years most common. There may be provisions for re-opening the contract during its life for renegotiation of certain issues.
2. Compensation, which includes wages, pensions, and other fringe benefits. In sports, there are several areas of individual compensation that are not covered in the negotiated agreement. Unions in sports negotiate the minimum standards, but supplements to the minimum are covered in the individual bargaining process.
3. Rules for the utilization of labor, such as length of the workday, work practices, overtime, and health and safety. In sports, the big issue is free agency for players, which allows them to move liberally among teams to command greater individual bargaining power.
4. Individual job rights in such areas as seniority and discipline. Concern in sports has centered on discipline for aberrant behavior such as violence, gambling, and drug abuse.
5. Rights of union and management in the bargaining relationship, such as a management rights clause and provision for union security (e.g., union shop, dues checkoff). The prevailing practice in sports is for negotiation of an agency shop. This requires players who elect not to join the union to pay a service fee to the union (usually the equivalent of union dues) for its bargaining, legal, and grievance handling services.
6. Methods for enforcing, interpreting, and administering the agreement terms on a day-to-day basis: for example, grievance procedures, grievance arbitration, and no-strike clauses.

The provisions of a collective bargaining agreement are applied to situations that arise in the employment relationship. Management and union representatives may differ in the meaning they attach to a particular contract clause. The typical pattern is for management to act on its interpretation. Then, if the union objects to management's action, a grievance will be filed and may later be decided by an arbitrator. These actions and reactions give vitality to the language of the agreement throughout its duration.

The collective bargaining process in professional sports is necessarily a multiparty phenomenon. Neither labor nor management are internally monolithic. A league is comprised of several franchises bearing few similarities, economically or otherwise. The diversity of owner personalities is remarkable. The player unions also are made up of varied personalities and interests. Players may range from the second string center to the all-pro running back. Joining the management and labor groups in the collective bargaining game is the league *qua* institution. The league role depends on the strength of the personality of the commissioner or president. Peter Uberroth, for example, is reported to have exerted great influence in the major league baseball bargaining process that resulted in the 1985 agreement. Hovering over the participants is the ever present shadow of the law. Litigation under the antitrust laws and labor statutes is common. Finally, the mediators and arbitrators, as well as other institutional personnel, add to the collective bargaining process. As you view the complexities of labor relations in professional sports, strive to understand the various forces at work within the process.

Both the labor team and the management team possess weapons for use in the process of collective bargaining. The player union may utilize the following tactics:

1. strikes with picketing;
2. formation of a new league;
3. generating a primary or secondary boycott of franchises.

The player strike may be supported by funding from other unions or a developed strike fund. The union is instrumental in economically supporting the striking players during the strike. Management possesses the following tactics:

1. lockouts;
2. using loyal management ("scab") players;
3. cancellation of the season.

Management is economically supported by strike insurance, a strike fund, or other reciprocal agreements among league franchise members. Employers may hire temporary replacement workers, even during a lockout. Employers also may hire permanent replacement workers and provide the replacement workers with priority over striking workers when the strike ends pursuant to the *Mackay Radio* Doctrine. *NLRB v. Mackay Radio & Telegraph Co.*, 304 U.S. 333 (1938). Striking workers, however, remain as "employees" under the National Labor Relations Act. The striking workers are entitled to full reinstatement upon the departure of the permanent replacement workers, unless they have acquired regular and substantially equivalent employment, or the failure to offer full reinstatement is for legitimate and substantial business reasons. *Laidlaw Corp.*, 171 N.L.R.B. 1366 (1968), *enforced*, 414 F.2d 99 (7th Cir. 1969), *cert. denied*, 397 U.S. 920 (1970). For an article arguing that the Mackay Radio Rule is not efficient, but imposes losses on permanent replacement workers, employers, striking workers, and consumers, *see* Harris, *Coase's Paradox & the Inefficiency of Permanent Strike Replacements*, 80 Wash. U. L.Q. 1185 (2002).

C. ANTITRUST LAW, LABOR, AND THE "NONSTATUTORY EXEMPTION"

The obvious restraints on player movement were historically challenged under the federal antitrust laws. Although professional baseball was held exempt from the reach of the antitrust statutes in the *Federal Baseball* and *Flood v. Kuhn* cases, Congress enacted the Curt Flood Act of 1998 to remove the exemption for major league labor purposes. *See* **Chapter 5, Section C**, *supra*.

Player restraints and other matters are regularly addressed through the collective bargaining process, pursuant to the National Labor Relations Act. A recurring question concerns whether traditional restraints and controls, including the free agent draft, are insulated from antitrust scrutiny due to a "labor exemption." Two types of labor exemptions exist: statutory and nonstatutory. "The statutory labor exemption removes from the coverage of the antitrust laws certain legitimate, albeit anticompetitive, union activities because they are favored by federal labor policy." *Powell v. National Football League*, 678 F. Supp. 777, 782 (D. Minn. 1988). Protected activities include secondary picketing and group boycotts. The source of the labor exemption is found in the Clayton Act, 15 U.S.C. §§ 17, 29, and the Norris-LaGuardia Act, 29 U.S.C. §§ 104, 105, 113. The provisions declare that union activities in furtherance of its own interests are exempt from the reach of the antitrust laws. The statutory exemption does not extend to agreements or actions between unions and non-labor groups, including employers. *See Bridgeman v. National Basketball Association*, 675 F. Supp. 960 (D.N.J. 1987).

The nonstatutory exemption excepts certain anti-competitive union-employer activities from antitrust liability. A union-employer agreement must meet three requirements to qualify for the exemption:

1. The restraint of trade primarily affects only the parties to the collective bargaining agreement;
2. The agreement concerns a mandatory subject of collective bargaining; and
3. The agreement is a product of bona fide arms'-length bargaining.

Powell v. National Football League, 930 F.2d 1293 (8th Cir. 1989), *cert. denied*, 498 U.S. 1040 (1991).

The United States Supreme Court, in *Brown v. Pro Football, Inc.* (**Case File**, *infra*), held that the nonstatutory labor exemption continues not only beyond the expiration of the collective bargaining agreement, but also beyond *impasse* in labor negotiations. A related question concerns whether management may unilaterally impose new or modified conditions of employment after expiration, or upon reaching impasse. Both inquiries are explored in the **Problem** and cases, below.

D. COMPETITIVE BALANCE — ECONOMIC PRINCIPLES

A basic premise in traditional professional sports league models is the "uncertainty of outcome" hypothesis. *See*, Neale, *The Peculiar Economics of Professional Sports*, 78 Quarterly J. of Econ. 1-14 (1964); Rottenberg, *The Baseball Player's Labor Market*, 64 J. Pol. Econ. 242, 255 (1956). Some economists contend that the prospect of winning a game motivates fan interest. El-Hodiri & Quirk, *An Economic Model of a Professional Sports League* 79 J. Pol. Econ. 1302 (1971). Others offer that it is the probability of winning a championship that drives the fan base. Whitney, *Winning Games Versus Winning Championships: The Economics of Fan Interest & Team Performance*, 26 Economic Inquiry 703-24 (1988). Another study analyzes the potential outcome further by examining the 1) short-run uncertainty of the result of an individual game; 2) uncertainty over a season regarding the eventual winners; 3) uncertainty during a season arising from play by teams in contention for a championship; and 4) long-run uncertainty arising from competition not being dominated by a single club. Cairns, Jennett & Sloane, *The Economics of Professional Team Sports: A Survey of Theory & Evidence*, 13 J. Econ. Studies 3-80 (1986). Yet, a countering theory argues that it is an overlapping mix of motivations that stimulates fan interest, including social and cultural factors over the long-run that result in habit persistence. Downward & Dawson, THE ECONOMICS OF PROFESSIONAL TEAM SPORTS 130-56 (2000). Jozsa and Guthrie conclude: "In the business of sports, successful teams create and sustain an illusion so potent and so deeply ingrained in the minds of many fans that after a certain point the attachment of fans becomes involuntary." RELOCATING TEAMS & EXPANDING LEAGUES IN PROFESSIONAL SPORTS: HOW THE MAJOR LEAGUES RESPOND TO MARKET CONDITIONS 136 (1999).

By whatever theory, competitive balance is acknowledged as a public good that is vulnerable to the occurrence of the tragedy of the commons phenomenon. Daly & Moore, *Externalities, Property Rights & the Allocation of Resources in Major League Baseball*, 19 Economic Inquiry 77, 80 (1981). Unrestricted competition in the market for players can result in domination by strong market clubs. Consequently, fan interest may wane with the attendant reduction in the market support infrastructure for the league as a whole. One writer makes a persuasive argument that the talent that turns an average team into a contender makes a disproportionately large contribution to the team's success. The intense market for star athletes, comprised of "have" and "have-not" clubs, generates an overbidding phenomenon which results in "destructive competition" whereby some participants abandon the market. Whitney, *Bidding Till Bankrupt: Destructive Competition in Professional Team Sports*, 31 Economic

Inquiry 100, 113 (1993). The tragedy occurs due to failure to take into consideration what economists refer to as a "limited positive production network externality." Rascher, *A Test of the Optimal Positive Production Network Externality in Major League Baseball*, in SPORTS ECONOMICS 27 (Fizel, Gustafson & Hadley, ed., 1999). *See also*, Bruggink & Zamparelli, *Emerging Markets in Baseball: An Econometric Model for Predicting the Expansion Teams' New Cities*, *Id.*, 49.

The primary scholarly and industry efforts focus upon league devices designed to impede the movement of players from weak market clubs to strong market teams: the reserve clause; amateur and professional drafts; waiver rules; salary caps; luxury and payroll taxes; and revenue sharing. A league's institutional mechanisms are intended to assure league-wide competitive balance. *See, e.g.*, Levin, Mitchell, Bolcker, & Will, *The Report of the Independent Members of the Commissioner's Blue Ribbon Panel on Baseball Economics* (2000). As is mentioned in **Chapter 5, Section C, Note 1**, *supra*, El-Hodiri and Quirk rely on Rottenberg's pioneering work to conclude that the combination of the reserve clause and amateur draft alone do not inhibit the feared movement of players from weak market teams to strong ones. El-Hodiri and Quirk, *Id.*, Rottenberg, *Id.* Where player talent can be bought and sold, the Coase Theorem assures that the assignment of property rights should not alter the allocation of resources. Coase, *The Problem of Social Cost*, 3 J. Law & Eco. 1 (1960). *See generally*, Demmert, THE ECONOMICS OF PROFESSIONAL TEAM SPORTS 36 (1973); Noll, *The Team Sports Industry: An Introduction*, in GOVERNMENT & THE SPORTS BUSINESS (Noll, ed. 1974). A recurring question concerns the necessary mix of additional devices needed to avoid the inevitable tragedy.

An empirical study of the effects of the draft and reserve clause on league balance in Major League Baseball from 1965-1976, however, concluded that the two devices together served as an effective restraint and the traditional views should be reconsidered. Daly & Moore, *Id.*, 94. Other scholars find that the improvement in competitive balance in Major League Baseball is attributable to the size of the talent pool population. Schmidt & Berri, 41 *Economic Inquiry* 692, 703 (2003). The effect of free agency on the efforts to assure competitive balance may be debated, although the Coase Theorem suggest there should be no impact. *See* Fishman, *Competitive Balance & Free Agency in Major League Baseball*, 14 Duke J. of Econ. 4 (2002). One writer questions whether the introduction of free agency into the mix has a negative sum effect on the quality of talent within a league, and that the attendant competitive balance is the result of "self-imposed mediocrity." Vrooman, *A General Theory of Professional Sports Leagues*, 61 So. Economic J. 971, 989 (1995). Andrew Zimbalist compares Major League Baseball's post-1995 competitive imbalance to the period of New York Yankees dominance in the 1950s and early 1960s to determine that "attendance (and revenue) today is more sensitive to team performance than it was forty and fifty years ago." Zimbalist, MAY THE BEST TEAM WIN: BASEBALL ECONOMICS & PUBLIC POLICY 51 (2003). Professor Anzivino uses eighteen correlations to calculate that "there is no question that high-payroll teams have a competitive advantage over low-payroll teams. Further, except for the NFL, the advantage is very significant, anticompetitive and unhealthy for the fans and the leagues." Anzivino, *The Correlation Between Team Payroll & Competitive Performance in Professional Sports Leagues*, 22-SUM Ent. & Sports Law. 1 (2004). Professor Fort concludes that the sharing of gate revenue and national media revenues, and the amateur draft do not work to eliminate the competitive imbalance problem, but that a combination of local revenue sharing, luxury tax on payroll, and salary cap can lead to successful results. Fort, SPORTS ECONOMICS 171-72 (2003).

PROBLEM

Teams in the Rugby League were originally composed of ex-NFL football players who turned to the game of rugby at the end of their careers. As both players and management were experienced in NFL matters, a collective bargaining agreement was adopted which was similar to previous NFL-NFLPA collective bargaining agreements. The agreement included the reserve system and free agent compensation scheme that enables the Commissioner to award draft choices, players, and cash as compensation for the loss of free agent players. The Rugby League teams draft players from college. The draft is part of the agreement, but eligibility for the draft is not specified. Ownership and management set the eligibility standards at each annual League meeting. The collective bargaining agreement between the RL and the RLPA expired by its own terms two years ago. The league has functioned as if the expired agreement remained in effect, but negotiations have stalled. Likelihood of further bargaining appears slight at best.

During the last negotiation meeting, the RL ownership representatives presented a written proposal that included the traditional draft rule which does not specify eligibility requirements. A representative mentioned orally during discussions that the owners likely would change the eligibility requirements of the draft to include foreign players. He also mentioned that the owners were in favor of limiting the signing of players to those 20 years of age and older. "In this way, we can avoid injuries. This is a game for men, not boys." Over the years, the team rosters have changed in nature from ex-NFL players to players selected in the amateur draft, or players from foreign jurisdictions hired as undrafted free agents. The modification provides for the drafting of players from "South Africa," "Australia," "England," "Scotland," "Wales," and "Ireland."

The Rugby League hired your firm as general counsel. It seeks your legal advice in planning for next year's season. The owners desire to unilaterally implement the "eligibility" modification. The owners proclaim that the league will be further stabilized by providing equal access among clubs for the services of foreign players. Under the present system, foreign players sign with the highest bidder, thus leaving the smaller market clubs with lesser rosters.

The RLPA does not favor the proposed draft eligibility rules. It threatens to challenge the draft eligibility restraints under the antitrust laws. The RLPA will "decertify," if necessary to bring the challenge. The Association will also file an unfair labor practice claim with the NLRB, if the RL unilaterally imposes the change. The senior partner instructed you as follows:

1. Assume the Rugby League is engaged in matters of interstate commerce.
2. Identify the existing legal rules governing the unilateral imposition of the "draft eligibility" standards by the RL.
3. Should the RL declare an *impasse* in negotiations at this time? Explain.
4. What arguments can you make that the nonstatutory labor exemption prevents adjudication under the antitrust laws? What arguments do you expect from counsel for the RLPA?
5. Assuming the court reaches the antitrust issues, what viable arguments can you make that the draft system of the Rugby League is valid under the antitrust laws? What counter arguments do you expect from opposing counsel? Do separate arguments apply to the reserve clause and free agent compensation system?

CASE FILE

BROWN v. PRO FOOTBALL, INC.

518 U.S. 231 (1996)

Justice BREYER delivered the opinion of the Court.

The question in this case arises at the intersection of the Nation's labor and antitrust laws.

A group of professional football players brought this antitrust suit against football club owners. The club owners had bargained with the players' union over a wage issue until they reached impasse. The owners then had agreed among themselves (but not with the union) to implement the terms of their own last best bargaining offer. The question before us is whether federal labor laws shield such an agreement from antitrust attack. We believe that they do. This Court has previously found in the labor laws an implicit antitrust exemption that applies where needed to make the collective-bargaining process work. Like the Court of Appeals, we conclude that this need makes the exemption applicable in this case.

I

We can state the relevant facts briefly. In 1987, a collective-bargaining agreement between the National Football League (NFL), a group of football clubs, and the NFL Players Association, a labor union, expired. The NFL and the Players

Association began to negotiate a new contract. In March 1989, during the negotiations, the NFL adopted Resolution G-2, a plan that would permit each club to establish a "developmental squad" of up to six rookie or "firstyear" players who, as free agents, had failed to secure a position on a regular player roster. *See* App. 42. Squad members would play in practice games and sometimes in regular games as substitutes for injured players. Resolution G-2 provided that the club owners would pay all squad members the same weekly salary.

The next month, April, the NFL presented the developmental squad plan to the Players Association. The NFL proposed a squad player salary of $1,000 per week. The Players Association disagreed. It insisted that the club owners give developmental squad players benefits and protections similar to those provided regular players, and that they leave individual squad members free to negotiate their own salaries.

Two months later, in June, negotiations on the issue of developmental squad salaries reached an impasse. The NFL then unilaterally implemented the developmental squad program by distributing to the clubs a uniform contract that embodied the terms of Resolution G-2 and the $1,000 proposed weekly salary. The League advised club owners that paying developmental squad players more or less than $1,000 per week would result in disciplinary action, including the loss of draft choices.

In May 1990, 235 developmental squad players brought this antitrust suit against the League and its member clubs. The players claimed that their employers' agreement to pay them a $1,000 weekly salary violated the Sherman Act. *See* 15 U.S.C. § 1 (forbidding agreements in restraint of trade). The Federal District Court denied the employers' claim of exemption from the antitrust laws; it permitted the case to reach the jury; and it subsequently entered judgment on a jury treble-damage award that exceeded $30 million. The NFL and its member clubs appealed.

The Court of Appeals (by a split 2-to-1 vote) reversed. The majority interpreted the labor laws as "waiv[ing] antitrust liability for restraints on competition imposed through the collective-bargaining process, so long as such restraints operate primarily in a labor market characterized by collective bargaining." 50 F.3d 1041, 1056 (D.C. Cir. 1995). The Court held, consequently, that the club owners were immune from antitrust liability. We granted certiorari to review that determination. Although we do not interpret the exemption as broadly as did the Appeals Court, we nonetheless find the exemption applicable, and we affirm that Court's immunity conclusion.

II

The immunity before us rests upon what this Court has called the "nonstatutory" labor exemption from the antitrust laws. . . . The Court has implied this exemption from federal labor statutes, which set forth a national labor policy favoring free and private collective bargaining, . . . which require good-faith bargaining over wages, hours and working conditions, . . . and which delegate related rulemaking and interpretive authority to the National Labor Relations Board . . . .

This implicit exemption reflects both history and logic. As a matter of history, Congress intended the labor statutes (from which the Court has implied the exemption) in part to adopt the views of dissenting justices in *Duplex Printing Press Co. v. Deering*, 254 U.S. 443 (1921), which justices had urged the Court to interpret broadly a different explicit "statutory" labor exemption that Congress earlier (in 1914) had written directly into the antitrust laws. . . . In the 1930's, when it subsequently enacted the labor statutes, Congress, as in 1914, hoped to prevent judicial use of antitrust law to resolve labor disputes — a kind of dispute normally inappropriate for antitrust law resolution. . . . The implicit ("nonstatutory") exemption interprets the labor statutes in accordance with this intent, namely, as limiting an antitrust court's authority to determine, in the area of industrial conflict, what is or is not a "reasonable" practice. It thereby substitutes legislative and administrative labor-related determinations for judicial antitrust-related determinations as to the appropriate legal limits of industrial conflict. . . .

As a matter of logic, it would be difficult, if not impossible, to require groups of employers and employees to bargain together, but at the same time to forbid them to make among themselves or with each other any of the competition-restricting agreements potentially necessary to make the process work or its results mutually acceptable. Thus, the implicit exemption recognizes that, to give effect to federal labor laws and policies and to allow meaningful collective bargaining to take place, some restraints on competition imposed through the bargaining process must be shielded from antitrust sanctions. . . .

The petitioners and their supporters concede, as they must, the legal existence of the exemption we have described. They also concede that, where its application is necessary to make the statutorily authorized collective-bargaining process work as Congress intended, the exemption must apply both to employers and to employees. . . . Nor does the dissent take issue with these basic principles. *See post,* at 2129. Consequently, the question before us is one of determining the exemption's scope: Does it apply to an agreement among several employers bargaining together to implement after impasse the terms of their last best good-faith wage offer? We assume that such conduct, as practiced in this case, is unobjectionable as a matter of labor law and policy. On that assumption, we conclude that the exemption applies.

Labor law itself regulates directly, and considerably, the kind of behavior here at issue — the postimpasse imposition of a proposed employment term concerning a mandatory subject of bargaining. Both the Board and the courts have held that, after impasse, labor law permits employers unilaterally to implement changes in preexisting conditions, but only insofar as the new terms meet carefully circumscribed conditions. For example, the new terms must be "reasonably comprehended" within the employer's preimpasse proposals (typically the last rejected proposals), lest by imposing more or less favorable terms, the employer unfairly undermined the union's status. . . . The collective-bargaining proceeding itself must be free of any unfair labor practice, such as an employer's failure to have bargained in good faith. . . . These regulations reflect the fact that impasse and an accompanying implementation of proposals constitute an integral part of the bargaining process. . . .

Although the caselaw we have cited focuses upon bargaining by a single employer, no one here has argued that labor law does, or should, treat multiemployer bargaining differently in this respect. Indeed, Board and court decisions suggest that the joint implementation of proposed terms after impasse is a familiar practice in the context of multiemployer bargaining. . . .

Multiemployer bargaining itself is a well-established, important, pervasive method of collective bargaining, offering advantages to both management and labor. . . . The upshot is that the practice at issue here plays a significant role in a collective-bargaining process that itself comprises an important part of the Nation's industrial relations system.

In these circumstances, to subject the practice to antitrust law is to require antitrust courts to answer a host of important practical questions about how collective bargaining over wages, hours and working conditions is to proceed — the very result that the implicit labor exemption seeks to avoid. And it is to place in jeopardy some of the potentially beneficial labor-related effects that multiemployer bargaining can achieve. That is because unlike labor law, which sometimes welcomes anticompetitive agreements conducive to industrial harmony, antitrust law forbids all agreements among competitors (such as competing employers) that unreasonably lessen competition among or between them in virtually any respect whatsoever. . . . Antitrust law also sometimes permits judges or juries to premise antitrust liability upon little more than uniform behavior among competitors, preceded by conversations implying that later uniformity might prove desirable, . . . or accompanied by other conduct that in context suggests that each competitor failed to make an independent decision . . .

If the antitrust laws apply, what are employers to do once impasse is reached? If all impose terms similar to their last joint offer, they invite an antitrust action premised upon identical behavior (along with prior or accompanying conversations) as tending to show a common understanding or agreement. If any, or all, of them individually impose terms that differ significantly from that offer, they invite an unfair labor practice charge. Indeed, how can employers safely discuss their offers together even before a bargaining impasse occurs? A preimpasse discussion about, say, the practical advantages or disadvantages of a particular proposal, invites a later antitrust claim that they agreed to limit the kinds of action each would later take should an impasse occur. The same is true of postimpasse discussions aimed at renewed negotiations with the union. Nor would adherence to the terms of an expired collective-bargaining agreement eliminate a potentially plausible antitrust claim charging that they had "conspired" or tacitly "agreed" to do so, particularly if maintaining the status quo were not in the immediate economic self-interest of some. . . . All this is to say that to permit antitrust liability here threatens to introduce instability and uncertainty into the collective-bargaining process, for antitrust law often forbids or discourages the kinds of joint discussions and behavior that the collective bargaining process invites or requires.

We do not see any obvious answer to this problem. We recognize, as the Government suggests, that, in principle, antitrust courts might themselves try to evaluate particular kinds of employer understandings, finding them "reasonable" (hence lawful) where justified by collective-bargaining necessity. But any such evaluation means a web of detailed rules spun by many different nonexpert antitrust judges and juries, not a set of labor rules enforced by a single expert administrative body, namely the Labor Board. The labor laws give the Board, not antitrust courts, primary responsibility for policing the collective-bargaining process. And one of their objectives was to take from antitrust courts the authority to determine, through application of the antitrust laws, what is socially or economically desirable collective-bargaining policy. . . .

III

Both petitioners and their supporters advance several suggestions for drawing the exemption boundary line short of this case. We shall explain why we find them unsatisfactory.

A

Petitioners claim that the implicit exemption applies only to labor-management agreements — a limitation that they deduce from caselaw language, . . . and from a proposed principle — that the exemption must rest upon labor-management consent. The language, however, reflects only the fact that the cases previously before the Court involved collective-bargaining agreements, . . . the language does not reflect the exemption's rationale. . . .

Nor do we see how an exemption limited by petitioners' principle of labor-management consent could work. One cannot mean the principle literally — that the exemption applies only to understandings embodied in a collective-bargaining agreement — for the collective-bargaining process may take place before the making of any agreement or after an agreement has expired. Yet a multi-employer bargaining process itself necessarily involves many procedural and substantive understandings among participating employers as well as with the union. Petitioners cannot rescue their principle by claiming that the exemption applies only insofar as both labor and management consent to those understandings. Often labor will not (and should not) consent to certain common bargaining positions that employers intend to maintain. . . . Similarly, labor need not consent to certain tactics that this Court has approved as part of the multiemployer bargaining process, such as unit-wide lockouts and the use of temporary replacements. . . .

Petitioners cannot save their consent principle by weakening it, as by requiring union consent only to the multiemployer bargaining process itself. This general consent is automatically present whenever multiemployer bargaining takes place. . . . As so weakened, the principle cannot help decide which related practices are, or are not, subject to antitrust immunity.

B

The Solicitor General argues that the exemption should terminate at the point of impasse. After impasse, he says, "employers no longer have a duty under the labor laws to maintain the status quo," and "are free as a matter of labor law to negotiate individual arrangements on an interim basis with the union." Brief for United States et al. as Amici Curiae 17.

Employers, however, are not completely free at impasse to act independently. The multiemployer bargaining unit ordinarily remains intact; individual employers cannot withdraw. . . . The duty to bargain survives; employers must stand ready to resume collective bargaining. . . . And individual employers can negotiate individual interim agreements with the union only insofar as those agreements are consistent with "the duty to abide by the results of group bargaining.". . . Regardless, the absence of a legal "duty" to act jointly is not determinative. This Court has implied antitrust immunities that extend beyond statutorily required joint action to joint action that a statute "expressly or impliedly allows or assumes must also be immune.". . .

More importantly, the simple "impasse" line would not solve the basic problem we have described above. . . . Labor law permits employers, after impasse, to engage in considerable joint behavior, including joint lockouts and replacement hiring. . . . Indeed, as a general matter, labor law often limits employers to four options at impasse: (1) maintain the status quo, (2) implement their last offer, (3) lock out their workers (and either shut down or hire temporary replacements), or (4) negotiate separate interim agreements with the union. . . . What is to happen if the parties cannot reach an interim agreement? The other alternatives are limited. Uniform employer conduct is likely. Uniformity — at least when accompanied by discussion of the matter — invites antitrust attack. And such attack would ask antitrust courts to decide the lawfulness of activities intimately related to the bargaining process.

The problem is aggravated by the fact that "impasse" is often temporary, . . . it may differ from bargaining only in degree, . . . it may be manipulated by the parties for bargaining purposes, . . . and it may occur several times during the course of a single labor dispute, since the bargaining process is not over when the first impasse is reached. . . . How are employers to discuss future bargaining positions during a temporary impasse? Consider, too, the adverse consequences that flow from failing to guess how an antitrust court would later draw the impasse line. Employers who erroneously concluded that impasse had not been reached would risk antitrust liability were they collectively to maintain the status quo, while employers who erroneously concluded that impasse had occurred would risk unfair labor practice charges for prematurely suspending multiemployer negotiations.

The Solicitor General responds with suggestions for softening an "impasse" rule by extending the exemption after impasse "for such time as would be reasonable in the circumstances" for employers to consult with counsel, confirm that impasse has occurred, and adjust their business operations, by reestablishing the exemption once there is a "resumption of good-faith bargaining,". . . and by looking to antitrust law's "rule of reason" to shield — "in some circumstances" — such joint actions as the unit-wide lockout or the concerted maintenance of previously-established joint benefit or retirement plans. . . . But even as so modified, the impasse-related rule creates an exemption that can evaporate in the middle of the bargaining process, leaving later antitrust courts free to second-guess the parties' bargaining decisions and consequently forcing them to choose their collective-bargaining responses in light of what they predict or fear that antitrust courts, not labor law administrators, will eventually decide. . . .

C

Petitioners and their supporters argue in the alternative for a rule that would exempt postimpasse agreement about bargaining "tactics," but not postimpasse agreement about substantive "terms," from the reach of antitrust. . . . They recognize, however, that both the Board and the courts have said that employers can, and often do, employ the imposition of "terms" as a bargaining "tactic." . . . This concession as to joint "tactical" implementation would turn the presence of an antitrust exemption upon a determination of the employers' primary purpose or motive. . . . But to ask antitrust courts, insulated from the bargaining process, to investigate an employer group's subjective motive is to ask them to conduct an inquiry often more amorphous than those we have previously discussed. And, in our view, a labor/antitrust line drawn on such a basis would too often raise the same related (previously discussed) problems. . . .

D

The petitioners make several other arguments. They point, for example, to cases holding applicable, in collective-bargaining contexts, general "backdrop" statutes, such as a state statute requiring a plant-closing employer to make employee severance payments, . . . and a state statute mandating certain minimum health benefits. . . . Those statutes, however, "'neither encourage[d] nor discourage[d] the collective-bargaining processes that are the subject of the [federal labor laws].'" . . . Neither did those statutes come accompanied with antitrust's labor-related history. . . .

Petitioners also say that irrespective of how the labor exemption applies elsewhere to multiemployer collective bargaining, professional sports is "special." We can understand how professional sports may be special in terms of, say, interest, excitement, or concern. But we do not understand how they are special in respect to labor law's antitrust exemption. We concede that the clubs that make up a professional sports league are not completely independent economic competitors, as they depend upon a degree of cooperation for economic survival. . . . In the present context, however, that circumstance makes the league more like a single bargaining employer, which analogy seems irrelevant to the legal issue before us.

We also concede that football players often have special individual talents, and, unlike many unionized workers, they often negotiate their pay individually with their employers. . . . But this characteristic seems simply a feature, like so many others, that might give employees (or employers) more (or less) bargaining power, that might lead some (or all) of them to favor a particular kind of bargaining, or that might lead to certain demands at the bargaining table. We do not see how it could make a critical legal difference in determining the underlying framework in which bargaining is to take place. . . . Indeed, it would be odd to fashion an antitrust exemption that gave additional advantages to professional football players (by virtue of their superior bargaining power) that transport workers, coal miners, or meat packers would not enjoy.

The dissent points to other "unique features" of the parties' collective bargaining relationship, which, in the dissent's view, make the case "atypical.". . . It says, for example, that the employers imposed the restraint simply to enforce compliance with league-wide rules, and that the bargaining consisted of nothing more than the sending of a "notice," and therefore amounted only to "so-called" bargaining. . . . Insofar as these features underlie an argument for looking to the employers' true purpose, we have already discussed them. . . . Insofar as they suggest that there was not a genuine impasse, they fight the basic assumption upon which the District Court, the Court of Appeals, the petitioners, and this Court, rest the case. . . . Ultimately, we cannot find a satisfactory basis for distinguishing football players from other organized workers. We therefore conclude that all must abide by the same legal rules.

* * *

For these reasons, we hold that the implicit ("nonstatutory") antitrust exemption applies to the employer conduct at issue here. That conduct took place during and immediately after a collective-bargaining negotiation. It grew out of, and was directly related to, the lawful operation of the bargaining process. It involved a matter that the parties were required to negotiate collectively. And it concerned only the parties to the collective-bargaining relationship.

Our holding is not intended to insulate from antitrust review every joint imposition of terms by employers, for an agreement among employers could be sufficiently distant in time and in circumstances from the collective-bargaining process that a rule permitting antitrust intervention would not significantly interfere with that process. . . . We need not decide in this case whether, or where, within these extreme outer boundaries to draw that line. Nor would it be appropriate for us to do so without the detailed views of the Board, to whose "specialized judgment" Congress "intended to leave" many of the "inevitable questions concerning multiemployer bargaining bound to arise in the future.". . .

The judgment of the Court of Appeals is affirmed.

It is so ordered.

* * *

MACKEY v. NATIONAL FOOTBALL LEAGUE

543 F.2d 606 (8th Cir. 1976)

LAY, Circuit Judge.

This is an appeal by the National Football League (NFL), twenty-six of its member clubs, and its Commissioner, Alvin Ray "Pete" Rozelle, from a district court judgment holding the "Rozelle Rule" to be violative of § 1 of the Sherman Act, and enjoining its enforcement.

This action was initiated by a group of present and former NFL players, appellees herein, pursuant to §§ 4 and 16 of the Clayton Act, 15 U.S.C. §§ 15 and 26, and § 1 of the Sherman Act, 15 U.S.C. § 1. Their complaint alleged that the defendants' enforcement of the Rozelle Rule constituted an illegal combination and conspiracy in restraint of trade denying professional football players the right to freely contract for their services. Plaintiffs sought injunctive relief and treble damages.

The district court, the Honorable Earl R. Larson presiding, conducted a plenary trial . . . and entered judgment in their favor on the issue of liability. This appeal followed.

The district court held that the defendants' enforcement of the Rozelle Rule constituted a concerted refusal to deal and a group boycott, and was therefore a *per se* violation of the Sherman Act. Alternatively, finding that the evidence offered in support of the clubs' contention that the Rozelle Rule is necessary to the successful operation of the NFL insufficient to justify the restrictive effects of the Rule, the court concluded that the Rozelle Rule was invalid under the Rule of Reason standard. Finally, the court rejected the clubs' argument that the Rozelle Rule was immune from attack under the Sherman Act because it had been the subject of a collective bargaining agreement between the club owners and the National Football League Players Association (NFLPA).

The defendants raise two basic issues on this appeal: (1) whether the so-called labor exemption to the antitrust laws immunize the NFL's enforcement of the Rozelle Rule from antitrust liability; and (2) if not, whether the Rozelle Rule and the manner in which it has been enforced violate the antitrust laws. . . .

HISTORY

* * *

For a number of years, the NFL has operated under a reserve system whereby every player who signs a contract with the NFL club is bound to play for that club, and no other, for the term of the contract plus one additional year at the option of the club. . . . Once a player signs a Standard Player Contract, he is bound to his team for at least two years. He may, however, become a free agent at the end of the option year by playing that season under a renewed contract rather than signing a new one. A player "playing out his option" is subject to a 10% salary cut during the option year.

Prior to 1963, a team which signed a free agent who had previously been under contract to another club was not obligated to compensate the player's former club. In 1963, after R.C. Owens played out his option with the San Francisco 49ers and signed a contract with the Baltimore Colts, the member clubs of the NFL unilaterally adopted the . . . Rozelle Rule, as an amendment to the League's Constitution and Bylaws:

> [W]henever a player, becoming a free agent in such manner, thereafter signed a contract with a different club in the League, then, unless mutually satisfactory arrangements have been concluded between the two League clubs, the Commissioner may name and then award to the former club one or more players, from the Active, Reserve, or Selection List (including future selection choices) of the acquiring club as the Commissioner in his sole discretion deems fair and equitable; any such decision by the Commissioner shall be final and conclusive.

* * *

During the period from 1963 through 1974, 176 players played out their options. Of that number, 34 signed with other teams. In three of those cases, the former club waived compensation. In 27 cases, the clubs involved mutually agreed upon compensation. Commissioner Rozelle awarded compensation in the four remaining cases. . . .

THE LABOR EXEMPTION ISSUE

* * *

To determine the applicability of the nonstatutory exemption we must first decide whether there has been any agreement between the parties concerning the Rozelle Rule.

* * *

Based on the fact that the 1968 agreement incorporated by reference the Rozelle Rule and provided that free agent rules would not be changed, we conclude that the 1968 agreement required that the Rozelle Rule govern when a player played out his option and signed with another team. Assuming, without deciding, that the 1970 agreement embodied a similar understanding, we proceed to a consideration of whether the agreements fall within the scope of the nonstatutory labor exemption.

Governing Principles

* * *

We find the proper accommodation to be: First, the labor policy favoring collective bargaining may potentially be given pre-eminence over the antitrust laws where the restraint on trade primarily affects only the parties to the collective bargaining relationship. . . . Second, federal labor policy is implicated sufficiently to prevail only where the agreement sought to be exempted concerns a mandatory subject of collective bargaining. . . . Finally, the policy favoring collective bargaining is furthered to the degree necessary to override the antitrust laws only where the agreement sought to be exempted is the product of bona fide arm's length bargaining. . . .

Application

Applying these principles to the facts presented here, we think it clear that the alleged restraint on trade effected by the Rozelle Rule affects only the parties to the agreements sought to be exempted. . . .

Mandatory Subject of Bargaining

Under § 8(d) of the National Labor Relations Act, . . . mandatory subjects of bargaining pertain to "wages, hours, and other terms and conditions of employment. . . ."

On its face, the Rozelle Rule does not deal with "wages, hours and other terms or conditions of employment" but with inter-team compensation when a player's contractual obligation to one team expires and he is signed by another. Viewed as such, it would not constitute a mandatory subject of collective bargaining. The district court found, however, that the Rule operates to restrict a player's ability to move from one team to another and depresses player salaries. There is substantial evidence in the record to support these findings. Accordingly, we hold that the Rozelle Rule constitutes a mandatory bargaining subject within the meaning of the National Labor Relations Act.

Bona Fide Bargaining

The district court found that the parties' collective bargaining history reflected nothing which could be legitimately characterized as bargaining over the Rozelle Rule; that, in part due to its recent formation and inadequate finances, the NFLPA, at least prior to 1974, stood in a relatively weak bargaining position vis-a-vis the clubs; and that "the Rozelle Rule was unilaterally imposed by the NFL and member club defendants upon the players in 1963 and has been imposed on the players from 1963 through the present date."

On the basis of our independent review of the record, including the parties' bargaining history as set forth above, we find substantial evidence to support the finding that there was no bona fide arm's-length bargaining over the Rozelle Rule preceding the execution of the 1968 and 1970 agreements. . . .

In view of the foregoing, we hold that the agreements between the clubs and the players embodying the Rozelle Rule do not qualify for the labor exemption. . . .

ANTITRUST ISSUES

We turn, then, to the question of whether the Rozelle Rule, as implemented, violates § 1 of the Sherman Act, which declares illegal "every contract, combination . . . or conspiracy, in restraint of trade or commerce among the several states." 15 U.S.C. § 1 . . . .

Players' Services as a Product Market

The clubs and the Commissioner first urge that the only product market arguably affected by the Rozelle Rule is the market for players' services, and that the restriction of competition for players' services is not a type of restraint proscribed by the Sherman Act. In support of this contention, defendants rely on § 6 of the Clayton Act, . . . and on language construing the statute in *Apex Hosiery Co. v. Leader* . . . .

On the surface, the language relied on by defendants lends merit to the defense. However, we cannot overlook the context in which the language arose. Section 6 of the Clayton Act was enacted for the benefit of unions to exempt certain of their activities from the antitrust laws after courts had applied the Sherman Act to legitimate labor activities. . . . In *Apex*, the Court condoned restrictions on competition for employee services imposed by the employees themselves, not by employers.

In other cases concerning professional sports, courts have not hesitated to apply the Sherman Act to club owner imposed restraints on competition for players' services. . . . In other contexts, courts have subjected similar employer imposed restraints to the scrutiny of the anti-trust laws. . . .

We hold that restraints on competition within the market for players' services fall within the ambit of the Sherman Act.

Per Se Violation

We review next the district court's holding that the Rozelle Rule is *per se* violative of the Sherman Act.

The express language of the Sherman Act is broad enough to render illegal nearly every type of agreement between businessmen. The Supreme Court has held, however, that only those agreements which "unreasonably" restrain trade come within the proscription of the Act. . . .

As the courts gained experience with antitrust problems arising under the Sherman Act, they identified certain types of agreements as being so consistently unreasonable that they may be deemed to be illegal *per se*, without inquiry into their purported justifications.

* * *

Among the practices which have been deemed to be so pernicious as to be illegal *per se* are group boycotts and concerted refusals to deal. . . . The term "concerted refusals to deal" has been defined as "an agreement by two or more persons not to do business with other individuals, or to do business with them only on specified terms.". . . The term "group boycott" generally connotes "a refusal to deal or an inducement of others not to deal or to have business relations with tradesmen.". . .

The district court found that the Rozelle Rule operates to significantly deter clubs from negotiating with and signing free agents. . . . The court concluded that the Rozelle Rule, as enforced, thus constituted a group boycott and a concerted refusal to deal, and was a *per se* violation of the Sherman Act.

There is substantial evidence in the record to support the district court's findings as to the effects of the Rozelle Rule. We think, however, that this case presents unusual circumstances rendering it inappropriate to declare the Rozelle Rule illegal *per se* without undertaking an inquiry into the purported justifications for the Rule.

First, the line of cases which has given rise to *per se* illegality for the type of agreements involved here generally concerned agreements between business competitors in the traditional sense. . . . Here . . . the NFL assumes some of the characteristics of a joint venture in that each member club has a stake in the success of the other teams. No one club is interested in driving another team out of business, since if the League fails, no one team can survive. . . . Although businessmen cannot wholly evade the antitrust laws by characterizing their operation as a joint venture, we conclude that the unique nature of the business of professional football renders it inappropriate to mechanically apply *per se* illegality rules here. . . .

Second, one of the underpinnings of the *per se* analysis is the avoidance of lengthy and burdensome inquiries into the operation of the particular industry in question. Here, the district court has already undertaken an exhaustive inquiry into the operation of the NFL and the effects of and justifications for the Rozelle Rule.

Rule of Reason

The focus of an inquiry under the Rule of Reason is whether the restraint imposed is justified by legitimate business purposes, and is no more restrictive than necessary. . . .

In defining the restraint of competition for players' services, the district court found that the Rozelle Rule significantly deters clubs from negotiating with and signing free agents; that it acts as a substantial deterrent to players playing out their options and becoming free agents; that it significantly decreases players' bargaining power in contract negotiations; that players are thus denied the right to sell their services in a free and open market; that as a result, the salaries paid by each club are lower than if competitive bidding were allowed to prevail; and that absent the Rozelle Rule, there would be increased movement in interstate commerce of players from one club to another.

We find substantial evidence in the record to support these findings. Witnesses for both sides testified that there would be increased player movement absent the Rozelle Rule. . . .

In support of their contention that the restraints effected by the Rozelle Rule are not unreasonable, the defendants asserted a number of justifications. First, they argued that without the Rozelle Rule, star players would flock to cities having natural advantages . . .; that competitive balance throughout the League would thus be destroyed; and that the distinction of competitive balance would ultimately lead to diminished spectator interest, franchise failures, and perhaps the demise of the NFL. . . . Second, the defendants contended that the Rozelle Rule is necessary to protect the clubs' investment in scouting expenses and player development costs. Third, they asserted that players must work together for a substantial period of time in order to function effectively as a team; that elimination of the Rozelle Rule would lead to increased player movement and a concomitant reduction in player continuity; and that the quality of play in the NFL would thus suffer, leading to reduced spectator interest, and financial detriment both to the clubs and the players. Conflicting evidence was adduced at trial by both sides with respect to the validity of these asserted justifications.

The district court held the defendants' asserted justifications unavailing. . . . The court further concluded that elimination of the Rozelle Rule would have no significant disruptive effects, either immediate or long term, on professional football. In conclusion, the court held that the Rozelle Rule was unreasonable in that it was overly broad, unlimited in duration, unaccompanied by procedural safeguards, and employed in conjunction with other anticompetitive practices such as the draft, Standard Player Contract, option clause, and the no-tampering rules.

We agree that the asserted need to recoup player development costs cannot justify the restraints of the Rozelle Rule. That expense is an ordinary cost of doing business and is not peculiar to professional football. Moreover, because of its unlimited duration, the Rozelle Rule is far more restrictive than necessary to fulfill that need.

We agree, in view of the evidence adduced at trial with respect to existing player turnover by way of trades, retirements and new players entering the

League, that the club owners' arguments respecting player continuity cannot justify the Rozelle Rule. . . .

In sum, we hold that the Rozelle Rule, as enforced, unreasonably restrains trade in violation of § 1 of the Sherman Act.

With the exception of the district court's finding that implementation of the Rozelle Rule constitutes a *per se* violation of § 1 of the Sherman Act and except as it is otherwise modified herein, the judgment of the district court is AFFIRMED.

ROBERTSON v. NATIONAL BASKETBALL ASSOCIATION

389 F. Supp. 867 (S.D.N.Y. 1975)

ROBERT L. CARTER, District Judge.

I. History of the Litigation

A. *Nature of the Action*

This action was instituted in 1970 pursuant to Sections 4 and 16 of the Clayton Act, 15 U.S.C. §§ 15 and 26, to recover treble damages, costs and injunctive relief for violation of Sections 1 and 2 of the Sherman Act, 15 U.S.C. §§ 1 and 2. . . .

B. *Background Facts*

This litigation began after reports in the spring of 1970 of a proposed merger between the NBA and the ABA. Plaintiffs' amended complaint charges defendants with conspiring to restrain competition for the services and skills of professional basketball players through such devices as the college draft, the reserve clause in the Uniform Player Contract (the Uniform Contract), the compensation plan attached to the reserve clause, and various boycott and blacklisting techniques. . . .

In May, 1970, this court (Tenney, J.) preliminarily enjoined the defendants from entering into "any merger, consolidation, or acquisition or combination by any means," except that defendants were permitted to negotiate a proposed merger for the sole purpose of petitioning Congress for antitrust exemption legislation. . . .

II. The Immediate Controversy

A. *Plaintiffs' Claims*

1. *Count 1*

Count One of the complaint alleges that at least since its inception in 1946, the NBA has engaged in a concerted plan, combination, or conspiracy to monopolize and restrain trade and commerce in major league professional basketball by: (1) controlling, regulating and dictating the terms upon which professional major league basketball is played in the United States; (2) allocating and dividing the market of professional player talent; and (3) enforcing its monopoly and restraint of trade through boycotts, blacklists and concerted refusals to deal. . . .

* * *

VI. The Motions for Summary Judgment

* * *

B. *The Labor Issues*

The two leagues claim that the complaint has tried to cast in antitrust terms a series of demands and issues which naturally and lawfully belong on the bargaining table. The intent of the suit is to increase plaintiffs' individual bargaining power. This, it is argued, conflicts with the policy announced in the National Labor Relations Act. The defendants' more fundamental contention, however, is that they are protected against the impact of the antitrust laws by a labor exemption.

1. *Plaintiffs' Standing to Sue Under the Antitrust Laws*

It is undoubtedly true that the intent of Congress was and is to encourage collective bargaining as the means of settling labor disputes. . . .

Section 4 of the Clayton Act, 15 U.S.C. § 15, grants standing for antitrust suits to any "person who shall be injured in his business or property by reason of anything forbidden in the antitrust laws." Courts have consistently allowed plaintiffs to sue their employers for alleged antitrust violations of the nature here asserted. . . .

In the sports area, the standing of players to assert antitrust violations similar to those alleged here has generally not been questioned. . . . Standing has been found to exist for hockey players challenging the reserve system, for a basketball player challenging the college draft system, for a golfer challenging a group boycott, for a football player challenging a blacklisting following a violation of the reserve clause. . . .

Plaintiffs have standing to bring this suit.

2. *Labor Exemption from Antitrust Laws*

There is no operative labor exemption barring or protecting the defendants from being sued for antitrust violations. The statutory bases for labor's exemption from the application of the antitrust laws are found in Sections 6 and 20 of the Clayton Act. A simple and concise answer to defendants' contention is that the exemption extends only to labor or union activities, and not to the activities of employers.

* * *

[I]n *United States v. Hutcheson*, 312 U.S. 219, the Court had declared that all three acts — Sherman, Clayton and Norris-LaGuardia — must be read in conjunction with each other to determine where concerted activities of unions are prohibited under the antitrust laws. . . .

Allen Bradley made clear that the "labor exemption" was created for the benefit of unions. While later cases revealed the possibility of a circumscribed exemption for employers, which might arise derivatively, and become effective when employers are sued by third parties for the activities of unions, the protection of the exemption is afforded only to employers who have acted jointly with the labor organization in connection with or in preparation for collective bargaining negotiations.

* * *

[D]efendants rely on a two-fold "test" which purports to determine when the exemption is available to employers. . . .

> 1) Are the challenged practices directed against non-parties to the relationship; if they are not, then 2) are they mandatory subjects of collective bargaining? If the answer to No. 1 is no, and to No. 2 yes, the practices are immune. . . .

* * *

In *Jewel Tea*, several unions had entered into identical collective bargaining agreements with all retail employers in the meat industry; the clause in dispute provided for uniform closing hours in all the meat departments. One employer attacked the clause arguing that he had only signed the agreement under threat of strike. As in *Pennington*, the fundamental question was whether the antitrust laws applied to the unions; could the agreement, obtained by the unions for their own benefit, be attacked, or was it exempt? No mention was made of labor exemption for employers. . . . The exemption was held applicable. . . .

Whatever support may be found in the *Jewel Tea* concurring opinion for defendants' test is completely undermined by the Court's explicit statement in *Pennington* that:

> [t]his is not to say that an agreement resulting from union-employer negotiations is automatically exempt from Sherman Act scrutiny simply because the negotiations involve a compulsory subject of bargaining, regardless of the subject or the form and content of the agreement. . . .
>
> [T]here are limits to what a union or an employer may offer or extract in the name of wages, and *because they must bargain does not mean that the agreement reached may disregard other laws.*

See Philadelphia Hockey, supra, 351 F. Supp. at 518. "Mandatory subjects of collective bargaining" do not carry talismanic immunity from the antitrust laws. . . .

Nor does the "test" which supposedly "flows" from *Pennington* and *Jewel Tea* find support in later decisions. . . .

The application of defendants' proposed "test" would result in an anomaly. The first question — whether the practices are addressed to third parties to the relationship — would be answered "yes." The second question — whether it was a mandatory subject of collective bargaining — is an irrelevance and was never asked. The basic inquiry must focus on determining whether the controverted practices or regulations were in the union's own interest. The test proposed by the NBA has no validity.

3. *Mandatory Subjects of Collective Bargaining*

The practices here under attack are not mandatory subjects of bargaining. . . .

I conclude at least tentatively since the record is not yet complete, that the reserve clause, the player draft, and the merger or non-competition agreement are not mandatory subjects of collective bargaining. Defendants' argument that the above cited cases and others require a contrary holding is wholly unpersuasive.

* * *

IN THE MATTER OF THE ARBITRATION BETWEEN MAJOR LEAGUE BASEBALL PLAYERS ASSOCIATION AND THE 28 MAJOR LEAGUE CLUBS

Opinion of the Chairman (Nicolau)

[T]he Association filed a grievance alleging that the Clubs' unilateral adoption of amendments to Major League Rules 3 and 4 on March 5, 1992 would, if implemented, constitute violations of Articles XVIII and XX of the Basic Agreement.

* * *

As relevant here, Major League Rules 3 and 4 deal with the June draft and the eligibility of certain amateur players to sign Major League or minor league contracts. Prior to the March 5 amendments, a Club drafting a player held exclusive negotiating rights to that player for approximately a year, after which the player, if unsigned, could re-enter the draft and be eligible for selection by another Club. However, if the player decided to enter college, the negotiating rights of the original drafting Club ended when that player entered his first college class. He was thereafter ineligible for re-entry into the draft until the conclusion of his junior year unless he dropped out of school at least seventy-five days prior to a draft and received authorization of eligibility from the Commissioner of Major League Baseball.

Essentially, the March 5, 1992 amendments extended a Club's exclusive negotiating rights to a player who entered college from a few months (early June to the beginning of classes in August or September) to five years, *i.e.,* one year after his projected graduation. Moreover, the dropout rule was changed. A player dropping out of school would not be eligible for reentry into the draft, but was still required to negotiate only with the Club that had previously drafted him. Moreover, the dropout waiting period was eliminated, thus allowing a player to complete a season with his college team and still sign with the Club holding rights to him in time to play rookie ball. As to drafted players who chose not to go to college, a drafting Club's exclusive negotiating rights were expanded to two years from the previous one.

Considerable testimony questioned the fairness of these amendments to amateur players. . . . However, both Parties recognized that the issue to be decided did not turn on those considerations, but was contractual, *i.e.,* whether the amendments violated the Basic Agreement.

The free agency provisions of that Agreement, found in Article XX, Reserve System, provide in B(4) that a Club signing a Type A Player (a free agent ranked in the upper 30% of his position group) must surrender to the Player's former Club its first or second "Regular Draft Choice," depending on the signing Club's order of finish the prior season. In addition, the former Club receives a "sandwich" pick to be selected between the draft's first and second rounds. For Type B free agents (those Players in the next 20% of their position group), a first or second Regular Draft Choice is surrendered, but there is no sandwich pick. Type C free agents (those in the next 10% of their position group) are also subject to compensation under limited circumstances, but that compensation is in the form of a sandwich pick between the second and third rounds and is thus not compensation directly from a signing Club. Unranked free agents, those statistically in the bottom 40% of their position group, are not subject to compensation, direct or otherwise.

As relevant, Article XVIII of the Basic Agreement, also implicated here, reads as follows:

ARTICLE XVIII — RULE CHANGES

> If during the term of this Agreement any Major League rule, Professional Baseball rule or rule or regulation of the American or National Leagues is proposed to be changed, the Clubs agree that they shall give the [MLBPA] notice thereof, and shall negotiate the proposed change with the [MLBPA], provided that the obligation to negotiate. . .shall apply only to (a) a change in a Player benefit under an existing rule or regulation and (b) the adoption of a rule or regulation which would change a Player benefit under an existing rule or regulation or impose an obligation upon the Players which had not previously existed. . . . [T]he right of the Clubs to make any rule change whatsoever shall not be impaired or limited in any way, provided that the Clubs shall not make any change which is inconsistent with the provisions of any then existing agreement between the Clubs and the [MLBPA].

Briefly stated, the Association contends that the draft rules at issue here are a mandatory subject of bargaining and must therefore be negotiated with the Union. It also contends that even if the draft is a permissive subject of bargaining, the amendments are inconsistent with Article XX and thus violate that portion of Article XVIII which forbids rule changes "inconsistent with the provisions of any then existing agreement between the Clubs and the Association."

In the latter argument, the Association asserts that the amendments to Rules 3 and 4 have changed the value of the draft choices a Club must surrender pursuant to Article XX B(4) in exchange for signing a Type A or B free agent and have thus improperly altered the economic bargain underlying that provision.

The Clubs, on the other hand, assert that the draft, which was unilaterally initiated in 1965 and periodically amended by the Clubs since that time, is not a mandatory subject of bargaining and has never been the subject of bargaining between the Parties; that some changes in the Major League Rules have been bargained, but only because those amendments, in the words of Article XVIII, directly affected Major League Players by changing a Player benefit or imposing a new obligation; but that the changes in Rules 3 and 4 are not of that character in that they only affect amateurs who are not and, under applicable law, could not be bargaining unit members.

As to the Association's Article XX argument, the Clubs assert that the Parties never agreed that the value of draft choices could not be changed; that, in any event, the amendments did not change the value of draft choices and even if they had, the extent or the effect of that change, if any, on future free agent markets is pure speculation. The Clubs also contend that by agreeing to tie free agent signings to a nonmandatory subject of bargaining such as the draft, the Association assumed the risk that the Clubs would unilaterally change the draft rules in a way that could potentially have an impact on some Major League Players. "Surely," the Clubs say, "they did not waive their statutory and contractual right to make unilateral changes in a permissive subject simply by agreeing that selections in that unilaterally implemented Draft would serve as free agent compensation."

Discussion

* * *

In that [Basic] Agreement and in all prior Agreements since 1976, the Association agreed, at the insistence of the Clubs, that free agent signings would be subject to compensation.

Over the years, the circumstances under which such compensation would be paid varied. [Recitation of varied arrangements: *Messersmith / McNally* period; 1981-1985; 1985-1990; 1990-present.]

The Clubs' insistence on compensation has been a subject of intense controversy between the Parties; the Clubs persistently maintaining that compensation was a necessary reimbursement to a Club "losing" a Player, while the Association argued that compensation was an unjustifiable impediment to Player movement. In fact, the Clubs' imposition of direct professional player compensation in 1981, as a result of the 1980 settlement, brought about a strike that lasted 50 days, ending only with agreement on the indirect professional player pool.

During the period since free agency and its system of compensation was incorporated into the Basic Agreement, there have been unilateral changes in the draft to which the Association raised no objection. . . .

On the other hand, various matters affecting the draft have been negotiated with the Association. [T]he sandwich picks for ranked players, which altered the structure of the draft itself, were agreed upon during Basic Agreement negotiations in 1981 and modified in 1985. Moreover, the Parties have negotiated a number of Basic Agreement provisions which affect players who have never been on a Major League roster and are thus not represented for collective bargaining purposes by the Association. . . .

Furthermore, the Parties have routinely negotiated provisions dealing with entry to and exit from the bargaining unit, *i.e.,* the movement of players into the Major Leagues, such as the Rule 5 draft agreement, and the movement of players back and forth between Clubs in those Leagues and affiliated clubs in the minor league system known as the National Association. . . .

Given this history, no waiver of the Association's right to challenge the changes in Rules 3 and 4 can be presumed and the Clubs do not seriously advance that contention. While the Association did not choose to assert bargaining rights or violations of contract over various changes in the draft, there is no indication that it abandoned its views any more than there is evidence that the Clubs abandoned theirs.

What the Clubs do argue, in answer to what is characterized as the Association's "novel concept," is that the free agency provisions in Article XX say nothing regarding the "value" of draft choices or suggest that the value must remain constant during the Basic Agreement's term. Therefore, even if the value of draft choices has been changed by the modification of the rules, . . . there is still no violation of the Agreement. The Clubs contend that the Parties have long recognized that they never agreed to a "static" free agency compensation system; and that this is evidenced by the above-referenced unilateral changes as well as changes wrought by external forces, such as payment of increased signing bonuses for amateurs, the upgrading of training in college baseball programs, etc.

* * *

The potential impact of forces not within the Parties' control is a risk both necessarily assume. But changes brought about by external factors cannot be equated with changes made by one of the parties to the bargain.

Here, the Parties agreed on March 19, 1990 to the continuation of draft choice compensation with one modification, that requiring a salary arbitration offer for compensation to attach in certain circumstances. At the time that agreement was made, at the conclusion of the negotiations during which the Association had previously suggested that the Parties might be better served if the link between compensation and free agency were severed. . . . [S]ome judgment could therefore be made on March 19, 1990 regarding the impediment to free agency movement rules of that nature might pose, thus providing a discernible basis for concluding what is essentially an economic bargain.

The changes made to the rules by the Clubs subsequent to the making of that bargain can properly be characterized as elemental and profound. Rather than losing the chance to sign an ostensibly college-bound player in a matter of weeks, a Club's right to that player was extended to five years. The pressure to sign a player on pain of losing him to another Club was gone. So, too, was the need to enhance an offer to induce a signature. . . . The Clubs could also wait for years to see if apparent promise was fulfilled before deciding whether to press for a contractual commitment or forego the signing and the expense associated with it.

The obvious effect of the changes was to dramatically shift leverage in the Clubs' favor and, as is quite apparent from the evidence, this is what the Clubs wanted to do. . . . If the time of exclusivity could be lengthened, those once passed over because they were deemed unsignable within a much shorter time frame could now perhaps be signed. Similarly, lengthened exclusivity reduced the need for added financial inducements.

While those objectives are understandable, they cannot be achieved if the means used are inconsistent with existing agreements. Here, there is no doubt, in my judgment, that such inconsistency exists. The rules are simply not the same as they were when the Parties agreed on their latest linking of compensation with free agency; the very nature of the amendments and the discussions and comments that preceded them make it abundantly clear that the value of draft choices to Clubs that hold them is significantly different from what it was before. Though the Association might reasonably expect and, as it has in the past, even accept minor variations in the underlying bargain, neither the Association nor the players it represents can be said to have willingly and knowingly assumed the risk of a change as striking as this.

One may dispute the value the amendments added to choices in the draft and whether that value may diminish in time. One may also dispute precisely how the change in draft choice value might affect particular free agent negotiations. What cannot be seriously disputed is that those free agents subject to compensation will carry a greater burden in negotiations by virtue of the change.

Thus, this is not a case that only affects non-employees not yet in the bargaining unit. It also affects bargaining unit employees because free agency and draft choices are, as of now, inseparable. Nor is this a case . . . where the connection with what was done . . . and free agency was less than readily apparent. Here, the connection is obvious; draft choices and free agency co-exist in the same contractual provision.

Exactly what that effect will be is not known with certainty, but, given the clear linkage between draft choice compensation and free agency, certainty as to the exact nature or level of that effect is not necessary.

The Clubs' assertion that they did not intend to affect free agency when adopting these far-reaching amendments is, in my judgment, unavailing. Of necessity, changes intended to make draft choices of greater worth to the Clubs, as these changes were, render free agent negotiations more difficult. . . .

In sum, the changes to Rules 3 and 4 were inconsistent with the bargain the Parties made in 1990. Thus, the amendments, found violative of the pledge embodied in Article XVIII, cannot stand. Given that pledge, it makes no difference, of course, whether the draft rules are a mandatory or only a permissive subject of bargaining. Whatever Board law may be with respect to the basis for finding an unfair labor practice, the Clubs, contrary to their assertion, have no "contractual" right to change a subject of bargaining by amendment of the Major League Rules, even if the subject is permissive. . . .

The remaining question, since the amendments must be rescinded, is whether the Clubs are obligated to bargain changes in the draft rules with the Association. The Parties vigorously advance conflicting answers to that question. . . .

There is some question, given the reading of the cases, as to how the Board might interpret the Act in the context of baseball if the statutory issue were put before it. But that is not the issue here. The question I must address is contractual. . . . As long as the contractual link between draft choice compensation and free agency continues, it's my judgment that unilateral changes in the draft rules are permissible only when the Association, after due notice of the proposed change as Article XVIII requires, fails to object.

SILVERMAN v. MAJOR LEAGUE BASEBALL PLAYER RELATIONS COMMITTEE, INC.

67 F.3d 1054 (2d Cir. 1995)

WINTER, Circuit Judge:

This is an appeal by the Major League Baseball Player Relations Committee, Inc. ("PRC") and the constituent member clubs of Major League Baseball ("Clubs") from a temporary injunction issued by Judge Sotomayor pursuant to section 10(j) of the National Labor Relations Act ("NLRA"), 29 U.S.C. § 160(j). The injunction is based on the district court's conclusion that appellants violated NLRA §§ 8(a)(1) and (5), 29 U.S.C. §§ 158(a)(1) and (5), by unilaterally implementing terms and conditions of employment that differed from those in the last collective agreement. It orders the PRC and the Clubs to: (i) abide by the terms of an expired collective agreement, (ii) rescind any actions taken that are inconsistent with that agreement and (iii) bargain in good faith with the Players Association . . . We affirm.

BACKGROUND

Article XX of the Basic Agreement that became effective in 1990 contains a series of provisions that govern free agency and reserve rights. Players with six or more years of major league service are free agents and may seek competing bids in an effort to obtain the best contract, which may of course give exclusive rights to the club for a stipulated number of years. *See Silverman*, 880 F. Supp. at 250. Free agency is guaranteed by an anti-collusion provision, Article XX(F), which prohibits the Clubs from acting in concert with each other with respect to the exercise of rights under Article XX. *See id.* Article XX(F) thus prevents the Clubs from agreeing either to refuse to bid for the services of free agents or to offer only low bids to them. Article XX(F) also prohibits players from acting in concert with regard to Article XX rights. *See id.*

Players with less than six years of service remain under reserve to their individual clubs, although a club may reserve a player only once. Although a minimum annual salary is provided, players with less than three years of major league service must negotiate with their clubs to determine their salary for the coming season. Article XX allows certain reserved players — generally those with more than three but less than six years of service — to demand salary arbitration. *See id.* at 251. Salary arbitration is a mechanism for determining the individual salaries for that group of reserved players if they cannot arrive at an agreement with their clubs. . . .

The Basic Agreement expired on December 31, 1993, pursuant to the PRC's notice of termination. Although negotiations for a successor agreement did not get underway until March 1994, the PRC and the Players Association continued to observe the terms of the expired Basic Agreement. Prior to the commencement of negotiations, the Clubs and the Players Association had completed individual salary arbitration hearings and had entered into individual player contracts for the 1994 baseball season, which began in April 1994. *See Silverman*, 880 F. Supp. at 251.

Negotiations for a new collective bargaining agreement continued unsuccessfully. The PRC offered its first formal economic proposal to the Players Association at a meeting on June 14, 1994. It included a "salary cap," a mechanism that establishes a ceiling on the total player salaries paid by each club. Generally, the aggregate salaries of each team are determined by an agreed upon formula and must remain above a minimum percentage of industry revenues, also determined by an agreed upon formula, but below a maximum percentage of those revenues. . . . The PRC proposal also eliminated the salary arbitration system and substituted restricted free agency rights for those reserved players previously eligible for salary arbitration. As an alternative to the PRC's proposed salary cap, the Players Association suggested a revenue sharing and luxury "tax" plan that would impose a tax on high-paying clubs. Subsequent proposals reflected disagreement over appropriate tax rates and payroll thresholds above which clubs would be subject to the tax.

The players struck on August 12, and the 1994 baseball season never resumed. On December 22, 1994, the PRC declared an impasse in negotiations and stated that it intended unilaterally to impose a salary cap and to implement other changes in the terms and conditions of employment, including the elimination of salary arbitration. The Players Association responded with a unilateral ban on players signing individual contracts with the Clubs.

On February 3, 1995, counsel for the PRC notified the NLRB General Counsel that the PRC would revoke the implementation of unilateral changes and restore the status quo ante. The General Counsel indicated that the Players Association charges would be dismissed as a result. Counsel for the PRC informed the General Counsel, however, that the PRC did not believe itself obligated to maintain provisions of the Basic Agreement that involved non-mandatory subjects of bargaining. He mentioned salary arbitration in that regard and also suggested that the Clubs might decide to bargain exclusively through the PRC. The NLRB General Counsel declined to offer an advisory opinion on these matters.

Three days later, by memorandum dated February 6, counsel for the PRC notified the Clubs that, until a new collective bargaining agreement was ratified or until further notice, individual clubs had no authority to negotiate contracts with individual players because the PRC was now the Clubs' exclusive bargaining representative. This amounted to an agreement among the Clubs not to hire free agents and thus was a departure from the anti-collusion provision, Article XX(F) of the Basic Agreement. It also amounted to an elimination of salary arbitration, because salary arbitration is a method of arriving at a wage for an individual player contract with a club.

The Players Association thereupon filed a new unfair labor practice charge, and the General Counsel issued a complaint alleging, *inter alia,* that the Clubs and the PRC had violated Sections 8(a)(1) and (5) of the NLRA by unilaterally eliminating, before an impasse had been reached, competitive bidding for the services of free agents, the anti-collusion provision, and salary arbitration for certain reserved players. The NLRB found that these matters were related to wages, hours, and other terms and conditions of employment and were therefore mandatory subjects for collective bargaining. It then authorized its General Counsel to seek an injunction under NLRA § 10(j). On March 27, the NLRB Regional Director filed a petition seeking a temporary injunction restraining the alleged unfair labor practices.

The district court agreed that the NLRB had reasonable cause to conclude that free agency and salary arbitration were mandatory subjects of bargaining and that the Clubs' unilateral actions constituted an unfair labor practice. The district court also concluded that injunctive relief was warranted. This appeal followed. We denied a stay on April 4.

DISCUSSION

. . . The petition invokes basic principles of labor law. Section 8(d) of the NLRA mandates that employers and unions bargain in good faith over "wages, hours, and other terms and conditions of employment." 29 U.S.C. § 158(d). These are so-called mandatory subjects of bargaining. Under caselaw, the parties may propose and bargain over, but may not insist upon, permissive subjects of bargaining. . . . When a collective agreement expires, an employer may not alter terms and conditions of employment involving mandatory subjects until it has bargained to an impasse over new terms. . . . Thereafter, it may implement the new terms. Generally, when an agreement expires, an employer need not bargain to an impasse over terms and conditions involving permissive subjects but may alter them upon expiration. . . .

The PRC and the Clubs argue that the anti-collusion and free agency provisions of the Basic Agreement do not involve mandatory subjects of bargaining and are therefore not subject to the *Katz* rule that unilateral implementation of new terms is an unfair labor practice unless the employer has bargained to an impasse over these new terms. . . . The PRC and the Clubs contend that an injunction compelling them to maintain the free agency and anti-collusion provisions undermines their right as a multi-employer group to bargain collectively through an exclusive representative. If so, they would be permissive subjects of bargaining. *See Borg Warner*, 356 U.S. at 349. With regard to salary arbitration, the PRC and the Clubs argue that it is the equivalent of interest arbitration — arbitration of the terms of a new collective agreement — and thus not a mandatory subject of bargaining. . . .

We are unpersuaded that an injunction compelling the PRC and the Clubs to observe the anti-collusion and free agency provisions of the Basic Agreement infringes on their right as a multiemployer group to bargain through an exclusive representative. Free agency and the ban on collusion are one part of a complex method — agreed upon in collective bargaining — by which each major league player's salary is determined under the Basic Agreement. They are analogous to the use of seniority, hours of work, merit increases, or piece work to determine salaries in an industrial context. The PRC and the Clubs describe free agency and the ban on collusion as provisions undermining their right to select a joint bargaining representative because those provisions entail individual contracts with clubs. However, the argument ignores the fact that free agency is simply a collectively bargained method of determining individual salaries for one group of players. The anti-collusion provision is not designed to prevent the PRC from representing the Clubs. Rather, that provision guarantees that free agency will be a reality when permitted by the Basic Agreement. The injunction thus does not in any way prevent the PRC from bargaining as the Clubs' exclusive representative with the Players Association over the elimination of free agency in its entirety or for a modified version of the same, and thereafter from implementing any proposals incorporated into a collective bargaining agreement.

The question, therefore, is whether the free agency, anti-collusion, and reserve issues are — or there is reasonable cause to believe they are — otherwise mandatory subjects of bargaining. Section 8(d) of the NLRA defines the duty to bargain as "the obligation . . . to meet . . . and confer in good faith with respect to wages, hours, and other terms and conditions of employment. . . ." In *Wood v. Nat'l Basketball Ass'n*, 809 F.2d 954 (2d Cir.1987), we noted that free agency and reserve issues are "at the center of collective bargaining in much of the professional sports industry," *id.* at 961, and that "it is precisely because of [free agency's] direct relationship to wages and conditions of employment that [it is] so controversial and so much the focus of bargaining in professional sports." *Id.* at 962.

[B]oth the leagues and the players unions view free agency and reserve issues as questions of what share of revenues go to the clubs or to the players. The more restrictive the reserve system is, the greater the clubs' share. The greater the role of free agency, the greater the players' share.

To hold that there is no reasonable cause for the NLRB to conclude that free agency and reserve issues are mandatory subjects of bargaining would be virtually to ignore the history and economic imperatives of collective bargaining in professional sports. A mix of free agency and reserve clauses combined with other provisions is the universal method by which leagues and players unions set individual salaries in professional sports. Free agency for veteran players may thus be combined with a reserve system, as in baseball, or a rookie draft, as in basketball, . . . , for newer players. A salary cap may or may not be included. To hold that any of these items, or others that make up the mix in a particular sport, is merely a permissive subject of bargaining would ignore the reality of collective bargaining in sports.

Indeed, free agency is in many ways nothing but the flip side of the reserve system. A full reserve system does not eliminate individual bargaining between teams and players. It simply limits that bargaining to one team. If free agency were a permissive subject of collective bargaining, then so would be the reserve system.

With regard to salary arbitration, we will assume, but not decide, that if it is a form of interest arbitration, it may be unilaterally eliminated. . . . Interest arbitration is a method by which an employer and union reach new agreements by sending disputed issues to an arbitrator rather than settling them through collective bargaining and economic force. . . . The salary arbitration provisions of the Basic Agreement are a method by which salaries for some players who are not eligible for free agency — those with three to six years of major league service — are set. The Basic Agreement sets forth criteria by which the arbitrator is to reach a decision. These criteria include the player's performance in the prior year, the length and consistency of career contribution, physical or mental defects, recent performance of the team on the field and at the gate, and salaries of certain comparable players. The Basic Agreement also forbids the arbitrator from considering certain facts that might otherwise be relevant.

Finally, the Basic Agreement requires that the arbitrator pick either the club's suggested salary or the player's.

We decline to analogize Article VI(F) of the Basic Agreement to interest arbitration. Salary arbitration provides limited discretion to the arbitrator to set salaries for designated players who are not eligible for free agency. The discretion afforded the arbitrator is arguably less than the discretion afforded arbitrators in grievance arbitration involving disputes arising under an existing collective agreement, which is beyond question a mandatory subject of bargaining. In grievance arbitration, an arbitrator may permissibly imply a term even though the term has no explicit support in the text of the collective agreement. . . . Similarly, a term may be implied from past practices even though somewhat inconsistent with the agreement. . . . We thus decline to analogize salary arbitration to interest arbitration, and, therefore, we hold that there is reasonable cause to believe that it is a mandatory subject of bargaining.

With regard to whether the granting of relief was "just and proper," 29 U.S.C. § 160(j), we review the district court's determination only for abuse of discretion. *Mego*, 633 F.2d at 1030; *Palby Lingerie*, 625 F.2d at 1051. We see no such abuse in the present matter. Given the short careers of professional athletes and the deterioration of physical abilities through aging, the irreparable harm requirement has been met. The unilateral elimination of free agency and salary arbitration followed by just three days a promise to restore the status quo. The PRC decided to settle the original unfair labor practice charges while embarking on a course of action based on a fallacious view of the duty to bargain. We see no reason to relieve it of the consequences of that course.

We therefore affirm.

CLARETT v. NATIONAL FOOTBALL LEAGUE

369 F.2d 124 (2d Cir. 2004),
cert. denied, 544 U.S. 961 (2005)

SOTOMAYOR, Circuit Judge.

Defendant-appellant National Football League . . . appeals from a judgment of the United States District Court . . . ordering plaintiff-appellee Maurice Clarett . . . eligible to enter this year's NFL draft on the ground that the NFL's eligibility rules requiring Clarett to wait at least three full football seasons after his high school graduation before entering the draft violate antitrust laws. In reaching its conclusion, the district court held, *inter alia*, that the eligibility rules are not immune from antitrust scrutiny under the non-statutory labor exemption. We disagree and reverse.

* * *

Clarett argues that he is physically qualified to play professional football and that the antitrust laws preclude NFL teams from agreeing amongst themselves that they will refuse to deal with him. . . . Such an arbitrary condition, he argues, imposes an unreasonable restraint upon the competitive market for . . . players' services, and, . . . constitutes a *per se* antitrust violation. The issue we must decide is whether subjecting the NFL's eligibility rules to antitrust scrutiny would "subvert fundamental principles of our federal labor policy." . . . For the reasons that follow, we hold that it would and that the non-statutory exemption therefore applies. . . .

Because the NFL players have unionized and have selected the NFLPA as its exclusive bargaining representative, labor law prohibits Clarett from negotiating directly the terms and conditions of his employment with any NFL club. . . .

In seeking the best deal for NFL players overall, the representative has the ability to advantage certain categories of players over others, subject of course to the representative's duty of fair representation. . . . The union representative may, for example, favor veteran players over rookies, . . . and can seek to preserve jobs for current players to the detriment of new employees and the exclusion of outsiders. . . .

Clarett's argument that antitrust law should permit him to circumvent this scheme established by federal labor law starts with the contention that the eligibility rules do not constitute a mandatory subject of collective bargaining and thus cannot fall within the protection of the non-statutory exemption. Contrary to the District Court, however, we find the eligibility rules are mandatory bargaining subjects. . . . [T]he eligibility rules for the draft represent a quite literal condition for initial employment and for that reason alone might constitute a mandatory bargaining subject. . . . But moreover, the eligibility rules constitute a mandatory bargaining subject because they have tangible effects on the wages and working conditions of current NFL players. . . . In *Silverman*, . . . we recognized that "[a] mix of free agency and reserve clauses combined with other provisions [such as a rookie draft and salary caps] is the universal method by which leagues and players unions set individual salaries in professional sports." . . . We therefore held that the issues of free agency, an anti-collusion provision in players' contracts, and major league baseball's reserve system are mandatory bargaining subjects. . . . Similarly, the complex scheme by which individual salaries in the NFL are set, which involves, *inter alia*, the NFL draft, league-wide salary pools for rookies, team salary caps, and free agency, was build around the longstanding restraint on the market for entering players imposed by the eligibility rules and the related expectations about the average career length of NFL players. The eligibility rules . . . cannot be viewed in isolation, because their elimination might well alter certain assumptions underlying the collective bargaining agreement. . . .

* * *

Clarett, however, argues that the eligibility rules are an impermissible bargaining subject because they affect players outside the union. But simply because the eligibility rules work a hardship on prospective rather than current employees does not render them impermissible. . . . The eligibility rules in this respect are not dissimilar to union demands for hiring hall arrangements that have been long recognized as mandatory subjects of bargaining. . . .

Clarett . . . stresses that the eligibility rules are arbitrary and that requiring him to wait another football season has nothing to do with whether he is in fact qualified for professional play. But Clarett is in this respect no different from the typical worker who is confident that he or she has the skills to fill a job vacancy but does not possess the qualifications or meet the requisite criteria that have been set. In the context of this collective bargaining relationship, the NFL and its players union can agree that an employee will not be hired or considered for employment for nearly any reason whatsoever so long as they do not violate federal laws such as those prohibiting unfair labor practices. . . . Any challenge to those criteria must be "founded on labor rather than antitrust law." . . .

[C]larett contends that the NFL clubs invited antitrust liability when they agreed amongst themselves to impose the same criteria on every prospective player. As a consequence of the NFL's unique position in the professional football market, . . . such joint action deprives Clarett of the opportunity to pursue. . . . the kind of high-paying, high-profile career he desires. In the context of collective bargaining, however, federal labor policy permits the NFL teams to act collectively as a multi-employer bargaining unit in structuring the rules of play and setting the criteria for player employment. Such concerted action is encouraged as a matter of labor policy and tolerated as a matter of antitrust law, . . . despite the fact that it "plainly involve[s] horizontal competitors for labor acting in concert to set and to implement terms of employement." . . . The fact that the challenged rules govern eligibility for the NFL draft, thereby excluding some potential employees from consideration, does not render the NFL's adherence to its eligibility rules as a multi-employer bargaining unit suspect.

The threat to the operation of federal labor law posed by Clarett's antitrust claims is in no way diminished by Clarett's contention that the rules were not bargained over during the negotiations that preceded the current collective bargaining agreement. The eligibility rules . . . were well known to the union, and a copy of the Constitution and Bylaws was presented was presented to the union during negotiations.

[T]he collective bargaining agreement itself makes clear that the union and the NFL reached an agreement with respect to how the eligibility rules would be handled. In the collective bargaining agreement, the union agreed to waive any challenge to the Constitution and Bylaws and thereby acquiesced in the continuing operation of the eligibility rules. . . .

* * *

Clarett would have us hold that by reaching this arrangement rather than fixing the eligibility rules in the text of the collective bargaining agreement or in failing to wrangle over the eligibility rules at the bargaining table, the NFL left itself open to antitrust liability. Such a holding, however, would completely contradict prior decisions recognizing that labor law policies that warrant withholding antitrust scrutiny are not limited to protecting only terms contained in collective bargaining agreements. . . . The reach of those policies, rather, extends as far as is necessary to ensure the successful operation of the collective bargaining *process* and to safeguard the "unique bundle of compromises" reached by the NFL and players union as a means of settling their differences. . . .

The disruptions to federal labor policy that would be occasioned by Clarett's antitrust lawsuit, moreover, would not vindicate any of the antitrust policies that the Supreme Court has said may warrant the withholding of the non-statutory exemption. This is simply not a case in which the NFL is alleged to have conspired with its players union to drive its competitors out of the market for professional football. . . . Nor does Clarett contend that the NFL uses the eligibility rules as an unlawful means of maintaining its dominant position in that market. . . . This lawsuit reflects simply a prospective employee's disagreement with the criteria, established by the employer and the labor union, that he must meet in order to be considered for employment. Any remedies for such a claim are the province of law.

NOTES AND COMMENTS

1. For coverage of labor law and professional sports, *see* STAUDOHAR, PLAYING FOR DOLLARS: LABOR RELATIONS AND THE SPORTS BUSINESS (1996); GREENBERG & GRAY, 1 SPORTS LAW PRACTICE ch. 1 (2d ed. 2005); Berry, *Collective Bargaining in Professional Sports, in* 1 LAW OF AMATEUR AND PROFESSIONAL SPORTS ch. 4 (Uberstine ed. 2005).

2. Review the three elements of the union-employer agreement essential to trigger the non-statutory labor exemption: 1) the restraint of trade primarily affects only the parties to the agreement; 2) the agreement concerns a mandatory subject of collective bargaining; and 3) the agreement is a product of bona fide arm's-length bargaining. In what manner can the players' association challenge one or more of the elements to fall outside of the exemption? Does the *Brown* opinion suggest an answer? Does the three prong test remain valid after *Brown*? Can matters concerning the draft, reserve clause, and free agent compensation systems be considered "permissive" subjects of bargaining after *Brown*?

3. Does there exist a difference in leverage possessed by the non-union employee and the member of a bargaining unit? The former, seemingly, faces no "nonstatutory" barrier to seeking antitrust reveiw of anticompetitive management behavior. Does *Brown* generate an incentive for player associations to "decertify"? Or, a disincentive for employees to organize, thus frustrating the intent of Congress? Are the implications of *Brown* greater than suggested by the holding? The public policy and underlying Congressional purpose are served by compelling both labor and management to utilize the labor law statutes rather than the antitrust statutes. Does the policy also demand that non-union employees utilize or "exhaust" the available labor law tools rather than antitrust litigation? For commentaries on the *Brown* case, *see* Kessler & Fehr, *What Justice Breyer Could not Know at his Mother's Knee: The Adverse Effects of* Brown v. Pro Football *on Labor Relations in Professional Sports,* 14-SPG ANTITRUST 14 (2000); Clark, Brown v. Pro Football, Inc.*: The Supreme Court Benches a Player's Right to Negotiate Salary*, 35 HOUS. L. REV. 571 (1998); Tyras, *Players versus Owners: Collective Bargaining and Antitrust After* Brown v. Pro Football, Inc., 1 U. PA. J. LAB. & EMPLOYMENT L. 297 (1998); Buchholz, *Run, Kick and (Im)passe: Expanding Employer's Ability to Unilaterally Impose Conditions of Employment After Impasse in* Brown v. Pro Football, 81 MINN. L. REV. 1201 (1997).

4. Justice Stevens, dissenting in *Brown*, notes that the NFL-NFLPA scenario allows for negotiation of individual salaries in a competitive market. He also reminds that exemptions should be construed narrowly. Does the majority utilize the appropriate standard in recognizing the exemption in the case? Is the sports league–labor model meaningfully different that the traditional industrial model? Justice Stevens states:

> [I] do not see why the employers should be entitled to a judicially crafted exemption from antitrust liability. We have explained that "[t]he nonstatutory exemption has its source in the strong labor policy favoring the association of employees to eliminate competition over wages and working conditions."... I know of no similarly strong labor policy that favors the association of employers to eliminate a competitive method of negotiationg wages that predates collective bargaining and that labor would prefer to preserve.

Brown v. Pro Football, Inc., 518 U.S. 231, 257 (Stevens, J., dissenting). For an article suggesting that fans will "lament" the *Brown* decision, *see* Harper, *Multiemployer Bargaining, Antitrust Law, and Team Sports: The Contingent Choice of a Broad Exemption*, 38 WM. & MARY L. REV. 1663 (1997).

5. The National Hockey League filed an action against the NHLPA seeking a declaratory judgment that NHL actions were shielded from challenge under the antitrust laws by the nonstatutory labor exemption. The NHL desired to remove the threat of an antitrust action from the NHLPA's collective bargaining arsenal. *See National Hockey League v. National Hockey League Players Association*, 789 F. Supp. 288 (D. Minn. 1993) (dismissed for lack of subject matter jurisdiction; possibility of antitrust litigation does not give rise to actual controversy). The NHL relied on the "unilateral change doctrine," in making its argument. The court described the doctrine as follows:

> Under the unilateral change doctrine, if an existing collective bargaining agreement has expired, and negotiations of a new contract have yet to be completed, an employer must bargain to impasse before it may unilaterally change an existing term or condition of employment. An employer's unilateral change, prior to bargaining impasse, results in a

> violation of the NLRA. *See Litton*, 111 S. Ct. at 2217; *Katz,* 369 U.S. at 747.

Id. at page 291, n.7.

6. As the court in *Clarett* indicated, the non-statutory labor exemption also bars suit under the antitrust laws by players who are not members of the union/bargaining unit. *See also Wood v. National Basketball Association,* 809 F.2d 954 (2d Cir. 1984) (NBA salary cap applied to rookies); *Zimmerman v. National Football League,* 632 F. Supp. 398 (D.D.C. 1986) (NFL supplemental draft applied to players who were not members of NFLPA). Can rookies and others sever ties with the player associations and the attendant barriers to litigation? The NLRA defines "employees" broadly to include workers outside the bargaining unit. 28 U.S.C. § 152(3). For analysis of the *Clarett* decision, *see* Champion, *Clarett v. NFL & the Reincarnation of the NonStatutory Labor Exemption in Professional Sports*, 47 S. Tex. L. Rev. 587 (2006).

In *National Football League Players Association v. Pro Football, Inc.*, 56 F.3d 1525 (D.C. Cir. 1995), thirty-seven Washington Redskin players refused to pay their union dues, arguing that the Redskins club is an employer in Virginia, a "right to work" state. The club's training facilities are located in Virginia. The players conduct more activities in Virginia than at RFK Stadium in Washington, D.C. The NFLPA notified the NFL that the players must be suspended under the terms of the CBA "agency shop" provision requiring all NFL players to pay dues within 30 days of employment. The National Labor Relations Act permits the "agency shop" provision, but also allows states to enact their own "right to work" laws. The matter proceeded to arbitration, federal district court, *National Football League Players Association v. Pro Football, Inc.*, 849 F. Supp. 1 (D.D.C. 1993) (NFLPA fails to gain TRO ordering Redskins to comply with arbitrator ruling that Virginia statute inapplicable), and to the D.C. Circuit (case dismissed as moot — season over).

To the extent that professional sports leagues expand operations beyond the borders of the United States, as has already been done in the case of the Canadian clubs, the labor laws of foreign jurisdictions may apply in specific contexts. *See* Lippner, Note, *Replacement Players for the Toronto Blue Jays?: Striking the Appropriate Balance Between Replacement Worker Law in Ontario, Canada and the United States*, 18 FORDHAM INT'L L.J. 2026 (1995).

7. The National Labor Relations Act provides three distinct rights: 1) right to self organization; 2) right to bargain collectively; and 3) right to engage in activities for the employees' mutual aid or protection.

The customary bargaining unit has developed on a "league-wide" basis. Thus, the NFLPA, NBPA, and MLBPA are typical of professional sports player associations. Would the structuring of bargaining units on a "craft" basis better represent the interests of certain player groups? For example, perhaps a "centers" unit could better compete with a "quarterback" unit for a distribution of the salary pool, than as a member of the "league-wide" unit. Should rookie first-year players form a unit to compete with veterans? Does this scenario differ from the traditional bargaining model under the National Labor Relations Act that results in worker advantages based on seniority? The notion of a "team-wide" unit was rejected in *Morio v. North American Soccer League*, 236 N.L.R.B. 1317 (1978), *aff'd*, 632 F.2d 217 (2d Cir. 1980). *See also North American Soccer League v. NLRB*, 236 N.L.R.B. 1312 (1978), *enforced*, 613 F.2d 1379 (5th Cir. 1980), *cert. denied*, 449 U.S. 889 (1980). *See generally* WEISTART & LOWELL, THE LAW OF SPORTS § 6.04 (1979).

8. Does the NBA possess a valid cause of action against agents allegedly interfering with the bargaining process between the agents' clients and management? Would the NFL possess a cause of action in antitrust against player agents acting in collusion, in the event of NFLPA decertification? *See The Five Smiths, Inc. v. National Football League Players Ass'n*, 788 F. Supp. 1042 (D. Minn. 1992). The court ruled the complaint, alleging that NFLPA and player agents' exchange of player compensation data and current offers information violated § 1 of the Sherman Act, failed to state a cognizable antitrust claim under either the *per se* or rule of reason test.

After the NBA-NBPA settlement, the NBPA decertified agent Wood who had challenged the NBPA during the negotiations. See materials at **Chapter 8** for a discussion of the agent certification process utilized by player associations.

9. Parties to the collective bargaining process possess the duties to bargain in good faith and provide information relevant to the mandatory bargaining issues. Must the league and the players association open the books for a full disclosure of the economic and financial status of the parties? For a decision rejecting arguments by the MLBPA placing a duty on the owners to provide economic information, *see Silverman v. Major League Baseball Player Relations Committee, Inc.*, 516 F. Supp. 588 (S.D.N.Y. 1981). The NLRB ruled that the NHL committed an unfair labor practice by refusing to provide the NHLPA with copies of trade memos relating to all player trades from the 1996-97 and following seasons, trade memos relating to trades of specified players, and information regarding subsidy payments received by clubs pursuant to the Supplemental Currency Equalization Plan. *National Hockey League and its Constituent Member Clubs and National Hockey League Players' Association*, before the National Labor Relations Board, Division of Judges (Kern, ALJ), 591 PLI/Pat 263.

10. Pursuant to most league constitutions, clubs in the league share revenues according to various formulas. The division of the proceeds is often changed by a vote of league directors. What arguments can be made pro and con that the implementation or modification of a revenue sharing arrangement between clubs is a mandatory subject of bargaining with the players' union under the National Labor Relations Act? In the *National Hockey League and its Constituent Members and National Hockey League Players' Association*, *supra* at **Note 9**, the NLRB determined that the NHL violated the National Labor Relations Act by failing and refusing to bargain with the NHLPA the implementation of a player payroll provision in the Supplemental Currency Assistance Plan (SCAP). SCAP, designed to assist those Canadian teams in the bottom half of League revenues, was to fund at 100 percent the difference between U.S. and Canadian dollars based on the difference between the average major league player salaries in U.S. dollars and an equivalent amount of Canadian dollars. An eligibility criterion was directly linked to player salaries, requiring that the team's player salaries must be at or below the average league salary (ALS) in order to receive full assistance.

Those clubs with above average salaries would have the assistance reduced at a rate of $2 of assistance for each dollar above the ALS. *See also*, Cohen, Note, *Sharing the Wealth: Don't Call Us, We'll Call You: Why Revenue Sharing is a Permissive Subject and therefore the Labor Exemption does not Apply*, 12 FORDHAM INTELL. PROP. MEDIA & ENT. L.J. 609 (2002).

11. A question of whether NBA clubs were obligated to compensate players with guaranteed salaries during the lockout period arose amidst the NBA-NBPA negotiations. The NBPA filed a grievance before Arbitrator Feerick, arguing that the absence of lockout language in the standard player contract meant that owners should be held liable for the payment of guaranteed salaries. Other circumstances in which salaries can be withheld are clearly specified. Lockout language also appears in the NBA's television and other contracts. The NBPA argued that the existence of the express clauses indicated that work stoppage was foreseeable and should have been included in player contracts. Arbitrator Feerick, Dean of Fordham Law School, rejected the NBPA's grievance arguments, holding that NBA clubs were not obligated to pay guaranteed salaries during the lockout.

A threshold question in the matter concerned the jurisdiction of the arbitrator which begins and expires with the collective bargaining agreement. Arbitrator Feerick ruled that the NBPA had filed the grievance hours before the imposition of the lockout on July 1, 1998, thus properly preserving the grievance arbitration. *See* Feerick, Arbitration Opinion at 548 PLI/Pat 87 (Feb-Mar 1999).

12. Drug testing exists as one of the most important issues confronting parties to future collective bargaining endeavors. Drug testing issues are discussed at **Chapter 15**, *infra*.

13. For cases concerning the discretion of leagues to establish eligibility requirements for the amateur draft, *see National Hockey League Players' Association v. Plymouth Whalers Hockey Club*, (*NHLPA II)* 419 F.3d 462 (6th Cir. 2005); (*NHLPA* I) 325 F.3d 712 (6th Cir. 2003); *Boris v. United States Football League*, 1984 WL 894 (C.D. Cal. 1984); *Linseman v. World Hockey Association*, 439 F. Supp. 1315 (1977); *Denver Rockets v. All-Pro Management*, 325 F. Supp. 1049 (C.D. Cal. 1971). *See also* McCann, Note, *Illegal Defense: The Law and Economics of Banning High School Players from the NBA Draft*, 1 VA. SPORTS & ENT. L.J. 295 (2002); Rosenthal, *the Amateur Sports Draft: The Best Means to an End?*, 6 MARQ. SPORTS L.J. 1 (1995). The drafting of high school players by NBA teams has generated considerable discussion regarding potential social impacts of the phenomenon. The NCAA Division I Board of Directors, in 2002, adopted a rule permitting high school athletes to maintain their college eligibility even if the players declare themselves eligible for a professional draft. The athlete loses amateur status by signing a contract or hiring an agent. The Board also adopted a rule to enable college football underclassmen to declare for the NFL draft and retain eligibility if they withdraw from the draft within 72 hours of the deadline for making the declaration. College basketball underclassmen may declare for the NBA draft and lose eligibility status only in the event they are actually drafted.

14. Problem: In 2001, the Commissioner of Baseball announced that MLB contemplated the contraction of two clubs, focusing primarily on the Minnesota Twins and Montreal Expos. The MLBPA challenged the managerial decision, arguing that the elimination of clubs is a mandatory subject of bargaining. Before a ruling was made in the grievance, the MLBPA and MLB negotiated a new collective bargaining agreement which barred contraction during the life of the CBA (2006). The MLBPA, however, agreed to waive any challenges pursuant to the NLRA regarding MLB elimination of troubled franchises for the 2007 season. The MLBPA reserved the right to challenge the "effects" of contraction, including the claim that the issue of "effects" is a mandatory subject of bargaining.

Is the contraction of a Major League team considered to be the closing of a business as a traditional entrepreneurial decision? Is the elimination tantamount to the "entire" closing of a business, or only a "partial" closing? Assuming that the players of the eliminated clubs are distributed to remaining teams, is contraction more akin to "relocation" of operations, rather than the closing of a business?

In *Textile Workers v. Darlington Co.*, 380 U.S. 263, 268 (1965), the United States Supreme Court held that an employer has the absolute right to permanently close the entire business, even if the liquidation is motivated by vindictiveness toward a union. A partial closing, however, is an unfair labor practice if motivated by a purpose to chill unionism in any of the remaining plants. *See also*, *Darlington Manufacturing Co. v. NLRB.*, 307 F.2d 760 (4th Cir. 1968). *Darlington*, by its own terms and subsequent decisions, is limited to the unique circumstance of the clear termination of a business and does not apply to discriminatory relocations or the subcontracting of work. *Lear Siegler, Inc.*, 295 N.L.R.B. 857 (1989). The United States Supreme Court, in *First National Maintenance Corp. v. NLRB*, 452 U.S. 666 (1981), held that the managerial decision to close part of a business for economic reasons was not a subject of mandatory bargaining, but bargaining over the "effects" of the decision must be conducted in a meaningful manner and at a meaningful time to satisfy the requirements of § 8(a)(5) of the National Labor Relations Act. In *Dubuque Packing Co.*, 303 N.L.R.B. 386 (1991), the Board established a test to determine whether an employer has the duty to bargain regarding plant relocations and transfers of work. The General Counsel possesses the burden to establish that the employer's decision concerned a relocation of work not accompanied by a change in the nature of the business operation. The employer may rebut a *prima facie* case by establishing that the work performed at the new location varies significantly from the work performed at the former plant, and that the work performed at the former plant is to be discontinued entirely and not transferred to the new location, or that the decision involves a change in the scope and direction of the enterprise. Alternatively, the employer may offer a defense that the labor costs were not a factor in the decision, or that if costs considered, the union could not have offered labor cost concessions that could have changed the employer's decision. Roger Noll contends that the Major League Baseball revenue sharing system creates incentives to contract clubs. Noll, *The Economics of Baseball Contraction* 2, 25-26 (2003), unpublished manuscript, Stanford Institute for Economic Policy Research. *See generally*, Rosner, *Squeeze Play: Analyzing Contraction in Professional* Sports, 10 VILL. SPORTS & ENT. L.J. 29, 42-43 (2003); Day, *Labor Pains: Why Contraction is not the Solution to Major League Baseball's Competitive Balance Problems*, 12 FORDHAM INTELL. PROP. MEDIA & ENT. L.J. 521, 547-52 (2002).

15. In *Bidwell v. Garvey*, 943 F.2d 498 (4th Cir. 1991), *aff'g*, 743 F. Supp. 393 (D. Md. 1990), the court ruled that NFL owners (management trustees) breached the 1982 collective bargaining agreement and were liable for $18 million plus interest in the Bert Bell Pension Plan. *See also Brumm* v. *Bert Bell NFL Retirement Plan*, 995 F.2d 1433 (8th Cir. 1993); *Bathgate v. NHL Pension Soc'y*, 11 O.R.(3d) 449 (1993).

16. Union membership, at times, may be dissatisfied with union leadership and performance in collective bargaining activities. Former National Hockey League players filed a class action against R. Alan Eagleson, past Executive Director of the NHLPA, and others, alleging RICO violations, including an alleged conspiracy between NHL defendants and Eagleson, by which Eagleson forsook the players' interests in collective bargaining with the NHL. The U.S. District Court granted summary judgment for defendants on the RICO claim, on the ground that the claim was time-barred. *Forbes v. Eagleson*, 19 F. Supp. 2d 352 (E.D. Pa. 1998), *aff'd*, 228 F.3d 471 (3rd Cir. 2000), *cert. denied* 533 U.S. 929 (2001). The court, however, allowed plaintiffs to file a fifth Amended Complaint to plead claims for injuries incurred after November 7, 1991. *Forbes v. Eagleson*, 183 F.R.D. 440 (E.D. Pa. 1998).

17. Examination of the history of labor battles between professional sports leagues and players unions provides insight into the workings of the collective bargaining agreements and the economic and other relationships between leagues and players. Roger Abrams concludes the collective bargaining relationship between baseball owners and players is dysfunctional. He recommends that the parties eschew traditional conflict bargaining for principled negotiations that result in partnership bargaining relationships. Abrams, *Partnership Bargaining in Baseball,* in LEGAL ISSUES IN PROFESSIONAL BASEBALL (Kurlantzick ed. 2005), ch. II.

For an analysis of the 2005 NHL-NHLPA collective bargaining agreement, *see* Jeglic, *Can the New Collective Bargaining Agreement Save the NHL?* 23-SUM Ent. & Sports Law. 1 (2005). For a discussion of the NHL-NHLPA bargaining efforts in years prior to 1995, *see* Dick & Sherman, THE DEFENSE NEVER RESTS (1994). Historical treatment of NFL labor matters may be found at Goplerud, *Collective Bargaining in the National Football League: A Historical & Comparative Analysis*, 4 Vill. Sports & Ent. L.J. 13 (1997); Heller, *Creating a Win-Win Situation Through Collective Bargaining: The NFL Salary Cap*, 7 Sports Law. J. 375 (2000). For discussion of labor issues in Major League Baseball, *see* Gould, *Labor Issues in Professional Sports: Reflections on Baseball, Labor and Antitrust Law*, 15 Stan. L. & Pol'y Rev. 61 (2004). An interesting analysis of baseball's "collusion clause" and the possible effect of a flooding of the market with free agents is presented at Edelman, *Has Collusion Returned to Baseball? Analyzing Whether a Concerted Increase in Free Agent Player Supply Would Violate Baseball's "Collusion Clause,"* 24 Loy. L.A. Ent. L. Rev. 159 (2004). For Professor Zimbalist's analysis of the impact of the NBA lockout and other factors on the 1999 CBA, *see* THE ECONOMICS OF SPORTS, ch. 5 (Kern ed. 2000). *See generally*, Weiler, LEVELING THE PLAYING FIELD: HOW THE LAW CAN MAKE SPORTS BETTER FOR FANS, 112-17 (2000).

18. The distinction between a "salary cap" and a "luxury or payroll tax" can be important. A "cap" restricts payroll, which truly affects salaries for all clubs. Some player salaries are necessarily curbed by the "cap." A "tax" does not restrict salaries, but adds a cost factor for clubs who spend above a threshold level. Although the "tax" may deter some club salary expenditures, it is likely to have very little effect on curbing player salaries so long as there exist owners who will spend at the free market level with little regard for tax consequences. The "tax," like the "cap," may be "soft" or "hard."

MLB's Blue Ribbon Panel determined that the "luxury tax" imposed by the 1996 Basic Agreement failed to moderate the rapid escalation of club payrolls. The "soft" tax weakness derived from the calculation of the tax threshold. The threshold was set as the mid-point between the fifth and six highest payroll clubs. Thus, the threshold was enabled to adjust upward in response to club behavior. "The flaw in the 'floating threshold' was obvious: the more the high payroll clubs spent on players, the higher the tax threshold and the less restraint on payroll escalation." The Panel recommended a "competitive balance tax" based on a "fixed" tax threshold that is joined with a minimum payroll requirement. The Panel concluded that the offsetting dynamics of the two features could result in a redistribution of, but no aggregate decrease in, the dollars devoted to player compensation. Levin, Mitchell, Volcker & Will, *The Report of the Independent Members of the Commissioner's Blue Ribbon Panel on Baseball Economics*, 39 (July 2000).

19. Terms of a collective bargaining agreement, of course, are subject to varying interpretations. Cases arise in all leagues concerning whether clauses in player contracts conform to CBA provisions. Creative efforts to avoid the restrictions of salary caps and luxury taxes also generate verbal agreements, side deals, and attempts to utilize loopholes and other circumvention techniques. The original NBA salary cap did not restrict a club's signing of its own free agents. Thus, a player arguably could agree to a lower salary in the initial contract, but recoup value through a second-year contract that was not limited by the salary cap. The use of "one-year opt-out" provisions was upheld in *Bridgeman v. National Basketball Association*, 838 F. Supp. 172 (D.N.J. 1993). Sometimes, incentive bonuses are not included in salary cap calculations. A question may arise whether the incentives were likely to be achieved and thus should be defined as "salary." For a discussion of circumvention techniques used in the NFL, and a suggestion that an implied covenant of good faith and fair dealing exists to counter attempts to avoid salary cap restrictions, *see* McPhee, Comment, *First Down, Goal to Go: Enforcing the NFL's Salary Cap Using the Implied Covenant of Good Faith and Fair Dealing*, 17 LOY. L.A. ENT. L.J. 449 (1997).

20. Rights of parties pursuant to the National Labor Relations Act may be waived by a failure to act in a timely and diligent manner. In 1997, the NHL unilaterally adopted a Deferred Compensation Program without bargaining with the NHLPA. The NHL stipulated that the issue was a mandatory subject of bargaining, but argued that the NHLPA waived its right to bargain over the implementation of the Program by its inaction following notice by telephone. The NHLPA answered that it did not receive adequate notice from the NHL, that the Program was presented as a *fait accompli* which made any request futile, and that it did as a matter of fact make a demand for bargaining. The NLRB rejected the NHLPA arguments and determined that the NHLPA failed to request bargaining in a timely fashion and thereby waived its right to bargain. *National Hockey League and its Constituent Members and National Hockey League Players' Association*, before the National Labor Relations Board, Division of Judges (Kern, ALJ), 591 PLI/Pat 263, 296.

21. Rights of the parties under the National Labor Relations Act may be waived by the express terms of a CBA. A typical waiver is made by use of the "no-strike" clause. Major League Umpires, as members of the Major League Umpires Association (MLUA), were faced with a "no-strike" clause in the collective bargaining agreement. Anticipating upcoming labor negotiations, the MLUA voted to submit resignations to the American and National Leagues. The organizational unity of the MLUA began to fail when some of the umpires did not submit resignation letters and others attempted to rescind their resignations. The American and National Leagues hired twenty-five replacement umpires and allowed some umpires, but not all, to withdraw their resignations. The MLUA filed suit in United States District Court to enjoin the Leagues from refusing to allow the withdrawal of all resignations. It also filed unfair labor practice claims before the NLRB. The MLUA contended, "The umpires never intended to sever their employment with the Leagues. Rather, they engaged in this mass resignation plant to publicize the dispute and to induce the Leagues to address the umpires' concerns. . . ." *Major League Umpires' Associ-*

ation v. The American League of Professional Baseball Clubs, et al., Complaint and Memorandum of Law in Support of Plaintiff, Page 17, 591 PLI/Pat 145, 174.

Pending a hearing on the grievance, a group of dissident umpires, the Major League Umpires Independent Organizing Committee (now World Umpires Association), was certified as the exclusive bargaining representative of major league baseball umpires after a contested election conducted by the NLRB. *See* 22 No. 4 ENT. L. REP. 8 (2000). As a condition of employment, all umpires must be members of the WUA or, in lieu of membership, must pay a financial core fee. Fifteen umpires challenged the validity of and calculation of the fee. *Bonin v. World Umpires Association*, 204 F.R.D. 67 (E.D. Pa. 2001) (court held that a protective order would issue limiting to the instant case the disclosure and use of any financial information produced by the WUA).

What bargaining tactics would you suggest that the MLUA could have utilized in place of the ill-fated resignation plan? Could the resignations be characterized as forced by management practices, so as to constitute "constructive firings?" *See NLRB v. Cosco Products Co.*, 280 F.2d 905 (5th Cir. 1960) (there is no basis in the National Labor Relations Act or law for recognition of constructive discharges). *See generally*, Franklin, *The Labor Strike: Is It Still a Useful Economic Weapon for Unions?*, 35 J. MARSHALL L. REV. 255 (2002); Insley, Comment, *Major League Umpires Association: Is Collective Bargaining the Answer to or the Problem in the Contractual Relationships of Professional Sports Today?* 29 CAP. U. L. REV. 601 (2001).

Chapter 7
ENFORCEMENT OF SPORTS CONTRACTS

A. INTRODUCTORY COMMENTS

This chapter focuses on judicial and nonjudicial enforcement of the professional sports contract, including threshold issues of *in personam* jurisdiction. The chapter first addresses equitable and legal remedies available to both the team and player as plaintiffs alleging breach of valid contracts. Of particular importance are the contractual provisions obligating the parties to submit any disputes arising under the contract to arbitration. The chapter next explores the availability of the equitable remedy of specific performance for the enforcement of facility leases. The Seattle Seahawks — King County, Washington (Kingdome) lease controversy is provided as a **Problem** of continuing importance.

Section C presents discussion of grievance arbitration, a feature of all professional sports bargaining agreements and uniform/standard player contracts. Recurring issues arising subsequent to the formation of the player-team contract are presented, including the ownership collusion case in major league baseball. Finally, the baseball salary arbitration mechanism is discussed and compared to the traditional arbitration model.

B. THE LAW OF CONTRACTS

1. Generally — Player and Club

The contract between the player and team, of course, must satisfy all legal requirements of the jurisdiction where the contract is formed, including the statute of frauds. Although form contracts are utilized by most professional sports leagues and other contracts are well drafted, disputes between parties arise under the terms of the contracts. Resolution of the disputes requires application of the general principles of the law of contracts and remedies.

A party seeking to enforce provisions of a contract necessarily argues that the contract is valid and the provisions should be construed as alleged. A party desiring to avoid the enforcement of a contract argues that the clauses should be read to reveal a different intention of the parties, or the contract is invalid and thus cannot be enforced. The attorney must remember that various canons of construction and other rules are used by courts to resolve contract issues. The rules differ among the jurisdictions. Generally, actions may be filed for construction or reformation.

A declaratory judgment action calling for judicial construction of contract provisions may be maintained where contract language is ambiguous. If the words are not ambiguous, the "plain meaning rule" prohibits judicial construction. Where the terms are ruled ambiguous, the court first looks within the four corners of the instrument to resolve the ambiguity by use of intrinsic evidence. If the ambiguity cannot be resolved by looking to the instrument as a whole, extrinsic evidence is utilized to determine the intentions of the parties. Canons of construction are also used, including the rule that ambiguities are resolved against the party drafting the instrument. Knowledge of the "parol evidence" rule is important, as is familiarity with other rules peculiar to the jurisdiction. For example, some jurisdictions possess statutes specifying that a contract which may be terminated at the will of one party may be terminated by the other. *See, e.g., Connecticut Professional Sports Corp. v. Heyman*, 276 F. Supp. 618 (S.D.N.Y. 1967).

An action for reformation requires a showing of mutual mistake, misrepresentation, fraud, duress, or other misconduct. A plaintiff bears the burden of proof by the "clear and convincing" evidence standard.

The usual contract remedies and defenses are available to parties litigating rights and duties under the terms of sports contracts. Thus actions for damages and/or equitable remedies are common. Cases have developed along two lines. Where ballclubs are attempting to restrain players from performing with other teams, courts readily adjudicate the matter under equity jurisdiction. Courts generally do not compel specific performance of personal service contracts. Courts, however, regularly enforce negative covenants, such as covenants in player-team contracts prohibiting the player from performing for another team during the contract period. A preliminary "negative injunction" will issue where the plaintiff satisfies four essential criteria as follows:

1. Irreparable injury to plaintiff/inadequate remedy at law;
2. Absence of substantial harm to defendant or other interested parties;
3. Absence of harm to the public interest; and
4. A likelihood that plaintiff will prevail on the merits.

See Cincinnati Bengals, Inc. v. Bergey, 453 F. Supp. 129 (S.D. Ohio 1985), *citing, Philadelphia World Hockey Club, Inc. v. Philadelphia Hockey Club, Inc.*, 351 F. Supp. 462 (E.D. Pa. 1972). The problem presented below is designed to acquaint you with the principles and elements of the negative injunction, as developed in the context of sports contracts.

Where players sue for alleged breach of the player team contract, courts deny judicial relief if the contract provisions enable the parties to resolve the issue through arbitration. Thus, the court initially determines whether a valid arbitration clause exists, and secondly, whether the dispute is within the scope of the clause. *See* discussion of grievance arbitration at **Section C**, *infra*.

2. Threshold Question: *In Personam* Jurisdiction

A plaintiff can obtain adjudication of a controversy only in a court which has personal jurisdiction over the defendant. The peculiar factual nature of sports employment generates several questions regarding the appropriate jurisdiction in which to file a lawsuit. The ballclub plays its home games in a specified locality. Road games are usually played in other cities and states. The broadcasting of games expands the areas in which the club operates. The player often maintains a permanent residence in one location and a temporary residence in another.

Practical considerations join jurisdictional questions to further complicate the decision regarding the appropriate forum for suit. Plaintiffs usually desire to file suit in a sympathetic jurisdiction. A relevant factor for a team filing suit for a negative injunction is whether the equitable decree will be enforced by sister state courts under the full-faith-and-credit clause of the U.S. Constitution, art. IV, § 1, cl. 1-2. Some courts refuse to enforce negative injunctions due to questions concerning continuing jurisdiction. *See* RESTATEMENT (SECOND) OF CONFLICTS OF LAW § 102 cmt. c (1971); Reese, *Full Faith & Credit to Foreign Equity Decrees,* 42 IOWA L. REV. 183 (1957).

A ballclub possesses several possibilities in filing suit against the player: 1) player's permanent residence; (2) player's temporary residence; and 3) situs of playerteam negotiations, usually location of college or high school. Although a defendant generally may be sued in the state of domicile, a player's contacts with the state may be in question. The defendant must have sufficient "minimum contacts" with the forum state in order to satisfy the due process standards set forth in *International Shoe Co. v. Washington*, 326 U.S. 310 (1945). Courts consider the following factors:

1. Length of time defendant spends in the state;
2. Nature of activities defendant undertakes in the state; and
3. Defendant's living arrangements in the state.

If little or no contact remains with the state subsequent to the negotiation of the contract, satisfaction of the minimum contacts standard is questionable.

The player-plaintiff also possesses alternatives in choosing the appropriate forum for litigation: 1) state where games are played; 2) state where revenues are derived; 3) state in which club is incorporated; 4) state where team is officed; and 5) state featuring broadcasts or recruiting efforts. The possible forums for litigation are analyzed under the *International Shoe* minimum contacts standard.

For detailed discussion of issues concerning the appropriate forum for sports contract litigation, *see* Uberstine, *The Enforceability of Sports Industry Employment Agreements, in* 2 LAW OF PROFESSIONAL & AMATEUR SPORTS ch. 10 (Uberstine ed. 2005).

PROBLEM

Chock Chiles is a person of tremendous athletic ability and talent. While in college, Chiles earned All-American honors in both football and baseball. Following his junior year, Chiles signed a professional baseball contract with the Detroit Tigers. He received a signing bonus of $100,000. He played in the Tigers' minor league system during the summer. In the fall, Chiles returned to college to complete his senior year of football eligibility. The Tigers expressly agreed to and otherwise permitted Chiles to play college football while under contract with the baseball club. Chiles made several All-America teams as a senior running back.

In the spring of his senior year, Chiles participated in the Tigers' major league training camp. At the completion of spring training, Chiles signed a new three-year contract and was placed on the active roster of the major league club. The contract included a clause stipulating that Chiles would not play football during the term of the contract. The clause was in all respects identical to Paragraph 5(b) of the Uniform Player Contract found at **Chapter 9**, *infra*. Chiles received a $100,000 bonus as compensation for agreeing to the clause prohibiting him from playing football.

Later in the spring, Chiles was chosen in the third round of the National Football League draft by the San Diego Chargers. (He would have been a first round choice but teams were hesitant, given the baseball contract.) Despite much pressure in the form of letters, phone calls, and personal visits from the Chargers, Chiles continued to play baseball and did not sign a football contract.

For the baseball season, Chiles hit .210, had 4 home runs, and 25 RBIs. All figures placed him among the worst in major league baseball. Chiles was mediocre, at best, as a defensive player. The Tigers were disappointed in Chiles' performance. Chiles vowed to work on several areas of weakness during the off-season. Chiles rejected further offers made by the Chargers at the end of the baseball season.

In the following spring, Chiles again made the major league club roster at the completion of spring training. Midway through the baseball season, Chiles was hitting .185 and had hit no home runs. On July 15th, Chiles announced his retirement from baseball. A news conference was held during which both the Tigers and Chiles remarked that the relationship of two and one-half years had been pleasant for both parties.

On August 15th, Chiles signed an NFL contract to play football for the Detroit Lions, who had gained rights to Chiles pursuant to NFL rules. Uncontroverted evidence indicates that the Lions had pressured Chiles to "jump" to football since April. Chiles initiated further negotiations with the Lions in early July.

Last week, Chock Chiles was served with a Complaint. The Plaintiff, Detroit Tigers, seek a "negative injunction" to prevent Chiles from performing with the Lions. Chiles retained the services of your law firm to represent him in the matter. The senior partner assigned the file to you. Assume that you are working on the case in August and that Chiles has not yet worked out or otherwise played with the Detroit Lions. The senior partner instructed you to complete the following tasks:

1. Outline the elements required for issuance of a "negative injunction."
2. Project the plaintiff's case from the evidence given in the problem text.
3. What defenses are available to Chiles? What evidence from the problem text supports Chiles' position?
4. What opportunities are likely available for compromise settlement?

Case File

MINNESOTA MUSKIES, INC. v. HUDSON

294 F. Supp. 979 (M.D.N.C. 1969)

Edwin M. Stanley, Chief Judge.

The plaintiffs seek by this action to enjoin the defendant, Louis C. Hudson, from playing professional basketball for any professional basketball team other than the plaintiff, Florida Professional Sports, Inc., for the term of an alleged contract he signed with the plaintiff, Minnesota Muskies, Inc., on May 3, 1967, and assigned to the plaintiff . . . on July 31, 1968. . . .

Facts

* * *

10. In the spring of 1966, Hudson was drafted by St. Louis in a player-draft held by the NBA, and on May 17, 1966, he signed an NBA Uniform Player Contract with St. Louis. The contract provided for the employment of Hudson as a basketball player for one year from October 1, 1966, with the following provision, known as a "reserve clause":

> "24. . . . If the Player fails, neglects, or omits to sign and return such contract to the Club so that the Club receives it on or before October 1st next succeeding, then this contract shall be deemed renewed and extended for the period of one year, upon the same terms and conditions in all respects as are provided herein, except that the compensation payable to the Player shall be the sum provided in the contract tendered to the Player pursuant to the provisions hereof, which compensation shall in no event be less than 75% of the compensation payable to the Player for the last playing season covered by this contract and renewals and extensions thereof.

> "The Club's right to renew this contract, as herein provided, and the promise of the Player not to play otherwise than for the Club and its assignees, have been taken into consideration in determining the amount of compensation payable under paragraph 2 hereof."

* * *

12. Hudson played for St Louis during the 1966-67 regular season, and during the NBA play-off games until St. Louis was eliminated from the play–off games on April 12, 1967. . . .

13. On or about March 4, 1967, Hudson borrowed $4,000.00 from St. Louis, for which he executed a promissory note. The note has typed on its face: "To be deducted from my 1967-68 contract with the St. Louis Hawks Basketball Club". . . .

* * *

15. On May 3, 1967, Hudson signed an ABA Uniform Player Contract with the Muskies. The contract provided for the employment of Hudson as a professional basketball player for a period of three years from October 2, 1967. . . .

* * *

17. The addendum to the contract between the Muskies and Hudson further provided as follows:

> "6. In the event legal proceedings be instituted to prevent and enjoin the Player from playing for the first year of this contract, and if the said legal proceeding be successful in that said Player be enjoined from playing for one year, then and in that event the Club will pay the Player the sum of $25,000.00 for the said year. The Player agrees to then play for the Club the next ensuing three years under the terms and conditions as set forth in Clause 1 of this Addendum . . . . "

18. The contract between Hudson and the Muskies also contains the following provision:

> "5. *Injunctive Relief.* The PLAYER hereby represents that he has special, exceptional and unique knowledge, skill and ability as a basketball player, the loss of which cannot be estimated with any certainty and cannot be fairly or adequately compensated by damages and therefore agrees that the CLUB shall have the right, in addition to any other rights that the CLUB may possess, to enjoin him by appropriate injunction proceedings against playing basketball, or engaging in activities related to basketball for any person, firm, corporation or institution, or injunction against any other breach of this contract."

19. As disclosed by the disposition testimony of the various individuals involved, the parties are in disagreement with respect to the details of the negotiations that led to the signing of the Hudson-Muskies contract. From the

conflicting testimony, it is found that sometime in March of 1967, at the time Hudson was still playing for St. Louis in playoff games, and while his contract with St. Louis was in full force and effect, Hudson was contacted by a representative of the Muskies for the purpose of determining whether he was interested in signing a professional basketball contract with the Muskies. After a series of telephone calls between Hudson and representatives of the Muskies organization, Hudson contacted his agent, Edward M. Cohen, an attorney in Minneapolis, and advised Cohen of his conversations with representatives of the Muskies and asked him to see what the Muskies had to offer . . . . Cohen immediately called to Hudson's attention the "reserve clause" in the contract, and questioned whether he would be a free agent at the end of the current basketball season. Nevertheless, it was decided that Cohen would continue his negotiations with the Muskies. . . . Cohen, Hudson, Barnett, Holman and Shields each attended some of the meetings, but all were not present at every meeting. The meetings culminated in Hudson and the Muskies signing the aforementioned contract on May 3, 1967.

20. All responsible officials of the Muskies, including Holman and Shields, were fully aware of the contract Hudson had with St. Louis before the contract between Hudson and the Muskies was prepared and signed, and had every reason to believe St. Louis would either exercise its options under the "reserve clause" of its existing contract or negotiate a new contract with Hudson. . . . Holman did not recognize any responsibility for conferring with St. Louis before executing the contract with Hudson, feeling that it was Hudson's duty to advise St. Louis as to the negotiations and the execution of the new contract.

21. Both parties to the Hudson–Muskies contract, as well as their attorneys, were uncertain as to the legal effect of the "reserve clause" in the St. Louis contract, and this uncertainty prompted Hudson to request that Paragraph 6 of the addendum be inserted in his contract with the Muskies. Further, it was Cohen's feeling that in the event St. Louis was successful in restraining Hudson from playing under his contract with the Muskies, Hudson was entitled to some financial protection.

22. On May 18, 1967, a press conference was held at the Leamington Hotel in Minneapolis, at which time the Muskies and Hudson announced that they had signed a contract. Following the press conference, a telegram, signed by Hudson, was sent to and received by Ben Kerner, the then owner of St. Louis, in which Kerner was advised that Hudson had signed with the Muskies and was not going to play with St. Louis. . . .

23. On May 25, 1967, one week after the Hudson-Muskies contract was publicly announced, St. Louis filed suit against the Muskies, all the other members of the ABA, and George Mikan, Commissioner of the ABA, in the United States District Court for the District of Minnesota, charging a conspiracy among the defendants, with respect to the Hudson-Muskies contract, to deliberately, maliciously, wrongfully and unjustifiably interfere with the contractual relation-

ship which existed between St. Louis and Hudson, and seeking actual damages in the sum of $2,000,000.00 and punitive damages in the sum of $1,000,000.00.

24. On May 25, 1967, St. Louis also filed suit against Hudson in the United States District Court for the District of Minnesota, seeking an injunction against Hudson from playing basketball for any other person, firm, or corporation, during the 1967-68 and the 1968-69 professional basketball seasons.

* * *

26. At the time Kerner received said telegram from Hudson, Ritchie Guerin, the St. Louis Coach, Bill Bridges, a member of the St Louis team and a roommate and close friend of Hudson, and some other St. Louis players, were in South America on a basketball tour. . . . Shortly thereafter, Hudson received a message at his home in Greensboro that Bridges was attempting to contact him by telephone from St. Louis. Before returning the call, Hudson called Cohen in Minneapolis and advised that certain St. Louis players, Bill Bridges for one, were desirous of seeking and talking with him. Cohen responded by telling Hudson that it was his personal business as to whether he talked with any of the St. Louis players, but reminded him of his contract with the Muskies. . . .

27. It is apparent that sometime during the early part of June of 1967 Hudson had become dissatisfied with the contract he had signed with the Muskies, and had decided to see if he could reach another agreement with St. Louis. . . . Hudson was in Atlanta on June 4, 1967, playing golf with Bridges and some other people. Either before or after his golf game, he wrote Kerner in St. Louis expressing regrets for the trouble he had caused St. Louis, and stating that he would like to continue with the St. Louis Club. . . .

28. On June 5, 1967, Hudson and St. Louis executed an NBA Uniform Player Contract covering a period of five years from October 1, 1967. . . .

* * *

30. Shortly after the signing of the Hudson-St. Louis contract on June 5, 1967, St. Louis submitted to a voluntary dismissal of the two actions it had brought in the United States District Court for the District of Minnesota against the Muskies, and others, and against Hudson. Answers had not been filed when the actions were dismissed.

31. Sometime in June or July of 1967, Hudson advised Cohen of the signing of the new St. Louis contract and instructed Cohen to return to the Muskies the $7,500.00 bonus the Muskies had paid him at the time he signed the Muskies contract. After receiving the instructions, Cohen called Holman and offered to return $5,000.00 of the $7,500.00 bonus, stating that this was all the money Hudson had at that time and that the balance would be paid "very shortly." Holman refused to accept the tender of $5,000.00, and also stated that he would refuse to take the full $7,500.00 should it be tendered.

* * *

33. On October 13, 1967, Holman wrote a letter to Hudson, in care of his attorney, Cohen, in which he stated that the Muskies were agreeable to Hudson playing out a one-year option with St. Louis, but that he was expected to perform under his contract with the Muskies at the end of the one-year option period, which was understood to be October 2, 1968. . . . The letter was received by Hudson, but he has never responded to same. . . . On May 3, 1968, in response to an inquiry, Cohen advised the Muskies that Hudson's position was that he did not have any contractual obligation to perform for the Muskies.

* * *

36. . . . There is no evidence that either Cousins or Sanders, or anyone else connected with the Atlanta purchase, had any knowledge of the Muskies having asserted a claim against Hudson until after the transaction with St. Louis had been closed. There is substantial evidence, however, that the transaction would not have been consummated, certainly not at the purchase price involved, if there had been any questions about the Hudson contracts.

* * *

40. On October 3, 1968, counsel for Hudson tendered to counsel for plaintiffs a certified check in the amount of $7,500.00, as reimbursement for the bonus paid Hudson by the Muskies. . . .

* * *

44. Hudson is highly skilled and talented, and possesses special, exceptional, and unique knowledge, skill and ability as a basketball player.

Discussion

The sole question presented for decision is whether the plaintiffs are entitled to an injunction restraining Hudson from playing professional basketball with any team or club other than Miami for the term of the contract he signed with the Muskies on May 3, 1967, and assigned by the Muskies to Miami on July 31, 1968. . . .

It is generally held that where a person agrees to render personal services to another, which require special and unique knowledge, skill and ability, so that in default the same services cannot easily be obtained from others, a court of equity is empowered to negatively enforce performance of the agreement by enjoining its breach. While acknowledging this principle of law, the defendants correctly assert that equitable relief should be denied to a suitor who comes into court with unclean hands. One of the most fundamental principles of equity jurisprudence is the maxim that "he who comes into equity must come with clean hands." Equity demands of suitors fair dealings with reference to matters concerning which they seek relief . . . .

Measured by these fundamental principles of equity jurisprudence, the conclusion is inescapable that the Muskies, in its dealings with Hudson, soiled the hands to such an extent that the negative injunctive relief sought should be denied. This is not to say that Hudson was an innocent bystander, or that he was an unwilling participant in his dealings with the Muskies. On the contrary, viewed strictly from the stand point of business morality, his position in this litigation, like that of the Muskies, is not an enviable one.

* * *

While not a controlling factor, the Court is convinced that the Muskies, admittedly desirous of acquiring a winning basketball team as quickly as possible, either contacted Hudson, or caused him to be contacted by someone on its behalf, while he was still actively engaged in the play-off games with St. Louis. Without this unwarranted interference on the part of the Muskies, there is every likelihood that Hudson would have fulfilled his contractual and moral obligations with St. Louis. . . .

Basically, the plaintiffs argue that Hudson's original contract with St. Louis, because it provides for perpetual service, and is lacking in the necessary qualities of definiteness, certainty, and mutuality, is void. The contract being void and unenforceable beyond the 1966-67 season, the plaintiffs contend that their contract with Hudson is in all respects valid, and that the Hudson-St. Louis contract executed on June 5, 1967, with knowledge of the existence of the Hudson-Muskies contract executed on May 3, 1967, is likewise void. Under these circumstances, plaintiffs assert that they are entitled to have their contract enforced in a court of equity. There is no merit to this argument. Even if the "reserve clause" in the St. Louis contract is of doubtful validity, the fact remains that the Muskies, knowing that Hudson was under a moral, if not a legal obligation to furnish his services to St. Louis for the 1967–68 and subsequent seasons, if St. Louis chose to exercise its option, sent for Hudson and induced him to repudiate his obligation to St. Louis. Such conduct, even if strictly within the law because of the St. Louis contract being unenforceable, was so tainted with unfairness and injustice as to justify a court of equity in withholding relief.

* * *

The Muskies chose to let Hudson return to St. Louis for the 1967-68 season rather than litigate the matter. The Muskies explained its inaction by stating that it recognized that Hudson was perhaps obligated to play for St. Louis for one more year. Notwithstanding its recognition of this obligation, the Muskies agreed to pay Hudson to sit out the 1967-68 season even if the Court should decree that the St. Louis contract was enforceable. This alone is sufficient for a court of equity to refuse relief.

Finally, plaintiffs insist that they are entitled to relief, notwithstanding their unfair and unjust conduct, because St. Louis was also guilty of inequitable and unlawful conduct in signing Hudson to a second contract on June 5, 1967, when it knew that Hudson had signed a valid contract with the Muskies on May 3, 1967. This argument is also lacking in merit. The doors of a court of equity are closed to one tainted with unfairness or injustice relative to the matter in which he seeks relief "however improper may have been the behavior of the defendant." . . .

The injunctive relief sought by the plaintiffs must be denied, not because the Hudson-St. Louis contract was of "any legal force and effect" or is one that "the courts will enforce," and not because the merits of the controversy are necessarily with St. Louis, "but solely because the actions and conduct of the (Muskies) in procuring the contract, upon which (its) right to relief is and must be founded, do not square with one of the vital and fundamental principles of equity which touches to the quick the dignity of a court of conscience and controls its decision regardless of all other considerations."

* * *

MUNCHAK CORP. v. CUNNINGHAM

457 F.2d 721 (4th Cir. 1972)

WINTER, Circuit Judge:

Plaintiffs, the owners and operators of the basketball club "The Carolina Cougars" sued to enjoin defendant, William John Cunningham, a professional basketball player, from performing services as a basketball player for any basketball club other than the Cougars. . . . The district court, finding that Cunningham had contracted to play for the Cougars, nevertheless concluded that even if Cunningham had failed and refused to perform his contract, plaintiffs had *unclean hands*. . . . It, therefore, denied injunctive relief.

In this appeal, we conclude that plaintiffs did not have *unclean hands*. . . . Accordingly, we reverse and remand the case for entry of an injunction restraining Cunningham from playing for any team other than the Cougars.

* * *

II

The principal reason why the district court refused equitable relief was that "the conclusion is inescapable that the Cougars, in its dealings with Cunningham, soiled its hands to such an extent that the injunctive relief sought should be denied." The *unclean hands* were found in the fact that the Cougars negotiated with Cunningham through intermediaries and agreed to pay him $80,000.00 if he did not play for the 76ers during his option year. We disagree.

In agreement with *Washington Capitols Basketball Club, Inc. v. Barry*, 419 F.2d 472 (9th Cir. 1969), we think that there was neither illegality nor *unclean hands* in the Cougars' contracting for Cunningham's services to be rendered *after* the term of his contract with the 76ers had expired, notwithstanding that the negotiations, whether directly or through intermediaries, took place while Cunningham's contract with the 76ers was still in full force and effect. As the *Washington Capitols* case stated, quoting from *Diodes, Inc. v. Franzen* "'no actionable wrong is committed by a competitor who solicits his competitor's employees or who hires away one or more of his competitor's employees who are not under contract, so long as the inducement to leave is not accompanied by unlawful action.'" Cunningham was under no obligation, option or restraint with respect to the 76ers after October 1, 1971, and the Cougars had a lawful right to bid and contract for his services to be rendered after that date.

* * *

DALLAS COWBOYS FOOTBALL CLUB, INC. v. HARRIS

348 S.W.2d 37 (Tex. Civ. App. 1961)

DIXON, Chief Justice.

Appellant Dallas Cowboys Football Club, Inc. . . . members of the National Football League, brought this action against James B. Harris for injunction to restrain Harris from playing professional football, or engaging in any activities related to professional football for anyone except the Club. Appellant alleged that Harris was bound by the terms of a written contract to play football for the Club and no one else, but that in violation of his contract he was playing football for the Dallas Texans Football Club, a member of the American Football League. . . .

In June 1958 James B. Harris for a consideration of $8,000.00 signed a contract to play football and to engage in activities related to football only for the Los Angeles Rams Football Club, a member of the National Football League. This contract covered a period of time beginning with the execution of the contract and extending to the first day of May following the 1958 football season, which latter date was May 1, 1959. The contract also included a clause providing that the Club at its option might renew the contract for an additional year. Both Harris and the Los Angeles Rams Football Club performed the primary contract which by its terms expired May 1, 1959. A controversy arose between the parties with reference, among other things, to the exercise by the Los Angeles Rams Club of its option on Harris' services for another year. As a result Harris chose not to play professional football during the 1959 season. Instead he reentered the University of Oklahoma as a student and also accepted a position as assistant football coach at the University.

In April 1960 Harris signed a contract to play football during the 1960 season for the Dallas Texans Football Club of the newly organized American Football League.

Harris' contract with the Los Angeles Rams was by its terms assignable. On July 22, 1960 the contract was assigned to the Dallas Cowboys Football Club, Inc., a new member of the National Football League. On the same date this suit was instituted against Harris by the latter club to restrain Harris from playing football for anyone except the Club.

Since the Club contends that Harris, as a matter of law, is bound by the terms of the 1958 contract and its option to play football only for the Club for an additional year, we deem it advisable to reproduce material parts of the contract:

> 2. The player agrees during the term of this contract he will play football and will engage in activities related to football only for the Club and as directed by the Club. . . .
>
> 3. For the Player's services . . . and for his agreement not to play football or engage in activities related to football for any other person, firm, corporation or institution during the term of this contract, and for the option hereinafter set forth . . . the Club promises to pay the Player . . . the sum of $8,000.00.
>
> 5. The player promises and agrees that during the term of this contract he will not play football or engage in activities related to football for any other person, firm, corporation or institution except with the prior written consent of the Club and the Commissioner. . . .
>
> 8. The Player hereby represents that he has special, exceptional and unique knowledge, skill and ability as a football player, the loss of which cannot be fairly or adequately compensated by damages and therefore agrees that the Club shall have the right, in addition to any other rights which the Club may possess, to enjoin him by appropriate injunction proceedings against playing football or engaging in activities related to football for any person, firm, corporation or institution and against any other breach of this contract. . . .

It is well established in this State and other jurisdictions that injunctive relief will be granted to restrain violation by an employee of negative covenants in a personal service contract if the employee is a person of exceptional and unique knowledge, skill and ability in performing the service called for in the contract.

But in this case there is a fact finding by a jury in answer to Special Issue No. 1 to the effect that at the time of the trial Harris did not have exceptional and unique knowledge, skill and ability as a football player. If the record reveals any evidence of probative force in support of this finding it was not error for the court to submit Special Issue No. 1 to the jury, nor was it error to overrule the Club's motions for summary judgment, directed verdict and judgment non obstante veredicto. If an issue of fact is raised by the evidence, it must go to the jury, though a verdict based on such evidence would have to be set aside as not supported by sufficient evidence.

In one of its points the Club takes the position that Harris by the express representations contained in his contract is estopped, as a matter of law, from disputing the fact that he possesses exceptional and unique knowledge, skill and ability as a football player.

We see no merit in the Club's claim of estoppel. We think the rule applicable here is stated correctly in 31 C.J.S. Estoppel § 79, p. 288: "To create an estoppel the representation relied on must be a statement of a material fact, and not a mere expression of opinion."

[In] this connection the testimony of Tom Landry, Head Coach of the Club, is of interest.

We quote from his testimony:

> "Q. . . . Paragraph 8 of the Plaintiff's contract says: "Player hereby represents he has special, exceptional and unique knowledge and skill and ability as a football player . . .? A. Well, I think the boy probably represents himself as being unique in that respect. Now, maybe he is not the best judge of his ability.
>
> "Q. Well, whether or not a man is unique is a matter of opinion, isn't it? A. I think that is probably true as far as forming a conclusion; yes."

The record discloses that appellee Harris himself on cross examination testified that he *thought* he had a certain amount of unique skill and ability.

But later a definition of the word "unique" was introduced without objection from appellant and in that connection Harris then testified as follows:

> "Q. Now, have you looked up the definition of "unique" in the dictionary? A. No, sir; I haven't.
>
> "Q. Well, I am reading from the New Century Dictionary here, and it says: "of which there is but one, or sole, or only"; Do you think you are the only defensive halfback? A. Not by any means of the imagination.
>
> "Q. It says, "Unparalleled or unequal" — you think you are unparalleled, or unequal? A. I wish I were, now.
>
> "Q. Do you think you are? A. No, sir; I am not. I know my own ability.
>
> "Q. It says, "something of which there is only one"; are you the only defensive halfback? A. No. I am not.
>
> "Q. "Something without parallel or equal of its kind"; are you that kind of a defensive halfback? A. No. I wish I was."

In view of the above testimony we are unable to agree with appellant Club that there is no evidence in the record of probative force to support the fact finding of the jury to the effect that Harris did not have exceptional and unique knowledge, skill and ability as a football player. Certainly we may not ignore the testimony, especially in view of the fact that it was admitted without objection. We overrule the Club's eight points on appeal in so far as they assert that the Club, under the record before us, was entitled to injunctive relief as a matter of law and that it was error for the court to submit Special Issue No. 1 and to overrule the motions for summary judgment, directed verdict and judgment non obstante veredicto.

Among the several grounds of error urged by the Club in its sixth point on appeal was this: the court erred in refusing to grant a new trial because the great weight and preponderance of the evidence showed that Harris did possess special, exceptional and unique knowledge, skill and ability as a football player, contrary to the answer of the jury.

* * *

As we said in substance earlier in this opinion, though there may be some evidence in the record which raises a fact issue necessitating the submission of the case to the jury, nevertheless it may be the duty of the court afterwards to grant a new trial if the record evidence is "insufficient" to support the jury verdict, that is, if the evidence is so against the overwhelming weight and preponderance of the evidence as to be manifestly wrong.

We think that is true in this case. The definition of the word "unique" introduced in evidence was too narrow and limited. We agree with the statement in *Philadelphia Ball Club v. Lajoie*, 202 Pa. 210, 51 A. 973, 58 L.R.A. 227, as follows:

> "We think, however, that in refusing relief unless the defendant's services were shown to be of such a character as to render it impossible to replace him he has taken extreme ground. It seems to us that a more just and equitable rule is laid down in Pom. Spec. Perf. p. 31, where the principle is thus declared: 'Where one person agrees to render personal services to another, which requires and presupposes a special knowledge, skill, and ability in the employee, so that in case of a default *the same service could not easily* be obtained from others, . . . its performance will be negatively enforced by enjoining its breach. . . .' WE have not found any case going to the [same] length of requiring, as a condition of relief, proof of the impossibility of obtaining equivalent service."

After a careful study of all the record evidence in this case we are of the opinion that the evidence is "insufficient" to support the jury finding.

All of those witnesses, whose testimony has any bearing on the question testified very positively that Harris was possessed of unique skill and ability. Prior to the introduction of the narrow and limited definition of "unique," Harris himself testified as follows:

> "Q. Jimmy, you signed contracts with both of them in which you represented that you did have unique skill and ability, didn't you? A. I thought I did.
>
> "Q. Well, you know that is in both of the contracts, don't you? A. That's right.
>
> "Q. . . . Then you know you do have unique skill and ability, don't you? A. I think I have a certain amount: yes.

"Q. You yourself told both clubs in your written contracts that you did have skill and ability, didn't you? A. That's right.

"Q. You now tell this jury that you have got that skill and ability, don't you? A. Right."

We also quote from the testimony of Don Rossi, General Manager of the Dallas Texans Football Club, who was a witness for Harris:

"Q. . . . In your opinion, Mr. Rossi, he does have exceptional skill and ability, doesn't he? A. Yes, sir.

"Q. Well, haven't you already testified that he was above the average? A. Well, yes, sir; average or above average.

"Q. That's right. A. Well, we will go along with that.

"Q. Well, he is above average, isn't he? A. We will buy that.

"Q. . . . Not buy it; you are just swearing to it? A. Yes sir."

The testimony of Schramm and Landry was even more positive. It is true that the witnesses named other professional football players who are "equal or better" than Harris as players, but the testimony was that players of Harris' ability were not available to the Club.

We sustain that part of the Club's sixth point on appeal wherein the Club asserts error in the court's refusing to grant a new trial because the great weight and preponderance of the evidence clearly showed that Harris did possess special, exceptional and unique knowledge, skill and ability as a football player, contrary to the answers of the jury.

In three cross-points Harris says that . . . the relief sought by the Club should be denied as a matter of law because (1) the contract was invalid not having been formed by a proper offer and acceptance; (2) the contract was not valid, having expired by its own terms, and (3) Harris had not retired from activities related to football.

We have concluded that these cross-points should be overruled.

We cannot support Harris' contention that the contract is so unreasonable and harsh as to be unenforceable in equity.

NOTES AND COMMENTS

1. The "negative injunction" was utilized early in cases concerning entertainment matters. *See Metropolitan Exhibition Co. v. Ewing*, 42 N.E. 198 (S.D.N.Y. 1890); *Metropolitan Exhibition Co. v. Ward*, 9 N.Y.S. 779 (1890). *See also Lumley v. Wagner*, 42 ENG. REP. 687 (1852). For general discussion of the negative injunction, including the historical basis, *see* GREENBERG & GRAY, 1 SPORTS LAW PRACTICE § 2.05 (2d ed. 2005); Uberstine, *The Enforceability of*

Sports Industry Employment Agreements, in 2 Law Of Professional & Amateur Sports ch. 10 (Uberstine ed. 2005).

2. *See Washington Capitols Basketball Club, Inc. v. Barry*, 419 F.2d 472 (9th Cir. 1969), for another instructive case regarding the negative injunction. Rick Barry began his professional basketball career in San Francisco playing for the NBAWarriors. At the termination of that contract, Barry signed with the ABA Oakland Oaks for three years. After the first year of the contract, the Oaks were sold and the franchise was moved to Washington, D.C. and renamed the Capitols. Upon receiving news of the franchise shift, Barry signed a contract with the NBA Warriors for a term overlapping with his ABA contract. The Capitols in turn brought suit to prevent Barry from playing for the Warriors and were successful in securing injunctive relief against Barry. Barry's allegation that the Oaks should not receive equitable relief because of "unclean hands" (for having lured Barry away from the Warriors) was unavailing. The court stated the principle that there is nothing "unclean" or tortious about negotiating for services to commence after the termination of a preexisting contract.

An annotation of negative injunction cases by sport is found at *Cincinnati Bengals v. Bergey*, 453 F. Supp. 129, 139 n.1 (S.D. Ohio 1985).

3. The "irreparable harm" requirement for the issuance of the negative injunction usually is determined by the "unique skills test." For a case departing from the test, *see Boston Professional Hockey Assoc., Inc. v. Cheevers*, 348 F. Supp. 261 (D. Mass. 1971), *remanded on other grounds*, 472 F.2d 127 (1st Cir. 1972) (district court assessed the effect on the team's economic position to deny the injunction on the irreparable harm issue, despite the fact that the player possessed unique skills).

4. Few cases are found involving professional sports athletes in which courts denied negative injunctions on the basis of inadequate or ordinary skills. Do professional players satisfy the test *per se*? For a case suggesting an answer in the affirmative, *see Central New York Basketball Club, Inc. v. Barnett*, 181 N.E.2d 506 (Ohio C.P. 1961). *But see, Matuszak v. Houston Oilers, Inc.*, 515 S.W.2d 725 (Tex. Civ. App. 1974) (question of skills depends on facts of each case).

The Albany Black Sox, a minor league baseball team, failed to satisfactorily establish "the unique and unusual" character of the services of its first baseman. Thus, the team's request for issuance of an injunction was denied. But, the court also found the player contract did not meet the requirement of mutuality of obligation. *Spencer v. Milton*, 287 N.Y.S. 944 (Sup. Ct. 1936). Can you adequately distinguish minor league ballplayers from major league players in terms of skill? Is the fact that only a small percentage of minor league players ever make the major leagues helpful in this regard? But, remember that only a minute percentage of amateur athletes are able to procure professional sports contracts, even at the minor league level.

For a case in which the court enjoined two rookies without any professional experience from jumping from a Canadian professional football club (CFL) to the

Cleveland Browns, *see Winnipeg Rugby Football Club v. Freeman & Locklear*, 140 F. Supp. 365 (N.D. Ohio 1955). For older cases of questionable authority finding that athletes did not have unique skills, *see Brooklyn Baseball Club v. McGuire*, 116 F. 782 (E.D. Pa. 1902); *American Base Ball and Athletic Exhibition Co. v. Harper*, 54 Cent. L.J. 449 (Cir. Ct. St. Louis 1902).

Perhaps it is helpful to review the basis of the negative injunction issued in *Philadelphia Ball Club v. Lajoie*, 51 A. 973 (Pa. 1902). The court enunciated the question as not whether the player was "irreplaceable," but whether replacement of the player on the playing field could be translated into money damages. Thus, the question was whether harm was irreparable, or the damage remedy at law inadequate.

5. Although problems with establishing "unique skill" may seem minimal, the attorney must, nevertheless, present the proof through direct evidence in the plaintiff's case. The task may prove interesting, as the *Harris* case, *supra*, illustrates.

6. Review the four essential elements of the action for a preliminary negative injunction set forth in *Bergey, supra*. Notice that the plaintiff has the burden of showing the absence of harm to the defendant. Is the court balancing the irreparable harm to the plaintiff under the *status quo* with the projected harm to the defendant in the event an injunction is issued? Is the court utilizing a test of reasonableness? How will you attempt to show absence of harm to a minor league player who desires to better the player's economic and professional opportunities by jumping to another club?

7. What arguments exist, pro and con, that the public is harmed if an injunction is granted? *See Cincinnati Bengals v. Bergey,* 453 F. Supp. 129, 147 (S.D. Ohio 1985).

8. A threshold question is whether the team possesses an exclusive right to the player's services. The terms drafted in the form contracts utilized by the major sports leagues clearly establish a team's exclusive right. The nature of the contract rights and duties may not be so clear in cases involving individual sports participants. *See, e.g., Madison Square Boxing, Inc. v. Shavers*, 434 F. Supp. 449 (S.D.N.Y. 1977) (Boxing); *Machen v. Johansson,* 174 F. Supp. 522 (S.D.N.Y. 1959) (Boxing).

9. Some courts require proof that defendant is or contemplates performing for an entity in direct economic competition with the plaintiff. The negative injunction, theoretically, enforces a negative covenant, not an affirmative promise. The New England Patriots of the NFL, for example, filed suit to enjoin Chuck Fairbanks, head coach, from making a career change to college coaching. *New England Patriots Football Club, Inc. v. University of Colo.*, 592 F.2d 1196 (1st Cir. 1979) (*See* **Case File** at **Chapter 12, Section F**, *infra*.) The coach–team contract included a negative covenant prohibiting Fairbanks from participating in "football" matters. A question arose whether the University of Colorado football program was in direct economic competition with the New England Patriots.

The competition may exist between teams in a league, teams in different leagues, or teams in different sports. Competition may occur on the ballfield for victories, or in the front office or TV studio for the fan market. Is the question in the *New England* case more appropriately phrased as a contract construction question, seeking the intent of the parties? Is the term "football," as used in the contract, ambiguous?

10. In the event a court awards damages, either in lieu of, or in addition to an injunction, what valuation methods exist to prove the damages with reasonable certainty? *See Eckles v. Sharman*, 548 F.2d 905 (10th Cir. 1977).

11. For every case of "team jumping," there exist at least two potential causes of action. The former team usually files an action against the player for a negative injunction, and a suit against the signing team for tortious interference with a valid business relationship. Does adjudication of one cause serve as collateral estoppel barring judicial resolution of the other? For discussion of intentional interference with contractual relations, *see* **Chapter 12, Section F**, *infra*.

12. For other cases in which the "clean hands" doctrine was used as a defense, *see Houston Oilers, Inc. v. Neely*, 361 F.2d 36 (10th Cir. 1966) (issued injunction, rejecting defense of unclean hands based on club signing college player prior to completion of eligibility in violation of NCAA rules); *New York Football Giants, Inc. v. Los Angeles Chargers Football Club, Inc.*, 291 F.2d 471 (5th Cir. 1961) (denied injunction on basis of defense of unclean hands resulting from club signing college player prior to completion of eligibility in violation of NCAA rules). For an analysis of the "clean hands doctrine" in the context of equitable remedies in sports cases, *see* Wichmann, *Players, Owners, and Contracts in the NFL: Why the Self-Help Specific Performance Remedy Cannot Escape the Clean Hands Doctrine*, 22 SEATTLE U. L. REV. 835 (1999).

13. What other contract defenses are available in addition to the defenses used in the cases found in the **Case File**, *supra*? *See, e.g., Boston Celtics v. Shaw*, 908 F.2d 1041 (1st Cir. 1990) (player argued promise to cancel a contract to play for an Italian basketball club is "null and void").

14. Player suits against teams or leagues for damages may be preempted by federal law. The United States Supreme Court has held that Section 301 of the Labor Management Act, 29 U.S.C. § 185, preempts state law claims that are substantially dependent upon analysis of a collective bargaining agreement. *Allis-Chalmers Corp. v. Lueck*, 471 U.S. 202, 220 (1985). The Act provides that contract actions between an employer and a labor organization may be brought in federal district court. If the conduct arises out of activities covered in the collective bargaining agreement, the matter is preempted. If the alleged conduct is unlawful or otherwise outside of activities contemplated by the agreement, state law claims are not preempted.

In *Smith v. Houston Oilers, Inc.*, 87 F.3d 717 (5th Cir.), *cert denied,* 117 S. Ct. 510 (1996), Sherman Smith and Tracy Smith sued the Houston Oilers and members of the staff, alleging that defendants required plaintiffs to participate in an abusive rehabilitation program, and made threats of dismissing the players and blackballing them with other NFL teams. Plaintiffs' state law tort claims arising out of the rehabilitation program were preempted by § 301 as a contract claim interpreting the CBA. Although the intentional infliction of emotional distress claim alleged activities not condoned by the CBA, the activities, if proven, constituted an unfair labor practice pursuant to §§ 7 and 8 of the National Labor Relations Act, and thus were preempted by federal law. *See also Hendy v. Losse*, 925 F.2d 1470 (9th Cir. 1991) (unpublished) (player suit against team physician for negligent and intentional withholding of medical information not preempted by CBA; physician duty to disclose arises from state law doctrine of informed consent).

15. In the Latrell Sprewell case concerning the proper NBA sanctions for violence in the workplace, the player physically attacked the coach during and after a practice session in 1997. The Golden State Warriors suspended Sprewell for a minimum of ten games and reserved the right to terminate his contract, which was later exercised. After investigation, the NBA suspended Sprewell for one year. The NBPA, on behalf of Sprewell, filed a grievance pursuant to the terms of the collective bargaining agreement. The arbitrator determined that the sanctions applied to Sprewell by the Warriors and NBA were permissible under the terms of the CBA, but that the Warrior's termination of Sprewell's contract was not supported by "just cause" and that the NBA's suspension should be limited to the remainder of the 1997-98 season. *In the Matter of Arbitration Between National Basketball Players Association on behalf of Player Latrell Sprewell and Warriors Basketball Club and National Basketball Association* (Feerick, Arb., March 4, 1998).

In May of 1998, Sprewell filed an action in federal district court alleging eleven causes of action, including a civil rights claim, and seeking vacatur of the arbitrator's decision. The court dismissed the Complaint without prejudice on July 30, 1998. Plaintiff filed an Amended Complaint on August 31. Plaintiff dropped antitrust and breach of contract claims, and introduced a new claim that defendants conspired to interfere with the arbitral process by producing false evidence. *Sprewell v. Golden State Warriors*, 1999 WL 179682, 1, 2 (N.D. Cal. 1999). The court granted Defendants' 12(b)(6) Motion to Dismiss the claims based on the civil rights allegations, and those attacking the propriety of the arbitration process. The court dismissed Plaintiff's state law claims as preempted by § 301 of the LMRA. The court explained the operative test for preemption as whether evaluation of the claim is "inextricably intertwined with consideration of the terms of the labor contract." *Id.* at 6. "If in the course of assessing the state law claim, the court must refer to the collective bargaining agreement in order to evaluate it, then that claim is preempted. . . ." *Id.* Plaintiff's claims were predicated upon the alleged impropriety of Defendants' actions concerning the suspension and contract termination, matters within the scope of the CBA's grievance and arbitration provisions. The court also granted Defendants' motion for sanctions pursuant to FRCP 11. *Id.* at 7.

The Court of Appeals for the Ninth Circuit affirmed the District Court's dismissal of Sprewell's claims related to the arbitration process, civil rights allegations, common law right of fair procedure, and the California Unruh Act as preempted by the National Labor Relations Act. The court reversed and remanded dismissal of state law claims for intentional interference with contract, intentional interference with business relations, civil conspiracy, and unfair business practices. The court stated, "[T]he alleged actions of the NBA and the Warriors, if proven true, would qualify as 'wrongful conduct' under California law independent of the rights and responsibilities set forth in the CBA." *Sprewell v. Golden State Warriors*, 266 F.3d 979, 991 (9th Cir. 2001), withdrawing 231 F.3d 520 (9th Cir. 2000), and amended at 275 F.3d 1187 (9th Cir. 2001).

C. GRIEVANCE ARBITRATION

1. Player-Team Contract Disputes — Generally

Conflicts regularly arise concerning the rights and duties of players and teams under the terms of collective bargaining agreements, player team contracts, and league constitutions and other governing documents. In professional sports, most conflicts between players and teams or leagues are resolved by arbitration rather than adjudication. The collective bargaining agreements of all major professional sports leagues contain provisions for arbitration of grievances. Baseball's salary arbitration system is presented in **Section D**, *infra*. Grievance arbitration in the sports industries, like arbitration in non-sports settings, is governed and otherwise established by the terms of contractual agreements, including collective bargaining agreements. Thus, the attorney must be well acquainted with the scope of the respective arbitration clauses, the procedures established by the various agreements, and the methods of selecting arbitrators.

2. Grievance Arbitration in Professional Sports

Arbitration in professional sports, arising from the collective bargaining agreements, is considered "labor" arbitration. Arbitration in other contexts is categorized as "commercial arbitration." For example, provisions in league constitutions requiring arbitration for the resolution of disputes between member ballclubs are classified as "commercial arbitration." Courts readily conclude that the subject matter of a dispute between player and team is within the scope of the arbitration clauses of the collective bargaining agreement and player team contract. Parties, however, may expressly or impliedly waive the right to arbitration. Strict time limitations appear as a matter of contract in the provisions of the collective bargaining agreements. As the problem below and **Case File** illustrate, the ballclub defendant to a suit by a player-plaintiff usually files a motion to dismiss and/or compel arbitration under the terms of the player contract. The right to rely on the arbitration provision may be waived by the defendant's unreasonable delay in making the motion. *See, e.g., Spain v. Houston Oilers, Inc.*, 593 S.W.2d 746 (Tex. Civ. App. 1979).

Judicial review of a labor arbitration decision is limited in scope, as indicated by the United States Supreme Court opinion in *Garvey*, **Case File**, *infra*. A court may overturn an arbitrator's ruling only when the arbitrator has strayed from application of the agreement and "dispensed his own brand of industrial justice." The scope of judicial review of commercial arbitration decisions is also limited by state and federal arbitration acts. *See Buzas Baseball, Inc. v. Salt Lake Trappers, Inc.*, 925 P.2d 941 (Utah 1996) (trial court inappropriately substituted its judgment for that of the arbitrator; arbitration panel did not exceed its authority; arbitration award did not represent material miscalculation; there was no manifest disregard of law; arbitration award was not made in violation of public policy; Federal Arbitration Act, which does not provide for attorney fees, does not preempt Utah Arbitration Act which does so provide). For arbitration that is mandated by statute, the standard of judicial review is *de novo*. *See Bowers v. Andrew Weir Shipping, Ltd.*, 27 F.3d 800 (2d Cir. 1994) (circuit courts apply *de novo* standard of review for statutorily mandated arbitration under 29 U.S.C. § 1401(a)).

In disciplinary cases, the arbitrator determines whether "just cause" exists to support the imposition of discipline for a particular offense, and the degree of penalty imposed. "Just cause" is evaluated according to the terms of the applicable agreement, existing rules and regulations, the circumstances attending the particular action under review, and the common law of the workplace. *See* Snow, *Contract Interpretation*, THE COMMON LAW OF THE WORKPLACE: THE VIEWS OF ARBITRATORS § 2.2 (St. Antoine ed. 2005), *citing Steelworkers v. Warrior & Gulf Navigation Co.,* 363 U.S. 574 (1960) (arbitrators possess knowledge of the "common law of the shop," in defining broad terms, such as "just cause").

Roger I. Abrams
Off His Rocker: Sports Discipline and Labor Arbitration

11 Marq. Sports L. Rev. 167 (2001)*

In his now famous December 27, 1999, *Sports Illustrated* story, reporter Jeff Pearlman revealed to the world the ugly side of Atlanta's hyperactive relief pitcher, John Rocker. . . .

Major League Baseball Commissioner Bud Selig suspended the "Mouth of the South," saying that his insensitive and inappropriate remarks "offended practically every element of society." Selig barred Rocker from spring training and playing the first month of the 2000 season and fined him $20,000.00. . . .

The Major League Baseball Players Association vowed to contest the Commissioner's penalty, as was its right under the terms of the collective bargaining agreement between Major League Baseball and the Association. . . .

At the arbitration hearing, the Commissioner's Office bore the burden of proving "just cause" for its discipline. Although Rocker's prominence in a major professional sport made his remarks and the resulting discipline national news, his case was not unlike hundreds of other discipline cases heard by labor arbitrators every year.

John Rocker and his fellow Major League ballplayers are employees of their respective clubs. . . . [T]hey are covered by the same protections, and subject to the same uncertainties, as factory workers. Like all employees, they have federally-protected rights to organize a union for purposes of collective bargaining. . . .

Baseball management and the Players Association select a permanent arbitrator to adjudicate disputes that arise during the term of the agreement. He serves at the pleasure of the parties and can be fired by either side. . . . During his service, the permanent arbitrator is expected to apply the generally understood principles of the common law of the collective bargaining agreement much as any appointed labor neutral.

Had John Rocker disparaged or verbally abused his manager or coaches in the clubhouse, a fairly easy case could be made that his aspersions would tend to undermine the authority of his supervisors. In fact, his intemperate language might even be considered "fighting words" worthy of serious discipline. Baseball players must conduct themselves in an appropriate manner toward their employer's representatives.

Rocker's ill-considered words were said away from the workplace, although one of his racist remarks concerned a teammate. In general, events away from the workplace are none of the employer's business, unless the employer can prove convincingly how the conduct would affect the employer's enterprise. The Union undoubtedly argued at the arbitration hearing that what this player said on his own time, away from the workplace, simply did not satisfy the high standard of proof.

In some instances, however, employee off-premises activities will lead to sustainable discipline. For example, an employee convicted of a notorious crime may bring harm to an employer's public image and thus affect a business' good will with actual and potential customers. An employee's legal, but disreputable, off-duty activities, for example, serving as the local commandant of a racist organization, may make it difficult for fellow employees to work with him productively or may result in a loss of business. Arbitrators have ruled that misbehavior away from work can implicate a legitimate employer interest justifying discipline or even discharge. . . .

At the Rocker hearing, the Commissioner's Office had to prove how the business of baseball was affected by Rocker's incendiary remarks. . . . [T]he Players Association undoubtedly pressed its claim that the Commissioner's penalty was unprecedented and draconian. . . . An unprecedented suspension is troubling, however, only if the discipline is unwarranted.

Parties to a collective bargaining agreement normally intend that management will follow progressive discipline in response to employee misconduct, imposing increasing penalties for repeated offenses in an effort to rehabilitate an employee and deter future misconduct. Under the contractual "just cause" standard, employers must use discipline to guide an employee toward improved performance. An employer has no legitimate parens patriae interest in punishing a misbehaving worker.

For relatively minor employee offense — poor work performance or tardiness, for example — an employer must first warn an employee of future disciplinary consequences if a misstep is repeated. Then, if necessary, the employer may impose more serious discipline — perhaps a suspension — in an effort to rehabilitate the worker. In the absence of proof of a cardinal sin — striking a supervisor, for example — an employer must try to teach a worker to do better and not repeat his misconduct. Especially in a tight labor market, it is to management's advantage to try to salvage a trained and experienced worker. In the process, an employer can seek to deter other employees from following the example of a disciplined employee. Ultimately, despite progressive discipline, if an employee proves incorrigible, dismissal would be warranted.

The Commissioner disciplined John Rocker to teach him the limits of his "lip." Other ballplayers certainly took notice of the suspension. . . . The question for the arbitrator was whether the penalty was more severe than necessary to accomplish these legitimate purposes of rehabilitation and deterrence. . . .

Arbitrator Das determined that the extent of discipline imposed by the Commissioner did not comport with the basic fairness due all employees. It was unduly harsh. . . . On the other hand, Das upheld the Commissioner's basic right, in appropriate circumstances, to discipline players for "pure speech" off the field that affects the business of baseball. . . . His conclusion . . . is well within the range of awards normally issued by labor arbitrators. . . .

PROBLEM

Tyrone Armstead was recently released by the Chicago Bulls of the National Basketball Association. Armstead is a ten year veteran. He was voted all-NBA forward on six occasions. One major publication selected Armstead as the "dream" power forward in the history of the NBA. The forward has never been injured or otherwise missed practice or a game. He is considered a leader by the other Bulls players, who regularly follow his advice. Armstead started for the Bulls last season. He was 7th in the NBA in scoring and 4th in rebounds. The player feels that he is in as good physical condition for the current season as he has been for any previous season.

Armstead was released pursuant to Article 20(b)(2) of the Uniform Player Contract:

> The club may terminate this contract upon written notice to the Player (but only after complying with the waiver procedure . . .) if the Player shall at any time: Fail, in the sole opinion of the Club's management, to exhibit sufficient skill or competitive ability to qualify to continue as a member of the Club's team. . . .

Armstead "cleared" waivers with no offers from other clubs in the NBA. He received written notice from the Bulls. All other procedural or technical requirements for termination of the contract under the governing documents of the NBA are satisfied.

Armstead was for two years the NBPA representative from the Bulls. Armstead, a college graduate with a degree in international relations, was instrumental in negotiations between management and labor of the current collective bargaining agreement. Armstead feels that his release was not made on the basis of skill or ability, but as retribution for his union activities. "The Bulls," Armstead said, "also do not want me around their younger players. I will tell them the truth about the flexibility of the salary cap." The Uniform Player Contract contains an arbitration clause, as follows:

> In the event of any dispute arising between the Player and the Club, relating to any matter arising under this contract or concerning the performance or interpretation thereof . . . , such dispute shall be resolved in accordance with the Grievance and Arbitration Procedure set forth in the Agreement currently in effect between the National Basketball Association and the National Basketball Players Association.

Armstead continues to work out and remains in good shape. But, he has received no phone calls or other contact from NBA teams. NBA scouts consider the lack of interest in Armstead a curiously odd phenomenon. One scout remarked, "There are eight teams in the NBA who need a player like Armstead. They could afford him, too." Armstead received two offers from Continental Basketball Association teams. One tentative offer was received from a European team. The NBPA is amenable to joining Armstead in any action against the NBA, but has made no effort to unilaterally challenge his release.

Armstead hired your law firm to represent him in the matter. The senior partner assigned the case to you. The partner requests that you respond to the following:

1. What arguments can you make that the release of Armstead constitutes a breach of the player-team contract? What counter-arguments do you expect from the Bulls?

2. How can you avoid the arbitration clause of the Uniform Player Contract? What are the arguments, pro and con?

3. In the event the matter is submitted to arbitration, what is the nature and scope of judicial review of an arbitrator's decision?

4. Develop a case based on the Baseball Collusion decision. What evidence above is useful? What additional evidence is needed?

CASE FILE

MAJOR LEAGUE BASEBALL PLAYERS ASS'N v. GARVEY

532 U.S. 504 (2001)

PER CURIAM.

The Court of Appeals for the Ninth Circuit here rejected an arbitrator's findings and then resolved the merits of the parties' dispute instead of remanding the case for further arbitration proceedings. . . .

In the late 1980's, petitioner Major League Baseball Players Association (Association) filed grievances against the Major League Baseball Clubs (Clubs), claiming the Clubs had colluded in the market for free-agent services after the 1985, 1986 and 1987 baseball seasons, in violation of the industry's collective-bargaining agreement. . . . In a series of decisions, arbitrators found collusion by the Clubs and damage to the players. The Association and Clubs subsequently entered into a Global Settlement Agreement (Agreement), pursuant to which the Clubs established a $280 million fund to be distributed to injured players. The Association also designed a "Framework" to evaluate the individual player's claims, and applying that Framework, recommended distribution plans for claims relating to particular season or seasons.

The Framework provided that players could seek an arbitrator's review of the distribution plan. The arbitrator would determine "only whether the approved Framework and the criteria set forth therein have been properly applied in the proposed Distribution Plan." (*Garvey I*). The Framework set forth factors to be considered in evaluating players' claims, as well as specific requirements for lost contract-extension claims. Such claims were cognizable "'only in those cases where evidence exists that a specific offer of an extension was made by a club prior to collusion only to thereafter be withdrawn when the collusion scheme was initiated.'"

Respondent Steve Garvey, a retired, highly regarded first baseman, submitted a claim for damages of approximately $3 million. He alleged that his contract with the San Diego Padres was not extended to the 1988 and 1989 seasons due to collusion. The Association rejected Garvey's claim in February 1996, because he presented no evidence that the Padres actually offered to extend his contract. Garvey objected, and an arbitration hearing was held. . . . He presented a June 1996 letter from Ballard Smith, Padres' President and CEO from 1979 to 1987, stating that, before the end of the 1985 season, Smith offered to extend Garvey's contract through the 1989 season, but that the Padres refused to negotiate with Garvey thereafter due to collusion.

The arbitrator denied Garvey's claim, after seeking additional documentation from the parties. In his award, he explained that " '[t]here exists . . . substantial doubt as to the credibility of the statements in the Smith letter.' " . . . He noted the "stark contradictions" between the 1996 letter and Smith's testimony in the earlier arbitration proceedings regarding collusion, where Smith . . . stated that the Padres simply were not interested in extending Garvey's contract. The arbitrator determined that, due to these contradictions, he must reject [Smith's] more recent assertion . . . , and found that Garvey had not shown a specific offer of extension. He concluded that:

> " '[t]he shadow cast over the credibility of the Smith testimony coupled with the absence of any other corroboration of the claim submitted by Garvey compels a finding that the Padres declined to extend his contract . . . as a baseball judgment founded upon [Garvey's] age and recent injury history.' "

Garvey moved in Federal District Court to vacate the arbitrator's award, alleging that the arbitrator violated the Framework by denying his claim. The District Court denied the motion. The Court of Appeals for the Ninth Circuit reversed by a divided vote. The court acknowledged that judicial review of the merits of the arbitrator's decision in a labor dispute is extremely limited. But it held that review of the merits of the arbitrator's award was warranted in this case, because the arbitrator " 'dispensed his own brand of industrial justice.' " The court recognized that Smith's prior testimony . . . conflicted with the statements in his 1996 letter. But in the court's view, the arbitrator's refusal to credit Smith's letter was "inexplicable" and "border[ed] on the irrational," because a panel of arbitrators, chaired by the arbitrator involved here, had previously concluded that the owners' prior testimony was false. The court rejected the arbitrator's reliance on the absence of other corroborating evidence, attributing that tact to Smith and Garvey's direct negotiations. The court also found that the record provided "strong support" for the truthfulness of Smith's 1996 letter. The Court of Appeals reversed and remanded with directions to vacate the award.

The District Court then remanded the case to the arbitration panel for further hearings, and Garvey appealed. The Court of Appeals, again by a divided vote, explained that *Garvey I* established that "the conclusion that Smith made Garvey an offer and subsequently withdrew it because of the collusion scheme was the only conclusion that the arbitrator could draw from the record in the proceedings. (*Garvey II*). . . . The Court of Appeals reversed the District Court and directed that it remand the case to the arbitration panel with instructions to enter an award for Garvey in the amount he claimed.

The parties do not dispute that this case arises under § 301 of the Labor Management Relations Act. . . . Although Garvey's specific allegation is that the arbitrator violated the Framework for resolving player's claims for damages, that Framework was designed to facilitate payments to remedy the Clubs' breach of the collective-bargaining agreement. Garvey's right to be made whole is founded on that agreement.

Judicial review of a labor-arbitration decision pursuant to such an agreement is very limited. Courts are not authorized to review the arbitrator's decision on the merits despite allegations that the decision rests on factual errors or misinterprets the parties' agreement. We recently reiterated that if an "'arbitrator is even arguably construing or applying the contract and acting within the scope of his authority,' the fact that 'a court is convinced he committed serious error does not suffice to overturn his decision.'" It is only when an arbitrator strays from interpretation and application of the agreement and effectively "dispense[s] his own brand of industrial justice" that his decision may be unenforceable. When an arbitrator resolves disputes regarding the application of a contract, and no dishonesty is alleged, the arbitrator's "improvident, even silly, factfinding" does not provide a basis for a reviewing court to refuse to enforce the award.

In discussing the courts' limited role in reviewing the merits of arbitration awards, we have stated that "'courts . . . have no business weighing the merits of the grievance [or] considering whether there is equity in a particular claim.'" When the judiciary does so, "it usurps a function which . . . is entrusted to the arbitration tribunal." Consistent with this limited role, we said in *Misco* that "[e]ven in the very rare instances when an arbitrator's procedural aberrations rise to the level of affirmative misconduct, as a rule the court must not foreclose further proceedings by settling the merits according to its own judgment. . . . That step, we explained, "would improperly substitute a judicial determination for the arbitrator's decision that the parties bargained for" in their agreement. Instead, the court should simply vacate the award, thus leaving open the possibility of further proceedings if they are permitted under the terms of the agreement.

To be sure, the Court of Appeals here recited these principles, but its application of them is nothing short of baffling. The substance of the Court's discussion reveals that it overturned the arbitrator's decision because it disagreed with the arbitrator's factual findings. . . . The Court of Appeals, it appears, would have credited Smith's 1996 letter, and found the arbitrator's refusal to do so at worst "irrational" and at best "bizarre." But even "serious error" on the arbitrator's part does not justify overturning his decision, where as here, he is construing a contract and acting within the scope of his authority.

In *Garvey II*, the court clarified that *Garvey I* both rejected the arbitrator's findings and went further, resolving the merits of the parties' dispute based on the court's assessment of the record before the arbitrator. For that reason, the court found further arbitration proceedings inappropriate. But again, established law ordinarily precludes a court from resolving the merits of the parties' dispute on the basis of its own factual determinations, no matter how erroneous the arbitrator's decision. Even when the arbitrator's award may properly be vacated, the appropriate remedy is to remand the case for further arbitration proceedings. . . . If a remand is appropriate *even* when the arbitrator's award has been set aside for "procedural aberrations" that constitute "affirmative misconduct," it follows that a remand ordinarily will be appropriate when the arbitrator simply made factual findings that the reviewing court perceives as "irrational." The Court of Appeals usurped the arbitrator's role by resolving the dispute and barring further proceedings, a result at odds with this governing law.

For the foregoing reasons, the Court of Appeals erred in reversing the order of the District Court denying the motion to vacate the arbitrator's award, and it erred further in directing that judgment be entered in Garvey's favor. The judgment of the Court of Appeals is reversed, and the case is remanded for further proceedings consistent with this opinion.

Justice GINSBURG, concurring in part and concurring in the judgment.

I agree with the Court that in . . . (*Garvey I*), the Ninth Circuit should not have disturbed the arbitrator's award. Correction of that error sets this case straight. I see no need to say more.

Justice STEVENS, dissenting.

It is well settled that an arbitrator "does not sit to dispense his own brand of industrial justice." We have also said fairly definitively, albeit in dicta, that a court should remedy an arbitrator's "procedural aberrations" by vacating the award and remanding for further proceedings. Our cases, however, do not provide significant guidance as to what standards a federal court should use in assessing whether an arbitrator's behavior is so untethered to either the agreement of the parties or the factual record so as to constitute an attempt to "dispense his own brand of industrial justice." Nor, more importantly, do they tell us how, having made such a finding, courts should deal with "the extraordinary circumstance in which the arbitrator's own rulings make clear that, more than being simply erroneous, his finding is completely inexplicable and borders on the irrational." . . . Because our case law is not sufficiently clear to allow me to conclude that the case below was wrongly decided — let alone to conclude that decision was wrong as to require the extraordinary remedy of summary reversal — I dissent from the Court's disposition of this petition.

Without the benefit of briefing or argument, today the Court resolves two difficult questions. First, it decided that even if the Court of Appeals' appraisal of the merits is correct — that is to say, even if the arbitrator did dispense his own brand of justice untethered to the agreement of the parties, and even if the correct disposition of the matter is perfectly clear — the only course open to a reviewing court is to remand the matter for another arbitration. That conclusion is not compelled by any of our cases, nor by any analysis offered by the Court. . . .

Second, without reviewing the record or soliciting briefing, the Court concludes that, in any event, "no serious error on the arbitrator's part is apparent in this case." At this stage in the proceedings, I simply cannot endorse that conclusion. After examining the record, obtaining briefing, and hearing oral argument, the Court of Appeals offered a reasoned explanation of its conclusion. Whether or not I would ultimately agree with the Ninth Circuit's analysis, I find the Court's willingness to reverse a factbound determination of the Court of Appeals without engaging that court's reasoning a troubling departure from our normal practice.

DRYER v. LOS ANGELES RAMS

709 P.2d 826 (Cal. 1985)

KAUS, Justice.

Defendant Los Angeles Rams (Rams) and individual codefendants appeal from an order to the Los Angeles Superior Court denying their petition to compel arbitration. . . .

I

Background

On April 1, 1980, plaintiff Fred Dryer and the Rams entered into an employment contract — a slightly modified version of the standard NFL player contract drafted pursuant to a collective bargaining agreement between the players' union and the NFL management. Alleging that the Rams removed him from the active roster in violation of his contract, Dryer sued in superior court. The Rams responded with a petition to compel arbitration.

Dryer's contract contains a standard provision calling for binding arbitration under the terms of the applicable collective bargaining agreement in the event a dispute involving interpretation or application of any provision of the contract. Article VII of the applicable collective bargaining agreement sets forth a grievance and arbitration procedure for general contract disputes. Replete with full panoply of due process safeguards — notice, representation, hearing, appeal to outside arbitrators, etc. — this basic arbitration machinery appears to be unobjectionable.

What the trial court did find offensive was a clause in Article VII which provides that matters which are filed as grievances and which involve "the integrity of, or public confidence in, the game of professional football" may be ordered withdrawn from the article VII procedure by the commissioner — after consultation with the player-club relations committee — and processed under article VIII ("Commissioner Discipline"). Once removed from the article VII grievance procedure, such matters are handled exclusively by the NFL commissioner, who hears both the dispute and any appeal arising from his own decision. The NFL commissioner is appointed and paid by the management of the member clubs.

The Superior Court's Opinion

The trial court denied defendants' petition to compel arbitration. Finding that the arbitration clause of the contract . . . is a contract of adhesion, the court further held that the contract is "unconscionable" in that it fails to meet the "minimum levels of integrity" standard required by *Graham v. Scissor-Tail, Inc.*, 623 P.2d. 165. This holding rests on the court's conclusion that under the collective bargaining agreement "all arbitration decisions can ultimately be vested in the League Commissioner at his discretion."

With regard to a possible federal preemption problem, the trial court did find that the collective bargaining agreement affects interstate commerce and is therefore subject to section 301(a) of the Labor Management Relations Act (29 U.S.C. § 185(a)). The court determined however, that applicable federal and state principles are compatible.

Finally, the court denied the petition to compel arbitration as to all defendants other than the Rams on the rationale that the individual defendants were not signatories to the contract.

II

Dryer's dispute with the Rams — centering on a provision of the NFL collective bargaining agreement — clearly falls within the ambit of section 301(a) of the Labor Management Relations Act . . . which pertains to "[s]uits for violation of contracts between an employer and a labor organization representing employees in an industry affecting commerce." This answers the threshold question of what law applies in this case, for it is firmly established that federal substantive law governs the validity and enforcement of contracts under the LMRA. . . .

Thus, while our jurisdiction over this suit is concurrent with that of the federal judiciary, federal law remains applicable, and "incompatible doctrines of local law must give way.". . .

After determining correctly that the NFL collective bargaining agreement is indeed subject to section 301(a) of the LMRA, the trial court expressed the view that "there is no incompatibility between federal and state principles as applied to this case." It then went on to apply principles of unconscionability and of adhesive contracts as embodied in *Graham v. Scissor-Tail, Inc.* (1981) 623 P.2d 165.

Our review of federal policy and case law strongly suggests that the principles of *Graham* — applied in the context of a motion to compel arbitration under a provision of a collective bargaining agreement subject to section 301(a) — are incompatible with federal law and national labor policy. To effectuate that policy, federal law appears to limit a court's inquiry to a few basic questions concerning arbitrability of the dispute and defenses, if any, based on allegations of a lack of fair representation. We find no federal precedent for a *Graham*-type inquiry into the fairness of the arbitration machinery itself as part of the court's role in considering a motion to compel arbitration under a bona fide collective bargaining agreement.

National labor policy favors arbitration. . . . Courts can best serve this policy by giving full effect to the means chosen by the parties for settlement of their differences under a collective bargaining agreement.

The United States Supreme Court has observed that state decisions contrary to this policy of full enforcement could have a "crippling effect" on grievance arbitration. Normally, a claim that the contract grievance procedures are unfair or inadequate cannot be asserted until the aggrieved party has attempted to implement the procedures and found them to be unfair. . . .

The judicial role in considering a motion to compel arbitration is thus quite limited. Indeed, the Ninth Circuit has noted that a district court's function is essentially ended "once it has found the collective bargaining agreement susceptible of an interpretation which would cover the dispute. . . ." (*Intern. Ass'n of Machinists v. Howmet Corp.* (9th Cir. 1972) 466 F.2d 1249, 1256 . . . .

In this case, Dryer's claims all arise from the contract and are thus subject to the contract provision mandating arbitration of "[a]ny dispute between Player and Club involving the interpretation or application of any provision of this contract. . . ."

Beyond the threshold determination of arbitrability of a dispute, a court may — consistent with federal law — consider the resisting party's allegations of breach of the duty of fair representation. Federal courts have held, for example, that an aggrieved employee may circumvent the arbitration procedures created in a collective bargaining agreement if the employee establishes that the union breached its duty of fair representation in processing the grievance. Dryer, however, has not shown a lack of fair representation. Rather, his argument concerns the inherent fairness of the arbitration machinery agreed upon by both union and management.

The limited role of the courts in this area has been underscored repeatedly by decisions to the effect that an order to arbitrate a particular grievance should not be denied unless it may be said with positive assurance that the arbitration clause is not susceptible of an interpretation that covers the asserted dispute and that all doubts are to be resolved in favor of coverage. . . . Federal case law, however, in no way suggests that a court may deny a motion to compel arbitration on the basis of a *Graham*-type analysis of the arbitration procedure itself. In fact, courts generally order arbitration despite objections concerning the arbitration procedures. For example, it is immaterial to a company's duty to arbitrate that the grievance procedure agreed to in the collective bargaining agreement is employee-oriented. (*Monongahela Power Co. v. Local No. 2332*

Intern. Broth. of Elec. Workers, AFL-CIO CLC (4th Cir. 1973) 484 F.2d 1209, 1214). Mere inequality of bargaining power between a union and an employer does not constitute unfairness which will permit either party to avoid a collective bargaining agreement. Also, under federal law, partisan arbitrators are generally permissible.

In short, when deciding whether to compel or deny arbitration, federal courts confine their inquiry to a few threshold issues; they do not consider the substance of the grieving party's claims, nor do they scrutinize the agreed-upon arbitration procedures for general fairness. Thus, although federal law does not expressly preclude the exercise of state powers with regard to arbitration procedures, we believe that to apply the reasoning of *Graham* in this context would frustrate rather than further the goals of national labor policy.[8] . . .

III

Federal law aside, we independently hold that arbitration should have been ordered in this case. The trial court concluded that the arbitration provisions tailed to meet "minimum levels of integrity" required by *Graham* solely because of the remote — indeed, speculative — possibility of commissioner intervention. However, neither the holding nor the reasoning of *Graham* dictates this result. . . .

Under the agreement's normal arbitration procedure — article VII — a grievance goes to the player-club relations committee, which is composed of two representatives from the players' union and two from the management council. If the disputants so desire, they may stipulate to bypass this stage and submit the matter directly to an outside arbitrator. Dryer's case is a contract dispute — not a disciplinary matter — and there is no indication that the intervention provision ever could be or would be invoked.

* * *

IV

The trial court also held that the individual defendants are not entitled to the benefit of arbitration because they are not parties to the contract between Dryer and the Rams. . . .

If, as the complaint alleges, the individual defendants, though not signatories, were acting as agents for the Rams, then they are entitled to the benefit of the

---

[8] In another context, we noted that federal labor legislation fostering collective bargaining could not be read to preempt state legislative efforts to prescribe minimum standards of wages, hours, and working conditions for the protection of employees. (*Industrial Welfare Com. v. Superior Court* (1980) 27 Cal. 3d 690, 727, 166 Cal. Rptr. 331, 613 P.2d 579.) State governmental entities retain broad authority to establish minimum standards related generally to the "welfare" of employees. . . . Nonetheless, as the foregoing review of federal law suggests, inquiry into the fairness of an arbitration procedure agreed to in a bona fide collective bargaining agreement does not appear to be consistent with the letter or spirit of federal law. Nor is such an inquiry — as part of a court's consideration of a motion to compel arbitration — a traditional exercise of the states police powers.

arbitration provisions. Thus, our conclusion that this entire dispute be referred to arbitration applies to the individual defendants as well as to the Rams.

For the foregoing reasons, the order is reversed. The trial court is directed to grant the petition to compel arbitration with respect to all defendants.

MOSK, BROUSSARD, REYNOSO, GRODIN and LUCAS, J.J., concur.

BIRD, Chief Justice, concurring and dissenting.

I agree with the majority's conclusion that *Graham v. Scissor-Tail* does not permit this court to invalidate an otherwise acceptable arbitration procedure on the "purely speculative possibility" that the Commissioner will intervene. I also join their decision to reserve judgment on whether *Graham* would control if the Commissioner were reasonably likely to intervene, or if it were shown that the possibility of intervention distorted the arbitration process.

I part company with their conclusion that section 301(a) of the federal Labor Management Relations Act (29 U.S.C. § 185(a)) forbids this court even to undertake a *Graham* inquiry. Nothing in the majority opinion persuades me that *Graham* was wrong on this score.

Here, this court is asked to review an arbitration procedure which appears to be fair at least as applied. The procedure is the result of a collective bargaining agreement. Under these circumstances, it is easy to forget that there may be arbitration procedures which, though contained in negotiated union contracts and governed by section 301(a), nonetheless "essentially preclude the possibility of a fair hearing." I would urge my colleagues not to jump to the conclusion that in all circumstances federal law will require us to enforce such agreements.

Graham reviewed the arbitration provisions of a union contract under which a union official would decide disputes between union members and employers. The decision was normally made without hearing, and no appeal to a neutral arbiter was available. In *Graham*, this court held that such procedures fell below "minimum levels of integrity" and denied the nonunion party "the common law right of fair procedure." The court went on to consider whether federal law nonetheless required enforcement of the arbitration agreement, since the action was arguably governed by section 301(a).

Graham found that federal law did not require this result. . . .

Today's majority reverse this holding of *Graham*. Yet in so doing, they fail to cite any federal case law which compels such a result. Since there appears to be none, I would affirm *Graham*'s holding.

* * *

I cannot find any federal law which requires the enforcement of arbitration procedures which are so unfair as to come under the *Graham* holding. On the contrary, as six members of this court found in *Graham*, "'Congress has put its blessing on private dispute settlement arrangements . . . , but it was anticipated, we are sure, that the contractual machinery would operate within some minimum levels of integrity.' "

The reason for the congressional blessing of arbitration agreements is the belief that they promote industrial peace. . . .

"A collective bargaining agreement is an effort to erect a system of industrial self-government . . . ."

None of these goals can be achieved if the parties perceive the arbitration machinery as fundamentally biased. Federal labor policy cannot demand enforcement of an arbitration agreement which Graham would otherwise invalidate.

* * *

[T]he problem then is to determine under what circumstances the individual employee may obtain judicial review of his breach-of-contract claim despite his failure to secure relief through the contractual remedial procedures. . . .

In Glover, the high court had refused to compel arbitration where the persons who would decide a grievance were inescapably biased about it . . . .

Other cases have recognized that arbitration procedures may be avoided when they require a party to submit to a decision-maker so biased as to be incapable of providing a fair hearing. . . .

It is to be hoped that arbitration machinery established through collective bargaining will seldom if ever run afoul of those "elementary requirements of impartiality taken for granted in every judicial proceeding." Yet, such situations can be imagined. . . . I fear the majority opinion sweeps so broadly that this court would henceforth be bound to enforce each of these contracts. I cannot agree that federal law requires us to do that.

MORRIS v. NEW YORK FOOTBALL GIANTS, INC.

150 Misc. 2d 271, 575 N.Y.S.2d 1013 (1991)

CAHN, J.

By separate motions, defendants New York Football Giants, Inc. (N.Y. Giants), New York Jets Football Club, Inc. (N.Y. Jets), and Paul Tagliabue (on behalf of the National Football League (NFL), an unincorporated association) seek for an order, pursuant to CPLR § 7503 and/or the Federal Arbitration Act, 9 U.S.C. § 1 *et seq.*, staying this action and compelling arbitration of all disputed claims. Plaintiffs Joseph Morris and Michael Shuler cross move for an order, in the event this court submits the dispute to arbitration, appointing a neutral and unbiased arbitrator.

This action arises out of a dispute between two professional football players and their former football clubs over the amount of compensation owed to the players for their services in 1990 prior to the start of the football season (1990 pre-season).

On or about May 30, 1989, Shuler signed a one year standard players contract with the N.Y. Jets pursuant to which he agreed to play for the Jets for the 1990 NFL season. On or about April 30, 1990, Morris executed a one-year standard players contract with the N.Y. Giants wherein he agreed to play for said team for the 1990 season. Paragraph 20 of each of said contracts expressly provided:

> DISPUTES. Any dispute between Player and Club involving the interpretation or application of any provision of the contract will be submitted to final and binding arbitration in accordance with the procedure called for in any collective bargaining agreement in existence at the time the event giving rise to any such dispute occurs. If no collective bargaining agreement is in existence at such time, the dispute will be submitted within a reasonable time to the League Commissioner for final and binding arbitration by him, except as provided otherwise in Paragraph 13 of this contract.

On September 4, 1990, after providing the pre-season services in accordance with their agreements, each of the players was released by their respective team and their contracts terminated. Thereafter, a dispute arose in connection with the amount due for players' compensation for the 1990 pre-season. . . .

Plaintiffs commenced this action alleging that the respective clubs have breached the terms of their individual player contracts with respect to compensation. . . .; they have also made a derivative claim against Paul Tagliabue and the NFL for tortious interference with their (players) contracts. . . . Thereafter, defendants brought on the instant motions alleging that the underlying dispute is not one for the courts, but for arbitration.

In support of the motions, defendants allege that the 1982 Collective Bargaining Agreement . . . contains a broad arbitration clause that embraces the underlying dispute, despite the CBA's formal expiration in August of 1987. Defendants contend that the player representatives, players and clubs, have, to date, continued to utilize grievance and arbitration machinery established by the CBA . . . .

In opposition to defendants' motion, plaintiff relies on, *inter alia, McNeil v. National Football League, et al,* . . . wherein, the court found that the . . . CBA expired on August 31, 1987. . . .

Hence, plaintiffs' post-expiration grievances are not subject to arbitration under the 1982 CBA. . . .

However, the plaintiffs' individual contracts expressly provide that "[I]f no collective bargaining agreement is in existence at such time, the dispute will be submitted within a reasonable time to the League Commissioner for final and binding arbitration. . . .

In opposition, plaintiffs argue that said arbitration clause of their contract should be stricken as an unenforceable adhesion contract because they had no opportunity to bargain or negotiate any contract terms other than compensation and length of contractual commitment.

Despite plaintiffs' contentions, the record clearly establishes that plaintiffs are highly paid, sophisticated professional athletes, who possessed considerable bargaining power over the terms of their contracts. They were represented by experienced agents and/or counsel during the negotiation and execution of their player contracts. Significantly, there is absolutely no evidence presented that the plaintiffs ever sought to delete or bargain over the arbitration clause. The arbitration clause is clearly prominently set forth, and is not a trap for the unwary. Nor is there any direct claim made by either plaintiff, by affidavit or otherwise, that they felt that their contracts were presented "on a take-it-or-leave-it basis." Further, the arbitration clause is not by itself "unreasonably favorable" to the defendants. Consequently, the court finds that the contracts at issue are not adhesion contracts. . . . Therefore, plaintiffs are bound by their agreements to resolve any disputes relating to their contracts by arbitration.

A very serious issue is raised as to who the arbitrator should be. The contracts expressly provide that the disputes be submitted to the Commissioner of the NFL. Plaintiffs allege . . . that Tagliabue . . . has an inherent interest in the outcome of the dispute, and is therefore biased and, consequently, should be replaced by a neutral and impartial arbitrator in advance of arbitration proceedings. As shall be discussed below, under both Federal and State law, it is this court's view that a neutral arbitrator should be substituted for the Commissioner in order to insure a fair and impartial hearing.

Regarding the Commissioner of the NFL, the Constitution of the NFL provides, . . . that the NFL . . . shall select and employ the Commissioner and shall determine his period of employment and his compensation. Article VIII, Section 8.4(b), provides that the Commissioner is the Chief Executive Officer of the NFL. Article II, Section 2.1, provides that the purposes and objectives for which the NFL is organized are to promote and foster the primary businesses of NFL members. . . . Moreover, prior to becoming Commissioner, Tagliabue was the chief outside legal counsel for the NFL. . . . In that capacity, he frequently represented NFL owners in disputes with players. . . . In addition, the complaint names Tagliabue as a defendant in connection with a claim of tortious interference of contract in issuing an edict "that no members of the NFL may pay their players the contractually provided 10% of the players negotiated salary for pre-season services, but instead must pay the fixed per diem wage." . . .

In opposition to plaintiffs' cross-motion, defendants allege, inter alia, that the Commissioner would not be arbitrating plaintiffs' suit against the NFL, but only the breach of contract claims alleged against the two teams. As a result, defendants contend, resolution of the underlying claims . . . would have no direct financial impact on the NFL.

The court finds that Tagliabue's position as Commissioner, together with his past advocacy of a position in opposition to plaintiffs' position herein, deprive him of the necessary neutrality to arbitrate these claims. To find for plaintiffs herein, the Commissioner would have to reverse certain positions he previously strongly advocated, and declare non-binding or void a certain directive he, through his office, issued to NFL clubs. Further, the determination of plaintiffs' claims may have a major financial impact on various NFL teams. . . . All of these factors dictate that the Commissioner can not be a neutral arbitrator herein.

Further, this court's authority to select a neutral arbitrator is "inherent when the potential bias of a designated arbitrator would make arbitration proceedings simply a prelude to later judicial proceedings challenging the arbitration award.". . .Thus, an arbitrator will be appointed by the court. . . .

Accordingly, defendants' motion staying this action and compelling arbitration is granted. Plaintiffs' cross motion for appointment of a neutral and impartial arbitrator is granted.

Summary of Arbitration Decisions

In re Matter of Arbitration between Detroit Lions and M. Hoopes

(Searce, arb., Sept. 2, 1978)

Detroit Lions head coach, Hudspeth, openly criticized the punting performance of Hoopes. Hudspeth later informed Hoopes that his statements placed "too much pressure" on Hoopes, thus Hoopes was being released and placed on waivers. No other club claimed Hoopes.

The Uniform Contract provided the Lions with authority to terminate the player-team contract on the basis of "lack of skill/performance." Hoopes argued that the termination resulted from the public comments of Hudspeth and the resultant pressure, not skill or ability. The arbitrator ruled in favor of Hoopes. The arbitrator concluded that the release was not motivated solely by the club's assessment of Hoope's skill and performance.

In re Matter of Arbitration between National Basketball Association (Atlanta Hawks) and NBPA (Ken Charles)

(Seitz, arb., June 22, 1978)

Charles was purportedly released on basis of lack of skill or ability to qualify as a member of the team. Charles was not advised of release by written notice as required by league rules and governing documents. Arbitrator held that club must establish and demonstrate a rational basis for its opinion that the player lacks the skill and ability to qualify for a roster position. The record indicates that statements were made that Charles was terminated for economic reasons. Statements also indicated that Charles no longer fit with the team's style of play. The arbitrator held that a veteran player with undiminished skills could be traded in the event the player ceased to be useful to the club due to revised style of play. Strong proof is required under the circumstances of the case to justify contract termination.

In re Elmer Nordstrom, Managing Partner, et al., d/b/a Seattle Seahawks and the National Football League Players Association (Sam McCullum)

National Labor Relations Board Division of Judges

Case No. 2-CA-19101, Washington, D.C. (Nov. 23, 1983)

(*See Nordstrom v. National Labor Relations Board*, at **Case File**, *infra*.)

Sam McCullem was a player representative to the NFLPA. McCullem was released by the Seattle Seahawks subsequent to his activities as player rep. The Seahawks argued that McCullum's release was based on several factors: (1) diminished skills; (2) more talented players available; and (3) team need for a more versatile player. McCullum argued that overt actions taken as a player rep were the impetus for his release.

Evidence revealed that the Seahawks replaced McCullum with a wide receiver three days after the release. McCullum was signed by and started for the Minnesota Vikings. McCullum testified that club personnel warned him of the "risk" of his actions as a union representative.

The judge ruled in favor of McCullum, deciding that the Seattle Seahawks violated Sections 8(a)(3) and (1) of the National Labor Relations Act.

In re Matter of Arbitration between the American and National Leagues of Professional Baseball Clubs (California Angels) and the Major League Baseball Players Association (B. Cowan) (1972)

Billy Cowan was the MLBPA representative from the California Angels during the 1972 players' strike. Cowan was released during the 1972 season. Cowan and the NLBPA filed a grievance, arguing that Cowan was released due to his union activities. The California Angels responded that Cowan was released pursuant to Section 7(b)(2) of the UPC, which provides that a club may terminate a contract where a player fails, within the opinion of the club, to exhibit sufficient skill or ability to continue as a member of the team.

The evidence showed that Cowan had completed three years on the active roster of the California Angels, prior to 1972. He received an increase in salary of $5,500 for the 1972 season. The club's general manager made statements to Cowan to the effect that Cowan was included in the team's plans for 1972.

The arbitrator ruled in favor of the California Angels. The arbitrator noted the lack of evidence supporting Cowan's position, stating, "[T]he opinions of Club Management as to the skill and ability of players should be, and normally will be, oriented to and based upon considerations which are relevant to the success of their respective teams."

In re Major League Players Association and the Twenty-Six Major League Baseball Clubs, Major League Baseball Arbitration Panel, Grievance No. 86-2

(T. Roberts, Chair, Sept. 21, 1987)

The MLBPA filed a grievance on January 31, 1986, asserting that the twenty-six Major League clubs had been acting in concert with respect to players who became free agents after the 1985 season. Paragraph H of Article XVIII of the Basic Agreement provides: "The utilization or non-utilization of rights under this Article . . . is an individual matter to be determined solely by each Player and each Club for his or its own benefit. Players shall not act in concert with other Players and Clubs shall not act in concert with other Clubs."

The grievance was heard over thirty-two days of presentation, with a total of 5,674 pages of verbatim transcript and 288 exhibits. Evidence revealed that following the 1984 season, sixteen of twenty-six major league clubs signed free agents who had been playing with other clubs. After the 1985 season, however, only Carlton Fisk received a *bona fide* offer from a club other than his former employer, while twenty-eight other free agents received no interest at any price until such time as their former clubs announced no desire to re-sign the players. Kirk Gibson received initial contact from three clubs, but no offers subsequent to an owners' meeting in October, 1985. The MLBPA alleged the owner actions within the free agent market as a "boycott." The clubs answered that the market actions were not a result of agreement between the clubs, but were individual club decisions based on legitimate factors, and were a culmination of a ten-year trend. All club representatives who testified at the hearing denied a common agreement or understanding.

During the off-season, several management meetings were convened, during which the clubs were admonished to exercise self-discipline in making operating decisions, and in resisting temptations to give in to unreasonable demands of experienced marginal players. The clubs were warned that rash moves to add free agents in hopes of a pennant resulted in negative financial results for clubs. The club representatives stated their intent to avoid long-term contracts in response to a poll conducted by the Commissioner. In a subsequent meeting, the Commissioner repeated his concerns regarding the financial commitment made by the clubs under "dumb" long-term contracts.

The arbitration panel found that the "distillation of the message of these meetings resulted in every major league club abstaining from the free agent market during that winter until an available free agent was 'released' by his former club. . . . The right of the clubs to participate in the free agency provisions of the Basic Agreement no longer remained an individual matter to be determined solely for the benefit of each club." The action constituted a violation of the prohibition of concerted conduct.

NORDSTROM v. NATIONAL LABOR RELATIONS BOARD

984 F.2d 479 (D.C. Cir. 1993)

D.H. GINSBURG, Circuit Judge:

The Seattle Seahawks petition for review of the amount of backpay that the National Labor Relations Board awarded to Sam McCullum, a former player whom the Seahawks unlawfully discharged. Finding that its backpay decision is supported by substantial evidence in the record, we uphold the Board in all respects.

I. Background

Sam McCullum began playing professional football as a wide receiver in 1974 and joined the Seattle Seahawks in 1976. It is undisputed that he was unlawfully released by the Seahawks in September 1982 for engaging in union-related activities. *See Elmer Nordstrom, Managing Partner, et al. d/b/a Seattle Seahawks*, 292 NLRB 899 (1989).

The Seahawks routinely notified all National Football League (NFL) teams of McCullum's availability. After trying out with the then-Oakland Raiders, McCullum accepted an offer of employment with the Minnesota Vikings. Minnesota released McCullum in May 1984, after McCullum rejected that team's offer of $203,500 for the 1984 season. McCullum, who had not received an offer for 1984 from any other NFL team, wrote the Vikings a formal letter of retirement in order to secure his pension benefits. In the letter he said that he did not intend to resume playing for the NFL.

The Board determined that McCullum's backpay period — that period during which he would have remained employed by the Seahawks but for the Employer's unlawful discrimination — extended through the end of the 1985 football season. The Board concluded, however, that the backpay award should run only through December 1984, because by that time McCullum had quit searching for suitable employment; he had thus failed to mitigate his damages beyond that point. *Elmer Nordstrom, Managing Partner, et al.*, Supp. Dec. and Order, 304 NLRB No. 78 (Aug. 27, 1991). In this regard, the Board reversed the

ALJ, who determined that McCullum had abandoned his search for employment in September 1984.

Players earn additional income when their team advances to the playoffs. The Vikings went to the playoffs in 1982; the Seahawks went in 1983. The Board found that McCullum's earnings from the Vikings' participation in the 1982 playoffs were the fruits of "interim employment" and thus were not deductible from the amount of backpay for which the Seahawks are liable to McCullum. The Board also ordered the Seahawks to compensate McCullum for income he would have received by reason of the Seahawks' participation in the 1983 playoffs.

The Seahawks seek review of the Board's determination that the backpay award should extend through the end of 1984 rather than ending in September of that year. The Employer also challenges the Board's refusal to deduct McCullum's 1983 playoff earnings from the amount of backpay due him.

II. Analysis

Section 10(c) of the National Labor Relations Act authorizes the National Labor Relations Board to award backpay in order to remedy the effects of unlawful discrimination. 29 U.S.C. § 160(c). The General Counsel bears the burden of proof in establishing the backpay period — in this case, the period during which McCullum would have continued to play for the Seattle Seahawks had he not been unlawfully discharged. . . . That determination need not be highly individualized; the Board need only apply "to particular facts a reasonable formula for determining the probable length of employment.". . . Because the length of a football player's career is highly variable with the individual player, however, the inquiry here was of necessity more detailed than in the usual industrial setting.

The General Counsel met his burden of establishing that McCullum would have played for the Seahawks through the 1984 season but for the unlawful discrimination. The Board affirmed the ALJ's determination that, looking at the Seahawks' roster, and McCullum's experience with Seattle, McCullum would have remained with that team in 1984. In support of its position that the Seahawks would not have retained McCullum for the 1984 season, the Employer argues simply that McCullum lacked the ability to play in the NFL after 1983. At least one team, however, thought otherwise: Minnesota offered to renew McCullum's contract for 1984, and McCullum failed to play that year only because he rejected Minnesota's offer as inadequate. We agree with the Board's determination that the Vikings' offer, combined with McCullum's experience with the Seattle system and Seattle's dearth of wide receivers suffices to establish that the backpay period should extend at least through the end of 1984.

The Employer also argues that because McCullum did not more actively look for employment after September 1984, he failed to mitigate his damages after that point. The Employer bears the burden of proof on this point. . . . McCullum's agent testified that he made inquiries regarding employment opportunities into the fall of 1984. McCullum's availability was widely known due to both these inquiries and Minnesota's earlier notice to all NFL teams that McCullum would no longer be playing for the Vikings.

Whether McCullum failed to exercise reasonable diligence in pursuing the various employment possibilities open to him is a closer question. McCullum did not try to find employment in the United States Football League, but that was not unreasonable because the 1984 USFL season was almost over when McCullum was released by the Vikings. We are more troubled by McCullum's failure to seek alternative employment in the Canadian Football League. We agree with the Board, however, that at least for the limited time between his waiver by the Vikings and the end of 1984 it was reasonable for McCullum to look for employment only in the NFL, where he had played his entire career and where his prospects seemed brightest. To be sure, an employee may need to lower his sights after a time, but the Board may resolve any reasonable doubt about the length of that time in favor of the innocent employee. . . .Thus, we need not decide today whether the duty of mitigation ever entails an obligation to seek employment in a foreign country. We therefore affirm the Board's determination that McCullum made "reasonable exertions" by indicating his desire for an NFL position and then, when no employment opportunities were immediately forthcoming, waiting as the season progressed to see whether any NFL team would hire him to replace an injured player. . . .

The Employer contends that McCullum effectively abandoned his search for employment when he sent his letter of resignation to the Vikings in August 1984. It is undisputed, however, that the letter was essentially a formality, "necessary," as the Board found, "to avoid a significant delay in obtaining severance pay," and revocable if McCullum received a contract offer from an NFL team. Supp. Dec. and Order at 5. While the retirement letter stated that McCullum did not intend to resume playing professional football, there is no evidence that the letter had any effect upon the NFL teams with whom McCullum continued to seek employment. Absent some evidence that sending the letter limited McCullum's prospects for re-employment, that letter cannot serve to terminate the Employer's liability. The Board's determination is supported by substantial evidence and we thus affirm it.

Finally, the Employer challenges the Board's refusal to deduct from its backpay liability the money McCullum earned when Minnesota went to the playoffs in 1982, although the Board included in the backpay award the money McCullum would have earned had he gone to the playoffs with Seattle in 1983. The Board treated McCullum's 1982 playoff earnings as supplemental income resulting from an additional two weeks of work over and above the time he would have worked for Seattle. In calculating backpay, the Board does not deduct supplemental income earned from a "moonlighting" job or from excess overtime even if the backpay claimant appears to be made "more than whole, [because] it is as a result of his extra effort above and beyond his performance of a full time job" that he secures the extra income. . . . McCullum worked an additional two weeks in order to secure his playoff pay. Therefore, the Board correctly determined that McCullum's 1982 playoff earnings represented supplemental income for a time during which he would not have been employed had he remained with Seattle because Seattle did not go the playoffs that year.

The Board's decision creates an apparent anomaly insofar as McCullum profits because the Seahawks and the Vikings went to the playoffs in different years. (If Seattle and Minnesota advanced to the playoffs during the same year, McCullum's playoff income could not properly be viewed as supplemental because McCullum would not have worked any days for Minnesota over and above the number of days he would have worked for Seattle in the relevant quarter.) The anomaly arises because the Board calculates backpay by calendar quarter, rather than by deducting the total amount earned in mitigation from the total amount of backpay otherwise due. Had the Board not used the calendar quarter system here, McCullum's 1983 playoff earnings might properly have been offset against his lost earnings from the 1982 playoffs; McCullum actually worked for Minnesota in the 1982 and 1983 seasons combined for the same number of hours he would have worked for Seattle over the same period. The Board's calendar quarter methodology is of longstanding and consistent application. . . . The Employer has not challenged the application of that methodology to professional football, and accordingly we make no judgment as to its propriety here.

III. Conclusion

For the foregoing reasons, the petition for review is in all respects denied and the crossapplication for enforcement is granted.

NOTES AND COMMENTS

1. For discussion of grievance arbitration in professional sports, *see* GREENBERG & GRAY, SPORTS LAW PRACTICE §§ 1.09, 2.03 (2d ed. 2005); Stiglitz, *Player Discipline in Professional Team Sports, in* 3 LAW OF PROFESSIONAL AND AMATEUR SPORTS, §§ 10.0 *et. seq.* For descriptions of the grievance arbitration mechanisms utilized in professional sports, *see* T. Steinberg, *Negotiating National Basketball Association Contracts, in* 2 LAW OF PROFESSIONAL AND AMATEUR SPORTS §§ 7.36-.39 (Uberstine ed. 2005); Kirke, *National Hockey League Contract Negotiations, Id.* §§ 9.21-9.25. For an insightful description of baseball grievance arbitration, *see* MILLER, A WHOLE DIFFERENT BALL GAME: THE SPORT AND BUSINESS OF BASEBALL 131-41 (1991).

2. What are the limits, if any, to the enforcement of the arbitration clause in professional sports player-team contracts? Must antitrust attacks first be decided by an arbitrator? Courts in commercial arbitration cases generally rule that arbitration provisions do not prevent initial adjudication of antitrust claims. *See, e.g., Cobb v. Lewis*, 488 F.2d 41 (5th Cir. 1974). *But see Orlando Thunder v. National Football League*, 45 F.3d 436, 1994 U.S. App. LEXIS 37261

(9th Cir. 1994) (unpublished) (Domestic antitrust claims are arbitrable; *Mitsubishi Motors Corp. v. Soler Chrysler–Plymouth*, 473 U.S. 614 (1985) (international antitrust claims are arbitrable); *Nghiem v. NEC Electronics*, 25 F.3d 1437 (9th Cir. 1994) (domestic antitrust claims are arbitrable).

3. What evidence supports a claim that a union breached the duty of fair representation in processing a grievance? Plaintiff, James Peterson, sued the NFLPA and two NFLPA attorneys for breach of the duty of fair representation in a grievance against the Tampa Bay Buccaneers. Peterson specifically alleged that the NFLPA and attorneys provided inaccurate advice in his pursuance of the grievance. The trial court granted a judgment notwithstanding the verdict (JNOV) in favor of the NFLPA defendants. The Ninth Circuit affirmed, stating:

> A union breaches its duty of fair representation only when its conduct toward a member of the collective bargaining unit is 'arbitrary, discriminatory, or in bad faith'. . .
>
> We have concluded repeatedly that mere negligent conduct on the part of a union does not constitute a breach of the union's duty of fair representation.
>
> . . . [U]nions are not liable for good faith, non-discriminatory errors of judgment made in the processing of grievances.

Peterson v. Kennedy, 771 F.2d 1244, 1253-54 (9th Cir. 1985). Could Peterson have gained *de novo* review of the arbitration decision on the basis of violation of the duty of fair representation? The trial court also ruled that Peterson failed to prove that he would have prevailed on the merits but for the alleged breach of duty. *Id.* at 1252.

4. Which opinion, majority or dissent, provides better reasoning regarding the appropriateness of the *Graham* analysis of the fairness of arbitration procedure in *Dryer, supra*? Does the *Morris* court utilize the *Graham* analysis in reaching its decision?

5. Can you enumerate or otherwise articulate standards that enable a court to determine whether an arbitrator has dispensed his "own brand of industrial justice," or is Justice Steven's dissent accurate in its criticism of the Court's majority opinion? *See* Byrnes & Prout, Comment, Major League Baseball Players Association v. Garvey*: Revisiting the Standard of Arbitral Review*, 7 HARV. NEGOT. L. REV. 389 (2002) (authors argue that the Court should clarify the principle by renaming it and providing review to determine whether the contract and governing laws are correctly applied).

The "industrial justice" doctrine was developed in the Steelworkers Trilogy in 1960. *United Steelworkers v. Enterprise Wheel & Car Corp.*, 363 U.S. 593 (1960); *United Steelworkers v. Warrior Gulf & Nav. Co.*, 363 U.S. 574 (1960); and *United Steelworkers v. American Mfg. Co.*, 363 U.S. 564 (1960). The parties having agreed to submit all questions of contract interpretation and application to the arbitrator, a reviewing court is confined to ascertaining whether the arbitration award draws its essence from the contract and does not simply reflect an arbitrator's own notions of industrial justice. The United States Supreme Court recognizes two exceptions to the general rule of deference. A court may review the arbitration ruling where there exists fraud and dishonesty, and where the arbitrator's award under a collective bargaining agreement is contrary to public policy. *United Paperworkers Int'l Union v. Misco*, 484 U.S. 29 (1987). A court's refusal to enforce an arbitrator's interpretation of a contract is limited to situations where the contract as interpreted would violate some explicit, well-defined, and dominant public policy that is ascertained by reference to laws and legal precedents and not from general considerations of public interests. *W.R. Grace & Co. v. Rubber Workers*, 461 U.S. 757, 766 (1983). Essentially, parties may not agree to violate public policy as determined by positive law principles. *See Eastern Associate Coal Corp. v. United Mine Workers of Am.*, 531 U.S. 57 (2000) (public policy considerations do not require courts to refuse to enforce an arbitration award ordering employer to reinstate an employee who twice tested positive in drug tests). *See generally* Huitsing, Note, *Retaining Bargained-For Finality and Judicial Review in Labor Arbitration Decisions: Dual Interests Preserved in* Major League Baseball Players Assn. v. Garvey, 2002 J. DISP. RESOL. 453 (2002).

6. Given the broad language of *Garvey* in limiting review of the arbitrator's award to the sole question of whether the ruling construed the agreed upon Framework and criteria applied in the proposed Distribution Plan, what arguments can you make on behalf of Steve Garvey?

The Framework required evidence of a "specific offer of an extension" made prior to collusion, only to be thereafter withdrawn when the collusion scheme was initiated. Garvey provided no evidence of the alleged offer in his filing, other than his own declaration. The MLBPA rejected his claim, and the matter proceeded to arbitration. At the hearing, Garvey testified that he received an offer and proffered a 1996 letter written by former Padres President and CEO, Ballard Smith, confirming the alleged 1985 offer, and the fact that the offer was withdrawn as a result of collusion between the clubs. The arbitrator, Thomas T. Roberts, granted a twenty-one day recess, admonishing each party to produce documentation to aid in ascertaining the facts in question. The MLBPA submitted answers of Garvey and his representatives to 1988 and 1991 questionnaires; a record of Smith's 1986 testimony in which he denied collusion; a letter from Garvey's agent, Jerry Kapstein, stating that (1) Garvey desired to handle extension negotiations with the Padres himself, (2) Smith told Kapstein that he hoped that the negotiations would result in an extension, (3) Garvey asked for Kapstein's help once negotiations stalled, and (4) when Kapstein talked with Smith, Smith reported that the Padres were not interested in talking about an extension, as club policy had changed; notes of MLBPA telephone conversations with Smith, during which Smith admitted to offering Garvey a contract extension in 1985, but withdrew the offer because of collusion.

After examining the evidence, the arbitrator denied Garvey's objection to the Plan of Distribution. The arbitrator, Thomas T. Roberts, rejected the probative value of the Smith letter and statements, doubting the credibility of Smith's assertions as indicated in the Supreme Court's opinion. Arbitrator Roberts had chaired the panel in *Collusion I*, which determined that the owners and representatives, including Ballard Smith, had not been truthful in denying collusion. He concluded that while Garvey and Smith may have discussed the possibility of a contract extension, there was inadequate evidence of a "specific offer" as required by the Framework. *Garvey v. Roberts*, 503 F.3d 580, 586 (9th Cir. 2000). For review of the facts in *Garvey*, *see* Perron, Note, 12 SETON HALL J. SPORT L. 131 (2002); Kaemmerer, Note, *Three Strikes and You're Out: The Supreme Court Reaffirmation of the Scope of Judicial Review of Arbitrators' Decisions*, 67 MO. L. REV. 635 (2002). Arbitrator Roberts utilized his experience and observations in *Collusion I*. Is there an "on the record" requirement in arbitration matters similar to the principle used in judicial and administrative proceedings? Can fundamental fairness notions of "neutrality" as explained in *Morris* be undermined by the experiences of a permanent arbitrator?

7. The arbitration clauses of collective bargaining agreements and form contracts utilized in professional sports leagues are generally written broadly to include all foreseeable disputes between players and management. *See Erving v. Virginia Squires Basketball Club*, 349 F. Supp. 716 (E.D.N.Y. 1972), *aff'd*, 468 F.2d 1064 (2d Cir. 1972) (court held that a broadly drafted arbitration clause included the issue of whether Julius Erving entered into the contract as a result of fraudulent inducement). For cases in which the disputes were held to exist outside the scope of the arbitration clauses, *see Pittsburgh Assocs. v. Parker*, No. 86-1084, slip op. at 6-9 (W.D. Pa., Aug. 5, 1986) (LEXIS, Gen-fed library, Dist. file) (issues related to payment of deferred compensation were not complaints involving the "interpretation of or compliance with" a player contract); *Johnson v. Green Bay Packers, Inc.*, 74 N.W.2d 784 (Wis. 1956) (language of 1947 NFL contract arbitration clause was qualified by preceding reference to NFL Constitution & By-laws which did not include disputes between club and player regarding whether compensation was made in accordance with the employment contract).

8. The collective bargaining agreements and uniform contracts of most major professional sports leagues provide economic protections for players suffering injuries in the course of employment. The agreements commonly provide: (1) the injury must be directly related to employment; (2) the club duty to pay the player's salary continues only so long as the player is injured; (3) the club duty to pay the player's salary continues only to the end of the contract year in which the player was injured; (4) strict procedural requirements, including duty of the player to report the injury; (5) a significant role of the team physician in deciding whether the professional athlete is physically fit to perform; and (6) a setoff of workers compensation received by the players. *See* 1985-1989

Basic Agreement (MLB), Article VIII(C); National Basketball Association Uniform Player Contract, Article 20(b)(2); NFL Player Contract, Article II.

9. Important factual and legal issues in injury grievance cases are identified by Professor Ensor, as follows:

(1) The date of the injury, and the status of the player with respect to the club at the time of the injury.

(2) How the injury occurred; the activity in which the player was engaged when injured.

(3) The effects of the injury; the extent to which the player was disabled or unable to perform at a competitive level.

(4) Whether the damage can be traced to a previous injury or a congenital condition.

Ensor, *Comparison of Arbitration Decisions Involving Termination in Major League Baseball, the National Basketball Association, and the National Football League*, 32 St. Louis L.J. 135, 150 (1987).

10. Evidentiary and procedural difficulties inherent in the injury grievance process are evident in *Peterson v. Kennedy, supra* at **Note 3**. Two important fact questions are whether the grievance should be filed pursuant to the non-injury or injury grievance procedures, and whether the grievance was filed within the time limits specified by the collective bargaining agreement. The court questioned the correctness of the arbitrator's decision (Decision of Arbitrator Volz, Nov 13, 1981, 1249-50) that Peterson's grievance was time-barred. The court recognized that the NFL and NFLPA both regularly fail to follow the strict time limits for handling grievances, and suggested there was no equitable reason to hold Peterson to the time limits. *Peterson v. Kennedy, supra*, 1250.

11. A substantive issue in injury cases is whether the player was terminated for lack of skill or due to the fact that the player was injured. The following problem is designed to acquaint you with a typical scenario.

Problem: Henry Summerall was a highly regarded professional athlete. Henry, however, was injured early in training camp. He was certified "fit to play" by the team physician late in the pre-season. Henry played in the last two pre season ballgames. He was released in the last cut of players from the team roster. Henry hired your firm to file a grievance challenging his release. The player is of the opinion that he would have made the team if he had not been injured. The injury prevented him from participating in the training camp, a crucial time for the development of the team as a team. Henry also feels that he was behind the other players in training and physical condition when called upon to perform in the games. His lack of fitness was a direct result of the injury. Thus, Henry contends that a clause in his contract, obligating the club to pay his salary for so long as a player is injured, protects him in this case.

What are the rights and duties of the respective parties? What evidence is relevant to the resolution of the issue? Several of the many grievance cases examining the issue are summarized below.

Injury Grievance Arbitration — Summary

In re the Arbitration between NFL Players Association (E. Harris) and NFL Management Council (St. Louis Cardinals and New Orleans Saints)

(Smith, Arb., Nov. 20, 1972)

Harris pulled his left hamstring muscle in training camp. After rehabilitation, Harris was examined by the team physician and pronounced ready to practice and able to play in two weeks. Harris was released on waivers due to lack of skill. He was claimed by the New Orleans Saints, but failed to pass the Saints' physical examination. A neutral physician concluded that Harris had recovered from his injury. Harris filed a grievance against both clubs.

The arbitrator phrased the issue as whether Harris would have made the team if he had not been injured. The arbitrator concluded that the club bears the burden of showing grounds for termination that are totally independent of the injury. The player, however, has the duty to mitigate.

The arbitrator ruled in favor of Harris. The measure of damages was established as the player's monetary loss. The arbitrator recognized that an arbitrator possesses broad discretion in setting the amount of recovery. Recovery was limited to 50% of the contract salary amount as the evidence was not clear that Harris would have "made the team" but for the injury.

In re the Arbitration between NFL Players Association (K. Lewis, E. Moore) and NFL Management Council

(Smith, Arb., Aug. 30, 1982)

The facts of *Lewis & Moore* are similar to the facts of the *Harris* case. The NFL Management Council contended that negotiations of the collective bargaining agreement modified the *Harris* doctrine. Council for the NFLPA presented evidence to the arbitrator that no mention was made during negotiations of a "skills" defense as an exception to the injury protection clause. The "skills" defense is an assertion that the player was terminated for the reason that he did not possess adequate playing skills, regardless of the factors contributing to the skill level. After reviewing the history of the negotiations, the arbitrator concluded that the "skills" defense was not available to the club.

In re the Arbitration between National Basketball Association (Seattle Sonics) and National Basketball Players Association (G. Edwards)

(May 9, 1978)

Edwards, a rookie, was injured in training camp. After resting for five days, Edwards resumed practice and played in two pre-season games. He was released for lack of playing skill. Edwards filed a grievance, alleging his termination was due to injury, and thus, he should be compensated under the injury protection clause of the contract.

The arbitrator ruled in favor of the Seattle Sonics, holding that the player possessed the burden of proving:

1. the termination was clearly without rational basis;
2. the termination was invidiously discriminatory; or
3. the termination was motivated by some wrongful or improper design or pretext.

12. The most reliable injury protection clause is the provision providing that the contract is "guaranteed." *See* **Chapter 9**, *infra*. The scope of the clause as intended by the parties is sometimes an issue in the dispute between the parties. *See, e.g., In the Matter of Arbitration between the National Football League Players Association and Dante Pastorini, Jr., and the National Football League Management Council and the Oakland Raiders* (Kagel, Arb., May 30, 1984).

The case of *In re the Arbitration of Thomas and the Los Angeles Raiders and the Los Angeles Rams*, is instructive. Thomas was entitled to "One Year Injury Guarantee" if he was unable to pass the club's physical examination for the year covered by the contract. Thomas passed the Rams' examination, despite the presence of considerable knee problems. He was traded to the Raiders. Thomas failed the Raider's physical examination. The arbitrator held that Thomas should not have passed the Rams' physical examination, based on the medical evidence in the record. The arbitrator ruled that the Rams and Raiders each were liable for one-half of the salary.

13. Sometimes negotiation of a player-team contract results in a provision shielding the team from liability under the injury protection clause due to aggravation of a prior-existing physical injury. A typical clause provides:

> I hereby waive and release the Club, the Club physician, its trainers, and the National Football League from any and all liability and responsibility in the event I become physically unable to perform the services required of me by my NFL Player Contract executed this date because of a deterioration or aggravation of the physical condition(s) set forth in Paragraph 1, above.

But see In the Matter of Arbitration Between National Basketball Association (Cleveland Cavaliers) and National Basketball Players Association (R. Cox) (Sept. 11, 1978) (rider in Cox's contract waiving injury compensation for injuries incurred prior to start of regular season was prohibited under Article 1, § 3 of the CBA).

14. Recurring issues in injury grievance arbitrations include off-season injuries, injuries sustained during rehabilitation, and alleged failure of professional athletes to disclose injuries. The issues perhaps can be avoided by gaining written permission from the club for any off-season workouts, disclosing all previous injuries, and keeping injury records similar to the records utilized by plaintiffs in tort suits.

15. What remedies are available to a party suing for breach of a contract? Under what circumstances may a party rescind or otherwise gain cancellation of a contract?

In the classic dispute between Jim "Catfish" Hunter and Charles Finley, Hunter utilized a contract provision allowing him to terminate the contract upon Finley's failure to pay required compensation. *In the Matter of the Arbitration between American and National Leagues of Professional Baseball Clubs (Oakland Athletics) and Major League Players Association* (*J. A. Hunter*) (Seitz, Arb. Chair., Dec. 13, 1974). *See also In the Matter of the Arbitration between Major League Baseball Clubs (Cleveland Indians) and Major League Baseball Players Association (J. Bibby)* (Porter, Arb. Chair., Apr. 3, 1978).

For judicial resolution of the rights and duties of the parties after breach of a contract, *see Alabama Football, Inc. v. Greenwood*, 452 F. Supp. 1191 (W.D. Pa. 1978); *Alabama Football, Inc. v. Stabler,* 319 So. 2d 678 (Ala. 1975).

16. Problem. Rob Timmons is a star pitcher for a professional baseball club and known to most baseball fans throughout the nation. He is outspoken on many social issues and plans to run for Congress at the conclusion of his baseball career. Timmons recently gained national headlines with his interview on ESPN in which he openly criticized the President and the United States' military actions abroad. He stated that he would refuse to stand for the National Anthem until the war ended. He also referred to the majority of his teammates as "sheep." Timmons wore his team jacket and cap during the interview.

Club representatives report that the public, fan-based, backlash has swamped the front office with telephone calls and letters objecting to Timmon's statements and the club's association with him. The General Manager responded, "We appreciate the conservative nature of our community and do not endorse Timmon's views. We have hereby canceled our 'Timmons bobble-head' promotion night, and have suspended Timmons for the 3-game series, as well as the 4-game series surrounding our 4th of July celebration promotions." The Commissioner of the League issued a statement supporting the club in its disciplinary actions, and further suspended Timmons from play until he assures he will stand for the

National Anthem played before each game. The Commissioner relies on his authority under the "best interests of baseball" standard.

The Players Association filed a grievance, asking the arbitrator to overturn the suspensions on the basis that the discipline was without "just cause" within the meaning of Article XII(A) of the Basic Agreement. Timmons argues that he has rights of free speech, especially on social issues as important as war, and should not be disciplined in any manner for exercising his rights and duties. In fact, the club actively encouraged players to interact with the media. He further contends that in the event any discipline is proper, the suspensions here are not proportionate to the alleged misconduct. He not only loses his salary for the games lost due to his suspension, but also forfeits a significant portion of his compensation that is based on incentive bonus clauses.

The team and Commissioner counter that Timmons violates Clause 3 of the Uniform Player's Contract whereby he "pledges himself to the American public and to the Club to conform to high standards of personal conduct. . . ." (*See* UPC at **Chapter 9**, **Section C**, *infra*). Respondents also contend that the suspensions are required for protection of the player and fans, as well as Timmons himself, and the game of baseball. Evidence indicates that the local public outrage is substantial. Some players have stated they do not want to play alongside Timmons and interact with him in the clubhouse. The "bobble-head night" must be canceled, the club reports, as a group of pro-war advocates have scheduled a demonstration at the ballpark that could disrupt the game and endanger patrons. The Commissioner is concerned that Timmons will utilize the 4th of July series to convert the game into a public forum for political expression.

The "just cause" standard is discussed as follows:

> [T]he burden of establishing just cause is on those imposing discipline. While the Commissioner has a "reasonable range of discretion" in such matters, the penalty he imposes in a particular case must be "reasonably commensurate with the offense" and "appropriate, given all the circumstances." . . . Moreover, "offenders must be viewed with a careful eye to the specific nature of the offense, and penalties must be carefully fashioned with an eye toward responsive, consistent and fair discipline." . . . There must, in other words, be "careful scrutiny of the individual circumstances and the particular facts relevant to each case."

In the Matter Between the Major League Players Association and the Commissioner of Major League Baseball (John Rocker), Decision of the Arbitration Panel (Das, Chair), 638 PLI/Pat 765, 804 (2001). What arguments can you make on behalf of Timmons and the Players Association? What arguments do you expect from the Respondents? *See generally* Kurlantzick, *John Rocker and Employee Discipline for Speech*, 16 LAB. LAW. 439 (2001).

17. Problem. Steve Howe, seven-time drug offender, successfully challenged his ban from baseball. Howe argued during grievance arbitration that his drug use was linked to a hyperactivity condition that was previously undiagnosed. In

1987, LaMarr Hoyt filed a grievance when the San Diego Padres sought to void his contract after a third drug-related incident. The arbitrator ruled that the Padres did not heed warning signs about Hoyt's behavior, or provide an adequate treatment alternative. In 1971, the California Angels placed Alex Johnson on the restricted list (suspension) as a disciplinary measure. Johnson submitted evidence of emotional illness during the arbitration hearing. The arbitrator found the actions of the Angels and the American League improper. The arbitrator believed that a player with emotional illness should be placed on the disabled list with full pay and credited service. *See generally* Hylton, *The Historical Origins of Professional Baseball Grievance Arbitration,* 11 MARQ. SPORTS L. REV. 175 (2001).

18. The NFL Standard Form Contract, Article 20, provides as follows:

> Any dispute between Player and Club involving the interpretation or application of any provision of this contract will be submitted to final and binding arbitration in accordance with the procedure called for in any collective bargaining agreement. . . . If no collective bargaining agreement is in existence at such time, the dispute will be submitted within a reasonable time to the League Commissioner for final and binding arbitration by him, except as provided otherwise. . . .

Remembering that the NFL-NFLPA collective bargaining agreement expired as discussed in *Brown, supra* at **Chapter 6**, what is the validity of the grievance arbitration procedures under the *Dryer* analysis? In most professional sports leagues, the commissioner possesses unfettered power in dealing with matters considered to imperil the sport, including disciplinary issues. How does the "commissioner's power" fare under the *Dryer* analysis? After *Morris*, may the commissioner act as arbitrator in any case? The authority of the commissioner's office is considered at **Chapter 5**, *supra*.

19. Steve Mattingly, a minor league umpire, was fired by the Pacific Coast League in mid-season. The PCL alleged that Mattingly had engaged in a fight with another umpire, had verbal altercations with airlines and rental car personnel, and possessed a history of not getting along with others. Branch Rickey, III, PCL President, concluded that Mattingly was not abiding by the "high standards" to which professional umpires are held, had caused the altercations, and engaged in conduct that was disruptive to the umpiring crew. Mattingly filed an unfair labor practice charge, claiming that his employment was terminated as a result of his efforts in union organization activities.

The NLRB utilized the "causation test," citing *NLRB v. Transportation Corp.*, 462 U.S. 393 (1983), as follows: The General Counsel must make a *prima facie* showing sufficient to support, by a preponderance of the evidence, the inference that protected conduct was a "motivating factor" in the employer's decision. Upon such a showing, the burden shifts to the employer to demonstrate that the same action would have taken place in the absence of the protected conduct.

The ALJ determined that the General Counsel failed to establish a *prima facie* case, but in the event the evidence is viewed as adequate, the evidence supports a finding that the League would have discharged Mattingly even in the absence of his protected activity. *Pacific Coast League of Professional Baseball Clubs, et al. and Steve W. Mattingly*, before the National Labor Relations Board, Division of Judges (Meyerson, ALJ), Sept. 28, 2001.

D. SALARY ARBITRATION

1. Introductory Comments

This section focuses upon baseball salary arbitration. Grievance arbitration, an element of all collective bargaining agreements in professional sports, is addressed in **Section C**, *supra*. The baseball salary arbitration process is distinguished from other forms of arbitration. The "final offer" format of baseball salary arbitration is explained in terms of traditional negotiation theory. The baseball salary arbitration process is compared to the salary arbitration model utilized by the National Hockey League in **Notes and Comments**, *infra*, **Note 6**.

2. Baseball Salary Arbitration — Generally

Arbitration is the submission of a dispute to a neutral, non-governmental decision maker. The arbitrator replaces the court as the third party external authority agent that decides rights and duties between parties. The baseball salary arbitration process, including eligibility and evidentiary criteria, is established according to the terms of the collective bargaining agreement between labor and management/ownership. The conventional arbitration process allows the arbitrator to adjudge the rights and duties from the evidence presented by the parties, fashioning the appropriate remedy. Baseball salary arbitration utilizes the "final offer" process described below.

On February 25, 1973, the MLBPA and MLB (Player Relations Committee) negotiated a collective bargaining agreement that contained a salary arbitration provision. The mechanism included a single arbitrator who, after hearing, selected either the offer of the club or player ("final offer process"), considering relevant evidence as specified in the collective bargaining agreement. The original salary arbitration model continued in use, with some modifications including eligibility standards, from 1973 through 1997. Salary arbitration and player "free agency," adopted during the 1976 negotiations, combine to produce a topic of controversy among owners and players, sportswriters, scholars, and fans.

The owners negotiated for and gained a "three-member panel" for salary arbitration in the 1997 Basic Agreement (CBA), rejecting the traditional "one-member" model. The "three-member panel" approach was retained in the 2003 CBA. The MLBPA and PRC utilize an agreed upon random selection method to determine the cases assigned to the respective models. For a comprehensive examination of the baseball salary arbitration process and dynamics, *see* ABRAMS, THE MONEY PITCH: BASEBALL FREE AGENCY AND SALARY ARBITRATION (2000).

Final Offer Process

Article VI of the Baseball Basic Agreement (CBA) provides for arbitration of disputes concerning a player's salary. The baseball salary arbitration process utilizes the "final offer" format. Each side, the player and club, submits to the arbitration panel its offer or demand in the form of a one year nonguaranteed salary figure. The panel must choose one or the other of the two figures submitted. No compromise or other modification of the submitted figures are allowed. The panel inserts the chosen figure in duplicate Uniform Player Contracts and forwards them to the appropriate League office. There is no opinion and no release of the arbitration award by the chair of the panel except to the club, player, MLBPA, and Player Relations Committee. Basic Agreement, art. VI(F)(5) (2003). The MLBPA and the Player Relations Committee select arbitrators on an annual basis. In the event the players association and ownership group are unable to agree by January 1 of any year, the arbitrators are chosen by the American Arbitration Association (AAA).

The player or the team can initiate the arbitration process. Where the team initiates the process, the player may refuse to arbitrate and the matter is removed from arbitration. The player files for arbitration by notifying the MLBPA, who in turn gives notice to the Player Relations Committee, representing ownership. The hearings are conducted on a private and confidential basis. Each of the parties is limited to one hour for presentation of evidence and one-half hour for rebuttal and summation. The time constraints may be extended by the arbitrator for good cause. The parties split the costs of the hearing and are responsible for their respective expenses.

Eligibility

Generally, players with at least three years major league service, however accumulated, but with less than six years experience are eligible for salary arbitration. A player gains one year of major league service for every 172 days on the active roster of a major league club. Parts of different seasons may be joined to equal a whole season. In 1991 and thereafter, a player with two but less than three years of major league experience is eligible for salary arbitration if the player has accumulated at least 86 days of service during the immediately preceding season, and ranks in the top seventeen percent (17%) in total service in the class of players who have at least two but less than three years of major league service, but with 86 days of accumulated service during the immediately preceding season. Basic Agreement, art. VI(F)(2) (2003). Parts of different seasons may be joined to equal a whole season.

Players with six or more years of major league service, and who do not qualify for free agency, may elect salary arbitration. The category includes players who have elected free agency within the previous five year period, and thus are ineligible for free agency. The club must consent to arbitration of the salary issue. In the event the club refuses, the player may elect free agency.

Players with six or more years of major league service, and who have completed the terms of their contracts, may elect free agency. The former club may offer to submit the salary issue to arbitration. If the club does not offer arbitration, the team may not negotiate with the player until May 1. The player, of course, may reject the offer and continue to negotiate with other major league teams. If the player accepts the offer of arbitration, the player relinquishes the free agency status for one year, and is bound with the club by the arbitrator's decision.

The Basic Agreement also provides, "The issue of a Player's salary may be submitted to final and binding arbitration by any Player or his club, provided the other party to the arbitration consents thereto." Baseball Basic Agreement, Article VI (F)(1) (2003).

Criteria/Evidentiary Constraints

The relevant criteria upon which the arbitrator bases the decision is set forth in the Basic Agreement, as amended, as follows:

1. Quality of the Player's contribution to his Club during the past season, including but not limited to:
   a. overall performance;
   b. special qualities of leadership;
   c. special qualities of public appeal;
2. Length and consistency of his career contribution;
3. Record of Player's past compensation;
4. Comparative baseball salaries;
5. Existence of physical or mental defects on the part of the player; and
6. Recent performance record of the Club, including but not limited to:
   a. league standing;
   b. attendance.

Any evidence may be submitted which is relevant to the stated criteria, with the exception of the following evidence which shall not be considered:

1. The financial position of the Player and the Club;

2. Press comments, testimonials or similar material bearing on the performance of either the Player or Club, except that recognized annual player awards for playing excellence shall not be excluded;
3. Offers made by either Player or Club;
4. The cost to the parties of their representatives, attorneys, etc.; and
5. Salaries in other sports or occupations.

The arbitrator is specifically instructed as follows:

> Effective with the 1987 Championship Season, the arbitrator shall, except for a Player with five or more years of Major League Service, give particular attention, for comparative salary purposes, to contracts of players with Major League Service not exceeding one annual service group above the Player's annual service group. Nothing herein shall limit the ability of a Player, because of special accomplishment, to argue the equal relevance of salaries of Players without regard to service, and the arbitrator shall give whatever weight to such argument as he (she) deems appropriate.

Basic Agreement, Art. VI(F)(12)(2003).

The following materials examine baseball salary final-offer arbitration from the perspective of traditional negotiation theory.

Howard Raiffa (with Richardson & Metcalfe) THE ART AND SCIENCE OF COLLABORATIVE DECISIONMAKING (2002)*

* * *

Final-offer arbitration has been used in the resolution of salary disputes in major league baseball. In 1973 it was agreed that, starting with 1974 contracts, final-offer arbitration could be invoked by either players or by clubs in an impasse over salaries; once invoked, it would be binding on both sides. The guidelines for arbitrators were established in the 1973 basic agreement, [*see* criteria above, including amendments subsequent to 1973] which states:

> The criteria will be the quality of the Player's contribution to his Club during the past season (including but not limited to his overall performance, special qualities of leadership and public appeal), the length and consistency of his career contribution, the record of the Player's past compensation, comparative baseball salaries, the existence of any

* Reprinted by permission of the publisher from THE ART AND SCIENCE OF NEGOTIATION: HOW TO RESOLVE CONFLICTS AND GET THE BEST OUT OF BARGAINING, by Howard Raiffa, pp. 110-115, 117-118, Cambridge Mass.: The Belknap Press of Harvard University Press, Copyright © 1982 by the President and Fellows of Harvard College.

> physical or mental defects on the part of the Player, and the recent performance record of the Club including but not limited to its League standing and attendance as an indication of public acceptance (subject to the exclusion stated in (a) below). Any evidence may be submitted which is relevant to the above criteria, and the arbitrator shall assign such weight to the evidence as shall to him appear appropriate under the circumstances. The following items, however, shall be excluded: (a) the financial position of the Player and the Club; (b) press comments, testimonials or similar material bearing on the performance of either the Player or the Club, except that recognized annual Player awards for playing excellence shall not be excluded; (c) offers made by either Player or Club prior to arbitration tration; (d) the cost to the parties of their representatives, attorneys, etc; (e) salaries in other sports or occupations.

Of special interest here is exclusion (c), which attempts to prevent concessions (or nonconcessions) made in Phase 1 negotiations from influencing the arbitrator in Phase 2 negotiations.

The rationale for final-offer arbitration. In practice, [f]inal-offer arbitration is quite effective in persuading parties to settle without an imposed, arbitrated solution. [L]et A be a maximizing female and B a minimizing male. In order for A to increase her chance of winning (which means, in this case, having the arbiter prefer her sealed bid), she should be less demanding and lower her contemplated offer or bid. There is a similar logic for B. So the perception is that there is motivation for both sides to be reasonable in submitting their sealed offers. But it's more complicated. Party A should be interested not only in her probability of winning but in the amount she wins, if she wins. Increasing A's contemplated offer decreases the chance of her winning, but increases the potential size of her winnings. . . .

All's Not Well with the Procedure

What are some of the strategic aspects of final-offer arbitration? Analysis of a sample negotiation will help here. Suppose that management (M) and the union (U) are at an impasse. They have negotiated without success, knowing full well that they will have to submit the determination of basic wage rate (a single number) for final-offer arbitration. Management submits a sealed final offer, m; the union submits a sealed offer, u. The arbitrator then selects one of these two offers, depending on which value seems more appropriate. How shall we formalize this?

Assume that the arbitrator, after determining the facts, has some ideal value, a, in mind. The arbitrator will elect whichever final offer, m or u, is closer to a. If we imagine m, u, and a to be plotted on some linear scale — say, dollar value (see Figure) — it would be easy to see which offer more closely approximates the ideal. It is possible, though. that the arbitrator might have different psychological measurement scales on either side of his ideal; m might be close to his ideal in terms of dollars, whereas u might be closer in terms of some other value. But this complicates our task prematurely. Let's just suppose that in terms of one linear scale, the arbitrator selects the offer that is closer to his ideal. Following is a discussion of three special cases of this situation: first, in which the value of the arbitrator's ideal is known; second, in which there is a commonly perceived probability distribution for the ideal; and third, in which there are differing probability distributions for the ideal.

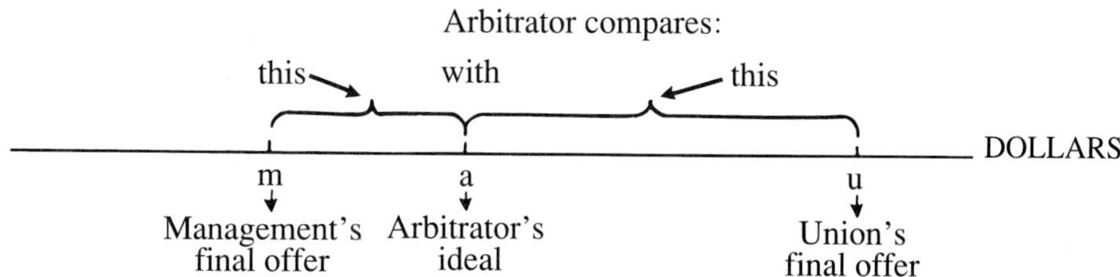

Idealized version of arbitrator's selection procedure in final-offer arbitration. (Arbitrator selects the final offer m or u closest to his ideal, a.)

Value of the Ideal is Known

Suppose that both M and U know the value of a before they submit their final offers. What is the best m against any given u? If, on a linear scale, m is quite a bit closer to a than is u, then the discrepancy between m and the ideal could be even slightly greater and m would still be the superior choice. So it is *not true* that the best retort for M against u is $m = a$. The best retort is to choose a value for m below a that is only slightly closer to a than the distance that u is above a.

To what extent can the parties be sure of their payoffs? If M chooses m below a on the linear scale, then M can guarantee a pay-off no worse than $a + (a\text{-}m)$. That value would be realized if u were selected at a distance above a that is equal to *m's* distance below a. Hence, to optimize M's security level (that is, to maximize M's minimum potential payoff), m should be set equal to a.

Let's now look at possible equilibria. If U selects $u = a$, then M's best retort is to select $m = a$; conversely, if M selects $m = a$, then U's best retort is to select $u = a$. Hence, the pair $m = a$ and $u = a$ are in equilibrium and, from the analysis above, it is clear that they are the only equilibrium pair.

If a were known, would the players choose their final offers equal to that value? Probably not all; but as the players become more experienced, a exercises a strong attraction.

Commonly Perceived Probability Distribution for the Ideal

To keep our case specific and simple, suppose that the annual wage rate for a starting fireman and the arbitrator's ideal value as perceived by M and U — which we will designate a — could be any value from 28 to 32 (in units of thousands of dollars). Both M and U perceive (and each knows that the other perceives) that all ideal values from 28 to 32 are equally likely for the arbitrator. The median and mean are both 30. Should M and U submit offers that are close to 30?

As a prelude to the analysis, we shall first determine the best retort for U against a known value of m — say, $m = 29$. . . . [I]f u were set at 30, then the outcome could either be 29 (at M's offer) or 30 (at U's offer), depending respectively on whether a were less than or more than 29.5. . . . So under our assumptions if u is chosen at 30, then U will be exposed to a lottery with payoffs 29 and 30 and probabilities of .375 and .625 respectively. An appropriate summary index for a risk-neutral U is the expected value: .375(29) + .625(30) = 29.625.

* * *

From Table . . . we observe the rather surprising fact that the best retort against $m = 29$ is $u = 32$ for an expected value of 30.125.

It's not difficult to show that to maximize expected monetary value, the best retort for U against any assumed value of m is the response $u = 32$. This is a strong and remarkable result. Analogously, the best retort for M against any assumed value of u is the response $m = 28$. The pair $m = 28$ and $u = 32$ are in equilibrium, but this is not nearly as strong as saying that $u = 32$ is a best response whether or not M plays its equilibrium value of 28; and $m = 28$ is a best response whether or not U plays its equilibrium value of 32.

If the commonly perceived distribution for the arbiter's ideal is not rectangular (that is, if all values are not equally likely between some lower and some upper value) but is a more natural, symmetrical, bell-shaped, distribution centered at a value, a, then against any assumed m the optimum retort [of U] . . . is higher than the mean of the distribution of the arbiter's uncertain value — surprisingly higher. And as m approaches the mean (central value), [the optimum retort] drifts further to the right. So it is not true that if M makes an offer close to the center of the distribution of a, that U should reciprocate. Intuitively, the higher value of m, the more U can afford to gamble. But also if U suspects that M is risk averse and will choose an m-value close to the mean, then U can afford to gamble with a higher u-value. All of this, of course, depends on U's being risk-neutral. If U is risk averse, then there will be an attractive force toward the center of the distribution a. Conversely, if U is risk prone, [the optimum retort of U] will be higher still.

An analogous story holds if we look at M's optimum retort. . . .

Table U's expected-value payoffs for selected values of u against $m = 29$ when all values for a from 28 to 32 are equally likely

Value of u	Possible outcomes	Probabilities	U's expected value
30	29	0.375	29.625
30		0.625	
31	29	0.5	30
31		0.5	
32	29	0.625	**30.125**
32		0.375	
33	29	0.75	30
33		0.25	
34	29	1	29
34		0	

Note: Boldface indicates maximum in column

Differing Probability Distributions for the Ideal

Some theoretical models show that with complete exchange of information M's and U's probablistic perceptions of the distribution of n should be identical. Empirically this does not turn out to be true, however, and very often the distributions are displaced in directions favoring each protagonist. All of this, of course, is speculative, and it is doubtful whether baseball players, ballclub owners, firemen's unions, or city managers formulate probability distributions. . . .

If U were to consciously calculate the best [retort] against a, then U would use its own assessment of a, and . . . there would be a vast discrepancy between m and [the best retort] (tempered somewhat by risk aversion). But now a further complication is introduced: U might suspect that M's assessment of a will be displaced to the left of U's own distribution, so that U might expect the possibility of very low m-values. Contrary to common wisdom, with the anticipation of low m-values and great uncertainty about a, U does not have much security and must be careful. With differing perceptions of a and differing perceptions of perceptions, with risk aversion and differing perceptions of the other party's risk aversion, with anticipated limited rationality and with expected miscalculations — in short, with full reality, this is a tremendously complicated problem.

Final-offer arbitration should have great appeal for the daring (the risk seekers) who play against the timid (the risk averse). It may be true that the proportion of cases going to final-offer arbitration is smaller than the proportion going to conventional arbitration. This of often cited as an advantage of final-offer arbitration. Of course, the logic is marred a bit, because conventional arbitration preceded by a round of Russian roulette would still do better.

Is it easier for an arbitrator to administer conventional or final-offer arbitration? In both cases he presumably would have to determine the facts. In conventional arbitration, he would have a continuum of choices; in final-offer arbitration, the adversaries — and in this case they really are adversaries — present the arbitrator with a dichotomous choice. It might be an easy choice: if the final offers are close together, it may not make much difference; if they are far apart and one seems ludicrous, again it's an easy matter. But if they are far apart and equally ludicrous, the task may be extremely difficult: the arbitrator might want to settle in the middle, but he can't. He does not have the luxury of being able to make fine distinctions in his judgments. On the other hand, if the arbitrator selects *m* or *u*, he does not have to publicly announce how he would have decided for every potential, embarrassingly difficult pair of offers.

NOTES AND COMMENTS

1. How does the description of the baseball salary arbitration process by Raiffa compare with your understanding? *See generally* 1 GREENBERG & GRAY, SPORTS LAW PRACTICE §§ 109(7)(d) *et seq.* (2d ed. 2005). For comparison of final offer arbitration with other models for dispute resolution, *see* Meth, *Final Offer Arbitration: A Model for Dispute Resolution in Domestic & International Disputes*, 10 AM. REV. INT'L ARB. 383 (1999). *See also*, Posthuma & Swift, *Legalistic vs. Facilitative Approaches to Arbitration: Strengths & Weaknesses*, 52 LABOR LAW J. 173 (2001). *See also* Chelius & Dworkin, *An Economic Analysis of Final-Offer Arbitration as a Conflict Resolution Device,* 24 J. OF CONFLICT RES. 293 (1980).

2. For views and comments on baseball salary arbitration, *see* Williams & Chambless, *Title VII and the Reserve Clause: A Statistical Analysis of Salary Discrimination In Major League Baseball*, 52 U. MIAMI L. REV. 461, 515 (1998) (suggests elimination of salary arbitration); Conti, *The Effect of Salary Arbitration on Major League Baseball*, 5 SPORTS LAW. J. 221, 222 (1998) (Salary arbitration is an effective compromise between reserve system and free agency).

Given the uncertainty of the arbitrator's decision making process, as expressed above, how should a party prepare for the arbitration hearing? The use of final offer arbitration, theoretically, motivates the parties to submit reasonable positions, rather than less than reasonable offers designed to compel the arbitrator to choose a position between the two. The motivating factor is the "fear" that the opposing party will be viewed by the arbitrator as being "more reasonable," and thus prevailing. Does final offer arbitration enhance negotiation between the parties, or does it have a chilling effect on negotiation?

3. Empirical examinations of the results of baseball's salary arbitration mechanism offer interesting insights into the process, including the strategies of bargainers and arbitrators. One study supports Professor Raiffa's projection that "[f]inal offer arbitration should have great appeal for the daring (the risk seekers) who play against the timid (the risk averse)." Using data from a sample of players eligible for arbitration in 1990-93, the authors find that more aggressive offers made by players are the primary determinant of which player/club pairs proceed to arbitration. But, the analysis indicates that the players fare worse when their aggression leads them to arbitration. On average, a player offer that is 10 percent higher than predicted results in a salary in excess of 9 percent below what would be predicted. The failure of the parties to achieve settlement through bargaining prior to arbitration is consistent with an "optimism" or "risk loving" model, where one or both parties exhibit excessive optimism about winning the case. Farmer, Pecorino & Stango, *The Causes of Bargaining Failure: Evidence from Major League Baseball*, 47 J.L. & ECON. 543 (2004).

Another study notes that final offer arbitration is designed to motivate bargainers to submit reasonable offers, as the arbitration panel cannot split the offers by selecting a compromise position, as is common in conventional arbitration. But, analysis of the data reveals that arbitrators in baseball's system may formulate preferred awards that compromise between bargainers' perspectives. Examination of the winning and losing offers implies that the arbitrators' preferred awards represent a weighted average of the player's salary in the previous season and the average free agent salary, a compromise between perspectives taken by the players and management. Marburger, *Arbitrator Compromise in Final Offer Arbitration: Evidence from Major League Baseball*, 42 Econ. Inquiry 60 (2004).

4. Notice the evidentiary constraints of the baseball arbitration process. What evidence is available for negotiation, but not proper for arbitration? Remember that the arbitrator does not issue an opinion or otherwise justify the decision. Can you explain the decision? Can you learn from the process? For analysis of the factors deemed to significantly influence the arbitrator's decision, *see* ABRAMS, THE MONEY PITCH: BASE BALL FREE AGENCY AND SALARY ARBITRATION (2000). *See also* Fizel, Krautmann & Hadley, *Equity and Arbitration in Major League Baseball*, 23 MANAGERIAL & DECISION ECONOMICS 427 (Oct.-Nov. 2002) (study indicates equity is a significant predictor of player's unilateral decision to file for arbitration, but an insignificant determinant of proceeding to hearing of offsetting responses by player and owner); Pikul & Mayo, *Performance and Eligibility for Arbitration or Free Agency and Salaries of Professional Major League Baseball Players, the 1994-1995 Experience*, 23 J. SPORT & SOCIAL ISSUES 353 (Aug. 1999) (study uses multiple regression to confirm that eligibility for arbitration or free agency and performance are positive predictors of players' salaries, a result consistent with theories of worker motivation).

5. Private parties formulate arbitration systems, as dispute resolution mechanisms, to gain various advantages that are not provided in judicial processes. Sports leagues and player associations traditionally seek the following values in design of arbitration methods:

1. Expeditious process;
2. Fair and equitable determination;

3. Low cost burdens; and
4. Preservation of League and Association integrity.

Does the "single offer" format accomplish the above objectives? Should the process include a single arbitrator, or a board of three or more members? Should the decision maker(s) possess authority to "split the baby," as opposed to selecting one of the two offers? Should the arbitrator be "permanent" or "specially appointed?" What are the benefits of each alternative arbitration mechanism?

6. The National Hockey League has utilized salary arbitration for a longer period of time than Major League Baseball, but uses the traditional arbitration model enabling the arbitrator to formulate an independent value determination, and issue an opinion explaining the choice. The 2005 NHL-NHLPA collective bargaining agreement made two changes to the arbitration process utilized in the previous CBA. Players are eligible for salary arbitration after four years of service instead of the three years previously required. Teams also possess the right to elect salary arbitration. Where a player earned more than $1.5 million in the prior year, the team may elect salary arbitration in lieu of making a "qualifying offer." Teams have the right to elect salary arbitration with respect to certain restricted free agents. The CBA retains the following innovative provisions for salary arbitration:

1. Owners have the right to reject an award in excess of average NHL salaries, which can be exercised a maximum of three times over two years;
2. Owners can elect to have the arbitrator establish the salary for two years, rather than one;
3. Owners may "walk-away" from an arbitration award, enabling the player to become a free agent; and
4. After the "walk-away" exercise, the player may "walk-back" and accept the last pre-arbitration offer made by the club, in the event the player does not receive a better offer.

See generally, Kirke, *National Hockey League Contract Negotiations*, *in* 2 Law Of Professional And Amateur Sports § 8.03(3) (Uberstine ed. 2005).

Chapter 8

REPRESENTATION OF PROFESSIONAL ATHLETES

A. INTRODUCTORY COMMENTS

As recently as thirty years ago, most professional athletes negotiated their own contracts. Today, professional sports have evolved into a multi-billion dollar industry, and athletes realize the need to hire professional sports agents to aid them in reaping the benefits of this increased wealth. Consider, for example, what a star amateur player will need in terms of representation and advice as he embarks on what is expected to be a lucrative NBA career in the path of Michael Jordan. This chapter focuses on the role of the player agent, first examining issues surrounding the legal capacity of a player agent to contract with a professional athlete for representation under existing state, player union, and other regulations. It next considers the questions confronting the player agent in the structuring of the sports agent practice, including the requisite player agent contracts. Finally, the chapter addressees common law and other duties imposed upon the player agent representing the professional athlete.

1. Player Agent Functions

The player agent performs myriad functions in representing the professional athlete. A single representative rarely performs all tasks. Some firms, through teamwork, provide a full-service package, but others concentrate on only singular acts, such as contract negotiation. Services provided by the attorney include the following:

1. Employment contract negotiation;
2. Legal counseling;
3. Obtaining and negotiation of endorsement contracts and other income opportunities;
4. Financial management and planning advice;
5. Career planning counseling;
6. Marketing of the athlete through public relations and other means; and
7. Resolution of disputes arising under an employment contract.

Professor Berry describes the various services and forms of business structure as follows:

Robert C. Berry
Representation of the Professional Athlete*

Functions of the Sports Representative Contract Negotiation

In addition to the player-team contract and endorsement contracts, the sports representative may also need to negotiate contracts related to special events, such as exhibitions, particularly in individual performer sports such as tennis or golf. In addition, when one represents athletes, one rarely stops negotiating. Even in relations with teams, the signed contract is only the first step. Numerous occurrences during the contract term may call for negotiation skill and tact. For instance, disputes may arise over a player's or a team's conduct. If possible, formal grievances should be avoided, and it may be left to the representative to negotiate a compromise. Another reality is that a contract can end at any time, but hopefully the player's skills will be wanted elsewhere. It is not unknown for a sports representative to negotiate three or four contracts with different clubs during the time period that was contemplated to be covered by the first contract.

Counseling

The remarks about negotiating should emphasize the importance of the counseling function. The client must be made to understand what may happen during negotiations and after a deal is signed. Counseling is an ongoing process, requiring empathy mixed with firmness. Sound counseling for the client provides protection for the client's best interests and, on a pragmatic note, is often the difference between retaining the client or losing the client to another representative.

Financial Management and Planning

Not all representatives undertake financial management and planning. When these are not offered directly, the sports representative often oversees the assigning of these tasks to others — accountants, marketing companies, investment advisors, and lawyer specialists, among many. These services can range from simple bookkeeping to advanced financial and tax planning.

Marketing

Extensive marketing of athletes to obtain endorsements and other sources of outside revenue is no easy task. The mistaken impression is that opportunities are boundless. This is far from the case. Except for certain stars, marketing opportunities are limited, and substantial efforts must be expended to realize a client's full potential. Marketing requires special skills, something that may

---

be beyond the capacity of the ordinary representative. Expert assistance may be advisable.

Dispute Resolution

Money breeds controversy and dispute. A sports representative must know that a signed contract is no guarantee of smooth relations from that point forward. When a dispute occurs, the sports representative must know what steps can be taken if a negotiated resolution is not achieved. In some situations, both arbitration and litigation are possibilities. In others, such as disputes falling under a league's collective bargaining provisions, arbitration preempts litigation. A sports representative must know when a matter is subject to arbitration, because filing deadlines are short and are easily waived. Thus, the collective bargaining agreement is an indispensable document in the representative's library, and the assistance of the players association may be essential. Other issues are still the province of litigation. If the representative is not equipped to litigate, assistance must be available.

Career Planning

The life of the professional athlete is, on average, a short one. It must be utilized to the fullest. At the same time, planning for a career after sports should be started as soon as possible. An athlete may profess to understand that his career in professional sports may be a short one, but the reality is, generally, that the athlete is not prepared for the day when his final release occurs. This is of course a type of counseling, but one so vital that it is listed separately to underscore its importance. Professional assistance by outside agencies is now increasingly made available through player associations and a limited number of private sources.

Models for a Sports Representation Business

In light of the many functions that a sports representative might undertake, this section considers the most popular ways in which sports representatives do in fact structure their businesses. These various models should be evaluated from several perspectives, not the least being the legal and ethical restrictions on sports lawyers and agents.

Free-Standing Sports Management Firms

This is probably the most popular model. The sports management firm is established as a business that offers a wide range of services to the athlete. A given business may not attempt to perform all of the services discussed in Section I above, but the likelihood is that the firm performs several of the functions, including contract negotiation and several types of financial management. The free-standing management firm in turn can be divided into two categories.

1. *Representation of Athletes Only*

These firms concentrate on the representation of the professional athlete and do not mix this with other undertakings, though some have branched into the representation of entertainers as well, particularly television talent.

2. *Combined Athlete Representation and Event Management*

A few large companies not only represent athletes but also help run events, often those in which some of their clients may participate. Event management may include a range from operating to underwriting to owning sports events.

Law Practice Only

Lawyer sports representatives often participate as principals in a sports management firm, but many opt to include this as just one aspect of their law practice. In this scenario, the lawyer performs the legal tasks needed for his client — including contract negotiation, preparation of tax returns, counseling and dispute resolution — but does not undertake financial management, marketing, investment advice or other ancillary functions. The sports lawyer practicing in a firm may, however, retain oversight as to the retention of other needed professionals.

Sports Management Firms Affiliated With Law Firm

Many lawyer sports representatives originally developed their practice simply as a law firm or sole practitioner. As their businesses developed, they saw the advantages of expanding the services offered the sports client. Some in this position abandoned the law firm title and moved wholly into a sports management posture. . . . Others chose to segregate functions. The law practice was retained, but a sports management firm was created to extend services that were not colorably the practice of law. Several examples of this type of bifurcated system, with a close affiliation between the law practice and the management firm, are still in existence.

A second type of affiliated business has more recently evolved. This is the sports management firm that continues its independence but has a working relationship with a law firm that does not otherwise involve itself in sports related matters. In this respect, the law firm is a backup to provide services that the management firm does not practice. Some sports management firms of this description even have offices within the law firm, but a clear demarcation between the sports business and the law firm is maintained.

* * *

2. Historical Overview

Athletes have received pay for play in the United States since the Civil War, but rarely utilized agent or other professional services until the mid-1960s. The player agent profession has grown tremendously from the 1970s until the present. Several reasons are cited for the evolution of the player agent relationship. First, players in most professional sports leagues possessed little bargaining power until recently. In the 1970s, players successfully challenged the reserve clauses of the traditional player contracts that bound the player to a team for life. Viable competing leagues formed during this period, resulting in increased leverage for the athlete. Player associations, struggling to become full fledged unions, emerged from the 1960s with the power to bargain collectively and strike in support of salary and other demands. As player salaries and other benefits increased, the need for professional services, including tax advice and financial planning, rose accordingly.

3. Professional Sports Today

The professional sports industry blossomed after World War II. Television and radio broadcasting served to expand the audience from the traditional ball-park or racetrack attendance to a national one. Increased gate and other receipts coupled with broadcast revenue enlarged the financial pie for distribution among the constituents of the professional sports environment. Also, national recognition of professional athletes joins media advertising patterns to generate off-the-field revenue opportunities for the players. The player agent functions in this context similarly to the traditional entertainment agent.

4. Need for Regulation

There is no doubt that development of the player agent profession has resulted in benefits for the players. However, severe criticism is focused upon some player agent practices and the unfortunate performances that have squandered athletes' lifetime earnings. The typical problem areas of agent practice include questions regarding:

1. unethical solicitation;
2. charging of excessive fees;
3. conflicts of interest;
4. general incompetence;
5. income mismanagement;
6. fraud; and
7. unauthorized practice of law.

A player agent is subject to laws of general applicability, such as contract, tort, agency, fraud, and criminal laws. In addition, player agents may be subject to state and federal regulation. For example, agents who provide advice in securities investment may be within the reach of the Federal Investment Advisers Act of 1940, 15 U.S.C. § 80b-1. Several states have statutes regulating persons who are in the business of procuring employment or engagement for entertainers. Attorneys, of course, are subject to the ethical rules of professional conduct governing lawyers.

The laws of general applicability are deemed inadequate to provide professional athletes with the needed protection. Many (perhaps most) agents are not attorneys. Some players represent themselves. Whether an agent's business advice falls within the reach of the Federal Investment Advisers Act is questionable. *See Zinn v. Parrish*, 644 F.2d 360 (7th Cir. 1981) (ruling that player agent who transmitted stock investment recommendations of others, provided advice on business investments, and invested funds on behalf of client, was not an "investment adviser" under the Act; isolated transactions were incident to the main purpose of the negotiating football contracts and did not constitute engaging in the business of advising others on investment securities so as to require registration under the Act). The talent and employment acts contain exemptions which arguably insulate player agents from the acts.

B. PLAYER AGENT: CAPACITY TO CONTRACT; ELIGIBILITY AND REGISTRATION UNDER REGULATIONS

More than one-half of the states and the respective NFL, NBA, NHL, and MLB player associations responded to the criticisms of player agent performance by enacting or otherwise promulgating regulations focusing directly upon player agents and agent practices. In 2004, Congress enacted the first federal statute directly regulating agent conduct. The Sports Agent Responsibility and Trust Act (SPARTA), 15 U.S.C. §§ 7801 *et seq.*, addresses agent contact with student athletes. Likewise, the Uniform Athlete Agents Act (2000) focuses solely upon agent practices in recruiting student athletes. Many regulations require registration or certification upon satisfactory review of qualifications and background. Importantly, the agent must comply with certification requirements of all mandatory regulations in order to possess the capacity to form a lawful contract with the player. The agent conduct prohibited and enforcement provisions vary from plan to plan. The National Conference of Commissioners on Uniform State Laws, in the Prefatory Note to the Uniform Athlete Agents Act (2000), states as follows:

> The [state] statutes differ greatly. About two-thirds of the statutes impose registration requirements. There are substantial differences in the registration procedures, disclosures required and requirements relating to record maintenance, reporting, renewal, notice, warning and security. . . . Conscientious agents operating in more than a single State must have nightmares caused by the lack of uniformity in the existing statutes, the difficulty in compliance and the severity of penalties which may be imposed for violations.

Registration schemes follow two distinct formats. Player associations and some states regulate all player agents' conduct associated with the negotiation of player-team contracts. The regulatory design attempts to protect rookie and veteran players from unscrupulous and incompetent player agent practice.

Other state statutes, including the Uniform Athlete Agents Act and the Sports Agent Responsibility and Trust Act, only govern agent contact with student athletes. Thus, the regulatory acts are intended to protect students and consequently, the rookie professional athletes, as well as the educational institutions and fans. The typical legislation requires certification prior to agent conduct to induce player-agent contracts, specifies terms which must be included in player-agent contracts, and contains enforcement provisions, including criminal and civil remedies.

The National Football League Players Association, in 2002, promulgated regulations governing player financial advisors. The voluntary program, the first of its kind in professional sports, attempts to pre-select and qualify financial advisors for service to NFL players. On January 25, 2003, the U. S. Securities and Exchange Commission issued a "No-Action Letter," at the request of the NFLPA, advising that the SEC would not recommend enforcement action for application of the Investment Advisors Act of 1940 to the NFLPA and investment advisors participating in the program.

The following **Problem** introduces the complexities of signing a player to a player-agent contract — the first step in representing a professional athlete. Cases, statutes, and other materials needed to complete the problem assignment are located in the **Case File**. As you work through the **Problem**, notice the differences between the various regulation schemes, and the overlapping jurisdictional reach.

Problem

Attorney James McNabb desires to become a full-time player agent. McNabb, confronted with important organizing questions, hired your law firm to advise and otherwise assist him in his endeavors.

McNabb is an active member in good standing of the California bar. He will locate his player agent office in Spokane, Washington. McNabb expects to represent the following athletes:

1. Jerome Jenkins, veteran member of the Oakland Raiders Football Club, residing in a state governed by the Uniform Athlete Agents Act, and currently represented by another agent;
2. Robert Newsome, rookie free agent (undrafted) football player, residing in Alabama; and
3. Larry Kinsella, NFL high round draft choice, residing in California.

McNabb desires to provide a full-service package to the athlete, including the hustling of endorsement contracts and investment counseling. A senior partner in your firm assigned the McNabb matter to you. She instructed you as follows:

1. Identify the regulation schemes in the **Case File** to which James McNabb is subject.
2. Outline the qualifications for agent eligibility under each regulatory plan.
3. Formulate suggestions for the preparation of an application package enabling your firm to adequately represent McNabb in making application for agent certification.
4. Identify the risks associated with representing Jerome Jenkins. Recommend actions available for resolving issues concerning Jenkins' current player agent contract.

Case File

NFLPA Regulations Governing Contract Advisors

(Regulations may be accessed at www.nflpa.org/agents/)

SECTION 1: SCOPE OF REGULATIONS

A. **Persons Subject to Regulations**

B. **Activities Covered**

SECTION 2: CERTIFICATION

A. **Application for Certification**

B. **Interim Certification**

C. . . .

D. Grounds for Denial of Certification

E. . . .

F. Suspension of Revocation of Certification

G. Provisional Certification

SECTION 3: STANDARD OF CONDUCT FOR CONTRACT ADVISORS

A. . . .

B. **Prohibited Conduct**

California Miller-Ayala Athlete Agents Act

Cal. Bus. & Prof. Code §§ 18895 et seq.

§ 18895.2 Definitions

§ 18896 Information regarding athlete agent filing with Secretary of State; contents

§ 18896.2 Revisesd information regarding athlete agent

§ 18896.3 Form statement

§ 18896.4 Exclusion from disclosure; other businesses of athlete agent

§ 18896.6 Written notification by athlete agent upon contact with athlete or family

Uniform Athlete Agents Act

(2000)

Section 2. DEFINITIONS. In this [Act]:

(1) "Agency contract" means an agreement in which a student-athlete authorizes a person to negotiate or solicit on behalf of the student-athlete a professional-sports-services contract or an endorsement contract.

(2) "Athlete-agent" means an individual who enters into an agency contract with a student-athlete or, directly or indirectly, recruits or solicits a student-athlete to enter into an agency contract. . . . The term does not include a spouse, parent, sibling, [or] grandparent[, or guardian] of the student-athlete or an individual acting solely on behalf of a professional sports team or professional sports organization. . . .

(4) "Contact" means a communication, direct or indirect, between an athlete agent and a student-athlete, to recruit or solicit the student-athlete to enter into an agency contract.

(5) "Endorsement contract" means an agreement under which a student-athlete is employed or receives consideration to use on behalf of the other party any value that the student-athlete may have because of publicity, reputation, following, or fame obtained because of athletic ability or performance. . . .

* * *

(7) "Person" means an individual, corporation, business trust, estate, trust, partnership, limited liability company, association, joint venture, government; governmental subdivision, agency, or instrumentality; public corporation, or any other legal or commercial entity.

(8) "Professional-sports-services contract" means an agreement under which an individual is employed, or agrees to render services, as a player on a professional sports team, with a professional sports organization, or as a professional athlete. . . .

* * *

(12) "Student-athlete" means an individual who engages in, is eligible to engage in, or may be eligible in the future to engage in, any intercollegiate sport. If an individual is permanently ineligible to participate in a particular intercollegiate sport, the individual is not a student-athlete for purposes of that sport.

Section 4. ATHLETE AGENTS: REGISTRATION REQUIRED; VOID CONTRACTS

(a) Except as otherwise provided in subsection (b), an individual may not act as an athlete agent in this State without holding a certificate of registration under Section 6 or 8.

(b) Before being issued a certificate of registration, an individual may act as an athlete agent in this State for all purposes except signing an agency contract, if:

(1) a student-athlete or another person acting on behalf of the student-athlete initiates communication with the individual; and

(2) within seven days after an initial act as an athlete agent, the individual submits an application for registration as an athlete agent in this State.

(c) An agency contact resulting from conduct in violation of this section is void and the athlete agent shall return any consideration received under the contract.

Section 5. REGISTRATION AS ATHLETE AGENT; FORM; REQUIREMENTS.

(a) An applicant for registration shall submit an application for registration to the [Secretary of State] in a form prescribed by the [Secretary of State]. . . . The application must . . . state or contain:

(1) the name of the applicant and the address of the applicant's principal place of business; . . .

* * *

(4) a description of the applicant's:

(A) formal training as an athlete agent;

(B) practical experience as an athlete agent; and

(C) educational background relating to the applicant's activities as an athlete agent; . . .

* * *

(6) the name, sport, and last known team for each individual for whom the applicant acted as an athlete agent during the five years preceding the date of submission of the application; . . .

* * *

(8) whether the applicant . . . has been convicted of a crime that, if committed in this State, would be a crime involving moral turpitude or a felony, and identify the crime;

(9) whether there has been any administrative or judicial determination that the applicant . . . has made a false, misleading, deceptive, or fraudulent representation;

(10) any instance in which the conduct of the applicant . . . resulted in the imposition of a sanction, suspension, or declaration of ineligibility to participate in an interscholastic or intercollegiate athletic event on a student-athlete or educational institution;

(11) any sanction, suspension, or disciplinary action taken against the applicant . . . arising out of occupational or professional conduct; and

(12) whether there has been any denial of an application for, suspension or revocation of, or refusal to renew, the registration or licensure of the applicant . . . as an athlete agent in any State.

* * *

Section 6. CERTIFICATE OF REGISTRATION; ISSUANCE OR DENIAL; RENEWAL.

(a) Except as otherwise provided in subsection (b), the [Secretary of State] shall issue a certificate of registration to an individual who complies with Section 5(a). . . .

(b) The [Secretary of State] may refuse to issue a certificate of registration if the [Secretary of State] determines that the applicant is engaged in conduct that has significant adverse effect on the applicant's fitness to act as an athlete agent. In making the determination, the [Secretary of State] may consider whether the applicant has:

(1) been convicted of a crime that, if committed in this State, would be a crime involving moral turpitude or a felony;

(2) made a materially false, misleading, deceptive, or fraudulent representation in the application or as an athlete agent;

(3) engaged in conduct that would disqualify the applicant from serving in a fiduciary capacity;

(4) engaged in conduct prohibited by [this Act];

(5) had a registration or licensure as an athlete agent suspended, revoked, or denied or been refused renewal or registration or licensure as an athlete agent in any State;

(6) engaged in conduct the consequence of which was that a sanction, suspension, or declaration of ineligibility to participate in an interscholastic or intercollegiate athletic event was imposed on a student-athlete or educational institution, or

(7) engaged in conduct that significantly adversely reflects on the applicant's credibility, honesty, or integrity.

(c) In making a determination under subsection (b), the [Secretary of State] shall consider:

(1) how recently the conduct occurred;

(2) the nature of the conduct and the context in which it occurred; and

(3) any other relevant conduct of the applicant.

(d) An athlete agent may apply to renew a registration by submitting an application for renewal in a form prescribed by the [Secretary of State].

Section 7. SUSPENSION, REVOCATION, OR REFUSAL TO RENEW REGISTRATION.

(a) The [Secretary of State] may suspend, revoke, or refuse to renew a registration for conduct that would have justified denial or registration under Section 6(b).

(b) The [Secretary of State] may deny, suspend, revoke, or refuse to renew a certificate of registration or licensure only after proper notice and an opportunity for a hearing. The [Administrative Procedures Act] applies to this [Act].

Alabama Athlete Agents Regulatory Act of 1987

Acts 1987, No. 87-628, § 1
Effective August 3, 1987

2- **Definitions.**

2- . . .

2- **Registration of athlete agents required.**

2- . . .

2- **Evaluation of applicant and principal place of business.**

2- **Grounds for refusal to grant registration; notice of refusal and opportunity for hearing; hearing procedure; determi-**

nation of commission; appeals; effective date of orders and judgments.

2- . . .

40- **Effect of failure to comply with § 8-26-4.**

COLLINS v. NATIONAL BASKETBALL PLAYERS ASSOCIATION

976 F.2d 740 (10th Cir. 1992) (unpublished), *aff'g*, 850 F. Supp. 1468 (D. Colo. 1991)

TACHA, Circuit Judge.

* * *

In summary, the NBPA is a labor union that the National Basketball Association (NBA) has recognized for over thirty years as the exclusive bargaining representative for all NBA players, pursuant to section nine of the National Labor Relations Act, 29 U.S.C. § 159. For over twenty years, the NBPA and the NBA have entered into collective bargaining agreements establishing the minimum salary an individual player must be paid, the maximum aggregate salary a team may pay all of its players, and other issues unique to professional sports. The NBPA, however, has always authorized the players or their individually selected agents to negotiate their individual compensation packages within the framework established by the collective bargaining agreements.

Player agents were unregulated before 1986. But in that year, in response to a growing number of player complaints about agent abuses — including violations of various fiduciary duties — the NBPA established the Regulations, a comprehensive system of agent certification. The Regulations permit only certified agents to represent NBPA members. The Regulations also establish the Committee, which is authorized to issue or deny certification of prospective player agents. The Committee may deny certification if it determines that the prospective agent has made a false statement of material fact in his application or that he has engaged in any conduct that significantly impacts on his credibility, integrity, or competence to serve in a fiduciary capacity. Any prospective agent whose application for certification is denied may appeal by filing a timely demand for final and binding arbitration.

Collins had been a player agent representing NBPA members since 1974. The Committee certified Collins as a player agent in 1986, the year the Regulations first took effect. However, Collins voluntarily suspended his activities as an agent during the pendency of a lawsuit filed by one of his clients, Kareem Abdul-Jabbar, and a corporation Abdul-Jabbar had established, Ain Jeem, Inc. Abdul-Jabbar alleged that Collins had breached a number of fiduciary duties when Collins mishandled Abdul-Jabbar's income tax returns, improvidently invested his money, mishandled his assets, and transferred funds from his accounts to the accounts of other players represented by Collins. The Ain Jeem lawsuit was settled in 1989, but in the interim the Committee had decertified Collins for violations of other regulations.

Collins reapplied for certification in 1990, and the Committee commenced an informal investigation into Collins' application. The Committee took testimony from both Collins and Abdul-Jabbar, and was provided with nonconfidential discovery material from the Ain Jeem suit. The Committee denied Collins' application because it found that Collins was unfit to serve in a fiduciary capacity on behalf of NBA players and that he had made false or misleading statements to the Committee during the investigation. It reached this conclusion after it found substantially all of Abdul-Jabbar's allegations to be true. The Committee informed Collins of his right to final and binding arbitration, but Collins did not demand arbitration and instead filed this lawsuit.

Before the district court, Collins claimed that the NBPA certification process violates the antitrust laws because it amounts to a group boycott. We agree with the district court's analysis of the labor and antitrust statutes and its conclusion that the statutory labor exemption from the Sherman Act permits the NBPA to establish a certification procedure for player agents. Specifically, we hold that the Regulations meet both prongs of the test established in *United States v. Hutcheson*, 312 U.S. 219 (1941), in which the Supreme Court held that labor unions acting in their self-interest and not in combination with nonlabor groups are statutorily exempt from Sherman Act liability. *Id.* at 232.

On appeal, Collins now acknowledges that the NBPA has the statutory authority to establish player agent regulations. But he maintains his attack on the Committee's decision to deny his certification because it was based in part on its finding that he had breached his fiduciary duty as an investment agent and money manager. He argues that his conduct outside of negotiations between players and their teams is not a legitimate interest of the union because it has no bearing on the union's interest in the wage scale and working conditions of its members.

The district court properly rejected this argument. The NBPA established the Regulations to deal with agent abuses, including agents' violations of their fiduciary duties as labor negotiators. It was entirely fair for the Committee to conclude that a man who had neglected his fiduciary duties as an investment agent and money manager could not be trusted to fulfill his fiduciary duties as a negotiator. The integrity of a prospective negotiating agent is well within the NBPA's legitimate interest in maintaining the wage scale and working conditions of its members.

Collins next contends that the district court erred in granting summary judgment because there still exists a genuine dispute over whether the NBPA intended to waive its statutory right to act as the exclusive bargaining agent of the NBA players. He argues that the fact that the NBPA permitted agents to negotiate individual salaries for over twenty years reasonably implies that the union intended to waive its exclusive right to bargain, and thereby waived its statutory exemption to the Sherman Act.

The district court was not in error because there is no genuine dispute over the NBPA's intent regarding its statutory exemption. "'[W]aiver is the intentional relinquishment of a known right.'" . . . A waiver of a right provided to a union by the labor statutes must be clear and unmistakable. . . . Collins has presented no evidence that the NBPA intended to waive its right other than the fact that the union did not seek to regulate player agents until the abuses came to its attention in the mid-1980s. Because no jury could reasonably infer from this fact that the NBPA clearly and unmistakably intended to waive its exclusive right to bargain on behalf of its members, there is no genuine issue of material fact. . . .

Finally, Collins contends that the district court erred in granting summary judgment because there still exists a genuine dispute over whether the NBPA estopped itself from failing to certify Collins as an agent. Collins argues that a reasonable jury could conclude that the NBPA's failure either to regulate agents for over twenty years or to inform him that it might someday regulate agents induced him to believe that it would never regulate agents.

The district court properly granted summary judgment because there is no genuine dispute over the factual elements of estoppel. The Tenth Circuit recently reiterated the four traditional elements of equitable estoppel: (1) the party to be estopped must know the facts; (2) the party to be estopped must intend that his conduct will be acted upon or must so act that the party asserting the estoppel has the right to believe that it was so intended; (3) the party asserting the estoppel must be ignorant of the true facts; and (4) the party asserting the estoppel must rely on the other party's conduct to his injury. . . . Collins has not established a genuine dispute over the third element because no reasonable jury could conclude that the NBPA intended to refrain from ever regulating agents or that Collins rightfully believed that the NBPA so intended.

For these reasons, we AFFIRM the district courts' order granting summary judgment. The mandate shall issue forthwith.

TOTAL ECONOMIC ATHLETIC MANAGEMENT OF AMERICA, INC. v. PICKENS

898 S.W.2d 98 (Mo. App. 1995)

ULRICH, Presiding Judge.

This anticipatory breach of contract case arose from a representation agreement signed by Bruce Evon Pickens and Total Economic Athletic Management of America, Inc., d/b/a Team America, a Nebraska Corporation. That representation agreement was to allow Team America to act as Mr. Pickens' contract advisor in negotiating his National Football League player contract. However, before negotiations, Mr. Pickens engaged another contract advisor who actually negotiated the NFL player contract. The ensuing litigation resulted in a $20,000 judgment entered on a jury verdict for Team America and against Mr. Pickens.

Both parties appeal. In its appeal, Team America claims that the trial court erred in restricting argument on damages, in denying its motion for additur, and in overruling its motion for a new trial on damages only. In his cross-appeal, Mr. Pickens contends that the trial court erred in giving and refusing instructions. The judgment is affirmed.

I. MR. PICKENS' CROSS-APPEAL

Mr. Pickens' cross-appeal is considered first. The cross-appeal asserts that the instructions misadvised the jury on the existence of a binding agreement and on the measure of damages. The following facts provide background on the representation agreement:

While a student at the University of Nebraska, Bruce Evon Pickens played football for the University's football team, a perennial National Collegiate Athletic Association (NCAA) Division I football power. Howard Misle is the president and owner of Total Economic Athletic Management of America, Inc., a corporation incorporated in Nebraska, d/b/a Team America. Mr. Misle apparently owns other businesses, including an automobile dealership in Lincoln, Nebraska. In behalf of Team America, Mr. Misle negotiates player contracts for athletes with professional football teams. Mr. Misle is a certified contract advisor by the National Football League Players' Association (NFLPA).

Trial evidence discloses that Mr. Misle and Mr. Pickens met when Mr. Pickens was a student at the University of Nebraska. On January 3, 1991, Mr. Pickens encountered Mr. Misle at Mr. Misle's automobile dealership. Mr. Pickens purchased a vehicle from the dealership, and Mr. Misle, in behalf of the dealership, advanced Mr. Pickens credit on a "house note." Mr. Pickens paid nothing for the automobile. Mr. Misle told Mr. Pickens that Mr. Pickens would be approached by many agents seeking to represent him in negotiations with a National Football League (NFL) professional football team to obtain a professional football player contract.

According to Mr. Misle's testimony, an agreement was signed by Mr. Pickens and Mr. Misle on January 18, 1991. The agreement bears the date January 20, 1991. Except for the deletion of paragraph 7, the agreement was a standard form entitled "Standard Representation Agreement Between NFLPA Contract Advisor and Player." Mr. Pickens was not given a copy of the document when it was signed.

Testimony differed about why the representation agreement was not dated when signed. Mr. Misle testified that he had inadvertently failed to date the agreement, and dated it sometime after the date the agreement was signed when he realized that failure. Mr. Misle also testified he explained to Mr. Pickens that sending the agreement to the NFLPA as provided in paragraph 7 was unnecessary because the organization was then a voluntary association and not a union. Mr. Misle also testified that he eventually gave a copy of the signed and dated document to Mr. Pickens.

Team America had representation agreements with other football players. Mr. Misle had sent those agreements to the NFLPA office as provided by paragraph 7 in the NFLPA form contract. In a letter submitted by Mr. Misle to the NFLPA office, he stated that as Team America continued to enter such agreements with athletes, he would submit copies of the agreements to NFLPA.

Mr. Pickens' testimony about signing the representation agreement differed from Mr. Misle's. Mr. Pickens stated that when he arrived home from the Orange Bowl game on January 3, 1991, an employee of Mr. Misle's automobile dealership was awaiting him at the airport. Mr. Pickens went to Mr. Misle's automobile dealership where he was shown several automobiles, including the vehicle that he chose. Mr. Misle provided the vehicle to him without Mr. Pickens' paying any money for its purchase. Mr. Misle then presented the NFLPA standard representation agreement saying to Mr. Pickens, "Since I'm putting myself out on a limb for you, why don't you show me a little bit of consideration and good faith by at least signing the document and letting me know that you are considering me for your agent." Mr. Pickens testified that Mr. Misle told him the document would not be dated and the agreement would not be binding until it was dated and sent to the NFLPA. According to Mr. Pickens, Mr. Misle stated that paragraph 7 of the agreement would be deleted because the document was not a binding agreement. Mr. Misle then stated to Mr. Pickens, according to Mr. Pickens, that when they reached agreement, the document would be dated and sent to the NFLPA to then become valid. Mr. Pickens then departed the dealership with the Audi automobile.

Sometime in early 1991, after Mr. Pickens and Mr. Misle signed the document at the automobile dealership, Mr. Pickens played in the East-West Shrine game. According to Mr. Pickens, sometime after the game a coach at Nebraska asked him if he had an agent, and when he replied that he did not, the coach suggested Tom Condon, a former Kansas City Chief professional football player and agent of numerous professional football players. Mr. Pickens met with Mr. Condon several times in Kansas City and in Lincoln. Mr. Pickens then signed a standard NFLPA representation agreement making Mr. Condon his contract advisor to negotiate a professional football player contract with an NFL team.

Mr. Pickens testified that he spoke to Mr. Misle after he signed the agreement with Mr. Condon. He informed Mr. Misle that he had signed the agreement with Mr. Condon and that he had decided that Mr. Condon would be his agent. Mr. Pickens informed Mr. Misle that he would return the Audi automobile, and would reimburse Mr. Misle for the money he periodically extended to him after January 18, 1991. The money consisted of numerous checks and goods totaling more than $2,900. The money and the automobile were provided to Mr. Pickens when he was a student at the University of Nebraska in 1991.

NCAA rules preclude giving things of value to athletes when they are undergraduates. Additionally, the NFLPA precludes giving athletes anything of value to induce them to sign an NFLPA representation agreement.

The Atlanta Falcons professional football team drafted Mr. Pickens. He was the number three selection in the first-round draft selections. Tom Condon conducted the negotiations. The Atlanta Falcons initially offered $2,700,000 in three one-year player contracts. Mr. Condon eventually negotiated five one-year contracts which Mr. Pickens signed on October 5, 1991. Those NFL player contracts for the 1991, 1992, 1993, 1994, and 1995 football seasons provided for total compensation and work-out bonuses of $4,100,000 and other incentive bonuses. Mr. Pickens' entitlement to compensation under each player contract depended on his making the Atlanta Falcons team for that year. The NFL player contracts also provided for a guaranteed signing bonus of $2,492,000 payable over five years.

ISSUES

* * *

I(A): The Verdict Director

In Point I, Mr. Pickens challenges the verdict director, Instruction 5, arguing that it improperly assumed facts in issue. Modeled in part on MAI 26.06, Instruction 5 provided:

> Your verdict must be for plaintiff if you believe: First, plaintiff agreed to serve as defendant's contract advisor in contract negotiations between defendant and a NFL club, and defendant agreed to allow plaintiff to be his contract advisor and to pay plaintiff a percentage of his NFL player contract, and Second, plaintiff was ready, willing and able to perform plaintiff's duties as defendant's contract advisor, and Third, defendant failed to perform his agreement, and Fourth, plaintiff was thereby damaged.

According to Mr. Pickens' argument, the verdict director confused the jury by assuming the validity of the agreement. He asserts that the words "agreed" and "agreement" conveyed to the jury the existence of a "binding agreement" with a "meeting of the minds" when evidence showed the invalidity of the agreement. He argues that, because the validity of the agreement was in issue, the verdict director improperly hypothesized that the agreement was binding.

Mr. Pickens fails to demonstrate either prejudicial or plain error. MAI 26.06 provides the pattern verdict director when the existence, terms, and breach of a contract are disputed. . . . Here, the verdict director was properly patterned on MAI 26.06 by following the approved language in hypothesizing that "plaintiff agreed to serve as defendant's contract advisor . . . and defendant agreed to allow plaintiff to be his contract advisor. . . ." Contrary to Mr. Pickens' claim, the verdict director did not assume a binding agreement; it required the jury to determine the existence of a binding agreement by finding that both plaintiff and defendant had agreed.

Further, the trial court submitted at Mr. Pickens' request a true converse instruction that reiterated each paragraph of Team America's verdict director. Under the circumstances, Mr. Pickens fails to establish that Team America's verdict director resulted in prejudice or manifest injustice. Point I is denied.

I(B): Affirmative Converses

* * *

Points II and III relate to proposed Instructions H and G:

Instruction H

Your verdict must be for defendant if you believe plaintiff and defendant agreed to be governed by the NFLPA code of conduct and that the written agreement was thereafter not sent to the NFLPA.

Instruction G

Your verdict must be for defendant if you believe that the NFLPA code of conduct for contract advisors was incorporated into the agreement between plaintiff and defendant and if you further believe that plaintiff failed to comply with the provisions of that code of conduct. Mr. Pickens maintains that his proposed affirmative converse Instructions H and G were appropriate because the verdict director failed to hypothesize contested issues of whether the NFLPA regulations were a part of the agreement and whether the NFLPA regulations had been complied with. Mr. Pickens submits that those affirmative converse instructions were supported by the evidence: (1) Paragraph 7 of the agreement form provided for submission of the completed agreement to the NFLPA; (2) Paragraph 7 of the agreement signed by Mr. Misle and Mr. Pickens had been crossed out; (3) Mr. Pickens testified that the agreement was not to be binding until dated and submitted to the NFLPA.

In Point VI, Mr. Pickens claims error in refusing Instruction C:

Instruction C

Your verdict must be for Defendant if you believe that the Plaintiff provided or offered to provide anything of significant value to Defendant in order to become the member contract advisor for the Defendant.

He contends that this affirmative converse instruction properly submitted the defense of illegality of the agreement. Arguing evidentiary support for Instruction C, Mr. Pickens points to testimony that Mr. Misle had provided him with an automobile to induce him to sign the agreement.

* * *

Here, Mr. Pickens, as proponent, fails to demonstrate the propriety of his proposed affirmative converse instructions. . . . Mr. Pickens fails to show how or why the facts hypothesized in Instructions H and G would have defeated Team America's claim of anticipatory breach of contract. He also fails to explain the theory underlying Instructions H and G that hypothesized facts on the applicability of and compliance with NFLPA regulations. Those failures hinder determining whether the facts submitted an ultimate issue or involved evidentiary facts. The facts in Instructions H and G appear to be evidentiary facts because those facts apparently refute the agreement propositions in the verdict director. Evidentiary facts are appropriately presented in argument to the jury, but are not properly submitted in an affirmative converse.

Similarly, Mr. Pickens fails to demonstrate that the facts in Instruction C would have defeated Team America's claim on the ground of illegality. The facts hypothesized in Instruction C concerned offering things of value to induce the agreement. Mr. Pickens makes no showing that those facts, even if found true, rendered the subject matter of the agreement illegal under either Missouri or Nebraska law.

Accordingly, no error, plain or otherwise, resulted from rejecting Mr. Pickens' alternative affirmative converse instructions. In this situation, the trial court appropriately allowed argument on the disputed matters; submitted the true converse, the approved method; and rejected the affirmative converses, the less favored method. Points II, III, and VI are denied.

I(C): Damage Instructions

In his Points IV and V, Mr. Pickens argues error in instructing the jury on damages. The trial court submitted Team America's Instruction 7 based in part on MAI 4.08:

Instruction 7

If you find in favor of plaintiff, then you must award plaintiff such sum as you believe is the sum which would have been due plaintiff under the agreement.

The court in turn refused Mr. Pickens' proposed Instruction B based in part on MAI 4.04:

Instruction B

If you find in favor of plaintiff, then you must award plaintiff the reasonable value of the services furnished.

Asserting error in giving Instruction 7 and in refusing Instruction B, Mr. Pickens contends that the proper measure of damages was quantum meruit, i.e., the reasonable value of the services furnished. Maintaining the propriety of instructing on quantum meruit, Mr. Pickens analogizes the agreement in this case with an attorney-client contract for a contingency fee. He asserts that the analogy is appropriate because both agreements involve contingent fees and fiduciary relationships. In support, Mr. Pickens cites *Plaza Shoe Store, Inc. v. Hermel, Inc.*, 636 S.W.2d 53, 60 (Mo. banc 1982), which limited the recovery of an attorney discharged from a contingent fee contract to the value of the services rendered.

Mr. Pickens' claimed entitlement to a damage instruction based on quantum meruit is unfounded. When the principal wrongly terminates an agency agreement, the agent may either sue in quantum meruit for the commissions due or sue for breach of contract for the commissions that would have been earned under the agreement. . . . Breach of contract and quantum meruit represent two separate causes of action that have different measures of damages. . . . The verdict director and the corresponding damage instruction must relate to the same cause of action. . . . Consequently, submission of a breach of contract verdict director and a quantum meruit damage instruction would result in prejudicial error. . . .

No error resulted from submitting the damage instruction based on breach of contract. In its amended petition, Team America, as a wrongfully-terminated agent, pleaded anticipatory breach of contract and sought damages based on the provisions of the representation agreement with Mr. Pickens. Team America proceeded on a breach of contract theory. The trial court submitted to the jury a verdict director and a damage instruction modeled in part on the breach of contract pattern instructions in MAI 26.06 and 4.08. The damage instruction submitted, therefore, was consistent with the cause of action pleaded and proved.

Further, Mr. Pickens' reliance on the *Plaza Shoe* holding is unavailing. That holding is restricted to actions to enforce attorneys' liens by attorneys employed under contingent fee contracts and discharged without cause; it should not be extended to contracts in ordinary trades. *Plaza Shoe*, 636 S.W.2d at 56. Points IV and V are denied.

II. TEAM AMERICA'S APPEAL

Team America's appeal asserts the inadequacy of the $20,000 damage award for the anticipatory breach of the representation agreement. . . .

* * *

In the context of professional sports, the player's breach of an agency agreement does not necessarily entitle the agent to commission. John C. Wienstart & Cym H. Lowell, The Law Of Sports § 3.18 (1979). Technically, the agent is only entitled to damages for breach of contract, *i.e.*, the value of the promised performance reduced by any expenses saved. *Id.* In addition, the agent is entitled to his commission only if he can show that, had he been permitted to continue performance, he would have been able to consummate the contracts upon which he claims commission. *Id.*

Contrary to Team America's assertions, it was not entitled to commissions based solely on the contracts negotiated by others. Although required to show what it would have negotiated, Team America points to no evidence showing its own past achievements in negotiating NFL player contracts. The jury was instructed to award Team America such sum as it believed to be the sum which would have been due Team America under the representation agreement. In determining damages, the jury could consider all evidence, including the contracts negotiated by others, and the backgrounds and experiences of the negotiators. Here, the $20,000 damage award appears to be within the range of the evidence, and is not unwarranted. The trial court's denial of a new trial on damages was not a clear abuse of discretion. Team America's Point II is denied.

Conclusion

Team America's appeal and Mr. Pickens' cross-appeal present no grounds for reversing the trial court's judgment. The judgment is affirmed.

All concur.

SPEAKERS OF SPORT, INC. v. PROSERV, INC.

178 F.3d 862 (7th Cir. 1999)

POSNER, Chief Judge

The Plaintiff, Speakers of Sport, appeals from the grant of summary judgment to the defendant, ProServ, in a diversity suit in which one sports agency has charged another with tortuous interference with a business relationship and related violations of Illinois law. The essential facts, construed as favorably to the plaintiff as the record will permit, are as follows. Ivan Rodriguez, a highly successful catcher with the Texas Rangers baseball team, in 1991 signed the first of several one-year contracts making Speakers his agent. ProServ wanted to expand its representation of baseball players and to this end invited Rodriguez to its office in Washington and there promised that it would get him between $2 and $4 million in endorsements if he signed with ProServ — which he did, terminating his contract (which was terminable at will) with Speakers. This was in 1995. ProServ failed to obtain significant endorsement for Rodriguez and after just one year he switched to another agent who the following year landed him a five-year $42 million contract with the Rangers. Speakers brought this suit a few months later, charging that the promise of endorsements that ProServ had made to Rodriguez was fraudulent and had induced him to terminate his contract with Speakers.

Speakers could not sue Rodriguez for breach of contract, because he had not broken their contract, which was, as we said, terminable at will. Nor, therefore, could it accuse Pro-Serv of inducing a breach of contract. . . . But Speakers did have a contract with Rodriguez, and inducing the termination of a contract, even when the termination is not a breach because the contract is terminable at will, can still be actionable under the tort law of Illinois, either as an interference with prospective economic advantage . . . or as in interference with the contract at will itself. . . .

There is in general nothing wrong with one sports agent trying to take a client from another if this can be done without precipitating a breach of contract. That is the process known as competition, which though painful, fierce, frequently ruthless, sometimes Darwinian in its pitilesssness, is the cornerstone of our highly successful economic system. Competition is not a tort, [citation omitted] but on the contrary provides a defense (the "competitor's privilege") to the tort of improper interference. . . . It does not privilege inducing the breach of a contract [citation omitted] — conduct usefully regarded as a separate tort from interfering with a business relationship without precipitating an actual breach of contract — but it does privilege inducing the lawful termination of a contract that is terminable at will. . . .

There would be few more effective inhibitors of the competitive process than making it a tort for an agent to promise the client of another agent to do better by him. . . . It is true the Speakers argues only that the competitor may not make a promise that he knows he cannot fulfill, may not, that is, compete by fraud. Because the competitor's privilege does not include a right to get business from a competitor by means of fraud, it is hard to quarrel with this position in the abstract, but the practicalities are different. If the argument were accepted and the new agent made a promise that was not fulfilled, the old agent would have a shot at convincing a jury that the new agent had known form the start that he couldn't deliver on the promise. Once a case gets to the jury, all bets are off. The practical consequence of Speakers' approach, therefore, would be that a sports agent who lured away the client of another agent with a promise to do better by him would be running a grave legal risk.

The threat to the competitive process is blocked by the principle of Illinois law that promissory fraud is not actionable unless it is part of a scheme to defraud, that is, unless it is one element of a pattern of fraudulent acts. [Citations omitted.] By requiring the plaintiff show a pattern, by thus not letting him rest on proving a single promise, the law reduces the likelihood of a spurious suit; for a series of unfulfilled promises is better (though of course not conclusive) evidence of fraud than a single unfulfilled promise.

* * *

Consider in this connection the characterization by Speakers' own chairman of ProServ's promise to Rodriguez as "pure fantasy and gross exaggeration" — in other words, as puffing. Puffing in the usual sense signifies meaningless superlatives that no reasonable person would take seriously, and so it is not actionable as fraud. [Citations omitted.] Rodriguez thus could not have sued ProServ . . . in respect of the promise of $2-$4 million in endorsements. If Rodriguez thus was not wronged, we do not understand on what theory Speakers can complain that ProServ competed with it unfairly.

The promise of endorsements was puffing . . . in the . . . sense of a sales pitch that is intended, and that a reasonable person . . . would understand, to be aspirational rather than enforceable. . . . It is not as if ProServ proposed to employ

Rodriguez and pay him $2 million a year. That would be the kind of promise that could found an enforceable obligation. . . .

It is possible to make a binding promise of something over which one has no control; such a promise is called a warranty. [Citations omitted.] But it is not plausible that this is what ProServ was doing. . . . So understood, the "promise" was not a promise at all. But even if it was a promise (or a warranty), it cannot be the basis for a finding of fraud because it was not a part of a scheme to defraud evidenced by more than the allegedly fraudulent promise itself.

It can be argued, however, that competition can be tortious even if it does not involve an actionable fraud . . . or other independently tortious act, such as defamation, or trademark or patent infringement, or a theft of a trade secret; that compaetitors should not be allowed to use "unfair" tactics; and that a promise known by the promisor when made to be unfulfillable is such a tactic, especially when used on a relatively unsophisticated, albeit very well to do, baseball player. . . . But the Illinois courts have not as yet embraced the doctrine, and we are not alone in thinking it pernicious. [Citations omitted.] The doctrine's conception of wrongful competition is ague — "wrongful by reasons . . . an established standard of a trade or profession." . . . We agree with Professor Perlman that the tort of interference with business relationships should be confined to cases in which the defendant employed unlawful means to stiff a competitor . . . and we are reassured by the conclusion of his careful analysis that the case law is generally consistent with this position as a matter of outcomes as distinct from articulation.

Invoking the concept of "wrongful by reason of . . . an established standard of a trade or profession," Speakers points to a rule of major league baseball forbidding players' agents to compete by means of misrepresentations. The rule is designed to protect the players, rather than their agents, so that even if it established a norm enforceable by law Speakers would not be entitled to invoke it; it is not a rule designed for Speakers' protection. In any event it violation would not be the king of "wrongful" conduct that should trigger the tort of intentional interference. . . .

It remains to consider Speakers' claim that ProServ violated the Illinois Consumer Fraud and Deceptive Practices Act. . . . Speakers is not a consumer, and while a competitor is permitted to bring suit under the Act as a representative of the consumer interest . . . , he must "prove, by clear and convincing evident, how the complained-of conduct implicates consumer protection concerns." [Citation omitted.] No effort at proving this was made here. . . .

The seller can be hurt even if the customer is not; but to allow the seller to obtain damages from a competitor when no consumer has been hurt is unlikely to advance the consumer interest. Allowing Speakers to prevail would hurt consumers by reducing the vigor of competition between sports agents. The Rodriguezes of this world would be disserved, as Rodriguez himself, a most reluctant witness, appears to believe. Anyway, we don't think that the kind of puffing in which ProServ engaged amounts to an unfair method of competition or an unfair act or practice. . . .

We add that even if Speakers could establish liability under either the common law of torts or the deceptive practices act, its suit would fail because it cannot possibly establish, as it seeks to do, a damages entitlement (the only relief it seeks) to the agent's fee on Rodriguez's $42 million contract. The contract was negotiated years after he left Speakers, and by another agent. Since Rodriguez had only a year-to-year contract with Speakers — terminable at will, moreover — and since obviously he was dissatisfied with Speakers at least to the extent of switching to ProServ and then when he became disillusioned with ProServ of not returning to Speakers' fold, the likelihood that Speakers would have retained him had ProServ not lured him away is too slight to ground an award of such damages. . . . Such an award would be the best example yet of puffing in the pie-in the-sky sense.

AFFIRMED.

NOTES AND COMMENTS

1. The definition of "practice of law" in the state of Washington is written broadly, as follows:

> The "practice of law" . . . is generally acknowledged to include not only the doing or performing of services in the courts of justice, throughout the various stages thereof, but in a larger sense includes legal advice and counsel and the preparation of legal instruments by which legal rights and obligations are established. Further, selection and completion of preprinted form legal documents has been found to be the "practice of law."

Hagan v. Kassler Escrow, Inc., 635 P.2d 73 (Wash. 1981).

McNabb, a California lawyer, is officed in Spokane, Washington. Are any of the player-agent services rendered by McNabb considered the practice of law as defined in Washington?

2. What advantages accrue from registering as an agent pursuant to any voluntary programs of the NCAA or professional organizations?

3. Problem. What review process or other remedies are available to an agent who is rejected for certification under those state regulatory schemes identified in the **Problem**? Does the agent possess due process rights in this context? *See Mathews v. Eldridge*, 424 U.S. 319 (1976); *Board of Regents v. Roth*, 408 U.S. 564 (1972). If so, what is the nature of the required hearing? Must the opportunity for hearing be provided prior to denial of certification? *See Cleveland Bd. of Education v. Loudermill*, 470 U.S. 532 (1985). Compare the hearing requirements of *Goldberg v. Kelly*, 397 U.S. 254 (1970).

States enact player agent regulatory legislation under the "police power" authority. Do the due process clauses of the United States Constitution and state constitutions impose limitations on the exercise of the police power? If so, what test is utilized to measure the constitutional validity of the legislation? What viable arguments exist that state regulation of sports agents is an undue fetter on interstate commerce? *See generally* TRIBE, AMERICAN CONSTITUTIONAL LAW ch. 8 (3d ed. 2000); Closius, *Hell Hath No Fury Like a Fan Scorned: State Regulation of Sports Agents*, 30 U. TOL. L. REV. 511 (1999) (state athlete agent statutes are of questionable validity due to concerns regarding legislative jurisdiction and the dormant Commerce Clause).

State regulation of non-residents must satisfy the "minimum contacts" test enunciated in *International Shoe Co. v. Washington*, 326 U.S. 310 (1945). Other jurisdictional questions may concern the proper reach of a state's long-arm statute. *See* Sudia & Remis, *The History Behind Athlete Regulation and the "Slam Dunking of Statutory Hurdles*, 8 VILL. SPORTS & ENT. L.J. 67, 87-88 (2001).

4. To the extent that player-agent relationships are matters included within the various collective bargaining agreements formed pursuant to the National Labor Relations Act, 29 U.S.C. § 141, is the regulatory power of states preempted by federal law? *See Amalgamated Association of Street Employees v. Lockridge*, 403 U.S. 274 (1971); *Hill v. Florida*, 325 U.S. 538 (1945).

5. Are the certification/registration schemes likely to achieve the protections for the professional and amateur athletes that are desired? *See*, Baker, *The Unintended Consequence of the Miller-Ayala Athlete Agents Act: Depriving Student Athletes of Effective Legal Representation*, 12 UCLA ENT. L. REV. 267 (2005); Willenbacher, *Regulating Sports Agents: Why Current Federal & State Efforts do not Deter the Unscrupulous Agent & How a National Licensing System may Cure the Problem*, 78 ST. JOHN'S L. REV. 1225 (2004). For comprehensive reviews scrutinizing the state regulatory acts, *see* Sudia & Remis, *Athlete Agent Legislation in the New Millennium: State Statutes and the Uniform Athlete Agents Act*, 11 SETON HALL J. SPORT L. 263 (2001); Sudia & Remis, *The History Behind Athlete Regulation and the "Slam Dunking of Statutory Hurdles*, 8 VILL. SPORTS & ENT. L.J. 67 (2001); Sudia & Remis, *Ethical and Statutory Limitations on Athlete Agent Income: Fees, Referrals, and Ownership Interests*, 27 FLA. ST. U. L. REV. 787 (2000); Sudia & Remis, *Athlete Agent Contracts: Legislative Regulation*, 10 SETON HALL J. SPORT L. 317 (2000); Sudia & Remis, *Statutory Regulation of Agent Gifts to Athletes*, 10 SETON HALL J. SPORT L. 265 (2000); Sudia & Remis, *Athlete Agent Solicitation of Athlete Clients: Statutory Authorization and Prohibition*, 10 SETON HALL J. SPORT L. 205 (2000); Remis & Sudia, *Escaping Athlete Agent Statutory Regulation: Loopholes and Constitutional Defectiveness Based on Tri-Parte Classification of Athletes*, 9 SETON HALL J. SPORT L. 1 (1999); Remis, *The Art of Being a sports Agent in More than One State: Analysis of Registration and Reporting Requirements and Development of a Model Strategy*, 8 SETON HALL J. SPORT L. 419 (1998); Remis, *Analysis of Civil and Criminal Penalties in Athlete Agent Statutes and Support for the*

Imposition of Civil and Criminal Liability Upon Athletes, 8 SETON HALL J. SPORT L. 1 (1998).

6. McNabb reports that he has signed Jerome Jenkins, the veteran NFL player in the **Problem** above, to a player-agent contract. Assuming McNabb is certified by the NFLPA, can he contract with Jenkins without becoming liable to Jenkins' prior agent under a claim for tortious interference with a business relationship? Is the answer dependent on whether the prior agent is registered or certified by the NFLPA? Would the answer differ in the case of a rookie player who had not yet signed an NFL contract? *See Pro Tect Management Corp. v. Worley*, 1990 WL 170358 (S.D.N.Y. 1990) (In breach of contract claim by one agent, whose contract with player made prior to NFL draft was terminated in favor of another, issues were not compelled to arbitration under the terms of the NFLPA Regulations). Can you formulate arguments that the Team America contract in the *Pickens* case is unenforceable? Explain the "competitor's privilege" defense as enunciated in *Speakers of Sport*. What type of and how many predicate acts are required to establish an interference case based on fraud? Compare the requirement of a case established pursuant to the Corrupt Organizations Act (RICO) based on wire and mail fraud. *See* general discussion of case elements in NHL players' civil RICO suit regarding alleged union mismanagement, *Forbes v. Eagleson*, 19 F. Supp. 352 (E.D. Pa. 1998). Can you reconcile the views of the *Pickens* court with the views of the *Speakers of Sport* court concerning the establishment of a case for damages?

7. Additional writings regarding players, agents, and the issues described above include: Sammataro, *Business and Brotherhood, Can They Coincide? A Search into Why Black Athletes Do Not Hire Black Agents*, 42 HOW. L.J. 535 (1999); Lock, *The Regulatory Scheme for Player Representatives in the National Football League: The Real Power of Jerry Maguire*, 35 AM. BUS. L.J. 319 (1998); Shropshire, *Sports Agency, Role Models and Race Consciousness*, 6 MARQ. SPORTS L.J. 267 (1996); GREENBERG & GRAY, 1 SPORTS LAW PRACTICE Ch. 10 (2d ed. 2002). *See also* SHROPSHIRE & DAVIS, THE BUSINESS OF SPORTS AGENTS (2002); Lipscomb & Titlebaum, *Selecting a Sports Agent: The Inside for Athletes and Parents*, 3 VAND. J. ENT. L. & PRAC. 95 (2001).

8. Congressional bills are drafted regulating player agents. A bill was introduced to the House Judiciary Committee on April 15, 1999, prohibiting influencing any student-athlete to end his or her collegiate eligibility. H.R. 1449. One previously proposed bill placed primary regulatory responsibilities with the Secretary of Commerce. The Secretary was directed to promulgate rules for the recognition of National Sports Agency Associations. A player agent, under the terms of the bill, must register with and be approved by a National Sports Agency Association prior to entering into a player-agent contract. Significantly, attorneys were included as sports agents under the coverage of the bill. *See also*, Rodgers, *The Need for Federal Agent Regulation*, XIII SPORTS LAW. 1 (Mar./Apr. 1995); Shefsky, *The Sports Agent Profession, Federal Legislation,* II SPORTS L. NEWSL. I (Spring 1985); Note, *Regulation of Sports Agents: Since at First it Hasn't Succeeded, Try Federal Legislation*, 39 HASTINGS LAW J. 1031 (1988).

For a description of the process utilized by the National Conference of Commissioners on Uniform State Laws to draft and adopt the Uniform Athlete Agents Act, *see* Davis, *Exploring the Contours of Agent Regulation: The Uniform Athlete Agents Act*, 8 VILL. SPORTS & ENT. L.J. 1 (2001).

9. Regulation of player agents by player associations, absent collective bargaining agreements, are subject to attack under antitrust laws. Sherman Act § 1, 15 U.S.C. § 1. Requirements imposed by unions in agreements between unions and employers are exempt from the reach of the antitrust statutes. *See Collins v. NBPA*, 976 F.2d 740 (10th Cir. 1992); **Case File**, *supra*. Union regulation of talent agents has received protection by the labor exemption. *H.A. Artists, Assoc. v. Actors Equity Association*, 451 U.S. 704 (1981).

10. Do any provisions of the player association plans exceed the scope of the labor exemption? The bases for the various player agent regulatory schemes differ among the player associations. For a description of each plan, *see* Curtis, *Regulation of Sports Agents, in* 1 THE LAW OF AMATEUR AND PROFESSIONAL SPORTS ch. 1 (Uberstine ed. 2005). For an argument in the affirmative, Note, *The NFL Players Association's Agent Certification Plan: Is It Exempt from Antitrust Review?*, 26 ARIZ. L. REV. 699 (1984).

11. Player associations have traditionally rested their authority to regulate agents on the basis that player agents are the agents of the unions. The player associations collectively bargain for minimum terms of employment, thus leaving the players free to bargain individually with their teams for additional compensation. In order to protect the integrity of the benefits obtained in collective bargaining, the player associations require certification of agents. Initially, concerns were expressed that the player associations perhaps lacked authority over agents representing rookies, who were not yet members of the unions, and that negotiation by an individual agent of the union arguably created a conflict of interest, or a breach of the unions' duty of fair representation. *See* GARVEY, THE AGENT GAME (1984).

It is now commonly recognized that player agents are permitted to negotiate player contracts solely because the player associations have delegated a portion of the exclusive representational authority to the agents. *White v. National Football League*, 92 F. Supp. 2d 918 (D. Minn. 2000); *Collins v. NBPA*, 976 F.2d 740 (10th Cir. 1992), **Case File**, *supra*. Arbitrator Nicolau stated, "When representing players, individuals certified by the NBPA do so in the Union's stead and as the NBPA's 'arm and extension.' They thus act as the NBPA's agent." *In the Matter of Arbitration Between NPBA Committee on Agent Regulation and Stephen M. Woods, Agent* (May 27, 1999) (Nicolau, arb.), 592 PLI/Pat 169 (Feb. 2000).

12. In *White v. National Football League*, *supra*, **Note 11**, three agents contended that they were not subject to penalty schemes established by the collective bargaining agreement as they were not parties to the CBA. The National Football League Management Council alleged that the San Francisco 49ers and player agents, Leigh Steinberg, Jeffrey Moorad, and Gary Wichard, had entered into undisclosed agreements concerning player compensation in violation of the NFL collective bargaining agreement and the previous settlement agreement (SSA) in *White*. The court addressed two issues: (1) whether the contracting parties intended to bind player agents to the CBA and SSA, and (2) whether the player agents were in fact bound. The court ruled in the affirmative on both issues, finding that parties clearly intended to bind agents to the agreements, and the agents impliedly manifested consent to comply with the terms of the agreement.

13. What review process or other remedies are available to a player agent who is rejected for certification by the NFLPA? A decertification process may be triggered by complaint by one agent against another. In January, 1999, Ray Anderson leveled charges against an alleged recruiter ("runner") for William "Tank" Black at the NFLPA Agents Advisory Committee meeting. Reportedly, Anderson claimed Randall "Banks" Menard had offered monetary remuneration to an assistant football coach for LSU to sway defensive tackle Anthony McFarland to sign with Black. According to reports, McFarland was committed to Anderson at the time of the alleged monetary offer. McFarland ultimately signed with a third agent, not associated with either Anderson or Black. The offering of a monetary inducement to any person for the purpose of encouraging the person to recommend the services of the agent is prohibited conduct under the NFLPA Regulations, § 3B(3), (**Case File,** *supra*). *See* Gotthelf, *NFLPA Launches Agent Probe*, 1 SPORTS BUS. J. 1, 47 (Feb. 8-14, 1999). Agent Black responded that Menard was not employed by his firm, Professional Management, Inc., that he is innocent of any charges, and that his accusers were using the publicity to attempt to sign his clients. The making of false accusations arguably violates § 3B(4), (**Case File,** *supra*), of the NFLPA Regulations that prohibit the providing of materially false or misleading information to any player in the context of recruiting the player as a client. The Regulations also prohibit an agent from soliciting another agent's client, except during the sixty days prior to a player's NFL contract expiring. *See* Gotthelf, *Agent Under Fire Charges Sabotage*, 1 SPORTS BUS. J. 1, 47 (Feb. 15-21, 1999). Andrew Joel, former agent of NFL star Michael Vick, sued Octagon for allegedly tampering with players under contract with other agents. *See* Mullen, *Octagon Faces Third Agent Suit,* 5 SPORTS BUS. J. 1, 34 (Feb. 3-9, 2003).

14. The NFLPA provides a test to agents that must be passed for certification purposes. In the event the agent fails the exam, the agent's certification is suspended, and the agent must pass the test at a future date for reinstatement. Reportedly, Leland Hardy, an agent working with Master P's "No Limit Sports," failed the 49-question exam. Agent Hardy and "No Limit Sports" were previously criticized for the deal negotiated on behalf of Ricky Williams, the New Orleans Saints' number one draft choice. Although the negotiated contract could be worth as much as $68.5 million, including a $8.64 Million signing bonus, Williams stood to collect less than $20 million over eight years if he was not one of the best performers in the NFL history. The test is a take-home, open book exam. Sources for the answers to the exam questions include the collective bargaining agreement, NFLPA Regulations Governing Contract Advisors, NFL Policy and Program for Substances Abuse, NFL Policy and Procedures for Anabolic Steroids and Related Substances, NFL Player Reserve Lists, current NFLPA Signals (newsletter), and Expansion Draft Documents. For a copy of ten of the forty-nine questions, *see* Gotthelf, *Criticized Agent Flunks Test*, 2 SPORTS BUS. J. 1, 45 (June 28-Jul 4, 1999).

15. Does an aggrieved player possess a cause of action against a player association, or tort claim against a state for negligent certification of an agent? *See*, **Section D, Note 8**, *infra*.

16. Does the NCAA have the authority to regulate agents? Note that the NCAA does not enjoy the labor exemption, but is subject to the antitrust laws. *See National Collegiate Athletic Association v. Board of Regents of The University of Oklahoma*, 468 U.S. 85 (1984).

C. PLAYER AGENT: REGULATORY LIMITATIONS ON FORMATION OF PLAYER AGENT SERVICES CONTRACTS; RESOLUTION OF DISPUTES BETWEEN PLAYER AND AGENT

The contract between player and agent, of course, must satisfy all legal requirements of the jurisdiction where the contract is formed, including the statute of frauds. Agents rarely use a single contract for all services provided as described above. The three basic contracts for agent services are: 1) contract for negotiation of player-team employment terms; 2) financial services contract; and 3) contract for the marketing of the player for endorsements and public appearances. Clauses commonly included within the three contracts are:

1. parties;
2. services;
3. term;
4. fee arrangement;
5. grounds for termination;
6. representations and warranties;
7. arbitration;
8. governing jurisdiction; and
9. explanatory and other clauses.

For a clause by clause description, including suggested clause provisions, *see* McAleenan, *Agent-Player Representation Agreements,* 1 LAW OF AMATEUR AND PROFESSIONAL SPORTS ch. 2 (Uberstine ed., 2005).

The player and agent are not free to negotiate all terms of the contracts. Player associations, states, attorney rules of professional conduct, and the general laws place limitations on contractual arrangements between players and agents. Regulatory limitations focus primarily upon fee arrangements, termination conditions, and procedures for the resolution of disputes arising under the contracts. The players associations generally require use of form contracts.

PROBLEM

Assume that James McNabb is certified by the NFLPA and is duly registered or certified under all relevant state regulation schemes. McNabb desires your firm to draft all needed player-agent contracts. He anticipates the signing of three athletes:

1. Jerome Jenkins, veteran NFL player;
2. Robert Newsome, rookie free agent (undrafted) football player, with college eligibility remaining; and
3. Larry Kinsella, NFL high round draft choice.

Your senior partner asks that you respond to the following:

1. What fees are allowed under NFLPA regulations?
2. Do the NFLPA Regulations and form contract govern McNabb's contractual arrangement with Robert Newsome?
3. What fee limitations are imposed by the attorney Rules of Professional Conduct?
4. Under what conditions may the NFLPA form contract be terminated by either party?
5. Outline the dispute resolution mechanisms required by the NFLPA.
6. Does the Uniform Athlete Agents Act apply to any of McNabb's prospective player-agent contracts? What requirements are imposed by the Uniform Athlete Agents Act? What risks are encountered by McNabb in the event he does not register pursuant to the Uniform Athlete Agents Act?
7. Draft a player-agent contract for a tennis player. The player does not reside in state that regulates the contract.

CASE FILE

NFLPA Regulations Governing Contract Advisors

(Regulations may be accessed at www.nflpa.org/agents/

SECTION 3: STANDARD OF CONDUCT FOR CONTRACT ADVISORS

A. . . .

B. **Prohibited Conduct**

SECTION 4: AGREEMENTS BETWEEN CONTRACT ADVISORS AND PLAYERS: MAXIMUM FEES

A. **Standard Form**

B. **Contract Advisor's Compensation**

SECTION 5: ARBITRATION PROCEDURES

A. **Disputes**

B. **Filing**

C. **Answer**

D. **Arbitrator**

E. **Hearing**

F. **Telephone Conference Call Hearings**

EXHIBIT C:

STANDARD REPRESENTATION AGREEMENT BETWEEN NFLPA CONTRACT ADVISOR AND PLAYER

Uniform Athlete Agents Act

(2000)

Section 10. REQUIRED FORM OF CONTRACT.

(a) An agency contract must be in a record, signed or otherwise authenticated by the parties.

(b) An agency contract must state or contain:

(1) the amount and method of calculating the consideration to be paid by the student-athlete for services to be provided by the athlete agent under the contract and any other consideration the athlete

agent has received or will receive from any other source for entering into the contract or for providing the services;

(2) the name of any person not listed in the application for registration or renewal of registration who will be compensated because the student-athlete signed the agency contract;

(3) a description of any expenses that the student-athlete agrees to reimburse;

(4) a description of the services to be provided to the student-athlete;

(5) the duration of the contract; and

(6) the date of execution.

(c) An agency contract must contain, in close proximity to the signature of the studentathlete, a conspicuous notice in boldface type in capital letters stating:

WARNING TO STUDENT-ATHLETE

IF YOU SIGN THIS CONTRACT:

(2) YOU MAY LOSE YOUR ELIGIBILITY TO COMPLETE AS A STUDENT-ATHLETE IN YOUR SPORT;

(3) IF YOU HAVE AN ATHLETIC DIRECTOR, WITHIN 72 HOURS AFTER ENTERING INTO THIS CONTRACT, BOTH YOU AND YOUR ATHLETE AGENT MUST NOTIFY YOUR ATHLETIC DIRECTOR; AND

(4) YOU MAY CANCEL THIS CONTRACT WITHIN 14 DAYS AFTER SIGNING IT. CANCELLATION OF THIS CONTRACT MAY NOT REINSTATE YOUR ELIGIBILITY.

(d) An agency contract that does not conform to this section is voidable by the student-athlete. If a student-athlete voids an agency contract, the student-athlete is not required to pay any consideration under the contract or to return any consideration received from the athlete agent to induce the student-athlete to enter into the contract.

(e) The athlete agent shall give a record of the signed or otherwise authenticated agency contract to the student-athlete at the time of execution.

Section 11. NOTICE TO EDUCATIONAL INSTITUTION.

(a) Within 72 hours after entering into an agency contract or before the next scheduled athletic event in which the student-athlete may participate, whichever occurs first, the athlete agent shall give notice in a record of the existence of the contract to the athletic director of the educational institution at which the student-athlete is enrolled or the athlete agent has reasonable grounds to believe the student-athlete intends to enroll.

(b) Within 72 hours after entering into an agency contract or before the next athletic event in which eh student-athlete may participate, whichever occurs first, the student-athlete shall inform the athletic director of the educational institution at which the student-athlete is enrolled that he or she has entered into an agency contract.

Section 12. STUDENT-ATHLETE'S RIGHT TO CANCEL.

(a) A student-athlete may cancel an agency contract by giving notice to the cancellation to the athlete agent in a record within 14 days after the contract is signed.

(b) A student-athlete may not waive the right to cancel an agency contract.

(c) If a student-athlete cancels an agency contract, the student-athlete is not required to pay any consideration under the contract or to return any consideration received from the athlete agent to induce the student-athlete to enter into the contract.

* * *

Section 14. PROHIBITED CONDUCT.

(a) An athlete agent, with the intent to induce a student-athlete to enter into an agency contract, may not:

(1) give any materially false or misleading information or make a materially false promise or representation;

(2) furnish anything of value to a student-athlete before the student-athlete enters into the agency contract; or

(3) furnish anything of value to any individual other than the student-athlete or another registered athlete agent.

(b) An athlete agent may not intentionally:

(1) initiate contact with a student-athlete unless registered under this [Act];

(2) refuse or fail to retain or permit inspection of the records to be retained by Section 13;

(3) fail to register when required by Section 4;

(4) provide materially false or misleading information in an application for registration or renewal of registration;

(5) predate or postdate an agency contract; or

(6) fail to notify a student-athlete before the student-athlete signs or otherwise authenticates an agency contract for a particular sport that the signing or authentication may make the student-athlete ineligible to participate as a student-athlete in that sport.

Section 15. CRIMINAL PENALTIES.

An athlete agent who violates Section 14 is guilty of a [misdemeanor] [felony]. . . .

Section 16. CIVIL REMEDIES.

(a) An educational institution has a right of action against an athlete agent or a former student-athlete for damages caused by a violation of this [Act]. In an action under this section, the court may award to the prevailing party costs and reasonable attorney's fees.

(b) Damages of an educational institution under subsection (a) included losses and expenses incurred because, as a result to the conduct of an athlete agent or former student-athlete, the educational institution was injured by a violation of this [Act] or was penalized, disqualified, or suspended from participation in athletics by a national association for the promotion and regulation of athletics, by an athletic conference, or by reasonable self-imposed disciplinary action taken to mitigate sanctions likely to be imposed by such an organization.

(c) A right of action under this section does not accrue until the educational institution discovers or by the exercise of reasonable diligence would have discovered the violation by the athlete agent or former student-athlete.

(d) Any liability of the athlete agent or the former student-athlete under section is several and joint.

(e) This [Act] does not restrict rights, remedies, or defenses of any person under law or equity.

Section 17. ADMINISTRATIVE PENALTY.

The [Secretary of State] may assess a civil penalty against an athlete agent not to exceed [$25,000] for a violation of this [Act].

IN THE MATTER OF THE ARBITRATION BETWEEN WILLIAM (BUCKY) WOY, GRIEVANT, AND BOB HORNER, RESPONDENT

Major League Baseball Players Association
Voluntary Arbitration Tribunal, Gr. No. 97-A-3

OPINION AND AWARD

ANTOINE, ARB.

FACTS

Grievant William (Bucky) Woy started out to become a professional golfer and wound up as one of the leading early sports agents. Respondent Bob Horner was the No. 1 pick in the 1978 amateur baseball draft. The two men got together and signed a "Salary Compensation Agreement" on June 15, 1978. . . .

* * *

Woy initially negotiated a contract on Horner's behalf with the Atlanta Braves. He continued to represent Horner for 10 or 11 years, up until a final contract with a club in 1989. Woy proposed changes in a new written agency agreement at the end of the first year, including a substitution of Woy's new business firm, but Horner never approved or signed it. Instead, the parties continued to operate all that time under an oral arrangement that may or may not have diverged from the terms of the original 1978 agreement. In any event a tabulation of agent's fees paid by Horner to Woy from 1978 through 1988 indicated payments amounting to 10.16% of Horner's salaries for those years. Apparently Horner never expressly terminated his contract with Woy.

Horner and his wife testified that Woy told him that the 10% fee was broken down into 3% for contract negotiations and 7% for money management and other financial services, but Woy, his son, and a business associate denied this. In Woy's 1988 application to the MLBPA for certification as a baseball agent, he stated that he charged 5% of the player's salary for contract negotiations. He emphasized that this was the first time anybody, including Horner, had asked for a breakdown, and so he "broke it 5 and 5 because I think that was recommended.

Horner had a notable career as a baseball player but he was plagued by injuries. Woy negotiated one-year agreements for Horner with Atlanta in 1978 and 1979; a three-year agreement with Atlanta in 1980 and a four-year agreement with Atlanta in 1983; a one-year agreement with a Japanese team in 1987; a one-year agreement with the St. Louis Cardinals in 1988; and a one-year nonguaranteed "catch-on" agreement with the Baltimore Orioles in 1989. In March 1989 Horner retired from baseball after an unsuccessful effort to come back from reconstructive surgery on a shoulder. . . .

According to Woy, Horner had a "great" season in 1985 and "performed admirably" in both 1985 and 1986. He was due to become an unrestricted free agent at the end of the '86 season. Woy began negotiating with the Atlanta management in late 1986 and initially they were receptive to a long-term contract. Then, as Woy described it, "suddenly there was like a complete turnover." Although Horner was "coming off a million eight" season, Atlanta started talking about a "million two" and eventually went "all the way down to like $900,000." Woy proceeded to "call . . . every club on the face of the earth . . . It was unreal. Nobody would even return calls." Finally, Woy and Horner "shook hands" with the San Diego Padres on what would have been about a five-year deal at $2 million a year. But some ten days later San Diego backed down to a one-year contract for about $800,000.

At this point Woy got Horner to agree to consider Japan. Woy worked out a one-year deal for 1987 with the Yakult, Japan, Swallows. It was in effect for $2 million, with Horner getting $1.9 million directly and with the Swallows paying half of Woy's fee or $100,000, in order to benefit Horner on his taxes. Woy also got Horner another three-quarters to a million dollars in endorsements, licensing, and a book deal. Horner and his family had an unhappy year in the foreign environment, however, and did not wish to return despite Woy's urging that there was good money available there, perhaps a three-year deal for between $10 and 12 million. The result of these differences of opinion was a souring of the previously close relationship between the two men, at least in Horner's eyes. Nonetheless, upon Horner's return to the United States, Woy negotiated a one-year contract for him with the St. Louis Cardinals, guaranteeing $950,000 for the 1988 season.

Woy retired from the professional representation of baseball players not long after Horner retired in 1989. . . .

In the meantime, the MLBPA had filed claims that the Major League Baseball Clubs had colluded with regard to free agents following the 1985, 1986, and 1987 playing seasons, in violation of the 1985 Basic Agreement between the Clubs and the Association. Woy provided over 140 pages of testimony on June 24, 1987 by telephone from Japan. On August 31, 1988, Chairman George Nicolau issued a liability finding in Collusion II, ruling that the Clubs had acted in concert against free agents by a boycott against them during the 1986-87 free agent market. On July 18, 1990 Chairman Nicolau held in Collusion III that the Clubs had further violated the Basic Agreement by creating a secret "information bank" for sharing information about offers to free agents during 1987-88. Subsequently, the Clubs agreed in a settlement agreement on December 21, 1990 to pay the Association $280 million plus interest on behalf of the injured players. Thereafter, in early 1991, the MLBPA distributed to players and their agents its "Proposed Framework for the Evaluation of Individual Claims.

Woy testified that he repeatedly indicated to Horner his readiness to pursue the collusion case for Horner, even for free, as an obligation under their agency contract. Woy also stated that he warned Horner that he would still be obligated to pay Woy his fees even if Horner hired someone else to represent him in the collusion case. Woy learned through his son, however, that Horner had engaged another agent to represent him. On April 15, 1991 the MLBPA sent Hendricks Sports Management at the latter's request the transcripts of the 1987 collusion testimony of Woy and Horner. Hendricks transmitted Horner's completed collusion claim questionnaire to the Players Association on May 17, 1991.

* * *

Grievant Woy filed an amended grievance with the MLBPA on July 18, 1997. A hearing was held before the undersigned on August 13-14, 1997 at the Dallas/Fort Worth Airport. All parties were present, examined and cross-examined witnesses, and submitted other evidence. Both parties submitted thorough post-hearing briefs and these have been duly considered.

ISSUES

1. Was there a valid agreement between the grievant Woy and respondent Horner to pay Woy an agent's fee for the collusion damages that Horner has received or will receive?

2. If so, what shall the remedy be for breach of that agreement by Horner?

3. If not, is there any other relief available to Woy from Horner for services rendered?

DISCUSSION

Although the hearing in this case extended over two days and delved into a multitude of facts, I consider the critical questions some rather simple issues of contract law — simple but not all that easy. The only written agreement between the two parties was signed on June 15, 1978 and expired June 12, 1979, except that its terms would continue for the duration of any professional baseball contract procured by the agent for the player (PA-1, ¶ III). After 1979 and for the next ten years, grievant agent and respondent player continued to operate year-by-year on the basis of a "handshake" or oral arrangement. Whether all the terms of the 1978 agreement were carried forward or to what extent they were modified is in dispute but I do not need to resolve that conflict. At least the parties abided by the clauses giving agent Woy exclusive representational rights and duties and requiring him to provide money management services, and obligating player Horner to pay for those in the amount of 10 percent of all baseball salary compensation received. For our purposes it makes no difference whether this is treated as an express oral contract or an implied-in-fact contract. *See* RESTATEMENT (SECOND) OF CONTRACTS §§ 22(2), 50(2) (1981).

I therefore conclude that a contract existed between the parties during the years 1986, 1987, 1988, and 1989. But the last contract came to an end in 1989, either when the "catch-on" contract with the Baltimore Orioles aborted and Horner retired from baseball, or at the latest in June 1989, a year after the last presumed extension in June 1988. *See also* Section 4(D) of the MLBPA Regulations Governing Player Agents, effective June 17, 1988: "A Player-Player Agent contract shall have a maximum duration of one year, and shall not contain automatic renewal provisions." By 1991 Horner was entitled to hire whomever he pleased to represent him in pursuing his collusion claim, unless it can be concluded that he had an obligation to Woy dating from 1986-88 because of Woy's efforts on his behalf at that time to obtain contracts from the Atlanta Braves, the San Diego Padres, and others.

As I see it, both Woy's exclusive right to represent Horner in the collusion case and his right to obtain a contract percentage of any collusion damages awarded Horner turn, viewed most favorably from Woy's perspective, on the terms of the 1978 agreement drafted by Woy. Paragraph II makes Woy . . . Horner's "sole and exclusive representative for the purpose of negotiating his compensation agreement (Player's Contract) to play professional baseball . . ." That says nothing about representing Horner in pursuing a collusion claim before some arbitral or judicial tribunal, which could call for an entirely different set of skills, including those of an experienced litigator.

On the crucial question of the agent's fee, the critical language is "10 per[c]ent (%) of the total aggregate amount of the [player's] original *compensation agreement*. The aggregate amount includes, but is not limited to the signing bonus, compensation due under the standard player's contract, collateral compensation, and collateral deferred compensation including performance bonus compensation." The key to the agent's fee is the player's *contractual* rights under his compensation *agreement*, regardless of whether the right to payment accrues immediately or is deferred. Woy's right to a contract fee depends, therefore, on whether Horner's right to collusion damages arises out of an *agreement* between him and a baseball club.

Neither the Atlanta Braves nor any other club had an obligation to enter into a player's contract with Horner for the 1987 season. They could unilaterally have declined to negotiate with him because they though him too prone to injury or because of almost any other nondiscriminatory reason. What they could *not* do was to collude with some 25 other Major League Clubs and boycott Horner in the free agent market. But Horner's resulting claim for damages did not arise out of any compensation agreement; it arose out of a violation of the Basic Agreement. . . . Horner would have been just as entitled to pursue a claim if he had never had a player's contract with Atlanta. He would have been just as entitled to pursue a claim against the other colluding clubs if Atlanta had gone bankrupt and could not pay him a cent. True, the *measure* of his damages would be determined by the likelihood of his obtaining a contract of a certain value, absent the boycott. But that is simply a yardstick for assessing the size of the loss — not the legal grounds for the claim. Grievant Woy is entitled to nothing from respondent Horner on the basis of the player-player agent contract as such.

Yet nonetheless agent Woy made a significant contribution to player Horner by his efforts in 1986 through 1988. His aborted attempts to secure a multiyear, multi-million dollar contract with the Atlanta Braves or the San Diego Padres laid the factual foundation for the collusion claim. . . . Woy conferred that benefit not as a volunteer but in performance of his ongoing contractual obligations to Horner at that time. It would be unfair — or "unjust enrichment" — to allow Horner to retain the benefit of Woy's contribution without some recompense. That is the very purpose of the action in restitution or *quantum meruit. See* RESTATEMENT (SECOND) OF CONTRACTS § 370 (1981).

Restitution in these circumstances may be measured either by the reasonable value of the services rendered in terms of the cost of obtaining them from a person in the claimant's position, or else by the extent to which the other parties' interests . . . have been advanced. Both approaches can be combined in this case, with the recognition that player Horner had to pay another party substantial sums to realize the gain for which agent Woy laid the groundwork. Ordinarily, I would have held further proceedings to go into such matters as the appropriate amount of set off and the like. But in light of the modest figures I am contemplating, I think it would serve everyone's best interest in avoiding further arbitration costs if I simply set forth a formula for measuring restitution and left it to the parties to apply, at least in the first instance.

Grievant Woy's traditional fee of 10 percent, if it were applied to representational services alone, would be totally out of line with current rates. I take judicial notice that in baseball today, at least for players in the higher salary ranges, the standard fee is likely to lie between 2.0 and 3.0 percent. I shall strike a middle ground and therefore set a reasonable value on Woy's negotiating services at 2.5 percent, assuming they had produced a contract. But Horner had to expend substantial amounts in pursuit of his collusion claim to actualize the potential value of Woy's services. It was probably not inappropriate for those charges to exceed the customary representational fees, in light of the considerable time and effort required to prepare and present a collusion claim. But, as I have indicated, I prefer not to get into the costly business of weighing through evidence the reasonableness of the particular fees charged Horner in order to arrive at some suitable setoff or deduction from the amount otherwise due Woy. One can say that Woy performed the first two necessary steps to create and collect a claim. On that theory, I shall simply halve the 2.5 percent figure I would have considered reasonable for a successful negotiation, and award grievant Woy, as his restitutional share, 1.25 percent of any collusion damages recovered by respondent Horner.

Understandably, Woy will feel this gravely undercompensates him for his loss. He would likely have received a full 10 percent of Horner's salary in a multiyear, multi-million dollar contract were it not for the collusion. But it was not Horner who caused this loss. It was the colluding baseball clubs. Conceivably Woy might have had some direct cause of action against the clubs for their wrongdoing. In any event, I am satisfied that he has no contractual claim against Horner, and that the modest remedy of restitution is his only recourse.

AWARD

* * *

2. Grievant Woy is entitled to receive in restitution from respondent Horner by January 1, 1998, 1.25 percent of the gross amount awarded Horner to date in collusion damages (presumably 1.25% of $1,324,249.79, or $16,553.12), with no deduction or set off for Horner's payment of professional fees to third parties. This was not a liquidated claim and there shall be no prejudgment interest.

3. Grievant Woy is entitled to receive in restitution from respondent Horner 1.25 percent of the gross amount awarded Horner in collusion damages in the future, . . . with no deduction or setoff. . . .

Notes and Comments

1. What law governs in the event of conflict between players association regulations and state regulations? *See Amalgamated Ass'n of Street Employees v. Lockridge*, 403 U.S. 274 (1971)

2. Problem: An important aspect of the player-agent contract is the time of the agent's receipt of the fee. What limitations in this regard are imposed by the NFLPA regulations?

Terry Williams, a former University of Alabama football star, hired Joseph Wilkins as his agent on June 1, 1988. Wilkins negotiated for Williams a player contract with the Chicago Bears. The contract package included a signing bonus of $150,000, and a series of one-year contracts. The first year salary was $100,000; the second year equaled $150,000; and a third year contract was for $245,000. Thus, the total package equaled $645,000. The player-agent contract provided for Wilkins to receive 3% of the gross dollar amount of contracts negotiated. Williams orally agreed to pay Wilkins up front. Wilkins received $19,350.00 when the Bears paid Williams the signing bonus. Unfortunately, the contracts were not guaranteed and Williams was cut from the squad at the completion of the rookie season.

Williams hired your firm to represent him for the purpose of securing a refund of a portion of the money paid to Wilkins. Wilkins feels that a "contract is a contract even if it is oral." What legal arguments do you have supporting a refund of compensation paid under the player-agent contract? What actions will you file?

3. Note that some questions regarding the player-agent contracts are no different than questions confronting the attorney in drafting the attorney retainer agreement. For example, a provision is sometimes used which requires client approval of any attorney expenditures that will be reimbursed by the client.

4. Problem: McNabb desires to sign Dominique Marquis, a foreign athlete, to a player-agent agreement. Marquis wishes McNabb to handle all matters for him, including the signing of the employment contract with the professional ballclub. Is McNabb allowed to sign for Marquis under "power of attorney" under the regulations?

5. An increasing number of athletes are playing in foreign sports leagues, such as the Federazione Italiana Pallacanestro in Italy. Japanese professional baseball attracts athletes each year. It is noteworthy that some foreign leagues are considered amateur leagues with special rules regarding American players with professional experience. Some foreign leagues do not have standard form contracts. Thus, the agent enjoys greater freedom in the negotiation of the terms of the employment contract.

6. The saga of Lloyd Bloom and Norby Walters produced two cases containing the issue of whether disputes arising under an approved NFLPA contract between agents and a non-member of the union are subject to the arbitration provision. The contracts under review were signed prior to completion of the athletes' college eligibility in violation of the rules of the NCAA and NFL.

In *Walters & Bloom v. Fullwood & Kickliter*, 675 F. Supp. 155 (S.D.N.Y. 1987), a federal judge refused to order arbitration, declaring the entire player agent contract unenforceable as an illegal contract under New York law. Conversely, a New York court ruled that the question of "arbitrability" was a matter of initial impression for the arbitrator. *Walters & Bloom v. Harmon*, 516 N.Y.S.2d. 874 (1987).

In the resulting arbitration, *Bloom & Walters d/b/a World Sports & Entertainment v. Harmon,* Case No. 11059-014, NFLPA, Culver Arbitrator, Hearing June 10, 1987, decided October 28, 1987, the arbitrator ruled the matter arbitrable and found a violation of the NFLPA regulations voiding the contract. The arbitrator, however, allowed the agents to recover the fair value of services rendered under a quantum meruit theory. *See also Pro Tect Management Corp. v. Worley*, 1990 WL 170358 (S.D.N.Y. 1990) (where contract made prior to draft, issues were not compelled to arbitration).

Agent, William "Tank" Black, challenged the arbitration proceeding in a NFLPA initiated action to revoke Black's certification. He argued that the disciplinary proceeding was based on race discrimination in violation of 42 U.S.C. § 1981, that the arbitration system was inherently biased, and that the arbitrator was not neutral. *Black v. National Football League Players Association*, 87 F. Supp. 2d 1 (D.D.C. 2000) (court determined that agent consented to arbitration as exclusive method of dispute resolution and peremptory challenge of arbitrator was improper before arbitration began).

7. What limitations are imposed by the NFLPA regulations and the Uniform Athlete Agents Act on service contracts for the marketing of the player for endorsement and other off-the-field revenue producing opportunities? How should the marketing agent-player contract differ from the NFLPA advisor contract?

8. Is the arbitrator in the *Woy* case accurate in adjudging that Horner's rights to collusion damages did not arise from his compensation agreement? Are the terms of the Basic Agreement incorporated into the compensation agreement? If so, is a breach of the terms of the Basic Agreement necessarily a breach of the terms of the compensation agreement? Should an implied covenant of "fair dealing," or implied duty to "act in a reasonable and prudent manner" be applied to each compensation agreement? Does Woy's argument depend on whether the implied covenant is implied "in fact" or "at law?" Is the contract between Woy and Horner enforceable under the requirements of the MLBPA Regulations Governing Player Agents? Given the "unjust enrichment" basis for the *Woy* decision, is an invalid player-agent agreement nevertheless enforceable if the player has received benefits as a result of the agent services?

9. The Sports Agent Responsibility and Trust Act (SPARTA), 15 U.S.C. §§ 7801 *et seq.*, categorizes three areas of agent conduct in the recruiting of student athletes as unfair and deceptive acts and practices: 1) giving false or misleading information, or making a false promise or representation; 2) providing anything of value to a student athlete or anyone associated with the athlete before the athlete enters into an agency contract, including any consideration in the form of a loan, or acting in the capacity of a guarantor or co-guarantor for any debt; 3) failing to disclose to the student athlete that the signing of an agency contract jeopardizes the athlete's amateur eligibility; and predating or postdating an agency contract. *Id.*, § 7802 (a).

The disclosure document must contain, in close proximity to the signature of the student athlete (or parent or legal guardian if less than 18 years of age) a conspicuous notice in boldface type stating:

> **"Warning to Student Athlete: If you agree orally or in writing to be represented by an agent now or in the future you may lose your eligibility to compete as a student athlete in your sport. Within 72 hours after entering into this contract or before the next athletic event in which you are eligible to participate, whichever occurs first, both you and the agent by whom you are agreeing to be represented must notify the athletic director of the educational institution at which you are enrolled, or other individual responsible for athletic programs at such educational institution, that you have entered into an agency contract."**

For a review of SPARTA, *see* Bogad, *Maybe Jerry Maguire Should Have Stuck with Law School: How the Sports Agent Responsibility and Trust Act Implements Lawyer-like Rules for Sports Agents*, 27 Cardozo L. Rev. 1889 (2006).

D. PLAYER AGENT: DUTIES IMPOSED BY COMMON LAW, STATUTES, AND REGULATIONS; REMEDIES

State and player association regulations join traditional common law remedies to govern player agent conduct, both during and subsequent to formation of the contract. Bar association rules of professional responsibility, of course, apply to the attorney agent. As noted above, the Federal Investment Advisers Act and state legislation regulating employment and entertainment agents may apply to the player agent. The cornerstone of common law principles relating to the player agent is found in the law of "agency." An agency relationship is defined as follows:

> § 1 Agency; Principal; Agent
>
> (1) Agency is the fiduciary relation which results from the manifestation of consent by one person to another that the other shall act on his behalf and subject to his control, and consent by the other so to act.

RESTATEMENT (SECOND) OF AGENCY § 1 (1958). Fiduciary duties are implied by law into the player (principal) agent contract. The primary duties are:

1. duty of loyalty;
2. duty of obedience; and
3. duty of care.

Available remedies include:

1. actions for breach of contract;
2. actions in tort;
   a. failure to perform;
   b. negligence;
   c. intentional tort;
3. restitution;
4. rescission;
5. accounting in equity;
6. fraud (actual); and
7. fraud (constructive).

The state legislation focusing directly upon player agents provides additional remedies. Some statutes provide for criminal liability and other civil penalties. Note that revocation or suspension of "certification" under the regulations is a popular statutory sanction.

PROBLEM

Johnny Jones is a superb athlete. He was the star football quarterback and baseball pitcher at the University. Sam Shepherd, a non-attorney player agent, approached Jones during his junior year to solicit his business. At the time, Shepherd represented a number of professional athletes, including major league baseball players, NFL players, and NBA players. Shepherd convinced Jones to sign a player-agent contract drafted by Shepherd's office. The player-agent contract was entitled, "OFFER SHEET," and specified that the agent could not as a "matter of law, or by intent of the parties," accept the offer until completion of Jones' college eligibility.

Johnny Jones was drafted in the third round of the Major League Baseball Draft in early June. Shepherd negotiated on behalf of Jones. Jones signed for a bonus of $17,000, and reported to the minor league training camp. After learning that the fourth round pick, Lewis, received a bonus of $40,000, Jones queried the Director of Minor League Personnel about the disparity. He was informed that his college baseball eligibility, under NCAA rules, ended when Shepherd negotiated his contract. Thus, Jones and Shepherd possessed little leverage in negotiating the bonus. Jones could either sign or seek a job in Japan. The fourth round choice, however, was a junior with a year of college eligibility remaining. Lewis bargained his value to $40,000 by threatening to return to college for his final year of baseball.

Jones received a letter from his college football coach in mid-July explaining that the "Offer Sheet" contract with Shepherd rendered him ineligible to participate in college football under NCAA rules.

Jones later signed to play pro football with the permission of the baseball club, but learned that his lost senior year cost him at least $200,000 of compensation. Jones is not satisfied with his football salary. Other players told Jones that Shepherd refused to negotiate for a figure higher than the salary of another Shepherd client playing for the same team.

Jones recently discovered that Shepherd commingled Jones' bonus payment with Shepherd's personal funds. Shepherd's funds are subject to a judicial garnishment proceeding. Shepherd apologized to Jones for the misfortunes.

Jones has retained the legal services of your law firm to bring an action against Shepherd. What causes of action exist at common law? Do the regulatory schemes add remedies?

CASE FILE

NFLPA Regulations Governing Contract Advisors

(Regulations may be accessed at www.nflpa.org/agents/)

SECTION 3: STANDARD OF CONDUCT FOR CONTRACT ADVISORS

A. . . .

B. **Prohibited Conduct**

SECTION 6: OVERSIGHT AND COMPLIANCE PROCEDURE

A. **Disciplinary Committee**

B. . . .

C. . . .

D. **Proposed Disciplinary Action**

E. **Appeal**

F. **Arbitrator**

California Miller-Ayals Athlete Agents Act

Cal. Bus. & Prof. Code §§ 18895 et seq.

§ 18897.7	**Notice of contract to elementary or secondary schools, colleges, universities, or other educational institutions; time of notice**
§ 18897.8	**Civil actions against athlete agents; presumptions; damages, costs and attorney's fees; legislative intent**
§ 18897.83	**Service of Process**
§ 18897.87	**Security for claims against agent or representatives or employees; amount and manner**
§ 18897.9	**Agent contracts; compliance with Miller-Ayala Athlete Agents Act**
§ 18897.93	**Violations; offenses; penalties**
§ 6106.7	**Violation of Miller-Ayala Athlete Agents Act by attorneys prohibited**

Alabama Athlete Agents Regulatory Act of 1987

Acts 1987, No. 87-628, § 1 (effective August 3, 1987)

§ 8-26-29	**Sale or transfer of athlete agent's interest in profits of the athlete agent**
§ 8-26-30	**Interest in entity directly involved in same sport prohibited**
§ 8-26-31	**Disclosure of athlete agent's interest in entity used in giving investment advice**
§ 8-26-32	**Contracts in violation of the law**
§ 8-26-33	**Publication of false, fraudulent, etc., information; advertisements or athlete agent; false information or promises concerning employment**
§ 8-26-36	**Parties to action against athlete agent; transfer and assignment of action; jurisdiction determined by damages claimed**
§ 8-26-41	**Penalties for violation of chapter**

DETROIT LIONS, INC. v. ARGOVITZ

580 F. Supp. 542 (E.D. Mich. 1984)

DeMascio, District Judge.

The plot for this Saturday afternoon serial began when Billy Sims, having signed a contract with the Houston Gamblers on July 1, 1983, signed a second contract with the Detroit Lions on December 16, 1983. On December 18, 1983, the Detroit Lions, Inc. (Lions) and Billy R. Sims filed a complaint in the Oakland County Circuit Court seeking a judicial determination that the July 1, 1983, contract between Sims and the Houston Gamblers, Inc. (Gamblers) is invalid because the defendant Jerry Argovitz (Argovitz) breached his fiduciary duty when negotiating the Gamblers' contract and because the contract was otherwise tainted by fraud and misrepresentation. Defendants promptly removed the action to this court based on our diversity of citizenship jurisdiction.

For the reasons that follow, we have concluded that Argovitz's breach of his fiduciary duty during negotiations for the Gamblers' contract was so pronounced, so egregious, that to deny rescission would be unconscionable.

Sometime in February or March 1983, Argovitz told Sims that he had applied for a Houston franchise in the newly formed United States Football League (USFL). In May 1983, Sims attended a press conference in Houston at which Argovitz announced that his application for a franchise had been approved. The evidence persuades us that Sims did not know the extent of Argovitz's interest in the Gamblers. He did not know the amount of Argovitz's original investment, or that Argovitz was obligated for 29 percent of a $1.5 million letter of credit, or that Argovitz was the president of the Gamblers' Corporation at an annual salary of $275,000 and 5 percent of the yearly cash flow. The defendants could not justifiably expect Sims to comprehend the ramifications of Argovitz's interest in the Gamblers or the manner in which that interest would create an untenable conflict of interest, a conflict that would inevitably breach Argovitz's fiduciary duty to Sims. Argovitz knew, or should have known, that he could not act as Sims' agent under any circumstances when dealing with the Gamblers. Even the USFL Constitution itself prohibits a holder of any interest in a member club from acting "as the contracting agent or representative for any player."

Pending the approval of his application for a USFL franchise in Houston, Argovitz continued his negotiations with the Lions on behalf of Sims. On April 5, 1983, Argovitz offered Sims' services to the Lions for $6 million over a four-year period. The offer included a demand for a $1 million interest-free loan to be repaid over 10 years, and for skill and injury guarantees for three years. The Lions quickly responded with a counter offer on April 7, 1983, in the face amount of $1.5 million over a five year period with additional incentives not relevant here. The negotiating process was working. The Lions were trying to determine what Argovitz really believed the market value for Sims really was. On May 3, 1983, with his Gamblers franchise assured, Argovitz significantly reduced his offer to the Lions. He now offered Sims to the Lions for $3 million over a four-year period, one-half of the amount of his April 5, 1983, offer. Argovitz's May 3rd offer included a demand for $50,000 to permit Sims to purchase an annuity. Argovitz also dropped his previous demand for skill guarantees. The May 10, 1983 offer submitted by the Lions brought the parties much closer.

On May 30, 1983, Argovitz asked for $3.5 million over a five-year period. This offer included an interest-free loan and injury protection insurance but made no demand for skill guarantees. The May 30 offer now requested $400,000 to allow Sims to purchase an annuity. On June 1, 1983, Argovitz and the Lions were only $500,000 apart. We find that the negotiations between the Lions and Argovitz were progressing normally, not laterally as Argovitz represented to Sims. The Lions were not "dragging their feet." Throughout the entire month of June 1983, Mr. Frederick Nash, the Lions' skilled negotiator and a fastidious lawyer, was involved in investigating the possibility of providing an attractive annuity for Sims and at the same time doing his best to avoid the granting of either skill or injury guarantees. The evidence establishes that on June 22, 1983, the Lions and Argovitz were very close to reaching an agreement on the value of Sims' services.

Apparently, in the midst of his negotiations with the Lions and with his Gamblers franchise in hand, Argovitz decided that he would seek an offer from the Gamblers. Mr. Bernard Lerner, one of Argovitz's partners in the Gamblers agreed to negotiate a contract with Sims. Since Lerner admitted that he had no knowledge whatsoever about football, we must infer that Argovitz at the very least told Lerner the amount of money required to sign Sims and further pressed upon Lerner the Gamblers' absolute need to obtain Sims' services. In the Gamblers' organization, only Argovitz knew the value of Sims' services and how critical it was for the Gamblers to obtain Sims. In Argovitz's words, Sims would make the Gamblers' franchise.

On June 29, 1983, at Lerner's behest, Sims and his wife went to Houston to negotiate with a team that was partially owned by his own agent. When Sims arrived in Houston, he believed that the Lions organization was not negotiating in good faith; that it was not really interested in his services. His ego was bruised and his emotional outlook toward the Lions was visible to Burrough and Argovitz. Clearly, virtually all the information that Sims had up to that date came from Argovitz. Sims and the Gamblers did not discuss a future contract on the night of June 29th. The negotiations began on the morning of June 30, 1983, and ended that afternoon. At the morning meeting, Lerner offered Sims a $3.5 million five-year contract, which included three years of skill and injury guarantees. The offer included a $500,000 loan at an interest rate of 1 percent over prime. It was from this loan that Argovitz planned to receive the $100,000 balance of his fee for acting as an agent in negotiating a contract with his own team. Burrough testified that Sims would have accepted that offer on the spot because he was finally receiving the guarantee that he had been requesting from the Lions, guarantees that Argovitz dropped without too much quarrel. Argovitz and Burrough took Sims and his wife into another room to discuss the offer. Argovitz did tell Sims that he thought the Lions would match the Gamblers financial package and asked Sims whether he (Argovitz) should telephone the Lions. But, it is clear from the evidence that neither Sims nor Burrough believed that the Lions would match the offer. We find that Sims told Argovitz not to call the Lions for purely emotional reasons. As we have noted, Sims believed that the

Lions' organization was not that interested in him and his pride was wounded. Burrough clearly admitted that he was aware of the emotional basis for Sims' decision not to have Argovitz phone the Lions, and we must conclude from the extremely close relationship between Argovitz and Sims that Argovitz knew it as well. When Sims went back to Lerner's office, he agreed to become a Gambler on the terms offered. At that moment, Argovitz irreparably breached his fiduciary duty. As agent for Sims he had the duty to telephone the Lions, receive its final offer, and present the terms of both offers to Sims. Then and only then could it be said that Sims made an intelligent and knowing decision to accept the Gamblers' offer.

During these negotiations at the Gamblers' office, Mr. Nash of the Lions telephoned Argovitz, but even though Argovitz was at his office, he declined to accept the telephone call. Argovitz tried to return Nash's call after Sims had accepted the Gamblers' offer, but it was after 5 p.m. and Nash had left for the July 4th weekend. When he declined to accept Mr. Nash's call, Argovitz's breach of his fiduciary duty became even more pronounced. Following Nash's example, Argovitz left for his weekend trip, leaving his principal to sign the contracts with the Gamblers the next day, July 1, 1983. The defendants, in their supplemental trial brief, assert that neither Argovitz nor Burrough can be held responsible for following Sims' instruction not to contact the Lions on June 30, 1983. Although it is generally true that an agent is not liable for losses occurring as a result of following his principal's instructions, the rule of law is not applicable when the agent has placed himself in a position adverse to that of his principal.

During the evening of June 30, 1983, Burrough struggled with the fact that they had not presented the Gamblers' offer to the Lions. He knew, as does the court, that Argovitz now had the wedge that he needed to bring finality to the Lions' negotiations. Burrough was acutely aware of the fact that Sims' actions were emotionally motivated and realized that the responsibility for Sims' future rested with him. We view with some disdain the fact that Argovitz had, in effect, delegated his entire fiduciary responsibility on the eve of his principal's most important career decision. On July 1, 1983, it was Lerner who gave lip service to Argovitz's conspicuous conflict of interest. It was Lerner, not Argovitz, who advised Sims that Argovitz's position with the Gamblers presented a conflict of interest and that Sims could, if he wished, obtain an attorney or another agent. Argovitz, upon whom Sims had relied for the past four years, was not even there. Burrough, conscious of Sims' emotional responses, never advised Sims to wait until he had talked with the Lions before making a final decision. Argovitz's conflict of interest and self dealing put him in the position where he would not even use the wedge he now had to negotiate with the Lions, a wedge that is the dream of every agent. Two expert witnesses testified that an agent should telephone a team that he has been negotiating with once he has an offer in hand. Mr. Woolf, plaintiffs' expert, testified that an offer from another team is probably the most important factor in negotiations. Mr. Lustig, defendant's expert, believed that it was prudent for him to telephone the Buffalo Bills and inform that organization of the Gamblers' offer to Jim Kelly, despite the fact that he believed the Bills had already made its best offer to his principal. The evidence here convinces us that Argovitz's negotiations with the Lions were ongoing and it had not made its final offer. Argovitz did not follow the common practice described by both expert witnesses. He did not do this because he knew that the Lions would not leave Sims without a contract and he further knew that if he made that type of call Sims would be lost to the Gamblers, a team he owned.

On November 12, 1983, when Sims was in Houston for the Lions game with the Houston Oilers, Argovitz asked Sims to come to his home and sign certain papers. He represented to Sims that certain papers of his contract had been mistakenly overlooked and now needed to be signed. Included among those papers he asked Sims to sign was a waiver of any claim that Sims might have against Argovitz for his blatant breach of his fiduciary duty brought on by his glaring conflict of interest. Sims did not receive independent advice with regard to the wisdom of signing such a waiver. Despite having sold his agency business in September, Argovitz did not even tell Sims' new agent of his intention to have Sims sign a waiver. Nevertheless, Sims, an unsophisticated young man, signed the waiver. This is another example of the questionable conduct on the part of Argovitz who still had business management obligations to Sims. In spite of his fiduciary relationship he had Sims sign a waiver without advising him to obtain independent counseling.

Argovitz's negotiations with Lustig, Jim Kelly's agent, illustrates the difficulties that develop when an agent negotiates a contract where his personal interests conflict with those of his principal. Lustig, an independent agent, ignored Argovitz's admonishment not to "shop" the Gamblers' offer to Kelly. Lustig called the NFL team that he had been negotiating with because it was the "prudent" thing to do. The Gamblers agreed to pay Kelly, an un-tested rookie quarterback \$3.2 million for five years. His compensation was \$60,000 less than Sims', a former Heisman Trophy winner and a proven star in the NFL. Lustig also obtained a number of favorable clauses from Argovitz; the most impressive one being that Kelly was assured of being one of the three top paid quarterbacks in the USFL if he performed as well as expected. If Argovitz had been free from conflicting interests he would have demanded similar benefits for Sims. Argovitz claimed that the nondisclosure clause in Kelly's contract prevented him from mentioning the Kelly contract to Sims. We view this contention as frivolous. Requesting these benefits for Sims did not require disclosure of Kelly's contract. Moreover, Argovitz's failure to obtain personal guarantees for Sims without adequately warning Sims about the risks and uncertainties of a new league constituted a clear breach of his fiduciary duty.

The parties submitted a great deal of evidence and argued a number of peripheral issues. Although most of the issues were not determinative factors in our decision, they do demonstrate that Argovitz had a history of fulfilling his fiduciary duties in an irresponsible manner. One cannot help but wonder whether Argovitz took his fiduciary duty seriously. For example, after investing approximately $76,000 of Sims' money, Argovitz, with or without the prior knowledge of his principal, received a finder's fee. Despite the fact that Sims paid Argovitz a 2 percent fee, Argovitz accepted $3800 from a person with whom he invested Sims' money. In March 1983, Argovitz had all of his veteran players, including Sims, sign a new agency contract with less favorable payment terms for the players even though they already had an ongoing agency agreement with him. He did this after he sold his entire agency business to Career Sports. Finally, Argovitz was prepared to take the remainder of his 5 percent agency fee for negotiating Sims' contract with the Gamblers from monies the Gamblers loaned to Sims at an interest rate of 1 percent over prime. It mattered little to Argovitz that Sims would have to pay interest on the $100,000 that Argovitz was ready to accept. While these practices by Argovitz are troublesome, we do not find them decisive in examining Argovitz's conduct while negotiating the Gamblers' contract on June 30 and July 1, 1983. We find this circumstantial evidence useful only insofar as it has aided the court in understanding the manner in which these parties conducted business.

We are mindful that Sims was less than forthright when testifying before the court. However, we agree with plaintiffs counsel that the facts as presented through the testimony of other witnesses are so unappealing that we can disregard Sims' testimony entirely. We remain persuaded that on balance, Argovitz's breach of his fiduciary duty was so egregious that a court of equity cannot permit him to benefit by his own wrongful breach. We conclude that Argovitz's conduct in negotiating Sims' contract with the Gamblers rendered it invalid.

* * *

Judgment will be entered for the plaintiffs rescinding the Gamblers' contract with Sims.

It is so Ordered.

BROWN v. WOOLF

554 F. Supp. 1206 (S.D. Ind. 1983)

Steckler, District Judge.

This matter comes before the Court on the motions of defendant, Robert G. Woolf, for partial summary judgment and for summary judgment. Fed. R. Civ. P. 56.

The complaint in this diversity action seeks compensatory and punitive damages and the imposition of a trust on a fee defendant allegedly received, all stemming from defendant's alleged constructive fraud and breach of fiduciary duty in the negotiation of a contract for the 1974-75 hockey season for plaintiff who was a professional hockey player. Plaintiff alleges that prior to the 1973-74 season he had engaged the services of defendant, a well known sports attorney and agent, who represents many professional athletes, has authored a book, and has appeared in the media in connection with such representation, to negotiate a contract for him with the Pittsburgh Penguins of the National Hockey League. Plaintiff had a professionally successful season that year under the contract defendant negotiated for him and accordingly again engaged defendant's services prior to the 1974-75 season. During the negotiations in July 1974, the Penguins offered plaintiff a two year contract at $80,000.00 per year but plaintiff rejected the offer allegedly because defendant asserted that he could obtain a better, long-term, no-cut contract with a deferred compensation feature with the Indianapolis Racers, which at the time was a new team in a new league. On July 31, 1974, plaintiff signed a five-year contract with the Racers. Thereafter, it is alleged the Racers began having financial difficulties. Plaintiff avers that Woolf continued to represent plaintiff and negotiated two reductions in plaintiffs compensation including the loss of a retirement fund at the same time defendant was attempting to get his own fee payment from the Racers. Ultimately the Racers' assets were seized and the organizers defaulted on their obligations to plaintiff He avers that he received only $185,000.00 of the total $800,000.00 compensation under the Racer contract but that defendant received his full $40,000.00 fee (5% of the contract) from the Racers.

Plaintiff alleges that defendant made numerous material misrepresentations upon which he relied both during the negotiation of the Racer contract and at the time of the subsequent modifications. Plaintiff further avers that defendant breached his fiduciary duty to plaintiff by failing to conduct any investigation into the financial stability of the Racers, failing to investigate possible consequences of the deferred compensation package in the Racers' contract, failing to obtain guarantees or collateral, and by negotiating reductions in plaintiff's compensation from the Racers while insisting on receiving all of his own. Plaintiff theorizes that such conduct amounts to a prima facie case of constructive fraud for which he should receive compensatory and punitive damages and have a trust impressed on the $40,000.00 fee defendant received from the Racers.

Defendant's motion for partial summary judgment attacks plaintiff's claim for punitive damages, contending that plaintiff has no evidence to support such an award and should not be allowed to rest on the allegations of his complaint. Further, he claims that punitive damages are unavailable as a matter of law in a constructive fraud case because no proof of fraudulent intent is required. By his motion for summary judgment, defendant attacks several aspects of plaintiff's claims against him. He argues (1) that plaintiff cannot recover on a breach of contract theory because Robert G. Woolf, the individual, was acting merely as the agent and employee of Robert Woolf Associates, Inc. (RWA), (2) that defendant's conduct could not amount to constructive fraud because (a) plaintiff alleges only negligent acts, (b) there is no evidence defendant deceived plaintiff or violated a position of trust, (c) there is no showing of harm to the public interest, and (d) there is no evidence that defendant obtained an unconscionable advantage at plaintiff's expense.

Turning first to the questions raised in the motion for partial summary judgment, the Court could find no Indiana case specifically discussing the availability of punitive damages in an action based upon the theory of constructive fraud. Cases from other jurisdictions reflect a division of authority. The Court concludes that Indiana courts would not adopt a *per se* rule prohibiting such damages in a constructive fraud action, but would rather consider the facts and circumstances of each case. If elements of recklessness or oppressive conduct are demonstrated, punitive damages could be awarded. *See Young v. Goodyear Stores*, 244 S.C. 493, 137 S.E.2d 578 (1964) (if defendant recklessly or heedlessly makes false statements, fact he was unaware of falsity does not defeat claim for punitive damages). *See also Logan v. Barge*, 568 F.2d 863 (Tex. Civ. App. 1978); *Harrington v. Holiday Rambler Corp.*, 176 Mont. 37, 575 P.2d 578 (1978); *contra, Logsdon v. Graham Ford Co.*, 54 Ohio St. 2d 336, 376 N.E.2d 1333 (1978) (*per se* rule).

Indiana cases contain several formulizations of the tort of constructive fraud. Generally it is characterized as acts or a course of conduct from which an unconscionable advantage is or may be derived, *Beecher v. City of Terre Haute*, 235 Ind. 180, 132 N.E.2d 141 (1956); *Hall v. Ind. Dept. of State Revenue*, 170 Ind. App. 77, 351 N.E.2d 35 (1976), or a breach of confidence coupled with an unjust enrichment which shocks the conscience, *Voelkel v. Tohulka*, 236 Ind. 588, 141 N.E.2d 344 (1957), or a breach of duty, including mistake, duress or undue influence, which the law declares fraudulent because of a tendency to deceive, injure the public interest or violate the public or private confidence, *Blaising v. Mills*, 374 N.E.2d 1166 (Ind.App.1978). Another formulization found in the cases involves the making of a false statement, by the dominant party in a confidential or fiduciary relationship or by one who holds himself out as an expert, upon which the plaintiff reasonably relies to his detriment. The defendant need not know the statement is false nor make the false statement with fraudulent intent. *Coffey v. Wininger*, 156 Ind. App. 233, 296 N.E.2d 154 (1973); *Smart & Perry Ford Sales, Inc. v. Weaver*, 149 Ind. App. 693, 274 N.E.2d 718 (1971).

The Court believes that both formulizations are rife with questions of fact, inter alia, the existence or nonexistence of a confidential or fiduciary relationship, and the question of reliance on false representations, as well as questions of credibility.

* * *

By reason of the foregoing, defendant's motions for partial summary judgment and for summary judgment are hereby DENIED.

IT IS SO ORDERED.

NOTES AND COMMENTS

1. The attorney Rules of Professional Conduct serve to govern most, if not all, of the problem areas of agent practice identified above:

a. Unethical Solicitation — MRPC § 7.3;

b. Charging of Excessive Fees — MRPC § 1.5;

c. Conflicts of Interest — MRPC2 §§ 1.7-1.9;

d. General Incompetence — MRPC §§ 1.1-1.3;

e. Income Mismanagement — MRPC § 1.15;

f. Fraud — MRPC § 8.1.

Do the state and player association regulatory schemes adequately govern nonattorney agent conduct?

2. Attorney agents are susceptible to the "malpractice" action. What are the distinctions between an attorney malpractice action and an action for breach of the duty of care, or negligence? Do the regulations create a cause of action for "agent malpractice"? If so, what standard should be utilized?

Under Illinois law, a sports agent fiduciary must treat the player with the "utmost candor, rectitude, care, loyalty, and good faith." *Jones v. Childers*, 18 F.3d 899 (8th Cir. 1994). *See also Bias v. Advantage International, Inc.*, 905 F.2d 1558 (D.C. Cir. 1990) (estate unsuccessful in attempt to recover in action for negligent performance of agent duties based on agent's failure to execute an insurance policy and endorsement contract prior to player's death).

See Carr v. CIGNA Securities, Inc., 1995 WL 680635 (N.D. Ill. 1995), for a case concerning statute of limitations bar to claims arising out of the investment of professional player's funds. *See also Buse v. The Vanguard Group of Investment Companies*, 1996 WL 369007 (E.D. Pa. 1996); 1995 WL 549014 (E.D. Pa. 1995), for a case involving the handling of pension plan and retirement program funds.

3. Does the violation of a provision of a regulatory scheme constitute a *per se* breach of a common law duty?

4. In the Johnny Jones problem above, the University lost the services of its star athlete due to the improper signing of the player agent contract. Does the University enjoy standing to sue Shepherd for damages? If so, explain the common law or statutory bases upon which the actions rest. *See* Uniform Athlete Agents Act, Section 16, **Case File, Chapter 8, Section B,** *supra*.

See TEX. CIV. PRAC. & REM. CODE §§ 131.001 to 131.008, for legislation enabling colleges to sue for the loss of player services. The Texas "NCAA-rule" Act applies to agents, attorneys, and boosters who violate NCAA rules, or encourage students to violate the rules. What is the nature of the damages sought in the action? Remember, the loss of a star player may not only result in lost gate receipts, but lost TV and bowl game revenues. *See* Meischen, *A Comparison of the Texas Athlete Agent Act and the Uniform Athlete Agent Act,* 2 TEX. REV. ENT. & SPORTS L. 89 (2001).

5. For what reasons would an attorney sue in contract rather than tort?

6. The Bloom & Walters saga, described above, includes criminal actions at both the state and federal levels. The state of Alabama successfully filed actions under the Deceptive Practices Act, Commercial Bribery, and illegal tampering with a sports contest. The United States attorney successfully prosecuted Walters and Bloom for RICO violations, obstruction of justice, mail fraud, and wire fraud. However, the conviction of Walters was ultimately overturned by the Seventh Circuit following several appeals and remands. The court determined that the prosecutor never proved the elements of mail fraud, the key aspect of the case. *Walters v. United States*, 997 F.2d 1219 (7th Cir. 1993). Anecdotal instances of agent misconduct involving both criminal and civil sanctions continue with the "Tank" Black saga, and the successful prosecution of Robert Walsh by the Alabama Attorney General's office.

7. For descriptions of unethical agent conduct, *see* RUXIN, AN ATHLETE'S GUIDE TO AGENTS (3d ed. 1998).

8. Note the remedy provided in the state and player association schemes declaring a contract void if negotiated prior to receiving certification or for failure to comply with the regulations.

Does an aggrieved player possess a cause of action against a player association, or tort claim against a state, for negligent certification of an agent?

A contract may also be declared void under common law principles. The distinction between contracts that are void and those that are voidable may be important. *See Jackson v. NFLPA*, 26 F.3d 122 (3rd Cir. 1994) (*aff 'd without opinion*) (no basis for cause of action against NFLPA).

9. Article III of the NCAA Constitution provides that an athlete is not eligible for participation if the player has taken or accepted the promise of pay for participation in that sport. Section l(a)(1). The player also is ineligible where the player enters into an agreement to negotiate a professional contract in the sport. Section l(a)(2). The declaring or making oneself available for the draft is tantamount to entering into an agreement to negotiate a professional contract.

Importantly, an amateur athlete who contracts with a player agent is considered a professional, thus losing college eligibility in the sport for which the service is performed. An agency contract not specifically limited in writing to a particular sport is deemed applicable to all sports. The player, however, is allowed to secure the advice of a lawyer concerning a proposed professional sports contract. But, the attorney cannot represent the player in negotiations concerning the contract. Section 1(c). Can you formulate a legal basis to challenge the NCAA rules? The NCAA and amateur sports are considered at **Chap-**

ter 2, *supra. See Shelton v. NCAA*, 539 F.2d 1197 (9th Cir. 1976) (unsuccessful challenge of NCAA rules).

See generally, Buckner, *University Liability in Florida when Coaches Refer Student Athletes to Sports Agents*, 73-APR FLA. B.J. 87 (1999); Arkell, *Agent Interference with College Athletics: What Agents Can and Cannot Do and What Institutions Should Do in Response*, 4 SPORTS LAW. J. 147 (1997).

10. The "Offer Sheet" (where a contract does not become valid until completion of a player's eligibility) is commonly used to circumvent the NCAA rules. The postdated contract or other arrangements are considered "agreements to be represented by an agent," and thus serve to destroy college eligibility. *See* Comment, *The Offer Sheet: An Attempt to Circumvent NCAA Prohibition of Representational Contracts*, 14 LOY. L.A. L. REV. 187 (1980).

11. For a case involving a claim by one agent against another for "subcontract" services in the negotiation of a player contract with the Phoenix Suns, *see Andrews v. Merriweather*, 1991 WL 38689 (N.D. Ill. 1991). *See also, Weinberg v. Silber*, 140 F. Supp. 2d 712 (N.D. Tex. 2001) (dispute of two sports agents arose from several oral joint venture agreements to recruit athletes and split fees and expenses). For a description of events that generate legal disputes among agents who have conducted partnership operations, see the "Findings of Fact" in *Steinberg, Moorad & Dunn v. Dunn*, 2002 U.S. Dist. LEXIS 26752 (C.D. Cal. 2002).

12. The Administer of the Bob Marley estate successfully maintained an action alleging fraud, breach of fiduciary duty, and violation of the Racketeer Influenced and Corrupt Organizations Act (RICO) against the singer's former legal and financial advisors. *Bingham v. Zolt*, 66 F.3d 553 (2d Cir. 1995). *See also Williams v. CWI, Inc.*, 777 F. Supp. 1006 (D.D.C. 1991) (Reggie and Kathy Williams recover $50,000 investment funds, $37,300 damages, and $50,000 punitive damages in breach of contract/fraud case).

13. Does the agent who represents two players competing for the same position possess a conflict of interest? Two players on the same team under the salary cap? Two players in the same draft? Two super stars competing for endorsement or appearance money? *See generally* Rosner, *Conflicts of Interest & the Shifting Paradigm of Athlete Representation*, 11 UCLA Ent. L. Rev. 193 (2004); Walton, *Conflicts for Sports and Entertainment Attorneys: The Good News, the Bad News, and the Ugly Consequences*, 5 VILL. SPORTS & ENT. L.J. 259 (1998); Brown, *The Battle the Fans Never See: Conflicts of Interest for Sports Lawyers*, 7 GEO. J. LEGAL ETHICS 83 (1994).

14. For an article questioning the propriety of an agent's "packaging" of clients in deals made with promoters or advertisers, *see* Newcomb & Comte, *Endorsement Tying Arrangements by Sports Agents Produces Growing Controversy Among Athletes*, FORBES MAGAZINE (November 23, 1992), *reprinted in* XI SPORTS LAW. 8 (July/Aug. 1993).

15. In 1995, professional golfer Lee Janzen signed a written three-year contract with his agent. Under the terms of the agreement, the agent was to serve as Janzen's exclusive representative in exchange for a fee of 20% of the value of endorsements and other opportunities generated by the agent. After two plus years, Janzen sought to terminate the agreement and recover documents from his file. The agent did not comply with Janzen's request, thus Janzen filed a lawsuit, seeking termination of the agreement, damages, attorneys fees and costs. Janzen alleged that the agent orally stated at the time of contract execution that Janzen could end the contract at any time that he was "unhappy." He further alleged that he executed the written agreement in reliance on the contemporaneous oral agreement. The Parole Evidence Rule generally prohibits introduction of evidence extraneous to the written words of the contract, including verbal promises prior to or contemporaneous with execution of the contract, to vary the plain meaning of the terms of the agreement in an action for judicial "construction." An exception to the Parole Evidence Rule exists in actions for "reformation" of the instrument to reflect the true intent of the parties that was not expressed in the instrument. Florida case law recognizes an exception that allows admission of an oral agreement which is shown by clear, precise, and undisputable evidence to establish a contemporaneous oral agreement which induced the execution of the written contract. Janzen seeks reformation of the contract to enable his termination based on alleged fraudulent inducement and deceptive and unfair practices in violation of Florida statutes.

Janzen also alleged a claim for breach of contract. The agent declared in a "Mission Statement" to be the preeminent marketing representative in the area of professional sports on a world-wide basis, providing excellent performance. The agent was bound by the contract to put forth "best efforts" to develop endorsement opportunities for Janzen. Plaintiff alleged that the agent presented only three endorsement contracts to the player, a number well below any level of "excellent performance." The complaint further alleged that the agent failed to keep Janzen properly informed of the agent's progress on his behalf, and engaged in a pattern of dishonesty towards Janzen and his wife concerning the nature and extent of the agent's communications with third parties concerning endorsement opportunities. Janzen also alleged that the agent breached an implied covenant to have available for the service of the player, personnel competent to discharge the various functions reasonably necessary to properly provide representation for a player of Janzen's ranking. Janzen is a seven-time winner on the PGA Tour, finished the 1997 season ranked 24th on the money list, earned in 1997 over $877,000, has career earnings of $5.33 million, and ranks 29th all-time earnings. *See Janzen v. Leader Enterprises, Inc.*, Case No. CI-97-9633 (Fla. 9th Cir. 1997).

Chapter 9

NEGOTIATION OF SPORTS CONTRACTS

A. INTRODUCTORY COMMENTS

In the book GETTING TO YES: NEGOTIATING AGREEMENT WITHOUT GIVING IN (1981), Fisher and Ury admonish that effective negotiators convert competitive positional bargaining to mutual joint problem solving, a search for beneficial results. The observation is particularly true for sports contract negotiation. This chapter first looks at negotiation as a discipline — a fundamental method of dispute resolution. The chapter next focuses upon the elements of sports employment contract negotiation. A matrix is developed to serve as a checklist for the attorney-agent. Materials provide the insight of practitioners in the field. Finally, the chapter views negotiation of the endorsement contract for off-the-field player revenue.

As you read the materials and work through the problems that follow, consider why negotiation may be better labeled as a science rather than an art. Do not forget the presence and limitations of the collective bargaining agreement, presented in **Chapter 6**. Also, keep in mind the function of the salary arbitration mechanism in major league baseball. Salary arbitration is the subject matter of **Chapter 7, Section D,** *supra*.

B. NEGOTIATION THEORY

Negotiation needs little definition. Attorneys, students, and others frequently utilize negotiation as a fundamental method of resolving disputes. Much of the written material concerning negotiation focuses on how to negotiate. When to pound your fist, when to walk out, how to manipulate the other parties, etc. Most successful negotiators, however, emphasize analysis and preparation as the key elements.

1. Structure of the Conflict

Conflicts, from the standpoint of bargaining, usually fit into one of three categories: two-party/single issue; two-party/multiple issue; and multi-party/multi-issue. The two-party single issue (distributive) bargaining is generally "zero sum" in nature. One party wins, the other loses. Thus, the more one party receives, the less the other receives or the more the other gives (the flip sides of the same coin). The stereotypical sale scenario is often used to depict the zero sum game.

CASE 1: PLAYER SALE

Assume that the New York Yankees club desires to sell a pitcher to the Texas Rangers. The Texas Rangers of the American League want to make a bid that the Yankees club is inclined to accept. Obviously, the Yankees want the price to be high and the Rangers want the price to be low. If negotiation is viewed as a series of decisions (decision tree analysis), one of the first decisions regards how much to offer/how much to demand. Both parties attempt to ascertain the other party's "reservation price," the minimum amount the seller will accept/the maximum amount the buyer will pay. The relative reservation price positions, in any given situation, depend on several factors.

The price the Yankees club is able to demand for the pitcher depends on the availability of other pitchers of equal quality on the market. The price the Rangers will pay is also a function of the Rangers' need for the pitcher. Theoretically, the pitcher has an intrinsic value based on ability or attained skill levels.

The Yankees club decided that the Yankees would accept at least $220,000 as the minimum price. The Yankees estimated the Rangers' range of reservation prices was between $250,000 and $475,000. The Yankees concluded that a reason able sales price was $350,000. The Rangers projected the Yankees' reservation price at $150,000. The Rangers, however, were willing to pay $320,000 for the pitcher.

The Yankees' general manager and the Rangers' GM met in New York to negotiate the deal. Neither party wanted to be the first to disclose his team's position. Finally, the Rangers put forth the offer of $130,000. The Yankees countered with a demand of $570,000. A split of the difference equaled the $350,000 figure projected by the Yankees. The "negotiation dance" continued with counter offer being matched against counter offer. Finally, the parties agreed to a price of $300,000.

The Yankees and Rangers reached an agreed sales price that satisfied the objectives of both parties. The agreement was made although both parties perceived the negotiation as a two party/single issue debate. The Rangers and Yankees were able to reach a settlement as both reservation price figures were within the "zone of agreement." The geometry of distributive bargaining is illustrated as follows:

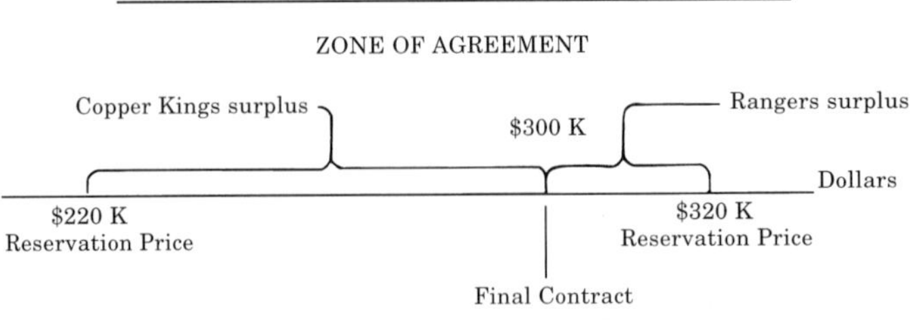

Note that it is impossible to reach agreement where one or both of the reservation prices are not within the zone of agreement. The parties also had numerous opportunities to walk away from the bargaining table with no agreement, although the reservation prices were within the zone. Misunderstandings, erroneous projections, ego trips, and greed are a few of the many barriers to a negotiated agreement in the zero sum game. Professor Raiffa quotes Benjamin Franklin as follows:

> "Trades would not take place unless it were advantageous to the parties concerned. Of course, it is better to strike as good a bargain as one's bargaining position permits. The worst outcome is when, by overreaching greed, no bargain is struck, and a trade that could have been advantageous to both parties does not come off at all."

Case 2: Player Sale

Assume that the Yankees and Rangers are negotiating the sale of the player as described in the Problem above. The Ranger reservation price, however, is only $200,000. As one of the reservation prices is not within the zone of agreement, successful bargaining is impossible. How can you move the parties from competitive positional bargaining to joint problem solving? One way is to introduce an additional issue, thereby converting a single-issue dispute to a multiple-issue problem. The two party/multiple issue (integrative) bargaining is not zero sum in nature. The parties can enlarge the pie in order that both gain more — a win-win scenario.

The Yankees have a program that aids the construction of public facilities for amateur baseball within the City. The Yankees plan to spend $20,000 to improve an amateur stadium and playing field, as the City does not have the funds to do so. The Rangers have a separate budget line item for charitable contributions. The Rangers can make a $20,000 tax deductible contribution to the City, thus relieving the Yankees of the expense burden. The Yankees net the $220,000 reservation price. The Rangers satisfy the team's budget constraints and purchase a pitcher for the $200,000 reservation price.

A commonly used means of expanding the menu of possible contracts is the introduction of contingency payments over periods of time. The Rangers and Yankees might reach agreement for a sales price of $200,000, with future payments based on the pitcher's performance. The parties could also agree that $200,000 is paid now, with other payments totaling $20,000 deferred to the future. As you will see *infra*, performance bonuses resulting from the use of the "incentive clauses" are popular in the negotiation of player-team contracts. The Dallas Cowboys and the Minnesota Vikings reached a trade agreement after protracted negotiation appeared to fail by expanding the issues to include contingency features. The Cowboys traded Herschel Walker for several players. If the Cowboys were to release any of the former Viking players at the end of the season, the Cowboys would receive draft choices from the Vikings.

The parties must adequately communicate the available issues in order to reach agreement. Importantly, the parties must work to identify and link issues together to move the debate from positional bargaining. Another significant factor is the relationship of the parties. Is the relationship continuous, or is it a one time affair? One party may wish to accommodate the other to further the continuous relationship. Persons, including artificial persons, treat each other differently when the relationship is ongoing rather than random.

CASE 3: PLAYER SALE

The Yankees and Texas Rangers are negotiating the sale of the pitcher as described in the **Problem** above. The Seattle Mariners express an interest in the player. The scenario becomes a multi-party/multi-issue problem. The Mariners and Rangers may bid against each other, thus enhancing the final sales price. The Rangers must consider not only the Yankees, but the Mariners as well. Sometimes in professional sports, teams will trade for or otherwise contract with a player to prevent a rival club from gaining the competitive benefits of the player. A creative way to satisfy all parties is to arrive at a three-way trade. The Rangers and Mariners could join to pay the Yankees the reservation or desired price for the pitcher. The Rangers would receive the pitcher. A player from the Rangers roster or farm system would transfer to the Mariners.

Another frequent scenario features the party that is not monolithic in nature. The general manager of a club may desire one or more players. The field manager or head coach may want a different player. Perhaps the owner possesses a completely distinct agenda. David Fishof recounts his experience in negotiating on behalf of Vince Farragamo with the L.A. Rams. Fishof was convinced that Rams General Manager, Don Klosterman, was not in control, but that the owner of the club was the actual decision maker. In short, the L.A. Rams were not internally monolithic, but were splintered. *See* FISHOF & SHAPIRO, PUTTING IT ON THE LINE: THE NEGOTIATING SECRETS, TACTICS, AND TECHNIQUES OF A TOP SPORTS AND ENTERTAINMENT AGENT (1983). Fishof brought another party into the scene by negotiating a deal with the Montreal club of the Canadian Football League.

The use of a third party to facilitate the bargaining process introduces another player to the negotiation game. In the late 1960s, Bowie Kuhn intervened in negotiations between the Houston Astros and the Montreal Expos. The Astros and Expos completed a trade sending Rusty Staub to the Expos and Donn Clendenon and others to the Astros. Clendenon retired rather than report to the Astros. Kuhn intervened to mediate a final solution. Staub remained in Montreal. The Astros received Jesus Alou and two pitchers, Skip Guinn and Jack Billingham. Importantly, the introduction of a third party to the negotiation changes the dynamics of the process. The multi-party/multiissue bargaining scenario usually produces the opportunity to expand the pie for allocation among the parties.

A "richer" class of multi-party/multi-issue disputes exists, however, when the participants are *bona fide* parties with identifiable interests at stake in the negotiation. A sports example would be the process utilized by sports leagues to choose commissioners.

The agonizing drama of the National Football League's selection of a successor to Pete Rozelle illustrates the complexity of multi-party negotiations.

In the non-sports area, environmental and land use disputes generally include many parties and multiple issues. An environmental matter may include one or more states, various federal agencies, state agencies, local governments, Indian tribes, economic interests, labor, homeowners, developers, and environmentalists of several varieties. International negotiations, of course, notoriously include multi-parties and multi-issues.

2. Best Alternative to Negotiated Agreement (BATNA)

The importance of formulating your client's best alternative to a negotiated agreement, and projecting the BATNA of your opponent, cannot be overstated. The BATNA is something that we all devise, usually without thinking of it in formal terms. Fisher and Ury in GETTING TO YES, *supra*, suggest that the negotiator make the BATNA decision a part of the planned preparation and analysis utilized during negotiation.

The BATNA is the standard against which any proposed settlement is measured. The deal must be better than the best alternative existing in lieu of the agreement. Otherwise the deal is unfavorable to your client. Note that the formulation of the BATNA must be realistic. It is not a "best of all worlds" concept. Knowing the BATNA of your client protects against making a bad deal. Formulation of the BATNA forces you to seek imaginative solutions.

Projection of the BATNAs of all parties to the negotiation is essential. Your proposed agreement must be better than the BATNAs of the other parties or settlement is unlikely. Communication is important. A party may overestimate the BATNA. Your task may include persuading a party to take a realistic view of the party's BATNA. Significantly, the BATNA of your client and the BATNAs of all parties may change during the negotiation process. Thus, the negotiator should constantly reevaluate the relative BATNAs of the parties to the negotiation.

3. Shadow of the Law

Negotiation of any kind takes place within the shadow of the law. The shadow may represent case law precedent defining the leverage of one party or another. The uncertainty of litigation exists as an incentive to bargain rather than adjudicate. The law is comprised of the constitution, statutes, agency regulations, agency decisions, and judicial case law. The shadow is cast also by limitations imposed on the negotiation process. For example, the structure of the bargaining process between labor and management is set by the labor laws. Agency regulations determined through negotiation ("reg neg") must be published and opened for public comment under the Administrative Procedure Act. Parties' approach to negotiation differs where a third party will determine the matter in the event the parties fail to reach agreement. In short, the dynamics of negotiation reflect the structure of the process established by the law.

The following analysis contrasts the effect of the process structure upon salary negotiation under the laws of Major League Baseball and the National Football League. Salary negotiation occurs within the framework established by the collective bargaining agreements, the uniform/standard player contracts, and the constitutions and by-laws of the professional leagues.

C. NEGOTIATION OF THE PLAYER-TEAM CONTRACT

Negotiation of player-team contracts requires preparation and analysis in two contexts. First, negotiators must fully understand the factual and legal backgrounds of the league and teams involved in the negotiation. Secondly, negotiators must adequately explore the complexities of each individual case scenario.

1. Background — The Paradigm

The negotiation of player team employment contracts in the various professional sports leagues bears some similarity of approach and undertaking. But, vast differences exist among the sports leagues. The paradigm within which the player and team management conduct the negotiation changes with each league in several ways: 1) shadow of the law; 2) economic realities; 3) custom and tradition. Thus, preparation by attorneys representing both players and management begins with an understanding of the paradigm.

2. Shadow of the Law

As discussed above, the process of negotiation in professional sports is structured according to a hierarchy of agreements. The collective bargaining agreement between labor and management is the supreme law for professional sports employment negotiation. The collective bargaining agreement controls in any conflict with the uniform/standard player contract. The uniform player contract is paramount to the league constitutions and governing documents.

The collective bargaining agreements generally establish the following:

1. minimum salaries, including the salary cap system of the NBA;
2. minimum rights and duties pursuant to uniform/standard player contracts;

3. policy regarding negotiable contract items (allowable amendments to UPC);
4. salary arbitration procedure, if any;
5. free agency system, including compensation arrangements;
6. time schedules for various undertakings; and
7. player eligibility rules, including draft systems.

3. Economic Realities

The economics of the leagues and of respective teams set the boundaries for employment negotiations between players and management. Attorneys representing the parties in player-team contract negotiation must have a working knowledge of economic realities to function adequately.

Economic disparities exist among leagues and teams within a league. Sometimes economic disparities are addressed by league constitutions or collective bargaining agreements. The NBA salary cap system, for example, is a direct offspring of the economic realities of the NBA. The revenue sharing and luxury tax of Major League Baseball enables the prosperous clubs in larger markets to carry, to some extent, weaker teams.

A professional sports team only has limited means of generating revenue. Gate receipts, broadcast revenue, concessions arrangements, advertising sales, marketing of publications, and merchandising are the common sources of team revenues. League rules regarding the division of gate receipts and broadcast revenue between teams are important in understanding the economics of your negotiation scenario. In the NFL, for example, visiting teams receive 40% of gate receipts for regular season games, 50% for pre-season games. Revenue from "luxury boxes" is not shared. Visiting major league baseball teams receive only 20% of the gate receipts. Gate revenue in the NBA and National Hockey League is not divided between the teams at all. Broadcast revenue is generated from national network TV and radio broadcasts, cable transmissions, and local market broadcasts. Network TV revenue is shared on a 50-50 basis. Local broadcast revenue is not split with the visiting club. A simple comparison of the potential of a weaker market as compared to the New York market illustrates the disparity existing between clubs.

4. Custom and Tradition

Professional sports leagues, like non-sports industries, operate partly from custom and tradition. Each league and team is a unique personality resulting from a wide array of experiences and other factors. Attorneys negotiating for players or ballclubs must learn the history of the league and teams within the league. A clear understanding of the demands and parameters of the sport is essential.

5. The Case

The contract matters that are subject to negotiation as amendments or additions to the form player contract differ among leagues and collective bargaining agreements. Generally, the following items are negotiable:

1. salary structure;
2. timing of salary payments;
3. signing or reporting bonuses:
4. roster bonus;
5. incentive and honors bonuses;
6. salary guarantees;
7. fringes and other benefits;
8. trade or no-trade provisions;
9. injury provisions;
10. options;
11. personal conduct provisions;
12. loans; and
13. other special provisions.

Bargaining over the contents of the negotiable items is conducted during the "negotiation dance" with the drama of offers, counter offers, walk outs, hold-outs, public demands, and other ploys. As noted above, most successful negotiators emphasize preparation and analysis as the key elements in the process. Negotiators should be wary of imitating the tactics of other successful agents. Negotiators, like trial attorneys, must operate within their own personalities.

6. Threshold Note — Use of Player Association Resources by Player Agent

The respective player associations possess a wealth of information for the agent representing the player. The management representative, of course, has even more data from league and club files. The availability of the player association data base, in sports terminology, serves to even the score. An efficient agreement cannot be reached unless both parties possess and utilize adequate data, according to traditional negotiation theory.

The player associations release data concerning employment matters in the leagues, including:

1. salary data;
2. bonus standards;
3. salary and other trends;
4. non-salary contract data;
5. information regarding team needs;
6. league and team revenue statistics; and
7. league and team background information.

Player associations also publish newsletters or other materials and conduct seminars for agents. The player agent should develop a working relationship with player association personnel.

7. Salary Matters

Representatives of both parties to the negotiation must possess complete data concerning the salary structure established by the collective bargaining agreement. General salary data, including average salary within the league and average salary by club, position, experience, etc., is available. The salary resulting from negotiation between the parties depends on numerous factors. The skill or ability of the player, needs of the team, and leverage due to free agency or other status combine to provide points of debate between the parties. For many players, the "zone of agreement" for salaries is narrow. Enhancement of compensation features stems from bonus provisions, discussed below. For the star or high draft choice, few limits exist apart from the realities of league and team economics.

Salary payments are sometimes deferred until future dates. The deferred payment plan may benefit the player or management, depending on the trade-offs generated by the negotiation. Knowledge of accounting and tax law is essential. Some agents or team representatives utilize tax consultants for advice concerning salary payment plans. Parties to the negotiation must be aware of league constraints on deferred payment plans.

Salary or contract guarantees are used to assure income in the event the player is injured, released from the team, or otherwise unable to play. The "guarantee clause" may be drafted broadly to cover any contingency, or narrowly to apply in only limited circumstances.

8. Bonuses

Bonus provisions are used to provide money up-front and/or adjust a player's salary according to performance. The various types of bonus provisions are as follows:

Signing or Reporting Bonuses

The signing or reporting bonus functions as an incentive to sign a contract with the team. The signing bonus is similar to the oil and gas lease bonus used to induce the mineral owner to sign the lease. The signing bonus is popular in all professional sports leagues.

Roster Bonuses

The roster bonus is commonly used in the NFL. The bonus is paid only if the player "makes the team" and is placed on the active roster. The roster bonus provision may be drafted broadly to assure payment in the event the player is active for a single game, or narrowly requiring the player to be on the roster for a specified number of games. The roster bonus often is included for non-drafted free agent or low round draft choice players trying-out with the club.

Incentive and Honors Bonuses

The incentive bonus is commonly used in non-sports employment contracts, as well as player-team contracts. The bonus is usually applied where a player reaches a performance standard. The standard may relate to quality or quantity of performance. The negotiating parties must be aware of the league rules regarding incentive bonuses. Major League Baseball, for example, does not allow incentive bonuses for quality of play, such as hits, home runs, etc., but approves bonuses based on quantity of play, including innings played, at bats, etc. Common clauses include bonuses based on the weight of players at a specified time. The clause, designed to provide the player with incentive to accomplish a physical objective or refrain from a physical activity, is similar to the "personal conduct" clause imposing a penalty or fine.

The honors bonus applies when a player receives awards or accolades. Typical bonus provisions apply when the player is voted to the league "All-Star" team, receives an award as "Most Valuable Player" or other honor. The honors bonus provision must be drafted with specificity to avoid future disputes between the parties concerning the scope of the clause.

Sometimes bonus provisions are included for team achievements. Thus, a player may receive a bonus if the team makes the playoffs, wins the World Series, etc. Some player-team contracts provide for bonuses based on fan attendance, a device that is particularly suitable for players possessing fan popularity.

All uniform/standard player contracts allow the club to freely assign the contracts of players. Sometimes, clubs agree to a "no-trade" provision or a clause providing for compensation for the player in the event the player is traded to another team. Importantly, the collective bargaining agreements may limit the issues for negotiation here. Some CBAs require trade approval by players with a specified number of years of service.

Special injury provisions include additional injury insurance for the player. The ballclub may attempt to secure a clause restricting club liability for injuries.

9. Matrix

The matrix is provided for use in working through the problems presented below in this chapter. You may add relevant factors as you discover them. You may wish to change the order of the matrix, or otherwise modify it. The matrix is not carved in stone, but is designed to direct your analysis in negotiating the player team contract.

Negotiation Analysis Matrix

1. The Parties
   a. Relationship of the Parties
   b. Potential Chaos/Past Friction
   c. Possible Cooperation/Future
   d. Options
   e. Incentives to Negotiate
   f. Economic and Other Profile
2. Are the Parties Monolithic?
   a. Potential Internal Conflicts
   b. Possibility of Synchronizing Internal-External Negotiations
   c. Necessity of Ratification
3. Linkage Effects
   a. Linkage with Other Actual Disputes
   b. Linkage with Other Potential Disputes
4. Issues
   a. Multiple/Single Issue
   b. Interacting Issues
   c. Range of Options/Choices
   d. Potential Trade-offs
   e. Flexibility of Parties

5. Time Factors
   a. Place on Salary Schedule
   b. Position re Free Agency
   c. Arbitration Posture
   d. Deadlines for Settlement-Formal
   e. Deadlines for Settlement-Informal
   f. Cost-Delay
6. Context of Negotiation
   a. Public
   b. Private
   c. Mixed
7. Group Norms
   a. Initial Positions
   b. Modified Positions
   c. Value Premises
   d. Negotiation Manners
   e. Attitude Toward Risk
   f. Ego Evaluation
8. Needed Data
   a. Existing Fact Data
   b. Needed Fact Data
   c. Technical/Statistical Analysis
   d. Expert Consultants
   e. Timeliness of Data
   f. Cost of Data Production
   g. Communication of Data
   h. Disputes re Data
9. Shadow of the Law
   a. Collective Bargaining Agreement
   b. Uniform/Standard Player Contract
   c. League Constitution & Governing Documents

   d. Probability Analysis

10. Prospect for Third Party Intervention

   a. Mediation-Externally

   b. Mediation-Internally

   c. Arbitration

   d. Other

11. BATNA of All Parties

Before working the problems, *infra*, consider the following advice:

Donald Dell
MINDING OTHER PEOPLE'S BUSINESS, 139-63 (1989)*

The Art of Negotiating

Twenty years ago the author John McPhee wrote a classic book about tennis called Levels of the Game, a title which referred not only to the levels of skill that separate one class of player from the next, but also to the many psychological levels — all the mental games — that go on during a match.

For me, nothing in business more closely parallels the psychological gamesmanship of competitive sports than negotiating. Perhaps because of my professional athletic back ground, nothing sets my competitive juices flowing faster than knowing I am about to go into a tough, important negotiation.

Whether I am negotiating for a client, for ProServ, or for myself, I find the nuances of the process — the gamesmanship involved — endlessly fascinating.

Donald Trump, for instance, has said that his constant courting of the media is just another negotiating practice: the bigger the "Trump" name becomes, the bigger percentage of deals his partners or adversaries expect him to get.

In my case, I have been accused, on occasion, of being less interested in the negotiating process than in merely getting my way — like a spoiled child who must be placated. This is what so intrigues me about the gamesmanship: If that's what an NBA owner must tell himself in order to justify paying more than he wanted for a player, that's fine with me. In the "inner game" of negotiating, his feeling that we don't "play nicely" becomes another weapon in our arsenal.

There is, however, one significant way in which gamesmanship in negotiating does differ from gamesmanship in sports. In sports there are two opposing general philosophies — that winning is everything" faction at one end of the spectrum and the "it's not whether you win or lose but how you play the game" faction at the other.

But in negotiations, winning or losing is determined by how you play the game.

It's All in the Preparation

I think having been a trial lawyer has helped me as a negotiator in any number of ways, but nothing so much as learning to appreciate that if you enter the courtroom properly prepared, the trial itself is that much easier.

Trials are won or lost in the preparation stage, and so are negotiations. Getting all your ducks in a row and preparing yourself for any eventuality is what wins negotiations, not tricks, artifice, or bluster. I believe so strongly in adequate preparation that when my colleague, David Falk, and I were preparing to negotiate Patrick Ewing's contract with the New York Knicks, we actually conducted several mock negotiation sessions in which we took turns playing Knicks management, each trying to top the other in coming up with the tough questions we thought we'd be asked.

In preparing for a negotiation, what are the kinds of things you should be looking for? First, you need all of the pertinent facts at your fingertips, all the facts, not just the ones that are easy to get.

The good attorney goes into a courtroom fully prepared. He or she knows everything there is to know about the witnesses and what questions to ask. The one thing that can turn around an otherwise winnable trial is the surprise fact or unanticipated answer from a witness. We have one rule around the office whenever anyone is briefing someone else for a meeting: no surprises.

Surprises can also kill you in a negotiation. Many times we will only know 90 percent of the story, and it turns out that the missing element is the one thing that jumps up and bites us later on. As a general rule, the most important facts in a negotiation are the ones known only to the other party, such as their absolute top dollar limit. They are certainly not obligated to reveal to you what you want to know. So you must deduce the facts that you don't know from the facts that you do know. It is the known facts that flush out the unknown facts. The more facts you have at your fingertips going in, the more you are naturally going to pick up along the way.

I can remember negotiating my very first basketball contract for Collis Jones in 1972. The owner of the Milwaukee Bucks said to me, "Our highest club salary is one hundred and fifteen thousand dollars." I said, "I don't believe you." He said, "I'll show you all my contracts."

He showed me three or four contracts, all of which were for under $115,000 a year. What I didn't know at that time (which I certainly have learned, of course) is that annual salary alone for a team sport athlete doesn't mean that much. You have to ask: How much money is deferred? What about loans and other forms of compensation? Is there a signing bonus? What are the incentive bonuses? The reporting bonuses? and so on down the list.

The only "defense" against this sort of ignorance is knowledge and experience — knowing the facts. Today, with the help of the players' association, we know what every basketball player is paid and how the compensation packages have been structured. There is a great power of precedent in any negotiation. If you know every salary in the league, you know almost as much as the owners do. Now we never have to guess about salaries anymore.

We also must know the facts that will justify our asking prices. What we try to do is take our figures out of the realm of subjective measurement of the athlete's talent and into a level of more objective criteria such as the player's value to the team and his or her name draw in bringing fans into the arena. In team sports, we have practically become economists in certain negotiations.

Becoming the equivalent of an "economist" in your area — a master of the facts, whatever they are — is crucial to your success. Although you might be concerned with banking or design or law or advertising, there is a body of specific information that could make you or break you.

For us, it's the difficult task of determining one man or woman's commercial worth. With an athlete such as a Michael Jordan, we will factor in his value to the franchise if Chicago Bulls owner Jerry Reinsdorf decides to sell the team. Additionally, Michael puts fans in the seats, brings PR value and excitement to the city of Chicago, allows the Bulls to raise ticket prices, and even lets them make better arena and concession deals for themselves. All these economic factors must be figured in to justify the player's value to and impact on the team — and therefore his or her real worth in that situation.

Though a client's value and impact is one way to measure a fair price, we must also rely on experience and instinct to determine what something is worth. I call it having a real "sense of the market" — the X factor. It's the same when an expert in real estate looks at a piece of property and says, "That's worth five hundred dollars an acre rather than one thousand dollars an acre." The expert is bringing all of his or her prior knowledge to bear on determining the value of that particular real estate. Anyone who represents clients in any field should have some sort of sense of his or her client's intrinsic market value. If the representative doesn't, he or she probably doesn't have the right "feel" for the business anyway.

Before going into any negotiation involving money, you also need to know all the factors relating to the size of the pot. No business can operate indefinitely at a loss. Whether that business is IBM or an NBA franchise, it can't afford to pay its employees more than it takes in in revenues.

Yet pro basketball owners, many of whom made their millions in some other business, were such profligate spenders that, in 1983, in order to protect themselves from themselves, they negotiated a player's salary cap with the NBA players' association. The problem is, the formula by which the cap is determined is so complicated that almost no one understands it or can figure it out

— especially the owners. As a result, the salary cap has had the ironic effect of giving us an edge in basketball negotiations.

David Falk, in our office, has an almost photographic memory of the salary cap of every NBA team. Since the salary cap was instituted, I doubt that we have had a player negotiation during which the owner hasn't said, usually as their first line of defense, "We can't do that because of the salary cap."

David will respond, "But if you trade so-and-so, as you plan to, then you can make the cap work." this puts us at a great advantage because the owners immediately know that we know as much (or even more) about their ultimate maneuverability under the salary cap rules as they do.

You also need to know the size of the pot because there is definitely such a thing as a "Pyrrhic" negotiating victory, which occurs when you get your price, but you so severely handicap the other party, he or she either can't or won't want to deal with you again. If we are negotiating with a local tennis promoter who is putting on a one-night exhibition, we can't very well insist on an extra 10 percent if his profit margin is so slim that it makes his whole effort a breakeven or loss proposition.

We want to make sure he makes money, because if he does, he will call us in six months or in a year to promote another event. If he loses money, we may never hear from him again. He'll be out of business, and we'll be chasing a debt we are never going to collect.

Sowing Some Seeds

Once you know all the facts you can possibly know, there are opportunities to put some of these facts to work even before you get down to the real nitty-gritty of negotiation. . . .

To use your known facts to "seed" a forthcoming negotiation obviously demands a certain amount of anticipation.

The year we represented UCLA basketball star Marques Johnson, we were fairly certain he would be drafted number three by the Milwaukee Bucks, who that year also held the number-one draft choice. That represented a problem for us because everyone knew that Indiana all-American Kent Benson would be drafted number one that year. Why was that a problem? Because Benson's agent wasn't very experienced and also had formerly worked for the Bucks organization, we were afraid that Benson was going to end up with a low contract. If they drafted Marques, they would expect him to accept an even lesser contract at the number-three position in the NBA draft.

To head off the trouble I was expecting, I called the Bucks owner, Jim Fitzgerald, the day before the draft. "Please don't draft Marques Johnson tomorrow," I said.

"Why?" he asked. I explained, "Please don't draft Marques Johnson because he's the best player in the draft, even though he won't go until the third or fourth pick. And I'm telling you right now that he's going to cost more money than Kent Benson because he's a much better player. If you choose to draft him, understand that we're going to demand more money than you are going to end up paying Benson. So what I'm suggesting is that if you're not prepared to do that, don't waste your number-three draft choice on Johnson."

With that call I was in a win/win position. If Milwaukee did draft Marques, I had the perfect argument: "I told you we were going to demand more than Benson got." If they didn't draft him, then we would go to Chicago, who needed him more than Milwaukee needed him anyway.

As it turned out, the Bucks drafted Marques. Sure enough, as we began negotiating, they trotted out Benson's contract to convince me. I pushed it back unread and when we set our price, Fitzgerald said, "That's crazy. How can you expect us to pay Johnson more than the very first player selected in the NBA draft?" I said, "I told you last week I was going to ask for more than you had to pay Benson."

Ultimately, four months later, he agreed to our price.

Cutting Off the Thems and Theys

The oldest negotiating trick in the world — so old, in fact, that it isn't even a trick anymore — is to go through the entire negotiating process and then have the other party say, "This looks fine, but now I've got to get the final okay from my president." The ploy is to come back and say apologetically, "My boss wouldn't accept these figures. I'm afraid we'll have to work out an agreement at a lower dollar amount."

One of the facts you need to know before going into a negotiation is who the ultimate decision maker is going to be and whether the person with whom you are negotiating has the authority to bind his organization. You need to cut off the "thems and theys."

If you suspect the other side will pull the old "I-have-to-check this-out-with-the boss" routine, you should spell it out at the outset: "I want to deal with the decision maker. If you're not the decision maker, let me talk to the right person. Who do I negotiate with — you or someone else?"

Actually the client manager has a very subtle advantage in that with rare exception he or she cannot bind the client. The knack is to keep the other party from having the same "out."

Naming Numbers

As negotiating has become an increasingly popular business subject, I have read and heard over and over again that the actual amount of money involved in a negotiation is only one of the crucial items that needs discussion and may indeed not even be among the most important items.

As a general rule, this is absolute hogwash! Obviously, any negotiation involves more than money. That's why agreements can often be thirty pages long rather than three pages or why negotiations can go on several months or even years rather than hours or days.

Most negotiated terms emanate from the size of the dollars. Paradoxically, I would bet in almost any business that the contracts with the biggest numbers attached to them are also the contracts with the best terms across the board and the most favorable language. This observation belies the conventional wisdom that negotiation is a process of trading off.

When it comes right down to it, there are really only two ways to negotiate numbers. Ninety percent of negotiations come down to a game of highball/lowball: You name this number, I name that number, and we end up somewhere in between. This to me is a lazy man's, ineffective way to negotiate.

The other way is to come in with your ducks in a row, set your price based upon justifiable facts, and stay there. Over the years we have had success in doing the latter, based largely on sound preparation — knowledge of the market — and coming in armed with a set of advantageous facts.

We may ask a large sum of money in some negotiations for our clients, but it will never be a number out of touch with reality, either for the player or for the marketplace. The offer will always be one that we can justify, not just to the other party, but in our own minds as well. When we explain why we think an athlete is worth X dollars, the club we're negotiating with may say, "I don't like your offer," but they can rarely say, "I think your offer is off the wall."

As anyone who has ever negotiated knows, if you're planning to name your number and stick to it, being able to justify your offer with tangible facts may get you, under ideal circumstances, as far as first base.

What we try to do is get all the way home. What we have done successfully in the past is to establish a presence, a palpable sense that we aren't kidding, that we mean what we say. If you choose to negotiate this way, there are no tricks, but there are certain rules and guidelines that you are best advised to follow.

• **You must be able to walk away.** The first rule of negotiation, any kind of negotiation, is that you have to be able to walk away from the table. You have to know before you sit down that you can say, "No, I'm not going to accept that." If you get into a situation where you **must** make a deal, it severely limits your ability to make the deal you want because you yourself know at the end of the day you can't pack up and walk away. Everything then becomes a bluff, and you never want to be in a situation where you are having to bluff your way through a negotiation.

There are times when I have been too reckless, when I've walked away from deals that maybe we should have done. But that might be the price you have to pay to get your clients what they deserve the other 95 percent of the time.

• **Use the power of precedent.** Let's say the other side offers $300,000 and you offer $800,000, and they say, "Can we compromise at six hundred thousand?" and you say, "No, we're going to be at eight hundred thousand four months from now because that's what we think the deal is worth." If you can then refer to five other negotiations in which you didn't budge from your number, your position carries more weight when it comes time for them to decide whether you are serious or not.

The power of precedent and presence is one of the real values of having someone with experience represent you in any sort of negotiation. The representative can point to his or her track record, even if it's in a different field or sport.

• **When to make the first offer.** The first offer from the other side is no more than a piece of information, and it can tell you volumes. Here's why: If our figure going into a negotiation is a million dollars a year, but the other side opens with an offer of $900,000, right away we know we may not be asking enough. If their opening offer is $200,000, that tells us that this is going to be a long, tough negotiation.

You force the other side to name their price first, not to be disagreeable, but because you want to know what their opening number is, which gives you a significant edge in the negotiations.

* * *

The one exception to having the other side go first would be if you suspect that their offer will be so low that you want to get yours on the table first. The idea is to "shame" the other side and discourage them from making such an "embarrassingly low" first offer.

* * *

Make Them Believe You

In order for a statement such as, "I'm not going to make an offer, not today, not tomorrow, not ever" to be effective the other side has to believe that you are serious. That is the essence of naming your number and getting it. Your credibility is on the line.

In many negotiations, there comes a **moment of truth**. There is a point where you come together and you say, "We're going to do X, and we're not going to do any more." They reply, "We're going to pay Y, and we're not going to pay more." The fundamental task is for me to know whether they mean it. Or for them to know whether we mean it.

When I say, "Our player is worth eight hundred thousand dollars, that's his market value, and here's why it's his market value, and we're not budging. Either pay the eight hundred thousand dollars or he's sitting out," the other side has to know that I'm dead serious, or else my client is going to end up with a lot less money.

* * *

Understand and Use Leverage

Leverage, or which side needs the deal more, is central to any negotiation and the price you are eventually going to get. The key is recognizing the leverage you have and not being afraid to use it.

Both professional basketball and football, for instance, instituted the player draft system to prevent bidding wars among the owners. What they failed to consider is that as a result, they are virtually obligated to sign their first draft choice. If they fail to do so, this sends an awful message to the fans and ticket holders and the advertisers who support the team locally. Appreciating the value of a first round draft choice is what I mean by recognizing leverage when you have it.

* * *

Outlast Them — and Don't Negotiate with Lamar Hunt

It often comes down to this, and the one advantage I find I have in negotiating is that I am extremely determined and sometimes a little stubborn.

What happens when both sides are equally stubborn? As the coach of Notre Dame once said, when asked what happens when Notre Dame plays Holy Cross and both teams pray in the locker room for victory, "Sit back and watch one hell of a ball game."

A number of years ago I was engaged in a marathon negotiating session in Washington, D.C., with Lamar Hunt, founder of the WCT Tennis Circuit and owner of the Kansas City Chiefs football team. The negotiations had gone on all day and had proceeded well into the night. It became obvious that Lamar was trying to outlast me in a battle of wills, and I was simply not going to give in. As the evening wore on, I found myself bordering on fatigue and incoherence.

At one point I excused myself to go to the bathroom, but my real mission was to splash cold water on my face to try to revive myself. When I returned to my office, I found Lamar on the floor doing push-ups!

* * *

When Opportunity Knocks . . .

Other than being well prepared and having all your facts and figures at your fingertips, perhaps nothing is more fundamental to successful negotiating than knowing how to be opportunistic.

What is opportunism? It is two things really. First, it is knowing how best to use any leverage you have going into a negotiation in a practical way. Second, like the good trial lawyer (or, as I mentioned earlier, a good salesperson), it is knowing how to take advantage of the informational crumbs that may inadvertently be tossed your way during the negotiation itself.

* * *

The Art of the Middleman

In order to represent your clients most effectively, you must also be cognizant and sensitive to the needs of the person to whom those interests are being represented. That is the art of being a middleman, the person charged with making the deal happen, but making it a deal that leaves both parties satisfied. Situation ethics comes into play; your judgment must constantly stand up to your own personal sense of what is right.

As a lawyer in a criminal case, the ethics are very clear; you do everything short of breaking the law to try to get your client off. But after the trial is over, the client does not then become partners with the prosecution. When you're representing a client in the sports business, that is exactly what happens. Often your client has to live in harmony with the "enemy" on the other side of the bargaining table once a deal is done.

This is one of the reasons we rarely tell our team sport clients what the clubs originally offered for their services. We don't want the client to hold a grudge against his prospective employer, if he would be upset or disappointed by it.

Most of the time, though, these "playing God" decisions are not so clear-cut. One time an advertising agency with whom we had done a lot of business had inadvertently used a photograph of Ivan Lendl in a print ad without permission or paying the normal fees. When we brought this to their attention, the agency said, "You're right. We did it. How can we settle this?" Here was our dilemma. On the one hand we had an obligation to Lendl to negotiate just as hard on his behalf as if this were a "clean deal." On the other hand, if we, in essence, forced the company into paying an unreasonably large fee, we would be earning their eternal enmity for Lendl.

Complicating the picture even further: Where did our own self-interest lie? If we did not have an ongoing relationship with this agency, would we be as likely to be agreeable? Having to answer these sort of questions isn't always fun. It helps to have certain guiding principles you can apply to these middleman situations.

In ProServ's case, we want to make a deal that we refer to as "the high end of fair." In other words, we want to get as much as we reasonably can for our client, but we also want to make a deal that is ultimately fair for both sides.

Sometimes I will say to one of our young guys, "You did a great job, but the company can't afford it. You made too good a deal for your client."

Even if the company is foolish enough to make the deal, it will come back to haunt you. They will get out of it legally or illegally at their first opportunity, and that will be the end of your relationship with that company. Part of knowing how to use leverage is knowing how **not** to overuse it. The other side knows when you have ramrodded a deal down their throats to meet a specific revenue objective for a client, and they will resent you for it. You may have won the battle, but you will have surely lost the war.

The better strategy is to get what you need out of the deal and to allow the other side to get what it needs out of the deal. Be fair and reasonable. That way, you will do business over and over again. Most often, the best deals are the fairest ones for both sides.

Which brings us back to the Lendl example above. What did we do? We settled for $40,000. The agency didn't feel like we had taken advantage of them and because we were paying attention to our client's interests, Lendl ended up with some money. When Lendl asked us where the money had come from, we said, "An ad agency inadvertently used your picture, and they're paying you forty thousand dollars for their mistake."

The Price You Sometimes Have to Pay

The one caveat to the preceding advice is that if you have to err, you must always err on the side of your client. Anyone who is going to be successful in the personal service business must accept up front that during the course of your business life, there are times when you are going to lose certain relationships if you are consistently serving your clients' best interests.

* * *

Try to Understand Where the Other Side Is Coming From

Sometimes the same deal can "smell" a lot better to the other side, simply by showing a little courtesy and sensitivity.

After months of agonizing back and forth while negotiating with the New Jersey Nets for all-star power forward Buck Williams, we were finally an inch away from making a deal that would pay Buck nearly $1.5 million per year. I was impatient to close this thing, as was Buck Williams. As we went into our umpteenth meeting, I figured the day had come when I could finally push them into signing the agreement.

I was pressuring them pretty hard when the Nets head owner said to me, "Donald, I don't want to seem personal, but do you make this kind of money in a year?" I looked at him like he was crazy. "Of course not," I said. "Not even close." The owner said, "Thanks, I was just curious."

After the meeting ended, I asked David Falk, who had been in the meeting with me, "What did he mean by that?" "What he meant," David chuckled, "is that one point five million dollars is a lot of money. They need another day to feel comfortable about paying somebody that much. They need another day to feel good about the deal." He was right, of course, and if I had been a little more sensitive about the situation, I could have figured that out for myself, for I had forgotten what the best negotiations are all about: striking a deal that everyone feels good about. Knowing from the start that there is such a point — where all interests converge and are served — is the secret of the best deal makers in business.

* * *

Michael Wheeler
First, Let's Kill All the Agents!
in NEGOTIATING ON BEHALF OF OTHERS, Ch. 8

(Mnookin & Susskind eds. 1999)*

Agents and Professional Sports

How much a given player earns depends in part on his skill and the demand for people who play his particular position, but the amount is also significantly influenced by legal factors. . . . The collective bargaining agreements impose constraints on both buyer and seller, so that very few of these transactions are really constructed at arm's length. Unlike the disgruntled customers in an automobile showroom, most players cannot simply walk away from an unsatisfactory offer and take their business to someone else down the street. Teams likewise are bound in varying degrees to their players.

The singular exception are so-called pure free agent players who, by virtue of their seniority, can sell their services to the highest bidder, leaving their previous team empty-handed. . . . In virtually all other instances, the no-agreement alternative still involves some kind of continuing rights or relationship, the contractual definition of which bears heavily on the balance of power between team and player. For example, the bargaining power of an unsigned amateur or collegiate player is severely constrained by the rules of governing professional drafts. . . . A young athlete has real leverage only if he plays two sports or if he is lucky enough to turn pro when an upstart league is offering competitive wages.

If anything, however, a player has even less bargaining power once he has signed a professional contract. Collective bargaining agreements typically require several years of major league service before a player qualifies even for arbitration rights. . . .

This option changes the player's best alternative to negotiated agreement (BATNA) and provides some cushion against unreasonable offers. . . . The respective expectations of team and player shape to some degree their demands at the bargaining table. Nevertheless, the team and the player remain tied together in an asymmetrical relationship; the player has nothing equivalent to the team's right to trade his contract to another team.

Salary is usually at the heart of contract negotiations, whatever the player's status and non-agreement alternatives, but other issues can have monetary, precedence-setting, and symbolic importance.

* * *

Standard Negotiation Analysis

The conventional way of understanding these negotiations would be to depict them as bargains within a zone of possible agreement (ZOPA) lying between the respective values that each party places on its perceived BATNA.

* * *

Strictly speaking, even with price the sole issue, this is not a zero-sum transaction. Instead, the amount represented by the difference between P [team's maximum price] and T [player's lowest acceptable price] is a surplus that is jointly generated if — and only if — the parties can come to an agreement. The resulting negotiation over how that surplus should be divided, however, is purely distributive. One side can gain only at the expense of the other.

Some might quarrel with characterizing sports contract negotiation as fundamentally distributive. The introduction of other issues (guarantees, contract extensions, etc.) supposedly should allow value-creating trades, at least if the parties' preferences, expectations, and risk profiles differ. . . .

The ZOPA . . . might be expanded by crafting a longer-term deal, spreading payments efficiently, or building in some contingencies. The question, however, is how much weight players and teams give these other factors, relative to the salary issue, and whether their preferences differ in such a way as to significantly expand the zone of possible agreement. There apparently has not been any rigorous analysis of this question, but there is little anecdotal evidence to support the belief in the possibility of tremendous mutual gains. After all, we do not hear stories of players and teams who were miles apart on salary yet managed to salvage agreement through ingenious deal structuring.

If anything, there is ample reason to conclude that opportunities for value creation are relatively limited in this domain. . . . In practice, however, incentive clauses are sometimes used, but they usually make up a small portion of the economic value of a contract. Thus, a player earning several million dollars in salary might be eligible for bonuses of 5% or 10% of that for being named most valuable player in the league. That teams and players do not make these a bigger element of their agreements likely says much about their relative preferences. Ancillary clauses likewise appear in contracts but typically as deal closers, a face-saving device to bridge relatively small salary gaps. . . .

In short, the persistence of hard bargaining over salary testifies to the relatively low importance of other common provisions. Sports contract negotiation appears to be fundamentally dollar-driven, hence largely distributive in both theory and execution. At first blush, it would seem easy to capture this dynamic in the familiar ZOPA model . . . , yet this may misrepresent the actual process. . . . The concept of a zone of possible agreement is crisp and familiar, so much so that we seldom consider the assumptions on which it is based.

* * *

This is a compelling model, to be sure, but it can trap us into examining only what occurs within the zone of possible agreement. . . . Instead of reasoning backward from the fact of final agreement to infer a latent zone of agreement, this chapter offers an alternative view of the process. . . . [I]t argues that when these negotiations begin, the reservation prices of teams and players are often far apart. Furthermore, agents and general managers often recognize that when they sit down to bargain, there may be no ZOPA. Such expectations would surely influence the ensuing negotiation process.

An Alternative Framework: From ZOPA to NOPA

Imagine a situation where a player's minimum acceptable salary is more than the maximum that his team is prepared to pay. Agreement would be possible only if at least one of those parties subsequently revises its reservation price (or if sufficient value can be created to bridge the gap by trading on other issues). . . . The outcomes . . . represent unacceptable compromises, with each side favoring nonagreement over any available option. We might call this the NOPA line for "no possible agreement."

There are compelling reasons to believe that this model more accurately depicts player contract negotiations. One is the peculiar nature of BATNA in professional sports, specifically the fact that the team and player are usually locked together contractually. The BATNA is not really "no deal"; it is the prospect of an agreement at a later point — when the other side finally comes to its senses or caves in. Players do not choose between a lucrative offer from the team and pumping gas . . . , but, instead, choose between that offer and the expected result of continued bargaining.

Interlocked BATNAs are not unique to sports. They are a basic feature of labor-management negotiation, of course, though in other industries, parties' expectations are usually bound by common understanding of market conditions. . . . In sports, by contrast, there is not the same kind of market discipline.

Comparability is a problem as well. The highest paid players are not necessarily the best performers, and their salaries become bones of contention in other negotiations. . . . The breadth of pay ranges compounds the problem. One player may earn 10 or even 100 times as much as some of his teammates. Emotion is surely a factor as well. The same kind of ego and drive that allow an athlete to excel at the highest level of competition probably correlates with a high sense of self-worth. General managers struggling to keep up with an inflationary market may likewise tend to be a day late and a pound short in terms of anticipating what their players will require. Role bias is common in many settings; the culture of sports may be an ideal medium where it can breed.

The NOPA gap may be deepened if parties start thinking in terms of right or wrong, not just economics. . . . Separating the people from the problem may be especially difficult in this kind of arena. Likewise, searching for underlying interests, creative options, and objective criteria may not get at the underlying dynamic of typical sports negotiations. In fact, there are several deep forces that tend to make the process adversarial.

First, the player's economic interests are inevitably bound up in his identity. . . . To concede on salary is to admit one's shortcomings to the world and oneself.

Second, the potential for creative deal structuring to bridge gaps is real but limited. The primacy of the salary issue makes it almost impossible to separate the expansion of the pie from its division.

Third, as already noted, attempts to use "comparables" might actually drive the negotiators farther apart if each sees the other's as self-serving. . . .

These contextual factors would be obstacles to interest-based negotiation even when a team is negotiating directly with a player. If anything, they may be amplified when agents sit at the bargaining table in place of players; specifically, agents may often have even less incentive to consider interests, options, and neutral criteria as means to joint problem solving.

First, as to underlying interests, agents typically compete for players by ambitious claims about what they can win for their clients. . . . An agent can subsequently get trapped by such promises, of course, but they also can become self-fulfilling commitments.

Second, differences between the agent's interests and those of his client can further inhibit value creation. . . .

Third, the agent must also take into account the collective interests of his stable of clients — particularly when their long-term financial success will redound to him personally. . . .

Finally, the fact that agents know that they may be called on to act as advocates when arbitration is a possibility may also make it hard for them to be dispassionate value creators at the bargaining table. (The same may be true for zealous litigators.) . . .

In short, strong institutional and social factors promote hard bargaining on the part of sports agents. This may not be inevitable, but practices and attitudes . . . are consistent with a view of negotiation *not* as moves in or toward a zone of possible agreement but, instead, as responses to genuine gaps between the expectations of players and their teams.

Furthermore, if parties see the bargaining game as one in which they have to significantly change the other side's reservation price, then communicating one's own unwillingness to budge becomes critical. (Again, this is particularly important where the BATNA is not a pure walkaway but the expectation of cutting a more favorable deal sometime in the future.) The temptation to issue threats and ultimatums may well be strong. Such tactics may lead to an uncontrolled escalation of hostilities in which pride and face loom large. Even without personal animosity, it may be difficult to pursue interest-based negotiation when offers and counteroffers are volleyed back and forth in the press.

Contract negotiations in these situations are not conducted along a bargaining range, with the parties moving from extreme positions to some intermediate zone of possible agreement. Instead, they constitute a dynamic process in which each side is trying to swing the line of *non*agreement . . . in its favor until it lies in acceptable territory.

Sports agents may be especially suited to this hardball task. As already noted, they have an ongoing professional interest in not appearing to be weak. Whereas a player might bargain once a year at most, agents build their reputations through multiple negotiations. Agents also offer tactical advantage. Because they do not suffer the consequences of a poor relationship, they can play the heavy, setting high demands and holding a player out while insulating the client from retaliatory threats.

Those who represent the players, however, are not the only agents in these transactions. The teams typically are represented by general managers (GMs) who are neither owners nor playing field coaches. The GMs have incentives and interests that are not perfectly parallel with those of others in their organizations, especially as they contend with conflicting mandates. . . .

The perceived toughness of a GM depends in part on the priorities of his employer. Some teams essentially operate as corporate franchises. . . . General managers in such situations may have a budget just as would the heads of any other business units. Whenever they negotiate one player's contract, they must be mindful of what will be left for others on the team.

Other general managers work for teams owned by wealthy individuals whose interests in profits may be dwarfed by a personal compulsion to be a "winner" or at least be in the media spotlight. . . .

Occasionally, one person holds the dual role of general manager and on-the-field coach. The usual practice, however, is to separate these functions, in part because they require different skills but also because of the perceived advantage of having one person hammer out the contracts while leaving the other to build successful working relationships with the players. This separation likewise may reinforce the tendency toward hard bargaining.

Problem

James Boyd is a left-handed pitcher with the Chicago White Sox. Boyd and the club's general manager will meet next week to negotiate Boyd's salary for next year.

The White Sox are tendering a one-year, nonguaranteed contract for the minimum salary allowed under the Basic Agreement.

Use the matrix, *supra*, to analyze the fact scenario and the following materials. Develop the initial positions of the two parties. What modifications are likely to occur during the negotiation process? What should be the final salary?

Biography of James Boyd

James P. Boyd

3-14-19____ 26 years of age

Experience: 1 year

Statistics: Last Season

Boyd was on the active roster for the full season. He pitched in 32 games/9 games started; 96 2/3 innings pitched; allowed 98 hits; walked 60 (9 intentional) and struck out 86. Boyd allowed 4.23 earned runs per nine innings. He won 1, lost 4, and saved 4 games.

Scouting Report: Last Season

Boyd has an 83 mph fastball (major league average = 85 mph); slider; curve; and change-up. Needs work on change-up to be effective. Boyd is the ninth pitcher on the White Sox roster of ten pitchers. White Sox have two pitchers at AAA who will challenge Boyd for the roster position. Three pitchers are at AA level and will be ready the year after next. Boyd is important to the White Sox while the team rebuilds its roster to championship quality, but he is unlikely to be around once it is rebuilt. However, Boyd can start or relieve. His control has improved. He has a variety of pitches. Attitude is good. Might be a good organization man for coaching later.

NOTES TO THE FILE

James Boyd is engaged to be married in June of next year. He is marrying the daughter of the owner of a restaurant chain in Chicago. Boyd's father-in-law told him that he could have a management job anytime he desires. The starting salary is $225,000. Boyd's projected restaurant income at the end of three years is $500,000, and the transfer of ownership interest that should enable him to buy the business over a ten-year period.

Boyd desires to play ball for as long as he can make a major league roster. He has no desire to return to the minor leagues as a player. He would consider coaching if the opportunity arose. Boyd has no college opportunities or desire.

Boyd feels that he has little security with the White Sox. He knows, however, that the White Sox pitching coach likes him and feels that Boyd is a reliable pitcher. Boyd's earned run average (earned runs per nine innings pitched) with runners in scoring position was 2.92. In short, he pitched well in the clutch. Boyd wants more than the minimum offered. He feels that the general manager remains irritated over the negotiations surrounding Boyd's signing with the White Sox after college five years ago.

The 2003-2006 Basic Agreement sets the minimum salary for 2003 and 2004 at the rate per season of $300,000. The 2005 minimum is established at $300,000, plus a cost of living adjustment, based on the Consumer Price Index for Urban Wage Earners and Clerical Workers published by the Bureau of Labor Statistics, and rounded to the nearest $500. To determine the rate, $300,000 is multiplied by a fraction, the numerator of which is the CPIW for November 2004, and the denominator for which is the CPIW for November 2002. The 2006 minimum salary is the 2005 rate per season plus a cost of living adjustment. The 2005 salary rate is multiplied by a fraction, the numerator of which is the CPIW for November 2005 and the denominator of which is the CPIW for November 2004. BASIC AGREEMENT, Art. VI(B). The Basic Agreement may be accessed at the official MLBPA site: www.mlbpa.com. Comparative player statistics and salaries are generally available via the internet and USA Today.

The Chicago White Sox player salaries are under the average for the league. The White Sox management vests large sums in several superstars, and does not anticipate paying greater than minimum-to-average salaries for support players. The management has the support of the Chicago community and surrounding areas. Progressive marketing joined with frugal operations result in a stable ballclub operation with a future. Reductions in TV contract revenue, however, offset the other financial advantages.

Major League
Uniform Player's Contract

Parties

Between ______________________________ herein called the Club, and

_________________________ of _________________________, herein called the Player.

Recital

The Club is, along with other Major League Cubs, signatory to the Major League Constitution and has subscribed to the Major League Rules.

Agreement

In consideration of the facts above recited and of the promises of each to the other, the parties agree as follows:

Employment

1. The Club hereby employs the Player to render, and the Player agrees to render, skilled services as a baseball player during the year(s) [20____] including the Club's training season, the Club's exhibition games, the Club's playing season, the League Championship Series and the World Series (or any other offi-

cial series in which the Club may participate and in any receipts of which the Player may be entitled to share).

Payment

2. For performance of the Player's services and promises hereunder the Club will pay the Player the sum of $____________________________________

____

____ in semi-monthly installments after the commencement of the championship season(s) covered by this contract except as the schedule of payments may be modified by a special covenant. Payment shall be made on the day the amount becomes due, regardless of whether the Club is "home" or "abroad." If a monthly rate of payment is stipulated above, it shall begin with the commencement of the championship season (or such subsequent date as the Player's services may commence) and end with the termination of the championship season and shall be payable in semi-monthly installments as above provided.

Nothing herein shall interfere with the right of the Club and the Player by special covenant herein to mutually agree upon a method of payment whereby part of the Player's salary for the above year can be deferred to subsequent years.

If the Player is in the service of the Club for part of the championship season only, he shall receive such proportion of the sum above mentioned, as the number of days of his actual employment in the championship season bears to the number of days in the championship season. Notwithstanding the rate of payment stipulated above, the minimum rate of payment to the Player for each day of service on a Major League Club shall be at the applicable rate set forth in Article VI(B)(1) of the Basic Agreement between the thirty Major League Clubs and the Major League Baseball Players Association, effective September 30, 2002 ("Basic Agreement"). The minimum rate of payment for Minor League service for all Players (a) signing a second Major League contract (not covering the same season as any such Player's initial Major League contract) or a subsequent Major League contract, or (b) having at least one day of Major League Service, shall be at the applicable rate set forth in Article VI(B)(2) of the Basic Agreement.

Payment to the Player at the rate stipulated above shall be continued throughout any period in which a Player is required to attend a regularly scheduled military encampment of the Reserve of the Armed Forces or of the National Guard during the championship season.

Loyalty

3.(a) The Player agrees to perform his services hereunder diligently and faithfully, to keep himself in first-class physical condition and to obey the Club's training rules, and pledges himself to the American public and to the Club to conform to high standards of personal conduct, fair play and good sportsmanship.

Baseball Promotion

3.(b) In addition to his services in connection with the actual playing of baseball, the Player agrees to cooperate with the Club and participate in any and all reasonable promotional activities of the Club and its League, which, in the opinion of the Club, will promote the welfare of the Club or professional baseball, and to observe and comply with all reasonable requirements of the Club respecting conduct and service of its team and its players, at all times whether on or off the field.

Pictures and Public Appearances

3.(c) The Player agrees that his picture may be taken for still photographs, motion pictures or television at such times as the Club may designate and agrees that all rights in such pictures shall belong to the Club and may be used by the Club for publicity purposes in any manner it desires. The Player further agrees that during the playing season he will not make public appearances, participate in radio or television programs or permit his picture to be taken or write or sponsor newspaper or magazine articles or sponsor commercial products without the written consent of the Club, which shall not be withheld except in the reasonable interests of the Club or professional baseball.

PLAYER REPRESENTATIONS

Ability

4.(a) The Player represents and agrees that he has exceptional and unique skill and ability as a baseball player; that his services to be rendered hereunder are of a special, unusual and extraordinary character which gives them peculiar value which cannot be reasonably or adequately compensated for in damages at law, and that the Player's breach of this contract will cause the Club great and irreparable injury and damage. The Player agrees that, in addition to other remedies, the Club shall be entitled to injunctive and other equitable relief to prevent a breach of this contract by the Player, including, among others, the right to enjoin the Player from playing baseball for any other person or organization during the term of his contract.

Condition

4.(b) The Player represents that he has no physical or mental defects known to him and unknown to the appropriate representative of the Club which would prevent or impair performance of his services.

Interest in Club

4.(c) The Player represents that he does not, directly or indirectly, own stock or have any financial interest in the ownership or earnings of any Major League Club, except as hereinafter expressly set forth, and covenants that he will not hereafter, while connected with any Major League Club, acquire or hold any such stock or interest except in accordance with Major League Rule 20(e).

Service

5.(a) The Player agrees that, while under contract, and prior to expiration of the Club's right to renew this contract, he will not play baseball otherwise than for the Club, except that the Player may participate in postseason games under the conditions prescribed in the Major League Rules. Major League Rule 18(b) is set forth herein.

Other Sports

5.(b) The Player and the Club recognize and agree that the Player's participation in certain other sports may impair or destroy his ability and skill as a baseball player. Accordingly, the Player agrees that he will not engage in professional boxing or wrestling; and that, except with the written consent of the Club, he will not engage in skiing, auto racing, motorcycle racing, sky diving, or in any game or exhibition of football, soccer, professional league basketball, ice hockey or other sport involving a substantial risk of personal injury.

Assignment

6.(a) The Player agrees that this contract may be assigned by the Club (and reassigned by any assignee Club) to any other Club in accordance with the Major League Rules. The Club and the Player may, without obtaining special approval, agree by special covenant to limit or eliminate the right of the Club to assign this contract

Medical Information

6.(b) The Player agrees:

(1) That the Club's physician and any other physician consulted by the Player pursuant to Regulation 2 of this contract or Article XIII(D) of the Basic Agreement may furnish to the Club all relevant medical information relating to the Player; and

(2) That, should the Club contemplate an assignment of this contract to another Club or clubs, the Club's physician may furnish to the physicians and officials of such other Club or clubs all relevant medical information relating to the Player.

No Salary Reduction

6.(c) The amount stated in paragraph 2 and in special covenants hereof which is payable to the Player for the period stated in paragraph 1 hereof shall not be diminished by any such assignment, except for failure to report as provided in the next subparagraph (d).

Reporting

6.(d) The Player shall report to the assignee Club promptly (as provided in the Regulation) upon receipt of written notice from the Club of the assignment of this contract. If the Player fails to so report, he shall not be entitled to any payment for the period from the date he receives written notice of assignment until he reports to the assignee Club.

Obligations of Assignor and Assignee Clubs

6.(e) Upon and after such assignment, all rights and obligations of the assignor Club hereunder shall become the rights and obligations of the assignee Club; provided, however, that

(1) The assignee Club shall be liable to the Player for payments accruing only from the date of assignment and shall not be liable but the assignor Club shall remain liable for payments accrued prior to that date.

(2) If at any time the assignee is a Major League Club, it shall be liable to pay the Player at the full rate stipulated in paragraph 2 hereof for the remainder of the period stated in paragraph 1 hereof and all prior assignors and assignees shall be relieved of liability for any payment for such period.

(3) Unless the assignor and assignee Clubs agree otherwise, if the assignee Club is a National Association Club, the assignee Club shall be liable only to pay the Player at the rate usually paid by said assignee Club to other Players of similar skill and ability in its classification and the assignor Club shall be liable to pay the difference for the remainder of the period stated in paragraph 1 hereof between an amount computed at the rate stipulated in paragraph 2 hereof and the amount so payable by the assignee Club.

Moving Allowances

6.(f) The Player shall be entitled to moving allowances under the circumstances and in the amounts set forth in Articles VII(F) and VIII of the Basic Agreement.

"Club"

6.(g) All references in other paragraphs of this contract to "the Club" shall be deemed to mean and include any assignee of this contract.

TERMINATION

By Player

7.(a) The Player may terminate this contract, upon written notice to the Club, if the Club shall default in the payments to the Player provided for in paragraph 2 hereof or shall fail to perform any other obligation agreed to be performed by the Club hereunder and if the Club shall fail to remedy such default within ten (10) days after the receipt by the Club of written notice of such default. The Player may also terminate this contract as provided in subparagraph (d)(4) of this paragraph 7. (*See* Article XV(I) of the Basic Agreement.)

By Club

7.(b) The Club may terminate this contract upon written notice to the Player (but only after requesting and obtaining waivers of this contract from all other Major League Clubs) if the Player shall at any time:

(1) fail, refuse or neglect to conform his personal conduct to the standards of good citizenship and good sportsmanship or to keep himself in first class physical condition or to obey the Club's training rules; or

(2) fail, in the opinion of the Club's management, to exhibit sufficient skill or competitive ability to qualify or continue as a member of the Club's team; or

(3) fail, refuse or neglect to render his services hereunder or in any other manner materially breach this contract.

7.(c) If this contract is terminated by the Club, the Player shall be entitled to termination pay under the circumstances and in the amounts set forth in Article IX of the Basic Agreement. In addition, the Player shall be entitled to receive an amount equal to the reasonable traveling expenses of the Player, including first class jet air fare and meals en route, to his home city.

Procedure

7.(d) If the Club proposes to terminate this contract in accordance with subparagraph (b) of this paragraph 7, the procedure shall be as follows:

(1) The Club shall request waivers from all other Major League Clubs. Such waivers shall be good for two (2) business days only. Such waiver request must state that it is for the purpose of terminating this contract and it may not be withdrawn.

(2) Upon receipt of waiver request, any other Major League Club may claim assignment of this contract at a waiver price of $1.00, the priority of claims to be determined in accordance with the Major League Rules.

(3) If this contract is so claimed, the Club shall, promptly and before any assignment, notify the Player that it had requested waivers for the purpose of terminating this contract and that the contract had been claimed.

(4) Within five (5) days after receipt of notice of such claim, the Player shall be entitled by written notice to the Club, to terminate this contract on the date of his notice of termination. If the Player fails to so notify the Club, this contract shall be assigned to the claiming Club.

(5) If the contract is not claimed, the Club shall promptly deliver written notice of termination to the Player at the expiration of the waiver period.

7.(e) Upon any termination of this contract by the Player, all obligations of both Parties hereunder shall cease on the date of termination, except the obligation of the Club to pay the Player's compensation to said date.

Regulations

8. The Player accepts as part of this contract the Regulations set forth herein.

Rules

9.(a) The Club and the Player agree to accept, abide by and comply with all provisions of the Major League Constitution, the Major League Rules, or other rules or regulations in effect on the date of this Uniform Player's Contract, which are not inconsistent with the provisions of this contract or the provisions of any agreement between the Major League Clubs and the Major League Baseball Players Association, provided that the Club, together with the other Major League Clubs and Minor League Baseball, reserves the right to modify, supplement or repeal any provision of said Constitution, Major League Rules, or other rules and regulations in a manner not inconsistent with this contract or the provisions of any then existing agreement between the Major League Clubs and the Major League Baseball Players Association.

Disputes

9.(b) All disputes between the Player and the Club which are covered by the Grievance Procedure as set forth in the Basic Agreement shall be resolved in accordance with such Grievance Procedure.

Publication

9.(c) The Club, the Vice-President, On-Field Operations and the Commissioner, or any of them, may make public the findings, decision and record of any inquiry, investigation or hearing held or conducted, including in such record all evidence or information, given, received, or obtained in connection therewith.

Renewal

10.(a) Unless the Player has exercised his right to become a free agent as set forth in the Basic Agreement, the Club may retain reservation rights over the Player by instructing the Office of the Commissioner to tender to the Player a contract for the term of the next year by including the Player on the Central Tender Letter that the Office of the Commissioner submits to the Players Association on or before December 20 (or if a Sunday, then on or before December 18) in the year of the last playing season covered by this contract. (*See* Article XX(A) of, and Attachment 12 to, the Basic Agreement.) If prior to the March 1 next succeeding said December 20, the Player and Club have not agreed upon the terms of such contract, then on or before ten (10) days after said March 1, the Club shall have the right by written notice to the Player at his address following his signature hereto, or if none be given, then at his last address of record with the Club, to renew this contract for the period of one year on the same terms, except that the amount payable to the Player shall be such as the

Club shall fix in said notice; provided, however, that said amount, if fixed by a Major League Club, shall be in an amount payable at a rate not less than as specified in Article VI, Section D, of the Basic Agreement. Subject to the Player's rights as set forth in the Basic Agreement, the Club may renew this contract from year to year.

10.(b) The Club's right to renew this contract, as provided in subparagraph (a) of this paragraph 10, and the promise of the Player not to play otherwise than with the Club have been taken into consideration in determining the amount payable under paragraph 2 hereof.

Governmental Regulation — National Emergency

11. This contract is subject to federal or state legislation, regulations, executive or other official orders or other governmental action, now or hereafter in effect respecting military, naval, air or other governmental service, which may directly or indirectly affect the Player, Club or the League and subject also to the right of the Commissioner to suspend the operation of this contract during any national emergency during which Major League Baseball is not played.

Commissioner

12. The term "Commissioner" wherever used in this contract shall be deemed to mean the Commissioner designated under the Major League Constitution, or in the case of a vacancy in the office of Commissioner, the Executive Council or such other body or person or persons as shall be designated in the Major League Constitution to exercise the powers and duties of the Commissioner during such vacancy.

Supplemental Agreements

The Club and the Player covenant that this contract, the Basic Agreement and the Agreement Re Major League Baseball Players Benefit Plan effective April 1, 2003, and applicable supplements thereto fully set forth all understandings and agreements between them, and agree that no other understandings or agreements, whether heretofore or hereafter made, shall be valid, recognizable, or of any effect whatsoever, unless expressly set forth in a new or supplemental contract executed by the Player and the Club (acting by its President or such other officer as shall have been thereunto duly authorized by the President or Board of Directors as evidenced by a certificate filed of record with the Commissioner) and complying with the Major League Rules.

Approval

This contract or any supplement hereto shall not be valid or effective unless and until approved by the Commissioner. Signed in duplicate this ____ day of _____ , A.D. [20__]

________________________ ________________________

(Player) (Club)

By

____________________________ ____________________________

(Home address of Player) (Authorized Signature)

Social Security No. ____________________________

Approved ____________________________, [20___]

____

Commissioner

REGULATIONS

1. The Club's playing season for each year covered by this contract and all renewals hereof shall be as fixed by the Office of the Commissioner.

2. The Player, when requested by the Club, must submit to a complete physical examination at the expense of the Club, and if necessary to treatment by a regular physician or dentist in good standing. Upon refusal of the Player to submit to a complete medical or dental examination, the Club may consider such refusal a violation of this regulation and may take such action as it deems advisable under Regulation 5 of this contract. Disability directly resulting from injury sustained in the course and within the scope of his employment under this contract shall not impair the right of the Player to receive his full salary for the period of such disability or for the season in which the injury was sustained (whichever period is shorter), together with the reasonable medical and hospital expenses incurred by reason of the injury and during the term of this contract or for a period of up to two years from the date of initial treatment for such injury, whichever period is longer, but only upon the express prerequisite conditions that (a) written notice of such injury, including the time, place, cause and nature of the injury, is served upon and received by the Club within twenty days of the sustaining of said injury and (b) the Club shall have the right to designate the doctors and hospitals furnishing such medical and hospital services. Failure to give such notice shall not impair the rights of the Player, as herein set forth, if the Club has actual knowledge of such injury. All workmen's compensation payments received by the Player as compensation for loss of income for a specific period during which the Club is paying him in full, shall be paid over by the Player to the Club. Any other disability may be grounds for suspending or terminating this contract.

3. The Club will furnish the Player with two complete uniforms, exclusive of shoes, unless the Club requires the Player to wear nonstandard shoes in which case the Club will furnish the shoes. The uniforms will be surrendered by the Player to the Club at the end of the season or upon termination of this contract.

4. The Player shall be entitled to expense allowances under the circumstances and in the amounts set forth in Article VII of the Basic Agreement.

5. For violation by the Player of any regulation or other provision of this contract, the Club may impose a reasonable fine and deduct the amount thereof from the Player's salary or may suspend the Player without salary for a period not exceeding thirty days or both. Written notice of the fine or suspension or both and the reason therefore shall in every case be given to the Player and the Players Association. (*See* Article XII of the Basic Agreement.)

6. In order to enable the Player to fit himself for his duties under this contract, the Club may require the Player to report for practice at such places as the Club may designate and to participate in such exhibition contests as may be arranged by the Club, without any other compensation than that herein elsewhere provided, for a period beginning not earlier than thirty-three (33) days prior to the start of the championship season, provided, however, that the Club may invite players to report at an earlier date on a voluntary basis in accordance with Article XIV of the Basic Agreement. The Club will pay the necessary traveling expenses, including the first-class jet air fare and meals en route of the Player from his home city to the training place of the Club, whether he be ordered to go there directly or by way of the home city of the Club. In the event of the failure of the Player to report for practice or to participate in the exhibition games, as required and provided for, he shall be required to get into playing condition to the satisfaction of the Club's team manager, and at the Player's own expense, before his salary shall commence.

7. In case of assignment of this contract the Player shall report promptly to the assignee Club within 72 hours from the date he receives written notice from the Club of such assignment, if the Player is then not more than 1,600 miles by most direct available railroad route from the assignee Club, plus an additional 24 hours for each additional 800 miles.

Post Season Exhibition Games. Major League Rule 18(b) provides:

> (b) **EXHIBITION GAMES**. No player shall participate in any exhibition game during the period between the close of the Major League championship season and the following training season, except that, with the consent of the Player's club and permission of the Commissioner, a player may participate in exhibition games for a period of not less than thirty (30) days, such period to be designated annually by the Commissioner. Players who participate in barnstorming during this period cannot engage in any Winter League activities. Player conduct, on and off the field, in connection with such post season exhibition games shall be subject to the discipline of the Commissioner. The Commissioner shall not approve of more than three (3) players of any one club on the same team. The Commissioner shall not approve of more than three (3) players from the joint membership of the World Series participants playing in the same game.
>
> No player shall participate in any exhibition game with or against any team which, during the current season or within one year, has had any

ineligible player or which is or has been during the current season or within one (1) year, managed and controlled by an ineligible player or by any person who has listed an ineligible player under an assumed name or who otherwise has violated, or attempted to violate, any exhibition game contract; or with or against any team which during said season or within one (1) year, has played against teams containing such ineligible players, or so managed or controlled. Any player who participates in such a game in violation of this Rule 18 shall be fined not less than Fifty Dollars ($50.00) nor more than Five Hundred Dollars ($500.00), except that in no event shall such fine be less than the consideration received by such player for participating in such game.

NOTES AND COMMENTS

1. For discussion of the negotiation of player team contracts in the major professional sports leagues, *see* GREENBERG & GRAY, 1 SPORTS LAW PRACTICE 2d §§ 3.01-5.25 (2d ed. 2005); Moorad, *Negotiating for the Professional Baseball Player, in* 1 LAW OF PROFESSIONAL AND AMATEUR SPORTS Ch. 5 (Uberstine ed. 2005); L. Steinberg, *Representing the Professional Football Player, id.*, Ch. 6; T. Steinberg, *Negotiating National Basketball Association Contracts, in* 2 LAW OF PROFESSIONAL AND AMATEUR SPORTS Ch. 7 (Uberstine ed. 2005); Chapman, *National Hockey League Contract Negotiations, in* 2 LAW OF PROFESSIONAL AND AMATEUR SPORTS Ch. 8.

2. For advice by practicing agents, *see* SHAPIRO, JANKOWSKI & DALE, THE POWER OF NICE (1998); HENDRICKS, INSIDE THE STRIKE ZONE (1994); SIMON, THE GAME BEHIND THE GAME: NEGOTIATING IN THE BIG LEAGUES (1993); Falk, *The Art of Contract Negotiation,* 3 MARQ. SPORTS L.J. 1 (1992); MCCORMACK, WHAT THEY DON'T TEACH YOU AT HARVARD BUSINESS SCHOOL 142-157 (1984). Excellent advice is found in MACKAY, SWIM WITH THE SHARKS WITHOUT BEING EATEN ALIVE 83-124 (1988).

3. Agent Leigh Steinberg, in WINNING WITH INTEGRITY (1998) at page 225, suggests the twelve essential rules of negotiation:

1. Align yourself with people who share your values.
2. Learn all you can about the other party.
3. Convince the other party that you have an option — even if you don't.
4. Set your limits before the negotiation begins.
5. Establish a climate of cooperation, not conflict.
6. In the face of intimidation, show no fear.
7. Learn to listen.

8. Be comfortable with silence.
9. Avoid playing split-the-difference.
10. Emphasize your concessions; minimize the other party's.
11. Never push a losing argument to the end.
12. Develop relationships, not conquests.

4. Problem: The topic of salary arbitration is addressed at **Chapter 7**, *supra*. Most arbitration cases are negotiated, as are law cases, until the actual hearing. Compare the leverage of a James Boyd who possesses rights to arbitrate the salary, with the leverage of the James Boyd in the problem. Assume that James Boyd has the right to seek salary arbitration. Attempt to negotiate a settlement. Utilize the Matrix to analyze the problem. For added facts, assume that the New York Giants are an affluent club in the National League. The Giants recently signed two pitchers with records and statistics almost identical with those of Boyd. The two pitchers received twice the amount that the White Sox are offering Boyd.

5. Professional baseball differs from football, basketball, and other professional sports. Players who are drafted or otherwise signed to an initial professional baseball contract rarely perform immediately for the club, but are assigned to minor league teams for further development. Thus, unlike football or basketball, what you see is not what you get. Baseball scouts and personnel evaluate the potential of the player to project the player's abilities and skills four to five years in the future.

6. Baseball's amateur free agent draft, held during the first week of June, allows major and minor league teams to select eligible amateur players. Eligible players include high school players, junior college players, and college players. *See generally* MLR 3; PBR 3; Moorad, *Negotiating for the Professional Baseball Player, supra* at **Note 1**.

Given leverage, the player/agent can demand that the player initially be assigned to a specified level of minor league baseball, or to the major league club at a specified point in time. Some players have secured agreements promising to invite the players to the major league spring training. Non-economic amendments to the form contract appear limited only by the creativity of the parties to the negotiation.

7. For discussion of the availability of "contractual bonus insurance," *see* Wright, *Obtaining Insurance for Contractual Bonuses*, UNDERWRITINGS (Summer 1994), *reprinted in* XII SPORTS LAW. 5 (Sep./Oct. 1994).

8. A common instruction for the attorney is, "Do not lose in the drafting stage what was gained in the negotiation stage!" What significance has the admonition for the attorney/agent?

9. Although the length of the contract is negotiable under most collective bargaining agreements, NFL contracts are customarily limited to one year in order to assure severability. Thus, a player contracting for four years signs a series of one year contracts. *Compare Chuy v. Philadelphia Eagles Football Club*, 595 F.2d 1265 (3rd Cir. 1979) (series of three one-year contracts intended by parties as a matter of fact to exist as one three-year contract), *with Sample v. Gotham Football Club*, 59 F.R.D. 160 (1973) (separate one-year agreements upheld).

10. The Players Associations prepare a wealth of information that is useful in negotiating on behalf of players. *See e.g.*, NFLPA website at www.nflpa.org (*A New Look at Guaranteed Contracts in the NFL*). Statistical analysis indicates that although guaranteed contracts, once a rare occurrence in the NFL, are increasing in number, a player gaining a signing bonus of $2 million or higher receives a *de facto* guaranteed contract.

11. Often, a professional sports team will maintain a player on the club roster for a longer tenure period, or invest more playing time in the player than the player's performance dictates. A study of NBA players revealed that a first-round draft pick stayed in the league approximately 3.3 years longer than a player drafted in the second round. The result is referred to as a "sunk-cost dilemma. Sunk costs influence personnel decisions, which sometimes reflect an escalating commitment to a losing course of action. *See* Barsade & Koput, *Escalation in Context: Testing Escalation Hypotheses on the Basketball Court and at the Credit Window*, in NEGOTIATION ECLECTICS 121 (Kolb, ed.).

D. NEGOTIATING THE ENDORSEMENT CONTRACT

The materials below address negotiation of the endorsement contract for off-the-field revenue. The notion of the endorsement contract covers activities from the promotional appearance for a local charity to the product endorsement by national television advertising. Obviously, the dynamics of negotiation change with the fact scenario presented. Read the following with care to prevent damage to your client in addition to a view toward "hyping" your player for sales purposes.

Robert C. Berry
Representation of the Professional Athlete*

Endorsement Opportunities for the Athlete

* * *

This brief outline covers league provisions as to endorsements, typical endorsement contracts, and what should be negotiated. . . .

League Provisions

If the athlete is on a professional sports team, it is likely that he is circumscribed in some fashion in the types of endorsements he can consider. In addition, there may be explicit restrictions on the extent to which he can use the team name or logo. . . .

Negotiation of the Endorsement Contract

The type of product to be endorsed of course influences the precise items to be negotiated. In addition, the respective leverage of the parties must be analyzed, as well as general market aims of both the company and the athlete. . . .

A. Grant of Rights

The territory involved and the products involved should be precisely defined. Athletes to their sorrow have discovered all too often that their names were used for purposes never envisioned by them, simply because insufficient care on the athlete's behalf was expended in defining the grant of rights. *See, e.g.*, *Cepeda v. Swift Co.*, 415 F.2d 1205 (8th Cir. 1969); and *Sharman v. C. Schmidt & Sons*, 216 F. Supp. 401 (E.D. Pa. 1963).

B. Length of Contract

Many factors affect the ultimate length agreed on by the parties. The company may have only short-term marketing plans. The athlete may be young and want to keep his/her options open. Multiyear contracts are the norm for major endorsement agreements, but many variables influence the final decisions.

C. Promotional Appearances

These should be as specific as possible, making certain they do not become unduly burdensome at a later time.

D. Guaranteed Compensation

One decision, in some negotiations, is how much to go for guaranteed income and how much to build upon a base with an attractive royalty or bonus package.

E. Royalties

As indicated in the foregoing, royalties, guaranteed compensation and bonuses are considered in tandem.

F. Performance Bonuses

These can be an acceptable form of income adjustment, geared to recognize the ascendant name recognition attached to the athlete who attains certain achievement levels.

G. Products for Player Use

The player may wish these to obtain free goods. The company may wish this to attempt to ensure that the player is in fact seen wearing or using company's products.

H. Labeling of Products

This is important, both for name recognition and also as to greatly affecting the levels of compensation under the endorsement agreement.

I. Retention of Rights in Player

In addition to a grant of rights, player wants to be certain that all remaining rights remain with him/her. It may also be necessary to specify certain rights retention and the ability to enter into certain contracts with other companies, to make certain there is no dispute over player's rights to do so.

J. Termination

Rights to terminate by both parties are important considerations. Companies increasingly are concerned about undesirable activities and attending notoriety visited on many celebrities. The company will want a wide ability to terminate. The player will want assurance of financial stability and best efforts to use player's grant of rights to greatest advantage. The player may also want to restrict language that company suggests as to termination rights under contentions (which is often the case) that the language is overly broad and overreaching.

K. Use of Endorsement on Termination

This important provision must be carefully drafted to allow a carryover period for the company to wind down the products endorsed by athlete during the term of the agreement. But it must be done in a way to allow both parties to proceed ahead with other deals.

L. Warranties and Indemnities

In certain instances, particularly with the veteran player who has endorsed other product lines, the company will want guarantees that no prior legal commitments affect player's ability to enter the current contemplated contract. Player obviously wants similar guarantees. The warranties should be as tightly drawn as possible.

M. Assignment

As with grant of rights, this holds pitfalls for the player in particular. Keep the rights to assign specific and minimal, if at all possible. . . .

Consider the following advice:

Donald Dell
MINDING OTHER PEOPLE'S BUSINESS, 124-38 (1989)*

A common myth created by the media is that most professional athletes earn millions of dollars from endorsements and other commercial activities. In truth, only a handful have the celebrity status and charisma to command national endorsement deals and even among this handful, there are only about a dozen superstars from any sports era — a Nicklaus and Palmer in golf, a Connors and Ashe in tennis, or a Jordan and Bird in basketball — who can literally name their price and pick their deals.

As a rule, most athletes earn far less from off-the-field business activities than the public believes. Yet the myth is so pervasive that many pro athletes themselves are stunned to learn the truth. On any number of occasions we have taken on clients who can't understand why they aren't swimming in a pool of endorsement deals immediately. Ironically, our job, in a way, is to perpetuate the myth by doing everything to make our clients the exceptions to the rule, rather than the examples of it.

As I said earlier, you earn the client's respect, first and foremost, through **performance**. This can mean different things to different people. In most client businesses, "getting the job done" ultimately comes down to the bottom line, either directly (such as with agents or brokers) or indirectly (such as with consultants and advertising firms). You can give a client the best advice in the world, and he or she may even take it, but at the end of the day it is salesmanship and results that make your relationship with your client succeed.

Persistence

* * *

When I have a front door slammed in my face, there is nothing I love more than the challenge of coming back at it through the side door or in the backdoor or down the chimney — whatever it takes. If I can turn a deal around with a "What about this . . .?" it is often more satisfying to me than a "yes" right out of the box.

Persistence is the groundwork that getting the job done for the client is based on. When persistence is combined with emotion, it leads to a kind of indomitability. . . . It is far better to be too persistent — to push too hard — on behalf of your clients than to risk losing the deal for not having been persistent enough.

More Than Money

During our first negotiation for Boomer Esiason of the Cincinnati Bengals, I said to Boomer as we began to get close to reaching a deal, "We're only twenty-five thousand dollars apart. We may get all of it, we may get none of it, but most likely we'll compromise. But I'd like your permission right now to try to finalize this thing."

Boomer hesitated, then said, "Can't we push a little harder? Twenty-five thousand is a lot of money. Remember you guys make a commission on that."

"Look Boomer," I said, "let me explain something to you. We've been negotiating this deal for two months now. It's been hardball. If you think that this is just a matter of making another phone call or that our fee on twenty-five thousand dollars is going to motivate us any more than we already are, then you don't really understand us very well. We want to get every penny of the twenty-five thousand dollars — out of pride. We want to feel we delivered the best possible contract for you, that we rolled up our sleeves and did our job well."

We ended up getting all the $25,000. And I tell this story to other players, because sometimes there is a perception in this business that we're in it strictly for the money, but it's much more than that.

Doing the best job possible is what is really important. As we enjoy more and more success, everybody wants to outshine us, and we want to outshine ourselves as well. We've arrived at the point where the real challenge becomes doing even better than we thought we could. Money — fees and commission — is just a way of keeping score.

Creative Positioning

Not only do you owe your clients your best efforts, you also owe them your best thinking.

Getting the job done for clients is not too different from getting clients in the first place. Much of what applies to recruiting clients and selling them on your services often applies to selling on their behalf. Not the least of these skills is making the best use of the facts available in order to position the client creatively in the marketplace.

The secret of creative positioning is opening up your mind to all possibilities. If you look at something from just one perspective, your mind gets "locked in" and it becomes more difficult to consider all the possibilities. There is a brain teaser represented here that illustrates this. The challenge is to connect all nine dots with just four lines without raising your pencil from the paper.

* * *

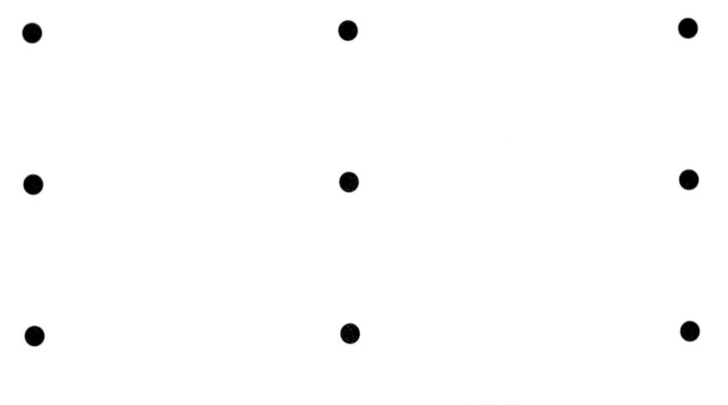

* * *

Give up? The secret is that you have to extend your thinking — and your lines — beyond the dots in order to do it. The difficulty that most people have in solving this is that they limit their thinking to the space circumscribed by the dots. For the solution, *see* [next page].

Solving problems in the business world also often involves solutions that are out of the ordinary. You constantly have to say to yourself, "Consider the unusual, even the outrageous. Go beyond the conventional borders." That's how some of the best creative thinking happens.

In the book where this puzzle appeared, the author reported that he has subsequently received many other correct solutions, including one from a clever fellow who drew enormous dots and connected them with three lines and from someone else who drew big dots, wadded up the paper and stuck his pencil through it, connecting all the dots with "one line."

How does this apply to clients? Creative positioning involves understanding your client's most marketable and attractive attributes, then opening your mind up to all the possibilities that their attributes might suggest.

This is not, by the way, the stuff of alchemy. You can't make the client into something he or she is not. But you do want to position the facts to present the client in the best possible light.

The solution:

* * *

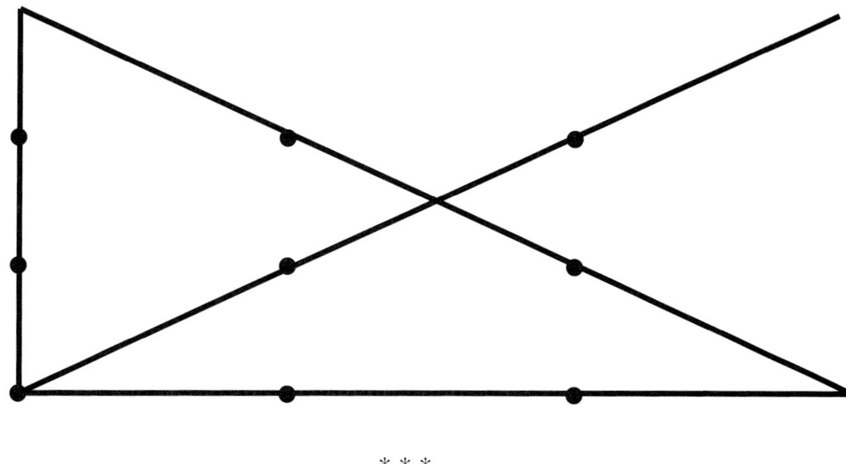

* * *

It pays to be creative and to pursue an alternate approach when your primary one is blocked.

Of course, you may not be in the business of positioning a client directly, but you should always keep in mind the image a client wants or ought to want. An architect who reads "traditional" into the trappings of a client's office might be missing the fact that the client is due or ready for a change. By the same token, a lawyer who is advocating this or that issue must know how strong he or she should come on and whether the client is best served by a hard-edged image or something softer. These choices, made consciously, give an edge to the kind of service you offer the client and help you to stand out from the competition.

Target Your Audience

An image is created in the eye of the beholder. You can have the greatest image in the world, but if you don't get it out in front of the target audience you want to convey that image to, it's all just a waste of time. As a result, you have to do two things with an image: You have to create it, and then you have to find ways to disseminate that image to the key groups that matter.

* * *

Selling the Client

As I mentioned earlier, creatively positioning the client works in much the same way as when you are recruiting clients: You sell yourself to the client by using the facts about yourself and your organization to your best possible advantage. Naturally, the same approach applies when selling your client to others.

A couple of years ago, we were trying to entice Seiko into sponsoring a challenge match between Ivan Lendl and Pat Cash in Hong Kong. Seiko initially turned us down because Cash and Lendl was not their idea of a dream matchup; at the time Cash wasn't even ranked in the top ten.

Our job, then, was to reposition the facts in order to make the match seem more attractive and exciting. We brought to their attention the fact that Cash had recently beaten Boris Becker, a world-class player, and gotten to the finals in a major tournament. We also told them, "Tennis fans remember the Lendl-Cash final match at Wimbledon," though in fact that final had been something of a disappointment. Just by recalling that match I was able to conjure up the Wimbledon mystique. After some further haggling, we were able to agree on the deal.

Obviously, if making deals for clients were always that simple then anyone would be crazy to be in any other business. This little back-and-forth with Seiko does illustrate a key point about sales: Selling of any kind requires — and handsomely rewards — the ability to think quickly on one's feet.

Getting to Know Them — Quickly

In many sales situations you do not have the luxury of a long-term courtship as you might when recruiting clients. You have to get to know your customers very quickly and make snap decisions based on what you can learn in a short period of time.

I used to think that the most effective selling was, "Have I got a client for you!" I would go into a meeting and immediately I would start to sell, sell, sell! The only problem was that I wasn't closing that many deals.

If there is one lesson I have finally learned over time, it's the importance in most sales situations of talking less, listening more, and asking intelligent questions. **Less** here is always **more**.

There was a time when I might have begun a sales pitch by saying, "I want to sell you a tournament in Orlando," and then would talk about twenty minutes, only to have the other party say, "We're not interested in tennis tournaments in Orlando because our entire business is in Portland, Oregon."

Now I am more likely to start off asking, "What is your core business? What are you looking for in sports promotion? What do you need to know about us? How do you think we might help you?" and so on. I will start to sell only after I have done a certain amount of intelligence gathering.

In selling situations you really do have to shut up and ask the right questions. It's not easy, particularly for the "born" salespeople who are naturally gregarious. It is something you have to be consciously aware of and work on all the time.

Even today, I will sometimes go into a meeting and get really excited about what's been discussed, and off I'll go. As a result, I will miss all but the most obvious of signals.

I once met with Michael Fuchs, the chairman of Home Box Office, to sell him on a musical show we were representing. After a few minutes, Fuchs, who is a friend, interrupted me and said, "I have to tell you something, Donald. I hate musicals. I would never put one on television. Our original programming needs are drama and sports."

Fortunately, Fuchs knew me well enough to stop me from running on at the mouth. If he had been someone else, I might have pitched him for twenty minutes, then he would have said, "Thanks a lot," and I never would have heard from him again.

Don't Feel Obligated to Reveal Your Ignorance

There is that old adage about it being better to be thought a fool than to open your mouth and remove all doubt. Even so, any of us can have a bad day.

I can remember a meeting about ten years ago when we were trying to sell a series of European clay court tennis events to PBS, the television network. I was well into my pitch when one of the PBS executives cut me off by saying, "We couldn't possibly do this deal. The cost of televising from Europe would be prohibitive."

Satellite technology was relatively new at the time, and in my defense I must say I wasn't involved in our day-to-day television operations. I responded to this executive by putting on my best know-it-all face and saying, "You're absolutely wrong about the cost. With these 'spoons' we can bring in the whole package from Europe for a lot less than you'd imagine."

Everyone in the room, including my colleagues, started looking quizzically at each other with, "What-in-the-world-is-he-talking-about?" expressions on their faces. Finally, one of my associates said somewhat sheepishly, "I think what Donald means is dishes — satellite **dishes** — not spoons."

Here I was, this supposed television expert, and I was rattling on about spoons. It was a classic case of trying to come across as knowing more than I actually knew — and getting caught at it.

Though these PBS executives knew me well enough that they didn't hold it against me, it was the kind of mistake you only have to make once to learn an unforgettable lesson in the limits of "winging it."

Thinking on Your Feet — Quickly

Talking less, listening more, and asking the right questions also gives you a chance to think on your feet and shift gears when necessary — which is most of the time. . . . But if most deals begin with a "no thanks," as I believe they do, then your ability to turn them around will depend almost entirely on your ability to think on your feet — to pick up on the subtle nuance or oddball fact, assimilate this immediately into your thinking, then shift gears accordingly and come back without missing a beat.

A Shot in the Dark

Although the specific reasons for talking less and listening more may be to gather information, to give yourself time to think, or simply to avoid putting your foot in your mouth, the overall desired effect is one of control — over the sales environment and the person to whom you are selling. In most business situations, the person who has learned more about the other and revealed less about him or herself will have a subtle yet distinct advantage over the other party, whether it's a matter of learning how best to position your client or product in terms of the buyer's desires, or figuring out just how far the other party can be pushed.

* * *

Hidden Agendas

No matter how good you may be at picking up subtle signals or reading between the lines, you must take what you learn with a grain of salt. In many sales situations in which you don't know the other party very well, there are often hidden agendas that you cannot possibly perceive. Indeed, one hidden agenda cost us a major deal for Tracy Austin.

We had spent four months negotiating with the Wilson Sporting Goods Company trying to conclude a racquet deal for Tracy, who had just won the U.S. Open at age sixteen. Two of our people had even spent several days with Wilson in Chicago trying to finalize contract terms but without much luck. Finally, Dick Calley, the president of Wilson Sporting Goods at that time, called to say that he and his general counsel were flying into Washington on the company jet to meet with me personally. "I want to wrap this thing up," he said, "even if it takes all weekend."

The next morning, the Saturday before Easter, we met in my office with Calley and Wilson's counsel Pam Nada. It was a very tough, unpleasant negotiation, and Calley's counsel was making it a lot more unpleasant than necessary. It was almost as though she were trying to sabotage the deal.

The final crucial issue came down to whether Tracy's name would be on the racquet face itself or on a hangtag attached to the racquet. We had insisted that the name be on the racquet itself. Though Calley fought me on this point, he relented in the end.

Finally, we had agreed to all terms — dollars, years, royalty, territory, and so forth. Calley said to his counsel, "Pam, why don't you and Tracy's lawyers go into the conference room and work out the final language?"

After they left, we sat in my office making small talk. While waiting for the others to finalize the language, we heard louder and louder voices coming from the adjoining conference room. It was Wilson's general counsel, who came running out yelling, "Dick, they are trying to change the deal." She was still insisting that Tracy's name be on the hangtag, not on the racquet face.

I was furious. We had made a deal, and she was now reneging. I said, "Dick, you have to control her. She is changing the deal and is very emotional about it."

Suddenly she burst into tears. "Also, they are being mean to me," Pam said, "and unfair to Wilson."

At that point Dick Calley totally overreacted. He turned to me and said, "That's it, forget the whole thing. The deal's off." Then turning to his counsel, he said, "Pam, dear, let's get out of here." They stormed out, the deal in shambles.

I was dumbfounded. As I stood there, I thought to myself: "Four months of negotiation down the drain." It made no sense whatsoever for this to happen over a resolvable issue.

Six weeks later I learned that the president of Wilson and his general counsel had both resigned and run off together to Mexico to get married! That's one hidden agenda I had totally missed — she was the boss!

NOTES AND COMMENTS

1. How does negotiation of the endorsement contract differ from negotiation of the player-team contract? Is the matrix useful in preparing for negotiation of the endorsement contract? Does there exist a meaningful difference between negotiation of contracts and sales?

2. For an example of a form endorsement contract, *see* XVII SPORTS LAW. 3-4 (Spring 1999); BERRY & WONG, I LAW AND BUSINESS OF THE SPORTS INDUSTRIES § 4.52 (1986).

3. *See generally* 1 GREENBERG & GRAY, SPORTS LAW PRACTICE §§ 7.01-7.10 (2d ed. 2005); Lester, *Marketing the Athlete; Endorsement Contracts, in* 3 LAW OF PROFESSIONAL AND AMATEUR SPORTS Ch. 27 (Uberstine ed. 2005).

4. Most players associations operate group licensing programs for players. The programs enable the associations or assigns to market promotions, endorsements, or other services of several players as a package. In the NFL, for example, when a player signs an NFLPA Group Licensing Agreement, or otherwise assigns his group licensing rights to the NFLPA, the NFLPAgains the exclusive right to use the player's name, likeness, voice, facsimile signature, photograph, picture and/or biographical information in licensed programs involving six or more players. The NFLPA assigns the rights to Players Inc. Revenues generated by the programs are utilized for various purposes. Excesses of revenues over expenses are disbursed to program participants according to association policy and procedures. *See* PLAYBOOK (NFLPA Publication).

Does a potential promoter or advertiser, as consumer, possess a valid complaint under Section 1 of the Sherman Antitrust Act? Is the group license agreement among the parties insulated from antitrust scrutiny by a recognized labor exemption?

Chapter 10

STADIUM AND ARENA ISSUES

A. INTRODUCTORY COMMENTS

The sports stadium and arena construction boom of the 1990s-2000s generates legal questions that accompany public participation in the economic ventures, creative public-private financing arrangements, and lease provisions. Local and regional communities join with leagues and franchise owners in ventures designed to provide reliable entertainment options for fans, while assuring recapture of both public and private expenditures over the life of the venue.

From 1990 through 1999, thirty-seven major league stadiums and arenas worth approximately $6.5 billion were constructed. Construction of stadiums between 1999-2003 reportedly cost approximately $13.5 billion. *See* Goodman, *The Public Financing of Professional Sports Stadiums: Policy and Practice,* 9 SPORTS LAW. J. 173 (2002). The major league "cathedrals" combine with the development of minor league venues and college and university developments to provide complex issues for the architectural, legal, and financial professionals.

While some legal questions do not change from one era to another, different issues necessarily arise within the context of new developments of the modern period. In the early 1900s, most stadium and arena projects were privately funded without considerable public participation. In the post-World War II years, perhaps peaking in the 1970s, most facilities were constructed at public expense without significant private contribution. Various stadium features initiated in the 1960-70s are enhanced today, such as the "suite/luxury box" component, utilized in the Houston Astrodome, and perfected by the Dallas Cowboys, and the "permanent seat license." Design specifications focus on venues for individual sports, replacing the multi-sport facilities of the last generation. Specialized amenities that maximize revenues enable smaller markets with newly styled stadiums/arenas to complete with larger demographic markets that do not have them. The venue-generated revenues traditionally have not been shared by the clubs in a league, and thus accrue to the benefit of the home team. Finally, the stadium/arena is utilized as the anchor for larger real estate projects, including the surrounding properties in mall developments, office park complexes, convention centers, and hotel/tourist districts. *See* Mitchell, *The New Urban Magnets: Stadiums and Arenas Eyed as Development Centerpieces*, 1 SPORTS BUS. J. 1, 44 (Nov. 30-Dec. 6, 1998).

B. PROLOGUE — ECONOMIC FEASIBILITY

Sports facility financing requires revenue streams to support multiple issues of debt. Potential sources include: sale of facility naming rights; rental payments; and revenue from stadium operations, such as concessions, novelties, parking, gate, luxury boxes, suites, and advertising. Bond issues are commonly backed by public sources, including general obligation pledges, annual appropriations, or specific taxes. Creative financing packages are likely to encompass the following elements: sales tax; hotel tax; tourist development tax; rental car tax; sin taxes on liquor and tobacco; airport departure tax; surcharge of ticket purchases; and special lottery and gaming revenues.

Some economists and others question whether professional sports operations and facilities generate adequate economic returns to justify the expenditure of public funds in the financing of stadium/arena construction. Sometimes the generalizations of the detractors fail in the face of historical data and related projections, similar to the Bank One Report, *infra*. Sports facility projects are supported by cost-benefit analyses that indicate a substantial positive return. Some costs and benefits are direct and can be measured accurately. The current value of a stream of lease rental payments made over the life of the lease, for example, can be ascertained. Other costs and benefits are projected by use of assumptions. Some are "qualitative," rather than "quantitative." Thus, the qualitative value of having a major league sports franchise, and other quality of life elements, including the avoidance of urban decay, are assigned values.

The process is essentially the same for any public decision to subsidize municipal golf courses, public parks, opera houses, convention centers, or the relocation of a factory (tax abatement, infrastructure costs, etc.) to the community. As Professor Zimbalist's testimony attests, "Depending on the assumptions, one can get wildly different estimates. . . ." And, of course, there exists the political element of the decision making process. Renewed scrutiny of public backing of sports stadium construction projects results in the creative joint venture arrangements that generate the present day issues.

PROBLEM

Your law firm is hired by a professional baseball club to advise and assist the club in its efforts to join with local, regional, and state governmental entities in the financing and construction of a new ballpark. The client asks that you specifically address the following:

1. Discuss whether the state, county, and municipal governmental entities may provide public funding (by whatever mechanism) for the construction of a stadium that will be utilized primarily by a private corporation;

2. Identify potential sources of revenue, both public and private, that could be utilized for repayment of construction costs, including debt service;

3. Analyze options for the joint funding of the envisioned stadium construction; and

4. Outline the legal challenges that likely will be pursued by opponents to the public funding of the stadium. What legal actions are available for use by the ballclub and public entities?

Case File

BROWER v. STATE

137 Wash. 2d 44, 969 P.2d 42 (1998),
cert. denied, 119 S. Ct. 1498 (1999)

Madsen, J.

This case concerns Laws of 1997, ch. 220, and Referendum 48, which provide for construction and financing of new stadium facilities for the Seattle Seahawks, a professional football team. Appellant Jordan Brower raises numerous constitutional challenges to the legislation, primarily in connection with provisions which conditioned referral of Referendum 48 to the people on the payment of costs of the referendum election by a private entity, the "team affiliate." Other challenges are that the Act violates the single subject rule of article II, section 19 of the Washington Constitution, and that it contains an invalid emergency clause. We conclude the legislation is valid and affirm summary judgment in favor of the respondents. In reaching this conclusion, we note that our recent decision in *CLEAN v. State*, 130 Wash. 2d 782, 928 P.2d 1054 (1996), dictates the result on a number of the issues Brower has raised.

FACTS

During the 19097 legislative session, the Legislature enacted a bill (the Act) providing for construction and financing of a new football and soccer stadium and exhibition center as a public-private enterprise. [Citation omitted.] At the time the legislation was considered, Respondent Football Northewest, Inc., had an option to purchase the Seattle Seahawks football team from its owner who wanted to move the team to California. Football Northwest declared it would not exercise the option to purchase, which was to expire unless exercised by July 1, 1997, unless the legislation was enacted.

The Legislature did not pass the bill outright, however. Instead, the Legislature referred sections 101 through 604 of the Act to the people. Among other things, this part of the Act authorizes creation of a public stadium authority by "any county that has entered into a letter of intent relating to the development of a stadium and exhibition center" with a team "affiliate" or entity with a contractual right to become a "team affiliate." [Citation omitted.] The stadium authority can then enter into agreements with a professional football team for development of a new stadium and exhibition center. [Citation omitted.]

Mr. Brower's constitutional challenges primarily concern sections 605 through 609 of the Act, which were not referred to the people. . . . Section 605 stated that "[t]he legislature neither affirms nor refutes the value of the proposal," set forth in the Legislature's intent that the voters be provided an opportunity to express their decision, and concluded by stating that "[I]t is also expressed that many legislators might personally vote against this proposal at the polls, or they might not." [Citation omitted.]

Section 606 provided that the Act would be null and void unless the team affiliate entered into an agreement with the Secretary of State to reimburse the state and counties for the cost of a special election to be held on Referendum 48. [Citation omitted.] A reimbursement agreement for costs of the election was entered into by the Secretary of State and the Seattle Seahawks, Inc. . . . The expenses have been paid.

Section 608 contained an emergency clause providing that sections 606 and 607 (the provisions for conducting the special election and for reimbursement of the costs of the election) should take effect immediately. . . .

On May 2, 1997, prior to the June 17 date set for the special election, Brower filed a complaint in Thurston County Superior Court against the State seeking an injunction to prevent the election on the basis that the Act contained an invalid emergency clause. In an amended complaint, he also sought declaratory relief, alleging that the Act is unconstitutional on numerous grounds. . . . [T]he Superior Court entered an order staying all proceedings until after the . . . special election. Referendum 48 was passed by a margin of 51.1% with a voter turnout of 51%.

Following the election, the parties filed cross-motions for summary judgment. The trial court granted summary judgment in favor of the State and Football Northwest. This court granted direct review of Brower's appeal. . . .

ANALYSIS

Authority to Submit Referendum 48 to the People

* * *

The people's power to legislate directly takes two forms, the initiative and the referendum. Const. Art. II, § 1. An initiative is a proposed law directly from the people through the filing of signed petitions with the Secretary of State. [Citation omitted.] An initiative may be an initiative to the people, or to the Legislature. The former is placed directly on the ballot for voter approval or rejection. The latter may be enacted by the Legislature, or the Legislature may decline to act on the measure, in which case it will be placed on the ballot, or the Legislature may enact an alternative to the initiative, in which case both the initiative and the legislative alternative will be placed on the ballot. [Citation omitted.]

The referendum is the second power reserved to the people, permitting the voters to approve or reject a measure which has been enacted by the Legislature. [Citation omitted.] A measure may be referred to the people in two ways. First, voters may refer a measure by submitting petitions singed by the required number of voters to the Secretary of State within 90 days of the end of the session in which the measure was enacted. [Citation omitted.] Second, the Legislature may refer a measure to the people without the voters petitioning for a referendum. [Citation omitted.] The case involves a measure referred to the people by the Legislature.

1. Conditioning Act on Agreement of Private Party to Reimburse Costs of Special Election

Mr. Brower maintains that the Legislature does not have general authority to refer a matter to the people, but instead has only that authority expressly set out in art. II, § 1(b). Here the Legislature provided that the Act would be null and void unless the team affiliate entered into an agreement . . . to reimburse . . . for the costs of the special election. This, Brower contends, illegally placed the power of referendum in the hands of a private party. . . . Brower further argues that aside from art. II, § 1(b), the Legislature does not have authority to grant a private party the power to perform a legislative act, particularly where, as here, the private party stands to benefit from the legislation. . . .

> The legislative authority of the State is vested in the Legislature . . .
>
> [H]owever, conditioning the operative effect of a statute upon a future event specified by the Legislature does not transfer the state legislative power to render judgment to the persons or entity capable of bringing about that event. [Citation omitted.]

Here, the Legislature determined that it was necessary to condition the Act on a requirement that the costs of the election be paid by the team affiliate in order to avoid the expenditure of any public funds in connection with a public stadium project unless the voters approved the Act. Because this judgment was made by the Legislature, no unconstitutional delegation of legislative authority occurred.

Brower contends, though, that while the Legislature may enact measures whose effectiveness is contingent upon a future event, it has not authority to condition the referral of a measure in such a manner.

The state constitution is not a grant but rather is a restriction on the lawmaking power. [Citation omitted.] "[T]he power of the legislature to enact all reasonable laws is unrestrained except where, either expressly or by fair inference, it is prohibited by the state and federal constitutions. [Citation omitted.]

* * *

The Legislature has authority both to refer a measure to the people and to condition the effectiveness of an enactment upon the happening of a future event, and nothing in art. II, § 1 restrains the Legislature from exercising the two powers in connection with one piece of legislation. . . .

2. Authority to Refer Only Part of an Act

Brower contends that the Legislature cannot refer only part of an act to the people. . . .This argument is based on a misreading of art. II, § 1(b). The provision states in relevant part that a referendum "may be ordered on any act, bill, law, or any part thereof passed by the legislature . . . either by petition . . . of the legal voters, or by the legislature as other bills are enacted. . . . [Citation omitted.] The language plainly means that a referendum may be ordered on a part of any act, bill, or law by either of two methods. . . .

3. Whether Legislation Can Be Referred to the People Where the Legislature Takes No Position on the Value of the Legislation

Mr. Brower also argues, as part of his claim that only a complete act can be referred to the people, that the Legislature cannot refer a measure on which it has refused to take a position. He maintains that Referendum 48 is unconstitutional because it is in fact an unlawful initiative to the people rather than a referendum. . . . Ordinarily, when a bill is passed by the Legislature, the Legislature affirmatively adopts the provisions of the bill. The Act is clearly an unusual piece of legislation because the Legislature deliberately took no position on the value of the legislation before referring it to the people. [Citation omitted.] Nevertheless, examination of the state constitution leads to the conclusion that, although unusual, Referendum 48 is a valid referendum.

The legislative rights of the people reserved in state constitutions are to be liberally construed in order to preserve them and render them effective. . . . Whether the Legislature takes a stand on the merits of the legislation or not, the Legislature must vote to send the matter to the people and the people then make the final decision as to whether the matter becomes law. . . .

Veto Power

Brower maintains that the Act unconstitutionally granted a veto power to Football Northwest in violation of art. III, § 12 of the Washington State Constitution which vests the right to veto legislation in the hands of the Governor. Brower apparently reasons that because the team affiliate could decline to agree to reimburse the costs of the special election, it had the power to veto the Act.

Brower cites no authority for the proposition that a third party's failure to act to bring about an event upon which the effectiveness of legislation is contingent would constitute a veto within the meaning of the constitution. . . . There is no merit to the argument. . . .

Special Legislation

Mr. Brower maintains that the referendum on sections 101 through 604 of the Act constitutes special legislation in violation of art. II, § 28 of the Washington State Constitution. He maintains that the Act provides that a single entity, the team affiliate, benefits from the legislation by agreeing to reimburse the costs of the special election. This challenge appears to relate to the entire Act.

* * *

Const. Art. II, § 28(6) provides in relevant part that "[t]he legislature is prohibited from enacting any private or special laws in the following cases . . . for granting corporate powers or privileges." Special legislation is legislation which operates upon a single person or entity while general legislation operates upon all things or people within a class. *CLEAN*, 120 Wash. 2d at 802, 928 P.2d 1054. . . . A class may consist of one person or corporation provided the law applies to all members of the class. [Citation omitted.] However, it is not what the law includes, but rather what it excludes, which is the test of special legislation. [Citation omitted.] "'Thus, to survive a challenge as special legislation, any exclusions from a statute's applicability, as well as the statute itself, must be rationally related to the purpose of the statute.'"

[Citation omitted.]

Mr. Brower argues the legislation applies to a single entity. He emphasizes language in the act defining "team affiliate" as "a" professional football team and any affiliate of the "team designated by the team, and stating that an "'affiliate of the team' means any person or entity that controls, is controlled by, or is under common control with the team." . . .

The Act is not special legislation. The Act allows for "any county" to create a public stadium authority if the county has entered into a letter of intent relating to the development of a stadium and exhibition center with a team affiliate or entity with a contractual right to become a team affiliate. [Citation omitted.] The stadium authority can then enter into agreements with a professional football team for development of a new stadium and exhibition center. [Citation omitted.] The definition of a "team affiliate" is "a professional football team that will use the stadium and exhibition center, and any affiliate of the team designated by the team. An 'affiliate of the team' means any person or entity that controls, is controlled by, or is under common control with the team." [Citation omitted.] A "professional football team" is "a team that is a member of the national football league or similar professional football association." [Citation omitted.]

The legislation applies to a class — any county is authorized to form a public stadium authority provided it satisfies the letter of intent requirement. *See CLEAN*, 130 Wash. 2d at 802, 928 P.2d 1054 (holding that legislation concerning construction and financing of a baseball stadium which applies only to counties of a certain size was not special legislation, even where only one county had a population of that size — possibility existed that another county could reach the given population in the future). Moreover, the term "team affiliate" also refers to a class, because it includes any national football league team or team of a similar association, and affiliates designated by such a team. Finally, the exclusions from the Act's provisions are rational. Counties which have not entered a letter of intent would not be in a position to have a professional football team playing its home games at a stadium in the county.

Lending of Credit

Mr. Brower contends that the state advanced funds and services to conduct the special election on Referendum 48, and this constituted lending of credit to a private party, the team affiliate, which was obliged to reimburse these costs. His premise is that the election was an election solely to benefit a private party, and the election costs were the costs of the private party.

Article VII, section 5 of the Washington State Constitution provides that "[t]he credit of the state shall not, in any manner be given or loaned to, or in aid of, any individual, association, company or corporation." The purpose of this provision is to "'prevent state funds from being used to benefit private interests where the public interest is not primarily served." [Citations omitted.] The first step in deciding whether a gift or loan of public funds has been made is to determine if the funds have been expended to carry out a fundamental purpose of government. [Citation omitted.] If so, no gift or loan of public credit has occurred.

As Respondents contend, there can be no doubt that a special election on a referendum measure is a governmental purpose. If there was any "lending" of credit, it was for a governmental purpose. However, it is difficult to agree that any lending of credit occurred, because the government generally bears the costs of special elections. . . . Here, a private entity agreed to reimburse the state and local governments for their costs. For these reasons, we hold that no lending of state credit occurred.

* * *

Emergency Clause

Mr. Brower contends that Section 608, the emergency clause relating to the reimbursement and election provisions, is invalid. He asserts that the purpose of the clause is to permit an election at a time dictated by the team affiliate. He argues that the clause is an obviously false and palpable attempt at dissimulation because the Legislature itself was neutral on the value of the Act and so no emergency existed. If an emergency had existed, Brower urges, the state would have paid the costs of the election.

Article II, section 1(b) provides in part that the power of referendum reserved by the people may be ordered on any legislation "except such laws a may be necessary for the immediate preservation of the public peace, health or safety. . . ." An emergency clause is tested against this standard. [Citation omitted.]

Mr. Brower's argument is not persuasive in light of *CLEAN*. The court there held that construction of a major public sports stadium is a proper exercise of the State's police power. [Citation omitted.] The court also held in that case that the stadium act concerning new baseball stadium facilities for the Seattle Mariners was necessary for the immediate preservation of the public peace, health or safety. The court noted that an emergency clause is given effect "'unless the declaration on its face is obviously false; and in determining the truth or falsity of the legislative declaration, [the court] will enter upon no inquiry as to the facts'" and will give the declaration every favorable presumption. [Citation omitted.] The court determined from the record in that case that a real emergency existed because the public purpose sought to be achieved by passage of the stadium act would be unattainable if the Mariners franchise was sold to investors before the Legislature could assure the owners that a new facility would be built in King County. [Citation omitted.]

In this case, submission of Referendum 48 clearly constitutes a public purpose because the state constitution expressly provides for the Legislature to refer enactments to the people at a special election. [Citation omitted.] The referendum itself concerns public sports stadium, also a public purpose. [Citation omitted.] The referral and election provisions were also necessary for the immediate preservation of the public peace, health, or safety. [Citation omitted.] The record shows that if these provisions had not been declared an emergency, they would not have taken effect until 90 days after the end of the legislative session, after Football Northwest's option to purchase the Seahawks expired. The then current owner of the Seahawks wanted to move the team from Washington. Football Northwest would help finance the cost of new facilities, but declared it would do so only if voters approved Referendum 48. In order for the legislation to achieve its purpose, the election had to be held before the option expired. . . . In other words, it was the need for an expeditious vote, not the need to construct a stadium, which constituted the emergency.

* * *

Conclusion

The trial court's grant of summary judgment in favor of Respondents is affirmed. . . .

DURHAM, C.J., and DOLLIVER, SMITH, GUY, JOHNSON, ALEXANDER and TALMADGE, JJ., concur.

KING COUNTY v. TAXPAYERS OF KING COUNTY

133 Wash. 2d 584, 949 P.2d 1260 (1997)

TALMADGE, Justice.

This is the third of a series of challenges to state legislation and local implementing ordinances for financing and constructing a new baseball stadium in

King County. We are asked in this action to determine if King County's issuance of $336 million in bonds to finance stadium construction is "valid" under RCW 7.25. To determine validity, we must decide if the lease between the Mariners and the public facilities district is an unconstitutional gift of public monies to a private organization; if the taxes authorized by the Legislature to pay for the stadium financing bonds are constitutionally imposed and properly collected; if the state unconstitutionally delegated legislative authority to the public facilities district; and if a proposed local initiative establishing more stringent debt limitations for King County than authorized by statute is applicable to the baseball stadium project.

We hold that the bonds issued by King County to finance stadium construction are valid because the use of public funds for a new baseball stadium here is not an unconstitutional gift of public monies to a private organization. Moreover, the taxes imposed to pay for the bonds are constitutionally imposed and properly collected. The state properly delegated authority to the public facilities district. The proposed local initiative is invalid insofar as it attempts to impose additional limitations on local debt not authorized by statute. We therefore affirm the trial court's declaratory judgment validating the $336 million in stadium construction bonds issued by King County.

* * *

FACTS

The Baseball Club of Seattle, L.P. (Mariners), is a Washington limited partnership formed in early 1992 for the express purpose of acquiring the Seattle Mariners Baseball Club to keep it in Seattle. Soon after acquiring the team, the Mariners began meeting with King County officials to modify the Kingdome lease and develop long-term capital plans. In 1994, a King County task force developed a plan for a new home for the Mariners, to be completed by 1999.

The 1995 Legislature considered legislation authorizing the financing of the new Mariners baseball stadium, ultimately enacting a baseball financing program at a special session. . . . The key provision of the Stadium Act permits the "legislative authority" of a county with a population on one million or more to impose a sales and use tax in addition to other taxes . . . not to exceed .017 percent of the selling price in the case of a sales tax, or value of the article used in the case of a use tax. [Citation omitted.]

Thereafter, Metropolitan King County Council (Council) . . . enacted Ordinance 12000, creating the Washington State Major League Baseball Stadium Public Facilities District (District), and imposing three special sales and use taxes the Stadium Act authorized, including a .017 percent special stadium sales and use tax, as special stadium sales and use tax on restaurants, bars, and taverns, and a special stadium sales and use tax on car rentals. The special stadium sales and use tax is a credit against the statewide sales and use tax. . . . Under the Stadium Act, the revenues from these taxes may be used only to finance the stadium. [Citation omitted.] The purpose of the District is to construct and operate the new stadium.

* * *

[T]he County filed a complaint seeking a declaratory judgment . . . validating the bonds. . . . [T]he trial court entered a declaratory judgment in favor of the County . . . , holding the bonds were valid and Initiative 16, if enacted, would "irreconcilably conflict" with state law. . . .

ANALYSIS

A. Declaratory Judgments of Local Bond Issues

This case is before us under RCW 7.25 providing for declaratory judgments as to local bond issues. . . . The statute, by its wording, contemplates an advisory opinion from a court as to the validity of an ordinance authorizing an issuance of bonds. Courts in other jurisdictions have articulated the purpose of statutory validation statutes. For instance, the Mississippi Supreme Court said:

> The main purpose of a statutory validation proceeding is to provide a forum and course of legal procedure to which a political district or subdivision may resort for the purpose of having the validity of the proposed bonds finally determined and adjudicated in advance of their issuance, "in order that the bonds so validated might be readily sold in the market, to create in the mind of the bond buyer a sense of security, in that by the decree of the court and the fiat of the Legislature there could be no further attack upon the validity of the bond issue."

Street v. Town of Ripley, 173 Miss. 225, 161 So. 855, 859, 102 A.L.R. 82 (1935) . . . *See also State v. City of Miami*, 113 Fla. 280, 152 So. 6, 8 (1933). . . .

* * *

A leading treatise on municipal law offers the following guidelines for testing the validity of a bond:

1. Is there legislative or constitutional authority delegated to the municipality to issue the bonds for the particular purpose?
2. Was the statute authorizing the bond issue constitutionally enacted? If not constitutionally enacted or if unconstitutional for any other reason, the issue is void and recitals are of no effect.
3. Is the purpose for which the bonds are issued, a public and corporate purpose, as distinguished from a private purpose?

15 EUGENE MCQUILLIN, MUNICIPAL CORPORATIONS § 43.04, at 575 (3rd ed. 1995).

* * *

For the purposes of determining the validity under RCW 7.25 of bonds issued by a local government, we expressly adopt the three-issue formulation for "validity" of bonds articulated in MCQUILLIN. Under RCW 7.25, our decision regarding the validity of bonds is conclusive as to any matter that is or should be brought within the ambit of the validity inquiry. . . . Moreover, we hold the burden of proving the validity of the bonds rests with King County and the District as the parties seeking to establish validity.

D. Use of Public Funds to Build a New Stadium Does Not Constitute Unconstitutional "Aid" to the Mariners

In applying the test for validity set forth above to this case, we note the Taxpayers do not challenge the legislative or constitutional authority of the County to issue the bonds. Moreover, we have already determined the bonds have a necessary public purpose. *Citizens for More Important Things*, 131 Wash. 2d at 416, 932 P.2d 135. Thus, the only item left to consider from the three-issue formulation is whether the statute authorizing the bond issue was constitutionally enacted.

The Taxpayers initially contend the bond issue violates Const. Art. VIII, §§ 5 and 7. "The 'aid' is in the form of construction at public expense of a new place of business for the [Mariners] to enhance its chance of making money."

At oral argument, counsel for the Taxpayers advanced the view that any benefit to a private organization may be violative of these constitutional provisions. We disagree. . . . An incidental benefit to a private individual or organization will not invalidate an otherwise valid public transaction. [Citation omitted.]

We held in *CLEAN* the stadium financing plan "does not amount to a gift of state funds nor a lending of the State's credit." *CLEAN*, 130 Wash. 2d at 800, 928 P.2d 1054. We suggested, however, that should the District "enter into an agreement with the Mariners that would permit the ball club to play its games in the stadium for only nominal rent, then the constitutional prohibitions against making a gift of state funds might be implicated." *Id.* This discussion in *CLEAN* is essentially the test for an unconstitutional gift of public funds. . . .

In deciding whether a public expenditure is a gift . . . , we have focused on two factors: consideration and donative intent. [Citation omitted.] Thus, to meet the burden of showing violation of the constitutional prohibition against gifts, the Taxpayers must show the lease amounts to "a transfer of property without consideration and with donative intent." [Citation omitted.]

In assessing consideration, courts do not inquire into the adequacy of consideration, but employ a legal sufficiency test. [Citations omitted.] We have been reluctant to engage in an in-depth analysis of the adequacy of consideration because such an analysis interferes unduly with governmental power to contract and would establish a "burdensome precedent" of judicial interference with government decisionmaking. [Citation omitted.]

Legal sufficiency "is concerned not with comparative value but with that which will support a promise." [Citation omitted.] . . . The adequacy of the consideration for the lease is a question of law. "Whether a contract is supported by consideration is a question of law and may be properly determined by a court on summary judgment." [Citation omitted.]

The Taxpayers now argue the lease agreement between the District and the Mariners for the use of the new stadium provides for only nominal rent and grossly inadequate consideration, thus implicating the constitutional concern. . . . The Taxpayers argue both donative intent and grossly inadequate return are present here.

A summary review of both the Stadium Act's requirements and the elements of the lease identifies the Mariners' obligations. The Stadium Act required (1) a commitment from the Mariners to play at least 90 percent of its games at the new stadium for the length of the term of the bonds; (2) a contribution of $45 million towards either preconstruction or construction costs of the stadium or associated facilities; and (3) profit-sharing with the District for the term of the bonds of profit earned after accounting for team losses after the effective date of the Act. . . .

The lease between the Mariners and the District contains the following additional obligations of the Mariners:

- payment of $700,000 in rent per annum
- payment of any construction cost overruns
- payment of any deficiencies on bonds for the parking facility
- maintenance and operation of the ballpark as a "first-class facility" in accordance with a management plan, and with oversight by the District, with enforcement mechanisms to ensure compliance
- making major repairs and capital improvements to the ballpark
- provision of insurance

Despite the Mariners' obligations under the lease, the Taxpayers call the lease "unconscionable," . . . arguing the consideration for the lease in favor of the County is so grossly inadequate the building of the stadium at public expense amounts to an unconstitutional gift.

The Taxpayers assert the County will receive nothing in return for its investment; thus, donative intent is present here. The assertion is simply another way of making their main point: that the lease is so much in favor of the Mariners, it amounts to a gift. In *CLEAN*, the Court said, "In our judgment, a plain reading of the Stadium Act reveals no intent by the Legislature to donate public funds to the Seattle Mariners." *CLEAN*, 130 Wash. 2d at 799, 928 P.2d 1054. . . . No donative intent is present here.

The Taxpayers assert the Mariners' obligations under the lease are a "sham and illusory," and do "truly do not give the public anything of value." [Citation omitted.] Their arguments do not bear close scrutiny in light of the Mariners' contribution of $45 million to the project, the profit-sharing provision, the 20-year lease obligation, the stadium maintenance requirement, and their obligations to pay insurance.

* * *

The Taxpayers claim that the profit sharing requirement in the lease is an "illusion," because the Mariners can doctor their books to pump up expenses as offsets to revenues in a way that will never show profit. [Citation omitted.] The County responds by noting the lease requires the Mariners' payments and expenses "be determined in accordance with generally accepted accounting principles[,]" [citation omitted] and that the County has the right to audit the Mariners' accounting to assure compliance with GAAP. Moreover, the mere possibility the Mariners may breach its promise in the future on its obligation to share profits with the County does not make this provision of the lease illusory. "An illusory promise is one which according to its terms makes performance optional with the promisor[.]" [Citation omitted.] The Mariners made an enforceable promise to share profits. The promise is not illusory.

The Taxpayers argue "the Club's promise to do business in the new ballpark is illusory because it has escape routes through the lease conditions[.]" [Citation omitted.] The Taxpayers' argument is disingenuous. The cited pages of the lease do not provide "escape" provisions that allow the mariners to leave of their own volition. They merely set forth certain obligations of the District, which, if not met, would allow the Mariners to terminate the lease. There are no escape routes that make illusory the Mariners' promise to play 90 percent of their games in the new stadium over the term of the lease. The Taxpayers neglect to mention the $70,000 annual rental due from the Mariners.

The Taxpayers contend the Mariners' agreement to be exclusively responsible for operations and maintenance of the ballpark is insignificant because the lease's definition of operations and maintenance does not include replacement or major repair. While the Operations and Maintenance section of the lease does not contain a repair obligation, the Major Maintenance and Capital Improvements section of the lease does. . . . "Major Maintenance and Capital Improvements" is defined to include "any work that is reasonably required to be performed . . . to repair, restore or replace components of the [Ballpark] necessitated by any damage, destruction, ordinary wear and tear, defects in construction or design, or any other cause to the condition required for consistency with [a first class facility]." [Citation omitted.] . . .

Finally, the Taxpayers assert without argument the requirement to maintain insurance is for the benefit of the Mariners. In fact, the insurance the lease requires . . . must protect the District "from all claims arising as a result of the ownership, use, management and operation of the [stadium]." [Citation omitted.] The Mariners are required to name the District as an additional insured on its liability policy. . . .

At its core, the Taxpayers' argument is the District and County made a bad deal. While that may or may not be true, "The wisdom of the King County plan is not for the consideration of this court — its constitutionality is." [Citation omitted.] The Taxpayers have failed to demonstrate a constitutional infirmity. . . . The Taxpayers' assertion that the Mariners' promises . . . are illusory is unsupported. In the absence of donative intent or grossly inadequate return, the Court's review is limited to the legal sufficiency of the consideration for the lease. [Citation omitted.] This lease met the test of legal sufficiency. . . .

G. The Collection of Stadium Sale and Use Tax Does Not Violate Constitutional Requirements

The Taxpayers make four arguments about the collection of the stadium sales and use tax. First, they argue the funding scheme is unconstitutional because it imposes a nonuniform state sales tax, requiring King County residents to pay state sales tax at a higher rate than residents of other counties. Second, they argue in the alternative the funding scheme is unconstitutional because King County residents pay less than their proportionate share of state sales tax. Third, they argue the .017 percent sales tax is being unconstitutionally diverted to the County, whereas the state constitution requires tax revenues to be deposited in the state treasury. Fourth, they argue the handling of the .017 percent sales tax violates the state constitution. . . .

The Taxpayers' argument is simply incorrect. The state sales tax is 6.5 percent. [Citation omitted.] The Taxpayers say the Stadium Act and Ordinance 12000 impose in King County a state sales tax .017 percent greater than in other counties. The Taxpayers ignore the provision of the Stadium Act that treats the .017 percent as a deduction against the 6.5 percent the King County taxpayers contribute to the state sales tax. . . . Thus, the taxpayers of King County do not pay more than 6.5 percent state sales tax.

Const. Art XI, § 9, reads, "No county, nor the inhabitants thereof, nor the property therein, shall be released or discharged from its or their proportionate share of taxes to be levied for state purposes, nor shall commutation for such taxes be authorized in any form whatever." If, the Taxpayers argue, the .017 percent is deducted . . . from the statewide 6.5 percent sales tax rate, then King County residents are paying only 6.483 percent sales tax for state purposes, and are essentially being unconstitutionally "released or discharged" from their fair share of taxes levied. . . .

This argument would have some force if the .017 percent were not being collected for a state purpose by a political subdivision of the state. . . . The building of the baseball stadium serves a state purpose, as we stated in *CLEAN*:

> If it is true that the existence of a major league baseball team in a city improves the economy of the state in which that city is located and

> enhances the fabric of life of its citizens, and we believe it is the prerogative of the Legislature to conclude that it does, it is certainly within the general police power of the State to construct a publicly owned stadium in order to promote those interests.

CLEAN, 130 Wash. 2d at 806, 928 P.2d 1054. . . .

* * *

Contrary to the Taxpayers' argument, the taxes are deposited in the State Treasury.

The Taxpayers also claim Const. Art. VIII, § 4 prevents the diversion of the .017 percent sales tax to the County. . . . "The object of the constitution . . . is to prevent expenditures of the public funds at the will of those who have them in charge, and without legislative direction." [Citation omitted.] The state treasurer cannot spend those funds "at will," because state statute prescribes the disposition of local sales and use taxes. . . . Moreover, the funds collected are paid into a special account in the state treasury whose sole purpose is the payment of the bonds. [Citation omitted.]

H. The Stadium Act Did Not Impermissibly Delegate Legislative Authority to the District

[Court held the Legislature properly delegated authority to a local municipal corporation to carry out a legislative determination.]

I. Initiative 16/Referendum

[Court held the constitutional and statutory grants of legislative authority to the counties to issue bonds preempts the field, leaving no room for concurrent jurisdiction pursuant to referendum or initiative.]

DURHAM, C.J., and DOLLIVER, SMITH, GUY, JOHNSON, and ALEXANDER, JJ., concur.

Economic and Fiscal Impact of BankOne Ballpark and Arizona Diamondbacks

Prepared for: **Downtown Phoenix Partnership**
Prepared by: **Elliott D. Pollack and Company**
September 10, 1998

* * *

1.02 SUMMARY OF FINDINGS AND CONCLUSIONS

Following are the primary findings and conclusions of this study.

1. The economic and fiscal impacts of the BankOne Ballpark and the Diamondbacks are significantly higher than originally anticipated in the 1993 Deloitte and Touche study. The increased cost of the stadium and higher than

anticipated levels of attendance at Diamondbacks' baseball games are the primary reasons for these higher impacts.

2. The total economic output of construction of the stadium is estimated at $693.6 million based on a construction cost of $354.5 million. Total annual employment over the two-year construction period is estimated at 4,626 jobs of which 1,775 are direct jobs and 2,851 indirect jobs (including induced jobs).

3. The City of Phoenix received a projected $4 million from various tax sources associated with the construction of the project and direct and indirect employment spending with the community. Maricopa County and all municipalities in the metro area, including Phoenix, received a combined $9.3 million. Excluding Phoenix, Maricipa County and the remaining cities received $5.3 million. Arizona state government received more than $19 million in revenue from the construction of the stadium.

4. Total 1998 direct revenues generated by the operation of the stadium and baseball team, which includes ticket sales, concessions, media, advertising and all other revenue, is projected at $129 million. Another $38 million in revenue is expected to be generated from out-of-stadium spending for restaurants, retail, parking and visiting baseball teams for a total of $167 million in direct spending. Using accepted economic multipliers, the total direct and indirect output of the stadium operations is $319 million. Total direct employment based on this level of sales activity is estimated at 1,716 jobs which includes the 738 employees directly employed by the Diamondbacks and stadium operator. Other direct jobs include those working in BOB's restaurants, media and advertising employees, and the employment supported by out-of-stadium spending. Another 2,394 indirect jobs have been created by the stadium operations for a total estimated employment impact of 4, 110 jobs.

5. For 1998, the City of Phoenix should receive over $2.3 million in tax revenue from stadium operations or approximately $1 million more than projected in 1993 study. Maricopa County, including all cities in the County, is projected to receive $5.7 million while the State of Arizona will collect over $9.1 million. Excluding Phoenix, Maricopa County and the remaining cities will receive $3.4 million. These are annual impacts that should recur each year assuming that attendance and spending patterns remain constant.

6. Based on data obtained from the Diamondbacks and the City of Phoenix, the stadium and its associated restaurants account for approximately 94% of the increase in Downtown restaurant sales, with most of the sale captured by the ballpark's concession stands. The convenience and broad selection of food options has assisted in this high capture rate of restaurant sales. Apparently, visitors to the stadium are not traveling far beyond the stadium proper itself, perhaps due to the closeness of parking facilities in the warehouse dis-

trict. Another factor that may limit walking to out-of-stadium restaurants is the summer heat.

7. Downtown Phoenix experienced a large 94% increase ($10.9 million) in the sale of retail goods in the first half of 1998. Virtually all of the increase during the first quarter of 1998, about $5 million, was unrelated to sporting or entertainment events, the Diamondbacks and BankOne Ballpark. In the second quarter, retail sales increased by nearly $6 million, $2 million of which was not related to sporting events. The remaining sales are primarily explained by the sale of Diamondbacks novelties and apparel at a variety of outlets.

8. BankOne Ballpark is a key component of Downtown cultural, hotel and sports facilities that are now reaching a critical mass. Two new hotels are planned for the area and a major new office complex is expected to break ground shortly. A number of residential projects are also on the drawing boards or already under construction. Attendance at Downtown Phoenix venues has been increasing over the past few years and the stadium will provide a significant influx of visitors to the area during the next few years. This synergy between public and private investment in the area will promote additional real estate development and assist in growing visitation to the Downtown as metro area residents and tourists become familiar with its cultural, entertainment, hotel, restaurant and sporting event offerings. Over time, BOB will contribute more to visitation in Downtown than just its 3 million annual baseball fans.

NOTES AND COMMENTS

1. Local governments regularly acquire stadium sites through use of the eminent domain power. For unsuccessful attempts to challenge condemnations under the "public use" standard, *see City of Arlington, Texas v. Golddust Twins Realty Corp.*, 41 F.3d 960 (5th Cir. 1994). General commitment of state and local funds to construct or improve sports facilities is traditionally considered a valid expenditure for a legitimate public purpose. The Illinois Supreme Court rejected a challenge to the public financing of improvements to Soldier Field, the home of the Chicago Bears, holding that the public assistance did not violate the provision of the Illinois Constitution requiring public funds be used only for public purposes. *Friends of the Parks v. The Chicago Park District*, 786 N.E.2d 161 (Ill. 2003). *See also CLEAN v. State*, 928 P.2d 1054 (Wash. 1997). The United States Supreme Court, in *Kelo v. City of New London, Connecticut*, 125 S. Ct. 2655 (2005), upheld under 5th Amendment analysis, a state statute authorizing the use of eminent domain to promote economic development. Is there a valid argument that the utilization of eminent domain for stadium purposes is unconstitutional?

2. Many professional sports facilities in the 1990s, as indicated by the Congressional testimony above, are underwritten either wholly or partially by public entities. *See generally*, Greenberg, *Sports Facility Financing & Development Trends in the United States*, 15 MARQ. SPORTS L. REV. 93 (2004); Fox, *Public Finance & the West Side* Stadium, 71 BROOK. L. REV. 477 (2005); Smith, *If You Build It, Will They Come? The Relationship Between Public Financing of Sports Facilities & Quality of Life in America's Cities*, 7 GEO. PUB. POL'Y REV. 45 (2001). Cities, counties, states, teams, and leagues must resolve issues of funding arrangements, design, and "obstructionist" lawsuits. *Tiger Stadium Fan Club, Inc. v. Governor,* 553 N.W.2d 7 (Mich. App. 1996) (Detroit); *Laramore v. Illinois Sports Facilities Authority*, 1996 WL 153672 (N.D. Ill. 1996) (Chicago); *Finlan v. City of Dallas*, 888 F. Supp. 779 (N.D. Tex. 1995) (Dallas). For description of a privately funded ballpark, *see* Schoenfeld, *Giants Defy Skeptics, Build New Ballpark on their Own Dime*, 2 SPORTS BUS. J. 1, 56 (Aug. 30-Sept. 5, 1999).

As in the *King County* case above, governmental entities sometimes file declaratory actions to determine the appropriateness of the public funding. The "validation lawsuits," by securing a judgment as to the lawfulness of the use of public funds, clears the way for issuance of bonds. Most states enable the joinder of all opposing parties and an expedited schedule. In a Florida case, the former Mayor of Tampa, William Poe, sought an injunction against the City of Tampa, Hillsborough County, and the Tampa Sports Authority preventing the construction of a stadium for the Tampa Bay Buccaneers. Plaintiff argued that defendants were using taxing power to aid a private entity, and thus violated the Florida Constitution. The trial court ruled that the bonds were invalid due to one provision of the financing plan. The Florida Supreme Court overruled, holding that although one clause benefited the private football club, the stadium served a "paramount public purpose," and was thus valid. *Poe v. Hillsborough County*, 695 So. 2d 672 (Fla. 1997). *See*, Acton & Campbell, *Public Funding of Sports Stadiums and Other Recreational Facilities: Can the Deal be "Too Sweet?"*, 27 STETSON L. REV. 877 (1998); Safir, *If You Build It, They Will Come: The Politics of Financing Sports Stadium Construction*, 13 J.L. & POL. 937 (1997).

3. Local or regional sports authorities are sometimes created by state legislation to facilitate the development, maintenance, and operation of sports facilities. The typical sports authority, a quasi-governmental agency, possesses the power to borrow money, issue bonds or notes, acquire land, charge rent, and otherwise oversee operations of the facility. *See generally* Stratos & Horrow, *Facility Development and the Sports Authority, in* 3 LAW OF PROFESSIONAL AND AMATEUR SPORTS ch. 22 (Uberstine ed. 2005). Prior to the enactment of the 1986 Tax Reform Act, facilities were publicly funded by issuance of tax exempt bonds. Since 1986, communities and club owners have joined to produce creative financing arrangements for the funding of facilities projects.

4. The concept of the luxury suite, first introduced by the Houston Astrodome in 1965, has evolved along with notions of club and premium seating to generate considerable revenue for the underwriting of stadium financing or club operations. As indicated in the Congressional testimony above, cities primarily compete for professional sports franchises on the basis of facility offerings. The "permanent" or "personal seating license" projects exist as an even greater source of capital. The "PSL" is the purchased right (and obligation) buy a season ticket for a specific seat in an arena or stadium for as long as the club plays in the facility. If the right exists for a limited period of time, the license is referred to as "personal" rather than "permanent." The cost of the yearly season ticket is additional. Importantly, the "PSL" is transferable. *See Permanent Seat Licenses*, KPMG'S FINANCIAL AND DEVELOPMENT ADVISORY NEWSLETTER FOR PROFESSIONALS SERVING THE SPORTS INDUSTRY 2 (Spring/Summer 1996); *Excerpts from Primer on Stadium and Arena Financing*, Smith Barney (Nov. 1995), *published in* Proceedings, *If You Build It, Will They Come?*, National Council for Urban Economic Development, Feb. 1-3, 1996. Is the "PSL" a security? Are the proceeds treated as taxable income if sold by a governmental entity? Private entity?

Contract questions sometimes arise between the team and fans regarding obligations incurred pursuant to PSL marketing schemes. *See Yocca v. Pittsburgh Steelers Sports Inc.*, 806 A.2d 936 (Pa. Cmwlth. 2002); *Reedy v. Cincinnati Bengals, Inc.*, 758 N.E.2d 678 (Ohio App. 2001). Rights and duties under ordinary season tickets plans may also be questioned. The New England Patriots terminated the season ticket privileges of a 20-year ticket holder. Words on the back of the Patriots' tickets states: "This ticket and all season tickets are revocable licenses. The Patriots reserve the right to revoke such licenses, in their sole discretion, at any time and for any reason." The season ticket holder claimed that the 20-year relationship created a contractual right to renew season tickets annually. Plaintiff also argued that the process used by the Patriots constituted a breach of the implied covenant of good faith and fair dealing. Held: Season ticket packages are revocable licenses, not contracts between teams and ticket holders. *Yarde Metals, Inc. v. New England Patriots*, 834 N.E.2d 1233 (Mass. App. Ct. 2005).

5. Some economists and others question the positive economic impact of professional sports teams and facilities on the community. *See* Parlow, *Publicly Financed Sports Facilities: Are They Economically Justifiable? A Case Study of the Los Angeles Staples Center*, 10 U. MIAMI BUS. L. REV. 483 (2002) (publicly financed sports facilities are rarely justifiable, but in certain circumstances, as with the Staples Center, financial deals can be structured with favorable benefits to both the team and governmental entity); Johnson & Whitehead, *Value of Public Goods from Sports Stadiums: The CVM Approach*, 18 CONTEMP. ECON. POL'Y 48 (2000) (utilizes contingent valuation method to measure the value of public goods generated by two proposed projects in Lexington, Kentucky); SHROPSHIRE, THE SPORTS FRANCHISE GAME: CITIES IN PURSUIT OF SPORTS FRANCHISES, EVENTS, STADIUMS, AND ARENAS (1995). *But see,* Sanderson, *In Defense of New Sports Stadiums, Ballparks, & Arenas*, 10 MARQ. SPORTS L.J. 173 (2000).

A collection of writings regarding the economic impact of sports teams and stadiums is found in SPORTS, JOBS AND TAXES (Noll & Zimbalist, ed.) (Brookings Inst., 1997). *See also*, Fraas, *"Bankers Up!" Professional Sports Facility Financ-*

ing and Other Opportunities for Bank Involvement in Lucrative Professional Sports, 3 N.C. BANKING INST. 201 (1999); A Report by the National Conference of State Legislatures: "Fiscal Affairs: Playing the Stadium Game," found at 549 PLI/Pat 375 (Feb.-Mar. 1999); New York State Independent Budget Office, *Double Play: The Economics and Financing of Stadiums for the Yankees and Mets* (April 30, 1998).

6. Are questions of financing and siting for a professional sports facility different from those for the funding and siting of a dam, power plant, or other project? Inevitably, a cost-benefit analysis is projected for the venture. Intangible costs and benefits are assigned values, usually by a team of economists. Which party is the proper one to decide the viability of the project? *See* Dorfman, *An Introduction to Benefit-Cost Analysis in* ECONOMICS OF THE ENVIRONMENT (3d ed. 1993). *Compare* Kelman, *Cost-Benefit Analysis: An Ethical Critique*, 1981 REGULATION 33 (Jan./Feb. 1981). The economists utilize an assumption that consumers "have only so much income . . . [to] . . . spend on leisure and entertainment activities," and thus ballpark spending diverts dollars otherwise spent elsewhere in the local economy. What is the nature of the factual predicate that supports the assumption? What other general assumptions are subject to question?

C. ASSURANCES — CONTRACTS BETWEEN CLUB AND FACILITY

Leases negotiated between clubs and governmental entities, or stadium authorities, sometimes include clauses enabling parties to seek a decree of specific performance of the lease where one party breaches or threatens to breach the lease. As the cases below indicate, the clauses as well as the general equitable principles may be judicially recognized. The legal issue becomes more important in the 1990s, as professional sports teams readily vacate traditional home territories for better financial opportunities elsewhere. Attorneys drafting lease documents consider various protective clauses in order to serve the public entity client, and preserve taxpayer interest.

The **Problem** below is based on the Spring 1996 dispute between the Seattle Seahawks and King County, Washington (Kingdome). The Seahawks and County sued each other on the same day, but in different counties. *Seattle Seahawks, Inc. v. King County*, 128 Wash. 2d 915, 913 P.2d 375 (Wash. 1996) (proper venue in King County).

PROBLEM

A club owner possesses an exclusive lease to operate a major league ballclub in the local stadium. The lease will not expire by its own terms for another two years. The owner desires to relocate the club to the Los Angeles area. She feels that she can gain league approval for the relocation, but seeks your advice concerning the burdensome lease. Lease paragraphs provide, as follows:

1. The Club shall play all regular season home games in the Stadium;
2. The Stadium Authority shall maintain the stadium as a "first class" sports facility;
3. Enforcement of this Agreement: It is recognized that the obligations of the parties to this Agreement are unique in nature and that it may be specifically or mandatorily enforced by either party.

The lease was renegotiated five years ago. Based on the lease promises, the City expended several million dollars to renovate the facility. Since that time regular maintenance has occurred, but no further capital improvements. The Stadium appears deficient as compared to recently built stadiums. For example, the Stadium is not constructed to generate maximum revenue from prime seating, permanent seating licenses, luxury suites, etc. The owner possesses a "seismic" study which indicates that the Stadium is unsafe in the event of an earthquake. The City, however, had a study which reaches an opposite conclusion.

What actions do you suggest the Owner initiate with regard to the scenario above? The City and Stadium Authority have filed suit seeking specific performance of the lease obligations. What are your defenses? What arguments do you expect from the City?

CASE FILE

CITY OF NEW YORK v. NEW YORK YANKEES

117 Misc. 2d 332, 458 N.Y.S.2d 486 (Sup. Ct. 1983)

RICHARD S. LANE, Justice:

On or about November 10, 1982 the New York Yankees told the City by telephone that the 1983 home opening series with the Detroit Tigers scheduled for the Stadium on April 11, 12 and 13 would be played in Denver. A day earlier renewal applications had been sent to box holders for a curtailed home schedule starting April 15.

The City promptly commenced an action seeking declaratory and injunctive relief, and moves herein for a preliminary injunction enjoining execution or implementation of any agreement with Denver pending trial.

The Yankees answered asserting failure to state a cause of action, waiver, estoppel and laches, and resisted the motion for a preliminary injunction on the basis of communications between the parties hereinafter described.

With the season only a few months off the motion may be the whole ball game.

Sometime after the extensive renovations to the Stadium undertaken by the City as the cornerstone of the 1972 lease with the Yankees, it was discovered there were certain structural flaws in the stands in lines abutting on left field and right field. Temporary repairs were made for several years; permanent repairs were scheduled to be made between the close of the 1982 season and the opening of the 1983 season; and plans and specifications were drafted, all with the participation and approval of the Yankees.

Came July 30, 1982 and the Deputy Commissioner of Parks wrote to the Yankees expressing confidence that the goal of completion prior to the beginning of the 1983 season could be achieved, but also expressing a caveat as follows: "However, in view of the magnitude of the project and the small time frame we would consider it prudent to establish a contingency schedule for Yankee games to be played at the Stadium during the early part of the season. While we will attempt to provide for contingencies in the contract itself, since a large part of the work will be accomplished in the winter it is conceivable that inclement weather and other unforeseeables may negatively affect our schedule. We would appreciate any thoughts and assistance you can give us in this connection. If you have any questions, please don't hesitate to call me." The City contends, and the Yankees on argument concede, that there had been ongoing discussions between the parties about problems created by the proposed construction work, and that this letter was written at the request of the Yankees as the basis for consultation with the Tigers and with the American League.

The Summer passed without any response from the Yankees to this July 30th letter. Meanwhile the plans and specifications were put out for bid, and a contract was let calling for completion by February 28. The contract included unusual provisions for overtime and enclosing the affected areas to protect against any interruption of the work as a result of adverse weather. In addition it was now understood with the contractor, as apparently it was not in the earlier discussions between the parties, that the playing field itself would not be affected in any way, thus saving about five weeks. The Yankees were fully briefed on this progress in early September.

Came October 8, 1982 and the Yankees at last replied to the July 30th letter requesting a guarantee of completion in a timely manner and an indemnification against any loss of revenue if the Stadium should not be available for opening day. The City's initial reaction was affirmative. However, on October 12 while the City's formal answer was allegedly awaiting the approval of the Corporation Counsel, the Yankees spelled out that the guarantee would have to extend to no debris or litter in view of fans and no seats unavailable on opening day. Scrapping the proposed guarantee and indemnification, if indeed it had ever been drafted, the Commissioner of Parks instead wrote personally to Mr. Steinbrenner on October 19, 1982. He adverted to the history of cooperation between them and to all of the efforts being made to assure timely completion, and suggested that, in the worst case, only 1000 to 2000 seats would be unavailable for which the Yankees would be compensated by abatement of rent pursuant to the lease.

Again there was no immediate response from the Yankees. Some three weeks later came the bombshell call about Denver.

There can be no dispute that playing in Denver would violate Section # 4.7 of the Lease requiring all home games to be played in the Stadium through the year 2002.

Is such violation justified in any way by the pas de deux between the parties during the Summer and early Fall?

The first possibility that comes to mind is anticipatory breach by the City. But clearly that possibility has to be rejected . . . .

In the first place nothing in the July 30th letter may be construed as a repudiation of the Lease. Implicit and explicit therein is the City's intention and expectation of being able to perform.

In the second place, even if a repudiation might be found lurking in the letter, it certainly does not go to the entire Lease. Partial repudiation is not sufficient. A distinction has to be drawn between anticipatory breach and just plain breach. The former entitles the other party to terminate, change position, and/or sue for damages before the time for performance has arrived. The latter merely allows the other party to sue for damages in the event of flawed performance.

In the third place, even if a repudiation might be found lurking in the letter and even if the principle of anticipatory breach might be stretched to encompass partial repudiation, the record establishes a retraction. By the early Fall the City is no longer talking about contingent scheduling, but merely of the possibility in the worst case of the unavailability of a couple of thousand seats. The threat to the Yankees' ability to open on April 11 in the Stadium, which may have been real enough in June, is substantially evaporated well before the consummation of negotiations with Denver. The chronology of those negotiations is not revealed in the papers, but the Court notes that the Denver Mile High Stadium user contract was not mailed to the Yankees until November 10.

Commendably recognizing the weakness of the anticipatory breach theory, the Yankees place greater reliance on the doctrine of waiver and estoppel. But these are equally tenuous reeds. Since there is no suggestion of any fraud or negligent misrepresentation by the City true estoppel or "estoppel in pais" is not involved here . . . . As used in defense here estoppel is just another way of saying waiver. It requires a showing that the City had intentionally and overtly abandoned its rights under the Section # 4.7 of the Lease or had agreed to excuse the failure of the Yankees to comply with their obligations thereunder — *i.e.,* to play the first scheduled home series in the Stadium; 1 WILLISTON ON CONTRACTS, (3rd Ed.) Section # 140; 5 WILLISTON ON CONTRACTS (3rd Ed.), Sections # 678 and 679; 22 N.Y.Jur. (2d), Contracts, Section # 330. No such showing may be found in the letter of July 30th, and it is certainly negatived by the City's subsequent communications and actions.

Nor may the City be charged with laches. It commenced this action within days after learning of the Yankees' intentions.

Accordingly the Court finds a strong likelihood of eventual success by the City in this action.

The Court also finds that the equities weigh on the side of the City. Viewed as objectively as possible it would appear that Mr. Steinbrenner, ignoring the good faith efforts by the City to satisfy his needs, was grabbing a pretext to take his team to greener pastures — i.e. a larger stadium and a populace with an unfulfilled yearning for major league baseball. Tending to demonstrate that concern about the conditions of the Stadium was not his only motivation are the following: a) He waited passively throughout the entire summer while the risk of non-availability of the Stadium was at its highest; b) He escalated his demand when it appeared that the City was about to give him the guarantee and indemnification he requested; c) He chose to negotiate with cities seeking a major league franchise while ignoring the obvious solutions — Shea Stadium or Tiger Stadium in Detroit; and d) In November looking forward, if the Stadium might not be ready on April 11, how could he assume that it would be ready on April 15?

Furthermore, to allow the Yankees to proceed to contract with Denver might open a real Pandora's Box. It would leave the Yankees with conflicting contract obligations. It would invite litigation in Colorado as well as New York with results in doubt throughout the winter not to mention the nightmare of possibly opposite results.

Finally the Court easily finds a threat of irreparable injury to the City . . . . Much more is at stake than merely the loss of direct and indirect revenue to the City.

The Yankee pin stripes belong to New York like Central Park, like the Statue of Liberty, like the Metropolitan Museum of Art, like the Metropolitan Opera, like the Stock Exchange, like the lights of Broadway, etc. Collectively they are "The Big Apple." Any loss represents a diminution of the quality of life here, a blow to the City's standing at the top, however narcissistic that perception may be.

"Big deal" argue the Yankees. We open in Seattle anyhow on April 5. We will have a New York opening with all the traditional hoopla on April 15. And it's only three games we are talking about which is proportionately a much smaller percentage of the season than the two games in the Jets case. However it is the symbolism of the act not the quantity which counts. Any reduction in the number of home games, especially if it involves the home opening games eagerly awaited by the real fans after a long winter in the hot stove league, erodes the ties of loyalty between the people of the City and their team. Dare one whisper the dreaded words: "The Denver Yankees"?

No money damages can measure or assuage this kind of harm.

Taking major league baseball on tour, Mr. Steinbrenner, is an idea whose time has not yet come. Perhaps it will come in due course. As the New York Times editorialized recently: "And however the Court rules in this case, fans accustomed to seeing players shift venue every season, had better get ready for the day when the whole team calls the whole country home." But if and when it does come, it should be institutionalized by the League so that no home stadium contracts are violated.

The motion for a preliminary injunction is granted.

CITY OF NEW YORK v. NEW YORK JETS FOOTBALL CLUB, INC.

90 Misc. 2d 311, 394 N.Y.S.2d 799 (1977)

HAROLD BAER, Justice:

This is a motion, brought on by order to show cause, for a preliminary injunction. The order of March 18, 1977 included a temporary restraining order pending the hearing. The order stayed the New York Jets Football Club, Inc. (Jets) and its acting president, Leon Hess, from breaching its lease agreement with the City of New York (City) by scheduling home football games at a place other than Shea Stadium. It stayed the New Jersey Sports and Exposition Authority (The Authority) and its Chairman, David Werblin, from inducing a breach of the Jets' contract with the City by arranging a lease whereby the Jets would play some home games in their facility (Meadowlands) in New Jersey. It enjoined the National Football League (N.F.L.) and its Commissioner, Pete Rozelle, from scheduling any Jets home games during the baseball season so as to violate the Jets-City lease agreement.

Shea Stadium, built by the City, was leased to the Metropolitan Baseball Club, Inc. (Mets) by agreement dated October 6, 1961. Later, on September 10, 1964, a lease agreement was entered into between the City and Gotham Football Club, Inc. predecessor of the Jets. No preliminary relief was requested in the original motion by the City against the Mets and its Chairman, M. Donald Grant. However, a later motion, by order to show cause, requested that they be stayed from failing to perform the agreement with the City. The Jets cross-moved for partial summary judgment. The Authority and Werblin cross–moved to dismiss the complaint on jurisdictional as well as on substantive grounds. The NFL and Rozelle likewise cross–moved for dismissal of the complaint on jurisdictional as well as on substantive grounds.

* * *

The Jets oppose the City's motion for a preliminary injunction on several grounds. They contend that no preliminary relief is warranted because the City has failed to establish irreparable injury or a meritorious action with likelihood of ultimate success. The Jets contend that a balancing of the equities would favor them. They claim that the agreement between the parties permits home games scheduled within the baseball occupancy period to be played elsewhere when there is a conflict (Sec. 4.2 agreement).

The Jet-City lease agreement requires that home games after September 1st of each year be played in Shea Stadium (Agreement § 4.7, § 38.1(b)). This requirement was a vital part of the consideration for the agreement. The City built the Stadium at great cost. It required state legislation to construct the Stadium (Chapter 729, Laws of 1961; Adm. Code § 532-15.0) and Board of Estimate approval of the lease agreements with the Mets and the Jets. The public interest and purpose of the stadium construction is detailed in the statute. The latter part is quoted: "It is hereby declared that all of the purposes referred to in this sub-division b are for the benefit of the people of the city and for the improvement of their health, welfare, recreation and prosperity, for the promotion of competitive sports for youth and the prevention of juvenile delinquency, and for the improvement of trade and commerce, and are hereby declared to be public purposes".

The City was not authorized to construct the stadium for the lease money consideration. The City, as a corporate body, has not, will not, nor was it intended to make a profit from stadium rental. It is the City as a community, "the people of the City" to quote the statute, who are here threatened with irreparable injury. The purpose of the construction and the leases, and the requirement that home games, both baseball and football, be played at Shea, are inextricably entwined with the vital public interest as quoted above from the enabling legislation. Every home game not played at Shea causes more than a loss of rental. That is only money. It results in injury to the welfare, recreation, prestige, prosperity and trade and commerce of the people of the City.

The Jets argue that "It's only two games. No big deal". Every business that leaves the City; every major corporate home office that departs for the suburbs; every drop in the number of people employed reported by the Bureau of Labor Statistics; every downward thrust in the City's credit standing; each team that leaves for a greener (larger) stadium is another drop of the City's life blood. Every reduction in the number of home games seriously adds to the cumulative effect upon the City's viability. Two games may sound small but they are an important part of the home game schedule. Such injuries are not measurable in money damages nor could money repair the harm. . . . The threat of irreparable injury has not merely been shown, it is self-evident.

Further, the lease agreement grants the City the right to injunctive relief against a threatened breach (27.7(a)). The Jets argue that the provision is mere "boilerplate", found in most leases and never enforced. The cases cited by defendants involving department stores and supermarkets as well as the personal service cases cited by the City are inapposite. Money damages may compensate a developer or manufacturer but money cannot compensate the people of this City for immeasurable, indirect and intangible damages.

The Jets have moved for what they call "partial" summary judgment. They assert that they are entitled to play home games away from Shea Stadium because of the Mets baseball schedule and request the court to so rule. In making the motion they go directly to the only vital issue between the Jets and the City. They recognize that issue is one of law, not of fact. They label their motion "partial" because they present it only in the context of the two games for this year scheduled in violation of the stay. In truth, the issue is not "partial" at all. Determination of the Jets' right to play those two games away from Shea requires interpretation of the Jets-City lease agreement and will fix their rights and their obligations for the balance of the lease as well. If they are correct in their contention that they may play those two games away from Shea not only will the temporary stay be terminated, this action will also be terminated. If they are wrong in their contention, the action will also be terminated. Since the only other issue, irreparable injury, has been determined as between the Jets and the City there are no issues to be resolved by trial between them.

The Jets' lease. In Section 38.1(b) the Jets agree that they will "not do or suffer to be done anything . . . to permit (them) to play home games in any such other city or location". There are exceptions to the home game requirement, specifically § 4.2 and § 4.7 to accommodate the prior lessee, the Mets, so as not to interfere with the baseball season. The Jets and the NFL were cognizant of the baseball schedule. For nine years and for four earlier years by the Jets' predecessors, schedules were promulgated so as not to interfere with the Mets' schedule. To schedule a game in direct conflict with the known baseball schedule does not permit the Jets to take advantage of § 4.2 or § 4.7, rather it is a breach of the agreement.

The Jets entered into this lease with full knowledge of, and subject to the Mets' lease. Section 1.1(a) requires that the Jets' lease "harmonize" with the Mets' lease; that to the extent necessary the Jets' lease "shall be deemed revised, rewritten or excised" to accomplish that result. Section 1.1(c) provides that any omission in the Jets' lease required to be made by the Mets' lease "shall be deemed to have been made". Lest there be any misunderstanding, two copies of the Mets' lease were initialed by the City and the Jets and incorporated, not merely by reference, but physically, in the Jets' lease.

The Mets' lease. The Mets are granted the priority right to play home games at Shea during the "baseball occupancy period", a time span which extends from seven days before the baseball season opens to the date of the last scheduled home game. During that period the City may authorize other uses of Shea such as Jets home games during Met road trips defined in the agreement as the period from a first away game to four days before the next scheduled home game. The lease, however, has a contingent definition: until the Mets are mathematically eliminated each year the "baseball occupancy period" is defined as ending "20 days after the end of the regular baseball season". The lease quite obviously attempts to reserve for the Mets the dates needed for play-off and World Series games. Whether it has done this with full effectiveness may be questioned but is not pertinent to determination of the Jets' motion for summary judgment and the City's motion against the Jets and the NFL.

After 13 years of scheduling home games to accommodate to the provisions of the Mets' lease, the Jets and the NFL, now schedule two home games, one patently impossible to be played at Shea because of a scheduled Met game (September 25, 1977) and the other (October 2, 1977) on a day, which rightly or wrongly, the Mets claim is a reserved day. In addition, the interpretation of the Jets' lease is aided by the constitution and by-laws of the National Football League. That 90 page document is replete with professional football's recognition of the need to schedule early season games around the late season baseball games to accommodate the 15 football teams that share stadia with baseball teams. Even the realignment of teams within the two football conferences is required to take into consideration "baseball conflicts involving clubs playing home games in baseball stadiums (sic)". (§ 4.4(h)).

The Jets insist, however, that §§ 4.2 and 4.7 justify their playing a home game away from Shea on September 25th. When the specific language of § 4.2 is examined, the Jets' reliance on it must be recognized as misplaced. The section is not an avoidance of § 38.1(b). It does not permit the Jets to effect advance scheduling of home games outside of Shea. It permits the City to cancel an already scheduled Jets' game. Similarly, § 4.7 read without reference to the rest of the lease, or to the Mets' lease, seems to excuse performance. However, neither of these sections are to be read in a vacuum. They must be read in the context of §§ 1.1 and 38.1(b) of the Jets' lease. They must be read in the context that both parties, when executing the lease, knew that when the football schedule is released in the spring of each year, the possibility always exists of the baseball teams requiring home dates in addition to the scheduled games, for playoff or World Series games. The Mets' lease anticipated that possibility, the NFL's constitution and By-Laws anticipated that possibility and § 4.2 and § 4.7 of the Jets' lease anticipated it. When read to "harmonize" with the Mets' lease (§ 1.1) and to afford the City its rights under § 38.1(b), it is evident that these sections are escapes for scheduling impossibilities, not excuses to leave for a larger stadium.

The performance required of the Jets under § 38.1(b) is not impossible so as to call into play either § 4.2 or § 4.7. A contractor is excused from performance when performance is impossible. That rule does not apply when performance is rendered impossible by the contractor's own act or failure to act, or the actions or failure of those bound to him. . . . Clearly under all the provisions of the Jets' lease, "harmonized" with the Mets' lease, the Jets and the NFL as will be shown, are required to schedule home games around the Mets instead of deliberately creating a conflict. It is their own act that is causing impossibility. The Jets' desire to play early season home games is understandable (even though manifested so threateningly for the first time only when a larger stadium is available), but that desire is not a substitute for actual impossibility which may excuse performance.

It may not be contended that an outside force, the NFL, makes performance excusably impossible. The NFL is not a stranger to the Jets' lease. The lease had long been in existence when the Jets joined the League. The lease was, and is, a public document. Even if it weren't, the Mets' use of Shea was open and notorious and the NFL had experience with shared stadia. The League knew or should have known that the Jets could not have free and totally unencumbered use of Shea. Even if it did not examine the lease, it accepted the Jets into the League subject to that existing lease. Moreover, contracts such as that between the Jets and the League or the television contracts cannot serve as the basis of an excuse of impossibility of performance. The Jets must take the risk of conflict between them and the pre-existing Jets' lease agreement (*Canadian I. A. Co. v. Dunbar, supra*).

The Jets' motion must be denied. As stated earlier there are no factual issues remaining. Summary judgment will be granted against the Jets and the NFL. Jets home games may be scheduled only on dates which "harmonize" with the Mets' schedule.

Irreparable injury and the threatened breach have been established. In fashioning its remedy a Court of Equity must weigh the effect on the parties. Enforcement of a contract which results in minimal benefit to one party while causing great harm to another cannot be countenanced in Equity. In balancing the equities among the parties involved, it should be noted that the Mets hold a prior lease; that the Jets and their predecessor were fully aware of the terms of the Mets' lease, in particular the definitions and Article V; that the Jets or their predecessor entered into their lease agreement with the City fully aware of those terms (*See* § 1.1 of Jets-City Agreement); they were in no way coerced. The Jets and the NFL adhered to the terms of the agreement for nine years and now for the first time set a home game on a scheduled baseball date during the baseball occupancy period. The Jets and the NFL have violated a restraining order. The Jets have available other early season home dates at Shea. Monday night September 26th, October 2nd, October 9th and October 16th are all available to satisfy that desire. The Court notes that only half the teams can ever open at home and only half the teams can ever play two or more of their first four games at home. Even with this years Mets' schedule the Jets and the NFL could have scheduled as many as three of the first four Jets' games at home. The Court notes, too, that elsewhere in the League the football schedule is set with knowledge of the potential for conflict with playoff and World Series games. Equity and good faith must be co-existent. Not only did the Jets and the NFL set conflict dates for the regular season games, they did the same for the two Jet exhibition home games. Both August 5th and August 20th are scheduled Met home dates. These were scheduled despite the fact that under the leases at least four other open dates are available. Although the City concedes that pre-season home games, under the lease, may be played away from Shea, one must wonder whether the 20,000 additional seats at the Meadowlands had anything to do with the dates chosen. When all of the foregoing, in particular the alternatives available to the Jets, are balanced against the nature of the injury to the City, the equities need be weighed no further. Injunctive relief is appropriate.

However, this court is aware of the desire of the Jets to play some of their early games at home. It is also aware of the preferential lease agreement held by the Mets. Accommodation can and should be made so that early games can be played at home by the Jets. This is for the future. At this time nevertheless the Jets can play some of their early games at the stadium. The Mets' last scheduled home game in 1977 falls on Sunday, September 25, 1977. They then leave on a road trip, ending the season on the road on October 2, 1977. They will not need use for the stadium except in the unlikely event of leading the Eastern division of the National League. Even if that should occur, they would not be scheduled to play at Shea until October 7, 1977 (more than four days after October 2nd). They cannot shift their last home game from September 25th. The Jets may utilize the stadium facilities, and the stadium can be made ready for football on Monday night, September 26, 1977, Sunday, October 2, 1977, Sunday, October 9, 1977 and each Sunday thereafter during the football season.

* * *

In lieu of further proceedings the Court suggests a meeting of all parties with the court prior to May 20, 1977 so as to avoid further litigation. The purpose of the meeting would be to attempt to harmonize the requirements of all parties and to formulate feasible joint use of the stadium. Such meeting may be held on May 17, 1977 at 2 P.M. o'clock if all parties agree and so inform the court.

At this time, judgment may be settled for injunctive relief as demanded against the Jets and NFL in accordance with this decision. Also, an order shall be settled dismissing the complaint against the Authority and Werblin and severing the action and the remaining motion against the Mets.

Notes and Comments

1. A New York state court issued a preliminary injunction preventing the NHL club, New York Islanders, from playing its home games anywhere other than the Nassau Veterans Memorial Coliseum. *County of Nassau v. New York Islanders Hockey Club*, Case No. 98-024330 (Sup. Ct. Nassau Co. 1998). The lease contains a provision that prohibits the team from doing anything "to cause . . . the franchise to be transferred to any location other than the coliseum." The Islanders earlier filed suit seeking an order enabling the club to leave the coliseum, citing safety concerns. *New York Islanders Hockey Club v. SMG*, Case No. CV-98-5698 (E.D.N.Y. 1998).

2. In the fall of 2001, the Commissioner of Baseball announced that MLB contemplated the contraction of the number of clubs for play in the following year, focusing primarily on the Minnesota Twins and Montreal Expos. Although the contraction did not occur and was barred by the subsequent collective bargaining agreement between MLB and the MLBPA, the Metropolitan Sports Facilities Commission gained an injunction preventing the Minnesota Twins from refusing to play in the Minneapolis ballpark in 2002. *Metropolitan Sports Facilities Comm'n v. Minnesota Twins Partnership*, 638 N.W.2d 214 (Minn. Ct. App. 2002). What arguments can be made in support of the action for injunction? For a description of both plaintiff and defendant arguments in the case, *see* Simon & Simon, *The Legal Dimension of Major League Baseball's "Contraction" Controversy*, 59 JUN BENCH & B. MINN. 21 (2002).

3. For detailed examination of facility lease provisions, *see* GREENBERG & GRAY, THE STADIUM GAME (1996). *See also*, Greenberg, *"Most Favored Nations" Clauses in Stadium and Arena Contracts*, XVII SPORTS LAW. 1, 8 (May-June 1999); Greenberg, *Force Majeure Clauses and the Obligation to Pay Rent During Labor Work Stoppages*, XVII SPORTS LAW. 9 (Mar.-Apr. 1999). *See also*, Negrin, Note, *If You Build It, They Might Stay: Unconscionability in Modern Sports Stadium Leases*, 30 PUB. CONT. L.J. 503 (2001).

4. For an interesting case in which a taxpayer files an action against the city and professional baseball team, challenging the city's failure to enforce its stadium lease agreement with the team, *see City of Cincinnati ex rel. Ritter v. Cincinnati Reds, L.L.C.*, 782 N.E.2d 1225 (Ohio App. 2002), *appeal denied*, 786 N.E.2d 901 (Ohio 2003).

PART III

ISSUES COMMON TO AMATEUR AND PROFESSIONAL SPORTS

Chapter 11

CRIMINAL LIABILITY OF SPORTS PARTICIPANTS

The primary focus of this chapter is upon the potential criminal liability of a participant for what can loosely be called "on the field" violence. In the additional notes section, other potential areas of criminal liability in the sports milieu are briefly explored.

In recent years, the problem of violence in sports has come under increasingly close scrutiny. The reason for this "closer look" is probably the result of a number of factors. First, violence is, in a very real sense, inherent in many sports activities. Many sports activities are, by nature, prone to violence. Secondly, the rising tide of professionalism in sports carries concomitant economic pressure to win. The pressure creates an environment which makes violence more likely to occur. Thirdly, violent episodes make "good copy." When violence does occur, it is likely that the media will help imprint it on the public conscience. This increased awareness of the problem has spawned several attempts to deal with it.

The problems and material that follow illustrate legislative and judicial responses to the problem of sports violence.

PROBLEM 1

You are a member of the United States House of Representatives and, as such, you are a member of a special ad hoc committee on sports violence. One of your colleagues has drafted a sports violence bill. Relevant provisions of the bill follow:

§ 115. *Excessive violence during professional sports events*

(a) Whoever, as a player in a professional sports event, knowingly uses excessive physical force and thereby causes a risk of significant bodily injury to another person involved in that event shall be fined not more than $5,000 or imprisoned not more than one year, or both.

(b) As used in this section, the term —

(1) "excessive physical force" means physical force that

(A) has no reasonable relationship to the competitive goals of the sport;

(B) is unreasonably violent; and,

(C) could not be reasonably foreseen, or was not consented to, by the injured person, as a normal hazard of such person's involvement in such sports event; and

(2) "professional sports event" means a paid-admission contest . . . of players paid for their participation.

The sponsor of the bill believes that the law would operate as an effective deterrent and would thus make sports safer for participants. Do you agree? Would you favor the enactment of such legislation? Why or why not? Be prepared to participate in a public committee meeting about the bill.

PROBLEM 2

The defense has just rested its case in *State v. Larke*, a criminal case tried before a judge and jury in the Superior Court of Spokane, Oklanois. An uncontroverted summary of the facts leading to the trial is as follows:

On November 20, one year past, a fighting incident occurred in a National Hockey League game in Spokane between the Spokane Bruins' Blaine Retchski and the Philadelphia Flyers' Robby Larke. As a result of that incident Blaine Retchski, a former star forward for the Bruins, is a quadriplegic. The Spokane District Attorney's office pressed criminal charges against Mr. Larke under the Sports Violence Bill, which had been recently enacted into law by the Oklanois Legislature. Mr. Retchski, as a prosecution witness, gave the following account of what transpired:

Q. Mr. Retchski, could you please tell the court what prompted the stick swinging incident?

A. Well, earlier in the first period Larke and I had been involved in some hard checking action down in the Philadelphia end of the rink.

Q. Excuse me, Mr. Retchski, were any penalties called for this "checking"?

A. No, they were not. The checks were hard but clean.

Q. Who in your opinion received the advantage from these checks?

A. On both occasions our team, the Bruins, scored, so I guess you would say we did.

Q. What was Mr. Larke's reaction to these encounters and subsequent scores?

A. He was angry, fighting mad, kept saying, "Retchski, I'm going to get you, I'm going to take your head off"; statements along those lines.

Q. At this time did you fear for your safety?

A. No, not really, Larke is known to have that kind of temper, guess I would have been a little hot too the way he was getting shown up.

Q. What then precipitated the stick swinging?

A. Well, later in the second period, we were up 6-0 and really making the Philadelphia defense look bad, Larke had the puck behind their net area and I came in hard pinning him against the boards trying to get the puck loose.

Q. What happened next?

A. Then Larke just seemed to sort of lose control. I raised my stick to protect myself. The next thing I knew I was in the hospital and it was three days later. Larke had severed my spinal column with the blade of his hockey stick.

On cross-examination, Retchski testified:

Q. Mr. Retchski how long had you been a professional hockey player?

A. Seven, going on eight years.

Q. So you would say you are well acquainted with all aspects of the game, is that correct?

A. Yes, sir, it is.

Q. Mr. Retchski do you consider hockey a violent game?

A. Not really violent, but we play hard and fast and tempers flare occasionally.

Q. But isn't it true that fights and hockey games are almost inseparable?

A. I don't think so.

Q. Did you realize when you skated out onto the ice each night that there was chance you'd fight or be challenged to fight?

A. Yes, there was that chance.

Q. But you voluntarily played anyway?

A. Hockey was my life. I couldn't let that chance of a little rough stuff keep me from making a living. But what Larke did to me I did not expect. If I did I would have never played.

The defendant, Robby Larke, testified in his own defense. On direct examination he testified as follows:

Q. Now Mr. Larke, when Mr. Retchski testified about the check that led to the stick swinging incident he characterized it as hard yet clean. Is that the way it occurred?

A. Only if clean is an elbow to the throat and hockey stick to the gut.

Q. Was this the first instance of this type of conduct in the game?

A. No, throughout the first and second periods, Retchski had been throwing elbows to my head, back and stomach. He kept jabbing at me with his stick handle every time we tied up on the boards.

Q. Going back to the incident of the night of the 20th, after Mr. Retchski tied you up, elbowed you and speared you with his stick butt, what did you do?

A. Well, I defended myself; he's been going after me all night, a man can only take so much.

Q. So you swung your stick at him?

A. No, not then, he raised his stick first, I swung in desperation, trying to protect myself. I thought he was going to swing first.

Q. In other words, Mr. Larke, you were only following the first law of nature — that of self-preservation?

A. That's right, I was only trying to defend myself.

On cross-examination, Larke testified as follows:

Q. Mr. Larke, isn't it true that you are known as a physical type of player, employed mostly for your intimidation of the opposing players instead of for your hockey ability?

A. No, that's just not true.

Q. Isn't it true that you were ejected from more games and drew more game misconduct penalties last year than anyone in the league?

A. (pause) Yes, that is true.

Q. Isn't it also true that you led the League in penalty minutes the last three years?

A. Hockey's a rough game, you can't let the other team skate all over you. I did what I had to do, most of the time it was in self-defense.

Q. Mr. Larke, would you relate your hockey nickname to the court?

A. Well, my given name is Robert, but all the players usually call me Rob or Robby.

Q. Isn't it also true that you are known as Larke the Shark for your overly aggressive play?

A. Well, the press uses that a lot, it's a lotta hype, I never liked it.

Assume the case has gone to jury. What would be the basis of your closing argument on behalf of the State? On behalf of the defendant? In preparing your closing arguments, assume that the following three cases are Oklanois cases.

CASE FILE

REGINA v. BRADSHAW

14 Cox Crim. Cas. 83 (Leicester Spring Assizes 1878)

WILLIAM BRADSHAW was indicted for the manslaughter of Herbert Dockerty at Ashby-de-la-Zouch, on the 28th day of February.

The deceased met with the injury which caused his death on the occasion of a football match played between the football clubs of Ashby-de-la-Zouche and Coalville, in which the deceased was a player on the Ashby side, and the prisoner was a player on the Coalville side.

The game was played according to certain rules known as the "Association Rules." [Footnote omitted.] After the game had proceeded about a quarter of an hour, the deceased was "dribbling" the ball along the side of the ground in the direction of the Coalville goal, when he was met by the prisoner, who was running towards him to get the ball from him or prevent its further progress; both players were running at considerable speed; on approaching each other, the deceased kicked the ball beyond the prisoner, and the prisoner, by way of "charging" the deceased, jumped in the air and struck him with his knee in the stomach. The two met, not directly but at an angle, and both fell. The prisoner got up unhurt, but the deceased rose with difficulty and was led from the ground. He died the next day, after considerable suffering, the cause of death being a rupture of the intestines.

Witnesses were called from both teams whose evidence differed as to some particulars, those most unfavorable to the prisoner alleging that the ball had been kicked by the deceased and had passed the prisoner before he charged; that the prisoner had therefore no right to charge at the time he did, that the charge was contrary to the rules and practice of the game and made in an unfair manner, with the knees protruding; while those who were more favorable to the prisoner stated that the kick by the deceased and the charge by the prisoner were simultaneous, and that the prisoner had therefore, according to the rules and practice of the game, a right to make the charge, though these witnesses admitted that to charge by jumping with the knee protruding was unfair. One of the umpires of the game stated that in his opinion nothing unfair had been done . . . .

BRAMWELL, L.J., in summing up the case to the jury said, "The question for you to decide is whether the death of the deceased was caused by the unlawful act of the prisoner. There is no doubt that the prisoner's act caused the death and the question is whether that act was unlawful. No rules or practice of any game whatever can make that lawful which is unlawful by the law of the land; and the law of the land says you shall not do that which is likely to cause the death of another. For instance, no persons can by agreement go out to fight with deadly weapons, doing by agreement what the law says shall not be done, and thus shelter themselves from the consequences of their acts. Therefore, in one way you need not concern yourselves with the rules of football. But, on the other hand, if a man is playing according to the rules and practice of the game and not going beyond it, it may be reasonable to infer that he is not actuated by any malicious motive or intention, and that he is not acting in a manner which he knows will be likely to be productive of death or injury. But, independent of the rules, if the prisoner intended to cause serious hurt to the deceased, or if he knew that, in charging as he did, he might produce serious injury and was indifferent and reckless as to whether he would produce serious injury or not, then the act would be unlawful. In either case he would be guilty of a criminal act and you must find him guilty; if you are of a contrary opinion you will acquit him." His Lordship carefully reviewed the evidence, stating that no doubt the game was, in any circumstances, a rough one; but he was unwilling to decry the manly sports of this country, all of which were no doubt attended with more or less danger.

Verdict, *Not guilty.*

REGINA v. MAKI

14 D.L.R.3d 164 (1970)

CARTER, PROV. CT. J.: — Mr. Maki is charged under § 231(2) of the *Criminal Code*: assault causing bodily harm. The case is basically a simple one factually but complicated to some extent in that the alleged assault occurred during the playing of a National Hockey League exhibition game and that there has not been such a prosecution in the past. The game was between the St. Louis Blues and the Boston Bruins, played at the Ottawa Civic Centre in the City of Ottawa on September 21, 1969.

I have considered the facts carefully and, although, as would be expected in such a fast moving situation, there are some inconsistencies in the evidence, the occurrence appears to have taken place in the following manner.

I might say in reviewing the facts I gave a great deal of weight to the evidence of the referee Mr. Bodenistel and of course to the evidence of Mr. Maki himself. I found both to be credible witnesses, as in fact were all the witnesses in the case.

At about the 11-minute mark of the first period St. Louis had shot the puck into the Boston zone and behind and to the left of the Boston net. Mr. Maki and Mr. Green followed the puck into the area and collided at this point. Mr. Green pushed or punched Mr. Maki in the face with his glove and, it would appear, caused some injury to his mouth. At this point the referee signaled a delayed penalty for an infraction by raising his arm and play continued. The two players, it would appear, broke apart at this juncture with Mr. Maki skating in the area in front of the Boston net and the puck was moved into the centre ice area. There is some evidence of spearing by Maki against Green, but this fact is in some considerable doubt. There is evidence that Mr. Maki was somewhat dazed as a result of the incident behind the net. This is borne out by evidence given by Mr. Maki and by Mr. Larkin.

At this point the two players came together again at some point in front of the Boston net, sticks swinging, and as a result Mr. Green's unfortunate injury occurred at this time. There is no doubt that Mr. Green swung at Mr. Maki first and struck him on the neck or shoulders. Mr. Maki states that Mr. Green then made another move or motion towards him with his stick and that Mr. Green's stick was above his shoulders and held by both hands. Mr. Maki then swung at Mr. Green and his stick hit Mr. Green's stick and glanced from there to the side of Mr. Green's head causing the injuries in question. It seems clear from the photographs filed that this was the case and that if Mr. Green's stick had not been raised as it was, the blow would probably have landed on Green's shoulder. Most witnesses testified that the blow struck by Mr. Maki was a chopping blow from a vertical position and was not, as one witness testified, a baseball-type swing. These are the main facts as I find them. There were other motions or movements by the players during this period, but these are the main facts upon which I base my decision. I might add at this point that the fact that Mr. Green indicated that he wanted no prosecution of Mr. Maki is of little or no interest in this case. The fact that he did not testify either for the Crown or defense is somewhat unusual, but I place no weight on that fact as well.

I will deal first with the law upon which I have based my decision — that is, self-defense, as put forward by defense counsel.

This whole affair took place in a matter of two to five seconds in a game noted for its speed and bodily contact. We have evidence to indicate that Mr. Green is a very aggressive, hard-hitting player, and Maki of course is fully aware of this.

Section 34 of the *Criminal Code* reads as follows:

> 34 (1) Every one who is unlawfully assaulted without having provoked the assault is justified in repelling force by force if the force he uses is not intended to cause death or grievous bodily harm and is no more than is necessary to enable him to defend himself.
>
> (2) Every one who is unlawfully assaulted and who causes death or grievous bodily harm in repelling the assault is justified if
>
> (a) he causes it under reasonable apprehension of death or grievous bodily harm from the violence with which the

assault was originally made or with which the assailant pursues his purposes, and

(b) he believes, on reasonable and probable grounds, that he cannot otherwise preserve himself from death or grievous bodily harm.

The law in this regard briefly stated therefor is that on a charge of this sort there must be an acquittal if the Court is left in any doubt as to whether the accused was acting in self-defense, that is, where self-defense is raised as a defense. The Court must also consider the reasonableness of the force used under the circumstances and the state of mind of the accused at the time in question.

Mr. Maki in his evidence states, and I am paraphrasing to some extent: "I was trying to protect myself"; "I didn't aim at any particular part of his body"; "I swung in desperation to protect myself." And in cross-examination he stated again that he was protecting himself "trying to ward off Green"; "I was not angry at Green, I was just protecting myself"; "I expected he would still come after me if I turned away"; "swung in desperation"; "I didn't know I would cause him serious injury", and so on. A number of witnesses including the referee could not assess clearly the severity of the blow. The referee also indicated in his evidence that Maki did not seem angry or to have lost his temper. He was the man who was watching the whole affair much more closely than anybody else. Mr. Finn, one of the linesmen, stated that he had no problem separating Maki from the fight area and that Maki did not appear to want to get back at Mr. Green.

It is to be emphasized that the paramount obligation is upon the Crown to have proved the guilt of the accused beyond all reasonable doubt. It is also important to note as in *R. v. Ogal*, 50 C.C.C. 71, [1928] 3 D.L.R. 676, 23 Alta.L.R. 511, cited by defense counsel, that where the means of defense used is not disproportionate to the severity of the assault a plea of self-defense is valid, although the defender, in this case Maki, fails to measure with nicety the degree of force necessary to ward off the attack and inflicts serious injury thereby. Green was the aggressor up to the point of Maki's blow to Green.

Can I, considering the fact situation as I have found it to be, find beyond any reasonable doubt that Maki intended to injure Green; that Maki should not have been under any reasonable apprehension of bodily harm, and that Maki used excessive force under the circumstances? I think not — I must have a doubt in my mind on all three points and the charge is dismissed.

I feel, however, that although it does not form part of my reasons for acquittal, I must comment on the merit of some of the Crown Attorney's submissions as to the defense of consent put forward by defense counsel. If the fact situation in this case had been such that no doubt was raised in my mind regarding self-defense, I would not have hesitated to convict the accused. The defense of consent would in my opinion have failed. Although no criminal charges have been laid in the past pertaining to athletic events in this country, I can see no reason why they could not be in the future where the circumstances warrant and the relevant authorities deem it advisable to do so. No sports league, no matter how well organized or self-policed it may be, should thereby render the players in that league immune from criminal prosecution. I agree with Mr. Cassells when he states that consent to bodily injury as a defense to criminal prosecution has its limitations. I refer to the words of Stephen, J., in *R. v. Coney, et al.* (1882), 8 Q.B.D. 534 at p. 549, when he states:

> In cases where life and limb are exposed to no serious danger in the common course of things, I think that consent is a defense to a charge of assault, even when considerable force is used, as, for instance, in cases of wrestling, single-stick, sparring with gloves, football, and the like; but in all cases the question whether consent does or does not take from the application or force to another its illegal character, is a question of degree depending upon circumstances.

Thus all players, when they step onto a playing field or ice surface, assume certain risks and hazards of the sport, and in most cases the defense of consent as set out in § 230 of the *Criminal Code* would be applicable. But as stated above there is a question of degree involved, and no athlete should be presumed to accept malicious, unprovoked or overly violent attack. Bastin, J., states it this way in *Agar v. Canning*, 54 W.W.R. 302 at p.305; affirmed 55 W.W.R. 384:

> But a little reflection will establish that some limit must be placed on a player's immunity from liability. Each case must be decided on its own facts so it is difficult, if not impossible, to decide how the line is to be drawn in every circumstance. But injuries inflicted in circumstances which show a definite resolve to cause serious injury to another, even when there is provocation and in the heat of the game, should not fall within the scope of the implied consent.

The adoption of such principals in the future would, I feel certain, be a benefit to the players, of course, to the general public peace and, in particular, to young aspiring athletes who look to the professionals for guidance and example. I would like at this point to thank counsel for the excellent manner in which the case was presented. Their arguments were extremely helpful to me and may form guide-lines in the future.

Charge dismissed.

REGINA v. GREEN

16 D.L.R.3d 137 (1970)

FITZPATRICK, PROV. CT. J. (orally): — Edward Joseph Green was charged that on or about September 21, 1969, at the City of Ottawa in the Regional Municipality of Ottawa-Carleton he unlawfully did assault one Wayne Maki, contrary to § 231(1) of the *Criminal Code* of Canada in such case made and provided.

The incident out of which this charge arose occurred on the evening of September 21, 1969, when an exhibition game involving two National Hockey League teams, the Boston Bruins and the St. Louis Blues, was being played at the Ottawa Civic Centre. Mr. Green was a member of the Boston Bruins and had for some time played for that team and was a defenseman. Mr. Maki was at that time a member of the St. Louis Blues.

The game was being refereed by Mr. Bodendistel, and the other officials employed were Ronald Finn and Robert John Waddel. All were relatively inexperienced in officiating at the National Hockey League level, but nevertheless they impressed me as alert and competent officials.

I think it necessary at this point to make a general statement of the facts as I find them to be surrounding and leading up to this incident. We heard from a great number of witnesses, both from the Crown and from the defense. I have examined all of this evidence and sifted it very carefully, and the facts that I am about to give are the facts as I have decided them to be on the evidence I have heard.

At approximately the 13-minute mark of the first period at the exhibition game (which time was established by the referee, Mr. Bodendistel), the puck came into the end that was being defended at that time by the Boston Bruins. Both Mr. Green and Mr. Maki were on the ice at that time. The puck went round behind the Boston net. Mr. Maki went in to attempt to get it out in front, and of course Mr. Green was there in his capacity as defenseman for the Boston Bruins in order to clear the puck out of his own zone if at all possible. A skirmish developed along the boards behind the Boston net, to the left of it, that is the goalie's left — a skirmish such as any one of a thousand skirmishes that occur during the course of the National Hockey League season. Somewhere in the skirmish, Mr. Green struck or pushed — and that is rather difficult to determine — Mr. Maki in the face with his glove. A penalty was signaled at that point, a delayed penalty which would be finally called when the whistle had blown when Boston had control of the puck. Shortly thereafter the players came off the boards and the sticks of both players were raised on high. There appeared to be a blow struck by Mr. Maki at Mr. Green, as a result of which Mr. Green was very seriously injured.

Now, at this particular point I have purposely not gotten into some of the other matters that happened on the boards. Neither the referee nor either of the linesmen made any reference to any spearing that may have been taking place on the boards; but there are competent witnesses — Mr. Larkin, Mr. Kealey, and Mr. Schmidt — who were there who stated that, while the two players were scuffling along the boards, Mr. Maki made a spearing motion, jabbed at Mr. Green, with the blade of his stick in the lower abdomen. Mr. Kealey, who was himself a hockey player, as far as at any rate A level, and whom I considered to be a very competent witness, saw this. Mr. Larkin, who was stationed immediately behind the Boston Bruins' net, and who has been a sports observer for many years, saw this. And Mr. Green in his own testimony stated that this in fact occurred.

It is interesting to note that Mr. Maki has no memory of this having happened; he does not remember spearing Mr. Green. But I note from his evidence that he was quite careful to say that he does not say that he did not spear him; he just does not remember whether he speared him or not. In any event, I find as a fact that on the evening around that time, the 13-minute mark, in the scuffle that took place, Mr. Green was in fact speared in the lower abdomen in the genital region by Mr. Maki.

I think it is necessary to say at this point that there is probably no more serious attack that can be made by one hockey player on another, in view of the hockey players themselves — and this is quite clear from the evidence — than the action of spearing. Mr. Kealey was asked in examination or cross-examination what he thought of spearing and he used the expression that in his opinion it was "dirty pool" and I think that pretty well defines the hockey players' attitude towards spearing. It is an extremely dangerous type of attack, directed as it very often is at the abdomen, which is relatively unprotected, and at the lower abdomen, and normally speaking it results in instant retribution, if the player who has been speared has not been hurt in the process and is unable to defend himself.

Now, we have to consider certain other facts. Mr. Green was at that time, and had been for a good many years, a member of the Boston Bruins. His reputation was well established.

He was, I suppose, what we would call a star in the hockey league. He had nothing to prove. He was merely, as he said himself in his own evidence, getting into shape for the season; he was using the exhibition game for that purpose. So we are not confronted with a young man who had to make his mark in the league and who had to prove something in order to obtain a place on the team once the season started.

I must also make this comment at this particular time. Because of the way the evidence had to be given, we would certainly get the impression that these events all happened in slow motion, but they took no considerable time. In fact, the whole incident probably did not consume more than 10 seconds. Hockey is a game that is played at great speed, and we are here dealing with players from the National Hockey League, who are, I think by common consent, the best trained and probably the best hockey players anywhere. We have here men wearing the very best equipment, with one notable and totally incomprehensible omission, and that is the fact that most players do not wear helmets. But apart from that they are very well equipped, they are very well trained, and they are playing in the best surroundings and on the best possible ice surface. They also in the very nature of the game assume certain risks.

I would like to read into the record § 230 of the *Criminal Code*:

> 230. A person commits an assault when, without the consent of another person . . .
>
> (a) he applies force intentionally to the person of the other, directly or indirectly.

I have left out the words "or with consent, where it is obtained by fraud."

There is not doubt that the players who enter the hockey arena consent to a great number of assaults on their person, because the game of hockey as it is played in the National Hockey League, which is the league I am dealing with, could not possibly be played at the speed at which it is played and with the force and vigor with which it is played, and with the competition that enters into it, unless there were a great number of what would in normal circumstances be called assaults, but which are not heard of. No hockey player enters on to the ice of the National Hockey League without consenting to and without knowledge of the possibility that he is going to be hit in one of many ways once he is on that ice.

I think it is notable that Mr. Maki in his evidence, when he was questioned about the fact that he was struck in the face by Mr. Green's glove, said this had happened to him hundreds of times. I think within our experience we can come to the conclusion that this is an extremely ordinary happening in a hockey game and the players really think nothing of it. If you go in behind the net with a defenseman, particularly one who is trying to defend his zone, and you are struck in the face by that player's glove, a penalty might be called against him, but you do not really think anything of it; it is one of the types of risk one assumes.

One now gets the most difficult problem of all, in my opinion: since it is assumed and understood that there are numerous what would normally be called assaults in the course of a hockey game, but which are really not assaults because of the consent of the players in the type of game being played, where do you draw the line? It is very difficult in my opinion for a player who is playing hockey with all the force, vigor and strength at his command, who is engaged in the rough and tumble of the game, very often in a rough situation in the corner of the rink, suddenly to stop and say, "I must not do that. I must not follow up on this because maybe it is an assault; maybe I am committing an assault." I do not think that any of the actions that would normally be considered assaults in ordinary walks of life can possibly be, within the context that I am considering, considered assaults at all.

I think it is necessary here to comment on several further points, the first of which is this. It is notable that the two most serious, grievous assaults that were committed that night — blows that caused most of the trouble, the blows that almost cost Mr. Green his life — were (a) the spearing of Mr. Green by Mr. Maki (which I have found to be a fact) and (b) the hitting of Mr. Green over the head by Mr. Maki.

I have to make this comment too. If that second blow had not been struck, if Mr. Maki had not struck Mr. Green, it is difficult for me to imagine that any charge would have been laid against Mr. Green. In other words, after the blow that was struck by Mr. Green on Mr. Maki, if that had been the end of the matter, if nothing else had happened, it would appear to me the necessary penalties would have been called (as they were in the process of being called) and that incident might have merited a line or two in the sporting pages the next day, and perhaps a comment or two in the sports telecasts and the radio sports broadcasts that evening. But that would have been the end of it and no more would have happened.

I now turn to the evidence of Mr. Green himself. Mr. Green gave his evidence in what I considered to be a very forthright way. It was the evidence of a man who is very experienced in his sport, a man who undoubtedly plays boisterously, as he is paid to; he is well known and his reputation is well known, and other players respect that reputation, as they have to in the circumstances. He gave substantially the account I have given of the facts, with this addition, that he said this fracas originally started when Mr. Maki grabbed him by the back of the sweater. No other witness gave that evidence, but I must make this comment, that Mr. Green was in fact in the best position to know this, because this would have been done at very close quarters, and I have no doubt that it was in fact what did start the fracas.

Mr. Green also said that when he had been speared, as he said, in the testicles by Mr. Maki, he then struck him a sort of half chop on the shoulder as a warning not to do it again, to desist, and this action happened almost simultaneously with or directly after the spearing by Mr. Maki. As I have previously said, this incident took place in a furious activity of a hockey game: it took place in a very few seconds; and I have no doubt from the evidence (which I have sifted and weighed) that the blow struck by Mr. Green was struck almost immediately after the blow — the much more serious blow in my opinion, the spearing — which had been struck at him by Mr. Maki. I do not think that Mr. Green was doing anything more in the circumstances than protecting himself. Mr. Maki himself said in his evidence that he did not remember spearing Mr. Green, but that if he had speared Mr. Green he would expect that Mr. Green would immediately retaliate.

We must remember that we are dealing with a hockey game. We are dealing with two competent hockey players at the peak of their form. We are not now dealing with the ordinary facts of life, the ordinary going and coming. We must remember that when we discuss the action of these men we are examining it within that forum and we are discussing it within the context in which the game is played, at high speed and obviously with people keenly on edge. In these circumstances I find as a fact that Mr. Green's action that night was instinctive and that all he was doing in effect was warning Mr. Maki not to do what he had done again.

Having said that I must also make this comment. Mr. Maki gave evidence that all he sustained in this matter was a sore neck and that quickly went away. I accept Mr. Green's evidence that what he directed at Mr. Maki was a half chop, which was directed at the upper arm in effect, where there is no padding, and that it was an instinctive motion of protection and warning, that he had no intent to commit an assault on Mr. Maki at that time, and certainly I have to find in all of the circumstances that no assault was in fact committed.

I want to make one thing quite clear. I am only deciding this particular case on this particular set of facts. It is quite probable that in other circumstances and given other sets of facts a charge of common assault might very well stand. However, I must make this comment, that given the permissiveness of the game and the risks that the players willingly undertake, I find it difficult to envision a circumstance where an offence of common assault as opposed to assault causing actual bodily harm could readily stand on facts produced from incidents occurring in the course of a hockey game played at that level. I am not talking about unprovoked savage attacks in which serious injury results. I am talking about these particular facts and these particular circumstances.

I must also make this comment. Counsel for both sides have been most meticulous in their preparation of arguments, and they have supplied me with an abundance of cases, which I have carefully examined, but I have to make the comment that, like so many other matters, this case has to be decided on its own facts. Though the law they quoted me was helpful, it really cannot be used in any sense in my decision here, because I am dealing with a particular set of facts in particular circumstances.

Having examined all the evidence very carefully, and having examined in particular the series of events that happened on the boards that night behind the Boston net, even though the original blow, if you will, was a hitting of Mr. Maki in the face by Mr. Green with the glove — a common action which happens hundreds of times — in my opinion the real cause of this altercation was the spearing of Mr. Green by Mr. Maki; Mr. Green's action was instinctive, and I find it was more protective in his own interests than anything else of his own safety. Having regard to those circumstances, I find Mr. Green not guilty.

Accused acquitted.

NOTES AND COMMENTS

1. Criminal prosecutions of athletes for on-the-field conduct have been only rarely undertaken. Most involve National Hockey League players and most of the prosecutions have been unsuccessful. Two grew out of one incident which you are already familiar with — the 1969 Maki-Green altercation. In 1975, Boston Bruin player Dave Forbes was tried in Minnesota for an attack on Minnesota player Henry Boucha. The case ended with a hung jury and the prosecutor decided not to retry Forbes. *State v. Forbes* (No. 63280 Minn. Dist. Ct., 4th. Jud. Dist., Judgment of mistrial entered August 12, 1975). A fourth reported case is *Regina v. Maloney*, 28 C.C.C.2d 323, Ont. Co. Ct. 1976. Dan Maloney, a Detroit Red Wing, was tried in Canada in connection with an attack on Brian Glennie, a player for the Toronto Maple Leafs. Maloney was acquitted by a Canadian jury.

Written accounts of the Forbes incident paint a sordid picture. (For a full and graphic account, *see* Mulvoy, *Hockey is Courting Disaster, Sports Illustrated*, January 27, 1975.) Forbes illegally checked Boucha. Boucha responded by punching Forbes. Both players were penalized for seven minutes and words were exchanged in the penalty box. Upon returning to the ice, Forbes struck Boucha in the face with his stick. Boucha fell to the ice and Forbes pummeled him until other players intervened. Boucha required twenty-five stitches to close a gash near his eye and surgery to repair a fractured eye socket.

The Maloney attack was equally savage. Newspaper accounts indicate that Maloney attacked Glennie from behind, punched him in the face and threw him down on the ice. Maloney then punched Glennie again and twice lifted him from the ice and dropped him. (*New York Times,* February 25, 1976, at 43, col. 5).

How do you explain (1) the fact that so few prosecutions are brought and (2) the fact that, when they are brought, they seemed doomed to fail?

In regard to (1), the prosecutor in *Forbes*, in declining to retry Forbes, stated that the expense of the trial, the likelihood of success on the merits, and the availability of a civil remedy contributed to his decision not to retry the case. (*New York Times*, August 12, 1975, at 24, col. 6). *See also* Kennedy, *Wanted: An End to Mayhem, Sports Illustrated*, November 17, 1975.

In a much celebrated case, Dino Ciccarelli became the first NHL player to go to jail for an "on-the-ice" incident. The following is reprinted from *Sports Illustrated,* September 5, 1988, at page 34.

North Star on Ice
by Austin Murphy

He did not particularly deserve the distinction, but last week Dino Ciccarelli became the first NHL player to go to jail for an on-ice assault. Dozens of NHLers, past and present, have committed barbarities as grave or graver than the one for which Ciccarelli was imprisoned last week. But none of them ever "did time."

Ciccarelli, 28, the Minnesota North Stars' all-time leading scorer, was convicted of assaulting Luke Richardson of the Toronto Maple Leafs during a game at Maple Leaf Gardens on Jan. 6. After twice clubbing Richardson in the head with his stick, Ciccarelli realized the futility of this exercise — thanks to his helmet, Richardson emerged unscathed — and proceeded to punch his adversary in the mouth. Traditionally in NHL towns, the long arm of the law withered when it came to enforcing laws in hockey arenas; police and the courts have almost always turned a blind eye to the game's violence.

That changed with this incident in Toronto. Two days after the game, officials announced they had issued a warrant tor Ciccarelli's arrest. In late May he appeared in provincial court in Toronto to plead not guilty to the assault charge, and he returned in July for a one-day non-jury trial. Last Wednesday, Judge Sidney Harris found Ciccarelli guilty. Citing the need to convey a message to the NHL that "violence in a hockey game or in any other circumstance is not acceptable in our society," Harris sent the North Star right wing to jail for a day and fined him $1,000.

Ciccarelli, who in January pleaded guilty to a misdemeanor charge of indecent exposure in Eden Prairie, Minn., was handcuffed and transferred to Toronto Jail, where he spent less than two hours. At first Ciccarelli was worried. "There were about 12 guys in the cell," he said, "But I ended up signing autographs." Ciccarelli, whose lawyer, Donald Houston, is appealing his conviction, was in custody for a total of four hours. Not exactly the rock pile.

Despite the brevity of Ciccarelli's incarceration, some hockey people were upset at the "meddling" from outside. "He already served a 10-game suspension. That cost him over $25,000," said North Star president Lou Nanne, referring to the action taken by the NHL last season. "That was punishment enough." Nanne said Ciccarelli was arrested only because "some politician" asked the Toronto police to press charges. "Now where do they draw the line?" It is a valid point. Hundreds of ugly, violent altercations break out in NHL games every season. Which ones merit police action?

"It seems to me that hockey has been able to police its own" said Minnesota general manager Jack Ferreira.

Here Ferreira runs into disagreement. Ontario attorney general Ian Scott said, "We have the perfect right to be in hockey rinks, particularly when those who administer professional hockey seem ill-equipped to curb this kind of incident."

While expressing disappointment with Judge Harris's verdict, NHL president John Ziegler did say, "It has long been our belief that sports are not above the law." That does not quite square with a new NHL bylaw, enacted in June, that imposes a $1 million fine on any club that leapfrogs the NHL's internal justice system and goes right to the courts, as the New Jersey Devils did during the Wales Conference finals in May, when they obtained a temporary restraining order against the suspension of Devils coach Jim Schoenfeld.

The problem is that society's and the NHL's ideas of justice are two different things. In a preseason game in Ottawa in 1969, St. Louis left wing Wayne Maki fractured the skull of Boston defenseman Ted Green during a vicious high-sticking joust. Both players were charged by local law enforcement officials with assault but both were acquitted in separate trials. The only time served by Maki or Green came in the form of 14- and 13-game suspensions, respectively. Before delivering more serious penalties, the NHL seems to be waiting for delivery of more serious injuries on ice. When such an injury happens, it may require a coroner.

The courts in at least one hockey town, however, are now apparently willing to give NHL justice a little boost into the 20th century.

On April 28, 1993, an incident during a Stanley Cup playoff game involving Dale Hunter of the Washington Capitals and Pierre Turgeon of the New York Islanders once again brought the NHL and "on-the-field" violence into the national limelight. Turgeon had just scored a goal to effectively eliminate the Capitals from the playoffs. As Turgeon celebrated the goal, Hunter chased him down, checked him from behind, and sent him flying into the boards. Turgeon suffered a separated shoulder which prevented him from playing in the next round of the playoffs. Hunter claimed to never have seen Turgeon score and simply thought play was still in progress when he hit Turgeon. However, videotape appeared to indicate that Hunter watched the puck as it entered the net.

Immediately after the incident, Turgeon's agent stated that a law firm had been hired to investigate the incident but that a claim for civil damages was the most likely course of action. Turgeon's agent also stated that, "This is a serious matter. No human being should be treated this way. Hunter has got to be made an example for the future." (*New York Times*, April 30, 1993, at B13, col. 2-4).

If this is the case, then why settle for civil damages? Will a monetary award really set an "example" in the world of million dollar professional athletes? Wouldn't a criminal action and a possible jail sentence be more of a deterrent? Could part of the reason that athletes do not press criminal charges for these incidents be the result of an attitude of, "It could be me next time"? Remember that the "victim" in *Regina v. Maki,* 14 D.L.R.3d 164 (1970), did not testify against Maki and did not wish to have anything to do with Maki's prosecution.

A recent and even more violent hockey incident occurred on April 17, 1998. During an Ontario Hockey League playoff game in Plymouth, Michigan, 19-year-old Jess Boulerice of the Plymouth Whalers struck 18-year-old Andrew Long of the Guelph Storm in the face. The blow broke Andrew's nose and caused multiple facial fractures, a Grade III concussion accompanied by seizure, a contusion of the brain, two black eyes, and a gash on the upper lip. Boulerice was suspended from the OHL for one year and the Wayne County prosecutors charged him with assault with intent to do great bodily harm less than murder. *See* Jeff MacGregor, *Less Than Murder*, *Sports Illustrated*, March 22, 1999, at 98. On May 8, 2004, Vancouver Canuck's forward Todd Bertuzzi landed a violent punch that cost the Colorado Avalanche's Steve Moore his career. The blow gave Moore a black eye and fractured two vertebrae. In addition to the NHL's twenty-game suspension, Bertuzzi pleaded guilty to assault causing bodily harm. He was sentenced to eighty hours of community service. *See* Michael Farber, *Scorecard: Skating On*, Sports Illustrated, November 1, 2005, at 20.

Why is it that a jury will often acquit a defendant of an attack on the hockey rink when the same attack on a street would probably not go unpunished? A sociological explanation resides with the "community subgroup" phenomenon. (W. LAFAVE, ARREST: THE DECISION TO TAKE A SUSPECT INTO CUSTODY, 110 (1965)). LaFave offers as an example of this phenomenon research data that indicates that in predominately black precincts, blacks are less likely to be arrested for assault than whites. The sociological explanation is that the police tolerate widespread illegal activity carried on by members of a definable minority when the effects of the activity are limited to the minority. Does this help explain the virtual immunity enjoyed by professional athletes for on-the-field behavior? *See* W. Kuhlman, *Violence in Professional Sports*, WIS. L. REV. 779 (1975); Hanson, Linda S. Calvert & Craig Dennis, *Revisiting Excessive Violence in the Professional Sports Arena: Changes in the Past Twenty Years?,* 6 SETON HALL J. SPORT L. 126 (1996).

It is also possible that the immunity of athletes reflects a shared psychological need. In a letter to the editor of TIME magazine, Dr. Walter Menninger wrote:

> Despite the recent indignation over violence in professional hockey, it should not be surprising that the spectator following should be so rabid, particularly in the congested metropolitan areas where legitimate expressions of violence are so limited. Many of the silent majority who feel so frustrated, angry and helpless today can readily identify with the beleaguered, assaulted hero of the "war on the ice." They experience a vicarious satisfaction from the open aggression and mayhem on the ice, and indeed, it is powerfully exhilarating to let one's emotions "all hang out." (TIME, March 3, 1975, at 51).

2. Those involved in extreme sports may also face criminal charges. Increasing numbers of charges are being brought against service providers of extreme sports (i.e. the individual who facilitates the bungee jumping or sky diving). However, prosecutors are still a bit apprehensive about prosecuting extreme sports participants. The prosecutions that do occur tend to be in non-contact sports that are inherently dangerous. *See* Carolyn B. Ramsey, *Homicide on Holiday: Prosecutorial Discretion, Popular Culture, and the Boundaries of the Criminal Law*, 54 HASTINGS L.J. 1641 (2003).

3. In the absence of a bill like the Sports Violence Bill, the overly zealous participant will most likely be charged, if he is to be charged at all, with assault and/or battery. What are the elements of criminal assault? Criminal battery? What defenses are available?

For example, a high school soccer player in Los Angeles was successfully prosecuted for kicking another player in the head. He was charged criminally with assault and battery and performed community service while under probation. *Prep Soccer Player Sentenced,* THE REPOSITORY, Wednesday, June 30, 1993, at C-2. Discuss the problem contained in this chapter as if Larke had been charged with assault and battery, as defined by your local jurisdiction.

4. Is it a particularly jaundiced view to say that criminal acts are commonplace in sports? Analyze the following fairly common situations as criminal cases. (If it helps, assume the victim has suffered grievous harm):

(a) the "brushback" pitch;

(b) the response to the brushback, where the batter runs towards the pitcher and punches him, or strikes him with the bat;

(c) the vintage baseball player's tantrum, in which the umpire has dirt kicked upon him, or tobacco juice sprayed in his face;

(d) the "spikes-up" slide;

(e) the "cheap-shot" in football, where a player is hit either out-of-bounds or after the whistle;

(f) the "clean but brutal" hit, where the tackler intends to cripple a vulnerable opponent;

(g) the "low-bridge" in basketball, where the perpetrator runs under the airborne opponent;

(h) the flagrant use of elbows to clear space after securing a rebound.

Are these acts not criminal because so commonplace or is it that they are common place because they are not effectively sanctioned?

One recent act which occurred in Division I college baseball was explained as part of the game by some, while being called a malicious, violent act by others. In a game on April 23, 1999, Wichita State pitcher Ben Christensen threw a ball at Evansville lead off man Anthony Molina while Molina was on deck approximately 30 feet away from the plate. Christensen explained that he thought Molina was "timing" his pitches, so he threw at Molina as he had been instructed by Wichita State pitching coach, Brent Kemnitz.

Molina was hit in the left eye where it took twenty-three stitches to close a one-inch gash. His vision in that eye has been reduced from 20/10 to 20/160. His playing career is in jeopardy. Christensen and Kemnitz were suspended for the rest of the season by the Missouri Valley Conference. Christensen was recently drafted with the 22nd pick in the first round of the Major League Draft. Kemnitz viewed the matter as a routine part of the game. He stated, "If the on-deck hitter is standing too close to home plate, you brush him back." *See A Purpose Pitch*, SPORTS ILLUSTRATED, May 17, 1999 at 24.

5. Can you make an argument that the league officials of the National Hockey League bear criminal responsibility for the criminal acts of the players? Obviously, you would need some evidence that the League "markets" violence. Assuming you came up with some convincing evidence of this kind of exploitation, are league officials vulnerable to criminal prosecution for the "on the field" criminal acts of participants? What about possible criminal liability for a coach who sends a known thug onto the field of play for the purpose of "enforcing"?

6. In recent years, we have seen that sports-related activities occasionally raise criminal law concerns.

For example, lengthy jail terms and substantial fines are mandated under a recently passed Texas law which forbids agents or boosters from using money or gifts to recruit college athletes. (Ironically, the statute was signed by Governor Bill Clements, who was personally involved in the 1987 SMU football scandal). *See* SPORTS INDUSTRY NEWS, May 19, 1989, at 147. Other states have passed legislation designed to control agents. Recently, the Federal government charged two overzealous agents with RICO violations. The following is reprinted from BACULUS, the law students' newspaper, at the University of Tulsa, April-May 1989, at page 7.

Whose Fraud Is It, Anyway?
by Professor Ray Yasser

A Federal District Court in Chicago is hearing evidence in the racketeering trial of former sports agents Norby Walters and Lloyd Bloom. The government prosecutors charge that Walters and Bloom effectively defrauded NCAA member schools by making under-the-table payments to scholarship athletes. The gist of the fraud counts is that the universities were duped into continuing scholarship payments to athletes who were theoretically ineligible because they were on the Walters-Bloom payroll. The athletes involved all acknowledged that they accepted the payments and gifts in violation of NCAA rules and continued to compete. The universities involved, since they presumably did not know about the illegal payments at the time they took place, continued to enjoy the athletic triumphs and financial rewards that were generated by the technically ineligible athletes. The NCAA has not penalized the universities, who after all, were "victims" of the conspiracy that existed between the unscrupulous agents and the greedy jocks.

The testimony at trial has produced evidence of even more egregious fraud, however; and the government is not going after the perpetrators. Former Iowa star running back Ronnie Harmon gave testimony under a grant of immunity to the effect that he remained "academically" eligible in the eyes of Iowa and the NCAA while making no progress toward any degree, taking courses such as bowling, soccer, history, football, and billiards during his freshman year. Other athletes testified to similar arrangements. In essence, the trial has shown that universities, when granting athletic scholarships, promise a real opportunity for a college education while knowing that, in many cases, they can't deliver. Now surely this is fraud too.

I'm not saying that Walters and Bloom are every-mother's-son type guys. But consider the fraud they perpetrated, and compare it to the fraud perpetrated by the NCAA in consort with its member schools. In the Walters-Bloom fraud case, if all we are talking about are under-the-table payments, how are the universities and the NCAA really harmed? Some harm to their integrity you say? Well this is harm to already severely damaged goods. Compare this harm to the harm caused by the fraud perpetrated by the NCAA and its member schools upon so many college athletes every year, who are promised an opportunity for a real college education and then systematically denied it.

Whose fraud is it, anyway?

For another view on agents and criminal liability, *see* Ricardo J. Bascuras, *Cheaters Not Criminals: Antitrust Invalidation of Statutes Outlawing Sports Agent Recruitment of Student Athletes,* 105 YALE L.J. 1603-37 (1996).

7. Tax evasion can also raise criminal issues. In an attempt to isolate daughter Steffi Graf from tax evasion charges, Peter Graf told prosecutors he was responsible for financial moves designed to avoid tax liability on an estimated $70 million in prize money and corporate endorsements for the star tennis player. Another more recent tax evasion which hits closer to home involved the referees of the National Basketball Association. In 1997-98, the IRS discovered that several referees were cashing in their first class plane tickets provided by the NBA for coach seats and not reporting the income to the IRS. They were arrested and fired by the NBA. Several referees were sentenced to house arrest and have not been rehired by the NBA.

8. Athletes have increasingly drawn media attention for alleged incidents of domestic violence. This issue, as well as other issues involving player misconduct, has given rise to the respective league commissioner also having the authority to discipline athletes for off-the-field misconduct, especially domestic violence. Most contracts now contain good behavior clauses. Improper conduct may portend more than criminal and team sanctions. It can also affect a player's endorsement opportunities and even an athlete's draft or trade value.

A rich body of excellent commentary is emerging concerning domestic violence and related issues in sports. *See, e.g,* Note, *Out of Bounds: Professional SportsLeagues and Domestic Violence*, 109 HARV. L. REV. 1048 (1996); MICHAEL MESSNER & DONALD SABO, SEX, VIOLENCE AND POWER IN SPORTS: RETHINKING MASCULINITY 53-65 (1994); Joan Ryan, *Why Sports Heros Abuse Their Wives*, REDBOOK, Sept., 1995, at 83; Donna Pazdera, *Spikes Must Avoid Wife, Get Counseling; Back Jailed for Night on Battery Charge, Shula Orders Probation,* SUN-SENTINAL Aug. 28, 1995, at 1C; JEFF BENEDICT, PUBLIC HEROES, PRIVATE FELONS: ATHLETES AND CRIMES AGAINST WOMEN, (Northeastern University Press, 1998); Ellen E. Dabbs, *Intentional Fouls: Athletes and Violence Against Women*, 31 COLUM. J.L. & SOC. PROBS. 167-99 (1998); Anna L. Jefferson, *The NFL and*

Domestic Violence: The Commissioner's Power to Punish Domestic Abusers, 7 SETON HALL J. SPORT L. 353-70 (1997); and Kevin Cook, *Crime and Banishment*, *Sports Illustrated*, November 17, 1998, at 3a.

These issues are not limited to professional sports. College athletes, and their schools, are being drawn into the foray. *See, e.g.,* Michael C. Griffaton, Note, *Forewarned is Forearmed: The Crime Awareness and Campus Security Act of 1990 and the Future of Institutional Liability for Student Victimization*, 43 CASE W. RES. L. REV. 525, 533-34 (1993); *see* 20 U.S.C. § 1232(g)(6) (1994); *see also* Linda J. Lacey, Book Review of Katie Roiphe's *We Have Nothing to Fear But Gender Stereotypes: Of Katie and Amy and "Babe Feminism": The Morning After: Sex, Fear, and Feminism on Campus,* 80 CORNELL L. REV. 612 (1995); Thomas N. Sweeney, *Closing the Campus Gates: Keeping Criminals Away From the University — The Story of Student-Athlete Violence and Avoiding Institutional Liability For the Good of All*, 9 SETON HALL J. SPORT L. 226-62 (1999). One recent example of this is the Duke Lacrosse debacle. Three Duke players were indicted on charges of rape, sexual offense, and kidnapping that allegedly occurred at an off-campus party. The incident resulted in a plethora of publicity and prompted university officials to cancel the 2006 lacrosse season. As of this writing, the case is unresolved, but the facts suggest that athletes also run the risk of being falsely targeted.

For some practical advice on prevention, *see* Jackson Katz, *Reconstructing Masculinity in the Locker Room: The Mentors in Violence Prevention Project*, 65 HARV. EDUC. REV. 163 (1995); and NORTHEASTERN UNIVERSITY'S CENTER FOR THE STUDY OF SPORT IN SOCIETY, THE MENTORS IN VIOLENCE PREVENTION PLAYBOOK (1994).

Recently, several instances of coaches abusing their players have come to light. *See*, Danielle Deak, *Out of Bounds: How Sexual Abuse of Athletes At the Hands of Their Coaches is Costing the World of Sports Millions*, 9 SETON HALL J. SPORT L. 171-95 (1999).

9. Fan violence often raises criminal law issues as well. The most notorious and shocking incident of fan violence against an athlete is the April 30, 1993 stabbing of Monica Seles, the reigning queen of women's tennis. Seles was stabbed in the back with a twelve centimeter long serrated steak knife by a rabid Steffi Graf fan during a tournament in Germany as she rested on a changeover. (*New York Times*, May 2, 1993, at 27, col. 1-5). A recent incident to note is the shirtless father and son tag team who slammed Kansas City Royals first base coach Tom Gamboa to the ground and started punching and kicking him during a game against the Chicago White Sox. The father and son initially contended that they were provoked before jumping onto the field during the ninth inning of the game and attacking Gamboa. They later apologized, blaming the incident on drug abuse and depression. Richard Zowie, CHI. TRIB., Sept. 29, 2002.

In addition to criminal charges against the fan, what other legal action might follow an attack of this nature? A civil action by Seles against her attacker?

A civil action against the event organizers for negligence due to a lack of adequate security for the players? *See, e.g.*, *A Survey of Domestic and International Sanctions Against Spectator Violence at Sporting Events,* 11 HOUS. J. INT'L L. 415-438 (1989). "Hooliganism" at soccer matches has on occasion resulted in criminal charges being brought.

In short, the whole panoply of sports-related activities probably ought to be subjected to criminal law scrutiny in much the same way as non-sports activities. Or are there valid reasons for giving sports-related activities a bit more breathing room?

10. From the Stands to the Penitentiary: Overzealous parenting in kids' sports is an issue in the criminal sports law arena. Although the screaming coach and angry parent have become typical fixtures in kids' sports, this behavior reached a dramatic peak in 2000, when one hockey father killed the father of another player. *The Rising Tide of Violence and Verbal Abuse by Adults at Youth Sports Events Reached Its Terrible Peak This Month When One Hockey Killed Another*, SPORTS ILLUSTRATED, July 24, 2000, at 86. *See* Dianna K. Fiore, *Parental Rage and Violence in Youth Sports: How Can We Prevent "Soccer Moms" and "Hockey Dads" from Interfering in Youth Sports and Causing Games to End in Fistfights Rather than Handshakes?*, 10 VILL. SPORTS & ENT. L.J. 103 (2003).

Chapter 12

TORTS AND SPORTS

Sports are rife with torts. This chapter addresses settings that have produced a large body of decisional law. First, **Part A** examines the tort liability of one participant to another. **Part B** explores the viability of the spectator's cause of action for injuries incurred at sporting events, as well as the spectator's potential liability for their misconduct. Medical malpractice in athletics and products liability for defective athletic equipment have been fertile litigation grounds, and the materials that follow explore these areas, too. Sports figures have been active as defamation and invasion of privacy plaintiffs, and this rich tradition is presented as well. Finally, since the tort of intentional interference with contractual relations is particularly relevant to the world of sports, this tort is examined in detail.

A. LIABILITY OF ONE PARTICIPANT TO ANOTHER

> Had the parties been upon the playgrounds of the school, engaged in the usual boyish sports, the defendant being free from malice, wantonness, or negligence, and intending no harm to plaintiff in what he did, we should hesitate to hold the act of the defendant unlawful, or that he could be held liable in this action. Some consideration is due to the implied license of the playgrounds.

Vosburg v. Putney, 50 N.W. 403, 404 (Wis. 1891)

> Playing at Hand-Sword, Bucklers, Foot-ball, Wrestling, and the like, whereby one of them receiveth a hurt . . . some are of the opinion that this is a [wrong] . . . some others are of opinion, that this is no [wrong] . . . but that they shall have their pardon, of course, as for misadventure, for that such their play was by consent, and again, there was no former intent to do hurt, or any former malice, but done only for disport, and trial of Man-hood.

M. Dalton, The Countrey Justice Cap, 96, 246 (1635).

Vosburg is a landmark torts case that has been used by law professors to confound and befuddle generations of law students by obfuscating the meaning of intent. Although it is not often cited in the sports law context, it is often used as the lead case in torts, and it seems natural to use it to kick off torts and sports. And, as you can see, the issue is not a new one.

Participation in sports is risky. It is probably fair to say that sports activities — baseball, basketball, football, tennis, racquetball, wrestling, and even jogging (not to mention Hand-Sword, Bucklers and the like) — create greater risks of physical harm than do most other human activities. Typically, injuries incurred in athletic participation are not of tortious origin, but they occur rather as a result of the normal risks associated with participation in the sport. For example, when a tennis player suffers a detached retina when struck by an opponent's all-too-powerful overhead smash, no lawyer worth his salt would be heard to argue that the opponent is a tortfeasor. However, injuries can occur as a consequence of arguably tortious behavior by a participant. This section explores the theories of tort liability that are available to one participant in a suit against a fellow participant for injuries that occur "in the heat of competition."

Generally, an athlete so injured can base an action to recover on three theories: (1) an intentional tort, such as battery or assault; (2) negligence; and (3) recklessness. The prevailing view appears to be that the participant to participant sports injury case requires at least recklessness.

Intentional Torts. A simple definition of battery is the intentional, unprivileged, harmful or offensive contact by the defendant with the person of another. An assault is committed when the defendant, without privilege, intentionally places the plaintiff in apprehension of an immediate harmful or offensive touching. Sports activities are rife with what can arguably be termed assaults and batteries. A review of the cases indicates that a defense of privilege is often the key issue in such litigation. The RESTATEMENT (SECOND) OF TORTS [hereinafter RESTATEMENT] categorizes privileges in terms of whether they are consensual or nonconsensual:

§ 10. PRIVILEGE

(1) The word "privilege" is used . . . to denote the fact that conduct which, under ordinary circumstances, would subject the actor to liability, under particular circumstances does not subject him to such liability.

(2) A privilege may be based upon (a) the consent of the other affected by the actor's conduct, or (b) the fact that its exercise is necessary for the protection of some interest of the actor or of the public which is of such importance as to justify the harm caused or threatened by its exercise.

Commonly accepted nonconsensual privileges include self-defense, defense of others, and defense of property. In sports, the consent privilege looms large. The courts are repeatedly faced with determining the scope of a participant's consent. The intentional tort theory is the clearest base of action, as the available defenses are well established and generally agreed upon.

The issue of intent in the assault and battery context is perplexing. The RESTATEMENT provides the following:

§ 8A. INTENT

The word "intent" is used throughout the Restatement of this Subject to denote that the actor desires to cause the consequences of his act, or that he believes that the consequences are substantially certain to result from it.

§ 16. CHARACTER OF INTENT NECESSARY

(1) If an act is done with the intention of inflicting upon another an offensive but not a harmful bodily contact, or of putting another in apprehension of either a harmful or offensive bodily contact, and such act causes a bodily contact to the other, the actor is liable to the other for a battery although the act was not done with the intention of bringing about the resulting bodily harm.

(2) If an act is done with the intention of affecting a third person in the manner stated in Subsection (1), but causes a harmful bodily contact to another, the actor is liable to such other as fully as though he intended so to affect him.

As you work through the problems in this section, apply these RESTATEMENT provisions to determine the presence or absence of the intent element.

Negligence. The basis of negligence as a cause of action is conduct that results in an unreasonable risk of harm to another. Of course, almost all human activities involve some risk of harm. The gist of a negligence-based claim is that the conduct involves a risk of harm that outweighs the benefits to be derived from engaging in the conduct. The RESTATEMENT provides:

§ 291. UNREASONABLENESS: HOW DETERMINED: MAGNITUDE OF RISK AND UTILITY OF CONDUCT

Where an act is one which a reasonable man would recognize as involving a risk of harm to another, the risk is unreasonable and the act is negligent if the risk is of such magnitude as to outweigh what the law regards as the utility of the act or of the particular manner in which it is done. When negligent conduct proximately causes harm, a *prima facie* case is established.

The main defenses to a negligence-based claim are contributory negligence and assumption of risk. Each of these defenses once operated as a complete bar to the negligence claim. Comparative negligence schemes now applicable in almost every state have changed this common law rule. Under comparative negligence, a contributorily negligent plaintiff is not necessarily precluded from recovery. Obviously, one must be familiar with the applicable comparative negligence scheme. A negligence-based claim in sports may be won or lost over the availability of an assumption of risk defense. As with consent in the intentional tort action, the assumption of risk defense will require the court to determine the nature of the risks that the willing participant assumes.

Recklessness. Recklessness is conduct that creates a higher degree of risk than that created by simple negligence. RESTATEMENT § 500 provides:

> The actor's conduct is in reckless disregard of the safety of another if he does an act or intentionally fails to do an act which it is his duty to the other to do, knowing or having reason to know of facts which would lead a reasonable man to realize, not only that his conduct creates an unreasonable risk of physical harm to another, but also that such risk is substantially greater than that which is necessary to make his conduct negligent.

Unlike the negligence cause of action, the plaintiff's contributory negligence does not operate as a defense to the defendant's reckless conduct. Whether comparative negligence principles apply to a recklessness-based claim is largely an open question. The defense of assumption of risk, however, may be a defense to the recklessness-based cause of action.

Vicarious Liability. The issue of vicarious liability often arises in sports injury cases. An injured participant may want to look beyond the tortfeasor for a defendant to whom the tortfeasor's acts properly can be imputed. Typically, the most significant basis for imputing liability is the employer-employee relationship. Generally, negligence committed by an employee within the scope of his employment may be imputed to the employer, who thus becomes vicariously liable for the damages caused. This principle is referred to as "respondeat superior" — literally, "let the master answer." A recurring question, however, is whether intentional torts are properly viewed as being within the scope of employment. The common law rule was that such wrongs were not within the scope of employment. The modern trend is that intentional torts can be regarded as being within the scope of employment if it can be shown that the act was closely connected to the employment. There is still considerable split of authority on this issue, and one must be familiar with the case law from the appropriate jurisdiction. Similar problems arise in regard to torts grounded on recklessness.

Negligent Supervision. It should also be remembered that employers might be liable because of their own tortious conduct, as distinguished from the tortious conduct of their employees. This is a newly emerging but increasingly viable cause of action. The thrust of the action is that the employer created unreasonable risks of harm by acting in such a way as to create an atmosphere in which the players believed that violence was an acceptable, if not a desirable, mechanism to ensure winning.

Availability of Punitive Damages. In *Sebastian v. Wood*, 66 N.W.2d 841, 844-45 (Iowa 1954), the Iowa Supreme Court articulated the rationale for permitting punitive damage awards:

> [The] main purpose [of punitive damages] . . . is that they are awarded under proper circumstances and conditions as a punishment for the particular party involved and as a warning and an example to him in

> the future, and to all others who may offend in like manner. . . . The allowance of such damages is wholly within the function and province of the jury, to be granted or denied in the exercise of a wise discretion, whether the moving cause be effected by malice, oppression, wantonness, recklessness, or gross negligence, and, if allowed, to fix the amount.

Ordinarily, punitive damages are available only if the conduct can be characterized as something worse than negligence. Again, counsel must consult the local jurisdiction for more specific guidance.

A related issue is whether the employer can be held liable for punitive damages in a case where the liability is established under principles of respondeat superior. Some states allow punitive damages without any showing of particular wrongdoing on the part of the employer. Other states require a showing of an intentional act or authorization or ratification on the part of the employer. And finally, whether punitive damages are appropriate in a case grounded on negligent supervision is problematic. As already noted, something worse than ordinary negligence is usually a necessary prerequisite for punitive damages. However, an argument could be made that negligent supervision, which creates the risk that the employee will act recklessly or with intent to injure, justifies the imposition of punitive damages.

PROBLEM

Dan Zomer has come to you to determine if he has a viable claim in connection with an injury he recently suffered. Zomer tells you that he is a major league baseball player who was "beaned" by a pitch thrown by Dickie Lane. At the time of the injury, Zomer was a 26-year-old shortstop for the Spokane Oilers earning $650,000 per year. The injury is likely to end his career. The beaning seriously impaired his vision and made him susceptible to brain damage. All three doctors he has consulted have recommended strongly that he retire from major league baseball. Zomer will be paid for the remainder of this year but he has no contract for the following year.

Zomer further explains to you that he would not even consider suing Lane if the whole thing was accidental. But Zomer is convinced that Lane intentionally threw at Zomer's head. Zomer bases his contention on a number of factors. First, two months before being beaned, Zomer was hit in the ribs by a pitched ball thrown by Lane. Zomer charged the mound and landed a solid right to Lane's jaw before being restrained. Secondly, Zomer maintains that Lane has a league-wide reputation as a "headhunter" — a pitcher who doesn't just use a "brushback" pitch to move batters away from the plate, but one who consciously throws at people. Finally, Zomer has provided you with a copy of an article about Lane which appeared in SPORTS GRAPHIC, the nation's most popular weekly sports magazine, just one week prior to the beaning. A copy of the relevant portions of that article is reprinted below.

Lane Lets Loose
By Rich Plimpton

The highest paid and most watched pitcher in New York is New York Tromps star Dickie "Fast Train" Lane. In an interview with Lane conducted last week, Lane talked about his much publicized personal life, his pitching philosophy, his strained relationship with Tromps owner Howard Tromp, and his plans for the future.

* * *

Lane's Pitching Credo

Lane: All I can say is I feel that home plate belongs to me. If a batter is too close to the plate, or appears to me to have too much confidence, I throw right at his ear. Pitching is about intimidation. Batting is about overcoming fear. . . .

* * *

Plimpton: Do you ever retaliate? For example, do you have any plans to get back at Zomer for that right cross he landed on your chin?

* * *

Lane: Zomer can expect one behind his ear sometime soon.

* * *

Lane: In the final analysis, I'm only doing what every great pitcher in baseball has done. I'm just more open and honest in talking about it. And the DH rule makes it just a little bit easier to do. (Laughter.)

The Lane-Tromp Love-Hate Relationship

Lane: For all the trouble I have had with Howard Tromp, I do have to say a few things in his defense. One, he pays me well and he pays me on time. Two, he does stand behind his players. Like last year, when I was suspended for two weeks for supposedly throwing at a batter and fined $30,000 by the league, Tromp paid my salary during the suspension and, contrary to league rules, even paid my fine, saying he didn't want me to change my pitching style. You see, in his own way, he understands the power and importance of striking fear into the hearts of your opponents. We're really soul brothers. It's just sometimes that I hate him.

Your own follow-up research indicates that Dickie Lane, Howard Tromp, and the New York Tromps organization all possess extremely deep pockets. Lane is currently the highest paid pitcher in baseball and, at age 27, is in the prime of his career. He is in the middle of a fully guaranteed 5 year contract which pays him $2.1 million per year. Tromp is a billionaire real estate and casino magnate.

The New York Tromps baseball organization is one of the most successful in professional baseball, earning an after-tax profit of 40 million dollars last year.

Based on these facts, prepare an analysis of all your causes of action. In preparing your analysis, assume that *Bourque, Nabozny,* and *Gauvin* are Oklanois cases and that *Hackbart* is a case in the federal circuit in which Oklanois is located, applying the law of Oklanois.

Case File

BOURQUE v. DUPLECHIN

331 So. 2d 40 (La. Ct. App. 1976)

WATSON, Judge.

Plaintiff, Jerome Bourque, Jr., filed this suit to recover damages for personal injuries received in a softball game. . . . [The defendant was Adrien Duplechin, a member of the opposing team, who inflicted the injury. The trial court rendered judgment in favor of Bourque. Duplechin appealed.]

[Duplechin contends] . . . that the trial court erred; in not finding that Bourque assumed the risk of injury by participating in the softball game; and in failing to find that Bourque was guilty of contributory negligence. Defendant Duplechin also contends that the trial court erred in finding him negligent and in finding that the injury to plaintiff Bourque occurred four to five feet away from the second base position in the general direction of the pitcher's mound.

On June 9, 1974, Bourque was playing second base on a softball team fielded by Boo Boo's Lounge. Duplechin, a member of the opposing team sponsored by Murray's Steak House and Lounge, had hit the ball and advanced to first base. A teammate of Duplechin's, Steve Pressler, hit a ground ball and Duplechin started to second. The shortstop caught the ground ball and threw it to Bourque who tagged second base and then stepped away from second base to throw the ball to first and execute a double play. After Bourque had thrown the ball to first base, Duplechin ran at full speed into Bourque. As Duplechin ran into Bourque, he brought his left arm up under Bourque's chin. The evidence supports the trial court's factual conclusion that the collision occurred four or five feet away from the second base position in the direction of the pitcher's mound. Duplechin was thrown out of the game by the umpire because of the incident.

Pertinent to the trial court's decision was the following testimony:

> Plaintiff Bourque, age 22 at the time of trial, testified that he is 5'7" tall. He was well out of the way when he was hit, standing four or five feet from second base and outside the base line. He knew there was a possibility of a runner sliding into him but had never imagined what

> actually happened, which he regarded as unbelievable under the circumstances.
>
> Gregory John Laborde, a student at Tulane Law School, testified that he witnessed the incident from the dugout along the first base line and saw Duplechin turn and run directly toward Bourque who was standing four or five feet from second base toward home plate. Duplechin did not attempt to slide or decrease his speed and his left arm came up under Bourque's chin as they collided. Duplechin had to veer from the base path in order to strike Bourque.

Donald Frank Lockwood, baseball coach at USL, testified as an expert witness that: softball is a noncontact sport; in a forced play to second such as this, the accepted way to break up a double play is by sliding.

Steve Pressler, who hit the ground ball that precipitated the incident, testified that the sides were retired as a result, because the collision was a flagrant violation of the rules of the game.

Duplechin admitted that he ran into Bourque while standing up in an attempt to block Bourque's view of first base and keep him from executing a double play. Duplechin also admitted that he was running at full speed when he collided with Bourque, a much smaller man. Duplechin attributed the accident to Bourque's failure to get out of the way.

Oral surgeon John R. Wallace saw Bourque following the accident and said the nature of the injury and the x-rays indicated that it was caused by a blow from underneath the jaw. Dr. Wallace characterized the injury as one that may have been common in football before the use of mouthpieces and face guards.

While other testimony was presented, both cumulative and contradictory, the evidence summarized above provides a reasonable evidentiary basis for the trial court's conclusions.

There is no question that defendant Duplechin's conduct was the cause in fact of the harm to plaintiff Bourque. Duplechin was under a duty to play softball in the ordinary fashion without unsportsmanlike conduct or wanton injury to his fellow players. This duty was breached by Duplechin, whose behavior was, according to the evidence, substandard and negligent. Bourque assumed the risk of being hit by a bat or a ball. [Citations omitted.] Bourque may also have assumed the risk of an injury resulting from standing in the base path and being spiked by someone sliding into second base, a common incident of softball and baseball. However, Bourque did not assume the risk of Duplechin going out of his way to run into him at full speed when Bourque was five feet away from the base. A participant in a game or sport assumes all of the risks incidental to that particular activity which are obvious and foreseeable. A participant does not assume the risk of injury from fellow players acting in an unexpected or unsportsmanlike way with a reckless lack of concern for others participating. [Citations omitted.] Assumption of risk is an affirmative defense which must be proven by a preponderance of the evidence, and the record here supports the trial court's conclusion that Bourque did not assume the risk of Duplechin's negligent act.

There is no evidence in the record to indicate contributory negligence on the part of Bourque. . . .

Duplechin was not motivated by a desire to injure Bourque. Duplechin tried to break up a double play with a reckless disregard of the consequences to Bourque. Duplechin's action was negligent but does not present a situation where the injury was expected or intended. . . .

The trial court awarded plaintiff Bourque $12,000 for his pain and suffering and $1,496.00 for his special damages. There is no dispute about the amount awarded. Bourque's jaw was fractured; his chin required plastic surgery; seven teeth were broken and had to be crowned; and one tooth was replaced by a bridge.

There is no manifest error in the trial court's conclusions which we summarize as follows:

> plaintiff Bourque's injuries resulted from the negligence of defendant Duplechin; Bourque was not guilty of contributory negligence and did not assume the risk of this particular accident. . . .

For the foregoing reasons, the judgment of the trial court is affirmed. . . .

AFFIRMED.

NABOZNY v. BARNHILL

31 Ill. App. 3d 212, 334 N.E.2d 258 (1975)

ADESKO, Justice.

Plaintiff, Julian Claudio Nabozny, a minor, by Edward J. Nabozny, his father, commenced this action to recover damages for personal injuries allegedly caused by the negligence of defendant, David Barnhill. Trial was before a jury. At the close of plaintiffs case on motion of defendant, the trial court directed a verdict in favor of the defendant. Plaintiff appeals from the order granting the motion.

Plaintiff contends on appeal that the trial judge erred in granting defendant's motion for a directed verdict and that plaintiffs actions as a participant do not prohibit the establishment of a prima facie case of negligence. Defendant argues in support of the trial court's ruling that defendant was free from negligence as a matter of law (lacking a duty to plaintiff) and that defendant was contributorily negligent as a matter of law. . . . [O]ur statement of facts reflects an examination of all of the evidence viewed in its aspect most favorable to plaintiff.

A soccer match began between two amateur teams at Duke Child's Field in Winnetka, Illinois. Plaintiff was playing the position of goalkeeper for the Hansa team. Defendant was playing the position of forward for the Winnetka team. Members of both teams were of high-school age. Approximately twenty minutes after play had begun, a Winnetka player kicked the ball over the mid-field line. Two players, Jim Gallos (for Hansa) and the defendant (for Winnetka) chased the free ball. Gallos reached the ball first. Since he was closely pursued by the defendant, Gallos passed the ball to the plaintiff, the Hansa goalkeeper. Gallos then turned away and prepared to receive a pass from the plaintiff. The plaintiff, in the meantime, went down on his left knee, received the pass, and pulled the ball to his chest. The defendant did not turn away when Gallos did, but continued to run in the direction of the plaintiff and kicked the left side of plaintiffs head causing plaintiff severe injuries.

All of the occurrence witnesses agreed that the defendant had time to avoid contact with plaintiff and that the plaintiff remained at all times within the "penalty area" a rectangular area between the eighteenth yard line and the goal. Four witnesses testified that they saw plaintiff in a crouched position on his left knee inside the penalty zone. Plaintiff testified that he actually had possession of the ball when he was struck by defendant. One witness, Marie Shekem, stated that plaintiff had the ball when he was kicked. All other occurrence witnesses stated that they thought plaintiff was in possession of the ball.

Plaintiff called three expert witnesses. Julius Roth, coach of the Hansa team, testified that the game in question was being played under "F.I.F.A." rules. The three experts agreed that those rules prohibited all players from making contact with the goalkeeper when he is in possession of the ball in the penalty area. Possession is defined in the Chicago area as referring to the goalkeeper having his hands on the ball. Under "F.I.F.A." rules, any contact with a goalkeeper in possession in the penalty area is an infraction of the rules, even if such contact is unintentional. The goalkeeper is the only member of a team who is allowed to touch a ball in play so long as he remains in the penalty area. The only legal contact permitted in soccer is shoulder to shoulder contact between players going for a ball within playing distance. The three experts agreed that the contact in question in this case should not have occurred. Additionally, goalkeeper head injuries are extremely rare in soccer. As a result of being struck, plaintiff suffered permanent damage to his skull and brain.

The initial question presented by this appeal is whether, under the facts in evidence, such a relationship existed between the parties that the court will impose a legal duty upon one for the benefit of the other. "[M]ore simply, whether the interest of the plaintiff which has suffered invasion was entitled to legal protection at the hands of the defendant."

There is a dearth of case law involving organized athletic competition wherein one of the participants is charged with negligence. There are no such Illinois cases. A number of other jurisdictions prohibit recovery generally for reasons of public policy. We can find no American cases dealing with the game of soccer.

This court believes that the law should not place unreasonable burdens on the free and vigorous participation in sports by our youth. However, we also believe that organized, athletic competition does not exist in a vacuum. Rather, some of the restraints of civilization must accompany every athlete onto the playing field. One of the educational benefits of organized athletic competition to our youth is the development of discipline and self control.

Individual sports are advanced and competition enhanced by a comprehensive set of rules. Some rules secure the better playing of the game as a test of skill. Other rules are primarily designed to protect participants from serious injury.

For these reasons, this court believes that when athletes are engaged in an athletic competition, all teams involved are trained and coached by knowledgeable personnel; a recognized set of rules governs the conduct of the competition; and a safety rule is contained therein which is primarily designed to protect players from serious injury, a player is then charged with a legal duty to every other player on the field to refrain from conduct proscribed by a safety rule. A reckless disregard for the safety of other players cannot be excused. To engage in such conduct is to create an intolerable and unreasonable risk of serious injury to other participants. We have carefully drawn the rule announced herein in order to control a new field of personal injury litigation. Under the facts presented in the case at bar, we find such a duty clearly arose. Plaintiff was entitled to legal protection at the hands of the defendant. The defendant contends he is immune from tort action for any injury to another player that happens during the course of a game, to which theory we do not subscribe.

It is our opinion that a player is liable for injury in a tort action if his conduct is such that it is either deliberate, willful or with a reckless disregard for the safety of the other player so as to cause injury to that player, the same being a question of fact to be decided by a jury.

Defendant also asserts that plaintiff was contributorily negligent as a matter of law, and, therefore, the trial court's direction of a verdict in defendant's favor was correct. We do not agree. The evidence presented tended to show that plaintiff was in the exercise of ordinary care for his own safety. While playing his position, he remained in the penalty area and took possession of the ball in a proper manner. Plaintiff had no reason to know of the danger created by defendant. Without this knowledge it cannot be said that plaintiff unreasonably exposed himself to such danger or failed to discover or appreciate the risk. The facts in evidence revealed that the play in question was of a kind commonly executed in this sport. Frank Longo, one of the plaintiff's expert witnesses, testified that once the goalkeeper gets possession of the ball in the penalty area, "the instinct should be there [in an opposing player pursuing the ball] through training and knowledge of the rules to avoid contact [with the goalkeeper]." All of plaintiff's expert witnesses agreed that a player charging an opposition goaltender under circumstances similar to those which existed during the play in question should be able to avoid all contact. Furthermore, it is a violation of the rules for a player simply to kick at the ball when a goalkeeper has possession in the penalty area even if no contact is made with the goalkeeper.

. . . [W]e conclude that the trial court erred in directing a verdict in favor of defendant. It is a fact question for the jury.

This cause, therefore, is reversed and remanded to the Circuit Court of Cook County for a new trial consistent with the views expressed in this opinion.

REVERSED AND REMANDED.

HACKBART v. CINCINNATI BENGALS, INC.

601 F.2d 516 (10th Cir. 1979)

WILLIAM E. DOYLE, Circuit Judge.

The question in this case is whether in a regular season professional football game an injury which is inflicted by one professional football player on an opposing player can give rise to liability in tort where the injury was inflicted by the intentional striking of a blow during the game.

* * *

[T]he judge resolved the liability issue in favor of the Cincinnati team and Charles Clark. Consistent with this result, final judgment was entered for Cincinnati and the appeal challenges this judgment. In essence the trial court's reasons for rejecting plaintiff's claim were that professional football is a species of warfare and that so much physical force is tolerated and the magnitude of the force exerted is so great that it renders injuries not actionable in court; that even intentional batteries are beyond the scope of the judicial process.

* * *

II

The evidence at the trial uniformly supported the proposition that the intentional striking of a player in the head from the rear is not an accepted part of either the playing rules or the general customs of the game of professional football. The trial court, however, believed that the unusual nature of the case called for the consideration of underlying policy which it defined as common law principles which have evolved as a result of the case to case process and which necessarily affect behavior in various contexts. From these considerations the belief was expressed that even intentional injuries incurred in football games should be outside the framework of the law. The court recognized that the potential threat of legal liability has a significant deterrent effect, and further said that private civil actions constitute an important mechanism for societal control of human conduct. Due to the increase in severity of human conflicts, a need existed to expand the body of governing law more rapidly and with more certainty, but that this had to be accomplished by legislation and administrative regulation. The judge compared football to coal mining and railroading insofar as all are inherently hazardous. Judge Matsch said that in the case of football it was questionable whether social values would be improved by limiting the violence.

Thus the district court's assumption was that Clark had inflicted an intentional blow which would ordinarily generate civil liability and which might bring about a criminal sanction as well, but that since it had occurred in the course of a football game, it should not be subject to the restraints of the law; that if it were it would place unreasonable impediments and restraints on the activity. The judge also pointed out that courts are ill-suited to decide the different social questions and to administer conflicts on what is much like a battlefield where the restraints of civilization have been left on the sidelines.

We are forced to conclude that the result reached is not supported by evidence.

III

Plaintiff, of course, maintains that tort law applicable to the injury in this case applies on the football field as well as in other places. On the other hand, plaintiff does not rely on the theory of negligence being applicable. This is in recognition of the fact that subjecting another to unreasonable risk of harm, the essence of negligence, is inherent in the game of football, for admittedly it is violent. Plaintiff maintains that in the area of contributory fault, a vacuum exists in relationship to intentional infliction of injury. Since negligence does not apply, contributory negligence is inapplicable. Intentional or reckless contributory fault could theoretically at least apply to infliction of injuries in reckless disregard of the rights of others. This has some similarity to contributory negligence and undoubtedly it would apply if the evidence would justify it. But it is highly questionable whether a professional football player consents or submits to injuries caused by conduct not within the rules, and there is no evidence which we have seen which shows this. However, the trial court did not consider this question and we are not deciding it.

Contrary to the position of the court then, there are no principles of law which allow a court to rule out certain tortious conduct by reason of general roughness of the game or difficulty of administering it.

Indeed, the evidence shows that there are rules of the game which prohibit the intentional striking of blows. Thus, Article 1, Item 1, Subsection C, provides that:

> "All players are prohibited from striking on the head, face or neck with the heel, back or side of the hand, wrist, forearm, elbow or clasped hands."

Thus the very conduct which was present here is expressly prohibited by the rule which is quoted above.

The general customs of football do not approve the intentional punching or striking of others. That this is prohibited was supported by the testimony of all of the witnesses. They testified that the intentional striking of a player in the face or from the rear is prohibited by the playing rules as well as the general customs of the game. Punching or hitting with the arms is prohibited. Undoubtedly these restraints are intended to establish reasonable boundaries so that one football player cannot intentionally inflict a serious injury on another. Therefore, the notion is not correct that all reason has been abandoned, whereby the only possible remedy for the person who has been the victim of an unlawful blow is retaliation.

* * *

V

The Restatement of Torts Second, § 500, distinguishes between reckless and negligent misconduct. Reckless misconduct differs from negligence, according to the authors, in that negligence consists of mere inadvertence, lack of skillfulness or failure to take precautions; reckless misconduct, on the other hand, involves a choice or adoption of a course of action either with knowledge of the danger or with knowledge of facts which would disclose this danger to a reasonable man. Recklessness also differs in that it consists of intentionally doing an act with knowledge not only that it contains a risk of harm to others as does negligence, but that it actually involves a risk substantially greater in magnitude than is necessary in the case of negligence. The authors explain the difference, therefore, in the degree of risk by saying that the difference is so significant as to amount to a difference in kind.

Subsection (f) also distinguishes between reckless misconduct and intentional wrongdoing. To be reckless the *act* must have been intended by the actor. At the same time, the actor does not intend to cause the harm which results from it. It is enough that he realized, or from the facts should have realized, that there was a strong probability that harm would result even though he may hope or expect that this conduct will prove harmless. Nevertheless, existence of probability is different from substantial certainty which is an ingredient of intent to cause the harm which results from the act.

Therefore, recklessness exists where a person knows that the act is harmful but fails to realize that it will produce the extreme harm which it did produce. It is in this respect that recklessness and intentional conduct differ in degree.

In the case at bar the defendant Clark admittedly acted impulsively and in the heat of anger, and even though it could be said from the admitted facts that he intended the act, it could also be said that he did not intend to inflict serious injury which resulted from the blow which he struck.

In ruling that recklessness is the appropriate standard and that assault and battery is not the exclusive one, we are saying that these two liability concepts are not necessarily opposed one to the other. Rather, recklessness under § 500 of the *Restatement* might be regarded, for the purpose of analysis at least, a lesser included act.

Assault and battery, having originated in common law writ, is narrower than recklessness in its scope. In essence, two definitions enter into it. The assault is an attempt coupled with the present ability to commit a violent harm against another. Battery is the unprivileged or unlawful touching of another. Assault and battery then call for an intent, as does recklessness. But in recklessness the intent is to do the act, but without an intent to cause the particular harm. It is enough if the actor knows that there is a strong probability that harm will result. Thus, the definition fits perfectly the fact situation here. Surely, then, no reason exists to compel appellant to employ the assault and battery standard which does not comfortably apply fully in preference to the standard which meets this fact situation.

* * *

In sum, having concluded that the trial court did not limit the case to a trial of the evidence bearing on defendant's liability but rather determined that as a matter of social policy the game was so violent and unlawful that valid lines could not be drawn, we take the view that this was not a proper issue for determination and that plaintiff was entitled to have the case tried on an assessment of his rights and whether they had been violated.

The trial court has heard the evidence and has made findings. The findings of fact based on the evidence presented are not an issue on this appeal. Thus, it would not seem that the court would have to repeat the areas of evidence that have already been fully considered. The need is for a reconsideration of that evidence in the light of that which is taken up by this court in its opinion. We are not to be understood as limiting the trial court's consideration of supplemental evidence if it deems it necessary.

* * *

GAUVIN v. CLARK

537 N.E.2d 94 (Mass. 1989)

Abrams, Justice

At issue is what standard of care participants in an athletic event owe one another. The plaintiff, Robert J. Gauvin, appeals from the Superior Court judgment entered in favor of the defendant, Richard Clark . . . . We hold that participants in an athletic event owe a duty to other participants to refrain from reckless misconduct and liability may result from injuries caused a player by reason of the breach of that duty. Because of the jury's determination that Clark did not act with reckless misconduct, we conclude that the judge correctly entered judgment for the defendant.

For purposes of this appeal, the parties agree to the following facts. On January 30, 1980, the varsity hockey team of Worcester State College played against the team from Nichols College.

Gauvin played center position for the Worcester State College team. Clark played center for the Nichols College team. During the second period, Gauvin was involved in a face-off with Clark, in which the referee dropped the puck, and both men vied for possession. Clark won the face-off. As the puck slid down the ice toward the Nichols College team's net, Gauvin felt a stick in his abdomen. Gauvin saw Clark's hockey stick coming away from Gauvin's abdomen, with the back of the hockey stick, called the "butt-end" protruding from Clark's hands. At trial, Harry Maxfield, a teammate of Gauvin, testified that he saw Clark give Gauvin a shot to the midsection after the puck slid down toward the Nichols goal. The blow to Gauvin's abdomen came after the face-off had been completed. The blow was struck when Gauvin and Clark were no longer competing for the puck.

As a result of the blow to his abdomen, Gauvin was hospitalized and underwent surgery. His spleen was removed. He missed seven weeks of school. Gauvin still suffers from bladder and abdominal pain.

The safety rules which govern the game of hockey prohibit "butt-ending." Butt-ending is the practice of taking the end of the stick which does not come into contact with the puck and driving this part of the stick into another player's body. Butt-ending is unexpected and unsportsmanlike conduct for a hockey game. The rules also prohibit a player, during a face-off, from making any physical contact with his opponent's body by means of his stick, except in the course of playing the puck. Butt-ending is penalized as a major penalty and also results in a disqualification of the penalized player.

Both Gauvin and Clark understood that the game was played according to a recognized set of rules, which prohibited butt-ending Clark understood that the prohibition on butt-ending was designed for the protection of the players. Gauvin's coach, John Laughlin, was knowledgeable about the game of hockey, and had trained Gauvin and his teammates. Clark's coaches, first Alan Kubicki and then the defendant, Mark Bombard, were both knowledgeable about the game of hockey. They had trained Clark and his teammates in the rules of hockey.

The case was tried to a jury. The case was submitted to the jury on special questions. The jury rendered a special verdict in which it answered six specific questions and found the following facts. Clark had butt-ended Gauvin. Clark had violated a safety rule, thus causing Gauvin's injuries. By playing hockey, Gauvin did not consent to the act which caused his injury.

The jury concluded, however, that Clark had not acted willfully, wantonly, or recklessly in causing Gauvin's injury. The jury assessed damages in the amount of $30,000. Based on the jury's answer to the question whether Clark acted willfully, wantonly, or recklessly, the judge entered judgment in favor of the defendant Clark.

Standard of Care. Gauvin argues that, since the jury found that Clark violated a safety rule, and Clark's action caused Gauvin's injury, judgment should have been entered in favor of Gauvin, despite the fact that the jury found that Clark had not acted recklessly. We do not agree.

The problem of imposing a duty of care on participants in a sports competition is a difficult one. Players, when they engage in sport, agree to undergo some physical contacts which could amount to assault and battery absent the players' consent. The courts are wary of imposing wide tort liability on sports participants, lest the law chill the vigor of athletic competition. Nevertheless, "some of the restraints of civilization must accompany every athlete on to the playing field." *Nabozny v. Barnhill*, 31 Ill. App. 3d 212, 215, 334 N.E.2d 258 (1975). . . .

The majority of jurisdictions which have considered this issue have concluded that personal injury cases arising out of an athletic event must be predicated on reckless disregard of safety. *See, e.g., Hackbart v. Cincinnati Bengals, Inc.*, 601 F.2d 516, 524 (10th Cir. 1979); *Nabozny v. Barnhill, supra*. . . .

We adopt this standard. Allowing the imposition of liability in cases of reckless disregard of safety diminishes the need for players to seek retaliation during the game or future games. *See Hackbart v. Cincinnati Bengals, Inc., supra* at 521. Precluding the imposition of liability in cases of negligence without reckless misconduct furthers the policy that "[v]igorous and active participation in sporting events should not be chilled by the threat of litigation." *Kabella v. Bouschelle*, [100 N.M. 461, 465, 672 P.2d 290 (1983)].

Gauvin reads the leading case of *Nabozny v. Barnhill, supra,* to mean that Clark should be held liable, because the jury found that Clark had violated a safety rule, even though the jury found that Clark had not acted wilfully, wantonly, or recklessly. Some of *Nabozny*'s language might seem to imply that all that is needed to establish an actionable tort is breach of a safety rule. However, "we see *Nabozny* as establishing the standard of conduct to be willfulness or a reckless disregard of safety. . . . " The judge below applied the proper rule of law in entering judgment in favor of Clark when the jury found that Clark had not acted recklessly.

* * *

Notes and Comments

1. If "participant" is defined broadly, it could include referees, cheerleaders, and coaches. A tort case against a referee might well involve a theory of negligent supervision.

Carraba v. Anacortes School District No. 103, 435 P.2d 936 (Wash. 1967) (referee's negligence in failing to detect an illegal wrestling hold). For example, a referee who permits a boxing match to continue when a reasonable referee would stop it might be named as defendant in a lawsuit by the injured boxer. On the other hand, a referee attacked by a disgruntled participant might initiate a lawsuit of his own on a battery theory. For a recent article on torts against sports officials, *see* Christopher M. Chiafullo, *From Personal Foul to Personal Attack: How Sports Officials are the Target of Physical Abuse from Players, Coaches, and Fans Alike*, 8 SETON HALL J. SPORT L. 201-28 (1998). For a list of ways sports officials can shield themselves from liability, *see* Richard J. Hunter, Jr., *An "Insider's" Guide to the Legal Liability of Sports Contest Officials*, 15 MARQ. SPORTS L. REV. 369 (2005).

The liability of the NFL as a result of referee negligence is a recent development in the area of participant vs. participant tort liability. On December 19, 1999, offensive tackle Orlando Brown suffered an injury when hit by a referee's penalty marker during a professional football game. Alan Rubin, *Ref Blamed For Eye Injury*, N.Y. DAILY NEWS, Mar. 30, 2001. Although the referee undeniably caused the injury, Brown has only brought suit against the NFL. Plaintiff's Petition at p. 1, *Brown v. NFL*, No. 1:01/CIV-4086 (S.D.N.Y. 2001). Brown could conceivably recover on a negligence theory if the referee acted negligently and the NFL, as the referee's employer, is liable under the respondeat superior doctrine. Additionally, the NFL could be liable for negligence in the training of its professional game officials.

2. A cheerleader who is injured when performing an acrobatic cheer may well be the victim of a tortfeasor-coparticipant, or of a negligent coach. The liability of coaches deserves special attention. In a negligence-based cause of action, the issue may be whether the coach fulfilled the duty to use reasonable care in protecting the athletes. In a series of reported cases, coaches were deemed to have fallen below that standard. Liability has been imposed, for example, when a coach plays an injured player, *Morris v. Union High School Dist. A*, 194 P. 998 (Wash. 1931), fails to direct the movement of an injured player properly, *Welch v. Dunsmuir Joint Union School Dist.*, 326 P.2d 633 (Cal. Dist. Ct. App. 1958), fails to acquire proper medical attention for heat stroke, *Mogabgab v. Orleans Parish School Bd.*, 239 So. 2d 456 (La. App. 1970), and fails to instruct adequately on safe techniques for participation, *Stehn v. Benarr McFadden Founds., Inc.*, 434 F.2d 811 (6th Cir. 1970). It is not difficult to imagine other contexts in which a coach might be liable for an injury to a player. The celebrated incident in which Coach Frank Kush grabbed and shook the facemask of his erring punter, Kevin Rutledge, indicates that sometimes overzealous, physical "coaching" takes on tortious dimensions. Here, liability would be based on an intentional tort rather than on negligence. Recently, two former New York high school football players were awarded $25,000 each in a suit against the coach and the school district as a result of the coaches' practice of hitting players in the head and body with a tackling dummy during practices. Situations in which a coach defames a player or invades a player's privacy by publicly disclosing private facts are certainly foreseeable. The nature of the player-coach relationship presents many possibilities for suits by players. *See* J. WEISTART & C. LOWELL, THE LAW OF SPORTS § 8.06 for a partial list of these cases. *See also* Ray Yasser, *Liability for Sports Injuries*, *in* LAW OF PROFESSIONAL AND AMATEUR SPORTS, § 14.05 (Uberstine ed. 1998); Anthony S. McCaskey & Kenneth W. Bredeynski, *A Guide to the Legal Liability of Coaches for a Sports*

Participant's Injuries, 6 SETON HALL J. SPORT L. 7-125 (1996); Janice Brown, *Legislators Strike Out: Volunteer Little League Coaches Should Not be Immune from Tort Liability*, 7 SETON HALL J. SPORT L. 559 (1997); and *McGurk v. Lincoln Community School District*, 677 N.E.2d 71 (Ill. App. 3d Dist. 1997).

Colleges and universities are potentially liable for the torts of their employees under the universally recognized principles of respondeat superior. The institution might also be liable for its own negligence in failing to take reasonable precautions against the risk of foreseeable life threatening injuries. In *Kleinknecht v. Gettysburg College*, 989 F.2d 1360 (3d Cir. 1993), the parents of a college lacrosse player who died of a heart attack during a practice session sued the college. The district court granted summary judgment for the college. The court of appeals reversed, noting that the college owed a duty of care based on the special relationship that exists between a college and its athletes. The court of appeals thought that the issue of whether the college took reasonable precautions to protect the student-athlete was a jury issue. The Third Circuit's decision provides an excellent review and analysis of many of the issues raised in connection with the duty owed by a college to its student athletes.

3. Many fairly common situations present interesting tort cases. Consider, for example, the situations listed in **Note 3** of **Chapter 11,** *supra,* as potential torts cases. In addition, as noted in the material on "recklessness," courts have at times gone out of their way to distinguish the cause of action in the contact as opposed to the non-contact sports injury case, by stating that "participants in bodily contact games such as basketball assume greater risks than do golfers and others in non-physical contact sports." *Oswald v. Township High School Dist. No. 214*, 406 N.E.2d 157 (Ill. App. Ct. 1980). There have been a multitude of golf cases in which action was brought for a variety of unique and innovative ways of inflicting serious injury (and not so serious general bonking) on fellow players, caddies, bystanders, and other innocent victims with the various paraphernalia of the game. Do you think that any of these cases belong in the context of a discussion involving participant to participant liability in sports? Do you think golf should be considered more of a game (like chess) than a sport (like football)? For a comprehensive survey of golf cases, *see* Ray Yasser, *In the Heat of Competition: Tort Liability of One Participant to Another: Why Can't Participants be Required to be Reasonable?*, 5 SETON HALL J. SPORT L. 267, n.77 (1995).

4. Although *Bourque* indicates that a negligence based claim of action is appropriate in the sports setting, the trend is away from the negligence claim. In fact, *Bourque* suggests as much when the court points out that the sports participant assumes "all risks incidental to that particular activity which are obvious and foreseeable" but does not assume "the risk of injury from fellow players acting in an unexpected or unsportsmanlike way with a reckless lack of concern for others participating." The thrust of *Bourque* is that the sports participant invariably assumes the risks created by the coparticipant's negligence but not necessarily by his recklessness. *Bourque* is really more accurately viewed as a case in which the defendant was liable because he was reckless and not because he was negligent.

5. *Nabozny* and *Hackbart* suggest also that the simple negligence claim will fail. Although negligence was pleaded in *Nabozny*, the court opinion stressed that "a player is liable if his conduct is such that it is either deliberate, willful or with a reckless disregard for the safety of the other player." The implication of *Nabozny* is that simple negligence will not suffice. The plaintiff in *Hackbart* did not even rely on a negligence theory. As the *Hackbart* court pointed out, "This [was] in recognition of the fact that subjecting another to unreasonable risk of harm, the essence of negligence, is inherent in the game of football."

Gauvin is an example of more recent cases which indicate that courts are rejecting negligence based claims and accepting recklessness as the appropriate minimum standard required. Other cases include: *Dotzler v. Tuttle*, 449 N.W.2d 774 (Neb. 1990) (participants are not liable for ordinary negligence but only conduct that is reckless); *Marchetti v. Kalish*, 559 N.E.2d 699 (Ohio 1990) (reckless disregard is the proper standard for both adult and child participants in recreational and sports activities); *Ginsberg v. Hontas*, 545 So. 2d 1154 (La. Ct. App. 1989) (duty of participants is to refrain from reckless conduct); *Lundrum v. Gonzalez*, 629 N.E.2d 710 (Ill. App. Ct. 1994) (plaintiff could not recover since he had not shown willful or wanton conduct on the part of the defendant); *Ordway v. Superior Court (Casella)*, 243 Cal. Rptr. 536 (Cal. Ct. App. 1988) (jockey assumes risk of negligence but not of recklessness). *See also Kiley v. Patterson*, 763 A.2d 583 (R.I. 2000); *Jaworski v. Kiernan*, 241 Conn. 399 (1997); *Phister v. Shusta*, 657 N.E.2d 1013 (Ill. 1995); *Hearon v. May*, 540 N.W.2d 124 (Neb. 1995); *McKichan v. St. Louis Hoelay Club, L.P.*, 967 S.W.2d 209 (Mo. Ct. App. 1998); and *Sicard v. University of Dayton*, 660 N.E.2d 1241 (Ohio Ct. App. 1995).

Still, a lawyer pleading a case arising out of a playing field incident ought to plead the negligence-based cause of action simply because the ground rules in such cases have not been clearly identified in all jurisdictions. The best advice to a practitioner representing an injured sports participant is to plead the three causes of action in the alternative. (This would be done in the same manner as one would plead breach of warranty, negligence, and strict liability on behalf of a consumer injured by a defective product.) The informed practitioner ought to recognize that the negligence-based claim probably will fail.

The outcome to the litigation might often depend on the availability of the defenses. In the recklessness context, the primary defense is akin to assumption of risk. It is interesting to note, however, that other defenses to a recklessness-based cause of action have not been clearly delineated. As *Hackbart* notes, the distinctions between recklessness and negligence and between recklessness and intentions are not brightline. As Oliver Wendell Holmes noted:

> If the manifest probability of harm is very great . . . we say that it is done intentionally; if not so great but still considerable, we say that the

harm is done negligently; if there is no apparent danger, we call it mischance.

Holmes, *Privilege, Malice, and Intent*, 8 HARV. L. REV. 1 (1894).

We might go on to say today that if the manifest probability of harm is not very great, but quite considerable, it is recklessness. The distinctions are not clear, and recklessness has only recently emerged as a separate and distinct cause of action. The available defenses to the recklessness claim, therefore, have not been clearly articulated. A practitioner would be well advised to plead the well established intentional tort defenses of consent, self-defense, defense of others, and defense of property, along with the well established negligence defenses of assumption of risk and contributory negligence, and let the court decide. *See* Ray Yasser, *In the Heat of Competition: Tort Liability of One Participant to Another: Why Can't Participants be Required to be Reasonable?*, 5 SETON HALL J. SPORT L. 267 (1995), and Barbara Svoranos, *Fighting? It's All in a Day's Work on the Ice: Determining the Appropriate Standard of a Hockey Player's Liability to Another Player*, 7 SETON HALL J. SPORT L. 487-512 (1997); Dean Richardson, *Player Violence: An Essay on Torts and Sports*, 15 STAN. L. & POLICY REV. 133 (2004).

6. Problem. You represent Kermit Washington and the Los Angeles Lakers in the following litigation. Do you recommend that the case be settled? How is it likely to be resolved?

The plaintiff in the case is Rudy Tomjanovich, a veteran professional basketball player, employed by the Houston Rockets, Inc., a professional basketball franchise based in Houston, Texas. The defendant is California Sports, Inc., which does business as the Los Angeles Lakers professional basketball team. The plaintiff's cause of action arose out of an altercation that took place during a basketball game between the Lakers and the Rockets. During the course of the game Tomjanovich was punched in the face by Kermit Washington, a Los Angeles Lakers player.

The undisputed facts reveal that the incident began with a fight between Kermit Washington and another Rockets player, Kevin Kunnert. A film of the incident showed that Washington grabbed Kunnert and blows were exchanged. Tomjanovich then approached and Washington punched him in the face with enough force to leave Tomjanovich with a fractured skull, nose and jaw, a brain concussion, facial lacerations, leakage of spinal fluid, and other serious complications.

The plaintiff offered a number of theories to support a cause of action against the Lakers. He alleged that Kermit Washington's attack was tortious and that the Lakers were vicariously liable for Washington's torts. The plaintiff contended that Washington was negligent, reckless and guilty of intentional wrongdoing. He asserted that no matter how Washington's tort was characterized, the Lakers were vicariously liable under the theory of respondeat superior. Tomjanovich also alleged that the Lakers were themselves negligent in their supervision of Washington. In this regard, the plaintiff claimed that the Lakers failed to control, train and discipline Washington. Punitive damages were requested for all causes of action.

Along with a general denial, the Lakers alleged, by way of affirmative defense, that insofar as the negligence-based cause of action was concerned, that Tomjanovich was contributorily negligent and assumed the risk. They further alleged that the recklessness-based cause of action was barred by Tomjanovich's reckless indifference to his own welfare and that the battery cause of action was defeated by the privileges of consent and self-defense.

The trial lasted 10 days, during which time the plaintiff and defendant introduced testimony from eyewitnesses and experts, and the jury viewed and reviewed films and photographs of the events surrounding the occurrence. What follows is the gist of what was established by the massive amount of evidence.

The plaintiff's evidence tended to establish that Tomjanovich was acting as a peacemaker when he approached Washington and Kunnert, who were scuffling. Tomjanovich appeared to be unprepared for the punch which floored him and was unable to defend himself from the blow. It appeared that he ran right into the punch. It was the kind of a blow that was unexpected in professional basketball; it was not customary and it was excessive in nature. Testimony was received concerning the vicious nature of the blow, with Kareem Abdul-Jabbar summing it up best by saying that, when he heard the impact of the punch, he thought that it sounded "like a watermelon being dropped on a cement floor." The plaintiff also offered evidence establishing the extensive damage caused by the blow. Evidence of the defendant's wealth was received as relevant to the issue of punitive damages. On the negligent supervision cause of action, Tomjanovich introduced evidence showing that the Lakers in fact encouraged overly-aggressive play, that they did not discipline and, in fact, paid the fines for players penalized for such play, that they encouraged Washington to be featured in a *Sports Illustrated* article on basketball's "enforcers," and that, subsequent to the Washington-Tomjanovich incident, they "ratified" Washington's conduct by paying his league imposed fine and by not disciplining him.

The defendant's evidence tended to show that professional basketball was an inherently "physical" game in which fights and scuffles were foreseeable. The Lakers' version of the incident was designed to show that Tomjanovich did not act reasonably in protecting himself, that he knew or should have known of the risks, and that Washington reasonably believed he was in danger when he glimpsed Tomjanovich approaching rapidly towards him. The Lakers presented evidence that they were indeed attempting to deal with the problem of on-court violence, and they threatened overly aggressive players with the loss of playing time and even with the loss of their spot on the roster, but that to a certain extent violence in pro basketball was to be expected, because, to a limited extent, it was an intrinsic part of the game.

7. In *Murphy v. Steeplechase Amusement Company, Inc.*, 250 N.Y. 479, 482, 166 N.E. 173, 174 (1929), Judge Cardozo stated: "One who takes part in . . . a sport accepts the dangers that inhere in it so far as they are obvious and necessary." Is this helpful? What dangers are "obvious and necessary" to a professional hockey player? To a professional football player? To a college football player? to a Little League baseball player? To participants in extreme sports? *See* Denise M. Yerger, *High-Risk Recreation: The Thrill that Creates a Statutory and Judicial Spectrum of Response and Drives the Dichotomy in Participant and Provider Liability*, 38 SUFFOLK U. L. REV. 687 (2005); David Horton, *Extreme Sports and Assumption of Risk*, 38 U.S.F. L. REV. 599 (2004).

In "the fireman's chair" case, *Arnold v. Schmeiser,* 34 A.D.2d 568, 309 N.Y.S.2d 699 (1970), it was held that the plaintiff assumed the risk that his fellow participants would fail to catch him when they tossed him in the air but that he did not assume the risk that his fellow participants would *refuse* to catch him. The case is an apt metaphor of the nature of the risks assumed. For more on assumption of risk in high school, college, and professional sports, *see* Keya Denner, *Taking One for the Team: The Role of Assumption of the Risk in Sports Torts Cases*, 14 SETON HALL J. SPORT L. 209 (2004).

8. The sports participant clearly does not enjoy talismanic immunity from tort liability. The obvious goal of any practitioner is to distinguish which cases have a reasonable chance of success. The materials in this section are ultimately designed to assist the practitioner in drawing that distinction. It does appear, however, that sports activity is one area of human behavior in which the participants are insulated from liability for ordinary negligence. Perhaps this is one thing that makes sports a special and unique form of human experience — participants are free to be unreasonable.

But the question of whether participants are required to be reasonable or are free to be unreasonable remains subject to some debate. Generally the courts have taken one of two positions: (1) that more than negligence is required to state a cause of action or (2) that negligence is sufficient for recovery. As already noted, the former view appears to be prevalent. Still, the matter is not entirely settled.

Nabozny, Hackbart, and Gauvin articulated the view that the simple negligence claim should fail. There are jurisdictions that have rejected this approach and allowed recovery on the basis of negligence. For example, in a 1993 decision, the Wisconsin Supreme Court ruled that liability in the sports injury case may be based on negligence, depending on the specific circumstances. *Lestina v. West Bend Mutual Insurance Co.*, 501 N.W.2d 28, 33 (Wis. 1993). Robert F. Lestina, the plaintiff, was injured in a collision with the defendant, Leopold Jerger. Lestina was playing an offensive position for his recreational soccer team and Jerger was the goal keeper for the opposing team. Jerger, the defendant, apparently ran out of the goal area and collided with the plaintiff. The plaintiff alleged that the defendant "slide tackled" him in order to prevent him from scoring. The plaintiff seriously injured his left knee and leg in the collision.

For a time, New Jersey also adopted the negligence standard for sports injury cases in *Crawn v. Campo*, 630 A.2d 368 (N.J. Super. Ct. App. Div. 1993). In *Crawn*, the appellate court held that ordinary negligence, rather than reckless conduct, was the appropriate standard to be applied in a participant-to-participant sports injury case. The Supreme Court of New Jersey, relying on *Nabozny*, rejected this reasoning and held that the duty of care required in establishing liability in recreational sports should be based on a standard of recklessness or intentional conduct, rather than negligence. *Crawn v. Campo*, 136 N.J. 494, 508 (1994).

In the professional arena, Connecticut joined the ranks of those jurisdictions allowing a negligence cause of action in *Babych v. McRae*, 567 A.2d 1269 (Conn. Super. Ct. 1989). The plaintiff, Wayne Babych, alleged that the defendant, Ken McRae, a fellow professional hockey player, struck the plaintiff across his right knee with a hockey stick during a game, causing the plaintiff to suffer personal injuries and financial losses. In holding that negligence is a legally sufficient cause of action when one professional sports participant is injured by another, the court rejected the New York decision in *Turcotte v. Fell*, 502 N.E.2d 964 (N.Y. 1986), which held that negligence was not actionable when one professional sports participant injured another. The Connecticut court in *Babych* found that there was no analogous case law barring a negligence cause of action in sports participant-to-participant cases.

A number of states appear to recognize negligence as a viable cause of action in the "heat of competition" context. In almost every area of our lives we are exposed to liability if we act in a negligent manner and cause harm to others. For the most part, our social compact says that unreasonable conduct which causes physical harm is actionable. This rule of liability is firmly grounded in social policy. The exposure to liability serves to deter unreasonably risky behavior and to compensate the injured.

There are a few limited areas where actors are insulated from liability for ordinary negligence. These exemptions, too, are rooted in public policy. For example, in the area of defamation law, a plaintiff who is a public person can ordinarily recover for injury to reputation only upon a clear and convincing showing of "knowledge or reckless disregard for truth or falsity." *New York Times v. Sullivan*, 376 U.S. 254 (1964). This solicitude for speech is grounded in strong social policy; we are as a people deeply committed to free speech and a wide-open, robust discussion of issues of public concern. In order to give speech the breathing room it needs to thrive, negligent speakers are insulated from liability.

Does it make sense, then, to insulate a negligent sports participant from liability to a physically injured co-participant? Is sports deserving of such solicitude? Are there really convincing policy reasons to insulate a sports participant from liability for physical harm caused by negligence?

The courts that require an injured sports participant to prove recklessness (and thus protect the "merely" negligent actor) do so on the theory that sports, like speech, needs "breathing room." But the evidence is accumulating that, on every level of competition, participants need to be restrained and not emboldened. From kids' sports to professional sports, it sometimes seems that sportsmanship, fair play and reasonable restraint are lost values. Grotesque showmanship, unethical means to win, and reckless unconcern mar the landscape of sport. Do you think that sports participants need breathing room or should they have their feet held to the liability fire? For more on whether sports violence should be civil or criminal, and if incidents should be left to the leagues or the law, *see* Matthew P. Barry, Richard L. Fox, & Clark Jones, *Judicial Opinion on the Criminality of Sports Violence in the United States*, 15 SETON HALL J. SPORT L. 1 (2005).

9. In *Benitez v. New York City Board of Education*, 530 N.Y.S.2d 825 (App. Div. 1988), a high school football player sued the school board on what can be loosely described as a "negligent scheduling" theory. Benitez suffered a fractured spine and a herniated disc when he was hit by an opponent during a high school football game. His suit alleged that the coaches and administrators were negligent in allowing the mismatch to occur.

The jury awarded Benitez $946,000 for loss of earnings and $304,000 for pain and suffering, but reduced the award by 30 percent as a result of Benitez's own negligence.

On appeal, the court reversed. The court held that a board of education was obligated to exercise ordinary reasonable care to protect student athletes in extracurricular sports from "unassumed, concealed or unreasonably increased risks." According to the court, Benitez failed to show that his injury resulted from a breach of that duty.

In *Avila v. Citrus Community College Dist.*, 38 Cal. 4th 148 (Cal. 2006), a college baseball player brought a negligence cause of action against the opposing team's school when he was intentionally hit in the head by a pitch during a scrimmage. *Id.* The California Supreme Court held that the host college had a duty not to increase the risks in the game. The court observed that being hit in the head by an intentional pitch was a risk inherent in baseball and that the rival college had not increased the risks by failing to stop its pitcher from intentionally throwing at the plaintiff. Accordingly, the case was dismissed. *Id.* at 165.

In *Kavanagh v. Trustees of Boston University*, 795 N.E.2d 1170 (Mass. 2003), a basketball player brought a negligence suit against Boston University and its coach after being punched in the face during a game by a BU player. The plaintiff claimed that Boston University was vicariously liable for the actions of its player and that the college and the coach acted negligently by not preventing the act. *Id.* at 1173.

The court held that the player who punched Kavanagh was not an agent or employee of the college. *Id.* at 1176. Furthermore, the court noted that neither

Boston University nor its coach owed a duty to Kavanagh because there was no special relationship between the parties. *Id.* at 1177. The court remarked that even if such a duty was present, that the assault and battery was not foreseeable. *Id.* The plaintiff's contention that the coach's aggressive style on the sidelines incited his player to attack also failed because the coach's actions did not amount to the requsite standard of recklessness. *Id.* at 1179.

10. Problem. You are a sole practitioner with special expertise in the area of sports-related torts. You have just received the following letter from California attorney James P. Carr. Prepare your response to Mr. Carr's letter. (Mr. Carr has agreed to pay your standard hourly rate for up to 10 hours of work).

Re: Buchan vs. United States Cycling Federation
Los Angeles County Superior Court Case
No. NWC 94943

We represent Ms. Barbara Buchan, who is the plaintiff in the above-referenced lawsuit being litigated in the Los Angeles County Superior Court and now on appeal to the Second District Court of Appeal of the State of California. The case went to trial in July, 1988, and a Los Angeles County jury awarded Barbara Buchan a verdict of approximately $2.3 million against the United States Cycling Federation.

I am taking the liberty of writing to you, since my research suggests that you are one of the recognized legal experts on the national scene with regard to sports law. There is what I believe a very interesting legal issue presented on appeal. I will briefly explain that issue in this letter, and would appreciate any insights or suggestions that you would like to offer. If there is any case authority closely on point that you are aware of, I would certainly appreciate any citations.

By way of background, my client, Barbara Buchan, was injured in July, 1982, while participating in the World Trials for Women, which were held in southern California. The World Trials were conducted by the United States Cycling Federation (U.S.C.F.), which is the national governing body for amateur cycling in the United States, sanctioned as such by the United States Olympic Committee.

Barbara was at the time of her injury a licensed Category II racer. Category II is the highest category for women within the U.S.C.F. In order to participate in this event, or any other U.S.C.F. event, it was necessary for Barbara to hold a valid racing license issued by the U.S.C.F. This was a point-to-point race from Malibu to Newbury Park, during which a major spill occurred involving as many as 20 racers. We presented evidence at the time of trial (which the jury obviously believed) that the cause of the spill was a first-year, inexperienced, and unqualified racer from San Diego. We contended and proved that the U.S.C.F. was negligent in permitting this woman to participate in the race, and that she caused this spill, which resulted in severe brain injuries to Barbara Buchan. We further contended that the helmet rule of the U.S.C.F. which existed in 1982 was inadequate, and that the U.S.C.F. was negligent for not implementing a better helmet rule prior to that time. The 1982 rule allowed the wearing of the so called "hairnet" helmet, which our evidence demonstrated is essentially worthless. The helmet regulation issue was, quite candidly, a secondary issue and does not appear to be the issue on which the jury found liability, although there was no specification in their special verdict.

The primary defense of the U.S.C.F. was based on two Release and Assumption of Risk Agreements executed by Barbara. The first of these was the document she signed in order to obtain a U.S.C.F. racing license. The second was the entry form for this series of races. Both included standard exculpatory language. On behalf of the plaintiff, we contended that these agreements were unenforceable as a matter of law under the rules for enforceability of adhesion exculpatory clauses.

As you might anticipate, counsel for the U.S.C.F. has argued that this verdict potentially opens some sort of "floodgate," thereby allowing a torrent of litigation in similar cases. In fact, the trial court's verdict has absolutely no precedential effect. It seems rather foolhardy for the U.S.C.F. and its insurance carrier to pursue this appeal, given the likelihood of creating bad law that will hurt them not only in California but elsewhere. However, they have filed their Notice of Appeal and appear bent on going forward. I should note as an aside that there is ample insurance coverage to pay the verdict.

I think that you may find that the release issue is truly an interesting one. I really would appreciate any insight or any suggestions that you might be able to offer. Thank you.

Very truly yours,

JAMES P. CARR

B. THE SPECTATOR AS PLAINTIFF

Spectators at sporting events are exposed to special risks. Racing cars occasionally hurtle over barriers and injure spectators. Foul balls, errant pucks, and misplayed golf balls strike spectators with some regularity. Spectators injure one another in their quest for souvenirs. On occasion, the spectator-heckler is injured by the short-tempered participant. This section focuses on those instances in which the spectator becomes a plaintiff in a civil suit.

Of primary concern here is the spectator's cause of action against the owner of the sports facility in which the event takes place. The owner's duty of care depends on the status of the plaintiff, who is traditionally categorized as a trespasser, a licensee, or an invitee. RESTATEMENT § 329 defines a trespasser as "a person who enters or remains upon land in possession of another without a privilege to do so created by the possessor's consent or otherwise." RESTATEMENT § 330 defines a licensee as "a person who is privileged to enter or remain on land only by virtue of the possessor's consent." RESTATEMENT § 332 defines an invitee as either a "public invitee" or a "business visitor." A public invitee is "a person who is invited to enter or remain on land as a member of the public for a purpose for which the land is held open to the public." A business visitor is "a person who is invited to enter or remain on land for a purpose directly or indirectly connected with business dealings with the possessor of land."

The trespasser is the least-protected class of plaintiffs. The traditional common law rule was that the possessor owed no duty to trespassers to make the premises safe. The only duty owed was to refrain from intentionally harming the trespasser. Over the years, a number of exceptions have been recognized. Although the precise nature of the duty owed varies from state to state, it is fair to say that a somewhat greater duty is owed when the presence of the trespasser is known or when the trespass is frequent over a limited portion of the land, or when the trespasser is a child endangered by an artificial condition (the so-called attractive nuisance doctrine).

The basic duty owed to a licensee is to warn of known dangers. The duty owed to an invitee is greater, encompassing those dangers which a reasonable inspection would have revealed. Furthermore, as far as an invitee is concerned, a warning is not sufficient if the condition is very dangerous. Thus, there is a duty to repair highly dangerous conditions to protect the invitee.

The ticket-holding spectator would clearly be an invitee to whom the highest duty of care is owed. A question arises as to the status of those who enter the facility without a ticket — for example, a spectator who enters at halftime of a game when the ticket-takers go off duty and the gates are opened. No reported cases address this issue. Rational arguments could be made that such a spectator fits any of the three categories.

Assumption of risk plays a vital role in cases involving injuries to spectators. Through a long line of cases, courts have generally agreed that spectators at sporting events assume the risks commonly associated with observing the sport. Weistart and Lowell, referring to this rule as the common knowledge rule, at 951, state that "spectators at sports activities assume, as a matter of law, all of the ordinary and inherent risks of the sport which they are observing." Thus, the baseball fan struck by a foul ball cannot recover. But the common knowledge rule is not so easy in cases involving less obvious assumptions of risk. The material that follows examines these cases, along with others, in which the defendant is not the owner of the sports facility but, rather, is another spectator or a participant.

PROBLEM

You are general counsel to the Spakone Huskies Professional Football Club, Inc. You recently received the following letter from Tex Marsh, the general manager of the club:

In some cases involving injured baseball spectators, it is claimed that the defendant is obligated to provide protective screening for all seats rather than for only the few seats located directly behind home plate. In *Fish v. Los Angeles Dodgers Baseball Club*, 128 Cal. Rptr. 807 (Cal. Ct. App. 1976), parents of a 14-year-old who died after being hit by a foul ball at a Dodgers game sued the Dodgers and a physician. The complaint asserted two theories: (1) failure to provide the boy "with a safe place to witness the ball game" and (2) negligent provision of emergency medical services. The first cause of action was dismissed by the trial court, and the dismissal was affirmed on appeal. The case was submitted to the jury solely on the second issue, which decided in favor of the defendant.

See also Mann v. Nutrilite, Inc., 289 P.2d 282 (Cal. Dist. Ct. App. 1955); *Hummel v. Columbus Baseball Club*, 49 N.E.2d 773 (Ohio Ct. App. 1942); *Cates v. Cincinnati Exhibition Co.*, 1 S.E.2d 131 (1939); *Shaw v. Boston Am. League Baseball Co.*, 90 N.E.2d 840 (Mass. 1950); *Anderson v. Kansas City Baseball Club*, 231 S.W.2d 170 (Mo. 1950). The majority of cases appear to hold, however, that the park owner is obligated to furnish just a reasonable number of protected seats and that a spectator assumes the risk by sitting elsewhere. *Dandoff v. Metropolitan Baseball Club, Inc.*, 92 A.D.2d 461, 459 N.Y.S.2d 2 (1983) (sitting in unscreened area where screened areas were available); *O'Bryan v. O'Connor*, 59 A.D.2d 219, 399 N.Y.S.2d 272 (1977) (bat flew out of batter's hands); *Leek v. Tacoma Baseball Club*, 229 P.2d 329 (1951) (perpendicular backstop screen sufficient). A contention that the entire park should be enclosed by a protective screen was rejected by a Wisconsin court as unreasonable because:

> [T]he interest, the popularity and the game of baseball as a national pastime would be doomed for the excitement and enthusiasm is so eloquently displayed to the Court's own eyes upon the chasing or retrieving of a foul ball in the stands and sometimes to the detriment of others, would be drastically curtailed and a thing of the past for our American souvenir loving sport spectators. *Powless v. Milwaukee County*, 94 N.W.2d 187, 190 (Wis. 1959).

If a spectator sits in an unprotected seat, he or she is deemed to have assumed the risk. Further, where a plaintiff was relegated to an unscreened seat even though she requested a protected seat, a subsequent injury was found to be noncompensable. *Schentzel v. Philadelphia Nat'l. League Club*, 96 A.2d 181 (Pa. Super. 1953). This case is representative of the hundreds of reported spectator versus owner cases. A woman attending a baseball game for the first time was struck by a foul ball and injured. Plaintiff Schentzel had contended that the owners of the club and field owed her a duty to exercise "exceptional precautions" since she was a woman and ignorant of the hazards of the game. The "exceptional precautions" included widening the coverage of the protective screening behind the batter's and catcher's positions, still leaving "a few sections" available for those preferring to watch the game from unprotected areas. She recovered a judgment in trial court.

The appeals court found no evidence that the ballpark's screening was insufficient in its coverage and no proof that the screening of a wider area would have prevented the plaintiff's injury. The court also agreed with the defendant that plaintiff had impliedly assumed the normal and ordinary risks of attending a baseball game, which included being struck by thrown or batted balls.

Consequently, judgment was reversed and entered for the defendant's ball club.

See Gill v. Chicago Park Dist., 407 N.E.2d 671 (Ill. App. Ct. 1980) (assault on way to washroom); *Uzdannies v. Metropolitan Baseball Club, Inc.*, 115 Misc. 2d 343, 454 N.Y.S.2d 238 (1982) (res ipsa loquitur applied where hole existed in netting behind home plate); *Jones v. Three Rivers Management Corp.*, 394 A.2d 546 (1979) (pre-game batting practice). *See also* WEISTART & LOWELL at 951-65 nn.52-86 (the footnotes list a good collection of spectator vs. owner cases). James G. Gaspard, *Spectator Liability in Baseball: Nobody Told Me I Assumed the Risk*, 15 REV. LITIG. 229-50 (1996); *Lowe v. California League of Professional Baseball*, 65 Cal. Rptr. 105 (4th Dist. Ct. App. 1997) (mascot distracted fan who was injured, court found no assumption of the risk); *Gil-De-Rebello v. Miami Heat Ass'n, Inc.*, 137 F.3d 56 (1st Cir. 1998) (Heat found liable under respondeat superior for injuries inflicted by mascot); and Roger I. Abrams, *Torts and Sports: The Rights of the Injured Fan: Two Sports Torts: The Historical Development of the Legal Rights of Baseball Spectators*, 38 TULSA L. REV. 433 (2003) (history of claims by baseball fans).

There is no assumption of risk when a ball passes through the protective screen and injures the spectator. The park owner will be held liable. *See, e.g., Edling v. Kansas City Baseball & Exhibition Co.*, 168 S.W. 908 (Mo. Ct. App. 1914) (if owner screens a part of a grandstand exposed to fly balls, seats behind screen are assumed to be protected; owner must exercise reasonable care to keep screen free of defects to avoid negligence). However, if a ball flies over, *see Hull v. Oklahoma City Baseball Co.*, 196 Okla. 40, 163 P.2d 982 (1945), or sails around, *see Wells v. Minneapolis Baseball & Athletic Ass'n*, 122 Minn. 326, 142 N.W. 706 (1913), the protective screening, the owner is generally not liable on the theory of assumption of risk, contributory negligence, or lack of proximate cause. For example, in *Jones v. Alexandria Baseball Ass'n, Inc.*, 50 So. 2d 93 (La. Ct. App. 1951), the ball sailed over the screen behind which the plaintiff was sitting. He watched the ball until it went beyond him and turned around to resume watching the game. The ball struck a light pole and shot back into the crowd, hitting and fracturing the plaintiffs jaw. The court denied recovery and stated, "It seems to us that one of the accepted maxims of the game of golf is most appropriate in this instance and that is that plaintiffs injury is attributable to his own fault in failing to 'keep his eye on the ball.'" *Id.* at 94.

See Stradtner v. Cincinnati Reds, Inc., 316 N.E.2d 924 (Ohio Ct. App. 1972) (affirming dismissal of personal injury suit by fan struck by batted ball); *O'Bryan v. O'Connor,* 59 A.D.2d 219, 399 N.Y.S.2d 272 (1977) (bat flew out of batter's hands). In an action based on an injury suffered from an errant baseball, no jury question is presented; there is no duty to warn of the obvious dangers, and as a matter of law, "a spectator familiar with the game assumes reasonable risks and hazards inherent in the game." *Shaw v. Boston Am. League Baseball Co.*, 90 N.E.2d 840, 842 (Mass. 1950).

Two recent Illinois cases explore the issues surrounding baseball stadium operators' liability to spectators. *See Yates v. Chicago Nat'l. League Ball Club*, 595 N.E.2d 570 (Ill. App. Ct. 1992) (upholds jury verdict for plaintiff against stadium operator — case includes lengthy discussion of evidence presented by both sides); *Coronel v. Chicago White Sox*, 595 N.E.2d 45 (Ill. App. Ct. 1992) (overturns summary judgment granted to defendant and sends back for fact finder to decide adequacy of screening and warnings). In addition, former California Angels pitcher Matt Keough recently sued the city of Scottsdale, Arizona, contending that the city was negligent in failing to provide adequate screens in front of the dugouts at Scottsdale Stadium. Keough alleges that he suffered a career-ending injury when he was struck by a foul ball during training camp. Since the incident, barriers have been installed. His case is still pending. For more suggestions on the duty that stadium owners owe to spectators, *see* David Horton, *Rethinking Assumption of Risk and Sports Spectators*, 51 UCLA L. Rev. 339 (2003).

Ice Hockey

Hockey is a relative newcomer on the American sporting scene. In a short time, hockey's inherent dangers have caused a great deal of litigation. *See Shurman v. Fresno Ice Rink*, 205 P.2d 77 (Cal. Dist. Ct. App. 1949); *Thurman v. Clune*, 125 P.2d 59 (1942); *Sutherland v. Onondonga Hockey Club*, 281 N.Y.S. 505 (1935); *Hammel v. Madison Square Garden Corp.*, 279 N.Y.S. 815 (1935). The question of owners' liability is not as well settled as in baseball. Many jurisdictions that have addressed this issue state that hockey, unlike baseball, is a new sport; therefore, inexperienced spectators cannot be held chargeable with knowledge of the game's dangers, and they do not assume the risk as a matter of law. *Thurman v. Ice Palace*, 97 P.2d 999 (1939); *Uline Ice, Inc. v. Neely*, 225 F.2d 540 (D.C. Cir. 1958); *Shanney v. Boston Madison Square Garden*

Corp., 5 N.E.2d 1 (Mass. 1936); *Oaser v. Charlotte,* 144 S.E.2d 610 (1965). *See also* Annotations, *Liability for Injury to One Attending Hockey Game,* 14 A.L.R.3d 1018 (2003).

Thus, while a spectator may not recover for a baseball injury, he may recover for an injury caused by a flying puck. *Morris v. Cleveland Hockey Club, Inc.*, states the majority's rationale: "There is sound reasoning for the baseball rule. Baseball is the national pastime of the U.S. . . . Although hockey is becoming ever more popular, it is not nearly so universally played as is baseball, and, as we have pointed out, its dangers are certainly not so obvious to a stranger to the game as would be the dangers incident to baseball." 105 N.E.2d 419, 426 (Ohio 1952).

A number of courts have adopted the "no assumption of risk" rule, including California, *see Shurman v. Fresno Ice Rink, Inc.*, 205 P.2d 77 (Cal. Dist. Ct. App. 1949), Massachusetts, *see Lemoine v. Springfield Hockey Ass'n*, 29 N.E.2d 716 (Mass. 1940) (plaintiff who had been attending games for 3-4 years struck by a puck while walking to restroom recovered in jury trial); *Shanney v. Boston Madison Square Garden Corp.*, 5 N.E.2d 1 (Mass. 1936), Nebraska, *see Tite v. Omaha Coliseum Corp.*, 12 N.W.2d 90 (Neb. 1943), and Rhode Island, *see James v. Rhode Island Auditorium, Inc.*, 199 A. 293 (R.I. 1938) (plaintiff seated in unscreened area and struck by puck justified in believing seat was reasonably safe), Minnesota, *see Modec v. City of Eveleth*, 29 N.W.2d 453 (Minn. 1947), Michigan, *see Wolf v. Olympia Stadium, Inc.*, Nos. 247-609, 247-610 (Wayne County Cir. Ct. Mich. 1949), and New York, *see Kaufman v. Madison Square Garden Corp.*, 246 A.D. 589, 284 N.Y.S. 808 (1935), however, have held that baseball and hockey are indistinguishable and that the spectator assumes the risk at both sporting events in these states. *Hammel v. Madison Square Garden Corp.* established this position. "There are, however, a number of cases where spectators at baseball games have been injured by batted balls coming into the stands. The consensus of opinion in those cases is that there is no liability; that spectators occupying seats that are not screened assume the risk incident thereto. The baseball cases seem to present the same legal question that confronts us here." 156 Misc. 311, 312, 279 N.Y.S. 815, 816 (1935). Minnesota, New York, and Michigan are clearly among the areas in which the sport of hockey has been established the longest. It is not surprising that hockey is treated in the same manner as baseball in these states. Hockey is a relatively new sport in many of the jurisdictions that do allow recovery. Thus, the essential problem may be in determining how prevalent hockey is in each jurisdiction. Because the cases that distinguish baseball and hockey are not recent, there may be some doubt as to their continued validity in light of the dramatic expansion of professional hockey. *See Benjamin v. State*, 115 Misc. 2d 71, 453 N.Y.S.2d 329 (1982) (failure to provide protection to spectator near player bench). *See also* C. Peter Goplerud III & Nicolas P. Terry, *Allo-*

cation of Risk between Hockey Fans and Facilities: Tort Liability after the Puck Drops, 38 TULSA L. REV. 445 (2003).

Injuries Caused by Unsafe Premises

Owners and operators of sporting arenas have the duty to maintain the premises in a reasonably safe condition and to supervise the conduct of spectators on the premises to prevent injury. *See* WEISTART & LOWELL at 956-57. Therefore, a spectator attending an athletic event may assume that the owner or operator has exercised reasonable care to make the facilities safe for the purposes of the invitation.

In *Rockwell v. Hillcrest Country Club, Inc.*, 181 N.W.2d 290 (Mich. Ct. App. 1970), a suspension bridge crossing a river on a golf course collapsed; its occupants dropped into the river below. At the time of the collapse, there were approximately 80 to 100 spectators watching a tournament being played on the course along with a golf cart on the bridge. Among the spectators were plaintiffs James and Ann Rockwell. Ann Rockwell fell 25 feet, struck the water, broke her back, and sustained permanent injuries.

The evidence produced at trial showed that the bridge was constructed to hold 25 people safely; when it collapsed, there were 80 to 100 people on the bridge; no sign was present warning those using the bridge of its safe capacity; and no supervisory personnel were present to oversee proper use of the bridge. In affirming a judgment for the plaintiffs, the court stated:

> The obligation of reasonable care is a full one, applicable in all respects, and extending to everything that threatens the invitee with an unreasonable risk of harm. The occupier must not only use care not to injure the visitor by negligent acts, and to warn him of latent dangers of which the occupier knows, but he must also take reasonable precautions to protect the invitee from dangers which are foreseeable from the arrangement or use. The obligation extends to the original construction of the premises, where it results in a dangerous condition.

Id. at 293. *See also Cachik v. United States*, 161 F. Supp. 15 (S.D. Ill. 1958) (bleacher blew over due to insufficient anchor); *Edling v. Kansas City Baseball & Exhibition Co.*, 168 S.W. 908 (Mo. Ct. App. 1914) (plaintiff struck in face by foul ball, which passed through hole in protective netting); *Kasper v. Buffalo Bills*, 42 A.D.2d 87, 345 N.Y.S.2d 244 (1973) (bleacher collapse); *Berrum v. Puwalisz*, 317 P.2d 1090 (1957) (holes in wire screen allowing passage of a part of a Little Leaguer's bat); and "Fans crushed in rush onto field lose appeal against Badger Stadium officials." SPORTS LAW, Spring 1998, at 7 (Stadium officials found not to be negligent in regular practice of locking gates to the field).

In the aftermath of September 11 and the Oklahoma City bombing, stadium owners should take every precaution possible to protect fans. A terrorist attack could injure thousands at any given sporting event. Those injured could potentially bring a negligence suit against the stadium owners. However, it may be difficult to prove every element of a negligence cause of action. In a major incident, the government could potentially step in and create an account similar to the September 11th Victim Compensation Fund. *See* Caitlin M. Piccarello, *Terrorism, Tourism, and Torts: Liability in the Event of a Terrorist Attack on a Sports or Entertainment Venue*, 12 VILL. SPORTS & ENT. L.J. 365 (2005).

The Waiver Issue

In many cases, the sponsors of sporting events draft waivers or releases by which they attempt to avoid liability. These exculpatory agreements are contractual and generally provide that the sponsor is not responsible for harm caused by negligence. Two strong public policies are in conflict here. One policy highly values freedom of contract, while the other expects individuals to be answerable for the consequences of their negligence. As might be expected, cases can be found on both sides. Those cases that uphold enforceability of exculpatory agreements: *Kotary v. Spencer Speedway, Inc.*, 341 N.Y.S.2d 45 (1973) (spectator in infield); *Lee v. Allied Sports Assocs., Inc.*, 209 N.E.2d 329 (Mass. 1965) (spectator in pits); *Winterstein v. Wilson*, 293 A.2d 821 (1972) (driver injured when racer struck object on the track). Those cases that do not uphold enforceability of exculpatory agreements: *Wade v. Watson*, 527 F. Supp. 1049 (N.D. Ga. 1981) (release may not as a matter of law apply to gross negligence); *Santangelo v. City of New York*, 66 A.D.2d 880, 411 N.Y.S.2d 666 (1978) (minor not bound by release signed by father in connection with ice hockey clinic); *Scheff v. Homestretch, Inc.*, 377 N.E.2d 305 (Ill. App. Ct. 1978) (release not effective to eliminate potential dram shop liability). It should also be noted that waivers and releases are often used to insulate the owner from liability to participants as well as to spectators. Here, too, the results are mixed. *See* WEISTART & LOWELL at 965-69 for more cases in this area.

Liability Based Upon Beer Sales

Some states impose strict liability upon the seller of intoxicating liquors when the sale is the proximate cause of harm to a third person. Liability is imposed even in the absence of negligence through the so-called "Dram Shop" statute. Fortunately for us, Oklanois has no dram shop statute.

In recent years, however, and perhaps as a reflection of the new temperance movement, negligence-based liability has been imposed on sellers of intoxicating beverages when the sale results in harm to the interests of a third person as a result of the intoxication of the buyer.

> The gist of such a suit is really negligence in making the sale to someone who the seller knew or reasonably should have known was intoxicated. If such a negligent sale can be said to be the proximate cause of injury to the plaintiff, a cause of action might be stated. We are potentially liable here and clearly ought to consider formulating a thoughtful policy in regard to beer sales. As of now, there is no relevant case precedent for or against such liability in Oklanois.

You have also discovered the following memorandum, written one month prior to the Sherman incident, by Chief of Stadium Security J.E. Glover, to Executive Vice President Dallas Brown.

> I am concerned that our failure to restrict beer sales is leading to some very serious security problems. Drunkenness among fans is a growing problem. Abusive language and fights are becoming increasingly commonplace in the stands and in the parking lot and I really can't imagine how some of these people drive home. The problem is most severe in the "cheap seats" in the north and south end zones. I would like for you to consider that we stop selling beer at halftime and/or we consider selling near beer (less than 3.2% alcohol) rather than the real stuff. We also should instruct vendors not to sell beer to the obviously drunk and provide prompt and efficient back-up when problems arise. In this regard, I would like authority to hire 10 additional security people for next week's game.

You have been unable to locate any response to the Glover memo. Brown remembers receiving it, but did not have time to fashion a reply.

Prepare for your meeting with Tex Marsh.

NOTES AND COMMENTS

1. Auto Racing. The danger involved in auto racing has been an important factor in its popularity. The spectators, of course, do not expect to share in this danger. The majority of American jurisdictions hold that the promoters of an auto race must provide adequate barriers for the protection of spectators. In *Saari v. State,* the court stated that because risk to spectators and participants from automobile races is high, "the standard of care must likewise be high. One who conducts or sponsors such an event is . . . negligent unless he uses a high degree of care to provide adequate safeguards against reasonably foreseeable dangers to spectators and enforces the observation of such safeguards and precautions both by participants and spectators." 119 N.Y.S.2d 507, 516 (N.Y. Ct. Cl. 1953). *See also Foode v. Elks Lodge 789*, 28 Cal. Rptr. 669 (1963) (no protection); *Capital Raceway Promotions, Inc. v. Smith*, 322 A.2d 238 (1974); *Regan v. Seattle*, 458 P.2d 12 (Wash. 1969) (hay bales not sufficient in "go cart" race); *Kaiser v. Cook*, 227 N.W.2d 50 (1975) (lack of sufficient seats to properly seat and protect all spectators); *Fitchett v. Buchanan*, 472 P.2d 623 (1970) (failure to provide barriers of sufficient strength to protect spectator). Are the dangers of auto racing obvious enough to the spectator? The majority of courts have held that injured spectators do not assume the risk. A landmark case in this area is *Arnold v. State*, 148 N.Y.S. 479 (N.Y. App. Div. 1914), in which a racer crashed through a wooden fence, killing eleven spectators and injuring several more. The court held that the State of New York, the race's sponsor, had breached its positive duty to guard against the possibility of a car leaving the track and had to compensate the victims for their injuries. Assumption of risk was not an effective defense. *Alden v. Norwood Arena, Inc.*, 124 N.E.2d 505 (Mass. 1955), confirmed this position in holding that the stock-car race promoter owed spectators a duty of due care to see that the premises were reasonably safe for their intended use and to warn of non-obvious dangers. Being hit by a flying automobile wheel was not a risk obvious to the spectator of ordinary intelligence; therefore, spectators who were injured while attending the stock-car race did not assume, as a matter of law, the risk of such injury. *Compare Blake v. Fried*, 95 A.2d 360 (Pa. Super. Ct. 1953).

A minority of jurisdictions have concluded that if the race track has made some provision for the safety of spectators, the spectator will be charged with assumption of risk. *Barrett v. Faltico*, 117 F. Supp. 95 (E.D. Wash. 1953) (spectator in dangerous spot); *Kelly v. Sportsman's Speedway*, 80 So. 2d 785 (1955) (in pits without permission); *Graham v. Northwest Sport*, 310 P.2d 306 (1957) (on racetrack at wrong time); *Mercurio v. Burrillille Racing Association,* 187 A.2d 665 (1963) (taking pictures in wrong place). In *Blake v. Fried*, 95 A.2d 360 (Pa. Super. Ct. 1953), the operators of a stockcar race track had encircled the track with a heavy guard rail three feet high and installed reinforced wire-mesh fence fourteen feet high around the track. The court held that because the defendants' conduct was reasonable in light of what they could anticipate, they were not negligent. Therefore, they were not liable for the injuries sustained by grandstand spectators when a wheel came off a stock car, hit a guard rail, and bounced over the fence into the grandstand.

2. Golf. The game of golf has generated an enormous amount of litigation, second only to baseball. *Outlaw v. Bituminous Ins. Co.*, 357 So. 2d 1350 (La. Ct. App. 1978) (adult owed child golfer duty not to drive ball in child's direction in playing through); *Carrigan v. Roussell*, 177 N.J. Super. 272, 426 A.2d 517 (1981) (duty to give warning when ball starting to hook); *Jackson v. Livingston Country Club, Inc.*, 55 A.D.2d 1045, 391 N.Y.S.2d 234 (1977) (driving without warning when plaintiff was walking away from green directly in intended flight of ball). Golf litigation arises under three basic sets of circumstances. First, the golfer who hits the ball in the intended direction is held to two duties: to make sure no one is within the area toward which he is aiming; and to give an audible warning prior to hitting the ball. Warning given after the ball is hit is insufficient. *See Biskup v. Hoffman*, 287 S.W. 865 (Mo. Ct. App. 1926). The second situation occurs when the defendant's shot "hooks" or "slices" in a completely unanticipated direction and strikes someone on the golf course. When this happens, the defendant who gives a warning as soon as the shot begins to deviate from the intended direction is not liable, and the injured plaintiff is held to have assumed the risk. *See Houston v. Escott*, 85 F. Supp. 59 (D. Del. 1949); *Carrigan v. Roussell*, 177 N.J. Super. 272, 426 A.2d 517 (1981). Finally, if a golf ball injures a person who is not on the golf course, such as on an adjoining roadway, the defendant owner of the golf course has exposure to liability. *See Westborough Country Club v. Palmer*, 204 F.2d 143 (8th Cir. 1953); *Townsley v. State*, 6 Misc. 2d 557, 164 N.Y.S.2d 840 (1957).

For a more complete survey of golf cases revealing a wide range of approaches to injuries caused by skilled and unskilled players, *see* Ray Yasser, *In the Heat of Competition: Tort Liability of One Participant to Another: Why Can't Participants Be Required to Be Reasonable?* 5 SETON HALL J. SPORT L., No. 1, 253 (1995); Michael A. Shadiack, *Does a Golf Course Owner and/or Operator Owe a Duty of Care to Their Patrons to Protect Them From Lightning Strikes*, 8 SETON HALL J. SPORT L. 301 (1998).

3. Wrestling. The sport of wrestling has created a surprising amount of litigation. *See, e.g., Davis v. Jones*, 112 S.E.2d 3 (1959) (wrestler dove through rope and injured timekeeper); *Parker v. Warren*, 503 S.W.2d 938 (Tenn. Ct. App. 1974) (collapse of bleachers at a wrestling match). In *Dusckiewicz v. Carter*, a spectator sued a promoter for injuries sustained when a wrestler was thrown from the ring into the spectator's lap. 52 A.2d 788 (Vt. 1947). The Vermont court, in holding that the defendant's motion for a directed verdict should not have been granted, stated, "An invitee at a place of amusement ordinarily assumes the risk of an obvious danger or one that is of common knowledge; conversely, such a person does not assume the risk of a hidden or undisclosed danger, not of common knowledge, in the absence of warning or personal knowledge." *Id.* at 791. Thus, the court followed the majority rule by holding that this type of risk is one that a spectator does not assume.

4. Vicarious Liability. A wholly separate category of cases involves situations in which the spectator is injured by the arguably tortious conduct of a participant. *Payne v. Maple Leaf Gardens, Ltd.*, 1 D.L.R. 369 (Ont. Can. 1949) (plaintiff struck by hockey stick during a fight between players could not recover from the team since fighting is outside the scope of employment). *Bonetti v. Double Play Tavern*, 274 P.2d 751 (Cal. Dist. Ct. App. 1954), involved an action against the sponsor of a baseball team for personal injuries sustained by the plaintiff. Evidence at the trial established that the operators of Double Play Tavern sponsored a semi-pro baseball team, appropriately named "Double Play." In the bottom of the ninth inning of the league championship game, with the score tied at zero and the bases loaded, Paul Hjort, the Double Play left fielder, dropped a high pop fly, and the winning run was scored. In anger, Hjort picked up the ball and threw it out of the park in the direction of a gas station. The plaintiff, who was walking across the station property to get into her fiancé's car, was struck on the side of her head and knocked to the ground.

The court held that the defendant, the Double Play Tavern, was liable because "in practically all jurisdictions the law is now settled that a master is liable for the willful and malicious acts of his servant when done within the scope of his employment." *Id.* at 754. In reasoning that Hjort's acts were within the scope of his employment, the court stated:

> Where the injury is suffered from a baseball thrown immediately after the player had dropped it, with the consequent loss of the game and championship, at a time when all the players were at a competitively high nervous pitch, in a sport where "hustle" and "fight" are fostered and encouraged, it is not too difficult to conclude that a player might well, in frustration, take the ball and heave it out of the lot, and that such conduct might well be expected by the master. The breaking of clubs, bats and sticks by excited players is a matter of common knowledge to all sportswise persons. *Id.* at 754.

In a vigorous dissent, Judge Molkenbuhr relied on Section 2338 of the California Civil Code, which reads in part: "A principal is responsible to third persons for . . . wrongful acts committed by such agent in and as part of the transaction of business." *Id.* at 755. Judge Molkenbuhr's opinion was that the act of the left fielder in deliberately throwing the ball out of the park was not an act "in and as a part of the principal's business — that of playing baseball." *Id.* The tort herein complained of was one that, under ordinary circumstances, could not have been anticipated. Consequently, the dissent claimed, the defendant tavern should not be held liable.

Contrast *Bonetti* with *Atlanta Baseball Co. v. Lawrence*, 144 S.E. 351 (Ga. Ct. App. 1928), in which a baseball player employed by the proprietor of a baseball park left his position in the field, entered the grandstand, and assaulted a spectator who had criticized his play. The court held that the assault was not committed within the scope of his employment nor in the pursuit of his master's business. The court reasoned that "if the defendant had good reason to apprehend that such a thing would probably happen, then it should have exercised reasonable care to prevent the occurrence, but it was not required to anticipate the improbable, nor to take measures to prevent a happening which no reasonable person would have expected." *Id.* at 353. *See also Wierson v. City of Long Beach*, 106 P.2d 42 (Cal. Dist. Ct. App. 1940) (wrestler who jumped out of ring and attacked plaintiff with a chair deemed to act outside scope of employment).

The cases have their own curious logic. For purposes of imposing vicarious liability, courts are guided by some notion of foreseeable participant behavior. While Hjort's post-game tantrum was foreseeable, the gratuitous violence in *Atlanta Baseball* arguably was not. Presumably, vicarious liability could be imposed even in cases in which participants are hurt by a players' fight, for instance, if the employer knew of the employee's propensity for such behavior. *See Payne v. Maple Leaf Gardens Ltd.*, 1 D.L.R. 369 (Ont. Can. 1949). Otherwise, such attacks likely will be viewed as outside the scope of employment, *see e.g.*, *Tomjanovich v. California Sports, Inc.*, No. H-78-243 (S.D. Tex. Oct. 10, 1979), appeal docketed, No. 79-3889 (5th Cir. Dec. 3, 1979), discussed in R. YASSER, TORTS AND SPORTS 21-22, 26 (1985).

5. Injuries Caused by Attacks from Participants. There are many occurrences of players "going after" spectators. Among Jimmy Piersall's many memorable antics were confrontations with heckling fans. Cesar Cedeno also ventured into the stands after a heckler who jabbered about an incident that has haunted Cedeno, when a young girl was found dead in his motel room. At the United States Open in 1983, John McEnroe threw sawdust in the face of a front-row fan who was rooting (perhaps too strongly) for McEnroe's opponent. The incident was captured by the television cameras. A subsequent lawsuit was settled for an undisclosed amount.

More recently, Albert Belle of the Cleveland Indians has been involved in a series of incidents which had the potential to expose him to liability to fans and members of the media. Vince Coleman's playful firecracker toss was another example of this genre. Vernon Maxwell's foray into the stands is further proof that we can expect these kinds of incidents to continue.

Readers are invited to share their own "participant bites spectator" stories.

6. The spectator who is denied admission. A related issue involves the rights of a spectator denied admission to a sporting event. The traditional common law rule gave the owner a broad power to exclude any person for any reason. The leading case is *Marrone v. Washington Jockey Club*, 227 U.S. 633 (1913), holding that a ticket does not create a property right and is not a conveyance of an interest in the race track. (The plaintiff was denied admission because of an alleged conspiracy to drug a horse.) The modern trend is to restrict this power, so that patrons are not arbitrarily excluded. Moreover, if the acts of the owner can be fairly regarded as "state action" for constitutional purposes, the power to exclude is further constrained by the constitutional rights of the spectators. The issue is addressed in detail in WEISTART AND LOWELL at 141-47, 190-95, and 963-65.

7. Stampedes and the duty to control crowds. It is surprising that more injuries are not incurred when crowds get out of control. Not long ago, a human stampede resulted in the loss of life at a "Who" concert in Cincinnati. Americans are used to reading about such tragedies at foreign soccer games. Our own national championship games, particularly if the home team wins, raise the specter of similar tragedies. When the Celtics won the 1984 NBA Championship Series at the Boston Garden, the ensuing melee was frightening. Mobs of spectators tearing down goalposts is a similarly potentially dangerous practice. It is simply a matter of time before Americans are beset by a stampede of epic proportions. What is the duty of the promoter to control the crowd under these circumstances?

An Indiana court has recently answered this question in *Hayden v. University of Notre Dame*, 716 N.E.2d 603 (Ind. Ct. App. 1999). *Hayden* involved a spectator who was injured as a result of another spectator going for a football that had landed in the stands after a field goal attempt. In reaching its decision, the court applied a totality of the circumstances test to determine if liability exists for the landowner. *Id.* at 605. Under the totality of the circumstances test, "the court considers all of the circumstances surrounding the event, including the nature, condition, and location of the land, as well as prior similar incidents to determine whether a criminal act was foreseeable." *Id.* The *Hayden* court determined that Notre Dame should have foreseen the injury and acted to prevent it. *Id.* This same rationale seems applicable to recent incidents in which fans get out of control and tear down the goal post after a big victory or loss. Tearing down goal posts after a big win may be customary, but event sponsors should not overlook its dangerousness. Similarly, the court in *Telega v. Security Bureau, Inc.*, imposed liability on a professional sports complex owner where the owner failed to protect a spectator from other spectators lunging for a souvenir football that was kicked into the stands. 719 A.2d 372 (Pa. Super. Ct. 1998). More college basketball fans are rushing the court after dramatic wins than ever before. For instance, on March 1, 2006, Coach Mike Krzyewski sent his players to the locker room with 1.7 seconds left on the clock after Florida State fans came pouring onto the court prematurely in what turned out to be a 79-74 FSU win. The win ended Duke's hopes of going undefeated in the ACC.

8. Medical assistance to spectators. In *Fish v. Los Angeles Dodgers Baseball Club*, 128 Cal. Rptr. 807 (Cal. Ct. App. 1976), parents of a 14-year-old who died after being hit by a foul ball while attending a Dodgers game sued the Dodgers and a physician. The complaint asserted two theories: (1) failure to provide the boy "with a safe place to witness the ball game," and (2) negligent provision of emergency medical services. The court's discussion of intervening causes in medical malpractice cases is especially noteworthy.

The point is that the failure to provide adequate emergency medical assistance to an injured spectator provides a viable cause of action to the injured spectator, at least to the extent it can be shown that the injuries were aggravated by the lack of such care.

9. The spectator as a defendant. Spectators could also find themselves on the receiving end of a summons and complaint in a number of situations. Overzealous fans are potential tortfeasors in a variety of fairly common situations, such as throwing debris on the playing surface or at the participants, including referees; fighting for souvenirs; and brawling with opposing fans. A number of years ago, it was quite popular at college football games for a group of fans to engage in what can be described as a "fan toss" wherein a fan was literally tossed about the crowd. If the human plaything is injured, are these fun-loving fans joint tortfeasors?

10. Spectator vs. Spectator. When Barry Bonds surpassed Mark McGuire's record by hitting his 73rd home run of the season, a battle for the ball ensued. Alex Popov initially retrieved the ball. However, immediately after retrieving the ball, Popov was thrown to the ground by at least ten fans, at which point another fan, Patrick Hayashi, emerged from the pile with the home run ball in hand. Neither Barry Bonds, nor the San Francisco Giants, claimed ownership of the ball and the battle line was drawn between the two fans. Popov sought an injunction, which the court granted, preventing Hayashi from selling the ball. The litigation was not about whether the team, the batter, or the fans owned the ball, but rather which fan owned the ball. Paul Finkelman, *Fugitive Baseballs and Abandoned Property: Who Owns the Home Run Ball?*, 23 CARDOZO L. REV. 1609 (2002). The case was tried in the fall of 2002, and, in Solomonic fashion, the judge ordered the litigants to split the proceeds from the sale of the baseball. *See* Ian Stewart, *Feud Over Home Run Ball Goes Into Extra Innings*, SAN JOSE MERCURY NEWS, Jan. 2, 2003.

11. An emerging trend? Traditionally, the courts have held that the owner of a sports complex has only a limited duty to protect the spectator from common hazards of the game. *Schneider v. American Hockey and Ice Skating Center, Inc.*, 342 N.J. SUPER. 527, 777 A.2d 380 (2001). Although courts have been reluctant to modify this limited duty, sports complex owners as well as league officials appear to be implementing new measures that recognize a broader duty for spectator safety. The recognition of a broader scope of duty was most recently seen after a 13-year-old girl received a fatal head injury as a result of an ice hockey puck being shot into the stands. *See* Jason Diamos, *Safety Netting at N.H.L. Rinks is Pressing Topic for Spectators*, N.Y. TIMES, Sept. 24, 2002. After the incident, the director of the NHL ordered all sports complexes in which NHL games are played to install and provide protective screening for spectator safety. *Id.* Although most NHL sports complexes provide some protective measures, almost every complex added additional safety measures by the start of the regular season. *Id.* These additional safeguards are clearly intended to protect spectators from injury, but are arguably also intended to shield owners from potential future liability. *See* C. Peter Goplerud III & Nicholas P. Terry, *Allocation of Risk Between Hockey Fans and Facilities: Tort Liability After the Puck Drops,* 38 Univ. Tulsa L. Rev. 445 (2003).

12. Contemporary changes in spectator viewing patterns. Spectators have always been held to assume the risk of being hit by a projectile that has left the area of play. This assumption is based on the notion that the spectator was, or at least should have been, paying attention to the game. But in today's sports complexes such things as massive video monitors, numerous mascots, advertising promotions, and liquor consumption can distract even the most responsible and attentive sports fan. The courts have recognized that a spectator assumes the inherent risks of attending a sporting event so long as the owner of the ballpark does not unduly enhance those risks. *Lowe v. California League of Professional Baseball*, 56 Cal. App. 4th 112 (1997). In *Lowe*, the court held that a spectator who was hit by a foul ball while being distracted by a team mascot standing directly behind him in the stands did not assume the risk. The court observed that allowing the mascot to enter the stands while the game was in progress increased the risk of injury to the plaintiff, and therefore the sports park owner was liable under a negligence theory. Under the holding in

Lowe, an increase in sports complex distractions will likely lead to a greater risk of owner liability.

In *Maisonave v. the Newark Bears Professional Baseball Club*, 881 A.2d 700 (N.J. 2005), a foul ball hit a fan while he was at the concession stand. He suffered extensive facial injuries. The spectator sued the stadium owner on a negligence theory, arguing that the concession stand should have been protected by netting. *Id.* at 703. The trial court dismissed the suit since the defendant had provided protection in the most dangerous areas of the park. *Id.* The appellate court overruled, distinguishing between fans actively watching the game and those occupied with other features of the ballpark, such as a concession stand. *Id.* at 704. On appeal, the New Jersey Supreme Court held that the chance of being struck by a foul ball was a risk inherent in baseball and that it would place undue hardship on stadium owners to ensure the safety of every spectator. *Id.* at 707. *See* Charles Toutant, *Play Ball! (Carefully): Ruling Erects Standard of Care for Sports Stadium Owners*, 181 N.J.L.J. 1065 (2005) (commentary on *Maisonave*).

C. MEDICAL MALPRACTICE IN ATHLETICS

The well-developed, negligence-based principles of medical malpractice also apply to sports medicine. As a general rule, the reasonableness of the medical care provided is measured against the minimum common skill of members in good standing of the profession. The "locality rule," which required a doctor to act only up to the standard of the locale in which he or she practiced, is largely a dead letter. The modern trend is to consider the locality of the practice as simply one factor to take into account in assessing the doctor's conduct. Additionally, doctors holding themselves out as specialists are held to a national standard. The issue of "informed consent" looms large. Although "informed consent" is technically an intentional tort defense, modern courts have translated the "informed consent" concept into negligence terminology. Cases thus turn on whether reasonable doctors would have disclosed certain risks. The following materials illustrate how these basic principles of medical malpractice apply in sports.

A number of problems, however, are peculiar to sports medicine. One perplexing problem arises out of the somewhat unusual relationships created by the common practice of employing a team doctor. The very term "team doctor" signals the problem. The team doctor owes sometimes conflicting duties to individual team members and the team. The problem manifests itself in situations in which a valuable player is injured before an important game, and the responsibility falls on the team physician to decide if the player can participate. This power to determine eligibility generates a host of issues. How, for example, is liability determined when a doctor permits an injured player to participate, and the injury is further aggravated or, worse, the athlete dies? Or suppose the doctor refuses to permit the athlete to participate; may the athlete claim a legal right to participate in the face of the medical prohibition?

A number of other problems are especially relevant to athletics. One concern is the extent to which a doctor may properly aid an injured player who wants to participate. To what extent should painkillers and the like be administered to willing athletes? And are the athletes really "willing" under the circumstances? Another problem concerns the use of chemicals to enhance performance. What is the doctor's proper role in this regard? This chapter explores these issues as well.

PROBLEM 1

You represent Tony Salano, a 15-year-old sophomore at Spakone High School. Tony has just been told that he will not be permitted to try out for the school's basketball team because he failed the team physical. Tony is a very promising basketball player, and, by all accounts, would have been selected for the team and would have seen considerable playing time as a sophomore. Tony has been told by the school's doctor that it is too dangerous for Tony to play basketball. Tony is blind in one eye and the doctor has refused to certify Tony for interscholastic competition.

Tony's parents support him fully in his desire to play and are willing to take legal action if that is necessary. At this point, the doctor's decision has been appealed to the local school board. Tony and his parents want you to argue his case before the school board. They are all willing to sign releases and Tony has agreed to wear an eye guard while playing, if that is required.

In your research, you discovered two arguably relevant cases, which you are to assume are Oklanois State Supreme Court cases. Those cases are reprinted below.

Prepare to make your argument on Tony's behalf.

PROBLEM 2

You are counsel for the Spakone City Orthopedic Clinic, a professional corporation. Dr. Robert Baker is a physician employed by the clinic. You have just learned that Dr. Baker and the clinic have been sued by Will Dalton, a star player for the Spakone Stuffers, the local N.B.A. franchise. A copy of the complaint is reproduced below. Review the complaint and prepare to meet with Dr. Baker to formulate your defense to the suit.

Plaintiff complains of Defendants, and each of them, and for a cause of action alleges:

I. At all times herein mentioned, the Defendant, SPAKONE CITY ORTHOPEDIC CLINIC, P.C., was, and now is, a business organization, which business organization was at all times herein doing business in the State of Oklanois.

II. At all times herein mentioned, Defendant ROBERT BAKER was a duly licensed physician and surgeon, and was engaged in the practice of medicine in the State of Oklanois.

III. At all times herein mentioned, the Defendants, and each of them, were the agents, servants and employees, each of the other, individually and collectively, and were acting within the course and scope of their agency, service and employment. DR. BAKER is also employed as the team physician for the Spakone Stuffers Professional Basketball Club.

IV. At all times herein mentioned, Plaintiff was, and continued to be, a medical patient of the Defendants ROBERT BAKER and SPAKONE CITY ORTHOPEDIC CLINIC, P.C. Said Defendants undertook to examine and treat, and to prescribe for, care for, diagnose for and provide medical care and attention for Plaintiff.

V. From February 28 until July, the Defendant SPAKONE CITY ORTHOPEDIC CLINIC, P.C., and its employee and agent, Defendant ROBERT BAKER, carelessly and negligently examined, diagnosed, treated, tested and cared for the Plaintiff in the following particulars:

1. In failing to diagnose the development and the eventual fracture of the tarsal navicular bone of the left foot at sometime between mid-February and April 22. At this time, the Plaintiff has been unable to ascertain from his doctors the exact date within that period that the fracture occurred. The Plaintiff complained to Defendant DR. BAKER of pain and discomfort in the left foot on the occasions that he visited his office on March 28, and April 20, and nearly every day from March 28 until April 22, when Plaintiff had contact with Defendant DR. BAKER at Spakone Stuffers' practices and games, and Plaintiff's apartment, in the City of Spakone, and at the Defendant DR. BAKER'S home. Additionally, Defendant DR. BAKER failed to diagnose said fracture on April 21 when Plaintiffs left foot was x-rayed at Spakone City Orthopedic Clinic.

2. The Defendant DR. BAKER prescribed oral doses of Butazolidin and Decadron during the period between February 28 and April 22 to be taken on a daily basis. On March 28 at the Memorial Coliseum, the Plaintiffs left foot received four injections of a mixture of Xylocaine and Decadron. On April 20, in the Defendant DR. BAKER'S offices, the Plaintiff received three injections in his left foot of Xylocaine and another drug, which Plaintiff believed to be a corticosteroid. On April 21, at the Memorial Coliseum, in the City of Spakone, the Plaintiffs left foot was injected twice with Xylocaine and a corticosteroid. Said medications were prescribed, administered and injected by Defendant DR. BAKER, and constituted wrongful and negligent therapy for Plaintiffs left foot condition.

3. Between March 28 and April 22, the Defendant DR. BAKER daily recommended and encouraged Plaintiff to bear weight on his left foot and attempt to use it in connection with engaging in basketball practice sessions, and professional basketball games for the Spakone Stuffers. Said recommendations were made both at DR. BAKER'S office and home, and at Plaintiff's apartment, the location of the Spakone Stuffers' practice sessions and the Memorial Coliseum. On April 20, following the aforesaid three injections on Plaintiffs left foot at DR. BAKER'S office, DR. BAKER recommended that Plaintiff place weight on and exercise his left foot, and on April 21 at the Memorial Coliseum, Defendant DR. BAKER gave Plaintiff medical clearance to participate in a professional basketball game following two injections of Xylocaine and a corticosteroid which had caused Plaintiffs left foot to become numb. The prescription and encouragement of the conduct and activity described above constituted negligent treatment.

4. Following the diagnosis of Plaintiffs left tarsal navicular fracture and at the time of removal of Plaintiffs case on June 2, at the offices of DR. BAKER, Plaintiff was negligently encouraged to resume weight-bearing on his left foot.

VI. As a direct and proximate result of the carelessness and negligence of Defendants described above, Plaintiff suffered a fracture of his left tarsal navicular bone, aggravation of said fracture, lengthening of his disability, permanent weakening of his left foot, increased vulnerability to subsequent fractures of the same and adjoining bones, and damage to the adjoining nerves, muscles and soft tissues of the left foot. As a further proximate result of the carelessness and negligence of the Defendants, Plaintiff has been deprived of his ability to engage in his professional basketball career, which resulted in substantial loss of future earning capacity.

VII. By reason of the premises, it became necessary for Plaintiff to incur expenses for doctors, hospitals, x-ray technicians, travel and other services required in the care and treatment of said injuries that were not paid for by a third party in the amount of $7,500.00.

VIII. By reason of the premises, Plaintiff has been unable to follow his regular employment, to his special damage in a sum of $624,500.00. Said loss is continuing and thus not yet fully determined.

IX. The Plaintiff remained under the medical care of Defendants ROBERT BAKER and SPAKONE CITY ORTHOPEDIC CLINIC, P.C., from February 28 and into July. During said period, he relied on the medical advice of the Defendants, and was not informed of the true nature and extent of his injury to his left foot and its negligent cause. The Plaintiff did not discover the nature and extent of his injury to his left foot and its negligent cause until July when he began consulting other doctors.

X. By reason of the premises, Plaintiff has been generally damaged in the sum of $5,000,000.00.

WHEREFORE, Plaintiff prays judgment against Defendants, and each of them, jointly and severally, as follows:

1. For general damages in the sum of $5,000,000.00;

2. For special damages in the sum of $632,000.00;

3. For costs and disbursements incurred herein.

CASE FILE

ROSENSWEIG v. STATE

5 A.D.2d 293, 171 N.Y.S.2d 912 (1958),
aff'd, 5 N.Y.2d 404, 158 N.E.2d 229 (1959)

COON, Justice.

[By statute in New York, all boxers must be examined by a physician. The physician files a report with the State Athletic Commission, which in turn must certify that the fighter is fit before the fighter will be permitted to box.]

On August 29, 1951, George Flores was knocked out in the eighth round of a fight at Madison Square Garden. He died four days later from cerebral hemorrhage and edema. Flores had fought on July 24 and August 14 of 1951, and in both those bouts, he lost by a technical knockout (T.K.O.). Before the August 29 bout, Flores was examined by a physician who certified his fitness to the Commission.

Flores' estate sued the State of New York, alleging that the negligence of the examining physician in certifying Flores' fitness could properly be imputed to the State of New York.

At the trial court level, Flores' estate prevailed. The intermediate appellate court reversed, and it is this decision that is excerpted here, because it is one of the few reported cases dealing directly with the liability of a doctor who certified an athlete as fit. It should be noted that New York's highest court affirmed the intermediate court, but without any discussion of the doctor's negligence. That court limited its discussion to whether the State was vicariously liable for the acts of the doctor, and concluded that, under the circumstances, it was not.]

* * *

Under these circumstances there is serious doubt as to whether the examining doctor is an employee of the State, but, even assuming employment by the State, claimant has not established negligence on the part of the examining doctor.

* * *

The doctor who examined decedent prior to the fatal fight had the benefit of the opinions of doctors who examined decedent after the two previous fights and who found no evidence of brain injury. A signed history given by decedent indicated no symptom of concussion or brain injury. A standard examination revealed no such symptom.

It is urged that there is evidence that some doctors believe it to be better medical practice to withhold permission to engage in another bout to a fighter who has received a severe beating about the head without a lay-off of from two to six months thereafter. It would, of course, be still safer to withhold permission forever. However, there was no official rule requiring a compulsory lay-off. . . .

For another reason the judgment may not be sustained. It is clear that the immediate proximate cause of the injury which resulted in death was the severe blow to the head which decedent suffered in the final fight. Claimant has failed to establish that this blow alone, irrespective of previous condition, would not have produced the fatal result.

Decedent was engaged in a concededly dangerous activity. From his experience he knew that he would likely be struck by blows to the head. In fact, the very objective of the contestants, well known in advance, is to "knock out" the opponent and cause him to fall to the floor in such condition that he is unable to rise to his feet for a specified time. Decedent assumed the risks known to be inherent in the fight. . . .

Judgment reversed and claim dismissed, without costs.

COLOMBO v. SEWANNAKA CENTRAL HIGH SCHOOL DISTRICT NO. 2

87 Misc. 2d 48, 383 N.Y.S.2d 518 (1976)

ALEXANDER BERMAN, Justice.

[John Colombo, a 15-year-old student, was barred from interscholastic participation in contact sports because of a hearing disability. Joined by his parents, he sought to overturn the ban on the ground that it was "arbitrary, capricious, and contrary to law." The court here held that the determination of the school district to follow the advice of its medical director was correct.]

* * *

On December 11, 1975, Dr. Nathan Samuels the duly designated medical officer for the school district, conducted a physical examination of the petitioner, John, Jr., to determine whether he should be permitted to participate in contact sports in the High School. . . .

The physical examination disclosed no abnormality other than a marked hearing deficiency, which petitioners concede, to wit: That John is totally deaf in his right ear and that he has a 50% loss of hearing in his left ear. This hearing problem has existed from birth. He wears a hearing aid in his left ear. . . .

By reason of this hearing deficit, Dr. Samuels determined that John should not be permitted to play football, lacrosse or soccer. He rationalized that John's hearing deficit leaves him with a permanent "auditory blind" right side and a diminished sound perception of his left side, even with the use of the hearing aid, and that "this inability to directionalize the source of sound leaves him at increased risk of bodily harm as compared with students with full sensory perception."

In reaching the conclusion that John should not be permitted to play such contact sports, Dr. Samuels, among other things, took into consideration guidelines published by the American Medical Association, Revised Edition 1972. . . .

Petitioners contend, however, that Dr. Samuels had not taken into consideration other factors which should have been weighed in his evaluation, such as: that both parents had given their unqualified consent to John's participation in these sports; that John is an all-around athlete of unusual and extraordinary talent; that John has demonstrated his ability to participate extensively in contact sports with his peers who had no hearing disability and that he had never sustained any injury during such competition; that he has actually played football with nonschool organizations under the strict supervision of organized athletic groups; and furthermore, that the prohibition against participation in these high school sports has had a damaging psychological effect upon this boy in that he has now lost interest in attending school and has been made to feel inferior to and different from the other children in school.

Both parents, it is true, not only joined in this petition, but testified that they were willing to assume the risk of additional injury to their son, even if same resulted in his becoming totally deaf. John's mother testified that another of her children, a daughter, is, in fact, totally deaf and although she would hope that John would not sustain such complete impairment of hearing, she believed that he could "live with it," and that he would, nevertheless, be able to function well "with such a handicap." John's father reiterated these feelings and added that he hoped John would he able to eventually obtain a college football scholarship as this would be of vital importance because of their limited financial resources. . . .

* * *

It is . . . clear that there are at least conflicting views with respect to whether John's participation in contact sports represents a danger to his physical wellbeing or to the safety of other students with whom he might participate in such games. A determination of an administrative body, made on a rational basis, should not be judicially set aside. . . .

* * *

The Court recognizes the psychological factors involved in the denial to John of the right to participate in contact sports and, indeed, has great concern for and sympathy with his plight. However, the medical determination of Dr. Samuels, the Court finds, was a valid exercise of judgment and was not arbitrary or capricious since: (a) there exists the risk of danger of injury to the ear in which there is only partial hearing and to which further injury could result in irreversible and permanent damage — in this case, total deafness; (b) aside from the risk of injury to his partially good ear, there also exists the possibility of injury to other parts of John's body by reason of his failure to perceive the direction of sound; and (c) there is the possibility of risk of injury to other participants. Even though these risks may all be minimal, in this Court's opinion it is sound judgment for the school district to follow the advice of its own medical director and the AMA Guide and prohibit John from participating in contact sports.

Respondent is entitled to judgment in its favor dismissing this proceeding.

NOTES AND COMMENTS

1. Note on *Rosensweig*. WEISTART & LOWELL are properly critical of the *Rosensweig* reasoning, at 994:

> The appellate court obviously disagreed with the trial court's conclusion that there was negligence, but the doctrinal basis for disagreement is not clear. The court stated that a "standard examination" had revealed no injury but gave no indication of what such a standard examination required or what facts indicated that such an examination had been given in the present case. It also noted that the boxer had signed a medical history that disclosed no brain injury, but surely this fact could have little relevance to the negligence of the doctors. . . . In short, the appellate court found no negligence but undertook almost no effort to indicate why it came to that conclusion. Its reasoning would appear to be that a doctor is required to give only a standard examination (which it did not define) and since such examinations had been given here (though it did not say why) there was no basis for a conclusion that the doctors had been negligent.

Also note that the court's glib conclusion that the proximate cause of death was the blow to the head does not preclude a finding that the doctor's negligence in certifying Flores' fitness was also a proximate cause of death.

2. Note on *Colombo*. A good argument can be made that *Colombo* was wrongly decided and that a court today, more sensitive to the issue of discrimination against people with disabilities, would overturn the school district. (Disabilities, the rights of athletes to participate, and the Americans with Disabilities Act (ADA) are discussed in **Chapter 14.**) Technically, this case is not a torts case at all but rather a constitutional law case dealing with the power of the state to regulate. It is useful, however, to consider the problem in a torts context. What tort cause of action, if any, would be available to Colombo? Malpractice? Intentional interference with prospective economic advantage?

3. Sports injuries and medical malpractice. As might be expected, a number of medical malpractice cases arise out of injuries incurred in sports. For example, in *Foster v. Englewood and Hospital Association,* 313 N.E.2d 255 (Ill. App. Ct. 1974), plaintiff was injured in a neighborhood football game and died during routine surgery. Affirming a trial court judgment in favor of the plaintiff, the court held the hospital, the surgeon, and the anesthetist liable for the death. In this category of cases, general medical malpractice principles apply.

4. In *Speed v. State,* 240 N.W.2d 901 (Iowa 1976), the plaintiff, a University of Iowa basketball player, brought a medical malpractice action alleging that doctors at the university hospital negligently failed to diagnose Speed's intracranial infection and that this resulted in Speed's blindness. The court affirmed the trial court judgment in Speed's favor, applying well-established medical malpractice rules.

5. Negligence might be found due to inadequate emergency medical services. In *Fish v. Los Angeles Dodgers Baseball Club*, 128 Cal. Rptr. 807 (Cal. Ct. App. 1976), parents of a fourteen-year-old who died after being hit by a foul ball while attending a Dodgers game sued the Dodgers and a physician. This case is discussed in **Note 8** of the "spectator as plaintiff" subsection of this chapter.

In *Stineman v. Fontbonne College*, 664 F.2d 1082, 1086 (8th Cir. 1981), the court relied on *Kersey v. Harbin*, 531 S.W.2d 76 (Mo. Ct. App. 1975), a decision which set forth certain elements necessary to impose a duty to provide medical assistance. (In *Stineman*, a college softball player was hit in the eye with a softball with enough force that the impact was heard one hundred yards away. The coach applied ice to the injury and sent Stineman home without even suggesting that she see a doctor. The case was complicated by the fact that the player was deaf and relied on her sight to read lips. She was later diagnosed with traumatic hyphema, a relatively common injury, which when treated promptly is repaired with a ninety percent or greater success rate. Ms. Stineman lost the vision in the eye and was forced to wear a prosthesis.)

"The first element under *Kersey* requires that the defendant must have been able to appreciate the severity of the plaintiff's injury." *Stineman* at 1086. Based on the facts in *Stineman*, the court ruled that Fontbonne should have appreciated the injury. "The second element of *Kersey* requires a determination that one or more of the defendants had the skill to provide adequate medical treatment. The only treatment required here was to get the injured person to a doctor." *Id.* at 1086. In this case, Fontbonne College's medical clinic was across the street from the softball field. "The third element of *Kersey* addresses whether providing medical attention would have avoided the injury's ultimate harm." *Id.* at 1086. This was established by expert testimony in this case. The satisfaction of these elements meant that the school had a duty to provide medical assistance.

Foreseeability has always been part of duty. But how far must one see? The question of foreseeability of serious harm is related to questions of medical malpractice. For example, the issue in *Kleinknecht v. Gettysburg College*, 786 F. Supp. 449, 452 (M.D. Pa. 1992), was whether the college "has a duty to anticipate cardiac arrest in a healthy young man showing no apparent illness whatsoever and guard against that possibility by having CPR trained individuals at hand or having some other way of providing treatment more promptly than he received." In this phase of the case the court determined that there was no duty. However, on appeal, *Kleinknecht v. Gettysburg College*, 989 F.2d 1360 (1993), the court determined that a duty was owed (in part because of the special relationship between the college and its student athletes); and that the college also had a duty to be reasonably prepared for handling medical emergencies that foreseeably arise during a student's participation in intercollegiate contact sports for which a student was recruited. *Id.* at 1369, 1371.

See Welch v. Dunsmuir Joint Union High School Dist., 326 P.2d 663 (Cal. Dist. Ct. App. 1958) (inadequate medical treatment caused permanent paralysis); *Mogabgab v. Orleans Parish School Bd.*, 239 So. 2d 456 (La. Ct. App. 1970) (failure to provide immediate medical assistance to heat stroke victim); *Guerriero v. Tyson*, 24 A.2d 468 (1942) (rendered unnecessary medical aid which injured child); *Wilson v. Vancouver Hockey Club*, 5 D.L.R. 4th 282 (1983) (failure to detect cancerous mole); *Orr v. Brigham Young University*, 960 F. Supp. 1522 (D. Utah 1994) (unauthorized practice of medicine by sports trainers); and *Daniels v. Seattle Seahawks*, 968 P.2d 883 (Wash. Ct. App. 1998) (claim against Seahawks' team physician). One of the issues in the litigation following the tragic death of Loyola Marymount University basketball player Hank Gathers was the adequacy of court-side medical care. The case has been settled.

Is there a duty to have Automatic External Defibrillator (AED) in high-risk locations? With energetic crowds in the thousands at sporting events or the rigorous workout regimes by many gym members, it is foreseeable that someone could suffer Sudden Cardiac Arrest (SCA). AED's retail for under $3,000 and increase the chances of surviving SCA from under 5% to over 50%. What is the extent of the duty that stadium owners or fitness clubs owe their patrons? *See Atcovitz v. Gulph Mills Tennis Club*, 571 Pa. 580 (Pa. 2002), holding that a tennis club did not have a duty to maintain an AED on its property. However, at least two states have mandated that AED's be placed in their public schools. *See* Ronald R. Gilbert & Wendy Wawryziak, *Does Ability to Save a Life Still Equal a Duty to Have an AED Despite Pennsylvania Supreme Court Decision Overruling Atcovitz?*, 17 The Sports, Parks, & Recreation L. Rep. 17 (2003).

6. The recurring issue of vicarious liability. In almost all of the cases in this chapter, vicarious liability has been an issue. More specifically, the issue raised is whether the doctor is properly viewed as an independent contractor (in which case there is generally no vicarious liability imposed on the employer) or an employee (in which case vicarious liability is imposed for torts committed in the scope of employment). In *Cramer v. Hoffman,* 390 F.2d 19 (2d Cir. 1968), the court held that the university doctor was an independent contractor whose negligence could not be imputed to the university. (Cramer was a college football player who was paralyzed after making a tackle during practice.)

The distinction between an independent contractor and an employee is not particularly clear.

RESTATEMENT § 220 provides in part:

> (2) In determining whether one acting for another is a servant or an independent contractor, the following matters of fact, among others, are considered:
>
> (a) the extent of control which, by the agreement, the master may exercise over the details of the work;
>
> (b) whether or not the one employed is engaged in a distinct occupation or business;
>
> (c) the kind of occupation, with reference to whether, in the locality, the work is usually done under the direction of the employer or by a specialist without supervision;
>
> (d) the skill required in the particular occupation;
>
> (e) whether the employer or the workman supplies the instrumentalities, tools, and the place of work for the person doing the work;
>
> (f) the length of time for which the person is employed;
>
> (g) the method of payment, whether by the time or by the job;
>
> (h) whether or not the work is a part of the regular business of the employer;
>
> (i) whether or not the parties believe they are creating the relation of master and servant; and
>
> (j) whether the principal is or is not in business.

One might well question whether the RESTATEMENT guidelines are particularly helpful.

Courts appear to be preoccupied with the "control" issue. Prosser and Keeton believe that it is accurate to say that "the person employed is a servant when, in the eyes of the community, he would be regarded as a part of the employer's working staff, and not otherwise." W. PAGE KEETON ET AL., PROSSER AND KEETON ON THE LAW OF TORTS at 501 (5th Ed. 1984)

Consider *Robitaille v. Vancouver Hockey Club Ltd.*, 124 D.L.R.3d 228, where the court held the NHL Club vicariously liable for the negligence of the team doctors. As is the case with many teams, the doctors were interested in sports medicine and received modest remuneration — season tickets, free parking, access to the lounge, and a $2500 bonus at the end of the season. *Id.* at 230. The court found that the defendant had the power to select, control, and dismiss the doctors, who were supplied to the team in furtherance of the defendants' business purposes. *Id.* at 243. The court further held that the degree of control exercised does not have to be complete to establish vicarious liability, and in the case of a professional person, the absence of control and direction over the manner of doing the work is of little significance. *Id.* at 243.

An interesting statistic illustrates the conflict that a team physician faces when dealing with the pressures from the "front office" and the adequate care of the player/patient. The statistic also reveals that doctors are fully aware of who butters their bread. During NFL arbitration hearings involving post-injury examinations to determine whether the team was liable for payment of a player's salary, the team physician testified on behalf of the team and against the player in each of sixty-seven hearings. *See* Charles V. Russell, *Legal and Ethical Conflicts Arising from the Team Physicians' Dual Obligations to the Athlete and Management,* 10 SETON HALL LEGIS. J. 299, 315-16 (1987). The teams were found liable in 39 of the 67 grievances filed. *Id.* at 316. Does this tend to show that "team doctors" are, in reality, employees of the team?

7. THE LAW REPORTER, a publication of the Association of Trial Lawyers of America, contains the following account from Chicago attorney Stephen I. Lane in the REPORTER'S June 1988 edition at page 215:

> Suit against football team physician was not barred by workers' compensation exclusivity rule.

Bryant v. Fox, 515 N.E.2d 775 (Ill. App. Ct. 1987).

Bryant and Edwards were playing football for the Chicago Bears when they suffered football-related injuries. Believing that they suffered additional injuries distinct from their football injuries as a result of treatment rendered by Fox, the team physician, they brought a medical negligence action against Fox. Fox moved to dismiss the claims, contending that since he was an employee of the Bears, plaintiffs' exclusive remedies were under the Illinois Workers' Compensation Act. The trial court granted defendant's motion, and the players appealed.

The court of appeals reversed, finding that an issue of law existed as to whether the team physician was an employee of the Bears or an independent contractor against whom the players had a common-law cause of action. The record contained the following facts: although Fox was supposed to attend all regular season games, he could send a substitute, subject to the Bears' approval. Fox was paid $12,000 annually for all treatment other than surgery, for which he received fees on an as performed basis. Fox had a busy medical practice, and this money represented less than ten percent of his total income. Unlike other Bears employees, Fox was not offered group medical insurance, life insurance, or paid vacations, and he was not a participant in the pension and profit-sharing plans. He was not provided with W-2 forms, and the Bears never made social security deductions from his compensation. Fox stated that he considered himself to be an employee of his orthopedic corporation and received W-2 forms from that organization.

Based on these facts, the appellate court believed that it could not, as a matter of law, rule that Fox was an employee of the Bears, immune from a negligence suit by the workers' compensation statute.

The court added that it was also unable, as a matter of law, to rule that football was an ultra-hazardous business, with automatic coverage under the Illinois Workers' Compensation Act.

8. Another recurring problem is one raised in **Problem 2** of this subsection concerning the duty of the team physician to provide information to players concerning the consequences of using pain killing drugs. In a case settled in 1976, it was reported that the Chicago Bears agreed to pay Dick Butkus $600,000. Butkus claimed that extensive injections of cortisone irreparably damaged his knee and that he had not been advised of the long-term effects. N.Y. TIMES, Sept. 14, 1976, at 50, col. 5.

9. One of the most recent highly publicized medical malpractice cases involved Marc Buoniconti. The following article by Ray Yasser is reprinted with the permission of BACULUS, the law student's newspaper at The University of Tulsa College of Law.

Torts in Sports: The Marc Buoniconti Case

It's tough to be the son or daughter of a star. Living up to the standard of a famous parent creates uniquely crushing pressures foreign to most of us. And it is particularly tough on the offspring who attempts to excel in or on the same field as the parent. But for Marc Buoniconti, son of football legend Nick Buoniconti, and only a short time ago a linebacker at The Citadel, that kind of pressure is a thing of the long-distant past, remembered now as trivial when compared to the pressure of just making it through another day. Marc Buoniconti is a quadriplegic. How he injured himself so nightmarishly, and what has happened to him since the injury, reveals a lot about our law and culture.

How It Happened

In the fall of 1985, Marc Buoniconti was a sophomore at The Citadel, a 150 year old military college in Charleston, South Carolina. Buoniconti was a linebacker who loved to hit. The coaches noticed. He became a starter. On October 5, in a game against Virginia Military Institute, he suffered a neck injury. Nonetheless, he played on October 12 against Davidson even though his neck was stiff and weak. He was tough. He took whirlpool treatments and played again on October 19 in a game against the University of Tennessee-Chattanooga. In that game he injured his neck again. He wore a soft-collar around campus and was excused from military drills and contact at football practice. X-rays were taken on Monday, the 21st, by the team doctor, Dr. E. K. Wallace, who found nothing that indicated that Buoniconti shouldn't play on the 26th. During the week The Citadel trainer, Andy Clawson, concocted a piece of equipment designed to prevent Buoniconti's head from bending backwards. He affixed an elastic strap to the face guard of Buoniconti's helmet, pulled it taut, and snapped it to the front of Buoniconti's shoulder pads. Dr. Wallace thought it would be okay for Marc to play on the 26th with this device to protect his neck.

In the game on the 26th against East Tennessee State, Marc Buoniconti, a guy who loved to hit, hit for the last time. The videotape shows a rather unremarkable play by football standards. As middle linebacker Buoniconti closes in on a running back running wide, and turning the corner up field, The Citadel's outside linebacker trips the runner up. Buoniconti dives in to finish him off — possibly "spearing" in the process. No penalty was called but the most serious penalty imaginable was exacted. The "hit" broke Buoniconti's neck, crushing the spinal cord. Since that time, Buoniconti has been unable to move any part of his body except his head.

The Law Suit

It had to be a gut-wrenching decision for the family to sue. In the controversy concerning whether Americans are overly litigious, it was clear where somebody like Nick Buoniconti probably stood. A lawyer himself, Nick Buoniconti has been for a time allied with tobacco interests, defending these interests from attacks by smokers, snuffers, and chewers. Here was a man who embodied the qualities of rugged individualism and individual responsibility — not your typical pro-plaintiff-let's-keep-the-doors-to-the-courthouse-wide-open-and-redistribute-some-wealth-while-we're-at-it type guy.

The negligence action was brought originally against The Citadel, trainer Andy Clawson, and Dr. Wallace. The insurer for The Citadel, which also insured Clawson as an employee of The Citadel, settled as the trial was in progress. (The insurer apparently recognized the vulnerable legal position of The Citadel in opting to settle.) The case went to the jury with Dr. Wallace as the sole defendant. After a five week trial, replete with warring experts, the jury deliberated three hours, found that Dr. Wallace was not liable, and awarded Buoniconti nothing.

The Jury Verdict

We can never be sure of a jury's reasoning. In our system, the jury room is sacrosanct. We trust the judgment of the jury, but we don't want to inquire into its reasoning (perhaps in fear of finding out the real basis for the group's decision). Absent a special verdict, it is most difficult to discern just what the jury's reasoning was. But the verdict itself reflects local law and prevailing community values, along with particular findings of fact.

It should be noted that South Carolina law applied to the case. South Carolina is one of a very few states remaining which has not adopted a comparative negligence scheme. South Carolina abides by the so-called common law rule. What this means is that the contributory negligence of the plaintiff operates as a complete bar to recovery. (In comparative negligence, the negligence of the plaintiff operates to diminish the recovery but it does not necessarily bar recovery. And under all types of comparative negligence schemes, a plaintiff who is less negligent than a negligent defendant recovers proportionately for the damages suffered). Moreover, at common law, and in South Carolina, the voluntary assumption of risk of a plaintiff absolutely bars recovery. These common law rules, noted for their harshness, appear to have operated most harshly to deny Marc Buoniconti compensation.

The jury applied this local law to particular findings of fact in concluding that Buoniconti recovered nothing. So what is it that this jury verdict says? In my mind, this jury verdict says that Marc Buoniconti knew and appreciated the risks he was confronting when he decided to play football that fateful day. It says that Marc Buoniconti was himself negligent in deciding to play and that this negligence ought to bar recovery. It says that he alone should bear the responsibility for that decision. This jury verdict says that Dr. Wallace was not negligent or that his negligence, if there was any, did not cause the harm. It says that Dr. Wallace breached no duty to Marc Buoniconti.

A more humane jury would have drawn starkly different conclusions. It would have said that Marc Buoniconti did not know and appreciate the risks that he was confronting in playing football that day. It would have recognized that powerful social forces combined to produce a youthful exuberance incapable of meaningful risk appreciation under these circumstances. It would have said that if Marc Buoniconti was negligent at all in playing, it was so minor in comparison to the negligence of Dr. Wallace as to justify the conclusion that Dr. Wallace ought to be held liable. A more humane jury would have found that Dr. Wallace had breached a duty to Marc Buoniconti to protect him from this kind of harm.

MARC BUONICONTI REVISITED . . .

In the eleven years since Marc Buoniconti's last "hit," Marc and his father Nick have proven to be winners after all. The original trial judge denied their request for a new trial and they filed an appeal with the South Carolina Supreme Court. In October 1988, almost three years to the day after the paralyzing injury, Marc and his family decided to abandon their appeal. The consent order of dismissal said Buoniconti agreed to drop his appeal and that Dr. Wallace agreed to waive his right to recover any costs. After three years of legal battles Marc recovered an $800,000 settlement from The Citadel's insurers for an estimated $16.5 million in costs for future medical care, actual medical bills, and estimated wage losses.

Marc, now 30, is pursuing a master's degree in psychology at the University of Miami. He and his father have been searching for a cure for spinal cord injuries. Their Buoniconti Fund has raised over $20 million for the Miami Project to Cure Paralysis at the University of Miami. They broke ground ten years to the day of the injury on a $30 million special research facility which is devoted entirely to spinal cord research. Some recent patients at the Miami Project include Mike Utley, former Detroit Lions guard who was paralyzed during a pass blocking accident; singer Gloria Estefan, who was paralyzed for over a month after a bus accident; and Superman himself, Christopher Reeve, paralyzed after falling from a horse.

In addition to their fundraising efforts, the Buonicontis advocate the "no practice, no play" rule to improve the safety of college and high school players. Nick Buoniconti suggests, "If a player can't practice during the week because of an injury, then he can't play on game day." As previously quoted, Marc was injured two weeks before the game injury that paralyzed him and did not practice the week of the game. However, like most young people on game day, Marc wanted to play, pain or no pain. Nick Buoniconti explains, "[a] kid 18, 19, or 20 wants to play regardless of his injury, [t]here has to be someone between the player and the field. That someone should be a doctor who'll make the decision."

However, as you can see in this chapter, the interaction between player, doctor, and team is far more complicated.

The issue of comparative negligence is still unresolved in South Carolina. The question appears to be whether the courts or the legislature should take the lead in adopting the doctrine. In *Langley v. Boyter*, 325 S.E.2d 550 (S.C. App. 1984), the Court of Appeals adopted comparative negligence but the Supreme Court reversed, holding that changing precedent was within the purview of the Legislature or the Supreme Court. *Langley v. Boyter*, 332 S.E.2d 101 (S.C. 1985). There is a statutory exception to the doctrine of contributory negligence but it is limited to railroad employees. S.C. CODE ANN. § 58-17-3730 (2002). The legislature also adopted a statute which states that contributory negligence shall not bar recovery in a motor vehicle accident. S.C. CODE ANN. § 15-1-300 (2002). However, the Court held that this statute violated the equal protection clause of both the South Carolina and United States Constitutions. In *Marley v. Kirby*, 245 S.E.2d 604, later appealed, 253 S.E.2d 370 (1978), the Court indicated that comparative negligence statutes of general application are valid, but if applied only to motor vehicle accidents they are constitutionally defective. (For a good discussion on comparative negligence in general and specifically as it relates to South Carolina, *see* Phillips, *The Case for Judicial Adoption of Comparative Fault in South Carolina,* 32 S.C. L. REV. 295. (1980).

10. The death of basketball player Hank Gathers from heart failure during a game produced several lawsuits. Gathers had collapsed earlier in the season, was put on medication and after several weeks away from basketball was allowed to return to competition. Following his death there was speculation surrounding the dosage of the medication, the advice given by the doctors, and the wisdom of his return to basketball. The litigation was settled in the spring of 1992. *See* Isaacs, *Conflicts of Interest for Team Physicians . . . in Light of Gathers*, 2 ALB. L.J. SCI. & TECH. 147 (1992). The death of Boston Celtics star Reggie Lewis reveals the recurring nature of these problems.

The case of Stephen Larkin and his quest to play college baseball, despite a serious medical condition, raised some of the same issues as the Gathers case. Larkin suffers from a heart ailment which had caused doctors at his high school and later at the University of Texas to withhold him from competition. In the spring of 1992 Larkin was successful in negotiations with the university and was allowed to return to competition. A carefully drafted release was apparently the key to the decision. *See* Note, *A High Price to Compete: the Feasibility . . . of Waivers . . . for Injuries to Athletes with High Medical Risks,* 79 KY. L.J. 867 (1990-1991).

In some situations a waiver or release may not succeed. But there are other players who have managed to "waive" their way on to the field despite serious medical conditions. (The reader should be convinced by now that the highly motivated athlete tests all boundaries in her desire to compete.) Stephen Hagins sued Arizona State University when it refused to medically clear Hagins to play baseball because of a congenital heart condition which ASU determined to be life threatening. Hagins' suit claimed ASU illegally discriminated against him because, according to ASU, he was physically handicapped. Although Hagins offered to waive liability, ASU refused due to concern that the waiver would not stand up to legal scrutiny. The case was settled when Hagins was released from his Letter of Intent and allowed to transfer without losing a year of eligibility. Hagins' key was finding other doctors who did not consider his condition as serious as the ASU doctors. Which approach would you recommend? Waiver or transfer?

In addition to liability waivers, two other methods have been used by athletes who have been advised not to compete by their doctors but are determined to compete regardless of the risk. Both of these tactics involve federal anti-discrimination law. The first, and most widely used by competitive athletes is to file a lawsuit based on a violation of § 504 of the Rehabilitation Act of 1973. Section 504 makes it unlawful for anyone receiving federal funding to discriminate against otherwise qualified individuals on the basis of a handicap. 29 U.S.C. § 701 et seq. In *Grube v. Bethlehem Area School District*, 550 F. Supp. 418 (1982), the court granted an injunction preventing the school district from precluding the student from playing high school football because he only had one kidney. The court stated that it was reluctant to reach its conclusion stating that it would disturb a well-intended decision of local school authorities. *Id.* at 423. The court reasoned that it was "bound to uphold an act of Congress which is specifically designed to protect Richard and the right he is asserting." *Id.* at 423.

However, in the case of *Pahulu v. University of Kansas*, 897 F. Supp. 1387 (D. Kan. 1995), Alani Pahulu, who had a football scholarship, was injured during a tackle and experienced "transient quadriplegia." Pahulu left the field under his own power and was subsequently examined by the team doctor who discovered that Pahulu had a congenitally narrow cervical canal. *Id.* at 1388. The team physician disqualified Pahulu, acknowledging that the decision was conservative. Pahulu tried to offer a waiver and release to no avail. *Id.* at 1388. He sued for injunctive relief and was denied. The court held that Pahulu was not "disabled" within the meaning of the Act even though intercollegiate football might be part of major life activity of learning. *Id.* at 1393. The court stated that Pahulu still had the opportunity to learn, still had his athletic scholarship, and still could participate in the football program in a role other than as a player. *Id.* at 1393. The court further held that even if the student was disabled, he was not "otherwise qualified," based on the physicians' reasonable and rational conclusion that Pahulu was at extremely high risk for subsequent and potentially permanent severe neurological injury. *Id.* at 1394. Will this case negate sports medicine physician shopping? *See also* David L. Herbert, *Athlete's Exclusion From Participation Does Not Violate Federal Rehabilitation Act,* 9 SPORTS PARKS & RECREATION L. REP. 49 (March 1996).

The second method is to file a lawsuit based on violation of the Americans With Disabilities Act of 1990, which makes it unlawful for a place of public accommodation or a public entity to discriminate against an individual on the basis of disability. 42 U.S.C. § 12101 et seq. Many of these cases deal with age discrimination caused by learning disability. *See Reaves v. Mills*, 904 F. Supp. 120 (W.D.N.Y. 1995) (age requirement did not violate ADA); *Dennin v. Connecticut Interscholastic Athletic Conference, Inc.*, 913 F. Supp. 663 (D. Conn. 1996) (age eligibility requirement must be waived for student with Down syndrome); *Sandison v. Michigan High School Athletic Association, Inc.*, 863 F. Supp. 483 (E.D. Mich. 1994) (learning disabled students granted injunction). These and related topics are covered more fully in **Chapter 14,** *infra.*

11. Doctors who provide performance enhancing drugs (like steroids) to athletes face a host of legal problems. The easiest suit to see is the personal injury lawsuit by an athlete who suffers side effects. The issue of informed consent would come into play here. These doctors might also expect to be professionally sanctioned or called before governmental investigative tribunals to testify. Moreover, it is foreseeable that sports organizations will attempt to fashion a cause of action against doctors who help to foist chemically enhanced athletes into otherwise legitimate competition. This note by no means exhausts the issues raised by drug use. **Chapter 15,** *infra,* is addressed entirely to the issue of drugs and drug-testing in athletics.

12. Doctors might also be potentially liable for fraudulent concealment of medical information. The elements of a cause of action for fraud or deceit are (1) a misrepresentation or suppression of a material fact, (2) knowledge of any falsity, (3) intent to induce reliance, (4) actual and justifiable reliance, and (5) resulting damages. According to Prosser, the athlete must also prove that he would not have played or undergone the medical treatment that caused the harm if he had been properly informed of the material risks of doing so, W. PAGE KEETON ET AL., PROSSER AND KEETON ON THE LAW OF TORTS § 105, at 728 (5th Ed., 1984).

In *Krueger v. San Francisco Forty Niners*, 234 Cal. Rptr. 579, 583 (1987) (ordered not published), the court held that "the duty of full disclosure within the context of a doctor/patient relationship defines the test for concealment or suppression of facts. A physician cannot avoid responsibility for failure to make full disclosure by simply claiming that information was not withheld." The court found that the team and the doctors knew the extent of the damage to Krueger's knee and in order to prolong his career and keep him on the field they regularly anesthetized him before and during games, administered questionable steroid treatments, and Krueger was even directed by a team physician to use amphetamines during games. *Id.* at 584. This showed the requisite intent. The court established reliance by holding that "patients are generally persons unlearned in the medical sciences, . . . and consequently are entitled to rely upon physicians for full disclosure of material medical information." *Id.* at 584. Finally, the court found that Krueger would have followed physician recommendations to discontinue playing football, which satisfied the necessary causal link between the nondisclosure of material risks and his harm. *Id.* at 584. In 1988, the California Superior Court ordered the 49ers to pay Charlie Krueger over $ 2.3 million in damages arising from the team's medical care of the former all pro defensive tackle.

The *Krueger* case also highlights the difficulty that doctors encounter when there is a conflict between the interests of the athlete/patient and the team.

13. In light of the experiences of Marc Buoniconti, Charlie Krueger, Hank Gathers and other motivated athletes, should the general legal principles used for resolving malpractice claims be applied to sports medicine? Or must special solicitude be provided the not-to-be-denied athlete?

The two leading articles which address this evolving topic use similar but different approaches to the issue. James H. Davis, in his article *"Fixing" the Standard of Care: Motivated Athletes and Medical Malpractice*, suggests that the traditional legal concepts of informed consent and assumption of the risk offer the best foundation upon which to formulate a standard for dealing with malpractice claims in the sports medicine field. 12 AM. J. TRIAL ADVOC. 215 (1988). On the other hand, Matthew J. Mitten advocates apportioning liability between the doctor and the athlete based on comparative responsibility principles. *Team Physicians and Competitive Athletes: Allocating Legal Responsibility for Athletic Injuries,* 55 U. PITT. L. REV. 129 (1993). A comparative approach leaves room for the perhaps overzealous athlete to recover in the face of his or her own negligence.

14. A rich body of excellent law review commentary is emerging concerning medical malpractice and related issues in sports. *See, e.g.,* Jones, *College Athletes: Illness or Injury and the Decision to Return to Play,* 40 BUFF. L. REV. 113 (1992); Mitten, *Amateur Athletes with Handicaps or Physical Abnormalities: Who Makes the Participation Decision?,* 71 NEB. L. REV. 987 (1992); Twila Keim, *Physicians for Professional Sports Teams: Health Care Under the Pressure of Economic and Commercial Interests*, 9 SETON HALL J. SPORT L. 196-225 (1999).

D. PRODUCTS LIABILITY FOR DEFECTIVE ATHLETIC EQUIPMENT

This section explores the legal theories available to sports participants injured by arguably defective sports equipment. Generally, a person injured by an arguably defective, commercially supplied product has available at least three separate and distinct causes of action — negligence, breach of implied warranty, and strict liability in tort. In some cases, a fourth cause of action, a breach of an express warranty, is available.

The negligence cause of action in the products liability context is not much different than the standard negligence-based cause of action. Manufacturers and sellers of products, like all others in the society, generally have a duty to act as reasonably prudent people would act under the same or similar circumstances. In the products liability setting, negligence typically takes one of three forms. One recurring form of negligence pertains to quality control. In this regard, an unreasonable failure to inspect for defects or to test the product is alleged. A second recurring form of negligence is that the design of the product is unreasonably unsafe. A third basis for showing negligent conduct is the manner in which the product is marketed. Here, the likely allegation is that there is a negligent failure to warn about dangers associated with the use of the product. Contributory negligence and assumption of risk are, of course, available as defenses, as they would be for any other negligence-based cause of action.

Under the Uniform Commercial Code, a warranty of merchantability accompanies the sale of goods by a merchant. This warranty assures that the goods are "of fair average quality" and "fit for the ordinary purposes for which such goods are used." (UCC 2-314.) Additionally, a warranty of fitness for a particular purpose is created if the buyer relies on the seller's judgment to furnish goods for a special purpose even if the seller is not a merchant. (UCC 2-315.) Under the UCC, such warranties may be disclaimed by the seller or lost by the buyer who fails to notify the seller of the breach within a reasonable time. (UCC 2-317 and 2-607.) Moreover, assumption of risk, misuse of the product, and failure to follow directions can defeat a breach of warranty claim. Finally, it should be noted that the UCC does not extend the warranty to all those who might foreseeably be expected to be affected by the goods. Rather, the UCC defines the classes of person to whom the warranty extends in three alternate versions of UCC 2-315. Under the version adopted in most jurisdictions, the seller is liable for personal injuries "to his buyer, members of his buyer's family, and guests in his buyer's home." (UCC 2-318, Alternative A.)

Both the UCC and the Restatement recognize the availability of causes of action based on express representations made concerning the nature or quality of the product. The UCC addresses the issue in terms of breach of an express warranty under 2-313. The Restatement addresses it under the rubric of tort misrepresentation in section 402B. The gist of each action is similar. The plaintiff must show a misrepresentation of a material fact regarding the nature or quality of the product which causes injury. Assumption of risk and misuse of the product are defenses to both causes of action. It should be noted, however, that under the RESTATEMENT, a commercial supplier is liable for injury to anyone who relied on the misrepresentation. Under the UCC, the injured person need not have relied on the express warranty. Instead, the UCC defines the classes of protected persons under the 2-318 alternatives previously mentioned.

Under the theory of strict liability in tort, a commercial supplier who sells a product "in a defective condition unreasonably dangerous to the user or consumer" is subject to liability for harm caused. (RESTATEMENT § 402A). Liability attaches even if the seller has exercised all possible care and even though the user or consumer has no contractual relation with the seller. The determination of whether a product is defective is made with reference to what a reasonable consumer would expect. Assumption of risk and misuse of the product are defenses.

The material that follows illustrates more fully the nature of the various products liability causes of action, and how such causes of action operate in regard to sports products.

PROBLEM

Your firm represents the McBride Protective Headgear Company (MPH) in an action recently brought against it by Dan Zomer. You have been assigned the role of lead defense attorney in the case and you are preparing to meet with Robert Johnson, the chief executive officer of MPH, to discuss litigation strategy. Zomer has also named Dickie Lane as a defendant in the suit. (*See* **Problem, Section A**, *supra*.)

MPH is the major manufacturer of protective headgear in the United States. It manufactures sports helmets for use in such varied activities as race-car driving, motorcycling, hockey, football, lacrosse, bicycling and baseball.

The complaint alleges four causes of action against MPH arising out of a beaning incident during the course of a major league baseball game. (The details of the incident are described in the problem presented in the earlier subsection and previously alluded to herein.) It is not disputed that Zomer was wearing a helmet manufactured and sold by MPH at the time of his injury. In the negligence based counts, Zomer contends that MPH maintained faulty quality control procedures, that the design of the helmet was defective and that MPH failed to adequately warn Zomer of the dangers associated with the use of the helmet. Zomer's second cause of action alleges a breach of implied warranty, and his third cause of action alleges a breach of an express warranty. Zomer's fourth cause of action is grounded upon strict liability in tort.

The beaning incident (which all the parties involved have on videotape) reveals that Zomer, a right-handed batter, was struck in the left cheek by a fast ball thrown by Dickie Lane. The film shows that the ball deflected off the edge of the protective headgear before striking Zomer in the cheek. Zomer was seriously injured by the force of the ball striking his cheek and eye.

To prepare for your meeting with Johnson, you met with Dr. Rhonda Ester, an engineer who is head of the design division at MPH, and Larry Boman, head of the marketing division.

Ester told you that the type of helmet Zomer wore met relevant government and industry safety standards in regard to head impact protection. She also told you that this type of helmet was tested through a series of "drop tests": a randomly selected 1% of the helmets of the type are strapped to a head form and released from distances varying between 3 and 9 feet onto a rounded plate. The test allows the engineers to determine the helmet's ability to minimize impact by absorbing energy. This particular helmet type, according to Dr. Ester, affords better impact protection than any other helmet on the market. Dr. Ester is concerned, however, about the helmet design. She has been in a battle with the marketing people, and others in the corporation, for some time about this issue. Ester forcefully contends that her department has developed a prototype for a much safer helmet, a helmet with a see-through plexiglass attachment that would protect the batter's eye and cheek from contact. She told you that she never has understood why this safer helmet has not been successfully marketed.

Boman has provided you with information concerning sales, including a copy of the brochure used to sell the helmet. The brochure includes language which describes the helmet as "state of the art, the most impact resistant helmet made and thus the safest for your players to wear." A label is affixed to the back of each helmet, however, which provides:

> Warning: This helmet cannot protect the wearer against all injuries caused by impact. The wearer expressly assumes the risk of injury caused by impact. It is expressly agreed that there are no warranties, expressed or implied, made by the manufacturer.

Boman recalls talking with Ester about her safer prototype but believes that such a helmet would not sell. Boman believes that ballplayers just don't like wearing it.

Boman is aware of another company which manufactures and sells such helmets, which are used mostly by the Little League and by players who have already been beaned who want special protection.

Your research file contains the following cases, all of which are cases decided by the Oklanois Supreme Court.

Case File

Negligence

McCORMICK v. LOWE & CAMPBELL ATHLETIC GOODS CO.

144 S.W.2d 866 (Mo. Ct. App. 1940)

CAMPBELL, Commissioner.

[The defendant, Lowe & Campbell Athletic Goods Company, supplied a vaulting pole which broke while the plaintiff, a high-school pole vaulter, was using it in vaulting. The plaintiff was seriously injured in the subsequent fall and brought a negligence-based cause of action to recover for his injuries. More specifically, the plaintiff alleged that the company was negligent in its failure to inspect and test the pole.

[At trial, the plaintiff introduced expert testimony which tended to show that a reasonable inspection would have revealed that the pole was brittle and susceptible to snapping off. The defendant's witness, an employee of the defendant, testified that he customarily tested a pole to make sure it would hold the person for whom it was intended by throwing his weight upon the pole in four different positions. The plaintiff prevailed at trial. The defendant appealed.]

From an examination of the numerous cases cited in the briefs relating to the so-called modern rule governing liability of a manufacturer in cases such as the present one, we conclude that a manufacturer of a product is under a duty to exercise ordinary care to test the product to determine whether or not it has a defect which would render it unsafe when applied to its intended use; that a failure to perform such duty renders the manufacturer liable to a person injured in consequence of such failure while using such article in the ordinary and usual manner.

* * *

The defendant insists . . . that its evidence "demonstrates" the pole was inspected and tested. There was evidence to the effect the pole "snapped off." This was sufficient . . . to enable the jury to find the pole brittle. The only evidence which it can be said tended to show the pole which broke was tested, was that of the defendant's employee, who stated the manner in which he customarily tested bamboo vaulting poles. . . .

Plainly, the court cannot say such a method of testing was a reasonably careful method. The question was one for the trier of the fact.

Defendant, in contending no case was made for the jury, says the plaintiff failed to prove any act or omission on its part was the proximate cause of his injuries; that plaintiff was guilty of contributory negligence "and had assumed the risk incident" to engaging in pole vaulting.

The facts stated above were sufficient to warrant the jury in finding . . . that if defendant had tested it in a reasonably careful manner the defect would have been discovered and the injury averted. Thus the failure of the defendant to properly test the pole was the direct cause of the accident.

Plaintiff assumed the ordinary risk of pole vaulting but he did not assume risks due to the negligence of the defendant. He did not, prior to the accident, know or have cause to believe the pole was not a safe one to use in vaulting. He vaulted . . . in the usual and skillful manner. This was not negligence as a matter of law. . . .

The judgment . . . is affirmed.

DUDLEY SPORTS CO. v. SCHMITT

279 N.E.2d 266 (Ind. Ct. App. 1972)

BUCHANAN, Judge.

[Danville High School purchased an automatic baseball pitching machine from Em-Roe Sporting Goods Company that carried the name, Dudley Sports Company. The machine was manufactured by Commercial Mechanisms Inc., but marketed by Dudley. Upon receipt of the machine by the high school, the vice principal, Gibbs, and the baseball coach, Trotter, uncrated it. The crate contained a parts list, assembly instructions, and a tag warning that the operation of the machine should be understood before uncrating. The tag referred to operating instructions, but no operating instructions were provided.

[Gibbs and Trotter uncrated the machine, assembled it, and used it. It was then placed in a storage room. Schmitt, a student at the school, was severely injured when he was struck by the pitching arm as he swept out the storage room.

[Schmitt brought an action against the high school, Em-Roe, and Dudley. In the suit against Dudley, which is the focus of our concern here, Schmitt alleged negligence in the design and manufacture of the machine. Schmitt won a $35,000 judgment at the trial level. Dudley appealed.]

* * *

. . . It is our opinion that a vendor who holds himself out as the manufacturer of a product and labels the product as such must be held to the same standard of care as if he were in fact the manufacturer. . . .

* * *

The reason for imposing such liability is not hard to find. When a vendor puts his name exclusively on a product, in no way indicating that it is the product of another, the public is induced to believe that the vendor was the manufacturer of the product. This belief causes the public to rely upon the skill of the vendor. When products are held out in this manner, the ultimate purchaser has no available means of ascertaining who is the true manufacturer. By this act of concealment, the vendor vouches for the product and assumes the manufacturer's responsibility as his own.

* * *

. . . It is our opinion that the evidence most favorable to Schmitt was sufficient for the jury to conclude that Dudley was negligent in the design, manufacture, and sale of the machine.

Point A

Schmitt contends that Dudley was negligent for failing to provide a shield around the pitching arm; for failing to provide a lock or catch mechanism on the machine by which the pitching arm could be locked; and for failing to give specific instructions as to the operation of the machine. Dudley replies that a manufacturer is under no duty to design an accident-proof product; that their duty was limited only to the use of reasonable care; that the danger from the lack of a protective shield around the throwing arm was an obvious danger, and therefore no warning was necessary.

While we recognize the validity of the argument that a manufacturer may not be liable for obvious dangers, it is also the law that a manufacturer and vendor are bound to avoid *hidden defects or concealed dangers* in their products. . . .

The lack of a guard around the arm was probably obvious to all potential users of the machine. But the extent of the hazards involved from the lack of a guard was not apparent. The potential risks of harm to the users of this machine lie first in its ability to deliver a swift, crippling blow even though unplugged. Secondly, whether connected or disconnected, if the throwing arm is in the ten o'clock position, a slight vibration or even a change in atmospheric conditions will trigger the throwing arm. This ability to operate while unplugged as a result of even a slight vibration is a latent danger which could only be discovered through an examination of the machine combined with knowledge of the engineering principles which produce the action of the machine. Such knowledge is not ordinarily possessed by a sixteen-year-old high school boy who had never seen the machine before.

In spite of these concealed dangers Dudley asserts that placing a screen around the throwing arm would create a false sense of security, thereby attracting curious persons to place their fingers inside the screen. We are not persuaded by this argument. The utilization of such a protective screen would, in fact, be actual notice of the danger. Those placing their fingers inside the screen would do so at their own risk, as would one who touches the blade of a power saw. Without a screen, however, there is no notice of, or protection from, the inherent dangers of this machine. As a result, the false sense of security is created when there is no screen.

* * *

Point B

The law requires a supplier of an imminently dangerous chattel to warn *all who may come in contact* with the chattel of any concealed danger, regardless of privily of contract.

Although a manufacturer or vendor is under no duty to warn of apparent dangers, this court has adopted the rule of *Campo v. Scofield* (1950), 301 N.Y. 468, 95 N.E.2d 802, which held that:

> ". . . in cases dealing with a manufacturer's liability for injuries to remote users, the stress has always been upon the duty of guarding against *hidden* defects and of giving notice of concealed *dangers*."

Dudley argues that because a general warning tag was sent to the High School, no liability can be attached to Dudley for Schmitt's injuries. Dudley did include a general warning tag in the shipping crate warning the High School to read the operating instructions before using the machine. However, this general warning tag hardly conveyed an implication that the machine would only be dangerous when in operation. No warning was given of the latent dangers of this machine. Nothing was mentioned about its triggering capabilities while unplugged. Thus, a more specific warning was required to fulfill Dudley's duty to warn.

The specific operating instructions referred to by the general warning tag were not included in the crate. Presumably, such instructions would have informed the purchaser as to the various positions of the throwing arm, the positions which were dangerous, that the machine was capable of being triggered even though unplugged, and that triggering the machine only required a slight vibration or change in atmospheric conditions.

* * *

Although a manufacturer may assume that the purchaser will properly use the product and avoid dangers, such reliance is improper if the product contains latent dangers and no notice is given thereof. Because no specific operating instructions were sent to the High School and no warning was given as to the specific latent dangers of the machine, it was reasonably foreseeable that a high school student might be the victim of such negligence. Thus, it was reasonable for the jury to find the evidence before them that Schmitt's injuries were the natural and probable consequence of Dudley's negligence.

There is no vitality in Dudley's argument that the machine was in keeping with modern scientific advancement in the baseball pitching machine industry and that it was an advancement when compared to the other models on the market. The fact that a particular product meets or exceeds the requirements of its industry is not conclusive proof that the product is reasonably safe. In fact, standards set by an entire industry can be found negligently low if they fail to meet the test of reasonableness.

* * *

The jury could well have found that Dudley violated its duty to notify the High School, and ultimately Schmitt, of the machine's inherent dangers.

* * *

The decision of the trial court is therefore affirmed.

Misrepresentation and Breach of Warranty

HAUTER v. ZOGARTS

534 P.2d 377 (Cal. 1975)

TOBRINER, Justice.

[The defendant manufactures and sells the "Golfing Gizmo" — a device designed to improve one's golf swing. The defendant marketed the Gizmo as a "completely equipped backyard driving range" which would permit the user to "drive the ball with full power." According to the defendant, the Gizmo was: "COMPLETELY SAFE BALL WILL NOT HIT PLAYER." Essentially, the Gizmo consisted of a golf ball attached to an elasticized cord secured to the ground by metal pegs.

[Louise Hauter purchased a Gizmo from the defendant and gave it to her 13-year old son, Fred, as a Christmas gift. Fred suffered permanent brain damage when he was struck on the head by the golf ball on the Gizmo. Causes of action were brought in Fred's name alleging false representation, strict liability in tort, and breaches of express and implied warranties. The jury returned a verdict for the defendant on each cause of action. The trial judge granted the plaintiff's motion for judgment notwithstanding the verdict. The defendant appealed. The court here affirmed. What follows is that portion of the opinion dealing with the false representation and warranty causes of action.]

Plaintiff's claim of false representation relies on common law tort principles reflected in section 402B of the Restatement Second of Torts. For plaintiffs to recover under this section, defendants' statement "COMPLETELY SAFE BALL WILL NOT HIT PLAYER" must be a misrepresentation of material fact upon which plaintiffs justifiably relied. (Rest. 2d Torts, § 402B, coms. f, g, and j.)

If defendants' assertion of safety is merely a statement of opinion — mere "puffing" — they cannot be held liable for its falsity. Defendant's statement is so broad, however, that it properly falls within the ambit of section 402B. The assertion that the Gizmo is completely safe, that the ball will not hit the player, does not indicate seller's subjective opinion about the merits of his product but rather factually describes an important characteristic of the product. Courts have consistently held similar promises of safety to be representations of fact.

These decisions evidence the trend toward narrowing the scope of "puffing" and expanding the liability that flows from broad statements of manufacturers as to the quality of their products. Courts have come to construe unqualified statements such as the instant one liberally in favor of injured consumers. Furthermore, the illustrations in the Restatement indicate that the assertion "COMPLETELY SAFE BALL WILL NOT HIT PLAYER" constitutes a factual representation. Defendants' statement parallels that of an automobile dealer who asserts that the windshield of a car is "shatter proof."

Moreover, the materiality of defendants' representation can hardly be questioned; anyone learning to play golf naturally searches for a product that enables him to learn safely. Fred Hauter's testimony that he was impressed with the safety of the item demonstrates the importance of defendants' statement. That Fred's injury occurred while he used the Gizmo as instructed proves the inaccuracy of the assertion on the carton.

Defendants, however, maintain that plaintiffs' reliance upon the assurance of safety is not justifiable. (*See* Rest. 2d Torts, § 402B, com. j.) Alluding to the danger inherent to the sport, defendants argue that the Gizmo is a "completely safe" training device only when the ball is hit squarely. Defendants repeatedly state that an improperly hit golf shot exposes the player, as well as others nearby, to a serious risk of harm; they point to testimony recounting how an experienced player once hit a shot so poorly that the ball flew between his legs. As a result, contend defendants, plaintiffs cannot reasonably expect the Gizmo to be "completely safe" under all circumstances, particularly those in which the player hits beneath the ball.

Defendant's argument does not withstand analysis. Fred Hauter was not "playing golf." He was home on his front lawn *learning* to play the game with the aid of defendants' supposedly danger-free training device. By practicing in an open, isolated area apart from other golfers and free of objects off which a poorly hit shot could ricochet, Fred Hauter *eliminated* most of the dangers present during a normal round of play. Moreover, even though certain dangers are inherent in playing golf, the risk that the golfer's own ball will wrap itself around his club and strike the golfer on the follow-through is not among those dangers. Fred Hauter's injury stemmed from a risk inherent in defendants' product, not a risk inherent in the game of golf.

Additionally, defendants' analysts would render their representation of safety illusory. Were we to adopt their analysis, the words "COMPLETELY SAFE BALL WILL NOT HIT PLAYER" would afford protection to consumers only in *relatively infrequent instances* in which the "duffers" using the Gizmo managed to hit the ball solidly. Yet defendants' instructions supplied with the Gizmo clearly indicate the defendants anticipated the users of their product would "hook," "slice" and "top" the ball. They expected their customers to commit the errors that normally plague beginning golfers. Thus, when they declared their product "completely safe," the only reasonable inference is that the Gizmo was a safe training device for all golfers regardless of ability and regardless of how squarely they hit the ball.

Although defendants claim they did not intend their statement to cover situations such as the one at bar, subjective intent is irrelevant. The question is not what a seller intended, but what the consumer reasonably believed. The rule "is one of strict liability for physical harm to the consumer, resulting from a misrepresentation of the character or quality of the chattel sold, even though the misrepresentation is an innocent one, and not made fraudulently or negligently." (Rest. 2d Torts, § 402B, com. a.)

We conclude that Fred Hauter reasonably believed he could use the Gizmo with safety and agree with the trial court that plaintiffs established all the elements of a cause of action for misrepresentation.

* * *

Defendants breached their express warranty that the Golfing Gizmo ball was "completely safe" and would "not hit Player," as well as their implied warranty of merchantability .

As an alternative cause of action, plaintiffs claim that defendants breached both an express warranty and an implied warranty of merchantability. [Footnote omitted.] In analyzing these claims, we confront for the first time the California Uniform Commercial Code provisions relating to warranties. (Cal. U. Com. Code, §§ 2313, 2314, and 2316.) The crucial issue here is not whether defendants created a warranty — as explained below, they clearly did. Rather, the bone of contention is whether they can escape liability by impliedly limiting the *scope* of their promise.

We first treat the claim for breach of express warranty, which is governed by California Commercial Code section 2313. The key under this section is that the seller's statements — whether fact or opinion — must become "part of the basis of the bargain." According to official Comment 3 to the Uniform Commercial Code following section 2313. "no particular reliance . . . need be shown in order to weave [the seller's affirmations of fact] into the fabric of the agreement. Rather, any fact which is to take such affirmations, once made, out of the agreement requires clear affirmative proof."

* * *

The trial court properly concluded . . . that defendants expressly warranted the safety of their product and are liable for Fred Hauter's injuries which resulted from a breach of that warranty.

The trial court also held for plaintiffs on the theory of breach of an implied warranty of merchantability. Unlike express warranties, which are basically contractual in nature, the implied warranty of merchantability arises by operation of law. "Into every mercantile contract of sale the law inserts a warranty that the goods sold are merchantable, the assumption being that the parties themselves, had they thought of it, would specifically have so agreed." Consequently, defendant's liability for an implied warranty does not depend upon any specific conduct or promise on their part, but instead turns upon whether their product is merchantable under the code. . . .

[T]he evidence shows that the Gizmo is not fit for the ordinary purposes for which goods are normally used. . . .

Defendants nevertheless seek to avoid liability by limiting the scope of their warranties. They claim that the box containing the Gizmo and the instructions pertaining to its use clarified that the product was "completely safe" only when its user hit the ball properly. They point to no language expressing such a limitation but instead claim that a drawing in the instructions depicting a golfer "correctly" using their product *implies* the limitation.

As we explained above in discussing the false representation claim, defendants' argument is wholly without merit. Furthermore, they fail to meet the stern requirements of California Uniform Commercial Code section 2315 [footnote omitted] which governs disclaimer and modification of warranties. Although section 2316 has drawn criticism for its vagueness, its purpose is clear. No warranty, express or implied, can be modified or disclaimed unless a seller *clearly* limits his liability. . . .

Because a disclaimer or modification is inconsistent with an express warranty, words of disclaimer or modification give way to words of warranty unless some clear agreement between the parties dictates the contrary relationship. At the very least, section 2316 allows limitation of warranties only by means of *words* that clearly communicate that a particular risk falls on the buyer.

Moreover, any disclaimer or modification must be strictly construed against the seller. Although the parties are free to write their own contract, the consumer must be placed on fair notice of any disclaimer or modification of a warranty and must freely agree to the seller's terms. "A unilateral nonwarranty cannot be tacked onto a contract containing a warranty."

In the instant case, defendants do not point to any language or conduct on their part negating their warranties. They refer only to a drawing on the box and to the notion that golf is a dangerous game; based on that meager foundation, they attempt to limit their explicit promise of safety. Such a showing does not pass muster under the code, which requires clear language from anyone seeking to avoid warranty liability. We conclude, therefore, that the trial court properly granted plaintiffs judgment notwithstanding the verdict with regard to the warranty causes of action.

Strict Liability in Tort

NISSEN TRAMPOLINE COMPANY v. TERRE HAUTE FIRST NATIONAL BANK

332 N.E.2d 820 (Ind. Ct. App. 1975)

LYBROOK, Judge.

[The defendant Nissen manufactured the "Aqua Diver" — a small circular trampoline to be used recreationally in lieu of a diving board. Nissen's literature described the Aqua Diver as "twice as much fun as an old fashioned diving board at half the cost." Southlake Beach purchased an Aqua Diver from Nissen and installed it upon a platform at its beach.

[Thirteen-year-old Bruno Garzolini, Jr. was injured while using the Aqua Diver at Southlake. The Terre Haute First National Bank, as guardian of Bruno's estate, initiated an action against Nissen and Southlake. Of concern here is the cause of action in strict liability against Nissen.

[At trial, Bruno testified that he was injured the first time he used the Aqua Diver when he attempted to jump from the designated platform onto the bed of the trampoline in order to catapult himself into the water. He landed with only one foot on the trampoline. His other foot became entangled in the elastic cables of the Aqua Diver which supported the bed of the trampoline. He then found himself suspended by his left leg, which was ensnarled in the cables. Eventually, Bruno's left leg had to be amputated above the knee. Other evidence at trial revealed that Nissen was aware of the danger that a user's foot could become entangled in the cables supporting the bed of the trampoline. The product was marketed without any warnings or instructions for use.

[The trial court jury returned a verdict for Nissen. The trial judge granted a new trial, pointing out that the jury verdict was against the weight of the evidence, which supported plaintiffs strict liability claim. Nissen appealed. The court here affirms the award of a new trial.]

I.

* * *

Initially, Nissen argues that the trial court's conclusion that the Aqua Diver was a defective product was not supported by substantial evidence. Nissen maintains that there was no evidence which established a defect in design or manufacture . . . .

Our analysis of the evidence reveals that, as Nissen maintains, no defect in design or manufacture has been shown. However . . . for reasons hereinafter stated, it is our opinion that . . . defectiveness is predicated upon Nissen's failure to warn of the known dangers in the use of the Aqua Diver.

Under the doctrine of strict tort liability as expressed in *Restatement* (2d) Torts, § 402A, and adopted in Indiana, it is well established that a product, although virtually faultless in design, material, and workmanship, may nevertheless be deemed defective so as to impose liability upon the manufacturer for physical harm resulting from its use, where the manufacturer fails to discharge a duty to warn or instruct with respect to potential dangers in the use of the product. Generally, the duty to warn arises where the supplier knows or should have known of the danger involved in the use of its product, or where it is unreasonably dangerous to place the product in the hands of a user without a suitable warning. However, where the danger or potentiality of danger is known or should be known to the user, the duty does not attach.

In the case at bar, the trial court's findings, which are supported by uncontradicted evidence, reveal that prior to marketing the Aqua Diver, Nissen had discovered through testing that it was possible for a user's foot to pass between the elastic cables connecting the bed of the trampoline to the circular frame and thereby cause injury. Additionally, the undisputed evidence reveals that notwithstanding the knowledge of this danger involved in the use of Aqua Diver, Nissen marketed the product without a warning. This undisputed evidence . . . is substantial evidence to support the trial court's conclusion that the Aqua Diver was a defective product dangerous to the user without a warning within the purview of § 402A. We therefore conclude that there were sufficient special findings to establish that Aqua Diver was defective.

II.

* * *

Clearly, under the doctrine of strict liability, an essential element of proof is that the defective condition of the product caused plaintiff's harm . . . .

The issue of causation in both negligence and strict liability cases wherein the defect is in design or manufacture differs fundamentally from causation in failure to warn cases. In the former, it is generally required that the plaintiff establish a causal connection in fact by proof that the harm resulted from the condition or ingredient that made the product defective. In the latter case, however, the difference arises in that the factor rendering the product defective is separable from the product itself. Applying the causation in fact test to the failure to warn case would give rise to a doctrine that liability is predicated upon a showing by the plaintiff that he would have suffered no injury but for the absence of warning. Stated differently, the plaintiff would be required to show that he would have heeded a warning had one been given. In our opinion, such an approach would undermine the purpose behind the doctrine of strict tort liability since any such testimony would generally be speculative at best. A more reasonable approach which represents a compromise within the framework of strict liability . . . is that the law should supply the presumption that an adequate warning would have been read and heeded, thereby minimizing the obvious problems of proof of causation. We find such an approach to be meritorious, workable, and desirable.

Comment j of *Restatement* (2d) Torts § 402A (1965), provides a presumption protecting the manufacturer where a warning is given: "Where warning is given, the seller may reasonably assume that it will be read and heeded. . . . "

However, where there is no warning as in the case at bar, the presumption of comment j that the user would have read and heeded an adequate warning works in favor of the plaintiff user. In other words, the presumption of causation herein is that Garzolini would have read an adequate warning concerning the danger of a user's foot slipping between the elastic cables of Aqua Diver and heeded it, resulting in his not using the Aqua Diver. This presumption may, however, be rebutted by the manufacturer Nissen with contrary evidence that the presumed fact did not exist. As the Texas Supreme Court said in *Technical Chemical Co. v. Jacobs,* [480 S.W.2d 602 (1972)]: "Depending upon the individual facts, this may be accomplished by the manufacturer's producing evidence that the user was blind, illiterate, intoxicated at the time of use, irresponsible or lax in judgment or by some other circumstance tending to show that the improper use was or would have been made regardless of the warning." 480 S.W.2d at 606.

Placing the burden of rebutting the presumption of causation on the manufacturer in failure to warn cases is not inconsistent with the policies behind strict liability. It would encourage manufacturers to provide safe products and to warn of the known dangers in the use of the product which might cause injury. Such a presumption would also discourage those manufacturers who would rather risk liability than provide a warning which would impair the marketability of the product. [Footnote omitted.] The presumption of causation in failure to warn cases is not to be taken as an abrogation of the issue of causation, thereby subjecting a manufacturer to liability for almost any injury caused by his product. Rather, it merely shifts to the manufacturer the burden of proof where the fact-finder could only speculate as to whether the injury could have been prevented by a warning.

* * *

Judgment affirmed.

NOTES AND COMMENTS

1. The negligence based cause of action. In *Filler v. Rayex Corp.*, 435 F.2d 336 (7th Cir. 1970), a manufacturer of sunglasses which shattered when struck by a baseball, causing the loss of the player's eye, was liable for negligent failure to warn users of the dangers of its product. Compare the result in *James v. Hillerich & Bradsby Company, Inc.*, 299 S.W.2d 92 (Ky. 1957), where a pitcher was struck by a piece of a baseball bat which had broken off when the batter swung. In denying recovery, the court pointed out that even though the bat may have been defective, the company was not negligent:

> It is our opinion that the ordinary risks of personal injury included in a baseball game, from the breaking of even a properly made bat are such that a defective bat cannot be said . . . to create an 'unreasonable risk.' It is common knowledge that bats frequently break, and we think it is immaterial that a properly made bat ordinarily will splinter with the grain while one made of defective wood may break across the grain. The risk of injury is not materially increased by the defect.

Id. at 94. Weistart and Lowell note that the result in *James* "may be subject to considerable question." (at 1000).

A recurring issue in the negligence cases concerns the effect of an intervening cause on the original tortfeasor's liability. For example, in *Dudley*, the defendant alleged that Gibbs and Trotter were negligent in failing to store the machine under lock and key, and that their negligence superseded or cut-off the liability of Dudley. This is a proximate cause issue. The court in *Dudley* correctly decided the issue, pointing out that, generally, an intervening act of negligence does not cut-off the liability of the original wrongdoer: "Where harmful consequences are brought about by intervening . . . forces, the operation of which should have been foreseen, the chain of causation extending from the original wrongful act to the injury is not broken by the intervening . . . force. The original wrongful act will still be treated as the proximate cause of the accident." 279 N.E. 2d 266, 276.

In *Fort Lauderdale Country Club v. Winnemore*, 189 So. 2d 222 (Fla. Dist. Ct. App. 1966), the plaintiff was injured when he was struck by a golf cart driven by his companion and provided by the country club. In his suit against the country club, the plaintiff contended that the cart was negligently maintained. The club contended that the negligent driving of the plaintiffs companion was the sole legal cause of the injuries. In affirming the plaintiff's judgment, the court noted that the conduct of the driver, even if negligent, "was not an intervening cause which breaks the chain of causation." *Id.* at 224. According to well-established tort principles, *Dudley* and *Fort Lauderdale* were correctly decided. As a general rule, intervening acts of negligence do not supersede or cut-off the liability of the original wrongdoer. Courts view such acts as foreseeable. On the other hand, intervening acts which can be characterized as grossly negligent, or intentional, ordinarily do supersede and cut off the liability of the wrongdoer. Thus, if Dudley's companion was drunk while driving the cart, a better case could be made that the country club was not liable.

2. The warranty based causes of action. It should be remembered that a breach of warranty cause of action is by nature contractual. Therefore, privity of contract is an issue. The traditional common law rule was that the plaintiff must have entered into some contractual relationship with the defendant in order to have a cause of action for breach of warranty. The matter is now largely governed by the UCC. The UCC defines classes of people protected in three alternative versions of § 2-318. Under Alternative A, the seller is liable for personal injuries to his buyer, members of his buyer's household, and guests in his buyer's home. As already noted, Alternative A has been adopted in most jurisdictions. Alternatives B and C provide broader warranties. Alternative B provides that a warranty extends to any natural person who could be expected to use, consume, or be affected by the goods and who is injured in person by the breach. Alternative C extends liability even further in that it covers property damage and is not confined to natural persons.

If the gravamen of the complaint is based on a misrepresentation, the cause of action sounds in tort. Under the RESTATEMENT § 402B, a commercial seller is potentially liable to anyone who relies upon the misrepresentation. Privity of contract is not an issue in the misrepresentation cause of action. In theory there is no liability for misrepresentation if the plaintiff has not relied upon it.

3. The strict liability in tort cause of action. As previously noted, RESTATEMENT 402A requires that the plaintiff show that the product was in a "defective condition unreasonably dangerous." In 1972, the California Supreme Court rejected the requirement that the plaintiff prove that the defect was "unreasonably dangerous" in *Cronin v. J.B.E. Olson Corp.*, 501 P.2d 1153 (Cal. 1972). The overwhelming majority of jurisdictions, however, adhere to the RESTATEMENT approach that the product must be both defective and unreasonably dangerous.

The determination of whether a product is in a defective condition unreasonably dangerous is made with reference to what a reasonable consumer would expect. By way of illustration, a cherry pie with a cherry pit in it would not be regarded as in a defective condition unreasonably dangerous. The reasonable consumer would expect to find a pit in a cherry pie every now and then. A review of the case law reveals that there are three basic types of defects — manufacturing flaws, design flaws, and marketing flaws. Manufacturing flaws can be described as individualized product imperfections. An example would be a coffee roll with a pebble in it. Design flaws impugn the entire product line. In litigation concerning the Ford Pinto, it was contended that all the Pintos of a given year were defective because Ford placed the gas tank in a dangerously vulnerable position behind the rear axle. This would be an example of an alleged design defect. Finally, marketing flaws arise when the seller fails to provide needed instructions regarding proper use, or to provide adequate warnings concerning not so obvious dangers. The Aqua Diver described in *Nissen* would be in this category.

It can be argued that a number of commonly used sports products are in defective conditions unreasonably dangerous to the user or consumer. The cases in this section dealt with a baseball pitching machine, a golf training machine, a vaulting pole, a helmet and a trampoline. There are reported cases dealing with baseball glasses, shotgun shells, ski boats, swimming pools, golf carts, snowmobiles, motorcycles, pool tables, bicycles, and elastic exercisers. Although there appear to be no reported cases, Astro Turf and its kissing cousins — Poly Turf and Tartan Turf — appear to be susceptible to attack on a products liability theory. New technologies make wooden bats and non-collapsible rims suspect. Baseball helmets without ear flaps and/or mouth guards are arguably defective. Even football goalposts may be susceptible. However, at least one case has held that a goalpost manufacturer was not liable on a products liability theory after a goalpost came crashing down on a college student in the wake of a post-game celebration. *Bourne v. Marty Gilman, Inc.*, No. 05-3300 (7th Cir. 2006). The point is, the possibilities are infinite. In any sports-related accident, a products liability suit which puts the sports equipment under scrutiny should at least be considered.

4. Artificial turf litigation. One of the most controversial issues in the sports arena today is whether the use of artificial turf as a playing surface should continue. Coaches and trainers report numerous artificial turf-related injuries including heat strokes and exhaustion, turf toe (*i.e.,* sprained great toe), concussions, ankle and knee injuries, first and second degree burns, secondary infections, blisters and dehydration. Despite these injuries, the use of artificial turf has been justified because it results in an increase in the players' speed, lowers maintenance costs, and increases utilization of the playing facilities.

As of this writing, there has been no litigation of this actual issue. But athletes are suing increasingly for injuries resulting from a defective product, so such a suit is likely to occur in the near future. If a player does decide to bring a products liability suit, he may have a cause of action under the theories of (1) negligence, (2) breach of warranty, and/or (3) strict liability.

Under a negligence theory, those responsible for the decision to use artificial turf could be held liable for an athlete's injuries for breach of duty to exercise reasonable care for the athlete's protection. Team owners, stadium owners, universities and colleges could be found negligent for breaching their duties to provide protection against any unreasonable risk of harm to the athlete. Finally, a manufacturer might be negligent for failing to exercise reasonable care in the manufacture and/or sale of the turf.

Warranty theories may be premised on two separate grounds. Manufacturers of artificial turf create an express warranty if they tell buyers that the turf is "safer than grass." An athlete who relies on this statement and is then injured may sue the manufacturer for breach of an express warranty. Athletes may also have a cause of action for breach of an implied warranty, if artificial turf is not suitable for the purpose for which it is sold.

Finally, a manufacturer is subject to a charge of strict liability for developing and selling a product which is unreasonably dangerous because of a defective condition. If the athlete is injured, the doctrine applies even if the manufacturer is not negligent. *See*, Bill Pennington, *Foes Aside, Artificial Turf is Players' No. 1 Enemy*, N.Y. Times, Sept. 9, 1998, at C24.

5. The bat is too good: Recent litigation has put the baseball bat industry on notice that players' safety, rather than bat performance, is the priority in bat design. In 2002, an eight-member panel in Oklahoma awarded damages to a high school pitcher who had been seriously injured by a batted ball. The plaintiff, Jeremy Brett, alleged that a high-performance aluminum bat known as the Air Attack 2, was defective because it allowed batted balls to reach dangerous speeds. Brett argued that the bat hits balls so hard and fast that pitchers are unable to react to protect themselves. This is the first verdict to hold a bat manufacturer liable for such injuries. *Brett v. Hillerich & Bradsby Co.*, No. CIV-99-981-C (W.D. Okla. 2002). As a result, several teams, leagues, and conferences in Massachusetts, New Jersey, New Mexico, New York, Pennsylvania, and other states have banned aluminum bats.

6. Athletes and liability surrounding performance-enhancing supplements: For years, athletes have used performance-enhancing supplements in hopes of competing at a higher level. Many of the supplements currently on the market contain the stimulant ephedra. This stimulant has allegedly been linked to the death of Steve Bechler and Korey Stringer, both young athletes competing at the professional level. Steve Bechler, a 23-year-old pitcher for the Baltimore Orioles, collapsed during conditioning practice and subsequently died at a Florida hospital. The Florida medical examiner indicated that he believed a performance-enhancing supplement containing ephedra contributed to Bechler's death. Bechler's widow, Kiley, has indicated that she will sue the manufacturer of the supplement containing ephedra. *See* Michael Kane, *Strictly Speaking about Ephedra: A Baseball Tragedy Helping to Define the Dynamic between Warning Defect and Design Defect,* 12 VILL. SPORTS & ENT. L.J. 97 (2005). Following on the heels of this announcement, the Minnesota Vikings filed court papers defending a $100 million wrongful death action on the grounds that ephedra, not the team's negligence, was the cause of offensive lineman Korey Stringer's sudden death during conditioning practice. Buster Olney, N.Y. TIMES, Feb. 26, 2003. Related issues are addressed in the drug testing materials in **Chapter 15**, *infra*.

E. DEFAMATION AND INVASION OF PRIVACY

1. Profile of the Tort of Defamation at Common Law: The Plaintiff's Prima Facie Case — A Strict Liability Tort

Defamation. The rules governing liability for defamation make about as much sense as the rules governing the conjugation of irregular verbs in French. What follows is an attempt to present, as clearly as possible, a picture of the current rules. The tort of defamation, as it existed at common law, can be defined as the unconsented to and unprivileged intentional communication to a third person of a false statement about the plaintiff which tends to harm the reputation of the plaintiff in the eyes of the community. Consent and privilege are affirmative defenses that must be pleaded and proved by the defendant. Once defamatory meaning is apparent, injury to reputation is generally presumed as a matter of law. Moreover, the plaintiff is given the benefit of a rebuttable presumption that the statement is false, thus making truth a defense to be pleaded and proved by the defendant. Therefore, the plaintiff's prima facie case consists of a simple allegation that the defendant intentionally communicated to a third person a statement about the plaintiff which tended to expose the plaintiff to such things as public hatred, shame, obloquy, contumely, odium, contempt, ridicule, aversion, ostracism, degradation or disgrace.

It should be noted that the tort of defamation is in substance one of strict liability. That is to say, the only intent that is required is the intent to communicate something to a third person. In the vast majority of cases, of course, the defendant clearly intends to communicate something to a third person even though she may not intend to defame or harm the plaintiff. In fact, it appears that the only type of case in which the courts are willing to concede that the requisite intent to communicate is lacking involves situations, for example, in which the defendant is alone with the plaintiff, defaming her to her face, and an unanticipated intruder overhears the defamatory utterance.

As to all other matters which conceivably could be either intended or negligently performed, the defendant is strictly accountable. It thus makes absolutely no difference that the defendant *does not intend* to lie, defame, or harm the plaintiff. Likewise, it is immaterial that the defendant *does not negligently* lie, defame, or harm the plaintiff. The defamer, in short, is strictly liable for whatever she intentionally communicates to a third person about the plaintiff if it turns out that what she said is false, injures the plaintiff's reputation in the eyes of the community, and is neither consented to by the plaintiff nor privileged. At common law, people communicate virtually at their own peril. The printed and written word is, in a legal sense, indistinguishable from nitroglycerin and dangerous animals — if someone is hurt by use of it, liability attaches.

The Libel/Slander Per Se/Per Quod Distinctions. Common law defamation consists of the two torts of libel and slander. Libel is written or printed defamation — defamation embodied in some tangible or permanent form and therefore generally subject to wide dissemination. Slander is oral defamation — fleeting and ephemeral and therefore generally not subject to wide dissemination. Any libel which is clearly defamatory, with no need to resort to extrinsic facts to show the defamatory meaning, is said to be actionable *per se*. The phrase "actionable *per se*" means that general damage to reputation will be presumed. Slander is actionable *per se* only if the slanderer says that the plaintiff: (1) committed a crime of moral turpitude, (2) has venereal disease or something equally loathsome and communicable, (3) is somehow unfit or not to be trusted in his or her occupation, or (4) is not chaste.

A libel that is not actionable per se is actionable per quod. The phrase "actionable *per quod*" means that there is no presumption of general damage to reputation and that the plaintiff must plead and prove "special damages" usually of a pecuniary nature. Libel *per quod* exists when the defamatory statement is innocent on its face but takes on a defamatory meaning when illuminated by proof of extrinsic facts. The extrinsic facts had to be pleaded by way of "inducement," "innuendo," or "colloquium." If the defamatory meaning could be established only by reference to facts not apparent on the face of the publication, the plaintiff had to show such facts by way of "inducement." The purpose of the requirement called "innuendo" was to explain the meaning of the words in light of the facts. So, for example, a false statement that the plaintiff had given birth to twins was not defamatory on its face since there was nothing there that would hold the plaintiff up to scorn or ridicule; but when it was pleaded by way of inducement that she was married one week at the time of the birth and by way of innuendo (for the slow to catch on) that she must have had premarital intercourse, a defamatory statement was made out. Libel *per quod,* however, can be magically transformed to libel *per se* if it turns out that the defamatory statement as illuminated by extrinsic facts falls within one of the four classes of slander actionable *per se.* Slander which does not fall into one of the four categories is only actionable *per quod.*

The requirement that the plaintiff plead and prove special pecuniary damages in cases which are only actionable per quod often proves to be a difficult obstacle to overcome. If, however, the plaintiff is successful in showing special pecuniary damage, general damages are then appropriate for presumed reputational injury along with nonpecuniary special damages, such as emotional distress or physical illness.

Available Defenses — Truth. Assuming that the plaintiff has made out a *prima facie* case, the defendant may escape liability by establishing that what was communicated was true or was either absolutely or conditionally privileged. Truth is a complete defense if the defendant can show that the imputation is substantially true. Generally, the defendant need not show literal truth but must establish that what was communicated was basically true as to the "sting" of the libel. Truth is generally a total defense regardless of the motives. Belief as to truth, however honest it may be, is no justification for defamation.

Privilege. Privilege, like truth, is a complete defense if it is established by the defendant. The rationale for the existence of privilege as a defense is that conduct which may otherwise impose liability is excusable if the defendant is acting in furtherance of some socially useful interest. That is to say, it is more desirable, from a social standpoint, to protect the defendant and allow the plaintiff to go uncompensated. If an absolute privilege is found to exist, the defendant is totally immune from liability. Absolute privilege arises when the defendant is acting in furtherance of some very important social interest — an interest so important that the court is willing to immunize the defendant from liability for false statements without regard to purpose, motive, or reasonableness. Absolute privilege is confined to the few situations where there are obvious strong policy reasons in favor of permitting unbridled speech. Thus, statements made in the course of judicial or legislative proceedings are absolutely privileged. Executive communications, arguably made in the discharge of official duties, are likewise absolutely privileged. The media are absolutely privileged for defamation uttered by political candidates who have been granted equal time under the Federal Communications Act.

Qualified privilege. The most common defense involves a claim of qualified privilege, which arises when the defendant is arguably justified in talking. It is somewhat difficult to define qualified privilege with any degree of precision; the cases reveal repeated reliance on Baron Parke's formulation that a statement is privileged when it is "fairly made by a person in the discharge of some public and private duty, whether legal or moral, or in the conduct of one's own affairs in matters where his interest is concerned." The immunity conferred on the defendant is conditioned on his or her good behavior; the defendant must act properly or else the privilege is defeated. In general, a qualified privilege is defeated by the existence of facts inconsistent with the purpose of the privilege. The common law qualified privilege includes the privilege to fairly comment on matters of public concern by offering opinion, but not false statement of fact, and to fairly and accurately report public proceedings.

2. The Matrix of Relevant Supreme Court Cases

NEW YORK TIMES CO. v. SULLIVAN
376 U.S. 254 (1964)

[In March of 1960, L.B. Sullivan was one of three elected commissioners to the city of Montgomery, Alabama. As such, he supervised the Montgomery police department, fire department, department of cemetery, and department of scales. On March 29, 1960, the *New York Times* ran a full page advertisement entitled *Heed Their Rising Voices.* The advertisement stated that thousands of Southern blacks, engaged in a nonviolent effort to secure constitutionally protected rights, were being met by an "unprecedented wave of terror" perpetuated by "Southern Violators," designed to prevent them from enjoying their constitutional rights. The Montgomery police were implicated on a number of occasions as "Southern Violators."

[It was uncontroverted that some statements in the advertisement were not accurate descriptions of events which occurred in Montgomery. The text of the advertisement concluded with an appeal for funds and appeared over the names of sixty-four persons — many widely known for accomplishments in religion, publications, trade unions, and the performing arts. L.B. Sullivan sued the *New York Times* and four black Alabama clergymen who signed the advertisement. A Montgomery County jury found that Sullivan was defamed and awarded him a half million dollars, the full amount claimed, against all the defendants. The Alabama Supreme Court affirmed, and the Supreme Court granted certiorari "because of the importance of the Constitutional issues involved."

[Although the Alabama law that was applied in *New York Times* did not differ significantly from the common law already described, the Supreme Court, with Justice Brennan writing the majority opinion, held "that the rule of law applied by the Alabama Courts is constitutionally deficient for failure to provide the safeguards for freedom of speech and of the press that are required by the First and Fourteenth Amendments in a libel action brought by a public official against critics of his official conduct." The Court went on to say that the evidence presented in the case was "constitutionally insufficient" to support the judgment for the respondent. The common law then, according to the Supreme Court, was inherently constitutionally defective.

[The Supreme Court considered the *New York Times* case "against the background of a profound national commitment to the principle that debate on public issues should be uninhibited, robust and wide-open, and that it may well include vehement, caustic and sometimes unpleasantly sharp attacks on government and public officials." The Court quoted Judge Learned Hand to the effect that the first amendment "presupposes that right conclusions are more likely to be gathered out of a multitude of tongues than through any kind of authoritative selection" and that although "[t]o many this is . . . folly" we have, nonetheless, as a society, "staked upon it our all." In view of this national commitment to robust, wide-open debate, Justice Brennan reasoned "that erroneous statement is inevitable in free debate and that it must be protected if the freedoms of expression are to have the 'breathing space' that they 'need . . . to survive.'" Brennan cited Judge Edgerton for the simple truth that "whatever is added to the field of libel is taken from the field of free debate."

[The Court then constructed legal rules to ensure that our national commitment was not compromised. According to the Court, the Constitution requires "a federal rule that prohibits a public official from recovering damages for a defamatory falsehood related to his official conduct unless he proves that the statement was made with 'actual malice'— that is, with knowledge that it was false or with reckless disregard of whether it was false or not." Moreover, the aggrieved official must prove "actual malice" with "convincing clarity" — a standard of proof which is arguably more demanding than proof by a mere preponderance of evidence.

[Thus was born the constitutional privilege in defamation cases. The original and exclusive owner of the privilege, it should be noted, was the "citizen critic" of government.]

CURTIS PUBLISHING CO. v. BUTTS

(and its companion case, *Associated Press v. Walker*)
388 U.S. 130 (1967)

[Three years after the landmark *New York Times* decision, a majority of the Supreme Court agreed to extend the constitutional privilege to defamatory criticism of "public figures." Although Justice Harlan announced the results in both *Butts* and *Walker*, a majority of the Court agreed with Chief Justice Warren's conclusion in his concurring opinion that the *New York Times* test would apply to criticism of "public figures" in addition to "public officials." The Court's extension of the constitutional privilege to defamatory criticism of public figures made the *New York Times* privilege available to those who defamed people "intimately involved in the resolution of important public questions" or who "by reason of their fame, shape events in areas of concern to society at large."

[The *Butts* case originated with an article in the *Saturday Evening Post* accusing Wally Butts of conspiring to "fix" a football game between the University of Georgia and the University of Alabama. At the time of the article, Butts was the athletic director of the University of Georgia. The article accused Butts of giving team secrets to the opposition. Butts brought a libel action in federal court against Curtis Publishing Company; the publisher of the *Saturday Evening Post*, seeking $5,000,000 compensatory and $5,000,000 punitive damages. At trial, the defendant relied on the defense of truth. The jury returned a verdict for $60,000 in general damages and $3,000,000 in punitive damages. The court reduced the total award to $460,000 by remittitur. The Court of Appeals for the Fifth Circuit affirmed, and the Supreme Court granted certiorari and affirmed the decision.

[*Walker*, the companion case to *Butts*, arose out of the distribution of a news story giving an eyewitness account of events on the campus of the University of Mississippi on the night of the now infamous riot which erupted as a consequence of federal efforts to enforce a judicial decree ordering the enrollment of James Meredith as the first black student at the University. The story stated that General Walker, a retired career soldier and staunch segregationist, personally led a charge against the federal marshals' attempt to carry out the court order. Walker sued the Associated Press in the Texas state courts and asked for $2,000,000 in compensatory and punitive damages. Walker denied taking part in any "charge" against federal officials. Although the Associated Press defended on the basis of truth, a verdict of $500,000 compensatory damages and $300,000 punitive damages was returned. The trial judge, however, refused to enter the punitive award on the ground that there was no evidence of "actual malice." Both sides appealed, and the Texas Court of Civil Appeals affirmed. After the Supreme Court of Texas denied a writ of error, the Supreme Court of the United States granted certiorari and reversed.

[The rationale used by the Chief Justice in his concurring opinion was that "differentiation between 'public figures' and 'public officials'. . .has no basis in law, logic or First Amendment policy." The same test should apply both to the public figure plaintiff and public official plaintiff; each must show "actual malice" in order to recover. "[W]alker was a public man in whose public conduct society and the press had a legitimate and substantial interest." Because he did not prove actual malice, Walker could not recover. Butts, too, was a public figure; but unlike Walker, Butts proved "actual malice," because the jury's punitive damage award was preceded by an instruction that such an award was appropriate only if "actual malice" was found. Butts, then, could recover. The result is that the privilege which once belonged only to the citizen critic of government is extended to the citizen critic of the public person.]

ROSENBLOOM v. METROMEDIA, INC.

403 U.S. 29 (1971)

[Approximately four years after *Butts* and *Walker*, the Supreme Court took the *New York Times* privilege one logical step further. Justice Brennan, writing for the plurality, concluded in *Rosenbloom* that the *New York Times* protection should extend to defamatory falsehoods relating to private persons, if the statements concerned matters of general or public interest.

[George Rosenbloom was a distributor of "nudist magazines" in the Philadelphia metropolitan area. During an obscenity crackdown, he was arrested for selling allegedly obscene material as he was making a delivery to a retail dealer. A few days after the arrest, the police obtained a search warrant to search Rosenbloom's home and warehouse and seized Rosenbloom's allegedly obscene inventory. Rosenbloom, who by this time was out on bail, was again arrested. Following the second arrest, a Metromedia, Inc. radio broadcast included an item about Rosenbloom. The report broadcast stated that obscene materials had been confiscated at Rosenbloom's home.

[Rosenbloom then sued various city and police officials and several local news media alleging that the material seized was not obscene. Rosenbloom asked for injunctive relief prohibiting further police harassment as well as further publicity of the arrests. Metromedia, in turn, reported that "girlie book peddlers" in the "smut literature racket" were seeking judicial relief. Rosenbloom, however, was not mentioned by name. Rosenbloom subsequently was acquitted of the criminal obscenity charge on the grounds that his magazines were not obscene. Following the acquittal, he filed a libel suit in federal district court, alleging that Metromedia's unqualified characterizations of his books as "obscene" and of him as a "girlie book peddler" in the "smut literature racket" were defamatory and constituted libel *per se*.

[At trial, Metromedia's defenses were truth and privilege. After receiving instructions which did not apply the *New York Times* privilege, but clearly articulated common law rules, the jury returned a verdict for Rosenbloom and awarded him $25,000 in general damages and $725,000 in punitive damages. The trial court then reduced the punitive damage award to $250,000 on remittitur. The Court of Appeals for the Third Circuit reversed, holding that judgment be entered for Metromedia because Rosenbloom's evidence did not reasonably support the conclusion that Metromedia had acted with "actual malice" as constitutionally defined. The Supreme Court granted certiorari and affirmed the judgment of the court of appeals.

[In affirming the lower appellate court, the Supreme Court in *Rosenbloom* extended the constitutional privilege to protect defamatory falsehoods concerning "private persons" if the statements concerned matters of "general or public interest." The Court focused on society's interest in learning about certain issues: "If a matter is a subject of public or general interest, it cannot suddenly become less so merely because a private individual is involved, or because in some sense the individual did not involuntarily 'choose to become involved.'" "Private individuals involved in an event of public interest" are the legal equivalents of "public officials" and "public figures." All have to prove "actual malice" to recover in a defamation action.

[The Court went on to carefully analyze the role of the free press, the public's right to know, and the importance of the First Amendment, concluding that the constitutional protection extended "to all discussion and communication involving matters of public or general concern, without regard to whether the persons involved are famous or anonymous." The critical inquiry concerns the subject matter of the discussion.]

GERTZ v. ROBERT WELCH, INC.
418 U.S. 323 (1974)

[By 1974, hundreds of post *New York Times* defamation cases had been before the courts. The result of this avalanche of litigation was a continuing struggle to find the appropriate balance between the rights of free speech and press and the right to be free from character attacks. In *Gertz v. Robert Welch, Inc.*, the Supreme Court reversed the trend by severely limiting, if not overruling, *Rosenbloom*.

[In 1968, a Chicago policeman named Nuccio shot and killed a youth named Nelson. The policeman was subsequently found guilty of second degree murder by state prosecutors. The Nelson family retained Elmer Gertz to represent them in civil litigation against Nuccio.

[Robert Welch published *American Opinion*, a monthly periodical of the John Birch Society. The magazine had long warned of a nationwide conspiracy to discredit local law enforcement agencies and create a national police force supporting a communist dictatorship. As a part of his effort to alert the public, Welch commissioned and published an article on the policeman's murder trial. In the article, Gertz was portrayed as a communist official with a criminal record. Statements made in the article contained serious factual inaccuracies.

[Gertz filed an action for libel in the United States District Court for the Northern District of Illinois, alleging injury to his reputation as a lawyer and citizen. Welch claimed that he was entitled to the constitutional privilege and asked for summary judgment on the grounds that Gertz would not be able to show "actual malice." The court denied the motion, concluding that Gertz might be able to prove "actual malice." After all the evidence was heard, the district court ruled that Gertz was not a public figure or public official and therefore did not have to prove "actual malice" to recover. The case was submitted to the jury, which determined the appropriate measure of damages was $50,000.

[Following the jury verdict and on further reflection, the district court entered judgment for the defendant notwithstanding the verdict, anticipating the *Rosenbloom* decision. The district court concluded that discussion of a public issue was constitutionally protected, that Welch's statements pertained to a public issue, and that Gertz had not met the *New York Times* "actual malice" standard. The *Rosenbloom* decision intervened, and the United States Court of Appeals for the Seventh Circuit then agreed with the district court and affirmed its judgment, citing *Rosenbloom*. The United States Supreme Court granted certiorari to reconsider the extent of a publisher's constitutional privilege against liability for defamation of a private citizen and reversed.

[The Supreme Court in *Gertz* carefully reviewed the development of the law of defamation through *New York Times* and *Rosenbloom* in light of the competing interests of free speech and press and of protecting an individual's reputation. The Court recognized the critical importance of free speech and press to robust debate; the Court also recognized that "absolute protection for the communications media would require a total sacrifice of the competing value served by the law of defamation," and that the "legitimate state interest underlying the law of libel is the compensation of individuals for the harm inflicted on them by defamatory falsehood." Balancing the interests, the Court concluded that the protection afforded the media under *Rosenbloom* was too broad: "[T]he extension of the *New York Times* test proposed by the *Rosenbloom* plurality would abridge this legitimate state interest to a degree that we find unacceptable."

[Thus the "public or general interest" test for determining the applicability of the *New York Times* standard was rejected as inadequately serving the competing values at stake. The Supreme Court concluded that the states should retain substantial latitude in their efforts to fashion a remedy for defamatory falsehoods about private individuals and that so long as liability was not imposed without fault, the states could define for themselves the appropriate standard of liability.

[To guard against the states using their new latitude to intrude upon the First Amendment, the Court then stated the requirement that state-proscribed remedies "reach no farther than is necessary to protect the legitimate interest involved" and concluded that "[i]t is necessary to restrict defamation plaintiffs who do not prove knowledge of falsity or reckless disregard for the truth to compensation for actual injury." Thus, presumed or punitive damages cannot be recovered by the private plaintiff who establishes liability under a less demanding standard than *New York Times*.

[The Court then turned its attention to the continuing dilemma of the "public person" as plaintiff. The *Gertz* Court endorsed its prior decisions in *Butts* and *Walker* and sought to further define the status of a public figure. Under *Gertz*, a public figure designation may rest on either of two alternatives:

> In some instances an individual may achieve such pervasive fame or notoriety that he becomes a public figure for all purposes and in all contexts. More commonly, an individual voluntarily injects himself or is drawn into a particular public controversy and thereby becomes a public figure for a limited range of issues. In either case such persons assume special prominence in the resolution of public questions.

[For the second category — public people for a limited range of issues — it "[i]s preferable to reduce the public figure question to a more meaningful context by looking to the nature and extent of an individual's participation in the particular controversy giving rise to the defamation." Public people in general enjoy "significantly greater access to the 'channels' of effective communication and hence have a more realistic opportunity to counteract false statements than private individuals normally enjoy." They typically also "invite attention and comment." In contrast, "private individuals are not only more vulnerable to injury than public officials and public figures; they are also more deserving of recovery."

[The Court concluded that Gertz was a private person and that the *New York Times* standard was not applicable. Because the jury was allowed to impose liability without fault and was permitted to presume damages without proof of actual injury, a new trial was ordered by the court.]

TIME, INC. v. FIRESTONE

424 U.S. 448 (1976)

[Less than two years later, in 1976, the Supreme Court added yet another link to the chain of defamation cases that began twelve years earlier with *New York Times v. Sullivan*. This time the Court was called on to refine its definition of "public figure" in *Time, Inc. v. Firestone*.

[In 1964, Mary Alice Firestone and Russell Firestone sought the dissolution of their marriage in Florida. Since Russell was heir to one of America's wealthiest industrial fortunes, the proceeding drew a great deal of attention in the Miami press. After judgment in the divorce proceeding was rendered, TIME magazine printed an item under its *Milestones* section, which stated that Russell Firestone had been granted a divorce based on the grounds of extreme cruelty and adultery. The article characterized the marriage as having "enough extramarital adventures on both sides to make Dr. Freud's hair curl."

[Within a few weeks of publication, Mary Alice Firestone demanded a retraction from TIME. When the magazine refused, a libel action was commenced against it in Florida circuit court. A jury ultimately awarded Ms. Firestone $100,000 in damages. The decision was reviewed by the Florida District Court of Appeals and ultimately affirmed by the Florida Supreme Court. The United States Supreme Court granted certiorari in 1975.

[Time, Inc. contended that as a publisher it was entitled to the *New York Times* conditional privilege and thus could not be found liable unless it was established that the article was published with "actual malice." In support of this contention, TIME argued that Ms. Firestone was a "public figure" and that the proceeding was of "a class of subject matter which . . . deserves the protection of the 'actual malice' standard." The Supreme Court rejected both propositions.

[The Court applied the *Gertz* criteria for defining a public figure and found that Ms. Firestone did not attain this status: "[r]espondent did not assume any role of especial prominence in the affairs of society . . . and she did not thrust herself to the forefront of any particular public controversy. . . ." The Court explained that Ms. Firestone did not voluntarily enter the public spotlight or freely choose to publicize issues concerning her married life. She had to use the courts to obtain a divorce. Time's attempt to "equate 'public controversy' with all controversies of interest to the public" failed. The Court noted that "[w]ere we to accept this reasoning, we would reinstate the doctrine advanced in the plurality opinion in *Rosenbloom v. Metromedia, Inc.*"

[Despite the fact that the *Firestone* Court rejected the argument that the *New York Times* privilege should extend to the TIME publisher, the Court nevertheless refused to affirm the Florida court and remanded the case for readjudication. The Court noted that the record did not indicate evidence of fault on the part of the defendant charged with publishing the defamatory material. Since "*Gertz* established . . . that not only must there be evidence to support an award of compensatory damages, there must also be evidence of some fault on the part of a defendant," the Court had no choice but to remand for further proceedings.]

DUN & BRADSTREET v. GREENMOSS BUILDERS, INC.

472 U.S. 749 (1985)

[Ten years after the decision in *Gertz*, the Supreme Court decided that the rule in *Gertz* was not applicable to all the defamation actions that were left uncovered by the *N.Y. Times* rule.

[Dun and Bradstreet (Dun) was a credit reporting agency which provided subscribers with financial and related information about businesses. All the information was confidential, and under the subscription agreement, the subscribers could not reveal it to anyone else. On July 26, 1976, Dun sent a report to five subscribers indicating that Greenmoss Builders, Inc. (Greenmoss), a construction contractor, had filed a voluntary petition for bankruptcy. This report was false and misrepresented Greenmoss's assets and liabilities. Greenmoss requested a corrective notice and Dun sent one to the five subscribers while refusing to divulge the five subscribers to Greenmoss. Greenmoss was dissatisfied with this corrective notice and brought a defamation action against Dun in Vermont state court.

[A jury verdict found for Greenmoss and awarded compensatory damages, presumed damages and punitive damages, but the trial court ordered a new trial because of dissatisfaction with its instructions to the jury. The Supreme Court of Vermont reversed, holding that the rule in *Gertz* which held that the First Amendment prohibits awards of presumed and punitive damages for false and defamatory statements unless the plaintiff shows actual malice, was not applicable to defamation actions against "nonmedia" defendants such as Dun. The Supreme Court, in a plurality opinion, affirmed.

[Five members of the Supreme Court agreed that the rule of *Gertz* did not apply where the false and defamatory statements involved do not involve matters of public concern. They also agreed that in the area of defamation law, the rights of institutional media under the First Amendment are no greater or no less than those enjoyed by other individuals or activities engaged in the same activities. In reaching its decision, the Court employed the approach approved in *Gertz* which balances the State's interest in compensating private individuals for injury to their reputation against the First Amendment interest in protecting this type of expression.

[The court found that the State's interest, as in *Gertz*, was "strong and legitimate" and bolstered by the fact that the "protection of private personality . . . is left primarily to the individual States under the Ninth and Tenth Amendments." The First Amendment interest, though, was not as important as the one in *Gertz*. Here, the Court found that the speech was of purely private concern. "Whether speech addresses a matter of public concern must be determined by the expression's content, form, and context as revealed by the whole record." The Court found that there was no credible argument that this type of credit reporting requires special protection to ensure that "debate on public issues will be uninhibited, robust, and wide-open." Therefore, while such speech is not totally unprotected by the First Amendment, its protections are less stringent.

[It was the disposition of the Supreme Court that permitting recovery of presumed and punitive damages in defamation cases absent showing of "actual malice" did not violate the First Amendment when the defamatory statements did not involve matters of public concern.]

MILKOVICH v. LORAIN JOURNAL CO.

497 U.S. 1 (1990)

[Over a quarter of a century after the Supreme Court's decision in *New York Times v. Sullivan*, the court in *Milkovich* clarified the fact-opinion distinction. Remember that the common law qualified privilege protected "opinions," but not false statements of fact.

[J. Theodore Diadum, a reporter for a newspaper owned by the Lorain Journal Co., authored an article in an Ohio newspaper which implied that Michael Milkovich (Milkovich), a local high school wrestling coach, lied under oath in a judicial proceeding about an incident involving Milkovich and his team which occurred at a wrestling match. Milkovich sued on a defamation theory. The trial court granted summary judgment for Lorain and the Ohio Court of Appeals affirmed. The judgment was based in part on the grounds that the article constituted an "opinion" protected from the reach of state defamation law by the First Amendment. The Supreme Court reversed, finding that the First Amendment does not prohibit the application of Ohio's defamation laws to the statement contained in the article.

[The issue before the Court was whether there was a constitutionally required "opinion" exception to the application of State defamation laws. The court discussed the common law. Lorain relied on dictum found in *Gertz* to support their argument that their "opinion" article was immune from the defamation laws. The court in *Gertz* had stated that, "[h]owever pernicious an opinion may seem, we depend for its correction not on the conscience of judges and juries but on the competition of other ideas." The Supreme Court here appears to retreat a bit from this notion.

[The court found that this passage from *Gertz* was not intended to create a wholesale defamation exception for anything that might be labeled "opinion." The court stated, "[n]ot only would such an interpretation be contrary to the tenor and context of the passage, but it would also ignore the fact that expressions of "opinion" may often imply an assertion of objective fact." Where a statement of "opinion" on a matter of public concern reasonably implies false and defamatory facts regarding public figures or officials, the speaker could be vulnerable if the plaintiff could show that the statement was made with actual malice. Here, the Court found that the article communicated the fact that Milkovich perjured himself. The Court did not believe that the speech here was the "sort of loose, figurative or hyperbolic language which would negate the impression that the writer was seriously maintaining petitioners committed the crime of perjury." The article conveyed a statement which was sufficiently factual to be susceptible of being proven true or false.]

3. Invasion of Privacy

It is generally accepted that invasion of privacy consists of four separate and distinct causes of action: (1) intrusion, (2) misappropriation, (3) public disclosure of private facts, and (4) "false light" invasion of privacy. All are especially relevant to sports.

The intrusion cause of action is stated when the plaintiff's right to solitude is invaded by the defendant in a manner that would be objectionable to a person of ordinary sensibilities. The classic intruder is the Peeping Tom. Intrusion might take place in the form of constant annoyance or excessive surveillance. Overzealous paparazzi may well be tortious intruders. This kind of intrusion is obviously relevant in sports. In a similar fashion, the overprotective team owner might intrude on a player's solitude in a desire to check on the player's drug habits.

Misappropriation occurs when the plaintiff's name or likeness is used for a primarily commercial advantage without the plaintiff's consent. Thus, marketing a Hank Aaron baseball glove without Hammerin' Hank's permission would be misappropriation. It should be pointed out that the media enjoys a broad privilege to report the news. Thus, photographs and stories in newspapers and magazines are generally not actionable even if they indirectly boost sales. The gist of the tort is commercially motivated misappropriation. In recent years, the law of misappropriation has taken on a more important role as the value of the right to exploit one's name or likeness continues to grow. To what extent does an athlete own his or her likeness? A good example of the contours of the dispute recently arose over Tiger Woods' fight to protect the use of his likeness. *See* Marcia Chambers, *Lawsuit Pits Artists' Rights vs. Athletes*, N.Y. TIMES, Feb. 16, 1999, C19. The law of intellectual property is as it relates to sports is fully explored in **Chapter 13**.

Perhaps the purest of the privacy torts is the public disclosure of true private facts in a way that offends a person of ordinary sensibilities. This so-called true privacy tort takes place when a disclosure is made of facts that a reasonable person would wish to keep private because of the embarrassment that the disclosure would create. Once again, newsworthiness operates in the manner of a defense. The cause of action may well turn on whether reasonable people agree that a certain piece of private information about a celebrity is newsworthy or not. As can be seen, the tort lacks a clear profile.

The final privacy tort is false light privacy, which occurs when the plaintiff has been placed in a false light in the public eye. This tort is closely related to defamation, and, although the Supreme Court has not entirely settled the issue, it would appear that the defamation rules previously discussed would apply to this tort as well. In fact, false light privacy appears capable of swallowing defamation entirely in that a cause of action is stated for false statements whether they are defamatory or not. Although the statements which place the plaintiff in a false light typically are defamatory, they need not be. For example, in *Spahn v. Julian Messner, Inc.*, 43 Misc. 2d 219, 250 N.Y.S.2d 529 (1964), the plaintiff Spahn was able to recover for false but laudatory statements about him. (The *Spahn* case is one of the landmark cases that follow.) In *Time, Inc. v. Hill*, 385 U.S. 374 (1967), the Supreme Court held that plaintiffs in such cases had to prove actual malice in order to recover.

Problem

You have just completed an interview with Dickie Lane, the major league baseball star who plays for the New York Tromps. Lane wants to sue Sports Graphic, the nation's most popular sports weekly magazine, because of a cover article that recently appeared in the magazine. A picture of Lane appeared on the cover with a full-sized caption that read: "The Fast Life of Dickie Lane." The feature-length article was written by Sports Graphic writer Rich Plimpton. Part of the article consisted of a transcript of an interview that Plimpton conducted with Lane. (*See* **Problem**, **Section A**, *supra*, for more background concerning this article.) Another part of the article was written by Plimpton and it is material in this part of the article that Lane finds objectionable, for a variety of reasons. The relevant portions of the article are reprinted below. . . .

Little Dickie Lane

One theory which explains Lane's thirst for recognition and acceptance is psychological. Lane is the biological son of a minor league baseball player with whom his mother had an affair during the period of time that her husband, a Naval officer named Tom Lane, was stationed aboard ship in the Mediterranean. To this day, Lane does not know the identity of his biological father, and he was raised, lovingly by all accounts, by his mom and Tom Lane, who had 4 children of their own. The family secret, that Dickie was not really Tom's boy, was one that has been jealously guarded by everyone in the family. But Dickie knew from the age of eight, and it must have affected him.

Another theory. . . .

Dickie the Philanderer

By trailing Dickie Lane for two weeks while he was on the road, our staff learned that Lane's tiresome public posturing about family values is just that — posturing. While on a road trip to California, Dickie received special permission from owner Howard Tromp to stay for three days at the home of an attractive, aspiring, 22-year-old model named Fawn Rice. Other Tromp players told us that Lane has a similar, quiet arrangement whenever the club visits Chicago. . . .

The Sports Graphic article included two photographs, one a posed family photo of Lane, his wife and two young children, the other a photo surreptitiously taken showing Lane hugging Fawn Rice as she greeted him at the door of her Beverly Hills condominium. The caption under the first photo said:

"Lane, baseball's most visible family man, shown here with wife Lola and children, Millie and Billie." The caption under the second photo said: "Lane, shown here, giving a warm greeting to Fawn Rice."

You have learned that in much of the promotional material designed to sell subscriptions, Sports Graphic utilizes the cover which features Dickie Lane.

The facts as you have learned them from talking with Lane are as follows. Indeed, Lane is the biological son of an unidentified minor leaguer. But this fact has been jealously guarded by all the Lanes. Dickie does not know how Plimpton found it all out. To his knowledge, this had never before been publicly revealed. It is also true that Dickie himself became aware of it at age eight. Lane swears that he has never cheated on his wife and is a committed family man. In fact, Fawn Rice is his sister. Moreover, his other sister lives in Chicago and Lane stays with her whenever the team is in Chicago. He has been very discreet about all this at the request of Howard Tromp, who much prefers for the team to stay together at the team's designated hotel. Tromp made a special concession to Lane during his last contract negotiation, at Lane's urging, to permit Lane to stay with his sisters during road trips to California and Illinois.

Based on your knowledge of defamation and privacy law, prepare for your second meeting with Lane. At this meeting be prepared to discuss with Lane all of the possible causes of action. (Assume that the cases that follow are part of your research file, that the state cases are Oklanois Supreme Court cases, and that the federal cases were decided by the circuit in which Oklanois is located. You may also assume that Oklanois has a privacy statute like the one referred to in *Spahn*.)

CASE FILE

Defamation

TIME, INC. v. JOHNSTON

448 F.2d 378 (4th Cir. 1971)

DONALD RUSSELL, Circuit Judge

The defendant is the publisher of *Sports Illustrated*, a weekly periodical devoted to sports and athletics. Annually, it features its selection of "Sportsman of the Year." In 1968, it chose Bill Russell, a star on the professional basketball team of the Boston Celtics, as its "Sportsman of the Year" and engaged George Plimpton, a well known writer, especially in the field of sports, to write the feature article. In developing his article, Plimpton quoted from interviews he had had with persons acquainted with Russell and his exceptional talents as a basketball player. In quoting an interview with Red Auerbach, Russell's coach, Plimpton included in his article the following paragraph:

> "That's a word you can use about him — he (Russell) 'destroyed' players. You take Neil Johnston — . . ., Russell destroyed him. He destroyed him psychologically as well, so that he practically ran him out of organized basketball. He blocked so many shots that Johnston began throwing his hook farther and farther from the basket. It was ludicrous, and the guys along the bench began to laugh, maybe in relief that they didn't have to worry about such a guy themselves."

The "Johnston" referred to in the quoted paragraph is the plaintiff. At the time of the incident referred to, he was an outstanding professional basketball player with the Philadelphia Warriors basketball team. He subsequently retired from professional basketball and is now the assistant basketball coach at Wake Forest University in Winston-Salem, North Carolina. Following the publication of the article, he sued the defendant, contending that he had been libeled in the quoted paragraph and had been "damaged in his chosen profession, that of coaching basketball."

After discovery was completed, both parties moved for summary judgment. . . . The District Court, after argument, denied both motions, 321 F. Supp. 837, and both parties have appealed.

Upon application under Section 1292(b), 28 U.S.C., this Court granted leave to the parties to take an interlocutory cross-appeal.

We reverse the denial of defendant's motion for summary judgment and dismiss plaintiff's cross-appeal.

The defendant invoked, in support of its motion, the constitutional rule of privilege, granted under the First Amendment, as applied in *New York Times Co. v. Sullivan* (1964). . . .

There can be no dispute that at the time of the events discussed in the challenged publication the plaintiff met the criteria of "a public figure." "Public figures," within the contemplation of the rule in *New York Times*, as enlarged by subsequent cases, are "those persons who, though not public officials, are 'involved in issues in which the public has a justified and important interest'" and "include artists, athletes, business people, dilettantes, anyone who is famous or infamous because of who he is or what he has done." Consonant with this definition, a college athletic director, a basketball coach, a professional boxer and a professional baseball player, among others, have all been held to be "public figures." The plaintiff, as he figures in the challenged publication, fits this definition of a "public figure.". . . He had offered his services to the public as a paid performer and had thereby invited comments on his performance as such. In a sense, he assumed the risk of publicity, good or bad, as the case might be, so far as it concerned his public performance. The publication in question related strictly to his public character. It made no reference to his private life, it involved no intrusion into his private affairs. It dealt entirely with his performance as a professional basketball player; it discussed him in connection with a public event in which the plaintiff as a compensated public figure had taken part voluntarily.

The plaintiff does not seriously question the defendant's premise that he was a "public figure" at the time of the event discussed in the publication; and the District Court apparently assumed in its decision that the plaintiff was such a "public figure." The plaintiff points out, though, that the event, to which the publication related, occurred twelve years before the publication and nine years after the plaintiff had retired as a professional basketball player. It is plaintiff's position that he had, at the time of publication, shed his character of "public figure" and that the *New York Times* standard was, therefore, inapplicable. This is the basic point of difference between the parties on this aspect of the case. The District Court accepted the plaintiff's view. In so doing, it erred.

The District Court relies for its conclusions primarily on a comment set forth in a note in *Rosenblatt v. Baer*, (1966) 383 U.S. 75, 87, note 14: "To be sure, there may be cases where a person is so far removed from a former position of authority that comment on the manner in which he performed his responsibilities no longer has the interest necessary to justify the *New York Times* rule." This, however, is not such a case as was envisaged by Justice Brennan. The claim that plaintiff had retired as a player in 1958, nine years before the publication, is misleading. While plaintiff did retire as a player in 1958, he, by his own affidavit, "remained in organized professional basketball, until 1966." He thus identifies himself with professional basketball up to approximately two years of the publication in question. And, at the time of the publication itself, he was a college basketball coach, still involved as a public figure in basketball. Perhaps as a college basketball coach, he was not as prominently identified with the sport as in his playing days. Neither was *Butts* as intimately identified with football as an athletic director as he had been as a coach but that did not make him an anachronism in football history any more than the plaintiff, with his outstanding record, had become a forgotten figure among the many devotees of the game of basketball.

That even the plaintiff did not reckon his career as a professional basketball player forgotten is demonstrated by his claim in this case that a reflection on that career and on his eminence as a player damages him in his present occupation as a college basketball coach. By his claim for damages here, he is contending that his standing as a college basketball coach rests substantially on the public recollection and estimation of his former career as a professional basketball player; and it is for that reason he sues. It is because he is still engaged in basketball and because of the effect that any adverse comment on his record and achievements as a basketball star may have on his present position in basketball that he claims damage herein. It is manifestly inconsistent for him to contend that, when his basis for damage is thus grounded, his "public figure" career has become so obscure and remote that it is no longer a subject of legitimate public interest or comment.

The event to which the publication related remained a matter of public interest not simply because of its relation to plaintiffs own public career; it had an equal or greater interest as marking the spectacular debut of Russell in a career that was still phenomenal at the time of the publication. It was an event that had, in the language of one sports writer reporting it, a "tremendous psychological effect on the league," It was an event that was vivid in the memory of Auerbach at the time of the publication and likely in that of other followers of the sport. It is fair to assume that in the memory of basketball fans, the event described was neither remote nor forgotten; nor was it devoid of newsworthiness.

Moreover, mere passage of time will not necessarily insulate from the application of *New York Times Co. v. Sullivan*, publications relating to the past public conduct of a then "public figure." No rule of repose exists to inhibit speech relating to the public career of a public figure so long as newsworthiness and public interest attach to events in such a public career. This issue of remoteness as providing a basis for casting a veil about "public figures" in "public events" has often arisen in privacy cases. There are, it is true, distinctions between actions for an invasion of privacy and suits for defamation [footnote omitted] but the same considerations it would seem would be present in either case in determining whether mere passage of time will remove the protection afforded by the constitutional privilege created by *New York Times* for a publication relating to a past event in the career of a "public figure." . . .

In summary, we conclude that . . . because of plaintiff's classification of a "public figure". . .the defendant was clearly entitled to invoke the constitutional privilege afforded by the rule in *New York Times Co. v. Sullivan* and related cases.

The plaintiff, by his cross appeal, however, has raised the point that, even if defendant be entitled to a First Amendment privilege, the motion for summary judgment should have been denied because there was sufficient evidence in the record that the defendant had published the challenged item with actual knowledge of its falsity, or recklessly without regard to whether it was true or not and thereby lost its constitutional privilege. The District Court concluded to the contrary. Recognizing that, if the *New York Times* immunity rule applies, "summary judgment, rather than trial on the merits, is a proper vehicle for affording constitutional protection," where there is no substantive basis for a finding of "knowing falsity or reckless disregard." [Footnote omitted.] It held "that if the plaintiff were a 'public figure' or if he were otherwise amenable to either standard as set out in *Curtis Publishing Company v. Butts, supra*, he could not, as a matter of law, recover in this action and summary judgment should be granted in favor of the defendant." There is nothing in the affidavits and depositions now before the Court which would give substance to a finding of actual malice, as defined in *New York Times v. Sullivan*, or an extreme departure from the standards of conduct of responsible publishers, as enunciated by Mr. Justice Harlan in *Curtis Publishing Company v. Butts*. We agree that there is no basis in the record to support a finding of "knowing falsehood or reckless disregard" on the part of the defendant.

It is undisputed that Auerbach, whose statement is quoted in the allegedly offensive statement, was correctly quoted. So long as the press correctly quotes another's statement about a matter of legitimate public interest, does not truncate or distort it in any way, and properly identifies the source, recent decisions indicate that it may properly claim the protection of *New York Times*. It is the plaintiff's contention, however, that the statement of Auerbach, though admittedly made by Auerbach and correctly quoted in the article, was known by the defendant to be false and defamatory and that, because of knowing falsity, the defendant is in no position to claim immunity under the doctrine of *New York Times*. To support such contention he points to two phrases as being knowingly false and defamatory. These phrases are "destroyed" and "psychologically destroyed" which he argues, taken in the context of the article and giving them their normal connotation, were libelous and were refuted by material in the defendant's own files. Manifestly, the challenged words were not used literally. No one reading the article would have assumed that Auerbach was stating that the plaintiff was actually and literally "destroyed" during the game being discussed. Auerbach was attempting to identify Russell's emergence as a star basketball player; he did that by recounting an event which, as he saw it, marked the beginning of Russell, the star, and incidentally, the eclipse of the plaintiff as star. In describing the event, he used phrases of some vividness, used them in a figurative, not literal, sense, used a form of hyperbole typical in sports parlance. *New York Times*, in its application, does not interdict legitimate or normal hyperbole. To deny to the press the right to use hyperbole, under the threat of removing the protecting mantle of *New York Times*, would condemn the press to an arid, desiccated recital of bare facts. . . . And the records available in the files of the defendant, so far from refuting this opinion that Russell had on the occasion in question "dominated" and outplayed the plaintiff, gave support to that conclusion and provided a rational basis for Auerbach's perhaps vivid characterization. Thus, in an interview with Russell reported earlier in *Sports Illustrated* Russell himself claimed that he had "psyched" Johnston in this their first encounter. And the comment of both Russell and Auerbach on the rivalry between Russell and the plaintiff on this occasion found confirmation in the account written contemporaneously by the sports reporter of The New York Times, an account which was in the files of the defendant. The article put it that, "Basketball fans all over the country buzzed about it (*i.e.,* Russell's 'defensive wizardry') for days afterward." The adjective "psychological" was used both in this article and in other newspaper accounts in describing the impact of Russell's defensive methods on this occasion. There was thus no basis for any conclusion that the defendant was in possession of any fact that would have justified on its part a "high degree of awareness of . . . probable falsity" of the statement made by Auerbach. The District Court was accordingly clearly right in concluding that the record included "nothing . . . which would give substance" to a finding of "knowing falsity or reckless disregard" on the part of the defendant.

Affirmed in part, vacated in part, and remanded with directions that judgment be entered for the defendant.

Privacy

SPAHN v. JULIAN MESSNER, INC.

43 Misc. 2d 219, 250 N.Y.S.2d 529 (1964)

JACOB MARKOWITZ, Justice.

[Sections 50 and 51 of Article 5 of New York's Civil Rights Law provide a cause of action for invasion of privacy when the plaintiff's "name, portrait or picture" is used for "advertising purposes, or for the purposes of trade," without the plaintiff's consent. Warren Spahn, one of the greatest left handed pitchers of all time, (of "Spahn and Sain and pray for rain" fame) brought an action against the defendant, the publisher of an unauthorized fictional biography of Spahn designed for juveniles, to enjoin publication and for compensatory damages for the invasion of privacy.]

[The trial court found that the "breadth and depth of the offending characteristics of the book are so all pervasive as to render impracticable their complete recitation . . . ." The court then outlined the "offending characteristics." It noted first that the whole tenor of the book projected a false intimacy with Spahn. Dialogue was invented. Events were fabricated. For example, two chapters of the book dealt with Spahn's experiences in World War II. The book erroneously decorates Spahn with a Bronze Star for heroic acts that Spahn did not perform. Similarly, chapters dealing with Spahn's boyhood and teenage years inaccurately portray the relationship between Spahn and his father. The book romanticized the relationship, referring to "daily baseball sessions with his father" which never took place. With respect to Spahn's courtship, marriage, and family life, events and dialogue were entirely made up. The same is true of Spahn's baseball career. Throughout the book, events were taken out of context.]

While the essence of the right of privacy eludes precise verbal definition, it comprehends, in its pure form, the individual's absolute dominion and control over his "inviolate personality" — the individual's property right in his very being, whether manifested by his actions, his thoughts, his character, his appearance, his name. Dean Prosser, a leading authority in the law of torts, defines the law of privacy as comprising "four distinct kinds of invasion of four different interests. . . . 1. Intrusion upon the plaintiff's seclusion or solitude, or into his private affairs. 2. Public disclosure of embarrassing private facts about the plaintiff. 3. Publicity which places the plaintiff in a false light in the public eye. 4. Appropriation, for the defendant's advantage, of the plaintiff's name or likeness." (Prosser, "Privacy" 48 Cal. L. Rev. 383, 386). . . .

During its early formative years, the right of privacy was shaped to meet the protection needed against the excesses of "yellow journalism" and the unauthorized practices of advertising, then in their embryonic stages. Today, the right must be construed in the context of a society that cannot cavalierly dismiss the pragmatic realities of our day. Scientific advances have multiplied the potential for infringement of the individual's sanctity, and the demands of our highly complex industrialized society dangerously engulf and threaten the perimeter of man's ever shrinking sphere of personal liberty. . . .

While untrue statements do not necessarily transform a book into the category of fiction, the all-pervasive distortions, inaccuracies, invented dialogue, and the narration of happenings out of context, clearly indicate, at the very least, a careless disregard for the responsibility of the press and within the context of this action, an abuse of the public's limited privilege to inquire into an individual's life. . . .

Although so tightly interwoven as to defy extrication of the one from the other, the offending characteristics of the book comprehend a non-factual novelization of plaintiffs alleged life story and an unauthorized intrusion into the private realms of the baseball pitcher's life — all to Spahn's humiliation and mental anguish.

The subject purported biography transgresses the bounds of legitimate public interest by its breadth of reportorial coverage of those areas of plaintiff's life which defy classification as public, *i.e.*, his deeply personal relationships with members of his immediate family and his introspective thoughts. Quantitatively, these trespasses upon plaintiff's private life represent a substantial portion of the book now under scrutiny. Qualitatively, the colorful portrayal of the intimate facets of Mr. Spahn's relationship with his father and his wife and the revelations of his innermost thinking . . . in many instances places the reader in the uncomfortable position of an embarrassed interloper upon another's private and personal domain.

Compounding the effect of these unlawful intrusions, plaintiffs uncontroverted testimony and evidence establish that factual errors so pervade and permeate these areas as well as the entire book as to render the whole story an "embroidered" and "embellished" version of Mr. Spahn's life.

In effect then, the defendants have used Spahn's name and pictures to enhance the marketability and financial success of the subject book of which approximately 16,000 copies were sold at the retail price of $3.25 per copy. . . .

To return to the four category definition of "Privacy" by Dean Prosser, defendants have (1) intruded upon the plaintiff's solitude and into his private affairs, (2) disclosed embarrassing "facts" about the plaintiff, (3) placed the plaintiff in a false light in the public eye, and (4) appropriated, for defendants' advantage, the plaintiff's name and likeness. Such intrusion, disclosure and appropriation for commercial exploitation are proscribed by . . . the Civil Rights Law.

Accordingly, plaintiff is entitled to the relief sought; to wit, injunctive relief preventing the further publication and distribution of the WARREN SPAHN STORY in all its aspects and phases and is entitled to damages against both defendants in the sum of Ten Thousand Dollars ($10,000) and costs.

[The decision of the trial court in *Spahn* was affirmed by New York's intermediate appellate court (23 A.D.2d 216, 260 N.Y.S.2d 451 (1965)). This decision in turn was affirmed, without opinion, by New York's highest court (18 N.Y.2d 324, 274 N.Y.S.2d 877, 221 N.E.2d 543 (1966)). The Supreme Court of the United States vacated the judgment and remanded the case for further consideration in light of *Time, Inc. v. Hill* (387 U.S. 239 (1967)). On remand, the New York Court of Appeals affirmed, pointing out that the record supported a finding of "malice," as required by *Time, Inc. v. Hill.* Mercifully, the case was closed when the Supreme Court of the United States dismissed the subsequent appeal (393 U.S. 1046 (1969)).]

NAMATH v. SPORTS ILLUSTRATED

48 A.D.2d 487, 371 N.Y.S.2d 10 (1975)

Before KUPFERMAN, J. P., and MURPHY, CAPOZZOLI, LAND and NUNEZ, JJ.

CAPOZZOLI, Justice:

[In one of the most memorable games in the history of professional football, Joe Namath led the upstart Jets to an upset victory over the Baltimore Colts in the 1969 Super Bowl, played in Miami on January 12. Namath's performance was highlighted with photographs in the January 20, 1969 issue of *Sports Illustrated* magazine. The magazine subsequently used one of the action photos of Namath in many of its advertisements to promote the sale of new subscriptions. In COSMOPOLITAN MAGAZINE, the photo was accompanied by the heading, "The Man You Love Loves Joe Namath." In LIFE magazine, the photo was accompanied by the heading, "How to Get Close to Joe Namath."

[Namath claimed that *Sports Illustrated* violated his right of privacy under New York's Civil Rights Law, the same law Spahn relied upon in the previous case. The defendant's motion to dismiss was granted at the trial court level. The court here affirms that dismissal.]

Plaintiff sought substantial compensatory and punitive damages by reason of defendants' publication and use of plaintiff's photograph without his consent. That photograph, which was originally used by defendants, without objection from plaintiff, in conjunction with a news article published by them on the 1969 Super Bowl Game, was used in advertisements promoting subscriptions to their magazine, *Sports Illustrated.*

The use of plaintiff's photograph was merely incidental advertising of defendants' magazine in which plaintiff had earlier been properly and fairly depicted and, hence, it was not violative of the Civil Rights Law. . . .

Certainly, defendants' subsequent republication of plaintiff's picture was "in motivation, sheer advertising and solicitation. This alone is not determinative of the question so long as the law accords an exempt status to incidental advertising of the news medium itself". . . . Again, it was stated, at 15 A.D.2d p. 350, 223 N.Y.S.2d p. 744 of the cited case, as follows: "Consequently, it suffices here that so long as the reproduction was used to illustrate the quality and content of the periodical in which it originally appeared, the statute was not violated, albeit the reproduction appeared in other media for purposes of advertising the periodical."

Contrary to the dissent, we deem the cited case to be dispositive hereof. The language from the Namath advertisements relied upon in the dissent, does not indicate plaintiff's endorsement of the magazine *Sports Illustrated.* Had that been the situation, a completely different issue would have been presented. Rather, the language merely indicates, to the readers of those advertisements, the general nature of the contents of what is likely to be included in future issues of the magazine. . . .

KUPFERMAN, Justice (dissenting).

It is undisputed that one Joseph W. Namath is an outstanding sports figure, redoubtable on the football field. Among other things, as the star quarterback of the New York Jets, he led his team to victory on January 12, 1969 in the Super Bowl in Miami.

This feat and the story of the game and its star were heralded with illustrative photographs in the January 20, 1969 issue of *Sports Illustrated,* conceded to be an outstanding magazine published by Time Incorporated and devoted, as its name implies, to the activities for which it is famous. Of course, this was not the first nor the last time that *Sports Illustrated* featured Mr. Namath and properly so.

The legal problem involves the use of one of his action photos from the January 20, 1969 issue in subsequent advertisements in other magazines as promotional material for the sale of subscriptions to *Sports Illustrated.*

Plaintiff contends that the use was commercial in violation of his right of privacy under §§ 50 and 51 of the Civil Rights Law. . . . Further, that because he was in the business of endorsing products and selling the use of his name and likeness, it interfered with his right to such sale, sometimes known as the right of publicity. . . . Defendants contend there is an attempt to invade their constitutional rights under the First and Fourteenth Amendments by the maintenance of this action and that, in any event, the advertisements were meant to show "the nature, quality and content" of the magazine and not to trade on the plaintiff's name and likeness.

Initially, we are met with the determination in a similar case, *Booth v. Curtis Publishing Co.*, 15 A.D.2d 343, 223 N.Y.S.2d 737 (1st Dept.) *aff'd without op.*

11 N.Y.2d 907, 228 N.Y.S.2d 468, 182 N.E.2d 812 (1962) relied on by Baer, J., in his opinion at Special Term dismissing the complaint.

The plaintiff was Shirley Booth, the well-known actress, photographed at a resort in the West Indies, up to her neck in the water and wearing an interesting chapeau, which photo appeared in *Holiday Magazine* along with photographs of other prominent guests. This photo was then used as a substantial part of an advertisement for *Holiday*.

Mr. Justice Breitel (now Chief Judge Breitel) wrote: "Consequently, it suffices here that so long as the reproduction was used to illustrate the quality and content of the periodical in which it originally appeared, the statute was not violated, albeit the reproduction appeared in other media for purposes of advertising the periodical." . . .

However, this situation is one of degree. A comparison of the Booth and Namath photographs and advertising copy shows that in the Booth case, her name is in exceedingly small print, and it is the type of photograph itself which attracted attention. In the Namath advertisement, we find, in addition to the outstanding photograph, in *Cosmopolitan Magazine* (for women) the heading "The Man You Love Loves Joe Namath." There seems to be trading on the name of the personality involved in the defendants' advertisements.

This distinction between actual advertising use and use to inform, *cf. Bigelow v. Virginia*, 421 U.S. 809 (1975) means that cases like *Time, Inc. v. Hill,* 385 U.S. 374 (1967) and *Cantrell v. Forest City Publishing Co.*, 419 U.S. 245 (1974) involving so called "false light" portrayal are of only incidental interest. It is also a distinction accepted by Mr. Justice Breitel in that he recognized a right "to have one's personality, even if newsworthy, free from commercial exploitation at the hands of another. . . . " *Booth v. Curtis Publishing Co, supra*, 15 A.D.2d at p. 351, 223 N.Y.S.2d at p. 745.

The complaint should not have been dismissed as a matter of law.

[*Namath* was affirmed again, this time with no written opinion, by New York's highest court at 39 N.Y.2d 897, 352 N.E.2d 584 (1976).]

NOTES AND COMMENTS

1. *Cepeda v. Cowles Magazines and Broadcasting Inc,* 392 F.2d 417 (9th Cir. 1968), *cert. denied,* 393 U.S. 840 (1968). The "Baby Bull" Orlando Cepeda was the plaintiff in a defamation law suit that took over 5 years to resolve. Cepeda found himself trapped in a legal "pickle," in which the rules of defamation changed from one inning to the next. Although *Look Magazine* defamed Cepeda by saying he was "not a team man" and that he was "temperamental, uncooperative and under-productive," Cepeda was unable to show actual malice and eventually lost the suit. Interestingly, when Cepeda first brought the suit, he was under no obligation to prove actual malice. Cepeda was recently selected to Baseball's Hall of Fame.

2. *Dempsey v. Time Inc.,* 43 Misc. 2d 754, 252 N.Y.S.2d 186 (1964). Heavyweight champion Jack Dempsey brought a defamation action in the wake of a *Sports Illustrated* article suggesting that Dempsey used "loaded gloves" when he beat Jess Willard for the heavyweight title in 1919. According to the report, Dempsey's gloves were loaded with plaster of Paris. The court denied the defendant's motion to dismiss, saying Dempsey introduced sufficient evidence of actual malice.

In June of 1999, former prizefighter and actor Randall "Tex" Cobb was awarded $8.2 million in a defamation suit against *Sports Illustrated* and its parent company Time Warner. Cobb brought the defamation action after the magazine printed an article in 1993 alleging that Cobb and his promoter conspired to fix one of his bouts and then after the fight the two men snorted cocaine.

3. The modern sports celebrity will probably be viewed as a public figure for defamation purposes in most cases. This is particularly true if the account relates to the athlete's performance, as was the case in *Cepeda, Dempsey,* and *Cobb.* But what if the defamatory material relates to an aspect of the performer's private life? For example, how would the courts view a report alleging that the athlete is a homosexual? Assuming the allegation is false, a good argument could be made that the plaintiff is a private figure for purposes of this litigation, and need not prove actual malice, according to *Gertz.* And if the report is true, the plaintiff's claim would be for public disclosure of private facts, not defamation.

4. Intrusion cases are relatively rare, but it is easy to see how the tort might arise in sports. Owners of clubs, eager to protect their investment, might be moved to unusual lengths to check on the activities of their players. The tort might thus arise in the manner of an overzealous bed check. In the early 1960s, it was reported that the Yankees hired private investigators to follow players. One perhaps apocryphal account had the Yanks following Tony Kubek and Bobby Richardson. Kubek and Richardson had squeaky clean reputations, and, as the story goes, the Yankees wanted to see if they were "for real." The erstwhile keystone combination proved that their reputations were well-deserved. The Yankees reportedly came up empty after repeatedly following the two into ice cream parlors and Disney movies.

Al Davis, the renegade owner of the Oakland (or is it Los Angeles?) Raiders has on occasion implied a willingness to closely monitor the activities of his players. In another context, an overzealous press seems quite capable of intruding on an athlete's solitude in the quest for new information.

5. Misappropriation cases are bountiful. One memorable case is the so called Human Cannonball case, *Zacchini v. Scripps-Howard Broadcasting,* 433 U.S. 562 (1977). Hugo Zacchini perfected a human cannonball act. Without his consent, a television station video taped and broadcast Zacchini's entire act. (The actual time elapsed from take-off to landing was less than 15 seconds.) The Supreme Court found that Hugo stated a cause of action, and had the right to control the viewing of his act. *Compare Gautier v. Pro-Football, Inc.,* 278 A.D. 431, 106 N.Y.S.2d 553 (1951). Arsene Gautier, an animal trainer, performed his act at halftime of a football game. He sued when the act was televised without his permission. The New York court dismissed his claim.

The more common misappropriation case in sports arises when the defendant makes use of the athlete's name for a purely commercial purpose, without the athlete's consent. *Uhlaender v. Henricksen*, 316 F. Supp. 1277 (D. Minn. 1970), is illustrative. In *Uhlaender*, the Major League Baseball Players'Association successfully enjoined the manufacturer of a table game from using players' names without consent. The court held that the players had proprietary interests in their names, likenesses, and accomplishments, significant enough in degree to justify the injunctive relief. *Palmer v. Schonhorn Enterprises,* 96 N.J. Super. 72, 232 A.2d 458 (1967), is very similar to *Uhlaender.* In *Palmer,* a group of golfers successfully enjoined the sale of a golf game. While the court recognized that a celebrity's right to privacy is somewhat limited, the use of a celebrity's name for a commercial purpose other than the dissemination of news or information is invasive.

Orlando Cepeda lost another tough one in *Cepeda v. Swift and Company,* 415 F.2d 1205 (8th Cir. 1969). In the nightcap of Cepeda's litigation doubleheader, the Baby Bull sued Swift, a meat company, for the unauthorized use of Orlando's name, likeness, photograph, and signature in an advertising campaign promoting the sale of hot dogs. Cepeda had an agreement with Wilson Sporting Goods Company by which Wilson had the exclusive right to commercially exploit the Cepeda name. Wilson struck an agreement with Swift by which Cepeda baseballs could be purchased with wrappers from Swift products. The court found that, in light of Cepeda's agreement with Wilson, he had no claim against Swift.

Uhlaender, Palmer and *Cepeda II* are offered as examples of the legion of misappropriation cases. The basic, well-established principle is that sports figures do possess a limited "right of publicity" — a right to control the manner in which their personalities are commercially exploited.

For scholarly treatment on the misappropriation of an athlete's right to publicity, *see* James M. Left, *Not for Just Another Pretty Face: Providing Full Protection Under the Right of Publicity*, 11 U. MIAMI ENT. & SPORTS L. REV. 321 (1994); Derek C. Crownover, *Minor League Rights of Publicity are Major League,* 2 SPORTS L.J. (1995); and Pamela Edwards, *What's the Score: Does the Right of Publicity Protect Sports Leagues?*, 62 ALB. L. REV. 579 (1998). As already noted, these issues will be dealt with more fully in **Chapter 13**.

6. The preoccupation of the modern press with the private lives of public figures creates fertile ground for public disclosure of private facts causes of action. This was especially evident at Wimbledon in 1984, where the players complained about the propensity of the English press to report about their private lives. It is not at all unreasonable to anticipate litigation in this area. The litigation, in turn, will help define the parameters of the tort, particularly if the scope of the "news" privilege is articulated with some degree of clarity.

7. It should be noted that the Supreme Court has not, as of this writing, clarified the false light privacy rules. In *Time Inc. v. Hill,* 385 U.S. 374 (1967), the Court ruled that the plaintiff in such a case had to show actual malice. In the wake of *Gertz,* the question is whether *Time, Inc.* is still good law. If the defamation rules apply in the false light context, it would appear that *Gertz* modifies *Time, Inc.* in regard to the private person plaintiff.

8. Doctors who reveal medical information about their athlete patients might find themselves defending defamation or privacy suits. Weistart and Lowell address the problem as a form of medical malpractice at 989-90.

9. Even though an abundance of information relates to defamation generally, there is a paucity of information concerning specific sports cases and sports figures, which is surprising because of the number of defamation cases arising in sports.

One law review article outlines the referees' defamation case. *See* Melvin Narol & Stuart Dedopolous, *Defamation: A Guide to Referees' Rights,* 16 TRIAL 42 (1980). The authors, both of whom are attorneys and basketball officials, predict an increase in defamation litigation by referees. They attribute this to the unwillingness of sports officials to continue to be subjected to verbal abuses and the like.

Although the authors list several issues to be considered in the referees' defamation case, they concentrate on one. In their opinion, the key issue is whether the sports official will be considered a "public figure." Because of the exposure through television, radio, and print media, the authors would regard an NBA referee as within the public figure category. On the other hand, they feel a professional boxing judge would not fall into that category because of limited media coverage of boxing.

Some factors to consider in evaluating whether the referee is a public official are the level of competition being officiated; the number of years the sports official has been officiating; whether the athletic contest was broadcast on radio or television; and the sports official's notoriety in the particular sports community. In light of these factors, the official will fall on a continuum between public figure and private individual. At the public figure end would be an NBA referee. Moving toward the middle, the authors place there the Amateur Athletic Union and semi professional and other similarly situated officials. In the middle falls the college sports official. The high-school official would fall into the private individual classification. And clearly, volunteer officials in Little League and community center games would be private individuals for defamation purposes.

A recent scholarly article details the status of persons who once may have been considered public figures but who have since faded from the spotlight. *See* Elsa Ransom, *The Ex-Public Figure: A Libel Without a Class*, 5 SETON HALL J. SPORT L. 389 (1995). The article "examine[s] how well erstwhile public figures have fared under the public figure doctrine in the years since *Gertz v. Robert Welch, Inc.*" The author finds that, although "[o]nce public status acquisition is established, public status retention is likely to be presumed," such a "presumption has no place in libel law." *Id.* at 417. *See also*, Stephen G. Strauss, *Defamation and the Collegiate Athlete: The Case of Failed Reporting and an NFL Drug Test,* 3 SPORTS LAW. J. 51 (1996); and Mark Gatto, *An Athlete's Statements Regarding the Conduct of His Agent Can be Actionable Under State Defamation Laws,* 9 SETON HALL J. SPORT L. 263 (1999).

10. Problem. A Case Study — *Virgil v. Time, Inc.*, 527 F.2d 1122 (9th Cir. 1975). The causes of action arise out of a *Sports Illustrated* article entitled *The Closest Thing to Being Born,* The article is about body surfing at the "Wedge," a public beach near Newport Beach, California, renowned for its dangerousness. The article, written by *Sports Illustrated* staff writer Thomas Curry Kilpatrick, focuses upon the body surfers at the Wedge. The plaintiff, Mike Virgil, a well-known body surfer at the Wedge, has the reputation of being the most daring of them all. Virgil was interviewed a number of times by Kilpatrick, and the article featured information from these interviews, along with photos of Virgil. In relevant part, the article provided:

> He is somewhat of a mystery to most of the regular personnel, partly because he is quiet and withdrawn, usually absent from their get-togethers, and partly because he is considered to be somewhat abnormal. Virgil's carefree style at the Wedge appears to have emanated from some escapades in his younger days, such as the time at a party when a young lady approached him and asked where she might find an ash tray. 'Why, my dear, right here' said Virgil, taking her lighted cigarette and extinguishing it in his mouth. He also won a small bet one time by burning a hole in a dollar bill that was resting on the back of his hand. In the process he also burned two holes in his wrist.

Prior to publication, the article was reviewed by a *Sports Illustrated* "checker," who called Virgil to verify certain information. Virgil indicated he no longer wanted to be mentioned in the article. Virgil did not dispute the truth of the article. He told the checker he thought the article was going to be about his ability as a body surfer and that he did not know that the article would contain references to incidents not directly related to his body surfing. *Sports Illustrated* published the article over Virgil's objections.

Discuss fully all of Virgil's possible causes of action.

F. INTENTIONAL INTERFERENCE WITH CONTRACTUAL RELATIONS

Extraordinarily talented people are often in demand. This is particularly true when the talent is marketable. When this is the case, it is not unusual to see employers vying for the services of the peculiarly gifted person. This in turn gives rise to the classic fact pattern out of which arises the intentional interference with contractual relations tort. The landmark case of *Lumley v. Gye*, 118 Eng. Rep. 749 (1853), is illustrative of the classic fact pattern. In that case, opera star Johanna Wagner had entered into an exclusive contract to perform for the Queen's Theatre. The Queen's Theatre alleged that the defendant, a rival employer, had attempted to induce Johanna Wagner to refuse to perform for the Queen's Theatre. In a case that broke new ground, the court recognized intentional interference with contractual relations as a viable cause of action. The tort today retains special vitality in the sports setting as rival employers compete for the special services of especially gifted athletes and coaches.

The tort's modern profile requires the plaintiff to show that the defendant intentionally interfered with an existing contractual relationship of the plaintiff. The defendant must do something that either prevents performance of the contract or makes performance substantially less likely. The defendant must have actual knowledge of the contract and must act with the intention of interfering with the contract. The defendant can justify the interference by showing that, on balance, his right to compete with the plaintiff for the personal services of others outweighs the plaintiff's interest in entirely stable contractual relations. Thus, the defendant might be justified in seeking to open negotiations with someone who is already employed. The cases and material which follow explore the parameters of the tort in greater detail.

Also, a separate cause of action against the employee often accompanies the claim of intentional interference with contractual relations. Typically, the plaintiff in the contractual relations claim will also seek to enjoin the employee from performing for someone else. This "negative injunction" is a standard remedial tool in the entertainment and sports industries. To illustrate, note that *Lumley v. Gye* had a companion, *Lumley v. Wagner,* 42 Eng. Rep. 687 (1852). In that case, the Queen's Theatre sought injunctive relief against Johanna Wagner to force her to perform her contract and to prevent her from performing elsewhere. The court held that while Johanna could not be compelled to perform for the Queen's Theatre, she could be prevented from performing elsewhere. This is generally true today in the sports industry.

PROBLEM

You are general counsel to Sunbelt University, a private university in the State of Oklanois. Although Sunbelt is a relatively small school, it has a big time intercollegiate sports program.

You have just left a meeting with the President of Sunbelt, J. Twyman Pasquale. Pasquale was extremely agitated — in fact, the word "livid" came repeatedly to mind during what an only be loosely described as a conversation — about what he refers to as the "Billy Day Fiasco." Pasquale wants you to meet with him tomorrow to outline Sunbelt's legal remedies arising out of the fiasco. The facts are as follows:

> Up until 4 years ago, Sunbelt had a mediocre basketball team. It then hired Coach Billy Day. (Pasquale has claimed credit for this move). Day had just won the National Junior College Championship while coaching Western Texas Junior College (WTJC). When Day came to Sunbelt, he brought with him four players from WTJC. The next year, Sunbelt became a credible team and each subsequent year has brought with it increasing success.
>
> In fact, last year, Sunbelt had an overall record of 28 wins and 7 losses, and made it to the "Sweet Sixteen" of the NCAA tournament, thus making it the most successful team in the history of Sunbelt.
>
> Following the tournament success in mid-March, Pasquale personally negotiated a new contract with Day. The contract was a 5 year contract which made Day the highest paid university employee, with the exception of Pasquale. The contract was signed on April 1.
>
> On April 15, Day came into Pasquale's office and told Pasquale that he had just agreed to coach at the University of Oklanois. Oklanois, it seems, had been wooing Day for the past three years without the knowledge or consent of Sunbelt. As a graduate and former star player there, Day felt a special bond with Oklanois, and, somewhat reluctantly, agreed to return to his alma mater. Upon hearing all this, Pasquale refused to accept Day's resignation and told Day to "get back to work." Day has refused and, on May 1, Day moved to Oklanois. Since that time Day has worked as the coach of Oklanois, making numerous public appearances on behalf of the Oklanois program and preparing for the coming season. (It is now mid June).

Your research has turned up the following two cases. Assume that *World Football League* was decided by the Oklanois Supreme Court and that the *New England Patriots* case was decided by the Federal Circuit in which Oklanois is located.

Be prepared to meet with President Pasquale.

CASE FILE

WORLD FOOTBALL LEAGUE v. DALLAS COWBOYS FOOTBALL CLUB, INC.

513 S.W.2d 102 (Tex. Civ. App. 1974)

BATEMAN, Justice.

[At the time of the lawsuit, the World Football League (WFL) was a newly organized professional football league attempting to compete with the well-established National Football League (NFL). The Dallas Cowboys, a franchised NFL team, sought injunctive relief against WFL recruiting practices which it characterized as "raiding." In particular, the Cowboys complained about letters and return postcards that were sent by the WFL to players under contract with the Cowboys, urging the players to consider signing with a WFL team. In pertinent part, the letter read as follows:

> Dear Player:
>
> The World Football League will begin play in 1974 with franchises in twelve areas, including New York, Chicago, Detroit, Toronto, New England, Southern California, Hawaii, and Florida. The remaining franchises will be awarded from some twenty applications for membership under consideration.
>
> It is the intention of the World Football League to be "Major League" in every way, particularly in signing the top professional players available. We feel strongly that every player should honor his present contractual obligation. However, we would very much like to talk with you about the possibility of joining our League at the expiration of your present contract.
>
> In order for us to know your status and to contact you, please fill out and return the enclosed post card as soon as possible.

The postcards asked for information about the player, including name, address, and number of years remaining on contract and asked the player to indicate if he was interested in hearing an offer from the WFL.

[Three Cowboys (Calvin Hill, Craig Morton, and Mike Montgomery) signed WFL contracts to perform for WFL teams following the completion of their contractual obligations to the Cowboys. The Cowboys argued that the WFL was guilty of tortious interference with contractual relations and were granted injunctive relief at the trial court level. The Court of Civil Appeals here dissolved the temporary injunction.]

The Club argues that WFL is guilty of "pirating" its players and that unless enjoined it will continue to do so, but the only evidence of any contact whatever between WFL and the Club's players is the above quoted letter and the post card enclosed therewith. These writings do not suggest an unlawful "raiding scheme." The letter plainly states that the player should honor his existing contractual obligations and inquires only about the possibility of the player's interest in joining one of the WFL teams after the expiration of his present contract. There was no evidence of legal malice or deceitful means used by WFL or any motive or effort on its part to interfere with the contractual relations between the Club and its players.

The Club also contends that WFL arranged for, and induced three players to participate in, press conferences and various publicity activities surrounding the signing of contracts with WFL teams by Hill, Morton and Montgomery, thus causing a breach of the contracts between said players and the Club. In each of those contracts the player agrees "that during the term of this contract he will play football and engage in activities related to football only for the Club. . . ."

The Club's principal contention is that the signing of the Cowboy players by WFL teams for services to be rendered after expiration of their present contracts is an unlawful interference with the Club's present contractual relations with its players, as defined by the above provision of its contracts, because the players so signing will not use their best efforts for the team under their current contracts, the morale of the entire team will suffer, the enthusiasm of the fans will wane, and the new employers will reap the benefits of any favorable publicity for outstanding performance of the players so signing. The Club argues further that publicity resulting from the signing of such contracts for future services is a breach of the present obligations which the players owe to the Club.

These facts, even if true, do not present grounds for equitable relief. We must consider the freedom of contract of the individual players as well as the rights of the Club under its present contracts. Bargaining for future services is a matter of economics. The Club can assure itself of the continued services and loyalty of its players by offering them long-term contracts and other financial inducements. If it chooses not to do so for economic reasons, it has no legal ground to complain if the players look elsewhere for their future careers and enter into contracts for services to be performed when their present contracts with the Club expire. Signing such contract is neither a breach of the contract by the players nor a tortious interference by the future employers, and the threat to enter into such contracts affords no ground for equitable relief. Neither does the publicity necessarily attendant upon the signing of contracts with well known players constitute a tort. An injunction restraining the signing of such contracts because of the attendant publicity would be an unreasonable restraint on the freedom of contract of the players and their prospective employers.

We should not be understood, however, as holding that other promotional and publicity activities for the benefit of future employers would not be subject to restraint as "activities relating to football," which the players are bound by their present contracts to reserve for the Club. No such limited equitable relief was sought either in the trial court or in this court. The Club has cast its entire case for injunctive relief on its contention that the signing of contracts for future services would in itself be a tortious interference with the players' performance of their obligations under their present contracts with the Club. Since the injunction cannot be sustained on that ground, it must be dissolved. . . .

The temporary injunction is dissolved.

NEW ENGLAND PATRIOTS FOOTBALL CLUB, INC. v. UNIVERSITY OF COLORADO

592 F.2d 1196 (1st Cir. 1979)

ALDRICH, Senior Circuit Judge.

[In 1973 Chuck Fairbanks contracted with the New England Patriots, a professional football club in the National Football League, to act as its general manager and head coach. In so doing, Fairbanks breached his then existing contract with the University of Oklahoma. In 1977, Fairbanks' contract with the Patriots was extended through 1983. The contract contained a provision that Fairbanks would not provide services connected with football to any entity other than the Patriots. It also contained a provision that Fairbanks would not render services to another not connected with football except with the permission of the Patriots. In November of 1978, Fairbanks was approached by agents of the University of Colorado to become its head football coach. At first, the negotiations were secret. When Fairbanks agreed to terms with the University of Colorado, he informed Sullivan, the owner of the Patriots, of his intention to leave the Patriots at the close of the 1978 season. Sullivan suspended Fairbanks and sought injunctive relief against the University of Colorado. The district court entered a preliminary injunction enjoining the University of Colorado from causing the university to employ Fairbanks as the university's coach. The university appealed and Fairbanks was given permission to file an amicus brief. The First Circuit here affirmed the district court.]

* * *

Although this is not our first experience with the athletic milieu's response to legal embroilment engendered by contract jumping, we set out the factual contentions in some detail in order to get in the mood. For this opportunity we are primarily indebted to the Fairbanks' amicus brief.

The extension of the contract to January 26, 1983 was agreed to on June 6, 1977. The briefs are silent as to this date, an understandable reticence in view of the fact that by that time Fairbanks had, apparently, already decided he might not keep his word.

"For a number of years, Fairbanks was extremely unhappy with remaining in professional football [and] . . . with his present location. . . . Fairbanks believed the health of his family, and a reassessment of career objectives, *mandated a change*. Accordingly, for a number of years, he had been investigating business opportunities outside football, as well as coaching at the college level . . . ." (Amicus br. 8)(Emphasis suppl.) . . .

[Because] in 1973 the Patriots allegedly had lured Fairbanks from the University of Oklahoma, inducing him to break his contract there, defendants conclude that the Patriots are barred from relief by the doctrine of unclean hands. We disagree. Both parties may have done the University of Oklahoma dirt, but that does not mean unclean hands with respect to "the controversy in issue.". . .

[Equally,] we are not taken by Fairbanks' claim that because, when he told Sullivan that he was leaving at the end of the season and Sullivan responded that he was "suspended," it was Sullivan who broke the contract.

"The simple fact is that Fairbanks was fired." (Amicus br. 11). Whatever may be thought the meaning in the trade of suspension, as distinguished from its commonly understood meaning, it is a novel concept that a contract-breaker had the option to require the other party to accept his choice of dates. At least until Fairbanks withdrew his unlawful announcement, the Patriots had a right not to accept the services of an unfaithful servant, or, as Sullivan put it to him at the time, one who had "his body in Foxboro and his heart in Colorado."

* * *

At the hearing Fairbanks testified that although the contract read "services directly connected with football . . . [or for] another entity not connected with football," this meant, simply, activities competitively connected with the Patriots. Apparently he has no more regard for the parole evidence rule forbidding the contradiction of unambiguous language than for other rules foisted upon him by legalisms. Parenthetically, having in mind, as sometimes helpless dial-spinners, that professional and prominent college football teams compete for TV viewers, and hence, presumably, for the advertising dollar, we may wonder whether we have to accept at face value the protestation of no competitive activity here. In any event, there is ample authority contradicting both aspects of defendants' legal position. Indeed, some courts have gone even further, and have enjoined the defaulting athlete himself from noncompetitive sport. *E.g., Munchak v. Cunningham*, 4th Cir., 1972, 457 F.2d 721 (ABA player enjoined from play with NBA, prior to merger); *Houston Oilers, Inc. v. Neely,* ante (AFL player enjoined from NFL play, prior to merger); *Nassau Sports v. Peters*, E.D.N.Y., 1972, 352 F. Supp. 870 (NHL player enjoined from play in fledgling WHA); *Winnipeg Rugby Football Club v. Freeman*, N.D. Ohio, 1955, 140 F. Supp. 365 (player under contract to Canadian team and NFL team enjoined); *see also Boston Professional Hockey Ass'n v. Cheevers*, ante (chance of irreparable harm shown by players under contract with NHL team jumping to WHA); *American League Baseball Club v. Pasquel,* Sup. Ct., 1946, 187 Misc. 230, 63 N.Y.S.2d 537 (Mexican League enjoined from inducing American League players from repudiating contracts). We would not distinguish between an athlete and a coach. To enjoin tortious interference by a third party, whether or not competitive, would seem a lesser step. *See Winnipeg Rugby Football Club v. Freeman,* ante; *Pino v. Trans-Atlantic Marine, Inc.,* 1970, 358 Mass. 498, 265 N.E.2d 583; *Moore Drop Forging Co. v. McCarthy*, 1923, 243 Mass. 554, 137 N.E. 919; *American League Baseball Club v. Pasquel*, ante.

* * *

We comment briefly on the self-serving statement in Fairbanks' amicus brief that he is "through with professional football." There is no such finding in the record, and even though that may now be the conventional wisdom, neither the Patriots nor the court are bound to accept it. At this stage Fairbanks could be expected to say no less. Defendants' constant stress that the injunction is unproductive, and nothing but "punishment" in light of the fact that a position with the University "is the only game in town," is a total non-sequitur that cuts the other way. If there may, in part, be a punitive effect, we could not avoid wondering how great a miscarriage that would be with respect to one who, on his own testimony, promised a longer term than he intended to keep, not only to afford himself sanctuary while he looked around, but, again on his own testimony, putting himself in line for higher pay meanwhile, and whose seeming only defense to his announced total breach is a claim that the Patriots grabbed the gun.

* * *

Notes and Comments

1. Is it an interference with existing contractual relations for the soon-to-be employer to publicize the fact that a player has agreed to "jump"? The issue was touched upon briefly in both *Dallas Cowboys* and *Bergey,* which is discussed in **Note 4**, below. Both courts thought that the publicity which necessarily flowed from the signing was unavoidable and obviously not tortious. But a number of questions remain. While the player would apparently be able to attend a press conference to announce his intention to play for the new club at some later date, may the new club enlist the player to promote ticket sales while the player is still under contract to his old club? May the new club prevail upon the player to attend promotional events? Or would this be a tortious interference with the existing contractual relations of the old club?

2. Thus far, the question of intentional interference has come up in the classic *Lumley v. Gye* context. That is to say, the basic ingredient is a rival, competing employer wooing away employees under contract. Is the context the same when it involves a rival employer who attempts to convince the employee to play a wholly different game? By way of illustration, take the Danny Ainge case. Ainge is under contract to play baseball for the Toronto Blue Jays. Red Auerbach, general manager of the Celtics, tries to convince Ainge to play basketball instead. Is Red's conduct to be evaluated as though he was trying to get Ainge to play baseball for him? Or is Red's competitive privilege broader in this context? *See Toronto Blue Jays Baseball Club v. Boston Celtics Corp.*, 81 Civ. 5263 (S.D.N.Y. 1981).

3. Most of the professional leagues have bylaws which prohibit a club from "tampering" with players on other teams. The standard provision makes it improper for a club to "tamper, negotiate with, or make an offer to" a player under contract with another club (NFL Constitution and Bylaws, Art. 9.2 (1972)). The typical sanctions are losses of draft choices and fines. With such rules, the leagues deter conduct which is legitimate under applicable tort principles. Note that the no tampering rules, for example, would prohibit negotiating for future services, which is clearly not tortious.

Whether the various no-tampering rules preclude tort claims is unclear. Recent moves by star coaches and players may prove ripe for the tort cause of action. For example the major deals involving Pat Riley, the Knicks and the Heat, and also Shaquille O'Neil's move to Los Angeles from Orlando could provide grist for interesting intentional interference claims.

4. Problem This problem is based on *Cincinnati Bengals, Inc. v. Bergey,* 453 F. Supp. 129 (S.D. Ohio, 1974), *aff'd,* Civil No. 74-1570 (6th Cir., Aug. 27, 1974). The case is in many ways similar to *World Football League v. Dallas Cowboys Football Club.* But the attack on the World Football League (WFL) recruiting practices by the National Football League (NFL) Cincinnati Bengals (Bengals) franchise has a broader base, and issues not addressed in the *Cowboys* case are confronted directly here.

Assume that the case has been tried to a federal judge sitting without a jury, and that the following facts were presented at trial. You are law clerk to the judge and she has asked you to be prepared to discuss all aspects of the case with her.

The Bengals' offense. On the field, the Bengals are noted for their creatively successful offense. This philosophy carries over to their litigation. The gist of the Bengals' claim is that the WFL, and its member teams, are tortiously invading the Bengals' ranks by signing players under existing Bengal contracts to contracts for future services. The Bengals seek injunctive relief, contending that the WFL is irreparably harming the Bengals by intentionally interfering with existing contractual relations. One key argument made by the Bengals is that a player who signs a contract for future services with the WFL is likely to "dog it" with the Bengals. Another key argument is that these signings adversely affect the performance of the rest of the team.

More particularly, the Bengals objected to the WFL's signing of two players, Steve Chomyszak and Bill Bergey. On April 9, 1974, Chomyszak signed a contract to play with the WFL Philadelphia Bell. The contract provided that Chomyszak would begin playing for the Bell at the conclusion of his contract with the Bengals following the 1974 season unless the Bengals released him, in which case the WFL contract would "accelerate." Since the Bell had agreed to pay Chomyszak more than the Bengals, the Bengals argued that Chomyszak had an incentive to be "cut" by the Bengals in order to start playing for the Bell.

Bergey was under contract with the Bengals through May 1976 at a salary of $38,750 per year. On April 17, 1974, Bergey signed with the WFL Virginia Ambassadors. The contract provided that Bergey would begin playing with the Ambassadors in May 1976, at a salary of $125,000 per year. Like Chomyszak's contract, Bergey's had an "acceleration" clause which provided: "However, should Bergey be released from his contract with The Cincinnati Bengals, Inc. so as to be available for the entire 1974 and 1975 football season, then, in such event, the term of this contract shall cover the 1974, 1975 and 1976 football seasons or the 1975, 1976 and 1977 football seasons, as the case may be. . . ." Additionally, Bergey's contract paid him a $150,000 bonus, in consideration of signing. And finally, it was a "no cut" contract, payable even in the event that Bergey was cut from the team for lack of skill. Once again, the Bengals argued that this contract substantially interfered with their contract with Bergey because of the strong incentive it provided Bergey to be released by the Bengals.

In order to show the full effects of these signings, the Bengals introduced evidence concerning the nature of professional football. Bengals' coach Paul Brown testified that the success of a football team "comes down to nothing, really, but people" and that "if they're ever a bad character or boozer or chaser or what not, we're that much farther away from winning what we're trying to win." Coach Mike McCormick, of the Philadelphia Eagles, testified that the "individual sometimes has to suppress himself for the good of the team." He further testified: "I believe it's a game where, as the immediate supervisor, the head coach has to have control. I believe if a man is under contract to someone else, then that leverage and control has been taken away from the head coach."

McCormick testified that he believed that Bergey would be a divisive force on the Bengals. Four assistant coaches for the Bengals and one player elaborated on the theme. Football was a unique sport with required emotional commitments from every player to play with desire as a member of a cohesive unit. Contractual commitments to WFL teams tended to destroy this commitment. The trial judge concluded: "From all this the Court can and does find that football is probably unique in that, to a greater degree than other professional sports, it is a team sport. Also it takes time and money to develop the players and 'units' so that they will be cohesive. In short, football is a scientific, sophisticated sport, and a delicate sort of mechanism."

In summary, the Bengals argued that these signings had a detrimental effect not only on Bergey's and Chomyszak's performances, but on the other members of the team as well.

The WFL defense. In an effort to disprove the requisite intent to interfere with contractual relations, the WFL offered testimony that the signing of name players to future contracts was essential to the WFL's success. The WFL was not trying to interfere with existing contractual relations; it was attempting to gain public acceptance as a bona fide professional football league. The court specifically acknowledged that "starting a new league is a risky business" and found that "the WFL's motive for signing established NFL players is not to cause any harm to the NFL teams in general or the Cincinnati Bengals in particular, but to further the competitive interests of the WFL."

The WFL also introduced evidence to offset the Bengals' claim that the signing had a detrimental effect on team performance. Several players testified specifically that Bergey's performance was not noticeably altered by his signing. The gist of the WFL testimony in this regard was that the signings had no appreciable detrimental effect on team performance. Assistant Coach Chuck Studley admitted that he perceived no animosity among the Bengals as a result of the lawsuit, and that neither team morale nor team performance had suffered.

5. The argument has been made that a good contractual interference cause of action exists against agents who violate NCAA eligibility rules by signing or compensating scholarship athletes. Evaluate the university's cause of action against the agent. *See* Richard P. Woods and Michael R. Mills, *Tortious Interference with an Athletic Scholarship: A University's Remedy For The Unscrupulous Sports Agent*, 40 ALA. L. REV. 141 (1988).

In *Davis v. Baylor University*, 976 S.W.2d 5 (Mo. Ct. App. 1998), Tyrone Davis was improperly recruited in violation of NCAA guidelines by Baylor University. When the violations came to light Davis was barred from playing the 1993-1994 season. He later transferred to Kansas State and played professionally in Japan. He felt his career was hindered by the violations. Davis sued the university and a number of its employees for interference with prospective business opportunities, contractual interference, false light defamation, negligent hiring, and other related causes of action. This case is still on appeal at the time of printing.

6. This cause of action may also be viable when the sale of a franchise is thwarted. The "Giants of Tampa Bay" and the City of St. Petersburg recently filed suit against the City of San Francisco and others, alleging tortious interference with contract and tortious interference with prospective economic advantage. The case arose out of the efforts of the owners of the San Francisco Giants to sell the Giants to a group of investors from the St. Petersburg area, who wished to relocate the team to play in the Florida Suncoast Dome. *See Giants of Tampa Bay Ltd . . . v. City and County of San Francisco*, in the Circuit Court of the Sixth Judicial Circuit in and for Pinellas County, Florida, Case No. 92-4972-CI-18.

Chapter 13

INTELLECTUAL PROPERTY ISSUES IN SPORTS

A. INTRODUCTION

Other than the occasional opportunity for a fan at a baseball game to take home a ball that has left the field of play from a foul or homerun, the fans who provide the revenue, directly or indirectly, to support both professional and amateur sports are paying for the right to consume an intangible good. These goods take numerous forms, such as the right to enter a stadium or arena to watch a game in action, to watch a broadcast image or description of a game, to purchase a garment or souvenir emblazoned with a logo or name of one's favorite team, or simply the knowledge and satisfaction that one is purchasing a product that his or her athletic hero uses and endorses.

The public fascination with sports and sports figures fuels an industry that garners millions — even billions — in revenue. The opportunities to market and commercially profit from sports go far beyond selling tickets for admission. In addition to their salaries, accomplished athletes have tremendous financial opportunities through endorsement contracts with companies eager to have the athletes promote their products. In some cases, players earn more through endorsement contracts than from salaries and team benefits. For professional and many collegiate sports teams, the most substantial sources of revenue lies in reaching a national, even international, audience through broadcasting coverage and the reporting of sporting events through audio, visual, print, and virtual mediums. Royalties from licensing authorized merchandise sales of sports memorabilia generates billions of dollars in additional revenue.

Sports also provides financial opportunities for enterprising businesses or individuals outside of those directly involved with a sports franchise — sports bars and restaurants, the hot dog vendor outside the stadium, and the merchants selling sports memorabilia are only a few examples. Cities have been willing to finance sports facilities on the expectation that the sporting events provide an economic benefit for community businesses and thus enhanced tax revenue. With the lucrative market sports provides, other businesses, entrepreneurs, and individuals are eager to capitalize on the public's interest by providing services, products, or information — sometimes in competition with those directly involved in the sports industry or simply because of the investment of the sports industry.

In the business of sports, the value the players, teams, and owners hold, and the product essentially sold, is intangible. An athlete's reputation and performance may enable a vast earning potential in endorsements. Returns on the investments made by the players, teams, and leagues in establishing quality sporting competitions and creating fan interest and loyalty are realized through valuable licensing contracts authorizing rights to broadcast team or league games and to market merchandise bearing the team's name, logo or distinctive style and through corporate sponsorships.

Protecting these intangible assets is of paramount concern for all involved in the sports business — the owners, athletes, teams, leagues, sponsors, event producers and player associations (sports industry). The valuable yet intangible rights of the sports industry are at risk when outsiders seek to profit unfairly from the sports industry's investments. Determining what constitutes a legitimate, as opposed to unlawful, commercial use by outsiders involves examining the legal rights of the various parties.

A body of law, broadly encompassed as intellectual property, has developed to establish the ownership and property rights in such intangible, yet extremely valuable, assets. This chapter focuses on three primary areas intersecting intellectual property issues and sports. **Section B** explores the question of whether and to what extent an individual athlete has a proprietary "right of publicity" to control and profit from the commercial use of the athlete's identity (*i.e.*, name, nickname, or image) and likewise to preclude others from such usage. **Section C** introduces a range of issues involving the scope of trademark protection for team names, logos, symbols and other distinctive marks in the areas of sports merchandising, advertising and naming rights. **Section D** addresses the highly lucrative area of sports broadcasting, examining issues of copyright protection and ownership of sports broadcast rights, as well as the scope of rights to restrict others from broadcasting, reporting or otherwise profiting from the sporting event. This issue has become increasingly more complicated and relevant with the emergence of new technologies.

Revenue shapes the game and competition. As players' and coaches' salaries continue to soar, as witnessed by Alex Rodriguez' historic ten-year $252 million contract with the New York Yankees and an increasing number of universities paying Division I college coaches in excess of $1 million a year, the ability of team owners to "show [them] the money" depends on securing the revenue and protecting the valuable, yet intangible, intellectual property rights. In reading the following cases, consider the competing interests underlying the particular disputes to intellectual property rights in sports and what interests are served by restricting dissemination of intellectual property rights.

B. INTELLECTUAL PROPERTY RIGHTS OF ATHLETES — RIGHTS OF PUBLICITY

Is image everything? Accomplished athletes and sports figures are celebrities, even heroes, in the public eye. These athletes often stand to profit as much or more from their image and fame through lucrative endorsement contracts as they do from their professional salaries. Michael Jordan, for example, more than doubled his $31 million salary in 1997 playing for the Chicago Bulls, earning $47 million in endorsement contracts with companies such as Nike, McDonalds, Gatorade, and MCI, to name a few. Upon announcing that he was leaving Stanford University to become a professional golfer, Tiger Woods signed endorsement contracts worth an estimated $70 million before he had played in his first tournament as a professional. LeBron James similarly began his NBA career out of high school with a $90 million shoe contract with Nike. Tiger is currently the best paid athlete whose numerous endorsement contracts garner him nearly $100 million annually. The sister act of tennis stars Venus and Serena Williams broke records for female athlete endorsement deals. In 2002, Venus Williams signed a $40 million contract with Reebok, the highest endorsement fee ever paid to a female athlete in the history of sports. A year later, Serena surpassed that record in a reported five-year, $50 million deal with Nike. Other female athletes with lucrative endorsement deals include Anna Kournikova and Maria Sharapova in tennis, and Mia Hamm in soccer. The demise of one's image leads to a correlative plummet in an athlete's commercial marketability. Using the extreme example involving O.J. "The Juice" Simpson, Hertz Rental Cars presumably no longer saw value in O.J. running through an airport to promote Hertz rental services after his infamous murder trial.

Sporting figures are concerned not only about maintaining a semblance of privacy but also protecting their image from exploitation by others. As seen from the following cases, state law generally provides some protection, under a "right of privacy" and a "right to publicity" to guard the names, reputations and identities of athletes from commercial exploitation. Consider, however, whether and to what extent the law limits the commercial use of an athlete's identity by others. Should an athlete who has become a public figure be entitled to preclude others from using his or her name, nickname, image, picture or distinctive reference (identity) without consent or remuneration to the athlete? If so, what is the proper scope of this right?

PROBLEM

Mark McGee, the baseball homerun king, is commonly recognized as the "Sultan of Swat" due to his superhuman ability to hit the long ball. One day, McGee went to the toy store to buy a gift for his son's birthday party. While walking through the store, McGee discovered his picture on the packaging of a bat and ball set. The picture was of McGee hitting his 71st homerun of the season. The superimposed picture showed McGee in his team uniform with his face and number clearly identifiable.

Lou Ruth, a homerun king in the 1970s, also goes by the nickname Sultan of Swat and has played professional baseball longer than McGee. This nickname originated with Ruth during his high school days and followed him through college and finally into his professional career. In fact, a movie titled "The Sultan of Swat: The Story of a Baseball Legend" was made about Ruth and his historic career.

McGee has just signed a contract with Big Shoe Company where he agreed to let Big Shoe use his nickname for advertising purposes. The Big Shoe Company has agreed to compensate McGee by paying him fifty percent of all profits resulting from the use of his nickname in association with Big Shoe products. Ruth hears of McGee's lucrative deal and is very upset that McGee is profiting off the use of Ruth's nickname.

Does Ruth have legal recourse against Big Shoe or McGee? Does the fact that Ruth had the nickname first have any effect on the outcome of the suit? Must Big Shoe obtain both Ruth's and McGee's consent to use the nickname — or neither? What are Ruth's damages, if any? Howard Cozmel was the sports broadcaster who coined the "Sultan of Swat" nickname for Ruth, what are his rights, if any?

McGee also files suit, but against the company that has used his picture to sell its product without his consent. What is McGee's cause of action, if any?

CASE FILE

HIRSCH v. S.C. JOHNSON & SON, INC.

280 N.W.2d 129 (Wis. 1979)

HEFFERNAN, Justice.

Elroy Hirsch, the plaintiff, seeks damages for the unauthorized use of his nickname, "Crazylegs," on a shaving gel manufactured by the defendant, S.C. Johnson & Son, Inc. Johnson admitted in its answer that it knew that Hirsch is nicknamed "Crazylegs" and admitted that it marketed a product, a moisturizing shaving gel for women, under the name of "Crazylegs." It acknowledged that it had not received Hirsch's consent for the use of this nickname but also alleged that the name, "Crazylegs," was not exclusively used with reference to the plaintiff; and it denied any misappropriation or damage to the defendant. The case was tried for five days, and the motion to dismiss was brought at the close of the plaintiff's case.

Two legal issues surfaced as being controlling and were the subject matter of the motion to dismiss. The first is whether a cause of action for appropriation of a person's name for commercial use exists as a matter of Wisconsin common law. Johnson asserts that the cause of action for the appropriation of a person's name for trade purposes is part and parcel of the law of privacy and makes the further undisputed contention that the right of privacy has never been accepted in Wisconsin as a matter of common law and on numerous occasions has been rejected. The second issue is whether the plaintiff established a *prima facie* case of common law trademark or tradename infringement when he failed to allege or prove that his name had ever been used to identify a product or service.

We conclude that the plaintiff's pleadings and proof were sufficient to state a cause of action upon which relief can be granted under both theories. A cause of action for the appropriation of a person's name for trade purposes is different in nature from other privacy torts, and prior decisions of this court are not controlling. The appropriation cause of action protects not merely the right to be let alone but, rather, protects primarily the property rights in the publicity value of aspects of a person's identity.

In respect to the second issue, we base our conclusion upon the rationale that the trial court failed to consider the common law of tradename infringement (as distinguished from trademark infringement) and that, under tradename law, there need be no evidence of the prior marketing of a product or service under the plaintiff's nickname, "Crazylegs." It is sufficient to allege and prove the cause of action to show that "Crazylegs" designated the plaintiff's vocation or occupation as a sports figure and that the use of the name on a shaving gel for women created a likelihood of confusion as to sponsorship. We therefore reverse and remand the cause for a new trial. . . .

It is undisputed that Elroy Hirsch is a sports figure of national prominence. The testimony showed that Hirsch was an outstanding athlete at the Wausau (Wisconsin) High School, and thereafter he entered the University of Wisconsin in 1942. From the outset he proved to be a superstar of the era. In the fourth game of his first season of play at Wisconsin, he acquired the name, "Crazylegs." In that game, Hirsch ran 62 yards for a touchdown, wobbling down the sideline looking as though he might step out of bounds at any moment. Hirsch's unique running style, which looked something like a whirling eggbeater, drew the attention of a sportswriter for the Chicago Daily News who tagged Hirsch with the nickname, "Crazylegs." It is undisputed that the name stuck, and Hirsch has been known as "Crazylegs" ever since. We take judicial notice of the fact that as recently as June 24, 1979, he was referred to as "Crazylegs" in the Madison newspaper, the "Wisconsin State Journal."

. . . He played football with the Los Angeles Rams from 1949 until 1957. During this period his professional achievements included 1951 All Pro NFL, 1952 Pro Ball Squad, 1953 All Pro NFL, and in 1970 he was named on the All Time All Pro Team for the first fifty years of football. He received numerous other athletic awards, and as recently as 1977 he received the Hickok Golden Link Award, one of the few recipients in history, on the basis of his outstanding traits of character, as well as for his athletic performance.

During his career as an athlete Hirsch did a number of advertisements, in all of which he was identified as "Crazylegs." After his active playing days, he was a general manager of the Rams football team and assistant to the president of the Rams organization. In 1969 he became athletic director of the University of Wisconsin.

In addition to there being evidence of numerous commercials which used the name, "Crazylegs," there was evidence introduced to show that a movie was made in the 1950s of his life called, "Crazylegs All American." This movie is still being shown on television. Hirsch stated that he had been protective of his name and what type product it was connected with. He stated that he refused to do cigarette advertising and that he declined to do any advertising for liquor and that he had a beer commercial withdrawn after he became the athletic director at the University of Wisconsin. In each case his nickname, "Crazylegs," was used to identify him.

There was evidence to show that the usual minimum compensation for the use of an athlete's name on an unrelated product was five percent of gross sales. Two expert witnesses testified, and it is undisputed that these witnesses were experts in the business of representing celebrities in the endorsement of products or in licensing the use of athletes' names for advertising purposes.

On the motion to dismiss, the defendants argued, and the court concluded, that a cause of action does not exist in Wisconsin for the unauthorized use of a person's name for the purposes of trade, even assuming, for the purpose of the motion, the factual finding that Johnson was using Hirsch's name without consent. The court also concluded, consistent with the defendants' argument, that an essential element of the cause of action for a common law trademark infringement was the prior use of the name, "Crazylegs," to identify goods or services and that Hirsch had not produced such proof.

We consider these causes of action separately.

The defendants conceded that "Crazylegs" is the plaintiff's nickname and that Johnson marketed a product under that name. It is clear from the record that the plaintiff presented sufficient credible evidence upon which a jury could find, as a matter of fact, that the name, "Crazylegs," identified Hirsch and that the use of that name had a commercial value to Johnson. The question dispositive of this appeal, although not of the case on retrial, is whether as a matter of law a cause of action exists for the unauthorized commercial use of the name, "Crazylegs." Subsequent to the operative facts in this case, the Wisconsin legislature in 1977 enacted sec. 895.50, Stats., under the general caption of the "Right of privacy." One of the definitions of "invasion of privacy" is included in the provisions of sec. 895.50(2)(b): "The use, for advertising purposes or for purposes of trade, of the name, portrait or picture of any living person, without having first obtained the written consent of the person. . . ."

Under the law enacted by the legislature in 1977, Hirsch would now have a cause of action. This statute, however, was enacted after Johnson's "Crazylegs" product was taken off the market, and the question here presented is whether plaintiff had a cause of action under the common law. We conclude that he did.

The defendants' basic argument is that the right of privacy was never recognized by this court as a part of the common law. The defendants fortify this argument by pointing out that the statute enacted in 1977 denominates the unconsented use of a person's name for advertising purposes as an "invasion of privacy." We conclude that the right of a person to be compensated for the use of his name for advertising purposes or purposes of trade is distinct from other privacy torts which protect primarily the mental interest in being let alone. The appropriation tort is different because it protects primarily the property interest in the publicity value of one's name. Because the previous decisions of this court declining to recognize a right of privacy have not dealt with the appropriation tort, they are not controlling. From almost the very outset of the recognition of the right of privacy, there has been an intermingling or confusion of the right of privacy and the right of control of the commercial aspects of one's identity.

The right of privacy was first extensively discussed in a law review article by Samuel D. Warren and Louis D. Brandeis in *The Right to Privacy,* 4 HARV. L. REV. 193 (1890). A reading of that article, which has been denominated as one of the most influential ever written, makes it clear that the authors were concerned not with the commercial exploitation of a celebrity's name, but were rather concerned with the right of a private individual to be left alone and not to have the private affairs of even public persons gossiped about in the press. It drew upon decisions based on principles of defamation and actions for breach of confidence.

. . . But Dean Prosser in his article has explained that the right of privacy as it has evolved is "not one tort but four," which are "distinct and only loosely related." He also states:

> What has emerged from the decisions is no simple matter. It is not one tort, but a complex of four. The law of privacy comprises four distinct kinds of invasion of four different interests of the plaintiff, which are tied together by the common name, but otherwise have almost nothing in common. . . .

The four torts Prosser lists are: "1. Intrusion upon the plaintiff's seclusion or solitude, or into his private affairs; 2. Public disclosure of embarrassing private facts about the plaintiff; 3. Publicity which places the plaintiff in a false light in the public eye; 4. Appropriation, for the defendant's advantage, of the plaintiff's name or likeness." The fourth tort the tort of appropriation alleged by Hirsch in the present case Prosser points out is "quite a different matter" from the other three, because the interest is not so much a mental one as a proprietary one in the exclusive use of one's name and likeness. Therein, in discussing the tort of appropriation, the author stated:

> The interest to be protected here deals primarily with the individual's 'right of publicity' and not the right to be let alone in the classical sense of privacy. This concept of appropriation sought to prevent the use of a celebrity's personality without consent. Thus, the tort represents the protection of a property interest.

The term, "right of publicity," was apparently first used by Judge Jerome N. Frank in *Haelan Laboratories, Inc. v. Topp's Chewing Gum, Inc.,* 202 F.2d 866 (2d Cir. 1953). Judge Frank wrote:

> (I)t is common knowledge that many prominent persons (especially actors and ballplayers), far from having their feelings bruised through public exposure of their likenesses, would feel sorely deprived if they no longer received money for authorizing advertisements, popularizing their countenances, displayed in newspapers, magazines, busses, trains and subways. This right of publicity would usually yield them no money unless it could be made the subject of an exclusive grant which barred any other advertiser from using their pictures.

Building upon the rationale of Haelan, Melville B. Nimmer wrote in *The Right of Publicity,* 19 Law and Contemporary Problems 203 (1954):

> Well known personalities connected with these industries do not seek the 'solitude and privacy' which Brandeis and Warren sought to protect. Indeed, privacy is the one thing they do 'not want, or need.' Their concern is rather with publicity, which may be regarded as the reverse side of the coin of privacy. However, although the well known personality does not wish to hide his light under a bushel of privacy, neither does he wish to have his name, photograph, and likeness reproduced and publicized without his consent or without remuneration to him. With the tremendous strides in communications, advertising, and entertainment techniques, the public personality has found that the use of his name, photograph, and likeness has taken on a pecuniary value undreamed of at the turn of the century.

Hence, Prosser, Frank, and Nimmer stress the significant distinction between the tort of appropriation and other torts involving invasion of privacy. The tort of appropriation protects a property right, not only the right of a person to be let alone or to live his life in seclusion without mention in the media. . . .

Because the right of publicity the right to control the commercial exploitation of aspects of a person's identity differs from other privacy rights, it is appropriate for this court to recognize a cause of action to protect this right, although other privacy rights were rejected in prior decisions of this court. Protection of the publicity value of one's name is supported by public-policy considerations, such as the interest in controlling the effect on one's reputation of commercial uses of one's personality and the prevention of unjust enrichment of those who appropriate the publicity value of another's identity. Moreover, where, as here, the record attempts to demonstrate that Hirsch over a period of years assiduously cultivated a reputation not only for skill as an athlete, but as an exemplary person whose identity was associated with sportsmanship and high qualities of character, and where the record demonstrates that much time and effort was devoted to that purpose, . . . [i]t is a form of commercial immorality to "reap where another has sown."

* * *

The record is replete with evidence from which a jury could conclude that Elroy Hirsch's name indeed had commercial value. There was testimony that he had been paid for the use of the name in the past, and there was expert testimony by qualified persons who stated the reasonable compensation for the authorized use of his name or identity. That the tort is compensable is clear. As the commentator in *The Tort of Misappropriation of Name or Likeness Under Wisconsin's New Privacy Law,* 1978 WIS. L. REV. 1029, stated: "The rule is fairly well established that well known athletes have a property right in their identities and are allowed to recover for wrongful appropriation."

The fact that the name, "Crazylegs," used by Johnson, was a nickname rather than Hirsch's actual name does not preclude a cause of action. All that is required is that the name clearly identify the wronged person. In the instant case, it is not disputed at this juncture of the case that the nickname identified the plaintiff Hirsch. It is argued that there were others who were known by the same name. This, however, does not vitiate the existence of a cause of action. It may, however, if sufficient proof were adduced, affect the quantum of damages should the jury impose liability or it might preclude liability altogether. Prosser points out "that a stage or other fictitious name can be so identified with the plaintiff that he is entitled to protection against its use." He writes that it would be absurd to say that Samuel L. Clemens would have a cause of action if that name had been used in advertising, but he would not have one for the use of "Mark Twain." If a fictitious name is used in a context which tends to indicate that the name is that of the plaintiff, the factual case for identity is strengthened.

. . . The question whether "Crazylegs" identifies Elroy Hirsch, however, is one of fact to be determined by the jury on remand, and full inquiry into that fact is not foreclosed by the defendants' concessions in the present procedural posture of the case.

Accordingly, we hold that a cause of action for appropriation of a person's name for trade purposes exists at common law in Wisconsin. The facts adduced in the plaintiff's case prima facie were sufficient for submission to the jury. . . .

Additionally, Hirsch argued that the facts adduced established a prima facie case of common law tradename infringement. The trial court also ruled on this question as a matter of law. It concluded that the case did not involve trademarks or tradenames because there was no evidence showing Elroy Hirsch's name or the name, "Crazylegs," had ever been connected with a service or a product. The position of the trial court and the position urged by the defendant on this appeal is that no cause of action for tradename infringement will lie unless it is alleged and proved that the alleged tradename, "Crazylegs," was used by the plaintiff to identify goods or services and distinguish them from others. We conclude that this is an erroneous view of the law.

The misuse of a tradename is a portion of the law of unfair competition . . . Common law trademark and tradename infringement is a branch of the law of unfair competition, and the principles used in each are substantially similar."Passing off," or misrepresenting one's goods or services as those of another, and direct competition are no longer considered to be essential elements of a cause of action for unfair competition. The modern approach to the law of unfair competition holds that: "(P)roperty rights of commercial value are to be and will be protected from any form of unfair invasion or infringement or from any form of commercial immorality. . . ."

As the discussion herein has demonstrated, the publicity value of a celebrity's name is built up by the investment of work, time, and money by the celebrity. The economic damage caused by unauthorized commercial use of a name may take many forms, including damage to reputation if the advertised product or service is shoddy and the dilution of the value of the name in authorized advertising.

The court reached its conclusion that Hirsch proved no cause of action for common law trademark infringement because he proved only that the name, "Crazylegs," was used to identify himself and not to identify goods or services. In that conclusion the court was correct in stating that there was no proof that the name was used to identify goods or services.

The definition of "trademark" . . . requires use in connection with goods and services. Such use, however, is not required where a name meets the definition of a tradename. The trial court failed to consider whether Hirsch's use of the name, "Crazylegs," met the definition of a tradename. Restatement 2d, Torts, sec. 716 . . . defined a tradename "[a]s a designation which is used by a person to identify his business, vocation, or occupation, provided such use is not prohibited by legislative enactment or by an otherwise defined public policy."

Sec. 717 of the Restatement provided that one infringes a trademark or tradename if: ". . .without a privilege to do so, he uses on or in connection with his goods, services or business a designation which so resembles the other's previously used mark or tradename as to be likely to (a) cause confusion, mistake or deception, or (b) cause prospective purchasers to believe that (i) the actor's goods or services are those of the other, or (ii) the actor's goods or services emanate from the same source as the other's goods or services, or (iii) the actor's goods or services are approved or sponsored by the other, or (iv) the actor's business is the business of, or is in some manner associated or connected with, the other, even though the actor does not use the designation with a purpose to deceive."

There was ample evidence for a jury to believe that "Crazylegs" designated Hirsch's vocation or occupation as a sports figure, first as a player and later in management and administration. There was also ample evidence to show the likelihood of confusion as to sponsorship of the product as the result of Johnson's use of the name, "Crazylegs."

Hirsch testified that there was actual confusion and that people told him that they assumed that he was sponsoring the product, and in fact he received orders for the product. For Hirsch to show that there was an infringement on the tradename, "Crazylegs," there was no necessity as a matter of law that the name had previously been identified with products and services. It was sufficient to show that the name was one used to identify Hirsch in his business or occupation and that the use of the name caused confusion or mistake in respect to the approval or sponsorship of the goods. The court erred in dismissing the cause of action for tradename infringement.

* * *

We conclude that Elroy Hirsch made out a prima facie case under two separate theories: The appropriation of his name for purposes of trade, and infringement of a tradename under the common law. . . . Upon retrial under the appropriation theory, Hirsch must prove that the name, "Crazylegs," identifies him and that he has suffered damages based either on his loss or Johnson's unjust enrichment. Under the common law tradename-infringement theory, he must prove that "Crazylegs" designates his vocation or occupation and that there is a likelihood of confusion tending to make the public believe that he sponsored the Johnson product. These are questions which must be determined by the jury. Because the plaintiff's complaint was dismissed prior to a jury determination of the factual issues, the cause must be remanded for a new trial.

ALI v. PLAYGIRL, INC.

447 F. Supp. 723 (S.D.N.Y. 1978)

GAGLIARDI, District Judge.

Plaintiff Muhammad Ali, a citizen of Illinois and until recently the heavyweight boxing champion of the world, has brought this diversity action for injunctive relief and damages against defendants Playgirl, Inc., a California corporation . . ., for their alleged unauthorized printing, publication and distribution of an objectionable portrait of Ali in the February, 1978 issue of Playgirl Magazine ("Playgirl"), a monthly magazine published by Playgirl, Inc., and distributed in New York State by Independent. The portrait complained of depicts a nude black man seated in the corner of a boxing ring and is claimed to be unmistakably recognizable as plaintiff Ali. Alleging that the publication of this picture constitutes, a violation of his rights under Section 51 of the New York Civil Rights Law (McKinney 1976) and of his related common law "right of publicity", Ali now moves for a preliminary injunction., directing defendants Playgirl, Inc. and Independent to cease distribution and dissemination of the February, 1978 issue of Playgirl Magazine, to withdraw that issue from circulation and recover possession of all copies presently offered for sale, and to surrender to plaintiff any printing plates or devices used to reproduce the portrait complained of. For the reasons which follow and to the extent indicated below, plaintiff's motion for a preliminary injunction is granted.

* * *

Liability on the Merits

In determining the issues of probable success on the merits or sufficiently serious questions going to the merits of this action, it is agreed that this court must look to the substantive law of New York. To be considered are plaintiff's claims that his statutory "right of privacy" under § 51 of the New York Civil Rights Law and his common law "right of publicity" have been violated.

Section 51 of the New York Civil Rights Law provides in pertinent part:

> Any person whose name, portrait or picture is used within this state for . . . the purposes of trade without the written consent (of that person) may maintain an equitable action . . . against the person, firm or corporation so using his name, portrait or picture, to prevent and restrain the use thereof; and may also sue and recover damages for any injury sustained by reason of such use . . .

Defendants do not, and indeed cannot, seriously dispute the assertion that the offensive drawing is in fact Ali's "portrait or picture." This phrase, as used in § 51, is not restricted to photographs, but generally comprises those representations which are recognizable as likenesses of the complaining individual. Even a cursory inspection of the picture which is the subject of this action strongly suggests that the facial characteristics of the black male portrayed are those of Muhammad Ali. The cheekbones, broad nose and wideset brown eyes, together with the distinctive smile and close cropped black hair are recognizable as the features of the plaintiff, one of the most widely known athletes of our time. In addition, the figure depicted is seated on a stool in the corner of a boxing ring with both hands taped and outstretched resting on the ropes on either side. Although the picture is captioned "Mystery Man," the identification of the individual as Ali is further implied by an accompanying verse which refers to the figure as "the Greatest". This court may take judicial notice that plaintiff Ali has regularly claimed that appellation for himself and that his efforts to identify himself in the public mind as "the Greatest" have been so successful that he is regularly identified as such in the news media.

It is also clear that the picture has been used for the "purpose of trade" within the meaning of § 51. In this regard it is the established law of New York that the unauthorized use of an individual's picture is not for a " trade purpose," and thus not violative of § 51, if it is "in connection with an item of news or one that is newsworthy." In the instant case there is no such informational or newsworthy dimension to defendants' unauthorized use of Ali's likeness. Instead, the picture is a dramatization, an illustration falling somewhere between representational art and cartoon, and is accompanied by a plainly fictional and allegedly libelous bit of doggerel. Defendants cannot be said to have presented "the unembroidered dissemination of facts" or "the unvarnished, unfictionalized truth." The nude portrait was clearly included in the magazine solely "for purposes of trade *e.g.*, merely to attract attention."

Finally, defendants concede that Ali did not consent to the inclusion of his likeness in the February, 1978 Playgirl Magazine. Defendants contend, however, that even if their use of Ali's likeness is determined to be unauthorized and for trade purposes, the statutory right of privacy does not extend to protect "someone such as an athlete . . . who chooses to bring himself to public notice, who chooses, indeed, as clearly as the plaintiff here does to rather stridently seek out publicity." Defendants are plainly in error in disputing liability on the basis of Ali's status as a public personality. Such a contention "confuses the fact that projection into the public arena may make for newsworthiness of one's activities, and all the hazards of publicity thus entailed, with the quite different and independent right to have one's personality, even if newsworthy, free from commercial exploitation at the hands of another . . . That (plaintiff) may have voluntarily on occasion surrendered (his) privacy, for a price or gratuitously, does not forever forfeit for anyone's commercial profit so much of (his) privacy as (he) has not relinquished."

Accordingly, this court is satisfied that plaintiff Ali has established probable success on the merits of his . . . claim that his right of publicity has been violated by the publication of the offensive portrait. This Circuit has long held that New York recognizes the common law property right of publicity in addition to, and distinct from, the statutory right under § 51.

It must be noted, however, that the courts of New York do not regularly distinguish between the proprietary right of publicity, and the § 51 right of privacy. The latter has been characterized as establishing and limiting the right of a person "to be left alone" and protecting "the sentiments, thoughts and feelings of an individual . . . from (unwanted) commercial exploitation," but numerous cases blend the concepts together and expressly recognize a right of recovery under § 51 for violations of an individual's property interest in his likeness or reputation.

The distinctive aspect of the common law right of publicity is that it recognizes the commercial value of the picture or representation of a prominent person or performer, and protects his proprietary interest in the profitability of his public reputation or "persona." [I]ndependent of his § 51 rights, "a man has a right in the publicity value of his photograph, *i.e.*, the right to grant the exclusive privilege of publishing his picture." . . . This common law publicity right is analogous to a commercial entity's right to profit from the "goodwill" it has built up in its name, and the interest which underlies protecting the right of publicity " 'is the straightforward one of preventing unjust enrichment by the theft of good will.' "

Accordingly, this right of publicity is usually asserted only if the plaintiff has "achieved in some degree a celebrated status." In the instant case, it is undisputed that plaintiff Ali has achieved such a "celebrated status" and it is clear to this court that he has established a valuable interest in his name and his likeness. [T] his court "can take judicial notice that there is a fairly active market for exploitation of the faces, names and reputations of celebrities." There can be little question that defendants' unauthorized publication of the portrait of Ali amounted to a wrongful appropriation of the market value of plaintiff's likeness. . . .

Irreparable Injury

As has been noted, in the course of his public career plaintiff has established a commercially valuable proprietary interest in his likeness and reputation, analogous to the good will accumulated in the name of a successful business entity. To the extent that defendants are unlawfully appropriating this valuable commodity for themselves, proof of damages or unjust enrichment may be extremely difficult. In virtually identical circumstances it has been observed that "a celebrity's property interest in his name and likeness is unique, and therefore there is no serious question as to the propriety of injunctive relief." Furthermore, defendants appear not only to be usurping plaintiff's valuable right of publicity for themselves but may well be inflicting damage upon this marketable reputation. As described previously, the "likeness" of Ali which has been published is a full frontal nude drawing, not merely a sketch or photograph of him as he appears in public. Damages from such evident abuse of plaintiff's property right in his public reputation are plainly difficult to measure by monetary standards. As this Circuit has noted in the preliminary injunction context, "difficulty (in computing damages) is especially common when damage to reputation, credibility or good will is present." Such difficulty in determining monetary damages leaves plaintiff without an adequate remedy at law and satisfactorily establishes irreparable injury for purposes for preliminary equitable relief.

* * *

Defendant Playgirl, Inc., is hereby enjoined from further distribution and dissemination of any copies of the February, 1978 issue of Playgirl Magazine containing the portrait complained of, and shall neither transfer nor remove from the jurisdiction any such copies presently in its custody, as well as the printing plates or devices used to reproduce the portrait, until further order of the court.

ETW CORPORATION, v. JIREH PUBLISHING, INC.

332 F.3d 915 (6th Cir. 2001)

GRAHAM, D.J., delivered the opinion of the court, in which SILER, J., joined.

Plaintiff-Appellant ETW Corporation ("ETW") is the licensing agent of Eldrick "Tiger" Woods ("Woods"), one of the world's most famous professional golfers. Woods, chairman of the board of ETW, has assigned to it the exclusive right to exploit his name, image, likeness, and signature, and all other publicity rights. ETW owns a United States trademark registration for the mark "TIGER WOODS" for use in connection with "art prints, calendars, mounted photographs, notebooks, pencils, pens, posters, trading cards, and unmounted photographs."

Defendant-Appellee Jireh Publishing, Inc. ("Jireh") is the publisher of artwork created by Rick Rush ("Rush"). Rush, who refers to himself as "America's sports artist," has created paintings of famous figures in sports and famous sports events. A few examples include Michael Jordan, Mark McGuire, Coach Paul "Bear" Bryant, the Pebble Beach Golf Tournament, and the America's Cup Yacht Race. Jireh has produced and successfully marketed limited edition art prints made from Rush's paintings.

In 1998, Rush created a painting entitled The Masters of Augusta, which commemorates Woods's victory at the Masters Tournament in Augusta, Georgia, in 1997. At that event, Woods became the youngest player ever to win the Masters Tournament, while setting a 72-hole record for the tournament and a record 12-stroke margin of victory. In the foreground of Rush's painting are three views of Woods in different poses. In the center, he is completing the swing of a golf club, and on each side he is crouching, lining up and/or observing the progress of a putt. To the left of Woods is his caddy, Mike "Fluff" Cowan, and to his right is his final round partner's caddy. Behind these figures is the Augusta National Clubhouse. In a blue background behind the clubhouse are likenesses of famous golfers of the past looking down on Woods. These include Arnold Palmer, Sam Snead, Ben Hogan, Walter Hagen, Bobby Jones, and Jack Nicklaus. Behind them is the Masters leader board.

The limited edition prints distributed by Jireh consist of an image of Rush's painting which includes Rush's signature at the bottom right hand corner. Beneath the image of the painting, in block letters, is its title, "The Masters Of Augusta." Beneath the title, in block letters of equal height, is the artist's name, "Rick Rush," and beneath the artist's name, in smaller upper and lower case letters, is the legend "Painting America Through Sports."

As sold by Jireh, the limited edition prints are enclosed in a white envelope, accompanied with literature which includes a large photograph of Rush, a description of his art, and a narrative description of the subject painting. On the front of the envelope, Rush's name appears in block letters inside a rectangle, which includes the legend "Painting America Through Sports." Along the bottom is a large reproduction of Rush's signature two inches high and ten inches long. On the back of the envelope, under the flap, are the words "Masters of Augusta" in letters that are three-eights of an inch high, and "Tiger Woods" in letters that are one-fourth of an inch high. Woods's name also appears in the narrative description of the painting where he is mentioned twice in twenty-eight lines of text. The text also includes references to the six other famous golfers depicted in the background of the painting as well as the two caddies. Jireh published and marketed two hundred and fifty 22½ x 30 serigraphs and five thousand 9 x 11 lithographs of The Masters of Augusta at an issuing price of $700 for the serigraphs and $100 for the lithographs.

ETW filed suit against Jireh, in the United States District Court for the Northern District of Ohio, alleging trademark infringement in violation of the Lanham Act, 15 U.S.C. § 1114; . . . unfair competition and false advertising . . .; and violation of Woods's right of publicity under Ohio common law. Jireh counterclaimed, seeking a declaratory judgment that Rush's art prints are protected by the First Amendment.

The district court granted Jireh's motion for summary judgment and dismissed the case. ETW timely perfected an appeal to this court. We review the district court's grant of summary judgment de novo.

II. Trademark Claims Based on the Unauthorized Use of the Registered Trademark "Tiger Woods"

ETW claims that the prints of Rush's work constitute the unauthorized use of a registered trademark in violation of the Lanham Act, and Ohio law. ETW claims that Jireh infringed the registered mark "Tiger Woods" by including these words in marketing materials which accompanied the prints of Rush's painting. The words "Tiger Woods" do not appear on the face of the prints, nor are they included in the title of the painting. The words "Tiger Woods" do appear under the flap of the envelopes which contain the prints, and Woods is mentioned twice in the narrative which accompanies the prints.

The Lanham Act provides a defense to an infringement claim where the use of the mark "is a use, otherwise than as a mark, . . . which is descriptive of and used fairly and in good faith only to describe the goods . . . of such party

A celebrity's name may be used in the title of an artistic work so long as there is some artistic relevance. The use of Woods's name on the back of the envelope containing the print and in the narrative description of the print are purely descriptive and there is nothing to indicate that they were used other than in good faith. The prints, the envelopes which contain them, and the narrative materials which accompany them clearly identify Rush as the source of the print. Woods is mentioned only to describe the content of the print.

The district court properly granted summary judgment on ETW's claim for violation of its registered mark, "Tiger Woods," on the grounds that the claim was barred by the fair use defense as a matter of law. . . .

IV. Lanham Act Unfair Competition and False Endorsement Claims, Ohio Right to Privacy Claims, and the First Amendment Defense

ETW's claims . . . include claims of unfair competition and false advertising in the nature of false endorsement. ETW has also asserted a claim for infringement of the right of publicity under Ohio law. The elements of a Lanham Act false endorsement claim are similar to the elements of a right of publicity claim under Ohio law. In addition, Jireh has raised the First Amendment as a defense to all of ETW's claims, arguing that Rush's use of Woods's image in his painting is protected expression. . . .

B. First Amendment Defense

The protection of the First Amendment is not limited to written or spoken words, but includes other mediums of expression, including music, pictures, films, photographs, paintings, drawings, engravings, prints, and sculptures. Speech is protected even though it is carried in a form that is sold for profit. The fact that expressive materials are sold does not diminish the degree of protection to which they are entitled under the First Amendment. Publishers disseminating the work of others who create expressive materials also come wholly within the protective shield of the First Amendment. Even pure commercial speech is entitled to significant First Amendment protection. Commercial speech is "speech which does 'no more than propose a commercial transaction [.]' "

Rush's prints are not commercial speech. They do not propose a commercial transaction. Accordingly, they are entitled to the full protection of the First Amendment. Thus, we are called upon to decide whether Woods's intellectual property rights must yield to Rush's First Amendment rights.

* * *

D. Right of Publicity Claim

ETW claims that Jireh's publication and marketing of prints of Rush's painting violates Woods's right of publicity. The right of publicity is an intellectual property right of recent origin which has been defined as the inherent right of every human being to control the commercial use of his or her identity. The right of publicity is a creature of state law and its violation gives rise to a cause of action for the commercial tort of unfair competition.

The right of publicity is, somewhat paradoxically, an outgrowth of the right of privacy. A cause of action for violation of the right was first recognized in *Haelan Laboratories, Inc. v. Topps Chewing Gum, Inc.*, 202 F.2d 866 (2nd Cir.1953), where the Second Circuit held that New York's common law protected a baseball player's right in the publicity value of his photograph, and in the process coined the phrase "right of publicity" as the name of this right. . . .

When the Ohio Supreme Court recognized the right of publicity, it relied heavily on the restatement (Second) Of Torts, § 652. The Restatement originally treated the right of publicity as a branch of the right of privacy and included it in a chapter entitled "Invasion of Privacy." In 1995, the American Law Institute transferred its exposition of the right of publicity to the restatement (Third) Of Unfair Competition, Chapter 4, in a chapter entitled "Appropriation of Trade Values." The current version of the Restatement (Third) Of Unfair Competition defines the right of publicity as follows:

> Appropriation of the Commercial Value of a Person's Identity: The Right of Publicity
>
> One who appropriates the commercial value of a person's identity by using without consent the person's name, likeness, or other indicia of identity for purposes of trade is subject to liability for the relief appropriate under the rules stated in §§ 48 and 49.

In § 46, Comment c, Rationale for Protection, the authors of the Restatement suggest that courts may justifiably be reluctant to adopt a broad construction of the right. The rationales underlying recognition of a right of publicity are generally less compelling than those that justify rights in trademarks or trade secrets. The commercial value of a person's identity often results from success in endeavors such as entertainment or sports that offer their own substantial rewards. Any additional incentive attributable to the right of publicity may have only marginal significance. In other cases the commercial value acquired by a person's identity is largely fortuitous or otherwise unrelated to any investment made by the individual, thus diminishing the weight of the property and unjust enrichment rationales for protection. In addition, the public interest in avoiding false suggestions of endorsement or sponsorship can be pursued through the cause of action for deceptive marketing. Thus, courts may be properly reluctant to adopt a broad construction of the publicity right. *See* § 47.

The authors of the Restatement note, "The right of publicity as recognized by statute and common law is fundamentally constrained by the public and constitutional interest in freedom of expression." In the same comment, the authors state that "[t]he use of a person's identity primarily for the purpose of communicating information or expressing ideas is not generally actionable as a violation of the person's right of publicity." Various examples are given, including the use of the person's name or likeness in news reporting in newspapers and magazines. The Restatement recognizes that this limitation on the right is not confined to news reporting but extends to use in "entertainment and other creative works, including both fiction and non-fiction." The authors list examples of protected uses of a celebrity's identity, likeness or image, including unauthorized print or broadcast biographies and novels, plays or motion pictures. According to the Restatement, such uses are not protected, however, if the name or likeness is used solely to attract attention to a work that is not related to the identified person, and the privilege may be lost if the work contains substantial falsifications.

We believe the courts of Ohio would follow the principles of the Restatement in defining the limits of the right of publicity . . . [and] give substantial weight to the public interest in freedom of expression when balancing it against the personal and proprietary interests recognized by the right of publicity. . . .

There is an inherent tension between the right of publicity and the right of freedom of expression under the First Amendment. This tension becomes particularly acute when the person seeking to enforce the right is a famous actor, athlete, politician, or otherwise famous person whose exploits, activities, accomplishments, and personal life are subject to constant scrutiny and comment in the public media. In Memphis Development Foundation, this court discussed the problems of judicial line drawing that would arise if it should recognize the inheritability of publicity rights, including the question "[a]t what point does the right collide with the right of free expression guaranteed by the First Amendment?"

* * *

In deciding where the line should be drawn between Woods's intellectual property rights and the First Amendment . . . [w]e turn now to a further examination of Rush's work and its subject.

E. Application of the Law to the Evidence in this Case

The evidence in the record reveals that Rush's work consists of much more than a mere literal likeness of Woods. It is a panorama of Woods's victory at the 1997 Masters Tournament, with all of the trappings of that tournament in full view, including the Augusta clubhouse, the leader board, images of Woods's caddy, and his final round partner's caddy. These elements in themselves are sufficient to bring Rush's work within the protection of the First Amendment. The Masters Tournament is probably the world's most famous golf tournament and Woods's victory in the 1997 tournament was a historic event in the world of sports. A piece of art that portrays a historic sporting event communicates and celebrates the value our culture attaches to such events. It would be ironic indeed if the presence of the image of the victorious athlete would deny the work First Amendment protection. Furthermore, Rush's work includes not only images of Woods and the two caddies, but also carefully crafted likenesses of six past winners of the Masters Tournament: Arnold Palmer, Sam Snead, Ben Hogan, Walter Hagen, Bobby Jones, and Jack Nicklaus, a veritable pantheon of golf's greats. Rush's work conveys the message that Woods himself will someday join that revered group.

* * *

In regard to the Ohio law right of publicity claim, we conclude that Ohio would construe its right of publicity as suggested in the restatement (Third) Of Unfair Competition, which articulates a rule analogous to the rule of fair use in copyright law. Under this rule, the substantiality and market effect of the use of the celebrity's image is analyzed in light of the informational and creative content of the defendant's use. Applying this rule, we conclude that Rush's work has substantial informational and creative content which outweighs any adverse effect on ETW's market and that Rush's work does not violate Woods's right of publicity.

We further find that Rush's work is expression which is entitled to the full protection of the First Amendment and not the more limited protection afforded to commercial speech.

When we balance the magnitude of the speech restriction against the interest in protecting Woods's intellectual property , . . . we note that Woods, like most sports and entertainment celebrities with commercially valuable identities, engages in an activity, professional golf, that in itself generates a significant amount of income which is unrelated to his right of publicity. Even in the absence of his right of publicity, he would still be able to reap substantial financial rewards from authorized appearances and endorsements. It is not at all clear that the appearance of Woods's likeness in artwork prints which display one of his major achievements will reduce the commercial value of his likeness.

While the right of publicity allows celebrities like Woods to enjoy the fruits of their labors, here Rush has added a significant creative component of his own to Woods's identity. Permitting Woods's right of publicity to trump Rush's right of freedom of expression would extinguish Rush's right to profit from his creative enterprise.

After balancing the societal and personal interests embodied in the First Amendment against Woods's property rights, we conclude that the effect of limiting Woods's right of publicity in this case is negligible and significantly outweighed by society's interest in freedom of artistic expression. In this case, we find that Woods's right of publicity must yield to the First Amendment.

NOTES AND COMMENTS

1. In both *Hirsch* and *Ali,* the courts recognized a common law "right of publicity." What are the distinctive elements of this claim and how does a "right of publicity" differ from the right of privacy? Is the right of publicity encompassed in the right to privacy? Why was did the court reject Tiger Woods's publicity claim?

2. Consider whether the right to publicity is violated in the following situations:

(a) A company manufactures and sells a baseball trivia board game that uses the names and statistical information (including team, uniform number, playing position, and career statistics) of hundreds of major league baseball players. *See Uhlaender v. Henricksen,* 316 F. Supp. 1277 (D. Minn. 1970); *Palmer v. Schornhorn Enterprises, Inc.,* 233 A.2d 458 (N.J. Super 1967) (professional golf).

(b) A seller of chewing gum includes trading cards with pictures of leading baseball players in its gum packets, without prior authorization by the players. *See Haelan Laboratories, Inc. v. Topps Chewing Gum, Inc.,* 202 F.2d 866 (2nd Cir. 1953).

(c) A national television advertisement for a cigarette manufacturer depicts a race car driver in a red and white racing car with racing number "11." Professional race car driver whose number "71" race car was always in red and white with the same pinstripe alleges a misappropriation of his right to publicity. *Motschenbacher v. R.J. Reynolds Tobacco Co.,* 458 F.2d 821 (4th Cir. 1974).

(d) A company produces trading cards with cartoon caricatures of baseball players who are renamed Cal Ripkenwinkle, Ken Spiffey, Jr., Treasury Bonds and play for teams such as the Seattle Mari-Nerds and St. Louis Credit Cards. *Cardtoons L.C. v. MLBPA,* 95 F.3d 959 (10th Cir. 1996).

(e) An automobile commercial advertisement during an NCAA basketball tournament uses the birth name, Lew Alcindor, of former professional basketball star Kareem Abdul-Jabbar as an answer to a "trivia" question posed by the announcer, without the athlete's consent. Abdul-Jabbar has not used or gone by the name Lew Alcindor for over ten years. *Abdul-Jabbar v. General Motors Corp.,* 85 F.3d 407 (9th Cir. 1995).

In all but one of the above scenarios, courts held that the players' rights to publicity and to control and profit from the commercial value of the players' identity were violated. In the cases finding a right to publicity, would it make a difference if the defendants' had used or published the same information but rather than sell, provided the publications, games, or products free to the public? Which case fails to constitute a right of publicity violation?

3. If a cause of action exists for violation of one's right of publicity, what are the remedies at law? Injunctive relief? Compensatory damages? Punitive damages? Must one be a celebrity to be entitled to the right of publicity? Is a celebrity's property interest in his or her name more unique than that of the average individual? What must one accomplish to be considered a celebrity in the eyes of the law? *See e.g., Uhlaender v . Henricksen,* 316 F. Supp. 1277 (D. Minn. 1970). How is the right of publicity lost? *See Pabst v. O'Brien,* 124 F.2d 167 (5th Cir. 1941) (rejecting an athlete's claim that use of his picture on a calendar amounted to an endorsement of Pabst beer where the athlete had authorized his team's publicity department to distribute pictures).

4. Does the "right of publicity" give players too much entitlement to restrict others from using any names, data, or features that reference the players? Does this right unduly restrict freedom of discussion, expression, or the public's access to information, names and products? At least two commentators contend the right of publicity creates tension with the First Amendment, as well as socially undesirable incentives, including the promotion, rather than prevention, of unjust enrichment. *See* Michael Madow, *Private Ownership of Public Image: Popular Culture and Publicity Rights,* 82 CAL. L. REV. 127 (1993); Roberta Rosenthal Kwall, *The Right of Publicity v. The First Amendment: A Property and Liability Rule Analysis,* 70 IND. L.J. 47 (1994) (asserting that courts lack a principled and consistent method of resolving conflict between right of publicity and First Amendment). Would these athletes be so famous and marketable without such press? Does the right to publicity threaten to "privatize" the public domain?

Consider this excerpt from the dissent in *Hirsch*:

> I would also hold that two simple words like "crazy" and "legs" whether spelled separately or as one word cannot as a matter of law under the facts here be regarded as the commercial "trade name" property of Mr. Hirsch. The record shows that other athletes have been so designated. If the name Elroy or Hirsch had been used with the crazy and legs, a different case would present itself because it would show that Elroy Hirsch was the person whose name was being used for commercial purposes. A gel for the shaving of women's legs has no association with football or any of the other athletic activities of Mr. Hirsch. Here again a close case might be presented if the subject of advertising was football helmets or football shoes but hardly women's leg shaving cream. One can recall "Crazy" Guggenheim on television a few years ago or the famous "Legs" Diamond. It would be reaching beyond reason to say either had a monopoly on the words "crazy" or "legs." This writer finds it hard to see how combining the two words in this context gives Mr. Hirsch a proprietary interest in the words.
>
> Counsel for Mr. Hirsch referred to an athlete called "Bulldog" Turner, but one could hardly claim the word "Bulldog" has become one person's property. There have been athletes known as "the horse," others known as "dizzy" and "daffy" but any of those names attached to a shaving cream for women's legs should not give rise to a cause of action for commercial exploitation of one's "name."

Hirsch, 280 N.W.2d at 141-42. Should the law grant star athletes such a monopoly over "words" or nicknames?

Judge Kozinsi, dissenting in *White v. Samsung Electronics America, Inc.*, 989 F.2d 1512 (9th Cir.1993), similarly observes that "Something very dangerous is going on here. . . . Overprotecting intellectual property is as harmful as underprotecting it. Creativity is impossible without a rich public domain. . . . "Intellectual property rights aren't free: They're imposed at the expense of future creators and of the public at large. . . . This is why intellectual property law is full of careful balances between what's set aside for the owner and what's left in the public domain for the rest of us[.]".

5. Under the scenario set forth in 2(d), above, First Amendment free expression and "fair use" considerations, as well as a parody exception to a state's publicity statute, were held to outweigh the major league baseball players' proprietary rights to publicity in *Cardtoons L.C. v. MLBPA,* 868 F. Supp. 1266 (N.D. Okla. 1994) (also noting no trademark infringement because no likelihood of confusion), *aff'd,* 95 F.3d 959 (10th Cir. 1996) (holding defendant's right to free expression outweighed MLBPA's proprietary right of publicity).

6. Does the right to publicity require player consent before a news entity can publish a story with an athlete's picture? *See Namath v. Sports Illustrated,* 363 N.Y.S.2d 276 (1976) (recognizing a "newsworthiness" permissible use of promotional materials for subscription applications of past edition showing quarterback's photograph on cover, noting "[f]reedom of speech and the press under the First Amendment transcends the right to privacy"). What is the difference between the use of an athlete's identity for news reporting versus for commercial exploitation? How is news reporting defined?

7. Teams, leagues, and producers of sporting events generally obtain consent to use the identity of athletes participating for advertising and promotional purposes by contractual agreements. In major league sports, players assign licensing rights to player associations, which negotiate licensing arrangements as well as authorize and police the use of player and group publicity rights. *See Uhleander v. Henricksen,* 316 F. Supp. 1277 (D. Minn. 1970).

8. The popularity of sports has seen the development of fan games such as "Fantasy Sports." The game is played whereby participants may choose a roster of players from a respective professional sport and earn points based on the play of the professional athlete's performance during the season. The participant with the most points at the end of the season wins. Does the use of professional athletes in fantasy sports violate their right of publicity? The increasing popularity of fantasy sports has spurred litigation as to who owns, or has the right to use for financial gain, a player's name, statistics, and identity. *Gionfirddo v. Major League Baseball* , 94 Cal. App. 4th 400 (2001) held that the players have no right to control the dissemination of factual data concerning their careers, performances, physical descriptions or statistics. Yet in a case filed by CDM Fantasy League against MLB, to establish its right to use sports statistics for financial gain, the players' union intervened asserting violations of the players' rights to publicity by using the players' likeness or identity for commercial advantage without consent. How should the court rule on these questions? *See CDM Distribution & Marketing v. MLB Advanced Media,* No. 4:05CV 22MLM (E.D. Mo. 2005). *See also infra* Section D, *NBA v. Motorola,* 105 F.3d 841 (2nd Cir. 1997).

9. Freedom of Expression and the Right of Publicity. Does an artist's rights to freedom of expression include painting pictures of great athletes participating in a public event and selling them without remuneration to or consent by the athlete? Do you agree with the outcome in *ETW Corp.v. Jireh Publishing,* 332 F.3d 915 (6th Cir. 2003), which dismissed Tiger Woods's request to enjoin the sports artists' sale of a series of prints called "The Masters of Augusta," depicting the elite professional golfers at the public event. Would the result be any different had the defendant been a photographer? Do, or should, athletes or celebrities have a right to a percentage of sales from magazines or newspapers that contain the athlete's photograph?

C. TRADEMARK PROTECTION IN SPORTS MERCHANDISING AND NAMING RIGHTS

As demonstrated by the "Crazylegs" and *Ali* cases, an athlete's name, image, or reputation can have significant commercial value. An athlete or sporting figure has often invested substantial time and resources in establishing such a reputation and justifiably resists others tarnishing or unfairly profiting from that "right of publicity."

Sports teams, leagues, player organizations, and conferences similarly invest substantial resources in developing fan loyalty and a national and international reputation for providing a quality sports experience and product. Many recognize the Master's golf tournament, with its signature Green Jacket award, played at Augusta, Georgia, as the premier golf tournament in the United States. Does Augusta National, therefore, have any recourse when a different company establishes and advertises the "Lady Masters at Moss Green Plantation" golf tournament or institutes a "Red Jacket" award? *See Augusta National, Inc. v. Northwestern Mutual Life Insurance Co.,* 192 U.S.P.Q. 210 (S.D. Ga. 1976).

As in *Hirsch,* teams and sporting events develop a proprietary interest in a team name, nickname, mascot, or other feature distinctive of a particular sport or sporting event — but do the Denver Broncos have the right to preclude a new sports team from adopting blue and orange uniforms (Denver Bronco colors) and calling themselves, for example, the Cleveland Broncos? Would it make a difference if the Cleveland team sought to participate in the NFL, the European Football League, or as a women's professional volleyball team?

Fans are eager to identify with their favorite teams, proudly wearing (until a demoralizing defeat) the jersey, t-shirt, cap, or jacket prominently displaying the team name, nickname, mascot, or logo. Sports merchandising has produced an amazing assortment of sports memorabilia, from clothing to coffee mugs, key chains, even pet bowls bearing the name or mark of one's favorite team. The market for sports merchandising generates billions of dollars annually in revenues. *See* 1 GREENBERG & GRAY, SPORTS LAW PRACTICE ch. 8 (2d ed. 1998) (reporting that the sale of collegiate sports merchandise generated sales in excess of $17 billion in 1997, while sales of licensed merchandise by NFL Properties produced over $3 billion). Sports teams, unions, conferences, and leagues share in this revenue through license agreements with manufacturers, retailers, and others authorizing the use and sale of products bearing team names, logos, or other distinctive features (sports trademarks) in exchange for a royalty fee or other revenue. Not surprisingly, these licensing parties urge consumers, in their sports merchandising purchase, to look for the tag indicating authenticity and official approval of the team, *i.e.,* the official Colorado Rockies sweatshirt contains the display tag "Congratulations on your selection of this genuine article — a product officially licensed by Major League Baseball. . . . Accept no substitute."

The possibility of consumers accepting "substitutes" and purchasing knock-offs or other unlicensed sports merchandise is of grave concern to the official licensing entities. Teams obviously want to protect their reputations, market share, and investments and vigilantly object to the marketing of counterfeit sports merchandise that suggests an association with the team or league. A related concern is "ambush marketing," which occurs when a business engages in a marketing strategy which falsely portrays itself as sponsoring, associated with, or approved by an official sporting event.

Federal trademark law under the Lanham Act, 15 U.S.C. §§ 1051-1127 (2006), recognizes the marketable property rights in licensed merchandise and the value of a sports entity's identity and reputation. The Act protects the sports industry, its licensees, and consumers by holding actionable the use or sale of goods or services that are likely to confuse or mislead the public as to their association with or endorsement by the sports industry. A **trademark** is defined as "any word, name, symbol, or device, or any combination thereof — (1) used by a person . . . to identify and distinguish his or her goods, including a unique product, from those manufactured or sold by others and to indicate the source of the goods, even if that source is unknown." 15 U.S.C. § 1127. Receiving equal Lanham Act protection, a **"service" mark** is defined as "any word, name, symbol, or service, or any combination thereof — (1) used by a person . . . to identify and distinguish the services of one person, including a unique service, from the services of others and to indicate the source of the services, even if that source is unknown." *Id.* "[A] trademark identifies and distinguishes the source and quality of a tangible product, a service mark identifies and distinguishes the source and quality of an intangible service." GREENBERG & GRAY, SPORTS LAW PRACTICE at ¶ 8.05(1). A **"trade name"** is "any name used by a person to identify his or her business or vocation." A trademark identifies a particular source of origin or ownership and often conveys a symbol of quality, goodwill, and origin. Because trademarks can consist of various words, symbols, or combinations thereof that distinguish the origin of a product or service, sport names, nicknames, logos, slogans, and other markers distinctive to a team, league, or event may qualify for trademark protection. Unlike copyrights, which protect original works of authorship for a period of time (*see* **Section D,** *infra*), trademark rights may be acquired through the use of names or designs in the public domain which come to symbolize a team or sporting event and are protected indefinitely. *See* Holly M. Burch, *A Sports Explosion: Intellectual Property Rights in Professional Athletic Franchises,* 5 SPORTS LAW. J. 29, 42 (1998). The monopoly in effect granted to trademark owners over the use of names and other symbols in the public domain has spawned litigation over the scope of trademark rights and the definition of what constitutes infringement.

CASE FILE

INDIANAPOLIS COLTS, INC. v. METROPOLITAN BALTIMORE FOOTBALL CLUB

34 F.3d 410 (7th Cir. 1994)

Before POSNER, Chief Judge, and BAUER and KANNE, Circuit Judges.

POSNER

The Indianapolis Colts and the National Football League, to which the Colts belong, brought suit for trademark infringement (15 U.S.C. §§ 1051 et seq.) against the Canadian Football League's new team in Baltimore, which wants to call itself the "Baltimore CFL Colts." (Four of the Canadian Football League's teams are American.) The plaintiffs obtained a preliminary injunction against the new team's using the name "Colts," or "Baltimore Colts," or "Baltimore CFL Colts," in connection with the playing of professional football, the broadcast of football games, or the sale of merchandise to football fans and other buyers. The ground for the injunction was that consumers of "Baltimore CFL Colts" merchandise are likely to think, mistakenly, that the new Baltimore team is an NFL team related in some fashion to the Indianapolis Colts, formerly the Baltimore Colts. From the order granting the injunction the new team and its owners appeal to us under 28 U.S.C. § 1292(a)(1). Since the injunction was granted, the new team has played its first two games — without a name.

A bit of history is necessary to frame the dispute. In 1952, the National Football League permitted one of its teams, the Dallas Texans, which was bankrupt, to move to Baltimore, where it was renamed the "Baltimore Colts." Under that name it became one of the most illustrious teams in the history of professional football. In 1984, the team's owner, with the permission of the NFL, moved the team to Indianapolis, and it was renamed the "Indianapolis Colts." The move, sudden and secretive, outraged the citizens of Baltimore. The city instituted litigation in a futile effort to get the team back — even tried, unsuccessfully, to get the team back by condemnation under the city's power of eminent domain — and the Colts brought a countersuit that also failed.

Nine years later, the Canadian Football League granted a franchise for a Baltimore team. Baltimoreans clamored for naming the new team the "Baltimore Colts." And so it was named — until the NFL got wind of the name and threatened legal action. The name was then changed to "Baltimore CFL Colts" and publicity launched, merchandise licensed, and other steps taken in preparation for the commencement of play this summer.

The defendants do not argue that the balance of irreparable harm is so one-sided against them that the preliminary injunction should not have been issued even if the plaintiffs have the stronger legal position.

* * *

It is as clear or clearer that [like personal jurisdiction] venue is proper in Indiana, *see* 28 U.S.C. §1391(b)(2); 3 J. THOMAS MCCARTHY, MCCARTHY ON TRADEMARKS AND INTELLECTUAL PROPERTY § 32.22(3)(b)(iii) (3d ed. 1994), so we can turn to the merits of the trademark dispute, cautioning the reader that the expression of views that follows is tentative, as we do not wish to prejudice the outcome of the trial on the merits.

The Baltimore team wanted to call itself the "Baltimore Colts." To improve its litigating posture (we assume), it has consented to insert "CFL" between "Baltimore" and "Colts." A glance at the merchandise in the record explains why this concession to an outraged NFL has been made so readily. On several of the items "CFL" appears in small or blurred letters. And since the Canadian Football League is not well known in the United States — and "CFL" has none of the instant recognition value of "NFL" — the inclusion of the acronym in the team's name might have little impact on potential buyers even if prominently displayed. Those who know football well know that the new "Baltimore Colts" are a new CFL team wholly unrelated to the old Baltimore Colts; know also that the rules of Canadian football are different from those of American football and that teams don't move from the NFL to the CFL as they might from one conference within the NFL to the other. But those who do not know these things — and we shall come shortly to the question whether there are many of these football illiterate — will not be warned off by the letters "CFL." The acronym is a red herring, and the real issue is whether the new Baltimore team can appropriate the name "Baltimore Colts." The entire thrust of the defendants' argument is that it can.

They make a tremendous to-do over the fact that the district judge found that the Indianapolis Colts abandoned the trademark "Baltimore Colts" when they moved to Indianapolis. Well, of course; they were no longer playing football under the name "Baltimore Colts," so could not have used the name as the team's trademark; they could have used it on merchandise but chose not to, until 1991 (another story — and not one we need tell). When a mark is abandoned, it returns to the public domain, and is appropriable anew — in principle. In practice, because "subsequent use of [an] abandoned mark may well evoke a continuing association with the prior use, those who make subsequent use may be required to take reasonable precautions to prevent confusion." This precept is especially important where, as in this case, the former owner of the abandoned mark continues to market the same product or service under a similar name, though we cannot find any previous cases of this kind. No one questions the validity of "Indianapolis Colts" as the trademark of the NFL team that plays out of Indianapolis and was formerly known as the Baltimore Colts. If "Baltimore CFL Colts" is confusingly similar to "Indianapolis Colts" by virtue of the history of the Indianapolis team and the overlapping product and geographical markets served by it and by the new Baltimore team, the latter's use of the abandoned mark would infringe the Indianapolis Colts' new mark. The Colts' abandonment of a mark confusingly similar to their new mark neither broke the continuity of the team in its different locations — it was the same team, merely having a different home base and therefore a different geographical component in its name — nor entitled a third party to pick it up and use it to confuse Colts fans, and other actual or potential consumers of products and services marketed by the Colts or by other National Football League teams, with regard to the identity, sponsorship, or league affiliation of the third party, that is, the new Baltimore team.

Against this the defendants cite to us with great insistence *Major League Baseball Properties Inc. v. Sed Non Olet Denarius, Ltd.*, 817 F. Supp. 1103 (S.D.N.Y. 1993), which, over the objection of the Los Angeles Dodgers, allowed a restaurant in Brooklyn to use the name "Brooklyn Dodger" on the ground that "the 'Brooklyn Dodgers' was a non transportable cultural institution separate from the 'Los Angeles Dodgers.'" The defendants in our case argue that the sudden and greatly resented departure of the Baltimore Colts for Indianapolis made the name "Baltimore Colts" available to anyone who would continue the "nontransportable cultural institution" constituted by a football team located in the City of Baltimore. We think this argument very weak, and need not even try to distinguish *Sed Non Olet Denarius* since district court decisions are not authoritative in this or any court of appeals. If it were a Supreme Court decision it still would not help the defendants. The "Brooklyn Dodger" was not a baseball team, and there was no risk of confusion. The case might be relevant if the Indianapolis Colts were arguing not confusion but misappropriation: that they own the goodwill associated with the name "Baltimore Colts" and the new Baltimore team is trying to take it from them. They did make a claim of misappropriation in the district court, but that court rejected the claim and it has not been renewed on appeal. The only claim in our court is that a significant number of consumers will think the new Baltimore team the successor to, or alter ego of, or even the same team as the Baltimore Colts and therefore the Indianapolis Colts, which is the real successor. No one would think the Brooklyn Dodgers baseball team reincarnated in a restaurant.

A professional sports team is like Heraclitus's river: always changing, yet always the same. When Mr. Irsay transported his team, the Baltimore Colts, from Baltimore to Indianapolis in one night in 1984, the team remained, for a time anyway, completely intact: same players, same coaches, same front-office personnel. With the passage of time, of course, the team changed. Players retired or were traded, and were replaced. Coaches and other nonplaying personnel came and went. But as far as the record discloses there is as much institutional continuity between the Baltimore Colts of 1984 and the Indianapolis Colts of 1994 as there was between the Baltimore Colts of 1974 and the Baltimore Colts of 1984. Johnny Unitas, the Baltimore Colts' most famous player, swears in his affidavit that his old team has no connection with the Indianapolis Colts, and he has even asked the Colts to expunge his name from its record books. He is angry with Irsay for moving the team. He is entitled to his anger, but it has nothing to do with this lawsuit. The Colts were Irsay's team, it was moved intact, there is no evidence it has changed more since the move than it had in the years before. There is, in contrast, no continuity, no links contractual or otherwise, nothing but a geographical site in common, between the Baltimore Colts and the Canadian Football League team that would like to use its name. Any suggestion that there is such continuity is false and potentially misleading.

Potentially; for if everyone knows there is no contractual or institutional continuity, no pedigree or line of descent, linking the Baltimore-Indianapolis Colts and the new CFL team that wants to call itself the "Baltimore Colts" (or, grudgingly, the "Baltimore CFL Colts"), then there is no harm, at least no harm for which the Lanham Act provides a remedy, in the new Baltimore team's appropriating the name "Baltimore Colts" to play under and sell merchandise under. If not everyone knows, there is harm. Some people who might otherwise watch the Indianapolis Colts (or some other NFL team, for remember that the NFL, representing all the teams, is a coplaintiff) on television may watch the Baltimore CFL Colts instead, thinking they are the "real" Baltimore Colts, and the NFL will lose revenue. A few (doubtless very few) people who might otherwise buy tickets to an NFL game may buy tickets to a Baltimore CFL Colts game instead. Some people who might otherwise buy merchandise stamped with the name "Indianapolis Colts" or the name of some other NFL team may buy merchandise stamped "Baltimore CFL Colts," thinking it a kin of the NFL's Baltimore Colts in the glory days of Johnny Unitas rather than a newly formed team that plays Canadian football in a Canadian football league. It would be naive to suppose that no consideration of such possibilities occurred to the owners of the new Baltimore team when they were choosing a name, though there is no evidence that it was the dominant or even a major consideration.

Confusion thus is possible, and may even have been desired; but is it likely? There is great variance in consumer competence, and it would be undesirable to impoverish the lexicon of trade names merely to protect the most gullible fringe of the consuming public. The Lanham Act does not cast the net of protection so wide. The legal standard under the Act has been formulated variously, but the various formulations come down to whether it is likely that the challenged mark if permitted to be used by the defendant would cause the plaintiff to lose a substantial number of consumers. Pertinent to this determination is the similarity of the marks and of the parties' products, the knowledge of the average consumer of the product, the overlap in the parties' geographical markets, and the other factors that the cases consider. The aim is to strike a balance between, on the one hand, the interest of the seller of the new product, and of the consuming public, in an arresting, attractive, and informative name that will enable the new product to compete effectively against existing ones, and, on the other hand, the interest of existing sellers, and again of the consuming public, in consumers' being able to know exactly what they are buying without having to incur substantial costs of investigation or inquiry.

To help judges strike the balance, the parties to trademark disputes frequently as here hire professionals in marketing or applied statistics to conduct surveys of consumers. The battle of experts that ensues is frequently unyielding. Many experts are willing for a generous (and sometimes for a modest) fee to bend their science in the direction from which their fee is coming. The constraints that the market in consultant services for lawyers places on this sort of behaviour are weak, as shown by the fact that both experts in this case were hired and, we have no doubt, generously remunerated even though both have been criticized in previous judicial opinions. The judicial constraints on tendentious expert testimony are inherently weak because judges (and even more so juries, though that is not an issue in a trademark case) lack training or experience in the relevant fields of expert knowledge. But that is the system we have. It might be improved by asking each party's hired expert to designate a third, a neutral expert who would be appointed by the court to conduct the necessary studies. The necessary authority exists, *see* Fed. R. Evid. 706, but was not exercised here.

Both parties presented studies. The defendants' was prepared by Michael Rappeport and is summarized in a perfunctory affidavit by Dr. Rappeport to which the district judge gave little weight. That was a kindness. The heart of Rappeport's study was a survey that consisted of three loaded questions asked in one Baltimore mall. Rappeport has been criticized before for his methodology, and we hope that he will take these criticisms to heart in his next courtroom appearance.

The plaintiffs' study, conducted by Jacob Jacoby, was far more substantial and the district judge found it on the whole credible. The 28-page report with its numerous appendices has all the trappings of social scientific rigor. Interviewers showed several hundred consumers in 24 malls scattered around the country shirts and hats licensed by the defendants for sale to consumers. The shirts and hats have "Baltimore CFL Colts" stamped on them. The consumers were asked whether they were football fans, whether they watched football games on television, and whether they ever bought merchandise with a team name on it. Then they were asked, with reference to the "Baltimore CFL Colts" merchandise that they were shown, such questions as whether they knew what sport the team played, what teams it played against, what league the team was in, and whether the team or league needed someone's permission to use this name, and if so whose. If, for example, the respondent answered that the team had to get permission from the Canadian Football League, the interviewer was directed to ask the respondent whether the Canadian Football League had in turn to get permission from someone. There were other questions, none however obviously loaded, and a whole other survey, the purpose of which was to control for "noise," in which another group of mallgoers was asked the identical questions about a hypothetical team unappetizingly named the "Baltimore Horses." The idea was by comparing the answers of the two groups to see whether the source of confusion was the name "Baltimore Colts" or just the name "Baltimore," in which event the injunction would do no good since no one suggests that the new Baltimore team should be forbidden to use "Baltimore" in its name, provided the following word is not "Colts."

Rappeport threw darts at Jacoby's study. Some landed wide. We are especially perplexed by the argument that survey research belongs to sociology rather than psychology (we leave the reader to guess the respective disciplines to which our rival experts belong); the courtroom is a peculiar site for academic turf wars. We also do not think it was improper for Jacoby to inquire about confusion between "Baltimore CFL Colts" and "Baltimore Colts," even though the Indianapolis Colts have abandoned "Baltimore Colts." If consumers believe that the new Baltimore team is the old Baltimore Colts, and the Indianapolis Colts some sort of upstart (the Johnny Unitas position), they will be less likely to buy merchandise stamped "Indianapolis Colts." But Rappeport was right to complain that the choice of "Horses" for the comparison team loaded the dice and that some of Jacoby's questions were a bit slanted. That is only to say, however, that Jacoby's survey was not perfect, and this is not news. Trials would be very short if only perfect evidence were admissible.

Jacoby's survey of consumers reactions to the "Baltimore CFL Colts" merchandise found rather astonishing levels of confusion not plausibly attributable to the presence of the name "Baltimore" alone, since "Baltimore Horses" engendered much less. . . . Among self-identified football fans, 64 percent thought that the "Baltimore CFL Colts" was either the old (NFL) Baltimore Colts or the Indianapolis Colts. But perhaps this result is not so astonishing. Although most American football fans have heard of Canadian football, many probably are unfamiliar with the acronym "CFL," and as we remarked earlier it is not a very conspicuous part of the team logo stamped on the merchandise. Among fans who watch football on television, 59 percent displayed the same confusion; and even among those who watch football on cable television, which attracts a more educated audience on average and actually carries CFL games, 58 percent were confused when shown the merchandise. Among the minority not confused about who the "Baltimore CFL Colts" are, a substantial minority, ranging from 21 to 34 percent depending on the precise sub-sample, thought the team somehow sponsored or authorized by the Indianapolis Colts or the National Football League. It is unfortunate and perhaps a bit tricky that the sub sample of consumers likely to buy merchandise with a team name on it was not limited to consumers likely to buy merchandise with a football team's name on it; the choice of the name "Baltimore Horses" for the comparison team was unfortunate; and no doubt there are other tricks of the survey researcher's black arts that we have missed. There is the more fundamental problem, one common to almost all consumer survey research, that people are more careful when they are laying out their money than when they are answering questions.

But with all this granted, we cannot say that the district judge committed a clear error in crediting the major findings of the Jacoby study and inferring from it and the other evidence in the record that the defendants' use of the name "Baltimore CFL Colts" whether for the team or on merchandise was likely to confuse a substantial number of consumers. This mean — given the defendants' failure to raise any issue concerning the respective irreparable harms from granting or denying the preliminary injunction — that the judge's finding concerning likelihood of confusion required that the injunction issue.

The defendants argue, finally, that, even so, the injunction is overbroad; it should not have forbidden them to use the word "Colts," but rather confined them to using it in conjunction with "Baltimore CFL." We are baffled by the argument. If they want to use "Colts" in conjunction with anything besides a Baltimore football team, there is nothing in this lawsuit to prevent them. The objection is precisely to their use of the word in a setting that will lead many consumers to believe it designates either the old Baltimore Colts (falsely implying that the Indianapolis Colts are not the successor to the Baltimore Colts or that the new Baltimore team is an NFL team or is approved by or affiliated with the NFL) or the Indianapolis Colts.

The defendants make some other arguments but they do not have sufficient merit to warrant discussion. The judgment of the district court granting the preliminary injunction is

AFFIRMED.

NOTES AND COMMENTS

1. Ownership of Team Name/Nickname. Judge Posner deemed insignificant the decision in *Major League Baseball Properties v. Sed Non Olet Denarius,* 817 F. Supp. 1103 (S.D.N.Y. 1993), which rejected a trademark infringement claim by the Los Angeles Dodgers against the Brooklyn Dodgers Sports Bar and Restaurant. Are the cases inconsistent?

The use of team nicknames has been the subject of much litigation. In *National Football League Properties, Inc. v. New Jersey Giants, Inc.,* 637 F. Supp. 507 (D.N.J. 1986), the NFL, on behalf of the New York Giants, obtained an injunction against a company selling "New Jersey Giants" merchandise. The Court found the defendant sought to capitalize on the confusion created by the New York Giants football team playing its home games in New Jersey and held the defendant's prominent use of the Giants name was confusingly similar to plaintiff's marks. *See also NFL v. Jacksonville Jaguars,* 886 F. Supp. 335 (S.D.N.Y. 1995) (disputing NFL use of team name "Jaguars" and the image of a jaguar resembling the emblem of Jaguar cars). Finding that the name "Redskins" is disparaging to Native Americans, *Harjo v. Pro-Football, Inc.*, 50 U.S.P.Q.2d 1705 (P.T.O. 1999), ordered cancellation of seven trademarks owned by the Washington Redskins football team.

In a case alleging "reverse confusion," which occurs when a "larger, more powerful junior user infringes on the trademark of a smaller, less powerful, senior user causing confusion as to the source of the senior user's goods and services," the court in *Harlem Wizards Entertainment Basketball, Inc. v. NBA Properties, Inc.,* 952 F. Supp. 1084, 1086 (D.N.J. 1997) dismissed the lawsuit by the Harlem Wizards, an entertainment basketball group similar to the Globetrotters, against the Washington Bullets which sought to change its name to the Washington Wizards, concluding consumer confusion was unlikely due to the different logos and type of entertainment. *Cf. DreamTeam Collectibles, Inc. v. NBA Properties, Inc.*, 958 F. Supp. 1401 (Mo. 1997) (holding actionable plaintiffs' claim of reverse confusion on defendant's use of the mark "Dream Team" to describe star basketball players competing in the Olympics where plaintiffs had previously registered the Dream Team trademark). Would the Harlem Globetrotters have a right under the Lanham Act to preclude the Harlem Wizards use of the name "Harlem"?

2. Trademark Infringement. What are the elements of a claim for **infringement** of a registered mark? Section 1114(a), 15 U.S.C., provides that:

> "(1) Any person who shall, without the consent of the registrant — (A) use in commerce any reproduction, counterfeit, copy, or colorable imitation of a registered mark in connection with the sale, offering for sale, distribution, or advertising of any goods or services on or in connection with which such use is likely to cause confusion, or to cause mistake, or to deceive . . . shall be liable in a civil action by the registrant for the remedies hereinafter provided."

Accordingly, a claimant must establish that the defendant used: a reproduction or imitation; of a registered mark, without consent; in commerce; for sale; and likely to cause confusion.

Section 1125 prohibits the false designation of origin, description, or representation of a registered or unregistered trademark. This section provides that:

> "(a)(1) Any person who, on or in connection with any goods or services, or any container for goods, uses in commerce any word, term, name, symbol, or device, or any combination thereof, or any false designation of origin, false or misleading description of fact, or false or misleading representation of fact, which (A) is likely to cause confusion, or to cause mistake, or to deceive as to the affiliation, connection, or association of such person with another person, or as to the origin, sponsorship, or approval of his or her goods, services, or commercial activities by another person, or (B) in commercial advertising or promotion, misrepresents the nature, characteristics, qualities, or geographic origin of his or her or another person's goods, services, or commercial activities, shall be liable in a civil action by any person who believes that he or she is or is likely to be damaged by such act."

As remedies for trademark infringement, the Lanham Act provides for injunctive relief, as well as the recovery of defendant's profits, plaintiff's damages, costs, and attorney fees. 15 U.S.C. §§ 1115 and 1116. What must an owner of an unregistered mark prove to prevail on an infringement claim?

3. Trademark law protects both against unfair competition and consumer confusion or deception by prohibiting the use of reproductions, copies, counterfeits, or colorable imitations of marks. Trademarks provide the consumer with information as to the source or origin and quality of a product or service, as well as protect the investments and goodwill of trademark owners in advertising and providing quality products. In *Indianapolis Colts,* Judge Posner stated that the test of infringement is "whether it is likely that the challenged mark if permitted to be used by the defendant would cause the plaintiff to lose a substantial number of customers." What factors are relevant for determining a likelihood of consumer confusion in sports trademark litigation? In addition to the factors cited in *Indianapolis Colts*, consider: "(1) the strength of the owner's mark; (2) relatedness of the goods; (3) similarity of the marks; (4) evidence of actual confusion; (5) marketing channels used; (6) likely degree of purchaser's care; (7) defendant's intent in selecting the mark." *Abdul-Jabbar v. General Motors Corp.*, 85 F.3d 407 (9th Cir. 1995).

4. What defenses are available to an infringement claim? *See* 15 U.S.C. § 1115(b) (recognizing defenses including trademark invalidity, abandonment, permission, individual's name, good faith and prior use, antitrust, and other equitable principles).

Words that are descriptive or merely functional are not registrable as trademarks. Why did the court in *Indianapolis Colts* not find abandonment?

5. What policy interests are served by according trademark protection to the use of words, such as team names, or to symbols or logos on sports merchandise? Do consumers benefit from the exclusive rights trademark protection provides to the sports industry — or pay more?

6. Acquired Distinctiveness/Secondary Meaning Infringement. Recall that a trademark does not necessarily have to be registered to receive trademark protection. Although registration of trademarks provides prima facie proof of trademark ownership, 15 U.S.C. § 1057(b), a trademark may also be acquired through the use of common words, names or symbols that the public comes to associate with a particular source. *NFLPI v. Wichita Falls Sportswear, Inc.*, 532 F. Supp. 651 (W.D. Wash. 1982), found "secondary meaning" infringement of Seattle Seahawk NFL trademark rights against a defendant who manufactured "Seattle" jerseys with official Seahawk blue and green team colors. In secondary meaning infringement, a plaintiff must prove that the public associates a defendant's products with the plaintiff and that the defendant's acts created a likelihood of confusion, demonstrated by plaintiff's distinctive marks and defendant's similar use. The court rejected defenses that the marks were functional or generic. To the court, the issue was whether there were trademark rights in the descriptive terms designating each team, when the terms were presented with the official team colors, large numerals, and sleeve designs. The court noted that while color was not capable of appropriation as a trademark, it could be an essential element in an arbitrary arrangement of symbols or words and could be protected in that context. Finding that the primary significance of the marks on the licensee's jerseys was source identification, the court stressed the physical similarities between the licensee's official jerseys and the manufacturer's jerseys. While there was some variation in design, striping, and color, these differences were not significant, the manufacturer's jerseys represented a calculated effort to create distinctions that had no real meaning in the minds of consumers.

7. Would (and should) trademark law protect slogans, such as ABC's Monday Night Football crowd-rousing question "Are you ready for some football?" Or announcer Michael Buffer's "Let's Get Ready to Rumble!"? Or Nike's "Just Do It"?

8. Trademark Licensing Arrangements. Sports teams often transfer trademark and licensing rights to a single corporation or trust, which represents an entire league, at the professional (properties divisions) and collegiate levels (*e.g.*, Collegiate Licensing Company). *See Boston Professional Hockey Association v. Dallas Cup & Emblem Mfgrs., Inc.*, 510 F.2d 1004 (5th Cir.), *cert. denied*, 423 U.S. 869 (1975) (describing NFL member clubs pooling of trademark rights into the NFL Trust, which manages licensing and policing of trademarks). Antitrust aspects of these agreements are explored in **Chapter 5,** *supra*.

9. Corporate Sponsorships and Naming Rights. Corporations have found sporting events an effective advertising medium and may sponsor a sporting event or product in which the corporate trademark is displayed. The sale of corporate naming rights to public and private sports facilities, stadiums, and arenas has become a significant new revenue source for financing sports facilities. *See* GREENBERG & GRAY, SPORTS LAW PRACTICE § 8.09 (describing corporate naming contracts such as America West Airlines' purchase of an arena for the Phoenix Suns and listing facilities across the country with corporate names). Stadium naming rights are also sold to finance university sports arenas, leading to some unusual names, including Coors Arena at the University of Colorado (later changed to the Colorado Arena in response to criticism of naming a university facility after an alcoholic beverage) and Value City Arena at Ohio State University.

D. SPORTS BROADCASTING: COPYRIGHT OWNERSHIP, PROTECTION, AND LIMITATIONS

A significant source of revenue for professional and many collegiate sports teams is derived from licensing exclusive rights to broadcast major sporting events. The value of these licensing rights is evident in the $3.1 billion dollars four major networks (FOX, NBC, ESPN, and CBS) agreed to pay each year for the rights to broadcast NFL games between years 2006-2012. The NCAA also has multi-billion dollar contracts with networks for the rights to broadcast major college sports. Local, national, and cable networks pay millions — even billions — for the rights to broadcast major sporting events and thereby to reach the vast sports advertising market and fan base.

The popularity of sports and its extraordinary revenue base is certainly attributable to the public's increased access to sports through media exposure and broadcasting. A fan who has never attended a live game has the opportunity to experience the game in action and usually for free by radio or network television broadcasts. Games not broadcast in a region may be accessed through satellite, cable, pay per view, and other forms of distribution, so a fan is rarely without access to follow his or her favorite team. The expansion of broadcasting medium from radio to television, cable, satellite, and now the internet has created an insatiable demand for content — a demand that sporting bodies, networks, and others are eager to supply. Sports events provide networks substantial programming content. For example, a professional baseball team plays a season of 162 games, each of which averages over three hours. Over the course of a season, this amounts to approximately 500 hours of broadcasting content. By comparison, a network situation comedy season, usually requiring a written script and rehearsals, produces approximately 26 half-hour shows for a total of only 13 hours (less commercial time) of content. For so much content, with a demonstrated ability to capture the public's attention, broadcasters are willing to pay seemingly exorbitant amounts for sports. ESPN offers two channels of continuous daily sports broadcasting. Every major newscast provides a sports segment, displaying game highlights and reporting on key aspects of play. The internet has numerous websites devoted to sports and offers audio and video capabilities to display plays and games and to provide instantaneous reports.

Technology continues to provide seemingly unlimited possibilities for fans to obtain up-to-the-minute and comprehensive access to sporting events. The obvious concern of the sporting bodies, however, is to protect the value of rights to license exclusive broadcasting. The value of the game rights is at its highest when the game is in progress. Networks risk losing viewers and commercial sponsors, and teams risk losing revenue from ticket sales, if the sporting event can be accessed elsewhere. *See* Holly M. Burch, *A Sports Explosion: Intellectual Property Rights in Professional Athletic Franchises*, 5 SPORTS LAW. J. 29, 38 (1998).

Federal copyright law protects the rights of the owner of the broadcast to use and authorize, by licensing, exclusive rights to the broadcast. The Copyright Act of 1976 confers upon copyright owners exclusive rights to reproduce, adapt, publish, and sell copyrighted work. 17 U.S.C. § 106. Copyright protection subsists in "[o]riginal works of authorship fixed in any tangible medium of expression." 17 U.S.C. § 102(a). Works of authorship include "audiovisual works." By this, the owner of the copyright to the sporting event has the exclusive right to use and authorize by licensing to broadcast the event. Congress' authority to enact this statute is derived from U.S. CONST. art. I, § 8 (providing Congress the power "to promote the progress of science and useful arts, by securing for limited times to authors and inventors the exclusive right to their respective writings and discoveries"). State common laws against commercial misappropriation may also entitle sports teams, owners, and leagues to limit others from reproducing or profiting from the broadcast, although there is some question about preemption by the federal copyright laws. *See NBA v. Motorola, infra.*

Technology presents increasingly complicated issues about the scope of rights afforded the copyright owner of a broadcast to restrict others' use of technology and media to use, reproduce, or otherwise profit from the sporting event. Sports leagues vigorously guard their broadcast rights, as evidenced by standard warnings to the effect that "This telecast is the property of [the NFL] . . . any rebroadcast, retransmission or other use of the events of this game, without the express written consent of the owner, is hereby prohibited. . . ."

What is the scope of protection for copyright holders? Does copyright ownership include restricting others from broadcasting the same event, showing game highlights, or reporting on the game? Does this preclude a local bar from showing "black out" or pay-per-view games to patrons via satellite interception? Or prohibit the same bar from allowing its customers to watch a game from the bar's rooftop overlooking the stadium? Is a sporting event even entitled to copyright protection? If so, who is the owner? What is the property? What constitutes infringement? The following cases examine these precise issues.

Problem

SPORTSPAGER is a new company offering real time scores and statistics on major league baseball games to those who are not able to watch the game live or on television. The concept is to provide sports enthusiasts real time scores and statistics via an electronic medium, a customized pager. SPORTSPAGER has its own employees watch the games, either live or on television, or listen to them on the radio. The employees simultaneously input current statistical information, such as the teams playing, current scores and score changes, team and player at bat, current pitcher, inning, and players on base. The statistical information is keyed into a computer, sent to the central computing system, and then relayed to the pagers.

The pager has become an overnight success. Thousands of sports fans have paid the $200 purchase price to keep them informed on the current scores of their favorite team. The service has become so profitable that SPORTSPAGER has decided to create a web-site offering the same services as the pager contemporaneous with a host of additional statistical information. The web-site also displays graphics drawings simulating game action with computer characters. The web-site now generates close to one hundred thousand hits per day. Advertising revenues for the web-site have increased dramatically with the site's popularity.

On behalf of its member teams, Major League Baseball (MLB) has filed a lawsuit against SPORTSPAGER, contending that the SPORTSPAGER product and website constitutes copyright and trademark infringement, as well as a misappropriation of MLB property. Explain the respective arguments of the parties. As the Court, how would you rule?

CASE FILE

Establishing Ownership of Copyrights in Sports Broadcasts

PITTSBURGH ATHLETIC CO. v. KQV BROADCASTING CO.

24 F. Supp. 490 (W.D. Pa. 1938)

SCHOONMAKER, District Judge.

This is an action in equity in which plaintiffs ask for a preliminary injunction to restrain defendant from broadcasting play-by-play reports and descriptions of baseball games played by the "Pirates," a professional baseball team owned by Pittsburgh Athletic Company, both at its home baseball park in Pittsburgh, known as "Forbes Field," and at baseball parks in other cities. . . .

The essential facts are not in dispute. The question at issue is primarily a question of law. Is the defendant within its legal rights in the practices thus pursued by it? The essential facts of the case may be briefly summarized as follows:

The plaintiff Pittsburgh Athletic Company owns a professional baseball team known as the "Pirates," and is a member of an association known as the "National League." With the several teams of the members of the League, the "Pirates" play baseball both at its home field and at the home fields of the other members of the League in various cities. The home games are played at a baseball park known as "Forbes Field" which is enclosed by high fences and structures so that the public are admitted only to the Park to witness the games at Forbes Field by the payment of an admission ticket, which provides that the holder of the admission ticket agrees not to give out any news of the game while it is in progress.

The Pittsburgh Athletic Company has granted by written contract, for a valuable consideration, to General Mills, Inc., the exclusive right to broadcast, play-by-play, descriptions or accounts of the games played by the "Pirates" at this and other fields. The National Broadcasting Company, also for a valuable consideration, has contracted with General Mills, Inc., to broadcast by radio over stations KDKA and WWSW, play-by-play descriptions of these games. The Socony-Vacuum Oil Company has purchased for a valuable consideration a half interest in the contract of the General Mills, Inc.

The defendant operates at Pittsburgh a radio broadcasting station known as KQV, from which it has in the past broadcast by radio play-by-play descriptions of the games played by the "Pirates" at Pittsburgh, and asserts its intention to continue in so doing. The defendant secures the information which it broadcasts from its own paid observers whom it stations at vantage points outside Forbes Field on premises leased by defendant. These vantage points are so located that the defendant's observers can see over the enclosures the games as they are played in Forbes Field.

On this state of facts, we are of the opinion that the plaintiffs have presented a case which entitles them under the law to a preliminary injunction. It is perfectly clear that the exclusive right to broadcast play-by-play descriptions of the games played by the "Pirates" at their home field rests in the plaintiffs, General Mills, Inc., and the Socony-Vacuum Oil Company under the contract with the Pittsburgh Athletic Company. That is a property right of the plaintiffs with which defendant is interfering when it broadcasts the play- by-play description of the ballgames obtained by the observers on the outside of the enclosure.

The plaintiffs and the defendant are using baseball news as material for profit. The Athletic Company has, at great expense, acquired and maintains a baseball park, pays the players who participate in the game, and have, as we view it, a legitimate right to capitalize on the news value of their games by selling exclusive broadcasting rights to companies which value them as affording advertising mediums for their merchandise. This right the defendant interferes with when it uses its broadcasting facilities for giving out the identical news obtained by its paid observers stationed at points outside Forbes Field for the purpose of securing information which it cannot otherwise acquire. This, in our judgment, amounts to unfair competition, and is a violation of the property rights of the plaintiffs. For it is our opinion that the Pittsburgh Athletic Company, by reason of its creation of the game, its control of the park, and its restriction of the dissemination of news therefrom, has a property right in such news, and the right to control the use thereof for a reasonable time following the games.

The communication of news of the ball games by the Pittsburgh Athletic Company, or by its licensed news agencies, is not a general publication and does not destroy that right. . . . On the unfair competition feature of the case, we rest our opinion on the case of *International News Service v. Associated Press,* 248 U.S. 215 (1918). In that case the court enjoined the International News Service from copying news from bulletin boards and early editions of Associated Press newspapers, and selling such news so long as it had commercial value to the Associated Press. The Supreme Court said:

> Regarding the news, therefore, as but the material out of which both parties are seeking to make profits at the same time and in the same field, we hardly can fail to recognize that for this purpose, and as between them, it must be regarded as quasi-property, irrespective of the rights of either as against the public. . . . The right of the purchaser of a single newspaper to spread knowledge of its contents gratuitously, for any legitimate purpose not unreasonably interfering with the complainant's right to make merchandise of it, may be admitted; but to

> transmit that news for commercial use, in competition with complainant — which is what defendant has done and seeks to justify — is a very different matter. . . .

* * *

Defendant contends it is not unfairly competing with any of the plaintiffs because it obtains no compensation from a sponsor or otherwise from its baseball broadcasts. It concedes, however, that KQV seeks by its broadcast of news of baseball games to cultivate the good will of the public for its radio station. The fact that no revenue is obtained directly from the broadcast is not controlling, as these broadcasts are undoubtedly designed to aid in obtaining advertising business.

Defendant seeks to justify its action on the ground that the information it receives from its observers stationed on its own property without trespassing on plaintiffs' property, may be lawfully broadcast by it. We cannot follow defendant's counsel in this contention for the reasons above stated.

* * *

2. The right, title and interest in and to the baseball games played within the parks of members of the National League, including Pittsburgh, including the property right in, and the sole right of, disseminating or publishing or selling, or licensing the right to disseminate, news, reports, descriptions, or accounts of games played in such parks, during the playing thereof, is vested exclusively in such members.

3. The actions and threatened actions of the defendant constitute a direct and irreparable interference with, and an appropriation of, the plaintiffs' normal and legitimate business; and said action is calculated to, and does, result in the unjust enrichment of the defendant at the expense of the plaintiffs and each of them.

4. The defendant's unauthorized broadcasts of information concerning games played by the Pittsburgh team constitute unfair competition with the plaintiffs and each of them. . . .

NOTES AND COMMENTS

1. *Pittsburgh Athletic* establishes that the team owns the property right to the broadcast of a sporting event. The Copyright Act codifies this by providing copyright protection for the broadcast of an athletic event. 17 U.S.C. § 102. But which team — the home team or visitor — owns the right to broadcast the event? Does a visiting team have the right to broadcast an away game so fans at home can watch? In most instances, broadcasting rights are addressed by contractual agreement or league or conference rules. The Sports Broadcasting Act, 15 U.S.C. §§ 1291-1295, provides a limited exemption from the antitrust laws allowing professional sports teams to pool team broadcasting rights and enter contracts with sponsored networks on behalf of an entire league. The Third Circuit has held, however, that this exemption does not extend to league contracts with companies or networks providing subscription or pay telecast services. *Shaw v. Dallas Football Club, Ltd.*, 172 F.3d 299 (3d Cir. 1999). *See* **Chapter 5, Section G, Note 12,** *supra.*

2. Athletes' Property Right in Performances? Do the players have ownership rights in their performances that are broadcast during the telecast of a sporting event? *See Baltimore Orioles, Inc v. Major League Baseball Players Association,* 805 F.2d 663 (7th Cir. 1986) (rejecting player claims of broadcast rights to their performances under a statutory "works for hire" presumption that works made within scope of employment belong to the employer, 17 U.S.C. § 201(b)), *cert. denied,* 480 U.S. 941 (1987). *Baltimore Orioles* also held that federal copyright law preempts players' rights of publicity in their game performance. *See also* Richard S. Robinson, *Preemption and the Right of Publicity and a New Federal Statute,* 16 Cardozo Arts & Ent. L.J. 183 (1998).

3. *Pittsburgh Athletic* found unlawful, under common law theories of unfair competition and unjust enrichment, defendant's practice of paying observers to relay play-by-play information about the game for the defendant's rebroadcast. Since *Pittsburgh Athletic,* Congress enacted the Copyright Act of 1976. In the following cases, consider whether the Copyright Act changes the basic holding of *Pittsburgh Athletic* and whether copyright protection includes the right to control others' use of replays, highlights, and other reporting of contemporaneous game information.

Case File

Scope of Copyright Protection and Ownership Rights

NATIONAL BASKETBALL ASSOCIATION v. MOTOROLA, INC.

105 F.3d 841 (2d Cir. 1997)

Van Graafeiland, Winter, and Altimari, Circuit Judges.

Winter.

Motorola, Inc. and Sports Team Analysis and Tracking Systems ("STATS") appeal from a permanent injunction entered by [District] Judge Preska. The injunction concerns a handheld pager sold by Motorola and marketed under the name "SportsTrax," which displays updated information of professional basketball games in progress. The injunction prohibits appellants, absent authorization from the National Basketball Association and NBA Properties, Inc. (collectively the "NBA"), from transmitting scores or other data about NBA games in progress via the pagers, STATS's site on America On-Line's computer dial-up service, or "any equivalent means."

The crux of the dispute concerns the extent to which a state law "hot-news" misappropriation claim based on *International News Service v. Associated Press,* 248 U.S. 215 (1918) ("*INS*"), survives preemption by the federal Copyright Act and whether the NBA's claim fits within the surviving *INS*-type claims. We hold that a narrow "hot-news" exception does survive preemption. However, we also hold that appellants' transmission of "real-time" NBA game scores and information tabulated from television and radio broadcasts of games in progress does not constitute a misappropriation of "hot news" that is the property of the NBA. . . .

I. BACKGROUND

The facts are largely undisputed. Motorola manufactures and markets the SportsTrax paging device while STATS supplies the game information that is transmitted to the pagers. The product became available to the public in January 1996, at a retail price of about $ 200. SportsTrax's pager has an inch-and-a-half by inch-and-a-half screen and operates in four basic modes: "current," "statistics," "final scores" and "demonstration." It is the "current" mode that gives rise to the present dispute. In that mode, SportsTrax displays the following information on NBA games in progress: (i) the teams playing; (ii) score changes; (iii) the team in possession of the ball; (iv) whether the team is in the free-throw bonus; (v) the quarter of the game; and (vi) time remaining in the quarter. The information is updated every two to three minutes, with more frequent updates near the end of the first half and the end of the game. There is a lag of approximately two or three minutes between events in the game itself and when the information appears on the pager screen.

SportsTrax's operation relies on a "data feed" supplied by STATS reporters who watch the games on television or listen to them on the radio. The reporters key into a personal computer changes in the score and other information such as successful and missed shots, fouls, and clock updates. The information is relayed by modem to STATS's host computer, which compiles, analyzes, and formats the data for retransmission. The information is then sent to a common carrier, which then sends it via satellite to various local FM radio networks that in turn emit the signal received by the individual SportsTrax pagers.

Although the NBA's complaint concerned only the SportsTrax device, the NBA offered evidence at trial concerning STATS's America On-Line ("AOL") site. Starting in January, 1996, users who accessed STATS's AOL site, typically via a modem attached to a home computer, were provided with slightly more comprehensive and detailed real-time game information than is displayed on a SportsTrax pager. On the AOL site, game scores are updated every 15 seconds to a minute, and the player and team statistics are updated each minute. . . .

The NBA's complaint asserted six claims for relief: (i) state law unfair competition by misappropriation; (ii) false advertising under Section 43(a) of the Lanham Act, 15 U.S.C. § 1125(a); (iii) false representation of origin under Section 43(a) of the Lanham Act; (iv) state and common law unfair competition by false advertising and false designation of origin; (v) federal copyright infringement; and (vi) unlawful interception of communications under the Communications Act of 1934, 47 U.S.C. § 605. Motorola counterclaimed, alleging that the NBA unlawfully interfered with Motorola's contractual relations with four individual NBA teams that had agreed to sponsor and advertise SportsTrax.

The district court dismissed all of the NBA's claims except the first — misappropriation under New York law. The court also dismissed Motorola's counterclaim. Finding Motorola and STATS liable for misappropriation, Judge Preska entered the permanent injunction, reserved the calculation of damages for subsequent proceedings, and stayed execution of the injunction pending appeal. Motorola and STATS appeal from the injunction, while NBA cross-appeals from the district court's dismissal of its Lanham Act false-advertising claim. The issues before us, therefore, are the state law misappropriation and Lanham Act claims.

II. THE STATE LAW MISAPPROPRIATION CLAIM

A. Summary of Ruling

Because our disposition of the state law misappropriation claim rests in large part on pre-emption by the Copyright Act, our discussion necessarily goes beyond the elements of a misappropriation claim under New York law, and a summary of our ruling here will perhaps render that discussion — or at least the need for it — more understandable.

The issues before us are ones that have arisen in various forms over the course of this century as technology has steadily increased the speed and quantity of information transmission. Today, individuals at home, at work, or elsewhere, can use a computer, pager, or other device to obtain highly selective kinds of information virtually at will. *International News Service v. Associated Press,* 248 U.S. 215 (1918) ("*INS*") was one of the first cases to address the issues raised by these technological advances, although the technology involved in that case was primitive by contemporary standards. *INS* involved two wire services, the Associated Press ("AP") and International News Service ("INS"), that transmitted news stories by wire to member newspapers. INS would lift factual stories from AP bulletins and send them by wire to INS papers. INS would also take factual stories from east coast AP papers and wire them to INS papers on the west coast that had yet to publish because of time differentials. The Supreme Court held that INS's conduct was a common-law misappropriation of AP's property.

With the advance of technology, radio stations began "live" broadcasts of events such as baseball games and operas, and various entrepreneurs began to use the transmissions of others in one way or another for their own profit. In response, New York courts created a body of misappropriation law, loosely based on *INS,* that sought to apply ethical standards to the use by one party of another's transmissions of events.

Federal copyright law played little active role in this area until 1976. Before then, it appears to have been the general understanding — there being no caselaw of consequence — that live events such as baseball games were not copyrightable. Moreover, doubt existed even as to whether a recorded broadcast or videotape of such an event was copyrightable. In 1976, however, Congress passed legislation expressly affording copyright protection to simultaneously recorded broadcasts of live performances such as sports events. *See* 17 U.S.C. § 101. Such protection was not extended to the underlying events.

The 1976 amendments also contained provisions preempting state law claims that enforced rights "equivalent" to exclusive copyright protections when the work to which the state claim was being applied fell within the area of copyright protection. *See* 17 U.S.C. § 301. Based on legislative history of the 1976 amendments, it is generally agreed that a "hot-news" *INS*-like claim survives preemption. However, much of New York misappropriation law after *INS* goes well beyond "hot-news" claims and is preempted.

We hold that the surviving "hot-news" *INS*-like claim is limited to cases where: (i) a plaintiff generates or gathers information at a cost; (ii) the information is time-sensitive; (iii) a defendant's use of the information constitutes free-riding on the plaintiff's efforts; (iv) the defendant is in direct competition with a product or service offered by the plaintiffs; and (v) the ability of other parties to free-ride on the efforts of the plaintiff or others would so reduce the incentive to produce the product or service that its existence or quality would be substantially threatened. We conclude that SportsTrax does not meet that test.

B. Copyrights in Events or Broadcasts of Events

The NBA asserted copyright infringement claims with regard both to the underlying games and to their broadcasts. The district court dismissed these claims, and the NBA does not appeal from their dismissal. Nevertheless, discussion of the infringement claims is necessary to provide the framework for analyzing the viability of the NBA's state law misappropriation claim in light of the Copyright Act's preemptive effect.

1. Infringement of a Copyright in the Underlying Games

In our view, the underlying basketball games do not fall within the subject matter of federal copyright protection because they do not constitute "original works of authorship" under 17 U.S.C. § 102(a). Section 102(a) lists eight categories of "works of authorship" covered by the act, including such categories as "literary works," "musical works," and "dramatic works." The list does not include athletic events, and, although the list is concededly non-exclusive, such events are neither similar nor analogous to any of the listed categories.

Sports events are not "authored" in any common sense of the word. There is, of course, at least at the professional level, considerable preparation for a game. However, the preparation is as much an expression of hope or faith as a determination of what will actually happen. Unlike movies, plays, television programs, or operas, athletic events are competitive and have no underlying script. Preparation may even cause mistakes to succeed, like the broken play in football that gains yardage because the opposition could not expect it. Athletic events may also result in wholly unanticipated occurrences, the most notable recent event being in a championship baseball game in which interference with a fly ball caused an umpire to signal erroneously a home run.

What "authorship" there is in a sports event, moreover, must be open to copying by competitors if fans are to be attracted. If the inventor of the T-formation in football had been able to copyright it, the sport might have come to an end instead of prospering. Even where athletic preparation most resembles authorship — figure skating, gymnastics, and, some would uncharitably say, professional wrestling — a performer who conceives and executes a particularly graceful and difficult — or, in the case of wrestling, seemingly painful — acrobatic feat cannot copyright it without impairing the underlying competition in the future. A claim of being the only athlete to perform a feat doesn't mean much if no one else is allowed to try.

For many of these reasons, NIMMER ON COPYRIGHT concludes that the "far more reasonable" position is that athletic events are not copyrightable. Nimmer notes that, among other problems, the number of joint copyright owners would arguably include the league, the teams, the athletes, umpires, stadium workers and even fans, who all contribute to the "work."

Concededly, caselaw is scarce on the issue of whether organized events themselves are copyrightable, but what there is indicates that they are not. In claiming a copyright in the underlying games, the NBA relied in part on a footnote in *Baltimore Orioles, Inc. v. Major League Baseball Players Assn.,* 805 F.2d 663, 669 n.7 (7th Cir. 1986), *cert. denied,* 480 U.S. 941 (1987), which stated that the "players' performances" contain the "modest creativity required for copyrightability." However, the court went on to state, "Moreover, even if the players' performances were not sufficiently creative, the players agree that the cameramen and director contribute creative labor to the telecasts." *Id.* This last sentence indicates that the court was considering the copyrightability of telecasts — not the underlying games, which obviously can be played without cameras.

We believe that the lack of caselaw is attributable to a general understanding that athletic events were, and are, uncopyrightable. Indeed, prior to 1976, there was even doubt that broadcasts describing or depicting such events, which have a far stronger case for copyrightability than the events themselves, were entitled to copyright protection. Indeed, as described in the next subsection of this opinion, Congress found it necessary to extend such protection to recorded broadcasts of live events. The fact that Congress did not extend such protection to the events themselves confirms our view that the district court correctly held that appellants were not infringing a copyright in the NBA games.

2. Infringement of a Copyright in the Broadcasts of NBA Games

As noted, recorded broadcasts of NBA games — as opposed to the games themselves — are now entitled to copyright protection. The Copyright Act was amended in 1976 specifically to insure that simultaneously-recorded transmissions of live performances and sporting events would meet the Act's requirement that the original work of authorship be "fixed in any tangible medium of expression." 17 U.S.C. § 102(a). Accordingly, Section 101 of the Act, containing definitions, was amended to read: "A work consisting of sounds, images, or both, that are being transmitted, is "fixed" for purposes of this title if a fixation of the work is being made simultaneously with its transmission." Congress specifically had sporting events in mind:

> The bill seeks to resolve, through the definition of "fixation" in section 101, the status of live broadcasts — sports, news coverage, live performances of music, etc. — that are reaching the public in unfixed form but that are simultaneously being recorded.

The House Report also makes clear that it is the broadcast, not the underlying game, that is the subject of copyright protection. In explaining how game broadcasts meet the Act's requirement that the subject matter be an "original work[] of authorship," 17 U.S.C. § 102(a), the House Report stated:

> When a football game is being covered by four television cameras, with a director guiding the activities of the four cameramen and choosing which of their electronic images are sent out to the public and in what order, there is little doubt that what the cameramen and the director are doing constitutes "authorship."

Although the broadcasts are protected under copyright law, the district court correctly held that Motorola and STATS did not infringe NBA's copyright because they reproduced only facts from the broadcasts, not the expression or description of the game that constitutes the broadcast. The "fact/expression dichotomy" is a bedrock principle of copyright law that "limits severely the scope of protection in fact-based works." "'No author may copyright facts or ideas. The copyright is limited to those aspects of the work — termed 'expression' — that display the stamp of the author's originality.'"

We agree with the district court that the "defendants provide purely factual information which any patron of an NBA game could acquire from the arena without any involvement from the director, cameramen, or others who contribute to the originality of a broadcast." Because the SportsTrax device and AOL site reproduce only factual information culled from the broadcasts and none of the copyrightable expression of the games, appellants did not infringe the copyright of the broadcasts.

C. The State-Law Misappropriation Claim

The district court's injunction was based on its conclusion that, under New York law, defendants had unlawfully misappropriated the NBA's property rights in its games. The district court reached this conclusion by holding: (i) that the NBA's misappropriation claim relating to the underlying games was not preempted by Section 301 of the Copyright Act; and (ii) that, under New York common law, defendants had engaged in unlawful misappropriation. We disagree.

1. Preemption Under the Copyright Act

a) Summary

When Congress amended the Copyright Act in 1976, it provided for the preemption of state law claims that are interrelated with copyright claims in certain ways. Under 17 U.S.C. § 301, a state law claim is preempted when: (i) the state law claim seeks to vindicate "legal or equitable rights that are equivalent" to one of the bundle of exclusive rights already protected by copyright law under 17 U.S.C. §106 — styled the "general scope requirement"; and (ii) the particular work to which the state law claim is being applied falls within the type of works protected by the Copyright Act under Sections 102 and 103 — styled the "subject matter requirement."

* * *

We hold that where the challenged copying or misappropriation relates in part to the copyrighted broadcasts of the games, the subject matter requirement is met as to both the broadcasts and the games. We therefore reject the partial preemption doctrine and its anomalous consequence that "it is possible for a plaintiff to assert claims both for infringement of its copyright in a broadcast and misappropriation of its rights in the underlying event." We do find that a properly narrowed *INS* "hot-news" misappropriation claim survives preemption because it fails the general scope requirement, but that the broader theory of the radio broadcast cases relied upon by the district court were preempted when Congress extended copyright protection to simultaneously recorded broadcasts.

b) "Partial Preemption" and the Subject Matter Requirement

The subject matter requirement is met when the work of authorship being copied or misappropriated "falls within the ambit of copyright protection." *Harper & Row, Inc. v. Nation Enter.,* 723 F.2d 195, 200 (1983). We believe that the subject matter requirement is met in the instant matter and that the concept of "partial preemption" is not consistent with Section 301 of the Copyright Act. Although game broadcasts are copyrightable while the underlying games are not, the Copyright Act should not be read to distinguish between the two when analyzing the preemption of a misappropriation claim based on copying or taking from the copyrightable work. . . .

Copyrightable material often contains uncopyrightable elements within it, but Section 301 preemption bars state law misappropriation claims with respect to uncopyrightable as well as copyrightable elements. In *Harper & Row,* for example, we held that state law claims based on the copying of excerpts from President Ford's memoirs were preempted even with respect to information that was purely factual and not copyrightable. . . .

Adoption of a partial preemption doctrine — preemption of claims based on misappropriation of broadcasts but no preemption of claims based on misappropriation of underlying facts — would expand significantly the reach of state law claims and render the pre-emption intended by Congress unworkable. It is often difficult or impossible to separate the fixed copyrightable work from the underlying uncopyrightable events or facts. Moreover, Congress, in extending copyright protection only to the broadcasts and not to the underlying events, intended that the latter be in the public domain. Partial preemption turns that intent on its head by allowing state law to vest exclusive rights in material that Congress intended to be in the public domain and to make unlawful conduct that Congress intended to allow. . . . We agree with Judge Easterbrook and reject the separate analysis of the underlying games and broadcasts of those games for purposes of preemption.

c) The General Scope Requirement

Under the general scope requirement, Section 301 "preempts only those state law rights that 'may be abridged by an act which, in and of itself, would infringe one of the exclusive rights' provided by federal copyright law." . . . However, certain forms of commercial misappropriation otherwise within the general scope requirement will survive preemption if an "extra-element" test is met. . . .

We turn, therefore, to the question of the extent to which a "hot-news" misappropriation claim based on *INS* involves extra elements and is not the equivalent of exclusive rights under a copyright. Courts are generally agreed that some form of such a claim survives preemption. This conclusion is based in part on the legislative history of the 1976 amendments. The House Report stated:

> "Misappropriation" is not necessarily synonymous with copyright infringement, and thus a cause of action labeled as "misappropriation" is not preempted if it is in fact based neither on a right within the general scope of copyright as specified by section 106 nor on a right equivalent thereto. For example, state law should have the flexibility to afford a remedy (under traditional principles of equity) against a consistent pattern of unauthorized appropriation by a competitor of the facts (i.e., not the literary expression) constituting "hot" news, whether in the traditional mold of *International News Service v. Associated Press,* 248 U.S. 215 (1918), or in the newer form of data updates from scientific, business, or financial data bases.

The crucial question, therefore, is the breadth of the "hot-news" claim that survives preemption.

In *INS,* the plaintiff AP and defendant INS were "wire services" that sold news items to client newspapers. AP brought suit to prevent INS from selling facts and information lifted from AP sources to INS-affiliated newspapers. One method by which INS was able to use AP's news was to lift facts from AP news bulletins. . . . Another method was to sell facts taken from just-published east coast AP newspapers to west coast INS newspapers whose editions had yet to appear. The Supreme Court . . . characterized INS's conduct as "amounting to an unauthorized interference with the normal operation of complainant's legitimate business precisely at the point where the profit is to be reaped, in order to divert a material portion of the profit from those who have earned it to those who have not; with special advantage to defendant in the competition because of the fact that it is not burdened with any part of the expense of gathering the news."

***

> Whether or not reproduction of another's work is "immoral" depends on whether such use of the work is wrongful. If, for example, the work is in the public domain, then its use would not be wrongful. Likewise, if, as here, the work is unprotected by federal law because of lack of originality, then its use is neither unfair nor unjustified.

[E]ven narrow "hot news" *INS*-type claims survive preemption. Moreover, the "extra element" test should not be applied so as to allow state claims to survive preemption easily. "An action will not be saved from preemption by elements such as awareness or intent, which alter 'the action's scope but not its nature'. . . . Following this 'extra element' test, we have held that unfair competition and misappropriation claims grounded solely in the copying of a plaintiff's protected expression are preempted by section 301." . . .

Our conclusion, therefore, is that only a narrow "hot-news" misappropriation claim survives preemption for actions concerning material within the realm of copyright. . . . The facts of the *INS* decision are unusual and may serve, in part, to limit its rationale. . . . The limited extent to which the *INS* rationale has been incorporated into the common law of the states indicate that the decision is properly viewed as a response to unusual circumstances rather than as a statement of generally applicable principles of common law. Many subsequent decisions have expressly limited the *INS* case to its facts.

In our view, the elements central to an *INS* claim are: (i) the plaintiff generates or collects information at some cost or expense, (ii) the value of the information is highly time-sensitive, (iii) the defendant's use of the information constitutes free-riding on the plaintiff's costly efforts to generate or collect it, (iv) the defendant's use of the information is in direct competition with a product or service offered by the plaintiff, (v) the ability of other parties to free-ride on the efforts of the plaintiff would so reduce the incentive to produce the product or service that its existence or quality would be substantially threatened. . . .

INS is not about ethics; it is about the protection of property rights in time-sensitive information so that the information will be made available to the public by profit-seeking entrepreneurs. If services like AP were not assured of property rights in the news they pay to collect, they would cease to collect it. The ability of their competitors to appropriate their product at only nominal cost and thereby to disseminate a competing product at a lower price would destroy the incentive to collect news in the first place. The newspaper-reading public would suffer because no one would have an incentive to collect "hot news."

We therefore find the extra elements — those in addition to the elements of copyright infringement — that allow a "hotnews" claim to survive preemption are: (i) the time-sensitive value of factual information, (ii) the free-riding by a defendant, and (iii) the threat to the very existence of the product or service provided by the plaintiff.

2. The Legality of SportsTrax

We conclude that Motorola and STATS have not engaged in unlawful misappropriation under the "hot-news" test set out above. To be sure, some of the elements of a "hot-news" *INS*claim are met. The information transmitted to SportsTrax is not precisely contemporaneous, but it is nevertheless time-sensitive. Also, the NBA does provide, or will shortly do so, information like that available through SportsTrax. It now offers a service called "Gamestats" that provides official play-by-play game sheets and half-time and final box scores within each arena. It also provides such information to the media in each arena. In the future, the NBA plans to enhance Gamestats so that it will be networked between the various arenas and will support a pager product analogous to SportsTrax. SportsTrax will of course directly compete with an enhanced Gamestats.

However, there are critical elements missing in the NBA's attempt to assert a "hotnews" *INS*-type claim. As framed by the NBA, their claim compresses and confuses three different informational products. The first product is generating the information by playing the games; the second product is transmitting live, full descriptions of those games; and the third product is collecting and retransmitting strictly factual information about the games. The first and second products are the NBA's primary business: producing basketball games for live attendance and licensing copyrighted broadcasts of those games. The collection and retransmission of strictly factual material about the games is a different product: *e.g.*, box-scores in newspapers, summaries of statistics on television sports news, and real-time facts to be transmitted to pagers. In our view, the NBA has failed to show any competitive effect whatsoever from SportsTrax on the first and second products and a lack of any free-riding by SportsTrax on the third.

With regard to the NBA's primary products — producing basketball games with live attendance and licensing copyrighted broadcasts of those games — there is no evidence that anyone regards SportsTrax or the AOL site as a substitute for attending NBA games or watching them on television. In fact, Motorola markets SportsTrax as being designed "for those times when you cannot be at the arena, watch the game on TV, or listen to the radio. . . ."

The NBA argues that the pager market is also relevant to a "hot-news" *INS*-type claim and that SportsTrax's future competition with Gamestats satisfies any missing element. We agree that there is a separate market for the real-time transmission of factual information to pagers or similar devices, such as STATS's AOL site. However, we disagree that SportsTrax is in any sense free-riding off Gamestats.

An indispensable element of an *INS* "hot-news" claim is free-riding by a defendant on a plaintiff's product, enabling the defendant to produce a directly competitive product for less money because it has lower costs. SportsTrax is not such a product. The use of pagers to transmit real-time information about NBA games requires: (i) the collecting of facts about the games; (ii) the transmission of these facts on a network; (iii) the assembling of them by the particular service; and (iv) the transmission of them to pagers or an on-line computer site. Appellants are in no way free-riding on Gamestats. Motorola and STATS expend their own resources to collect purely factual information generated in NBA games to transmit to SportsTrax pagers. They have their own network and assemble and transmit data themselves.

To be sure, if appellants in the future were to collect facts from an enhanced Gamestats pager to retransmit them to SportsTrax pagers, that would constitute free-riding and might well cause Gamestats to be unprofitable because it had to bear costs to collect facts that SportsTrax did not. If the appropriation of facts from one pager to another pager service were allowed, transmission of current information on NBA games to pagers or similar devices would be substantially deterred because any potential transmitter would know that the first entrant would quickly encounter a lower cost competitor free-riding on the originator's transmissions.

However, that is not the case in the instant matter. SportsTrax and Gamestats are each bearing their own costs of collecting factual information on NBA games, and, if one produces a product that is cheaper or otherwise superior to the other, that producer will prevail in the marketplace. This is obviously not the situation against which *INS* was intended to prevent: the potential lack of any such product or service because of the anticipation of free-riding.

For the foregoing reasons, the NBA has not shown any damage to any of its products based on free-riding by Motorola and STATS, and the NBA's misappropriation claim based on New York law is preempted.

* * *

Notes and Comments

1. In *Pittsburgh Athletic,* the defendant paid observers, sitting outside of the stadium but within viewing range of the game, to relay game information for the defendant's unauthorized radio broadcast of play-by-play game action. The court held that this conduct violated the team's exclusive property right to control rights to broadcast the game played in the team stadium and also held defendant liable on common law theories of unjust enrichment and unfair competition. *See also Zacchini v. Scripps-Howard Broadcasting Co.*, 433 U.S. 564

(1977) (holding that the "owner" of an event, a 15-second human cannonball act, had a right of publicity to control distribution and that the First Amendment did not confer a right to broadcast an entire event without consent); *New Boston Television v. ESPN*, 215 U.S. P.Q. 755 (D. Mass. 1981) (holding that ESPN's videotaping from public airways, excerpting and rebroadcasting "highlights" of copyrighted broadcasts was not 'fair use' under Copyright Act). How does the *Motorola* pager case differ, if at all? What were the key factual distinctions in *Motorola* which led the court to rule in Motorola's favor? Do you agree with the Court's ruling?

2. If copyright law prohibits the copying of the broadcast and does not extend to the underlying game, could another party tape and broadcast a game using a sophisticated camera from a roof overlooking a sports stadium? How would the scenario in *Pittsburgh Athletic* be resolved under the Copyright Act? In 2002, the Chicago Cubs sued a group of rooftop bar owners who charged fans to watch Cubs games from their rooftops, which had a clear view of the ballpark. The Cubs alleged that the game itself was copyrighted, and that the defendants were profiting from the team's name, players, trademarks, copyrighted telecasts and images without the Cubs' consent. *Chicago NL Club v. Sky Box on Waveland*, No. 02 C 9105 (N.D. Ill.). The parties reached a settlement agreement that the rooftop owners would pay the Cubs 17% of their annual profits for 20 years. Would a court have ruled differently, particularly if the rooftop owners did not charge to watch the game?

3. Would a different result in *New Boston* ensue if the games are played in a publicly financed stadium? *WCVB-TV v. Boston Athletic Ass'n*, 926 F.2d 42 (1st Cir. 1991) held that, although the event sponsor had an exclusive licensing agreement with one network, another network's simultaneous broadcasting of a sports event occurring in public was permissible. Moreover, the station's use of the words "Boston Marathon" did not violate trademark law because the use merely described the event to be broadcast and did not indicate sponsor's approval: "[t]he use of words for descriptive purposes is called a 'fair use,' and the law usually permits it even if the words themselves also constitute a trademark." *See* Anne M. Wall, *Sports Marketing and the Law: Protecting Proprietary Interests in Sports Entertainment Events*, 7 MARQ. SPORTS L.J. 77, 147 (1996) (suggesting that exclusive broadcast rights may not preclude another's simultaneous broadcast of an event held in public).

4. Copyright Law Limitations. To establish copyright infringement, two elements must be proven: (1) ownership of a valid copyright, and (2) copying of copyrighted work. The Copyright Act does not define infringement, but 17 U.S.C. § 102(b) provides that a copyright "does not extend to any idea, procedure, process, system, method of operation, concept, principle, or discovery, regardless of the form in which it is described, explained, illustrated, or embodied in such work." Thus, the law makes a distinction between facts or ideas and expressions. The Act also recognizes that the "fair use" of a copyrighted work is not infringement where it is for purposes such as criticism, news reporting, teaching, scholarship, or research. *Id.* at § 107.

5. In *New Boston*, ESPN argued "fair use" and newsworthiness defenses to plaintiff's claim of copyright infringement. If Motorola's use of game information is lawful, why was ESPN's use deemed a copyright violation? Do copyright holders have the right to restrict local news networks or organizations from showing highlights or otherwise reporting on sporting events? What are the damages? *See NFL v. Rondor*, 840 F. Supp. 1160 (N.D. Ohio 1993) (local bar and restaurant infringed upon NFL's copyright in unauthorized interception of blacked-out television broadcast by use of special antenna).

6. If a primary objective of the Copyright Act is to encourage the production of original creative works, including sports broadcasts as audio-visual works, does this protection impair technological advances to provide real-time services available with the Internet, electronic or video conferencing? How does the public benefit from copyright law?

7. Live games or performances. In *Motorola*, why did the Court find no copyright violation by the SPORTSTRAX pager product or the AOL web site services? The Court distinguished copyright protection for broadcasts, as opposed to underlying sporting events. Judge Winter stated, "Sports events are not 'authored' in any common sense of the word. . . . What 'authorship' there is in a sports event, moreover, must be open to copying by competitors if fans are to be attracted." 105 F.3d at 846.

8. Sports "Moves" as Intellectual Property? Do you agree with Judge Winter's suggestion that sports "moves" cannot be copyrighted? Could an athlete claim a copyright or trademark in his or her signature move, such as in Abdul-Jabbar's skyhook, Chris Evert's two-handed backhand, or Dick Fosberry's high-jumping flop? *See e.g.*, Robert M. Kundstadt, *et. al.*, *Are Sports Moves Next in IP Law?*, NAT'L L.J. C2 (May 20, 1996) (proposing that distinctive sports "moves" are protectable as intellectual property rights); and Jefferey A. Smith, Comment: *It's Your Move — No It's Not! The Application of Patent Law to Sports Moves*, 70 U. COLO. L. REV. 1051 (1999) (analyzing application of intellectual property laws to sports moves).

9. Preemption and State Law Claims. The Second Circuit held that the Copyright Act preempts state law misappropriation claims, yet also ruled that the Copyright Act does not apply to the games themselves. Notwithstanding, the Court acknowledges that a narrow *INS* 'hot news' misappropriation claim survives preemption. Is this analytically consistent? Do state claims survive preemption of the Copyright Act? If so, when? Would it make a difference if the defendants had gathered and transmitted game information from inside the sports arena, rather than by watching or listening to broadcasts? Suppose the admission ticket prohibited any reproduction or transmission of play?

10. "Hot News" Misappropriation. In analyzing the NBA's claim that defendants unlawfully misappropriated "hot news" rights to their games, the

Court considered (1) the plaintiff's investment in generating or collecting information; (2) the time-sensitive value of the factual information; (3) the free riding by a defendant; (4) direct competition; and (5) the threat to the very existence of the product or service provided by the plaintiff. Why did the Court reject the NBA's "hot news" misappropriation claims? *See also Morris Communications, Inc. v. PGA Tour*, 235 F. Supp. 2d 1269 (M.D. Fla. 2002) (ruling the PGA Tour justified in restricting newspaper corporation from publishing "real time" golf scores obtained from the tournaments' on-site media centers because (1) the newspaper sought to free-ride on the PGA Tour's efforts, and (2) the PGA Tour has a property right in the scores before they are in the public domain, distinguishing *Motorola*'s "hot news" that could be acquired independently).

11. How does the protection under copyright (original works of authorship embodied in a tangible form of expression), over trademark (type of symbol to identify a particular set of goods), law differ?

Chapter 14

HEALTH AND DISABILITY ISSUES IN SPORTS LAW

A. INTRODUCTION

When thinking about athletes participating in competitive or organized sports, typically the public rarely contemplates the inclusion of players with medical impairments or other physical, mental, and learning disabilities. Yet many athletes with disabilities, whether visible or hidden, have achieved success in both amateur and professional sports. Although deaf, Kenny Walker attained All-American status as a defensive tackle at the University of Nebraska and went on to play professionally with the Denver Broncos. Jim Abbot, who has only one arm as a result of a birth defect, successfully pitched in the professional baseball leagues. The sporting public has applauded the accomplishments of these athletes who are able to compete presumably "despite" their disabilities or by "overcoming" them. The awe turned to apprehension when Hank Gathers, who was medically cleared to play college basketball despite a heart rhythm disorder, died on the court, or when twelve-year old Michael Montalvo, who has AIDS, sought to enroll in karate classes, and even when Magic Johnson returned to professional basketball after revealing that he was HIV positive.

The rights of athletes with medical impairments or disabilities to participate in competitive sports are also increasingly controversial. Because of a medical impairment or disability, some athletes cannot satisfy certain eligibility requirements set by the governing sporting organizations or they need accommodation in order to participate. National attention focused on Casey Martin, who suffers from a severe congenital disability affecting his right leg, in his lawsuit seeking to compel the PGA Tour to permit Martin to ride a cart during competitions although all other players are required to walk.

Athletes who have been effectively excluded from sports participation because of a medical impairment or disability have invoked the stringent anti-discrimination standards of federal disability laws in asserting rights to participate and to reasonable modifications of eligibility standards in sports programs at the interscholastic, intercollegiate, and professional levels.

Federal disability legislation, primarily through the Rehabilitation Act of 1973, which applies to federally funded programs, and the Americans with Disabilities Act of 1990 (ADA), whose broader coverage reaches most private employers and private entities constituting places of public accommodations, prohibits discrimination on the basis of disability and further obligates these entities to provide reasonable accommodations, modifications, or auxiliary aids that will enable qualified individuals with disabilities to access and to participate in the program or activity. 29 U.S.C. § 794; 42 U.S.C. § 12101. In enacting the ADA, Congress found, *inter alia*, that individuals with disabilities continually encounter various forms of discrimination, including "outright intentional exclusion, the discriminatory effects of architectural, transportation, and communication barriers, overprotective rules and policies, failure to make modifications to existing facilities, programs and practices, exclusionary qualification standards and criteria, segregation, and relegation to lesser services, programs, activities, benefits, jobs or other opportunities." 42 U.S.C. § 12101(b). A goal of these laws, which apply to virtually all sports teams and organizations, is to assure the equality of opportunity and full participation for individuals with disabilities.

Federal disability laws have had and continue to have a significant impact in sports, raising complicated and controversial medico-legal questions surrounding the rights of individuals with disabilities to participate in athletics and the concomitant rights and obligations of the entities regulating athletic competition to set and enforce eligibility and safety rules. Many of the cases involving disability law in sports have garnered intense public attention, raising questions about the impact on the competitive nature of sports and the ability of sporting organizations to enforce rules of participation.

This chapter addresses the legal issues and major litigation involving health and disability issues in sports. **Section B** sets forth the key statutory provisions and framework for analyzing claims and defenses under the federal disability laws. Thereafter, the primary areas explored involve issues relating to athletes with high medical risk of injury or death and athletes who fail to meet neutral eligibility rules and standards, determining what constitutes reasonable modification of competition rules for athletes with disabilities, and defining obligations for stadium facility and arena physical accessibility.

B. FEDERAL DISABILITY LEGISLATION — KEY STATUTORY DEFINITIONS AND PROVISIONS

Much of the litigation involving disability issues in sports has focused on whether the athlete is protected by, or a sports organization subject to, federal legislation. The following statutory definitions and provisions are generally at issue.

1. The Americans with Disabilities Act of 1990

The ADA is codified under five titles. Relevant here are Title I applying to employment, Title II to public programs and services, and Title III to private entities constituting places of public accommodation. Applicable to all subchapters of the ADA is the important definition of "disability."

42 U.S.C. § 12101(2) **Disability.** The term "disability" means, with respect to an individual —

(A) a physical or mental impairment that substantially limits one or more of the major life activities of such individual;

(B) a record of such impairment; or

(C) being regarded as having such an impairment.

Title I

(Employment)

42 U.S.C. § 12112(a) **Discrimination.** "No covered entity shall discriminate against a qualified individual with a disability because of the disability of such individual in regard to job application procedures, the hiring, advancement, or discharge of employees, employee compensation, job training, and other terms, conditions or privileges of employment."

42 U.S.C. § 12113(b) **Qualification Standards.** "The term 'qualification standards' may include a requirement that an individual shall not pose a direct threat to the health and safety of other individuals in the workplace."

Title II

(Public Services)

42 U.S.C. § 12132 **Discrimination.** "[N]o qualified individual with a disability shall, by reason of such disability, be excluded from participation in or be denied the benefits of the services, programs, or activities of a public entity, or be subject to discrimination by any such entity."

42 U.S.C. § 12131(2) **Qualified Individual with a Disability.** "The term 'qualified individual with a disability' means an individual with a disability who, with or without reasonable modifications to rules, policies, or practices, . . . meets the essential eligibility requirements for the receipt of services or the participation in programs or activities provided by the public entity."

Title III

(Public Accommodations)

42 U.S.C. § 12182 **Prohibition of Discrimination by Public Accommodations.**

"No individual shall be discriminated against on the basis of disability in the full and equal enjoyment of the goods, services, facilities, privileges, advantages or accommodations of any place of public accommodation by any person who owns, leases (or leases to) or operates a place of public accommodation."

42 U.S.C. § 12182(b)(1)(B) **Integrated Settings.** "Goods, services, facilities, privileges, advantages, and accommodations shall be afforded to an individual with a disability in the most integrated setting appropriate to the needs of the individual."

42 U.S.C. § 12182(b)(2) **Specific Prohibitions.** "(A) Discrimination — includes [*inter alia*] (i) the imposition or application of eligibility criteria that screen out or tend to screen out an individual with a disability or any class of individuals with disabilities from fully and equally enjoying any goods, services, facilities, privileges, advantages, or accommodations, unless such criteria can be shown to be necessary for the provision of the goods, services, facilities, privileges, advantages, or accommodations being offered; [and] (ii) a failure to make reasonable modifications in policies, practices, or procedures, when such modifications are necessary to afford such goods, services, facilities, privileges, advantages, or accommodations to individuals with disabilities, unless the entity can demonstrate that making such modifications would fundamentally alter the nature of such goods, services, facilities, privileges, advantages, or accommodations. . . ."

2. The Rehabilitation Act of 1973

29 U.S.C. § 794(a) **Nondiscrimination under Federal grants and programs.**

"No otherwise qualified individual with a disability . . . shall, solely by reason of his or her disability, be excluded from the participation in, be denied the benefits of, or be subjected to discrimination under any program or activity receiving federal financial assistance. . . ."

Prior to the enactment of the federal disability legislation, athletes with medical impairments and disabilities seeking rights to participate in sports met limited success in raising Constitutional claims against exclusion. In *City of Cleburne v. Cleburne Living Center*, 473 U.S. 431 (1985), the Supreme Court held that individuals with disabilities are not a suspect or quasi-suspect class. As a result, public schools and institutions (as "state actors") may discriminate against or exclude disabled athletes from participation if rationally related to a legitimate objective, such as to guard the health and safety of athletes. On a due process level, there is no fundamental or constitutional right to participate in competitive sports. *See* Matthew J. Mitten, *Sports Participation by "Handicapped" Athletes*, 10 SPG-ENT. & SPORTS LAW 15 (1992). By contrast, the Rehabilitation Act and the ADA provide athletes with disabilities substantial protection. Accordingly, most disability discrimination claims are based on the federal statutes rather than on the U.S. Constitution. Recourse may also be available under some state anti-discrimination laws.

In analyzing an issue involving an athlete's rights under federal disability law, consider: (1) Is the athlete "disabled" within the meaning of the statute? More specifically, is an athlete "substantially limited" in a "major life activity"? Is sports participation a "major life activity"? (2) Is the athlete "otherwise qualified" to participate in the sports program with or without reasonable accommodations? (3) Was the athlete discriminated against or excluded "because of" the person's disability? and (4) Would the requested accommodation or modification be unreasonable, require the elimination of essential eligibility requirements or fundamentally alter the nature of the sport or competition? To determine the applicable statutory coverage, ask whether the defendant is: a recipient of federal funds (Rehabilitation Act); a public entity (ADA Title II); a place of public accommodation (ADA Title III); or an employer of the potential plaintiff (ADA Title I).

C. PARTICIPATION RIGHTS AND RESPONSIBILITIES: ELIGIBILITY OF ATHLETES WITH HIGH MEDICAL RISK; PROTECTIVE ISSUES

Problem

Mia Bently is a sophomore basketball player on athletic scholarship at Middleton University, a private university and Division I member of the NCAA. Last year, Mia was seriously injured in an automobile accident, resulting in the loss of a kidney and some vision in her right eye. As basketball season approaches, she is concerned that the school officials are not going to clear her to participate this season. Mia's personal physician has assured her that she will be perfectly healthy by that time and that the loss of vision and the kidney should not impact her playing ability. Mia's doctor cleared her to participate. The university team physician, however, refused to clear Mia to participate in team competitions, citing safety and liability concerns.

1. Mia seeks your advice as to what her legal recourse might be against the school. She desperately wants to play this year. Her fear is that the loss of playing opportunities will jeopardize her scholarship and prevent her from playing professionally when she has completed her eligibility at the collegiate level.

2. You are general counsel at Middleton University. Mia Bently has filed a lawsuit seeking a preliminary injunction order that she be permitted to play on the school basketball team. You are concerned about the potential liability the school might encounter by allowing athletes with serious medical conditions or disabilities to compete, and you believe the university has an independent obligation to guard all athletes' health and safety and to abide by the team physician's recommendation. The student and her parents have expressed a willingness to sign a liability waiver. How do you respond to Mia Bentley's request and motion for injunctive relief?

CASE FILE

KNAPP v. NORTHWESTERN UNIVERSITY

101 F.3d 473 (7th Cir. 1996), *cert. denied*, 520 U.S. 1274 (1997)

Before BAUER, DIANE P. WOOD, and EVANS, Circuit Judges.

TERRANCE T. EVANS, Circuit Judge.

Nicholas Knapp wants to play NCAA basketball for Northwestern University — so badly that he is willing to face an increased risk of death to do so. Knapp is a competent, intelligent adult capable of assessing whether playing intercollegiate basketball is worth the risk to his heart and possible death, and to him the risk is acceptable. Usually, competent, intelligent adults are allowed to make such decisions. This is especially true when, as here, the individual's family approves of the decision and the individual and his parents are willing to sign liability waivers regarding the worst-case scenario should it occur.

Northwestern, however, refuses to allow Knapp to play on or even practice with its men's basketball team. Knapp, currently a sophomore at Northwestern, has the basketball skills to play at the intercollegiate level, but he has never taken the court for his team. Although Northwestern does not restrict him from playing pick-up basketball games, using recreational facilities on campus, or exerting himself physically on his own, the university disqualified Knapp from playing on its intercollegiate basketball team. The issue in this case boils down to whether the school — because of § 504 of the Rehabilitation Act of 1973, as amended, 29 U.S.C. § 794 — will be forced to let Knapp don a purple uniform and take the floor as a member of Northwestern's basketball team.

Prior to his senior year of high school Knapp was rated among the best basketball players in Illinois. He was recruited by numerous universities, including Northwestern. At the end of Knapp's junior year at Peoria's Woodruff High School, Northwestern orally offered him an athletic scholarship to play basketball. Knapp orally accepted the offer.

A few weeks into his senior year, Knapp suffered sudden cardiac death — meaning his heart stopped — during a pick-up basketball game. Paramedics used cardiopulmonary resuscitation, defibrillation (*i.e.*, electric shocks), and injections of drugs to bring Knapp back to life. A few weeks later, doctors implanted an internal cardioverter-defibrillator in Knapp's abdomen. The device detects heart arrhythmia and delivers a shock to convert the abnormal heart rhythm back to normal. In other words, if Knapp's heart stops again the device is supposed to restart it.

On the day following his sudden cardiac death, Northwestern informed Knapp and his family that whatever the ultimate medical decision, Northwestern would honor its commitment for a scholarship. Seven weeks after his collapse Knapp signed a national letter of intent to attend Northwestern.

Knapp did not play basketball during his senior year in high school, but he was always a superb student, and in June 1995 he graduated as the valedictorian of his class. In September 1995 he enrolled as a Northwestern student.

On November 7, 1995, Dr. Howard Sweeney, Northwestern's head team physician, declared Knapp ineligible to participate on Northwestern's men's basketball team for the 1995-96 school year.[1] Dr. Sweeney based his decision on Knapp's medical records in which several treating physicians recommended that Knapp not play competitive basketball, the report of team physician Dr. Mark Gardner following a physical examination of Knapp, published guidelines and recommendations following two national medical conferences known as the Bethesda Conferences[2] regarding eligibility of athletes with cardiovascular abnormalities, and recommendations of physicians with whom Dr. Gardner and Dr. Sweeney consulted. After the basketball season ended, Northwestern and the Big Ten declared Knapp permanently medically ineligible to play basketball. Northwestern's athletic director, Rick Taylor, later confirmed that Northwestern will never voluntarily let Knapp play intercollegiate basketball as a Wildcat.

As a result, Knapp has never practiced with the Northwestern team nor played in a college game. His scholarship nevertheless continues and he attends practices (though he is not allowed to do anything but watch, apparently). He also receives other benefits afforded to athletes (such as tutoring, counseling, and training table), in addition to the full range of academic and nonacademic offerings the university provides to all students.

On the same day Dr. Sweeney declared him ineligible, Knapp filed a complaint in federal district court asserting that Northwestern's actions violated the Rehabilitation Act. The suit sought declaratory relief, preliminary and perma-

---

1 Northwestern's Presidential Directive on Self-Regulation of Intercollegiate Athletics, the Big Ten Conference's Handbook Agreements for Men's Programs, and the NCAA's Constitution and Sports Medicine Handbook all give the team physician sole responsibility to decide whether a student is medically eligible to compete on the basketball team.

2 Two national medical conferences were held in Bethesda, Maryland, for the specific purpose of establishing prudent consensus recommendations among cardiologists and sports medicine physicians regarding the eligibility of athletes with cardiovascular abnormalities to compete in sports. . . . The 26th Bethesda Conference's task force on arrhythmias addressed conditions like Knapp's and implanted cardioverter-defibrillators. This task force recommended that athletes with ventricular fibrillation "that result in cardiac arrest in the presence or absence of structural heart disease cannot participate in any moderate or high intensity competitive sports." 24 JOURNAL OF THE AMERICAN COLLEGE OF CARDIOLOGY 845, 897 (1994). "For athletes with implantable defibrillators . . . all moderate and high intensity sports are contraindicated." *Id.*

nent injunctive relief, and compensatory damages. Knapp's undisputed goal is to force Northwestern to allow him to play varsity basketball.

In May 1996 Northwestern filed a motion for summary judgment, and Knapp thereafter requested a permanent injunction. The district court held a hearing on September 6, 1996, solely to determine whether Knapp presently is medically eligible to play intercollegiate basketball. Presented with conflicting evidence, the district court found Knapp medically eligible and Northwestern in violation of the Rehabilitation Act. After subsequent hearings on the issue of reasonable accommodation, the district court denied Northwestern's motion for summary judgment and entered a permanent injunction prohibiting Northwestern from excluding Knapp from playing on its basketball team for any reason related to his cardiac condition.

The district court's decision was based on the affidavit of Knapp and the testimony and affidavits of two experts presented by Northwestern and three experts presented by Knapp. All the experts agreed Knapp had suffered sudden cardiac death due to ventricular fibrillation; even with the internal defibrillator, playing intercollegiate basketball places Knapp at a higher risk for suffering another event of sudden cardiac death compared to other male college basketball players; the internal defibrillator has never been tested under the conditions of intercollegiate basketball; and no person currently plays or has ever played college or professional basketball after suffering sudden cardiac death and having a defibrillator implanted. Northwestern's experts, cardiologists who participated in at least one of the Bethesda conferences, testified that playing intercollegiate basketball significantly and unacceptably increases Knapp's risk of death. At least one of Northwestern's experts stated that individuals with internal defibrillators should not play intercollegiate basketball. Knapp's expert cardiologists, one of whom, Dr. Lawrence Rink, is Knapp's treating cardiologist and an Indiana University basketball team physician, testified that although Knapp is at an increased risk for sudden cardiac death, that risk, especially with the internal defibrillator in place, is insubstantial or at least acceptable.

After tasting defeat in the district court, Northwestern filed an emergency notice of appeal [and] sought a stay of enforcement of the injunction. . . .

We review the district court's grant of a permanent injunction for abuse of discretion . . . Interpretation of the Rehabilitation Act presents legal questions calling for de novo review.

The Rehabilitation Act, which is the sole basis for Knapp's claim, ensures that:

> no otherwise qualified individual with a disability . . . shall, solely by reason of her or his disability, be excluded from the participation in, be denied the benefits of, or be subjected to discrimination under any program or activity receiving Federal financial assistance. . . .

29 U.S.C. § 794(a). To prevail on his claim for discrimination under the Act, Knapp must prove that: (1) he is disabled as defined by the Act; (2) he is otherwise qualified for the position sought; (3) he has been excluded from the position solely because of his disability; and (4) the position exists as part of a program or activity receiving federal financial assistance. Northwestern does not dispute that it receives federal financial assistance and that it has excluded Knapp from its intercollegiate basketball program solely because of his cardiac condition, so our focus is on whether Knapp is an "otherwise qualified individual with a disability."

> To show that he is disabled under the terms of the Act, Knapp must prove that he (i) has a physical . . . impairment which substantially limits one or more of [his] major life activities, (ii) has a record of such an impairment, or (iii) is regarded as having such an impairment.

29 U.S.C. § 706(8)(B). Knapp satisfies the first element of part (i) of this definition. A cardiovascular problem constitutes a physical impairment under § 706(8)(B). Northwestern does not dispute this fact, but it instead zeros in on the second element of the disability definition: whether playing intercollegiate basketball is part of a major life activity and, if so, whether its diagnosis of Knapp's cardiac condition substantially limits Knapp in that activity.

In determining whether a particular individual has a disability as defined in the Rehabilitation Act, the regulations promulgated by the Department of Health and Human Services with the oversight and approval of Congress are of significant assistance. Those regulations define "major life activities" as basic functions of life "such as caring for one's self, performing manual tasks, walking, seeing, hearing, speaking, breathing, learning, and working." 34 C.F.R. § 104.3(j)(2)(ii). Regulations regarding equal employment opportunities under the Americans with Disabilities Act, adopt the same term and definition and an interpretive note provides a bit more guidance: "'Major life activities' are those basic activities that the average person in the general population can perform with little or no difficulty."

The regulations promulgated pursuant to the Rehabilitation Act do not define "substantial limitation". . . . The court must ask "'whether the particular impairment constitutes for the particular person a significant barrier to [a major life activity].'"

This case is difficult because it does not fit neatly under the Rehabilitation Act. The "disability" Knapp claims is the basis for discrimination against him is not a continuing one like blindness or deafness. At any given moment in time when Knapp's heart is functioning properly his disability does not affect him. He is truly disabled only when his heart stops, which may or may not happen to him again. The disability regarding which Northwestern allegedly discriminates, therefore, actually is the greater risk of harm for Knapp than the risk faced by other male college basketball players. In addition, other impairments usually do not have as severe a result as is possible in this case. A person who is deaf, for instance, will not suddenly die on the basketball court because of that disability. Here, Knapp's disability is all or nothing. Finally, because Knapp's disability affects one of the most central organs of the body, his disability to some extent affects all major life activities — if his heart stops, he will not breathe, see, speak, walk, learn, or work. Once again it is all or nothing — either his heart is functioning and no major life activities are limited at that moment, or it has stopped and the most major life activity of all — living — has been affected.

In any event, the parties here have framed their arguments as involving solely the major life activity of learning. Knapp contends that playing an intercollegiate sport is an integral part of his major life activity of learning and that his education will be substantially limited if he cannot play on the team. He states that he does not believe he can obtain confidence, dedication, leadership, perseverance, discipline, and teamwork in any better way. The district court agreed with him, determining that for Knapp, playing on the Northwestern basketball team was part of the major life activity of learning and that he was substantially limited from such learning by the university. . . .

We think this same interrelationship applies regarding learning. If playing NCAA basketball reaches a major life activity, then it is likely that deprivation of that activity would, for the individual basketball player, be a substantial limitation. Likewise, if playing intercollegiate basketball does not reach the status of major life activity, then it is most likely that deprivation will not be a substantial limitation.

We do not think that the definition of "major life activity" can be as particularized as Knapp wants it to be. [*See Jasany v. United States Postal Service*, 755 F.2d 1244 (6th Cir. 1985) (An impairment that affects only a narrow range of jobs can be regarded either as not reaching a major life activity or as not substantially limiting one.).] Playing intercollegiate basketball obviously is not in and of itself a major life activity, as it is not a basic function of life on the same level as walking, breathing, and speaking. Not everyone gets to go to college, let alone play intercollegiate sports. We acknowledge that intercollegiate sports can be an important part of the college learning experience for both athletes and many cheering students — especially at a Big Ten school. Knapp has indicated that such is the case for him. But not every student thinks so. Numerous college students graduate each year having neither participated in nor attended an intercollegiate sporting event. Their sheepskins are no less valuable because of the lack of intercollegiate sports in their lives. Not playing intercollegiate sports does not mean they have not learned. Playing or enjoying intercollegiate sports therefore cannot be held out as a necessary part of learning for all students.

* * *

Because intercollegiate athletics may be *one part* of the major life activity of learning for *certain* students, the parties here have framed the analysis of what constitutes a major life activity into a choice between a subjective test or an objective test — whether we look at what constitutes learning for Nick Knapp or what constitutes learning in general for the average person. The Rehabilitation Act and the regulations promulgated under it give little guidance regarding whether the determination of what constitutes a major life activity turns on an objective or subjective standard. And while we have previously said that whether a person is disabled is "an individualized inquiry, best suited to a case-by-case determination," we have also indicated that "the definition of 'major life activity' in the regulations 'cannot be interpreted to include working at the specific job of one's choice.'" Other courts have been across the board on whether the test is objective or subjective. *Compare Pahulu v. University of Kansas*, 897 F. Supp. 1387, 1393 (D. Kan. 1995) ("for Pahulu, intercollegiate football may be a major life activity, *i.e.*, learning"), and *Sandison v. Michigan High School Athletic Ass'n*, 863 F. Supp. 483, 489 (D. Mich. 1994) (participation on high school teams is "as to them a major life activity"), with *Welsh v. City of Tulsa, Okla.*, 977 F.2d 1415 (10th Cir. 1992) (major life activity of working does not necessarily mean working at the job of one's choice).

We decline to define the major life activity of learning in such a way that the Act applies whenever someone wants to play intercollegiate athletics. A "major life activity," as defined in the regulations, is a basic function of life "such as caring for one's self, performing manual tasks, walking, seeing, hearing, speaking, breathing, learning, and working." These are basic functions, not more specific ones such as being an astronaut, working as a firefighter, driving a race car, or learning by playing Big Ten basketball. . . . An impairment that interferes with an individual's ability to perform a particular function, but does not significantly decrease that individual's ability to obtain a satisfactory education otherwise, does not *substantially* limit the major life activity of learning.

Because learning through playing intercollegiate basketball is only one part of the education available to Knapp at Northwestern, even under a subjective standard, Knapp's ability to learn is not substantially limited. Knapp's scholarship continues, allowing him access to all academic and — except for intercollegiate basketball — all nonacademic services and activities available to other Northwestern students, in addition to all other services available to scholarship athletes. Although perhaps not as great a learning experience as actually playing, it is even possible that Knapp may "learn" through the basketball team in a role other than as a player. Knapp is an intelligent student and athlete, and the inability to play intercollegiate basketball at Northwestern forecloses only a small portion of his collegiate opportunities. Like the firefighter in *Welsh*, who did not show that his education and training limited him to being a firefighter, Knapp has not shown that his education and training limit him to do nothing but play basketball. The fact that Knapp's goal of playing intercollegiate basketball is frustrated does not substantially limit his education. The Rehabilitation Act does not guarantee an individual the exact educational experience that he may desire, just a fair one. Consequently, we hold that Knapp as a matter of law is not disabled within the meaning of the Rehabilitation Act.

Even if we were inclined to find Knapp disabled under the Rehabilitation Act, he would still come up short because we also hold as a matter of law that he is not, under the statute, "otherwise qualified" to play intercollegiate basketball at Northwestern. A qualified disabled person, with respect to postsecondary education services, is a "person who meets the academic and technical standards requisite to admission or participation in the [school's] education program or activity." An explanatory note to the regulations states that the term "technical standards" means "all nonacademic admissions criteria that are essential to participation in the program in question."

Section 794 does not compel educational institutions to disregard the disabilities of disabled persons. It requires only that an "otherwise qualified" disabled person not be excluded from participation in a federally funded program solely because of the disability. In other words, although a disability is not a permissible ground for assuming an inability to function in a particular context, the disability is not thrown out when considering if the person is qualified for the position sought. "An otherwise qualified person is one who is able to meet all of a program's requirements in spite of his handicap," with reasonable accommodation.

Legitimate physical qualifications may in fact be essential to participation in particular programs. . . . Although blanket exclusions are generally unacceptable, legitimate physical requirements are proper.

A significant risk of personal physical injury can disqualify a person from a position if the risk cannot be eliminated. But more than merely an elevated risk of injury is required before disqualification is appropriate. Any physical qualification based on risk of future injury must be examined with special care if the Rehabilitation Act is not to be circumvented, since almost all disabled individuals are at a greater risk of injury.

In *Mantolete*, the Ninth Circuit addressed the standard to apply in determining if an individual is otherwise physically qualified to perform an activity when the possibility of future injury exists:

> [I]n some cases, a job requirement that screens out qualified handicapped individuals on the basis of possible future injury is necessary. However, we hold that in order to exclude such individuals, there must be a showing of a reasonable probability of substantial harm. Such a determination cannot be based merely on an employer's subjective evaluation or, except in cases of a most apparent nature, merely on medical reports. The question is whether, in light of the individual's work history and medical history, employment of that individual would pose a reasonable probability of substantial harm. . . . In applying this standard, an employer must gather all relevant information regarding the applicant's work history and medical history, and independently assess both the probability and severity of potential injury. This involves, of course, a case-by-case analysis of the applicant and the particular job.

767 F.2d at 1422. We agree this is the appropriate standard. We now turn, however, to who should make such an assessment.

In this case, the severity of the potential injury is as high as it could be — death. In regard to the probability of injury, Dr. John H. McAnulty, one of Knapp's experts, testified at the injunction hearing that the annual risk of death to Knapp as a result of his cardiac condition under a worst-case scenario is 2.4 percent and that playing intercollegiate basketball would elevate this annual risk to 2.93 percent, or 1 in 34. In other words, if 34 Nick Knapps played basketball for a year, chances are one would die. Dr. Brian Olshansky, another expert for Knapp, put Knapp's risk of death for the 1996-97 basketball season at no greater than 1 in 100. These estimates took into account Knapp's internal defibrillator, apparently the only "accommodation" possible for Knapp's condition. Although the doctors indicated that these numbers were merely estimates, all agreed that the risk to Knapp is higher than to the average male collegiate basketball player. Knapp's experts believed it was an acceptable level of risk.

Northwestern's experts agreed with the school's team doctors that Knapp's participation in competitive Big Ten basketball presented an unacceptable level of risk. According to Dr. Barry J. Maron, one of Northwestern's experts, based on a 10-year study, the risk of nontraumatic death for the average male college basketball player is 1 in 28,818. Dr. Maron further testified that participation in intercollegiate basketball significantly increases Knapp's risk of death, although he believed the precise risk could not be quantified. Dr. Douglas J. Zipes agreed. According to both Drs. Zipes and Maron, the most important fact in assessing Knapp's current risk of sudden cardiac death while playing intercollegiate basketball is the fact that his previous sudden cardiac death was induced by playing basketball.

Knapp's and Northwestern's experts disagreed on the effect of the passage of time on the likelihood that Knapp would suffer another sudden cardiac death. Almost all experts agreed that the internal defibrillator had never been tested under conditions like an intercollegiate basketball game or practice and that it was unclear whether the device would actually work under the stress and physical conditions of a high-intensity sport. Dr. Olshansky, though, indicated that biweekly "interrogations" of the defibrillator would minimize the risk of its failure. Knapp has had his defibrillator checked on a regular basis and has had no problems with it.

The district court judge in this case believed that in the face of conflicting opinion evidence regarding risk, and the fact that no scientific data existed to quantify that risk, the decision on whether Knapp should play falls in the lap of the court:

> We have nothing more exotic here than highly qualified experts, in agreement on all the basic scientific principles and differing only in their medical judgment on the final question. . . . All possess the education, training and experience required to become experts and none dis-

> putes the expertise of the others. The range of disagreement is extremely narrow, confined only to the dimensions of the risk of recurrence and the effect of the passage of time on that risk. . . . My task is to consider all the opinions and determine which are most persuasive. It is what the trial of disputes such as this will sometimes require. It might have been better to have left the choice to a panel of physicians, but Congress left it with the courts and the random assignment of this case has left it here with me.
>
> . . . I again find the opinions of Drs. McAnulty, Rink and Olshansky to be persuasive and I find that the risk to Nicholas Knapp of a repeat episode is not substantial.

We disagree with the district court's legal determination that such decisions are to be made by the courts and believe instead that medical determinations of this sort are best left to team doctors and universities as long as they are made with reason and rationality and with full regard to possible and reasonable accommodations. In cases such as ours, where Northwestern has examined both Knapp and his medical records, has considered his medical history and the relation between his prior sudden cardiac death and the possibility of future occurrences, has considered the severity of the potential injury, and has rationally and reasonably reviewed consensus medical opinions or recommendations in the pertinent field — regardless whether conflicting medical opinions exist — the university has the right to determine that an individual is not otherwise medically qualified to play without violating the Rehabilitation Act. The place of the court in such cases is to make sure that the decision-maker has reasonably considered and relied upon sufficient evidence specific to the individual and the potential injury, not to determine on its own which evidence it believes is more persuasive.

* * *

We do not believe that, in cases where medical experts disagree in their assessment of the extent of a real risk of serious harm or death, Congress intended that the courts — neutral arbiters but generally less skilled in medicine than the experts involved — should make the final medical decision. Instead, in the midst of conflicting expert testimony regarding the degree of serious risk of harm or death, the court's place is to ensure that the exclusion or disqualification of an individual was individualized, reasonably made, and based upon competent medical evidence. So long as these factors exist, it will be the rare case regarding participation in athletics where a court may substitute its judgment for that of the school's team physicians.

. . . Because we hold today as a matter of law that a court must allow Northwestern to make its own determinations of substantial risk and severity of injury if they are based on reliable evidence, the district court's order forcing Northwestern to let Knapp play must be reversed.

In closing, we wish to make clear that we are *not* saying Northwestern's decision necessarily is the right decision. We say only that it is not an illegal one under the Rehabilitation Act. On the same facts, another team physician at another university, reviewing the same medical history, physical evaluation, and medical recommendations, might reasonably decide that Knapp met the physical qualifications for playing on an intercollegiate basketball team. Simply put, all universities need not evaluate risk the same way. What we say in this case is that if substantial evidence supports the decision-maker — here Northwestern — that decision must be respected.

Section 794 prohibits authorities from deciding without significant medical support that certain activities are too risky for a disabled person. Decisions of this sort cannot rest on paternalistic concerns. Knapp, who is an adult, is not in need of paternalistic decisions regarding his health, and his parents — more entitled to be paternalistic toward him than Northwestern — approve of his decision. In regard to cases involving risk of future injury, a school's perception of the threat of such injury cannot be based on unfounded fears or stereotypes; it must be based on objective evidence. But here, where Northwestern acted rationally and reasonably rather than paternalistically, no Rehabilitation Act violation has occurred. The Rehabilitation Act "is carefully structured to replace . . . reflexive actions to actual or perceived handicaps with actions based on reasoned and medically sound judgments. . . ."

For these reasons, the district court's grant of the permanent injunction and denial of Northwestern's motion for summary judgment are reversed and the case is remanded with instructions to enter summary judgment in favor of Northwestern.

REVERSED.

NOTES AND COMMENTS

1. The court holds that although Knapp was medically ineligible, he was not "disabled." Why?

2. The court focused on the arguments of whether participation in intercollegiate athletics is a major life activity and if this determination is a subjective or objective one. The district court in *Knapp* found that intercollegiate sports play an important part of a student's education and learning process, and, at a minimum, constituted a major life activity for Nick Knapp. By affidavit, Knapp stated, "My participation in competitive basketball has provided me and could continue to provide me with a unique experience that I have not encountered in any other extracurricular activity in which I have been involved. . . . Among other things, competitive basketball has helped to instill in me the following character traits: confidence, dedication, leadership, teamwork, discipline, perseverance, patience, the ability to set priorities, the ability to compete, goal-setting and the ability to take coaching, direction and criticism. . . ." 942 F. Supp.

1191 (N.D. Ill. 1996). Northwestern argued that exclusion from a single activity is not a substantial limitation because he could participate in other extracurricular activities, such as band. The Seventh Circuit reversed the district court. Do you agree? Would it have made a difference if Northwestern refused to extend Knapp the basketball scholarship?

3. If Nick Knapp were a professional athlete would his "disability" status differ? Should a professional athlete be bound by his or her team's physician's opinion of medical disqualification due to risk of harm? Does a professional athlete have a stronger interest in participation because her livelihood is at stake? *See* **Section E**, *infra*.

4. When Experts Conflict — Who Decides? The parties implicitly agreed that a person is not "qualified" if there is a substantial risk of injury to the student or others. Assuming that some medical risk of injury or death is unacceptable, whose assessment of medical risk governs when the opinion of the team physician and the player's medical experts conflict — the player, the team, or the court? *See* Matthew J. Mitten, *Enhanced Risk of Harm to One's Self as a Justification for Exclusion from Athletics*, 8 MARQ. SPORTS L.J. 189, 213-15 (1998) (asserting that a model according deference to the team physician's decision, if supported by a reasonable medical basis, appropriately balances an athlete's interest in participation and the team or sponsor's interests in protecting the health and safety of participants). The court in *Wright v. Columbia University*, 520 F. Supp. 789, 794 (E.D. Pa. 1981), however, ordered the university to allow a student with sight in one eye to play football, accepting the player's ophthalmologist's opinion that participation did not pose a substantial risk of serious eye injury and rejecting team physician's contrary opinion. The court noted that the university's laudable concern for student safety cannot derogate from a student's rights under the Rehabiliation Act, "which prohibits 'paternalistic authorities' from deciding that certain activities are 'too risky' for people with disabilities." Do you agree that deference to the school's decision is warranted or that a court should independently weigh the evidence?

5. Attention became squarely focused on the safety of athletes competing with serious medical conditions following the death of basketball star Hank Gathers. He had collapsed once during the season, was placed on medication for a heart problem, and eventually returned to the court. Sadly, Gathers collapsed again during a game and died. In the wake of his death, schools have been far more cautious about allowing athletes with medical problems to compete. Gathers' family sued his treating physicians, claiming failure to fully inform Gathers of the seriousness of his heart condition and risks of playing, and asserting that he should not have been medically cleared to continue playing college basketball. Sports programs are in a tenuous liability situation in these cases, considering the refusal to permit an athlete with high medical risks to play may also result in litigation. For example, team doctors at Florida State University refused medical clearance for Devard Darling to continue to play football after his twin brother, Devaughn, died during conditioning drills because Devard also has a sickle cell trait, which can sometimes cause danger during physical exertion but was not determined to be the cause of Devaughn's death. Devard transferred to Washington State and had an outstanding season in 2002. Was FSU justified in denying clearance? Is this a case of genetic discrimination? Should the NCAA be required to waive its transfer rules allowing Devard to play at Washington State without sitting out one year as an accommodation under the ADA?

6. Efficacy of Liability Waivers. If an athlete who does not obtain medical clearance of physical qualifications is fully informed of, and consents to, the risks of participation, should the school be required to permit the athlete to play? Some schools have reluctantly allowed athletes with heart and other ailments to compete, but only after negotiating carefully drafted waivers of liability. Athletes, including Stephen Larkin of the University of Texas and Monty Williams of Notre Dame, went on to compete as professionals. In *Wagenbalst v. Odessa School District*, 758 P.2d 968 (Wash. 1988), however, exculpatory releases of the school district's negligence, signed as a condition of participation in interscholastic sports, were held invalid as contrary to public policy. *See also* Andrew Manno, Note, *A High Price to Compete: The Feasibility and Effect of Waivers Used to Protect Schools From Liability for Injuries to Athletes with Medical High Risks*, 79 KY. L.J. 867 (1991) (asserting that waivers may inadequately protect schools from liability if later challenged on grounds of misrepresentation, fraud, incapacity, or contrary to public policy).

7. Risk of Injury to Self vs. to Others. The *Knapp* court justified exclusion based on the risk of harm that participation would pose to Nick Knapp himself. The ADA provides a defense when the disabled person poses a risk of harm to others, yet says nothing regarding when the risk of harm is to one's self. Courts and the EEOC regulations, however, appear to recognize the defense. *See Devlin v. Arizona Youth Soccer Ass'n,* 1996 WL 118445 (D. Ariz. 1996) (refusing to dismiss the defense of risk of direct harm to self as justification to exclude player); *Columbo v. Sewannaka Central High School District No. 2*, 383 N.Y.S.2d 518 (Sup. Ct. 1976) (deferring to the judgment of the team physician that a deaf student was ineligible to participate in team sports where his participation posed a risk of injury to the boy and to other team members).

The "direct threat to self" issue was somewhat resolved in *Chevron U.S.A. Inc. v. Echazabal*, 122 S. Ct. 2045 (2002), which held that EEOC regulations authorizing the refusal to hire an individual whose performance on the job would endanger his own health, due to a disability, did not exceed the scope of permissible rule-making under the ADA. Exclusion on the basis of direct threat must be based on an individualized and scientific determination, and not merely a subjective good faith belief. *Bragdon v. Abbott*, 524 U.S. 624 (1998); *Anderson v. Little League Baseball, Inc.*, 794 F. Supp. 342 (D. Ariz. 1992) (finding an ADA violation because no proof that on-field coaching in a wheelchair poses a direct threat to others' health and safety).

8. Athletes with AIDS. *Montalvo v. Radcliffe*, 1999 WL 65624 (4th Cir. 1999), held it permissible to exclude a boy who was HIV positive from participation in full contact karate classes because of the significant risk to other participants' health and safety. The issue of mandatory AIDS testing in sports is also controversial. Though some view testing as a violation of privacy, others see it as protecting the right of healthy players not to be exposed to infectious and contagious diseases. This debate resurfaced when Earvin "Magic" Johnson announced he was returning to professional basketball after having contracted HIV, the virus that causes AIDS. *See* Anthony DiMaggio, *Mandatory HIV Testing of Athletes as a Health and Safety Issue*, 8 SETON HALL J. SPORT L. 663 (1998); John T. Wolohan, *An Ethical and Legal Dilemma: Participation in Sports By HIV Infected Athletes*, 7 MARQ. SPORTS L.J. 373 (1993).

9. This area of the law has produced numerous scholarly articles. *See e.g.*, Matthew J. Mitten, *Amateur Athletes With Handicaps or Physical Abnormalities: Who Makes the Participation Decision?*, 71 NEB. L. REV. 987 (1992); Adam Milani, *Can I Play? The Dilemma of the Disabled Athlete in Interscholastic Sports*, 49 ALA. L. REV. 817 (1998); Matthew J. Mitten, *Team Physician & Competitive Athletes: Allocating Legal Risks for Athletic Injuries*, 55 U. PITT. L. REV.129 (1993).

D. PARTICIPATION RIGHTS AND RESPONSIBILITIES: ELIGIBILITY STANDARDS AND RULES

In competitive sports, the governing athletic organizations, teams, and schools establish eligibility criteria intended to protect the health and safety of athletes and to maintain the integrity of the competition. This section examines litigation brought by athletes with disabilities challenging seemingly neutral eligibility standards, which negatively impact disabled student-athletes.

1. Interscholastic Competition Rules — Age/Semester Limits on Participation

PROBLEM 1

The Hagan family has come to your office for advice. Joseph Hagan, 6 foot, 225 pounds, is a defensive lineman on the high school football team. Joseph has been a starter on the team for his freshman through junior year. Shortly before football season began, the team coach regretfully informed Joseph that he was ineligible to compete in athletics during his senior year because he turns age 19 before September 1 of the current school year. The state high school athletic association strictly enforces the age-limitation rule, regarding the rule as essential to the safety and integrity of interscholastic sports programs. Joseph explains that due to a learning disability, he repeated two grades in elementary school. The Hagan family wants to know whether federal disability laws entitle Joseph to force the high school athletic association to allow him to play. As his counsel, what arguments and specific evidence would you present in seeking to enjoin the enforcement of the age-limitation rule to Joseph? What arguments are likely to be made in response by the athletic association?

Problem 2

Because of his learning disability, Joseph also has a specialized high school curriculum, in which he takes several remedial and special education courses. He has a cumulative GPA of 2.0. Joseph has received an offer of a full collegiate athletic scholarship provided he attain NCAA "qualifier" certification. Joseph took the SAT under non-standard conditions which allowed him unlimited time and a large-print test. Unfortunately, even after three attempts, Joseph has not made the required minimum test score. Although Joseph was accepted to Kanarado State University under the regular admissions process, the NCAA has declared Joseph "ineligible." As a result, Joseph cannot compete in intercollegiate athletics or receive the athletic scholarship. Please advise Joseph whether he has any recourse under federal disability laws.

Case File

SANDISON v. MICHIGAN HIGH SCHOOL ATHLETIC ASSOCIATION, INC.

64 F.3d 1026 (6th Cir. 1995)

Nelson and Ryan, Circuit Judges; Echols, District Judge.

Ryan, Circuit Judge.

Ronald Sandison and Craig Stanley, two recent graduates of Michigan public high schools, filed this action against their respective high schools and the Michigan High School Athletic Association (MHSAA) alleging claims under, *inter alia*, the Rehabilitation Act of 1973, 29 U.S.C. § 794, and titles II and III of the Americans with Disabilities Act (ADA), 42 U.S.C. §§ 12132, 12182. Each student suffers from a learning disability, and before reaching high school each fell behind the typical school grade for children of his age. The plaintiffs started their senior years in Fall 1994, but by then had turned nineteen years old. The MHSAA, of which the plaintiffs' high schools are members, prohibits students who turn nineteen by September 1 of the school year to compete in interscholastic high school sports. In the district court, the plaintiffs won preliminary injunctive relief. . . .

I.

When he was four years old, Ronald Sandison was placed in a special preschool program for learning disabled children because he had difficulty processing speech and language. Sandison started ungraded kindergarten at age six, rather than at the usual age of five, and it was not until age seven that Sandison was considered a student in graded kindergarten. This two-year delay placed Sandison two school grades behind his age group. At age eleven, Sandison was diagnosed with auditory input disability, which hampers Sandison's ability to distinguish between similar sounds. With the help of special education support, Sandison attended Rochester Adams High School in regular classrooms and graduated in June 1995. Sandison ran on Adams's cross-country and track teams during his first three years of high school. He turned nineteen years old in May 1994, a few months before starting his senior year.

Due to a learning disability in mathematics, Craig Stanley repeated kindergarten and then spent five years in a special education classroom. Stanley made the transition into regular classrooms by entering the fourth grade, rather than the fifth grade, after those five years in special education. Accordingly, Stanley is two school grades behind his age group. With the help of special education support, Stanley has attended Grosse Pointe North High School in regular classrooms and graduated in June 1995. Stanley ran on his high school's cross-country and track teams during the first three years. He turned nineteen years old in May 1994, a few months before starting his senior year.

Like most high schools in Michigan, Rochester Adams and Grosse Pointe North are members of the MHSAA. Members of the MHSAA agree to adopt the MHSAA's rules governing interscholastic sports. MHSAA Regulation I § 2 forbids students over nineteen years old from playing interscholastic sports:

> A student who competes in any interscholastic athletic contests must be under nineteen (19) years of age, except that a student whose nineteenth (19th) birthday occurs on or after September 1 of a current school year is eligible for the balance of that school year. Any student born before September 1, 1975, is ineligible for interscholastic athletics in Michigan. No waiver of the age requirement is permitted. MHSAA Handbook, Art. VII, § 4E.

On August 18, 1994, the plaintiffs sued the Rochester and Grosse Pointe school systems, and the MHSAA, under the Rehabilitation Act of 1973; the Americans with Disabilities Act, 42 U.S.C. §§ 12132, 12182; the federal Constitution, 42 U.S.C. § 1983; and the Michigan Handicappers' Civil Rights Act. Sandison and Stanley alleged that excluding them from playing interscholastic sports amounted to unlawful disability discrimination. In late August 1994, the district court granted the plaintiffs a temporary restraining order permitting the students to run in immediately upcoming interscholastic cross-country races. The plaintiffs then moved in early September for a preliminary injunction, which the district court entered.

First, the district court restrained all three defendants from preventing the plaintiffs from participating in interscholastic cross-country and track competition. Second, the district court enjoined the MHSAA from sanctioning Rochester Adams and Grosse Pointe North for permitting the plaintiffs to participate in interscholastic meets. The district court explained that it relied only on the Rehabilitation Act and the ADA to support the preliminary injunction.

The district court first reasoned that two titles of the ADA, as well as the Rehabilitation Act, applied to the claim against the MHSAA. The district court held that, by managing interscholastic athletic events, the MHSAA operated "places of education" and "places of entertainment" under title III of the ADA, which generally prohibits disability discrimination in places of "public accommodation." In addition, the district court relied on Michigan law and the MHSAA's membership to conclude that the MHSAA was a "public entity" under title II of the ADA. Finally, the district court held that the MHSAA indirectly received federal financial assistance under the Rehabilitation Act, § 794.

As for the remaining elements of a disability discrimination claim under the Rehabilitation Act and the ADA, the district court held that the plaintiffs were disabled, "otherwise qualified," and discriminated against solely on the basis of their disabilities. The MHSAA does not dispute the finding of "disability" on appeal. The district court concluded that the plaintiffs were "otherwise qualified" because permitting the plaintiffs to participate would not thwart the purposes of the age restriction. The district court reasoned that the age limit had two purposes: (1) to safeguard other athletes against injuries arising from competing against overage, and thus oversized, athletes; and (2) to prevent overage athletes from gaining an unfair competitive advantage. Accordingly, waiver of the age limit for Sandison and Stanley was a "reasonable accommodation" because the plaintiffs played a noncontact sport and were not "'star' players." The MHSAA appealed the issuance of the preliminary injunction. However, neither Rochester Adams nor Grosse Pointe North appealed; both schools have supported the plaintiffs' position from the start.

II.

A. Mootness

Before reviewing the preliminary injunction, we point out that the controversy over the first part of the preliminary injunction — requiring the defendants to permit Sandison and Stanley to participate in track meets — is moot. The 1995 track season has ended, and thus the plaintiffs will have no more races to run. The "capable of repetition yet evading review" exception to mootness does not apply to these plaintiffs because the exception requires not only that "'the challenged action was in its duration too short to be fully litigated prior to its cessation or expiration,'" but also that "'there was a reasonable expectation that the same complaining party would be subjected to the same action again.'" At oral argument, we learned that Sandison and Stanley graduated from high school in June 1995, which precludes the repetition of another controversy over whether these same plaintiffs may run on their high school teams.

However, the second part of the preliminary injunction — ordering the MHSAA to refrain from penalizing the high schools for permitting the plaintiffs to compete — is not moot. When an age-ineligible player competes on a high school team, MHSAA Regulation 5 § 4(B), (D) provide for penalties such as forfeiture of team victories and erasure of individual performances. Sandison and Stanley of course still have an interest in preventing the MHSAA from erasing their teams' victories and their own performances. Accordingly, this controversy remains live.

B. Standard for Reviewing Preliminary Injunctions

[W]e consider four factors in determining whether the district court abused its discretion in issuing the preliminary injunction: (1) whether the movant has a "strong" likelihood of success on the merits; (2) whether the movant would otherwise suffer irreparable injury; (3) whether issuance of a preliminary injunction would cause substantial harm to others; and (4) whether the public interest would be served by issuance of a preliminary injunction. . . .

III. Rehabilitation Act of 1973

We first discuss the plaintiffs' claim under section 504 of the Rehabilitation Act of 1973. In its current form, the section provides in pertinent part:

> No otherwise qualified individual with a disability . . . shall, solely by reason of his or her disability, be excluded from the participation in, be denied the benefits of, or be subjected to discrimination under any program or activity receiving Federal financial assistance. . . . 29 U.S.C. § 794(a) (as amended 1992).

A cause of action under section 504 comprises four elements: (1) The plaintiff is a "handicapped [disabled] person" under the Act; (2) The plaintiff is "otherwise qualified" for participation in the program; (3) The plaintiff is being excluded from participation in, being denied the benefits of, or being subjected to discrimination under the program solely by reason of his handicap [disability]; and (4) The relevant program or activity is receiving Federal financial assistance. In this case, the plaintiffs are unlikely to succeed on the merits of the second and third elements.

A. "Solely by Reason of" Disability

Taking the latter element to start, we hold that the plaintiffs are not, in the words of the statute, "being excluded from the participation in . . . any program or activity" "solely by reason of . . . his disability." 29 U.S.C. § 794(a). . . . [U]nder a "natural reading" of section 504, the MHSAA's disqualification of students who reach nineteen years of age by the specified date "cannot readily be characterized as a decision made," "solely by reason of" each student's respective learning disability. Regulation I § 2 is a "neutral rule" — neutral, that is, with respect to disability — and as far as the record shows, is neutrally applied by the MHSAA. Throughout the plaintiffs' first three years of high school, Regulation I § 2 did not bar the students from playing interscholastic sports, yet the students were of course learning disabled during those years. It was not until they turned nineteen that Regulation I § 2 operated to disqualify them. Accordingly, we must conclude that the age regulation does not exclude students from participating "solely by reason of" their disability. The plain meaning of section 504's text does not cover the plaintiffs' exclusion.

* * *

[A]bsent their respective learning disability, Sandison and Stanley still fail to satisfy Regulation I § 2. The plaintiffs' respective learning disability does not prevent the two students from meeting the age requirement; the passage of time does. We hold that, under section 504, the plaintiffs cannot meet the age requirement "solely by reason of" their dates of birth, not "solely by reason of [disability]." . . .

B. "Otherwise Qualified"

We also hold that the district court clearly erred by finding that the plaintiffs are likely to show that they are "otherwise qualified" to participate in interscholastic track and cross-country competition. Specifically, after finding that the plaintiffs are not "star" players and are not an injury risk to other competitors, the district court found that the MHSAA must waive Regulation I § 2 as to Sandison and Stanley in order to reasonably accommodate the plaintiffs. We disagree.

Under section 504, a disabled individual is "otherwise qualified" to participate in a program if, with "reasonable accommodation," the individual can meet the "necessary" requirements of the program.

* * *

Aside from the necessity of the program's requirement, the other question in the otherwise qualified inquiry is "'whether some "reasonable accommodation" is available to satisfy the legitimate interests of both the grantee and the handicapped person. . . . Generally, an "accommodation is not reasonable if it either imposes 'undue financial and administrative burdens' on a grantee, or requires 'a fundamental alteration in the nature of [the] program.'" *School Bd. of Nassau County v. Arline*, 480 U.S. 273 (1987).

We join the only other circuit that has decided the "otherwise qualified" question on similar facts, and hold that the MHSAA's age regulation is "necessary" and that waiver of the regulation is not a "reasonable accommodation." In *Pottgen v. Missouri High School Activities Association*, 40 F.3d 926 (8th Cir. 1994), the plaintiff suffered from a learning disability, forcing him to repeat two grades in elementary school. After playing interscholastic baseball during his first three years of high school, the plaintiff turned nineteen before his senior year. An under-nineteen age requirement imposed by Missouri's high school athletic association disqualified the plaintiff from playing in his senior year.

In rejecting the student's claim that the Missouri association's age restriction violated section 504, the Eighth Circuit first found that the restriction constituted "an essential eligibility requirement," citing four reasons: "An age limit helps reduce the competitive advantage flowing to teams using older athletes; protects younger athletes from harm; discourages student athletes from delaying their education to gain athletic maturity; and prevents over-zealous coaches from engaging in repeated red-shirting to gain a competitive advantage." Next, the court in *Pottgen* found that, given the plaintiff's age, "the only possible accommodation is to waive the essential eligibility requirement itself." The Eighth Circuit rejected waiver as a reasonable accommodation, concluding that "waiving an essential eligibility standard would constitute a fundamental alteration in the nature of the baseball program."

We hold that the district court did not clearly err in finding that Regulation I § 2 is "necessary." In defending against the preliminary injunction motion, the MHSAA proffered testimony from an expert in physical growth and development. The testimony supports the district court's conclusions that the age restriction advances two purposes: (1) "safeguards against injury" to other players; and (2) "prevents any unfair competitive advantage that older and larger participants might provide." The age restriction is a necessary requirement of the interscholastic sports program.

But the district court erred in finding that waiver of Regulation I § 2 constituted a reasonable accommodation. First, we agree with the court in *Pottgen* that waiver of the age restriction fundamentally alters the sports program. Due to the usual ages of first-year high school students, high school sports programs generally involve competitors between fourteen and eighteen years of age. Removing the age restriction injects into competition students older than the vast majority of other students, and the record shows that the older students are generally more physically mature than younger students. Expanding the sports program to include older students works a fundamental alteration.

Second, although the plaintiffs assert that introducing their average athletic skills into track and cross-country competition would not fundamentally alter the program, the record does not reveal how the MHSAA, or anyone, can make that competitive unfairness determination without an undue burden. The MHSAA's expert explained that five factors weigh in deciding whether an athlete possessed an unfair competitive advantage due to age: chronological age, physical maturity, athletic experience, athletic skill level, and mental ability to process sports strategy. It is plainly an undue burden to require high school coaches and hired physicians to determine whether these factors render a student's age an unfair competitive advantage. The determination would have to be made relative to the skill level of each participating member of opposing teams and the team as a unit. And of course each team member and the team as a unit would present a different skill level. Indeed, the determination would also have to be made relative to the skill level of the would-be athlete whom the older student displaced from the team. It is unreasonable to call upon coaches and physicians to make these near-impossible determinations.

Finally, we note that there is a significant peculiarity in trying to characterize the waiver of the age restriction as a "reasonable accommodation" of the plaintiffs' respective learning disability. Ordinarily, an accommodation of an individual's disability operates so that the disability is overcome and the disability no longer prevents the individual from participating. In this case, although playing high school sports undoubtedly helped the plaintiffs progress through high school, the waiver of the age restriction is not directed at helping them overcome learning disabilities; the waiver merely removes the age ceiling as an obstacle.

Accordingly, we conclude that the plaintiffs are unlikely to succeed in pursuing their section 504 claim. The plaintiffs are excluded from participating in interscholastic track and cross-country competition "solely by reason of" age, not disability. Furthermore, waiver of the "necessary" age restriction does not constitute a "reasonable accommodation."

* * *

[T]he plaintiffs are not subjected to "discrimination on the basis of disability," and waiver is not in this case a "reasonable modification[]." Furthermore, the age restriction does not prevent the plaintiffs from "fully and equally" enjoying the interscholastic sports program; Regulation I § 2 equally excludes overage, nondisabled students. . . .

V.

Accordingly, the plaintiffs are unlikely to succeed on the merits of their section 504 and ADA claims. We DISMISS as moot the appeal from that portion of the preliminary injunction ordering that the high schools and the MHSAA permit the plaintiffs to run on the cross-country and track teams; and we REVERSE that portion of the preliminary injunction ordering the MHSAA to refrain from entering penalties for the plaintiffs' performance.

JOHNSON v. FLORIDA HIGH SCHOOL ACTIVITIES ASSOCIATION, INC.

899 F. Supp. 579 (M.D. Fla. 1995)

SUSAN C. BUCKLEW, United States District Judge.

Facts

The plaintiff, Dennis Johnson, is a nineteen year old senior at Boca Ciega High School in St. Petersburg, Florida. At approximately nine months, Dennis contracted meningitis, losing all hearing in one ear and substantially all hearing in the other. Because of this disability, Dennis' parents elected to wait a year before enrolling him in kindergarten. According to Dennis' mother, Gail M. Johnson, the decision to wait a year was made by her and her husband and was based upon their beliefs that Dennis was not "up to par" with the other children his age. Gail Johnson stated that Dennis was not talking very well for his age and that she and her husband attributed his deficiency to his hearing impairment.

Dennis progressed adequately in kindergarten. However, the school system decided to hold Dennis back in first grade because of his performance in reading and language. Once again, Dennis' deficiencies were attributed to his hearing impairment. Dennis was placed in special education classes in second grade and remained there until his sophomore year, when he entered Boca Ciega High School. He is provided an interpreter, notetaker and itinerant teacher at Boca Ciega. Additionally, just prior to entering eighth grade, Dennis lost all hearing in both ears.

Although a senior in high school, Dennis turned nineteen on June 29, 1995. According to the rules of the FHSAA, Dennis is ineligible to participate in high school athletics. FHSAA By-Law 19-4-1 (prohibiting anyone who turns age nineteen before September 1 of the current school year from participating in interscholastic sports). Dennis has played football and wrestled for the last three years. Unlike most of the other athletes, however, Dennis did not start playing organized sports until he entered high school. Dennis contacted the FHSAA about receiving a "hardship" exception due to the fact that Dennis' "ineligible age" was a result of his disability. The FHSAA responded that the Executive Committee of the FHSAA "does not have the authority to waive the age eligibility rule." The Court notes, however, that the rules of the FHSAA do provide for "undue hardship" exceptions as to the FHSAA's other rules, but that the age requirement is "unwaivable" because it is deemed an essential eligibility requirement by the FHSAA. Thus, Dennis is currently precluded from participating in high school athletics. Additionally, the Court notes that if Dennis did participate, the rules of the FHSAA would result in Boca Ciega High School forfeiting those games in which Dennis participated. FHSAA By-Law 19-1-2.

Dennis is five foot nine inches and weighs 250 pounds and plays defensive tackle. Last year he weighed approximately 230 pounds and played the same position. According to the affidavit of Dennis' coach, Dennis is not considered a "star" player and is not "larger" than the other players. Additionally, a review of the rosters from two of Boca Ciega's opponents reveals that while Dennis is large, he is not the largest student to play defensive line. The Court notes that one of Boca Ciega's opponents lists a junior linemen as six foot four inches and 260 pounds. Additionally, as a wrestler, Dennis wrestles in the heavy weight division. This division limits competitors to a maximum of 275 pounds.

Discussion

(A) Substantially Likelihood of Prevailing on the Merits

Dennis' claim is premised upon the Rehabilitation Act, 29 U.S.C. § 794 and the Americans with Disabilities Act ("ADA"), 42 U.S.C. § 12101, *et. seq*. In order to establish a claim under the Rehabilitation Act, the Plaintiff must prove: (1) he has a disability as defined by the Act; (2) he is "otherwise qualified" to participate in interscholastic high school athletics as regulated by the FHSAA or that he may be "otherwise qualified" via "reasonable accommodations;" (3) he is being excluded from participating in interscholastic high school athletics solely because of his disability; and (4) the FHSAA receives federal financial assistance. *Sandison v. Michigan High Sch. Athletic Ass'n*, 863 F. Supp. 483 (E.D. Mich. 1994).

In order to establish a claim under Title II of the ADA, 42 U.S.C. § 12132, the Plaintiff must prove: (1) the FHSAA is a "public entity;" (2) he is a "qualified individual with a disability;" and (3) he has been excluded from participation from or denied the benefits of the activities of the public entity. Alternatively, in order to establish a claim under Title III of the ADA, 42 U.S.C. § 12182, the Plaintiff must prove: (1) he is disabled; (2) the FHSAA is a "private entity" which operates a "place of public accommodation;" and (3) he was denied the opportunity to "participate in or benefit from services or accommodations on the basis of his disability," and that reasonable accommodations could be made which do not fundamentally alter the nature of FHSAA's accommodations.

As for the requirements under the Rehabilitation Act, FHSAA concedes all elements except for the "otherwise qualified" requirement. Citing to the Eighth Circuit opinion in *Pottgen v. Missouri State High Sch. Activities Ass'n*, 40 F.3d 926 (8th Cir. 1994), FHSAA contends that the Plaintiff is not "otherwise qualified" and that no "reasonable accommodations" can be made so as to make the Plaintiff "otherwise qualified." Specifically, FHSAA contends that the Plaintiff is too old and that the "reasonable accommodation" of waiving the age requirement fundamentally alters the purpose of the rule and is therefore an "unreasonable" accommodation. Accordingly, since waiving the age requirement is the only available "accommodation," and since this "accommodation" is unreasonable, the Plaintiff is not "otherwise qualified." Thus, he cannot participate in high school sports.

As for Plaintiff's Title II ADA claim, FHSAA argues that it is not a "public entity" as defined by section 12131(1) of the ADA and that the Plaintiff is not a "qualified individual with a disability" as defined by section 12131(2) of the ADA. Alternatively, FHSAA challenges Plaintiff's Title III claim, arguing that as a private entity, FHSAA does not operate a place of "public accommodation" as defined by section 12181(7) of the ADA. Additionally, FHSAA contends that no "reasonable accommodation" can be made because waiving the age requirement constitutes a "fundamental alteration." Once again, FHSAA cites to *Pottgen*.

In deciding whether the Plaintiff has established "a substantial likelihood of prevailing on the merits," the most important issue is the "otherwise qualified" requirement as supplemented by the "reasonable accommodation" requirement. The Court rejects FHSAA's argument that FHSAA is not subject to the ADA. The Court finds that the FHSAA is a "public entity" as defined by the ADA. The Court notes that section 12131(1)(B) of the ADA defines "public entity" as any "other instrumentality of the state . . . or local government." The FHSAA is a non-profit corporation which regulates the interscholastic activities of Florida high school students. As the regulatory arm for Florida high schools, its actions have been deemed state actions. *The Florida High Sch. Activities Ass'n, Inc. v. Thomas*, 434 So. 2d 306 (Fla. 1983). The *Thomas* court specifically noted that since the FHSAA has "exclusive authority and responsibility for controlling all aspects of interscholastic activities in both public and private high schools throughout Florida," its actions constitute state action. Thus, since its actions are deemed state action, it follows that the FHSAA is an "instrumentality of the state" and is therefore a "public entity." *See also Sandison*, 863 F. Supp. at 487 (holding that state athletic association was a public entity). Having determined that the FHSAA is a public entity, the Court refrains from addressing all issues pertaining to Plaintiff's alternative claim that FHSAA is a "private entity" which operates a "place of public accommodation."

The Court also finds that the Plaintiff is a "qualified individual with a disability.". . . [A] "qualified individual with a disability" means: "an individual with a disability who, with or without reasonable modifications to the rules, . . . meets the essential eligibility requirements for the receipt of services or the participation in programs or activities provided by a public entity." § 12131(2). Boiled down, the dispositive issue before the Court is whether waiving the age requirement constitutes a "fundamental alteration" to the purposes of the rule. Resolution of this issue requires an examination of the purposes of the age requirement as applied to the instant case and as noted by the courts in *Pottgen* and in *Sandison*.

The purposes of the age requirement as promulgated by the FHSAA are two-hold. First, the rule promotes safety. By prohibiting players who turn age nineteen prior to September 1st of the current year from participating in interscholastic athletics, the rule liberally regulates the size and strength of the players. The second purpose is fairness, *i.e.*, to create an even playing field. The rule prevents schools from "redshirting" their players so as to build a better program. These are admittedly salutary purposes.

In *Pottgen*, the Eighth Circuit provided a simple three step analysis as to the "otherwise qualified" requirement under the Rehabilitation Act. First, the court articulated the general rule that the disabled individual must be "otherwise qualified." In other words, the disabled individual must meet all of the essential eligibility requirements in spite of his disability. Translated to the instant case, Dennis must be under age nineteen on September 1, 1995. Second, the court noted that the rule had an exception. If the disabled individual cannot meet all the essential eligibility requirements because of his disability, then the Court must determine whether "reasonable accommodations" might be made thereby enabling the disabled individual to become "otherwise qualified." As applied to Dennis, FHSAA must waive the age requirement. Third, the court noted that there was an exception to the exception. An "accommodation" is not "reasonable" if it "fundamentally alters the nature of the program." The *Pottgen* court went on to hold that the age requirement was a fundamental eligibility requirement which could not be waived. Thus, since no other "reasonable accommodation" was available, Pottgen failed the "otherwise qualified" requirement. Accordingly, the Eighth Circuit reversed the district court, holding that it was error to grant the preliminary injunction.

A review of the *Pottgen* opinion, however, reveals that the Court provided no analysis as to the relationship between the age requirement and the purposes behind the age requirement. Rather, the court accepted the Missouri State High School Activities Association's assertion that the age requirement was an essential eligibility requirement. This is most evident from the dissent.

> In other words, the age requirement could be modified for this individual player without doing violence to the admittedly salutary purposes underlying the age rule. But instead of looking at the rule's operation in the individual case of Ed Pottgen, both the Activities Association and this Court simply recite the rule's general justifications (which are not in dispute) and mechanically apply it across the board. But if a rule can be modified without doing violence to its essential purposes . . . I do not believe that it can be "essential" to the nature of the program or activity to refuse to modify the rule. . . . In determining this issue, it seems to me entirely appropriate to focus on the effect that modification of the requirement for the individual in question would have on the nature of the program. When the case is looked at from this point of view, it becomes clear that the Association could easily bend to accommodate Ed Pottgen without breaking anything essential. 40 F.3d at 932-33.

Unlike the *Pottgen* court, the district court in *Sandison* addressed the purposes of the age requirement and whether those purposes would be undermined if the age requirement was waived for the particular plaintiffs. In concluding that the age requirement could be waived, the court stressed that waiving the age requirement would not thwart those purposes. As in the instant case, the purposes of the age requirement were safety and fairness. The *Sandison* court specifically noted that the goal of safety was not thwarted because the plaintiffs sought to participate in two non-contact sports, cross-country and track. Additionally, since the plaintiffs were mid-level competitors and not "star" players, the court stated that their participation would not "provide any unfair competitive advantage to their respective teams." Thus, the court concluded that waiving the age requirement constituted a "reasonable accommodation" by which the plaintiffs became "otherwise qualified." . . . The fact that the FHSAA deems the age requirement essential does not make it so. Rather, the relationship between the age requirement and its purposes must be such that waiving the age requirement in the instant case would necessarily undermine the purposes of the requirement.

In the instant case, the Court finds that the purposes of the age requirement are not undermined by allowing Plaintiff to participate in interscholastic athletics. The Court emphasizes that while the Plaintiff is large, he is not the largest football player playing his position. There are individuals larger than him on the playing field. Thus, accepting the fact that football is a contact sport in which injuries do occasionally occur, the Court finds that allowing this individual to play does not facilitate or exacerbate the potential for injury. Additionally, the weight divisions in wrestling eliminate any safety concern as to that sport. Moreover, the Court finds that Boca Ciega High School does not gain an unfair advantage through the play of the Plaintiff. The Court notes that the Plaintiff is considered a mid-level player and not a "star." Furthermore, the Plaintiff is no more experienced than the other players. Rather, in comparison to some players he is less experienced. The plaintiff has only played organized football for three years.

In conclusion, the Court finds that the plaintiff has demonstrated a "likelihood of success on the merits." The Plaintiff has established the essential elements required to assert claims under the Rehabilitation Act and the ADA. Specifically, the Court finds that waiving the age requirement in the instant case does not fundamentally alter the nature of the program. Allowing Dennis Johnson to participate in interscholastic athletics in no way undermines the purposes of safety and fairness. The Court stresses that its holding is limited to the facts before it.

(B) Irreparable Injury if the Injunction Does Not Issue

The Court finds that irreparable injury will result to the Plaintiff if the injunction is not granted. There is no doubt that playing interscholastic athletics has changed the Plaintiff's life. As a direct result of his participation, the Plaintiff has gained friends and confidence. Prior to playing sports he had few hearing friends. Since playing he has become more social and has been recognized not as a deaf student, but as a student who participates in high school athletics. During the hearing, the Plaintiff specifically commented on how important athletics is to his life. He enjoys showing people that a deaf person can play sports. Given that this is the Plaintiff's senior year, to prohibit him from playing would undermine any gains he has made.

(C) A Threatened Injury to Him That is Greater Than Any Damage the Preliminary Injunction Would Cause to FHSAA

There is no risk of harm to the FHSAA or others if the injunction is issued. As previously noted, allowing the Plaintiff to participate does not create an additional safety concern. His presence alone does not exacerbate the potential for injury. Additionally, granting the injunction does not subject the FHSAA to "numerous frivolous lawsuits" as it suggests. Rather, the Court's granting of the injunction is limited to the narrow case before it. Moreover, the Court rejects FHSAA's argument that waiving the age requirement forces FHSAA to undertake a comparative analysis of all the athletes in the league. FHSAA suggests that to determine whether the goals of safety and fairness are undermined by letting the "disabled individual" play, the FHSAA would have to impanel a group of expert educators and physicians. This panel would examine the "disabled student" as against the other players on his or her team and on the opponents' team, comparing strength and ability. Simply stated, FHSAA's argument makes a mountain out of a mole hill. Strength and size disparities already exist throughout the league and yet no comparative analysis is undertaken. This Court finds that no such analysis is needed to determine whether an average size and average skilled disabled nineteen year old defensive linemen and wrestler can participate in interscholastic athletics when there is no indication that the student has held back or "reshirted" so as to better the program. Accordingly, the Court finds that the threatened injury to the Plaintiff is greater than any damage or injury the FHSAA might suffer as a result of the issuance of the injunction.

(D) The Absence of Any Adverse Effect on the Public Interest if the Injunction Issues

The Court finds that the public interest is advanced by issuing the injunction and allowing the Plaintiff to participate in interscholastic athletics. Congress' concern to eliminate intentional and benign discrimination against disabled individuals in evident in the findings and purpose of the ADA. The purpose of the ADA and the Rehabilitation Act is "to include persons with disabilities in society equal to those without disabilities by addressing discrimination against persons with disabilities." Thus, there is a significant public interest in eliminating discrimination against individuals with disabilities and issuing the injunction advances this interest. The injunction enables the Plaintiff to enjoy high school fully and to show to his fellow classmates that deaf persons can play sports.

Conclusion

Plaintiff's Motion for Preliminary Injunction is GRANTED. The Defendant FHSAA is enjoined from enforcing its rules prohibiting the Plaintiff from playing interscholastic athletics and penalizing Boca Ciega High School for allowing the Plaintiff to play.

NOTES AND COMMENTS

1. The federal courts are divided on whether interscholastic age eligibility rules violate the federal anti-discrimination laws when applied to students who exceed the age limits and were held back in school because of a disability. The Sixth and Eighth Circuits have upheld age-limitation rules, reasoning in part that such rules are essential to promote the safety of younger athletes and to maintain a competitive balance in interscholastic athletics by precluding physically more mature students. According to these courts, waiver of the rule would fundamentally alter the nature of interscholastic competition and pose an undue administrative burden on the associations to assess competitive fairness in individual cases. *See Sandison v. Michigan High School Athletic Association, Inc.*, 64 F.3d 1026 (6th Cir. 1995) and *Pottgen v. Missouri State High School Activities Association*, 40 F.3d 926 (8th Cir. 1994) (holding the age limit rule was an essential eligibility requirement supported by health and safety concerns and that modification would be unreasonable). However, the individualized analysis approach used in *Johnson* has gained recognition. *See Washington v. Indiana High Sch. Ath. Ass'n*, 181 F.3d 840 (7th Cir. 1999) (requiring individualized determination of waiver of eight-semester rule); *Cruz v. Pa. Interscholastic Ath. Ass'n*, 157 F. Supp. 2d 485 (E.D. Pa. 2001) (concluding that waiver of the maximum age rule for a learning disabled student would not fundamentally alter high school sports program); *Dennin v. Connecticut Interscholastic Athletic Conf., Inc.*, 913 F. Supp. 663 (D. Conn. 1996) (noting that age rule, although facially neutral with regard to disabilities, is discriminatory when applied to a particular student whose disability was the sole reason he was held back in school), *vacated*, 94 F.3d 96 (2d Cir. 1996) (vacating appeal as moot because plaintiff had participated under district court's injunction and graduated). As a practical matter, what impact does *Sandison* have on disabled student-athletes in the Sixth Circuit?

2. "Solely by reason of" disability. *Sandison* emphasized that the age requirement was a neutral rule applicable to all students and that the plaintiffs were excluded from participation only in their senior years and "solely by reason of" their age, not disability. The Court did not find it relevant that the plaintiffs were delayed in their schooling as a result of their learning disabilities. *Johnson,* operating under Title II of the ADA, did not address this element but focused on whether waiving the requirement fundamentally alters the purposes of the rule. The ADA prohibits discrimination "on the basis of disability" and defines discrimination to include the imposition of eligibility criteria that screen out or tend to screen out individuals with disabilities, unless the criteria is necessary to the program. *See* 42 U.S.C. § 12182(b)(2)(A). Under what circumstances could a "facially neutral requirement" discriminate "on the basis of disability"? Is *Sandison's* construction of the term correct, or too narrow?

3. Individualized Waiver Inquiry. *Sandison* and *Johnson* differ on whether an athletic association is obligated under federal law to conduct an individualized evaluation of whether waiver of the age limit rule is a reasonable accommodation to a particular student. *Johnson* conducted an individualized inquiry, analyzing whether granting a waiver in the plaintiff's individual case would undermine the legitimate purposes of the age limit rule. A number of commentators analyzing this issue have argued that the individualized approach taken by *Johnson* is more consistent with the purpose of the ADA and legislative intent. *See e.g.,* Adam Milani, *Can I Play?: The Dilemma of the Disabled*

Athlete in Interscholastic Sports, 49 ALA. L. REV. 817 (1998); John T. Wolohan, *Are Age Restrictions a Necessary Requirement for Participation in Interscholastic Athletic Programs?*, 66 UMKC L. REV. 345 (1997); Katie M. Burroughs, *Learning Disabled Student Athletes: A Sporting Chance Under the ADA?*, 14 J. CONTEMP. H.L. & POL'Y 57 (1997); Colleen M. Evale, Sandison v. Michigan High School Athletic Association*: The Sixth Circuit Sets Up Age Restrictions as Insurmountable Hurdles for Learning Disabled High School Student-Athletes*, 5 SPORTS LAW. J. 109 (1998).

4. Not that good or strong anyway? *Johnson* acknowledged the salutary purposes served by the age limitation rule, but determined, based on an individualized assessment, that in Johnson's case, waiver of the age rule was a reasonable accommodation. The court cited to factors, such as the plaintiff was of average size and ability and did not intentionally delay his education to get an athletic advantage. The district court in *Dennin* used similar reasoning in ordering a waiver of the age restriction to allow a 19-year-old student with Down's Syndrome to participate in intercollegiate swimming. The court ruled that a waiver would not undermine the purposes of the rule, given that the student was not a safety risk in competitive swimming, a noncontact sport, and did not have a competitive advantage, as one of the slowest swimmers on the team. 913 F. Supp. 663 (D. Conn. 1996), *judgment vacated on other grounds, appeal dismissed by*, 94 F.3d 96 (2d Cir. 1996). *Cf. Sandison*, (requiring individual competitive fairness determinations is an undue administrative burden). How do "star" student-athletes with disabilities who are exceptionally skilled, strong, large, or talented, fare under even the individualized standard?

5. Preliminary Injunctions. Claims by student-athletes seeking rights to participate are usually made in the context of a motion for preliminary injunction. Because of the short timing of the sports season, the plaintiffs' claims may quickly become moot whether injunctive relief is granted or not. Accordingly, the courts test whether the plaintiff can demonstrate irreparable harm and a substantial likelihood of success on the merits of an ADA or Rehabilitation Act claim. The appeal in *Sandison* was not mooted as to the penalty imposed on schools, such as forfeiture of season games, for allowing students who exceed the age limit to participate.

2. Academic Requirements for Athletic Eligibility

Another area in which student-athletes with disabilities may be excluded from participation is in the context of academic eligibility requirements. For example, the NCAA has established and enforced minimum initial academic eligibility requirements, which entering freshman must meet in order to participate in Division I and II intercollegiate athletics. To qualify under NCAA standards, students must complete a certain number of high school "core" academic courses and attain a minimum score based on grade point average in these courses and on national standardized exams. The stated purpose of these requirements is to protect the integrity of intercollegiate athletics and to ensure, by uniform standards, that student-athletes are academically prepared to succeed in college.

Student-athletes with learning disabilities have claimed that the NCAA's initial eligibility standards discriminate against them in violation the federal disability discrimination laws. Because of their learning disabilities, many students have specialized high school curriculum, which does not meet the NCAA's definition of "core" academic courses. Many of these students contend the NCAA's imposition of a minimum grade point average and testing score penalizes them due to their learning disabilities.

The question raised in these cases is whether the ADA precludes organizations, such as the NCAA, from enforcing academic eligibility requirements as a condition for participating in intercollegiate athletics.

PROBLEM

Kingston University, a private university and member of NCAA Division I, offered a full athletic scholarship to C.C. Stewart, a highly recruited high school swimmer, provided she attain "qualifier" certification under the initial academic eligibility requirements set by the NCAA. Stewart, however, failed to achieve the minimum test score on the SAT college entrance exam required for NCAA eligibility. In the Spring of her senior year, a psychologist diagnosed Stewart as learning disabled, determined she also had test anxiety disorder, and recommended that she re-take the SAT with the accommodations of an untimed test with larger print. After her third test taken under non-standard conditions, Stewart made the qualifying score. The NCAA's learning disabilities specialist also evaluated Stewart, opined that she did not have a learning disability, and recommended that she spend more time committed to her studies. (Stewart spent five hours daily in training). The NCAA rejected Stewart's non-standard test scores. As a result, Stewart was deemed ineligible to participate in athletics or to receive the athletic scholarship. Stewart has been accepted for admission to Kingston University, which has a special program for students with learning disabilities. Stewart seeks your advice as to whether she has any recourse against the NCAA or Kingston University under federal disability laws.

Case File

BOWERS v. NATIONAL COLLEGIATE ATHLETIC ASSOCIATION

9 F. Supp. 2d 460 (D.N.J. 1998)

Stephen M. Orlofsky, United States District Judge.

This case is about Plaintiff's eligibility to participate in intercollegiate athletics during his freshman year of college. The National Collegiate Athletic Association, the governing body of intercollegiate athletics, has promulgated regulations which determine whether a student-athlete is a "qualifier," "partial qualifier," or "nonqualifier," and thereby whether a student-athlete is eligible to compete in intercollegiate athletics during his or her freshman year. Plaintiff, a promising football player, was determined to be a "nonqualifier," and therefore ineligible for intercollegiate football competition during his freshman year of college. Plaintiff then filed this action claiming, among other things, that his status as a "nonqualifier" was assigned in a fashion that discriminates against the learning disabled in violation of several federal and New Jersey statutes, in particular, the Americans with Disabilities Act, the Rehabilitation Act, and the New Jersey Law Against Discrimination.

* * *

I. Facts and Procedural History

* * *

B. Michael Bowers

Bowers is a resident of Palmyra, New Jersey and currently a student at Temple. Throughout his primary and secondary school education, Bowers received special education and related services as a result of a learning disability. Bowers' learning disability, identified more formally as a perceptual impairment, "affects his ability to achieve in spite of his intellectual ability, and . . . interferes with his reading and writing skills." Bowers is also a talented football player and during high school was heavily recruited by several Division I and II colleges and universities to play football at the collegiate level, including Temple, Iowa, and AIC.

C. The NCAA

The NCAA is a not-for-profit unincorporated association of approximately 1,200 educational institutions in the United States with its principal place of business in Kansas. The NCAA is the "predominant governing body in college sports" and one of its stated purposes is to "maintain intercollegiate athletics as an integral part of the educational program and the athlete as an integral part of the student body and, by so doing, retain a clear line of demarcation between intercollegiate athletics and professional sports." The members of the NCAA (the "member-institutions") are grouped into distinct divisions. The distinctions among the divisions determine, *inter alia*, the scope of the athletic program, the level of competition, and the amount of financial aid distributable through its athletic program. For example, Division I members "recruit[] regionally and nationally" and sponsor "one or both of the traditional spectator-oriented, income producing sports of football and basketball" "at the highest feasible level of intercollegiate competition." Among the member-institutions of the NCAA are Temple, Iowa, and AIC. . . . Temple and Iowa are Division I members, and AIC is a Division II member.

Since 1969, the NCAA has received federal funds for its National Youth Sports Program. Also, "member-institutions pay the NCAA dues from revenues obtained from the tuition and activity fees of the student body, including money paid in whole or part with federal funds."

D. Initial Eligibility Status and the Clearinghouse

Among its other activities, the NCAA establishes the standards to determine whether an incoming freshman student is eligible to participate in intercollegiate athletics at the Division I or Division II level. This determination is known as a student's "initial eligibility." There are three possible initial eligibility statuses: "qualifier," "partial qualifier," or "nonqualifier." In combination with whether or not a student has been recruited by a member-institution, a student's initial eligibility status determines, *inter alia*: whether and when he or she may compete in intercollegiate athletics; whether, when, and with whom he or she may practice or engage in conditioning; and whether and from what sources of funds a student may receive institutional financial aid or an athletic scholarship. These requirements are separate from and in addition to the individual member-institutions' requirements for admission.

Initial eligibility status is a function of a number of factors, including, whether a student has graduated from high school, a student's Scholastic Aptitude Test ("SAT") score, and a student's grade-point average in "core courses," of which the student must pass a total of thirteen. For Division I eligibility, the core course requirements are four units of English, two units of mathematics, two units of science, two units of social science, one additional unit of English, mathematics, or science, and two additional units of core courses in certain areas. The Division II core course requirements vary slightly from those for Division I.

Under NCAA rules, courses which "are taught at a level below the high school's regular instructional level (*e.g.*, remedial, special education, or compensatory) [are not] considered core courses regardless of course content." However, courses for students with learning disabilities may be accepted as core courses if "the high school principal submits a written statement to the NCAA indicating that students in such classes are expected to acquire the same knowledge, both quantitatively and qualitatively, as students in other core courses."

* * *

E. Bowers' Application to the Clearinghouse

On or about September 13, 1995, Bowers paid an $18 fee to ACT in order for the Clearinghouse to evaluate his initial eligibility application. This evaluation included an evaluation of Bowers' high school transcript which denominated Bowers' special education courses as such. On April 16, 1996, the Clearinghouse informed Bowers' high school, Palmyra High School, of the procedures it would employ to "approve the use of nonstandard tests . . . and use high school courses designated for students with learning disabilities to satisfy core course requirements." The Clearinghouse requested, among other things, a copy of the application to take a standardized test under non-standard conditions and a copy of the student's IEP,[4] as well as descriptions of his learning disabled courses, course syllabi, and information from the high school principal regarding the relationship between "regular academic course[s]" and the "comparable learning disabled course[s]."

Shortly thereafter, Palmyra High School began to provide that information to the Clearinghouse. On April 25, 1996, the principal of Palmyra High School informed the Clearinghouse that "students in [special education] classes are expected to acquire the same knowledge, both quantitatively and qualitatively, as students in comparable course(s). The same grading standards are employed in such classes as those utilized in this (these) course(s)." On May 17, 1996, Dori Levy, the Director of Special Services of Palmyra Public Schools, identified Bowers as a student with an IEP and informed the Clearinghouse that she administered an untimed SAT exam for him. At some point before June 7, 1996, "information about all of [Bowers'] courses including table[s] of contents and course descriptions, proficiencies, outlines, and objectives" was submitted to the Clearinghouse.

On July 30, 1996, "the NCAA through its Clearinghouse" notified Bowers of the final determination that he was a nonqualifier. Among various deficiencies, the Clearinghouse determined that Bowers lacked two years of social studies, three years of English, and the requisite additional core courses, and that his application lacked documentation required to accept standardized test scores achieved under non-standard testing conditions. Bowers was only given core course credit for three of his high school courses.

As a result of his status as a nonqualifier, Bowers "is ineligible to compete in intercollegiate football" for some period of time, may not practice or condition with qualifiers, may not compete in intercollegiate football for the maximum number of seasons, and may not receive an athletic scholarship. In the Spring

[4] IEP stands for individualized education program and is "a statement of the student's instructional guide and basic plan which [a] school district uses to determine placement and participation in regular education and/or special education programs with the appropriate curricular or instructional modifications." Under the Individuals with Disabilities Education Act (IDEA), 20 U.S.C. §§ 1400-1485, students with specific learning disabilities are entitled to an individualized special education program at the primary and secondary educational levels.

of 1997, Bowers enrolled at Temple as a full-time student. Bowers received $2,275 in need-based financial aid from Temple.

F. Efforts to Recruit Bowers

Among other schools, Temple, Iowa, and AIC were interested in recruiting Bowers for their football programs. All of the efforts to recruit Bowers hinged, to some extent, on his attaining qualifier status. After Temple requested an unofficial copy of Bowers' high school transcript, Temple's football recruiter determined that the Clearinghouse would not deem Bowers to be a qualifier. Accordingly, Temple discontinued its efforts to recruit Bowers for its football program, thereby effectively ending his chances of receiving an athletic scholarship from Temple. Similarly, after some initial recruiting contacts with Bowers, a representative of Iowa assured Bowers' mother that, if the Clearinghouse identified Bowers as a qualifier, he would receive a full scholarship. After Bowers was designated a nonqualifier, Iowa terminated its efforts to recruit Bowers. Finally, after some initial contacts with Bowers, AIC discontinued its interest in Bowers as a football recruit once Bowers was designated a non-qualifier. . . .

II. Standards on Motions to Dismiss and for Summary Judgment

The NCAA, ACT and the Clearinghouse, and Iowa have all moved to dismiss Bowers' various claims or, in the alternative, for summary judgment. . . .

[Discussion of procedural standards omitted.]

III. Discussion

I review each of Bowers' five claims seriatim to determine whether Bowers has stated a claim and, if so, whether any of the moving Defendants is entitled to summary judgment on the claim. . . .

B. Americans with Disabilities Act (Count I)

Bowers asserts his ADA claim against the NCAA, ACT and the Clearinghouse, Temple, Iowa, and AIC. There are two basic provisions of the ADA under which Bowers sues. The first is section 12132:

> [N]o qualified individual with a disability shall, by reason of such disability, be excluded from participation in or be denied the benefits of the services, programs, or activities of a public entity, or be subjected to discrimination by any such entity.

42 U.S.C. § 12132. This provision applies to Bowers'ADA claim against Iowa and Temple and not to his ADA claim against the NCAA, ACT and the Clearinghouse, and AIC. A "public entity" is defined, in relevant part, as "any department, agency, special purpose district, or other instrumentality of a State or States or local government." 42 U.S.C. § 12131(1)(B). Conversely, a private entity is "any entity other than a public entity." *Id.* at § 12181(6). Thus, regardless of Bowers' assertion to the contrary, Iowa and Temple, to the extent they are instrumentalities of the states of Iowa and Pennsylvania, are both potentially subject to Title II of the ADA, but not Title III.

The second provision of the ADA under which Bowers sues is section 12182(a) which applies to Bowers' claim against the NCAA, ACT and the Clearinghouse, and AIC. This section provides as a general rule that:

> No individual shall be discriminated against on the basis of disability in the full and equal enjoyment of the goods, services, facilities, privileges, advantages, or accommodations of any place of public accommodation by any person who owns, leases (or leases to), or operates a place of public accommodation.

42 U.S.C. § 12182(a). Notwithstanding Bowers' allegation and argument to the contrary, Title III, not Title II, applies to the NCAA. An unincorporated association of many colleges and universities, some of the members of which are state colleges and universities, does not fit at all neatly within the definition of "public entity" as defined by section 12131(1)(B). Because "private entity" is defined to capture everything which is not a "public entity," the NCAA fits much more cleanly and logically within the language of section 12181(6).

* * *

1. Title II Claim as Against Iowa

In order to state a claim under Title II, Bowers must allege that: 1) he is a qualified individual; 2) with a disability; 3) he was excluded from participation in or denied the benefits of the services, programs, or activities of a public entity, or was subjected to discrimination by any such entity; 4) by reason of his disability.

Iowa attacks Bowers'ADA claim on numerous prongs. On the "disability" prong, Iowa adopts the arguments of ACT and the Clearinghouse that Bowers is not disabled. Iowa also argues that playing intercollegiate football — Bowers' ultimate goal — is not a major life activity and that, therefore, Bowers cannot be disabled. On the "qualified individual" prong, Iowa argues that Bowers is not a "qualified individual" within the meaning of section 12132 because the modification of the initial eligibility rules requested by Bowers would not be reasonable. Iowa also argues that Bowers was not qualified to play football at Iowa as evidenced by the fact that he was not given a football scholarship for reasons independent of his nonqualifier status. Iowa's arguments fail, and its motion to dismiss the ADA claim or, in the alternative, for summary judgment will be denied.

a. Disability under the ADA

The ADA defines "disability" as:

> (A) a physical or mental impairment that substantially limits one or more of the major life activities of such individual;
>
> (B) a record of such an impairment; or
>
> (C) being regarded as having such an impairment.

42 U.S.C. § 12102(2). For the purposes of both Titles II and III, the term "major life activities" "means functions such as caring for one's self, performing manual tasks, walking, seeing, hearing, speaking, breathing, learning, and working." 28 C.F.R. §§ 35.104, 36.104. Bowers has adequately alleged that he has a disability within the meaning of the ADA. . . . Iowa adopts the arguments of ACT and the Clearinghouse that as a factual matter Bowers is not disabled because, *inter alia*, he has achieved a laudable level of success in his college courses at Temple. The fact that Bowers may have completed a substantial amount of high school mathematics within a relatively short amount of time and that he may be doing well at Temple are simply not inconsistent, on the record before me, with his being disabled within the meaning of the ADA. Assuming, *arguendo*, that Bowers should be compared to the average unimpaired student, Iowa has not shown, sufficient to support a summary judgment motion, that Bowers is not impaired in his ability to learn as compared to the average student. The factual support adduced in support of that proposition, the two facts alluded to above, is at best flimsy. . . .

. . . Unlike the plaintiff in *Knapp v. Northwestern Univ.*, 101 F.3d 473 (7th Cir. 1996), *cert. denied*, 520 U.S. 1274 (1997), Bowers is not claiming a disability because of a limitation on his ability to play college sports. *See* 101 F.3d at 479-82 (holding that student's heart condition did not constitute disability because student was only limited in playing intercollegiate sports which, by itself, is not a major life activity). Rather, Bowers alleges that: 1) he is limited in his capacity to learn; 2) therefore, he is disabled within the meaning of the ADA; and 3) he was denied the ability to participate in, among other things, intercollegiate football.

b. By Reason of Such Disability

Iowa next argues that Bowers was not discriminated against "by reason of [his] disability" within the meaning of section 12132. This, Iowa asserts, is because Bowers was determined to be a nonqualifier as a result of his failure to satisfy the NCAA's core course requirements, not because of his disability. . . .

Iowa has not shown that these two methods — acceptance of a principal's certification that learning disabled courses are as demanding as "regular" core courses and a waiver procedure — sufficiently accommodate the learning disabled such that the NCAA's requirements as administered do not actually violate Title II's antidiscrimination principle. In the more penetrating light of fully-conducted discovery, it may very well be that these accommodations or modifications are insufficient.

For example, as counsel for the United States eloquently explained at oral argument, the timing of the waiver procedure may preclude it from being an acceptable modification or accommodation. The United States argued first that, if the waiver procedure may only be initiated after a student has already graduated from high school, then it may do little to help the learning disabled student because college recruiting will generally have been completed by that time. Second, the waiver procedure, even if successful from the student's perspective, may be completed so late that a student cannot involve himself or herself in fall collegiate athletic programs.

The same may also be true for the acceptance of a principal's certification about the nature of courses for learning disabled. For example, Bowers was not finally notified of his nonqualifier status until July 30, 1996, well after his high school graduation, and he may not have had any inkling of a problem with his high school transcript until late December, 1995, or early January, 1996. Also, an individual student may not have notice of NCAA policies sufficiently early in his or her high school career such that he or she can make affirmative efforts to improve his or her odds of being deemed a qualifier. Finally, without discovery as to the nature of the waiver procedure and its functioning, in general and specifically with respect to Bowers, it is impossible to ascertain whether the waiver procedure or the acceptance of principal certifications are meaningful accommodations or modifications. . . .

c. Qualified Individual with a Disability

The ADA defines "qualified individual with a disability," in relevant part, as:

> an individual with a disability who, with or without reasonable modifications to rules, policies, or practices . . . or the provision of auxiliary aids and services, meets the essential eligibility requirements for the receipt of services or the participation in programs or activities provided by a public entity.

42 U.S.C. § 12131(2).

[K]nowing that Bowers has avoided dismissal and summary judgment on the question of whether he has a disability within the meaning of section 12102, I must determine whether Iowa would be entitled to summary judgment on the question of whether Bowers is a "qualified individual." To do so, I evaluate Iowa's entitlement to summary judgment based upon two criteria: 1) whether the eligibility requirements imposed upon Bowers are essential; and 2) if so, whether Bowers meets these requirements with or without a modification.

At the outset, I note that Iowa must shoulder the burden of showing that "the making of modifications would fundamentally alter the nature of the service, program, or activity," and the burden of showing that eligibility criteria which might otherwise "screen out or tend to screen out . . . a class of individuals with disabilities" are necessary for the provision of the service, program, or activity offered,"

After a review of only the first of these questions — the necessity of the NCAA's initial eligibility standards — I find that there are substantial questions of fact which preclude the entry of summary judgment. First, it is not at all clear that the initial eligibility requirements are essential or necessary to the maintenance of intercollegiate athletics since the NCAA itself provides for the waiver of the initial eligibility standards at the request of a member-institution and now, the student. *See, e.g.*, NCAA Manual § 14.3.1.7. Additionally, Iowa has offered no evidence to show that waivers are so infrequently granted that the initial eligibility criteria cannot be deemed anything but essential. Nor has Iowa adduced any evidence suggesting that the NCAA so rarely accepts a high school principal's submission that students with learning disabilities are expected to acquire the same knowledge, both quantitatively and qualitatively, as students in other core courses that the non-acceptance of courses for learning disabled students as core courses can be deemed, at this point, essential or necessary. Finally, Iowa has presented no evidence to show that the NCAA's standards could not be modified in such a way that the goals of the initial eligibility requirements could not be achieved without the use of the current initial eligibility criteria, for example, by implementing a more nuanced, individualized assessment of a disabled student's ability to manage the pressures of intercollegiate athletics and college academics rather than applying a purely numerical assessment of a high school student's academic record and standardized test scores. *See Bowers I*, 974 F. Supp. at 461 (noting that goals of initial eligibility requirements are "to assure proper emphasis on educational objectives, to promote competitive equity among institutions, and to prevent exploitation of student athletes"); *cf. Pottgen*, 40 F.3d at 929-30 (finding that no reasonable accommodation to age limit requirement existed and that therefore plaintiff was not qualified).

* * *

Bowers has specifically responded to this affidavit with far more than a "mere scintilla" of evidence and his affidavit shows the existence of a question of fact as to when and why he was eliminated as a potential scholarship recipient . . . [i]t is reasonable to infer, based on the facts contained in Bowers' affidavit and on a motion for summary judgment, that Iowa considered Bowers' academic record inadequate, at least in part, because of the presence of numerous special education courses on his transcript and/or because of Iowa's expectation, after reviewing Bowers' academic record, that he would not be assigned qualifier status by the Clearinghouse. There is also a genuine issue of material fact as to whether Bowers was not offered an athletic scholarship by Iowa because of his learning disability or whether it was because Iowa did not think sufficiently of his prospects as a football player. Thus, genuine issues of material fact exist as to whether Bowers is a "qualified individual." Accordingly, Iowa is not entitled to summary judgment on the question of whether Bowers is a "qualified individual with a disability."

2. Title III Claim as Against the NCAA, ACT, and the Clearinghouse

* * *

In order to state a claim under Title III of the ADA, Bowers must allege that: 1) he was discriminated against on the basis of disability; 3) in the full and equal enjoyment of the goods, services, facilities, privileges, advantages, or accommodations of any place of public accommodation; 4) by any person who owns, leases (or leases to), or operates a place of public accommodation.

a. ACT and the Clearinghouse

In order to be subject to Title III of the ADA, a potential defendant must be "[a] person who owns, leases (or leases to), or operates a place of public accommodation." 42 U.S.C. § 12182(a). The statutory language prohibits discrimination by certain persons and extends no further than to actions by those persons.

The question I must answer is: Does Bowers properly allege that ACT and the Clearinghouse are such persons and, if so, are ACT and the Clearinghouse entitled to summary judgment on that question? ACT and the Clearinghouse argue that Bowers cannot avoid a dismissal for failure to state a claim because ACT is not a public accommodation. I find that, taking the facts as alleged in the First Amended Complaint as true, Bowers fails to state a claim under the ADA against ACT and the Clearinghouse.

Of course, I must begin my analysis by examining the language of the statute itself. The ADA defines "public accommodation" in the following fashion:

> The following private entities are considered public accommodations for purposes of [Title III], if the operations of such entities affect commerce —
>
> (A) an inn, hotel, motel, or other place of lodging, except for an establishment located within a building that contains not more than five rooms for rent or hire and that is actually occupied by the proprietor of such establishment as the residence of such proprietor;
>
> (B) a restaurant, bar, or other establishment serving food or drink;
>
> (C) a motion picture house, theater, concert hall, stadium, or other place of exhibition or entertainment;
>
> (D) an auditorium, convention center, lecture hall, or other place of public gathering;
>
> (E) a bakery, grocery store, clothing store, hardware store, shopping center, or other sales or rental establishment;
>
> (F) a laundromat, dry-cleaner, bank, barber shop, beauty shop, travel service, shoe repair service, funeral parlor, gas station, office of an accountant or lawyer, pharmacy, insurance office, professional office of a health care provider, hospital, or other service establishment;
>
> (G) a terminal, depot, or other station used for specified public transportation;
>
> (H) a museum, library, gallery, or other place of public display or collection;

(I) a park, zoo, amusement park, or other place of recreation;

(J) a nursery, elementary, secondary, undergraduate, or postgraduate private school, or other place of education;

(K) a day care center, senior citizen center, homeless shelter, food bank, adoption agency, or other social service center establishment; and

(L) a gymnasium, health spa, bowling alley, golf course, or other place of exercise or recreation.

42 U.S.C. § 12181(7). The term "place" as used in the statutory language "place of public accommodation" is not defined by the ADA. I am guided by the Department of Justice regulations, the promulgation of which was expressly authorized by the statute, to the extent those regulations are not arbitrary, capricious, or manifestly contrary to the statute. The regulations slice the statutory language in a confusing fashion, but ultimately end up at the same place as the statute: only those who own, lease (or lease to), or operate a place of public accommodation are subject to Title III. *See, e.g.*, 28 C.F.R. pt. 36, app. B at 613.

Perhaps recognizing this fatal flaw, Bowers argues, albeit obliquely, that the "Clearinghouse is a joint venture of the NCAA and ACT," and ACT and the Clearinghouse are, therefore, somehow subject to Title III of the ADA. The language of the ADA does not support this extension of liability to those who merely contract with someone who ultimately may be subject to Title III. . . . Bowers' other argument, advanced in an equally oblique fashion, is that ACT is covered by the ADA because it is "a national testing service that leases facilities to administer college achievement test [*sic*]." I note first that this "allegation" is not included in the First Amended Complaint. Much more fundamentally, however, Bowers'ADA claim as alleged in the First Amended Complaint has nothing at all to do with testing facilities and his enjoyment thereof. The allegations of the First Amended Complaint do not suggest that he was denied the enjoyment of those (unspecified) testing facilities. Rather, Bowers' claim relates to the NCAA's initial eligibility requirements, ACT and the Clearinghouse's application thereof, and ultimately Bowers' enjoyment of, among other things, intercollegiate football. Thus, Bowers still does not allege that ACT and the Clearinghouse own, lease (or lease to), or operate a place of public accommodation in such a way that they could modify that place of public accommodation to grant Bowers the enjoyment he alleges he was denied.

Stated another way, to the extent ACT actually does own, lease, or operate a place of public accommodation in connection with a national testing service, ACT and the Clearinghouse are subject to the ADA's anti-discrimination principles only in the operation of that place of public accommodation. Mere operation of one place of public accommodation does not by itself subject every other aspect of the operator's business to Title III. . . . Accordingly, because Bowers has not alleged sufficient facts to subject ACT and the Clearinghouse to liability under Title III of the ADA, the ADA claim as alleged against ACT and the Clearinghouse will be dismissed.

b. The NCAA

The NCAA argues that Bowers'ADA claim fails for three reasons. First, it argues that it is not a place of public accommodation and that it does not own, lease, or operate a place of public accommodation. Second, the NCAA argues that Bowers has not alleged that he was denied access to a place of public accommodation. Finally, the NCAA argues that it does not discriminate against the learning disabled. These arguments in support of the motion to dismiss and, when matters outside the pleadings are considered, in support of the motion for summary judgment, are without merit.

With respect to the first argument — that the NCAA itself is not a place of public accommodation. . . . As I have repeatedly stated, the critical question for liability under section 12182 is whether the NCAA owns, leases (or leases to), or operates a place of public accommodation. . . .

ii. Operates a Place of Public Accommodation and Enjoyment of a Place of Public Accommodation

* * *

[B]owers has alleged . . . that the NCAA at least operates the place or places of public accommodation of which Bowers was allegedly denied enjoyment in such a way that the NCAA manages, regulates, or controls discriminatory conditions of that place or those places of public accommodation. In particular, Bowers alleges . . . that the NCAA operates such places of public accommodation as team training, dining, living, playing, practice, and meeting facilities, and colleges and universities more generally. Bowers also alleges . . . that the NCAA operates these places of public accommodation in such a way that it manages, regulates, or controls the allegedly discriminatory conditions of these places.

In particular, Bowers alleges that a student's initial eligibility status, which is assigned strictly according to criteria promulgated by the NCAA, determines, for example, whether and how much financial aid a student-athlete may receive from a college or university, and whether and to what extent a student-athlete may practice, train, dine, live, and compete with a particular team. All of these are within the broad swath carved out by "goods, services, facilities, privileges, advantages, or accommodations of a place of public accommodation." 42 U.S.C. § 12182(a).

While at times the First Amended Complaint is framed in terms of the NCAA's control over, and Bowers' enjoyment of, something as ethereal as "intercollegiate athletics," there is a clear and sufficient nexus between what Bowers alleges he was denied and various public accommodations. That is, what Bowers alleges he was denied is most certainly "of a place of public accommodation." The First Amended Complaint is more than sufficient to satisfy the standard explicated above. . . .

* * *

The NCAA's initial eligibility requirements determine whether and to what extent a particular student can participate in intercollegiate athletics and can receive institutional financial aid. And participation in intercollegiate athletics and receipt of financial aid from a member-institution are really just shorthand for a set of goods, services, facilities, privileges, advantages, or accommodations of specific places of public accommodation, such as undergraduate schools generally, food service establishments, stadia or other places of exhibition, gymnasia or other places of exercise or recreation, all of which the NCAA's regulations clearly treat. Accordingly, for these reasons the NCAA's motion for summary judgment will be denied.

iii. Discrimination under Title III

Finally, the NCAA claims that it does not discriminate against the learning disabled. For the same reasons that Iowa is not entitled to summary judgment on this question, *see* Part III.B.1, supra, the NCAA's motion will be denied.

* * *

[Portion of opinion denying summary judgment on Rehabilitation Act claims omitted.]

IV. Conclusion

For the reasons set forth above, the ADA claim (Count I) will be dismissed with prejudice as to ACT and the Clearinghouse. The Sherman Act claim (Count III) will be dismissed with prejudice as to ACT, the Clearinghouse, the NCAA, and Iowa, as well as non-moving Defendants, Temple and AIC. In all other respects, Defendants' motions will be denied.

NOTES AND COMMENTS

1. Application of Title III to Sporting Associations. Title III specifically applies to places of public accommodations and does not identify membership organizations or standard-setting associations in the listed categories of public accommodations. The NCAA argued that, as a private association, it was not subject to Title III. The NCAA also argued it was not a place of public accommodation and did not own, lease, or operate such a place, and that Bowers was not denied access to any "place." The PGA makes a similar argument in *PGA Tour, Inc. v. Martin, infra*. According to the court in *Bowers*, what was the critical inquiry in determining whether the NCAA is subject to Title III?

2. The NCAA may also be subject to the Rehabilitation Act. Although the NCAA is not a "recipient" of federal funds by its receipt of dues from member institutions receiving federal funds, the NCAA's connection with the National Youth Sports Program, which receives federal funds, may render it subject to the Rehabilitation Act. *See NCAA v. Smith,* 525 U.S. 459 (1999).

3. ADA Prima Facie Claim. The University of Iowa, which allegedly stopped recruiting Bowers after it received his transcripts indicating special education courses, asserted that Bowers was not a "qualified individual with a disability." As Northwestern successfully asserted in *Knapp*, Iowa argued that Bowers was not disabled simply because he could not participate in intercollegiate sports. Iowa also argued that Bowers was not discriminated against "because of" his learning disability but was denied eligibility due to his failure to fulfill the core course and GPA requirements. The court rejected both arguments. Why?

4. In *Ganden v. NCAA*, 1996 WL 680000 (N.D. Ill. 1996), a highly recruited swimmer diagnosed with a learning disability since second grade sought to compel the NCAA to modify its core course criteria to accept remedial courses taken as part of his special education curriculum and to modify its GPA criteria. In rejecting this request as unreasonable and as a fundamental alteration, the court stated "[w]hatever criticism one may level at GPA and the national standardized tests, these provide significant objective predictors of a student's ability to succeed at college. The 'core course' criteria further serves the dual interests of insuring the integrity of the GPA and independently insuring that the student has covered the minimum subject matter required for college." The court added, "Title III does not require the NCAA to simply abandon its eligibility requirements, but only to make reasonable modifications to them." When is modification to academic standards "reasonable"?

5. Consent Decree. The United States Department of Justice (DOJ), charged with enforcement of Title III of the ADA, investigated the NCAA's initial eligibility certification process in response to several discrimination complaints filed by student-athletes with learning disabilities. The DOJ determined that "several aspects" of the NCAA's initial eligibility requirements violate Title III of the ADA, in particular the "core course" definition explicitly excluding any remedial, special education, or compensatory courses. On May 26, 1998, the NCAA entered into a Consent Decree with the DOJ, agreeing to revise certain procedures and policies with respect to student-athletes with learning disabilities. *United States v. NCAA*, Consent Decree (D.D.C. May 26, 1998) <www.usdoj.gov/crt/adm/ ncaa>. Under the Decree, the NCAA agreed to: certify classes designed for students with disabilities as "core courses" if they provide them with the same type of "knowledge and skills as other college-bound students," permit ineligible learning disabled students to earn a fourth year of eligibility by making "substantial progress" towards an academic degree; include experts on learning disabilities in evaluating waiver applications; and to pay $35,000 to four student athletes who had filed complaints with the DOJ. The NCAA entered the Consent Decree even though no court had yet ruled that a learning disabled student had a reasonable probability of succeeding on the merits of a disability discrimination claim against the NCAA. Expressly in the Consent Decree, however, the NCAA maintains that it is not subject to Title III of the ADA and denies any liability under the ADA. *Cf. Matthews v. NCAA*, 179 F. Supp. 2d 1209 (E.D. Wash. 2001) (holding that waiver for learning disabled student of NCAA rule requiring 75% credit hours be taken during the school year, so long as the plaintiff maintains the minimum grade point average and progression toward his degree, constitutes a necessary and reasonable modification of NCAA bylaws and does not fundamentally alter the NCAA's purpose).

6. Learning Disabilities. Learning disabilities are neurological disorders that cause difficulties in learning which cannot be attributed to poor intelligence, poor motivation, inadequate teaching, or environmental, cultural, or economic disadvantages. Learning disabilities encompass a wide range of learning impairments with dyslexia the most common form. Unlike most physical disabilities, learning disabilities are usually hidden and may go undetected. For example, among the waiver applications filed with the NCAA, some learning disabled students were diagnosed at an early age and received special education throughout schooling (*Ganden, Bowers*). Others were not diagnosed until later in high school or even after having failed to meet NCAA requirements. Michelle Huston, a state champion in gymnastics, was not diagnosed as learning disabled until late in her sophomore year when she had a 1.1 grade point average. Since then, Michelle has performed well academically but failed to meet NCAA eligibility because of the first two years' grades. In *Tatum v. NCAA*, 992 F. Supp. 1114 (E.D. Mo. 1998), experts issued conflicting diagnoses as to whether the student was learning disabled and entitled to receive accommodation, the court agreed with the NCAA's rejection of Tatum's learning disability diagnosis. The Association on Higher Education and Disabilities (AHEAD) has developed guidelines to assist post-secondary institutions in verifying learning disabilities diagnoses and accommodation requests, including guidance on evaluator qualifications and appropriate clinical documentation to substantiate a learning disability. *See* Maureen A. Weston, *Academic Standards or Discriminatory Hoops? Learning Disabled Student Athletes' Challenge to NCAA Initial Eligibility Requirements*, 66 TENN. L. REV. 1049 (1999).

E. RULES OF PLAY AND REASONABLE ACCOMMODATIONS

The previous sections of this chapter have examined judicial resolution of sports "eligibility" issues under the federal disability laws. Note, however, that the courts did not intervene in the actual rules of play and competition. Application of the Americans with Disabilities Act and the Rehabilitation Act becomes more controversial when the laws appear to require modifications or accommodations for athletes with disabilities in competition, particularly at the professional level. Most professional teams or organizations do not receive federal financial assistance and are not covered by the Rehabilitation Act. In the few disability discrimination cases brought by professional athletes, the athletes have invoked Title I (employment) and Title III (public accommodations) of the ADA to seek legal relief.

Problem

Phil Luna, as a straight-on placekicker for the University of Texoma, set a new record in NCAA Division I football for field-goals. When he was five years old, the front half of Luna's right (kicking) foot was severed in a lawnmower accident. Since then he has worn a specially designed shoe to play sports. For placekicking, Luna wears a specially designed extra-wide cleat, featuring a square toe with wood at the half end of the shoe and padding to keep his foot from hitting the wood. Despite complaints by other teams and players in college that the shoe provides a competitive advantage, Luna was allowed to wear the special shoe. Luna seeks to play professionally and has been highly recruited by several NFL teams. However, the NFL has a rule prohibiting the use of special equipment by players. The NFL had the special cleat X-rayed, weighed, and inspected by several officials. Thereafter, the NFL denied Luna's request to play with his square-toed wooden shoe, maintaining that such use violates the special equipment prohibition. Luna seeks your advice regarding whether federal disability laws require the NFL to permit him to wear the specially designed kicking shoe.

Case File

PGA TOUR, INC. v. MARTIN

532 U.S. 661 (2001)

Justice Stevens delivered the opinion of the Court.

This case raises two questions concerning the application of the Americans with Disabilities Act of 1990, 42 U.S.C. § 12101 *et seq.*, to a gifted athlete: first, whether the Act protects access to professional golf tournaments by a qualified entrant with a disability; and second, whether a disabled contestant may be denied the use of a golf cart because it would "fundamentally alter the nature" of the tournaments, § 12182(b)(2)(A)(ii), to allow him to ride when all other contestants must walk.

I

Petitioner PGA TOUR, Inc., a nonprofit entity formed in 1968, sponsors and cosponsors professional golf tournaments conducted on three annual tours. About 200 golfers participate in the PGA TOUR; about 170 in the NIKE TOUR and about 100 in the SENIOR PGA TOUR. PGA TOUR and NIKE TOUR tournaments typically are 4-day events, played on courses leased and operated by petitioner. The entire field usually competes in two 18-hole rounds played on Thursday and Friday; those who survive the "cut" play on Saturday and Sunday and receive prize money in amounts determined by their aggregate scores for all four rounds. The revenues generated by television, admissions, concessions, and contributions from cosponsors amount to about $300 million a year, much of which is distributed in prize money.

There are various ways of gaining entry into particular tours. For example, a player who wins three NIKE TOUR events in the same year, or is among the top-15 money winners on that tour, earns the right to play in the PGA TOUR. Additionally, a golfer may obtain a spot in an official tournament through successfully competing in "open" qualifying rounds, which are conducted the week before each tournament. Most participants, however, earn playing privileges in the PGA TOUR or NIKE TOUR by way of a three-stage qualifying tournament known as the "Q-School."

Any member of the public may enter the Q-School by paying a $3,000 entry fee and submitting two letters of reference from, among others, PGA TOUR or NIKE TOUR members. The $3,000 entry fee covers the players' greens fees and the cost of golf carts, which are permitted during the first two stages, but which have been prohibited during the third stage since 1997. Each year, over a thousand contestants compete in the first stage, which consists of four 18-hole rounds at different locations. Approximately half of them make it to the second stage, which also includes 72 holes. Around 168 players survive the second stage and advance to the final one, where they compete over 108 holes. Of those finalists, about a fourth qualify for membership in the PGA TOUR, and the rest gain membership in the NIKE TOUR. The significance of making it into either tour is illuminated by the fact that there are about 25 million golfers in the country.

Three sets of rules govern competition in tour events. First, the "Rules of Golf," jointly written by the United States Golf Association (USGA) and the Royal and Ancient Golf Club of Scotland, apply to the game as it is played, not only by millions of amateurs on public courses and in private country clubs throughout the United States and worldwide, but also by the professionals in the tournaments conducted by petitioner, the USGA, the Ladies' Professional Golf Association, and the Senior Women's Golf Association. Those rules do not prohibit the use of golf carts at any time.

Second, the "Conditions of Competition and Local Rules," often described as the "hard card," apply specifically to petitioner's professional tours. The hard cards for the PGA TOUR and NIKE TOUR require players to walk the golf course during tournaments, but not during open qualifying rounds. On the SENIOR PGA TOUR, which is limited to golfers age 50 and older, the contestants may use golf carts. Most seniors, however, prefer to walk.

Third, "Notices to Competitors" are issued for particular tournaments and cover conditions for that specific event. Such a notice may, for example, explain how the Rules of Golf should be applied to a particular water hazard or man-made obstruction. It might also authorize the use of carts to speed up play when there is an unusual distance between one green and the next tee.

The basic Rules of Golf, the hard cards, and the weekly notices apply equally to all players in tour competitions. As one of petitioner's witnesses explained with reference to "the Masters Tournament, which is golf at its very highest level . . . the key is to have everyone tee off on the first hole under exactly the same conditions and all of them be tested over that 72-hole event under the conditions that exist during those four days of the event."

II

Casey Martin is a talented golfer. As an amateur, he won 17 Oregon Golf Association junior events before he was 15, and won the state championship as a high school senior. He played on the Stanford University golf team that won the 1994 National Collegiate Athletic Association (NCAA) championship. As a professional, Martin qualified for the NIKE TOUR in 1998 and 1999, and based on his 1999 performance, qualified for the PGA TOUR in 2000. In the 1999 season, he entered 24 events, made the cut 13 times, and had 6 top-10 finishes, coming in second twice and third once.

Martin is also an individual with a disability as defined in the Americans with Disabilities Act of 1990 (ADA or Act). Since birth he has been afflicted with Klippel-Trenaunay-Weber Syndrome, a degenerative circulatory disorder that obstructs the flow of blood from his right leg back to his heart. The disease is progressive; it causes severe pain and has atrophied his right leg. During the latter part of his college career, because of the progress of the disease, Martin could no longer walk an 18-hole golf course. Walking not only caused him pain, fatigue, and anxiety, but also created a significant risk of hemorrhaging, developing blood clots, and fracturing his tibia so badly that an amputation might be required. For these reasons, Stanford made written requests to the Pacific 10 Conference and the NCAA to waive for Martin their rules requiring players to walk and carry their own clubs. The requests were granted.

When Martin turned pro and entered petitioner's Q-School, the hard card permitted him to use a cart during his successful progress through the first two stages. He made a request, supported by detailed medical records, for permission to use a golf cart during the third stage. Petitioner refused to review those records or to waive its walking rule for the third stage. Martin therefore filed this action. A preliminary injunction entered by the District Court made it possible for him to use a cart in the final stage of the Q-School and as a competitor in the NIKE TOUR and PGA TOUR. Although not bound by the injunction, and despite its support for petitioner's position in this litigation, the USGA voluntarily granted Martin a similar waiver in events that it sponsors, including the U.S. Open.

III

In the District Court, petitioner moved for summary judgment on the ground that it is exempt from coverage under Title III of the ADA as a "private clu[b] or establishmen[t]," or alternatively, that the play areas of its tour competitions do not constitute places of "public accommodation" within the scope of that

Title. The Magistrate Judge concluded that petitioner should be viewed as a commercial enterprise operating in the entertainment industry for the economic benefit of its members rather than as a private club. Furthermore, after noting that the statutory definition of public accommodation included a "golf course," he rejected petitioner's argument that its competitions are only places of public accommodation in the areas open to spectators. The operator of a public accommodation could not, in his view, "create private enclaves within the facility . . . and thus relegate the ADA to hop-scotch areas." Accordingly, he denied petitioner's motion for summary judgment.

At trial, petitioner did not contest the conclusion that Martin has a disability covered by the ADA, or the fact "that his disability prevents him from walking the course during a round of golf." Rather, petitioner asserted that the condition of walking is a substantive rule of competition, and that waiving it as to any individual for any reason would fundamentally alter the nature of the competition. Petitioner's evidence included the testimony of a number of experts, among them some of the greatest golfers in history. Arnold Palmer, Jack Nicklaus, and Ken Venturi explained that fatigue can be a critical factor in a tournament, particularly on the last day when psychological pressure is at a maximum. Their testimony makes it clear that, in their view, permission to use a cart might well give some players a competitive advantage over other players who must walk. They did not, however, express any opinion on whether a cart would give Martin such an advantage.

Rejecting petitioner's argument that an individualized inquiry into the necessity of the walking rule in Martin's case would be inappropriate, the District Court stated that it had "the independent duty to inquire into the purpose of the rule at issue, and to ascertain whether there can be a reasonable modification made to accommodate plaintiff without frustrating the purpose of the rule" and thereby fundamentally altering the nature of petitioner's tournaments. The judge found that the purpose of the rule was to inject fatigue into the skill of shot-making, but that the fatigue injected "by walking the course cannot be deemed significant under normal circumstances." Furthermore, Martin presented evidence, and the judge found, that even with the use of a cart, Martin must walk over a mile during an 18-hole round, and that the fatigue he suffers from coping with his disability is "undeniably greater" than the fatigue his able-bodied competitors endure from walking the course. As the judge observed: "[P]laintiff is in significant pain when he walks, and even when he is getting in and out of the cart. With each step, he is at risk of fracturing his tibia and hemorrhaging. The other golfers have to endure the psychological stress of competition as part of their fatigue; Martin has the same stress plus the added stress of pain and risk of serious injury. As he put it, he would gladly trade the cart for a good leg. To perceive that the cart puts him — with his condition — at a competitive advantage is a gross distortion of reality." As a result, the judge concluded that it would "not fundamentally alter the nature of the PGA Tour's game to accommodate him with a cart." The judge accordingly entered a permanent injunction requiring petitioner to permit Martin to use a cart in tour and qualifying events.

On appeal to the Ninth Circuit, petitioner did not challenge the District Court's rejection of its claim that it was exempt as a "private club," but it renewed the contention that during a tournament the portion of the golf course "'behind the ropes' is not a public accommodation because the public has no right to enter it." The Court of Appeals viewed that contention as resting on the incorrect assumption that the competition among participants was not itself public. The court first pointed out that, as with a private university, "the fact that users of a facility are highly selected does not mean that the facility cannot be a public accommodation." In its opinion, the competition to enter the select circle of PGA TOUR and NIKE TOUR golfers was comparable because "[a]ny member of the public who pays a $3000 entry fee and supplies two letters of recommendation may try out in the qualifying school." The court saw "no justification in reason or in the statute to draw a line beyond which the performance of athletes becomes so excellent that a competition restricted to their level deprives its situs of the character of a public accommodation." Nor did it find a basis for distinguishing between "use of a place of public accommodation for pleasure and use in the pursuit of a living." Consequently, the Court of Appeals concluded that golf courses remain places of public accommodation during PGA tournaments.

On the merits, because there was no serious dispute about the fact that permitting Martin to use a golf cart was both a reasonable and a necessary solution to the problem of providing him access to the tournaments, the Court of Appeals regarded the central dispute as whether such permission would "fundamentally alter" the nature of the PGA TOUR or NIKE TOUR. Like the District Court, the Court of Appeals viewed the issue not as "whether use of carts generally would fundamentally alter the competition, but whether the use of a cart by Martin would do so." That issue turned on "an intensively fact-based inquiry," and, the court concluded, had been correctly resolved by the trial judge. In its words, "[a]ll that the cart does is permit Martin access to a type of competition in which he otherwise could not engage because of his disability."

The day after the Ninth Circuit ruled in Martin's favor, the Seventh Circuit came to a contrary conclusion in a case brought against the USGA by a disabled golfer who failed to qualify for "Ama's greatest — and most democratic — golf tournament, the United States Open." *Olinger v. United States Golf Assn.*, 205 F.3d 1001 (7th Cir. 2000). The Seventh Circuit endorsed the conclusion of the District Court in that case that "the nature of the competition would be fundamentally altered if the walking rule were eliminated because it would remove stamina (at least a particular type of stamina) from the set of qualities designed to be tested in this competition." In the Seventh Circuit's opinion, the physical ordeals endured by Ken Venturi and Ben Hogan when they walked to their Open victories in 1964 and 1950 amply demonstrated the importance of stamina in such a tournament. As an alternative basis for its holding, the court also concluded that the ADA does not require the USGA to bear "the administrative burdens of evaluating requests to waive the walking rule and permit the use of a golf cart."

Although the Seventh Circuit merely assumed that the ADA applies to professional golf tournaments, and therefore did not disagree with the Ninth on the threshold coverage issue, our grant of certiorari encompasses that question as well as the conflict between those courts.

IV

Congress enacted the ADA in 1990 to remedy widespread discrimination against disabled individuals. In studying the need for such legislation, Congress found that "historically, society has tended to isolate and segregate individuals with disabilities, and, despite some improvements, such forms of discrimination against individuals with disabilities continue to be a serious and pervasive social problem. . . ."

In the ADA, Congress provided that broad mandate. In fact, one of the Act's "most impressive strengths" has been identified as its "comprehensive character," and accordingly the Act has been described as "a milestone on the path to a more decent, tolerant, progressive society." To effectuate its sweeping purpose, the ADA forbids discrimination against disabled individuals in major areas of public life, among them employment (Title I of the Act), public services (Title II), and public accommodations (Title III). At issue now, as a threshold matter, is the applicability of Title III to petitioner's golf tours and qualifying rounds, in particular to petitioner's treatment of a qualified disabled golfer wishing to compete in those events.

Title III of the ADA prescribes, as a "[g]eneral rule":

> "No individual shall be discriminated against on the basis of disability in the full and equal enjoyment of the goods, services, facilities, privileges, advantages, or accommodations of any place of public accommodation by any person who owns, leases (or leases to), or operates a place of public accommodation."

42 U.S.C. § 12182(a).

The phrase "public accommodation" is defined in terms of 12 extensive categories, which the legislative history indicates "should be construed liberally" to afford people with disabilities "equal access" to the wide variety of establishments available to the nondisabled.

It seems apparent, from both the general rule and the comprehensive definition of "public accommodation," that petitioner's golf tours and their qualifying rounds fit comfortably within the coverage of Title III, and Martin within its protection. The events occur on "golf course[s]," a type of place specifically identified by the Act as a public accommodation. In addition, at all relevant times, petitioner "leases" and "operates" golf courses to conduct its QSchool and tours. As a lessor and operator of golf courses, then, petitioner must not discriminate against any "individual" in the "full and equal enjoyment of the goods, services, facilities, privileges, advantages, or accommodations" of those courses. Certainly, among the "privileges" offered by petitioner on the courses are those of competing in the Q-School and playing in the tours; indeed, the former is a privilege for which thousands of individuals from the general public pay, and the latter is one for which they vie. Martin, of course, is one of those individuals. It would therefore appear that Title III of the ADA, by its plain terms, prohibits petitioner from denying Martin equal access to its tours on the basis of his disability.

Petitioner argues otherwise. To be clear about its position, it does not assert (as it did in the District Court) that it is a private club altogether exempt from Title III's coverage. In fact, petitioner admits that its tournaments are conducted at places of public accommodation. Nor does petitioner contend . . . that the competitors' area "behind the ropes" is not a public accommodation, notwithstanding the status of the rest of the golf course. Rather, petitioner reframes the coverage issue by arguing that the competing golfers are not members of the class protected by Title III of the ADA.

According to petitioner, Title III is concerned with discrimination against "clients and customers" seeking to obtain "goods and services" at places of public accommodation, whereas it is Title I that protects persons who work at such places. As the argument goes, petitioner operates not a "golf course" during its tournaments but a "place of exhibition or entertainment," and a professional golfer such as Martin, like an actor in a theater production, is a provider rather than a consumer of the entertainment that petitioner sells to the public. Martin therefore cannot bring a claim under Title III because he is not one of the "'*clients or customers* of the covered public accommodation.'" Rather, Martin's claim of discrimination is "job-related" and could only be brought under Title I — but that Title does not apply because he is an independent contractor rather than an employee. . . .

We need not decide whether petitioner's construction of the statute is correct, because petitioner's argument falters even on its own terms. If Title III's protected class were limited to "clients or customers," it would be entirely appropriate to classify the golfers who pay petitioner $3,000 for the chance to compete in the Q-School and, if successful, in the subsequent tour events, as petitioner's clients or customers. In our view, petitioner's tournaments (whether situated at a "golf course" or at a "place of exhibition or entertainment") simultaneously offer at least two "privileges" to the public — that of watching the golf competition and that of competing in it. Although the latter is more difficult and more expensive to obtain than the former, it is nonetheless a privilege that petitioner makes available to members of the general public. In consideration of the entry fee, any golfer with the requisite letters of recommendation acquires the opportunity to qualify for and compete in petitioner's tours. Additionally, any golfer who succeeds in the open qualifying rounds for a tournament may play in the event. That petitioner identifies one set of clients or customers that it serves (spectators at tournaments) does not preclude it from having another set (players in tournaments) against whom it may not discriminate. . . .

Our conclusion is consistent with case law in the analogous context of Title II of the Civil Rights Act of 1964. Title II of that Act prohibits public accommodations from discriminating on the basis of race, color, religion, or national origin . . . as a public accommodation during its tours and qualifying rounds, petitioner may not discriminate against either spectators or competitors on the basis of disability.

V

As we have noted, 42 U.S.C. § 12182(a) sets forth Title III's general rule prohibiting public accommodations from discriminating against individuals because of their disabilities. The question whether petitioner has violated that rule depends on a proper construction of the term "discrimination," which is defined by Title III to include:

> "a failure to make reasonable modifications in policies, practices, or procedures, when such modifications are necessary to afford such goods, services, facilities, privileges, advantages, or accommodations to individuals with disabilities, *unless the entity can demonstrate that making such modifications would fundamentally alter the nature* of such goods, services, facilities, privileges, advantages, or accommodations."

§ 12182(b)(2)(A)(ii) (emphasis added).

Petitioner does not contest that a golf cart is a reasonable modification that is necessary if Martin is to play in its tournaments. Martin's claim thus differs from one that might be asserted by players with less serious afflictions that make walking the course uncomfortable or difficult, but not beyond their capacity. In such cases, an accommodation might be reasonable but not necessary. In this case, however, the narrow dispute is whether allowing Martin to use a golf cart, despite the walking requirement that applies to the PGA TOUR, the NIKE TOUR, and the third stage of the Q-School, is a modification that would "fundamentally alter the nature" of those events.

In theory, a modification of petitioner's golf tournaments might constitute a fundamental alteration in two different ways. It might alter such an essential aspect of the game of golf that it would be unacceptable even if it affected all competitors equally; changing the diameter of the hole from three to six inches might be such a modification. Alternatively, a less significant change that has only a peripheral impact on the game itself might nevertheless give a disabled player, in addition to access to the competition as required by Title III, an advantage over others and, for that reason, fundamentally alter the character of the competition. We are not persuaded that a waiver of the walking rule for Martin would work a fundamental alteration in either sense.

As an initial matter, we observe that the use of carts is not itself inconsistent with the fundamental character of the game of golf. From early on, the essence of the game has been shotmaking — using clubs to cause a ball to progress from the teeing ground to a hole some distance away with as few strokes as possible. That essential aspect of the game is still reflected in the very first of the Rules of Golf, which declares: "The Game of Golf consists in playing a ball from the *teeing ground* into the hole by a *stroke* or successive strokes in accordance with the rules." Rule 1-1, Rules of Golf, App. 104 (italics in original). Over the years, there have been many changes in the players' equipment, in golf course design, in the Rules of Golf, and in the method of transporting clubs from hole to hole. Originally, so few clubs were used that each player could carry them without a bag. Then came golf bags, caddies, carts that were pulled by hand, and eventually motorized carts that carried players as well as clubs. "Golf carts started appearing with increasing regularity on American golf courses in the 1950's. Today they are everywhere. And they are encouraged. For one thing, they often speed up play, and for another, they are great revenue producers." There is nothing in the Rules of Golf that either forbids the use of carts, or penalizes a player for using a cart. That set of rules, as we have observed, is widely accepted in both the amateur and professional golf world as the rules of the game. The walking rule that is contained in petitioner's hard cards, based on an optional condition buried in an appendix to the Rules of Golf, is not an essential attribute of the game itself.

Indeed, the walking rule is not an indispensable feature of tournament golf either. As already mentioned, petitioner permits golf carts to be used in the SENIOR PGA TOUR, the open qualifying events for petitioner's tournaments, the first two stages of the Q-School, and, until 1997, the third stage of the Q-School as well. Moreover, petitioner allows the use of carts during certain tournament rounds in both the PGA TOUR and the NIKE TOUR. In addition, although the USGA enforces a walking rule in most of the tournaments that it sponsors, it permits carts in the Senior Amateur and the Senior Women's Amateur championships.

Petitioner, however, distinguishes the game of golf as it is generally played from the game that it sponsors in the PGA TOUR, NIKE TOUR, and (at least recently) the last stage of the QSchool — golf at the "highest level." According to petitioner, "[t]he goal of the highest-level competitive athletics is to assess and compare the performance of different competitors, a task that is meaningful only if the competitors are subject to identical substantive rules." The waiver of any possibly "outcome-affecting" rule for a contestant would violate this principle and therefore, in petitioner's view, fundamentally alter the nature of the highest level athletic event. The walking rule is one such rule, petitioner submits, because its purpose is "to inject the element of fatigue into the skill of shot-making," and thus its effect may be the critical loss of a stroke. As a consequence, the reasonable modification Martin seeks would fundamentally alter the nature of petitioner's highest level tournaments even if he were the only person in the world who has both the talent to compete in those elite events and a disability sufficiently serious that he cannot do so without using a cart.

The force of petitioner's argument is, first of all, mitigated by the fact that golf is a game in which it is impossible to guarantee that all competitors will play under exactly the same conditions or that an individual's ability will be the sole determinant of the outcome. For example, changes in the weather may produce harder greens and more head winds for the tournament leader than for his closest pursuers. A lucky bounce may save a shot or two. Whether such happenstance events are more or less probable than the likelihood that a golfer afflicted with Klippel-Trenaunay-Weber Syndrome would one day qualify for the NIKE TOUR and PGA TOUR, they at least demonstrate that pure chance may have a greater impact on the outcome of elite golf tournaments than the fatigue resulting from the enforcement of the walking rule.

Further, the factual basis of petitioner's argument is undermined by the District Court's finding that the fatigue from walking during one of petitioner's 4-day tournaments cannot be deemed significant. The District Court credited the testimony of a professor in physiology and expert on fatigue, who calculated the calories expended in walking a golf course (about five miles) to be approximately 500 calories — "nutritionally . . . less than a Big Mac." 994 F. Supp. at 1250. What is more, that energy is expended over a 5-hour period, during which golfers have numerous intervals for rest and refreshment. In fact, the expert concluded, because golf is a low intensity activity, fatigue from the game is primarily a psychological phenomenon in which stress and motivation are the key ingredients. And even under conditions of severe heat and humidity, the critical factor in fatigue is fluid loss rather than exercise from walking.

Moreover, when given the option of using a cart, the majority of golfers in petitioner's tournaments have chosen to walk, often to relieve stress or for other strategic reasons. As NIKE TOUR member Johnson testified, walking allows him to keep in rhythm, stay warmer when it is chilly, and develop a better sense of the elements and the course than riding a cart.

Even if we accept the factual predicate for petitioner's argument — that the walking rule is "outcome affecting" because fatigue may adversely affect performance — its legal position is fatally flawed. Petitioner's refusal to consider Martin's personal circumstances in deciding whether to accommodate his disability runs counter to the clear language and purpose of the ADA. As previously stated, the ADA was enacted to eliminate discrimination against "individuals" with disabilities, and to that end Title III of the Act requires without exception that any "policies, practices, or procedures" of a public accommodation be reasonably modified for disabled "individuals" as necessary to afford access unless doing so would fundamentally alter what is offered. To comply with this command, an individualized inquiry must be made to determine whether a specific modification for a particular person's disability would be reasonable under the circumstances as well as necessary for that person, and yet at the same time not work a fundamental alteration.

To be sure, the waiver of an essential rule of competition for anyone would fundamentally alter the nature of petitioner's tournaments. As we have demonstrated, however, the walking rule is at best peripheral to the nature of petitioner's athletic events, and thus it might be waived in individual cases without working a fundamental alteration. Therefore, petitioner's claim that all the substantive rules for its "highest-level" competitions are sacrosanct and cannot be modified under any circumstances is effectively a contention that it is exempt from Title III's reasonable modification requirement. But that provision carves out no exemption for elite athletics, and given Title III's coverage not only of places of "exhibition or entertainment" but also of "golf course[s]," its application to petitioner's tournaments cannot be said to be unintended or unexpected. Even if it were, "the fact that a statute can be applied in situations not expressly anticipated by Congress does not demonstrate ambiguity. It demonstrates breadth."

Under the ADA's basic requirement that the need of a disabled person be evaluated on an individual basis, we have no doubt that allowing Martin to use a golf cart would not fundamentally alter the nature of petitioner's tournaments. As we have discussed, the purpose of the walking rule is to subject players to fatigue, which in turn may influence the outcome of tournaments. Even if the rule does serve that purpose, it is an uncontested finding of the District Court that Martin "easily endures greater fatigue even with a cart than his able-bodied competitors do by walking." The purpose of the walking rule is therefore not compromised in the slightest by allowing Martin to use a cart. A modification that provides an exception to a peripheral tournament rule without impairing its purpose cannot be said to "fundamentally alter" the tournament. What it can be said to do, on the other hand, is to allow Martin the chance to qualify for and compete in the athletic events petitioner offers to those members of the public who have the skill and desire to enter. That is exactly what the ADA requires. As a result, Martin's request for a waiver of the walking rule should have been granted.

The ADA admittedly imposes some administrative burdens on the operators of places of public accommodation that could be avoided by strictly adhering to general rules and policies that are entirely fair with respect to the able-bodied but that may indiscriminately preclude access by qualified persons with disabilities. But surely, in a case of this kind, Congress intended that an entity like the PGA not only give individualized attention to the handful of requests that it might receive from talented but disabled athletes for a modification or waiver of a rule to allow them access to the competition, but also carefully weigh the purpose, as well as the letter, of the rule before determining that no accommodation would be tolerable.

The judgment of the Court of Appeals is affirmed.

Justice SCALIA, with whom Justice THOMAS joins, dissenting.

In my view today's opinion exercises a benevolent compassion that the law does not place it within our power to impose. The judgment distorts the text of Title III, the structure of the ADA, and common sense. I respectfully dissent.

* * *

II

[S]ince it has held (or assumed) professional golfers to be customers "enjoying" the "privilege" that consists of PGA TOUR golf; and since it inexplicably regards the rules of PGA TOUR golf as merely "policies, practices, or procedures" by which access to PGA TOUR golf is provided, the Court must then confront the question whether respondent's requested modification of the supposed policy, practice, or procedure of walking would "fundamentally alter the nature" of the PGA TOUR game. The Court attacks this "fundamental alteration" analysis by asking two questions: first, whether the "essence" or an "essential aspect" of the sport of golf has been altered; and second, whether the change, even if not essential to the game, would give the disabled player an advantage over others and thereby "fundamentally alter the character of the competition." It answers no to both.

Before considering the Court's answer to the first question, it is worth pointing out that the assumption which underlies that question is false. Nowhere is it written that PGA TOUR golf must be classic "essential" golf. Why cannot the PGA TOUR, if it wishes, promote a new game, with distinctive rules (much as the American League promotes a game of baseball in which the pitcher's turn at the plate can be taken by a "designated hitter")? If members of the public do not like the new rules — if they feel that these rules do not truly test the individual's skill at "real golf" (or the team's skill at "real baseball") they can withdraw their patronage. But the rules are the rules. They are (as in all games) entirely arbitrary, and there is no basis on which anyone — not even the Supreme Court of the United States — can pronounce one or another of them to be "nonessential" if the rulemaker (here the PGA TOUR) deems it to be essential.

If one assumes, however, that the PGA TOUR has some legal obligation to play classic, Platonic golf — and if one assumes the correctness of all the other wrong turns the Court has made to get to this point — then we Justices must confront what is indeed an awesome responsibility. It has been rendered the solemn duty of the Supreme Court of the United States, laid upon it by Congress in pursuance of the Federal Government's power "[t]o regulate Commerce with foreign Nations, and among the several States," to decide What Is Golf. I am sure that the Framers of the Constitution, aware of the 1457 edict of King James II of Scotland prohibiting golf because it interfered with the practice of archery, fully expected that sooner or later the paths of golf and government, the law and the links, would once again cross, and that the judges of this August Court would some day have to wrestle with that age-old jurisprudential question, for which their years of study in the law have so well prepared them: Is

"nonessential" rules of a made-up game; and its Animal Farm determination that fairness and the ADA mean that everyone gets to play by individualized rules which will assure that no one's lack of ability (or at least no one's lack of ability so pronounced that it amounts to a disability) will be a handicap. The year was 2001, and "everybody was finally equal." K. Vonnegut, Harrison Bergeron, in Animal Farm and Related Readings 129 (1997).

NOTES AND COMMENTS

1. PGA Subject to the ADA. The Supreme Court determined that the PGA was a "public accommodation" subject to the ADA, rejecting the PGA's argument that the law protected only "customers or clients" of a public accommodation and not Martin, who was a competitor or provider of entertainment services. The Court reasoned that, even if Title III's protected class were limited to clients and customers, "it would be entirely appropriate to classify the golfers who pay petitioner $3,000 for the chance to compete in the Q-School and if successful, in the subsequent Tour events as petitioner's clients and customers." Would Martin be protected under Title III of the ADA if the PGA eliminated the registration fee and instead treated all competitors as independent contractors? (Note that Title I of the ADA protects employees, which can include professional athletes employed by sporting organizations, but does not extend to cover independent contractors.) If this were a lawsuit alleging racial discrimination, would the PGA argue it was not a public accommodation subject to the Civil Rights laws?

2. According to *Martin,* "the court has the independent duty to inquire into the purpose of the rule at issue, and to ascertain whether there can be a reasonable modification made to accommodate the plaintiff without frustrating the purpose of the rule. . . ." The PGA argued that the no-cart rule was necessary to competition fairness and a level playing field, the purpose of the walking rule is to inject the element of fatigue into the skill of shot-making, and a change in the rule would fundamentally alter the competition. Did the court properly consider the PGA's explanation of the purpose of the rule? Upon what factors did the court rely in holding that the purpose of the rule would not be frustrated by permitting Casey Martin to ride?

3. Discrimination and Rules of the Game. The PGA argued that the law should distinguish between rules defining who is eligible to compete from rules governing how the game is played, with any modification to the latter "substantive" rules a *per se* fundamental alteration. Justice Scalia, joined by Justice Thomas, argued in dissent that sport is different from other enterprises which are subject to the ADA and that no court, "not even the Supreme Court of the United States," can pronounce one or another of the competitive rules of sport nonessential if the rulemaker deems them otherwise. As posed by Justice Scalia, "why must the PGA play traditional golf?" How does a sporting entity or a court determine whether the rule or policy which a disabled athlete seeks to modify would alter a fundamental aspect of the competition? What is discrimination on the basis of disability when it comes to sports and athletic competition?

4. Accommodation or Competitive Advantage? The *Martin* case received national media attention, and the public, as well as professional golfers, honed in on the debate: Was Martin getting an unfair advantage? Is walking integral to the game? What is a level playing field? Where do we draw the line? *See* W. Kent Davis, *Why is the PGA Teed Off at Casey Martin? An Example of How the Americans with Disabilities Act (ADA) Has Changed Sports Law*, 9 MARQ. SPORTS L.J. 1, 33-42 (1998) (citing the varied comments of professional golfers responding to the Casey Martin accommodation issue). How do you respond to the scenario posed by the dissent where a Little League player with attention deficit disorder, whose disability "makes it at least 25% more difficult to hit a pitched ball," should receive the accommodation of four strikes (absent "a judicial determination that, in baseball, three strikers are metaphysically necessary")?

5. Athletic competition is inherently discriminatory — there are winners and losers, only the best play. The PGA argued that its rules of competitive play provide the framework for a level playing field for all competitors, but when the rules for one player are changed in a competitive sport, the landscape of the competition is inherently changed. Does the *Martin* decision open the door for judicial intrusion on athletic competition? Was the ADA really intended to apply to professional sporting competitions? Was the playing field under the PGA rules "even" for Casey Martin?

6. The central issue, according to *Martin*, was "whether allowing the plaintiff, given his individual circumstances, the requested modification of using a cart in tournament competition would fundamentally alter PGA and Nike Tour golf competitions." The court in *Ganden* similarly noted, "the ADA does not require [the sporting organization] to simply abandon its eligibility requirements, but only to make reasonable modifications to them." A modification is unreasonable "if it imposes an 'undue financial and administrative burden' or requires a 'fundamental alteration' in the nature of the privilege or program." *See also Montalvo* (holding karate school was not required to change its group lessons to a softer, less rigorous style for child with AIDS and stating that private lessons are a reasonable accommodation). Disputes arise, however, in defining when a requested accommodation would be unreasonable, require elimination of an essential eligibility requirement, or fundamentally alter the nature of the sport or competition. Are the courts the best arbiters of these determinations?

7. *Martin* illustrates that sporting organizations should be prepared to explain the purpose of its eligibility requirements and rules of competition, to articulate the connection between the requirements and purpose, and to evaluate on an individual basis, whether modification of such rules can be made without undermining legitimate purposes or fundamentally altering the nature of the game. Yet, based on *Martin*, the Court summarily vacated the Seventh Circuit Court of Appeals's ruling, which denied the request by Ford Olinger, a professional golfer with a degenerative hip disorder, injunctive relief to ride a cart in the U.S. Open. *Olinger v. USGA*, 18 Fed. Appx. 409 (7th Cir. 2001). The Seventh Circuit had affirmed the district court's ruling that "the nature of the competition would be fundamentally altered" if the walking rule were eliminated because it would "remove stamina (at least, a particular type of stamina) from the set of qualities designed to be tested in this competition." The court also agreed that the administrative burdens of evaluating requests to waive the walking rule were undue, in that, the USGA "would need to develop a system and a fund of expertise to determine whether a given applicant truly needs, or merely wants, or could use but does not need, to ride a cart to compete." 205 F.3d 101 (stating "the decision on whether the rules of the game should be adjusted to accommodate him is best left to those who hold the future of golf in trust."). Should *Olinger* have come out the same as *Martin*? How should future requests to waive the walking rule, or any other rule of competition, be evaluated? The *Martin* ruling has not created a significant change in rules of sport as was anticipated by some. For example, the requested modification for a wheelchair user to be permitted two bounces in racketball competition with footed players was denied as a fundamental alteration of the nature of the sporting competition in *Kuketz v. Petronelli,* 821 N.E.2d 473 (Mass. 2005).

F. EMPLOYMENT

With respect to its employees, sports organizations are also subject to the nondiscrimination and reasonable accommodations mandates of Title I of the ADA, 42 U.S.C. §§ 12111-12116. Under Title I, employers are prohibited from discriminating against qualified employees on the basis of disability in employment provided the individual does not pose a direct threat to the health and safety of other individuals in the workplace. *See Anderson v. Little League Baseball*, 794 F. Supp. 342 (D. Ariz. 1992) (holding league rule prohibiting base coach in wheelchair from the playing field was invalid under the ADA absent an individualized determination of direct threat). *Cf. Maddox v. University of Tennesee*, 642 F.3d 843 (6th Cir. 1995) (upholding university's termination of assistant football coach for misconduct [public drunkenness] despite coach's argument the conduct was caused by an alcoholism disability protected under the ADA).

Student-athletes at the interscholastic or intercollegiate levels are not considered "employees," thus precluding Title I relief to them. Professional athletes may assert Title I claims as "employees" of their respective teams. However, exclusion from play (or work to the professional) alone may not be sufficient to state a Title I claim. A professional athlete must be disabled, defined as having (or regarded as having) a physical or mental impairment that substantially limits in a major life activity. 42 U.S.C. § 12112. Guidelines promulgated by the Equal Employment Opportunity Commission (EEOC) under Title I provide that a person is not substantially limited in working simply because the person is "unable to perform a specialized job or profession requiring extraordinary skill, prowess, or talent," such as a baseball pitcher with a bad elbow who cannot throw. 29 C.F.R. § 1630.2(j)(3)(i). *See also Knapp, supra.* As a result, professional athletes must show their disability substantially limits a major life activity other than working as a professional athlete, such as walking in Casey Martin's case.

A professional athlete's Title I claim against a professional sports league or association is less tenable. Without explanation, the *Martin* court agreed that the PGA was not subject to the employment provisions of Title I of the ADA as Martin's "employer." One commentator has suggested an employment relationship did not exist between Martin and the PGA, which did not exercise control over Martin in terms of requiring him to play particular tournaments, controlling the player's schedule, or providing him with wages or insurance or withholding taxes. *See* Davis, 9 MARQ. SPORTS L.J. at 38. The Davis article proposes that the analysis for determining whether a sports association is an employer under the ADA is a two-part test: (1) is the defendant a covered employer under the ADA (more than 15 employees); and (2) does an employment relationship exist between the plaintiff and defendant? 9 MARQ. SPORTS L.J. at 38 (by analogy to Title VII, citing *Graves v. Women's Professional Rodeo Association, Inc.,* 708 F. Supp. 233 (W.D. Ark. 1989) (holding rodeo association to whom members pay dues and which promulgates competition rules is not an "employer" to its members), *aff'd,* 907 F.2d 71 (8th Cir. 1990)). A professional athlete's employment claim against a sports association would likely fail absent a showing of an employment relationship.

G. PHYSICAL ACCESS TO STADIUMS, FACILITIES, AND SPORTS ARENAS

Under Title III of the ADA, places of public accommodation, including sports facilities, stadiums, and arenas, must be physically accessible and usable by people with disabilities in the most integrated setting possible. 42 U.S.C. § 12181(a)(b)(1). The Department of Justice guidelines set forth standards applicable to sports facilities requiring the removal of architectural barriers to access and the provision of wheelchair accessible parking, entrances, seating, restrooms, public telephones, drinking fountains, signs, and assistive listening devices. ADAAccessibility Guidelines (ADAAG), 28 C.F.R. Pt. 36, App. A (1996). Under these guidelines, stadiums constructed after 1993 are also required to provide at least one percent of total seating for wheelchair users and one accompanying companion seat. The regulation that has generated the most litigation is Section 4.33.3, which provides that: "Wheelchair areas shall be an integral part of any fixed seating plan and shall be provided so as to provide people with physical disabilities a choice of admission prices and lines of sight comparable to those for members of the general public."

A number of lawsuits have been filed by or on behalf of spectators with disabilities against stadium owners, operators, and architects to require that newly constructed stadiums provide unobstructed lines of sight for wheelchair seating locations when spectators stand or do the "wave." Stadium access litigation has also raised issues of whether seating is sufficiently integrated and dispersed. For a detailed discussion, *see* Mark A. Conrad, *Wheeling Through Rough Terrain — The Legal Roadblocks of Disabled Access in Sports Arenas*, 8 MARQ. SPORTS L.J. 263 (1998) (discussing stadium sight-line access litigation); Adam A. Milani, *Oh Say Can I See — and Who Do I Sue if I Can't?: Wheelchair Users, Sightlines Over Standing Spectators, and Architect Liability Under the Americans with Disabilities Act,* 3 FLA. L. REV. 523 (2000).

Chapter 15

DRUG TESTING

A persistent and recurring sports law topic concerns the drug testing of athletes. From a legal standpoint the problem is of recent vintage. The rules are very much in the process of being defined. So it is not surprising that a good deal of uncertainty still exists about what can and cannot be done. Adding to the problem inherent in the newness of it all is the fact that so many different organizations have adopted so many different drug testing schemes. This significantly adds to the problem of defining rules with some degree of specificity and predictability. To evaluate the legality of any drug testing scheme, it is important to consider who the tester is, why the test is to be conducted, who the test is to be conducted upon, how the test is to be administered, what drugs are to be tested for, and what procedures are to be triggered if someone "fails" the test, just to name a few of the variables.

Recently, the Supreme Court supplied a degree of certainty. In *Earls*, reprinted below, the Court deals with drug testing of middle school and high school students involved in competitive extracurricular activities. While *Earls* answers some questions, it leaves many others open. The problem that follows *Earls* is designed to address some of those still-open questions.

BOARD OF EDUCATION v. EARLS

122 S. Ct. 2559 (2002)

JUSTICE THOMAS delivered the opinion of the Court.

The Student Activities Drug Testing Policy implemented by the Board of Education of Independent School District No. 92 of Pottawatomie County (School District) requires all students who participate in competitive extracurricular activities to submit to drug testing.

Because this Policy reasonably serves the School District's important interest in detecting and preventing drug use among its students, we hold that it is constitutional.

I

The city of Tecumseh, Oklahoma, is a rural community located approximately 40 miles southeast of Oklahoma City. The School District administers all Tecumseh public schools. In the fall of 1998, the School District adopted the Student Activities Drug Testing Policy (Policy), which requires all middle and high school students to consent to drug testing in order to participate in any extracurricular activity. In practice, the Policy has been applied only to competitive extracurricular activities sanctioned by the Oklahoma Secondary Schools Activities Association, such as the Academic Team, Future Farmers of America, Future Homemakers of America, band, choir, pom pon, cheerleading, and athletics. Under the Policy, students are required to take a drug test before participating in an extracurricular activity, must submit to random drug testing while participating in that activity, and must agree to be tested at any time upon reasonable suspicion. The urinalysis tests are designed to detect only the use of illegal drugs, including amphetamines, marijuana, cocaine, opiates, and barbituates, not medical conditions or the presence of authorized prescription medications.

At the time of their suit, both respondents attended Tecumseh High School. Respondent Lindsay Earls was a member of the show choir, the marching band, the Academic Team, and the National Honor Society. Respondent Daniel James sought to participate in the Academic Team. Together with their parents, Earls and James brought a 42 U.S.C. § 1983 action against the School District, challenging the Policy both on its face and as applied to their participation in extracurricular activities. They alleged that the Policy violates the Fourth Amendment as incorporated by the Fourteenth Amendment and requested injunctive and declarative relief. They also argued that the School District failed to identify a special need for testing students who participate in extracurricular activities, and that the "Drug Testing Policy neither addresses a proven problem nor promises to bring any benefit to students or the school."

Applying the principles articulated in *Vernonia School Dist. 47J v. Acton*, 515 U.S. 646 (1995), in which we upheld the suspicionless drug testing of school athletes, the United States District Court for the Western District of Oklahoma rejected respondents' claim that the Policy was unconstitutional and granted summary judgment to the School District. The court noted that "special needs" exist in the public school context and that, although the School District did "not show a drug problem of epidemic proportions," there was a history of drug abuse starting in 1970 that presented "legitimate cause for concern." The District Court also held that the Policy was effective because "it can scarcely be disputed that the drug problem among the student body is effectively addressed by making sure that the large number of students participating in competitive, extracurricular activities do not use drugs." *Id.*

The United States Court of Appeals for the Tenth Circuit reversed, holding that the Policy violated the Fourth Amendment. The Court of Appeals agreed with the District Court that the Policy must be evaluated in the "unique environment of the school setting," but reached a different conclusion as to the Policy's constitutionality. Before imposing a suspicionless drug testing program, the Court of Appeals concluded that a school "must demonstrate that there is some identifiable drug abuse problem among a sufficient number of those subject to the testing, such that testing that group of students will actually redress its drug problem." The Court of Appeals then held that because the School District failed to demonstrate such a problem existed among Tecumseh students participating in competitive extracurricular activities, the Policy was unconstitutional. We granted certiorari, and now reverse.

II

The Fourth Amendment to the United States Constitution protects "the right of the people to be secure in their persons, houses, papers, and effects, against unreasonable searches and seizures." Searches by public school officials, such as the collection of urine samples, implicate Fourth Amendment interests. *See Vernonia, supra*, at 652. We must therefore review the School District's Policy for "reasonableness," which is the touchstone of the constitutionality of a governmental search.

In the criminal context, reasonableness usually requires a showing of probable cause. The probable-cause standard, however, "is peculiarly related to criminal investigations" and may be unsuited to determining the reasonableness of administrative searches where the "Government seeks to *prevent* the development of hazardous conditions." The Court has also held that a warrant and finding of probable cause are unnecessary in the public school context because such requirements " 'would unduly interfere with the maintenance of the swift and informal disciplinary procedures [that are] needed.' "

Given that the School District's Policy is not in any way related to the conduct of criminal investigations, *see* Part II-B, *infra*, respondents do not contend that the School District requires probable cause before testing students for drug use. Respondents instead argue that drug testing must be based at least on some level of individualized suspicion. It is true that we generally determine the reasonableness of a search by balancing the nature of the intrusion on the individual's privacy against the promotion of legitimate governmental interests. But we have long held that "the Fourth Amendment imposes no irreducible requirement of [individualized] suspicion." "In certain limited circumstances, the Government's need to discover such latent or hidden conditions, or to prevent their development, is sufficiently compelling to justify the intrusion on privacy entailed by conducting such searches without any measure of individualized suspicion." Therefore, in the context of safety and administrative regulations, a search unsupported by probable cause may be reasonable "when 'special needs, beyond the normal need for law enforcement, make the warrant and probable-cause requirement impracticable.' "

Significantly, this Court has previously held that "special needs" inhere in the public school context. While schoolchildren do not shed their constitutional rights when they enter the schoolhouse, "Fourth Amendment rights . . . are different in public schools than elsewhere; the 'reasonableness' inquiry cannot disregard the schools' custodial and tutelary responsibility for children." *Vernonia, supra*. In particular, a finding of individualized suspicion may not be necessary when a school conducts drug testing.

In *Vernonia*, this Court held that the suspicionless drug testing of athletes was constitutional. The Court, however, did not simply authorize all school drug testing, but rather conducted a fact-specific balancing of the intrusion on the children's Fourth Amendment rights against the promotion of legitimate governmental interests. *See* 515 U.S. at 652-653. Applying the principles of *Vernonia* to the somewhat different facts of this case, we conclude that Tecumseh's Policy is also constitutional.

A

We first consider the nature of the privacy interest allegedly compromised by the drug testing. As in *Vernonia*, the context of the public school environment serves as the backdrop for the analysis of the privacy interest at stake and the reasonableness of the drug testing policy in general.

A student's privacy interest is limited in a public school environment where the State is responsible for maintaining discipline, health, and safety. Schoolchildren are routinely required to submit to physical examinations and vaccinations against disease. Securing order in the school environment sometimes requires that students be subjected to greater controls than those appropriate for adults. See *T. L. O., supra,* 469 U.S. at 350 (Powell, J., concurring) ("Without first establishing discipline and maintaining order, teachers cannot begin to educate their students. And apart from education, the school has the obligation to protect pupils from mistreatment by other children, and also to protect teachers themselves from violence by the few students whose conduct in recent years has prompted national concern").

Respondents argue that because children participating in nonathletic extracurricular activities are not subject to regular physicals and communal undress, they have a stronger expectation of privacy than the athletes tested in *Vernonia*. This distinction, however, was not essential to our decision in *Vernonia*, which depended primarily upon the school's custodial responsibility and authority.

In any event, students who participate in competitive extracurricular activities voluntarily subject themselves to many of the same intrusions on their privacy as do athletes. Some of these clubs and activities require occasional off-campus travel and communal undress. All of them have their own rules and requirements for participating students that do not apply to the student body as a whole. For example, each of the competitive extracurricular activities governed by the Policy must abide by the rules of the Oklahoma Secondary Schools Activities Association, and a faculty sponsor monitors the students for compliance with the various rules dictated by the clubs and activities. This regulation of extracurricular activities further diminishes the expectation of privacy among schoolchildren. *Cf. Vernonia*, 515 U.S. at 657 ("Somewhat like adults who choose to participate in a closely regulated industry, students who voluntarily participate in school athletics have reason to expect intrusions upon normal rights and privileges, including privacy." We therefore conclude that the students affected by this Policy have a limited expectation of privacy.

B

Next, we consider the character of the intrusion imposed by the Policy. Urination is "an excretory function traditionally shielded by great privacy." But the "degree of intrusion" on one's privacy caused by collecting a urine sample "depends upon the manner in which production of the urine sample is monitored." *Vernonia*, 515 U.S. at 658.

Under the Policy, a faculty monitor waits outside the closed restroom stall for the student to produce a sample and must "listen for the normal sounds of urination in order to guard against tampered specimens and to insure an accurate chain of custody." The monitor then pours the sample into two bottles that are sealed and placed into a mailing pouch along with a consent form signed by the student. This procedure is virtually identical to that reviewed in *Vernonia*, except that it additionally protects privacy by allowing male students to produce their samples behind a closed stall. Given that we considered the method of collection in *Vernonia* a "negligible" intrusion, the method here is even less problematic.

In addition, the Policy clearly requires that the test results be kept in confidential files separate from a student's other educational records and released to school personnel only on a "need to know" basis. Respondents nonetheless contend that the intrusion on students' privacy is significant because the Policy fails to protect effectively against the disclosure of confidential information and, specifically, that the school "has been careless in protecting that information: for example, the Choir teacher looked at students' prescription drug lists and left them where other students could see them." But the choir teacher is someone with a "need to know," because during off-campus trips she needs to know what medications are taken by her students. Even before the Policy was enacted the choir teacher had access to this information. In any event, there is no allegation that any other student did see such information. This one example of alleged carelessness hardly increases the character of the intrusion.

Moreover, the test results are not turned over to any law enforcement authority. Nor do the test results here lead to the imposition of discipline or have any academic consequences. Rather, the only consequence of a failed drug test is to limit the student's privilege of participating in extracurricular activities. Indeed, a student may test positive for drugs twice and still be allowed to participate in extracurricular activities. After the first positive test, the school contacts the student's parent or guardian for a meeting. The student may continue to participate in the activity if within five days of the meeting the student shows proof of receiving drug counseling and submits to a second drug test in two weeks. For the second positive test, the student is suspended from participation in all extracurricular activities for 14 days, must complete four hours of substance abuse counseling, and must submit to monthly drug tests. Only after a third positive test will the student be suspended from participating in any extracurricular activity for the remainder of the school year, or 88 school days, whichever is longer. Given the minimally intrusive nature of the sample collection and the limited uses to which the test results are put, we conclude that the invasion of students' privacy is not significant.

C

Finally, this Court must consider the nature and immediacy of the government's concerns and the efficacy of the Policy in meeting them. This Court has already articulated in detail the importance of the governmental concern in preventing drug use by schoolchildren. The drug abuse problem among our Nation's youth has hardly abated since *Vernonia* was decided in 1995. In fact, evidence suggests that it has only grown worse. As in *Vernonia*, "the necessity for the State to act is magnified by the fact that this evil is being visited not just upon individuals at large, but upon children for whom it has undertaken a special responsibility of care and direction." The health and safety risks identified in *Vernonia* apply with equal force to Tecumseh's children. Indeed, the nationwide drug epidemic makes the war against drugs a pressing concern in every school.

Additionally, the School District in this case has presented specific evidence of drug use at Tecumseh schools. Teachers testified that they had seen students who appeared to be under the influence of drugs and that they had heard students speaking openly about using drugs. A drug dog found marijuana cigarettes near the school parking lot. Police officers once found drugs or drug paraphernalia in a car driven by a Future Farmers of America member. And the school board president reported that people in the community were calling the board to discuss the "drug situation." We decline to second-guess the finding of the District Court that "viewing the evidence as a whole, it cannot be reasonably disputed that the [School District] was faced with a 'drug problem' when it adopted the Policy."

Respondents consider the proffered evidence insufficient and argue that there is no "real and immediate interest" to justify a policy of drug testing nonathletes. Brief for Respondents 32. We have recognized, however, that "[a] demonstrated problem of drug abuse . . . [is] not in all cases necessary to the validity of a testing regime," but that some showing does "shore up an assertion of special need for a suspicionless general search program." The School District has provided sufficient evidence to shore up the need for its drug testing program.

Furthermore, this Court has not required a particularized or pervasive drug problem before allowing the government to conduct suspicionless drug testing. For instance, in *Von Raab* the Court upheld the drug testing of customs officials on a purely preventive basis, without any documented history of drug use by such officials. In response to the lack of evidence relating to drug use, the Court noted generally that "drug abuse is one of the most serious problems confronting our society today," and that programs to prevent and detect drug use among customs officials could not be deemed unreasonable. Likewise, the need to prevent and deter the substantial harm of childhood drug use provides the necessary immediacy for a school testing policy. Indeed, it would make little sense to require a school district to wait for a substantial portion of its students to begin using drugs before it was allowed to institute a drug testing program designed to deter drug use.

Given the nationwide epidemic of drug use, and the evidence of increased drug use in Tecumseh schools, it was entirely reasonable for the School District to enact this particular drug testing policy. We reject the Court of Appeals' novel test that "any district seeking to impose a random suspicionless drug testing policy as a condition to participation in a school activity must demonstrate that there is some identifiable drug abuse problem among a sufficient number of those subject to the testing, such that testing that group of students will actually redress its drug problem." Among other problems, it would be difficult to administer such a test. As we cannot articulate a threshold level of drug use that would suffice to justify a drug testing program for schoolchildren, we refuse to fashion what would in effect be a constitutional quantum of drug use necessary to show a "drug problem."

Respondents also argue that the testing of nonathletes does not implicate any safety concerns, and that safety is a "crucial factor" in applying the special needs framework. They contend that there must be "surpassing safety interests," or "extraordinary safety and national security hazards," in order to override the usual protections of the Fourth Amendment. Respondents are correct that safety factors into the special needs analysis, but the safety interest furthered by drug testing is undoubtedly substantial for all children, athletes and nonathletes alike. We know all too well that drug use carries a variety of health risks for children, including death from overdose.

We also reject respondents' argument that drug testing must presumptively be based upon an individualized reasonable suspicion of wrongdoing because such a testing regime would be less intrusive. In this context, the Fourth Amendment does not require a finding of individualized suspicion, and we decline to impose such a requirement on schools attempting to prevent and detect drug use by students. Moreover, we question whether testing based on individualized suspicion in fact would be less intrusive. Such a regime would place an additional burden on public school teachers who are already tasked with the difficult job of maintaining order and discipline. A program of individualized suspicion might unfairly target members of unpopular groups. The fear of lawsuits resulting from such targeted searches may chill enforcement of the program, rendering it ineffective in combating drug use. *See Vernonia*, 515 U.S. at 663-664 (offering similar reasons for why "testing based on 'suspicion' of drug use would not be better, but worse"). In any case, this Court has repeatedly stated that reasonableness under the Fourth Amendment does not require employing the least intrusive means, because "the logic of such elaborate less-restrictive-alternative arguments could raise insuperable barriers to the exercise of virtually all search-and-seizure powers."

Finally, we find that testing students who participate in extracurricular activities is a reasonably effective means of addressing the School District's legitimate concerns in preventing, deterring, and detecting drug use. While in *Vernonia* there might have been a closer fit between the testing of athletes and the trial court's finding that the drug problem was "fueled by the 'role model' effect of athletes' drug use," such a finding was not essential to the holding. *cf. id.*, at 684-685 (O'CONNOR, J., dissenting) (questioning the extent of the drug problem, especially as applied to athletes). *Vernonia* did not require the school to test the group of students most likely to use drugs, but rather considered the constitutionality of the program in the context of the public school's custodial responsibilities. Evaluating the Policy in this context, we conclude that the drug testing of Tecumseh students who participate in extracurricular activities effectively serves the School District's interest in protecting the safety and health of its students.

III

Within the limits of the Fourth Amendment, local school boards must assess the desirability of drug testing schoolchildren. In upholding the constitutionality of the Policy, we express no opinion as to its wisdom. Rather, we hold only that Tecumseh's Policy is a reasonable means of furthering the School District's important interest in preventing and deterring drug use among its schoolchildren. Accordingly, we reverse the judgment of the Court of Appeals.

It is so ordered.

JUSTICE BREYER, concurring.

I agree with the Court that *Vernonia School Dist. 47J v. Acton*, 515 U.S. 646 (1995), governs this case and requires reversal of the Tenth Circuit's decision. The school's drug testing program addresses a serious national problem by focusing upon demand, avoiding the use of criminal or disciplinary sanctions, and relying upon professional counseling and treatment. In my view, this program does not violate the Fourth Amendment's prohibition of "unreasonable searches and seizures." I reach this conclusion primarily for the reasons given by the Court, but I would emphasize several underlying considerations, which I understand to be consistent with the Court's opinion.

I

In respect to the school's need for the drug testing program, I would emphasize the following: First, the drug problem in our Nation's schools is serious in terms of size, the kinds of drugs being used, and the consequences of that use both for our children and the rest of us. Second, the government's emphasis upon supply side interdiction apparently has not reduced teenage use in recent years.

Third, public school systems must find effective ways to deal with this problem. Today's public expects its schools not simply to teach the fundamentals, but "to shoulder the burden of feeding students breakfast and lunch, offering before and after school child care services, and providing medical and psychological services," all in a school environment that is safe and encourages learning. The law itself recognizes these responsibilities with the phrase *in loco parentis* — a phrase that draws its legal force primarily from the needs of younger students (who here are necessarily grouped together with older high school students) and which reflects, not that a child or adolescent lacks an interest in privacy, but that a child's or adolescent's school-related privacy interest, when compared to the privacy interests of an adult, has different dimensions. A public school system that fails adequately to carry out its responsibilities may well see parents send their children to private or parochial school instead — with help from the State.

Fourth, the program at issue here seeks to discourage demand for drugs by changing the school's environment in order to combat the single most important factor leading school children to take drugs, namely, peer pressure. It offers the adolescent a nonthreatening reason to decline his friend's drug use invitations, namely, that he intends to play baseball, participate in debate, join the band, or engage in any one of half a dozen useful, interesting, and important activities.

II

In respect to the privacy-related burden that the drug testing program imposes upon students, I would emphasize the following: First, not everyone would agree with this Court's characterization of the privacy-related significance of urine sampling as "negligible." Some find the procedure no more intrusive than a routine medical examination, but others are seriously embarrassed by the need to provide a urine sample with someone listening "outside the closed restroom stall." When trying to resolve this kind of close question involving the interpretation of constitutional values, I believe it important that the school board provided an opportunity for the airing of these differences at public meetings designed to give the entire community "the opportunity to be able to participate" in developing the drug policy. The board used this democratic, participatory process to uncover and to resolve differences, giving weight to the fact that the process, in this instance, revealed little, if any, objection to the proposed testing program.

Second, the testing program avoids subjecting the entire school to testing. And it preserves an option for a conscientious objector. He can refuse testing while paying a price (nonparticipation) that is serious, but less severe than expulsion from the school.

Third, a contrary reading of the Constitution, as requiring "individualized suspicion" in this public school context, could well lead schools to push the boundaries of "individualized suspicion" to its outer limits, using subjective criteria that may "unfairly target members of unpopular groups," or leave those whose behavior is slightly abnormal stigmatized in the minds of others. If so, direct application of the Fourth Amendment's prohibition against "unreasonable searches and seizures" will further that Amendment's liberty-protecting objectives at least to the same extent as application of the mediating "individualized suspicion" test, where, as here, the testing program is neither criminal nor disciplinary in nature.

* * *

I cannot know whether the school's drug testing program will work. But, in my view, the Constitution does not prohibit the effort. Emphasizing the considerations I have mentioned, along with others to which the Court refers, I conclude that the school's drug testing program, constitutionally speaking, is not "unreasonable." And I join the Court's opinion.

JUSTICE O'CONNOR, with whom JUSTICE SOUTER joins, dissenting.

I dissented in *Vernonia School Dist. 47J v. Acton*, 515 U.S. 646 (1995), and continue to believe that case was wrongly decided. Because *Vernonia* is now this Court's precedent, and because I agree that petitioners' program fails even under the balancing approach adopted in that case, I join JUSTICE GINSBURG's dissent.

JUSTICE GINSBURG, with whom JUSTICE STEVENS, JUSTICE O'CONNOR, and JUSTICE SOUTER join, dissenting.

Seven years ago, in *Vernonia School Dist. 47J v. Acton*, 515 U.S. 646 (1995), this Court determined that a school district's policy of randomly testing the urine of its student athletes for illicit drugs did not violate the Fourth Amendment. In so ruling, the Court emphasized that drug use "increased the risk of sports-related injury" and that Vernonia's athletes were the "leaders" of an aggressive local "drug culture" that had reached "'epidemic proportions.'" Today, the Court relies upon *Vernonia* to permit a school district with a drug problem its superintendent repeatedly described as "not . . . major," to test the urine of an academic team member solely by reason of her participation in a nonathletic, competitive extracurricular activity — participation associated with neither special dangers from, nor particular predilections for, drug use.

"The legality of a search of a student," this Court has instructed, "should depend simply on the reasonableness, under all the circumstances, of the search." Although "'special needs' inhere in the public school context," those needs are not so expansive or malleable as to render reasonable any program of student drug testing a school district elects to install. The particular testing program upheld today is not reasonable, it is capricious, even perverse: Petitioners' policy targets for testing a student population least likely to be at risk from illicit drugs and their damaging effects. I therefore dissent.

I

A

* * *

In short, *Vernonia* applied, it did not repudiate, the principle that "the legality of a search of a student should depend simply on the reasonableness, *under all the circumstances*, of the search." Enrollment in a public school, and election to participate in school activities beyond the bare minimum that the curriculum requires, are indeed factors relevant to reasonableness, but they do not on their own justify intrusive, suspicionless searches. *Vernonia,* accordingly, did not rest upon these factors; instead, the Court performed what today's majority aptly describes as a "fact-specific balancing." Balancing of that order, applied to the facts now before the Court, should yield a result other than the one the Court announces today.

B

Vernonia initially considered "the nature of the privacy interest upon which the search [there] at issue intruded." The Court emphasized that student athletes' expectations of privacy are necessarily attenuated:

> "Legitimate privacy expectations are even less with regard to student athletes. School sports are not for the bashful. They require 'suiting up' before each practice or event, and showering and changing afterwards. Public school locker rooms, the usual sites for these activities, are not notable for the privacy they afford. The locker rooms in Vernonia are typical: No individual dressing rooms are provided; shower heads are lined up along a wall, unseparated by any sort of partition or curtain; not even all the toilet stalls have doors. . . . There is an element of communal undress inherent in athletic participation."

Competitive extracurricular activities other than athletics, however, serve students of all manner: the modest and shy along with the bold and uninhibited. Activities of the kind plaintiff-respondent Lindsay Earls pursued — choir, show choir, marching band, and academic team — afford opportunities to gain self-assurance, to "come to know faculty members in a less formal setting than the typical classroom," and to acquire "positive social supports and networks [that] play a critical role in periods of heightened stress."

* * *

The Vernonia district, in sum, had two good reasons for testing athletes: Sports team members faced special health risks and they "were the leaders of the drug culture." No similar reason, and no other tenable justification, explains Tecumseh's decision to target for testing all participants in every competitive extracurricular activity.

Nationwide, students who participate in extracurricular activities are significantly less likely to develop substance abuse problems than are their less-involved peers. Even if students might be deterred from drug use in order to preserve their extracurricular eligibility, it is at least as likely that other students might forgo their extracurricular involvement in order to avoid detection of their drug use. Tecumseh's policy thus falls short doubly if deterrence is its aim: It invades the privacy of students who need deterrence least, and risks steering students at greatest risk for substance abuse away from extracurricular involvement that potentially may palliate drug problems.

To summarize, this case resembles *Vernonia* only in that the School Districts in both cases conditioned engagement in activities outside the obligatory curriculum on random subjection to urinalysis. The defining characteristics of the two programs, however, are entirely dissimilar. The Vernonia district sought to test a subpopulation of students distinguished by their reduced expectation of privacy, their special susceptibility to drug-related injury, and their heavy involvement with drug use. The Tecumseh district seeks to test a much larger population associated with none of these factors. It does so, moreover, without carefully safeguarding student confidentiality and without regard to the program's untoward effects. A program so sweeping is not sheltered by *Vernonia;* its unreasonable reach renders it impermissible under the Fourth Amendment.

II

* * *

It is a sad irony that the petitioning School District seeks to justify its edict here by trumpeting "the schools' custodial and tutelary responsibility for children." In regulating an athletic program or endeavoring to combat an exploding drug epidemic, a school's custodial obligations may permit searches that would otherwise unacceptably abridge students' rights. When custodial duties are not ascendant, however, schools' tutelary obligations to their students require them to "teach by example" by avoiding symbolic measures that diminish constitutional protections. "That [schools] are educating the young for citizenship is reason for scrupulous protection of Constitutional freedoms of the individual, if we are not to strangle the free mind at its source and teach youth to discount important principles of our government as mere platitudes."

* * *

For the reasons stated, I would affirm the judgment of the Tenth Circuit declaring the testing policy at issue unconstitutional.

PROBLEM

You are a law clerk to the Oklanois state court judge who has been assigned the following case (the complaint, answer and appropriate exhibits are reproduced below). She has asked you to review the case file materials, to read the Supreme Court case touching upon drug testing (reproduced earlier herein) and to be ready to discuss the case with her.

SPAKONE DISTRICT COURT, COUNTY OF SPAKONE, OKLANOIS

DAVID HAMMOND, individually and on behalf of all others similarly situated, Plaintiffs,

v.

UNIVERSITY OF OKLANOIS, SPAKONE, through its Board, THE REGENTS OF THE UNIVERSITY OF OKLANOIS, a body corporate; STEPHEN DEE, as President of the [U]niversity of Oklanois, Spakone, and; WILLIAM BOLT as Athletic Director, Department of Intercollegiate Athletics, Defendants.

VERIFIED CLASS ACTION COMPLAINT
FOR DECLARATORY AND INJUNCTIVE RELIEF

INTRODUCTION

1. This is a class action complaint for declaratory and injunctive relief challenging the constitutionality of the drug screening program of the University of Oklanois's Department of Intercollegiate Athletics.

PARTIES

2. The named plaintiff class representative ("plaintiff") is a full time undergraduate student athlete currently enrolled at the University of Oklanois, Spakone, who is subject to the University's drug screening program.

3. Plaintiff is and has been a member of the track and field and cross-country athletic programs since the middle of last season.

4. Defendant University of Oklanois ("University") is a state institution of higher education established and regulated by Article IX, §§ 12 and 13, Oklanois Constitution and state statutory law, O.R.S., § 23-20-101, *et seq.* (Cum. Supp. 1986).

5. The University is ultimately governed by the defendant body corporate, known as "The Regents of the University of Oklanois" (the "Regents").

6. Defendant Stephen Dee is President of the University and has been elected as such by the Regents. As President, defendant Dee is the chief executive officer of the University and is responsible for the operation of the University and the departments which comprise it.

7. Defendant William Bolt is Athletic Director of the Department of Intercollegiate Athletics.

8. Athletic Director Bolt is responsible for the promulgation and enforcement of the University's drug screening program.

CLASS ACTION ALLEGATIONS

9. Plaintiff brings this suit as a class action pursuant to O.R.C.P. 23(a) and (b)(2).

10. The plaintiff class consists of all University students who have participated, currently participate or will participate in intercollegiate athletics and who have been, are or will be subject to defendants' drug screening program, which is part of defendant University's "Intercollegiate Athletics Drug Education Program."

11. The plaintiff class consists of well in excess of 200 students and is thus so numerous that joinder of all class members would be impracticable.

12. The questions of law and fact at issue here are common to all class members, to wit: does the University's drug screening program violate the constitutional rights of the plaintiff class?
13. The claims of the plaintiff are typical of the claims of all other class members since the drug screening program operates against all class members in an identical fashion.
14. The plaintiff will fairly and adequately protect the interests of all class members since his interests are not in conflict with those of the class members, the plaintiff is fully committed to carrying the case through for the benefit of the class and the class is represented by counsel which are experienced and competent in prosecuting such cases.
15. The defendants have acted on grounds generally applicable to the class since they have applied the allegedly unconstitutional drug screening program to all class members and accordingly, final injunctive and declaratory relief is appropriate with respect to the class as a whole.

FACTUAL ALLEGATIONS

16. Starting in the last academic year the University's Athletics Department instituted what it referred to as the "University of Oklanois Intercollegiate Athletics Drug Education Program" ("education program") (attached as Appendix 1).
17. The heart of this education program is a drug screening program.
18. Under the drug screening program student intercollegiate athletes are required to give samples of their urine to be tested for drugs which are listed in the drug screening program.
19. Drugs tested for include amphetamines, barbiturates, cocaine, tetrahydrocannabinol (THC or marijuana), methaqualudes, opiates, morphine, codeine, PCP ("angel dust," and analogues), and under certain conditions anabolic steroids.
20. Student athletes are tested even though defendants may have no reason at all to believe the plaintiff class members have used or are under the influence of the drugs for which they are being tested.
21. Testing is done first at an annual physical at the beginning of the academic year.
22. Thereafter, all class members are subject to regular urine testing on a schedule, and by a selection system, unknown to plaintiff, but which is purported to be random.
23. Urine testing is carried out in the following manner:
    a. Upon reporting to athletic practice certain students are informed that they have been picked to give a urine sample.

b. These students are given until the end of the athletic practice session to provide such sample.

c. Students picked to give urine samples are required to undress and bare their genitals in front of a student trainer or other athletic department staff member ("observer").

d. Students must then urinate into a container while the observer actually watches the urine leave the student's bodily orifice and enter the collection container.

e. If a student is unable to provide a sample as ordered, the student is required to wait and encouraged to drink liquids to stimulate the production of urine.

f. Inability or refusal to give a sample is considered by defendants to be equivalent to a positive test for proscribed drugs.

24. Such samples are then split and sent to an outside contract laboratory for chemical testing.

25. Defendant's policy requires that initial positive test results be confirmed by another testing method on the split sample.

26. A double positive test is then reported by the laboratory to the defendants' team physician, head athletic trainer, head coaches, athletic director, student athlete and his or her parents or legal guardian.

27. After receiving a double positive a student who wishes to continue in the athletic program is first suspended from play and practice for the current competitive season and then required to successfully complete a drug abuse counseling program, during which time such student is subject to periodic drug screening at defendants' pleasure.

28. If any student receives a second double positive urine test for proscribed drugs, the same individuals as set out in Paragraph 26 above are again notified, the student is permanently suspended from all of defendants' athletic program activities and his or her financial aid is revoked.

29. All intercollegiate athletes are required to execute a consent form "voluntarily" agreeing to participate in the above described program. This consent is unenforceable.

30. While student athletes are told that they may refuse to sign such consent form, refusal results in ineligibility to participate in intercollegiate athletics.

31. Such consent form includes an authorization for release of information concerning drug screening results to those individuals listed in Paragraph 26 as well as substance abuse counseling personnel.

FIRST CLAIM FOR RELIEF

42 U.S.C. § 1983

32. Defendants' promulgation and enforcement of the drug screening program described herein constitutes state action under 42 U.S.C. § 1983.

33. The drug screening program described herein represents official governmental policy as adopted by all defendants.

34. Defendants' collection and testing of student athletes' urine is a search within the meaning and protection of the Fourth Amendment to the United States Constitution.

35. This search is unreasonable under the Fourth Amendment for the following reasons:

    a. it is not supported by individualized, adequate suspicion or cause;

    b. it is a highly intrusive and unjustified interference with the legitimate expectation of privacy plaintiff class members have in their privacy and bodily fluids and;

    c. the privacy interests of the plaintiff class members outweigh the governmental interests in performing such searches and tests.

36. Information disclosed to defendants and their agents by way of the defendants' drug testing program includes personal and highly sensitive confidential medical information irrelevant to the concerns of defendants, such as whether plaintiff class members are taking birth control medication, medication for the control of sexually transmitted diseases, or genetic or seizure disorder medication, etc.

37. By requiring the disclosure of highly personal and confidential medical information irrelevant to defendants' concerns about illicit drug use, defendants are violating the plaintiff class members' constitutional right to privacy guaranteed under the First, Ninth and other Amendments to the United States Constitution.

38. By disseminating information gained about plaintiff class members in the drug screening program to the wide range of individuals called for in the policy defendants are further violating plaintiff class members' constitutional right to privacy.

39. On information and belief plaintiffs allege that the testing and confirmation procedures utilized by defendants are not sufficiently accurate and thereby violate the rights of the plaintiff class members to substantive due process.

40. Defendants' unsupported decision to test only intercollegiate athletes and not other students, some of whom may for example be engaged in scientific research touching on matters of national security, violates the principles of equal protection and due process.

41. The constitutional rights of the plaintiff class members to their privacy, to be free from unreasonable searches and seizures, to substantive due process and equal protection of the laws apply to the state and are guaranteed to plaintiffs through the Fourteenth Amendment to the United States Constitution.

42. The plaintiff class has been damaged by defendants' promulgation and enforcement of its drug screening program by having to submit to an unconstitutional violation of their rights as described above.

SECOND CLAIM FOR RELIEF

OKLANOIS CONSTITUTION

43. Plaintiffs here incorporate the allegations of Paragraphs 33 through 39 and 41 of the complaint above.

44. Defendants' actions in promulgating and enforcing its drug screening program violate plaintiffs' rights under Art. II, § 7 and Art. II, § 25 of the Oklanois Constitution, which provide as follows:

> Section 7. Security of person and property — searches — seizures — warrants. The people shall be secure in their persons, papers, homes and effects, from unreasonable searches and seizures; and no warrant to search any place or seize any person or things shall issue without describing the place to be searched, or the person or thing to be seized, as near as may be, nor without probable cause, supported by oath or affirmation reduced to writing.
>
> Section 25. Due process of law. No person shall be deprived of life, liberty or property, without due process of law.

REQUEST FOR PRELIMINARY INJUNCTIVE RELIEF

45. Based on the overwhelming weight of authority on the subject, governmental urine testing programs such as defendants' are violative of civil rights and accordingly plaintiffs can demonstrate a reasonable probability of success on the merits of this action.

46. If defendants' drug screening program is allowed to continue pending a final judgment in this case, real, immediate and irreparable injury will occur in the interim to each of the plaintiff class members tested in violation of their constitutional rights.

47. There is no plain, speedy or adequate remedy that plaintiffs have at law to protect their civil rights pending final resolution of this case.

48. The granting of a preliminary injunction prohibiting defendants from enforcing their drug screening program during pendency of this action will in fact serve the public interest in preserving and protecting the civil rights of the plaintiff class.

49. The balance of equities favors the plaintiff class and the granting of a preliminary injunction since it is always more equitable to preserve than to violate constitutionally guaranteed rights of fundamental importance.

50. The granting of a preliminary injunction will preserve the status quo that existed prior to the establishment of defendants' unconstitutional policy ("status quo ante") and put the parties back on a neutral footing pending final resolution of the matter.

PRAYER FOR RELIEF

WHEREFORE, the plaintiff class seeks an order granting to them the following relief:

51. That the court:

    a. Certify that this matter may be prosecuted as a class action as set out above;

    b. Declare, pursuant to Rule 57, O.R.C.P. and 42 U.S.C. § 1983, that defendants' drug screening program violates the state and federal constitutional rights of the plaintiff class;

    c. Issue preliminary and permanent injunctive relief pursuant to Rule 65, O.R.C.P. and 42 U.S.C. § 1983 ordering defendants to cease enforcement of their drug screening program;

    d. Order that all members of the plaintiff class who have suffered suspension from athletic programs or other penalties by virtue of the enforcement of defendants' drug screening program be reinstated into such athletic programs and be reinvested with all benefits, credits and the like to which they would have been entitled along with any financial aid which has been taken from them;

    e. Grant the plaintiffs their reasonable costs and attorney's fees pursuant to O.R.S. § 13-17-101, et seq. and 42 U.S.C. § 1988;

    f. Grant to plaintiffs such other and further relief to which they may be entitled.

Appendix 1

UNIVERSITY OF OKLANOIS
INTERCOLLEGIATE ATHLETICS
DRUG EDUCATION PROGRAM

The Department of Intercollegiate Athletics at the University of Oklanois, Spakone, its coaching personnel and administrators, strongly believe that the use and/or abuse of drugs (excluding those drugs prescribed by a physician to treat a specific medical condition) can:

1. Be detrimental to the physical and mental well-being of its student-athletes, no matter when such usage should occur during the year;

2. Seriously interfere with the performance of individuals as students and as athletes; and,

3. Be extremely dangerous to the student-athlete and his/her teammates, particularly with regard to participation in athletic competition or practice.

Therefore, the Athletic Department has implemented a mandatory program of drug education, testing, and counseling/rehabilitation efforts to assist and benefit the men and women athletes of the University of Oklanois, Spakone.

Purpose of the Program

The purpose of the University of Oklanois Intercollegiate Athletic Drug Education Program is not to unduly interfere with the private lives of the student athletes. The sole purpose of the Program is to aid and assist the student-athletes of the University of Oklanois, Spakone.

Specific goals of the Program are as follows:

1. To generally educate University of Oklanois athletes concerning the associated problems of drug abuse;

2. To prevent any drug use and/or abuse by University of Oklanois athletes;

3. To identify any athlete who may be using drugs and to identify the drug;

4. To educate any athlete so identified regarding such usage as it may affect the athlete and his/her team and teammates;

5. To see that any chronic dependency is treated and addressed properly;

6. To provide reasonable safeguards that every athlete is medically competent to participate in athletic competition;

7. To encourage discussion about any questions the athlete may have, either specifically or generally, about usage of drugs; and

8. To attempt to assure that athletes are physically and mentally fit for the rigors of intercollegiate athletic participation in an effort to minimize the risks of serious injury to the athlete and/or his/her teammates.

Implementation of Program

At the beginning of the academic year, a presentation will be made to all intercollegiate athletic squads at the University of Oklanois, Spakone, to outline and review the Intercollegiate Athletic Drug Education Program, its purposes and implementation. A copy of the Program will be given to each athlete. A copy of the Program will also be mailed to all parent(s) or legal guardian(s) of athletes. Each athlete will thereafter be asked to sign a form acknowledging receipt and understanding of the Program and providing voluntary consent to the administration of the urinalysis testing required by the Program and a release of testing information to a limited and select group.

Any athlete who does not wish to sign the Consent Form may choose not to do so and forego participation in intercollegiate athletics. In this case, the terms of the athlete's Athletic Award Notification would be controlling.

Athletes and parents or legal guardians are encouraged to ask questions or make suggestions at any time with reference to the Program and athletes will be asked to participate in ongoing reviews and revision of the Program. The Athletic Department is very serious about this Program and its success and expects the athletes to be equally interested and concerned.

This program and its administration/operation is subject to change/modification at any time. However, any change/modification will only be implemented by action of the District of Intercollegiate Athletics and will not be applied retroactively if that would adversely affect an athlete's rights. Any athlete who has been requested to provide a specimen for testing purposes and who fails to comply with such a request will be deemed to have tested positive.

The Drug Screening Program

As part of the annual physical at the beginning of the academic year, athletes will be subject to a drug screening to test for the following substances:

Amphetamines	Methaqualudes
Barbiturates	Opiates, morphine,
Cocaine	codeine
Tetrahydrocannabinol (THC or Marijuana)	PCP (Angel Dust) and Analogues

NOTE: While anabolic steroids are not within the parameters of this Drug Education Program, studies indicate that usage of such substances may be extremely detrimental to the health and well-being of the users of such substances. Therefore, selective anabolic steroid screening will be done by the Team Physician(s) as a part of the regular physical examination/evaluations of athletes for educational and medical reasons only. If it is determined that an athlete is utilizing anabolic steroids for purposes other than for treatment of a specific illness or injury as authorized or approved by the Team Physician or the Head Athletic Trainer, the athlete's head coach and Athletic Director will be counseled and the athlete may be found in violation of team training regulations. Infractions of team training regulations could result in suspension and possible loss of financial aid. The University of Oklanois Intercollegiate Athletic Department discourages the usage of anabolic steroids.

Thereafter, all athletes will be regularly tested during the academic year (tests will not be administered to athletes upon completion of eligibility for intercollegiate athletics). Those who at any time experience positive testing can expect further screenings to be done on a more regular basis.

The drug screening shall consist of the collection of a urine sample from the athlete under the supervision of Team Physician(s), Wardenburg Student Health Center Staff, the athletic training staff or other Athletic Department staff. The sample will be split for verification purposes and donors' names will be replaced with coded designations prior to sending the sample to the outside agency for testing. The collection of the specimen will be observed, and the athlete may be asked to disrobe in order to protect the integrity of the testing procedure. Each urine sample shall be analyzed for the presence of the above drugs by an outside agency contracted by the University to provide such service. The outside agency shall report all test results to the Team Physician(s) within 24-48 hours, who in turn will review such results to determine which, if any, of the test results are positive. For purposes of this Program, a positive result shall mean a test result which indicates, in the opinion of the outside agency performing such testing, the presence of one or more of the above listed drugs in the athlete's urine. The Athlete will be immediately notified of a positive test result. Whenever a confirmed positive test result occurs, the athlete will be given a reasonable opportunity to provide additional information as desired.

All athletes who have a confirmed positive test also may be required to undergo a physical assessment prior to any further participation in practice or a competitive event. Additionally, the Team Physician(s) may prohibit athletic competition/participation by any athlete for such time as deemed medically necessary should it reasonably appear that the athlete's condition would present a health danger to himself/herself or his/her teammates.

Every possible step will be taken to assure and maintain the accuracy and confidentiality of the test results including the maintenance of a documented chain of specimen custody to insure the identity and integrity of the sample throughout the collection and testing process.

Additionally, precautions will be taken to assure the randomness of the subsequent testing, including having selections for testing made by computer.

Any student-athlete who is notified of a confirmed positive result may, within five (5) days of being so notified, request the Athletic Director to meet with the student athlete to review the test procedures used, to discuss the situation with the student athlete and/or to allow the student athlete to provide any pertinent facts or mitigating circumstances. This meeting will occur as soon as possible.

Effect of Positive Test Results

First Positive: A split specimen of the individual athlete will be retested immediately, utilizing an alternate method of testing, to assure no error has occurred. A double positive test of a split specimen will be accepted as a confirmed positive result. If the positive result is thus verified and confirmed by the outside testing agency, the Team Physician is advised. The Team Physician will advise the athlete of the confirmed positive result. The Team Physician will inform the Head Athletic Trainer. The Head Athletic Trainer will advise the Athletic Director. The Athletic Director will notify the athlete's Head Coach(es). Additionally, the athlete will be required to, as promptly as possible, participate in a conference telephone call between the athlete and his/her parent(s) or legal guardian(s), notifing them of the positive test results.

The athlete will be required to participate in counseling as directed by a substance abuse counselor at the Wardenburg Student Health Center. The athlete shall also be suspended from play and practice for the current competitive season. The athlete will retain his/her scholarship for the remainder of the suspension period. The athlete may be reinstated at the termination of the suspension at the discretion of the Head Coach if the following conditions have been met:

1. The athlete must show proof of the successful completion of a substance abuse rehabilitation program approved by the Wardenburg Student Health Center. Said rehabilitation program to be at the sole expense of the athlete. (The initial counseling session conducted at Wardenburg will be an Athletic Departmental expense).
2. The athlete will subject himself/herself to periodic drug screening tests throughout the suspension.
3. The athlete signs the consent for urinalysis screening form.

REFUSAL TO PARTICIPATE AS SET FORTH IN THIS PARAGRAPH WILL RESULT IN INELIGIBILITY FOR THE ATHLETE TO ASSOCIATE WITH THE UNIVERSITY OF OKLANOIS ATHLETIC DEPARTMENT. In this case, the terms of the athlete's Athletic Aid Award Notification would be controlling.

Second Positive: A split specimen of the individual athlete will be retested immediately, utilizing an alternate method of testing, to assure no error has occurred. A double positive test of a split specimen will be accepted as a confirmed positive result. If the positive result is thus verified and confirmed by the outside testing agency, the Team Physician is advised. The Team Physician will advise the athlete of the confirmed positive result. The Team Physician will inform the Head Athletic Trainer. The Head Athletic Trainer will advise the Athletic Director. The Athletic Director will notify the athlete's Head Coach(es). Additionally, the athlete will be required to, as promptly as possible, participate in a conference telephone call between the athlete and his/her parent(s) or legal guardian(s), notifying them of the positive test results.

The athlete will be suspended permanently from further participation in any activity sponsored by the University of Oklanois Athletic Department. Additionally, the athlete will lose his/her financial aid in accord with the terms of the

Financial Aid Agreement (as set forth in the Athletic Aid Award Notification) between the athlete and the University and in accord with University, NCAA and Big Nine Conference Rules.

Prior to the implementation of the suspension or permanent suspension period, the athlete has the opportunity to fully discuss the matter with the Athletic Director and present evidence of any mitigating circumstances which he/she feels important.

Conclusion

It is believed and hoped that the implementation of this University of Oklanois Intercollegiate Athletics Drug Education Program will serve to benefit all connected with intercollegiate athletics at the University of Oklanois, Spakone. While ultimate decisions with reference to drug usage and/or substance abuse are dependent upon the interests, values, motivations, and determinations of the individual involved, it is believed and hoped that participation in this Program will make the men and women who participate in intercollegiate athletics at the University of Oklanois, Spakone, and represent the University in various areas of athletic competition, better students, better athletes, and better able to make individual, informed, and intelligent decisions with reference to drug usage, both now and in the future.

CONSENT TO TESTING OR URINE SAMPLE AND AUTHORIZATION FOR RELEASE OF INFORMATION

TO: TEAM PHYSICIANS

WARDENBURG STUDENT HEALTH CENTER

UNIVERSITY OF OKLANOIS, SPAKONE

I hereby acknowledge that I have received a copy of the University of Oklanois Intercollegiate Athletics Drug Education Program. I further acknowledge that I have read said Program, that it has been outlined to me, that I fully understand the provisions of the Program and that I agree to voluntarily participate in the Program as described. I understand that I may choose not to sign this Form and forego participation in intercollegiate athletics at the University of Oklanois.

I hereby consent to have a sample of my urine collected this ______ day of ________ , 20___, and tested for the presence of certain drugs or substances in accordance with the provisions of the University of Oklanois Intercollegiate Athletics Drug Education Program, and at such other times as urinalysis testing is required under the Program during the academic year.

I further authorize you to make a confidential release to the Head Athletic Trainer at the University of Oklanois, Spakone; my parent(s) or legal guardian(s) or spouse; the head coach of any intercollegiate sport in which I am a team member; the Athletic Director of the University of Oklanois, Spakone; and the Drug Counseling Program at the Wardenburg Student Health Center, of all information and records, including test results, you may have relating to the screening or testing of my urine sample(s) in accordance with the provisions of the University of Oklanois Intercollegiate Athletics Drug Education Program which is applicable to all intercollegiate athletes at the University of Oklanois, Spakone. I waive any privilege I may have in connection with such information only to the limited extent set forth in this document.

I understand that any urine samples will be sent to ANALYTAOX LAB in Spakone, Oklanois, for actual testing.

The University of Oklanois, its Board of Regents, its officers, employees and agents are hereby released from legal responsibility or liability for the release of such information and records as authorized by this form.

____________________________ ____________________________

Parents Signature (if athlete is under 18 years) (Print Name)

____________________________ ____________________________

(Date) (Signature)

____

Witness

____

(Date)

DISTRICT COURT, COUNTY OF SPAKONE, STATE OF OKLANOIS
Case No. 20-CV-2Y45-3

ANSWER

DAVID HAMMOND, individually and on behalf of all others similarly situated, Plaintiffs,

v.

UNIVERSITY OF OKLANOIS, Spakone, through its Board, THE REGENTS OF THE UNIVERSITY OF OKLANOIS, a body corporate; STEPHEN DEE, as President of the University of Oklanois, Spakone, and; WILLIAM BOLT as Athletic Director, Department of Intercollegiate Athletics,

Defendants.

The Regents of the University of Oklanois, a body corporate, Stephen Dee and William Bolt, the Defendants in the above-captioned action, by and through their undersigned attorneys, answer the Plaintiffs' Complaint as follows:

1. Upon information and belief the allegations of paragraph 1 of the Complaint relating to the Drug Education Program of the University of Oklanois do not require an answer by these Defendants.

2. Defendants admit that Plaintiff is a full-time undergraduate student athlete currently enrolled at the University of Oklanois, Spakone, who voluntarily participates in the University's Drug Education Program. Except as herein specifically admitted, the allegations of paragraph 2 are denied.

3. Defendants admit that Plaintiff has been a member of the track and field and cross country athletic programs since the middle of the 1985-86 athletic season. Except as herein specifically admitted, the allegations of paragraph 3 are denied.

4. Admitted.

5. Admitted.

6. Defendant Stephen Dee is President of the University of Oklanois and its Chief Executive Officer. Except as herein specifically admitted, the allegations of paragraph 6 are denied.

7. Admitted.

8. As Director of the Department of Intercollegiate Athletics, of which the Drug Education Program is a component, Defendant Bolt is responsible for the implementation and operation of the Drug Education Program. Except as herein specifically admitted, the allegations of paragraph 7 are denied.

9. Upon information and belief the allegations of paragraph 9 of the Complaint do not require an answer by these Defendants.

10. Defendants deny the existence of a class as set forth in O.R.C.P. 23 (a) and (b)(2).

11. Denied.

12. Denied.

13. Defendants admit that the Drug Education Program of the Department of Intercollegiate Athletics of the University of Oklanois is administered in a fair and impartial manner to the students who voluntarily participate in Intercollegiate Athletics at the University of Oklanois. Except as herein specifically admitted, Defendants deny the allegations set forth in paragraph 13 of the Complaint.

14. Defendants deny the existence of a class which meets the requirements of law, and therefore deny the allegations of paragraph 14.

15. Denied.

16. Admitted.

17. Denied.

18. As part of the Drug Education Program, student intercollegiate athletes voluntarily consent to provide urine samples to be tested for the drugs set forth in the written description of the program.

19. Admitted.

20. Defendants admit that in general student athletes are randomly tested, and that such random tests are not administered in response to a suspicion or belief that said athletes have used or are under the influence of the drugs for which tests are conducted. Except as herein specifically admitted, the allegations of paragraph 20 are denied.

21. Admitted.

22. Defendants admit that student athletes, as a part of their voluntary participation in the Drug Education Program, consent to random urine testing. Except as herein specifically admitted, the allegations of paragraph 22 are denied.

23. Defendants admit that the testing component of the Drug Education Program is generally characterized by the following aspects:

    a. Certain student athletes are informed that they have been randomly selected to provide a urine sample on that day.

    b. Said student athletes are required to provide the sample by the time of closing of the training room.

    c-d. Student athletes randomly selected to provide urine samples may either disrobe and provide a specimen in an enclosed area, or not disrobe and provide a specimen in the presence of a staff member of the Department of Athletics or the Wardenburg Student Health Center.

    e. Denied.

    f. Refusal to provide a urine sample will result in the same procedural consequences as a first positive test, as set forth in the Drug Education Program.

Except as herein specifically admitted, Defendants deny the allegations of paragraph 23 and each of its subparagraphs.

24. Defendants admit that immediately after production, urine samples are sealed by the staff member in the presence of the student athlete and sent to an outside contract laboratory where the samples are split for chemical testing. Except as herein specifically admitted, the allegations of paragraph 24 are denied.

25. Admitted.

26. Defendants admit that a confirmed positive test is then reported by the laboratory, pursuant to the written Drug Education Program, to the team physician and/or the head athletic trainer. Except as herein specifically admitted, the allegations of paragraph 26 are denied.

27. Defendants admit that a student athlete who receives a confirmed positive and who wishes to continue to participate in the athletic program must also continue to participate in the Drug Education Program, pursuant to which the athlete, if mitigating or exculpatory circumstances are not presented, will: participate in counseling as directed by a substance abuse counselor at the Wardenburg Student Health Center, be suspended from play and practice for the current competitive season, be subject to further non-random testing at the discretion of the team physician, and successfully complete a substance abuse rehabilitation program approved by the Wardenburg Student Health Center. Except as herein specifically admitted, the allegations of paragraph 27 are denied.

28. Defendants admit that if any student athlete receives a second confirmed positive urine test for proscribed drugs that is established to be unrelated to the first confirmed positive, the team physician and head athletic trainer are notified and the student athlete is permanently suspended from all athletic program activities. Except as herein specifically admitted, the allegations of paragraph 28 are denied.

29. Defendants admit that any student athlete who does not wish to provide a written consent to drug testing as a part of the Drug Education Program may choose not to do so and forego participation in the University of Oklanois Intercollegiate Athletic Program. Except as herein specifically admitted, the allegations of paragraph 29 are denied.

30. Defendants admit that participation in the Drug Education Program and execution of a written consent to drug testing as set forth in the description of the program is a prerequisite to participation in the Intercollegiate Athletic Program at the University of Oklanois. Except as herein specifically admitted, the allegations of paragraph 30 are denied.

31. Defendants admit that the consent form (*see* Exhibit A attached hereto and incorporated herein by reference) provides an authorization for confidential release of test results to parents and/or legal guardians, the head coach of the program in which the student athlete participates, the athletic director, and the Drug Counseling Program at the Wardenburg Student Health Center.

32-39. Denied.

40. Defendants admit that all students at the University of Oklanois are entitled to the same rights under the Oklanois and United States Constitutions as any other citizen. Except as herein specifically admitted, the allegations of paragraph 40 are denied.

41-49. Denied.

AFFIRMATIVE DEFENSES

1. Plaintiffs' individual claims fail to state a claim upon which the relief can be granted.
2. Plaintiffs' individual claims are barred by virtue of Plaintiffs' contractual agreement to participate in said program as a condition of receipt of financial aid and participation in intercollegiate athletics (*see* Exhibit B attached hereto and incorporated herein by reference).
3. Plaintiffs' individual claims are barred by the doctrine of estoppel.
4. Plaintiff, by virtue of having not been subject to any disciplinary or enforcement processes of the Drug Education Program, lacks standing to challenge certain aspects of the Program.

WHEREFORE, Defendants request the following relief from the Court:

a. That the Plaintiffs' complaint be dismissed.

b. That class certification be denied.

c. That Plaintiffs' prayer for injunctive relief be denied.

d. That Defendants be awarded their costs, and such other and further relief as to the Court is deemed just and proper.

EXHIBIT A

CONSENT TO TESTING OF URINE SAMPLE AND AUTHORIZATION FOR RELEASE OF INFORMATION

[Same as shown in Appendix I of the Complaint]

EXHIBIT B

UNIVERSITY OF OKLANOIS, SPAKONE

ATHLETIC AID AWARD NOTIFICATION

( ) New ( ) Renewal

Dated Typed _________ SPORT ________ ( ) Transfer

____ STUDENT #: ____________

NAME (LAST, FIRST)

____________________________________ CLASS: __________________________

HOME ADDRESS

________________________________ HOUSING: ___ On-Campus ___ Off-Campus

CITY, STATE, ZIP

Length of Award: From ________________ through ____________________

AID OFFERED Fall Amount Spring Amount Total Amount Award Code

Tuition and Fees $_________ $_________ $_________ $_________

Room and Board $_________ $_________ $_________ $_________

Books $_________ $_________ $_________ $_________

Total Value $_________ $_________ $_________ $_________

Comments:

____

____

____

This award is contingent upon your eligibility status based on University of Oklanois, Big Nine Conference, and National Collegiate Athletic Association (NCAA) rules and regulations.

This award is also contingent upon your participation in the Drug Education Program of the University of Oklanois, Spakone Intercollegiate Athletic Department.

Recommended by: _________________________ ______________________

Approved: ______________________________ ________________________

Approved: ______________________________ ________________________

I have read, understand, and accept the athletic aid offered under the terms stated above.

My signature represents my intention to participate in intercollegiate athletics at the University of Oklanois. My signature also indicates that I have received a copy of the above referenced Drug Education Program and that I have read and understand the Program. I understand that noncompliance with the Program will be a breach of this financial aid agreement which would permit the University of Oklanois to remove me from participation and/or void this financial aid agreement in accord with NCAA and Big 9 Conference Rules.

________________________________ ______________________________

Student Athlete Signature Date

For use by Office of University

Registrar

______ Fall-Spring/Cumulative G.P.A. ______ White original to File

______ Green copy to Athlete

______ Fall-Spring/Cumulative Hours ______ Yellow copy to Athletic Business

Passed Office

______Pink copy to Registrar

______ Eligible ______ Not Eligible ______ Gold copy to Financial Aid

______ Blue copy to Athletic Business

Office

______ White copy to Head Coach

Certified by: ______________________ ________________________________

Registrar Date

Notes and Comments

1. It seems that just about every entity with control over athletics and athletes has decided to test athletes for drugs. (It wouldn't be totally surprising to read the paper tomorrow and learn that the Little League has adopted a drug testing program). High schools, high school athletic associations, colleges, universities, leagues, conferences, amateur athletic associations, the United States Olympic Committee, the NCAA, the NAIA, and professional leagues all have adopted drug testing procedures of their own. The result is a crazy-quilt.

In sorting through the various schemes, it is important to classify the organization doing the testing as either a state actor or a private entity. At least in so far as state actors are concerned, the law is settled around the guidelines established by the Supreme Court in *Earls*. However, the Supreme Court has not spoken on the issue of how private drug testing is to be evaluated. And given the Supreme Court's now somewhat cramped view of state action, this is an extremely important area. Private high schools, private colleges, the NCAA (according to *Tarkanian*), and even the USOC (according to *DeFrantz*), are all probably private actors. According to fairly well-established principles, these schemes would not be subjected to Fourth Amendment scrutiny, but would be evaluated under the more permissive rubric of private associational law. In the world of professional sports, drug testing schemes imposed upon union members by management would be evaluated according to labor law principles. A substantial body of law review literature is emerging in these areas. *See, e.g.*, Alan Fecteau, *NCAA State Action: Not Present When Regulating Intercollegiate Athletics — But Does That Include Drug Testing Student-Athletes?*, 5 Seton Hall J. Sport L. 291 (1995); Samantha Osheroff, *Drug Testing of Student*

Athletes in Vernonia School District v. Acton*: Orwell's* 1984 *Becomes Vernonia's Reality in 1995*, 16 LOY. L.A. ENT. L.J. 513 (1995); Donald Crowley, *Student Athletes and Drug Testing*, MARQ. SPORTS L.J. 65 (1995); Michael Hallam, *A Casualty of the "War On Drugs": Mandatory, Suspicionless Drug Testing of Student Athletes in . . .* Vernonia, 74 N.C. L. REV. 833 (1996); Carla E. Laszewski, *Gone to Pot: Student Athletes Fourth Amendment Rights after . . .* Vernonia, 40 ST. LOUIS U. L.J. 575 (1996); Nancy D. Wagman, *Are We Becoming a Society of Suspects? Examining Random Suspicionless Drug Testing of Public School Athletes*, 3 VILL. SPORTS & ENT. L.J. 325 (1996); Robert L. Roshkoft, *The Constitutionality of Random, Suspicionless Urinalysis Drug Testing of College Athletes*, 3 VILL. SPORTS & ENT. L.J. 361 (1996); Lynn Crossett, *Do Public School Athletes Shed Their Constitutional Rights at the Locker Room Door?*, 27 TEX. TECH. L. REV. 327 (1996); Samantha Elizabeth Shutler, *Random, Suspicionless Drug Testing of High School Athletes*, 86 J. CRIM. L & CRIMINOLOGY 1265 (1996); Eric N. Miller, *Suspicionless Drug Testing of High School and College Athletes after* Acton*: Similarities and Differences,* 45 U. KAN. L. REV. 301 (1996); Barry R. Ervy, *Drug Dispensing in Athletic Departments of Colleges and Universities: A New Proposal*, 7 SETON HALL J. SPORT L. 371 (1997).

The USOC established the United States Anti-Doping Agency (USADA) in 2000 to supervise the doping activities of Olympians. The USADA implemented the World Anti-Doping Agency (WADA) code which accepts a "comfortable satisfaction" standard instead of the higher "beyond a reasonable doubt" threshold that is common in American criminal courts. *See* Laura S. Stewart, *Has the United States Anti-Doping Agency Gone Too Far? Analyzing the Shift From 'Beyond a Reasonbale Doubt' to 'Comfortable Satisfaction'*, 13 VILL. SPORTS & ENT. L.J. 207 (2006); John T. Wendt, *The Year of the Steroid: Are New Testing Regimes Enough?*, 22 ENT. & SPORTS LAW. 8 (WTR 2005). This topic is discussed in Chapter 16, *infra*.

2. The California Supreme Court has held that the NCAA's drug testing program is consistent with the privacy provisions of the California Constitution. *Hill v. NCAA*, 865 P.2d 633 (Cal. 1994). Although a lower California appellate court had ruled that drug testing by the NCAA violated the California Constitution, the court reversed and reasoned that, although the athletes had significant privacy interests, the interest of the NCAA in protecting the safety and health of athletes and in maintaining the reputation of its programs outweighed the students' interests. *See* Anthony Cruz Jr., *After Ten Years of Litigation, NCAA Drug Testing is Upheld by California Supreme Court,* SPORTS LAW., July/Aug. 1994, at page 1; Karen E. Crummy, Note, *Urine or You're Out: Student-Athletes' Right of Privacy Stripped in* Hill v. NCAA, 29 U.S.F. L. REV. 197 (1994); Stephen M. Kennedy, Note, *Emasculating a State's Constitutional Right to Privacy: The California Supreme Court's Decision in* Hill v. NCAA, 68 TEMP. L. REV. 1473 (1995). *See also,* Ted O'Neal, *The Constitutionality of NCAA Drug Testing: A Fine Specimen for Examination,"* 46 SMU L. REV. 513 (1992).

3. The Colorado Supreme Court struck down the drug testing scheme of the University of Colorado finding that the testing violated both the United States and Colorado Constitutions. *University of Colorado v. Derdeyn*, 863 P.2d 929 (Colo. 1993). The extent to which the principles announced in *Earls* would change the holding in *Derdeyn* is unclear since (1) *Derdeyn* was based in part upon state constitutional principles and (2) *Derdeyn* was a college situation while *Earls* involved a high school. There is also a distinction between *Derdeyn* and *Hill* because the University of Colorado is clearly a state actor while the *Hill* Court found that the NCAA was not a state actor.

4. When union and management collectively bargain over and agree to a drug testing scheme, a strong presumption supports the legality of the scheme. After all, the union is well-positioned to represent the interests of its members. But an entirely different problem arises when management unilaterally implements a drug testing program. Management's right to implement random drug testing will turn on whether drug testing is considered a mandatory or non-mandatory collective bargaining topic. If mandatory, unilateral implementation would probably be impermissible. In *The Legality Under the National Labor Relations Act of Attempts by Owners to Unilaterally Implement Drug Testing Programs,* 39 U. FLA. L. REV. 1 (1987), Professor Ethan Lock argues convincingly that drug testing is a mandatory topic, while recognizing that neither the NLRB nor the courts have yet addressed the issue. If the NFLPA does challenge management when it unilaterally implements a drug testing scheme, how will the NLRB be likely to respond?

In 1998, Mark McGwire came under scrutiny while setting the single season home run record. A reporter discovered the muscle-building supplement androstenedione (andro) in his locker. Andro had been banned by every major sports governing body except for Major League Baseball. Andro is similar to steroids in its effects on the human body. Major League Baseball continues to face an onslaught of criticism regarding its steroid policy, or lack thereof. With homerun sluggers such as Barry Bonds, Sammy Sosa, and Rafael Palmero at the forefront of the controversy, MLB is tightening its antisteroid rules. In late 2005, MLB implemented is new steroid policy requiring players to be suspended for 50 games for testing positive once, 100 games for a another positive test, and a banned lifetime ban for testing positive three times. Still, as of this writing the problem of steroid use continues to plague baseball. Commissioner Selig has asked George Mitchell to lead a rather ill-defined probe of the issue.

5. Reliability questions plague many drug testing schemes. The obvious danger of false positive readings necessitates safeguards which include a second phase of testing. Nonetheless, errors will be made. Part of the problem is that legal substances sometimes produce false readings. Another part of the problem is that labs competing for business sometimes make cost-cutting decisions which undermine reliability. And still another problem is raised by false negatives. For a more complete look at the very perplexing problem of reliability, *see* Lawrence Miike & Maria Hewitt, *Accuracy and Reliability of Urine Drug Tests*

36 KAN. L. REV. 641 (1988). *See also* SPORTS INDUSTRY NEWS, Sept. 19, 1986, at page 296.

A major dilemma occurs when the substances being tested for are undetectable. This is a growing problem in sports. Two solutions exist. One method is to rely on non-analytical positive evidence, such as documents revealing the purchase of banned substances. The other option is athletic profiling. Here, a physical profile of an athlete would be created. A major departure from that profile would serve as evidence that the athlete is using banned substances. *See* James A. R. Nafziger, *Circumstantial Evidence of Doping: BALCO and Beyond*, 16 MARQ. SPORTS L. REV. 45 (2005).

Several athletes, especially Olympic athletes, have spoken out about faulty drug testing. In 1998, soon after setting the world record of 43.29 seconds in the 400 meters, Butch Reynolds was found to have tested positive for steroids. Reynolds has repeatedly claimed his innocence but nonetheless was forced to miss the 1988 Olympic Games where he was a heavy favorite to win a gold medal. Other prominent Olympic athletes such as Ben Johnson, Mary Decker Slaney, and Michelle Smith have been banned from competition for taking banned substances. Johnson has admitted to his cheating, while Slaney and Smith have both denied use of banned substances but both lost their appeals. At the 1998 Tour de France an entire cycling team was removed from competition for using banned substances. Peter Korda, the 1998 Australian Open winner tested positive for steroids at Wimbledon in 1998 and was suspended. His ranking went from #2 to #102, and he retired from tennis after failing to qualify for the 1999 Wimbledon. He denies taking steroids to this day. Reliability questions continue to plague many drug-testing schemes.

6. *Drug Testing Legislation: What Are The States Doing?,* 36 KAN. L. REV. 919 (1988), surveys state legislative responses to the problem of drugs in the workplace. The comment explores the justifications for drug testing generally, and analyzes seven state drug testing statutes which authorize private employers to test employees. The comment also examines pending legislation.

7. The following is reprinted from THE PHYSICIAN AND SPORTS MEDICINE, Vol. 14, No. 11, November 1986 at page 47-48.

Drug Testing and Moral Responsibility

by Thomas H. Murray, Ph.D.

Opposing drugs today is as American as apple pie, motherhood, and baseball. Politicians are trampling each other in a stampede to be seen as "tougher" on drugs than their opponents. Peeing has apparently replaced flag-waving as the most important test of a politician's loyalty to God and country. But not all is well. The American Heart Association cautions us about the shortening and sugar in apple pie, Newsweek tells us that great numbers of Americans are rejecting parenthood, and baseball has a drug problem, for which the currently fashionable solution seems most decidedly un-American. As Judge Sarokin noted in throwing out a government plan for mass drug screening: "The public interest in eliminating drugs in the workplace is substantial, but to invade the privacy of the innocent in order to discover the guilty establishes a dangerous precedent, one which our Constitution mandates be rejected."

In recent decades drug use has been a substantial problem in sports, and testing programs have sprung up to deal with it. But the moral justification for drug tests such as those given to Olympic athletes is vastly different from the rationale behind the current flurry of drug screening in the workplace — even when the workplace is a football field, baseball diamond, or basketball court. The principal differences lie in the purpose of the drug use and the reasons for wanting to discourage it. Olympic athletes often face great pressure to use drugs — not for pleasure, but to enhance their athletic performance. Anabolic steroids are probably the best known performance-enhancers, but the list of stimulants and other performance-enhancing drugs is long and growing. Using drugs to gain a performance edge is a form of cheating and distorts the nature of sport. Athletes become trapped in a system in which they must either use drugs (thus risking their health and facing possible disqualification) or concede an advantage to their competitors.

A fair and effective drug screening program, with sanctions for those who are caught, seems the only feasible way to discourage the use of performance enhancers. Such screening must be done to protect the integrity of sport as well as to ensure that the athletes compete fairly — that is, against their opponents' talents rather than their pharmacies.

In contrast, the new screening proposals for the workplace come with a confusing hodgepodge of rationales. Is drug screening intended to protect workers from themselves? Except for addicts who need help breaking their habit, this is a dubious reason. Is it to protect others? This is a valid reason, but relevant to only a small percentage of jobs — airline pilots, bus drivers, crane operators, etc. Of course, when a worker's job performance is clearly impaired, it is reasonable to investigate the source of the impairment. . . . But testing individuals when there is no reasonable cause for suspicion does not justify mass screening.

Probably the most influential rationale for screening is to try to reduce the demand for drugs by increasing the social risks of drug use. We have no idea whether it will work, and as Judge Sarokin noted, it is a curious method for a society such as ours, which is strongly committed to the freedom and dignity of individuals.

For example, recent proposals by major league baseball and the National Collegiate Athletic Association to screen athletes appear to confuse the two purposes of drug testing. Are we trying to ensure fair competition? Then test for performance-enhancers. But if we are trying to prevent athletes from using drugs for pleasure, what right do we have to insist that they submit to mass screening? (Remember that impaired performance is always a prima facie reason to test an individual.) Why are we any more justified in testing the football team for marijuana than the debate team, the band, or everyone taking freshman English?

Explanations for this phenomenon are easier to find than justifications. One reason for the lack of protest is that screening for one category of drugs in sports was already established and accepted. Failing to keep the rationales distinct, we slid all too easily from testing for performance-enhancers to testing for pleasure-enhancers. A second factor may be that athletes are accustomed to having their lives regulated by other people — coaches, for instance — to a degree far in excess of what most of us would tolerate in everyday life. To an athlete, drug testing may seem no more intrusive than a dozen other aspects of their routine.

Third, and I think most important in the larger problem of drug use among athletes, is that athletes are often treated like children — large and physically gifted children, but children nonetheless. The dark side of our desire to glorify athletes is that we may shield them from the cold realities of adult life. In how many ways are college and professional athletes protected from the consequences of their actions? What lessons does a young man learn when, because he can do marvelous things with a football or basketball, he is permitted to ignore his academic responsibilities, have transgressions hushed up, and receive gifts and money under the table?

Recall the public reaction when Mike Ditka, coach of the Chicago Bears, was cited for driving while intoxicated (DWI). To its credit, the judicial system treated Ditka as they would any other DWI, and Ditka accepted their decision. But the sports fans of Chicago became enraged at the police and courts for punishing their hero. How many of those fans understand the childishness of their own behavior, or the underlying insult to Mike Ditka — the implication that he was not a strong enough person to accept the consequences of his actions?

We do a great disservice to athletes when we expect less from them than from their nonathlete peers. We stunt the growth of their character and delude them into thinking they need not be responsible for their own actions. Could it be that the tragic death of Len Bias was due in part to a feeling that he was invulnerable, that he could do things others could not? He *could* do extraordinary things on the basketball court. But the bulk of life is lived elsewhere, even for such an enormously talented athlete.

Done properly, screening athletes for performance-enhancing drugs is well justified. But screening them for the so-called drugs of abuse may not be. There is no more reason to screen college or professional athletes than any other students or employees. Drug education, voluntary testing, and counseling are as appropriate for athletes as for anyone else. But if we genuinely want to help athletes make good moral decisions in their lives — including the decision not to use drugs — then we ought to stop treating them as if they were not morally accountable adults. Screening for pleasure drugs is just one more way of telling them that they are not, and cannot be, responsible individuals.

8. Problem. You are the general counsel to the University of Oklanois, and you have just received the following letter from the general counsel of the American Council on Education along with the accompanying materials. Prepare to discuss your response.

Dear Counsel:

In the course of the past several months, college and university administrators have become increasingly concerned about drug use by student athletes. The recent action by the NCAA convention calling for drug testing prior to bowl and championship games has expanded awareness of the issue and created a movement to promulgate institutional student athlete drug testing policies.

In view of the growing interest in the subject and in an effort to aid institutions that have not developed drug testing policies, the American Council on Education plans to issue a paper outlining in general terms some of the policy issues and broad guidelines that should be considered in developing a drug testing program. Attached is a first draft of such a paper. It is designed to provide general advice and guidance without impairing the ability of institutions to adopt standards and procedures that best suit their individual circumstances. The document is based on several articles written on the subject and a number of existing institutional drug testing policies.

Since ACE does not have a football or basketball team, I am unsure how these proposed guidelines will work in practice. I am therefore asking you to please review the attached paper.

Once again, I appreciate your help with this important project. Your advice and guidance on past matters has been invaluable in shaping the development of policy statements that have aided the higher education community.

With warmest regards,

Sincerely,

General Counsel, ACE

DRAFT

POLICY CONSIDERATIONS

Colleges and universities may justifiably be concerned about use of drugs by student athletes. Use of performance-enhancing drugs undermines the integrity of athletic competition, which is grounded on the principle that athletic achievement is the result of individual and team ability, training and motivation. Tolerance of this sort of drug abuse encourages others to use drugs to equalize the competition. Drug use may also pose a risk of injury or even long-term harm to the drug user. Additionally, student athletes represent the institution in competition with other institutions and in the eyes of the public.

Many colleges and universities have undertaken, or are considering, routine testing (usually urinalysis) to detect whether college athletes are using drugs. Against the interests of the school must be balanced the interests of students in avoiding or minimizing such intrusive and unpleasant testing. Such tests unquestionably involve some invasion of students' privacy and in effect require students to prove their innocence through a procedure subjecting them to some indignity. There are, in addition, the risks of mistaken test results, intentional or unintentional misuse of confidential testing information and "leaks" of information to third parties.

Colleges and universities must not approach drug testing proposals casually. Drug testing should only be undertaken where schools intend to abide by the letter of formal, written procedures established to govern the program. Schools should be aware that any departure from the procedures — or any mistaken imposition of penalties, leak of confidential information, or failure to afford "due process" procedures before taking adverse action — can embroil the school in protracted and costly litigation having the prospect of a substantial award of damages to a wronged student. It is also possible that at least some courts will strike down testing programs that are not so closely related to important school interests as to justify the associated invasion of student privacy.

Without attempting to resolve the unsettled legal issues surrounding drug testing programs, the American Council on Education's Guidelines seek to formulate a common sense approach that balances the interests of colleges and universities with those of the students who would be subject to drug testing. The Guidelines also try to anticipate principal danger areas where the risk of legal liability may be especially great.

A key feature of the Guidelines is their singling out of performance-enhancing drugs as the appropriate focus of drug testing programs. It is abuse of these drugs that most threatens the integrity of athletic competition; to tolerate such abuse only encourages others to misuse drugs in order to redress a real or imagined competitive imbalance. Testing for the presence of these drugs has a direct and immediate connection to the interests of college athletes and the welfare of students as athletes; for these reasons, well conceived testing programs focusing on performance-enhancing drugs should not be regarded as intruding unjustifiably into the private lives of student athletes.

The justification for including recreational drugs in a test program is not nearly so strong. The connection to the integrity of college athletics is weaker. That is particularly so of testing during the off season or at other times removed from a student's actual participation in athletic competition. It is not apparent why schools have a greater interest in testing athletes than in testing students in general for use of recreational drugs. There are other complications — such as law enforcement issues — which arise if a school obtains (and maintains) incriminating information about students' use of illegal recreational drugs. It might be said, in defense of a broad testing program embracing recreational drugs, that detecting all kinds of drug abuse may help protect the health of athletes. But in most cases, that argument is really a rationalization for an overbroad testing program. It is likely that health-threatening drug abuse would be detected in the course of routine physical examinations or by the coaching staffs' day-to-day observations of the athletes under their supervision.

Consistent with the goal of avoiding unnecessary intrusion into students' private lives, testing programs should be sport specific — *i.e.*, each athlete should be tested for drugs reasonably suspected of enhancing performance in his or her sport(s). Cross-country runners, for example, are unlikely to use steroids to improve their performance. Testing should also be scheduled so as to detect drug use likely to affect athletic performance, not merely any use of drugs at anytime by an athlete.

No school should institute a drug testing program without first conferring with its legal counsel. Schools and their counsel will wish to consider the following points in devising any program:

Need to Follow Written Rules. Each program should be set forth fully and completely in writing. Each element of the testing program should be covered, including the responsibilities of all persons administering the program, the persons entitled to receive confidential information and the procedures to be followed to preserve the confidentiality of the information. These procedures must always be followed to the letter; any deviation would subject a school (and individuals) to possible liability for failing to uphold the safeguards protecting student participants.

Need for Informed Consent. Each student subject to drug testing should receive a copy of the written rules, together with written materials explaining how the program is to operate. There must be clear and unambiguous disclosure of all elements of the program, including such risks as there may be of disclosure of information to third parties. Participants should sign acknowledgments that they have received the pertinent materials, had the opportunity to ask questions, and decided to participate in the program. New students should be made aware of the program before they enroll and the program should be described in the school's catalog or official bulletin. Special efforts should be made to disclose all aspects of the program to those who are being recruited as likely athletes before they decide to enroll. Some courts hold that materials provided to prospective students *before* they enroll constitute a "contract" governing the student-college relationship; every effort must be made to avoid charges that a school failed to make timely disclosure of its policies.

Due Process. Even if test data indicates an extremely high probability that a student has used a prohibited drug, he or she should still be afforded reasonable notice and an opportunity to be heard before sanctions are imposed. The formality of the hearing procedure that is required depends on the seriousness of the threatened sanction; a student facing loss of an athletic scholarship, for example, should be afforded the opportunity to present evidence to a neutral hearing panel and confront the opposing evidence and witnesses. Most university counsel are familiar with the requirements of due process in student disciplinary cases and they should be consulted about the procedures that should be established and followed in cases involving positive drug tests.

Encouragement of Drug Abuse. A well-conceived drug abuse program is not complete unless there is some channel by which student athletes may complain about circumstances in which they are encouraged or induced to use performance-enhancing drugs. Ideally, such complaints could be submitted to school authorities who are independent of the athletic department and fully authorized to investigate the allegations. Such procedures should be a well-publicized part of the drug testing program. Such a complaint procedure not only provides further protection to the integrity of college athletics, but it also imposes on student athletes a responsibility to come forward and report violations of school policy. In the final analysis, such a procedure protects athletic staffs against untrue allegations of complicity made after a student has tested positive on a drug test: in such a case, the student would have to explain why he or she had not previously reported violations of the school's policy against performance-enhancing drugs.

AMERICAN COUNCIL ON EDUCATION DRAFT GUIDELINES STUDENT ATHLETE DRUG TESTING PROGRAM GUIDELINES

1. The purpose of programs for testing intercollegiate athletes for use of drugs should be to prevent use of performance-enhancing drugs that undermine the integrity of athletic competition. It is undesirable to employ drug testing programs as a means of detecting use of recreational drugs, whether their use is legal or illegal, that are not used to enhance athletic performance.

2. Drug testing programs should be sport-specific. Tests should focus upon drugs whose abuse can reasonably be anticipated because they are used to enhance performance in specific kinds of competition. Testing should also be scheduled to detect use of drugs affecting athletic competition, rather than any use of drugs at any time.

3. The drug testing program should incorporate procedures guaranteeing the accurate identification of each individual's test results and provide for additional verification of initial positive test results through extremely reliable test procedures.

4. The drug testing program should provide students for whom test results are positive with adequate notice and the right to a hearing prior to any adverse action based on the test. The more severe the potential sanction, the more formal must the hearing procedures be in affording the student the opportunity to present information in his or her defense and to challenge evidence and testimony against him or her before neutral hearing officers. Procedures should incorporate a right of review and appeal prior to the imposition of severe sanctions, such as loss of eligibility or rescission of an athletic scholarship.

5. The drug testing program should include procedures protecting the privacy of all athletes. Information disclosed by testing must be restricted to personnel responsible for administering the program. No other release of the information can be authorized without the athlete's written consent or appropriate judicial process.

6. The drug testing program should include written rules governing each step of the program, including: means of selecting students for testing; scheduling and collection of samples; testing of samples; determination that a test result is positive; means of verification of positive results; communication with students and third parties about positive tests results; counseling to be provided; sanctions to be imposed for violations of the drug use policy; applicable hearing/due process procedures; and schedule of penalties imposed for particular violations or cumulative violations.

7. The drug testing program should require students to give their written consent to the program prior to their participation in any intercollegiate athletic program. There must at this time be full disclosure to athletes of all facts surrounding the program so that each student can give his or her informed consent.

8. Any college with a testing program should provide full and complete information about the program to all intercollegiate athletic recruits early in any recruitment process (and certainly before any recruit makes a decision upon any offer from the college) and to all students prior to their enrollment.

9. The information provided to students should at a minimum include the written program itself; a full description of the purposes of the drug testing program; the procedures for collecting samples; procedures upon determination that a test result is positive, including both verification of the result and the hearing procedures; and sanctions to be imposed for the first and subsequent violations of the drug use policy as determined by the testing program. The information should be clear, complete and accurate, and acknowledge the risk that information from the testing program may be accessible to third parties.

10. The drug testing program should include procedures for training (and regularly monitoring or retraining) college personnel in all aspects of their responsibilities related to the program, including: testing techniques; the need to adhere to the governing rules and procedures; legal rights and responsibilities implicated by the program; the overriding need for confidentiality of information about drug testing results; and who is to be consulted in the event of any questions or controversies that may arise.

11. Any college with a student athlete drug testing program should also have a policy forbidding any college personnel from providing performance-enhancing drugs or encouraging or otherwise inducing student athletes to use drugs, except as specific drugs may be prescribed by qualified medical personnel for treatment of individual students. The college should also establish and publicize its procedures for handling complaints that staff or faculty have encouraged or induced use of performance enhancing drugs. Such complaints should be

processed by school personnel that are independent of the athletic department and who have full authority to investigate such allegations.

9. A body of law will no doubt develop around the problems connected with HIV testing of athletes. The issue has been raised as four high-profile athletes have disclosed that they are HIV-positive. The first athlete was basketball superstar Magic Johnson who announced that he was HIV-positive in November of 1991. Magic sat out the 1991-92 season but played in the 1992 NBA All-Star Game and in the 1992 Summer Olympics. He attempted to return to the NBA for the 1992-93 season but decided to stop his comeback after other NBA players voiced their concerns of contracting HIV from Magic. After sitting out four seasons, Magic finally returned to play basketball with the Los Angeles Lakers in February of 1996.

Professional tennis player Arthur Ashe, winner of the 1968 U.S. Open and Wimbledon in 1975, also announced that he was HIV-positive in April of 1992. Although he had known that he was HIV-positive since 1988, Ashe did not reveal his condition. However, Ashe made the announcement when he learned that news media had learned of his condition. Ashe believed that he contracted HIV from a blood transfusion during a heart operation in 1983. Ashe died from complications resulting from AIDS in 1993. *See* Sally Jenkins, *Another Battle Joined, Sports Illustrated*, April 20, 1992, at page 24; Donald L. Dell, *A Tribute to Arthur Ashe,* 3 SETON HALL J. SPORT L. 1 (1993).

Olympic diving gold-medalist Greg Louganis is another athlete who made the disclosure. Louganis' participation in the 1988 Summer Olympics evoked controversy. Louganis knew that he was HIV-positive but did not reveal it to anyone. At the Olympics, he cut his head on the diving board during a preliminary dive, blood got in the pool water thereby exposing other divers' and the U.S. team physician stitched up Louganis' cut without wearing rubber gloves. The controversy stems from the extent and degree to which other individuals could have contracted HIV and whether Louganis had a duty to reveal his condition to prevent possible transmission of the virus.

Most recently, heavyweight boxer Tommy Morrison revealed that he is HIV-positive. Morrison had been scheduled to fight in Las Vegas on February 10, 1996. The Nevada State Athletic Commission requires all boxers to be tested for HIV before fighting. When test results were positive, the fight was called off. A few days later, Morrison made an official announcement.

These athletes and their situations have raised awareness of HIV and AIDS in intercollegiate and professional athletics. Two main legal issues that are raised for athletics are (1) whether it is legally permissible to test an athlete for HIV and (2) whether it is legally permissible to prevent an athlete who is HIV-positive from participating. For scholarly treatment of these issues, *see* Tracey E. George, *Secondary Break: Dealing With AIDS in Professional Sports After the Initial Response to Magic Johnson,* 9 U. MIAMI ENT. & SPORTS L. REV. 215 (1992); Matthew J. Mitten, *AIDS and Athletics*, 3 SETON HALL J. SPORT L. 5

(1993); Daniel M. Webber, *When the 'Magic' Rubs Off: The Legal Implications of AIDS in Professional Sports,* 2 SPORTS LAW. J. 1 (1995); Roger S. Magnusson, and Hayden Opie, *HIV and Hepatitis in Sports: An Australian Legal Framework for Resolving Hard Cases,* 5 SETON HALL J. SPORT L. 69 (1995). *See also* Dan O'Kane, *HIV Tests for NCAA?,* THE TULSA WORLD, FEB. 13, 1996, at page B1.

There may be some related problems arising in connection with gender testing. *See* Pamela B. Fastiff, *Gender Verification Testing: Balancing the Rights of Female Athletes with a Scandal-Free Olympic Games,* 19 HASTING CONST. L.Q. 937 (1992).

Chapter 16

OLYMPIC AND INTERNATIONAL SPORTS RULES AND PROCEDURES

A. INTRODUCTION

The study of sports law in this casebook primarily focuses on the application of state and federal laws to individuals and sports organizations within the United States. Many amateur and professional athletes, however, also participate in international sports competitions. Elite American athletes compete with athletes from around the world in numerous international sporting competitions, including the FIFA World Cup, Wimbledon, the Tour de France, the British Open, and, of course, the Olympics. Sports leagues also include foreign teams, such as the Canadian teams which have played within the National Hockey League and Major League Baseball for years. Some sports leagues are expanding operations into foreign countries, such as the NFL's establishment of the NFL Europe football league. The growth in international sports is accompanied by lucrative financial opportunities for athlete endorsements, corporate sponsorships, merchandising, and broadcasting contracts. Accordingly, the sports lawyer must also understand the laws, governing bodies, and dispute resolution procedures for sports in the international context.

From a legal standpoint, determining the rights of athletes participating in international sports can get extremely complicated. An athlete who has intensely trained his or her entire life aspiring to compete in the Olympics or world-class competitions may be excluded, stripped of a gold medal, even banned for life from competition based on the decision of a non-governmental national or international sporting organization. In *DeFrantz v. United States Olympic Committee*, athletes argued that the USOC's boycott of the 1980 Olympics in Moscow for political reasons violated their constitutional and statutory rights to compete. The Court's response, in dismissing the lawsuit, stated that "Many of life's disappointments, even major ones (like not having the opportunity to participate in the Olympics), do not enjoy constitutional protection. This is one such instance." 492 F. Supp. 1181 (D.D.C.).

What are an athlete's legal rights to challenge decisions involving international sporting events? Do the laws of the United States have any application to protect American athletes participating in (or unlawfully excluded from) the Olympics or international competitions? Does a judgment rendered by a court in the United States bind an international sporting entity? Should a court within the United States apply domestic or foreign law in a case involving international sports? Does any court, in the U.S. or a foreign country, have a right to invalidate decisions or rules promulgated by an international sporting body? Where may (or must) an aggrieved athlete bring a complaint involving an international sporting event? Are athletes bound by rules set by an international sporting body prohibiting athletes from filing lawsuits? Who are the decision makers? The organizational structure of the Olympics and international competitions is complex, with the regulating sporting bodies operating at various national and international levels. As seen from the following cases involving several Olympic athletes, these sporting bodies often issue conflicting decisions regarding an athlete's eligibility. Determining the proper appeals process and which entity has jurisdiction and final authority has confounded and consumed the time of many.

Controversy is not new to the Olympics and international sports scene. Highly publicized issues involving athlete eligibility, drug testing and doping scandals, misconduct, discrimination, violence or other infractions, the end of amateurism, alleged corruption within certain governing sporting bodies or Olympic Host Cities, and the expanding commercialization and influence of TV and corporate sponsors, often mar or detract from the celebration of athletic contests. A major issue involving the eligibility of athletes to compete in the Olympics and in most international sports competitions concerns drug-testing and the use of performance-enhancing drugs (doping). Deciding these and other recurring eligibility issues has typically involved jurisdictional conflicts among national and international governing sporting entities.

This Chapter introduces the predominant players, legal issues, and dispute resolution processes in Olympic and international sports. In your analysis of an issue involving Olympic and international sports, consider the relationship among the various governing entities, the jurisdiction of a particular court or entity to adjudicate a dispute or to review a decision, and the procedure for seeking redress of an adverse eligibility ruling.

B. THE OLYMPIC MOVEMENT

The most prominent and long-standing international sporting competition is the Olympics. Athletes from around the world participate in the Summer or Winter Olympic Games held every four years (the Olympiad) at a different host city. While some might assert that the Olympics has become an intensely competitive and hugely commercial event, the stated purpose of the Games is to promote international understanding, diplomacy, and peace. The Olympic Games have occurred since ancient times, originally held in Olympia, Greece, from 776 B.C. until A.D. 393, and revived in 1896. According to the Olympic Charter, "the goal of the Olympic Movement is to contribute to building a peaceful and better world by educating youth through sport practised without discrimination of any kind and in the Olympic spirit, which requires mutual understanding with a spirit of friendship, solidarity, and fair play." The Olympic Charter, Fundamental Principles ¶ 6. The amateurism concept of the Olympics was modified in 1994 to permit international federations to decide whether professional athletes are eligible to compete. As of 1996, the Summer and Winter games were no longer held in the same year but two years apart.

The Olympic Movement consists of several governing bodies in an elaborate international and domestic organizational structure. At the pinnacle of this structure is the International Olympic Committee (IOC), a non-profit, non-governmental organization formed and operating in Lausanne, Switzerland under Swiss law. Under the Olympic Charter, the IOC possesses the rights to and governs the operation of the Olympics and is the "final authority on all questions concerning the Olympic Games and the Olympic Movement." Olympic Charter ¶ 23. The IOC recognizes, *inter alia*, two governing bodies which play a prominent role in the Olympic movement. International Sports Federations (IFs) administer Olympic programs for a particular sport, conduct international competitions, and define eligibility and technical rules for international competition. For each country participating in the Olympics, the IOC also recognizes a National Olympic Committee (NOC) as the "sole authorities responsible for the representation of their respective countries at the Olympic Games as well as at other events held under the patronage of the IOC." *Id.* ¶ 24(B). These NOCs in turn recognize separate national governing bodies (NGBs) within their countries responsible for each Olympic sport and the selection of athletes. NGBs are also members of their respective sport's international federation. *See* http://www.olympic.org.

The national representative of the United States to the IOC is the United States Olympic Committee (USOC), chartered by Congress under the Amateur Sports Act of 1978, to act as the exclusive governing body for U.S. participation in the Olympic and Pan-American Games. Pursuant to the Act, the USOC recognizes an amateur sports organization to act as the NGBs for each sport. In 1998, the Act was amended and renamed as the Ted Stevens Olympic and Amateur Sports Act, 36 U.S.C. § 22051 *et seq.,* available at http://www.olympic-usa.org.

Olympic athletes are subject to the rules, standards, and procedures of the IOC and the respective IF, NOC, and NGB. These entities and over 80 countries have also adopted the World Anti-Doping Code (WADA Code), administered by the World Anti-Doping Agency, increasingly prominent in the fight against doping in sport internationally. NOCs typically provide for internal dispute resolution procedures and arbitration options. The Amateur Sports Act charges the USOC "to establish and maintain provisions . . . for the swift and equitable resolution of disputes" involving athletes and its member organizations, yet precludes a court from granting injunctive relief within 21 days of the start of an Olympic event. The Act also requires that the USOC hire an ombudsman to provide independent advice to athletes, at no cost, about applicable laws and procedures. *Id.* § 220509. The Act authorizes an aggrieved party to appeal an NGB or USOC determination to the American Arbitration Association (AAA) for a binding determination. *Id.* § 220529. As a prerequisite, an athlete must usually comply with NGB rules for challenging eligibility decisions. Recourse through the judicial system provides a limited option, as applicable administrative remedies must generally be exhausted. While Congress may have envisioned a streamlined procedure for dispute resolution, Olympic athletes and the USOC must operate in a larger international arena. It is within this larger context of overlapping jurisdictions that the potential for conflict between athletes and governing bodies reaches its peak. For example, the IF, which autonomously supervises a particular sport at the international level (subject only to the limitations in the Olympic Charter), may have different rules, procedures, or sanctions, which vary or operate independently from the domestic process. The IOC also has established the Court of Arbitration for Sport (CAS), an international arbitration tribunal based in Switzerland and operating under Swiss law, to adjudicate sports-related disputes in accordance with the Code of Sports-related Arbitration. To an athlete with eligibility concerns, seeking recourse within the Olympic Movement may appear to be a bad game of Abbott & Costello's "Who's on First?" Could this be said of Butch Reynolds, *infra*?

C. ADJUDICATION OF OLYMPICS-RELATED DISPUTES PROBLEM

Jerry Billings is a junior at Middle State University, a Division I member of the NCAA, and a world class swimmer. Last year he won the United States Swimming National Championships in the 100 and 200-meter butterfly. However, in the recently completed Olympic Trials he failed to qualify in either event. He finished third in the 200-meter race, .01 second behind the second place finisher. The top two finishers qualified to go to the Olympics. Billings is convinced that he should have qualified for the team and has come to your law firm seeking legal assistance. He believes that the winner of the 200 used an "illegal" kick en route to his victory. He lodged a complaint with race officials, but it was rejected. He also questions the accuracy of the electronic touch pad at the finish point of the race. He maintains that the video of the race shows that he actually finished second. What advice do you give to Billings as to his options?

CASE FILE

REYNOLDS v. INTERNATIONAL AMATEUR ATHLETIC FEDERATION

23 F.3d 1110 (6th Cir.), *cert. denied*, 513 U.S. 962 (1994)

KENNEDY and MILBURN, Circuit Judges; and LIVELY, Senior Circuit Judge.

LIVELY, Senior Circuit Judge.

The International Amateur Athletic Federation (IAAF) appeals the district court's denial of its motion to quash garnishment proceedings and vacate a default judgment and permanent injunction previously entered by the district court. As it did before the district court, the IAAF argues on appeal that the district court had neither subject matter jurisdiction nor personal jurisdiction over the IAAF in the proceedings resulting in the default judgment and permanent injunction.

I.

A.

Harry "Butch" Reynolds is a world-class sprinter who regularly participates in international track and field meets. Reynolds currently holds the individual world record in the 400 meters, is a member of the world record holding 4x400 relay team, and is a gold and silver medalist from the 1988 Olympics.

On August 12, 1990, Reynolds ran in the "Hercules '90" meet in Monte Carlo, Monaco. Immediately after the competition, Reynolds was tested for illegal performance-enhancing drugs as part of a random drug test conducted after all international track meets. Two different samples of Reynolds' urine were sent to Paris for analysis. Each sample contained trace amounts of the steroid Nandrolone, a drug banned by international track regulations created by the IAAF.

The IAAF is an unincorporated association based in London, England, and is made up of track and field organizations representing 205 nations and territories. Its purpose is to coordinate and control track and field athletes and competitions throughout the world. The IAAF has no offices in the United States, and holds no track meets in Ohio, where Reynolds brought this action. One member of the IAAF is The Athletics Congress of the United States, Inc. (TAC) [now USA Track & Field], the United States national governing body for track and field. . . .

After Reynolds' positive drug test, the IAAF banned him from all international track events for two years, thereby eliminating his hopes for competing in the 1992 Olympics in Barcelona.

The IAAF issued a press release on November 5, 1990, stating that Reynolds was tested following the Monte Carlo meet and that "the Paris laboratory revealed metabolites of the banned substance Nandrolone and a second analysis carried out on the 12th October 1990 confirmed their presence." The release went on to say that Reynolds had been suspended and offered a hearing by TAC, the date of which had not been set. American sports publications and newspapers picked up the release and reported Reynolds' suspension as news items.

B.

Reynolds immediately brought suit in the Southern District of Ohio, arguing that the drug test was given negligently, and provided an erroneous result. The court dismissed one claim and stayed the remainder of the case after finding that Reynolds failed to exhaust administrative remedies provided by the Amateur Sports Act, 36 U.S.C. §§ 371-396 and TAC. Reynolds appealed the district court's decision. This court agreed with the exhaustion requirement but vacated the judgment and directed that the entire case be dismissed for lack of subject matter jurisdiction. *Reynolds v. TAC*, 935 F.2d 270 (6th Cir. 1991).

In an attempt to exhaust his administrative remedies, Reynolds participated in an independent arbitration before an AAA panel in June of 1991. Reynolds took this action under the Amateur Sports Act and the United States Olympic Committee Constitution. The AAA arbitrator rendered a decision fully exonerating Reynolds; the arbitrator found strong evidence that the urine samples provided to the Paris laboratory were not Reynolds'. However, the IAAF refused to acknowledge the arbitrator's decision because the arbitration was not conducted under IAAF rules. Accordingly, the IAAF refused to lift Reynolds' two year suspension.

Reynolds then appealed his suspension to TAC, as required by IAAF rules. TAC held a hearing on September 13, 1991. After thoroughly examining the evidence and deliberating for two weeks, the TAC Doping Control Review Board completely exonerated Reynolds, stating that:

> after hearing the matters before it, the testimony of witnesses and expert witnesses of both sides, documents and exhibits, [we] find that Mr. Harry "Butch" Reynolds has cast substantial doubt on the validity of the drug test attributed to him.

Still not satisfied, the IAAF reopened Reynolds' case pursuant to IAAF Rule 20(3)(ii), which allows the IAAF to conduct an independent arbitration where it appears that one of its member foundations such as TAC has "misdirected itself." The IAAF arbitration was held on May 10 and 11, 1992, in London, England (the London Arbitration). The parties to the arbitration proceeding were the IAAF and TAC. Reynolds attended and testified at the hearing, and Reynolds' attorneys participated in the proceedings before the IAAF arbitration board, including examining and cross-examining witnesses. At the conclusion of the hearing, the IAAF arbitral panel found that the drug tests were valid, and that there was "no doubt" as to Reynolds' guilt. As a result, the panel upheld Reynolds' two year suspension.

II.

A.

Soon after the IAAF made its final decision, Reynolds filed the present action in the Southern District of Ohio alleging four different state law causes of action: breach of contract, breach of contractual due process, defamation, and tortious interference with business relations. Reynolds sought monetary damages, and a temporary restraining order that would allow him to compete in races leading to the U.S. Olympic trials on June 20, 1992. The IAAF refused to appear in the case, stating in a letter to Reynolds' attorney that the district court had no jurisdiction over the IAAF. The district court issued a temporary restraining order that prevented the IAAF from interfering with Reynolds' attempt to make the Olympic tryouts. Despite IAAF threats to both Reynolds and TAC, Reynolds ran in a few races and qualified to compete in the U.S. Olympic trials in New Orleans.

On June 17, 1992, the district court held a preliminary injunction hearing to decide if Reynolds should compete in the June 20 Olympic trials. The IAAF refused to appear, but TAC intervened to oppose Reynolds. On June 19, the district court issued a preliminary injunction after finding that it had personal jurisdiction over the IAAF and that Reynolds was likely to succeed on the merits of his claims. That afternoon, TAC filed a motion with the Sixth Circuit Court of Appeals, asking for an emergency stay of the district court's decision. At 7:00 that evening, Judge Siler granted the stay. The next morning, Reynolds filed an emergency motion with Supreme Court Justice John Paul Stevens, asking for an order vacating Judge Siler's emergency stay. Justice Stevens granted Reynolds' request, finding that the District Court's opinion was "persuasive." *Reynolds v. IAAF*, 112 S. Ct. 2512 (1992).

Despite these rulings, the IAAF announced that every athlete who competed with Reynolds at the U.S. Olympic trials would be ineligible to compete in the Barcelona Olympics. Reynolds' events were temporarily postponed while TAC filed an application to the full Supreme Court to vacate Justice Stevens' stay. The Court denied TAC's request, and Reynolds was eventually allowed to compete in the Olympic trials, after an agreement was reached between the U.S. Olympic Committee and the IAAF. Reynolds made the Olympic team as an alternate for the 400 meter relay. However, the IAAF refused to let Reynolds compete at the 1992 Olympics, and TAC removed him from the U.S. Olympic team roster. Moreover, the IAAF increased Reynolds' two year suspension by four months as punishment for participating in the U.S. Olympic trials.

B.

On September 28, 1992, Reynolds filed a supplemental complaint with the district court, outlining the above events. The IAAF did not respond to Reynolds' complaint and TAC did not appear in the default proceedings. After the IAAF was given full notice, the court entered a default judgment in Reynolds' favor. Soon afterward, the district court held a hearing to determine damages. Again, the IAAF was provided notice but refused to appear. On December 3, 1992, the district court issued an opinion awarding Reynolds $27,356,008, including treble punitive damages. The district court found that the IAAF "acted with ill will and a spirit of revenge towards Mr. Reynolds." Particular acts by the IAAF cited by the district court included "the suppression of evidence, threats levied against Reynolds and his fellow athletes, and the extension of Reynolds' suspension for an additional four months." More than $20,000,000 of the award was punitive damages for these acts.

The district court found that it had diversity jurisdiction in this case because Reynolds is a citizen of Ohio and the IAAF is a foreign association. The IAAF is an unincorporated association, and the district court reasoned that the IAAF is deemed to be a citizen of all states where its members are domiciled. The court held that diversity jurisdiction was proper because no IAAF members are citizens of Ohio. The district court also found that it had personal jurisdiction over the IAAF. The court held that the Ohio long-arm statute was satisfied because the IAAF transacted business with Reynolds in Ohio, and the IAAF's public announcement of Reynolds' positive drug test adversely affected Reynolds in Ohio. The court held that the IAAF had the required minimum contacts with Ohio after finding that TAC acted as the IAAF's agent in the United States.

C.

On February 17, 1993, Reynolds began garnishment proceedings against four corporations with connections to the IAAF. The IAAF finally appeared at a garnishment hearing before the district court, and later filed a "Motion to Quash Garnishment Proceedings and To Vacate the Default Judgment" pursuant to FED. R. CIV. P. 60(b)(4). In its motion, the IAAF contended that the court lacked personal and subject matter jurisdiction. Before the motion was decided, the IAAF filed a recusal motion, arguing that previous opinions by the court put the district judge's impartiality into question.

The district court denied all motions on July 13, 1993. The court found that it had jurisdiction to overturn the IAAF's arbitration decision despite the United States' participation in the United Nations Convention on the Recognition and Enforcement of Foreign Arbitral Awards (the Convention). *See* 9 U.S.C. § 201, *et seq*. The text of the Convention appears following 9 U.S.C.A. § 201. The Convention provides that recognition and enforcement of an award may be refused if it "has been set aside or suspended by a competent authority of the country in which, or under the law of which, that award was made." Convention, Article V 1(e). The district court found that the Convention only applies where an agreement to arbitrate is in writing and signed by both parties — preconditions not present in the instant case.

The IAAF appeals from denial of its motions. Because it contends that the district court lacked jurisdiction in the earlier proceedings, the IAAF seeks to reverse the money judgment and injunction as well.

III.

Because we have concluded that the district court lacked personal jurisdiction over the IAAF, the sole defendant in this case, it is not necessary to consider the other issues presented and argued by the parties.

A.

The district court found that it had personal jurisdiction over the IAAF under Ohio's longarm statute. Under this statute a nonresident may be sued in an Ohio court on a cause of action arising from the nonresident's:

(1) Transacting any business in this state . . .;

(3) Causing tortious injury by an act or omission in this state . . .;

(6) Causing tortious injury in this state to any person by an act outside this state committed with the purpose of injuring persons, when he might reasonably have expected that some person would be injured thereby in this state. . . .

Ohio Revised Code (O.R.C.) § 2307.382. The district court found the IAAF amenable to suit under subsection (1) on Reynolds' contract claims and under subsections (3) and (6) on his claims of defamation and tortious interference with business relations.

* * *

B.

When determining whether there is personal jurisdiction over a defendant, a federal court must apply the law of the state in which it sits, subject to constitutional limitations. . . .

* * *

Under the Constitution, personal jurisdiction over a defendant arises from "certain minimum contacts with [the forum] such that maintenance of the suit does not offend 'traditional notions of fair play and substantial justice.'" *International Shoe Co. v. Washington*, 326 U.S. 310 (1945). Depending on the type of minimum contacts in a case, personal jurisdiction can be either general or specific. Reynolds relies on specific jurisdiction because he claims that jurisdiction arose out of the IAAF's alleged wrongful acts in Ohio.

The Sixth Circuit has established a three-part test for determining whether specific jurisdiction may be exercised: First, the defendant must purposefully avail himself of the privilege of acting in the forum state or causing a consequence in the forum state. Second, the cause of action must arise from the defendant's activities there. Finally, the acts of the defendant or consequences caused by the defendant must have a substantial enough connection with the forum to make the exercise of jurisdiction over the defendant reasonable.

* * *

IV.

This court reviews issues of personal jurisdiction de novo. Nevertheless, this appeal is from denial of the IAAF's Rule 60(b) motion to set aside a default judgment. We review the denial of that motion under the abuse of discretion standard.

A.

The district court held that TAC was the agent of the IAAF and that TAC had sufficient minimum contacts with Ohio to bring the IAAF under the "transacting business" provisions of the Ohio long-arm statute. The IAAF insists that

TAC, though a member of the IAAF, is an autonomous body that acts for itself within the United States. The record is to the contrary. TAC represents the IAAF in dealings with American athletes who participate in international events. Its bylaws state that "the purposes of this Congress are to act as the national governing body for athletes in the United States, and to act as the IAAF member in the United States." TAC's president, Frank Greenberg, testified that TAC is "the exclusive representative of [the IAAF] in this country," and that "part of that obligation, part of being the named representative is that [TAC] must follow [IAAF] rules."

Furthermore, the facts in this case demonstrate the IAAF's control over TAC. After receiving the results of the two urine tests and after suspending Reynolds, the IAAF did not notify Reynolds. Instead it told TAC to notify Reynolds and look into the matter, even though the meet involved was sponsored by the IAAF. Reynolds requested documents directly from the IAAF, but the IAAF told Reynolds that all document requests must be made through TAC. As a result, all IAAF documents that Reynolds received came through TAC. Moreover, after the Supreme Court held that Reynolds could compete in the U.S. Olympic Trials, the IAAF told TAC to "take all necessary steps to ensure that Mr. Reynolds does not so compete." While it is true that TAC supported Reynolds at the London Arbitration, it was not there on his behalf, but as a member of the IAAF that was responding under the IAAF's rules. Thus, we agree with the district court that TAC is an agent of the IAAF.

Nevertheless, unless TAC had minimum contacts with Ohio in relation to the "contract" between the IAAF and Reynolds, the court erred in premising jurisdiction of TAC's agency.

B.

The Supreme Court has spoken with respect to the significance of a contractual relationship between an in-state plaintiff and an out-of-state defendant. The Court has held that a contract with an out-of-state party, standing alone, is not sufficient to establish minimum contacts. Instead, to determine whether a party purposefully availed itself of a forum a court must evaluate "prior negotiations and contemplated future consequences, along with the terms of the contract and the parties' actual course of dealing. . . ." In the instant case, there were no negotiations between Reynolds and the IAAF prior to "execution" of the contract. The IAAF arguably had a minimal course of dealing with Reynolds in Ohio, providing money to Reynolds in Ohio to travel to track events. However, there is no real evidence that a contract was negotiated in Ohio, created in Ohio, performed in Ohio, or breached in Ohio.

Without further evidence concerning the purported contract, we are unable to agree that the district court had personal jurisdiction over the IAAF on the contract claims, either based on its own activities or those of TAC.

Moreover, the IAAF could not reasonably anticipate being sued in Ohio because of its alleged business dealings with Reynolds. It did not regularly transact or solicit business in Ohio or engage "in any other persistent course of conduct" there. The IAAF cannot foresee being required to defend in every forum where one of its athletes is present. Reynolds' Ohio residence is merely fortuitous and "unilateral activity of [the plaintiff] is not an appropriate consideration when determining whether a defendant has sufficient contacts with a forum State to justify an assertion of jurisdiction." Instead, minimum contacts can only be formed by "an action of the defendant purposefully directed toward the forum State."

The IAAF's contact with Ohio through letters and phone calls was also insufficient to support jurisdiction. Reynolds asked the IAAF for information, but such unilateral action by a plaintiff does not render the defendant amenable to suit in the plaintiff's home forum. Moreover, "the use of interstate facilities such as the telephone and mail is a 'secondary or ancillary' factor and 'cannot alone provide the minimum contacts required by due process.'" Although various IAAF officials sent correspondence or made telephone calls to Ohio, these communications are insufficient to establish purposeful availment. It is the "quality" of such contacts, "not their number or their status as pre- or post-agreement communications" that determines whether they constitute purposeful availment. That quality is missing here.

In short, the IAAF is based in England, owns no property and transacts no business in Ohio, and does not supervise U.S. athletes in Ohio or elsewhere. Its contacts with Reynolds in Ohio are superficial, and are insufficient to create the requisite minimum contacts for personal jurisdiction.

Even if the IAAF purposefully availed itself of Ohio privileges, the claims against the IAAF must arise out of the IAAF's activities in Ohio. In general, "an action will be deemed not to have arisen from the defendant's contacts with the forum state only when they are unrelated to the operative facts of the controversy." The controversial urine sample was taken in Monaco, analyzed in France, and confirmed by an arbitration hearing in England. The district court found that the IAAF breached Reynolds' contract in Ohio, but there is no evidence of a contract made, performed, or breached in Ohio. Accordingly, Reynolds' contract claim did not arise out of the IAAF's contacts with Ohio. All of the activities relied upon by the district court as taking place in Ohio occurred after the activities in Europe upon which Reynolds bases his contract claims. These activities do not constitute a basis for finding personal jurisdiction under subsection (1) for "transacting business" in Ohio.

V.

The district court found that the IAAF was subject to personal jurisdiction under the provision of the Ohio long-arm statute which provides that a party is amenable to suit by "causing tortious injury in this state . . . by an act outside this state." O.R.C. § 2307.382(A)(6). A tort action can be brought in the location where the injury is suffered. Reynolds claimed a loss of more than $4,000,000 in Ohio because of the IAAF's false press release and the district court specifically found that the injury to Reynolds was in Ohio, holding "the IAAF intentionally and purposefully directed their tortious acts toward Plaintiff, and such acts had a devastating effect upon Plaintiff." More needs to be demonstrated, however. The question remains whether the IAAF, in making the alleged defamatory statement in England, had minimum contacts with Ohio.

The leading case on this issue is *Calder v. Jones*, 465 U.S. 783 (1984). In *Calder*, a professional entertainer sued the writers and editors of a Florida magazine for libel in a California court. . . . Because the defendants' intentional actions were aimed at California and the brunt of the harm was felt there, the Court concluded that the defendants could reasonably anticipate being haled into court in California.

We find *Calder* distinguishable for several reasons. First, the press release concerned Reynolds' activities in Monaco, not Ohio. Second, the source of the controversial report was the drug sample taken in Monaco and the laboratory testing in France. Third, Reynolds is an international athlete whose professional reputation is not centered in Ohio. Fourth, the defendant itself did not publish or circulate the report in Ohio; Ohio periodicals disseminated the report. Fifth, Ohio was not the "focal point" of the press release. The fact that the IAAF could foresee that the report would be circulated and have an effect in Ohio is not, in itself, enough to create personal jurisdiction. Finally, although Reynolds lost Ohio corporate endorsement contracts and appearance fees in Ohio, there is no evidence that the IAAF knew of the contracts or of their Ohio origin. Calder is a much more compelling case for finding personal jurisdiction.

Reynolds argues, however, that his claims arose out of the IAAF's connection with Ohio because the IAAF intentionally defamed him and interfered with his Ohio business relationships. Under this theory, the IAAF knew that the worldwide media would carry the report and that the brunt of the injury would occur in Ohio.

Even accepting that the IAAF could foresee that its report would be disseminated in Ohio, however, the IAAF would not be subject to personal jurisdiction in Ohio. The press release that the IAAF issued in London did not directly accuse Reynolds of using forbidden substances. It recited the fact that the Paris laboratory had reported a positive drug test and that Reynolds had been suspended and offered a hearing. We cannot hold that this act of the IAAF satisfied the requirements of the Ohio statute, or that permitting the IAAF to be sued in Ohio for the press release would comport with due process.

VI.

Relying on F.R.C.P. § 12(h)(1) (waiver of defenses), the district court found that the IAAF waived its right to contest personal jurisdiction. We do not agree. Under F.R.C.P 12(h), a party waives the right to contest personal jurisdiction by failing to raise the issue when making a responsive pleading or a general appearance. However, courts have generally held that "defects in personal jurisdiction . . . are not waived by default when a party fails to appear or to respond." The IAAF did not file a responsive pleading or enter a general appearance. Accordingly, the district court incorrectly decided that the IAAF waived its personal jurisdiction defense by failing to appear until after the default judgment was entered.

The district court also held that the IAAF waived its objection to personal jurisdiction by reason of TAC's intervention in this action. After Reynolds lost in the London arbitration proceeding, he filed a motion for preliminary injunction to let him race in the United States Olympic Trials. The IAAF did not respond and did not appear at the injunction hearing, but TAC intervened as a defendant.

The key to determining whether the IAAF waived its personal jurisdiction defense through TAC's intervention is whether the IAAF authorized TAC to appear in its place. In its request to intervene, TAC argued that it was required to uphold IAAF regulations, and contended that: TAC, a member of the IAAF . . . is bound by the decision declaring plaintiff ineligible; and thus under the Amateur Sports Act, TAC may not permit him to participate in the Olympic Trials.

TAC was carrying out its statutory duty under the Amateur Sports Act and was not acting as the IAAF's agent when it intervened. There is no indication that the IAAF authorized or even requested TAC to appear. Indeed, the IAAF had consistently refused to appear and had taken the position that the district court lacked jurisdiction over the entire proceeding. We conclude that TAC appeared solely in its role as the national governing body under the Amateur Sports Act.

CONCLUSION

In conclusion, we do not believe that holding the IAAF amenable to suit in an Ohio court under the facts of this case comports with "traditional notions of fair play and substantial justice." The IAAF stated in its brief and at oral argument that it will not challenge the jurisdiction of English courts to determine the validity of the London Arbitration award if Reynolds seeks to have it set aside in the courts of that country.

* * *

WALTON-FLOYD v. UNITED STATES OLYMPIC COMMITTEE

965 S.W.2d 35 (Tex. App. 1998)

Eric Andell, Justice.

The appellant, Delisa Walton-Floyd, appeals a summary judgment granted in favor of the United States Olympic Committee (USOC). We are asked to determine whether the USOC owed Mrs. Floyd a duty pursuant to federal statutory law and under Texas common law. In seven points of error, Walton-Floyd asserts: 1) the USOC's summary judgment motion did not address all her causes of action making the final summary judgment granted in this case inappropriate, 2) the Amateur Sports Act of 1978, 36 U.S.C. §§ 371-96 (1988) (the Act) creates an implied right of action for damages, 3) the USOC assumed a duty to Floyd through a voluntary course of action, 4) the USOC negligently misrepresented the nature of a drug when Floyd made an inquiry about it to the USOC's drug hotline, 5) damages are not limited based on the USOC's status as a charitable organization, and 6) the USOC was grossly negligent and thus liable for exemplary damages. We affirm.

Factual Summary

The USOC serves as the coordinating body for amateur athletics in the United States for international amateur athletic competitions. It represents the United States concerning Olympic activity with the International Olympic Committee and the Pan-American Sports Organization. 36 U.S.C. § 375(1) & (2). It has the power to recognize amateur sports organizations as National Governing Bodies (NGB's) for any sport in the Olympics or Pan-American games. *Id.* § 375(4). The USOC is designed to resolve disputes among athletes and sports organizations or between competing sports organizations and provide uniformity in the area of amateur athletics, thus protecting the rights of amateur athletes to compete. Furthermore, it has the power to sue and be sued.

The USOC recognizes The Athletic Congress (TAC) as the NGB in the area of track and field. TAC coordinates and conducts track and field competitions to ensure these competitions are in compliance with the rules and regulations promulgated by the International Amateur Athletic Federation (IAAF). In order to ensure fair competition, the IAAF implemented rules that restrict athletes participating under its auspices from using certain performance enhancing drugs. The IAAF created a list of prohibited substances. An athlete who tests positive for one of the banned substances is subject to harsh penalties, including the suspension of the athlete from all IAAF events. The USOC issued a card listing many of the more common substances on the banned list. A warning is included on this card stating:

> This list is not complete. It is the athlete's responsibility to check the status of all medications. CALL THE USOC HOTLINE 1-800-233-0393.

This warning is the gravamen of Walton-Floyd's complaint. In theory, the USOC established the drug hotline so athletes may discover whether the IAAF prohibits certain medications. The record is unclear whether the USOC reports directly from the IAAF's list, some other list, or a list of its own creation.

Walton-Floyd is a middle-distance runner whose specialty is the 800 meters. During the 1980's, she consistently ranked among the top 10 in the United States for the 800 meters. In 1988, she placed fifth in the Seoul Olympic Games. After the 1988 Olympics, Walton-Floyd took a year off from training and competing to have a child. Sometime after her pregnancy, she resumed training with her husband, Stanley Floyd, as her coach.

Once a track and field athlete, Mr. Floyd was familiar with the track circuit. From his years of traveling to track events and exposure to other athletes, he had become aware of a drug called Sydnocarb. Mr. Floyd wanted to find a carbohydrate supplement for his wife as he was concerned that such a high-carbohydrate diet might cause weight problems.

While in Germany in January 1991, Mr. Floyd met with a man known as Hans. Mr. Floyd traded some vitamin B12 to Hans for a box of Sydnocarb. Mr. Floyd testified the box contained the label "Sydnocarbi" and that below this word appeared some writing, which he believed to be Russian, along with the letters "CCCP." Mr. Floyd testified he could not read this writing and he did not have it translated. He also stated the box did not otherwise contain instructions on how to use the medication or a list of ingredients comprising each Sydnocarb pill. The box of Sydnocarb contained fifty white pills, each about the size of an Actifed, wrapped in plastic bubbles sealed by aluminum. The box contained five plastic sheets with ten pills per sheet. Mr. Floyd testified this was the only box of Sydnocarb he bought.

Mr. Floyd testified that at some point around the time he acquired the Sydnocarb, he called the USOC hotline to inquire about its status. He asserts that the USOC operator told him Sydnocarb was not on the banned list. The operator told him Sydnocarb was a carbohydrate supplement, thus confirming what he knew about the drug. The hotline operator, however, did not specifically tell Mr. Floyd that Sydnocarb was safe to use, nor did she give him any other assurances about it. Stanley recommended to his wife that she supplement her workout with Sydnocarb. She testified she also called the hotline. The USOC operator essentially repeated the same assurances communicated to Mr. Floyd — that Sydnocarb was not on the banned list and represented a carbohydrate supplement. She did not receive any further assurances about Sydnocarb from the USOC. As a result of her husband's recommendation and this phone call to the hotline, Walton-Floyd began using Sydnocarb. She and her husband testified they called the hotline on other occasions during the spring and summer of 1991 to inquire about the status of Sydnocarb. Each time, the USOC operator told them the banned list did not contain Sydnocarb, confirming their previous inquiries. Once when Walton-Floyd was suffering from severe menstrual cramping, she called the hotline to inquire about Midol and also whether Sydnocarb could be the cause of her severe cramping. The hotline operator assured her that Sydnocarb was not producing her symptoms.

In 1991, Walton-Floyd won the national championship for the 800 meters, qualifying her for the 1992 Olympic trials in New Orleans. In August 1991, Walton-Floyd competed in the IAAF World Championships in Tokyo, Japan. After her semi-final heat in the 800 meters, she took a drug test. She provided the meet officials with a urine sample, which was divided into an A sample and a B sample. The A sample tested positive for amphetamines, a prohibited substance. IAAF officials informed Walton-Floyd of the test results and invited her to attend a second testing of the B sample. The B sample also resulted in a positive test for amphetamines. The IAAF conveyed the test results to TAC, which suspended Walton-Floyd from further competition. Though the TAC appeals board recommended her immediate reinstatement, the appeals board could not reinstate Walton-Floyd without ignoring the IAAF "contamination rule," which denies eligibility to any athlete who has used a prohibited substance. Consequently, TAC suspended Walton-Floyd from amateur track and field for four years. Sometime after the drug test, she discovered not only that Sydnocarb was the apparent source of the amphetamines in her system but also that Sydnocarb was a type of antidepressant.

Walton-Floyd filed this lawsuit alleging negligence on the part of USOC for the following acts and omissions:

(a) providing her with erroneous and false information through the hotline;

(b) failing to properly inform and warn her of the possible effect of ingesting Sydnocarb;

(c) failing to advise her that the use of Sydnocarb would result in the failure of the IAAF drug test;

(d) providing her with the information that Sydnocarb was a carbohydrate supplement and not a substance on the banned list;

(e) failing to inform and educate its hotline personnel concerning Sydnocarb and the risk involved in using it;

(f) failing to keep its list of banned substances up to date to include Sydnocarb despite actual knowledge and industry knowledge concerning Sydnocarb and the fact that it represented an amphetamine derivative;

(g) failing to test or research the drug Sydnocarb despite calls from athletes inquiring whether or not the drug could be used; and

(h) failing to maintain a system that would accurately identify the composition of drugs brought to its attention by athletes inquiring through the hotline.

Furthermore, she alleged negligence on the part of USOC for breaching various duties prescribed by the Act. Finally, she alleged that the USOC owed her a duty, because the USOC represented itself as an expert in the field of illegal substances, and it instructed athletes to use its hotline to obtain information on those substances, provide them with accurate information, and not intentionally or negligently mislead them in regard to the risk of taking a possible prohibited substance.

In response, the USOC moved for summary judgment based on the following grounds:

(1) the Act does not permit a private cause of action for damages, and it does not create any legal duties to prevent an athlete from experimenting with drugs; therefore, federal law precludes such actions;

(2) Floyd's cause of action for negligent misrepresentation is barred because no evidence exists as to whether the USOC possessed a pecuniary interest in the hotline;

(3) the damages asserted by Floyd are limited under Texas law, because the USOC represents a charitable organization;

(4) no evidence of malice exists to support Floyd's claim for punitive damages.

The USOC filed a brief outlining its arguments in regard to these grounds contemporaneously with this motion for summary judgment. Walton-Floyd filed a response to this motion asserting, with respect to the duties owed to her by the USOC, that the Act: 1) creates an implied cause of action for damages, and even absent such a private right of action in the Act, one who voluntarily undertakes an affirmative course of action for the benefit of another owes a duty of reasonable care, and 2) a negligent misrepresentation claim does not require a pecuniary interest if the defendant conveys the information in the course of business. The USOC filed a reply to this response addressing Walton-Floyd's arguments.

Standard of Review

Summary judgment is proper only when a movant establishes that there is no genuine issue of material fact and that the movant is entitled to judgment as a matter of law. . . .

Discussion

In seven points of error, Floyd asserts: 1) the USOC owed her a duty pursuant to federal statutory law and Texas common law, 2) fact issues exist whether the USOC had breached those duties, 3) fact issues exist whether damages can be limited, and 4) fact issues exist whether the USOC was grossly negligent. Because we hold that the USOC did not owe Floyd a duty under any of the theories pled, we do not address her remaining points of error concerning the existence of factual issues.

Private Right of Action Under the Amateur Sports Act

In her first point of error, Walton-Floyd maintains the Act provides for an implied private cause of action that permits the recovery of monetary damages based upon the failure of the USOC to comply with the duties imposed upon it by Congress. Walton-Floyd contends the Act adopted and incorporated these duties and that Congress would not have supplied the Act with the specific provision that the USOC could be sued if it did not intend to create a private cause of action. 36 U.S.C. § 375(a)(6). The USOC argues the Act does not imply a private cause of action based on the Act's legislative history, underlying purposes, and caselaw.

To determine whether a statute contains an implied cause of action, the Supreme Court prescribes four factors: (1) whether the plaintiff is a member of a class for whose special benefit the statute was enacted, (2) whether there is an indication of Congress' intent to create or deny a private remedy, (3) whether a private remedy would be consistent with the statute's underlying purposes, and (4) whether the cause of action traditionally is relegated to state law. *Cort v. Ash*, 422 U.S. 66 (1975). The above factors do not require the same weight, and the central inquiry remains whether Congress intended to create, either expressly or by implication, a private cause of action. Once Congress' intent is determined, there is no need to work through all four of the factors in *Cort*.

No Texas court has considered this issue and we turn to federal caselaw on this subject. Federal courts that have interpreted the Act and its legislative history have held no private cause of action exists against the USOC. *Oldfield v. The Athletic Congress*, 779 F.2d 505 (9th Cir. 1985); *Michels v. United States Olympic Committee*, 741 F.2d 155 (7th Cir. 1984); *DeFrantz v. United States Olympic Committee*, 492 F. Supp. 1181 (D.D.C. 1980); *Martinez v. United States Olympic Committee*, 802 F.2d 1275 (10th Cir. 1986).

In analyzing the legislative history of the Act, these courts have looked to the following four factors to determine that Congress did not intend to imply a private cause of action:

1) There is a strong preference that athletes resolve their disputes through the internal mechanisms provided by the USOC rather than the judicial system.
2) There are express provisions for causes of actions for certain violations set out within the Act.
3) The right to a private cause of action against the USOC is set out in the USOC Constitution, which is not part of the Act and is not what Congress approved.
4) The original Act was designed to settle disputes between organizations seeking recognition as NGB's for a particular sport and shield amateur athletes from suffering harm because of these internal conflicts. When it was rechartered in 1978, the Act outlined internal grievance procedures for athletes.

In *Oldfield*, TAC denied an amateur shot put athlete, who signed a professional contract . . ., the attempt to reestablish amateur status four years later [and] deemed Oldfield ineligible to compete in the 1984 Olympic Trials. *Oldfield*, 779 F.2d at 506. Oldfield brought suit for an injunction and damages against TAC and USOC, alleging that the two organizations had arbitrarily denied him the right to compete in violation of the Act. While the plaintiff conceded no express right existed, he contended that an inferred right allowing a private cause of action existed.

The Ninth Circuit affirmed the summary judgment in favor of the USOC. In its reasoning the court considered the legislative history of the Act and Congress's intent in implementing it. The court believed the Act, as originally proposed, contained a provision referred to as the "Amateur Athletes' Bill of Rights," which expressly granted athletes the power to contest in federal court the actions of any sports organization that threatened to deny them the opportunity to participate. The court noted that on the final version of the Act, Congress withdrew the provision allowing athletes to sue in federal court from the bill and inserted it in the USOC Constitution. The court in *Oldfield* noted the USOC Constitution is not part of the Act, and thus, the provision allowing suits cannot be construed as allowing private individuals to litigate in federal court.

In *Michels*, the International Weightlifting Federation (IWF) suspended a weightlifter for two years because drug test results revealed an impermissible testosterone level. The plaintiff brought suit against the IWF, the U.S. Wrestling Federation, and the USOC, contending the USOC violated the Act. The plaintiff claimed the test results were invalid and he had a right to a hearing on the matter. Based on the Act's legislative history, the Seventh Circuit held that the Act contained no private right of action to require the USOC to hold a hearing. The court noted that Congress's refusal to insert the bill of rights provision into the final version indicates that it considered and then rejected a cause of action for athletes to enforce the Act's provisions. In his concurring opinion, Judge Richard Posner suggested that in light of the Act's provisions to resolve disputes internally, the Act is better equipped to handle disputes involving athletes. "There can be few less suitable bodies than the federal courts for determining the eligibility or the procedures for determining eligibility, of athletes to participate in the Olympic Games."

The court in *DeFrantz* considered the case of twenty-five athletes and one executive member of the USOC who filed a claim against the USOC for an injunction prohibiting the USOC from implementing a USOC House of Delegates resolution to decline a 1980 Moscow Summer Olympics invitation. The Court held the Act did not confer an enforceable right to an amateur athlete to compete in Olympic competition as the Act confers the broad authority to the USOC to make all decisions regarding competitions and participation. Furthermore, even if such a right to compete existed, the court noted that the Act does not imply a private cause of action to enforce such a right. In its reasoning, the court noted that the Act sought to protect the opportunity for athletes to compete and prevent rivalries between sports organizations. The court looked to 36 U.S.C. § 395 and found established procedures for the internal consideration and resolution of jurisdictional and eligibility issues. The court also cited 36 U.S.C. § 395(c)(1), which grants any aggrieved party the right to review by arbitration after exhaustion of other USOC remedies, as confirming the Act's intent to handle disputes internally.

Finally, in *Martinez*, a personal representative of the estate of an amateur boxer, who died from injuries sustained in a boxing tournament, filed a wrongful death action against the USOC and other various organizations responsible for the event. The Tenth Circuit, relying on the analysis of the Act's legislative history in *DeFrantz*, dismissed the suit for failure to state a federal cause of action. The Court found no indication in the Act that Congress intended the USOC to be liable to athletes injured while competing in events not fully controlled by the USOC.

Walton-Floyd attempts to distinguish the above cases on the basis of the remedy sought by the plaintiff and scope of USOC control of the events. First, Walton-Floyd asserts that, with the exception of *Martinez*, all the cases cited by the USOC stand only for the proposition that Congress did not intend to create an implied right of action in favor of an athlete to enjoin the USOC or one of the NGBs from restricting that athlete's right to participate in amateur sporting events. In doing so, Walton-Floyd attempts to distinguish her situation, where she has brought suit for damages, from those cases where athletes seek to enjoin the USOC from denying their right to participate.

However, Walton-Floyd does not present any cases in support of her position; instead, she directs the Court's attention to certain alleged duties conferred upon the USOC by the Act and to the fact that the USOC may be sued. To permit Walton-Floyd to bring forth a private claim for damages would directly contravene *Oldfield*, where the Ninth Circuit expressly denied the plaintiff a cause of action for his damages claim. The legislative history of the Act indicates that Congress did not intend to provide individual athletes a private cause of action. If Congress had, then it would not have removed the bill of rights from the original version of the Act. Moreover, if Congress desired to differentiate between monetary claims and injunctions, then it could have so provided in the Act. Congress devised the statute, including its emphasis on internal dispute mechanisms, and thus it should have the authority to amend it. In fact, Congress expressly reserves itself this right. . . . Finding there is no implied private right of action against USOC, we overrule the appellant's first point of error.

Voluntary Assumption of a Duty Under State Law

In point of error two, Walton-Floyd argues the Act imposes a duty upon the USOC or a duty exists through voluntary assumption of the hotline service. Since we have held there is no private cause of action under the Act, we must determine whether the USOC assumed a duty under state tort law. Walton-Floyd maintains that even absent a statutory duty under the Act, the USOC voluntarily undertook an affirmative course of action for her benefit. Walton-Floyd asserts the USOC thereby concurrently assumed the obligation to exercise reasonable care. The USOC claims it does not owe the appellant any duty under Texas tort law, because: 1) statutory goals and objectives cannot form the basis of a common law negligence action, 2) the USOC did not voluntarily assume a duty to the appellant, and 3) the Act pre-empts any common law negligence action. . . .

We agree [that] the Act, thereby enabling an individual athlete to bring suit, threatens to override the intent of Congress and open the door to inconsistent interpretations of the Act.

We hold Congress did not intend to create an implied right of action for damages in favour of an athlete in light of precedent and the Act's legislative history and underlying purposes. Since we conclude that Walton-Floyd does not maintain a right to a private cause of action and that the USOC does not owe Walton-Floyd a duty under the Act or Texas common law, we do not address Walton-Floyd's other points of error regarding the existence of factual issues. We therefore affirm the court's grant of summary judgment.

NOTES AND COMMENTS

1. *Reynolds* illustrates the procedural quagmire athletes may confront in challenging an eligibility decision rendered by an international or national sporting body. Note that the district court could not accept the case initially until Reynolds had exhausted internal administrative remedies. Courts consistently hold athletes to the requirement to exhaust administrative remedies before accepting jurisdiction to hear a case. *See Barnes v. International Amateur Athletic Fed'n*, 862 F. Supp. 1537 (S.D. W. Va. 1993) (dismissing athlete's claim contesting ineligibility under the Amateur Sports Act (ASA) where the USOC has established procedures to resolve disputes regarding an athlete's participation in international competition). While Reynolds did so, the remedies provided under the ASA and international federation rules appeared to conflict. Under the Act, the national governing body, TAC [now USA Track & Field], was required to submit to binding arbitration "in accordance with the commercial rules of the American Arbitration Association [AAA] in any controversy involving . . . the opportunity of any amateur athlete . . . to participate in amateur athletic competition. . . ." 36 U.S.C. § 391(b)(3). The independent AAA arbitrators "fully exonerated"Reynolds, finding strong evidence the urine samples were not his. The IAAF disregarded the AAA decision, the same conclusion reached by TAC, and the United States Supreme Court's ruling that Reynolds could compete in the Olympics Trials.

The IAAF required Reynolds to appear before an arbitration panel appointed by the IAAF (the same body filing the accusation) in London, England. After pursuing all administrative procedures, where could Reynolds have filed suit, if at all? What issues and claims could be raised in the judicial proceeding?

2. Would a court have jurisdiction to review (or vacate) an arbitration decision rendered either by the IAAF, the London tribunal, the AAA, or the Court of Arbitration for Sport? What law would apply? *See* James A.R. Nafziger, *Sympo-*

sium: Sports Law in the 21st Century: Globalizing Sports Law, 9 MARQ. SPORTS L.J. 225 (1999) (questioning why the *Reynolds* courts did not consider application of foreign or international law or the binding effect of the foreign arbitral award). Note that both domestic and arbitral awards may be judicially enforced, and such awards may be vacated only upon limited grounds, such as arbitral fraud, corruption or bias. 9 U.S.C. § 10.

3. Does the Sixth Circuit's decision in *Reynolds* mean that an international sports federation may never be subject to personal jurisdiction in a court in the United States? Is the IAAF insulated from suit in any country but England? The IAAF argued that it was not subject to jurisdiction in the U.S. and not required to comply with national laws. Do you agree with the IAAF's argument that subjecting it to suit anywhere in the world an athlete resides would hinder international competition? Is that sufficient justification? The IAAF received half of its $174.5 million budget from U.S. corporations and exerted substantial control over TAC, as a member of the IAAF. In what situations could the IAAF be sued in the U.S.? Why wasn't the court's finding that TAC was an agent of the IAAF grounds for personal jurisdiction? In the wake of the judging scandal that marred the figure skating competition at the 2002 Winter Olympics in Salt Lake City, Utah, a number of participants in the sport, including athletes, coaches, and judges, formed the WSF, a "not-for-profit international sports federation incorporated in the state of Nevada, whose stated goal was the restoration of "merits-based competition to figure skating events." The WSF sought the IOC to recognize it as the international federation for the sport of figure skating and thus to oust the ISU, claiming that ISU has violated US antitrust laws in order to maintain its stranglehold over the sport of figure skating. *World Skating Federation v. International Skating Union*, 357 F. Supp. 2d 661 (S.D.N.Y. 2005) (dismissing claims against ISU based on lack of personal jurisdiction).

4. Should an international federation be able to disregard or trump the decision of a National Olympic Committee or a national governing body? The concern in giving final decision-making authority to a national governing body is that a domestic tribunal may be more lenient in enforcing doping or other eligibility restrictions in order to present the most competitive athletes at international competitions. What is the risk, however, of having final resolution under the control of an international federation or foreign arbitral body?

5. Limited Rights? Athletes seeking to invoke due process or equal protection rights under the U.S. Constitution against the USOC have met a *Tarkanian* problem, by judicial rulings that the USOC, despite its extensive regulation and powers under the Amateur Sports Act, is not a state actor whose decisions must meet the Constitutional standards. *See San Francisco Arts & Athletes, Inc. v. United States Olympic Committee*, 483 U.S. 522 (1987); *DeFrantz v. USOC*, 492 F. Supp. 1181 (D.D.C. 1980). Although the Amateur Sports Act provides that the USOC has the power to sue and be sued, 36 U.S.C. § 375(a)(6), *Walton-Floyd* reflects the prevalent judicial view that the Act does not provide a private right of action to individual athletes and preempts state tort law. What is an athlete to do? To maintain a legal action in a U.S. court, athletes have had to rely on other legal theories in suing the USOC, such as claims raised in *Reynolds* for breach of contract, defamation, and tortious interference. Would Walton-Floyd have sustained summary judgment by asserting a contract claim (rather than statutory or negligence) based on the USOC's hotline service?

6. Discrimination Claims. In *Martin v. IOC*, 740 F.2d 670 (9th Cir. 1984), women runners from 27 countries unsuccessfully invoked the anti-discrimination laws under the U.S. Constitution and California state law to require the 1984 Olympic Games to include 5,000 and 10,000-meter track events for women (part of the men's events since 1923). The court agreed that the plaintiffs had shown a historical pattern of gender discrimination but was reluctant to impose U.S. Constitutional or state laws on an international athletic event and deferred to the procedures under the Olympic Charter. The dissent thought that at least state law should apply, stating that

"When the Olympics move to other countries, some without America's commitment to human rights, the opportunity to tip the scales of justice in favor of equality may slip away." Is the judicial reluctance to intervene in an international sporting event, particularly those held in the United States, appropriate? What laws apply to international sporting organizations? In recent years, professional women tennis players have alleged sex discrimination by the prize money disparities at premier events such as Wimbledon. Do they have rights against gender discrimination? Assuming similar pay disparity, would they have a stronger claim at the U.S. Open? Lee v. USTU, 331 F.Supp.2d 1252 (D. Hawaii 2004) held that the ASA pre-empted a US Olympic taekwando coach's state claims, but not his federal claims alleging race discrimination).

7. The Harding Saga. At the time the *Reynolds* case was tied up in various proceedings (and before the Sixth Circuit had reversed the $27 million verdict against the IAAF), the United States Figure Skating Association (USFSA) was faced with the bizarre eligibility question as a result of Tonya Harding's alleged involvement in a "clubbing attack" on her national rival Nancy Kerrigan. One might wonder why, after Reynolds, Harding was able to compete in the 1994 Olympics in Norway when criminal charges were pending against her. Harding was able to use the administrative procedural scheme to buy enough time to compete in the Olympics. After the USFSA charged Harding with violation of USFSA ethics rules less than three weeks prior to the competition, Harding filed a lawsuit to enjoin the USFSA from holding a disciplinary hearing that could result in her expulsion from the Olympics. As part of a settlement, with Harding dropping her damages suit, the USOC (perhaps mindful of Reynolds' $27 million judgment) allowed her to compete in the Olympics. Following the Olympics, Harding continued to fight the USFSA in its efforts to hold a disciplinary hearing prior to the March 1994 World Championships. The court granted a temporary injunction requiring the USFSA to abide by its rules which entitle athletes a minimum of 30 days to respond to disciplinary charges and a reasonable time to prepare for a hearing. *Harding v. United States Figure Skat-*

ing Ass'n, 851 F. Supp. 1476 (D. Or. 1994). The case was mooted when Harding pled guilty to criminal charges. The USFSA ultimately banned Harding for life for violating a code of conduct. Should a sporting body defer sanctioning an athlete until criminal charges are resolved? Suppose Harding had been acquitted?

8. 1998 Restrictions on Injunctive Relief. Judicial reluctance to intervene is in resolving sporting disputes is particularly heightened in the international context. The court in *Harding* expressed that: "The courts should rightly hesitate before intervening in disciplinary hearings held by private associations. . . . Intervention is appropriate only in the most extraordinary circumstances, where the association has clearly breached its own rules, that breach will imminently result in serious and irreparable harm to the plaintiff, and the plaintiff has exhausted all internal remedies. Even then, injunctive relief is limited to correcting the breach of the rules. The court should not intervene in the underlying dispute." 851 F. Supp. at 1479. Congress apparently agrees, as it is amended to the Amateur Sports Act in 1998 to provide that a court shall not grant injunctive relief against the USOC within 21 days before the start of the Olympic Game. 36 U.S.C. § 220509. The 1998 Amendments also provide for an ombudsman who, at the expense of the USOC, provides independent advice to athletes about the applicable laws and procedures for appealing and resolving Olympic-related disputes. Suppose the ombudsman or NGB provides the wrong advice? Canadian sprinter Ben Johnson was stripped of his Olympic gold medal after testing positive for steroids at the 1988 Seoul Games and later banned for life after a second positive drug test. A Canadian arbitrator had ruled that Johnson be reinstated because the Canadian federation did not properly inform Johnson of his appeal options and Johnson did not knowingly take drugs because of a test showing that he had an elevated testosterone level. The IAAF, however, convened its own panel which rejected the arbitrator's decision and ordered Johnson banned for life.

D. ARBITRATION OF OLYMPIC DISPUTES

As a result of limited judicial remedies and a strong emphasis on resolving disputes through internal administrative procedures and arbitration, fewer lawsuits involving Olympic athletes are filed in the court system. Whether this trend is good or bad is still subject to debate. According to Judge Richard Posner, "There can be few less suitable bodies than the federal courts for determining the eligibility, or the procedures for determining eligibility, of athletes to participate in the Olympic Games." *Michels v. United States Olympic Committee*, 741 F.2d 155 (7th Cir. 1984). Do you agree? In 1992, Professor Nafziger noted that "although this trend seems to offer a welcome alternative to executive fiat, on the one hand, and litigation, on the other, these tribunals are controversial. Reliance on them may deter athletes from seeking alternatives such as adjudication, they may sometimes be little more than executive panels in disguise. . . ." James A.R. Nafziger, *International Sports Law: A Replay of Characteristics and Trends*, 86 AM. J. INT'L L. 489, 506 (1992).

The *Reynolds* and *Harding* cases demonstrate the need for an alternative to protracted litigation and the need to be free from the influence of a particular national or international sporting federation. The Amateur Sports Act requires that the USOC create a dispute resolution process which entitles an athlete to appeal to the American Arbitration Association (AAA) for final and nonbinding arbitration. 36 U.S.C. § 220529. However, the international federation may not recognize AAA decisions. Given the timing and nature of international sporting competitions, the need for swift resolution of eligibility disputes is critical. In recent years, dispute resolution procedures have developed to provide more efficient resolution of disputes and to mitigate overlapping jurisdictional problems. In many instances, consent to arbitration and waiver of the right to file a lawsuit is mandatory for athlete participation. For example, as a condition of participating in the Olympics, athletes must sign a Court of Arbitration for Sport Waiver form. As of 1995, the Olympic Charter has provided that "any dispute arising on the occasion of or in connection with the Olympic Games shall be submitted exclusively to the Court of Arbitration for Sport, in accordance with the code of Sports-Related Arbitration." Olympic Charter ¶ 74.

In 1984, the IOC created the Court of Arbitration for Sport (CAS) to provide a forum where parties, by agreement, would submit to arbitration to resolve Olympic sports-related disputes. To provide an arbitration forum independent of the IOC (which had created, funded and selected CAS members essentially from its own ranks), the International Council of Arbitration for Sport (ICAS) was established in 1994 to administer and fund CAS, to select neutral CAS arbitrators, and to protect the rights of the parties, particularly the athletes. CAS is structured into three divisions: (1) The Olympic Division, or *Ad Hoc* Division, first used in the 1996 Atlanta Games, is on-site to handle disputes which occur during the games; (2) the Ordinary Arbitration Division hears disputes arising out of commercial contracts related to sport; and (3) the Appeals Arbitration Division, which after internal remedies are exhausted, deals with challenges involving decisions of sports federations or other sports bodies. CAS is headquartered in Lausanne, Switzerland, but has additional offices in Sydney, Australia and New York. ICAS operates pursuant to a Code of Sports-Related Arbitration. The CAS arbitrators review each case "in light of the Olympic Charter, the applicable rules of each sport and general principles of law. . . ." Ad Hoc Rules, Art. 17. Absent the consent of parties otherwise, the choice of law is Swiss or the law of the country in which the federation, association, or sports body is domiciled. The CAS proceedings are typically confidential, more expeditious than court proceedings, but final and binding on the parties. *See* http://www.tas-cas.org.

Case File

U.S. Domestic Arbitration Under the Amateur Sports Act

LINDLAND v. UNITED STATES OF AMERICA WRESTLING ASSOCIATION, INC.

227 F.3d 1000 (7th Cir. 2000)

EASTERBROOK.

Readers of our prior opinions (or the sports pages) know that Keith Sieracki and Matt Lindland both believe that they are entitled to be the U.S. entrant in the 76 kilogram weight class of Greco-Roman wrestling at the 2000 Olympic Games. They have met twice in championship bouts where the Olympic spot was the victor's reward: Sieracki won the first by a score of 2-1; Lindland won the second by a score of 8-0. Each claims that his victory entitles him to the slot in Sydney. Lindland protested the result of the first match through the hierarchy of USAWrestling, the national governing body for amateur wrestling. After USAWrestling rejected his protests, Lindland commenced arbitration, which was his right under the Ted Stevens Olympic and Amateur Sports Act. *See* 36 U.S.C. § 220529(a). Arbitrator Burns ordered the rematch, which Lindland won. USA Wrestling was unwilling to accept this outcome; instead of sending Lindland's name to the United States Olympic Committee (USOC) as its nominee for the Games, it told the USOC to send Sieracki and listed Lindland only as a person eligible to compete in the event of injury. Lindland then sought confirmation of the Burns Award under § 9 of the Federal Arbitration Act, and in an opinion issued on August 24 we held that Lindland is entitled to that relief — which, we pointedly added, means that he is entitled to be USAWrestling's nominee to the USOC.

Later that day, USAWrestling informed the USOC that Sieracki remained its nominee. Its explanation for this defiance was that a second arbitrator, in a proceeding initiated by Sieracki, had disagreed with Arbitrator Burns and directed USA Wrestling to make Sieracki its nominee on the basis of his victory in the first match. USAWrestling had no excuse for following Arbitrator Campbell's unreviewed award rather than a decision of a federal court confirming Arbitrator Burns's award, and on August 25 we issued a writ of mandamus requiring the district court to ensure that USAWrestling implemented the Burns Award "immediately and unconditionally." On August 26 USAWrestling finally complied, but the USOC then refused to accept Lindland as a member of the team, asserting that USA Wrestling's nomination of Lindland was untimely because Sieracki's name already had been sent to the International Olympic Committee (IOC) in Lausanne, Switzerland.

Lindland then returned to the district court, asking it to compel the USOC to send his name to the IOC. Sieracki fought back by asking a different district court (in Denver, Colorado) to confirm the Campbell Award. The district judge in Denver sensibly transferred that request to the Northern District of Illinois, consolidating all proceedings arising out of the dispute. The Northern District ordered the USOC to request the IOC to substitute Lindland for Sieracki. The USOC has done so, and the IOC has made the substitution. The Northern District also denied Sieracki's petition to confirm the Campbell Award. Two appeals ensued. We expedited the briefing and affirmed both decisions on September 1, promising that this opinion would follow with an explanation.

Although Lindland now is a member of the U.S. team, and the IOC's deadline for making changes has expired, the dispute is not moot. The Games begin at 4 a.m. on September 15 (Chicago time), and the 76 kilogram classification in Greco-Roman wrestling does not get underway until September 24. The IOC accepted a substitution of Lindland for Sieracki after its deadline, remarking that it was willing to make the change because the USOC acted under judicial order. This implies that if we now confirmed the Campbell Award (including its provision annulling the Burns Award) and directed the USOC to substitute Sieracki for Lindland, the IOC would accept that change as well. We therefore address the merits — starting with what is logically the first issue, whether to confirm the Campbell Award.

Lindland had argued to Arbitrator Burns that USA Wrestling's grievance proceedings were flawed. Arbitrator Burns agreed and ordered the rematch as a remedy in lieu of directing USAWrestling to reconsider Lindland's protest to the judging of his match with Sieracki. Arbitrator Campbell went over the same ground, disagreeing with Arbitrator Burns about the adequacy of USAWrestling's processes and adding that, in his view, the result of the first match (which everyone calls "Bout # 244") had not been affected by any errors in applying the scoring rules for Greco-Roman wrestling. It is not a surprising view for Arbitrator Campbell to have taken, because the proceedings began amicably. Sieracki initiated the arbitration to defend his initial victory, and USAWrestling, the respondent, likewise defended both the scoring of the match and the conduct of its internal appeals. (Lindland intervened to defend the Burns Award, but, having already won the rematch, was more interested in preserving that victory than in litigating from scratch.) What is surprising was that Arbitrator Campbell not only approved the result of the original Bout # 244 and the adequacy of USAWrestling's grievance procedures but also directed it to ignore the result of the rematch — that is, Arbitrator Campbell directed USAWrestling not to implement the Burns Award.

Sieracki argues that the Campbell Award is no less confirmable under the standards of the Federal Arbitration Act than was the Burns Award, and if he is entitled to confirmation of the Campbell Award then we should set aside the confirmation of the Burns Award (because relief from the Burns Award is part of the Campbell Award). Certainly there is no evidence that the Campbell Award is the result of "corruption," "fraud," "evident partiality," or any similar bar to confirmation. The district court refused to enforce the Campbell Award because the Burns Award had been enforced already, and it read *Consolidation Coal Co. v. United Mine Workers*, 213 F.3d 404 (7th Cir. 2000), as precluding enforcement of incompatible awards. Only one of these athletes can be on the Olympic Team, and the district judge thought that federal courts should not order the USOC to send both. Sieracki replies that arbitrators need not follow judicial notions of preclusion — a good point about arbitrators, but not about judges. Once the Burns Award was confirmed, it was no longer simply the view of a fellow arbitrator with which Campbell could disagree. But this may not be a complete answer. If the Campbell Award is understood to vacate the Burns Award, then confirmation of the Campbell Award logically entails vacating the prior confirmation of the Burns Award. That step would not leave USAWrestling under conflicting judicial instructions. (Nor is it clear that conflict is an irremediable evil.) Injunctions create property rights, which may be altered by private agreements. Bargaining among Sieracki, Lindland, and USA Wrestling could lead to a settlement that would relieve USAWrestling of any incompatible obligations.

Definitive resolution of the right way to handle conflicting awards, after one has been confirmed, may await another day. The Campbell Award could not be confirmed even if it were the sole award. It is doubly flawed: first, the entire proceeding appears to have been ultra vires; second, the award violates the Commercial Rules of the American Arbitration Association, under which the proceeding was conducted. Because Arbitrator Campbell exceeded his powers, his award cannot be confirmed.

Sieracki initiated an arbitration not to contest a final decision by USAWrestling but to protest the Burns Award. Sieracki filed his demand for arbitration on August 11, two days after the Burns Award and three days before his rematch with Lindland (and thus before any issues associated with that bout could have arisen). The Stevens Act does not authorize arbitration about the propriety of another arbitrator's decision. Section 220529(a) provides:

> A party aggrieved by a determination of the corporation under section 220527 or 220528 of this title may obtain review by any regional office of the American Arbitration Association.

[L]indland exhausted his remedies within USA Wrestling and obtained "a determination of the corporation under section 220527 . . . of this title", and thus was entitled to arbitrate his grievance. Sieracki, by contrast, did not initiate any proceedings within the scope of § 220527. . . . Sieracki did not have such a claim and therefore was not entitled to arbitration under the Stevens Act even if it was proper to pretermit administrative remedies. No other provision of which we are aware supports arbitration whose sole subject is the decision of a prior arbitrator. The Stevens Act would be self-destructive if it authorized such proceedings, which would lead to enduring turmoil (as happened here) and defeat the statute's function of facilitating final resolution of disputes.

Even if the second arbitration had been authorized, however, the outcome would have been forbidden by the rules under which it was conducted. Rule 48 of the AAA's Commercial Rules provides that an "arbitrator is not empowered to redetermine the merits of any claim already decided." Sieracki stresses, as our opinion of August 24 acknowledged, that judicial ideas about issue and claim preclusion need not apply in arbitration. But arbitrators assuredly are bound by the contracts and other rules that give them power to act. An arbitrator who throws aside those rules and implements his "own brand of industrial justice" oversteps his powers, and the resulting award must be set aside. *Steelworkers v. Enterprise Wheel & Car Corp.*, 363 U.S. 593 (1960). What the Steelworkers Trilogy declared about "industrial justice" is equally true of commercial or athletic justice. Arbitrators are not ombudsmen; they are authorized to resolve disputes under contracts and rules, not to declare how the world should work in the large. Arbitrator Campbell did not misinterpret Rule 48; he decided to ignore it utterly. . . . By the time Campbell acted, the Burns Award had "already decided" that the nomination to the Olympic Team would depend on a rematch between Sieracki and Lindland. Whatever powers Campbell possessed vis-à-vis Sieracki, he lacked the power to order USAWrestling to nominate anyone other than the winner of the rematch. The Campbell Award therefore is not entitled to confirmation.

This conclusion makes it unnecessary to decide whether, by participating in the Campbell proceedings, Lindland waived or forfeited his entitlement to the benefits of the Burns Award. The Campbell Award is invalid, so it does not bind Lindland or anyone else. . . . Lindland is entitled to USAWrestling's nomination because (a) Arbitrator Burns ordered USAWrestling to hold a rematch, and (b) Lindland won that rematch. If Sieracki had prevailed in the rematch, he would be on the Olympic Team today. Athletic disputes should be settled on the playing field — as the Burns Award provided.

For completeness, we add that none of the parties' arguments persuades us that the order confirming the Burns Award should be reconsidered. Sieracki, USAWrestling, and the USOC continue to assert that the Burns proceedings were flawed because Sieracki was not a party to them. These submissions ignore the language of the Stevens Act, which provides for arbitration between an aggrieved athlete and the national governing body, not for arbitration among athletes. In arbitration the national governing body, by defending its decision (as USAWrestling vigorously did), also defends the interests of the winning athlete. Doubtless the constitution or bylaws of the USOC or USAWrestling could designate as additional parties those athletes potentially affected by the proceedings, but they do not do so. . . .

Briefing the "active concert or participation" issue at our instructions, the USOC contends that it is an independent organization, entitled to make the final decision. No one doubts this, but the "active concert or participation" clause supposes legal distinctiveness; if USAWrestling and the USOC were the same party, the order would be binding directly. The "active concert or participation" clause is designed to prevent what may well have happened here: the addressee of an injunction, eager to avoid its obligations, persuades a friendly third party to take steps that frustrate the injunction's effectiveness. The USOC has given every indication of willingness to lend a hand. For example, it responded to the initiation of the Campbell proceedings by promising to respect their outcome — which entails a promise to ignore the outcome of the Burns proceedings. The events of August 24 also imply that USA Wrestling and the USOC acted in concert. On the evening of August 24 USAWrestling sent the USOC one document "notifying" it of this court's decision and a second document nominating Sieracki. The USOC decided to accept the nomination of Sieracki, knowing full well that this nomination violated a decision of this court. The inference that USA Wrestling and the USOC undertook a joint effort to defeat the Burns Award (and our decision) is very strong.

That inference could be overcome by a demonstration that the USOC had an independent ground of decision. No one doubts that the USOC may adopt its own criteria and make its own selections. Thus if, for example, Lindland failed a drug test, or if his behavior at past international competitions had brought shame on the team (as the U.S. Olympic hockey team did en masse in 1998), then the USOC could have sent Sieracki to the Games. Similarly, if the USOC regularly made its own judgments about athletic prowess, then a determination that Sieracki is the wrestler most likely to succeed in Sydney would be respected by the federal judiciary. Yet in response to a question posed by this court (and a similar one posed by the district court), the USOC failed to identify even a single instance in which it has not forwarded to the IOC the nomination of a national governing body such as USAWrestling. Its promise to send whichever athlete Arbitrator Campbell selected abjures any independent role; indeed, that promise is the best evidence that USAWrestling and the USOC have acted jointly to implement the Campbell Award despite judicial enforcement of the Burns Award. . . . .

Under the USOC's own rules, Lindland is entitled to the position on the Olympic Team. This makes it very hard to understand the USOC's position as anything other than a continuation of the view disparaged in our August 24 opinion: a belief by the USOC that athletes who pursue their rights under the Stevens Act should be penalized. The district court was entitled to prevent the USOC from carrying out that view under the pretext that USAWrestling's nomination of Lindland arrived too late.

Nonetheless, the USOC insists, it is entitled to do as it pleases — defying injunctions to its heart's content — if it manages to stall until only three weeks remain before the Games. For this proposition it relies on another part of the Stevens Act, 36 U.S.C. § 220509(a):

> The corporation shall establish and maintain provisions in its constitution and bylaws for the swift and equitable resolution of disputes involving any of its members and relating to the opportunity of an amateur athlete, coach, trainer, manager, administrator, or official to

> participate in the Olympic Games, the Paralympic Games, the Pan-American Games, world championship competition, or other protected competition as defined in the constitution and bylaws of the corporation. In any lawsuit relating to the resolution of a dispute involving the opportunity of an amateur athlete to participate in the Olympic Games, the Paralympic Games, or the Pan-American Games, a court shall not grant injunctive relief against the corporation within 21 days before the beginning of such games if the corporation, after consultation with the chair of the Athletes' Advisory Council, has provided a sworn statement in writing executed by an officer of the corporation to such court that its constitution and bylaws cannot provide for the resolution of such dispute prior to the beginning of such games.

Saturday, August 26, was the 21st day before the "beginning" of the Sydney Olympics. The USOC filed in the district court an affidavit parroting the statutory terms and insists that, as a result, the district court was powerless to enforce the Burns Award.

Section 220509(a) is designed to prevent a court from usurping the USOC's powers when time is too short for its own dispute-resolution machinery to do its work. The premise of the USOC's argument is that the dispute among Lindland, Sieracki, and USAWrestling is one to be resolved by the USOC's internal processes, which can't be done at this late date. This is just another variation of the USOC's misunderstanding about the genesis of the district court's order. Lindland has not asserted a private right of action to enforce the Stevens Act, nor has he attempted to initiate a new dispute-resolution process before the USOC. His claim depends on the Burns Award, which was issued on August 9, well outside the 21-day window, and the decision of this court, also issued before the 21st day. The only question on the table is whether USAWrestling and the USOC will comply with obligations that had been established before that three-week period. The USOC's liability stems from its obligation as an entity "in active concert or participation with" USA Wrestling to avoid frustrating the order enforcing the Burns Award.

We do not for one second believe that Congress set out to reward intransigence, so that the USOC can protect scofflaws among the national governing bodies, or itself defy judicial orders if, on the 21st day before the Olympic torch enters the stadium, the President of the USOC is not already in prison for contempt. There is no dispute for the USOC to resolve, so its inability under its constitution and bylaws to act on short notice is not important. All the USOC had to do was implement this court's decision of August 24 (enforcing the Burns Award of August 9); all we hold is that delay in compliance with an obligation judicially articulated before the 21st day does not entitle the USOC to escape that obligation. To put this in the statutory language, the prohibition applies only if "such dispute" — that is, a dispute to be handled under the USOC's procedures — can't be resolved in the time remaining before the games. When no "such dispute" survives into the three-week period (because it had been resolved earlier), § 220509(a) does not preclude enforcement of the outstanding decision.

Senator Stevens himself may have a different view about the effect of § 220509(a). At the behest of the USOC, he wrote a letter asking the district judge to vacate its order. Our reading of the letter implies that the USOC misinformed the Senator about the nature of the controversy and the reason the district judge had ordered the USOC to send Lindland's name to the IOC, but no matter. Legislative history is a chancy subject; subsequent legislative history is weaker still, indeed is an oxymoron, and a letter or affidavit written as a form of constituent service is the bottom of the pecking order. Letters written after a statute's enactment were not presented in the course of debate and so are not the sort of views that may be credible because other members of the legislature rely on them and may impose penalties on those who misrepresent, or misunderstand, the text.

A letter from a Member of Congress telling a judge how to decide a pending case reflects a misunderstanding of the difference between legislative and judicial functions. Senator Stevens played a leading role in the creation of § 220509, but he has no role in adjudication. Giving weight to such a letter would only invite other litigants to pester Members of Congress for expressions of support — or Members of Congress to pester the courts with their latest views about how laws should be implemented and cases decided. It is best, we think, for each institution to hew to its constitutional function.

AFFIRMED.

International Arbitration in the Court of Abitrator for Sport In the Arbitration Between: United States Anti-Doping Agency — and — Tim Montgomery Arbitral Award delivered by The Court of Arbitration for Sport (CAS)

Lausanne, 13 December, 2005 (CAS 2004/O/645)

I. INTRODUCTION

1. This Award is the culmination of an exhaustive process of briefings and hearings, discussions amongst the parties, and numerous interventions by the Panel.

2. At issue is the charge by the United States Anti-Doping Agency ("USADA") that Tim Montgomery violated applicable IAAF anti-doping rules, notwithstanding that Mr. Montgomery never tested positive in any in-competition or out-of-competition drug test. As such, the issues raised in this so-called "non-analytical positive" case are, if not wholly novel, certainly not in the nature of issues arising in a typical "adverse analytical finding" (or "analytical positive")

doping case. However . . . "the straightforward application of legal principles to essentially undisputed facts leads to a clear resolution of this matter."

3. USADA seeks a four-year sanction of Tim Montgomery for participating in a wideranging doping conspiracy implemented by the Bay Area Laboratory Cooperative ("BALCO"). USADA charges that, for a period of several years, Mr. Montgomery used various performance-enhancing drugs provided by BALCO. As noted, Mr. Montgomery has never had a single drug test found to be a positive doping violation, but USADA's charges are based, in part, on all of the blood and urine tests at IOC-accredited and non-IOC-accredited laboratories that he has had in recent years. USADA also relies, among other things, on documents seized by the U.S. government from BALCO that have been provided to USADA; statements made by BALCO officials; and other documents.

4. According to USADA, BALCO was involved in a conspiracy the purpose of which was the distribution and use of doping substances and techniques that were either undetectable or difficult to detect in routine drug testing. BALCO is alleged to have distributed several types of banned doping agents to professional athletes in track and field, baseball and football. Among these were tetrahydrogestrinome ("THG"), otherwise known as "the Clear" by BALCO and its users. THG is a designer steroid that could not be identified by routine anti-doping testing until 2003, when a track and field coach provided a sample of it to USADA. It is undisputed that the Clear is a prohibited substance under the IAAF Rules.

5. On 3 September 2003, FBI agents searched BALCO's premises pursuant to search warrants. Approximately twenty-four agents searched BALCO's offices and seized hundreds of documents there and at other locations maintained by BALCO. The agents also seized samples of the Clear and other substances distributed by BALCO. During this raid, agents interviewed the company's President, Victor Conte, and other BALCO officials, who spoke about its activities and its customers. Mr. Conte named fifteen track and field athletes whom he alleged were clients of BALCO, including Mr. Montgomery, as well as other athletes from the NFL and Major League Baseball.

6. Following the BALCO raid, government agents obtained other documents, such as emails, through the use of subpoenas and other law enforcement mechanisms. Additional records were produced and created as part of the Grand Jury investigation, which resulted in the indictment of Mr. Conte, along with several alleged co-conspirators. None of the evidence in this case derives from the Grand Jury proceedings. However, the BALCO documents were obtained by the U.S. Senate, which subsequently provided them to USADA.

7. [T]the Panel's determination of the case against Mr. Montgomery turns on certain statements made by the Respondent himself which make it unnecessary for the Panel to determine whether the mass of other evidence adduced by USADA and derived in large measure from the BALCO documents, is also conclusive of the doping charges brought against him. . . .

II. THE PARTIES

9. The Claimant, USADA, is the independent Anti-Doping Agency for Olympic sports in the United States and is responsible for managing the testing and adjudication process for doping control in that country. In that capacity, USADA conducts drug testing and results management for participants in the Olympic movement within the United States.

10. The Respondent, Tim Montgomery ("**Mr. Montgomery**" or the "**Athlete**"), is an elite and highly successful American track and field athlete. As a sprinter, Mr. Montgomery has won numerous track and field titles, including World Championship and Olympic gold medals, as well as a world record.

11. On 17 September 2004, The International Association of Athletics Federations (the "**IAAF**"), the international federation responsible for the sport of athletics worldwide, requested permission to appear in the arbitration as a party (i.e., as an intervener). In its request, the IAAF stated that, under IAAF Rules, should the Panel allow it to appear as a party, the Panel's award ". . . will be final and binding and no further reference may be made to the CAS" and, further, that "the IAAF is content for this to be the final decision on [the Athlete's] eligibility."

III. PROCEDURAL BACKGROUND

A. USADA's "Charging Letter"

13. On 7 June 2004, USADA informed Respondent that it had received evidence which indicated that Mr. Montgomery was a participant in a doping conspiracy involving various elite athletes and coaches as well as BALCO. On the same date, USADA submitted the matter to its Anti-Doping Review Board (the "**Review Board**") pursuant to the USADA Protocol. In accordance with the provisions of that paragraph, the Athlete also submitted a lengthy and detailed submission on the matter to the Review Board.

14. By letter dated 22 June 2004 (the so-called "**Charging Letter**"), USADA informed Mr. Montgomery that, after consideration of the documents submitted to it by USADA and Mr. Montgomery, the Review Board had determined that there existed "sufficient evidence against you to proceed with the adjudication process as set forth in [the USADA Protocol]." The charges against Respondent were set out in the Charging Letter, and reiterated in USADA's Statement of Claim, as follows: "[A]t this time, and reserving all rights to amend the charge, USADA charges you with violations of the IAAF Anti-Doping Rules. (. . .) USADA charges that your participation in the Bay Area Laboratory Cooperative ("BALCO") conspiracy, the purpose of which was to trade in doping substances and techniques that were either undetectable or difficult to detect in routine testing, involved your violations of the following IAAF Rules that strictly forbid doping."

* * *

Specifically, the evidence confirms your involvement with the following prohibited substances and prohibited techniques: one or more substances belonging to the prohibited class of "Anabolic Steroids;" Testosterone/Epitestosterone Cream; EPO; Growth Hormone; and Insulin.

B. The Decision to Proceed Directly to CAS

16. In response to the Charging Letter, Mr. Montgomery notified USADA that he elected to "bypass the domestic hearing process" and "proceed directly to a single final hearing before the Court of Arbitration for Sport." [U]pon an athlete making such an election, "[t]he CAS decision shall be final and binding on all parties and shall not be subject to further review or appeal."

* * *

H. The Hearing on the Merits (6 - 10 June 2005)

39. At the hearing, the Panel heard oral argument from both parties. It also heard the evidence of [several] witnesses.

40. Although Mr. Montgomery's counsel cross-examined each of the witnesses produced by USADA, the Athlete called no fact witnesses of his own nor did he himself give evidence.

IV. THE CASE AGAINST MR. MONTGOMERY

J. USADA's 7 Types of Evidence

43. As presented by USADA at the hearing, the evidence of doping by Mr. Montgomery consisted of what Claimant referred to as 7 types of evidence:

(1) Blood test results from a Mexican laboratory in February 2000 which allegedly show Mr. Montgomery's testosterone level doubling in the course of one day;

(2) Documents extracted from the files seized from BALCO which, according to USADA, "individually or when linked together established Montgomery's doping";

(3) Evidence of the suppression and rebound of endogenous steroids in Respondent's urine, as shown in a table depicting test results reported by IOC-accredited and BALCO Laboratories on 56 occasions between March 1999 and September 2004;

(4) Alleged abnormal blood test results on 5 occasions between November 2000 and July 2001;

(5) Respondent's alleged admission to Kelli White that he had used a prohibited substance known colloquially as the "Clear";

(6) So-called admissions against interest, which implicated Mr. Montgomery, made by the President of BALCO, Victor Conte, in interviews with investigative authorities as well as the media; and

(7) Reports in the San Francisco Chronicle supposedly based on secret grand jury testimony by Mr. Montgomery in which he admits to using various prohibited substances.

44. All of the foregoing evidence was challenged by the Respondent. . . .

45. The Panel has wrestled with the question whether, in the circumstances, it should address in this Award each element of USADA's case against Mr. Montgomery, including each of what USADA calls its "7 types of evidence" of doping by the Athlete. On balance, the Panel has determined not to do so for the simple reason that it is unnecessary. This is because the Panel is unanimously of the view that Mr. Montgomery in fact admitted his use of prohibited substances to Ms. White, as discussed in more detail below, on which basis alone the Panel can and does find him guilty of a doping offence. The fact that the Panel does not consider it necessary in the circumstances to analyse and comment on the mass of other evidence against the Athlete, however, is not to be taken as an indication that it considers that such other evidence could not demonstrate that the Respondent is guilty of doping. Doping offences can be proved by a variety of means; and this is nowhere more true than in "nonanalytical positive" cases such as the present.

46. As mentioned, Ms. White has admitted to doping and has accepted a two-year sanction as a result.

47. According Ms. White's evidence, in March 2001, while at an international meet in Portugal (no exact date was provided by the witness) she and Mr. Montgomery had "a small discussion about whether or not the Clear made our calves tight." Mr. Montgomery asked Ms. White, "Does it make your calves tight?" Ms. White responded in the affirmative. Mr. Montgomery, still in her presence, then placed a telephone call to someone who may or may not have been Mr. Conte (Ms. White believes that it was Mr. Conte) to whom he relayed the information that "she said that it makes her calves tight too". According to Ms. White, there was not the slightest doubt as to the substance about which she and Mr. Montgomery were speaking and which they both acknowledged had the effect of making their calves tight: they were talking about the Clear.

48. It is essential to note that this evidence of what USADA claims constitutes a direct admission of Mr. Montgomery's guilt, is uncontroverted.

49. Counsel for Respondent may have questioned Ms. White's motives in offering her testimony concerning Mr. Montgomery's use of the Clear and, more generally, his relationship with BALCO. They may have sought (without success) to impugn her honesty and to draw attention to the witness' own history of involvement with BALCO and her efforts to conceal that involvement. However, the Panel has already declared its finding with respect to Ms. White's credibility as a witness in these proceedings and its view that she is telling the truth.

L. Mr. Montgomery's Decision Not to Testify

51. Of course, as noted by USADA's counsel during closing argument: "It would be a real different issue if Tim Montgomery took the stand and said '*no, no, when I said "it" I meant something else'.*" It might indeed have affected the Panel's appreciation of Ms. White's evidence had Respondent chosen to provide the Panel with a different explanation of their March 2001 conversation or had he denied that the conversation took place as described by the witness. The fact remains that he did not.

52. [I]t is common ground that Mr. Montgomery was fully within his rights to testify in his own defence, or not, as he saw fit. Where the parties differ, however, is with respect to the question whether the Panel has the authority to draw an adverse inference from Mr. Montgomery's decision not to testify in the arbitration; and, if it does have the power to do so, whether such an inference should be drawn in this case.

53. On 17 September 2005, the Panel advised the parties that, having considered their written and oral arguments and the legal authorities filed by them for and against the drawing of an adverse inference, and after deliberation, it found that "it does have the right and power to draw an adverse inference from Mr. Montgomery's refusal to testify. More particularly, it may draw adverse inferences in respect of allegations regarding which USADA has presented evidence that would normally call for a Response from the Respondent himself, and nor merely from his experts or counsel."

55. Mr. Montgomery has been provided every conceivable opportunity to provide an exculpatory explanation of his own statements evidencing his guilt. He has had ample opportunity to deny ever making such statements. But because he has not offered any evidence of his own concerning his admission to Ms. White of his use of the Clear, the Panel can only rely on the testimony of Ms. White. That testimony is more than merely adverse to Mr. Montgomery; it is fatal to his case. In the circumstances, faced with uncontroverted evidence of such a direct and compelling nature, there is simply no need for any additional inference to be drawn from the Respondent's refusal to testify. The evidence alone is sufficient to convict.

V. DECISION

M. The Doping Offence

56. USADA bears the burden of proving, by strong evidence commensurate with the serious claims it makes that the [Respondent] committed the doping offences in question."

57. USADA has met this standard. The Panel has no doubt in this case, and is more than comfortably satisfied, that Mr. Montgomery committed the doping offence in question. It has been presented with strong, indeed uncontroverted, evidence of doping by Mr. Montgomery, in the form of an admission contained in his statements made to Ms. White and to others while in her presence. On

this basis, the Tribunal finds Respondent guilty of a doping offence. In particular, the Panel finds Mr. Montgomery guilty of the offence of admitting having used a prohibited substance. . . .

N. The Sanction

60. In the circumstances, the Panel finds that Mr. Montgomery's admission of his use of prohibited substances merits a period of ineligibility under IAAF Rules of two years.

62. In addition to the two-year sanction already discussed, the Panel orders the retroactive cancellation of all of Mr. Montgomery's results, rankings, awards and winnings as of 31 March 2001 (as noted above, Ms. White did testify as to the exact date during the month of March, 2001 on which Mr. Montgomery admitted his use of the Clear, and the Panel thus considers it reasonable that the last day of the month in question be selected for this purpose).

In this regard, IAAF Rule 60.5 provides: "Where an athlete has been declared ineligible he shall not be entitled to any award or addition to his trust fund to which he would have been entitled by virtue of his appearance and/or performance at the athletics meeting at which the doping offence took place, or at any subsequent meetings."

In the Arbitration Between: Mr. Dmitry Vlasov, Russia and ATP Tour Inc., United States Arbitral Award delivered by The Court of Arbitration for Sport (CAS)

Lausanne, 23 August, 2005 (CAS 2005/A/873)

1.1 This is an appeal by Dmitry Vlasov ("the Player") against the decision of an ATP Tour Tribunal ("the Tribunal") finding him guilty of a doping offence and imposing, *inter alia* a period of ineligibility for one year.

2.1 According to the Code of Sports-related Arbitration (the "Code"), decisions of sports federations may be appealed to the Court of Arbitration for Sport ("CAS") insofar as their statutes or regulations provide for such appeal. . . . the seat of the Panel is established at Lausanne, Switzerland.

BACKGROUND FACTS

6.2 The Player is a professional tennis player from Russia. He has been a member of the ATP since 2 May 2001. Before the events that form the subject of this appeal he had not been found guilty of any other offences.

6.3 The ATP Tour is a non-for-profit membership organisation composed of male professional tennis players and tournament organisers. The ATP sanctions tennis tournaments and provides league governance and support to its member tournaments and players. In fulfilment of this role the ATP has adopted rules for the conduct of tournaments and players. The Rules are applicable to this case.

6.4 On 14 September 2004 the Player attended the outpatient Department of the Moscow Scientific and Development Research Institute of Psychiatry of the RF Ministry of Health ("the Department"). He testified that he had back pain that had been troubling him for some time and had not slept for 3 days previously. He complained generally of problems with sleep, appetite reduction, irritation and loss of performance capacity.

6.5 The attending physician, Dr Malin, attributed the Player's depression to breach of relations with his sponsor, which was aggravated by worsening relationships with a female companion. He had also been given anti-inflammatory injections for back pain. He was diagnosed with a depressive syndrome. Dr Malin advised the Player on various recuperative activities and provided a medical prescription to the Player for his depression, who was accordingly given *Dynamin* to take 3 times a day for 3 weeks.

6.6 The leaflet for *Dynamin* that accompanied the pills was in Spanish and listed its ingredients including *Pemolina de Magnesio 10mg*. There is also a warning in Spanish on the leaflet, which (in liberal translation) states: Notice to Sportsmen that this medicine may contain components which would cause a positive drug test for athletes.

6.7 On 9 October 2004 the Player provided a urine sample pursuant to the Anti-Doping Rules during the ATP sanctioned tournament the "Kremlin Cup" at Moscow, Russia. The urine sample provided was analysed by a World Anti-Doping Agency ("WADA") accredited laboratory, located in Point Claire, Quebec, Canada. . . . Richard Ings ("Mr Ings") notified the Player on behalf of the ATP that he had committed a Doping Offence. He was advised of his right to appeal, which he duly exercised.

THE ANTI-DOPING RULES

8.1 The AD Rules provide, so far as material, as follows:

A. Introduction

1. *The purpose of the Tennis Anti-Doping Program ("the Program") is to maintain the integrity of tennis and protect the health and rights of all tennis players.*

C. Doping Offences

Doping is defined as the occurrence of one or more of the following (each, a "**Doping Offence**"):

1. ***The presence of a Prohibited Substance or its Metabolites or Markers in a Player's Specimen, unless the Player establishes that the presence is pursuant to a therapeutic use exemption granted in accordance with Article E.***

a. It is each Player's personal duty to ensure that no ***Prohibited Substance*** *enters his body. A Player is responsible for any* ***Prohibited Substance*** *or its* ***Metabolites*** *or* ***Markers*** *found to be present in his Specimen. Accordingly, it is not necessary that intent, fault, negligence or knowing Use on the Player's part be demonstrated in order to establish a Doping Offence under Article C.1; nor is the* ***Player's*** *lack of intent, fault, negligence or knowledge a defence to a charge that a Doping Offence has been committed under Article C.1 . . .*

SUMMARY OF EVIDENCE

9.4 The Player in his statement to the Tribunal noted that Dr Malin was not a specially trained sports doctor. He states that he was given urgent medical care and offered a drug that in fact contains Pemoline. It was for that reason that on receipt of the adverse analytical finding, he decided that he would not have the B sample analysed. He testified that he had not slept for 3 to 4 days prior to seeing Dr Malin. He had been depressed for several months preceding his unscheduled examination by Dr Malin that he described as being an urgent and emergency treatment for his insomnia, back pain and depression. He candidly admitted that he did not tell Dr Malin he was a professional tennis player nor that he was subject to an anti-doping control regimen as a professional athlete.

9.5 When questioned on the urgency of the treatment, the Player testified that the culmination of his maladies combined with lack of sleep for several days had brought him to see Dr Malin. He testified further that he relied upon the doctor and his treatment and did not make any inquiries about the medicines he was to take. He never made any examination of the leaflet accompanying the pills because it was in Spanish and was therefore in a language that he did not speak or understand. He made no subsequent attempt to check the ATP prohibited list or consult a sports doctor for the 21 days that he was taking the pills. However, on learning of his positive analytical result in December he had no difficulty in learning through visiting the ATP website that the prohibited list included Pemoline which was the stimulant in the pills he had been taking.

9.6 In the Notice of Appeal and letter the Player made the following points of fact or comment:

(i) Although he had acknowledged receipt of the Rules he got no text of the Anti-Doping Program and knew nothing about the Anti-Doping Program and knew nothing either about the Anti-Doping Program itself or the sanctions for offences.

(ii) ATP representatives should give common instructions to tennis players at least on the Anti-Doping Program existence and necessity to study it.

(iii) He consulted the only Doctor available for his depression.

(iv) The Doctor had successfully prescribed Dynamin on many occasions and was unaware that it can not be prescribed for sportsmen.

(v) Neither he nor the Doctor could read Spanish.

ANALYSIS

11.1 It is not disputed that there was a **Prohibited Substance** Pemoline in the Player's urine specimen. Therefore, a **Doping Offence** under AD Rule C.1 has been established.

11.2 The establishment of a Doping Offence *prima facie* required a sanction of a period of **Ineligibility** under AD Rule M.2. for a First Offence of two years.

11.3 The ATP is empowered to list as a specified substance one that is either particularly susceptible to unintentional anti-doping violation because of its general availability in medicinal products or is less likely to be successfully abused as a doping agent. Whether or not the ATP could or even should have listed Pemoline as a prohibited substance is not to the point. The ATP do not do so. This Panel is not itself empowered to rewrite the Rules or (unless they contravene the general principles of the lex sportiva) to ignore or set them aside. In any case the Panel is not institutionally qualified to make judgments on appropriate controls of an anti-doping policy in terms of what substances should or should not be used by players.

11.4 The Player is right to assert that the list of specified substances is open, not closed in the sense that it is capable of expansion (or contraction); but wrong to assert that this Panel can deal with the list other than as it stood at the material time.

11.5 As to (ii) to be within the parameters of **Exceptional Circumstances. . . .** the Player must establish *how the **Prohibited Substance** entered his or her system in order to have the period of **Ineligibility** eliminated or reduced*. It is not disputed that the Player has discharged the burden of proof in this regard. Dr. Malin recommended to the Player a therapeutic course of medical treatment (associated with a medical diagnosis of depression) of which Pemoline was a component in the over the counter medicine *Dynamin*. Therefore, the Player has established a necessary precondition of engagement of the **Exceptional Circumstances** provision.

11.6 AD Rule M.5. a. is triggered when the proven circumstances are such that **No Fault or Negligence** has occurred. The definition requires that the Player *did not know or suspect, and could not reasonably have known or suspected even with the exercise of the utmost caution, that he had used. . . .* [a] ***Prohibited Substance. . . .***

11.7 The Panel cannot in this context improve on the analysis of the Tribunal:

(i) *Throughout that 3 week period hereto open to discussion the Player did not at any time consult with a sports medicine doctor or review the Prohibited List of Appendix Three.*

(ii) *He certainly found the substance in December by examining the ATP web site for the list of prohibited substances. He could have done that search and inquiry in the 21-day period he took the medicine.*

(iii) *Yet he knew Dr Malin was not a sports medicine doctor.*

(iv) *He did not tell Dr Malin that he was a professional athlete who plays tennis under the ATP Anti-Doping Program.*

(v) *When he needed medical help he knew enough to contact a sports doctor who was at the Olympic Games in Athens at the time.*

The Anti-Doping Rules are very explicit in Rule C.1.a. in stating that "It is each Player's personal duty to ensure that no ***Prohibited Substance*** *enters his body." We found in Player's suggestion that he was not fully appraised of the anti-doping policy unconvincing in the light of the documentation exhibit to the ATP Defence. The Panel has no reason to doubt that the Player did not know that he was using a prohibited substance: but we cannot acquit him of fault or negligence."* So the Panel agrees with the Tribunal that there was fault and negligence.

NOTES AND COMMENTS

1. Race to the Arbitral Forum? *Lindland* demonstrates the process provided by the Amateur Sports Act to appeal a decision of a NGB to the American Arbitration Association (AAA), a private non-profit arbitration organization. The case also illustrates how the private arbitration process for resolving Olympic-related disputes can result in conflicting arbitration decisions and perhaps create an incentive to race to the courthouse to confirm a favorable award, whereby a non-party may be bound by adverse arbitration decision. On the other hand, the domestic arbitration award is not always respected by the international sporting tribunals.

2. Field-of-Play Challenges. The situation raised in *Lindland*, including the AAA's order that Sieraki and Lindland re-wrestle, prompted the USOC to amend its rules. The USOC bylaws now also provide that after a competition, an arbitrator cannot review field of play decisions of on-site officials, unless the decision is (1) outside the authority of the referee to make or (2) the product of fraud, corruption, partiality or other misconduct of the referee. On such basis, CAS refused the request by South Korean gymnast Tae Young to overturn a confirmed erroneous judges' scoring decision, which left US gymnast Paul Hamm with the gold medal and Young the bronze in Athens Summer 2004, because a formal challenge had not been timely raised and because such a quasi field-of-play call by officials must be challenged solely through procedures set by the governing body.

3. Compulsory Arbitration. Athletes are required to arbitrate their eligibility disputes under provisions of the U.S. Amateur Sports Act and as a condition of participating in the Olympic Games, by which athletes must agree to CAS jurisdiction. CAS jurisdiction is also provided for in the bylaws or regulations of many international sports federations, as well as the IOC. The viability of judicial recourse is thus extremely limited. *Slaney v. Int'l Amateur Ath. Fed'n*, 244 F.3d 580 (7th Cir. 2001) upheld dismissal of the former Olympic runner's suit challenging an IAAF arbitration panel's finding that she had committed a doping offense on the grounds that the Convention on the Recognition and Enforcement of Foreign Arbitral Awards (New York Convention) barred Slaney's state and federal claims against the IAAF because those claims had been the subject of a valid arbitration decision. Additionally, the Seventh Circuit upheld dismissal of Slaney's state law claims against the USOC regarding administration of its drug testing program, finding that the Amateur Sports Act gave the USOC the "exclusive" right to determine disputes over athlete eligibility and "does not create" a private right of action under which Slaney could seek to have those claims addressed by the district court. Does this decision leave without a remedy American athletes who are harmed by the manner in which International Olympic federations carry out their drug testing activities? *See also* Gahan v. US Amateur Conf. of Roller Skating, 382 F. Supp.2d 1127 (D. Neb. 2005) (denying request to postpone arbitration held in the United States by athlete, who would be in China, to challenge drug testing procedures).

4. The CAS Olympic *ad hoc* Division convenes (at any hour) to resolve disputes arising during the Games. Article 19(4) of the Olympic Charter provides that "The decisions of the IOC, taken on the basis of the Olympic Charter, are final. Any dispute relating to their application or interpretation may be resolved solely by the IOC Executive Board and, in certain cases, by arbitration before the Court of Arbitration for Sport (CAS)."

5. Doping Controversies. The most publicized and hotly contested Olympic eligibility cases have involved doping and drug-testing. The use of performance-enhancing drugs among elite athletes is thought to be wide-spread. WADA is organized to coordinate at the international level the fight against doping in all forms and monitors compliance with the World Anti-Doping Code, the worldwide standard for anti-doping regulations. The Prohibited List identifies banned substances and is updated annually. Athletes are personally responsible to ensure compliance with the Code. Although the adoption of the World Anti-Doping Code has helped to streamline doping standards and procedures, the reliability of drug-testing procedures remained subject to challenge and maintaining a complete list of prohibited drugs (and masking agents) difficult. Ambiguity is rarely resolved in the athlete's favor. The CAS decision in *Vlasov v. ATP* suggests that the Tribunal is limited to enforcing the strict doping codes as written, even where the equities appear to lie with the athlete. What are an athlete's options in challenging overly broad doping rules? What should be the standard for qualifying as a banned substance? Should this include medications such as insulin which may be needed by an athlete with diabetes? With the vast spectrum of Olympic events including baseball, which traditionally has not prohibited or tested for steroids, to snowboarding, table tennis, handball, and bobsledding, should the same doping policy apply to all sports? Should a sports doping policy include substances which are performance-neutral or performance-inhibiting?

6. Commentary on Olympic Arbitration. *See* James A.R. Nafziger, *Dispute Resolution in the Arena of International Sports Competition*, 50 AM. J. COMP. L. 161 (2002); Nancy K. Raber, *Dispute Resolution in Olympic Sport: The Court of Arbitration for Sport*, 8 SETON HALL J. SPORT L. 75 (1998).

7. IOC Scandal. While the pressure to be faster, stronger and go for the gold has tempted some athletes to violate doping rules, the IOC itself is alleged to have succumbed to temptations of bribery and other payoffs in the process of selecting host cities for the Olympic Games. Scandal erupted in early 1998 with reports of bribery of certain IOC officials in connection with the selection of Salt Lake City, Utah, for the 2002 Winter Olympic Games. According to some, this is not an isolated occurrence. *See e.g.*, VYY SIMPSON & ANDREW JENNINGS, DISHONORED GAMES: CORRUPTION, MONEY AND GREED AT THE OLYMPICS (1992) ("This is our discovery about the world of modern Olympic sport: it is a secret, elite domain where the decisions about sport, our sport, are made behind closed doors, where money is spent on creating a fabulous life style for a tiny circle of officials rather than providing facilities for athletes, where money destined for sport has been siphoned away to offshore bank accounts and where officials preside forever, untroubled by elections").

E. OLYMPIC TRADEMARK AND INTELLECTUAL PROPERTY ISSUES; COMMERCIALISM

An area of substantial Olympic-related litigation involves trademark and intellectual property. In its role as the exclusive national coordinator for U.S. participation in the Olympic Games, the USOC assists in the funding of U.S. participation in the Olympic Games. Although chartered by Congress, the USOC is a private non-profit entity and does not receive governmental financial support. The USOC raises funds to promote the United States' Olympic efforts through arrangements for corporate sponsorship, licensing of the USOC logos for merchandising, and revenues from television broadcasting.

In the Amateur Sports Act, Congress conferred upon the USOC exclusive trademark rights to the "Olympic" name, the Olympic symbol consisting of five interlocking rings, the emblem of the USOC, and the words "Olympic", "Olympiad", the motto "Citius Altius Fortius" (meaning "Faster, Higher, Stronger"), or any combination or simulation thereof, subject to the preexisting rights usage prior to September 21, 1950. The Act also grants the USOC exclusive rights to license commercial and promotional use of Olympic trademarks, as a means to enable the USOC to raise funds to support the United States' participation in the Olympics Games and the Pan-American Games. Such licenses are a substantial inducement for contributions from commercial corporations. 36 U.S.C. § 220502(b) ("The [USOC] may authorize contributors and suppliers of goods or services to use the trade name of the [USOC] as well as any trademark, symbol, insignia, or emblem of the International Olympic Committee or of the [USOC] in advertising that the contributions, goods or, services were donated, supplied, or furnished to or for the use of, approved, selected, or used by the [USOC] or the United States Olympic or Pan-American team or team members."). The Act grants USOC remedies of commercial trademark and imposes civil liability upon any person who uses the Olympic name or symbol without USOC consent. *See* Erinn M. Batcha, Comment, *Who are the Real Competitors in the Olympic Games? Dual Olympic Battles: Trademark Infringement and Ambush Marketing Harms Corporate Sponsors — Violations Against the USOC and its Corporate Sponsors*, 8 SETON HALL J. SPORT L. 229, 230 (1998). As the following demonstrates, the USOC vigilantly protects against unauthorized use of Olympic marks.

PROBLEM

Athena Socrates, an owner of a small Greek restaurant in Salt Lake City has operated "The Olympic Restaurant" since 1983. She has just received a demand letter by the USOC stating that she must immediately cease and desist from using the name "Olympic," rename her restaurant immediately, and discontinue selling onion rings in the Olympic ring formation. She consults you for advice.

CASE FILE

O-M BREAD, INC. v. UNITED STATES OLYMPIC COMMITTEE

65 F.3d 933 (Fed. Cir. 1995)

Before ARCHER, Chief Judge, NEWMAN and SCHALL, Circuit Judges.

NEWMAN

This trademark opposition was filed by the United States Olympic Committee ("USOC") against the application of Roush Products Company, Inc., the successor in interest to O-M Bread, Inc., (together "Roush") to register the mark OLYMPIC KIDS for bakery goods. The application to register OLYMPIC KIDS was filed on March 5, 1991, based on the "intent to use" provision of the Trademark Act. The Trademark Trial and Appeal Board of the United States Patent and Trademark Office ("the Board") sustained the opposition, interpreting the Amateur Sports Act of 1978 to mean that Roush's grandfathered rights to continue to use its OLYMPIC marks for bread and bakery products do not extend to the registration of OLYMPIC KIDS for bakery products. We affirm the Board's decision.

The "Olympic" Statutes

In 1950, as part of "An Act to Incorporate the United States Olympic Association," the Association (predecessor of the USOC) was granted certain exclusive rights to use of the word "Olympic." The Act recognized the "grandfather" rights of prior users:

> § 9 Provided, however, That any person, corporation, or association that actually used, or whose assignor actually used, the said emblem, sign, insignia, or words ["Olympic," "Olympiad," "Citius Altius Fortius", or any combination thereof] for any lawful purpose prior to the effective date of this Act, shall not be deemed forbidden by this Act to continue the use thereof for the same purpose and for the same class or classes of goods to which said emblem, sign, insignia, or words had been used lawfully prior thereto. Pub. L. No. 81-805 (1950) (current version at 36 U.S.C. § 380).

The 1950 statute was succeeded by the Amateur Sports Act of 1978, (codified with some differences at 36 U.S.C. § 371 *et seq.*). Section 110(c) of the 1978 Act grants the USOC certain exclusive rights to the use of the word "Olympic":

> § 110(c) The Corporation [USOC] shall have exclusive right to use . . . the words "Olympic", "Olympiad", "Citius Altius Fortius" or any combination thereof subject to the preexisting rights described in subsection (a). (codified at 36 U.S.C. § 380(c)).

Section 110(a) of the Act continues to prohibit unauthorized uses and to grandfather pre-existing rights, including preexisting trademark use, and provides for remedy by civil action:

> § 110(a) Without the consent of the Corporation, any person who uses for the purpose of trade, to induce the sale of any goods or services, or to promote any theatrical exhibition, athletic performance, or competition — . . . (3) any trademark, trade name, sign, symbol, or insignia falsely representing association with, or authorization by, the International Olympic Committee or the Corporation; or (4) the words "Olympic", "Olympiad", "Citius Altius Fortius", or any combination or simulation thereof tending to cause confusion, to cause mistake, to deceive, or to falsely suggest a connection with the Corporation or any Olympic activity; shall be subject to suit in a civil action by the Corporation for the remedies provided in the Act of July 5, 1946 (popularly known as the Trademark Act of 1946). However, any person who actually used . . . the words, or any combination thereof, in subsection (a)(4)

> of this section for any lawful purpose prior to September 21, 1950, shall not be prohibited by this section from continuing such lawful use for the same purpose and for the same goods or services. In addition, any person who actually used, or whose assignor actually used, any other trademark, trade name, sign, symbol, or insignia described in subsections (a)(3) and (4) of this section for any lawful purpose prior to enactment of this Act shall not be prohibited by this section from continuing such lawful use for the same purpose and for the same goods or services. (Codified with some differences at 36 U.S.C. § 380(a).)

This opposition to registration of OLYMPIC KIDS was brought in accordance with this statutory provision.

The Roush "Olympic" Trademarks

In 1938 Roush registered the trademark OLYMPIC for bakery products including bread, asserting first use in 1931. In 1947 Roush commenced use of the trademark OLYMPIC MEAL on bread mix and other bakery products, and in 1979 registered this mark, over the opposition of the USOC, based on the grandfathered use of OLYMPIC MEAL. Roush owns two other relevant registrations, design marks for OLYMPIC MEAL and OLYMPIC MEAL SPECIAL FORMULA. None of these registered marks is at issue here, although Roush points out that the two latter registrations are based on use after the Olympic statutes were enacted, arguing that this fact supports its entitlement to register the mark OLYMPIC KIDS.

Roush's argument is that since it is authorized to use its marks containing the word OLYMPIC for bakery products, this extends to the proposed use of OLYMPIC KIDS for bakery products. Roush states that OLYMPIC KIDS simply comprises the word "Olympic," in which Roush has grandfather rights for bakery products, and the word "kids," which Roush states is descriptive of the target users and in any event not subject to any rights of the USOC. Roush states that it is not enlarging its grandfather rights, but is simply exercising them.

Roush stresses that the rights and interests of prior users of "Olympic" words and marks were recognized and preserved by Congress, and states that the Board's denial of registration deprived Roush of the property interests that the grandfather provision was enacted to protect. Roush argues that the USOC's only ground of objection to registration of OLYMPIC KIDS for bread products is the presence of the word "Olympic," and that Roush's use of "Olympic" is grandfathered for bakery products. Roush argues that it is irrelevant whether it used OLYMPIC KIDS before 1950, because its grandfather rights to the word "Olympic" preclude any holding that OLYMPIC KIDS violates § 110(a).

The Board recognized Roush's rights to use OLYMPIC for bakery products, but held that these rights do not confer any grandfather benefit on Roush's proposed use of OLYMPIC KIDS, which the Board held was a "different" mark from OLYMPIC. The Board also rejected Roush's "prior registration defense," on the ground that this equitable defense is not available to overcome a statutory prohibition.

The Statutory Purpose

A "grandfather" provision in a statute is "an exception to a restriction that allows all those already doing something to continue doing it even if they would be stopped by the new restriction." BLACK'S LAW DICTIONARY 699 (6th ed. 1990). Roush states that the Board's ruling frustrates the purpose of the grandfather provision, by narrowing Roush's preexisting rights and limiting Roush's normal commercial use of its grandfathered rights to "Olympic." In response, the USOC foresees dire consequences should Roush be permitted a broadened use of "Olympic," such as in combination with other words, instead of being limited strictly to the actual uses during the grandfathered period.

We look first to the statute for guidance to the interpretation of the grandfather provision. The question before us impinges on both § 110(a) and § 110(c) and the policies they implement. The statutory provisions are not ambiguous. On one hand, there is a clear intent to reserve to the USOC all remaining rights to use and profit from the "Olympic" name and symbols; § 110(c) so provides. On the other hand, it is clear that Congress intended to protect prior users, and did so in § 110(a). Cogent arguments are made by both parties as to the dominance of the rights of each, in this region of conflicting interests wherein each side invokes the protection of statutory purpose.

A statute is interpreted on the plain meaning of its provisions in the statutory context, informed when necessary by the policy that the statute was designed to serve. A statute must be construed to give effect to all of its provisions, and not to diminish any of them. Thus both § 110(a) and § 110(c) must accommodate the overall policy and purpose of the enactment.

On review of the statute and the history of its enactment, it is apparent that the primary purpose of these provisions is to secure to the USOC the commercial and promotional rights to all then-unencumbered uses of "Olympic" and other specified words, marks, and symbols, *see United States Olympic Committee v. Intelicense Corp., S.A.*, 737 F.2d 263, 266 (2d Cir.), *cert. denied*, 469 U.S. 982 (1984), but subject to the commercial rights that existed at the time of enactment. The interest in facilitating United States participation in the Olympic games by enhancing the USOC's opportunity to profit from licensing and sales of goods and services that derive their value from the Olympic connection is not in overt conflict with the obligation to safeguard the property rights of prior users. However, while the rights of prior users are protected from diminution, they are also restricted from enlargement.

Roush argues that OLYMPIC KIDS represents normal commercial growth of its OLYMPIC-styled bakery products. However, commercial growth into new "Olympic"-based marks is outside the letter of the statute, as well as outside its spirit. The statutory balance that limited prior users to the words, marks, goods and services in use before enactment, and thus limited potential expansion, is not an unreasonable implementation of the legislative policy. This conclusion accords with the spirit of the Supreme Court's observation, on review of the legislative history, that the statute provides broader protection to the USOC than would, simply, trademark rights in the Olympic words and symbols:

The protection granted to the USOC's use of the Olympic words and symbols differs from the normal trademark protection in two respects: the USOC need not prove that a contested use is likely to cause confusion, and an unauthorized user of the word does not have available the normal statutory defenses. *San Francisco Arts & Athletics, Inc. v. United States Olympic Committee*, 483 U.S. 522, 531 (1987). This explanation is in harmony with the USOC's argument that the purpose of the Act is to secure all commercial and promotional uses of "Olympic" to the USOC, except for those uses that are grandfathered.

The Board's Decision

The Board found that OLYMPIC and OLYMPIC KIDS are different marks, based primarily on their different commercial impressions. On this ground the Board denied to OLYMPIC KIDS the benefit of Roush's grandfather rights in OLYMPIC.

Whether marks are "different" is a less stringent criterion than whether the marks are likely to cause confusion. Further, as in determining likelihood of confusion, it is not relevant whether a portion of the mark is disclaimed or does not have strong trademark significance, such as the word "kids." No part of the mark can be ignored in comparing the marks as a whole. *Specialty Brands, Inc. v. Coffee Bean Distributors, Inc.*, 748 F.2d 669, 672-73,(Fed. Cir. 1984). The Board correctly determined that the marks were different, based primarily on their differing commercial impression.

We have also considered the criteria for determining whether marks may be linked for purposes of continuity. As summarized in *Van Dyne-Crotty, Inc. v. Wear-Guard Corp.*, 926 F.2d 1156 (Fed. Cir. 1991), to be linked or "tacked" for purposes of continuity the marks must create the same commercial impression, and the later mark must not be materially different from or alter the character of the earlier mark. These criteria are not met by OLYMPIC and OLYMPIC KIDS. We take note that Roush states that it "does not contend that the use of the mark OLYMPIC KIDS is equivalent to the use of the mark OLYMPIC," instead arguing that this is not an issue of legal equivalence. We agree. However, when different marks present a different commercial impression and are not legal equivalents, it would be an incorrect interpretation of the Amateur Sports Act to hold that they are nonetheless grandfathered under § 110. Thus we affirm the Board's ruling that the proposed use of OLYMPIC KIDS for bakery products is not a permitted extension of Roush's grandfathered rights to the mark OLYMPIC, and not independently registrable.

* * *

The Board's decision, sustaining the USOC's opposition to the registration of OLYMPIC KIDS, is AFFIRMED.

NOTES AND COMMENTS

1. In *San Francisco Arts & Athletes, Inc. v. United States Olympic Committee*, 483 U.S. 522 (1987), the Supreme Court upheld the USOC's right to prohibit a nonprofit corporation from using the phrase "The Gay Olympic Games" to promote the athletic association's games or products. The Court held that the USOC's exclusive rights in the word "Olympic" do not violate freedom of speech, as the plaintiffs had alternative means to express opposition to the Olympics, and that there is no First Amendment right to use the Olympic phrase or symbols. The Court also ruled that the Act incorporates the remedies but not defenses under the Lanham (Trademark) Act, and thus the USOC was not required to show that unauthorized use was likely to cause consumers to confuse the event as associated with the USOC. *See* **Chapter 13**, *supra*.

2. The USOC permits use of the trademark Olympic name only to a few organizations that sponsor athletic competitions consistent with USOC purposes, such as the "Special Olympics" for athletes with disabilities, and "Junior Olympics" for youth. 36 U.S.C. § 347(7) (13). The USOC has barred usage to other groups. *See San Francisco Arts*, 483 U.S. at 543 (describing USOC cases against the March of Dimes Birth Defects Foundation, and Golden Age Olympics, Inc.).

3. Non-commercial use exception? The use of the Olympic name and symbol in signs by a citizen's group named "Stop the Olympic Prison," in protesting the conversion of the former Lake Placid, New York Olympic facilities to a prison, was held not to violate § 380 because they were not sold or distributed commercially and were not likely to confuse as an endorsement by the USOC. *Stop the Olympic Prison v. United States Olympic Committee*, 489 F. Supp. 1111 (S.D.N.Y. 1980).

4. Ambush Advertising. Corporate sponsors pay millions for the rights to sponsor the Olympic Games and to use Olympic trademarks. The value of these rights is diluted when actions or advertising by other parties creates the impression as officially associated with the Olympics. In 1996, Eastman Kodak paid $40 million for corporate sponsorship rights to the Summer Olympic Games. Days before the Games, Fuji displayed a photo exhibit honoring Olympic track and field athletes in Atlanta. For a discussion of the ambush marketing problem and the Olympics, *see* Robert N. Davis, *Ambushing the Olympic Games*, 3 VILL. SPORTS & ENT. L.J. 423 (1996).

5. The Olympic Charter provides that "all rights to the Olympic symbol, the Olympic flag, the Olympic motto and the Olympic anthem belong exclusively to the IOC." Article 17. National Olympic Committees, however, may use and license the Olympic trademarks for non-profit-making Olympic fundraising and activities. The Charter directs each NOC to protect the use of the Olympic flag, symbol, flame, and motto from unauthorized use. *Id.* Other countries such as Canada, Great Britain, Australia and Japan have similarly strong national intellectual property laws protecting Olympic trademarks. *See* Ronald T. Rowan, *Legal Issues and the Olympic Movement: Speech: Legal Issues and the Olympics*, 3 VILL. SPORTS & ENT. L.J. 395 (1996).

F. OTHER INTERNATIONAL SPORTS

Issues of international sports governing bodies' decisions, with attendant jurisdictional questions, have also come before foreign courts. Consider the European Court of Justice's ruling in *Union Royale Belge des Societes de Football Ass'n ASBL v. Bosman*, E.C.R. I-5040 (1995) (holding that the soccer sporting association's ruling requiring the payment of a transfer and development fee in order to employ a professional footballer with a club in another member state upon expiration of his contract violated European Community Treaty provisions regarding the free movement of workers). For an interesting discussion of international sports issues, *see* James A.R. Nafziger, *Symposium: Sports Law in the 21st Century: Globalizing Sports Law*, 9 MARQ. SPORTS L.J. 225 (1999).

WEB DIRECTORY

AMATEUR SPORTS GOVERNING BODIES

www.ncaa.org	National Collegiate Athletic Association
www.naia.org	National Association of Intercollegiate Athletics
www.njcaa.org	National Junior College Athletic Association
www.nfhs.org	National Federation of State High School Associations
www.aausports.org	Amateur Athletic Union

OLYMPIC SPORTS GOVERNING BODIES

www.usoc.org	United States Olympic Committee (Site also includes links to web sites for the National Governing Bodies (NGB) of the 48 recognized Olympic sports)

PROFESSIONAL SPORTS LEAGUES

www.nfl.com	National Football League
www.mlb.com	Major League Baseball
www.nba.com	National Basketball Association
www.nhl.com	National Hockey League
www.wnba.com	Women's National Basketball Association
www.minorleaguebaseball.com	Minor League Baseball
www.cfl.ca	Canadian Football League
www.arenafootball.com	Arena Football League
www.premierleague.com	F.A. Premier League

PROFESSIONAL SPORTS GOVERNING BODIES

www.pgatour.com	PGA Tour
www.lpga.com	LPGA Tour
www.atptennis.com	ATP Tour
www.wtatour.com	WTA Tour
www.nascar.com	NASCAR

PLAYERS ASSOCIATIONS

www.nflpa.org	National Football League Players Association
www.mlbplayers.mlb.com	Major League Baseball Players Association
www.nhlpa.com	National Hockey League Players Association
www.nbpa.com	National Basketball Players Association

TRADE ASSOCIATIONS/ADVOCACY GROUPS

http://nacda.cstv.com/	National Association of Collegiate Directors of Athletics
www.nabc.org	National Association of Basketball Coaches
www.afca.com	American Football Coaches Association
www.womenssportsfoundation.org	Women's Sports Foundation
www.wbca.org	Women's Basketball Coaches Association
www.bcasports.org	Black Coaches Association

PROFESSIONAL ORGANIZATIONS

www.sportslaw.org	Sports Lawyers Association
www.abanet.org/forums/entsports	ABA Forum on Entertainment and Sports Industries

SPORTS MEDIA

www.espn.com

www.usatoday.com

www.foxsports.com

www.sportingnews.com

www.cnnsi.com

SPORTS LAW JOURNALS

www.law.du.edu/sportsjournal/inthenews.htm	Denver Sports and Entertainment Law Journal

www.law.depaul.edu/students/organizations_journals/student_orgs/lawslj/Home.asp	DePaul Journal of Sports and Contemporary Problems
http://law.shu.edu/journals/sportslaw/	Seton Hall Journal of Sports and Entertainment Law
www.law.villanova.edu/scholarlyresources/journals/sportsandentlj/	Villanova Sports and Entertainment Law Journal
www.student.virginia.edu/~vase/	Virginia Sports and Entertainment Law Journal

BLOGS

http://sports-law.blogspot.com/	Sports Law Blog

SPORTS LAW EDUCATIONAL PROGRAMS

www.fcsl.edu/centers/LawAndSports/	Center for Law and Sports, Florida Coastal School of Law
http://law.marquette.edu/cgi-bin/site.pl?2130&pageID=160	National Sports Law Institute, Marquette University Law School
www.law.tulane.edu/prog/index.cfm?d=specialty&main=specsport.htm	Sports Law Program, Tulane University Law School
www.law.duke.edu/sportscenter/	The Center for Sports Law and Policy, Duke University School of Law
http://faculty.lls.edu/sli/	Sports Law Institute, Loyola Law School, Loyola University Los Angeles
http://www.valpo.edu/law/sportsclinic/	Sports Law Clinic, Valparaiso University School of Law

Table of Cases

References are to pages. Locations of principal cases appear in italics.

A

B

C

D

E

F

G

H

N

O

P

Q

R

V

W

Y

Z

INDEX

[References are to pages.]

A

B

C

[References are to pages.]

[References are to pages.]

[References are to pages.]

U

W